The Armagh Guardian, 1844 – 1852
(Volume I.)
Births, Marriages, and Deaths

THE ARMAGH GUARDIAN, 1844 – 1852
(VOLUME I.)
BIRTHS, MARRIAGES, AND DEATHS

COMPREHENDING

Transcripts of
Birth, Marriage, and Death Notices,
gleaned from historical editions of
The Armagh Guardian newspaper,
as published by John Thompson
between
December 3, 1844 – December 25, 1852,
at the city of Armagh, county Armagh,

WITH

Indexes of
Surnames, Place Names, and
Institutions & Publications.

COMPILED AND EDITED BY

Alison Kilpatrick

Copyright © Alison Joan Kilpatrick, 2015.
All rights reserved.

No part of this publication may be copied, reproduced, or transmitted in any form or by any means, electronic or mechanical, including photocopying, recording, extraction, re-use or storage in any retrieval system, or scanning, uploading, or any other transmission via the Internet, without the prior written permission of the publisher.

This volume consists of data that were: selected for transcription or extraction; entered, catalogued, indexed, and stored in a relational database created by the compiler; output, assembled, and articulated for publication as an historical reference and finding aid; and, supplemented by the editor with interpretive remarks, research notes, statistics, and annotations.

The compiler's database contains detailed fields for: publication references (date, page, column, type of notice); surnames, forenames, and titles; institutions and publications; cause of death*; occupations, including rank*; place names (country, county, city or townland, and civic address, where stated). *Not indexed in this volume.

Permission to reproduce material from this publication is granted, subject to the following:

1. The use must be for a non-commercial, educational or private research purpose.
2. A maximum of 10 index entries or 300 transcribed words may be used in a non-commercial, private research publication or presentation. If your proposed project requires more than this allowance, write to the publisher at the address given below.
3. Provide an appropriate bibliographic citation, for example: "Transcription of this article previously published in *The Armagh Guardian, 1844-1852: Transcripts and Indexes*, compiled and edited by Alison Kilpatrick (St. Thomas, Ontario: Quercus Arborealis Publications, 2015)."
4. This permission is not extended to transmissions, look-ups, or postings to newsgroups, bulletin boards, mailing lists or any other forum, web page, etc. on the Internet or any other sharing, social network, electronic, digital or similar media or network logically or reasonably anticipated by this exclusion.

> Under no circumstances may any portion of or extract from this book be published to any medium associated with commercial interests or solicitations of any kind including, but not limited to, advertising, requests for donations, or references or links to same or similar, whether the purpose, enterprise, or activity is conducted for profit or not-for-profit.

For information regarding permissions, write to the publisher at:
Quercus Arborealis Publications
e-mail: editor@quercus-arborealis.ca
web: www.quercus-arborealis.ca

This book is for genealogists, local historians, and those who love reading stories from the past.

Some articles contain language and characterizations which may have been in common use at the time the articles or stories were written, but which are no longer acceptable. These articles do not reflect the opinions of the compiler, editor, or publisher of this book.

ISBN 978-0-9868873-5-2

Second Edition

*Dedicated to the memory of
Dorothy May Causton née Kilpatrick (1922–2003),
whose maternal grandparents,
John Flavell (1834–1888)
and
Rachel Mary Gilmore (1855–1930),
emigrated from
the county Armagh to Toronto, Canada.*

∷ ∷ ∷

TABLE OF CONTENTS

List of countries and Irish counties indexed in this volume	ix
1. Introduction	1
Surnames	1
Place names	2
Causes of death	2
Notable notices	4
How to use this book	7
Abbreviations and acronyms	9
2. Transcripts	11
Editorial from inaugural edition of *The Armagh Guardian*	296
3. Index of Surnames	299
4. Index of Place Names	343
5. Institution & Publication Index	415
6. John Thompson, Proprietor and Editor	425
Bibliography	429

List of Countries and Irish Counties Indexed in this Volume.

Country and county not named	343	Ireland, continued:	
At Sea	343	Louth, county of	391
Australia (Note 1)	343	Mayo	392
Belgium	343	Meath	392
Canada East. *See also* Québec.	343	Monaghan	393
Canada West. *See also* Upper Canada.	343	Queen's. *See also* Laois.	396
Cape of Good Hope	344	Roscommon	396
China	344	Sligo	396
East Indies. *See also* India.	344	Tipperary	397
England	344	Tyrone	398
France	350	Waterford	407
Germany	350	Westmeath	407
India. *See also* East Indies.	351	Wexford	407
Ireland:		Wicklow	407
County and townland not named	351	Isle of Man	408
County not named	351	Italy	408
Antrim, county of	353	Jamaica	408
Armagh	356	N.B. (New Brunswick)	408
Carlow	366	N.B. (North Britain) *var.* Scotland	408
Cavan	366	N.S. Wales. *See also* New South Wales.	408
Clare	368	North America	409
Cork	369	North Britain *var.* Scotland	409
Derry	369	Portugal	409
Donegal	373	Québec. *See also* Canada East.	409
Down	376	Russia	409
Dublin	380	Scotland	409
Fermanagh	383	South Africa	410
Galway	389	South Australia	410
Kerry	389	South Wales. *See also* Wales.	411
Kildare	389	Spain	411
Kilkenny	389	Tasmania. *See also* Van Dieman's Land.	411
King's (Offaly)	390	United States of America	411
Laois. *See also* Queen's.	390	Upper Canada. *See also* Canada West.	412
Leitrim	390	Van Dieman's Land. *See also* Tasmania.	412
Limerick	391	Wales. *See also* South Wales.	412
Longford	391	West Indies. *See also* Jamaica.	413

Notes:
(1) *See also* N.S. Wales, New South Wales, and South Australia.
(2) The index of place names, given in Chapter 4, includes a number of entries for Irish dioceses and for several countries, for which one to three entries, only, were represented in this run of the *Armagh Guardian*. Examples of the former include the Dioceses of Ardagh, Ardfert and Aghadoe, Armagh, Cashel, Clogher, Clonfert, Clonmacnoise, Cloyne, Connor, &c.; and of the latter: Antigua, the Arctic, Australasia, Austria, Batavia, Bermuda, Brazil, British Guyana, Ceylon, &c.

1. INTRODUCTION

This book presents two related compilations: first, transcriptions of Birth, Marriage and Death (BMD) notices from historic issues of *The Armagh Guardian* newspaper, published between the years, 1844–1852; and second, indexes to serve as finding aids for those articles.

John Thompson, the proprietor and editor of *The Armagh Guardian*, commenced publication of his newspaper at Armagh, with the December 3, 1844 edition. Between 1844–1852, Mr. Thompson published a total of 6,453 birth, marriage and death notices, as summarized in Table 1. This period of publication corresponds with that dark age in Irish history known as the Great Famine—from the earliest reports of disease found in the potato crops in late 1844, to the dénouement of this tragedy in the early 1850s—in an Ireland permanently altered by the consequences of mass hunger, disease, death, and emigration.

Table 1. Summary of notices of vital events by type.

Births	1,118
Marriages	1,860
Deaths	3,475
Total no. notices	6,453

Surnames—This series of BMD notices contains 14,534 surname references. The surnames occurring most frequently were Johnson, Wilson, Hamilton, Armstrong, Smith, Irwin, Moore, and Stewart. Table 2 provides details of the distribution of those surnames occurring most frequently, and some of the spelling variants found.

Table 2. Surnames most frequently reported in BMD notices, 1844–1852, in rank order.

Surname	No.	Surname	No.
1. Johnson, Johnston, Johnstone	197	21. Porter	52
2. Wilson	142	22. Rodgers, Rogers	51
3. Hamilton	141	23. Alexander	50
4. Thompson, Thomson	130	24. Buchanan, Buchannon, Buchanon	50
5. Armstrong	127	25. Henderson	50
6. Smith, Smyth, Smythe	122	26. Allan, Allen	49
7. Irwin, Irwine	106	27. Atkinson	49
8. Moore	104	28. Kidd, Kydd	49
9. Stewart, Stuart	101	29. White, Whyte	48
10. Bell	87	30. Crawford	47
11. Brown, Browne	83	31. Young	47
12. Clark, Clarke	75	32. Dobbin	45
13. Graham, Greame, Greham	72	33. Fleming, Flemming	45
14. Anderson	69	34. Elliot, Elliott	44
15. Robinson	69	35. Knox	44
16. Campbell, Cambell	66	36. Millar, Miller	44
17. Irvin, Irvine	64	37. Read, Reade, Reed, Reid	44
18. Hughes	59	38. Beattie, Beatty, Beaty	42
19. Scott	59	39. Martin	40
20. Porter	52	40. Montgomerie, Montgomery	39

Place names—This series of BMD notices contains 25,982 references to place names: 22,353 within Ireland, and 3,629 in other parts of the world. Table 3 provides a summary of these place name references, sorted by Country, while Table 4 summarizes Irish place names by County.

Table 3. Number of references to place names, sorted by Country, and in rank order.

Place name	No.	Per cent
Ireland	22,353	86.0%
England	1,963	7.6%
Scotland	402	1.6%
USA	391	1.5%
Canadian provinces	169	0.7%
East Indies	115	0.4%
France	71	.3%
Australia	47	.2%
New Brunswick	44	.2%
Wales	41	.2%
Spain	38	.2%
Germany	31	—
Belgium	21	—
Italy	20	—
Portugal	20	—
At sea	19	—
Jamaica	19	—
China	14	—
Isle of Man	13	—
Van Dieman's Land	12	—
West Indies	11	—
Jersey	10	—
Cape of Good Hope	9	—
Rivers (various)	8	—
Africa	8	—
Ceylon	7	—
Greece	6	—
New Zealand	6	—
Trinidad	6	—
Antigua	5	—
Holland	4	—
Russia	4	—
Other	58	—
Total, all places	25,982	100.0%

Table 4. Number of references to place names in Ireland, sorted by County.

Place name	No.	Per cent
Antrim	1,791	8.0%
Armagh	4,788	21.4%
Carlow	27	0.1%
Cavan	795	3.6%
Clare	38	0.2%
Cork	211	0.9%
Derry	1,145	5.1%
Donegal	1,265	5.7%
Down	1,613	7.2%
Dublin	2,117	9.5%
Fermanagh	1,804	8.1%
Galway	130	0.6%
Kerry	65	0.3%
Kildare	34	0.2%
Kilkenny	52	0.2%
King's	42	0.2%
Leitrim	186	0.8%
Limerick	103	0.5%
Longford	63	0.3%
Louth	305	1.4%
Mayo	66	0.3%
Meath	94	0.4%
Monaghan	1,049	4.7%
Queen's	65	0.3%
Roscommon	53	0.2%
Sligo	252	1.1%
Tipperary	99	0.4%
Tyrone	3,410	15.3%
Waterford	55	0.3%
Westmeath	66	0.3%
Wexford	70	0.3%
Wicklow	95	0.4%
County not stated	398	1.8%
Total, Irish references	22,353	100.0%

Causes of death—Of the 3,475 death notices published in *The Armagh Guardian* during this period, 1,719 recorded the cause of death. Table 5 provides an outline of these, grouped according to similar ailments, with details as to the various phrases and terms employed by the writers of these notices.

Table 5. Causes of death reported in death notices, *The Armagh Guardian*, 1844–1852.

Cause of death	No.	Per cent	Details
Accident	23	1.3%	Accident, Drowned, Suffocation
Apoplexy	38	2.2%	Apoplexy, Paralysis, Paralytic
At sea	3	0.2%	After a severe passage at sea, Sea sickness, Ship lost at sea
Bowel/intestinal	30	1.8%	Refer to (1), below.
Brain ailments	21	1.2%	Refer to (2), below.
Brief illness	145	8.4%	After a brief illness/suffering, After a short but painful illness
Burns, fire	2	0.1%	Fire
Cardiac	42	2.4%	Refer to (3), below.
Childbirth	6	0.4%	Childbirth, Puerperal fever
Cholera	56	3.3%	Cholera, Asiatic cholera, English cholera
Contagious disease	40	2.3%	Refer to (4), below.
Consumption	66	3.9%	Consumption; or, Acute, rapid, or pulmonary Consumption
Ear, nose, throat	4	0.2%	Having swallowed a copper coin, Laryngitis, Lock-jaw
Fever	133	7.7%	Refer to (5), below.
Inflammation	6	0.4%	Inflammation
Kidney disease	2	0.1%	Inflammation of the kidneys
Liver disease	10	0.6%	Abscess on/disease of the liver, Bilious attack, Jaundice
Long illness	164	9.5%	Refer to (6), below.
Lung disease	38	2.2%	Refer to (7), below.
Old age and decline	746	43.4%	Decay of nature, Decline, Old age, Rapid decline
Other illness	5	0.3%	Refer to (8), below.
Smallpox	5	0.3%	Confluent smallpox, Small pox
Suddenly	78	4.5%	Refer to (9), below.
Suicide	1	0.1%	Suicide
Typhus	41	2.4%	Typhus fever, Malignant/Spotted typhus fever
Other	14	0.8%	Refer to (10), below.
Total no. references	1,719	100.0%	

1. Bowel/intestinal ..	Diarrhoea, Dysentery, Gastric fever, Inflammation in the bowels or stomach
2. Brain ailments ...	Brain fever, Cerebral fever, Congestion of the brain, Epilepsy, Hydrocephalus, Water in the head, Water on the brain
3. Cardiac	Bursting of a blood-vessel, Disease of the heart, Dropsy, Effusion of blood on the brain, Internal hemorrhage, Palpitation of the heart, Rheumatic attacks, Rheumatism in the heart, Rupture of a blood vessel, Sudden hemorrhage
4. Contagious disease	Malignant measles, Malignant scarletina, Measles, Of the prevailing epidemic, Virus
5. Fever	Country fever, Fever, Malignant fever, Putrified fever, Spotted fever, Yellow fever
6. Long illness	After a lengthened illness, After a lingering and painful/severe illness, After a lingering illness, After a long and lingering/painful/protracted/severe/tedious illness, After a long confinement, After a long illness, After a painful and protracted illness, After a painful illness, After a protracted illness, After a severe and lingering illness, After a tedious illness, After a tedious and painful illness, After a very protracted and trying illness, After an illness of several months
7. Lung disease	Bronchitis, Disease of the chest, Disease of the lungs, Effusion of water on the chest, Inflammation of the lungs, Inflammatory croup, Influenza, Inveterate bronchitis, Pleurisy, Pneumonic infection, Water on the chest, Whooping cough
8. Other illness	After a severe and tedious illness, After severe suffering, After tedious bad health
9. Suddenly	Died rather suddenly, Died unexpectedly, Died suddenly, Died suddenly
10. Other	After sleeping in a damp bed, Dog bite, Excessive ball playing, Exhaustion, Exposure to damp, Gangrene, Gout, Indisposition, Lightning, Mortification, Painter's colic

Notable Notices—The following paragraphs highlight those notices which may strike the reader as remarkable or extraordinary, either by the nature of their content, or the style employed to emphasize certain aspects of the notice (with references to the numbers of those notices, as published in this compilation, in parentheses):

- Abundant numbers of children born to families, ranging from 12 to 27 (notices no. 359, 2343, 3487, 4089, 4318, 5292, 5683, 5906, 6170). One death notice (no. 4318) observed the demise of James Stewart, of Killymore, county Tyrone, who "left behind him a numerous offspring, consisting of 53 children and grandchildren, all of whom with the exception of one, reside in the same townland."

- Multiple births, varying in number from twins to quadruplets (notices no. 56, 204, 575, 1528, 1649, 1718, 1903, 1904, 1971, 2075, 2388, 3324, 4410, 4567, 4895, 5179, 5180, 5225, 5353, 5488, 6170, 6236, 6327, 6378).

- Childbirth under the newly discovered anaesthetic, chloroform (notices no. 1567, 5837).

- The birth of a child to a seventy-one-year old woman in Highland county, Ohio, USA, in 1851 (notice no. 5024).

- The report of the birth of a child to an emigrant family bound from Belfast for San Francisco, giving the precise latitudinal and longitudinal coordinates (notice no. 5106).

- Marriages involving elderly brides and grooms (notices no. 1475, 1690, 1862, 1939, 2172, 3307, 3559, 4205, 4434, 4435) or, alternatively, "May-December" romances (nos. 1569, 4151, 5432, 5627).

- A marriage occurring after a courtship of only thirty-five days, in Ballymena, county Antrim (no. 4307).

- An attempt at wit, on the occasion of the marriage of John Frederick Pike, Esq., to Dorothea Fisher, of Sibton in the county of Suffolk, England (notice no. 4116), by the inclusion of the following poetic ditty:

   For years the Fisher tried with line and hook
   To take the finny tyrant of the brook;
   He nibbled—bit; the bait he seemed to like;
   He bit again and she secured the Pike.

- The expression of hope for better times, as the sufferings and misfortunes of the Great Famine diminished, in the notice (no. 4583) of the marriage of James Elden, of Clonmacash, to Esther M'Cadim, of Cloncore: "The splendid turnout of the wedding party brought to the recollection of the inhabitants of the parish the prosperous days of bygone times, and was considered by them a certain indication of returning prosperity to the country."

- An allusion to scandal in the notice for the marriage (no. 4574), in January 1851, at Niagara, Canada West, of G.G. Granville Munro, Esq. to Annie Hamilton, daughter of Captain George Vallancey Hamilton: "It will be remarkable in the recollection of newspaper readers, that a very remarkable and painful paragraph, involving the relatives of the parties whose union is here noticed, went the rounds of the entire press, a few months since." A later article, published in the December 12, 1850 edition of *The Armagh Guardian*, reveals the nature of this "painful" episode. It appears that Lieutenant Munro was attached to

Chapter 1: Introduction

Capt. Hamilton's company, and whilst stationed in Montreal, he paid marked attention to the Captain's daughter, eventually declaring his intention to marry her. After about three months, the Lieutenant disavowed his earlier promise, making quick his escape upon learning that the young lady, who was not only broken-hearted and wretched, but also confined to her bed, as an expectant mother. The case went to trial and, the jury finding a verdict of guilty, awarded £700 damages.

- Death notices that marked the passing of persons at a venerable old age (notices no. 224, 383, 515, 770, 838, 878, 1297, 1462, 1604, 1644, 2004, 2163, 2254, 2444, 2508, 2540, 2619, 2653, 2665, 2705, 2767, 2818, 2936, 2938, 2960, 3526, 3589, 3717, 3817, 3860, 4052, 4142, 4260, 4404, 4459, 4578, 4686, 4882, 4917, 4939, 4980, 5057, 5211, 5212, 5321, 5377, 5445, 5456, 5590, 5596, 5683, 5768, 5772, 5958, 5973, 6062, 6066, 6086, 6114, 6182, 6336, 6341, 6420). While most of these notices reported the deaths of centenarians between the ages of 100–110, three reported exceptional longevity of 145–150 years, which defies belief (notices no. 1297, 2767, 5596). Centenarianism has long been a source of fascination. The 1851 Census of Ireland recorded 711 persons aged 100 years and upwards. In 1861, Irish centenarians numbered 765 in a population of 5,798,967, whilst only 201 were counted in England in a population of 20,066,224—a ratio of nearly 14 centenarians in Ireland to just 1 in England. In 1851, the greatest age reported was 121 years, and in 1861, 120 years. After civil registration of vital events was introduced into Ireland in 1864, these deaths would continue to fascinate readers, and to warrant investigation and corroboration by the Registrars.

- Multiple deaths in families, within short periods of time (notices no. 1397, 1593, 2055, 2464, 2465, 2466, 2696, 2871, 2995, 3165, 3631, 3920, 4138, 4403, 4460, 4730, 5073, 6183, 6419). Causes of death were various: in 1849 near Belfast, a man and his wife, son, brother-in-law, nephew, and sister, of causes not reported (no. 2871); in 1849 at Clontarf, near Dublin, a man and his wife, and their servant, after a brief illness (no. 2995); in 1850 at Killygordon, county Donegal, two children, of scarletina (no. 3631); in 1850 at Portpatrick, Scotland, a man, his wife and two daughters, in the wreck of the ship, *Orien* (no. 3920); in 1850 at Derryvale, county Tyrone, two infant children, of scarletina (no. 4138); in 1850 at Sacramento, California, USA, eleven people, all natives of Ireland—five of cholera, two of diarrhoea, and four of unreported causes (no. 4460); in 1851 at New York, three children, of malignant scarletina (4730); and, in 1852 at Gayfield, county Derry, a woman and her two daughters, of causes not reported (no. 6183).

- The burial of a man, clad, at his request, in his first wife's wedding gown, at Kewstoke, Somerset, England (notice no. 4261).

- The curious cause of death recorded for a schoolmaster, of "cholera, brought on by excessive ball playing" (notice no. 2977).

- The death of a woman at Sheffield, England, while in receipt of parochial relief—yet who had property of £1,000 (notice no. 6128); and similarly, the death of a farmer at Greet, Gloucestershire, who appeared to live in poor circumstances yet, by the legacies of "some maiden ladies" had "managed to accumulate a large fortune, worth more than £100,000" (notice no. 5153).

- Arguably, the most poignant death notice (no. 3418) published in this run of *The Armagh Guardian*: "On 21st Dec. [1850], Samuel, youngest and last surviving child of Mr. Samuel Keightly, of Ballybofey, aged 18 years."

- Obituaries for persons of note in the county Armagh, including Samuel Magee, Esq., M.D., Medical Officer of the Dispensary at Keady (notice no. 24); Samuel M'Dowel, Esq., M.D., Surgeon to the Gaol and infirmary of county Monaghan (no. 25); Miss Mary Ann Waugh, of Armagh, a charitable benefactor (no. 41); the Rev. Bernard Loughran, P.P., of Annslough, near Middletown (no. 174); Dr. Oakman, of Ardross, a famous practitioner of medicine, who employed the mystery of charms; William Blacker, Esq. (no. 4274); and, Major Robert Innes Thornton (no. 4363).

- The death of an eccentric character, Hugh M'Culla, in College-street Armagh (no. 3683).

- A reference in the death notice (no. 5212) for Robert Porter, of Leckpatrick, co. Tyrone, to the notorious murder of Miss Mary Anne Knox, of Prehen, county Londonderry, who was shot by her lover, John MacNaughten, in 1761—as a means of fixing the year of Mr. Porter's birth and thus, his age at the time of his death in 1851, at 105 years.

- The passing of particularly industrious people, including: Samuel Parr, of Bolton, Lancashire, who, "during his leisure hours ... made 578 balloons, 103 pairs of small scales ... 1153 walking sticks, and 73 violins (notice no. 2543); Robert Rolston, at Callin-Turlagh, near Charlemont, who employed "upwards of 600 families in the different branches of the linen trade" (no. 2615); Arthur Mercer, a linen manufacturer of Portadown, who employed "upwards of 500 families" (notice no. 2788); and Elizabeth Porter, of Clones, county Monaghan, who taught the system of muslin embroidery, and worked as agent to the warehouse of Messrs. Hugh Brown & Co., of Glasgow, paying nearly £10,000 to women for work done in the neighbourhood of Clones (no. 3648).

- A genealogical outline for Robert Forrester, of Cloverhill, county Derry, dating to the siege of Derry in 1688, and further, to Scotland (notice no. 3651).

- Great respect accorded on the occasion of the funeral for Margaret M'Closkey, of Dungiven, county Derry, evidenced by a procession of 174 young women, who accompanied the remains of the deceased to the place of interment (notice no. 3061).

- Kindness of expression in the death notice (no. 4312) for John Cuming, of Leeson Terrace, Dublin: "A man of more amiable character, or one more generally esteemed, never breathed."

- A mysterious reference to court-room proceedings in the death notice (no. 5934) for A. Thompson, Esq., of Willoughby place, Enniskillen: "In 1830, Mr. Thompson was an extensive tobacco manufacturer, but having served as a juror after the Macken fight, in which a conviction was obtained, exclusive dealing induced him to give up business and retire into private life." This probably refers to a party, or sectarian, conflict that occurred at Macken, near Enniskillen, in July, 1829, three months after the passage of the *Catholic Emancipation Act*. As a result of this incident, several cases were tried. Arthur Thompson's name was recorded as one of the Petit Jurors, in the *King against Francis M'Brien, Ignatius M'Manus otherwise Storey*; a verdict of *Guilty* was returned against M'Manus, of *Not Guilty* for M'Brien.

- A public rebuke to the Queen, or her Government, or both, in the death notice (no. 5925) published for Jeffrey Hart Bent, Chief Justice, who died June 29, 1852 at Georgetown, Demerara: "So long a career of service, unrewarded by any mark of distinction from the Sovereign, is totally unprecedented."

Chapter 1: Introduction

- The death at Pas de Calais, France, of a man, aged 91 years, whose daily habits included imbibing an average of ten litres of beer (notice no. 4909).

- A death notice worthy of envy, that is, the retraction of the announcement of the death of William Kernaghan, formerly of Sligo, who was reported later by a relative to be "alive and well" (notice no. 6407).

- The apparent unlikelihood that a man was a medical doctor at the age of sixteen years, as reported in the death notice, published in December 1852, for John Smyth, Esq., M.D., of Belmont House, Stillorgan, county Dublin (notice no. 6423). A small monument in Irishtown Church contains the following inscription: "S.M. of John Smyth, A.M., M.D., T.C.D., of Belmont House, Stillorgan, Co. Dublin. Esteemed by his acquaintances, endeared to his friends, beloved by his family, through a life of varied usefulness his path was that of the just, 'as the shining light that shineth more and more unto the perfect day.' Released from his labours, he rested with his Redeemer, December 4th, 1852." A final clue is gleaned from death notices published in the *Medical Directory for Scotland*, in which John Smyth was recorded as having earned his B.M. and M.D. degrees in 1819 and 1832, respectively. It appears, therefore, that either the age of sixteen years, as reported by *The Armagh Guardian*, was a typographical error, or the age was communicated incorrectly to the editor.

- To conclude this list of "notable notices," the editor's favourite death notice (no. 3363), published January 7, 1850: "On 31st ult., Mr. James Kennedy, of Lurgan, famed for his good humour, and an inexhaustible fund of wit."

HOW TO USE THIS BOOK:

Transcripts—One of the objectives in the production of this volume was to produce faithful transcriptions from the newspaper record. This work includes just two exceptions to that rule: the insertion of transcriber's notes and editorial remarks, which are enclosed within [square parentheses]; and, editorial amendments, as discussed in the paragraph, *Editing and layout*.

Each transcript or extract in **Chapter 2, *Transcripts***, includes a reference, or unique identifier, to the original publication in the following format:

Article no. :: Ref. Date of issue (year-month-day); page & column numbers; D, M, or B.

The letter 'D' signifies a death notice, 'M' a marriage, and 'B' a birth. For example, the reference for the first notice in Chapter 2 is **No. 1 :: Ref. 1844-12-03, 2:3, M**—indicating that the compiler has assigned the number 1 to this Article, a marriage notice that was published in the December 3, 1844 edition, on page 2, column 3.

Indexes—The second objective in this work was to formulate convenient and useful finding aids, in the form of indexes, to assist readers in locating notices quickly and reliably. These indexes are sorted in three ways: by surname (**Chapter 3, *Index of Surnames***); by place name (***Chapter 4, Index of Place Names***); and, by institution or publication name (**Chapter 5, *Institution and Publication Index***). Given the number of spelling variants extant for many townlands, the place name index is offered as a finding aid. Not every BMD notice stated the county to which a townland belonged. For this, considerable use was made of the 1851 Townland

Index and other resources. Where there is doubt, readers should undertake their own study to ascertain county–townland combinations.

A wide array of institutions was indexed in this volume including asylums, banks and loan funds, boards of poor law guardians, canal companies, consulates and embassies, coach companies, convents, courts, gaols, government boards and departments, hospitals and infirmaries, hotels, inns and taverns, medical dispensaries, mercantile and industrial concerns, regiments of the British Army and of the Hon. East India Company, railway companies, the Royal Navy, schools and universities, ships, societies and associations, theatres, workhouses, and other organizations. Publications that were indexed include books, journals, legislation, newspapers (Irish, English, Canadian, and American), poems, and songs.

Please note that the numbers appearing in the indexes, i.e., in Chapters 3, 4, and 5, refer to Article numbers in **Chapter 2, *Transcripts***, not to page numbers.

Editing and layout—Simplicity, ease of reference, and readability were the primary rules used to produce and format these transcripts and indexes. The layout of the notices, as rendered in the original newspaper record, has not been reproduced in this book. For example, while the original newspaper record contains occasional capitalization of surnames, e.g., BURKE, this volume employs plain type for surnames, e.g., Burke. In addition, this compilation of transcripts italicizes the names of published works and of ships, a practice not always followed in the original newspaper record.

The compiler has exercised occasional editorial license. Examples include: the use of the editorial mark, [sic]; insertion of punctuation to improve readability (most often, in the form of a comma to separate the names of cities and counties); suggestions of alternative spellings within [square brackets]; clarification of the meaning of the phrases "same date" and "same place"; and, [illegible] or [?] to indicate uncertainty about the spelling of a word where, on occasion, the text was barely legible.

Errors and omissions—The vital events of only those who could afford to pay for a notice, or who were otherwise considered noteworthy, were recorded in *The Armagh Guardian* and other newspapers of the day. Thus, this work is neither either a complete survey or a representative sample of all the births, marriages, and deaths occurring in the county of Armagh between the years 1844–1852.

Great care and every reasonable effort have been taken to produce a comprehensive and reliable set of transcripts and indexes, supported by useful research notes, statistics and editorial annotations. However, because this work required analysis, interpretation and judgment, errors may have occurred, for which the compiler apologizes in advance. No matter how carefully designed and assembled, this book constitutes a secondary source. When in doubt, the original source record should be consulted as the final authority.

:: :: ::

Whether employed in the pursuit of family or local history research, or perused at leisure in an armchair, may this book also serve as a tribute to the memory of the people who were born in the county of Armagh, in neighbouring counties, and in Ireland generally—and perhaps, especially—the multitude who suffered during the famine years and whose names were not immortalized in *The Armagh Guardian* or other contemporary newspapers.

Chapter 1: Introduction

ABBREVIATIONS AND ACRONYMS:

A.B.	Bachelor of Arts degree, *Artium Baccalaureus*
A.C.	Assistant-Commissary (as in, Assistant-Commissary General)
A.D.C.	Aide-de-Camp
A.M.	Master of Arts degree, *Artium Magister*
B.D.	Bachelor of Divinity degree, *Baccalaureus Divinitatis*
Bart.	Baronet
C.B.	Companion of the Bath
C.C.	Catholic Curate
C.E.	Civil Engineer
C.P.	Constable of the Police (?) [ref. no. 3955]
Capt.	Captain
co., or Co.	County, or Company
Col.	Colonel
D.C.L.	Doctor of Civil Law degree; or, Doctor of Canon Law degree
D.D.	Doctor of Divinity degree, *Doctor Divinitatis*
D.E.	District Engineer?
D.L.	Deputy Lieutenant
E.I.C.	East India Company
Esq.	Esquire
F.R.C.S.	Fellow of the Royal College of Surgeons
F.R.C.S.I.	Fellow of the Royal College of Surgeons of Ireland
F.R.S.E.	Fellow of the Royal Society of Edinburgh
F.R.S.L.	Fellow of the Royal Society of London
F.S.A.	Fellow of the Society of Antiquities
F.T.C.D.	Fellow of Trinity College Dublin
G.C.B.	Knight (or Dame) Grand Cross
H.B.M.	Her Britannic Majesty's
H.E.I.C.S.	The Honourable East India Company's Service
H.M.	Her Majesty's
H.M.C.	Her Majesty's Customs
H.M.S.	Her Majesty's Ship
H.P.	Half-Pay
Hon.	The Honourable
I.R.	Inland Revenue
inst.	instant
J.P.	Justice of the Peace
K.C.B.	Knight Commander of the Bath
K.C.H.	Knight Commander of the Royal Guelphic Order
K H	Knight
K.R.	King's Royal (as in, King's Royal Rifles)
K.T.S.	Knights Templar Society (?) [ref. no. 6216]
Ky.	Kentucky
LL.B.	Bachelor of Laws degree, *Legum Baccalaureus*
LL.D., or L.L.D.	Doctor of Laws degree, *Legum Doctor*
L.R.C.S.I.	Licentiate of the Royal College of Surgeons of Ireland
Lieut.	Lieutenant
Lieut.-Col.	Lieutenant-Colonel
M.A.	Master of Arts degree, *Magister Artium*
M.B.	Bachelor of Medicine degree, *Medicinae Baccalaureus*
M.D.	Medical Doctor, *Medicinae Doctor*

Abbreviations and acronyms, continued:

M.N.I.	Madras Native Infantry
M.P.	Member of Parliament
M.R.C.S.	Member of the Royal College of Surgeons
M.R.C.S.E.	Member of the Royal College of Surgeons of Edinburgh
M.R.C.S.I.	Member of the Royal College of Surgeons of Ireland
M. Inst. C.E.	Member of the Institution of Civil Engineers
Maddle.	Mademoiselle
mercht.	merchant
Mus.Bac.	Bachelor of Music degree, *Musicae baccalaureus*
Mus.D.	Doctor of Music degree, *Musicae doctor*
N.B.	New Brunswick; or, North Britain (a 19th century appellation for Scotland)
N.H.	New Hampshire (USA)
N.I.	Native Infantry (of the Hon. East India Company Army)
Nn. Cunningham	Newtowncunningham (County Donegal)
Nn-Limavady	Newtownlimavady (County Derry)
Oxon.	Oxonia (University of Oxford)
P.L.C.	Poor Law Commissioner
P.L.G.	Poor Law Guardian
P.P.	Parish Priest
Pa.	Pennsylvania
Q.C.	Queen's Counsel
R.A.	Royal Artillery
R.C.	Roman Catholic
R.C.C.	Roman Catholic Curate
R.C.S.	Royal College of Surgeons
R.E.	Royal Engineers, Corps of
R.E.D.	?? [ref. no. 2859]
R.F.B.	Republican Flute Band (?) [ref. no. 757]
R.H.A.	Royal Horse Artillery
R.M.	Resident Magistrate
R.N.	Royal Navy
R.N.B.	Royal North Britain (as in, R.N.B. Regiment)
Regt.	Regiment
S.C.	Staff Corps
S.I.	Sub-inspector (Constabulary)
S.L.C.S.	?? [*See article no.* 3118]
Sergt.	Sergeant
sic	a Latin adverb, meaning 'as written', or 'intentionally so written'
T.C.D.	Trinity College Dublin
U.C.	Upper Canada (or, Canada West)
ult.	ultimo
V.G.	Vicar-General
V.S.	Veterinary Surgeon
Va.	Virginia

2. TRANSCRIPTS

No. 1 :: Ref. 1844-12-03, 2:3, M.
On Tuesday last, in the Parish Church of Kilmore, by the Rev. Edward M. Taylor, Wm. Langtry, of Moyallen, in the County of Down, Esq., to Catherine Isabella, youngest daughter of the late George Walker, of Annahill, in this county, Esq.

No. 2 :: Ref. 1844-12-03, 2:3, M.
On the 28th ult., by the Rev. Mr. O'Brian, R.C.C., Mr. John Fannon, of Monaghan, Merchant, to Miss Hughes, Thomas-street, Armagh.

No. 3 :: Ref. 1844-12-03, 2:3, M.
On the 25th ult., in Kilmore Church, by the Rev. E. M. Taylor, Mr. William Langtry, Strabane, to Catherine Isabella, only surviving daughter of the late George Walker, Annahilt, county Armagh, Esq.

No. 4 :: Ref. 1844-12-03, 2:3, D.
On the 27th ult., at the Savings' Bank, in her 82d year, Anne, relict of the late Christopher Christian, Esq., of this city.

No. 5 :: Ref. 1844-12-24, 3:1, B.
On the 16th instant, at 55, Mount-street, Park Lane, the Countess of Enniskillen of a son and heir.

No. 6 :: Ref. 1844-12-24, 3:1, B.
In Dublin, the lady of the Rev. John Stone, of a son.

No. 7 :: Ref. 1844-12-24, 3:1, D.
On the 15th instant, at Dungannon, of disease of the heart, aged 26 years, Anne, the beloved wife of Mr. George Moon, and daughter of Mr. Joseph Irvine.

No. 8 :: Ref. 1844-12-24, 3:1, D.
At Ballyshannon, on Sunday, the 15th instant, of typhus fever, Mr. William Beatty, for many years an active and zealous preacher in the Primitive Wesleyan Methodist connexion.

No. 9 :: Ref. 1844-12-31, 2:6, B.
On the 29th instant, Mrs. Gray, Vicar's Hill, of a daughter.

No. 10 :: Ref. 1844-12-31, 2:6, B.
December 29, at Hazlewood, the Lady Anne Wynne, of a son, still-born.

No. 11 :: Ref. 1844-12-31, 2:6, M.
On Thursday, the 24th instant, in the parish Church of Ramelton, by the Rev. William Welsh, the Rev. Edmund Maturin, Curate of Tartarahan, in the diocese of Armagh, to Elizabeth Catherine, second daughter of Dominick Persse, Esq., of Ramelton.

No. 12 :: Ref. 1844-12-31, 2:6, M.
On Sunday, the 29th instant, in Lurgan, by the Rev. Doctor O'Brien, P.P., Mr. John Hughes, of Armagh, to Eliza, daughter of the late Ephraim Byrne, of Lurgan.

No. 13 :: Ref. 1844-12-31, 2:6, M.
On the 24th instant, by the Rev. Henry Wallace, Mr. William L. Warnock, of Fountain-street, Londonderry, to Ellen, relict of the late Mr. John Campbell, of Coleraine.

No. 14 :: Ref. 1844-12-31, 2:6, M.
On the 19th instant, by the Rev. J. Thompson, Raphoe, Mr. John Duncan, to Mary, second daughter of Mr. Robert Craig, both of the Common.

No. 15 :: Ref. 1844-12-31, 2:6, D.
At Caledon, on Thursday, the 19th instant, Elizabeth A., youngest daughter of Mr. James Galbraith.

No. 16 :: Ref. 1844-12-31, 2:6, D.
December 18, at her residence, No. 6, Mortimer-street, Cavendish-square, London, Sarah, widow of the Right Hon. John Philpot Curran, some time Master of the Rolls in Ireland, at the advanced age of eighty-nine years.

No. 17 :: Ref. 1844-12-31, 2:6, D.
On the 20th instant, aged 23 years, at the residence of her father (Doctor Foster, Ballybofey,) Mary Annabella, the beloved wife of Robert Barclay, Esq., Ardarva-House, county Tyrone. Her entire life was devoted to the service of her God and Saviour. During a very protracted and trying illness she evidenced growing preparation for a blissful eternity; and she now, (it is assuredly hoped,) is employed in the pure devotions of the Church on high, clothed in robes washed and made white in the blood of the Lamb.

No. 18 :: Ref. 1845-01-07, 2:5, B.
In Moy, on Friday, the 3d instant, the lady of Thomas Martin, Esq., M.D. of a daughter.

No. 19 :: Ref. 1845-01-07, 2:5, M.
On the 31st December, by the Rev. James Wilson, Presbyterian Minister, Magherafelt, Mr. Lyttle Black, of Curnavathan, Cookstown, to Margaret Jane, eldest daughter of Mr. James Cathcart, Spring-lane, Magherafelt.

No. 20 :: Ref. 1845-01-07, 2:5, M.
On the 1st instant, by the Rev. James Morgan, Mr. James Glenn, merchant, Belfast, to Jane, third daughter of the late Mr. Robert Allen, Ann-street, Belfast.

No. 21 :: Ref. 1845-01-07, 2:5, D.

In Drumacmay, parish of Aghaloo, and county of Tyrone, on the 3d instant, at a very advanced age, Mrs. M'Kenna, mother of the Rev. John M'Kenna, the highly estimable Catholic Curate of Clonfeele.

No. 22 :: Ref. 1845-01-07, 2:5, D.

On Tuesday, 31st December last, the infant daughter of Mr. W. S. Hughes, of this city.

No. 23 :: Ref. 1845-01-07, 2:5, D.

On the 31st ultimo, Sarah, the beloved wife of Wm. Frazer, of Rushen, county Fermanagh, deeply and deservedly regretted by a numerous circle of friends and acquaintances.

No. 24 :: Ref. 1845-01-07, 2:5, D.

Death of Samuel Magee, Esq., M.D.—Suddenly, at his residence in Keady, on the 1st instant, Samuel Magee, Esq., M.D., aged 51, who for upwards of 29 years filled the responsible situation of Medical Officer to the Dispensary of that town, the arduous duties of which, he performed with skill and talent. The numerous concourse of persons, (from the High Sheriff of the county to the most humble individual,) that attended his remains to the grave, sufficiently attested the great estimation in which this lamented gentleman was held by all classes of society. In him the poor have indeed lost a considerable friend—and the gentry in the neighbourhood a Medical adviser in whom they reposed unbounded confidence; and with respect to the domestic circle, language fails to convey any idea of the grief there felt; where it need scarcely be said, his virtues were revered and his worth appreciated.

No. 25 :: Ref. 1845-01-07, 2:5, D.

Death of Dr. M'Dowel.—At his residence Townview, Monaghan, Jan. 2, Samuel M'Dowel, Esq., M.D., Fellow of the College of Physicians, Edinburgh, aged 77 years; during 40 of which he discharged the important duties of Surgeon to the county Gaol and infirmary. The permanent and valuable testimonials publicly conferred upon him by the guardians of these institutions, strongly attest their sentiments of respect, admiration, and esteem; to the afflicted inmates of these asylums he was the harbinger of consolation—the dispenser of relief and comfort—soothing the lot of the wretched, and mitigating the miseries of humanity; and oft did the faultering voice which wafted the accents of thanksgiving and adoration to the eternal throne of Grace and Mercy, commingle its holy aspirations in favour of him who was father, friend. In the walks of private life his unostentatious, yet periodic charities evinced a benevolent and humane mind, and long shall the widow and the the orphan deplore the loss they have sustained. Varied as were his qualities of head and heart, (and to the lot of few was assigned the happy combination,) pre-eminently was he distinguished in the hallowed circle of domestic life—in manners bland, in address urbane, courteous and dignified, a perfect exemplification of the gentleman of *"olden times"*—at his festive board did he draw from his rich and diversified intellectual store, to the improvement, gratification, and delight of his guests; the professional man retired truly proud of such a member, while all vied in collation of the virtues that adorned the character, and shed a lustre upon a life full of years and of honours.

"Esse, quam videri, maluet."

In accordance with a wish expressed by the deceased, his remains were borne to the grave by his brethren of the Masonic Order, amongst whom were the Rev. Allan Mitchel, Rector of Drumsna; John Johnstone, Esq., J.P., Thornhill; Mr. Temple, M.D; Thomas J. Tenison, Esq., J.P., Past Grand Aide-Camp of Knights Templars in Ireland; T. E. Wright, Esq., No. 50, Dublin, &c.—(*From a Correspondent.*)

No. 26 :: Ref. 1845-01-14, 2:6, M.

On Friday, the 10th instant, Mr. Ralph Dermott, to Miss M. Matchett, both of this city.

No. 27 :: Ref. 1845-01-14, 2:6, M.

December 25, at Moira Cottage, near Coburg, Canada, Thomas V. Tupper, Esq., of Cavanville, to Anna Sophia, daughter of Morgan Jellet, Esq., of Ballymena, county Antrim.

No. 28 :: Ref. 1845-01-14, 2:6, M.

December 14, at New York, by the Rev. Mr. May, Mr. Chas. E. Edgeworth, Dublin, to Miss Sara Parry, of Liverpool.

No. 29 :: Ref. 1845-01-14, 2:6, D.

At her residence, Northland row, Dungannon, on the 8th instant, Miss Isabell Graves, only surviving sister of the late Admirals Samuel, Sir Thomas, John, and Richard Graves.

No. 30 :: Ref. 1845-01-14, 2:6, D.

January 4, at his residence, Auburn, county Dublin, Andrew Crawford, Esq., most sincerely and deservedly lamented.

No. 31 :: Ref. 1845-01-14, 2:6, D.

November 10, at Nolapore, India, of cholera, after three days' illness, Ensign George John Weld, of her Majesty's 22d Regiment of Infantry, second son of George Weld, Esq., of Leagram Hall, near Preston, Lancashire, and nephew of Joseph Weld, Esq., of Lulworth Castle.

No. 32 :: Ref. 1845-01-14, 2:6, D.

At Blackrock, Cork, aged 72 years, George Foot, Esq., barrister-at-law.

No. 33 :: Ref. 1845-01-14, 2:6, D.

January 6, in Lower Dominick-street, Dublin, Alexander, the infant son of Daniel Auchinleck, Esq., of Crevenagh House, Omagh.

No. 34 :: Ref. 1845-01-14, 2:6, D.

At St. John's [sic], New Brunswick, on the 7th December, after a long and painful illness, Mr. William Wilson, in the 82d year of his age. He was a native of St. Johnston, county Donegal, Ireland.

No. 35 :: Ref. 1845-01-14, 2:6, D.

On Friday, the 10th instant, in Shipquay-street, after an illness of less than 24 hours, most deeply and deservedly regretted by a large circle of friends and acquaintances, Eliza, eldest daughter, unmarried, of David Webster, Esq., Manager of the Provincial Bank, Derry.

No. 36 :: Ref. 1845-01-14, 2:6, D.

In the 79th year of his age, Michael Meegan, of Mount-stewart, near Clogher, in the county of Tyrone.

No. 37 :: Ref. 1845-01-14, 2:6, D.

At Milltown, parish of Ardstraw, David Love, Esq., Lieutenant of the 1st Strule corps of Yeomanry, who loved him for his straightforward, upright, liberal principles. He was a sound Protestant, orthodox Presbyterian, and a lover of truth, and spurned the idea of contending about Church ceremonies and creed; in a word,

He was the staunch unflinching friend,
Whose object was truth's holy word to read,
When bigots raged against each other's creed.

No. 38 :: Ref. 1845-01-21, 2:4, M.

January 14, in St. Anne's Church, by the Rev. Mr. Bredin, Mr. Charles Graham, of Enniskillen, to Sarah, youngest daughter of Mr. John Green, of Wicklow-street, Dublin.

No. 39 :: Ref. 1845-01-21, 2:4, D.

In this city, on the 14th instant, aged 9 years, Margaret Alicia, daughter of Mr. Grattan, Surgeon Dentist. She was a child possessed of great amiability and sweetness of temper, and her loss is severely felt by her sorrowing parents.

No. 40 :: Ref. 1845-01-21, 2:4, D.

Yesterday evening, aged 19, Miss Anne Rickards, second daughter of James Rickard, of this city, Esq.

No. 41 :: Ref. 1845-01-21, 2:4, D.

On yesterday morning, at 11 o'clock, Miss Mary Anne Waugh, of this city, aged 58. Few persons have departed this life of late years in Armagh whose loss will be so severely felt as that of Miss Waugh. Possessing, in a great degree, the means of doing good, she practically enforced the doctrine—"*where there is much, much should be given*"—and seemed to derive her greatest happiness from sharing the wealth which Providence allotted her, with the needy and the destitute; nor did her desire to do good rest with the mere exercise of her many unostentatious charities. The humble and struggling artisan—the industrious widowed mother, the child of better days, but of fortune's reverses, had but to make their wants known to her to obtain the means of relief. To all our public charities and institutions she was a most munificent contributor; and as a landlady she was kind and considerate. As a neighbour, the marks of general sympathy throughout the city attest how much she is regretted. For a length of time previous to her death, Miss Waugh endured great bodily suffering with Christian fortitude, and in her latest breath testified a lively hope of a glorious immortality through faith in the Lord Jesus. Her labours of love [are] now ended; but it is consoling to know that a rich reward awaits her in another and a better world, whither she has gone to prove how truly "*Blessed are the dead which die in the Lord.*"

No. 42 :: Ref. 1845-01-21, 2:4, D.

Suddenly, in Newry, on last Monday evening, Mr. Daniel Bannon, owner of the *Shamrock* Steamer.

No. 43 :: Ref. 1845-01-28, 2:5, B.

On the 27th inst., the lady of James Stanley, Esq., of this city, of a daughter.

No. 44 :: Ref. 1845-01-28, 2:5, B.

At Enniskillen, the lady of Captain Ovens, 57th Regiment, of a daughter.

No. 45 :: Ref. 1845-01-28, 2:5, M.

January 23, in York-street Chapel, by the Rev. Dr. Urwick, the Rev. Samuel Shaw, of Moy, to Jane, fourth daughter of the late Richard Milliken, Esq.

No. 46 :: Ref. 1845-01-28, 2:5, D.

On the 17th inst., in her 69th year, Ellen, relict of the late Rev. Doctor Henry of Randalstown, daughter of the late Pooley Shuldham, Esq., Moigh House, county Longford, and mother of the present Rev. Dr. Henry of this city. Her remains have been interred in the grave of her well known and highly respected husband.

No. 47 :: Ref. 1845-01-28, 2:5, D.

January 23, at Lough Eske, Donegal, the residence of her nephew, Thomas Brooke, Esq., Mrs. Young, relict of the Rev. John Young, Killishil, county Tyrone.

No. 48 :: Ref. 1845-01-28, 2:5, D.

At his residence in Verner-street, Belfast, on the 21st inst., Mr. John M'Leod, aged 64 years.

No. 49 :: Ref. 1845-01-28, 2:5, D.

Of inflammation of the lungs, at the age of three years and five months, Albert, son of the Rev. James Beatty, Dundalk.

No. 50 :: Ref. 1845-01-28, 2:5, D.
After a protracted illness, the wife of Dr. Joseph Murphy, of Clones.

No. 51 :: Ref. 1845-01-28, 2:5, D.
At Aughareny, near Dungannon, Mr. Henry Irwin, in the 84th year of his age. He was a consistent member of the Wesleyan Methodist Society for upwards of 60 years.

No. 52 :: Ref. 1845-01-28, 2:5, D.
At Markethill, on the 24th inst., Mr. John Archer, aged 69 years.

No. 53 :: Ref. 1845-02-04, 2:6, B.
January 25, in St. George's-place, Dublin, Lady Ernest Bruce, of a son.

No. 54 :: Ref. 1845-02-04, 2:6, B.
At Kilbride, the Lady of the Rev. Ogle Moore, Vicar of Blesinton, of a daughter.

No. 55 :: Ref. 1845-02-04, 2:6, B.
On Tuesday morning, the 28th ult., the Lady of John Stanley, jun., Esq., of a daughter.

No. 56 :: Ref. 1845-02-04, 2:6, B.
At Dungannon, county Tyrone, the lady of Edward Sinclair, Esq., of twins.

No. 57 :: Ref. 1845-02-04, 2:6, B.
Jan. 27, at Fort William, county of Cavan, the Lady of T. Coote, Esq., D.L., of a son.

No. 58 :: Ref. 1845-02-04, 2:6, M.
On the 30th ult., at St. Patrick's Cathedral, in this city, by the Rev. Richard Quin, Hugh Boyle, of Killeen Cottage, Esq., to Jane Josephine, eldest daughter of Osborne Kidd, Esq. Immediately after the ceremony the happy couple set off for Dublin to spend the honeymoon.

No. 59 :: Ref. 1845-02-04, 2:6, M.
Jan. 30, in St. Thomas's Church, Dublin, by the Venerable Archdeacon Magee, John Baird, of Ballymena, in the county of Antrim, merchant, to Frances, daughter of the late Alexander Sheane, Esq., of Roscrea, in the county of Tipperary, deceased.

No. 60 :: Ref. 1845-02-04, 2:6, M.
On the 1st inst., by the Rev. Richard O'Brien, P.P., Mr. Bernard Branigan, merchant of this city, to Margaret, daughter of Mr. James Salley, of Tullynickle, in this county.

No. 61 :: Ref. 1845-02-04, 2:6, M.
In Charlemont Church, by the Rev. James Disney, Mr. John Craig, of Cor, to Catherine, youngest daughter of Mr. Daniel Wilson, of Legor Hill.

No. 62 :: Ref. 1845-02-04, 2:6, D.
January 30, at Fitzgibbon-street, Dublin, aged 17 years, Katherine, second daughter of John Irvine of Rockfield, county Fermanagh, Esq.

No. 63 :: Ref. 1845-02-04, 2:6, D.
January 26, suddenly, at Crofton Terrace, Kingstown, aged 73 years, Martha, relict of Rev. John Alexander, of Drumreany Glebe, in the county of Westmeath.

No. 64 :: Ref. 1845-02-04, 2:6, D.
At Elm Cottage, Portadown, Ann, wife of Lieut. Hickland.

No. 65 :: Ref. 1845-02-04, 2:6, D.
At Annaguinea, near Dungannon, on Friday, the 24th inst., aged 16 years, John, third son of James Young, Esq.

No. 66 :: Ref. 1845-02-11, 2:6, B.
February 7, at Fox-hall, in the county of Donegal, the lady of John Chambers, Esq., of a son.

No. 67 :: Ref. 1845-02-11, 2:6, B.
February 7, the lady of Captain A. L. Corry, of H.M.S. *Superb*, of a daughter.

No. 68 :: Ref. 1845-02-11, 2:6, M.
February 7, at St. Mark's Church, by the Rev. Robert Haig, Mr. James Nugent, to Miss Elizabeth Irwin, both of this city.

No. 69 :: Ref. 1845-02-11, 2:6, M.
January 27, in Castleblayney, by the Rev. J. Black, the brother-in-law of the bride, Alexander William Lee, of Ivey Farm, Esq., nephew of William Lee, of Cloghog House, in the county Tyrone, Esq., to Charlotte, second daughter of the late Alexander Neale Little, of Stewartstown, Esq.

No. 70 :: Ref. 1845-02-11, 2:6, D.
February 7, at Moy, after a lingering and severe illness, borne with christian fortitude and pious resignation, Annabella, the beloved wife of Robert Crothers, Esq., Surgeon, and daughter of the late Alexr. Maclaurin, Esq., of Greenock.

No. 71 :: Ref. 1845-02-11, 2:6, D.
January 31st, at the residence of his brother-in-law, Morris Wilson Knox, Esq., Littlemount, Francis White, Esq., in the 26th year of his age.—He was a gentleman of the most amiable disposition—his premature removal has been the source of great regret to a numerous circle of friends and acquaintances.

No. 72 :: Ref. 1845-02-11, 2:6, D.
February 8, at his residence, Tanagh, county Monaghan, Captain Charles Dawson, D.L., J.P.

No. 73 :: Ref. 1845-02-18, 2:6, B.
In this city, on the 16th inst., the Lady of John Cuming, Esq., Berresford Row, of a daughter.

No. 74 :: Ref. 1845-02-18, 2:6, D.
On Sunday morning, the 16th inst., after a long and painful illness which she bore with christian fortitude

and patient resignation, Mrs. Jane Reilly, widow of the late Mr. William Reilly, of Drummond, near this city.

No. 75 :: Ref. 1845-02-25, 2:6, M.
Feb. 13, in the parish Church of Cappagh, by the Rev. H. H. Harte, Rector, Montgomery Armstrong, of the Island of Innishmore, Lough Erne, county Fermanagh, Esq., to Sarah, daughter of John Buchanan, Esq., Bunnynubber, near Omagh.

No. 76 :: Ref. 1845-02-25, 2:6, M.
Feb. 13, at the parish Church of Forkhill, by the Rev. Dr. Campbell, Henry Stanley, Esq., M.D., fourth son of John Stanley, Esq., of Armagh, to Francis Grace, only daughter of Captain Robinson, Sub-Inspector of Revenue Police.

No. 77 :: Ref. 1845-02-25, 2:6, M.
In St. Mark's Church, yesterday, by the Rev. Robert Haig, Mr. James Stoops of Killuney, to Miss Isabella Elliott, Palace, Armagh.

No. 78 :: Ref. 1845-02-25, 2:6, D.
On the 9th inst., at 12, Holland-street, Westminster, London, Mr. William Jackson, Merchant, late of Moy, county Tyrone.

No. 79 :: Ref. 1845-02-25, 2:6, D.
On the 10th inst., at Caledon, Jane, widow of the late Mr. Thomas Moore.

No. 80 :: Ref. 1845-02-25, 2:6, D.
Feb. 7, at Southampton, Charlotte, daughter of Charles Leslie, Esq., formerly of Glasslough, County Monaghan, aged 66.

No. 81 :: Ref. 1845-03-04, 3:5, M.
On the 24th ult., by the Rev. Robert Shields, Mr. David Shields, Killycairn, to Mary Anne, daughter of Mr. William Barber, Tyronesditches.

No. 82 :: Ref. 1845-03-04, 3:5, M.
On Thursday the 27th ult., in Charlemont Church, by the Rev. James Disney, Isabella, daughter of Robert Corrigan, of Moss-spring, Charlemont, Esq., to George Wilford, of ... [illegible].

No. 83 :: Ref. 1845-03-11, 3:1, B.
On the 5th inst., in this City, the lady of Alexander Lane, Esq., M.D., R.N., of a daughter.

No. 84 :: Ref. 1845-03-11, 3:1, M.
At Richhill, by the Rev. Mr. Hogan, Mr. Wm. Donaldson, to Mary Jane, daughter of Constable Holland, both of Richhill.

No. 85 :: Ref. 1845-03-11, 3:1, M.
In same place, by the Rev. Mr. Hogan, Thomas Cully, Esq., to Jane, daughter of Mr. George Rowan.

No. 86 :: Ref. 1845-03-11, 3:1, M.
On the 4th inst., in St. George's Church, Dublin, by the Rev. Gibson Black, the Rev. Joseph Druit, incumbent of Clope, County Meath, only son of the late Rev. Joseph Druit, Vicar of Denn, County Cavan, to Jane Anne, eldest daughter of Charles Thorp, Esq., of Nelson-street, Dublin.

No. 87 :: Ref. 1845-03-11, 3:1, D.
On the 25th ult., at his residence, Warrington, England, in the prime of life, James Clarke Reid, Esq., merchant, formerly of the county Armagh.

No. 88 :: Ref. 1845-03-11, 3:1, D.
On Sunday the 2nd inst., aged 13 months, Margaret, youngest daughter of Francis Carvill, Esq., Newry.

No. 89 :: Ref. 1845-03-18, 3:1, D.
On Saturday, the 5th inst., at the residence of her son, Thomas A. Prentice, Esq., of this City, Eliza, relict of the late George Prentice, Esq., and daughter of the Rev. Archibald Kidd, late rector of Jonesborough.

No. 90 :: Ref. 1845-03-18, 3:1, D.
On the 7th inst., in Derry, Elizabeth, relict of the late Rev. John Graham, of Magilligan Glebe.

No. 91 :: Ref. 1845-03-18, 3:1, D.
On the 12th inst., at Trevor Hill, Captain Ogle, aged 70 years, late Paymaster of the Armagh Militia.

No. 92 :: Ref. 1845-03-18, 3:1, D.
At Firgrove, Tanderagee, aged 55 years, Jane, relict of the late Robert Henderson, Esq.

No. 93 :: Ref. 1845-03-18, 3:1, D.
On the 11th inst., at her residence, of puerperal fever, Jane, the beloved wife of Dr. Collins, of Keady.

No. 94 :: Ref. 1845-03-18, 3:1, D.
On the 11th inst., William Henry, Esq., of Islandbridge, Dublin.

No. 95 :: Ref. 1845-03-25, 2:6, M.
On the 18th instant, at Kilkeel Church, by the Rev. J. F. Close, Rector, Mr. George M'Cracken, Newry, to Jane, eldest daughter of the late Mr. John Wright, Kilkeel.

No. 96 :: Ref. 1845-03-25, 2:6, M.
On the 17th instant, at Killyman Church, by the Rev. Wm. Quain, George Stewart, Esq., Belfast, to Elizabeth, daughter of the late David Scott, Esq., Dublin.

No. 97 :: Ref. 1845-03-25, 2:6, M.
On the 12th instant, at Hillsborough church, by the Venerable Archdeacon Mant, Mr. Richard Evans, chemist, Manchester, to Eliza, youngest daughter of the late Mr. Joseph Gilmore, Belfast.

No. 98 :: Ref. 1845-03-25, 2:6, M.
On the 15th instant, by the Rev. A. G. Ross, of Markethill, Mr. William Kitson, of Brackley, to Miss Turner, of Corhammock, county Armagh.

No. 99 :: Ref. 1845-03-25, 2:6, M.

March 20, in Middletown Church, by the Rev. Thos. Jervis White, Thomas, eldest son of the late James Wensley Bond, of Cartronard, in the county of Longford, Esq., to Charlotte Stanley, eldest daughter of Henry Coote Bond, of Bondville, in the county of Armagh, Esq.

No. 100 :: Ref. 1845-03-25, 2:6, D.

On the 11th inst., Mrs. Stewart, of Hillhall, near Lisburn. The deceased was the daughter of the late Rev. S. Edgar, of Loughagery, and sister to the Rev. S. Edgar, of Armagh.—The disorder, which terminated in her dissolution, was tedious and distressing. This, however, she bore with distinguished resignation, founded on the atonement of Emanuel, the only ground of hope, and on the prospect of immortality, the only source of consolation in the hour of death. In her life, she was cheerful, pious, and affectionate, full of information, and excelling in conversation. She was, in consequence, the delight of her many friends and acquaintances. She has escaped through the dark portals of death to the regions of endless life, and light, and glory.

No. 101 :: Ref. 1845-03-25, 2:6, D.

Suddenly, at Armagh, on the 20th instant, Hesse Jane, the beloved wife of Robert Turle, Esq., organist of the Armagh Cathedral and daughter of the late Thomas Greer, of Belfast, Esq., deeply and sincerely regretted by a numerous circle of sorrowing friends.

No. 102 :: Ref. 1845-04-01, 3:6, B.

March 25, at No. 6, Mountjoy-square, East, the lady of Wm. Humphreys, Esq., of Ballyhaise House, county of Cavan, of a daughter.

No. 103 :: Ref. 1845-04-01, 3:6, M.

On the 29th ult., at Maguiresbridge, by the Rev. T. W. Rowe, John Nixon, Esq., Garrohill, to Miss Margaret Smyth, Littlehill, near Maguiresbridge.

No. 104 :: Ref. 1845-04-01, 3:6, M.

On the 27th ult., by the Rev. Wm. Sweeney, Presbyterian Minister of Croghan, Wm. C. M'Bride, Esq. of Alistragh, Armagh, to Mary Jane, daughter of Charles Magee, Esq., Tully, Killesandra.

No. 105 :: Ref. 1845-04-01, 3:6, M.

On the 26th ult., in the parish church of Kilmore, by the Rev. Henry Cobb, Mr. John Hutchinson, eldest son of Mr. Samuel Hutchinson, Fruithill, to Miss Maria, only daughter of Mr. William Morison, Willmount, both of the county Armagh.

No. 106 :: Ref. 1845-04-01, 3:6, M.

On the 19th ult., in Templemahery Church, by the Rev. M. Burke, Mr. James Jones, of Drumboe, near Lowtherstown, to Elizabeth, youngest daughter of Mr. Robert Evans, of Glenarn, near Lack.

No. 107 :: Ref. 1845-04-01, 3:6, M.

March 22, in Tynan Church, by the Rev. Thomas Gervis White, Robert Todd Houston, Esq., Fellow of the Royal College of Surgeons in Ireland, to Mary, widow of the late Dr. Allan, and only child of the late Captain Moore, of Drummond, county of Tyrone.

No. 108 :: Ref. 1845-04-01, 3:6, M.

On the 25th ult., at Honeybark, by the Rev. William Emslie, of the Free Church, Inch, George Troup, Esq., of the *Banner of Ulster*, to Helen, third daughter of William Emslie, Esq., merchant, Aberdeen.

No. 109 :: Ref. 1845-04-01, 3:6, M.

On the 27th ult., at Keady, by the bride's father, the Rev. Henry Jackson Dobbin, of Ballymena, to Anne, daughter of the Rev. Joseph Jenkins.

No. 110 :: Ref. 1845-04-01, 3:6, M.

On the 25th ult., by the Rev. Dr. Edgar, William Moffat, Esq., M.D., of Belfast, to Mary, eldest daughter of the Rev. Thomas Heron, of Springbank, County Derry.

No. 111 :: Ref. 1845-04-01, 3:6, M.

On the 24th inst., in the Cathedral of Lisburn, by the Very Rev. the Dean of Ross, Mr. Arthur Morgan, to Catherine, daughter of Mr. James Vernon, both of Lisburn.

No. 112 :: Ref. 1845-04-01, 3:6, D.

On the 31st ult., at Avon Lodge, Armagh, Major Thomas Shaw, aged 75 years, universally respected and regretted.

No. 113 :: Ref. 1845-04-01, 3:6, D.

On Friday last, in Thomas-street, in this city, Mr. Hans Gordon, after an illness of only two days.

No. 114 :: Ref. 1845-04-15, 3:5, B.

On the 6th inst., at Armagh, the lady of Henry H. Dickson, Esq., of a daughter.

No. 115 :: Ref. 1845-04-15, 3:5, M.

In St. Patrick's Cathedral, Armagh, on Wednesday, 9th inst., John, fourth son of Wm. Armstrong, Esq., of Lurgan, to Marian, eldest daughter of John Cardwell, Esq., of Tullyelmer, in this county.

No. 116 :: Ref. 1845-04-15, 3:5, M.

On the 10th instant, by the Rev. S. Edgar, Minister of the Second Presbyterian Congregation of Armagh, Mr. W. Platt, to Martha, daughter of Mr. J. Brooks, both in the vicinity of Armagh. This license was the first granted by the Rev. L.D. Elliot, Licenser to the Presbytery of Armagh, and the marriage, it appears, was the first celebrated according to the new marriage act in the Presbyterian Church of Ireland.

No. 117 :: Ref. 1845-04-15, 3:5, M.

On the 2d inst., at St. Peter's church, Dublin, by the Rev. Elias Handcock, the Rev. Benedict Arthure, rector of St. Laurence, Isle of Wight, to Bessie Maria, daughter of the late B. Dillon of Ballyquin house, county of Kilkenny, Esq.

No. 118 :: Ref. 1845-04-15, 3:5, M.
In the parish church, Ballyshannon, on Monday last, by the Rev. Mr. Tuthill, Henry Lipsett, Esq., to Mary, third daughter of Andrew Macintyre, Esq., both of Ballyshannon.

No. 119 :: Ref. 1845-04-15, 3:5, D.
At his father's house, Bloomvale near Lurgan, John, only son of Mr. Robert Gaskin, after a lingering illness, which he bore with exemplary patience, and pious resignation to the Divine will.

No. 120 :: Ref. 1845-04-15, 3:5, D.
April 4, at Merrion-avenue, county Dublin, Meriel Anne, relict of James Kearney, Esq.

No. 121 :: Ref. 1845-04-15, 3:5, D.
On the 27th ult., at Loughlan House, county Cavan, Robert Algeo, Esq., after a short illness.

No. 122 :: Ref. 1845-04-22, 3:2, B.
At Rokeby-green, Mall, in this city, on the morning of Monday the 14th inst., Mrs. John M'Connell of a daughter.

No. 123 :: Ref. 1845-04-22, 3:2, M.
April 12, in Donaghmore Presbyterian meeting-house, by the Rev. Verner M. White, of Liverpool, Maxwell, youngest son of the late Thomas Simpson, Esq., Beechhill, county of Armagh, to Mary, second daughter of the late Samuel Martin, Esq., of Longhorne, county of Down.

No. 124 :: Ref. 1845-04-22, 3:2, M.
April 15, in St. Thomas's church, Thomas Smyth, Esq., Solicitor, to Alicia Rachel, eldest daughter of the late Jeremy Marsh, Esq., Captain, 90th regiment.

No. 125 :: Ref. 1845-04-22, 3:2, M.
April 16, at Clonakilty Church, by the Rev. John Quarry, the Rev. Horace J. Townsend, of Seagoe, in this county, to Agnes, youngest daughter of the late Richard N. Somerville, Esq., of Baltimore, county Cork.

No. 126 :: Ref. 1845-04-22, 3:2, D.
On the 16th inst., at Woodpark, Lucinda Margaret, eldest daughter of Acheson St. George, Esq., Treasurer of this County.

No. 127 :: Ref. 1845-04-22, 3:2, D.
On the 17th inst., in Lower English-street, in this city, Dr. Bampfield, Surgeon in the 32d regiment of foot, aged 64 years, leaving a widow and four children, one of whom is in the first royals. His remains were yesterday conveyed to the grave yard of St. Mark's, and interred with military honours.

No. 128 :: Ref. 1845-04-22, 3:2, D.
On the 20th inst., after a short illness, at Tullymacone House, near Keady, in the 77th year of her age, Miss Ann M'Bride. She was a steady and consistent member of the Wesleyan Methodist Society, and received the inestimable blessing of redemption in the blood of Jesus—the forgiveness of sins—lived under its salutary and saving influence for the space of 50 years, and died rejoicing, with the assured confidence and blooming hope of a glorious immortality.

No. 129 :: Ref. 1845-04-22, 3:2, D.
On the 21st inst., at Portadown, Mary Anne, the beloved wife of Mr. Thomas Sinnamon, Merchant, aged 73 years; deservedly regretted by a numerous circle of friends and relatives.

No. 130 :: Ref. 1845-04-29, 3:5, M.
On the 19th inst., in St. Anne's Church, Belfast, by the Rev. R. Oulton, James Hamilton Stitt, grandson of the late Rev. William Stitt, Dungannon, to Catherine, eldest daughter of the late John Porter, Belfast.

No. 131 :: Ref. 1845-04-29, 3:5, M.
At Lurgan Church, by the Rev. William Falloon, Incumbent of St. John's, Liverpool, Edward Leslie Falloon, Esq., Surgeon &c., 17, Stafford-street, Liverpool, third son of the Rev. M. Falloon, Rector of Layde, Cushendall, to Eliza, third daughter of Joseph Breedon, Esq., Surgeon, R.N., Standstead-plain, Canada.

No. 132 :: Ref. 1845-04-29, 3:5, M.
In St. Peter's Church, on the 23d inst., by the Rev. J. Quinn, Robert Gee, of Hollywood, Cheshire, Esq., to Elizabeth, daughter of the late Trevor Corry, of Newry, Esq.

No. 133 :: Ref. 1845-04-29, 3:5, M.
At St. Mary's Church, on the 23d instant, by the Rev. James Wilson, D. D., Precentor of St. Patrick's Cathedral, William Palmer, Esq., Stock Broker, fourth son of Abraham Palmer, Esq., of Lower Dominick-street, Dublin, to Emma Margaret, only daughter of William Burnside, Esq., Stratford, Co. Wicklow, and niece of John Henderson, Esq., Agnesville, Co. Down.

No. 134 :: Ref. 1845-04-29, 3:5, M.
In Clones Church, on the 18th inst., by the Rev. Charles Welch, Mr. James Elliot, only son of Mr. Andrew Elliot, of Rosbick, to Mary Anne, third daughter of Mr. Wm. Kenedy, deceased, of Carneyharne, county Fermanagh.

No. 135 :: Ref. 1845-04-29, 3:5, D.
On Friday, the 25th inst., at half-past three p.m., Master Charles George Jackson, aged 14 years, third son of Thomas Jackson, Esq., Asylum, Armagh. For some time past the deceased had suffered much affliction, which he bore with Christian fortitude and resignation, so much so that the bereavement of his sorrowing parents is in a great degree alleviated by the consoling thought that he is gone to show *"how sweet the flower in Paradise would bloom."*

No. 136 :: Ref. 1845-04-29, 3:5, D.
Suddenly on Monday last, in this town, aged 23 years, of disease of the heart, Eliza, eldest daughter of Mr. Patrick M'Sharry, of Callon-street.

No. 137 :: Ref. 1845-04-29, 3:5, D.
On the 23d inst., at Tandragee, Mary, relict of the late Mr. James Acheson, in the 74th year of her age.

No. 138 :: Ref. 1845-04-29, 3:5, D.
In this city, aged 42 years, Mr. John Gribben, builder, and proprietor of the marble-yards and quarries in the vicinity of this city.

No. 139 :: Ref. 1845-04-29, 3:5, D.
April 20, after a long and painful illness, George Beresford Dawson, late of the Rifle Brigade, and second son of the Right Hon. George R. Dawson.

No. 140 :: Ref. 1845-04-29, 3:5, D.
April 21, at Manor Highgate, county Fermanagh, Kate Isabella, daughter of Captain W. B. M'Clintock, R.N., aged one year and five months.

No. 141 :: Ref. 1845-04-29, 3:5, D.
On Friday, the 18th inst., Mr. William Maxwell, of Glasmullagh, near Lowtherstown.

No. 142 :: Ref. 1845-04-29, 3:5, D.
On the 18th inst., at Blackwatertown, aged 30 years, Jane, wife of Mr. Wm. Elliott, Primitive Wesleyan Missionary and Teacher, late of Ballsmill.

No. 143 :: Ref. 1845-04-29, 3:5, D.
On the 14th inst., at Forquay [sic], in the 34th year of his age, Daniel Wilson, Esq., Solicitor, eldest son of the late James Wilson, Esq., Clerk of the Crown, county Tyrone.

No. 144 :: Ref. 1845-05-06, 3:1, B.
April 22d, at Portadown, the lady of Robert Ball Colhoun, Esq., M.D., of a son.

No. 145 :: Ref. 1845-05-06, 3:1, B.
April 25, the lady of Thomas Henry Harpur, Esq., of Goerstown, Moy, of a son.

No. 146 :: Ref. 1845-05-06, 3:1, B.
April 25, in Enniskillen, the lady of Wm. Ovenden, Esq., of a son, still-born.

No. 147 :: Ref. 1845-05-06, 3:1, B.
April 29, at Stewartstown, the lady of John Little, Esq., of a son.

No. 148 :: Ref. 1845-05-06, 3:1, B.
April 29, at Lurgan, the lady of William Armstrong, jun., Esq., of a daughter.

No. 149 :: Ref. 1845-05-06, 3:1, M.
On the 22d. ult., in Connor Church, by the Rev. Mr. Hobson, Mr. Alexander Harman, Merchant, of Enniskillen, to Mary, youngest daughter of Henry Martin, Esq., Aughnacloy, county Tyrone.

No. 150 :: Ref. 1845-05-06, 3:1, D.
April 26, at Portadown, of apoplexy, Robert Ball Calhoun, Esq., M.D.

No. 151 :: Ref. 1845-05-06, 3:1, D.
On Sunday, the 27th of April, in Eden, Enniskillen, Mr. Cockran, aged 60 years.

No. 152 :: Ref. 1845-05-06, 3:1, D.
On the 26th ult., at Bell-Hill, after a short illness, John Armstrong, Esq., in the 76th year of his age.

No. 153 :: Ref. 1845-05-06, 3:1, D.
In his 37th year, Mr. John Lipsett, son of Mr. Thomas Lipsett, Ballyshannon—a gentleman universally regretted by all who knew him.

No. 154 :: Ref. 1845-05-06, 3:1, D.
At the residence of her son, Dr. Mervyn Crawford, Upper Berkeley-street, London, aged 78 years, Elizabeth, relict of Alexander Crawford, Esq., formerly of Miltown House, near Dublin, and of Millwood, county Fermanagh.

No. 155 :: Ref. 1845-05-06, 3:1, D.
Deeply regretted, Jane Maria, the wife of Mr. Wm. Scott, draper, Omagh, in the county of Tyrone, and fourth daughter of the late Jerald Lloyd, Esq., Munville, in the county of Fermanagh, in the 27th year of her age.

No. 156 :: Ref. 1845-05-13, 3:2, B.
On Wednesday, the 30th April, the lady of James M. Ross, Esq., Church-square, Monaghan, of a daughter.

No. 157 :: Ref. 1845-05-13, 3:2, M.
On the 2nd inst., at Ballynahinch Church, by the Rev. Charles Boyd, Mr. William Davison, of Banbridge, to Miss Isabella Chambers, daughter of the late Robert Chambers, Esq., of Ballynahinch.

No. 158 :: Ref. 1845-05-13, 3:2, D.
Yesterday, in Russell-street, Mr. John Noble, aged 19 years. The death of this promising young man is a source of deep regret to a numerous circle of friends and acquaintances.

No. 159 :: Ref. 1845-05-13, 3:2, D.
On Wednesday, the 7th inst., suddenly, at his residence, Gorthaloghan, near Enniskillen, Mr. Crozier Beatty, a highly respectable farmer, and much esteemed. He was advanced in years, and was in perfect health a few moments previous to his death.

No. 160 :: Ref. 1845-05-13, 3:2, D.
In Dungannon, on Thursday, the 8th inst., Mrs. M'Gerr, wife of Mr. John M'Gerr, of that town, and daughter of Mr. Matthew Vallely, Monaghan.

No. 161 :: Ref. 1845-05-20, 3:3, M.
On the 18th inst., in Caledon Church, by the Rev. J. Chamley, Mr. Andrew Bampton, of Strabane, to

Frances Elizabeth, fourth daughter of Henry Pilkington Ogle, Furz Park, County Meath.

No. 162 :: Ref. 1845-05-20, 3:3, M.

In Benburb Church, on Tuesday, the 13th inst., by the Rev. Richard Wrightson, Mr. Andrew Wilson, of the Ordnance Survey department, to Miss Caldwell, of this City.

No. 163 :: Ref. 1845-05-20, 3:3, M.

On Friday, the 9th inst., in Portadown Church, Thomas Sinnamon, jun., Esq., to Margaret Maria, eldest daughter of James Kinkead, Esq., of Tandragee, and sister to G. Kinkead, Esq., of Portadown.

No. 164 :: Ref. 1845-05-20, 3:3, M.

On the 14th inst., in the Wesleyan Chapel, Sandys-street, by the Rev. Mr. Carey, Mr. Isaac Glenny, to Miss Anna Harcourt, third daughter of the late Mr. Richard Harcourt, both of Newry.

No. 165 :: Ref. 1845-05-20, 3:3, M.

On the 12th inst. in Portadown Church, Robert Wilson, Esq., of Lisburn, to Susanna, only daughter of David Hammond, Esq., of the Excise.

No. 166 :: Ref. 1845-05-20, 3:3, D.

Yesterday, in Scotch-street, at the house of her son, Mr. Robert Barnes, Mrs. Barnes, relict of the late Wm. Barnes, Esq., of this City, in the 71st year of her age, much and deservedly regretted.

No. 167 :: Ref. 1845-05-20, 3:3, D.

At the residence of her uncle, in Dobbin-street, Armagh, aged 16 years, Isabella, daughter of the late Mr. James Star, of this City.

No. 168 :: Ref. 1845-05-20, 3:3, D.

On the 10th inst., in the 88th year of her age, at the house of her son, Mr. Archibald Johnston, of Middletown, Mrs. Rachel Johnston, widow of the late Mr. M. Johnston, of Derryhaw, near Tynan. In all the relations of life she was most exemplary, meek, and humble; she enjoyed comfort in death, and fell asleep in Jesus, in true and certain hope of a glorious resurrection.

No. 169 :: Ref. 1845-05-20, 3:3, D.

On Wednesday, the 14th instant, at Summer Hill, in this county, the residence of her mother, Jane Anne, wife of Mr. Richard C. Vogan, of this City, Merchant, in the 28th year of her age.

No. 170 :: Ref. 1845-05-20, 3:3, D.

At Caledon, on Wednesday, the 14th inst., Anne, eldest daughter of Mr. John Taggart.

No. 171 :: Ref. 1845-05-20, 3:3, D.

On the 15th of March, at Meerat, Eliza Euphemia, wife of Lieutenant Frederick Thornton Raikes, of her Majesty's 62d Regiment, and second daughter of John Hamilton, Esq.

No. 172 :: Ref. 1845-05-20, 3:3, D.

May 11, in Stephen's-green, Dublin, Rev. James M'Kee, Wesleyan minister, aged twenty-eight years. He was a young man of humble piety, fervent zeal, and much usefulness.

No. 173 :: Ref. 1845-05-20, 3:3, D.

On the 9th inst., at Caledon, Mr. Marcus M'Clean.

No. 174 :: Ref. 1845-05-20, 3:3, D.

On the 15th inst., at his residence, Annslough, near Middletown, of a tedious and painful illness, which he bore with the most Christian patience and resignation, the Rev. Bernard Loughran, P.P., of Tynan. The Rev. deceased commenced his clerical career under the late venerated R. C. Primate, Dr. Curtis, as curate, in Drogheda, where his mission is still remembered with unabated affection and attachment by all who shared the benefit of his care and example. He was subsequently—after some other changes in Louth—appointed to the parochial charge of Camlough, near Newry, from whence he was removed, on the death of the Rev. Mr. Lappan, by cholera, in 1834, to his late parish, Tynan. For the well-known faithful discharge of his onerous duties eulogium may, perhaps, be uncalled for; but for the practice of every social quality that can endear man to man, he was pre-eminent, and deserves our kindest remembrances. In private life, the wide circle of his numerous and attached friends will best attest the steadiness of his friendships, which, when once formed, no reverse of fortune or change of circumstances could lessen or abate. By old and young he was equally beloved; and the friendly violence manifested by his parishioners to retain his remains among them, when his relatives, with a natural desire wished to inter him with his ancestors, is a sufficient evidence that he was to them a true and acceptable pastor. As a scholar and theologian, his attainments were varied and extensive, and as a patriot, whilst his opinions were most decided and uncompromising in the cause of his country, he secured by his urbanity of manner and toleration for those who differed with him, the warmest regards of all. The numerous attendance at his funeral of his dissenting brethren is the strongest proof of their esteem, and his own liberality. By all who (like the writer) enjoyed the happiness of a long intimate acquaintance with him, his loss will be severely felt; but whilst we mourn his departure from amongst us, we have the consolation to know that if we discharge our various duties as he has done, and live as he lived, we may again be united with him for a happy eternity. *Requiescat in pace.—(Communicated.)*

No. 175 :: Ref. 1845-05-27, 2:3, B.

On the 21st inst., at Chantilly Lodge, the lady of Ralph Smith Obre, Esq., of a son and heir.

No. 176 :: Ref. 1845-05-27, 2:3, M.
At Tempo Church, on Tuesday, 20th May, by the Rev. John Whittaker, Mr. John Lemon, merchant, Enniskillen, to Jane, daughter of the late Mr. Robert Armstrong, of Brookeborough.

No. 177 :: Ref. 1845-05-27, 2:3, D.
May 21, at Vicar's Hill, in this city, Mrs. George Benson.

No. 178 :: Ref. 1845-05-27, 2:3, D.
On the 15th inst., Miss E. Tuthill, daughter of the Rev. Mr. Tuthill, curate of Ballyshannon.

No. 179 :: Ref. 1845-05-27, 2:3, D.
February 28, at St. Helena, on his passage home from China, aged 21 years, Henry William, third son of Samuel T. Potter, Esq., of Bundoran.

No. 180 :: Ref. 1845-05-27, 2:3, D.
March 19, of cholera, Lieutenant and Adjutant John James Ochiltree Stuart, 5th Regiment M.N.I., third son of the Hon. A. G. Stuart, Lisdhu, county of Tyrone. By his death the service has lost a bright ornament. He lived beloved and respected, and his death is lamented by all who knew him.

No. 181 :: Ref. 1845-05-27, 2:3, D.
On the 16th instant, of consumption, at his residence in Ireland's entry Belfast, Mr. Thomas M'Ilwee, foreman, *Protestant Journal*, aged 25 years, much and deservedly regretted.

No. 182 :: Ref. 1845-06-03, 3:1, B.
On Monday, Mrs. Wm. Armstrong, (Imperial Hotel,) Enniskillen, of a daughter.

No. 183 :: Ref. 1845-06-03, 3:1, M.
On the 23d ult., at St. George's Church, Dublin, James Power, Esq., of Colehill-house, county of Longford, to Eliza, second daughter of the late Alexander Nixon Montgomery, Esq., of Bessmount-park, county of Monaghan.

No. 184 :: Ref. 1845-06-03, 3:1, M.
May 21, by the Rev. John Rutherford, Ballydown, Mr. Jas. Withers, editor of the *Ulster Conservative*, to Agnes, daughter of Captain Crawford, Mutton-hill, Banbridge.

No. 185 :: Ref. 1845-06-03, 3:1, D.
On Saturday last, at Blackwatertown, Margaret, wife of John Crothers, Esq., aged 26 years, seized by a fatal disease in the midst of youth and great usefulness.—She was enabled to commit herself with complete resignation to the will of God, and has, through his Grace, exchanged the varied relationships of life, which she eminently adorned, for the rest of a glorious immortality.

No. 186 :: Ref. 1845-06-03, 3:1, D.
May 28, at Newry, in the 59th year of his age, Mr. Arthur Russell, of Rostrevor—and who was for many years a respectable inhabitant of Newry.

No. 187 :: Ref. 1845-06-03, 3:1, D.
May 25, at 18, Kildare-street, Elizabeth, relict of William Studdert, Esq., of Clonlohan House, in the King's county, and only sister of the late Rev. Launcelot Dowdall, D.D., of Dungannon.

No. 188 :: Ref. 1845-06-03, 3:1, D.
In Omagh, on Thursday, the 29th ult., of gastric fever, Mr. James Morrow, Primitive Wesleyan Methodist Preacher, in the 46th year of his age, and 21st year of his itinerancy. He has left a large family to deplore his loss, and is deeply regretted by a numerous circle of friends and acquaintances. His end was peace.

No. 189 :: Ref. 1845-06-03, 3:1, D.
March 16, at Hullyhall, near Darwar, Madras Presidency, Ensign John Edgar Leslie, of the 35th Native Infantry, eldest son of Major-General John Leslie, K.H., of her Majesty's service commanding at Bellary.

No. 190 :: Ref. 1845-06-03, 3:1, D.
In Belfast, on the 25th ult., Fanny, daughter of the late Daniel Donelly, Esq., of Monaghan.

No. 191 :: Ref. 1845-06-03, 3:1, D.
On the 18th April, at Kingston, Jamaica, Isabella, wife of William Henry Harrison, Esq., formerly of Belfast.

No. 192 :: Ref. 1845-06-03, 3:1, D.
On the 23d ult., Miss Catherine Morrison, third daughter of Mr. Charles Morrison, of Cullentree-road, in the 10th year of her age.

No. 193 :: Ref. 1845-06-03, 3:1, D.
On the 22d ult., at her mother's house, at Kingstown, Margaret, relict of Philip Geraghty, late of Dungannon, Esq.

No. 194 :: Ref. 1845-06-03, 3:1, D.
May 21, at Newcastle, after a few days' illness, deeply regretted by his brother officers, and all who knew him, Colonel Archibald Montgomery Maxwell, K.H., Lieutenant-Colonel commanding the 36th Regiment.

No. 195 :: Ref. 1845-06-10, 3:4, B.
June 2, at Clonervy, county Cavan, the lady of the Rev. Thomas Fetherston, of a daughter.

No. 196 :: Ref. 1845-06-10, 3:4, M.
On the 4th inst., in St. Anne's Church, Dublin, Mr. John Wilson, of Rockcorry, county of Monaghan, to Sarah Jane, daughter of the late Mr. Patrick Shaw, of Newtownhamilton, in this county.

No. 197 :: Ref. 1845-06-10, 3:4, M.

On Friday, the 23d ult., in the cathedral of Derry, by the Rev. John Kincaid, Mr. John Montgarret, printer, to Elizabeth, eldest daughter of Mr. William Mooney, both of Derry.

No. 198 :: Ref. 1845-06-10, 3:4, M.

On Tuesday, the 28th ult., by license, in the Presbyterian Church, Dundonald, by the Rev. E.T. Martin, John Nicholson, Newcastle-on-Tyne, to Isabella Girvan, Dundonald.

No. 199 :: Ref. 1845-06-10, 3:4, D.

In this city, on Sunday the 8th inst., at the residence of her nephew, John Stanley, jun., Esq., at an advanced age, and after a useful and well spent life,—Mary, daughter of the late Robert Crooks, Esq., of Clogher, county Tyrone. She has left a numerous circle of sorrowing friends, who, however, "*mourn not as those without hope.*" Her remains will be interred in St. Mark's Church-yard on to-morrow (Wednesday) at 10 o'clock.

No. 200 :: Ref. 1845-06-10, 3:4, D.

On Saturday, the 7th inst., at Dundrum, near Keady, Alicia, wife of Samuel Kidd, sen., Esq., aged 55 years.

No. 201 :: Ref. 1845-06-10, 3:4, D.

At Corn Market, Dublin, aged twenty-eight years, Mr. W.L. Fletcher, printer. He was the author of many poems, amongst which was one published entitled the "*Frequented Village.*"

No. 202 :: Ref. 1845-06-10, 3:4, D.

On the 29th ult., Doctor Oakman, of Ardross, county of Armagh. This practitioner acquired his entire medical knowledge by *inspiration*, although he preferred the mystery of charms to the regular medical agents, and, occasionally confounded the maladies of his patients with the distempers of cattle. Although no sepruchal structure marks the spot sacred to his repose, his fame among the surrounding peasantry will prove, no doubt, a monument more lasting than brass, and more enduring than sculptured marble.

No. 203 :: Ref. 1845-06-10, 3:4, D.

On the 1st inst., at Mountpleasant-square, Dublin, of consumption, which she bore with Christian patience and meekness, Rachel, youngest daughter of the late Doctor Currie, of Ballyconnel, county Cavan; sincerely regretted by all who knew her.

No. 204 :: Ref. 1845-06-17, 2:5, B.

On Monday se'nnight, the wife of a man named Golland, living at Ferry, was delivered of four fine children, two boys and two girls, all of whom are, with the mother, doing well.

No. 205 :: Ref. 1845-06-17, 2:5, M.

June 12, by the Rev. Mr. O'Brien, P.P., Mr. Wm. Brickley, officer of Excise, to Mary Anne, eldest daughter of Mr. Peter Downey, Desert, Armagh.

No. 206 :: Ref. 1845-06-17, 2:5, M.

On the 11th inst., in Charlemont Church, by the Rev. James Disney, Thomas Dawson, Esq., late Portrieve of that Town, son of the late Captain Dawson, of Bovain House, County of Tyrone, and brother to William Dawson, of Dungannon, Esq., M.D., to Frances, youngest daughter of the late Mr. Robert Brown, of Lurgan Cot, near Richhill.

No. 207 :: Ref. 1845-06-17, 2:5, M.

On the 6th inst., by the Rev. G. Jamison, of Glastry, Mr. William Cavan, of Ballee, to Miss Ann Warnock, of Ballyesborough.

No. 208 :: Ref. 1845-06-17, 2:5, M.

On the 6th inst., by the Rev. G. Jamison, of Glastry, Mr. John Brown, of Ballyhalbert, to Miss Mary Fullerton, of Ballyesborough.

No. 209 :: Ref. 1845-06-17, 2:5, D.

June 10, in Willoughby-place, Enniskillen, Mrs. Stewart, wife of Captain Stewart.

No. 210 :: Ref. 1845-06-17, 2:5, D.

At Belfast, on Friday, the 13th inst., the Rev. Matthew Tobias, Wesleyan Minister, in the 54th year of his ministry, and 75th year of his age. The deceased was a native of Charlemont, in this County, and at an early age embraced the principles of the venerable Wesley, having had the high privilege of attending his last sermon in Charlemont in 1789. He was a man of distinguished abilities and sincere piety, and possessed of great influence among his brethren.

No. 211 :: Ref. 1845-06-17, 2:5, D.

At his villa residence, Blackrock, Dundalk, on the 8th inst., after a tedious illness, Alex. Shekleton, Esq., of Dundalk, in the 58th year of his age. He was for several years Secretary to the Grand Jury of the county of Louth, and was the founder of the extensive establishment in Dundalk for the manufacture of machinery, &c.

No. 212 :: Ref. 1845-06-17, 2:5, D.

On the 4th inst., at Broomhill, the residence of his brother-in-law, Mr. Joseph Snowdon, formerly of Killinchy, aged 83 years.

No. 213 :: Ref. 1845-06-17, 2:5, D.

At Stamford, Niagara, Maria, wife of Dr. Corry, of Rockcorry, County Monaghan, and daughter of the late Major Baylis, formerly Deputy Assistant Adjutant-General in Dublin.

No. 214 :: Ref. 1845-06-17, 2:5, D.

June 10, at 7, Fitzgibbon-street, Robert Colville Jones, aged sixteen months, son of James Jones, Esq., Mount Edward, county of Sligo.

No. 215 :: Ref. 1845-06-17, 2:5, D.
June 6, in London, William John Story, second son of the late Rev. Joseph Story, of Bingfield, in the county of Cavan.

No. 216 :: Ref. 1845-06-17, 2:5, D.
June 3, suddenly, at Hollybrook, the seat of Colonel Dickson, Lisnaskea, county Fermanagh, much regretted, Charlotte, relict of Colonel Johnstone, Buttevant Barracks.

No. 217 :: Ref. 1845-06-24, 2:6, B.
June 11, at the Parsonage, Newbliss, the lady of the Rev. Wm. Deering, of a daughter.

No. 218 :: Ref. 1845-06-24, 2:6, M.
On the 18th inst., at Derrycortrevy church, by the Rev. Mr. Major, Alfred Sotheren, of Bray, Esq., to Ellen, fourth daughter of the late John Gilmore, of Lisrone, County Tyrone, Esq.

No. 219 :: Ref. 1845-06-24, 2:6, M.
Same day [18th inst.], in St. Patrick's Cathedral, Armagh, James Gardner, Esq., to Miss Anne Scott, niece of George Scott, Esq., of Vicar's-Hill.

No. 220 :: Ref. 1845-06-24, 2:6, M.
June 18, in St. Peter's Church, Dublin, the Rev. J. North, only son of Roger North, of Kilduffe House, King's County, Esq., to Emma, daughter of the late John Deering, Esq., of Derrybrusk, county Fermanagh.

No. 221 :: Ref. 1845-06-24, 2:6, M.
June 12, by the Rev. Mr. Cummins, Parish Priest of Ballyshannon; and afterwards by the Rev. Mr. Tuthill, in the Church of Ballyshannon, John Allingham, Esq., of Willsbrook, near Ballyshannon, to Mary Ann, daughter of the late Doctor Sheil, and Niece to the late O'Connor Don, M.P.

No. 222 :: Ref. 1845-06-24, 2:6, M.
June 14, in Kilkenny, Wm. F. Winslow, Esq., second son of the late Captain Winslow, of Dresternan, in the county of Fermanagh, to Nannie, second daughter of James Poe, Esq.

No. 223 :: Ref. 1845-06-24, 2:6, D.
On Sunday evening last, in Beresford place, Armagh, at the house of her aunt, Catherine Elizabeth Swan, aged 19 years, second daughter of Thomas Swan, Curlough, near Caledon, Esq.

No. 224 :: Ref. 1845-06-24, 2:6, D.
On Friday, the 20th inst., Christina Brockey, of this city, aged 106.

No. 225 :: Ref. 1845-06-24, 2:6, D.
At Caen, where he had resided more than twenty years, J. S. Smith, Esq., brother of the late Admiral Sir Sidney Smith, and formerly Ambassador at Constantinople. He was well known as a learned antiquary, and for his general literacy attainments.

No. 226 :: Ref. 1845-07-01, 2:1, M.
June 24, in St. Mary's Church, Newry, by the Rev. Dr. Campbell, Rector of Forkhill, George Casey, Esq., of Liverpool, to Mercy Boursequot, eldest daughter of George Glenny, Esq., late of Moorvale, in the county of Armagh.

No. 227 :: Ref. 1845-07-01, 2:1, D.
On the 25th ult., in Moy, at the residence of her brother, Dr. Crothers, in her 16th year, Susan, daughter of the late George Crothers, Esq., of Aughnacloy, county Tyrone.

No. 228 :: Ref. 1845-07-01, 2:1, D.
At Toronto, on the 24th of May, Mr. John Walker, aged 67 years, formerly of Culkearn, Moy, Ireland.

No. 229 :: Ref. 1845-07-01, 2:1, D.
On the 24th ult., of typhus fever, at Nelson-Street, Dublin, William Stone, Esq., aged 27 years, second son of the late Major Stone, of Mount Zion, Jamaica.

No. 230 :: Ref. 1845-07-01, 2:1, D.
At the house of her brother-in-law, the Rev. R. G. Dickson, in Drumnakilly, Jane, wife of Mr. John Orr, merchant, of Omagh.

No. 231 :: Ref. 1845-07-01, 2:1, D.
June 19, at the residence of her grand-mother, Mrs. Walker, of Donegal, where she had been on a visit for a few weeks, aged 19 years, Elizabeth, relict of Mr. John W. Davidson, of this City. Her remains were accompanied to the family vault of her late grandfather by a numerous and respectable concourse of deeply afflicted relations and friends.

No. 232 :: Ref. 1845-07-08, 2:5, B.
June 30, at Castle Coole, the Countess of Belmore of a son.

No. 233 :: Ref. 1845-07-08, 2:5, B.
On the 2d inst., at Lisburn, the lady of William Whitla, Esq., of a son.

No. 234 :: Ref. 1845-07-08, 2:5, B.
On the 25th ult., at Killishil Cottage, county Tyrone, the lady of the Rev. Christopher Graham, of a daughter.

No. 235 :: Ref. 1845-07-08, 2:5, M.
On Saturday last, in St. Mark's Church, in this city, by the Rev. Robert Haig, Mr. Edward Taylor, of North-street, Belfast, formerly of Caledon, seedsman, to Miss Annie, second daughter of the late Mr. George Penton, of Thomas-street, Armagh.

No. 236 :: Ref. 1845-07-08, 2:5, M.
On the 10th ult., at Philadelphia, Thomas Richardson, of New York, son of James N. Richardson, of Glenmore, near Lisburn, to Anna C., daughter of Richard Price, of that city.

No. 237 :: Ref. 1845-07-08, 2:5, M.

July 2, in St. George's Church, by the Rev. Richard Connolly, brother to the bridegroom, Francis West Connolly, Esq., of Ballinamore, county Leitrim, to Elizabeth, second daughter of the late Thomas Fleming, Esq., of the Ordnance Department, Dublin.

No. 238 :: Ref. 1845-07-08, 2:5, M.

June 27, in Cavan Church, by the Rev. Decimus William Preston, A.B., Wadham Wyndham Bond, Esq., Lieutenant 4th King's Own Regiment, son of H. C. Bond, Esq., of Bondville, county of Armagh, to Catherine Charlotte, daughter of the late William Wilkins, Esq.

No. 239 :: Ref. 1845-07-08, 2:5, M.

July 1, in Trory Church, by his brother, the Rev. George Stone, Mr. Ralph Stone, of Enniskillen, to Catherine, third daughter of the late Acheson Irvine, Esq., of Derrygore, in county Fermanagh.

No. 240 :: Ref. 1845-07-08, 2:5, M.

June 18, in St. Peter's, Dublin, by the Rev. W.W. Deering, the Rev. Joseph North, only son of Roger North, of Kilduff House, in the King's county, Esq., to Emma, daughter of the late John Deering, Esq., Q.C., of Derrybrusk, county of Fermanagh.

No. 241 :: Ref. 1845-07-08, 2:5, D.

On the 30th ult., at Lurgan, at an advanced age, Dorothea, relict of the late John Hazlett, Esq., of that town.

No. 242 :: Ref. 1845-07-08, 2:5, D.

At Summer-hill, on Monday last, of inflammation of the stomach, Joseph Richardson, Esq., J.P., eldest son of the Rev. John Richardson, of Kesh Glebe.

No. 243 :: Ref. 1845-07-08, 2:5, D.

On Friday last, at the house of Mr. Andrew M'Farland, of Glencoppagagh, near Plumbridge, where she had been on a visit, Rachel, the beloved wife of Mr. John M'Farland, watchmaker, Omagh.

No. 244 :: Ref. 1845-07-08, 2:5, D.

On the 6th May last, at Ottamby, Upper Canada, Hannah, wife of T. Shaw, Esq., the only daughter of the late William Carlow, Esq., of Callanbridge, Armagh.

No. 245 :: Ref. 1845-07-08, 2:5, D.

July 2, at Coagh, county Tyrone, Elizabeth, youngest daughter of the late Rev. Thomas Paul.

No. 246 :: Ref. 1845-07-08, 2:5, D.

At Corgariff, county Cavan, Mr. George B. Harman, brother to Mr. Alexander Harman, merchant, Enniskillen.

No. 247 :: Ref. 1845-07-08, 2:5, D.

In Enniskillen, on Wednesday last, James, youngest son of Mr. William Hall, New Market.

No. 248 :: Ref. 1845-07-15, 3:2, M.

July 7, in Slane Church, by the Rev. John Disney, the Rev. Richard Hamilton, of Bedford, in the county of Donegal, to Jane, eldest daughter of the late Rev. Barry M'Gusty, Rector of Rathkenny, county of Meath.

No. 249 :: Ref. 1845-07-15, 3:2, D.

In Montreal, on the 16th April, aged 39 years, Mr. William Addy, of that city, grocer. He was a native of Loughgall, in the County of Armagh, but had resided at Montreal from early youth, and was much praised by the citizens for his personal worth and unsullied public and private character.

No. 250 :: Ref. 1845-07-15, 3:2, D.

On the 2d instant, at Northland Row, Dungannon, Mary, wife of John Brydge, Esq., and daughter of the late Rev Doctor Shuter, of Ballinderry.

No. 251 :: Ref. 1845-07-15, 3:2, D.

July 6th, at Greenmount, near Omagh, aged 21 years, William Thomas, third son of the Rev. S. G. Rogers.

No. 252 :: Ref. 1845-07-15, 3:2, D.

July 6th, Mr. Hugh M'Mahon, Hotel-keeper, Clones. He was a man respected by all who knew him, and the attendance of persons of all religious persuasions at his funeral showed how much he was regretted.

No. 253 :: Ref. 1845-07-22, 3:6, M.

At Dr. Henry's Church, Armagh, by the Rev. Mr. Elliott, Portadown, John Hanna, of Terryskean, county Armagh, Esq., to the second daughter of the late William Wilson, Esq., of Blackwatertown, and niece of the late Sir Isaac Wilson, Knight, Surgeon in Ordinary to the late Duke of Sussex.

No. 254 :: Ref. 1845-07-22, 3:6, M.

On the 17th inst., in Charlemont Church, by the Rev. James Disney, Joseph Patterson, Esq., Moy, to Susan, fifth daughter of Robert Corrigan, of Moss-spring, Esq., and niece of John Corrigan, Esq., of this City.

No. 255 :: Ref. 1845-07-22, 3:6, M.

In Clones Church, by the Rev. Charles Welsh, Mr. Robert Irwin, merchant, Clones, to Louisa Maria, second daughter of the late John Clarke, Esq., Postmaster, of same place.

No. 256 :: Ref. 1845-07-22, 3:6, M.

July 10, Captain William Lacey, late of the 46th Regiment, and son of Colonel Lacy, Royal Artillery, to Georgiana, widow of the Rev. James Henville, M.A., of Wymering, Hants, and daughter-in-law of Sir Charles Napier, K.C.B., of Merchistoun-hall, Hants.

No. 257 :: Ref. 1845-07-22, 3:6, D.

On the 16th instant, in this city, of consumption, Jane, the beloved wife of Mr. Daniel M'Allen, aged 27 years.

No. 258 :: Ref. 1845-07-22, 3:6, D.

Yesterday morning, in this city, Elizabeth, fourth daughter of Mr. John Douglas, of Scotch-street, aged 11 years.

No. 259 :: Ref. 1845-07-22, 3:6, D.

At Blackwatertown, of hooping-cough, on the 13th instant, aged three months, James, second son of James Hanna, Esq., of same place, and grand-nephew of the late Sir Isaac Wilson, Knight, Surgeon in Ordinary to His Royal Highness the late Duke of Sussex.

No. 260 :: Ref. 1845-07-22, 3:6, D.

July 13, after a few days' illness, at Charlestown Glebe, county of Louth, the residence of her father, the Rev. Richard Olpherts, Eliza Jane, relict of the late Rev. Theodore Dunkin, late Chaplain in the Hon. the East India Company's Service. Her remains were interred in St. Mark's Church-yard, in this city, on Thursday last.

No. 261 :: Ref. 1845-08-05, 2:6, M.

In Clennanese Presbyterian Church, county Tyrone, Hamilton Boyd, Esq., of Lynchburgh, Virginia, North America, to Margaret, eldest daughter of the Rev. James Kinnear, of Lower Clennanese, near Dungannon.

No. 262 :: Ref. 1845-08-05, 2:6, D.

At Charlemont-place, Armagh, on Tuesday, 29th ult., Miss Jessie Paton, second daughter of James Paton, Esq., of Ayr, Scotland, aged 22. Her remains were taken to Ayr for interment.

No. 263 :: Ref. 1845-08-05, 2:6, D.

On the 29th ult., at Brookeborough, aged 84 years, Doctor John West, the oldest medical practitioner in Fermanagh.

No. 264 :: Ref. 1845-08-05, 2:6, D.

On Monday evening, 29th ult., at Willoughby-place, Enniskillen, at an advanced age, Mrs. Betty, relict of the late John Betty, Esq., Cappy.

No. 265 :: Ref. 1845-08-12, 2:5, B.

On the 25th ult., at the Parsonage, Moy, the Lady of the Rev. John Leech, of a son.

No. 266 :: Ref. 1845-08-12, 2:5, M.

In Loughgall Church, by the Rev. Savage Hall, Mr. J. Benson, of Annahue Cottage, to Ruth, eldest daughter of the late Mr. George Palmer of Whengrove, both of this county.

No. 267 :: Ref. 1845-08-12, 2:5, M.

On the 6th inst., in Jonesborough Church, by the Rev. R. Henry, Mr. George Dick, of Forkhill, to Miss Eliza Carpenter, of Jonesborough.

No. 268 :: Ref. 1845-08-12, 2:5, D.

On Sunday evening last, Mr. Thomas Joshua Jackson, son of Thomas Jackson, Esq., governor of the asylum, Armagh, aged sixteen years, sincerely and deservedly regretted.

No. 269 :: Ref. 1845-08-12, 2:5, D.

In Enniskillen, aged 44 years, Jane, the beloved wife of Wm. Trimble, Esq., Proprietor and Editor of the *Fermanagh Reporter*. Throughout life her acts of charity to the needy and Christian kindness to all, endeared her to an extensive circle of friends and acquaintances. In her character shone those superior graces which adorn the sex—she was kind, humane, tender, affectionate, and her loss is a source of sorrow to many who experienced her maternal care. In the more important relations of life she acquitted herself honourably—attached, as a wife; loving, as a parent; sincere, as a friend. During the last two hears her health was delicate: and on Saturday morning at one o'clock, that God whom she served so steadily on earth, called her to himself in heaven. Released from pain, she has entered upon an everlasting reward, and happy is she that believed.

No. 270 :: Ref. 1845-08-15, 2:5, M.

On the 7th inst., in the Lisburn Cathedral, by the Rev. P. Neilly, the Rev. Thomas Fitzgerald, to Lilly Ann Maxwell, step-daughter of William Thompson, Esq., M.D., and Physician to the County Antrim Infirmary.

No. 271 :: Ref. 1845-08-19, 3:2, B.

August 3, at Wall-end, Warwickshire, the lady of John Hancock, Esq., of Lurgan, county Armagh, of a son.

No. 272 :: Ref. 1845-08-19, 3:2, B.

August 10, in Enniskillen, Mrs. W. Alexander, of a son.

No. 273 :: Ref. 1845-08-19, 3:2, M.

On the 13th inst., in St. Mark's Church, Dublin, by the Rev. Mr. O'Meara, Mr. Samuel Lindsay, of William-street, to Lydia Matilda, second daughter of Mr. John Barret, Westmorland-street.

No. 274 :: Ref. 1845-08-19, 3:2, D.

On Tuesday the 12th inst., Thomas Kennedy, of Brackagh, county Tyrone, Esq., aged 43 years. For his steadiness, benevolence, and urbanity of manner, he is most deservedly lamented by a numerous circle of friends, whose only consolation is, that he sleeps with the Lord Jesus, on whom he placed his hope.

No. 275 :: Ref. 1845-08-19, 3:2, D.

On Thursday last, at Belleek, color-sergeant Digby, 5th Fusileers, sincerely regretted by the officers and men of the regiment.

No. 276 :: Ref. 1845-08-26, 3:1, D.

On the 20th inst., at Clogher, Mr. James M'Quade, Innkeeper.

No. 277 :: Ref. 1845-08-26, 3:1, D.
On Monday the 18th inst., of apoplexy, Mr. Robert Kidney, merchant, Enniskillen. And on Tuesday, his brother, Thomas who had been ill of decline for some time.

No. 278 :: Ref. 1845-09-02, 2:6, B.
On the 21st ult., in this city, the Lady of the Rev. Richard Quin, of a daughter.

No. 279 :: Ref. 1845-09-02, 2:6, B.
On the 27th at Portadown, the lady of John Overend, Esq., of a son.

No. 280 :: Ref. 1845-09-02, 2:6, B.
On the 6th ult., at Charlemont-place, Armagh, the Lady of George C. G. Wray, Esq., of Ardnamona, in the county of Donegal, of a son.

No. 281 :: Ref. 1845-09-02, 2:6, B.
On Tuesday the 16th ult., at the house of her father, George Chapman, Esq., Tromara, near Moira, the lady of the Rev. Robert Jones, Wesleyan Minister of a son.

No. 282 :: Ref. 1845-09-02, 2:6, M.
On the 20th ult., at Derrygortreavy Church, by the Rev. Wm. Mayor, Mr. Thomas Davidson, of Ardress, county Armagh, to Miss Jane Shillington, third daughter of the late Mr. Joseph Shillington, Clew Bridge county, Tyrone.

No. 283 :: Ref. 1845-09-02, 2:6, M.
On the 21st ult., in Tartaraghan Church, by the Rev. James Sullivan, Mr. William Johnston, Tullybrone, near Keady, to Mary, second daughter of Mr. Robert Woodhouse, Drummanon.

No. 284 :: Ref. 1845-09-02, 2:6, M.
On the 14th ult., in the parish Church of Strabane, by the Rev. Edward Atkinson, Mr. Robert Hall, to Margaret, daughter of Mr. Nicholas Sims, of the Abercorn Arms Hotel, Strabane.

No. 285 :: Ref. 1845-09-02, 2:6, M.
In Pettigo Church, by the Rev. Charles Lucas Bell, on the 16th ult., Mr. Joseph Collins, Sergeant of Police, Kilmore, to Anna, eldest daughter of Mr. William Black, High-Constable of the Barony of Kilmacrenan, county Donegal.

No. 286 :: Ref. 1845-09-02, 2:6, M.
August 21, at Colebrook Church, by the Rev. J.M. Roe, George Booker, of Bensfort House, county Meath, Esq., to Margaret Clarke, daughter of the late Jonathan Clarke, Esq., of Maguiresbridge, county Fermanagh.

No. 287 :: Ref. 1845-09-02, 2:6, M.
On the 14th ult., in Sancho [sic] Errigle-Church, J. Leeper, Esq., Surgeon, Keady Dispensary, to Margaret Jane, second daughter of the late R. Anketell, Ivy-hill, county Monaghan, Esq.

No. 288 :: Ref. 1845-09-02, 2:6, D.
On Friday, the 29th ult., at Russell-street, in this city, Lucy, fifth daughter of J.T. Noble, Esq., aged 6 years.

No. 289 :: Ref. 1845-09-02, 2:6, D.
August 12, at Lough Glore, near Castlepollard, Charles Mills, Esq., late of the Common Pleas Office.

No. 290 :: Ref. 1845-09-02, 2:6, D.
On Monday, the 25th ult., after a lengthened illness, Mr. J. Bryden, cabinet-maker, Basin-walk, Newry, aged 74 years, an old and much-respected inhabitant of the town.

No. 291 :: Ref. 1845-09-02, 2:6, D.
On the 21st ult., at Sandville, in her 75th year, Catherine, relict of the late John Crozier, Gortra House, County Fermanagh, Esq.

No. 292 :: Ref. 1845-09-02, 2:6, D.
August 13, at Benmore, Churchhill, county Fermanagh, Isabella, second daughter of the late Right Rev. Hugh Hamilton, Bishop of Ossory, aged 68 years.

No. 293 :: Ref. 1845-09-02, 2:6, D.
August 15, Mr. Hugh Beattie, eldest son of Mr. Jas. Beattie, of Tyregarty, near Blackwatertown, in the 22d year of his age.

No. 294 :: Ref. 1845-09-02, 2:6, D.
August 15, at Cloverhill, county Monaghan, Alexander Waddell, Esq., aged 78. Mr. Waddell was one of the celebrated Volunteers of '82.

No. 295 :: Ref. 1845-09-09, 2:5, B.
September 3, at Crewe Cottage, Ballygauley, the wife of the Rev. H.L. Baker, B.A., Incumbent of Ballygauley, diocese of Armagh, of a daughter.

No. 296 :: Ref. 1845-09-09, 2:5, B.
August 31, at 26, Dorset-street, Dublin, the lady of John Peebles, M.D., of a son.

No. 297 :: Ref. 1845-09-09, 2:5, M.
On the 2d inst., in the Cathedral of Clogher, by the Rev. Wm. B. Ash, Mr. James Stinson, of Altnaveagh, to Miss Elizabeth M'Clelland, Fimore.

No. 298 :: Ref. 1845-09-09, 2:5, M.
September 2, at Carnmoney Church, by the Rev. Dr. Drew, Henley R. Bass, Esq., of Glasgow, to Julia Vincent Duff, youngest daughter of the late William Duff, Esq., Mount Caulfield, in this county.

No. 299 :: Ref. 1845-09-09, 2:5, M.
September 4, in Clontibret Church, by the Venerable the Archdeacon of Clogher, the Rev. John Evans Lewis, Rector of Moynagh, in this county, eldest son of the late Wm. Lewis, Esq., of Sligo, to Margaret Jane, youngest daughter of the late Henry Swanzy, Esq., of Rockfield, county Monaghan.

No. 300 :: Ref. 1845-09-09, 2:5, M.

September 2, in the First Presbyterian Church, Derry, by the Rev. Peter Dale, of Houston, Renfrewshire, George Hay, Esq., Barrister, to Margaret, second daughter of James Thompson, Esq., of Derry.

No. 301 :: Ref. 1845-09-09, 2:5, M.

On the 25th ult., in the parish church of Clondevanddock, by the Rev. Thomas Fullerton, Henry Lathem, of Fanet, in the county of Donegal, Esq., to Harriet Barbara, youngest daughter of the late Major Barton, of Derryhallagh, in the county of Monaghan.

No. 302 :: Ref. 1845-09-09, 2:5, M.

On the 27th ult., in the 2d Drumbanagher Presbyterian Church, by the Rev. Robert M'Clean, Mr. Richard Hudson, Fourtowns, to Isabella, only daughter of Mr. John Porter, Kilrea, and sister to the Rev. H. Porter, Coleraine.

No. 303 :: Ref. 1845-09-09, 2:5, D.

On Tuesday, the 2d inst., Margaret, wife of Mr. Walsh Linton, of Armagh, in the 72d year of her age, sincerely regretted, by all who had the pleasure of her acquaintance.

No. 304 :: Ref. 1845-09-09, 2:5, D.

At Keady Cottage, on the 1st inst., Miss Rebecca Simpson, aged 40 years.

No. 305 :: Ref. 1845-09-09, 2:5, D.

At Plumtree Cottage, Mullaghmore, Mr. Thomas White, aged 80 years.

No. 306 :: Ref. 1845-09-09, 2:5, D.

At Seskinore, on the 3d inst., Mr. Mathew Brown, aged 87 years, for many years permanent Sergeant of Seskinore yeomanry. His remains were followed by the following Orange Lodges, with their colours and music playing the dead march, viz.:—Seskinore, Gortaclare, Tullyarm, and Beragh. The coffin was decorated with an orange sash, and the members wore white scarfs.

No. 307 :: Ref. 1845-09-09, 2:5, D.

On Friday last, in Enniskillen, Mr. George Faulkner, boot and shoe maker, aged 73 years. He was an old inhabitant, and much respected by all who knew him.

No. 308 :: Ref. 1845-09-16, 2:6, M.

On the 9th inst., at the office of the District Registrars, Lisburn, the Rev William John Pettigrew, Baptist Missionary, to Miss Anna Shaw, daughter of the late Rev. John Shaw, of Drumbo.

No. 309 :: Ref. 1845-09-16, 2:6, M.

On the 8th inst., at Tubrid Church, by the Rev. Thomas Stack, Rector of Lower Badony, the Rev. Richard Stack, Curate of Saint Peter's, Dublin, third son of the Rev. Edward Stack, of Tubrid, in the county Fermanagh, to Annabella Elizabeth, eldest daughter of the late William Stack, of the city of Dublin, Esq., M.D.

No. 310 :: Ref. 1845-09-16, 2:6, D.

On the 10th inst., at Nockmany, Mr. Thomas Scarlett, in the 20th year of his age.

No. 311 :: Ref. 1845-09-23, 3:2, B.

On the 15th inst., at Phoenix-park, the Lady of Captain Larcom, Royal Engineers, of a daughter.

No. 312 :: Ref. 1845-09-23, 3:2, M.

September 17, in Newmills Church, by the Rev. James Mauleverer, Incumbent of Middletown, diocese of Armagh, John Graves Thompson, Esq., of Armagh, to Sarah Henrietta Caroline Sophia, second daughter of the Hon. Andrew Godfrey Stuart, of Lisdhu, county Tyrone, and niece to the Earl of Castlestuart.

No. 313 :: Ref. 1845-09-23, 3:2, M.

On Wednesday, 17th inst., in the Presbyterian Church, Lurgan, Mr. John Fulton, merchant, to Margaret, daughter of the late Mr. John Chisholm, Edinburgh.

No. 314 :: Ref. 1845-09-23, 3:2, M.

September 16, in Portadown Church by the Rev. C. Pepper, Caulfield, third son of the late Robert Atkinson, Esq., of Green Hall, county of Armagh, to Anne, second daughter of the late George Pepper, Esq., of Ballyworkan House, same county.

No. 315 :: Ref. 1845-09-23, 3:2, D.

On Sunday evening last, Leland Hutchinson, Esq., of Ballyrath, near Armagh, aged 42 years. His remains will be interred on Wednesday morning at half-past 7 o'clock.

No. 316 :: Ref. 1845-09-26, 3:1, B.

On Sunday, the 10th inst., in College-street, Armagh, the lady of J. Lester, Esq., Principal of the Armagh Boarding and Day School, of a daughter.

No. 317 :: Ref. 1845-09-30, 2:6, B.

On the 22d instant, at Newtownhamilton, the lady of Henry R. Barker, Esq., Solicitor, of a daughter.

No. 318 :: Ref. 1845-09-30, 2:6, B.

September 23, at No. 2, Upper Brook-street, the Hon. Lady Brooke, of a son.

No. 319 :: Ref. 1845-09-30, 2:6, B.

September 24, at Rutland square, Dublin, the lady of Dr. White, Inspector General of Prisons, of a son.

No. 320 :: Ref. 1845-09-30, 2:6, M.

On the 18th inst., at Acton Church, by the father of the bride, M. Fleming Handy Esq., of New Haggard Cottage, in the County of Meath, to Isabella Sarah, daughter of the Rev. H. Gamble, of Drumnargoole-house, county Armagh.

No. 321 :: Ref. 1845-09-30, 2:6, M.

In Rossory Church, on Monday last, by the Rev. J. Taylor, Dr. A. Nixon, of Willoughby Place, Enniskillen, to Matilda Susanna, only daughter of Capt. Stewart of same place.

No. 322 :: Ref. 1845-09-30, 2:6, D.

On the 15th inst. at Rostrevor, at an advanced age, deeply regretted, Constantia, relict of William Blacker Bennett, of Castlerea, in the county of Limerick, Esq.

No. 323 :: Ref. 1845-09-30, 2:6, D.

September 20, at Bath, aged 38 years, Mrs. Elizabeth Close, last surviving sister of the late Sir Barry Close, and of the late Rev. Samuel Close, of Elmpark, county Armagh.

No. 324 :: Ref. 1845-09-30, 2:6, D.

September 21, at Bundoran, where he had gone for the benefit of his health, Alexander Hassard, Esq., J.P., and formerly captain in the Inniskilling dragoons. He was a brave and distinguished officer, and an upright magistrate.

No. 325 :: Ref. 1845-09-30, 2:6, D.

September 20, in his 64th year, Hugh Mulreany, Esq., of Mountcharles.

No. 326 :: Ref. 1845-09-30, 2:6, D.

September 25, at his residence, Summerhill-parade, Dublin, aged 65 years, Marmaduke J. Richardson, Esq., formerly a Lieutenant in her Majesty's Rothsay and Caithness Regiment, and youngest son of John Richardson, of Furlough House, county Tyrone, Esq., deceased, sometime High Sheriff of that county, and Captain of the Dungannon Volunteers.

No. 327 :: Ref. 1845-09-30, 2:6, D.

On Wednesday, the 17th instant, at Dunleer, universally regretted, Arlminte Sophia, the beloved wife of H. M. Blackwell, Esq., M. D.

No. 328 :: Ref. 1845-09-30, 2:6, D.

In Dublin, Robert Haig, Esq., of Dodderbank.

No. 329 :: Ref. 1845-09-30, 2:6, D.

At his residence, in Omagh, after a protracted illness, Mr. C. W. Klophel, aged 65, Professor of Music, and formerly Master of the band in H.M. 50th Regiment of Foot.

No. 330 :: Ref. 1845-09-30, 2:6, D.

Death of the Rev. John Fitzgerald.—This respected minister died suddenly on Monday morning at Tullybracky Rectory, in this county, of effusion of water on the chest.—*Limerick Chronicle.*

No. 331 :: Ref. 1845-10-07, 3:1, M.

On the 1st of Oct., in St. Mark's Church, by the Rev. W. Jones, and afterwards by the Rev. Dr. Croly, Mr. John M'Donell, merchant, Belfast, to Margaret, third daughter of John Adams, Esq., Rosebrook, near Armagh.

No. 332 :: Ref. 1845-10-07, 3:1, M.

On the 30th ult., in the Presbyterian Church, Whiteabbey, by the Rev. Henry Cooke, D.D., LL.D.., Charles Mathews, Esq., Glasgow, to Caroline Mary, eldest daughter of the late William Duff, Esq., formerly of Mount Caulfield, county Armagh.

No. 333 :: Ref. 1845-10-07, 3:1, M.

On the 29th ult., at St. Mary's Church, by the Rev. Gibson Black, A.M., Richard Hassard, of Bawnboy House, in the county of Cavan, Esq., to Eliza Maria, youngest daughter of the late Michael Nolan, of Fitzroy-square, London, Esq.

No. 334 :: Ref. 1845-10-07, 3:1, M.

On the 1st inst., in Carntall Meeting-house, by the Rev. James Phillips, Mr. George Spence, of Fivemiletown, merchant, to Eliza, youngest daughter of the late William Glenn, Esq., of said town.

No. 335 :: Ref. 1845-10-07, 3:1, M.

On the 10th inst., in Warrenpoint Church, by the Rev. John Davis, Mr. Robt. Stewart Riddall, sixth son of the late James Riddall, Esq., of Barn Hill, County of Armagh, to Mary Olivia, youngest daughter of the late Rev. Samuel Alcorn, Wesleyan minister.

No. 336 :: Ref. 1845-10-07, 3:1, D.

On the 30th ult., rather suddenly, at Portadown, Mary, relict of the late Christopher Armstrong, Esq., aged 74 years. She was a woman of unbending integrity, remarkable for spiritual mindedness, which endeared her to an extensive and respectable circle of friends and acquaintances. Her remains were interred in Drumcreve [sic] Church-yard, on Friday last, and were attended to their last resting place by a large concourse of sorrowing friends.

No. 337 :: Ref. 1845-10-07, 3:1, D.

At Glinn House, Carlingford, Sarah Anne, relict of James Fforde, Esq., of Raughlan, county of Armagh.

No. 338 :: Ref. 1845-10-14, 2:6, B.

October 8, at Anketell Grove, county Monaghan, the lady of Mr. Mathew John Anketell, of a daughter.

No. 339 :: Ref. 1845-10-14, 2:6, M.

October 2, in Portadown Church, by the Rev. H. De'L. Willis, the Rev. John Oliver, of Tandragee, to Elizabeth H., youngest daughter of Mr. Hugh Mathews, Anagh, Portadown.

No. 340 :: Ref. 1845-10-14, 2:6, M.

On the 1st inst., in Carntall Meeting-house, by the Rev. Jas. Phillips, Mr. Geo. Spence, of Fivemiletown, merchant, to Eliza, youngest daughter of the late Wm. Glenn, Esq., of said town.

No. 341 :: Ref. 1845-10-14, 2:6, M.

On the 30th ult., in the Presbyterian Church, Whiteabbey, by the Rev. Henry Cooke D.D., LL.D., Charles Mathews, Esq., Glasgow, to Caroline Mary, eldest daughter of the late W. Duff, Esq., formerly of Mount Caulfield, county Armagh.

No. 342 :: Ref. 1845-10-14, 2:6, D.
On Sunday morning, the 12th inst., at her son's house in this city, Mrs. Anne Riddall, relict of the late Mr. Walter Riddall, of Blackwatertown.

No. 343 :: Ref. 1845-10-14, 2:6, D.
At his residence, in this city, on Thursday morning, after a long illness, Mr. James Greacen, Printer, eldest son of Mr. Nathaniel Greacen, of Monaghan.

No. 344 :: Ref. 1845-10-14, 2:6, D.
At Belfast, on Friday, the 3rd of October, after a brief illness of two days, the Rev. Charles Oulton, Vicar of Kilmore, in the Diocese of Down, aged 73, and for 50 years a pious and active Minister of the Lord Jesus.

No. 345 :: Ref. 1845-10-14, 2:6, D.
September 27, at the residence of his brother, Hugh Lyle, Esq., of Carnagrave, county Donegal.

No. 346 :: Ref. 1845-10-14, 2:6, D.
On the 20th ult., at Lydia Villa, Sarah, eldest daughter of Mr. Joseph Dudgeon, Postmaster of Stewartstown, and grand-daughter of the late Anthony M'Reynolds, Esq., Solicitor, Stewartstown.

No. 347 :: Ref. 1845-10-21, 2:5, M.
On the 15th inst., in Mullabrack Church, by the Rev. Charles Seaver, Mr. David Watson, of Lurgaboy, to Mary Jane, eldest daughter of the late Mr. Alexander Spence of Drumatee.

No. 348 :: Ref. 1845-10-21, 2:5, M.
On Tuesday, 14th inst., at St. Mary's Church, Newry, by the Rev. D. Boyd, Peter Sheriff, Esq., Liverpool, to Anna, eldest daughter of William Cowan, Esq., Newry.

No. 349 :: Ref. 1845-10-21, 2:5, M.
August 19th, at Trelawney, Jamaica, the Rev. Charles Alfred Cooper, Minister of St. Mary's Chapel, St. Thomas in the East, to Harriet, third daughter of Francis Sanderson, Esq., of Prospect House, Tandragee, county Armagh.

No. 350 :: Ref. 1845-10-21, 2:5, D.
Oct. 13, at Clontarf, where he had been ordered by his physician for the benefit of sea air, Lieutenant-Colonel Moore, K. H., 54th regiment, only son of the late John Moore, Esq., of Drumbanagher, county of Armagh. The demise of the gallant and most amiable colonel has caused deep sorrowing to his disconsolate widow and a numerous circle of friends, by whom he was beloved and admired for his many endearing qualities of head and heart.

No. 351 :: Ref. 1845-10-21, 2:5, D.
On the 11th instant, at his residence, Willoughby-place, Enniskillen, Frederick Geddings, Esq., aged 62, Ordnance storekeeper, and acting Barrack-master, deservedly and deeply regretted by a large circle of friends.

No. 352 :: Ref. 1845-10-21, 2:5, D.
On Sunday, of inflammation, Mr. James Innes, of Enniskillen, merchant. He enjoyed, apparently, perfect health throughout the week.

No. 353 :: Ref. 1845-10-21, 2:5, D.
On the 8th instant, at Mullaghmore, in the county of Sligo, in the 52d year of his age, Michael Hugh Tutthill, Esq., late Assistant Surgeon in the Royal Artillery.

No. 354 :: Ref. 1845-10-21, 2:5, D.
On the 14th inst., at Derrybrusk Glebe, Francis Tuthill, aged 76, relict of the Rev. Tutthill, late Rector of the parish of Drumkeeran.

No. 355 :: Ref. 1845-10-28, 2:5, M.
On Thursday 23d inst., in Ballymena Church, by the Rev. William Reeves, John Kerr, Esq., Parkmount, Dungannon, to Eliza, daughter of Mr. Brangan, Ballymena.

No. 356 :: Ref. 1845-10-28, 2:5, M.
On Tuesday morning last, in Omagh Church, by the Rev. T.L. Stack, Mr. John Robinson, master-tailor, to Charlotte, daughter of Mr. John M'Farland, both of Omagh.

No. 357 :: Ref. 1845-10-28, 2:5, D.
October 19, at "*Telegraph*" Court, Newry, in the 8th year of her age, Margaret, daughter of Mr. James Henderson.

No. 358 :: Ref. 1845-10-28, 2:5, D.
At Annacramp, near Grange, on Tuesday last, after a lingering illness, which he bore with Christian fortitude, Mr. Adam Sloane, aged 56 years, much regretted by all who were acquainted with him. He was for 35 years master of Lodge No. 86, Loughgall district. On Friday last his remains were brought into this city for interment, accompanied by a large body of the brethren of the above district, amounting to about 500—men of the most intelligent appearance, and respectability.

No. 359 :: Ref. 1845-11-04, 3:5, B.
October 26, at Dungannon, the lady of William Dawson, Esq., of a daughter, her fourteenth child.

No. 360 :: Ref. 1845-11-04, 3:5, M.
October 30, in the Cathedral, Armagh, by the Rev. James Mauleverer, Samuel, eldest son of Nicholas Delacherois Crommelin, Esq., of Carradare Castle, County Down, to Anna Maria, only daughter of the late John Thompson, Esq., of Dublin.

No. 361 :: Ref. 1845-11-04, 3:5, M.
October 27, in the parish church of Aughnacloy, by the Rev. A.M. Pollock, Manly Power Dudden, Esq., of Lara Vale, youngest son of the late Jacob Dudden, Esq., 32d regiment of foot, to Susan, ninth daughter of the late Mr. John Beggs, Merchant, Aughnacloy.

No. 362 :: Ref. 1845-11-04, 3:5, M.
At Magherafelt, by the Rev. John Quinn, Robert Collins, Esq., Saltertown-house, to Miss Nancy M'Ilwee, eldest daughter of the late Mr. Michael M'Ilwee, of Magherafelt.

No. 363 :: Ref. 1845-11-04, 3:5, M.
In Magherafelt Church, by the Rev. C.K. Irwin, Mr. John G. Adams, merchant, Magherafelt, to Eliza, youngest daughter of the late Moses Barrett, Esq., Black-causeway, Strangford, County Down.

No. 364 :: Ref. 1845-11-11, 3:6, B.
Nov. 5, at Armagh, the wife of the Rev. Alexander Irwin, of a son.

No. 365 :: Ref. 1845-11-11, 3:6, M.
On the 6th inst., in St. Mark's Church, by the Very Rev. Lord Montmorres, his brother-in-law, Joseph Shaw, Esq., of Celbridge, to Margaret, eldest daughter of the Rev. Dr. Henry.

No. 366 :: Ref. 1845-11-11, 3:6, M.
On the 3d inst., by the Rev. John M'Kenna, Catholic Curate of Clonfeacle, Mr. Francis Donaghy, of Eglish Mills, county Tyrone, to Eliza, daughter of the late Mr. James Malone, of Clonfeacle.

No. 367 :: Ref. 1845-11-11, 3:6, D.
On Saturday the 8th inst., in Dublin, J. T. Andrews, Esq., of this city, after a lingering illness, aged 35 years.

No. 368 :: Ref. 1845-11-11, 3:6, D.
In London, on the 6th inst., Sarah, the second daughter of John Hardy, Esq., Loughgall.

No. 369 :: Ref. 1845-11-11, 3:6, D.
On the 22d of August last, at Etobicoke, near Toronto, Upper Canada, Phoebe, wife of Dr. Thistle, formerly of Benburb, county Tyrone, aged 49 years.

No. 370 :: Ref. 1845-11-18, 2:6, M.
In Mullabrack church, on the 12th inst., by the Rev. Charles Seaver, Mr. James Todd, of Markethill, to Jane, eldest daughter of Mr. Matthew Black, of Cabra, both of the county Armagh.

No. 371 :: Ref. 1845-11-18, 2:6, M.
November 5, in St. Peter's Church, Lucius H. Deering, Esq. youngest son of the late John Deering, Esq., of Derrybrusk, county Fermanagh, to Caroline, daughter of the late Anthony Gildea, Esq., of Cloncormick House, county Mayo.

No. 372 :: Ref. 1845-11-18, 2:6, M.
On the 15th inst., at the house of the lady's father, by the Rev. Michael O'Brian, C.C., John M'Avoy, Esq., Bealmount, Dungannon, to Jane, third daughter of Wm. Carpenter, Esq., Armagh.

No. 373 :: Ref. 1845-11-18, 2:6, D.
Nov. 13, in this city, Miss Catherine Cuming, at an advanced age.

No. 374 :: Ref. 1845-11-18, 2:6, D.
At his residence, near Omagh, on the 11th inst., very suddenly, of disease of the heart, George Dick, Esq., aged 66 years, most deservedly regretted.

No. 375 :: Ref. 1845-11-18, 2:6, D.
At Ballygawley, on the 11th inst., Mrs. Mortimer, aged 80 years.

No. 376 :: Ref. 1845-11-18, 2:6, D.
At Ballycastle, on the 2d inst., at the house of her brother-in-law, the Rev. Patrick M'Menamy, Georgina, daughter of the late John Elder, Esq., J.P., of Knock, Isle of Skye, Scotland. Besides other donations to benevolent purposes she bequeathed the sum of £40 to the Home Missions of the Presbyterian church in Ireland.

No. 377 :: Ref. 1845-11-18, 2:6, D.
At Kilwaughter near Larne, on the 26th ult., Mr. Samuel Fullerton, aged 78 years. He has bequeathed £200 to the Missions of the General Assembly.

No. 378 :: Ref. 1845-11-25, 2:5, B.
Nov. 21, at Enniskillen, Mrs. William Quinton, of a son.

No. 379 :: Ref. 1845-11-25, 2:5, M.
On the 18th inst., in Armagh, by the Rev. Mr. M'Alister, Mr. William M'Murry, of Cavanagh-grove, to Miss Anne Jane, youngest daughter of Mr. M'Lochlin, of Killylea, county Armagh.

No. 380 :: Ref. 1845-11-25, 2:5, M.
In Lisnaskea Church, on Friday, the 21st inst., by the Rev. A. Hurst, Mr. James Noble, Shoemaker, of Lisnaskea, to Miss Margaret Gardner, of same place.

No. 381 :: Ref. 1845-11-25, 2:5, D.
Nov. 19, at Enniskillen, Miss Jane Irvine, aged 67, much regretted by a large circle of friends and acquaintances.

No. 382 :: Ref. 1845-11-25, 2:5, D.
Nov. 17, at Greenhill, aged 30 years, Hamilton John Irvine, Esq., second son of Major Hamilton Irvine.

No. 383 :: Ref. 1845-11-25, 2:5, D.
Nov. 18, at Glentimon, in the parish of Urney, at the advanced age of 105 years, Mrs. Knox, relict of the late Mr. Hugh Knox, of said place.

No. 384 :: Ref. 1845-11-25, 2:5, D.
Nov. 14, at Oundle, in Northamptonshire, Hariette, relict of the late Rev. John Stack, Rector of Dromaid, county of Sligo.

No. 385 :: Ref. 1845-11-25, 2:5, D.
At Drumcondra Hill, Dublin, after a lingering illness, which he bore with christian fortitude, the Rev. John S. Wilson, Wesleyan Methodist Minister.

No. 386 :: Ref. 1845-12-02, 3:4, B.

Nov. 29, in Abbey-street, in this city, the wife of the Rev. G. Grant, Wesleyan Minister, of a son, which survived but a few hours.

No. 387 :: Ref. 1845-12-02, 3:4, B.

Nov. 21, at Rathfriland, county Down, the lady of James Ponsonby Hill, Esq., sub-inspector of constabulary, of a son.

No. 388 :: Ref. 1845-12-02, 3:4, B.

At Dunfanaghy, county Donegal, the lady of the Rev. Edmund Maturin, of a son.

No. 389 :: Ref. 1845-12-02, 3:4, M.

Nov. 24, at Rosstrevor, by the Rev. P. M'Evoy, P.P., Thomas Whittington, Egan, [sic] Esq., eldest son of the late Thomas Egan, Esq., Solicitor, Dublin, to Miss Kate, only daughter of the late Mark Devlin, Esq., Solicitor, Newry.

No. 390 :: Ref. 1845-12-02, 3:4, M.

Nov. 27, at St. Ann's Church, by the Rev. William M'Ilwaine, Mr. Robert Atkinson, eldest son of Mr. John Atkinson, Portadown, to Susanna, daughter of the late James Bryson, Esq., Waring-street, Belfast.

No. 391 :: Ref. 1845-12-02, 3:4, M.

Nov. 20, at Plumstead Church, Robert Ramsay Pringle, Esq., Deputy Ordnance Store-keeper and Barrack-master at Enniskillen, to Harriette, third daughter of Joseph Cheetham, Esq., Ordnance Store-keeper, Windsor.

No. 392 :: Ref. 1845-12-02, 3:4, M.

On Wednesday morning last, in Ballyshannon Church, by the Rev. Mr. White, curate, Mr. Robert Kerr, Primitive Wesleyan Methodist Minister, to Miss Charlotte Patience Hardinge, youngest daughter of Captain Hardinge, Donegal Militia.

No. 393 :: Ref. 1845-12-02, 3:4, M.

Nov. 18, by the Rev. James White, Mr. Richard Apsley, Steward of the ship *Sea-King*, to Miss Margaret M'Dowell, both of Carrickfergus.

No. 394 :: Ref. 1845-12-02, 3:4, D.

Nov. 23, at the residence of her father, Jane, third daughter of Mark Berry, Esq., of Richmount, in the 21st year of her age. She was amiable in health—patient in affliction—and triumphant in death. Her mortal remains were conveyed on Tuesday last, to Drumcree graveyard, the family burying-place, attended by the parish clergyman and a numerous circle of respectable sorrowing friends and acquaintances.

No. 395 :: Ref. 1845-12-02, 3:4, D.

At Agean, in France, the Honourable George Hely Hutchinson, nephew of the late, and brother of the present Earl of Donaghmore.

No. 396 :: Ref. 1845-12-02, 3:4, D.

Nov. 23, suddenly, at Arthurstown, Wexford, Edward Sweeney, Esq., Sub-Inspector of Police, and nephew of Daniel O'Connell, Esq., M.P.

No. 397 :: Ref. 1845-12-09, 2:5, B.

On Saturday the 6th instant, the lady of the Rev. Henry de Laval Willis, Incumbent of Portadown, of a daughter.

No. 398 :: Ref. 1845-12-09, 2:5, B.

Nov. 24, at Fair View, Dungannon, the lady of the Rev. John Vigneles Brabazon, of a daughter.

No. 399 :: Ref. 1845-12-09, 2:5, B.

Nov. 25, at Portadown, the lady of John Obins Woodhouse, Esq., of a daughter, still-born.

No. 400 :: Ref. 1845-12-09, 2:5, M.

Nov. 25, in the Office of the District Register, Castleblayney, by the Rev. Thomas Cathcart, Mr. Robert Crane of Tullycahey, farmer, to Miss Agnes M'Kee, of Tullynaglush, county Armagh.

No. 401 :: Ref. 1845-12-09, 2:5, M.

Dec. 2, by the Rev. Edward Harvey, Mr. John Campbell, of Cootehill, Woollendraper, to Miss Sarah M'Elwain, of Coleraine.

No. 402 :: Ref. 1845-12-09, 2:5, M.

Nov. 27, in Loughgall Church, John, eldest son of the late Robert Langtry, of Bellview, in the county of Armagh, Esq., to Sarah, third daughter of Mr. William Orr, of Ballymagerney, linen merchant.

No. 403 :: Ref. 1845-12-09, 2:5, D.

Suddenly, at Charlemont, on the 3d instant, Mr. Joseph M'Mullan of that town, aged 62 years.

No. 404 :: Ref. 1845-12-16, 2:6, B.

At Coleraine, on the 7th inst., the lady of the Rev. Dr. Appelbe, Wesleyan Minister, of a son.

No. 405 :: Ref. 1845-12-16, 2:6, M.

On Friday, the 12th inst., at the Second Presbyterian Meeting-house, of this City, by the Rev. S. Edgar, Mr. James Johnston, of Ballinagaragh, to Martha, second daughter of Mr. William Couser, of Achavilly, in this County.

No. 406 :: Ref. 1845-12-16, 2:6, M.

Dec. 5, at Aughavea Church, Mr. Alexander Irvine, of Enniskillen, Woollen-draper, to Jane, eldest daughter of W.S. Armstrong, Esq., Brookeborough.

No. 407 :: Ref. 1845-12-16, 2:6, M.

On the 1st inst., in Aghadoey Meeting-house, by the Rev. Dr. Brown, Mr. James Duncan, eldest son of Mr. William Duncan, Head-Constable of Police, Clogher, county Tyrone, to Miss Ann M'Cloy, eldest daughter of Mr. William M'Cloy, farmer, county Derry.

No. 408 :: Ref. 1845-12-16, 2:6, M.

Dec. 11, in Fisherwick-place Church, by the Rev. James Morgan, James Alexander Henderson, Esq., eldest son of James Henderson, Esq., Newry, to Agnes, daughter of the late Alexander Mackay, jun., Esq., Mount Collyer Park.

No. 409 :: Ref. 1845-12-16, 2:6, M.

Dec. 6, at the Wesleyan Chapel, Great Homer-street, Liverpool, by the Rev. C.M. Birrill, Baptist Minister, the Rev. Camillo Pietro Vincenzo Melchiorre Baldassarro Mapei, D.D., formerly a Roman Catholic Priest, Canon of the Cathedral, Examiner of the Clergy, and Professor of Theology, at Penne, in the kingdom of Naples, to Caroline, third daughter of John R. Burrowes, Esq., Surgeon, Great Oxford-street.

No. 410 :: Ref. 1845-12-16, 2:6, D.

On the 10th inst., Jane, the beloved wife of the Rev. Samuel Shaw, of Moy, deeply lamented by a large and affectionate circle of friends. Her remains were interred on the 13th in the burial ground of the parish Church of that town. The kindest spirit of sympathy was manifested, in the attendance of the Clergymen of the Church of England, the Roman Catholic Clergy, the Presbyterian, the Wesleyan and Congregational Ministers, with many of their respective flocks. The solemn ceremony of burial was performed by the Rev. J.D. Smyth, of Newry, who, also, on the following Sabbath, improved the event of this afflictive bereavement, to the sympathising congregation over which the sorrowing Pastor presides.

No. 411 :: Ref. 1845-12-16, 2:6, D.

In this City, on Sunday evening, the 10th inst., of decline, Mary Jane, the beloved wife of Mr. Robert Gilmore, merchant, aged 25 years.

No. 412 :: Ref. 1845-12-16, 2:6, D.

Dec. 6, at her residence, in Upper Dorset-st., Dublin, in her eighty-second year, Mary, relict of Hamilton Cross, Esq., late of this city, and formerly of Clones, county of Monaghan.

No. 413 :: Ref. 1845-12-23, 3:1, B.

On the 9th instant, at Annesley Lodge, Coal Island, the lady of Robert Stewart Wilberforce King, Esq., of a daughter.

No. 414 :: Ref. 1845-12-23, 3:1, M.

On the 17th inst., in the Cathedral, Armagh, by the Rev. Mr. Haig, Thomas Greer, Esq., of Belfast, to Sarah Jane, second daughter of Thomas Scott, Esq., Grange, and niece of George Scott, Esq., Armagh.

No. 415 :: Ref. 1845-12-23, 3:1, M.

On the 16th inst., at Bryansford Church, by the Rev. Christopher Ussher, Henry L. Lindsay, Esq., Melbourne Terrace, Armagh, to Helena, third daughter of the late Christopher Crawley, of Bryansford, in the County of Down, Esq.

No. 416 :: Ref. 1845-12-23, 3:1, M.

On the 11th inst., in the Presbyterian Meeting-house, Cookstown, by the Rev. Thomas Miller, Mr. Robert Henry, of Stewartstown, merchant, to Marianne, fourth daughter of Mr. Joseph Dudgeon, Postmaster, Stewartstown.

No. 417 :: Ref. 1845-12-23, 3:1, M.

On the 11th instant, by the Rev. A. Symington, D. D., Paisley, the Rev. William S. Ferguson, of Grange, County Tyrone, to Sarah Jane, second daughter of Alexander Ferguson, Esq., of Ardtrea, near Cookstown.

No. 418 :: Ref. 1845-12-23, 3:1, D.

On the 18th instant, at his house in Scotch-street, in this City, aged 31 years, Mr. Alexander Davidson. By an humble reliance on the great Atonement, he was enabled to meet death with much calmness and resignation.

No. 419 :: Ref. 1845-12-23, 3:1, D.

At Dungannon, on the 19th inst., Mr. Thomas M'Adam, Druggist and Apothecary, formerly of Loughgall. His remains were interred in St. Mark's Church-yard on yesterday.

No. 420 :: Ref. 1845-12-23, 3:1, D.

On the 8th instant, at Clones, after giving birth to two daughters, Sophia Anne, the beloved wife of Mr. Joseph Crowe.

No. 421 :: Ref. 1845-12-23, 3:1, D.

December 15, in Fitzwilliam-square, Wm. Alexander, Esq.

No. 422 :: Ref. 1845-12-23, 3:1, D.

December 15, in Waterford, the Rev. Francis Newport, Vicar of Poleroan, diocese of Ossory.

No. 423 :: Ref. 1845-12-23, 3:1, D.

November 29, near Florence, the Hon. Colonel Hughes, brother to Lord Dinorben.

No. 424 :: Ref. 1845-12-30, 3:3, B.

December 17, at Brighton, the Marchioness of Abercorn, of a son.

No. 425 :: Ref. 1845-12-30, 3:3, B.

December 21, at Florencecourt, the Countess of Enniskillen, of a son.

No. 426 :: Ref. 1845-12-30, 3:3, B.

December 19, at Belmont, Forkhill, the lady of Henry Stanley, Esq., of a daughter.

No. 427 :: Ref. 1845-12-30, 3:3, M.

December 27, at Stewartstown, in the Parish Church of Donaghendry, by the Rev. J.J. Jackson, the Rev. Charles Ward, of Wadworth, Yorkshire, to Mary, daughter of the late Very Rev. J.E. Jackson, Dean of Armagh.

No. 428 :: Ref. 1845-12-30, 3:3, M.

December 15, in Ballinamallard Church, by the Rev. Thomas Ovenden, Mr. William Anderson, son of William Anderson, Esq., of Lowtherstown, to Jane, daughter of William Armstrong, Esq., of Kilgartnaleague.

No. 429 :: Ref. 1845-12-30, 3:3, M.

At Killult Church, on Thursday, the 18th instant, by the Rev. David Irwin (father of the bride), John Walker Benson, Esq., eldest son of Richard Benson, of Carrowcannon, Esq., to Jane, eldest daughter of the Rev. David Irwin, Rector of the parish of Tulloughobegley, county Donegal.

No. 430 :: Ref. 1845-12-30, 3:3, D.

On Friday, 26th instant, at the Deanery, Armagh, Mr. Sam Hawkins, aged 35 years, Land-Steward to the Rev. Dr. Elrington. He was a faithful servant, and the respectable concourse which attended his remains to their last resting-place, showed how much he was esteemed in life. The burial service was read by Dr. Elrington, who seemed deeply affected while performing the solemn rite.

No. 431 :: Ref. 1845-12-30, 3:3, D.

On the 10th instant, at Cordrummond, near Markethill, Mr. William Redmond, in the 85th year of his age.

No. 432 :: Ref. 1845-12-30, 3:3, D.

December 10, at Lakefield, Mohill, Duke Crofton, Esq., one of the oldest magistrates, and a D.L. of the county of Leitrim.

No. 433 :: Ref. 1846-01-06, 2:6, B.

On the 22d of December, at Tynan, the lady of Dr. Huston, of a son.

No. 434 :: Ref. 1846-01-06, 2:6, B.

Dec. 25, at Riverstown, county of Fermanagh, the lady of Robert Archdall, Esq., of a daughter.

No. 435 :: Ref. 1846-01-06, 2:6, M.

Dec. 31, in Carrickmacross Church, by the Rev. William Thompson, Mr. John C. Adams, of the city of Armagh, to Eliza, second daughter of Mr. Geo. Rennick, of Carrickmacross.

No. 436 :: Ref. 1846-01-06, 2:6, M.

Dec. 15, by the Rev. William Ferguson, Mr. John Johnston, Donagh, Monaghan, to Lydia Anne, daughter of Mr. John Curry, Halftown, Aughnacloy.

No. 437 :: Ref. 1846-01-06, 2:6, M.

Dec. 26, in the Cathedral Church of Clogher, by the Rev. Mr. Ash, Mr. George Alexander, of Breakly, to Jane, eldest daughter of Mr. William Killen, of Mullaghmore.

No. 438 :: Ref. 1846-01-06, 2:6, M.

Dec. 26, in Longford Church, by the Rev. J. Le Poer Trench, Mr. William Bredin, of Maguiresbridge, County of Fermanagh, to Catherine Anne, third daughter of Mr. H. Needham, of Longford.

No. 439 :: Ref. 1846-01-06, 2:6, D.

On Friday, the 2nd inst., at Ballyhaise, county Cavan, William Adams, Esq.

No. 440 :: Ref. 1846-01-06, 2:6, D.

At his residence, Victoria-place, Belfast, Samuel B. Greer, Esq., son of the late Thomas Greer, Esq., Belfast, formerly of Armagh.

No. 441 :: Ref. 1846-01-06, 2:6, D.

On Thursday, the 1st instant, at Belfast, Mr. Thomas Wilson, linen merchant.

No. 442 :: Ref. 1846-01-13, 2:2, B.

January 6th, at Gardiner's-place, Dublin, the lady of Joseph Nelson, Esq., Q.C., of a son.

No. 443 :: Ref. 1846-01-13, 2:2, M.

On the 8th inst., in St. Ann's Church, Belfast, by the Rev. Wm. Campbell, Mr. John Stanley, Merchant, Portadown, to Ann Jane, eldest daughter of the late Mr. John Coates, Belfast.

No. 444 :: Ref. 1846-01-13, 2:6, M.

In the First Presbyterian Meeting House, Monaghan, by the Rev. John Bleckley, William Kinkead, Esq., of the Belfast Bank, Newry, to Margaretta, third daughter of the late David Horner, Esq., of Monaghan.

No. 445 :: Ref. 1846-01-13, 2:6, D.

On the 6th inst., at Annagh, near Portadown, Mr. William Church, aged 85 years.

No. 446 :: Ref. 1846-01-13, 2:6, D.

January 6, at his residence, in Great Ship-street, in the 70th year of his age, deeply regretted, Mr. Francis Priestly, upwards of forty-five years compositor on *Saunders's News Letter*.

No. 447 :: Ref. 1846-01-13, 2:6, D.

On the 25th December, at his residence, John M'Clintock, Esq., eldest son of the late Alexander M'Clintock, Esq., of Mountain House, county Louth.

No. 448 :: Ref. 1846-01-20, 3:4, B.

On the 6th inst., at Melbourne-terrace, in this city, the lady of James Trewman Bell, Esq., of a daughter.

No. 449 :: Ref. 1846-01-20, 3:4, B.

On the 13th inst., at Markethill, the lady of the Rev. Chas. Seaver, Curate of Mullabrack, of a daughter.

No. 450 :: Ref. 1846-01-20, 3:4, B.

On the 16th inst., in the townland of Derrypubble, Mrs. Thomas Stafford, of a son.

No. 451 :: Ref. 1846-01-20, 3:4, M.

On the 14th inst., at the District Registrar's Office, Dungannon, John Avil, Esq., of Northampton, England, to Eliza, eldest daughter of Mr. James Duncan, Academy, Dungannon.

No. 452 :: Ref. 1846-01-20, 3:4, M.
On the 14th inst., at the bride's father's, by the Rev. Eugene Troy, R.C.C., Mr. James Magill, Innkeeper, Dungannon, to Jane, eldest daughter of Mr. James Dixon, Coreany, Dungannon.

No. 453 :: Ref. 1846-01-20, 3:4, M.
On the 13th inst., at Dungannon, by the Rev. Eugene Troy, R.C.C., Mr. William Griffith, to Anne, only daughter of Mr. Patrick Begley, farmer, Clonor.

No. 454 :: Ref. 1846-01-20, 3:4, M.
On the 14th inst., at Tallaght Church, by the Rev. William Robinson, William Irwin, Esq., Captain 88th Regiment, to Elizabeth, only surviving daughter of the late Joshua Crump, Esq., of Carland, near Dungannon.

No. 455 :: Ref. 1846-01-20, 3:4, M.
In Tynan Church, on the 9th inst., by the Rev. T.J. White, Mr. Daniel M'Caul, of Middletown, Master-taylor, to Miss Mary Anne Morrison, of Limnagore, daughter of Mr. James Morrison, Builder, of same place.

No. 456 :: Ref. 1846-01-20, 3:4, M.
On the 8th inst., in Moy Church, by the Rev. Mr. Leeche, Mr. William Weir, third son of Mr. Henry Weir, Tullamore, to Martha, second daughter of Mr. Thomas Wilson, Derryscholop.

No. 457 :: Ref. 1846-01-20, 3:4, M.
On the 12th instant, in Armaghbreague Church, by the Rev. D. Donaldson, A.M., Wm. Tenison Collyns, Esq., M.R.C.S., to Emma, third daughter of the late Samuel Magee, Esq., M.D. of Keady, County Armagh.

No. 458 :: Ref. 1846-01-20, 3:4, M.
On the 8th instant, in Richhill Church, by the Rev. James Hogan, Mr. William Hewett, near Portadown, to Miss Anne Jane, third daughter of Mr. Wm. Sinton, near Richhill.

No. 459 :: Ref. 1846-01-20, 3:4, M.
On the 11th instant, in Killyleagh Church, by the Rev. Edward Hincks, D.D., Mr. Joseph Henry Martin, of Birkenhead, to Maryann, eldest daughter of Mr. Henry Girvin, of Killyleagh, county Down.

No. 460 :: Ref. 1846-01-20, 3:4, M.
Jan. 13, in St. Peter's Church, by the Rev. Mr. Griffith, S. Rutherford Moorhead, Esq., of Clones, in the county of Monaghan, to Mary Elizabeth, only daughter of Henry Barton, Esq., of Clanbrassil-terrace, and grand-daughter of the late Thomas Hamilton Ennis, formerly of Dublin.

No. 461 :: Ref. 1846-01-20, 3:4, M.
On the 16th inst., in Benburb Church, by the Rev. Richard Writeson, Mr. Robert Osburn, son of Mr. Osburn, near Aughnacloy, to Miss Jane Bleeks, eldest daughter of Mr. Thomas Bleeks, of Curren.

No. 462 :: Ref. 1846-01-20, 3:4, D.
On the 15th inst., at Portarlington, Frances, daughter of the late Rev. Richard Clarke, of Portarlington, and sister of Dr. Clarke, of Blackwatertown.

No. 463 :: Ref. 1846-01-20, 3:4, D.
On the 13th inst., in this city, John Morris, fourth son of Mr. Nicholas Colvan, Actuary, Armagh Loan Fund, aged 13 years.

No. 464 :: Ref. 1846-01-20, 3:4, D.
On the 15th inst., at Larch Mount, Dungannon, the residence of his son-in-law, Wm. Robson, Esq., Samuel King, Esq., of the firm of King & Newton, Coalisland Mills, and for many years a leading merchant in Dungannon, much and deservedly regretted.

No. 465 :: Ref. 1846-01-20, 3:4, D.
On the 13th inst., at Lurgan, James Morrison, Esq., Manager of the Ulster Branch Bank.

No. 466 :: Ref. 1846-01-20, 3:4, D.
On the 7th inst., at Outerarde, Margaret, the beloved wife of J.D. M'Illre, Esq, of Cnlturbet [sic], county of Cavan.

No. 467 :: Ref. 1846-01-20, 3:4, D.
January 7, at his residence, Lower Fitswilliam street, after a painful and tedious illness, Robert S. Irvine, Esq., only surviving son of the late Doctor Irvine, of Johnstown, county Fermanagh, aged 73 years.

No. 468 :: Ref. 1846-01-20, 3:4, D.
In the nineteenth year of her age, Mary, the only daughter of Mr. John Jenkins, Altinamorichan, Newtownhamilton.

No. 469 :: Ref. 1846-01-20, 3:4, D.
On the 5th November, at Cape Town, in the 23d year of her age, Anna, second daughter of the late Captain John Scott, of Umgola, county Armagh, Ireland.

Safe on the bosom of thy God,
Fair Spirit rest thee now;
E'en while with us thy footsteps trod,
His seal was on thy brow.
Dust, to its narrow house beneath,
Soul, to its seat on high;
Who that hath seen thy look in death,
They need not fear to die.
—Sly's African Journal.

No. 470 :: Ref. 1846-01-27, 3:2, M.
On the 14th instant, at the Registry Office, Dungannon, by the Rev. Mr. Bates, the Rev. Mr. Aveo, Baptist Minister, to Miss Elizabeth Duncan, eldest daughter of Mr. James Duncan, Perry Street, Dungannon.

No. 471 :: Ref. 1846-01-27, 3:2, M.
January 20, at Cabra House, county Down, George H. Gartlan, Esq., of Carrickmacross, to Mary, eldest daughter of Alexander M'Mullen Esq.

No. 472 :: Ref. 1846-01-27, 3:2, D.
On the 19th instant, at Aughataragh, Mr. James Allen, aged 80 years. The respect in which the deceased was held was amply testified by the very numerous concourse of friends and neighbours who accompanied his remains to *"that bourne from whence no traveller returns."*

No. 473 :: Ref. 1846-01-27, 3:2, D.
At Shanmullagh, near Ballycassidy, county Fermanagh, on the 20th instant, aged 66, Mr. James Armstrong, very deservedly regretted.

No. 474 :: Ref. 1846-01-27, 3:2, D.
On the 18th instant, in Aughnacloy, James W. Spear, Esq., eldest son of W. Spear, late of Belnesagart, county Tyrone, Esq., very much regretted by many relatives and acquaintances.

No. 475 :: Ref. 1846-01-27, 3:2, D.
On the 13th inst., at his residence, Marorkin, County Armagh, Mr. Daniel Black, aged 90 years.

No. 476 :: Ref. 1846-01-27, 3:2, D.
On the 15th inst., at his residence, Dungannon, Mr. Arthur Devlin, aged 73 years.

No. 477 :: Ref. 1846-01-27, 3:2, D.
June 18, at Mountpleasant, Ballyconnell, Bedel Benison, Esq, aged 73 years, deeply and universally regretted.

No. 478 :: Ref. 1846-01-27, 3:2, D.
January 12, at Carnagh House, in the county of Armagh, John Robert, third and youngest son of John Robert Irwin, Esq., aged fourteen months.

No. 479 :: Ref. 1846-01-27, 3:2, D.
On the 19th instant, at Ballinahatty, Mr. Ebenezer Rogers, at the advanced age of 95 years.

No. 480 :: Ref. 1846-02-03, 3:1, B.
Jan. 23, at Mountnorris, the lady of the Rev. Richard Verschoyle, of a son.

No. 481 :: Ref. 1846-02-03, 3:1, B.
At Keady Rectory, county Armagh, the lady of the Rev. Samuel Simpson, of a son.

No. 482 :: Ref. 1846-02-03, 3:1, M.
Jan. 28, in St. Thomas's Church, by the Rev. J.J. Molloy, William Auchinleck Dane, fourth son of the late Richard Dane, Esq., D.L. and J.P., of Killyhevlin, in the county of Fermanagh, to Sarah, daughter of the late Benjamin Friel Foster, of Drumloo Cottage, in the county of Monaghan.

No. 483 :: Ref. 1846-02-03, 3:1, D.
Jan. 27, in Belfast, at the residence of her son-in-law, Mr. Alexander Forrester, Mrs. Brown, aged 60, only sister of the late Mr. George Corry, Merchant, Armagh.

No. 484 :: Ref. 1846-02-03, 3:1, D.
Jan. 28, at her residence at Kingstown, Mrs. Henrietta Spear, widow of Frederick Spear, Esq., of College-green, Dublin.

No. 485 :: Ref. 1846-02-10, 2:6, B.
February 3, at Enniskillen, the lady of the Rev. Newport White, of a son.

No. 486 :: Ref. 1846-02-10, 2:6, B.
January 28, at Corry-square, Newry, the lady of M. Singleton, Esq., R.M., of a son.

No. 487 :: Ref. 1846-02-10, 2:6, M.
On the 5th inst., in Tartaraghan Church, by the Hon. and Rev. Francis Clements, Mr. Charles Dunlop, Clanacle, to Anne Thistle, only Daughter of Mr. John Woodhouse, Foxpark, Loughgall.

No. 488 :: Ref. 1846-02-10, 2:6, M.
On the 4th inst., at Monkstown Church, by the Rev. Hans Atkinson, brother to the bridegroom, Charles Atkinson, of Green Hall, county of Armagh, Esq., to Rebecca Sarah, only child of the late Henry Kyle, of Mountpelier-parade, county of Dublin, Esq., and niece to the Right Rev. the Lord Bishop of Cork.

No. 489 :: Ref. 1846-02-10, 2:6, M.
On the 29th ult., the Rev. Stewart Fullerton, of Ahoghill, to Miss Barnett, daughter of Thomas Barnett, Esq., Ballough, Clogher, county Tyrone.

No. 490 :: Ref. 1846-02-10, 2:6, D.
On Sunday, 25th January, at Manchester, after a short illness, which he bore with Christian fortitude, Mr. Thomas Callison, late of Drumorgan, county Armagh, aged 39 years. Beloved by all that knew him and by them sincerely regretted, his end was peaceful and triumphant.

No. 491 :: Ref. 1846-02-10, 2:6, D.
At Ballintagert, near Portadown, Mr. Robert Hewitt, aged 47 years, much and deservedly regretted.

No. 492 :: Ref. 1846-02-10, 2:6, D.
On the 30th ult. at Tyrrels-Pass, in his 19th year, of bilious fever, George, eldest son of Thomas Somers, Esq., of that place, and grandson of the late Dr. Armstrong of Clones.

No. 493 :: Ref. 1846-02-10, 2:6, D.
January 28, at Killevie Castle, county Armagh, the residence of Powell Foxall, Esq., Sarah Selina Welsh, aged 81 years, relict of Robert Welsh, of Dublin, Esq., Barrister-at-law.

No. 494 :: Ref. 1846-02-17, 2:6, B.
On the 12th inst., the lady of Dr. Henry, Pomeroy Dispensary, of a son.

No. 495 :: Ref. 1846-02-17, 2:6, M.
On Thursday, the 12th instant, in the Red Rock Presbyterian meeting-house, by the Rev. James Hervey, Mr. Hans Hamilton, of Derryran, to Sarah, second daughter of Mr. Nathaniel M'Clure, of Killycopple, both of the county of Armagh.

No. 496 :: Ref. 1846-02-17, 2:6, D.
On Tuesday, the 10th inst., in this city, Mrs. Margaret Wright, wife of Mr. Thomas Wright, aged 50 years, much and deservedly regretted.

No. 497 :: Ref. 1846-02-17, 2:6, D.
On Saturday, the 7th instant, aged 23 years, Mr. William Scott, of Lake View, in the County of Armagh. Though cut off in the prime of life, yet his sorrowing friends are consoled with the assurance that he sleeps in Jesus.

No. 498 :: Ref. 1846-02-17, 2:6, D.
Death of Rear-Admiral Edward S. Clay.—We have to record the decease of the above flag officer, who expired on Tuesday last, at Southwell, Notts, at the advanced age of 78 years. He had been nearly 63 years in the service, having entered the navy in 1783.

No. 499 :: Ref. 1846-02-17, 2:6, D.
At Barrackpore, Bengal, Major Robert Verner, of her Majesty's 61st regiment. His horse rearing up, fell back, and killed him on the spot.

No. 500 :: Ref. 1846-02-24, 3:3, B.
At Kircubbin, the lady of Rev. W.H. Brett, of a son.

No. 501 :: Ref. 1846-02-24, 3:3, B.
Feb. 17, at Madden, near Armagh, the lady of the Rev. S. Mangan, of a son.

No. 502 :: Ref. 1846-02-24, 3:3, M.
Feb. 12, in St. George's Church, Dublin, John Miller, Esq., Barrister-at-Law, to Frances, Dianna [sic], daughter of the late Richard R. Lodge, of Caledon, county Tyrone, Esq.

No. 503 :: Ref. 1846-02-24, 3:3, M.
Feb. 13, in the Cathedral, Derry, by the Rev. John Kincaid, Mr. James Fowler, late of Newry, to Sarah, eldest daughter of Mr. John Laverty, of Derry.

No. 504 :: Ref. 1846-02-24, 3:3, M.
Feb. 12, in St. Peter's Church, Dublin, Wm. A. Williams, Esq., of Mount Carmel, county Monaghan, to Frances Beasley, youngest daughter of the late R. Beasley, Esq., Lieutenant in the 9th Light Dragoons.

No. 505 :: Ref. 1846-02-24, 3:3, M.
Feb. 12, in the Parish Church of Tullyneskin, Courtenay, eldest son of Andrew Newton, Esq., of Dungannon, to Anne, daughter of the late Richard Howard, Esq., of Phipsbridge, Mitcham, Surrey.

No. 506 :: Ref. 1846-02-24, 3:3, M.
Feb. 18, in Coolock Church, by the Rev. W. Machoney, William Edwin Clarke, Esq., of Liverpool, son of George R. Clarke, Esq., to Fanny, eldest daughter of James Kerr, Esq., of Larchhill, Santry, and Capel-street, Dublin.

No. 507 :: Ref. 1846-02-24, 3:3, D.
Feb. 17, in this City, Mr. Charles Forster, sen., in his 67th year, deeply and deservedly regretted by a numerous circle of friends and acquaintances.

No. 508 :: Ref. 1846-02-24, 3:3, D.
Feb. 11, at 120, Summer-hill, Dublin, Elizabeth, the beloved wife of Mr. George M'Mullen, formerly of Lurgan.

No. 509 :: Ref. 1846-02-24, 3:3, D.
Feb. 16, in Enniskillen, George Spear, Esq., of apoplexy, at the advanced age of 82, a magistrate for three counties, Cavan, Fermanagh, and Tyrone, for the last 50 years.

No. 510 :: Ref. 1846-02-24, 3:3, D.
Feb. 18, at Willoughby-place, Enniskillen, Captain Stewart, aged 70 years.

No. 511 :: Ref. 1846-02-24, 3:3, D.
Feb. 19, at Enniskillen, Mr. William Kitson, merchant.

No. 512 :: Ref. 1846-02-24, 3:3, D.
Feb. 18, at Harmony Avenue, Donnybrook, aged 71 years, the Rev. William Kidd, Wesleyan Methodist Minister.

No. 513 :: Ref. 1846-02-24, 3:3, D.
Feb. 12, at Portadown, Jane, eldest daughter of Henry Stanley, Esq.

No. 514 :: Ref. 1846-02-24, 3:3, D.
Feb. 13, at Carrig Glebe, county Cavan, aged 71 years, the Rev. Thomas Skelton, Vicar for 39 years of the parish of Kildrumferton, in the diocese of Kilmore.

No. 515 :: Ref. 1846-02-24, 3:3, D.
Feb. 14, at 105, Lower Baggot-street, Miss Moore, sister of the Poet, Thomas Moore, Esq., greatly beloved and respected by a numerous circle of friends.

No. 516 :: Ref. 1846-03-03, 2:5, B.
On Friday, 20th ultimo, at Vicar's Hill, in this city, Mrs. George Allen, of a daughter.

No. 517 :: Ref. 1846-03-03, 2:5, M.
On the 27th ult., in St. Mary's Church, Newry, by the Rev. W.R. Williams, Edward D. Atkinson, Esq., of Tandragee, to Georgina, third daughter of the late James Searight, Esq., of Newry.

No. 518 :: Ref. 1846-03-03, 2:5, M.
On the 1st inst., in Moy Church, by the Rev. John Leech, Mr. Joseph Kidd, of Culkeeran, to Arabella, daughter of Mr. James Pillar, formerly of same place.

No. 519 :: Ref. 1846-03-03, 2:5, M.
On 27th ult., in 2nd Presbyterian Church, Armagh, by the Rev. S. Edgar, Mr. Henry Stewart, to Jane, daughter of Mr. Joseph Redman, both of Lisnadill, in this county.

No. 520 :: Ref. 1846-03-03, 2:5, M.
In Lisnaskea Church, on Tuesday, 24th ult., by the Rev. William Dickson, Mr. Thomas Russell, of Belfast, to Miss Catherine Wade, of Lisnaskea, third daughter of the late Mr. Francis Wade, of Fivemiletown, county Tyrone.

No. 521 :: Ref. 1846-03-03, 2:5, D.
Feb. 26, at his residence, Maydown, Richard Cross, Esq., aged 63.

No. 522 :: Ref. 1846-03-03, 2:5, D.
On Tuesday morning last, 24th ult., in Abbey-street, Mr. Alexander Baxter, Builder, aged 39 years, much and deservedly regretted.

No. 523 :: Ref. 1846-03-03, 2:5, D.
On the 26th ult., at his residence Rockland, near Carlingford, in the 70th year of his age, after a lingering illness, George Farley, Esq., esteemed and lamented by all who had the happiness of his acquaintance.

No. 524 :: Ref. 1846-03-10, 3:6, D.
March 1, at Crossmaglen, Samuel Ball, Esq., only son of the late Captain Ball, Royal Marines.

No. 525 :: Ref. 1846-03-17, 3:1, M.
On the 6th inst., at the Stone-bridge Presbyterian Meeting-house, by the Rev. Wm. White, Mr. James Armstrong, of Kalmacklay, to Miss Anne Armstrong, Drummullen, both of the county Monaghan.

No. 526 :: Ref. 1846-03-17, 3:1, M.
March 5, in Clones Register office, Mr. George Pogue, of Clinculland, to Miss Jane Little, of Clough, eldest daughter of the late Mr. Wm. Little, both of the county Monaghan.

No. 527 :: Ref. 1846-03-17, 3:1, M.
On the 12th inst., at Druminis Presbyterian Meeting-house, by the Rev. Mr. Kidd, Mr. John Bell, of Derryrane, to Miss Ferguson, daughter of Mr. Hugh Ferguson.

No. 528 :: Ref. 1846-03-17, 3:1, D.
On Monday, the 9th inst., at the residence of her father, Charlemont Place, Armagh, Elizabeth, second daughter of William Lodge Kidd, Esq., M.D.

No. 529 :: Ref. 1846-03-31, 2:6, B.
At Clones, on the 24th inst., the lady of M. William Jordan, Cabinet-maker of a son.

No. 530 :: Ref. 1846-03-31, 2:6, B.
On Monday last, at Dundiven glebe, the lady of the Rev. Thomas Maunsell, of a son.

No. 531 :: Ref. 1846-03-31, 2:6, M.
March 23, in Ballinode church, county of Monaghan, the Rev. Edward O'Bryen Pratt, Curate of Killymard, in the diocese of Raphoe, to Geraldine Caulfield, relict of Thomas C. Hanington, Esq., and youngest daughter of James Murray Gordon, Esq., of Balmaghie House, Kircudbrightshire, Captain in the Royal Navy.

No. 532 :: Ref. 1846-03-31, 2:6, D.
On the 13th inst., at 10, Corn-market, Dublin, of inflammation of the lungs, Grace Bell, youngest daughter of Mr. Letford M'Clelland, Dungannon.

No. 533 :: Ref. 1846-03-31, 2:6, D.
At his residence, Ballycushy, near Fintona, aged 36, Mr. Joseph Moore, sincerely and most deservedly regretted by a numerous circle of friends and acquaintances, to whom he was deservedly dear.

No. 534 :: Ref. 1846-03-31, 2:6, D.
March 25, at her residence, Cobourg-place, Miss Jane Sewell, in the 85th year of her age.

No. 535 :: Ref. 1846-03-31, 2:6, D.
At Island view, Enniskillen, on the 26th inst., Mr. Robert Frith, at the advanced age of 86 years.

No. 536 :: Ref. 1846-03-31, 2:6, D.
March 16, at Kilcronaghan Glebe, county Derry, after a long and painful illness, borne with Christian patience and submission to the will of his Heavenly Father, the Rev. George Harris, eldest son of the late Hugh Harris, Esq., of Ashfort, county Armagh. In all relations of life, as husband, father, and friend, he was deservedly beloved and regretted.

No. 537 :: Ref. 1846-04-07, 2:6, B.
On the 1st inst., the lady of William Walker, Esq., Architect, 8, Apsley-place, Belfast, and Monaghan, of a son.

No. 538 :: Ref. 1846-04-07, 2:6, M.
On the 30th ult., in St. Patrick's Church, Dublin, Mr. James Williams, of that city, to Miss Martha Hamilton, eldest daughter of Mr. George Hamilton, Farmer, of Gortanelly, near Caledon.

No. 539 :: Ref. 1846-04-07, 2:6, M.
On the 1st inst., in the parish church, Carrickfergus, by the Very Rev. the Dean of Connor, the Rev. Jonathan Lovett Darby, of Acton Glebe, county of Armagh, to Anne Catherine, eldest daughter of Alexander Johns, Esq., of Carrickfergus.

No. 540 :: Ref. 1846-04-07, 2:6, D.
On the 29th ult., at his residence in Dublin, Jonathan David Clarke, Esq., Q.C., of Merrion-square, Dublin, and La Bergerie, Portarlington, aged

75, for many years Father of the Home Bar, and father of Francis Clarke, Esq., M.D., Blackwatertown, county of Armagh.

No. 541 :: Ref. 1846-04-07, 2:6, D.
On the 24th ult., at the residence of her mother, Savilla, wife of Mr. John Turner, and youngest daughter of the late Mr. William Osborne, of Newry.

No. 542 :: Ref. 1846-04-07, 2:6, D.
On the 31st ult., in Chichester-street, Belfast, of decline, Letitia, youngest daughter of the late Wm. Richardson, Esq., Moy, county Tyrone. Her remains were interred in the family burying place, in Moy Church-yard, on the 2d inst.

No. 543 :: Ref. 1846-04-07, 2:6, D.
On the 26th ult., in Thomas-street, in this City, after a protracted illness aged 45 years, Rose, wife of Mr. Arthur Conry.

No. 544 :: Ref. 1846-04-07, 2:6, D.
On the 13th ult., at 10, Corn-market, Dublin, of inflammation of the lungs, Grace Bell, youngest daughter of Mr. Letford M'Clelland, Dungannon.

No. 545 :: Ref. 1846-04-07, 2:6, D.
On the 18th ult., at an advanced age, Mrs. Hassard, wife of George Hassard, Esq., J.P., of Skea House, county Fermanagh.

No. 546 :: Ref. 1846-04-07, 2:6, D.
February 15, on board the Royal Mail steamer *Thames*, on passage from Bermuda to Jamaica, of rapid consumption, Lieutenant Edward Warwick Harvey, of the 36th Regiment, youngest son of Major-General Sir John Harvey, Governor of Newfoundland, and nephew of Lord Lake.

No. 547 :: Ref. 1846-04-07, 2:6, D.
On the 29th ult., in Dublin, Sophia Willoughby, wife of Thomas Tilson Magan, Esq., and daughter of the late W. Humphreys, Esq., of Ballyhaise House, county of Cavan.

No. 548 :: Ref. 1846-04-07, 2:6, D.
On the 28th ult., in Monaghan, of dropsy and decline, which he bore with resignation to the Divine will, Mr. John Graham, aged 26 years. He left a wife and two young children to lament the loss of a kind husband and good father, and is deservedly regretted by all who knew him.

No. 549 :: Ref. 1846-04-07, 2:6, D.
In this city, on the 1st inst., James Rickard, Esq., aged 49 years, much and deservedly regretted by all who knew him.

No. 550 :: Ref. 1846-04-21, 2:6, B.
March 27, at Glenaghy, Portadown, the lady of Rev. Simon Foot, of a daughter.

No. 551 :: Ref. 1846-04-21, 2:6, B.
April 17, at Avon Lodge, Armagh, the lady of Wm. H. Davis, Esq., of a son.

No. 552 :: Ref. 1846-04-21, 2:6, B.
April 11, at Gardiner's-place, Dublin, the lady of Leonard Dobbin, Esq., of a son.

No. 553 :: Ref. 1846-04-21, 2:6, M.
On the 15th instant, in St. Mark's Church, Armagh, by the Rev. Robert Haig, Robert Riddall, of Armagh, Esq., to Harriet, second daughter of Samuel Gardner, of Armagh, Esq.

No. 554 :: Ref. 1846-04-21, 2:6, M.
On the 14th instant, John S. Mulvany, Esq., to Eleanor, daughter of Joseph Burke, Esq., of Culloville, Co. Armagh.

No. 555 :: Ref. 1846-04-21, 2:6, M.
In the Parish Church, Carrickferguss, by the Very Rev. the Dean of Connor, the Rev. J.L. Darby, of Acton Glebe, county of Armagh, to Anne Catherine, eldest daughter of Alexander Johns, Esq., of Carrickferguss.

No. 556 :: Ref. 1846-04-21, 2:6, M.
On Tuesday, 14th inst., by the Rev. Michael Lennon, P.P., John Skipton Mahony, Esq., to Eleanor, daughter of Joseph Burke, Esq., of Culloville, county Armagh.

No. 557 :: Ref. 1846-04-21, 2:6, D.
In King William-street, Keady, on the 17th inst., Mr. James Scott, in the 98th year of his age, sincerely and deservedly regretted.

No. 558 :: Ref. 1846-04-21, 2:6, D.
At Beacho, on Monday the 6th of March, inst., aged 66, Anne, the beloved wife of Mr. Thomas Wilkin.

No. 559 :: Ref. 1846-04-21, 2:6, D.
At Dungannon, on the 9th inst, at an advanced age, Ellen, relict of the late Jeremiah Coffey, Esq., Surveyor of Excise, formerly of Cashel, County Tipperary.

No. 560 :: Ref. 1846-04-21, 2:6, D.
April 2, at Monkstown House, the residence of Euseby S. Kirwan, Esq., at an advanced age, Emilia, relict of the late Rev. Robert Evans, of Dungannon, county of Tyrone.

No. 561 :: Ref. 1846-04-21, 2:6, D.
At Clenanees, Carnteel, on the 18th inst., the Rev. John Lowry, for nearly half a century Presbyterian minister of Upper Clenanees Congregation.

No. 562 :: Ref. 1846-04-21, 2:6, D.
February 15 and 18, at Secunderabad, Madras Presidency, of cholera, Captain Osborne, 40th Native Infantry (2d son of Sir Toler Osborne, Bart., and the Lady Harriette Osborne), Anne, his wife, and their youngest child. They all three lie buried in one grave.

No. 563 :: Ref. 1846-04-28, 2:6, B.
April 12, at Lurgan, the lady of Christopher Crowe, Esq., Ballintate House, county Armagh, of a daughter.

No. 564 :: Ref. 1846-04-28, 2:6, B.
April 17, at Bellevue, county Tyrone, the lady of A.W. Cole Hamilton, Esq., of a son.

No. 565 :: Ref. 1846-04-28, 2:6, B.
April 18, the lady of the Rev. James Geraghty, rector of Donaghendry, diocese of Armagh, of a son.

No. 566 :: Ref. 1846-04-28, 2:6, M.
On the 20th inst., at St. Peter's church, Dublin, by the Rev. H.C. Keogh, uncle to the bride, Shapland Swiny, of Clohamon house, county of Wexford, Esq., J.P., to Georgiana Mary, second daughter of George Rous Keogh, of Kilbride, county of Carlow, Esq., D.L., and niece to Sir George A. Molyneux, Bart. of Castledillon, county Armagh.

No. 567 :: Ref. 1846-04-28, 2:6, M.
On Wednesday, the 22d inst., in St. Mark's church, Armagh, by the Rev. E.O. Disney, Rector of Newtownhamilton, Henry Davison, Esq., eldest son of the late Thomas Davison, Esq., of Glenarm, to Alicia, eldest daughter of the late Robert Cope Hardy, Esq., of Armagh. Immediately after the ceremony, the happy couple left for Bryansfort, to spend the honey moon.

No. 568 :: Ref. 1846-04-28, 2:6, M.
March 13, at Toronto, the Rev. A. Little Hamilton Hunter, Esq., Superintendent of Education of the Home District, to Sarah, fifth daughter of Francis Mulligan, Esq., of Banbridge, Ireland.

No. 569 :: Ref. 1846-04-28, 2:6, D.
On the 20th inst., at Lurgan, Mary, third daughter of Robert Bell, Esq., M.D.

No. 570 :: Ref. 1846-04-28, 2:6, D.
On the 17th inst., at Castleblayney, Maryanne, wife of S. Smith, Esq., Sub-Inspector of Constabulary.

No. 571 :: Ref. 1846-04-28, 2:6, D.
In Laraghshankle, near Blackwatertown, on Friday, the 17th inst., Mr. James Dougan, aged 90 years.

No. 572 :: Ref. 1846-04-28, 2:6, D.
April 20, at 5, Sandford Terrace, Ann, relict of James Molyneux, Esq.

No. 573 :: Ref. 1846-04-28, 2:6, D.
April 22, at Killashee, of measles, Louisa Margaret, relict of the Rev. William Digby, in the 47th year of her age.

No. 574 :: Ref. 1846-05-05, 2:6, B.
At the residence of her father, Beresford-row, Armagh, on the 28th ult., the lady of M.B. Meredith, Esq., of a son.

No. 575 :: Ref. 1846-05-05, 2:6, B.
April 23, at Corkhill, in the county of Tyrone, the lady of James Lendrum, Esq., D.L., of twin sons.

No. 576 :: Ref. 1846-05-05, 2:6, M.
April 28, by special license, in Taney church, by the Venerable the Archdeacon of Dublin, the Rev. Launcelot Dowdall, Vicar of Ballyhalbert, to Maria, fourth daughter of John Downing, of Rowesgift, Esq., and niece of George A. Downing Fullerton, of Ballintoy castle, county Antrim, and of Tockington, in Gloucestershire, Esq.

No. 577 :: Ref. 1846-05-05, 2:6, M.
In the Scots church, Kingstown, by the Rev. Richard Dill, the Rev. John Dill, of Clonmel, to Sarah, only daughter of the late Wentworth Paul, Esq., of Armagh, county Armagh.

No. 578 :: Ref. 1846-05-05, 2:6, D.
On Monday, 20th ult., Ann Workman, relict of John Workman, late of Richmount, near Portadown, Esq., rendered up the charge which she had given her from a gracious Creator for more than 85 years. Her mortal remains [were] conveyed to the family burying place, Drumcree, on the 23d ult., attended by a numerous circle of respectable sorrowing friends.

No. 579 :: Ref. 1846-05-05, 2:6, D.
On the 16th instant, at Milton, near Gravesend, in his 69th year, Adam Park, surgeon, brother of Mungo Park.

No. 580 :: Ref. 1846-05-05, 2:6, D.
On the 21st inst., in the 72d year of his age, Mr. Thos. Tegg, of Cheapside, London, publisher.

No. 581 :: Ref. 1846-05-05, 2:6, D.
On the 22d inst., aged 29, Alfred Byron Tegg, of Pembroke College, Oxford, youngest son of the late Thomas Tegg, Esq., of Cheapside, London.

No. 582 :: Ref. 1846-05-05, 2:6, D.
On Tuesday, the 21st ult., at his residence, Mountnorris, Thos. Ingram, Esq., M.D.

No. 583 :: Ref. 1846-05-05, 2:6, D.
At Jennymount, on the 27th ult., in the 18th year of her age, Elizabeth Ellen Blacker, eldest daughter of the late Rev. James S. Blacker.

No. 584 :: Ref. 1846-05-12, 3:1, B.
May 6, at Beresford Place, in this city, the lady of Captain Donelan, Staff Officer, of a son.

No. 585 :: Ref. 1846-05-12, 3:1, B.
May 4, in Upper Mount-street, Dublin, the lady of A.E. Gayer, Esq., Q.C., LL.D., of a daughter.

No. 586 :: Ref. 1846-05-12, 3:1, M.
May 3, at St. Mary's Church, Newry, by the Rev. W.R. Williams, Andrew James Newton, Esq., of Cookstown, in the county of Tyrone, to Mary Jane, second daughter of the late James Searight, Esq.

No. 587 :: Ref. 1846-05-12, 3:1, M.

In Aughnacloy Church, by the Rev. A.M. Pollock, Mr. Robert Robinson, near Dungannon, to Sarah, fourth daughter of the late John M'Williams, Esq., Cairnteel House, county Tyrone.

No. 588 :: Ref. 1846-05-12, 3:1, D.

On the 4th inst., at Marlycoo, in this county, James Boyde, Esq., aged 73.

No. 589 :: Ref. 1846-05-12, 3:1, D.

On the 2d instant, David Millar, Esq., of Burnside, near Antrim, aged 76 years.

No. 590 :: Ref. 1846-05-19, 2:5, B.

May 16, at Cookstown, the wife of Mr. William Allan, of a son.

No. 591 :: Ref. 1846-05-19, 2:5, M.

On the 12th instant, at Derryvoland church, by the Rev. A.H. Irvine, John Caldwell Bloomfield, Esq., of Castle Caldwell, eldest son of John C. Bloomfield, Esq., and grandson of the late Sir John Caldwell, Bart., to Elizabeth, eldest daughter of William D'Arcy, Esq., of Necairn Castle, and niece of Sir Arthur Brooke, Bart., Colebrooke.

No. 592 :: Ref. 1846-05-19, 2:5, M.

On Friday last, in Tempo church, by the Rev. John Whittaker, Mr. William Hurst, Merchant, Enniskillen, to Elizabeth, second daughter of the late Mr. James Gamble, of same place.

No. 593 :: Ref. 1846-05-19, 2:5, D.

On Wednesday, the 13th instant, in this city, Wm. M'Williams, Esq., aged 89 years. He was one of the oldest and most respectable inhabitants of the city, and had been one of the volunteers of 1780.

No. 594 :: Ref. 1846-05-19, 2:5, D.

On the 17th inst., in this city, John Stanley, Esq., at the age of 67, after a long illness which he bore with a truly christian resignation. Few have lived more respected, and has left this for a better world sincerely and deservedly regretted.

No. 595 :: Ref. 1846-05-19, 2:5, D.

On the 14th inst., at Charlemont, aged 42 years, Frances, wife of Thomas Dawson, Esq.

No. 596 :: Ref. 1846-05-19, 2:5, D.

On the morning of the 12th inst., at Tandragee, Mr. Robert Hardy, aged 23 years, eldest son of the late Mr. George Hardy, of Tandragee.

No. 597 :: Ref. 1846-05-19, 2:5, D.

On the 15th instant, in the 27th year of his age, in Barrack-street, Armagh, Mr. Charles Brown, for many years the proprietor of the Commercial Hotel. He bore his protracted illness with Christian fortitude, and through life sustained a character which for unimpeachable moral excellence will long be remembered by his numerous surviving friends and acquaintances.

No. 598 :: Ref. 1846-05-19, 2:5, D.

On the 12th inst., at Drumneil, county Monaghan, in the 42d year of his age, Mr. John Maclin.

No. 599 :: Ref. 1846-05-26, 3:3, M.

On the 21st inst., by the Rev. Samuel Blair Shaw, Registrar, Bloomfield, Castleblayney, A.G. Hewitt, Esq., Richmount, Portadown, to Mary Ann, second daughter of the late Thomas Glasgow, of Lislea, near Keady, Esq., and grand-daughter to the Rev. Henry M'Ilree, Keady. After the ceremony the bridal party spent a few days at Mountainview, the residence of the Rev. Samuel Dunlop, the bride's uncle.

No. 600 :: Ref. 1846-05-26, 3:3, M.

On the 22d inst., by the Rev. Mr. Morell, first Presbyterian House, Dungannon, Uriah Gaut [Gant?] Esq., Killyman House, county Tyrone, to Miss Jane, eldest daughter of Mr. Samuel Sterling Boland, near Dungannon.

No. 601 :: Ref. 1846-05-26, 3:3, M.

In Keady, by the Rev. Mr. Carson, Mr. Hugh M'Burney, to Mary Jane, eldest daughter of the late Mr. John Eccles of same place.

No. 602 :: Ref. 1846-05-26, 3:3, M.

On the 20th inst., in London, Robert Aldridge, Esq., late Captain in the 60th Rifles, to Olivia, fourth daughter of the late David Verner, Esq.

No. 603 :: Ref. 1846-05-26, 3:3, M.

On the 19th inst., at St. Mark's Church, Armagh, by the Rev. Mr. Haig, Mr. William Glenn, Fivemiletown, merchant, to Ann, daughter of the late Oliver Vance, Esq., Dungannon.

No. 604 :: Ref. 1846-05-26, 3:3, M.

May 21, in Dublin, William Trimble, Esq., Editor and proprietor of the "*Fermanagh Reporter*," Enniskillen, to Anne, relict of John Farrell, Esq., merchant, late of Westport.

No. 605 :: Ref. 1846-05-26, 3:3, M.

May 19th, at Nn-Limavady church by the Rev. John Olphert Rector of Drumachose, George Claudius Beresford Stirling, eldest son of the Rev. Blair Stirling, of Gardiner's-place, Dublin, to Sally, eldest daughter of Marcus Gage, Esq., of Strieve, in the county of Londonderry.

No. 606 :: Ref. 1846-05-26, 3:3, D.

Yesterday, at Vicar's-hill, in this city, Mr. Charles Subsole, aged 21 years.

No. 607 :: Ref. 1846-05-26, 3:3, D.

At Moyard, Benburb, on the 18th instant, in the 67th year of her age, Mary, relict of the late Nathaniel Holmes of Moyard Esq.

No. 608 :: Ref. 1846-05-26, 3:3, D.
On the 1st ult., at Quebec, Mr. Joseph Brackenridge, aged 42 years, a native of Armagh, Ireland.

No. 609 :: Ref. 1846-05-26, 3:3, D.
On the 21st October, 1845, at an advanced age, at Hemmingford, Canada, Mary, wife of Mr. Joseph Hall, formerly of Charlemont, and daughter of the late Mr. Patrick Marshall, of Toll Bridge, County of Armagh.

No. 610 :: Ref. 1846-05-26, 3:3, D.
At Lurgan, on the 9th inst., in the 81st year of his age, the Rev. Thomas Kerr, Wesleyan minister.

No. 611 :: Ref. 1846-06-02, 3:3, B.
May 19, at Whitecastle, county of Donegal, the lady of Alexander Curry, Esq., of a daughter.

No. 612 :: Ref. 1846-06-02, 3:3, M.
May 12, at Benburb, by the Rev. Richard Wrightson, Mr. Thomas Smyth, Linen Draper, to Jane, eldest daughter of Jas. Whiteside, Esq., of Derrygonan House. After the ceremony the happy pair set off for the Giant's Causeway to spend the honeymoon.

No. 613 :: Ref. 1846-06-02, 3:3, M.
May 14, at Kilmore church, county Armagh, by the Rev. Henry Cobb, Mr. Corry Sinton, of Ash trees, near Tandragee, to Mary, third daughter of Mr. Henry Lamb, Drumart.

No. 614 :: Ref. 1846-06-02, 3:3, M.
Same day [May 14], in this city, by the Rev. Mr. Fleming, Mr. John Dalrymple Wyllie, carpenter, at Castle Dillon, (late of Montrose, Scotland,) to Mary, youngest daughter of Mr. Alexander Langlands, of Maines of Brighton, near Montrose.

No. 615 :: Ref. 1846-06-02, 3:3, D.
On the 25th ult., at Vicar's-hill, in this city, of consumption, Mr. Charles B. Srubsole, deeply and deservedly regretted by his numerous friends. During a period of 13 years he had been a member of the cathedral choir. He was called away in the bloom of youth, in his twentieth year, and exalted to the choir above, there to sing with all God's ransomed throng everlasting praises and hallelulahs to Him who sitteth upon the throne, and to the Lamb for ever and ever.

No. 616 :: Ref. 1846-06-02, 3:3, D.
In Scotch-street, on Saturday night last, in the 22d year of his age, of consumption, Mr. Andrew David Henry, fourth son of Mr. John Henry, Cabinet-maker and Upholsterer, sincerely regretted by a large circle of friends and acquaintances.

No. 617 :: Ref. 1846-06-02, 3:3, D.
On the 22d ult., at Leamington, the Rev. William Newcome, son of the late Primate of Ireland, of Hockwold Hall, in the county of Norfolk, and vicar of Surton, in the Isle of Ely.

No. 618 :: Ref. 1846-06-02, 3:3, D.
May 25, at his residence, Green Hill, near Brookeborough, Mr. Hamilton Irvine, in his 78th year. Deceased was Major of the Fermanagh Militia, and had served with his Regiment since before the Rebellion, in both England and Ireland, up to the last disembodment. He was the oldest Grand Juror of the county; was deputy-Lieutenant and Justice of the Peace; and for many years—up to his death—Provost of the Borough of Enniskillen.

No. 619 :: Ref. 1846-06-02, 3:3, D.
May 3, at Pau, in France, aged seventy, M. Patrick O'Quin, Knight of the Legion of Honor, and of the Order of Saint Louis. The deceased was the lineal descendant of an illustrious Irish family, who left their native land on the fall of the Stuarts. He served under the Empire in various military capacities; and in consideration of his literary talents, was appointed Commandant Reporteur in the army. He subsequently attained the rank of Sous-Intendant, and retired in 1831. His only son, M. Patrick O'Quin, has distinguished himself in the literary world by the translation of Dr. Taylor's *Treatise on the Climate of Pau.*

No. 620 :: Ref. 1846-06-02, 3:3, D.
In some oversight we omitted last week to notice the death of Robert M'Endow, Esq., sen., which took place in this city on the 24th ult. Mr. M'Endow was a man greatly respected through life, and the large and respectable concourse who accompanied his remains to the church-yard proved how much in death he was lamented.

No. 621 :: Ref. 1846-06-09, 3:4, B.
June 2, at Clontarf, the lady of Robert Disney, Esq., of a son.

No. 622 :: Ref. 1846-06-09, 3:4, M.
June 3, at St. Anne's Church, by the Rev. H.E. Prior, the Rev. Thomas Power, younger son of the late Rev. William Power, of Affane, county of Waterford, to Dorothea Edie, fifth daughter of William Edie, of Thornhill, county Tyrone.

No. 623 :: Ref. 1846-06-09, 3:4, D.
In Glasslough, at an advanced age, of apoplexy, Miss Rawdon, a respected inhabitant of that town.

No. 624 :: Ref. 1846-06-09, 3:4, D.
On the 30th ult., Jane, relict of the late Mr. John Shields, of Tullycairn, Markethill, aged 78 years.

No. 625 :: Ref. 1846-06-09, 3:4, D.
June 1, at Moyle Glebe, county Tyrone, after a protracted illness, Mary, eldest daughter of the Rev. R.H. Nash, Ex. F.T.C.D.

No. 626 :: Ref. 1846-06-09, 3:4, D.
On Thursday last, in Enniskillen, of decline, Mr. William Elliott, aged 26 years, eldest son of Mr.

Thomas Elliott, Civil Engineer. He was a young man much esteemed and beloved by a large circle of friends and acquaintances.

No. 627 :: Ref. 1846-06-09, 3:4, D.
On the 5th inst., at Moy, Mrs. Barret, aged 92 years.

No. 628 :: Ref. 1846-06-09, 3:4, D.
June 5, at Moy, aged 13 years, Anna, sister of Dr. Crothers, of that town.

No. 629 :: Ref. 1846-06-09, 3:4, D.
June 5, at Tullyrone, aged 15 years, Eliza Jane, third daughter of Simon Sinclair, Esq.

No. 630 :: Ref. 1846-06-09, 3:4, D.
On the 3d inst., at Furze Lodge, Glenavy, county Antrim, Helena, eldest daughter of the late Robert Stewart, Esq., 19th regiment.

No. 631 :: Ref. 1846-06-09, 3:4, D.
At Presteign, Radnorshire, on the 28th of April, after a few days illness, Mr. Alexander Beatty, in the 32d year of his age, son of Mr. John Beatty, of Tyregarty, county Armagh. From the earliest dawn of reason his mind was deeply impressed with the all-importance of religion, and throughout his short career made it his constant study and delight, well aware that all terrestrial things in comparison are but as a feather in the balance. Perfectly resigned to the will of his heavenly Father, he evinced at that last and awful hour a mind solely devoted to the all-sustaining power of His Redeemer—his aspirations were constant and fervent; and he died in the full assurance of a blessed Resurrection.

No. 632 :: Ref. 1846-06-16, 3:2, M.
June 11, in St. Peter's Church, by the Venerable the Archdeacon of Dublin, the Rev. Lord Adam Loftus, Rector of Ballibay, county of Monaghan, third son of the late Marquess of Ely, to Margaret, fourth daughter of the late Robert Fannin, Esq., of Leeson-street, Dublin.

No. 633 :: Ref. 1846-06-16, 3:2, M.
On the 13th inst., at St. Mark's church, by the Rev. Mr. Haig, and afterwards at the house of the lady's father, by his Grace the Most Rev. Dr. Crolly, Catholic Primate, David Hillyard, Esq., of Killarney, to Kate Frances, fourth daughter of William Carpenter, of Armagh, Esq.

No. 634 :: Ref. 1846-06-16, 3:2, D.
Deeply and sincerely regretted by her friends and acquaintances, Mrs. Mary Holmes, relict of the late Nathaniel Holmes, Esq., of Moyard, county Tyrone.

No. 635 :: Ref. 1846-06-16, 3:2, D.
On Monday se'nnight, in Tullycalliday, Mary, relict of Mr. Thomas Donaldson, aged 54 years. She died in hope of a glorious resurrection.

No. 636 :: Ref. 1846-06-16, 3:2, D.
On Tuesday last, in Drumetre, Mr. Wm. M'Mullen, at the advanced age of 98 years, eighty of which he received pay from the government, having enlisted in the 5th Dragoons at the age of eighteen.

No. 637 :: Ref. 1846-06-16, 3:2, D.
On the 6th inst., Pauline Henrietta Maria, the infant daughter of Wm. Macartney, Esq., S.L. [S.I.?], of Constabulary, Newry.

No. 638 :: Ref. 1846-06-16, 3:2, D.
On the 8th inst., Mr. John Little Allen, aged 21, eldest son of the Rev. Robert Allen, Stewartstown.

No. 639 :: Ref. 1846-06-16, 3:2, D.
On the 5th inst., at the house of her son-in-law, Mr. John Porter, Ballyrussell, Comber, Mary, relict of the late Mr. John Dunlop, of Balloo, Bangor, in the 95th year of her age.

No. 640 :: Ref. 1846-06-23, 3:4, M.
On the 16th instant, in the Presbyterian church, Aughnacloy, by the Rev. William M'Ilwain, William Cochrane, Esq., of Annaro, to Nannie, eldest daughter of James Montgomery, Esq., of Garvey.

No. 641 :: Ref. 1846-06-23, 3:4, M.
On the 11th inst., at Killyman, by the Rev. J.R. Darley, Wm. Carr Boyd, Esq., T.C.D., to Charlotte Marianne, second daughter of B. M'Avoy, Esq., Surgeon, R.N., of Twyford, county Tyrone.

No. 642 :: Ref. 1846-06-23, 3:4, M.
On 11th instant, by the Rev. J.H. Moore, Connor, the Rev. S.J. Moore, Donaghmore, to Mary, daughter of Mr. D. Carmichael, Millisle.

No. 643 :: Ref. 1846-06-23, 3:4, M.
On the 11th instant, in the Monkstown Church, by the Rev. Mr. Williams, John O'Richards, Esq., of Elm Grove county of Dublin, and Tempo, County of Fermanagh, to Susan, eldest daughter of Richard Saunders, Esq., of Largay, County of Cavan.

No. 644 :: Ref. 1846-06-23, 3:4, D.
On Sunday, the 14th inst., at her son's residence in Derryhaw, Letitia, relict of the late Mr. James Johnston, of same place, aged 79 years. She died rejoicing in hope of a glorious immortality.

No. 645 :: Ref. 1846-06-23, 3:4, D.
On the 11th inst., at Coslett's-bridge, near Lisburn, Jane Toan, relict of Robert Toan, aged 72.

No. 646 :: Ref. 1846-06-23, 3:4, D.
On the 12th inst., at Ballyhagan, County Armagh, aged 77 years, Elizabeth, relict of the late Mr. John Keegan.

No. 647 :: Ref. 1846-07-07, 3:1, B.
At Grange, Armagh, on July 1st., the wife of the Rev. J.W.H. Molyneux, of a son.

No. 648 :: Ref. 1846-07-07, 3:1, B.
June 21, at Drumnargoole House, county Armagh, the residence of her father, the Rev. H. Gamble, the lady of M. Fleming Handy, Esq., of a son.

No. 649 :: Ref. 1846-07-07, 3:1, B.
On the 5th inst., the wife of Mr. David Barry, merchant, Moy, of a daughter, still-born.

No. 650 :: Ref. 1846-07-07, 3:1, B.
On the 5th inst., the wife of Mr. Thomas M'Kell, Moy, of a son.

No. 651 :: Ref. 1846-07-07, 3:1, B.
On the 2d inst., in Abbey-st., in this city, Mrs. M'Neale Johnston, of a son.

No. 652 :: Ref. 1846-07-07, 3:1, D.
On Thursday, the 2d inst., in this city, Miss Catherine Fitzpatrick, aged 44 years.

No. 653 :: Ref. 1846-07-07, 3:1, D.
June 22, at her residence, Upper Rutland-street, Martha Maria, relict of the Rev. William Magee, Presbyterian Minister of Lurgan, and sister of the late Major-General Stewart, of the Royal Horse Artillery.

No. 654 :: Ref. 1846-07-07, 3:1, D.
In May last, at Ann Arbor, Michigan, Mrs. Cross, formerly Mrs. Conolly, of Clones, sister of the late Samuel Hanna, Esq., of Newry. Her last words were, "*Oh, Lord receive my soul. Oh, take me home.*"

No. 655 :: Ref. 1846-07-14, 3:6, D.
July 1, Eby Stinson, of Kilturk, aged ninety-nine years, one of the oldest Orangemen of the county of Fermanagh, deeply regretted by all who knew him.

No. 656 :: Ref. 1846-07-14, 3:6, D.
At Barrack hill, in this city, yesterday, Mrs. Benson, wife of Mr. Jonathan Benson, late Sergeant-Major of 20th Light Dragoons, aged 60 years.

No. 657 :: Ref. 1846-07-14, 3:6, D.
In this city, on Friday last, John M'Allen, son of Mr. David M'Allen, aged 12 years and 6 months.

No. 658 :: Ref. 1846-07-21, 3:2, B.
On the 11th inst., at No. 5, Carlton Terrace, London, the Countess of Caledon, of a son.

No. 659 :: Ref. 1846-07-21, 3:2, B.
On the 11th inst., at Lakeview House, near Magherafelt, the lady of William Magill, Esq., M.D., of a daughter.

No. 660 :: Ref. 1846-07-21, 3:2, M.
At St. George's, Hanover-square, by the Rev. M.D. French, M.A., M.G. Laing Meason, Esq., of Lindertis, North Britain, and Hydepark-gate, to the Hon. Eliza Molyneux, relict of Lieutenant-Colonel the Hon. G.B. Molyneux, of Seafield-lodge, Hove.

No. 661 :: Ref. 1846-07-21, 3:2, M.
July 14, at Moy Church, by the Rev. Frederick Cavendish, Robert Staples, Esq., of Donmore, Queen's County, to Mary Isabella, eldest daughter of W.M. Bond, Esq., of the Argory, county Armagh.

No. 662 :: Ref. 1846-07-21, 3:2, M.
On the 7th inst., in the Second Presbyterian Meeting House, Markethill, by the Rev. R. Morrison, Mr. Joseph Burns, Brackley, to Miss Margaret Gibson, Lattery.

No. 663 :: Ref. 1846-07-21, 3:2, M.
July 14, at St. Mary's Church, Dublin, by the Rev. Robert A. Irwin, A.M., Curate of Madden, in the Diocess of Armagh, Henry Irwin, Esq., Bengal Army, F.R.C.S.I., fourth son of William Irwin, of Mount Irwin, county of Armagh, Esq., to Harriette Josephine, only daughter of the late George Ogle Jacob, Esq., Bengal Medical Service.

No. 664 :: Ref. 1846-07-21, 3:2, D.
On the 16th inst., in this city, at the house of her son-in-law, John Cuming, Esq., Mrs. Tate, aged 66 years.

No. 665 :: Ref. 1846-07-21, 3:2, D.
On Thursday, the 16th inst., Mr. Henry Porter, of Campstown, near Cootehill, aged 72 years, much, and deservedly, respected by all who knew him.

No. 666 :: Ref. 1846-07-21, 3:2, D.
In Market-hill, on Friday, Mrs. Ashton, in the full assurance of faith, aged 31 years.

No. 667 :: Ref. 1846-07-21, 3:2, D.
In same place [Market-hill], on Wednesday, Mrs. Kearney, aged 71 years.

No. 668 :: Ref. 1846-07-21, 3:2, D.
On the 7th inst., at Cootehill, aged 76, Mrs. S. Macfadden.

No. 669 :: Ref. 1846-07-21, 3:2, D.
On the 9th inst., at his father's residence, Cloncorie, county Fermanagh, Mr. Robert Farley, aged 22 years, who had completed his third session at college as a student of the general Assembly of the Presbyterian Church of Ireland. Mr. Farley was the first student from county Fermanagh, who attended Belfast College. He rendered himself distinguished in the Hebrew class, and was a young gentleman of the most gentle and kind manners, and most benevolent disposition. The congregration of Ballyhobridge, to which he belonged, have sustained a serious bereavement in his death.

No. 670 :: Ref. 1846-07-21, 3:2, D.
On the 8th inst., Jane the beloved wife of Mr. Robert Johnson, Killyfaddy, near Magherafelt, aged 34 years.

No. 671 :: Ref. 1846-07-28, 3:1, B.
July 23, at Cookstown, the wife of Mr. Mark Devlin, of a daughter.

No. 672 :: Ref. 1846-07-28, 3:1, B.
July 20, at Kinsale, the lady of Captain Fleury, 36th Regiment, of a son.

No. 673 :: Ref. 1846-07-28, 3:1, M.
July 21, in the Presbyterian Church, Magherafelt, by the Rev. James Wilson, Mr. John M'Keown, merchant, Louisiana, U.S., to Miss Shannon, daughter of Dr. Shannon, of Magherafelt.

No. 674 :: Ref. 1846-07-28, 3:1, D.
In Dobbin-street, aged 18 years, Miss Eliza, daughter of Mr. James Devlin, late of Loughgall, much regretted by a large circle of friends.

No. 675 :: Ref. 1846-07-28, 3:1, D.
In the island of Rathlin, on the 21st inst., Miss Amelia, fourth daughter of the Rev. Robert Gage. She died in sure hope of a blessed immortality.

No. 676 :: Ref. 1846-07-28, 3:1, D.
At Richmond-street, Dublin, on the 21st inst., at an advanced age, Miss Lillias Anne Norris, formerly of Caledon, in the county of Tyrone.

No. 677 :: Ref. 1846-07-28, 3:1, D.
On Tuesday last, after a few minutes illness, Cole Fitzgerald, Esq., of Lisabuck, near Clones.

No. 678 :: Ref. 1846-07-28, 3:1, D.
On 21st at Enniskillen, Mr. Robert Armstrong, jun., after a long illness.

No. 679 :: Ref. 1846-07-28, 3:1, D.
On Friday, 17th July, William, youngest son of Mr. Robert Fairley, of Lisdown, near Armagh, aged five years and four months.

No. 680 :: Ref. 1846-08-04, 3:2, B.
July 27, at Drumbraine House, county Monaghan, the lady of A. Bernard Bleazby, Esq., of a son.

No. 681 :: Ref. 1846-08-04, 3:2, M.
At Shaw-place, Greenock, on the 21st inst., by the Rev. J. Sinclair, Robert Crothers, Esq., Surgeon, Moy, County Tyrone, to Jessie, youngest daughter of the late William Murdock, Esq., same place.

No. 682 :: Ref. 1846-08-04, 3:2, M.
July 20, at Silso, Bedfordshire, Langford Kennedy, Esq., of Devonshire-place, London, to Alicia, relict of Handcock Montgomery, Esq., of Bessmount Park, county Monaghan

No. 683 :: Ref. 1846-08-04, 3:2, M.
On the 13th inst., at the house of the bride's father, by the Rev. Mr. O'Tool, P.P., Dungannon, Mr. Francis Campbell, Coal Island, to Miss Bidilla Finn, daughter of Mr. John Finn, Clanmore, county of Armagh.

No. 684 :: Ref. 1846-08-04, 3:2, D.
On Thursday last, at the residence of her brother, Market-street, Armagh, Miss Mary Anne Corry, after a long and severe illness, which she bore with christian patience, in a sure hope of a blessed immortality, much regretted by a large circle of her friends.

No. 685 :: Ref. 1846-08-04, 3:2, D.
On the 27th ult., at Drumgrannon, near Moy, Elizabeth, relict of the late Mr. John Bull, aged 74 years.

No. 686 :: Ref. 1846-08-04, 3:2, D.
On the 29th ult., Sarah, relict of the late Mr. Wm. Forest, Moy, in her 70th year. She was for many years a pious and consistent member of the Methodist Society, and her *"behaviour (such as becometh holiness)"* long *"adorned the doctrine of God our Saviour in all things."* To her, *"to live was Christ, and to die gain."*

No. 687 :: Ref. 1846-08-11, 3:2, M.
On Saturday morning, August 1, in the Presbyterian church, Aughnacloy, by the Rev. William M'Ilwain, Mr. William Brown, Dungannon, to Ann Eliza, only daughter of Mr. Timothy Loughead, Aughnacloy, merchant.

No. 688 :: Ref. 1846-08-11, 3:2, M.
August 5, at Warrenpoint Church, by the Rev. John Tottenham, of Rathangan, the Rev. William Shepphard, eldest son of James Shepphard, of Clifton, county Tipperary, Esq., to Bithia, eldest daughter of Leonard Watson, of Warrenpoint, county Down, Esq.

No. 689 :: Ref. 1846-08-11, 3:2, M.
In Omagh church, on Wednesday, 5th instant by the Rev. J. Hill, Royal Hospital, Greenwich, brother-in-law of the bridegroom, Mr. Wm. M'Cullough, manager of the Provincial Bank of Ireland, Newry, to Eleanor Jane, eldest daughter of Mr. Joseph M'Knight, Omagh.

No. 690 :: Ref. 1846-08-11, 3:2, M.
August 6, in Delgany church, by the Rev. Alexander Hudson, Rector of Outeragh, Francis Charles Hassard, eldest son of the late Sir F. Hassard, of the city of Waterford, to Margaret Frances, eldest daughter of Richard Hudson, of Spring Farm, county Wicklow, Esq.

No. 691 :: Ref. 1846-08-11, 3:2, M.
And at same time [August 6] and place [Delgany church], Michael D. Hassard, Esq., only son of the late Capt. Richard Hassard, of the city of Waterford, to Anne, only daughter of Sir Francis Hassard, deceased.

No. 692 :: Ref. 1846-08-11, 3:2, D.
In London, Catherine Louisa D'Arcy Irvine, eldest daughter of Sir Georges Irvine, Bart., of Castle Irvine, county Fermanagh, and niece of John Caulfield Irvine, of Grove-hill, Esq. This lamented lady was sister to Viscountess Dungannon, and the Marchioness Incoutri.

No. 693 :: Ref. 1846-08-11, 3:2, D.
On the 8th inst., in the 20th year of his age, sincerely and deservedly regretted by his numerous friends and acquaintances, Beatty Irvine, third son of Wilkin Irvine, Esq., of Feglish, near Lowtherstown, county Tyrone.

No. 694 :: Ref. 1846-08-18, 2:6, M.
On the 11th instant, in the Presbyterian Meeting-house, Keady, by the Rev. Joseph Jenkins, Mr. Thos. James Manson, of Rockmount, Keady, to Jane, eldest daughter of Mr. John Dobbin, of same place.

No. 695 :: Ref. 1846-08-18, 2:6, M.
In the city of Toronto, on the 7th ult., at the residence of the bride's father, by the Rev. J. Harris, Richard Robinson, Esq., of Baltimore, United States, to Margaret, daughter of the Rev. Samuel Cuthberston [sic], formerly of Omagh.

No. 696 :: Ref. 1846-08-18, 2:6, M.
In Ballygawly Meeting-house, on Tuesday, the 11th inst., by the Rev. Wm. Ferguson, Mr. Wm. Neely, of Ballygawley, to Miss Mary Anne Neely, daughter of Wm. Neely, Esq., Grange House, county of Monaghan.

No. 697 :: Ref. 1846-08-18, 2:6, M.
In Mountfield Church, on the 13th instant, by the Rev. Wm. Samuel Cuthbert, John M'Cay, Esq., Kilrail House, to Margaret eldest daughter of John Fullerton, Esq., Mayne House, County Tyrone.

No. 698 :: Ref. 1846-08-18, 2:6, M.
On the 5th inst., at Acton Church, Poyntzpass, by the father of the bride, Henry Frederick, son of the late Captain Hole, R.M., of Newport, Devonshire, and grandson of the late Rev. Wm. Hole, Incumbent of Swimbridge, Devonshire, to Anne Hester, eldest daughter of the Rev. H. Gamble, of Drumnargoole-House, County of Armagh.

No. 699 :: Ref. 1846-08-18, 2:6, D.
On the 6th instant, at Parsonstown, of gastric fever, Maria, relict of the late Marcus Longford M'Causland, of Roe Park, county of Londonderry, deeply regretted by her family and friends.

No. 700 :: Ref. 1846-08-25, 3:1, B.
At Palace-row, in this city, on Tuesday, the 25th instant, Mrs. R. Lilburn, of a son.

No. 701 :: Ref. 1846-08-25, 3:1, B.
On the 15th instant, at the residence of her uncle, W.W. Algeo, Esq., Armagh, the lady of T. Delacherois Crommelin, Esq., of a son.

No. 702 :: Ref. 1846-08-25, 3:1, M.
On the 12th instant, by the Rev. James Wilson, Mr. George Brown, Ballymoughan, to Miss Jane Parks, of Ballinderry, near Magherafelt.

No. 703 :: Ref. 1846-08-25, 3:1, M.
August 18, at St. Peter's church, by the Hon. and Very Rev. the Dean of Clogher, Sir Edward Synge, of Leslee Court, county Cork, Bart., and D.L., to Anne, only daughter of Henry Irwin, of Streamstown, county of Sligo, and Ray, county of Donegal, Esq.

No. 704 :: Ref. 1846-08-25, 3:1, M.
At Tandragee, by the Rev. Henry Burdett, John Thomas Hinds, Esq., of Waterloo Lodge, Trim, to Emma, fifth daughter of the Very Rev. the Dean of Tuam.

No. 705 :: Ref. 1846-08-25, 3:1, M.
August 13, in Enniskillen church, by the Rev. Newport B. White, James Jasper Macaldin, Esq., M.D., Coleraine, to Mary Jane, eldest daughter of Thomas Kernahan, Esq., Enniskillen.

No. 706 :: Ref. 1846-08-25, 3:1, D.
At Killowen, near Rosstrevor, on the 16th instant, Henry, second son of Henry Stanley, Esq., merchant, Portadown.

No. 707 :: Ref. 1846-09-01, 2:3, B.
On the 23d instant, at Castlebellingham, the lady of Sir Alan E. Bellingham, Bart., of a son and heir.

No. 708 :: Ref. 1846-09-01, 2:3, B.
August 20, at Banbridge, the lady of the Rev. Wm. Metge, of a son, which survived only a few hours.

No. 709 :: Ref. 1846-09-01, 2:3, B.
August 18, at Donoughmore Rectory, the lady of the Rev. E.P. Hodgens, of a son.

No. 710 :: Ref. 1846-09-01, 2:3, B.
August 17, at Baden Baden, the Lady Augustus Loftus, of a daughter, still-born.

No. 711 :: Ref. 1846-09-01, 2:3, M.
On the 21st instant, in St. Ann's Church, by the Reverend Thomas Walker, Vicar, Mr. John Reid, Glasgow, to Eliza, eldest daughter of Mr. W. Hunter, Springvale, Ballyclare.

No. 712 :: Ref. 1846-09-01, 2:3, M.
On the 22d instant, by the Rev. W. Blackwood, Moderator of the Presbyterian Synod of England, the Rev. T. Knox Anderson, to Jane, youngest daughter of the late W. Knox, Esq., Newcastle-upon-Tyne.

No. 713 :: Ref. 1846-09-01, 2:3, M.
August 27, in St. Nicholas's Church, Robert, eldest son of the late Isaac Powell, Esq., of Riversdale, county Sligo, to Isabella, youngest daughter of the late Joseph Mortimer, Esq.

No. 714 :: Ref. 1846-09-01, 2:3, M.
At Duntogher, Scotland, on the 25th August, by the Rev. John Lin Templeton, Mr. Matthew Taylor, Scotch Establishment, Armagh, to Helen, seventh daughter of the late James Bryson, Esq.

No. 715 :: Ref. 1846-09-01, 2:3, D.
In this city, on the 30th August, after a long and severe illness, Mr. Robert Stubbs, aged 52 years. For 24 years he filled the situation of clerk to the late James Wilson, of Omagh, Esq. Throughout life he was an honest and upright man, but through reverse of circumstances, being deprived of a comfortable home, he was unable to bear up, and died of a broken heart.

No. 716 :: Ref. 1846-09-01, 2:3, D.

August 26, Mrs. Roberts, wife of Stephen Roberts, Esq., Moy, aged 48 years, deservedly regretted for her many virtues, by a large circle of friends and acquaintances.

No. 717 :: Ref. 1846-09-01, 2:3, D.

On the 3d inst., at Fowey, Joseph Dickson Thornley, Esq., Collector of her Majesty's Customs at that port. This much lamented gentleman was a native of Ballyshannon, county Donegall.

No. 718 :: Ref. 1846-09-01, 2:3, D.

On the 22d inst., at her residence, near Muckamore, Miss Margaret Bruce, at the advanced age of 98 years.

No. 719 :: Ref. 1846-09-01, 2:3, D.

August 23, at Cashel, aged 70 years, Benjamin Newport White, Esq., J.P., and Deputy Mayor of Cashel.

No. 720 :: Ref. 1846-09-08, 3:1, D.

On the 29th ult., after a short illness, in her 67th year, Sarah, the beloved wife of William Irwin, Esq., of Mount Irwin, in this county.

No. 721 :: Ref. 1846-09-08, 3:1, D.

On the 1st inst., at his residence, Cloverhill, near Loughbrickland, Mr. George M'Clelland, in his 51st year.

No. 722 :: Ref. 1846-09-08, 3:1, D.

August 27, at Glasgow, Theodosia Elizabeth Gage, youngest daughter of the late Marcus Gage, Esq., of Bellarena, county of Londonderry.

No. 723 :: Ref. 1846-09-08, 3:1, D.

On the 1st inst., at his residence at Malahide, John Bell, Esq., late of Omeath, near Newry, very suddenly, from the rupture of a blood-vessel.

No. 724 :: Ref. 1846-09-08, 3:1, D.

On the 2nd inst., of water on the brain, aged nine years, Mary second daughter of Richard William Beaty, Esq., Blessington-street, Dublin.

No. 725 :: Ref. 1846-09-08, 3:1, D.

On Wednesday, the 2nd inst., aged 40 years, Mary Anne, the affectionate and beloved wife of Mr. William Carroll, of Upper Dorset-street, Dublin, deeply lamented by a large circle of friends.

No. 726 :: Ref. 1846-09-08, 3:1, D.

On the 27th ult., at Loughgall, Mr. George Walker, aged 32 years.

No. 727 :: Ref. 1846-09-22, 2:4, B.

September 6, at Fairview, county of Monaghan, the lady of Rev. J.H. Morell, of a daughter.

No. 728 :: Ref. 1846-09-22, 2:4, B.

On Sunday last, the 13th inst. at Drumnakilly, the lady of Alexander M'Causland of a daughter.

No. 729 :: Ref. 1846-09-22, 2:4, B.

September 11, at Enniskillen, the lady of Dr. William C. Ovenden, of a son.

No. 730 :: Ref. 1846-09-22, 2:4, M.

On the 10th inst., in Loughgall Church, by the Rev. Francis John Crawford, Alexander John Pringle, only son of the late Michael Pringle, Esq., Sally Vale, to Miss Martha, second daughter of William Jackson, Esq., Ballymagerney.

No. 731 :: Ref. 1846-09-22, 2:4, M.

On the 15th instant, in St. Mark's Church, Armagh, by the Rev. Robert Haig, Mr. John Smith, A.M., Principal of the Diocesan School, Abbey-street, to Miss Mary Power, of the Model School, Armagh.

No. 732 :: Ref. 1846-09-22, 2:4, M.

Sept. 10, Thomas Austin, Esq., 44th Foot, to Charlotte Agnes Florence Turner, niece of Samuel B. Ralph, late of Harold's-cross, Esq.

No. 733 :: Ref. 1846-09-22, 2:4, M.

In Castlecaulfield Church, by the Rev. W. Paul, William, eldest son of James Burns, of Killymaddy House, near Dungannon, Esq., to Mary, daughter of Joseph Irwin, Esq., of Dungannon, merchant.

No. 734 :: Ref. 1846-09-22, 2:4, M.

September 9, in St. Peter's Church, Dublin, by the Rev. Mark Perrin, Rector of Atherney, in the Diocess of Tuam, John Perrin, Esq., Barrister-at-law, eldest son of the Right Honourable Louis Perrin, of Rutland-square, one of the Judges of the Court of Queen's Bench, in Ireland, to Penelope, eldest daughter of John Hatchell, of Merrion-square, Esq., one of her Majesty's Counsel at Law.

No. 735 :: Ref. 1846-09-22, 2:4, M.

September 15, in the parish church of Ardagh, by the Very Rev. Dean of Ardagh, uncle to the bride, the Rev. David T. Barry, to Anne Elizabeth, daughter of the late Alexander M'Kee, Esq., M.D., of Moneymore, Derry.

No. 736 :: Ref. 1846-09-22, 2:4, M.

September 14, in George's Church, Thomas Dawson, Esq., of Belvidere-place, eldest son of the late John Dawson of Annamartin, county Fermanagh, Esq., to Susan Frances, eldest daughter of Edward Moore, of Lower Gardiner-street, Solicitor.

No. 737 :: Ref. 1846-09-22, 2:4, M.

At Carntall Meeting-house, by the Rev. John Hannagh, Mr. John Henderson, of Sherrygroom, to Margaret, daughter of Thomas Barnette, Esq., of Clogher.

No. 738 :: Ref. 1846-09-22, 2:4, D.

On the 16th inst., at Clark's bridge, near Newtownhamilton, the beloved wife of the Rev. William M'Alister, Presbyterian Minister, sincerely and deservedly regretted.

No. 739 :: Ref. 1846-09-22, 2:4, D.

On Sunday, the 20th inst., at Magarity, in this county, after a long and tedious illness, Mr. William Dunlop, aged 39 years, deeply and sincerely regretted by a numerous circle of friends and acquaintances.

No. 740 :: Ref. 1846-09-22, 2:4, D.
On the 7th inst., after a few days' illness, Maria Sydney, aged 16 years, third daughter of the late Mr. Robert Reid, of Balleer.

No. 741 :: Ref. 1846-09-22, 2:4, D.
On the 7th instant, at Dundalk, aged 60 years, Arabella, widow of the late John Martin, Esq., of that town.

No. 742 :: Ref. 1846-09-22, 2:4, D.
September 6, in France, in her 73d year, Anne, widow of Thomas Ormsby, Esq., of Cummin, in the county of Sligo, and sister to the Dowager Lady Gore Booth, of Lissadill House, county Sligo.

No. 743 :: Ref. 1846-09-22, 2:4, D.
At Monkstown, in the 17th year of her age, Jane Charlotte, youngest daughter of the Rev. Hamilton Stuart, of Rochfort, Buncrana, in the County of Donegal.

No. 744 :: Ref. 1846-09-22, 2:4, D.
September 7, at Tullamore, of apoplexy, in the prime of life, Joseph Metcalf, Esq., Supervisor of Excise.

No. 745 :: Ref. 1846-09-22, 2:4, D.
August 3, at Tobago, West Indies, of yellow fever, James Wilson, Esq., aged 25 years, second son of the late James Wilson, Esq., Clerk of the Crown for the county of Tyrone.

No. 746 :: Ref. 1846-09-22, 2:4, D.
On Wednesday last, at Carndaisy, county Derry, (the residence of his brother,) the Rev. Francis Quin, P.P., of Drumsagh [?], after a lingering illness, aged 48 years.

No. 747 :: Ref. 1846-09-29, 2:5, M.
On the 12th inst., in St. Thomas's Church, Dublin, by the Rev. W.J. Mulloy, George Walter Young, of Knockbawn, in the County of Armagh, Esq., to Jane, only daughter of David Leslie, of Leslie Hill, in said County, Esq.

No. 748 :: Ref. 1846-09-29, 2:5, M.
September 19, in the Scots Church, Enniskillen, by the Rev. A.C. Maclatchy, M.A., William, son of the late Captain M'Leod, R.M., to Bessie, third daughter of Charles Gerrard, Esq., of Bushhill.

No. 749 :: Ref. 1846-09-29, 2:5, D.
On the 15th instant, at Willowbank, Keady, aged 62 years, Jane, wife of the Rev. Joseph Jinkins.

No. 750 :: Ref. 1846-09-29, 2:5, D.
On the 15th inst., Mrs. Lowry, relict of the late Rev. J. Lowry, of Upper Clennanees, after a tedious and painful illness.

No. 751 :: Ref. 1846-09-29, 2:5, D.
Died, September 28, at Armagh, Sarah Anne, wife of Captain Donnelan, Staff officer, sincerely and deservedly regretted.

No. 752 :: Ref. 1846-09-29, 2:5, D.
Died, on Tuesday morning last, at Charlemont, Mr. Thomas Dawson.

No. 753 :: Ref. 1846-10-06, 3:1, B.
September 29, at Greenfield, Coolock, the lady of Benjamin G. Darley, Esq., M.D., of a daughter.

No. 754 :: Ref. 1846-10-06, 3:1, B.
Sept. 28, at 2, Abercomby-square, Liverpool, the lady of Mark Seton Synnot, Esq., of a daughter.

No. 755 :: Ref. 1846-10-06, 3:1, B.
On the 29th ult. at Clounagh, near Portadown, Mrs. W. Langtry of a daughter.

No. 756 :: Ref. 1846-10-06, 3:1, M.
On the 1st inst., in St. Mark's Church, Armagh, by the Rev. Stephen Radcliffe, Edward Anderson, Esq., of Moygannon, Rosstrevor, to Georgina, daughter of the late George Prentice, Esq.

No. 757 :: Ref. 1846-10-06, 3:1, M.
September 28, at St. Paul's, Wilton-place, by the Rev. Wm. Bennett, A.M., Gore Somerset D'Arcy Irvine, Esq., R.F.B., youngest son of Sir George Irvine, Bart., of Castle Irvine, county Fermanagh, to Emblyn, youngest daughter of T. Knox Hannyngton, Esq., of Dungannon Castle, county Tyrone, and niece of Major-General Caulfield, C.B.

No. 758 :: Ref. 1846-10-06, 3:1, M.
October 1, at Fintona Church, by the Rev. John Grey Porter, Rector of Kilskeery, William Woolsey, Esq., eldest son of J. Woolsey, Esq., of Milesdown, county Louth, to Francis Rose, second daughter of Samuel Vessey, Esq., D.L., of Derrabard House, county Tyrone.

No. 759 :: Ref. 1846-10-06, 3:1, M.
In Benburb Church, by the Rev. Richard Wrightson, Curate of Clonfeacle, Mr. David M'Dowal, Serjeant 54th Regiment, to Miss Eliza Jane Hutchinson, of Benburb.

No. 760 :: Ref. 1846-10-06, 3:1, D.
On the 28th ult., at the residence of his mother, Kilmorey street, Newry, in the 25th year of his age, Mr. Wm. Gordon, printer.

No. 761 :: Ref. 1846-10-06, 3:1, D.
On the morning of the 27th ult., of apoplexy, Mary, the beloved wife of James Maclannahan, Esq., of Waring Bank, Clogher.

No. 762 :: Ref. 1846-10-06, 3:1, D.
September 29, at his residence, Leeson-street, Thomas Quinan, Esq., formerly Chief Examiner of Her Majesty's High Court of Chancery, Ireland.

No. 763 :: Ref. 1846-10-06, 3:1, D.
September 30, in Jail-street, Ennis, at an advanced age, Mrs. Frances Knox, relict of Mr. Thomas Saunders Knox, proprietor of the *Clare Journal* newspaper.

No. 764 :: Ref. 1846-10-06, 3:1, D.
On the 24th ult., at the house of her son-in-law, Mr. George Burnett, near Poyntzpass, County Armagh, Louisa, relict of the late Mr. Charles Magarry, and daughter of the late Hubert Kelly, of Killybrook, County Westmeath, Esq.

No. 765 :: Ref. 1846-10-06, 3:1, D.
On the 22d ult., at Armagh, Anne, wife of Mr. Edward Butt, aged 38 years.

No. 766 :: Ref. 1846-10-13, 2:3, M.
At Drumsallen Church, on 2nd inst., by the Rev. Mr. Waring, Mr. John Frazier of Killymadday, to Jane, third daughter of Mr. James Wilson, of Tullylern, near Benburb, Co. Tyrone.

No. 767 :: Ref. 1846-10-13, 2:3, M.
At St. George's Church, G.W. Leech, Esq., to Catherine, daughter of H.W. Chambre, Esq., Hawthorn Hill, Armagh, and North Great George's-street, Dublin.

No. 768 :: Ref. 1846-10-13, 2:3, M.
October 8, at Monkstown Church, by the Rev. Richard Mauleverer, Rector of Tipperary, Alexander Montgomery, Esq., of Clonmannon, county Wicklow, eldest son of the late Alexander Nixon Montgomery, of Bessmount Park, county Monaghan, Esq., to Henrietta, daughter of Major Stafford, of Tully, county Cavan.

No. 769 :: Ref. 1846-10-13, 2:3, D.
October 7, in Upper Mount-street, Friddy A.H. Armstrong, only daughter of the late Captain Armstrong, of Hilltown, county Wexford, aged 25 years.

No. 770 :: Ref. 1846-10-13, 2:3, D.
August 24, at Niagara, Wm. Finch, a native of Kilkenny, Ireland, at the advanced age of 102 years.

No. 771 :: Ref. 1846-10-13, 2:3, D.
On the 2d inst., at Greenhill, in the county of Donegal, Elizabeth Fenwick, relict of William Fenwick, Esq., and sister of the late Bishop of Raphoe, in the 90th year of her age.

No. 772 :: Ref. 1846-10-13, 2:3, D.
At St. John's [sic], N.B., on September 3, Mr. James Schoales, aged 25 years, son of the late Mr. John Schoales, Tempo, county Fermanagh. Mr. Schoales was a young man much respected in life, and his premature demise is lamented by a large circle of friends and acquaintances in Fermanagh.

No. 773 :: Ref. 1846-10-13, 2:3, D.
On the 9th inst., at Moyard, Benburb, in the 43rd year of his age, W. Robert Holmes.

No. 774 :: Ref. 1846-10-13, 2:3, D.
On the 7th inst., at Miltown, near Newtownbutler county Fermanagh, Rosanna, relict of the late Wm. Adams, Esq., aged 80 years.

No. 775 :: Ref. 1846-10-20, 2:3, M.
On Tuesday, the 13th inst., in the Presbyterian Church, Enniskillen, by the Rev. Robert Holmes, Coagh, the Rev. A.T. Holmes, Tempo, to Sara M'Ilwaine, Tettymacall, near Enniskillen, youngest daughter of John M'Ilwaine, Esq., Strabane.

No. 776 :: Ref. 1846-10-20, 2:3, D.
On the morning of the 18th inst., at Maydown, near Benburb, at an advanced age, Benjamin Eyre, Esq., uncle of Thomas Eyre, Benburb Castle, and James Eyre Jackson, Tullydoey, Esqrs., J.P.s.

No. 777 :: Ref. 1846-10-27, 3:1, M.
On the 20th, in St. Mark's Church, of this city, Christopher Caldwell, Esq., to Miss Turner, eldest daughter of the late Mr. J. Turner of this city.

No. 778 :: Ref. 1846-10-27, 3:1, M.
Oct. 21, in Aghavea Church, in the county of Fermanagh, by the Rev. Henry Lucas St. George, father of the bridegroom, Henry Lucas St. George, Esq., of Dromore Rectory, in the county of Tyrone, to Harriet Charlotte Rebecca Sterne, only child of William Sterne, Esq., of the city of Bristol, and Gola House, of the county of Fermanagh, (formerly Captain in the 52d Regiment of Foot during the Peninsular war,) and lineal descendant of Richard Sterne, Archbishop of York, who attended the unfortunate Charles to the scaffold. There were present on the occasion—Capel and Edward St. George, Esqrs., brothers to the bridegroom; and Anne and Henrietta, sisters; together with Rev. William and Mrs. Burnside, and other Irish friends. Sir Hugh and Lady Stewart, sister, were prevented by the various duties which Sir Hugh and other good, honourable, and proper landlords have to attend to at their respective posts during the present period of distress amongst the poor. The happy pair drove off from the church immediately after the ceremony to Dromore Rectory, that residence having been allotted to them to pass the honeymoon.

No. 779 :: Ref. 1846-10-27, 3:1, D.
On the 23rd inst., in the eighth year of his age, William Cross, eldest son of Thos. H. Harpur, Esq., Gorestown, Moy.

No. 780 :: Ref. 1846-11-03, 3:1, B.
The lady of Robert Burrowes, Esq., of Stradone House, county Cavan, of a son.

No. 781 :: Ref. 1846-11-03, 3:1, B.
At Orange Lodge, the lady of Rev. Arthur Irwin, of a son.

No. 782 :: Ref. 1846-11-03, 3:1, M.
October 28, in St. Thomas's Church, by the Rev. William Magee, William Overend, Esq., Barrister-at-Law, second son of the late William Overend, Esq., of Edenderry-House, Portadown, to Louisa, eldest daughter of John M'Mahon, Esq., of Gloucester-street, Dublin, and Donard, county of Wicklow.

No. 783 :: Ref. 1846-11-03, 3:1, M.

October 22, at the Cathedral Church, Clonfert, John, eldest son of John Eyre, Esq., of Eyrecourt, county Galway, to Eleanor Maria, eldest daughter of Hubert B. Moore, Esq., of Shannon View, in same county.

No. 784 :: Ref. 1846-11-03, 3:1, D.

At Moy, on 31st ult., in the 45th year of his age, Mr. Thos. Walker, of this city, Builder.

No. 785 :: Ref. 1846-11-03, 3:1, D.

Oct. 24, at Tivoli House, Kingstown Hill, Sarah, wife of J. Jackson, Esq.

No. 786 :: Ref. 1846-11-03, 3:1, D.

October 25, at De Vesci Terrace, Kingstown, Ada Augusta daughter of Thomas J. Quinton, Esq.

No. 787 :: Ref. 1846-11-10, 2:5, M.

At Derryvoland Church, on the 6th inst., by the Rev. Mr. Bradshaw, Mr. Wm. C. Bracken, merchant, Black-Lion, co. Cavan, to Jane, youngest daughter of the late Wm. Armstrong, Esq., Drummee, Inishmore Island, co. Fermanagh.

No. 788 :: Ref. 1846-11-10, 2:5, M.

On the 5th instant, in St. Mark's Church, Armagh, by the Rev. Robert Haig, Mr. Robert White, of Fivemiletown, to Mary Jane, youngest daughter of the late Mr. John Bell, of Scotch-street, in this city.

No. 789 :: Ref. 1846-11-10, 2:5, M.

On the 22d inst. in Caledon Church, Mr. Robert Marshall, of that town, to Henrietta, eldest daughter of William Lundie, Esq., Adjutant of the Royal Tyrone Militia.

No. 790 :: Ref. 1846-11-10, 2:5, M.

Oct. 22, in Sandys'-street Presbyterian Church, Newry, by the Rev. J.A. Canning, of Morne, Nathaniel Weir, Esq., of Newry, in the county of Down, to Anne, eldest daughter of M. Singleton, Esq., R.M.

No. 791 :: Ref. 1846-11-10, 2:5, M.

On Thursday, the 5th inst., at Warrenpoint church, by the Rev. John Davis, John Fleming, Esq., of the Hill, Monaghan, to Mary, third daughter of Benjamin Atkinson, Esq., of Ballymoney, co. Antrim.

No. 792 :: Ref. 1846-11-10, 2:5, M.

October 22, in the Cathedral Church of Clonfert, by the Rev. Mark Perrin, Rector of Atherney, John, eldest son of John Eyre, Esq., of Eyrecourt Castle, in the county of Galway, to Eleanor Maria, eldest daughter of Hubert Moore, Esq., of Shannon View, in the same county.

No. 793 :: Ref. 1846-11-10, 2:5, D.

Of decline, at Caledon, on 6th inst., Wm. Pettigrew, Esq., aged 18 years.

No. 794 :: Ref. 1846-11-10, 2:5, D.

At Moy, on the 3d inst., in the 58th year of her age, Hester, daughter of the late Thomas Hawkins, Esq., Captain 3d Buffs.

No. 795 :: Ref. 1846-11-10, 2:5, D.

Oct. 25, at Mrs. Annesley's, Castleblayney, Robert M'Cord, aged fourteen, only son of William M'Cord, Esq., Ohoghill [sic], county of Antrim, deeply regretted by his friends.

No. 796 :: Ref. 1846-11-10, 2:5, D.

On the 23d ult., at Ramsey, Isle of Man, Robert Hunter, Esq., manager of the Provincial Bank of Ireland in Limerick.

No. 797 :: Ref. 1846-11-10, 2:5, D.

On the 28th September, at Petersburgh, Canada West, in the 59th year of her age, Isabella, relict of the late Mr. David Dickson, merchant, Dungannon, County Tyrone, Ireland.

No. 798 :: Ref. 1846-11-10, 2:5, D.

On the 25th ult., John Ward, Lower Malone, aged 82. He was upwards of 42 years a pensioner from the 6th Royal Enniskillen Dragoons.

No. 799 :: Ref. 1846-11-10, 2:5, D.

Death of Lady Manners.—The Dowager Lady Manners, formerly the Hon. Jane Butler, expired on the 2d instant, at Farnham Hall, near Bury St. Edmund's, aged 68. She was daughter of James, eleventh Lord Caher, and sister to the late Earl of Glengall. In 1815 her ladyship was married to the first Lord Manners, who at that time was Lord Chancellor of Ireland.

No. 800 :: Ref. 1846-11-17, 2:6, M.

On the 10th inst., by the Rev. Alexander Strain, Alexander M'Donald, Esq., Bovain, near Moy, to Anna, daughter of the late Rev. Joseph Crawford, of Cremore.

No. 801 :: Ref. 1846-11-17, 2:6, D.

On Saturday the 7th inst., in London, Arthur Walter Cope, of Drummilly, in this county, Esq.

No. 802 :: Ref. 1846-11-17, 2:6, D.

Nov. 8, at his residence, 29, Lower Leeson-street, Dublin, after a long and painful illness, Martin Keene, Esq., in the 66th year of his age, deeply and deservedly regretted.

No. 803 :: Ref. 1846-11-17, 2:6, D.

On the 7th inst., at his residence, Hill Cottage, Monaghan, Mr. John Rowland, in the 78th year of his age.

No. 804 :: Ref. 1846-11-17, 2:6, D.

At Thistleton, near Hull, in his 80th year, Mr. John Perkins. Deceased was proprietor and publisher of the *Hull Rockingham* newspaper upwards of thirty years. He was an officer on board his Majesty's ship *Buffalo* in the year 1782, and was an eye-witness to the unfortunate catastrophe of the sinking of the *Royal George*, at Spithead.

No. 805 :: Ref. 1846-11-24, 2:6, M.
At Charlemont church, on the 19th inst., by the Rev. James Disney, Mr. Robert Cherry, of Derrycary, Verner's bridge, to Mary, daughter of the late Mr. John Madden, of Corr and Dunavally.

No. 806 :: Ref. 1846-11-24, 2:6, M.
On the 17th inst, in Benburb church, by the Rev. Richard Wighton, curate of Clonfeacle, Miss Marianne Neely, of Tullygoney, to Mr. James Hogan, of Benburb.

No. 807 :: Ref. 1846-11-24, 2:6, M.
At Magherafelt, on the 18th inst., by the Rev. C.K. Irwin, Mr. Thomas York, to Miss Jane Williamson.

No. 808 :: Ref. 1846-11-24, 2:6, M.
On the 5th inst., in the Ahorey Meeting-house, by the Rev. Thomas Kilpatrick, Mr. James Lafferty, to Miss Mary Wallace, both near Tandragee.

No. 809 :: Ref. 1846-11-24, 2:6, M.
On the 5th inst., in the Ahorey Meeting-house, by the Rev. Thomas Kilpatrick, Mr. A. Wilson, of Ballynewry, to Miss Sarah Lewis, of Ahorey.

No. 810 :: Ref. 1846-11-24, 2:6, M.
On the 9th inst., at the family residence of the lady, by the Rev. Hugh Magauran, Catholic curate of Kinawley, Nathaniel, only surviving son of Patrick Maguire, Esq., of Bonebrooke, county Cavan, to Anna Alicia, fourth daughter of the late Dan Tighe Winslow, Esq., of Dresternan House, county Fermanagh.

No. 811 :: Ref. 1846-11-24, 2:6, D.
At Vicar's Hill, in this city, on Monday, the 16th inst., after a long and protracted illness, Mr. Richard Rogers, aged 67 years.

No. 812 :: Ref. 1846-11-24, 2:6, D.
In this city, on the 19th inst., at the residence of her son, Agnes, relict of the late Mr. Charles Keys, at the advanced age of 84 years,—55 of which she was a consistent member of the Wesleyan Methodist Society. She died as she had lived, peaceful and happy, with full confidence in her Redeemer.

No. 813 :: Ref. 1846-11-24, 2:6, D.
On the 11th inst., at Drumcree, near Portadown, Mr. Geo. Scott, aged 89.

No. 814 :: Ref. 1846-11-24, 2:6, D.
On the 10th inst., at Lurgan, in the 31st year of his age, Mr. Wm. Wells, woollendraper.

No. 815 :: Ref. 1846-11-24, 2:6, D.
At Monaghan, at the residence of his brother, the Rev. H. Maffet, on the 15th inst., Richard Maffet, Esq., M.D., F.R.C.S.I., of Glasslough, in the 35th year of his age.

No. 816 :: Ref. 1846-11-24, 2:6, D.
On the morning of the 4th inst., at Dundalk, of dysentery, Mr. Wm. Gunne, Primitive Wesleyan Methodist preacher, aged 20 years.

No. 817 :: Ref. 1846-11-24, 2:6, D.
On Saturday, at his residence in Dublin, George Rankin, Esq., of Enniskillen, solicitor, aged 53.

No. 818 :: Ref. 1846-11-24, 2:6, D.
On the 28th of September, at Peterborough, Canada West, in the 59th year of her age, Isabella, relict of the late Mr. D. Dickson, merchant, Dungannon, county Tyrone.

No. 819 :: Ref. 1846-11-24, 2:6, D.
On the 6th inst., of typhus fever, at Lurgan, Mr. J. Mason, Master of the Workhouse, in the 28th year of his age.

No. 820 :: Ref. 1846-12-01, 2:6, B.
Nov. 25, in this city, the lady of John Clarke Adams, Esq., of a daughter.

No. 821 :: Ref. 1846-12-01, 2:6, B.
Nov. 19, at Kilmore, county Monaghan, the lady of Captain Herbert Schomberg, Royal Navy, of a son.

No. 822 :: Ref. 1846-12-01, 2:6, M.
At the Parish Church of Wrodwardine, Shropshire, by the Rev. Charles Clifton, Edward Archdall, Esq., Captain 14th Regiment, third son of Edward Archdall, Esq., of Riversdale, county Fermanagh, to Caroline Anne, widow of John Starke, Esq., of Lougharne, Carmarthenshire, third surviving daughter of the late C.C. Clifton, Esq., of Tymaur, Breconshire.

No. 823 :: Ref. 1846-12-01, 2:6, M.
November 26, in Enniskillen Church, by the Rev. John Brien Frith, James Bryden, Esq., of Regent-street, London, to Anne Jane, eldest daughter of William Frith, Esq., of The Cross, in the County of Fermanagh.

No. 824 :: Ref. 1846-12-01, 2:6, M.
On Tuesday, the 24th ult., in the First Presbyterian Church, Derry, by the Rev. Henry Wallace, Jas. M'Neight, Esq., editor of the *Londonderry Standard*, to Catherine, second daughter of Joseph Macpherson, Esq., Ballongery, near that city.

No. 825 :: Ref. 1846-12-01, 2:6, M.
On Thursday, the 26th ult., at Moy Church, by the Rev. Mr. Leech, Mr. John Gunning, of Donaghadee, to Miss Isabella Sinclair, daughter of the late Mr. John Sinclair, Kinneary, near this city.

No. 826 :: Ref. 1846-12-01, 2:6, D.
Suddenly, in this city, on the 24th ult., Jane, the beloved wife of Mr. John Kitson, of Barrickhill, deeply lamented by a numerous circle of friends.

No. 827 :: Ref. 1846-12-01, 2:6, D.
On the 24th ultimo, at Killay, near Pomeroy, Mr. Henry Glasgow, aged 24 years. The deceased bore a protracted illness with Christian fortitude, and died with a hope full of immortality.

No. 828 :: Ref. 1846-12-08, 2:5, M.

On the 4th inst., in Tandragee Church, by the Rev. Henry Burdett, Mr. William Matthews, of Rathfriland, to Susanna, sister of Mr. Richard Greenaway of Athol Cottage, near Tandragee.

No. 829 :: Ref. 1846-12-15, 2:5, M.

At Simla, Bengal Presidency, on the 16th of October, by the Rev. John Vaughan, A.B., Major Thomas Young, 2d Grenadiers, to Mary Anne, second daughter of Lawford Tronson, Esq., Newry, Ireland, and relict of the late William Egerton, Esq., of the 2d Grenadiers.

No. 830 :: Ref. 1846-12-22, 2:6, B.

December 13, at Poplar Vale, county Monaghan, the lady of John Richardson, Esq., of a son.

No. 831 :: Ref. 1846-12-22, 2:6, M.

On the 15th inst., at St. Peter's Church, by the Rev. Harry Disney (uncle to the bride,) William Beauchamp Clayton, M.D., to Sarah, relict of the late Robert Robinson, Esq., and second daughter of the late Thomas Waters, M.D., Parsonstown.

No. 832 :: Ref. 1846-12-22, 2:6, M.

Dec. 17, in St. George's Church, by the Rev. Charles Miller, Hall Stirling, Esq., son of the Rev. J.B. Stirling, to Elizabeth, eldest daughter of Leonard Dobbin, Esq., of Gardiner's-place.

No. 833 :: Ref. 1846-12-22, 2:6, M.

On the 9th inst., in Kells Church, by the Rev. Hans Caulfield, the Rev. Abraham St. George Caulfield, to Mary Ann, eldest daughter of the late W. Waring, Esq.

No. 834 :: Ref. 1846-12-22, 2:6, M.

On the 11th inst., in the Presbyterian Church, Fourtowns, Robert Paul, Esq., Ballymagorman House, county Armagh, to Sarah Ann, second daughter of Joseph Hawthorne, Esq., Whitehill, Poyntzpass.

No. 835 :: Ref. 1846-12-22, 2:6, D.

On the 18th inst., of scarlet fever, at 5, Gloucester place, Portman-square, George Molyneux, youngest son of Sir George Molyneux, of Castledillon, Bart., aged 2 years and 8 months.

No. 836 :: Ref. 1846-12-22, 2:6, D.

On the 18th inst., Mr. Edward Parkinson of this city, aged 86 years. He had been writing master in the Royal School of this city for upwards of 40 years, and nearly 60 years a consistent member of the Methodist Society. His end was peace.

No. 837 :: Ref. 1846-12-22, 2:6, D.

On the 15th inst., in Armagh jail, Mr. William Brown, turnkey, aged 31 years.

No. 838 :: Ref. 1846-12-22, 2:6, D.

On the 19th inst., at Teagury, near Loughgall, in this county, Mr. Wm. Benson, at the advanced age of 101 years—for many years of which he was a steady member of the Primitive Wesleyan Methodist connexion, and retained the possession of his faculties to the period of his departure.

No. 839 :: Ref. 1846-12-22, 2:6, D.

On the 10th inst., at Stewardstown, Martha, widow of the late Mr. John Park, aged 88 years.

No. 840 :: Ref. 1846-12-22, 2:6, D.

On the 12th ult., at Madeira, in his 21st year, Samuel John, youngest son of the Hon. Judge Torrens.

No. 841 :: Ref. 1846-12-22, 2:6, D.

On the 10th ult., at New York, Jane, relict of the late Thos. Addis Emmett, Esq.

No. 842 :: Ref. 1846-12-22, 2:6, D.

In Dublin, on the 11th inst., in the 76th year of his age, J. Wemys Disney, Esq., formerly of the 2d Garrison Battalion, nephew of the late Colonel Wemys, of Danesfort, Kilkenny, and of the late Colonel Arthur Disney, of the E.I.C. Service.

No. 843 :: Ref. 1846-12-22, 2:6, D.

December 11, at the residence of his uncle, Samuel Wauchob, Esq., 73, Lower Mount-street, Daniel, only son of Daniel Baird, Esq., Mayor of the city of Londonderry, aged 20 years.

No. 844 :: Ref. 1846-12-29, 3:4, M.

On the 15th inst., at Inver Church, Mr. James Neill, of Londonderry, to Catherine Anne, second daughter of Robert Larmour, Esq., Bonny Glen, Donegal.

No. 845 :: Ref. 1846-12-29, 3:4, D.

On the 25th inst., in this city, Mr. George Penton, aged 26 years.

No. 846 :: Ref. 1846-12-29, 3:4, D.

On the 22d inst., at Tandragee, in sure and certain hope of the resurrection to eternal life, Jane, widow of the late William Guy, of Ballymore, aged 95 years.

No. 847 :: Ref. 1846-12-29, 3:4, D.

At Dunfanaghy, on Sunday, the 13th inst., Mr. John Irvine, aged 43. As a charitable friend and kind neighbour he will long be remembered by the poor of the town and its vicinity. He died as he lived, at peace with God and man.

No. 848 :: Ref. 1846-12-29, 3:4, D.

At Coleraine, on the 19th inst., Samuel Ogle, Esq., Collector of Customs, late of Newry, aged 45 years.

No. 849 :: Ref. 1846-12-29, 3:4, D.

December 17, at Strandtown, near Belfast, Mary, youngest daughter of the late John Murray, Esq., of Creevy, county Down.

No. 850 :: Ref. 1847-01-05, 2:5, B.

Dec. 25th, at Enniskillen, Mrs. Thomas Wood, of a son.

No. 851 :: Ref. 1847-01-05, 2:5, B.

On the 26th inst., at Kells, the lady of Henry L. Lindsay, Esq., of a son.

No. 852 :: Ref. 1847-01-05, 2:5, B.
On the 22d inst., the lady of James Harden, of Harrybrook, Esq., of a son.

No. 853 :: Ref. 1847-01-05, 2:5, B.
Dec. 26, the lady of Robert Hassard, of Cookstown, Esq., of a daughter.

No. 854 :: Ref. 1847-01-05, 2:5, M.
On the 4th inst., at Donaghmore Church, by the Rev. Thos. Carpendale, brother of the bride, Capt. Donnelan, Staff-officer, to Elizabeth, widow of the late Major Shaw, both of this city.

No. 855 :: Ref. 1847-01-05, 2:5, M.
On the 28th inst., in St. Ann's Church, Mr. Henry Love, merchant, Belfast, to Elizabeth, third daughter of the late Lieutenant S.G. Victor, R.N.

No. 856 :: Ref. 1847-01-05, 2:5, D.
At the residence of her granddaughter, Mrs. A. Davidson, Thomas-street, Ann Waddle, relict of the late Daniel Waddle, builder, formerly of Paisley, Scotland, at the advanced age of 89 years—her end was peace.

No. 857 :: Ref. 1847-01-05, 2:5, D.
December 24, at Cottage-hill, Aughnacloy, Mrs. Moore, wife of Hugh Moore, Esq., J.P., whose loss will be severely felt by the poor in the neighbourhood, to whom she was the kind and generous assistant.

No. 858 :: Ref. 1847-01-05, 2:5, D.
December 24, at Cookstown, aged one year and five months, Fanny, daughter of Robert Hassard, Esq.

No. 859 :: Ref. 1847-01-05, 2:5, D.
December 27, at Saul Rectory, in the county of Down, Catherine Darnley Byrne, daughter of the late Thomas Byrne, of Lurgan, Esq., deeply and sincerely regretted.

No. 860 :: Ref. 1847-01-12, 2:5, B.
On the 1st inst., at Portadown, the lady of John Overend, Esq., of a son.

No. 861 :: Ref. 1847-01-12, 2:5, B.
On the 31st ult., at Rossfad, County Fermanagh, the lady of H M Richardson, Esq., of a daughter.

No. 862 :: Ref. 1847-01-12, 2:5, M.
On Wednesday, the 6th inst., in the First Presbyterian Church of this city, by the Rev. Mr. Fleming, Mr. Wm. R. Ferris, of the firm of M'Culla and Ferris, merchants, Armagh, to Maria, second daughter of Mr. Arthur Hughes, of Scotch-street.

No. 863 :: Ref. 1847-01-12, 2:5, M.
On the 31st ult., in Drumcree Church, by the Rev. David Babington, Mr. William Sweany, of Foy, to Fanny third daughter of Mr. Benjamin Huniford, Corneymuckley.

No. 864 :: Ref. 1847-01-12, 2:5, M.
On the 2d inst., in St. Mary's Church, Newry, by the Rev. Daniel Bagot, Richard Jebb Brown, Esq., to Miss Kate Brown Dickenson.

No. 865 :: Ref. 1847-01-12, 2:5, M.
On the 5th instant, at Dungannon, by the Rev. Dr. Monteague, Mr. John Doherty, of Portballyraine, Letterkenny, county Donegal, to Catherine, only daughter of the late Mr. Patrick Feeny, Commercial hotel, Dungannon.

No. 866 :: Ref. 1847-01-12, 2:5, M.
On the 6th inst., at Lislooney Meeting House, by the Rev. Paul Borland, Mr. James Little of Breaky, to Ellen, oldest daughter of Mr. James Howey of Coolkiln, Middletown.

No. 867 :: Ref. 1847-01-12, 2:5, D.
Dec. 31, at Kilfane Glebe, county of Kilkenny, in the seventy-seventh year of his age, John Irvin, Esq., of Tanragee, Colonel of the Sligo Regiment.

No. 868 :: Ref. 1847-01-12, 2:5, D.
On the 31st ult., at Rossory Glebe, the Rev. John Taylor, Rector, after a protracted illness.

No. 869 :: Ref. 1847-01-12, 2:5, D.
On the 5th instant, at Cootehill, Samuel Macfadin, aged 77 years.

No. 870 :: Ref. 1847-01-12, 2:5, D.
On the 26th Dec., at Newry, Mr. Samuel Wallace, merchant, aged 52 years.

No. 871 :: Ref. 1847-01-19, 2:6, B.
On the 10th inst, at 59, Blessington-street, Dublin, the lady of Arthur Sharman Crawford, Esq., of a son.

No. 872 :: Ref. 1847-01-19, 2:6, M.
January 11, at the Presbyterian Meeting-house, Fintona, T. Wilson, Esq., of Newry, to Marianne, eldest daughter of J. Sherrard, Esq., of Fintona.

No. 873 :: Ref. 1847-01-19, 2:6, M.
January 13th, 1847, at Stone-Bridge, Presbyterian Meeting-house, by the Rev. Wm. White, John Crumley, Esq., to Jane, eldest daughter of Mr. George Elliott, merchant, both of Clones.

No. 874 :: Ref. 1847-01-19, 2:6, D.
On Sunday, 17th instant, in Thomas-street, Armagh, Miss Frances Ball, aged 70 years, whose long and useful life was devoted to education. Her remains will be interred in St. Mark's Church yard, to-morrow at 11 o'clock, a.m.

No. 875 :: Ref. 1847-01-19, 2:6, D.
At Moy, on the 14th inst., of consumption, Jane, eldest daughter of A. Nepean Molesworth, Esq., formerly of Fairlawn House, in this county.

No. 876 :: Ref. 1847-01-19, 2:6, D.
At Tandragee, on the 5th inst., aged 69 years, Sarah, wife of Mr. James Craig.

No. 877 :: Ref. 1847-01-19, 2:6, D.
On the 6th inst., at Crosshill, near Crumlin, Mr. J. Owens, teacher, formerly of Belfast, aged 67 years.

No. 878 :: Ref. 1847-01-19, 2:6, D.
On the 30th ult., at Artabracken, Portadown, Mr. Henry Thornton, aged 102 years.

No. 879 :: Ref. 1847-01-19, 2:6, D.
In Dublin, on the 11th inst., Mr. Samuel Matthews, printer, formerly of Belfast, sincerely and deservedly regretted.

No. 880 :: Ref. 1847-01-26, 2:6, M.
On the 20th inst., in St. Mark's Church, Armagh, by the Rev. Thomas Jones, William Leebody, Esq., M.D., to Eliza, youngest daughter of the late John Stanley, Esq., of this city.

No. 881 :: Ref. 1847-01-26, 2:6, M.
At Fintona Presbyterian Church, on the 11th inst., by the Rev. R. Chambers, Marianne, eldest daughter of J. Sherrard, Esq., to Thomas Wilson, Esq., Newry.

No. 882 :: Ref. 1847-01-26, 2:6, M.
In Belfast on Friday, 22nd inst., by the Rev. David Hamilton, the Rev. J. Bennet, of Tassagh, near Keady, to Mary Jane, daughter of Mr. John Scott, of Belfast, and grand-daughter of the late Rev. James Garraway, Rector of Ahanloo, Newtownlimavady.

No. 883 :: Ref. 1847-01-26, 2:6, M.
On the 20th inst., in Drumsallon Church, by the Rev. C. Waring, and afterwards in the parish Chapel by the Rev. Hugh Murphy, Mr. P. Malone, of Clonfecle, county Tyrone, to Elizabeth, eldest daughter of the late John Wilson, Esq., of Drumrush, and grand-niece, to the late Sir I. Wilson, knight, Surgeon in Ordinary to Her Royal Highness the Duchess of Kent.

No. 884 :: Ref. 1847-01-26, 2:6, M.
January 21, at Castleblaney Church, by the Rev. J.T. Whitestone, J. Fitzstephen Creagh, Esq., of Glin, county of Limerick, to Catherine Jane, youngest daughter of the late Andrew F. Macmath, Esq., of Thornford House, county of Monaghan.

No. 885 :: Ref. 1847-01-26, 2:6, M.
On Jan. 22, in the Presbyterian Meeting House, Auchnacloy, by Rev. William M'Ilwain, Mr. James M'Chappan, Corderry, to Sarah, second daughter of Mr. James M'Clery, merchant, Aughnacloy.

No. 886 :: Ref. 1847-01-26, 2:6, M.
On the 19th inst., by the Rev. Robt. Wallace, Minister of the Reformed Presbyterian Congregation of Newry, Mr. Robert S. M'Clelland, Newry, to Agnes, youngest daughter of the late Mr. Robert M'Alister, Buskhill, Donaghmore.

No. 887 :: Ref. 1847-01-26, 2:6, D.
On Tuesday the 19th instant, in the 64th year of her age, Martha, the beloved wife of Mr. Robert Little, of Monaghan, in the certain hope of Eternal Life. Truth and religion found in her at all times, a zealous and steady supporter. The several virtues she possessed as a friend, wife and mother, obtained the esteem of all her acquaintances, and her death inflicts the deepest sorrow on her bereaved husband and family.

No. 888 :: Ref. 1847-01-26, 2:6, D.
On the 9th inst., at Dungannon, in the 44th year of his age, after a few days' illness, Mr. Peter Rocks, Innkeeper.

No. 889 :: Ref. 1847-01-26, 2:6, D.
On the 16th inst., at Moyle Glebe, County Tyrone, in the 76th year of his age, the Rev. R. Herbert Nash, D.D., for some time senior Fellow of Trinity College, Dublin, and for 27 years Rector of the Parish of Ardstraw, near Newtownstewart, Diocese of Derry.

No. 890 :: Ref. 1847-01-26, 2:6, D.
On the 23d inst., at Dungannon, William Dawson, Esq., M.D., of Typhus Fever, caught while in attendance on his professional duties.

No. 891 :: Ref. 1847-01-26, 2:6, D.
Of measles, at Castleblaney, Maria, only child of Mr. Wm. Twible.

No. 892 :: Ref. 1847-01-26, 2:6, D.
Jan. 7, at Ringrove House, near Kingsbridge, the Right Hon. John Stapleton DeCourcy, Baron Kinsale, aged 42. His lordship was the premier Baron of Ireland, and had the privilege (which was appertained to the Barons of Kinsale for some centuries) of wearing his hat in the Royal presence. He is succeeded in his title and estates by his eldest son, now in his minority.

No. 893 :: Ref. 1847-01-26, 2:6, D.
At Fivemiletown, on the 20th inst., Sarah, relict of the late M.J. Alexander, of that town, aged 92 years.

No. 894 :: Ref. 1847-01-26, 2:6, D.
January 16, at his residence, Mount Salem, Clones, the Rev. Adam Averell, in the 93d year of his age, and 70th of his ministry. This venerable servant of the Lord was ordained by the Bishop of Clonfert, but like Mr. Wesley, he subsequently confined his labours to the promotion of religion amongst the Methodists, and for about 60 years, his time, property, influence, and talent, were devoted to advance the cause of God through the instrumentality of that society. His strong attachment to the Established Church led him, at the time of the division in the Methodist body, to connect himself with those who adhered to primitive principles, and so long as his health permitted, he presided at the Annual Conference of the Methodists who continue in communion with the Church. His end was that of holy joy and triumph.

No. 895 :: Ref. 1847-01-26, 2:6, D.
January 13, at Waltham Terrace, Blackrock, Catherine, wife of R.B. Blackwood, Esq., and sister of the late Colonel Madden, of Hiltown, county Monaghan.

No. 896 :: Ref. 1847-01-26, 2:6, D.
In Enniskillen, on Friday, William Gabbett, Esq., late Capt. in the Fermanagh Militia, aged 82. Mr. Gabbett, was for many years, a most active magistrate for Fermanagh, and took part in all our local institutions and affairs, until age unfitted him.

No. 897 :: Ref. 1847-01-26, 2:6, D.
At the house of her son, (Doctor George Alcock Nixon,) Enniskillen, aged 64, Mrs. Nixon, relict of the late Thomas Nixon, Esq.

No. 898 :: Ref. 1847-01-26, 2:6, D.
On Monday, the 4th instant, at Bristol, in the 78th year of her age, Miss Susannah Sterne, only surviving relative by his father's side, of Major Sterne of Gola, county Fermanagh.

No. 899 :: Ref. 1847-01-26, 2:6, D.
At Benburb Castle, on the morning of the 25th inst., after an illness of only two days, Thomas Eyre, Esq., J.P. for the Counties of Armagh and Tyrone.

No. 900 :: Ref. 1847-02-02, 2:6, M.
On the 27th Jan., at St. Mary's Colton, by the Rev. J.O. Oldham, the Rev. Robert Haig of Armagh, son of the late R. Haig, Esq., of Dublin, and grandson of the late Sir Wm. Wolseley, Bart., of Wolseley, Staffordshire, to Matilda, daughter of James Oldham Oldham [sic], Esq., of Bellamour Hall in the same county, and late of the Bengal Civil Service.

No. 901 :: Ref. 1847-02-02, 2:6, M.
On the 28th ultimo, in Aughnacloy Church, by the Rev. Edward Newenham, Mr. Thomas M'Mahon, Ballymacone, near Keady, in the County Armagh, to Isabella, youngest daughter of the late John M'Williams, of Carnteel House, in the County Tyrone, Esq.

No. 902 :: Ref. 1847-02-02, 2:6, M.
At Castleblaney Church, J. Fitzstephen Creagh, Esq., of Glin, county Limerick, to Catherine Jane, daughter of the late Andrew F. Macmath, Esq., of Thornford House, county Monaghan.

No. 903 :: Ref. 1847-02-02, 2:6, M.
On the 20th Jan., at St. Hilda's Catholic Church, Hartlepool, Durham, by the Rev. Wm. Knight, and subsequently on the same day at the Parish Church, Stranton, Stockton on Tees, by the Rev. Rowland Webster, George Duggan, D.E., Birmingham, to Harriette Anne, second daughter of Thomas Casebourne, Esq., M. Inst. C.E., Resident Engineer at Hartlepool West Harbour and Docks.

No. 904 :: Ref. 1847-02-02, 2:6, D.
Jan. 28th, at her residence, Main-street, Enniskillen, Margaret, relict of the late John Irwin, Esq. She bore a tedious and protracted illness with patience and resignation, and died in the hope of eternal life.

No. 905 :: Ref. 1847-02-02, 2:6, D.
Suddenly, on the 10th Jan., at Ballyhagan, near Loughgall, Mr. Wm. Charles Keegan, aged 34 years, sincerely regretted.

No. 906 :: Ref. 1847-02-02, 2:6, D.
At Fivemiletown, on the 20th ult., Sarah, relict of the late Mr. James Alexander, of that town, aged 92 years.

No. 907 :: Ref. 1847-02-02, 2:6, D.
Jan. 22, at Swanlinbar, at the advanced age of 88, Mary, relict of the late Rev. William Johnston, Vicar of Innismagrath, whom she survived 33 years.

No. 908 :: Ref. 1847-02-02, 2:6, D.
January 22, in Lowtherstown, Mr. James Johnston, merchant, in the 25th year of his age, after a long and painful illness.

No. 909 :: Ref. 1847-02-09, 2:6, B.
At the Provincial Bank of Ireland, Fermoy, the lady of James M'Creery, Esq., of a daughter.

No. 910 :: Ref. 1847-02-09, 2:6, D.
On 1st instant, Charles Haig, Esq., Lower Gardiner-street Dublin.

No. 911 :: Ref. 1847-02-09, 2:6, D.
On the 3d instant, in Irish-street, Mary, relict of the late Mr. Thomas Healy, and Mother of the late Revds. John and Charles Healy, at the advanced age of 93 years. She lived an exemplary life.

No. 912 :: Ref. 1847-02-09, 2:6, D.
On the 23d ult., at George's place, Dublin, Mrs. E. Moore, daughter of the late Robert Moore, Esq., of Moorvale, county Armagh, aged 82 years.

No. 913 :: Ref. 1847-02-09, 2:6, D.
On the 27th Jan., Mr. Archibald Campbell, of Newry, aged 78 years.

No. 914 :: Ref. 1847-02-09, 2:6, D.
On Monday, 1st instant, at Derrybrusk, County Fermanagh, Glebe, Rev. G. Harris, aged 67.

No. 915 :: Ref. 1847-02-09, 2:6, D.
Lost, in the ship "*Mayda,*" supposed to have foundered on her passage from Van Dieman's Land, Robert Dwarris, third son of George Bicknell, Esq., of the Manor House, Kilrea.

No. 916 :: Ref. 1847-02-16, 2:5, B.
On the 7th inst., at Rosstrevor, the lady of Alexander Lane, Esq., M.D., R.N., of her fifth son.

No. 917 :: Ref. 1847-02-16, 2:5, B.
At Mount Collyer Park, on the 10th inst., Mrs. J.A. Henderson, of a daughter.

No. 918 :: Ref. 1847-02-16, 2:5, B.
At Lurgan, on the 8th instant, the lady of John Hancock, Esq., of a son.

No. 919 :: Ref. 1847-02-16, 2:5, M.

On Saturday, February 13, at the Cathedral, Armagh, by the Rev. R. Allott, Precentor and Sub-Dean, John Livington Campbell, Esq., of Achrader, of Perthshire, to Miss Geraldine Julia St. Felix.

No. 920 :: Ref. 1847-02-16, 2:5, M.

On the 8th inst., in Madden Church, by the Rev. Robert A. Irwin, A.M., Mr. Geo. Tecey, of Drumgreenah, to Mary, eldest daughter of the late Mr. John Turner, of Armagh.

No. 921 :: Ref. 1847-02-16, 2:5, M.

On the 16th August last, by special license, at Perth Church, Jamestown, Van Dieman's Land, David Gibson, Esq., of Glasslough, South Esk, to Caroline, third daughter of George R. Clarke, Esq., Boyne Lodge, Drogheda.

No. 922 :: Ref. 1847-02-16, 2:5, M.

On the 8th instant, at the residence of her mother, Whitehall, Blackrock, Susan, fifth daughter of the late Philip Hughes, Esq., of Newry, to Charles Gavan Duffy, Esq.

No. 923 :: Ref. 1847-02-16, 2:5, M.

Feb. 10, in the Parish Church of Dundalk, by the Rev. Elias Tackeray, a.m., Vicar, Richard, eldest son of Thomas Richard Needham, Esq., of St. Edmondsbury, county Dublin, to Mary, eldest daughter of John Townley, Esq., of Dundalk, county Louth.

No. 924 :: Ref. 1847-02-16, 2:5, D.

In Russell-street, Armagh, on the 11th instant, Mrs. Noble, aged 46 years, sincerely regretted by a large circle of friends.

No. 925 :: Ref. 1847-02-16, 2:5, D.

At Beith, on Monday, the 8th instant, Jane, daughter of James Faulds, Esq., Merchant.

No. 926 :: Ref. 1847-02-16, 2:5, D.

On the 2d inst., at Killinure, county Cavan, the residence of Mrs. Bell, Mrs. Margaret Smyth aged 83, upwards of sixty years housekeeper in the family of the late George Bell, Esq., Barrister at law. The undeviating fidelity and devotion with which she discharged the duties of her station, as well as the strict integrity of her character in every relation of life, have rendered her decease a source of sincere regret to all who were acquainted with her worth.

No. 927 :: Ref. 1847-02-16, 2:5, D.

On the 7th instant, at the house of his mother, 5, Chichester-street, Belfast, on his return from Africa, of a rapid consumption, Latimer Barklie, third son of the late James Barklie, linen merchant, Linenvale, County Armagh, aged 28.

No. 928 :: Ref. 1847-02-16, 2:5, D.

On the 9th inst., at Ballybay, in the 30th year of his age, Mr. Samuel Foster; deeply and deservedly regretted.

No. 929 :: Ref. 1847-02-16, 2:5, D.

On the 15th Feb. at Clones, of consumption, in the 19th year of her age, Anna Maria Lions, youngest daughter of the late William Lions, Primitive Wesleyan Methodist Preacher.

No. 930 :: Ref. 1847-02-23, 2:6, M.

On the 16th inst., at the lady's residence, Donegall-street, Belfast, by the Rev. P. Dorrian, N. M'Devitt, Esq., Editor of the *Vindicator*, to Eliza, daughter of the late John Magennis, Esq., Ballymacilreny.

No. 931 :: Ref. 1847-02-23, 2:6, M.

On the 12th inst., in Antrim Church, by the Rev. William Greene, Vicar, Mr. Robert Mathers, of Lurgan, to Anne, eldest daughter of Mr. Joseph M'Lorinan, of Antrim.

No. 932 :: Ref. 1847-02-23, 2:6, M.

On the 10th inst., in the Presbyterian Church, Magherafelt, by the Rev. James Wilson, Mr. Wm. Ekin, to Miss Eliza M'Lernon, of Ballymulderg, near Magherafelt.

No. 933 :: Ref. 1847-02-23, 2:6, M.

On the 11th inst., by the Rev. Robert Morrison, Markethill, Mr. Robert Morrison, Kingston, Upper Canada, to Amelia, daughter of Mr. Alexander M'Cullagh, Dennyhara.

No. 934 :: Ref. 1847-02-23, 2:6, M.

On the 16th inst., in Caledon Church by the Rev. Mr. Chamly, Mr. Andrew Simpson, Surgeon, to Susan Seers, Lady Caledon's nursery maid.

No. 935 :: Ref. 1847-02-23, 2:6, M.

On the 17th inst., in Bantry Church by the Rev. Godfrey Alexander, Wm. Bell, Esq., Christian's town County Louth, to Mary, only daughter of Henderson Crozier, Esq., H.P. 22d Regiment.

No. 936 :: Ref. 1847-02-23, 2:6, D.

On the 16th inst., at his residence Mountain-lodge, county Armagh, Hugh Garmany, Esq., aged 85 years.

No. 937 :: Ref. 1847-02-23, 2:6, D.

On the 14th inst., at Newry, Mr. John Moore, Merchant, in the 51st year of his age. He died of malignant fever—caught, it is believed, in attending at the Union Workhouse, of which he was a most zealous and efficient Guardian.

No. 938 :: Ref. 1847-02-23, 2:6, D.

Lieutenant-Colonel Ratcliffe, K.H., late of the Inniskilling Dragoons and 2d Dragoons, died on the 9th instant. He served in the Peninsula with the 2d Dragoons, from June, 1811, to the end of the war in 1841, including the battles of Salamanca, Vittoria, Pyrenees, and Toulouse.

No. 939 :: Ref. 1847-03-02, 2:6, B.

On the 20th ult., in Northland-row, Dungannon, the lady of James Hamilton, Esq., Surgeon, of a daughter.

No. 940 :: Ref. 1847-03-02, 2:6, D.

On Saturday morning last, at the advanced age of 79 years, 52 of which he was Rector of the parish of Kilmore, county Monaghan, Rev. G.H. Schomberg, lineal descendant of the celebrated Duke Schomberg.

No. 941 :: Ref. 1847-03-02, 2:6, D.

Of fever, on Tuesday, the 23d ult., at his residence, Ballintra, in the county of Donegal, Arthur Corscaden, Esq., in the 49th year of his age, much and deservedly regretted by a very large circle of friends and acquaintances.

No. 942 :: Ref. 1847-03-02, 2:6, D.

At his residence in Middletown, on Saturday the 27th Feb. of Fever, caught in the discharge of his arduous professional duties, David Smyth, Esq., M.D., Medical Superintendent of the Middletown Infirmary and Fever Hospital. The universal, and uncontrollable wail of the poor, and the deep, though silent, grief of his friends and acquaintances, not only attest what were his merit as a successful practitioner, but also proclaim how dearly he was beloved; and how severely his loss is felt by all classes of the community. Let them not mourn—his indeed, will be a rich reward, for *"Blessed are the dead that die in the Lord"* &c. Surely do they rest *"and their works do follow them."*

No. 943 :: Ref. 1847-03-09, 3:5, M.

On the 4th inst., at New Mills Church, by the Rev. James Mauleverer, the Rev. George Robinson, only son of George Robinson, Esq., of Armagh, to Charlotte Augusta, eldest daughter of the Hon. and Rev. Godfrey Stuart, of Lisdhu, County of Tyrone, and niece to the Earl of Castle-Stuart.

No. 944 :: Ref. 1847-03-09, 3:5, M.

In St. James's Church, London, on the 22nd February, Lieutenant-Colonel Sir George A.F. Houston, Bart., Grenadier Guards, to Euphemia Boswell, Blackadder Castle, and daughter of the late Thomas Boswell, Esq.

No. 945 :: Ref. 1847-03-09, 3:5, M.

On the 1st inst., in St. Mary's Church, Newry, by the Rev. Daniel Bagot, Vicar of Newry, Mr. Edward Hyde, of Newry, to Jane, only daughter of the late Thos. Oakman, Esq., Portadown.

No. 946 :: Ref. 1847-03-09, 3:5, M.

On the 27th Feb., in St. Ann's Church, Mr. William John Coburn, of Newry, to Catherine, eldest daughter of Mr. Walter Wheeler, Belfast.

No. 947 :: Ref. 1847-03-09, 3:5, M.

At Clones, on the 22d ult., by the Rev. C. Welsh, Matilda, second daughter of Mr. David Thompson, of Gortnawinny Cottage, to Mr. Charles Graham, of Clones.

No. 948 :: Ref. 1847-03-09, 3:5, D.

At Bath, of scarlet fever, Thomas Molyneaux, eldest son of Sir George K. Molyneaux, of Castle-dillon, Bart., aged 10 years.

No. 949 :: Ref. 1847-03-09, 3:5, D.

Suddenly, in this city, yesterday morning, Mr. William Hamilton, publican.

No. 950 :: Ref. 1847-03-09, 3:5, D.

On the 22d., Feb., at Banbridge, the Rev. David Waugh, Wesleyan Minister, aged 72 years.

No. 951 :: Ref. 1847-03-09, 3:5, D.

Feb. 25, at Lucan, aged 81 years, Louisa, relict of Charles Lucas, Esq., of Castleshane, county Monaghan.

No. 952 :: Ref. 1847-03-09, 3:5, D.

Suddenly, in Liverpool, John Donnelly, Esq., one of the most extensive butter merchants in the United Kingdom.

No. 953 :: Ref. 1847-03-09, 3:5, D.

On the 23d Feb., at his daughter's residence, Talbot-street, Mr. James Hainen, aged 71 years.

No. 954 :: Ref. 1847-03-16, 2:5, B.

March 5, at Tartaraghan Rectory, the lady of the Hon. and Rev. Francis Clements, of a son.

No. 955 :: Ref. 1847-03-16, 2:5, D.

In this city, on Wednesday last, of fever, caught in the discharge of his ministerial duty, the Rev. Robert Haig, aged 30 years. Mr. Haig was first curate in this parish; and never did a minister of the Gospel perform more faithfully the high and important functions of his office—the constant aim and end of his life being the advancement of that great glory, which in his own spirit he is now enjoying. His remains were interred in St. Mark's church-yard, on Friday last; and the large and respectable funeral procession attests how sincerely he is regretted by the community at large.

No. 956 :: Ref. 1847-03-16, 2:5, D.

At 3, North Patterson-Street, Glasgow, on the 11th instant, Catherine, infant daughter of Mr. Daniel T. Jackson, Bookseller and Publisher.

No. 957 :: Ref. 1847-03-16, 2:5, D.

On the morning of the 8th inst., at the residence of his mother, Windsor Hill, Newry, after a tedious illness, the Rev. Wm. Carr, A.M., formerly pastor of the Berry Street Presbyterian Church, Belfast.

No. 958 :: Ref. 1847-03-23, 2:6, B.

On the 21st instant, at Belmount, Forkhill, the lady of Henry Stanley, Esq., M.D., of a daughter.

No. 959 :: Ref. 1847-03-23, 2:6, B.

On Monday last, the 15th inst., in Scotch-street, the lady of Joseph Matthews Esq., of a son.

No. 960 :: Ref. 1847-03-23, 2:6, B.

On the 12th inst., at Castleblaney, the lady of William Parker, Esq., Solicitor of a daughter.

No. 961 :: Ref. 1847-03-23, 2:6, B.

On the 15th inst., at Lower Gardiner-street, the lady of William Auchinleck Dane, Esq., of a son.

No. 962 :: Ref. 1847-03-23, 2:6, M.
On Thursday, the 18th inst., in St. Mark's Church, in this city, by the Rev. Alexander Irwin, Mr. John Reilly, to Miss Margaret Robinson, both of Armagh.

No. 963 :: Ref. 1847-03-23, 2:6, M.
On the 9th inst., in Seago Church, by the Rev. Archdeacon Saurin, Mr. A.J. Lutton, of Fairview, to Sarah, third daughter of Mr. Thomas Porter, Derryvore House, Portadown.

No. 964 :: Ref. 1847-03-23, 2:6, M.
On the 11th inst., in St. George's Church, Dublin, by the Rev. John Gregg, the Rev. Robert Warren Wolsley, youngest son of Major R.B. Wolsley, of Russell-place, Dublin, to Georgina, seventh daughter of the late James Nixon, Esq., Prospect, county Fermanagh.

No. 965 :: Ref. 1847-03-23, 2:6, D.
On Saturday last, in this city, of fever, caught in the discharge of his duty, as medical attendant to the Armagh Workhouse, James Leslie, Esq., M.D., much regretted by a large number of friends and acquaintances.

No. 966 :: Ref. 1847-03-23, 2:6, D.
On the 22d instant, in this city, Mr. John Vallely, merchant, of fever.

No. 967 :: Ref. 1847-03-23, 2:6, D.
On the 19th instant, at Dartry, county Armagh, at an advanced age, Mrs. Macartney, relict of the late Doctor Macartney, Professor of Anatomy, &c., Trinity College, Dublin.

No. 968 :: Ref. 1847-03-23, 2:6, D.
In this city, on Thursday, the 18th inst., after suffering acutely, John, eldest son of James Bowman, Esq., of the Provincial Bank of Ireland, aged 10 years. He was endowed with superior intellect, and by his amiability won the affectionate esteem of the teachers and fellow-pupils, who followed his remains to their resting-place in mournful silence. Cut off in the morning of his days, he finished his brief career in the confident expectation of inheriting everlasting happiness.

No. 969 :: Ref. 1847-03-23, 2:6, D.
In Upper Rutland-street, Dublin, after a lingering illness, Mary, the beloved wife of James Irwin, Esq., of Dungannon, and daughter of the late Rev. O. Ormsbey, Rector of Balymascanlon, in this diocese.

No. 970 :: Ref. 1847-03-23, 2:6, D.
On Monday, the 15th inst., at Coolkill, near Dungannon, Jane Eliza, eldest daughter of Mr. Wm. Stinson, aged 2 years and 8 months.

No. 971 :: Ref. 1847-03-23, 2:6, D.
In Lucan, Louisa, relict of Charles Lucan, Esq., Castleshane, county Monaghan.

No. 972 :: Ref. 1847-03-23, 2:6, D.
In Fitzwilliam-square, Elizabeth, widow of the late J. Pringle, Esq., Caledon.

No. 973 :: Ref. 1847-03-23, 2:6, D.
On the 15th inst., after a lingering illness, Jane, widow of the late Rev. Robert Campbell, in her 88th year. She was upwards of half a century residing on Vicar's Hill, and one of the oldest inhabitants of this city.

No. 974 :: Ref. 1847-03-23, 2:6, D.
On the 15th inst., at the house of her brother, Sinclair Carroll, Esq., Armagh, Eliza, youngest daughter of the late John Carroll, of Moy, in the humble hope of a happy immortality, much and deservedly regretted by all her sorrowing friends.

No. 975 :: Ref. 1847-03-23, 2:6, D.
On the 6th inst., at his residence, North Queen-street, Belfast, Mr. Richard May, aged 50 years.

No. 976 :: Ref. 1847-03-23, 2:6, D.
In Fintona, on Sunday, the 11th inst., Andrew, son of Andrew Allen, Esq., surgeon, R.N., aged 11 years.

No. 977 :: Ref. 1847-03-23, 2:6, D.
At Strabane, on Sunday morning last, Mr. Charles Kelly, innkeeper.

No. 978 :: Ref. 1847-03-23, 2:6, D.
At Donegal, on the 10th instant, aged 52 years, Ellen, wife of Mr. Richard Corscaden, merchant.

No. 979 :: Ref. 1847-03-23, 2:6, D.
March 5, of Typhus fever, caught in the discharge of his ministerial duties, in the workhouse, the Rev. David Bennett, Presbyterian Minister of Dungannon, in the 66th year of his age, and 42d of his ministry.

No. 980 :: Ref. 1847-03-23, 2:6, D.
March 12, at Silverhill, county Fermanagh, Noble Weir, Esq.

No. 981 :: Ref. 1847-03-23, 2:6, D.
On Friday the 12th inst., at the residence of her son-in-law, Mr. James Montgomery, Oakfield, Margaret, relict of the late James Williamson, Esq., Manorhamilton.

No. 982 :: Ref. 1847-03-30, 2:6, B.
On the 22d inst., at Magherafelt, the lady of the Rev. Samuel Twigg, of a son.

No. 983 :: Ref. 1847-03-30, 2:6, B.
At Thornhill, county Cavan, on the 23rd instant, the wife of William Nixon, Esq., of a daughter.

No. 984 :: Ref. 1847-03-30, 2:6, M.
On the 11th inst., in St. George's Church, Dublin, by the Rev. John Gregg, the Rev. Robert Warren Wolsley, youngest son of Major R.B. Wolsley, of Russell-place, Dublin, to Georgina, seventh daughter of the late James Nixon, Esq., Prospect, county Fermanagh.

No. 985 :: Ref. 1847-03-30, 2:6, M.

March 23, St. Thomas's Church, by the Rev. William Molloy, Alexander Henry, Esq., of Stickillen, county of Louth, to Jane, youngest daughter of John Sheckleton, Esq., of Drumnahall, county of Down.

No. 986 :: Ref. 1847-03-30, 2:6, D.

On the 22nd inst., at Segahan, near Armagh, of Inflammation on the Lungs Mr. John M'Clure, Poor-law Guardian for the Lisnadill Electoral Division of Armagh Union.

No. 987 :: Ref. 1847-03-30, 2:6, D.

On the 22nd inst., at Edenderry, near Benburb, Margaret, eldest daughter of Mr. Joseph Wilson, of decline, deeply regretted by a large circle of friends and acquaintances.

No. 988 :: Ref. 1847-03-30, 2:6, D.

On the 22nd inst., at Mullalagon, near Blackwatertown, Miss Martha Trotter aged 70 years.

No. 989 :: Ref. 1847-03-30, 2:6, D.

At Lisburn, on Saturday last, after a few days illness of malignant fever, caught in the discharge of his ministerial duty, the Rev. Bernard Dowan, P.P., of that town, universally regretted by all classes of the community.

No. 990 :: Ref. 1847-03-30, 2:6, D.

On Thursday 18th inst., at Caledon, Michael Bragan—a miser, who through life had managed to scrape together a good deal of money. Previous to his death he had a horse and cart brought to his house and was conveyed to a neighbouring grove to get his money—an hour before death he took a hearty meal of bread and tea.

No. 991 :: Ref. 1847-03-30, 2:6, D.

On the 21st inst., at Lurgan, Robert, youngest son of Mr. J. Gaskin, Kilvergan.

No. 992 :: Ref. 1847-03-30, 2:6, D.

In Abbey-yard, Newry, on the 18th inst., Fanny Cotton, youngest daughter of the late Hugh Carlile, Esq.

No. 993 :: Ref. 1847-03-30, 2:6, D.

On the 22nd March, Jane, relict of the late James Dane, Esq., Drumard, aged 76.

No. 994 :: Ref. 1847-03-30, 2:6, D.

On the 16th inst., Mrs. Forster, wife of Mr. William Forster, Maguiresbridge.

No. 995 :: Ref. 1847-03-30, 2:6, D.

On Tuesday, the 16th inst., Amelia Jane, youngest daughter of the late James Kidney, Esq., of Enniskillen, aged 14 years.

No. 996 :: Ref. 1847-03-30, 2:6, D.

On the 11th inst., of fever, Mr. Robert Carse, Master of the Magherafelt Workhouse, aged 35.

No. 997 :: Ref. 1847-04-06, 2:6, B.

In Charlemont-place, Armagh, on the 2nd inst., the lady of J. Lester, Esq. A.B., Master of the Academical Institution, of a daughter.

No. 998 :: Ref. 1847-04-06, 2:6, B.

March 25, at Dungannon, the lady of Courtenay Newton, Esq., of a daughter.

No. 999 :: Ref. 1847-04-06, 2:6, B.

March 28, at 19, Lower Pembroke-street, the lady of Lucius H. Deering, Esq., of a son.

No. 1000 :: Ref. 1847-04-06, 2:6, M.

On the 25th ult., in the Presbyterian Church, Kingsmill, Alexander Arbuthnot, Esq., merchant, Newry, to Agnes, second daughter of W. Harpur, Esq., Lisnadian.

No. 1001 :: Ref. 1847-04-06, 2:6, D.

On Good Friday, in the triumph of faith, Elizabeth relict of the late Mr. Edward Parkinson, of this city, aged 77 years, during 60 of which she was a member of the Methodist Society. Her love to all who loved the Saviour, and especially to the messengers of the Gospel, has caused her removal to be deeply regretted by all who knew her.

No. 1002 :: Ref. 1847-04-06, 2:6, D.

On the 31st ult., of inflammation of the lungs, Anna, daughter of Mr. John Kennedy, Armagh.

No. 1003 :: Ref. 1847-04-06, 2:6, D.

Of fever on Tuesday, the 19th March, Anne, wife of Mr. Wm. Montgomery, master of the Clones workhouse, aged 44 years. She was appointed matron of the establishment on its first opening, and always discharged the arduous duties of the situation to the entire satisfaction of the Board of Guardians, and the comfort of those placed under her care. Her character may be summed up in one word—a sincere Christian, and as such her end was peace, the estimation in which she was held, was manifested by the unusually large and respectable attendance at her funeral.

No. 1004 :: Ref. 1847-04-06, 2:6, D.

March 31, Mr. George M'Williams, Glencull, Aughnacloy, universally regretted by a large circle of acquaintances.

No. 1005 :: Ref. 1847-04-06, 2:6, D.

March 31, Messrs [sic] M'Cormick, of Armagh, aged 90 years.

No. 1006 :: Ref. 1847-04-06, 2:6, D.

On the 27th ult., William James Campbell, of measles, aged 7 years, son to William Campbell, Auctioneer, of this city.

No. 1007 :: Ref. 1847-04-06, 2:6, D.

March 18, at Dartry, in the county of Armagh, the residence of William Olpherts, Esq., Sarah, relict of Doctor Macartney, Professor of Anatomy and Surgery, Trinity College, Dublin.

No. 1008 :: Ref. 1847-04-06, 2:6, D.
At her residence, Warrenpoint, on the 26th ult., Mrs. Mary Black, eldest daughter of the late Robert M'Bride, Esq.

No. 1009 :: Ref. 1847-04-06, 2:6, D.
On Sunday, the 28th ultimo, at his residence near Newry, William Henry Quinn, Esq., J.P., for the Counties of Down and Armagh, aged 38 years.

No. 1010 :: Ref. 1847-04-13, 2:6, B.
March 30, the lady of James Lendrum, Esq., of Corkhill, County of Fermanagh, of a daughter.

No. 1011 :: Ref. 1847-04-13, 2:6, M.
April 7, in St. George's Church, Dublin, by the Rev. William Robinson, Rector of Tallaght, J.H. Workman, of Upper Rutland-street, Esq, Barrister-at-Law, to Mary, daughter of Richard Barker, Esq., of Gardiner's-row, Dublin, and Stirling House, County Meath.

No. 1012 :: Ref. 1847-04-13, 2:6, M.
At St. Peter's Church, Dublin, by the Rev. Abraham Hamilton, Rector of Manorhamilton, John Elliott, Esq., Royal Marines, son of the late Captain Sir William Elliott, R.N., to Georgina Francis, fourth daughter of the late Lieutenant-Colonel Cullen, of Skreeny, County Leitrim.

No. 1013 :: Ref. 1847-04-13, 2:6, D.
On the 2nd inst., at Blackwatertown, at an advanced age, Elizabeth, relict of the late John Crothers, Esq.

No. 1014 :: Ref. 1847-04-13, 2:6, D.
On the 25th ultimo, at the School for the sons of the Clergy, Lucan, of effusion on the brain, the dregs of scarlatina, Maxwell Close, youngest son of the Rev. Maxwell Carpendale, of Tamlaght, County Tyrone.

No. 1015 :: Ref. 1847-04-13, 2:6, D.
On the 20th ult., at the residence of his son, Bush Mount, near Dungannon, Samuel Hughes, Esq., late of Strabane.

No. 1016 :: Ref. 1847-04-13, 2:6, D.
On the 6th inst., Mr. Andrew Smith, of Mossvale, aged 68 years.

No. 1017 :: Ref. 1847-04-13, 2:6, D.
On the 10th instant, at Drumlargue, near Keady, of fever, Mr. Thomas Stuart, aged 46 years. Mr. Stuart had just disposed of his land and effects, for the purpose of emigrating to America with his wife and nine children, when he was seized with the sickness which ended mortally.

No. 1018 :: Ref. 1847-04-13, 2:6, D.
Of fever, at the Enniskillen Workhouse, Mr. David Vaughan, where he had filled the office of Wardmaster, to which situation he had been but recently elected.

No. 1019 :: Ref. 1847-04-20, 2:6, B.
On the 9th instant, at 30, Charles-street, St. James's-square, London, the residence of his Grace the Lord Primate, the lady of George Dunbar, Esq., of a daughter.

No. 1020 :: Ref. 1847-04-20, 2:6, B.
April 14, at Richmond-place, Mountjoy-square, Dublin, the lady of John Stanley, Esq., of a son and heir.

No. 1021 :: Ref. 1847-04-20, 2:6, B.
In College-street, in this city, on the 11th instant, the lady of James Stanley, Esq., of a son.

No. 1022 :: Ref. 1847-04-20, 2:6, D.
In Armagh, on the 19th instant, Miss Jane Nicholson, daughter of the late James Nicholson, Esq., of Grange, county Tyrone.

No. 1023 :: Ref. 1847-04-20, 2:6, D.
On the 13th instant, at Markethill, at the residence of their brother, the Rev. C. Seaver, Alicia and Nicholina, daughters of the late Jonathan P. Seaver, late Lieutenant in the 15th Regiment of Foot. *"They were lovely and pleasant in their lives, and in their death they were not divided."*

No. 1024 :: Ref. 1847-04-20, 2:6, D.
On the 7th instant, at Lurgan, of typhus fever, Sarah, wife of W. Thompson, Esq., aged 54 years.

No. 1025 :: Ref. 1847-04-20, 2:6, D.
In Armagh, on the 17th instant, aged 76 years, Mr. John Stewart, late of the *Belfast News-Letter*, where he had been a pressman for upwards of 30 years.

No. 1026 :: Ref. 1847-04-20, 2:6, D.
In this city, on the 17th inst., at the residence of her son, Elizabeth, relict of the late Mr. George Matchett, aged 67 years.

No. 1027 :: Ref. 1847-04-20, 2:6, D.
On the 14th instant, in Enniskillen, Elizabeth, daughter of the late William Whittaker, Esq., Stamp-distributor, Enniskillen.

No. 1028 :: Ref. 1847-04-20, 2:6, D.
On the 14th instant, in Enniskillen, Mrs. Armstrong, wife of Mr. William Armstrong, Pawnbroker, much regretted.

No. 1029 :: Ref. 1847-04-20, 2:6, D.
On the 7th instant, at Rockmount, near Keady, in the 64th year of her age, Jane Aiken, wife of Mr. John Manson, writing clerk, formerly of Larne, in the county of Antrim.

No. 1030 :: Ref. 1847-04-27, 2:5, M.
On the 20th inst., in St. Mark's Church, Portadown, by the Rev. Arthur Malony, Rector of Derryloran, Cookstown, James, youngest son of the late James Searight, of Newry, Esq., to Elizabeth, youngest daughter of William Paul, of Portadown, Esq.

No. 1031 :: Ref. 1847-04-27, 2:5, D.

On the 20th inst., at the residence of his brother, Doctor Clarke, Blackwatertown, Edward Clarke, Esq., aged 23 years, youngest son of the late Rev. Richard Clarke, of Portarlington.

No. 1032 :: Ref. 1847-04-27, 2:5, D.

April 18, aged 86, the Very Rev. Henry Roper, D.D., Dean of Clonmacnoise, and Rector of Clones.

No. 1033 :: Ref. 1847-04-27, 2:5, D.

On Sunday last, of fever, Mr. Thomas Morrow, of Thomas-street, in this city, aged 40 years.

No. 1034 :: Ref. 1847-04-27, 2:5, D.

In this city, on Friday last, of fever, Anne, wife of Mr. William Hughes, aged 70 years. She was for upwards of 25 years matron of Armagh gaol.

No. 1035 :: Ref. 1847-04-27, 2:5, D.

At Moy, on the 22d instant, of typhus fever, in the 61st year of his age, Mr. Owen Tomney, universally and deservedly regretted.

No. 1036 :: Ref. 1847-04-27, 2:5, D.

On the 24th inst., at Tullymacone House, Keady, of hooping cough, Thomas M'Bride, eldest son of Thomas G. M'Bride, Engineer and Land Surveyor, of Armagh.

No. 1037 :: Ref. 1847-04-27, 2:5, D.

On Thursday, the 22d inst., of fever, aged 48 years, Sarah Anne, wife of Mr. Mathew Johnston, of Middletown. A numerous circle of friends and acquaintances, to whom she was justly dear, from her kindness and amiability, sympathize with her afflicted family, who will long deeply deplore her loss.

No. 1038 :: Ref. 1847-05-04, 2:2, M.

April 27, in Rostrevor Church, by the Rev. Edward Ogle Disney, Rector of Newtownhamilton, Thomas Disney, jun., Esq., of Ballygallbeg, in the county of Dublin, to Dorothea Jane, only daughter of the Rev. Edward John Evans, Vicar of Kilbroney, Rostrevor.

No. 1039 :: Ref. 1847-05-04, 2:2, M.

In Dublin, on Friday, the 23d ult., by the Rev. R. Masaroon, Wesleyan Minister, Mr. John Ranson, of Belfast, to Miss Charlotte Brown, of Dublin.

No. 1040 :: Ref. 1847-05-04, 2:2, D.

April 25, at her residence, 52, Dorset-street, Dublin, Miss Catherine Miller, sister of the Rev. Doctor Miller, of Armagh, in the seventy-ninth year of her age.

No. 1041 :: Ref. 1847-05-04, 2:2, D.

On the 1st of May, at Melbourne Terrace, in this city, Emily Elizabeth, youngest daughter of James T. Bell, Esq., aged 15 months.

No. 1042 :: Ref. 1847-05-04, 2:2, D.

On the 23d April, at Lisnadill, near this city, Lucretia, youngest daughter of J.D. Evlyn, Esq. Throughout a tedious and painful illness, she manifested "*the fruits of the spirit,*" and died "*rejoicing in God her Saviour,*" leaving to her sorrowing parents and relatives, the comfortable assurance that she has gone "*to be for ever with the Lord.*"

No. 1043 :: Ref. 1847-05-04, 2:2, D.

April 24, at Cookstown House, Ardree, Catherine, relict of the late Patrick Carroll, Esq., eldest daughter of the late Owen Caraher, Esq., of Cardistown.

No. 1044 :: Ref. 1847-05-04, 2:2, D.

April 32 [sic], at his residence, Northland-row, Dungannon, county of Tyrone, Mrs. Henry Goold, widow of the late Henry Michael Goold, Esq., brother to the present Sir George Goold, Bart.

No. 1045 :: Ref. 1847-05-04, 2:2, D.

April 12, suddenly, at Bobmischdorf, in Austrian Silesia, Thos. Joplin, Esq., well known for his introduction of joint-stock banking into England, and his numerous works on banking and the currency.

No. 1046 :: Ref. 1847-05-04, 2:2, D.

On the morning of Saturday, the 24th ult., at his residence, Lisnamallard, aged 69 years, Joseph Orr, Esq., of fever, caught in the discharge of his duties as coroner, at an inquest held in Fintona, on the body of a poor traveller, at which the verdict was "*died of typhus fever.*"

No. 1047 :: Ref. 1847-05-04, 2:2, D.

April 21, at his residence, Tegnavin, Lurgan, Mr. Johnston M'Caw.

No. 1048 :: Ref. 1847-05-04, 2:2, D.

April 17, at Ballyclare, of pulmonary consumption, Eliza, wife of the Rev. R.A. Devers, Wesleyan Minister.

No. 1049 :: Ref. 1847-05-04, 2:2, D.

The demise of the recently-appointed Bishop of Sodor and Man, Dr. W.A. Shirley, took place on Wednesday last. His lordship was the Bampton lecturer of the present year, and has delivered only two of the lectures. His illness was occasioned by sleeping in a damp bed at Liverpool, on his last journey from Oxford to the Isle of Man.

No. 1050 :: Ref. 1847-05-11, 2:6, B.

On the 9th inst., at Goerstown house, Moy, the lady of Thomas A. Harper Esq., of a son.

No. 1051 :: Ref. 1847-05-11, 2:6, B.

On the 7th inst., at Markethill, the lady of P. M'Shane, Esq., Surgeon, of a son.

No. 1052 :: Ref. 1847-05-11, 2:6, D.

On the 8th inst., at her residence, at the Arran Arms Hotel, Donegal, after an illness of only a few days, Ann, relict of the late — Dillon, Esq., universally beloved and regretted by all who had the pleasure of her acquaintance.

No. 1053 :: Ref. 1847-05-11, 2:6, D.
At Fellows-hall, near Tynan, on the 9th inst., after a lingering illness, Eliza, wife of Mr. Robert Clarke, aged 48 years.

No. 1054 :: Ref. 1847-05-11, 2:6, D.
On Friday the 7th inst., the Rev. James Patterson, Minister of the Presbyterian Congregation of Richhill. The disease which caused his removal from this earthly scene, was fever of a very malignant kind. He has left a young widow, and an infant child, and a wide circle of friends to lament their bereavement. The congregation also mourn, in deep sorrow, the loss of an able, attentive, and useful pastor. The partiality of friendship, on these occasions, sometimes portray the character of the departed, in too flattering colours, but the subject, in this instance, receives neither flattery nor exaggeration, he was, in the strictest truth, an amiable man, a warm friend, a kind husband, and a faithful minister of the gospel.

No. 1055 :: Ref. 1847-05-11, 2:6, D.
April 28, at Market Hill, county Armagh, after a short but severe illness, which she bore with Christian fortitude, Elizabeth, eldest daughter of the late John Stuart, Esq., of Limerick, and niece to the late General Charles Stuart, of the Honourable East India Company's service.

No. 1056 :: Ref. 1847-05-18, 2:6, B.
May 10, at Florence Court, the Countess of Enniskillen, of a daughter.

No. 1057 :: Ref. 1847-05-18, 2:6, B.
On the 14th instant, Mrs. O'Neile, wife of Mr. D. O'Neile, Civil Engineer, 26, Dobbin-street, Armagh, of a son.

No. 1058 :: Ref. 1847-05-18, 2:6, M.
At Magherafelt, on the 10th inst., by the Rev. James Wilson, John Graves, Esq., of her Majesty's Customs, Jamaica, to Eliza, youngest daughter of John Duncan, Esq., Manager, Northern Bank Branch, Magherafelt.

No. 1059 :: Ref. 1847-05-18, 2:6, M.
On the 11th inst., at Castleblayney, by the Rev. T.J. Whitestone, Mr. Joseph Crowe, Dundalk, to Jane Eliza, youngest daughter of William Molloy, Esq., Castleblayney.

No. 1060 :: Ref. 1847-05-18, 2:6, M.
May 11, in Monkstown Church, by the Hon. and Very Rev. the Dean of Leighlin, Arthur, eldest son of the late Hugh Faulkner, Esq., of Fort Faulkner, county of Wicklow, to Louisa Anne, eldest daughter of John Downing, Esq., of Rowesgift, formerly Judge of the Supreme Court of the Canadian Provinces.

No. 1061 :: Ref. 1847-05-18, 2:6, D.
At his residence, Glenaule, on the 15th May, of a malignant fever which he caught in the discharge of his duty as a member of the Relief Committee of the district, Joseph Johnston, Esq., aged 54 years.

No. 1062 :: Ref. 1847-05-18, 2:6, D.
On the 29th ult., in the house of her son-in-law, the Earl of Ranfurley, 40, Berkeley-square, London, the Hon. Sophia Margaret Stuart, grand daughter of the celebrated Wm. Penn, founder and proprietor of Pennsylvania, and widow of the Hon. and Rev. W. Stuart, D.D., late Lord Primate of all Ireland, aged 83.

No. 1063 :: Ref. 1847-05-18, 2:6, D.
On the 11th inst., at Newbliss, in the sixty-fifth year of her age, Elizabeth, relict of the late Alex. Donaldson, Esq., of Tullyvallen, county Armagh.

No. 1064 :: Ref. 1847-05-18, 2:6, D.
At his residence, Glenmore, near Lisburn, on the 13th inst., James Nicholson Richardson, Esq., aged 64 years.

No. 1065 :: Ref. 1847-05-18, 2:6, D.
May 9, at Castle-street, Lisburn, James Hogg, Esq., aged ninety-three years.

No. 1066 :: Ref. 1847-05-18, 2:6, D.
On the 20th ultimo, at his residence, Tempo House, Killyman, William M'Ilroy, Esq., aged 88 years. After five weeks' illness, he calmly sank to rest, relying confidently on the merits of the Redeemer.

No. 1067 :: Ref. 1847-05-18, 2:6, D.
In Scotch-street, in this city, Charles, fourth son of Mr. Charles Keys, aged 18 years.

No. 1068 :: Ref. 1847-05-18, 2:6, D.
At Enniskillen, on the 12th instant, of fever, Stewart Betty, Esq.

No. 1069 :: Ref. 1847-05-18, 2:6, D.
At Pettigo, of fever, the Rev. Simon Nelson, Presbyterian Minister.

No. 1070 :: Ref. 1847-05-18, 2:6, D.
May 12, at Kilmashogue Cottage, in the 24th year of his age, Isaac Newton, fifth son of the late Thomas Bewley, of Palmyra, county Dublin.

No. 1071 :: Ref. 1847-05-18, 2:6, D.
In London, on the 29th April, Henrietta Gartwood, second daughter of Wm. Walker, Esq., Architect, Monaghan.

No. 1072 :: Ref. 1847-05-18, 2:6, D.
On Wednesday evening, of fever (after an illness of three days), Richard Jackson, Esq., seneschal of the manor court of Rosslea.

No. 1073 :: Ref. 1847-05-25, 2:6, B.
May 14, at Cookstown, county Tyrone, the lady of A.J. Newton, Esq., of [a] son.

No. 1074 :: Ref. 1847-05-25, 2:6, B.
May 20th, in Cootehill, the lady of Thomas Fitzgerald, Esq., of a son.

No. 1075 :: Ref. 1847-05-25, 2:6, M.
In Lisnaskea church, on the 14th inst., by the Rev. John M. Graydon, Mr. William Armstrong of Coxtown, county Donegal, to Anne, only daughter of Mr. William Beatty of Lisnaskea.

No. 1076 :: Ref. 1847-05-25, 2:6, D.
In this city, on Saturday, Mr. Robert Davison, after an attack of most malignant fever, which carried him off on the 14th day, at the early age of 31 years. Mr. Davison was a young man who was rapidly rising in respectability and esteem. He was a man of the highest moral and religious character, and his premature loss is universally felt and deplored. He was a member and deacon of the Independent church of this city. His remains will be interred this day, at 9 o'clock.

No. 1077 :: Ref. 1847-05-25, 2:6, D.
On Sunday, the 23d instant, in this city, of disease of the heart, after a lingering illness, Mr. Arthur Hughes, aged 66 years.

No. 1078 :: Ref. 1847-05-25, 2:6, D.
In Keady, on the 12th May, Mary, relict of the late Mr. James Scott, aged 98 years.

No. 1079 :: Ref. 1847-05-25, 2:6, D.
On the 20th inst., of malignant fever, Miss Cardwell, Moy, aged 50 years.

No. 1080 :: Ref. 1847-05-25, 2:6, D.
At Portadown, on Wednesday, 12th inst., Elizabeth, fourth daughter of Thomas Sinnamon, Esq.

No. 1081 :: Ref. 1847-05-25, 2:6, D.
On the 11th inst., at Clontibret, county Monaghan, at an advanced age, after a protracted illness, which he bore with christian resignation, M.J. Niblock, deeply regretted.

No. 1082 :: Ref. 1847-05-25, 2:6, D.
May 15, at the Cove of Cork, Mary Stuart, second daughter of the Rev. Hamilton Stuart, of Rockfort, Buncrana, county of Donegal.

No. 1083 :: Ref. 1847-05-25, 2:6, D.
To the inexpressible grief of her family and friends, Alethea, the beloved wife of Major Edward Bond, of Her Majesty's 39th Regiment.

No. 1084 :: Ref. 1847-05-25, 2:6, D.
May 16, in Sligo, of fever caught in the performance of his duty, John Loftus Griffin, Esq., Sub-Inspector of Constabulary.

No. 1085 :: Ref. 1847-05-25, 2:6, D.
On Tuesday, the 18th inst., at Shanklen, in the Isle of Wight, whither he had repaired for the benefit of his health, R.H. Sheehan, Esq., of Mespil House, Dublin, for twenty-five years Editor and joint Proprietor of the *Dublin Evening Mail*.

No. 1086 :: Ref. 1847-06-01, 3:1, B.
May 20, at Anketell Grove, the lady of Mathew John Anketell, Esq., of a daughter.

No. 1087 :: Ref. 1847-06-01, 3:1, B.
May 23, at Muff Glebe, Cookstown, the lady of the Rev. William J. Irvine, of a daughter.

No. 1088 :: Ref. 1847-06-01, 3:1, B.
On the 25th ult., at Tandragee, the lady of E.D. Atkinson, Esq., of a daughter.

No. 1089 :: Ref. 1847-06-01, 3:1, M.
On the 20th ult., at Portadown, Mr. W.P. Adshead, of Denby, Derbyshire, eldest son of the Rev. C.L. Adshead, Wesleyan Minister, to Sarah, eldest daughter of Mr. Thomas May, Portadown.

No. 1090 :: Ref. 1847-06-01, 3:1, M.
May 27, in St. Anne's Church, Dublin, by the uncle of the bride, the Rev. William Maclean, Prebendary of Tynan, in the diocese of Armagh, the Rev. Robert V. Dickson, F.T.C.D., to Kate, second daughter of Samuel Maclean, Esq., of Stephen's-green, Dublin.

No. 1091 :: Ref. 1847-06-01, 3:1, M.
On the 20th ult., in Belturbet church, by the Very Rev. Dean of Cashel, Theophilus Thompson, Esq., of Cavan, county Cavan, to Isabella Olivia, second daughter of George Marshall Knipe, Esq., of Erne Hill, county Cavan.

No. 1092 :: Ref. 1847-06-01, 3:1, M.
May 26, in the Wesleyan Centenary Chapel, Stephen's-green, by the Rev. William Ferguson, Henrietta M'Kee, eldest daughter of the Rev. Robert Masaroon, Dublin, to the Rev. John Donald, Wesleyan Minister, Maryborough.

No. 1093 :: Ref. 1847-06-01, 3:1, D.
May 30, in College-street, Armagh, after a tedious illness, in the 49th year of his age, Mr. Joseph Henry Soden, Editor of the *Ulster Gazette*.

No. 1094 :: Ref. 1847-06-01, 3:1, D.
On the 16th ult., of typhus fever, at her residence in Lurgan, aged 45 years, Anne, relict of the late John Paul, Esq., and eldest daughter of Thos. Sinnamon, of Portadown, Esq.

No. 1095 :: Ref. 1847-06-01, 3:1, D.
On the 26th ult., at the residence of his father, Lisdown, in the 21st year of his age, Mr. James Fairley, theological student of the Dublin Independent College. He possessed talents of the highest order, with literary attainments extensive and varied. To know him was to esteem and love him; for his heart, naturally gentle and affectionate under the abiding influence of the Gospel of truth and love, *(cont'd...)*

No. 1095, cont'd: ... his deportment exemplary and kind—his society instructive and delightful, consequently, that inscrutable Providence which removed him at such a season, when his studies for the ministry of the Gospel were on the point of being completed, and a long and extensive career of usefulness was naturally anticipated, has, in addition to his bereaved family, left numbers who enjoyed the privilege of his friendship to mourn his loss. If his course here has been short, his trials have been proportionably few; and having run with patience the race set before him, looking unto Jesus, he has left to his friends the blessed assurance that he has now attained to *"the mark for the prize of the high calling of God in Christ Jesus"* his Lord.

No. 1096 :: Ref. 1847-06-01, 3:1, D.
At Kinneary, near Charlemont, on the 24th May, of consumption, William, youngest son of the late Mr. John Sinclair. During his affliction (which he bore with Christian resignation) he was often visited by many who felt an interest in his soul's salvation, and for some time previous to his death he was enabled to rejoice in hope of the glory of God.

No. 1097 :: Ref. 1847-06-01, 3:1, D.
On Tuesday, the 27th ult., of fever, Mr. James Mills, master of Drelincourt school, Armagh, in the 55th year of his age, deeply lamented.

No. 1098 :: Ref. 1847-06-01, 3:1, D.
At Warrenpoint, on the 19th May, of bilious fever, Mr. George Ferguson, Officer of Excise, aged 29 years, leaving a wife and family to deplore his loss, as well as a numerous circle of friends and acquaintants.

No. 1099 :: Ref. 1847-06-01, 3:1, D.
At Willoughby-place, Enniskillen, on Wednesday, the 26th May, Captain Rodney Bell, aged 69 years, late of the 87th Regiment.

No. 1100 :: Ref. 1847-06-01, 3:1, D.
On Saturday, the 22d May, in Enniskillen, of fever, Hugh Collum, Esq., apothecary to the workhouse, and also county coroner. Mr. Collum was a gentleman esteemed and respected for his many estimable qualities. His loss will be long and sincerely deplored by a numerous circle of friends and acquaintances. Mr. Collum was 47 years of age.

No. 1101 :: Ref. 1847-06-01, 3:1, D.
On the 12th ult., at Roslea, in the county Monaghan, of fever, in the 53d year of his age, Richard Jackson, Esq., Seneschal of the Collegiate Manor of Slatmulrony.

No. 1102 :: Ref. 1847-06-01, 3:1, D.
On the 22d ultimo, of fever, caught in the discharge of his duties, Mr. Babington, Apothecary to the Union Workhouse at Cavan.

No. 1103 :: Ref. 1847-06-01, 3:1, D.
On the 22d ult., at his father's residence, Donegall-street, Belfast, William Ewing, M.D., aged 24 years.

No. 1104 :: Ref. 1847-06-01, 3:1, D.
In Belfast, on Tuesday last, Sir Arthur Chichester, Bart. He was unmarried and the title is now extinct.

No. 1105 :: Ref. 1847-06-01, 3:1, D.
On the 20th of May, at his residence, 11, College-square, Belfast, Richard Barnsley, Esq., M.D., aged 30 years.

No. 1106 :: Ref. 1847-06-01, 3:1, D.
At Bath, on the 21st ult., Lieutenant-General Sir Thomas Pearson, K.C.H., Colonel of the 85th Regiment of Foot.

No. 1107 :: Ref. 1847-06-01, 3:1, D.
May 27, at his residence in Upper Baggot-street, Dublin, in the 84th year of his age, Thomas Dickson, Esq., LL.D., Q.C., and Father of the Irish Bar.

No. 1108 :: Ref. 1847-06-01, 3:1, D.
On the 25th ult., at his residence, No. 7, Gardiner's-place, Dublin, Joseph Nelson, Esq., Q.C., Assistant-Barrister for the county of Longford.

No. 1109 :: Ref. 1847-06-08, 3:2, B.
On the 27th ult., at the Crescent, Portstewart, the lady of John H. Lawlor, Esq., Provincial Bank of Ireland, Coleraine, of a daughter.

No. 1110 :: Ref. 1847-06-08, 3:2, B.
May 28, at Warrenpoint, county Down, the lady of Rev. Wm.. Sheppard, of a daughter.

No. 1111 :: Ref. 1847-06-08, 3:2, B.
May 29, at 212, Great Brunswick-street, Dublin, Mrs. Holland, of three daughters, all alive and healthy. In her last accouchement, two years ago, she was confined of two sons.

No. 1112 :: Ref. 1847-06-08, 3:2, M.
At Simla, on the 23d March, by the Rev. John Vaughan, A.B., brother-in-law to the bride, Lieutenant Southwell Greville, 1st Bengal Fusiliers, to Jane, youngest daughter of Lawford Tronson, Esq., Newry.

No. 1113 :: Ref. 1847-06-08, 3:2, M.
May 30, in Lurgan Church, by the Rev. William Platt Oulton, Curate of the parish of Shankhill, Mr. James Hammond, of Lurgan, builder, to Rebecca, eldest daughter of Mr. John Warren, of Lurgan.

No. 1114 :: Ref. 1847-06-08, 3:2, M.
May 24, in the Presbyterian Meeting-house, Carland, Letitia, youngest daughter of the late Huggins Marshall, Esq., Solicitor, Dungannon, to Samuel Morrow, jun., Esq., Kilmaslee.

No. 1115 :: Ref. 1847-06-08, 3:2, M.
May 27, in Athboy Church, by the Rev. Henry Hugh O'Neill, Rector of Munterconnaught, county of

Cavan, Ferdinand M'Veagh, only son of Ferdinand M'Veagh, Esq., of Drewstown, in the county of Meath, to Maria, only daughter of Thomas Rotherham, Esq., of Friermore, in the same county.

No. 1116 :: Ref. 1847-06-08, 3:2, M.
At Drumsallan, on the 3d instant, by the Rev. Charles Warring, Eliza, relict of the late Mr. Joseph Allen, of Milburn Cottage, Carmagh, to Mr. Joseph Turner, of Tanagh, Killalea.

No. 1117 :: Ref. 1847-06-08, 3:2, M.
In the parish Church of Killyman, on the 2d instant, by the Rev. Mortimer O'Sullivan, D.D., Mr. Robert Corrigan, jun., of Moss Spring, near Charlemont, to Elinor, youngest daughter of Mr. Bugloss, of Trew, Killyman, and sister of the Rev. Doctor Bugloss, of Dublin.

No. 1118 :: Ref. 1847-06-08, 3:2, M.
At Aughinunshin Church, on Thursday, the 3d of June, by the Rev. John Irwin, the Rev. C. Faussett, son of Robert Faussett, of Lisbofin, in the county of Fermanagh, to Ann Jane, eldest daughter of the late William Wray, of Oak Park, in the county of Donegal, Esq.

No. 1119 :: Ref. 1847-06-08, 3:2, D.
On the 6th inst., at Armagh, in the 48th year of her age, Anne, the beloved wife of Mr. William Boyd, merchant. She suffered a long and painful illness with patience and resignation to the Divine will.

No. 1120 :: Ref. 1847-06-08, 3:2, D.
On the 2d instant, at Ballytyrone, near Loughgall, Mr. George Walker. He had been an active young man in looking out for those persons in the townland who required relief, and took fever, which terminated in death.

No. 1121 :: Ref. 1847-06-08, 3:2, D.
At Markethill, on the 31st May, Reford Woodhouse, and Mary Jane, his wife, both of fever.

No. 1122 :: Ref. 1847-06-08, 3:2, D.
May 26, in Lurgan, after a short illness, Arabella Ballantine, in her 66th year.

No. 1123 :: Ref. 1847-06-08, 3:2, D.
May 23, at his father's residence, in Dungannon, John G. Dickson, late a Student of Belfast College, aged 18 years.

No. 1124 :: Ref. 1847-06-08, 3:2, D.
May 25, at his residence, Greenvale, Keady, James Girvin, Esq., in the 78th year of his age.

No. 1125 :: Ref. 1847-06-08, 3:2, D.
May 30, at his father's residence, Tullybrick Nursery, near Middletown, of consumption aged 25 years, David, fourth son of Mr. Daniel Anderson. He was a young man of great promise,—deservedly loved and esteemed by all with whom he was acquainted. He bore a long and trying illness with pious resignation to his Maker's will, and left this transitory life with a firm reliance on his blessed Redeemer, and in the sure but humble hope of a joyful resurrection.

No. 1126 :: Ref. 1847-06-08, 3:2, D.
On the 26th ult., at Abbey-yard, Charlotte, fourth daughter of the late Isaac Corry, J.P., of Newry.

No. 1127 :: Ref. 1847-06-08, 3:2, D.
June 4, at Saintfield House, county Down, Nicholas Price, Esq., D.L. and J.P., aged 97 years.

No. 1128 :: Ref. 1847-06-08, 3:2, D.
May 26, at his residence, Clontibret, county Monaghan, after a few days illness, of a malignant fever, the Rev. Mr. Lewis, curate of the above parish.

No. 1129 :: Ref. 1847-06-08, 3:2, D.
In Bennet-street, Bath, at an advanced age, Jane, relict of the Rev. William Maxwell, D.D., of Falkland, county of Monaghan.

No. 1130 :: Ref. 1847-06-08, 3:2, D.
May 28, at his residence in Hereford-street, London, the Hon. and Very Rev. William Herbert, Dean of Manchester, aged 69.

No. 1131 :: Ref. 1847-06-08, 3:2, D.
On the 28th ult., at Ballyshannon, of malignant fever, Mr. John Earls, merchant, aged 49.

No. 1132 :: Ref. 1847-06-08, 3:2, D.
May 28, at Dullaghy, the residence of her uncle, Arthur Church, Esq., Elizabeth, relict of the late Mr. Archibald Fullerton, Lisaghrin, and third daughter of Henry Hunter, Esq., Castledawson.

No. 1133 :: Ref. 1847-06-08, 3:2, D.
May 28, in Ballyshannon, of spotted fever, Anne, the beloved wife of Mr. William Stephens, jun., of that town, deservedly regretted.

No. 1134 :: Ref. 1847-06-08, 3:2, D.
In Sligo, on 3d instant, of spotted typhus fever, the Rev. Mr. Tackaberry, Wesleyan Minister.

No. 1135 :: Ref. 1847-06-15, 2:6, M.
June 2, in Bellaghy Church, by the Rev G H Ashe, R.H. Gordon, Esq., M.D., to Mabella Hemsworth, second daughter of John Hill, Esq., Bellaghy Castle, county of Londonderry.

No. 1136 :: Ref. 1847-06-15, 2:6, M.
On the 1st inst., in St. Anne's Church, Belfast, Mr. Joseph Conn, travelling clerk, to Miss Crawford, both of Lurgan.

No. 1137 :: Ref. 1847-06-15, 2:6, D.
On the 7th instant, at his residence, near Lurgan, Mr. William Anderson, in the 58th year of his age.

No. 1138 :: Ref. 1847-06-15, 2:6, D.
On the 1st instant, at Dungannon, Mr. William Rodgers, merchant, in the 56th year of his age, deeply and deservedly lamented by his family and numerous friends.

No. 1139 :: Ref. 1847-06-15, 2:6, D.
At Belturbet, on the 1st instant, of typhus fever, James Finlay, Esq., aged 39 years.

No. 1140 :: Ref. 1847-06-15, 2:6, D.
On the 6th instant, of fever, Mark Hall, Esq., of Moneymakin. Mr. Hall was an active Guardian of the Poor, for the Lisnaskea Union, at which, it is thought, he caught the disease. He is very much regretted.

No. 1141 :: Ref. 1847-06-15, 2:6, D.
At his residence, Pound-hill, Clones, of typhus fever, in the 23d year of his age, Mr. James Gray, much and generally regretted.

No. 1142 :: Ref. 1847-06-15, 2:6, D.
On Thursday last, at Camus, near Strabane, Mr. William Elliott, jun., son of William Elliott, Esq., aged 24 years.

No. 1143 :: Ref. 1847-06-15, 2:6, D.
In Bishop street, Derry, of jaundice, on the 7th instant, Sarah, youngest daughter of the late Benjamin Greer, of Moy, Esq.

No. 1144 :: Ref. 1847-06-15, 2:6, D.
On the 12th instant, of fever, at Timmakeel, near Portadown, Mr. William Templeton, aged 50 years, leaving a wife and three young children, all dangerously ill of the disease, to lament his loss.

No. 1145 :: Ref. 1847-06-15, 2:6, D.
June 11, of dysentery, at Derrigolin Glebe, Carrickmacross, James, the beloved child of the Rev. William Thompson, aged six years.

No. 1146 :: Ref. 1847-06-22, 3:2, M.
On the 10th instant, by the Rev. Thomas Greer, at Annahilt Meeting-house, county Down, Robert Samuel Jebson, to Sarah, only daughter of the late Wm. Cordner, of Newry.

No. 1147 :: Ref. 1847-06-22, 3:2, M.
In the Registrar's Office, Dungannon, on Monday, the 14th inst., Mr. Thomas Pillar, of Drumanney, to Miss Esther Kidd, of Culkeeran, near Moy.

No. 1148 :: Ref. 1847-06-22, 3:2, M.
On the 10th instant, at Welgrave, Northamptonshire, by the Rev. John Cox, M.A., G.V. Wilson, Esq., of the White House, Killybegs, county Donegal, to Sophia, youngest daughter of S. Sheldon, Esq.

No. 1149 :: Ref. 1847-06-22, 3:2, M.
On the 16th inst., in St. Thomas's Church, Dublin, by the Rev. Josiah Lowe, A.B., Alexander Crothers, Esq., Blackwatertown, to Eliza, only daughter of the late Andrew Wilson, Esq., Solicitor, Lower Gardiner-street, Dublin.

No. 1150 :: Ref. 1847-06-22, 3:2, M.
On the 17th instant, in Castleblayney Church, by the Rev. J.T. Whitestone, B.V. Cumming, M.D., to Ann, second daughter of Edward Hunter, merchant, both of Castleblayney.

No. 1151 :: Ref. 1847-06-22, 3:2, D.
On the 15th instant, of disease of the heart, Mr. William M'Cleery, son of Mr. James M'Cleery, merchant, Aughnacloy, in the 24th year of his age. To enumerate the many virtues and endearing qualities of this young man would trespass too far on the columns of a newspaper. Some idea of them may be formed by representing to ourselves everything that is estimable in the kind affectionate brother—the loving and dutiful son, in whom all were happily blended. The closed windows and shops of the town for two entire days—the very large and respectable funeral procession that accompanied his remains to their last resting place at Caledon, proclaim but too sensibly that society has lost in him an ornament of no ordinary character.—*A Correspondent.*

No. 1152 :: Ref. 1847-06-22, 3:2, D.
On the 17th instant, at Westport, of brain fever, Mr. Matthew Milling, jun., formerly of Thomas-street, Armagh, aged 20 years. His remains were brought to St. Mark's Church on Saturday last.

No. 1153 :: Ref. 1847-06-22, 3:2, D.
On the 16th ult., at Oyden, Monroe County, State of New York, Mr. James Birch, brother of Mr. Robert Birch, Post-master of this city, aged 37 years.

No. 1154 :: Ref. 1847-06-22, 3:2, D.
On the 12th instant, at Warrenpoint, after a short illness, much regretted, Mr. Moses Searight, aged 48 years.

No. 1155 :: Ref. 1847-06-22, 3:2, D.
On the 11th instant, at Lisburn, aged 40 years, Mr. Stewart Magee, of fever.

No. 1156 :: Ref. 1847-06-22, 3:2, D.
On the 20th instant, of typhus fever, Mr. William Hyde, porter to Armagh Union Workhouse. He was a respectable and worthy officer.

No. 1157 :: Ref. 1847-06-22, 3:2, D.
On the 13th inst., at Coleraine, at the house of her son-in-law, A. M'Ilwaine, Esq., in the 76th year of her age, Sarah, relict of the late Thomas Shillington, Esq., Portadown.

No. 1158 :: Ref. 1847-06-22, 3:2, D.
June 11, in Ballyshannon, Bessy, second daughter of the late William Carson, Esq.

No. 1159 :: Ref. 1847-06-22, 3:2, D.
At Killybegs, on the 2d June, of typhus fever, caught whilst administering to the wants of the poor, Margaret, wife of Alexander Browne, Esq., commander of the *Racer*, Revenue Cutter, stationed there.

No. 1160 :: Ref. 1847-06-22, 3:2, D.
June 14, at Rockdale House, county Tyrone, James Lowry, Esq., aged sixty years.

No. 1161 :: Ref. 1847-06-22, 3:2, D.
In Clones, of fever, deservedly regretted, Mr. Thomas Hanna, merchant.

No. 1162 :: Ref. 1847-06-22, 3:2, D.
In Clones, Margaret, wife of the Rev. J.E.H. Simpson.

No. 1163 :: Ref. 1847-06-29, 3:1, M.
June 22, in Lurgan, by the Rev. Hamilton Dobbin, Mr. Girwood, of Belfast, to Bessie, eldest daughter of Henry Mercer, Esq., Farm Lodge, Lurgan.

No. 1164 :: Ref. 1847-06-29, 3:1, M.
June 16, by the Rev. S.J. Moore, at Donoughmore, county Down, Robert Ross Todd, of North Great George's-street, Dublin, Esq., Solicitor, to Elizabeth, third daughter of the late Samuel Martin, of Loughborne, in the county of Down, Esq.

No. 1165 :: Ref. 1847-06-29, 3:1, M.
June 17, in St. Anne's Church, Dublin, by the Rev. Charles Dickenson, Francis Fawcett, Esq., of Mullyare, county Fermanagh, to Eliza, youngest daughter of the late Edward Fawcett, Esq., of Rowantree Hill, county Donegal.

No. 1166 :: Ref. 1847-06-29, 3:1, M.
June 16, at Castle Archdall Church, by the Rev. Charles Wellington Welsh, John Maguire, Esq., of Broughas, county Fermanagh, to Catherine, eldest daughter of James Coulson, Esq., Rossinin.

No. 1167 :: Ref. 1847-06-29, 3:1, D.
June 21, at his residence near Clones, in the 35th year of his age, after a short illness, William Mayne Clarke, Esq., Inspector for the Ulster Canal Carrying Company, for the Western District.

No. 1168 :: Ref. 1847-06-29, 3:1, D.
May 7, at New Orleans, William J. Bryan, Esq., eldest son of the late Josiah Bryan, Esq., Rose Lodge, Magherafelt.

No. 1169 :: Ref. 1847-06-29, 3:1, D.
June 12, Mrs. M'Dowal, the beloved wife of Alexander M'Dowal, postmaster of Emyvale, aged 30 years.

No. 1170 :: Ref. 1847-06-29, 3:1, D.
June 18, Mr. Andrew Kidney, of Enniskillen.

No. 1171 :: Ref. 1847-07-06, 3:2, B.
On the 29th ult., Mrs. William Hamilton, of Kesh, of a son.

No. 1172 :: Ref. 1847-07-06, 3:2, B.
June 25, the lady of J.J. Macaldan, Esq., M.D., Coleraine, of a daughter.

No. 1173 :: Ref. 1847-07-06, 3:2, M.
June 16, at the parish church, Halifax, by the Rev. John Hope, Mr. Edward Irwin, merchant, of Leeds, and formerly of Derrygore, county Fermanagh, to Hannah, daughter of Thomas Baines, Esq., of Leeds.

No. 1174 :: Ref. 1847-07-06, 3:2, D.
June 23, at Liverpool, Robert Tronson, Esq., second son of the late Rev. Robert Tronson, many years Rector of Newtownhamilton, Diocese of Armagh.

No. 1175 :: Ref. 1847-07-06, 3:2, D.
In Derry, on the 1st instant, Mr. Robert E. Hughes, of Armagh, second son of the late Mr. Arthur Hughes.

No. 1176 :: Ref. 1847-07-06, 3:2, D.
At Enniskillen, on Tuesday last, the 29th ult., of fever, Mary, the beloved wife of John Wood, Esq. Mrs. Wood's demise has cast a gloom over the circle in which she moved. In her, the poor have lost a kind benefactor, and society has sustained an irreparable loss.

No. 1177 :: Ref. 1847-07-06, 3:2, D.
At Enniskillen, on Sunday, the 27th ult., Mr. James Crooke, an old and respectable inhabitant of Enniskillen, deeply regretted by a large and respectable connexion of friends in Fermanagh. He was one of the Enniskillen Protestant Yeomen, who, in 1798, took up arms against the insurgents of his country.

No. 1178 :: Ref. 1847-07-06, 3:2, D.
June 29, in Enniskillen, Mrs. Hugh Kittson, relict of the late Mr. Hugh Kittson, of Dublin, and daughter of the late Wm. Crooke, Esq., of Silverhill, near Enniskillen.

No. 1179 :: Ref. 1847-07-06, 3:2, D.
At Ballyshannon, on Saturday 26th ult., Mrs. Earls.

No. 1180 :: Ref. 1847-07-06, 3:2, D.
At Farnacassidy, county Fermanagh, on the 19th ult., Margaret, fourth daughter of James Teevan, Esq., aged 15 years.

No. 1181 :: Ref. 1847-07-06, 3:2, D.
In Maguiresbridge, of fever, on the 26th ult., in the prime of life, Mr. John Pott.

No. 1182 :: Ref. 1847-07-13, 3:2, B.
July 3, at Eaton-square, the Lady Claud Hamilton, of a daughter.

No. 1183 :: Ref. 1847-07-13, 3:2, B.
July 3, at Sharavogue, the Hon. Mrs. Westenra, of a daughter.

No. 1184 :: Ref. 1847-07-13, 3:2, B.
June 27, at Mount-Louise, county Monaghan, the lady of S.R.B. Evatt, Esq., of a son.

No. 1185 :: Ref. 1847-07-13, 3:2, B.
June 29, in Monaghan, the lady of Henry P. Lennon, Esq., of a son.

No. 1186 :: Ref. 1847-07-13, 3:2, M.

July 7, in the Church of Killylea, by the Rev. John C. M'Causland, Incumbent, William G. Murray, Esq., Lower Gardiner-street, Dublin, to Mary Anne, only daughter of the late James Craig, Esq., Barrister-at-Law.

No. 1187 :: Ref. 1847-07-13, 3:2, M.

July 1, at Monaghan, James A. Ross, Esq., of that town, to Anne, only daughter of the late Captain Alexander Waddel, of Lisnavane.

No. 1188 :: Ref. 1847-07-13, 3:2, M.

June 28, at Glasgow, William Verner E. Reynolds, Esq., of Dublin, to Julia, second daughter of Thomas Seaver, Esq., Heath Hall, county Armagh.

No. 1189 :: Ref. 1847-07-13, 3:2, D.

On the morning of the 8th inst., at the house of her son-in-law, Mr. Richard Barry, of Trew Cottage, Mrs. White, relict of the late Mr. David White, of Copney, county Armagh, in the 84th year of her age.

No. 1190 :: Ref. 1847-07-13, 3:2, D.

At Fivemiletown, on the 6th instant, of water on the brain, in the 9th year of his age, Joseph, only son of Mr. John Nelson. Few had at any age, and still fewer at his, shown so evidently that though in the world he was not of it.—Regretted exceedingly by a numerous circle of friends and acquaintances, they mourn not as those without hope. That he had in no ordinary way endeared himself to all who had known him was evinced by the immense concourse of people who attended his remains to Clogher, the family burying ground. In front of the hearse walked two-by-two, accompanied by the teacher, the boys, his companions at school, where he had very much distinguished himself. May our last end be like his.— *A Correspondent.*

No. 1191 :: Ref. 1847-07-13, 3:2, D.

On the 5th instant, James Verner, Esq., formerly Captain in the 19th Dragoons.

No. 1192 :: Ref. 1847-07-13, 3:2, D.

July 2, at Edinburgh, aged 29, Mr. Robert Hodgens, formerly of Rich-Hill, county Armagh.

No. 1193 :: Ref. 1847-07-13, 3:2, D.

July 4, of fever, John M'Elwee, Esq., Excise Officer, Portadown.

No. 1194 :: Ref. 1847-07-13, 3:2, D.

On the morning of the 3d inst., of typhus fever, Mr. John Bennie, proprietor of the Eagle Iron Foundry.

No. 1195 :: Ref. 1847-07-13, 3:2, D.

In Newry, on the evening of the 3d inst., Mr. Adam Ledlie, merchant.

No. 1196 :: Ref. 1847-07-13, 3:2, D.

On the 2d of April last, on board H.M.S. *Bombay*, homeward bound from India, G.W. Joyce, Brookeborough.

No. 1197 :: Ref. 1847-07-13, 3:2, D.

On the 7th July, Mr. Joseph Whitley, of Enniskillen, aged 65 years.

No. 1198 :: Ref. 1847-07-20, 2:2, B.

On the 9th instant, at the Rectory, Castleblayney, the wife of the Rev. T. Whitestone, of a son.

No. 1199 :: Ref. 1847-07-20, 2:2, B.

In Willoughby-place, Enniskillen, on the 30th ult., while dangerously ill in fever, Mrs. Frederick Nixon, of a son, who survived only a few hours.

No. 1200 :: Ref. 1847-07-20, 2:2, M.

On Friday 16th instant, by the Rev. A. Fleming, in the first Presbyterian Church, Armagh, the Rev. Henry William Carson, of Hermitage, Keady, to Susan, daughter of the late Dr. King, of Moy.

No. 1201 :: Ref. 1847-07-20, 2:2, M.

July 7, at Ebenezer Chapel, Newry, the Rev. Hugh Martin, Independent Minister, Clonmel, to Eliza, only daughter of the late George Newell, Esq., of Rathfriland, County Down.

No. 1202 :: Ref. 1847-07-20, 2:2, M.

In the Church of Lisnaskea, on the 15th instant, by the Rev. John Flanagan, Thomas William M'Cartney, of Drumcrew, Esq., to Margaret, second daughter of Charles Moorhead, of Ballymakenny, Esq., county Fermanagh.

No. 1203 :: Ref. 1847-07-20, 2:2, M.

On the 29th ult, in Carntall Presbyterian Church, by the Rev. Jas. Phillips, Mr. Thomas R. Clements, of Beragh, merchant, to Charlotte, third daughter of Mr. William Alexander, of Fivemiletown, merchant.

No. 1204 :: Ref. 1847-07-20, 2:2, D.

At Barrie, Upper Canada, Ellen, the beloved wife of Thomas Dallas, Esq., one of her Majesty's Judges for Canada, East; daughter to the late Rev. Arthur Ardagh, for upwards of 30 years Rector of Moyglere, in the county of Meath; and sister to Dr. Ardagh, Medical Superintendent of the Verner's-bridge Dispensary, county Armagh.

No. 1205 :: Ref. 1847-07-20, 2:2, D.

At Trillick, on the 4th instant, Mr. Francis Crawford, aged 27 years. He was of sterling worth, and his pious example will be long cherished by the rising generation. He died in peace.

No. 1206 :: Ref. 1847-07-20, 2:2, D.

July 11, after a long illness, of consumption, Mr. Thomas Simpson, aged 14 years, eldest son of Hugh Simpson, Esq, Mill View, Aughnacloy. This promising youth is sincerely regretted by his friends and acquaintances. When 13 years of age, he weighed 12 stone 8 lbs.

No. 1207 :: Ref. 1847-07-20, 2:2, D.

On the 18th instant, at Drumcullen, near Blackwatertown, James, son of Mr. Robert Morrow, aged 16 years, after a lingering illness.

No. 1208 :: Ref. 1847-07-20, 2:2, D.

On the 6th instant, of congestion of the brain, at Derrykeighan Glebe, county Antrim, Richard D'Evlyn, student of the University of Dublin. He was a young man of considerable promise—patient and persevering in his studies—amiable and beloved in life—in death he resigned his spirit into the hands of his merciful Redeemer, in sure and certain hope of a joyful resurrection to everlasting life; deeply and deservedly regretted by all who knew him.

No. 1209 :: Ref. 1847-07-20, 2:2, D.

July 4, of fever, at Lodge, county Louth, the residence of her son-in-law, William Baille, Esq., Jane Carlow, late of Armagh, aged 43 years.

No. 1210 :: Ref. 1847-07-20, 2:2, D.

On the 10th instant, at Forkhill, the residence of his father, Mr. Charles Murdock, aged 24 years.

No. 1211 :: Ref. 1847-07-27, 3:5, B.

On the 16th instant, at 76, Cadogan-place, Belgrave-square, London, the lady of Robert Synnot, Esq., of a daughter.

No. 1212 :: Ref. 1847-07-27, 3:5, B.

At Markethill, on the 26th inst., the lady of the Rev. Mr. Seaver, of a daughter.

No. 1213 :: Ref. 1847-07-27, 3:5, M.

On Thursday, the 22d inst., in the first Presbyterian Church of Derry by the Rev. Wm. M'Clure, Mr. Charles Morrison, to Margaret, second daughter of Mr. Dawson Bell, Omagh.

No. 1214 :: Ref. 1847-07-27, 3:5, M.

On the 22d inst., in the Presbyterian Church of Ballylennon, by the Rev. George Hanson, the Rev. John M'Carter, of Nn-Stewart, to Margaret, only daughter of the late William Brown, of the Waterside, Esq.

No. 1215 :: Ref. 1847-07-27, 3:5, M.

On Tuesday, the 20th inst., at Killaghtee Church, by the Rev. James Ovens, A.M., Rector of Inniskeel, Hamilton Porter, Esq., of Swanmount, county of Donegal, to Ellen, eldest daughter of the late Francis Hamilton Nesbitt, Esq.

No. 1216 :: Ref. 1847-07-27, 3:5, D.

On the 18th instant, Miss Eliza Smyth, of Scotch-street, Armagh.

No. 1217 :: Ref. 1847-07-27, 3:5, D.

July 17, at Warrenpoint, aged 69 years, Mrs. Elizabeth Fivey, relict of the late Robert Fivey, Esq., and eldest daughter of the late Wolsey Atkinson, Esq., of Eden Villa, Portadown.

No. 1218 :: Ref. 1847-07-27, 3:5, D.

July 18, at Ballibay, in her 26th year, Miss Margaret Gray.

No. 1219 :: Ref. 1847-07-27, 3:5, D.

July 19, of water on the brain, Samuel Harpur May, son of Mr. George May, Donegall street, Belfast, aged 2 and a-half years.

No. 1220 :: Ref. 1847-07-27, 3:5, D.

July 9, at Maguiresbridge, Mr. William Forster, sen., aged 80 years.

No. 1221 :: Ref. 1847-07-27, 3:5, D.

July 16, of fever, Miss Frances Beatty, Matron of the Lisnaskea Union Workhouse, aged 44 years; and on the 27th of April last, her sister, Miss Beatty, School-mistress in the same establishment, aged 46 years.

No. 1222 :: Ref. 1847-07-27, 3:5, D.

July 16, at Churchhill, of fever, in the 67th year of his age, Mr. Wm. Nelson.

No. 1223 :: Ref. 1847-07-27, 3:5, D.

July 18, at Parkmore, Cushendall, the residence of her brother, Jane, daughter of the late Jason Hassard, of Levaghy, county Fermanagh, Esq.

No. 1224 :: Ref. 1847-07-27, 3:5, D.

At the residence of his father, in the Diamond, Clones, of a lingering illness, Mr. Jonathan Burns, aged 19 years, much and deservedly regretted.

No. 1225 :: Ref. 1847-07-27, 3:5, D.

At New Haven, Connecticut, on 10th of June, 1847, aged 70 years, Mrs. Frances Martin, relict of Abraham Martin, of Screen, county Sligo, Ireland, sister of Mr. Richard Smith, formerly merchant of Sligo.

No. 1226 :: Ref. 1847-07-27, 3:5, D.

At Cheltenham, 17th July, 1847, Mr. Hugh Henry Hunter, formerly of Ballybritton, county Derry, Linen Merchant, aged 47 years.

No. 1227 :: Ref. 1847-07-27, 3:5, D.

On the 17th inst., in the 37th year of her age, after a lingering illness, which she bore with Christian fortitude and resignation, Sarah, the beloved wife of Mr. James Cairnes, of Derry.

No. 1228 :: Ref. 1847-07-27, 3:5, D.

On the 23d inst., of typhus fever, at Tartlogue, in the 43d year of her age, Martha, the beloved wife of Mr. Thomas Johnston. She has left a large family and numerous circle of friends to mourn her loss.

No. 1229 :: Ref. 1847-07-27, 3:5, D.

At Aughnacloy, on the 18th inst., Mr. William M'Cully, aged 56 years,—Cousin to the late Mr. Sergeant Corry, M.P. for this borough (Armagh).

No. 1230 :: Ref. 1847-08-03, 3:3, M.

On the 21st ult., in the Presbyterian Church, Benburb, by the Rev. Mr. Montgomery, Mr. Matthew Bell, merchant of Armagh, to Sarah Ann, daughter of the late Mr. J. Crosier, of New York.

No. 1231 :: Ref. 1847-08-03, 3:3, M.
On the 27th ult., in the meeting-house of the Presbyterian Church, Clare, by the Rev. Alexander G. Ross, Mr. Thomas Dalzell, merchant, Market-hill, to Eliza, eldest daughter of the late Robert Orr, Esq., Course Lodge, near Richhill.

No. 1232 :: Ref. 1847-08-03, 3:3, M.
July 27, in the parish Church, Killyman, by the Rev. Mortimer O'Sullivan, D.D., Mr. John Kerr, of Charlemont, to Anne, second daughter of the late Mr. William Bewglass, of Killyman, county Tyrone.

No. 1233 :: Ref. 1847-08-03, 3:3, M.
July 27, in the Presbyterian Church, Mountnorris, by the Rev. W.H. M'Ewen, Mr. Robert Irvine, of Ballynerary, to Miss Prudence M'Mullen, of Cladybegg.

No. 1234 :: Ref. 1847-08-03, 3:3, M.
July 27, by the Rev. Dr. Montague, Vicar-General, John Donnelly, Esq., of Omagh, to Mary Jane, only daughter of the late J. Hughes, Esq., of Dungannon.

No. 1235 :: Ref. 1847-08-03, 3:3, D.
Suddenly, at his residence, Northumberland-street, Strand, London, Captain William Molyneux, R.N., son of the late General Sir Thomas Molyneux, Bart., of Castle Dillon, county Armagh, in his 46th year.

No. 1236 :: Ref. 1847-08-03, 3:3, D.
In this city, on 20th ult., Mr. James Bennett.

No. 1237 :: Ref. 1847-08-03, 3:3, D.
On Thursday, 22d July, at his residence, Tullybrick Nursery, near Middletown, Mr. Daniel Anderson, aged 75 years. He was a native of Tain, in Rosshire; and after having served as head-gardener to several noblemen in his own country, and in Ireland, for some years of his early life, finally settled in Tullybrick, in the year 1801—married and reared a large family respectably. He was noted for his social, hospitable, and benevolent disposition, as well as for his strict integrity. He bore with Christian resignation many of the afflictions of his life: the greatest, perhaps, of which was the loss of his two legs in the year 1818, by amputation, from the effects of malignant typhus fever. His loss is deeply regretted by all who knew him.

No. 1238 :: Ref. 1847-08-03, 3:3, D.
On Friday, the 30th ult., at his residence, Ardmore, near Derry, John A. Smyth, J.P., D.L., aged 75.

No. 1239 :: Ref. 1847-08-03, 3:3, D.
On Monday, the 19th ult., at his residence in Cookstown, Mr. Wm. Brown, at the advanced age of 86.

No. 1240 :: Ref. 1847-08-03, 3:3, D.
July 20, of fever, Margaret, the beloved wife of Mr. Robert Birch, Anglies, near Cookstown.

No. 1241 :: Ref. 1847-08-03, 3:3, D.
July 23, at Allan Park, Stirling, the residence of his father-in-law, John Galbraith, Esq., Solicitor, Enniskillen, in the 35th year of his age.

No. 1242 :: Ref. 1847-08-10, 2:3, B.
On the 31st ult., Mrs. John Keys, of Great James-street, Derry, of a daughter.

No. 1243 :: Ref. 1847-08-10, 2:3, M.
At Magherally Presbyterian Church, on the 31st ult., by the Rev. James Thomson, David Lockhart, Esq., Tullylish, to Miss Jane Barr, Lurgan.

No. 1244 :: Ref. 1847-08-10, 2:3, D.
On Friday, the 30th ult., at Caledon, Bridget, wife of Mr. James Keenan, innkeeper, aged 40 years.

No. 1245 :: Ref. 1847-08-10, 2:3, D.
In Lurgan, on the 2d inst., of fever, Sarah Ann, wife of Mr. James M'Kee, of that town, aged 26 years.

No. 1246 :: Ref. 1847-08-10, 2:3, D.
On the 31st ult., of dropsy, Eliza, eldest daughter of Mr. Wm. Vint, North-street, Belfast, aged 24 years.

No. 1247 :: Ref. 1847-08-10, 2:3, D.
On the 2d inst., of fever, at his residence in Clones, to the inexpressible grief of a large circle of sorrowing and deeply-afflicted relatives and friends, James T. Hurst, Esq., M.D., aged 53 years.

No. 1248 :: Ref. 1847-08-10, 2:3, D.
On the 7th inst., in Enniskillen, Mr. William Stinson.

No. 1249 :: Ref. 1847-08-17, 2:6, B.
August 10, at Hollybrook, county Fermanagh, the lady of Lieutenant Col. Dickson, of a son.

No. 1250 :: Ref. 1847-08-17, 2:6, M.
On the 9th inst., in St. Anne's Church, Belfast, Edward Rodgers, Esq., Vicar-Choral, Cathedral, Armagh, to Charlotte, daughter of William Campbell, Esq., late of her Majesty's 38th Regiment of Foot.

No. 1251 :: Ref. 1847-08-17, 2:6, M.
August 10, at St. Peter's Church, by the Rev. Charles Alexander, Rector of Drumcree, county of Armagh, Alan O'Bryan Bellingham, Esq., of Dunneny-House, county of Louth, to Sophia Florence, eldest daughter of the late Col. Heyland, of Glendarragh, county Antrim.

No. 1252 :: Ref. 1847-08-17, 2:6, D.
On the 15th inst., after a long and severe illness, Mrs. Hall, of Copney, near Moy, aged 52 years.

No. 1253 :: Ref. 1847-08-17, 2:6, D.
August 9, at 18, North Earl-street, Dublin, aged seventy years, Mr. Benjamin Stokes, Printer.

No. 1254 :: Ref. 1847-08-17, 2:6, D.
August 10, of water on the chest, George Hassard, Esq., of Skea, county Fermanagh, in his 78th year.

No. 1255 :: Ref. 1847-08-17, 2:6, D.

August 5, at Gallina, Monaghan, at the residence of his father, Alexander Fleming, Esq., Ex-Scholar of T.C.D., Barrister-at-Law, aged 31 years.

No. 1256 :: Ref. 1847-08-17, 2:6, D.

At his residence, in Pike township, Knox, county Ohio [sic], America, on Wednesday, 2d June last, in the 48th year of his age, Mr. Edward Cooke, formerly of Enniskillen and Crievehill, county Fermanagh.

No. 1257 :: Ref. 1847-08-24, 3:1, B.

At Armagh, on the 19th instant, the lady of the Rev. James Hardy, of a daughter.

No. 1258 :: Ref. 1847-08-24, 3:1, B.

At Middletown, on the 19th inst., the lady of Dr. Clarke, of a son.

No. 1259 :: Ref. 1847-08-24, 3:1, M.

By the Rev. John R. M'Alister, on 23d August, in the First Presbyterian Church of Keady, Mr. James Montgomery, Civil Engineer, to Miss M'Endow, daughter of the late Mr. Robert M'Endow, merchant, Armagh.

No. 1260 :: Ref. 1847-08-24, 3:1, M.

On Monday, the 11th inst., at Letterkenny Church, by the Rev. Richard Smith, Mr. Andrew M'Neely, merchant, Dunkaneely, to Jane, youngest daughter of Mr. Benjamin Maddock, Limerick.

No. 1261 :: Ref. 1847-08-24, 3:1, M.

On the 20th inst., in Drumsullin Church, this county, by the Rev. Charles Warren, Thomas, second son of William Anderson, Esq., Bracknagh Hill, to Phebe, second daughter of Samuel Knipe, Esq., Balaghey, both of this county.

No. 1262 :: Ref. 1847-08-24, 3:1, M.

In the Registrar's Office, Dungannon, on Monday the 16th inst., Mr. John Henry, to Miss Jane M'Cracken, both of Moy.

No. 1263 :: Ref. 1847-08-24, 3:1, M.

On the 10th inst., by the Rev. William White, Downpatrick, Mr. Robert Nesbit, of Belfast, woollen-draper, to Sarah, second daughter of Mr. William Rowan, Downpatrick.

No. 1264 :: Ref. 1847-08-24, 3:1, D.

In Derryfubble, on Sunday, the 15th instant, Mr. William Wiley, aged 55 years. He was through life an upright man, and in death is mourned by numerous friends and acquaintances, by whom his remains were attended to their resting place.

No. 1265 :: Ref. 1847-08-24, 3:1, D.

August 14, at Woodstock, county of Wicklow, Lieutenant William Tottenham, R.N., fifth son of Lord R.P. Tottenham, Lord Bishop of Clogher.

No. 1266 :: Ref. 1847-08-24, 3:1, D.

On the 6th inst., at Portadown, Roger Marley, Esq., at an advanced age of 88 years.

No. 1267 :: Ref. 1847-08-24, 3:1, D.

On the 17th inst., at Fairlawn, near Moy, after a short illness, Thomas Sinclair, Esq., aged 70 years. His character through life was such as gained him many friends, by whom he is deeply and deservedly regretted.

No. 1268 :: Ref. 1847-08-24, 3:1, D.

At Enniskillen, on the 19th inst., of fever, Miss Rebecca Sharpe.

No. 1269 :: Ref. 1847-08-31, 2:5, B.

On 22nd inst., at Toam, near Blacklion, county Cavan, the wife of Mr. William Copeland Brackin, merchant, of a daughter.

No. 1270 :: Ref. 1847-08-31, 2:5, B.

On the 26th inst., at Annaroe house, the lady of William Cochrane, Esq., of a son.

No. 1271 :: Ref. 1847-08-31, 2:5, M.

In the Cathedral, Armagh, on Thursday, 26th inst., Mr. George Benson, to Miss Millar.

No. 1272 :: Ref. 1847-08-31, 2:5, M.

On the 27th inst., in Seagoe church, by the Venerable the Archdeacon of Dromore, Mr. Benjamin Robb, merchant of Tandragee, to Jane, second daughter of Wilson Irwin, Esq., of Kearn House.

No. 1273 :: Ref. 1847-08-31, 2:5, M.

In the Parish Church of St. Nicholas, Dundalk, by the Rev. Dr. Thackeray, Alexander Shekleton, Esq., to Mary Anne, only daughter of James Knowles, Esq., of Dundalk.

No. 1274 :: Ref. 1847-08-31, 2:5, M.

At Glasgow, on the 18th instant, by the Rev. W.H. Cornforth, Mr. James Coutts, merchant, Enniskillen, to Eliza, daughter of the late Mr. Charles Mackay, Edinburgh.

No. 1275 :: Ref. 1847-08-31, 2:5, M.

On the 26th instant, at Cookstown church, by the Rev. Richard Stewart, rector of Kildress, the Rev. Thomas O'Rourke, incumbent of Loughcrew, diocese of Meath, to Mary, eldest daughter of the late Major Charles Richardson, [of] Armagh House, in the county of Tyrone.

No. 1276 :: Ref. 1847-08-31, 2:5, D.

At her residence, Mall, on the 27th inst., Rossanne, fourth daughter of the late Mr. Archibald M'Connell of Armagh, aged 32 years.

No. 1277 :: Ref. 1847-08-31, 2:5, D.

On the 18th instant, at Drumbane, near Moira, Ann, wife of Mr. Mark Berry, aged 65 years.

No. 1278 :: Ref. 1847-08-31, 2:5, D.

On the 24th instant, of fever, in Castle-street, Enniskillen, Mrs. Emily Fitzgerald, deeply regretted by a number of friends.

No. 1279 :: Ref. 1847-08-31, 2:5, D.

August 24, of acute consumption, at the Beresford Arms, in this city, on his way home from Dublin to Moneymore, Robert M'Kee, Esq., youngest son of the late David M'Kee, Esq., of Greenview, Castledawson, in the county of Londonderry.

No. 1280 :: Ref. 1847-08-31, 2:5, D.

At Tullymore Park, the seat of the Earl of Roden, on the 25th inst., of malignant typhus fever, Cecilia, the beloved wife of the Hon. Captain Augustus Jocelyn, of the Carbineers, and second daughter of Lieutenant General Sir Neil Douglas, K.C.B., in the 25th year of her age.

No. 1281 :: Ref. 1847-09-07, 3:1, B.

August 30th, at Newry, the lady of William Stitt, Esq., of a son.

No. 1282 :: Ref. 1847-09-07, 3:1, B.

August 28, in Upper Charlemont-street, the lady of Charles Coote, Esq., of a daughter.

No. 1283 :: Ref. 1847-09-07, 3:1, M.

In Coleraine church, by the Rev. F. Ould, the Rev. G.V. Chichester, son of the Rev. Edward Chichester, of Kilmore, diocese of Armagh, to Harriet Eleanor, third daughter of Hugh Lyle, Esq., of Knocktarns, county of Londonderry.

No. 1284 :: Ref. 1847-09-07, 3:1, D.

August 30th, at Templecarne glebe, near Pettigo, of malignant fever, which he caught in the discharge of his duty, the Rev. Thomas Birney, in the 66th year of his age; he was Rector of that Parish for seven years; during which period, he was highly esteemed by all classes, and is universally lamented by a large circle of friends.

No. 1285 :: Ref. 1847-09-07, 3:1, D.

At Enniskillen, on the 2d. inst., the wife of Stewart Whittaker, Esq., Stamp Distributor for Fermanagh and Cavan.

No. 1286 :: Ref. 1847-09-07, 3:1, D.

At Lurgan, at his residence, on Saturday, 28th ult., Henry Gilbert, aged 90 years, the last of the old Irish Volunteers.

No. 1287 :: Ref. 1847-09-07, 3:1, D.

August 24th Rothsay, Isle of Bute, the Rev. Robert Jessop, of Bath.

No. 1288 :: Ref. 1847-09-07, 3:1, D.

In Strabane, on the 29th ult., Mr. Charles Sproule, aged 39 years.

No. 1289 :: Ref. 1847-09-07, 3:1, D.

In Ballyshannon, on the 30th ult., of fever, Mr. James M'Gonigle, Apothecary.

No. 1290 :: Ref. 1847-09-07, 3:1, D.

On 29th ult, at his residence, Omagh, after a short illness, Francis Meahan, Esq., merchant, aged 86 years.

No. 1291 :: Ref. 1847-09-07, 3:1, D.

Of a rapid decline, William, eldest son of Mr. James Henry, of Hill-head, Tynan, aged 20 years, nephew of Mr. John Kyle, of same place, and Student of the Belfast College.

No. 1292 :: Ref. 1847-09-07, 3:1, D.

On the 30th inst., at his residence, 10, Prussia-street, Dublin, the Rev. John Stone, aged 28 years, of fever, caught in the discharge of his duties. He has left a wife and two children to deplore his loss.

No. 1293 :: Ref. 1847-09-14, 3:2, B.

On the 4th inst., at Grove Cottage, Fulham road, London, Mrs. George Gray, of a son.

No. 1294 :: Ref. 1847-09-14, 3:2, B.

September 3, in Ballina, the lady of the Rev. George Read, of a daughter.

No. 1295 :: Ref. 1847-09-14, 3:2, M.

On the 7th inst., in the Scots Church, Bandon, by the Rev. William Hogg, the Rev. David Coote, minister of the Presbyterian Church, Killalea, Armagh, to Anne, second daughter of the late Thomas Fuller, Esq., Bandon.

No. 1296 :: Ref. 1847-09-14, 3:2, M.

On the 7th inst., by the Rev. Michael M'Glinchy, Charles Mulreny, Esq., Donegal, to Margaret, eldest daughter of the late William M'Hugh, Esq., Castlederg.

No. 1297 :: Ref. 1847-09-14, 3:2, D.

On the 30th June, at Kippet, Peeblesshire, in his 150th year, Mr. David Roe, shepherd.

No. 1298 :: Ref. 1847-09-14, 3:2, D.

On the 3d inst., at Edinburgh, John Hamilton, Esq., Advocate, Editor of *The Scottish Guardian*.

No. 1299 :: Ref. 1847-09-14, 3:2, D.

At his brother's in Philadelphia, on the 26th July, of fever, contracted on the 5th day before arrival of the vessel in which he went from this country, Mr. Samuel Marshall, of Lisnagir, near Omagh.

No. 1300 :: Ref. 1847-09-14, 3:2, D.

On the 9th inst., at 5, Fitzwilliam Square East, Dublin, the Right Hon. Edward Pennefather.

No. 1301 :: Ref. 1847-09-14, 3:2, D.

On the 2d inst., of fever, in London, Hercules, third son of the late Mr. Thomas M'Comb, merchant, Belfast.

No. 1302 :: Ref. 1847-09-14, 3:2, D.

On the 3d inst., of typhus fever, in the 63d year of her age, Jane, the beloved wife of Wm. M'Caldin, Tinary, Newbliss.

No. 1303 :: Ref. 1847-09-14, 3:2, D.

At the residence of his brother, East-road, City-road, London, William, third son of the late John Young, of Cookstown, in the county of Tyrone, Esq., Surgeon in the Royal Navy.

No. 1304 :: Ref. 1847-09-14, 3:2, D.
At her residence, Newtownstewart, county of Tyrone, Isabella Alexander, widow of Joseph Alexander, Esq., aged 40 years, deservedly regretted by all who knew her.

No. 1305 :: Ref. 1847-09-21, 3:2, B.
September 8, the lady of the Rev. Alexander Lowry, Presbyterian Minister, Ballyshannon, of a daughter.

No. 1306 :: Ref. 1847-09-21, 3:2, B.
September 6, at Enniskillen, the lady of Captain Gordon Tidy, of a son.

No. 1307 :: Ref. 1847-09-21, 3:2, M.
On the 2d inst., at Lara Church, county Cavan, by the Rev. Mr. Erskine, James George Lepper, Esq., of Monaghan, to Eliza, only daughter of Robert Thompson, Esq., of Ravenswood.

No. 1308 :: Ref. 1847-09-21, 3:2, M.
In the Registrar's Office, Cookstown, by the Rev. John W. Graham, on the 14th inst., Mr. James Hamilton, of Ballysudden, near Cookstown, to Miss Jane Irwin, of Brackaville, near Coalisland.

No. 1309 :: Ref. 1847-09-21, 3:2, M.
On Friday, the 17th inst., in Belnaleck Church, by the Rev. N. Baker, James Armstrong, Esq., of Ross, county Fermanagh, to Jane, third daughter of Mr. Wm. Armstrong, Enniskillen.

No. 1310 :: Ref. 1847-09-21, 3:2, M.
In Kingstown, N.H., Colonel William Webster, aged sixty-seven, to Miss Martha Winslow, aged nineteen. By the above union, the bridegroom has married his sister's grand-daughter, which makes the bride a wife to her great uncle, sister to her grandfather and grandmother, aunt to her father and mother, and great aunt to her brothers and sisters. She is a stepmother to five children, fourteen grand children, and one great grandchild.

No. 1311 :: Ref. 1847-09-21, 3:2, D.
On the 12th inst., at Drumnasoo, near Loughgall, Mr. Robert Orr, aged 70 years.

No. 1312 :: Ref. 1847-09-21, 3:2, D.
At Spike Island, Cove, on Monday last, after a very brief illness, Mr. John Donally, Deputy-governor of the Island, and late deputy-governor of the gaol of Omagh, aged 32 years.

No. 1313 :: Ref. 1847-09-21, 3:2, D.
At Bundoran, on the 17th inst., of inflammation, Mrs. Beatty, wife of Thos. Beatty, Esq., Newtownbutler, county Fermanagh, in the 68th year of her age and also, upon the following morning, her husband, Thomas Beatty, Esq., aged 74. Mr. Beatty was for a considerable length of time previous, indisposed from rheumatic attacks, on account of which he had that day week arrived at Bundoran, for the benefit of the salt water, accompanied by Mrs. Beatty, who was in her usual state of health until the morning on which she died. The two coffins were conveyed in the same hearse to Newtownbutler, to be deposited in the family burying place.

No. 1314 :: Ref. 1847-09-21, 3:2, D.
September 13, in Kinsale Barracks, of dysentery, aged twenty-one years, John Jackson Hall, Esq., A.B., T.C.D., Ensign in her Majesty's 54th Regt., youngest son of Perry Hall, Esq., Tully House, Monaghan.

No. 1315 :: Ref. 1847-09-28, 3:2, B.
On the 22d inst., at Chatham, the Lady of W.W. Bond, Esq., 4th (King's Own) Regiment, of a son.

No. 1316 :: Ref. 1847-09-28, 3:2, B.
Sept. 19, at Ballyconnell House, county of Donegal, the lady of Wybrants Olphert, Esq., of a son.

No. 1317 :: Ref. 1847-09-28, 3:2, B.
Sept. 17, at Carnagh House, county Armagh, the lady of John Robert Irwin, Esq., of a son.

No. 1318 :: Ref. 1847-09-28, 3:2, B.
September 19, at Woodeaton, Oxfordshire, the Countess of Verulam, prematurely, of a daughter.

No. 1319 :: Ref. 1847-09-28, 3:2, D.
At Donoughmore, on Sunday the 19th inst., Elizabeth Ann, relict of the late Charles Colhoun, Esq., of Sixmilecross, aged 75 years.

No. 1320 :: Ref. 1847-09-28, 3:2, D.
In College-street, on Sunday morning, 26th inst., aged 32 years, Mary, the beloved wife of Mr. James Lee, of the Cathedral Choir, Armagh. The deceased was a very exemplary character, possessed of many virtues, religious, social, and domestic, which endeared her to all her acquaintances and friends. She died the second day after giving birth to a still born male child.

No. 1321 :: Ref. 1847-09-28, 3:2, D.
On the 21st inst., of apoplexy, Mr. George Rodgers, of Cookstown, in the 56th year of his age. He was for many years a valued elder of the 1st Presbyterian Congregation of Cookstown, where the deep, active, and unwearied interest which he took in all that affected the prosperity of the Church will be long remembered.

No. 1322 :: Ref. 1847-09-28, 3:2, D.
On the 13th inst., in his 21st year, at the residence of John G. Copley, Esq., Richmond Hill, Manchester, William, youngest son of the late Samuel King, Esq., of Coalisland Mills, Dungannon.

No. 1323 :: Ref. 1847-09-28, 3:2, D.
In Linen-hall-street, Dundalk, in the 2d year of his age, John Charles, youngest son of J.C. Fitzgerald, Esq., Editor of the *Newry Examiner* and *Louth Advertiser*.

No. 1324 :: Ref. 1847-09-28, 3:2, D.
Sept. 18, at Keadue, Mrs. Tenison, relict of Thomas Tenison, Esq., of Castle Tenison, county of Roscommon.

No. 1325 :: Ref. 1847-09-28, 3:2, D.
Sept. 21, at Antrim, Andrew Annesley Molyneux, surgeon.

No. 1326 :: Ref. 1847-09-28, 3:2, D.
At his residence, Middletown Glebe, on Sunday, 26th inst., the Rev. James Mauleverer, Incumbent, of fever caught in the faithful discharge of his ministerial duties.

No. 1327 :: Ref. 1847-09-28, 3:2, D.
On the 20th instant, of typhus fever, at Drumnasoo, near Loughgall, Ann, relict of the late Mr. Samuel Orr, aged 70 years.

No. 1328 :: Ref. 1847-10-05, 3:1, B.
September 29, at Broomfield, county Cavan, the lady of the Rev. Arthur Monypeny, of a daughter.

No. 1329 :: Ref. 1847-10-05, 3:1, B.
On the 22d ult., at Ray, near Manorcunningham, county Donegal, Mrs. John Montgomery, jun., of a daughter.

No. 1330 :: Ref. 1847-10-05, 3:1, M.
On the 30th ult., at Mullabrack church, in this county, A. M'Anally, Esq., surgeon, second Grenadiers, Bengal army, to Jane, second daughter of Barnet M'Kee, Esq., J.P., Markethill.

No. 1331 :: Ref. 1847-10-05, 3:1, M.
In Richhill Church, on Monday, the 27th ult., by the Rev. James Hogan, Mr. John Harris, to Miss Sophia Disney Kirwan, both of Richhill.

No. 1332 :: Ref. 1847-10-05, 3:1, M.
September 23, at Omagh, Peter Keegan, Esq., of Belfast, to Bessie, daughter of the late James Quinn, Esq., of Omagh.

No. 1333 :: Ref. 1847-10-05, 3:1, D.
At Caledon, on the 24th ult., Mrs. Humphries, wife of Dr. Humphries.

No. 1334 :: Ref. 1847-10-05, 3:1, D.
On the 27th ult., at Belfast, Mr. John Breen, head porter of the Belfast Banking Company.

No. 1335 :: Ref. 1847-10-05, 3:1, D.
September 28, at a very advanced age, Margaret wife of William Slacke, of Annadale, Esq., county Leitrim.

No. 1336 :: Ref. 1847-10-05, 3:1, D.
On the 27th ult., at Ballyhomra, near Hillsborough, very suddenly, Caroline Susan, eldest daughter of Marcus Corry, Esq., and grand-daughter of the late Isaac Corry, sen., Esq., of Newry.

No. 1337 :: Ref. 1847-10-12, 3:2, B.
At Avon Lodge, Armagh, on the 8th inst., the lady of W.H. Davis, Esq., of a daughter.

No. 1338 :: Ref. 1847-10-12, 3:2, B.
October 6, at Fitzwilliam-square, West, the lady of Charles Eccles, Esq., of a son and heir.

No. 1339 :: Ref. 1847-10-12, 3:2, B.
October 1, at the Infirmary House, this city, the lady of Dr. Robinson, of her eighth son.

No. 1340 :: Ref. 1847-10-12, 3:2, B.
October 2, at Swanlinbar, the lady of John Johnston, Esq., of a son.

No. 1341 :: Ref. 1847-10-12, 3:2, M.
October 4, in St. George's Church, Allan O'Neill, Esq., of Manorhamilton, in the county Leitrim, to Anne Sophia, youngest daughter of the late Henry H. Bell, Esq., of Warwick Lodge, in the county of Derry.

No. 1342 :: Ref. 1847-10-12, 3:2, M.
On the 17th ult., in Killymard Church, by the Rev. Wm. Ewing, Vicar of Donegal, Robert, son to Mr. John Scott, merchant, Donegal, to Eliza Ritchie, niece to the Rev. Wm. Niblock.

No. 1343 :: Ref. 1847-10-12, 3:2, M.
On the 17th ult., in the Covenanting Church, Gortlee, by the Rev. Dr. Henry, Wm. Bates, Esq., merchant, Strabane, to Miss Jane Buchannn [sic], second daughter of Mr. Alexander Buchanan, Drumquin.

No. 1344 :: Ref. 1847-10-12, 3:2, M.
October 2, in the Parish Church of Kingscourt, by the Rev. Robert Winning, Rector of Enniskeen, and father of the bridegroom, William Alexander Winning, Esq., to Sarah Jane, youngest daughter of the late Philip Ward, Esq., of Kingscourt.

No. 1345 :: Ref. 1847-10-12, 3:2, M.
At Madras, 3rd of August last, Capt. J.W.G. Kenny, of the 13th Native Infantry, to Margaret Rosborough, third daughter to the late Major A. Rennick, of Derryargan, County Fermanagh, and formerly of the honourable East India company's service.

No. 1346 :: Ref. 1847-10-12, 3:2, M.
On the 27th August, at the residence of the bride's father, by the Rev. Wm. M'Cullough, Mr. Ezekiel James Nesbitt, Peterboro', third son of the Rev. John Nesbitt, Wesleyan Minister, Enniskillen, Ireland, to Mary, eldest daughter of Walter Sheridan, Esq., of Peterboro', clerk of the Colborne district.

No. 1347 :: Ref. 1847-10-12, 3:2, D.
On the 4th inst., at Beech Hill, the residence of his brother-in-law, John M'Causland, Esq., aged 40 years.

No. 1348 :: Ref. 1847-10-12, 3:2, D.
On the 2d inst., Robt. Waddell, Esq., of Drumcree, formerly of Lisnavane, county of Monaghan.

No. 1349 :: Ref. 1847-10-12, 3:2, D.
At Strabane, on Wednesday week, Mrs. Adams, relict of the late Mr. James Adams, Canal basin.

No. 1350 :: Ref. 1847-10-12, 3:2, D.
October 3, at Carrickmacross, to the deep regret of her family and friends, Catherine, the beloved wife of Wm. Moore, Esq., aged 25 years.

No. 1351 :: Ref. 1847-10-12, 3:2, D.
September 26, of fever, in the 22d year of his age, William, fifth son of the late Edward Kellett, Esq., Rantavan, county Cavan.

No. 1352 :: Ref. 1847-10-12, 3:2, D.
October 3, at Whitepark, the residence of Charles Ovenden, Esq., of fever, James Haughton, Esq., M.D., Physician to the Brookborough Dispensary and Fever Hospital.

No. 1353 :: Ref. 1847-10-12, 3:2, D.
At Dromard, County Fermanagh, on Friday morning last, of gout in the stomach, Dr. William Dane, in the 38th year of his age. Mr. Dane was a gentleman of consistent and sturdy principles, who was inclined to serve his fellow man where he conceived that he needed it, and possessed ample means.—Many of the poor and destitute often experienced his relieving kindness and generosity.

No. 1354 :: Ref. 1847-10-19, 2:6, B.
On the 7th inst., at Drumart, the lady of Henry Hardy, Esq., of a daughter.

No. 1355 :: Ref. 1847-10-19, 2:6, B.
On the 11th inst., at Elsinore, Rostrevor, the lady of Henry I. Algeo, Esq., of a daughter.

No. 1356 :: Ref. 1847-10-19, 2:6, B.
On the 8th inst., at Barford House, Bridgewater, the Countess of Cavan, of a daughter.

No. 1357 :: Ref. 1847-10-19, 2:6, M.
On the 12th inst., in the Independent Chapel, Donoughmore, by the Rev. James Hanson, Mr. William Duff Gibson, of Ballywhilon, to Miss Hanson, of Charlemont.

No. 1358 :: Ref. 1847-10-19, 2:6, M.
On Tuesday the 12th inst., in Rossorry Church, by the Rev. John C. Hudson, the Rev. George W. Welsh, incumbent of Castlearchdall, to Catherine, eldest daughter of the late Alex. Hudson, J.P., of Clintivern, in the County of Fermanagh, Esq.

No. 1359 :: Ref. 1847-10-19, 2:6, M.
October 12, at Magherafelt Church, by the Rev. William Mortimer, Richard Wilson, Esq., eldest son of the late William Wilson, Esq. of Maxwell Court, county of Down, to Henrietta, daughter of the late Rev. Mark Cassidy, Chancellor of Kilfenora and Incumbent of Newtownards.

No. 1360 :: Ref. 1847-10-19, 2:6, M.
On the 14th inst., in the Cathedral, by the Rev. George Smith, Edwin S. Maxwell, Esq., Benburb, Surgeon, to Ellen, third daughter of Mr. Dawson Bell, Omagh.

No. 1361 :: Ref. 1847-10-19, 2:6, M.
In the Scotch Church, Enniskillen, on the 16th inst., by the Rev. A.C. Maclatchy, Mr. Archibald Elliott, of Waterford, to Ann Jane, eldest daughter of Wm. Trimble, Esq., proprietor of the *Fermanagh Reporter*.

No. 1362 :: Ref. 1847-10-19, 2:6, M.
On Tuesday, the 12th inst., at St. John's Point Wesleyan Methodist Chapel, Co. Donegal, by the Rev. John Walker, Richard Corscadden, Esq. merchant, Donegal, to Miss Nesbitt, daughter of John Nesbitt, Esq., Woodend, and sister to the late Captain Nesbitt, of Londonderry.

No. 1363 :: Ref. 1847-10-19, 2:6, D.
On the 4th inst., at Mullaghboy, near Moy, of small pox, Mr. Thos. Reilly, aged 29 years. His remains were attended by a large body of Orangemen to the place of interment, Benburb.

No. 1364 :: Ref. 1847-10-19, 2:6, D.
Lately, at Kinsale, county Cork, of fever, in the 26th year of her age, Mrs. Eliza Jane M'Dowall, wife of Sergt. M'Dowall, 54th Regt. foot. A few days afterwards, Sergt. David M'Dowall, in the 25th year of his age.

No. 1365 :: Ref. 1847-10-19, 2:6, D.
At Ballyshannon, on Saturday last, Mary the beloved wife of Mr. Moffit, Primitive Wesleyan Methodist Minister.

No. 1366 :: Ref. 1847-10-19, 2:6, D.
On Wednesday, the 6th inst., at his residence, in Gracehill, near Ballymena, the Rev. John Willey, Moravian Minister, in the 66th year of his age.

No. 1367 :: Ref. 1847-10-19, 2:6, D.
In Curran, on the 11th inst., in the 52d year of his age, Mr. John Burton, after tedious bad health for 12 years, caused by paralytic. His remains were conveyed to the family burying ground, in Benburb, by a large and respectable number of his relations and friends.

No. 1368 :: Ref. 1847-10-26, 2:4, B.
On the 14th inst., at Kilmore House, county Cavan, the lady of John Edward Vernon, Esq., of a daughter.

No. 1369 :: Ref. 1847-10-26, 2:4, M.
On the 12th inst., at Coalisland church, by the Rev. Isaac Ashe, Robert M'Cracken, Esq., of Belfast, to Sarah Elizabeth, eldest daughter of James Gray, Esq., Coalisland-house.

No. 1370 :: Ref. 1847-10-26, 2:4, M.
On the 18th inst., at Monkstown Church, Kingstown, Mr. John M'Dowall, Merchant, Everton, to Bessie Ann, only daughter of William Forster, Streamstown, Ballinamore, County Leitrim.

No. 1371 :: Ref. 1847-10-26, 2:4, D.
On the 13th instant, at Loughgall, in consequence of a fall from his horse, which he survived only two days, John Shegog, Esq., M.D., M.R.C.S.I.; for 19 years Medical Attendant of the Loughgall Dispensary.

No. 1372 :: Ref. 1847-10-26, 2:4, D.
On the 19th inst., in this city, Rebecca, relict of the late Mr. James Dickson, aged 47 years, deservedly regretted.

No. 1373 :: Ref. 1847-10-26, 2:4, D.
On the 14th inst., of fever, caught in the discharge of his duties, as Clerk to the Board of Guardians of the Coleraine Union, Mr. Edward Fleming, aged fifty-five.

No. 1374 :: Ref. 1847-10-26, 2:4, D.
At his residence, Beragh, on the 8th inst., the Rev. R. M'Aleer, P.P., Ballintockan, in the 45th year of his age, and 18th of his ministry.

No. 1375 :: Ref. 1847-10-26, 2:4, D.
On the 5th inst., Esther, wife of Mr. John Mitchell, Inspecting Officer of the Coast Guards, Rathmullan, aged 55 years.

No. 1376 :: Ref. 1847-10-26, 2:4, D.
Oct. 11, at Lifford, county Donegal, Mary, the beloved wife of Capt. Clifford Henry, 48th Regiment, aged 25.

No. 1377 :: Ref. 1847-10-26, 2:4, D.
On the 13th inst., at Pultney-street, Bath, after a long and tedious illness, Miss Mary Thompson, daughter of the late Mr. Joseph Thompson, of Enniskillen, and sister to Captain Thompson, 51st Regiment, deeply regretted by all who knew her.

No. 1378 :: Ref. 1847-10-26, 2:4, D.
On the 24th inst., at Vicar's Hill, Armagh, Mr. James Groves, Principal of the Cathedral School.

No. 1379 :: Ref. 1847-11-02, 3:1, B.
October 26, at Drumshambo Glebe, county Tyrone, the lady of the Rev. Richard Johnston, of a son.

No. 1380 :: Ref. 1847-11-02, 3:1, M.
On the 30th October, in Dromore Church, by the Rev. H.L. St. George, Wm. James Moffit, Dromore, county Tyrone, to Margaret, youngest daughter of the late Mr. John Johnston, Lack, county Fermanagh.

No. 1381 :: Ref. 1847-11-02, 3:1, M.
Oct. 23, in Ballyshannon, by the Rev. John Shoales, E. Atthill, Esq., J.P., fourth son of the late Rev. W. Atthill, of Ardress, county Fermanagh, to Jane, eldest daughter of the late L. Brien, Esq., of Ardverney, county Fermanagh.

No. 1382 :: Ref. 1847-11-02, 3:1, M.
On the 7th ult., by the Rev. Doctor Hetherington, at Spalding House, the residence of the bride's brother-in-law, Walter F. Ireland, Esq., the Rev. John C. Quin, Free Church of Scotland's Assembly's Missionary to Canada, to Catherine, daughter of the late Rev. Thos. Gillespie, LL.D., Professor of Humanity in the United Colleges of St. Salvador and St. Leonard's, St. Andrew's, and grand-daughter to the late Principal, Dr. John Hunter, of the same place.

No. 1383 :: Ref. 1847-11-02, 3:1, M.
On the 16th ult., in Padztow Church, Cornwall, by the Rev. Mr. Tyke, Dr. John Caruthers, to Amelia, eldest daughter of Capt. Clements, formerly of Londonderry.

No. 1384 :: Ref. 1847-11-02, 3:1, M.
October 20th, in Broghan Presbyterian church, by the Rev. William Sweeney, Mr. Henry Faris, of Killeshandra, Merchant, to Isabella, sixth daughter of James Barry, Esq., of Broghan House, County Cavan.

No. 1385 :: Ref. 1847-11-02, 3:1, M.
On the 27th ult., in the Presbyterian church, Tempo, by the Rev. Mr. Holmes, Mr. William Johnston, of Trillic, merchant, to Prudence, eldest daughter of the late Mr. James Rutledge, of Badony.

No. 1386 :: Ref. 1847-11-02, 3:1, M.
On the 28th ult., in the Cathedral, Derry, by the Rev. John W. Loughlin, Frederick H. M'Causland, Esq., merchant, to Mary, eldest daughter of David Gilmour, Esq., Pump-street.

No. 1387 :: Ref. 1847-11-02, 3:1, M.
October 19, at St. Jame's [sic] Fryern Barnet, Massy Herbert Morphy, Esq., of Enniskillen, to Anna, daughter of the late John Hawks, Esq., of Gateshead, Durham.

No. 1388 :: Ref. 1847-11-02, 3:1, M.
At Lifford, on the 25th ult., by the Rev. Mr. M'Crossan, Mr. Edward M'Kenney, innkeeper, Strabane, to Maria, daughter of the late Mr. Monaghan, Mountcharles.

No. 1389 :: Ref. 1847-11-02, 3:1, D.
In Thomas-street, Armagh, on Sunday evening, of hooping-cough, aged 3 years, Thomas, second son of Mr. Samuel Magowan, Tailor.

No. 1390 :: Ref. 1847-11-02, 3:1, D.
Of malignant fever, at the Island Mills, Lisburn, on the 27th ult., Samuel Richardson, the senior partner of the firm, aged 30 years, after a brief illness of only five days duration. Deceased attended the market in Armagh, on the 19th, and in Tandragee, in his usual good health, on the 20th ult.

No. 1391 :: Ref. 1847-11-02, 3:1, D.

On the 11th ult., at Lifford, county Donegal, Mary wife of Captain Clifford Henry, 48th Regiment, aged 25 years.

No. 1392 :: Ref. 1847-11-02, 3:1, D.

On the 25th of October, Capt. Joseph C. Laidler, of the barque *Envoy*, of Londonderry.

No. 1393 :: Ref. 1847-11-02, 3:1, D.

At Gortmesson, Fermanagh, on the 23d ult., Thomas Ramsay, Esq., aged 68 years.

No. 1394 :: Ref. 1847-11-02, 3:1, D.

On the 24th ult., in Derry, Michael M'Goldrick, aged 66 years. He was a servant in the employment of the Londonderry and Dublin Coach Company for upwards of forty years; and (most singular) during that period, he was never one day absent from business. He lived to see the demise of four successive mail contractors; and never, during his recollection, had he a day's sickness.

No. 1395 :: Ref. 1847-11-02, 3:1, D.

On Monday, the 18th ult., at Miltown, Ballymagorry, near Strabane, Mr. Benjamin Boyd, aged 51 years, after a few days' illness. Mr. Boyd is sincerely regretted by a numerous circle of relations and friends.

No. 1396 :: Ref. 1847-11-02, 3:1, D.

On the 22d ult., in the 45th year of her age, after a lingering illness which she bore with Christian fortitude and resignation, trusting in her Redeemer, Sarah, the beloved wife of Mr. Wm. Rosborough, of Lisbuney.

No. 1397 :: Ref. 1847-11-02, 3:1, D.

On Monday, the 25th ult., of malignant fever, Jane, relict of the late John Creighton, Esq., of Castlemunay, near Dunkaneely, county Donegal. The mortality in this family has been remarkable severe, two of her sisters, a son, and herself having all paid the debt of nature within the last three weeks.

No. 1398 :: Ref. 1847-11-02, 3:1, D.

In Great James Street, Derry, on the 28th ult., of scarletina, Robert, the beloved and only son of John Keys, Esq.

No. 1399 :: Ref. 1847-11-02, 3:1, D.

On the 12th ult., Mrs. Macartney, relict of the late Francis Macartney, Esq., and mother of Thomas Macartney, Esq., of Drumcrew House, Lisnaskea.

No. 1400 :: Ref. 1847-11-02, 3:1, D.

On the 23d ult., at Berney Glebe, Strabane, after a long and painful illness, Cecilia Ann, eldest daughter of the Rev. James Smith.

No. 1401 :: Ref. 1847-11-02, 3:1, D.

On the 18th ult., of typhus fever, Hugh Lyle, of Knockintern, in the county of Londonderry, Esq., aged 56 years.

No. 1402 :: Ref. 1847-11-09, 2:6, B.

On Wednesday, in Ballymacone, Mrs. Thomas M'Mahon, of a daughter.

No. 1403 :: Ref. 1847-11-09, 2:6, M.

On the 5th inst., in St. Mark's Church, Armagh, by the Rev. B. Wade, Color Sergeant W.H. Morton, 44th Regiment, to Elizabeth, eldest daughter of Mr. R. Wiggins.

No. 1404 :: Ref. 1847-11-09, 2:6, M.

On the 5th inst., in the first Presbyterian Church, Monaghan, by the Rev. John Bleackey, Mr. Robert Black, merchant, Dungannon, to Rachel, sixth daughter of Mr. Nathaniel Greacen, Printer, Armagh, formerly of Monaghan.

No. 1405 :: Ref. 1847-11-09, 2:6, M.

On the 1st instant, in Middletown Church, by the Rev. Robert Arthur Irwin, Mr. Robert Rolestone, of Blackwatertown, to Miss Fanny Connor, of Middletown.

No. 1406 :: Ref. 1847-11-09, 2:6, M.

By the Rev. David Watson, in the Presbyterian Meeting-house of Clough, on the 2d inst., Mr. John Ochiltree, Ballyward, Parish of Drumgooland, to Miss Bell, Castlewellan.

No. 1407 :: Ref. 1847-11-09, 2:6, M.

In Padztow Church, Cornwall, by the Rev. Mr. Tyke, Dr. John Carruthers, to Amelia, eldest daughter of Captain Clement, formerly of Derry.

No. 1408 :: Ref. 1847-11-09, 2:6, M.

On 28th ult., in Mullaghdun Church, Co. Fermanagh, by the Rev. Alex. Staples Clarke, Alexander Flood, Esq., Blacklion, Co. Cavan, Surgeon, to Rebecca, daughter of Robert Fawcett, Esq., Mullyare, county Fermanagh.

No. 1409 :: Ref. 1847-11-09, 2:6, M.

On the 28th ult., in Ansty Church, Leicestershire, by the Rev. Edward Gibson, William Bosworth, Esq., of Charely hall, Leicestershire, to Sophia, eldest daughter of the late Henry Nugent Bell, of Bellevue, County of Fermanagh, Esq.

No. 1410 :: Ref. 1847-11-09, 2:6, D.

The Rev. Bartholomew Campbell, R.C.C., Forkhill, County Armagh, after only a few days' illness, from fever.

No. 1411 :: Ref. 1847-11-09, 2:6, D.

In Thomas-street, Armagh, on the 3d inst., after a painful and protracted illness, Ellen, wife of Mr. Thomas Murray, bootmaker, aged 62 years.

No. 1412 :: Ref. 1847-11-09, 2:6, D.

October 21, in London, Bertha, wife of Michael M'Donald, Esq., and daughter of the late Richard Mitchell, Esq., of Monaghan.

No. 1413 :: Ref. 1847-11-09, 2:6, D.
Of lock-jaw, caused from the effects of an explosion of gunpowder while blasting, Mr. Francis M'Hugh, of Clonghore, near Castlederg, aged 35 years. Deceased has left a wife and four children.

No. 1414 :: Ref. 1847-11-09, 2:6, D.
At Montreal, after having reached the residence of their uncle, Samuel Matthewson, Esq., John James and Oliver, the eldest and third sons of Mr. Andrew Elder, of Roughan, in the Parish of Allsaints; the former of fever, on the 26th of July; and the latter of dysentery, on the 29th of September last. Both these young men left their native land with superior talents and high hopes, respected by a numerous circle of relatives and acquaintances, by whom their early fate will be long lamented.

No. 1415 :: Ref. 1847-11-16, 2:6, M.
On the 5th inst., in St. Mark's Church, Armagh, by the Rev. B. Wade, Color Sergeant W.H. Morton, 44th Regiment, to Elizabeth, eldest daughter of Mr. R. Wiggins.

No. 1416 :: Ref. 1847-11-16, 2:6, M.
On the 5th inst., at Birkenhead, Liverpool, William Barton, Esq., of Church-street, Dungannon, to Ann Jane, eldest daughter of P. Kirk, Esq., of same place.

No. 1417 :: Ref. 1847-11-16, 2:6, M.
On the 9th instant, at Middletown Presbyterian Church, by the Rev. Robert P. Borland, Mr. James Wilson, of Donaghmore, County Tyrone, to Ann Jane, youngest daughter of the late Mr. John Murdock, of Middletown.

No. 1418 :: Ref. 1847-11-16, 2:6, M.
On the 2d inst., by the District Registrar, Banbridge, Robert Halliday, Esq., to Mrs. Young, of Kate's-bridge. The bridegroom is in the seventieth year of his age.

No. 1419 :: Ref. 1847-11-16, 2:6, M.
At Bangor, on Thursday, the 11th inst., in the Second Presbyterian Church, by the brother of the bride, the Rev. W. Patteson, Mr. Matthew J. Alexander, of Londonderry, to Margaret, daughter of Mr. Matthew Patteson, Bangor, county Down.

No. 1420 :: Ref. 1847-11-16, 2:6, M.
November 3, in Cootehill Church, by the Rev. Charles Walsh, of Clones, St. John Purcell, Esq., of Sligo, to Louisa, youngest daughter of M. Walsh, Esq., M.D., of Cootehill.

No. 1421 :: Ref. 1847-11-16, 2:6, D.
At Carrick, on the 4th inst., at the house of Mr. Beatty, her son-in-law, Mrs. Breaden, relict of the late Mr. Edward Breaden, Head-Constable for Magherestaphena, Fermanagh.

No. 1422 :: Ref. 1847-11-16, 2:6, D.
November 1, in Bundoran, Miss Forde, sister of Captain Forde, of Ballyshannon.

No. 1423 :: Ref. 1847-11-23, 2:6, B.
On the 12th inst., the lady of Mr. John Allen, jun., Prospect Hill, Cookstown, of a son.

No. 1424 :: Ref. 1847-11-23, 2:6, B.
November 13, at Castletown House, county Tyrone, the lady of George Bestall, Esq., of a daughter.

No. 1425 :: Ref. 1847-11-23, 2:6, M.
November 13, at Monkstown Church, the Rev. Thomas Jebb, son of the late Hon. Judge Jebb, to Catherine Letitia, eldest daughter of the late Rev. James M'Creight, Rector of Keady, of this county.

No. 1426 :: Ref. 1847-11-23, 2:6, M.
On the 28th ult., at Peter's Church, Dublin, by the Rev. Mr. Burton, John H. Halliday, Esq., Surgeon, Belfast, second son of John Halliday, Esq., of Ballicassidy, county Fermanagh, to Sarah Eliza, third daughter of Abraham Briscoe, Esq., of Rathmines, Dublin.

No. 1427 :: Ref. 1847-11-23, 2:6, M.
November 5, at Clare Church, near Tandragee, by the Rev. James Wilson, John Stephenson, Esq., Tandragee, to Harriet, second daughter of the late Rev. Thomas Walsh, Rector of Tartaraghan, near Loughgall.

No. 1428 :: Ref. 1847-11-23, 2:6, M.
In Moneymore Church, on the 16th inst., by the Rev. Mr. Molony, Mr. Robt. Stanley, merchant, Lurgan, to Ann Eliza, eldest daughter of James Staunton, Esq., of Tullybuoy, county Derry.

No. 1429 :: Ref. 1847-11-23, 2:6, M.
On Wednesday, 21st April, in St. James Church, Sydney, by the Right Rev. the Lord Bishop of Australia, Samuel James Ussher, Esq., fifth son of the late Rev. Dr. Henry Ussher, of Ramelton, county Donegal, Ireland, to Margaret Lillias, youngest daughter of David Chambers, Esq., formerly of Magherafelt, in the county of Londonderry, Ireland, and now of Macquarrie Street, Sydney, New South Wales.

No. 1430 :: Ref. 1847-11-23, 2:6, D.
On the 17th inst., Mrs. Carson, of Belfast, mother of the Rev. John Carson, Templepatrick, in the 86th year of her age.

No. 1431 :: Ref. 1847-11-30, 2:6, B.
At Park View, Tandragee, on Sunday last, the lady of the Rev. George Robinson, of a daughter.

No. 1432 :: Ref. 1847-11-30, 2:6, B.
On the 21st inst., at Sandford Grove, the lady of Samuel Bewley, Esq., of a son.

No. 1433 :: Ref. 1847-11-30, 2:6, B.
Nov. 21, at Mountnorris, county Down, the lady of the Rev. Richard Verschoyle, of a daughter.

No. 1434 :: Ref. 1847-11-30, 2:6, B.
At Letterkenny, on the 20th inst., the lady of Henry M'Cay, Esq., LL.B., of a son.

No. 1435 :: Ref. 1847-11-30, 2:6, B.
On the 19th inst., at Letterkenny, Margaret, wife of Mr. Michael M'Cann, Excise Officer, of a daughter.

No. 1436 :: Ref. 1847-11-30, 2:6, B.
November 24, at Hazlewood, the Lady Anne Wynne, of a son.

No. 1437 :: Ref. 1847-11-30, 2:6, B.
November 21, at Cloncovie, county Cavan, the lady of the Reverend Thos. Fatherston, of a son.

No. 1438 :: Ref. 1847-11-30, 2:6, M.
On Tuesday, the 23d inst., in Benmore church, by the Rev. Hugh Hamilton, Rector of Innismacsaint, Mr. James Rankin, late of the Constabulary, to Mary Jane, eldest daughter of Mr. Francis Graham, of Sandhill-cottage, near Derrygonnelly, county Fermanagh.

No. 1439 :: Ref. 1847-11-30, 2:6, M.
November 17, in Bandon, the Rev. Anketell M. Henderson, Wesleyan Minister of Belfast to Mary, eldest daughter of Robert Edwards, Esq., of Bandon.

No. 1440 :: Ref. 1847-11-30, 2:6, M.
On the 16th inst., at Lower Longfield Church, by the Rev. Mr. Hamilton, Curate, Charles Caldwell, Esq., of Killen, county Tyrone, to Jane Caldwell, eldest daughter of the late Andrew Caldwell, Esq., of Lackaugh.

No. 1441 :: Ref. 1847-11-30, 2:6, M.
On the 18th inst., at Upper Chelsea, the Rev. Edward Mayne, of Lakeview, County of Monaghan, to Anna, relict of H.O. Smith, Esq., of the 42d Native Infantry, Madras Army, and grand-daughter of the late Warden Flood, Judge of the High Court of Admiralty.

No. 1442 :: Ref. 1847-11-30, 2:6, M.
Nov. 18, by the Rev. Mr. Burningham, Michael George Burke, Esq., eldest son of the Rev. Henry A. Burke, Rector of Magheracross, to Eliza, youngest daughter of Jas. Beatty, Esq., M.D., Enniskillen.

No. 1443 :: Ref. 1847-11-30, 2:6, D.
On the 8th inst., at Omagh, in the 104th year of her age, Isabella Johnston, mother to Mr. Hugh Johnston, late of Omagh, merchant, and now of St. Clair, province of Canada, North America. Her end was peace.

No. 1444 :: Ref. 1847-11-30, 2:6, D.
November 21, in Waterford, of typhus fever, William, second son of the Rev. C. Hardcastle, Baptist Minister, of that city.

No. 1445 :: Ref. 1847-11-30, 2:6, D.
On the 24th inst., at Mullaghbawn, near Blacklion, at the house of his son-in-law, Thomas Elliot, Esq., at an advanced age, Mr. M'Donald.

No. 1446 :: Ref. 1847-11-30, 2:6, D.
Oct. 9, of fever, at Port Antonio, in Jamaica, aged twenty-nine years, Chas. John, the second son of David Gaussen, Esq., Lakeview House, county of Londonderry.

No. 1447 :: Ref. 1847-11-30, 2:6, D.
At her residence, Drumlogher, on Thursday, the 25th inst., Mary, relict of the late Mr. John Glen, at the advanced age of 83 years.

No. 1448 :: Ref. 1847-11-30, 2:6, D.
On the 16th inst., at St. Helier's, Jersey, in the 14th year of his age, after a short but severe illness, George, second son of the late Sir Geo. Hill, Bart., of St. Columb's, Londonderry.

No. 1449 :: Ref. 1847-11-30, 2:6, D.
Nov. 17, Humphrey Bevan, son of Humphrey Semple, Esq., of Dunmore Cottage.

No. 1450 :: Ref. 1847-11-30, 2:6, D.
Nov. 22, at Chichester-street, Belfast, the Rev. John Davison, Presbyterian Minister of Cookstown, county Tyrone, in the seventy-ninth year of his age and fiftieth of his Ministry.

No. 1451 :: Ref. 1847-12-07, 3:1, B.
At Ballyshannon, on Wednesday last, the lady of the late Henry Lipsett, Esq., of a son.

No. 1452 :: Ref. 1847-12-07, 3:1, M.
On the 1st inst., by the Rev. Alexander Fleming, in the First Presbyterian Church, Armagh, the Rev. Robert P. Borland, Presbyterian minister of Lislooney, to Mary Jane, daughter of the late Thomas Wynne, Esq., of Lislea house, Armagh.

No. 1453 :: Ref. 1847-12-07, 3:1, M.
On Wednesday 1st inst., by the Rev. J. Keatinge, P.P., Mr. Patrick Mallin, of Killyquin, to Margaret, second daughter of the late Mr. James Hughes, Builder, Charlemont.

No. 1454 :: Ref. 1847-12-07, 3:1, M.
On the 23rd ult., in Glenfin Church, parish of Kelteevack, by the Rev. Thos. Ramsey, Mr. Robert Donaldson of Caldwell view cottage, county Fermanagh, to Elizabeth, second daughter of Alexander Donaldson of Welshtown cottage, county Fermanagh.

No. 1455 :: Ref. 1847-12-07, 3:1, M.

At Gretnagreen, on the 11th of November, and subsequently at the Cathedral, Manchester, on the 27th, by the Rev. Mr. Wilson, George Alcock Nixon, Esq., M.D., Enniskillen, to Frances Willoughby, eldest daughter of the late Sir Thomas and Lady Yates. The happy couple are at present sojourning in Dublin.

No. 1456 :: Ref. 1847-12-07, 3:1, D.

At her residence in this city, on Tuesday, November 30, Martha, eldest surviving daughter of the late Robert Poolar, Esq., of Tyross, county Armagh.

No. 1457 :: Ref. 1847-12-07, 3:1, D.

On the 26th November, in the 88th year of her age, at the residence of her son-in-law, Mr. Mathew Johnson, of Middletown, Martha Little, relict of the late Mr. Nicholas Little of Kiltubride.

No. 1458 :: Ref. 1847-12-07, 3:1, D.

At Mount Irwin, near Tynan, county Armagh, on the 30th ult., William Irwin, Esq., aged 78 years.

No. 1459 :: Ref. 1847-12-07, 3:1, D.

On 28th ult., at Artigarvon, near Strabane, Mr. Wm. Boyd.

No. 1460 :: Ref. 1847-12-07, 3:1, D.

On the 29th of September, at the residency, Hyderabad, East Indies, in the 33d year of his age, after a protracted illness, of abscess on the liver, Dr. Wm. Morehead, late Assistant-Surgeon, 37th Grenadiers, and formerly of Dungannon, County Tyrone, Ireland.

No. 1461 :: Ref. 1847-12-07, 3:1, D.

On the 26th ult., aged thirty-one years, Mr. John Hill, of Lambeg, engineer to Messrs. Richardson & Co. Mr. Hill was a young man of remarkably fine abilities.

No. 1462 :: Ref. 1847-12-07, 3:1, D.

At Omagh, on Monday, the 8th of November, at the advanced age of 104 years, Mrs. Isabella Johnston. Her end was peace.

No. 1463 :: Ref. 1847-12-07, 3:1, D.

In Coleraine, on Sunday the 21st ult., aged 27, of disease of the heart, Marianne, daughter of the late Rev. John Remington, Wesleyan Minister.

No. 1464 :: Ref. 1847-12-07, 3:1, D.

At his residence, in Bishop-street without, on Saturday, the 27th ult., after a brief illness, Mr. William Hamerton, aged 38 years. He filled the situation of a confidential clerk in the Londonderry Branch of the Bank of Ireland for sixteen years.

No. 1465 :: Ref. 1847-12-14, 3:1, M.

At Holbeach, Lincolnshire, England, on the 8th inst., by the Rev. J. Morton, B.D. Vicar, Thomas A. Prentice, Esq., of Armagh, to Mary, daughter of J. Johnton, Esq., of the former place.

No. 1466 :: Ref. 1847-12-14, 3:1, M.

December 7, in the church of Lisnaskea, by the Rev. Archibald Crawford, Incumbent of Trinity Church, Crom, and Chaplain to the Right Hon. the Earl of Erne, the Rev. John Flanagan, Perpetual Curate of Lisnaskea, to Sarah, second daughter of the late Robert Moorhead, Esq., of Carnalay, in the county of Tyrone.

No. 1467 :: Ref. 1847-12-14, 3:1, M.

In Clones Church, on the 6th inst., by the Rev. Charles Walsh, Mr. Francis Gee, constable of the Drum station of Police, county Monaghan, to Catherine Anne, youngest daughter of Mr. James Porter, boot and shoe maker, late of Drum, and now of No. 81 Adelaide-street, Toronto, U.C. America.

No. 1468 :: Ref. 1847-12-21, 3:1, B.

December 12, at the Rectory, Bailieborough, the lady of the Rev. Charles Beresford, of a daughter.

No. 1469 :: Ref. 1847-12-21, 3:1, M.

At Aughadrum, on the 25th ult., by the Rev. Mr. Kerr, Catherine, only daughter of Patrick Gartland, Esq., merchant, Augher, to Mr. Owen M'Anally, brother to the Right Rev. Dr. M'Anally, Roman Catholic Bishop of Clogher.

No. 1470 :: Ref. 1847-12-21, 3:1, M.

On the 25th ult., Mary, daughter of the late Mr. Thomas M'Lean, to Mr. Thomas Dale, Augher.

No. 1471 :: Ref. 1847-12-21, 3:1, M.

On the 14th instant, in the First Presbyterian Church, Stranorlar, by the Rev. James Steele, Mr. John Barr, Admirand, to Eliza, daughter of Mr. G. Griffith, Doolish.

No. 1472 :: Ref. 1847-12-21, 3:1, M.

In Castledawson Presbyterian Church, by the Rev. John Radcliffe, Mr. Hugh Miller, Greenhill, to Miss Martha Brown, Magherafelt.

No. 1473 :: Ref. 1847-12-21, 3:1, M.

December 16, at St. Peter's Church, Dublin, by the Rev. Cadwallader Wolseley, the Rev. Capel Wolseley, of Seagoe, county of Armagh, to Ann Jane, daughter of the late Nathaniel Proctor, of Carlow, Esq.

No. 1474 :: Ref. 1847-12-21, 3:1, M.

At the Scots church, Enniskillen, on the 14th instant, by the Rev. A.C. Maclatchey, Mr. William White, Veterinary Surgeon, Enniskillen, to Mary Jane, only daughter of the late John Baird, Esq., Strabane.

No. 1475 :: Ref. 1847-12-21, 3:1, M.

On the 7th instant, in Bovea Meeting-house, by the Rev. Mr. M'Gill, register of marriages, Mr. John Wilson, Derrylane, near Dungiven, to Miss Sarah Smyth, Mulkereagh. The united ages of the happy couple was about 130 years.

No. 1476 :: Ref. 1847-12-21, 3:1, M.

December 7, at St. George's Church, Newcastle, Staffordshire, by the Rev. Samuel Minton, Henry Graves, of Cookstown, in the county of Tyrone, M.D., youngest son of the late Captain Thomas Graves, R.N., to Mary Lee, the only child of the late Charles Dyer, Esq., of Wotton-under-Edge, in the county of Gloucester.

No. 1477 :: Ref. 1847-12-21, 3:1, M.

Mr. George Rutledge, of Ennis, to Rebecca, daughter of Henry Leech, Esq., of Sligo.

No. 1478 :: Ref. 1847-12-21, 3:1, M.

Dec. 14, at the parish church of Raymochey, Manorcunningham, by the Rev. W.A. Butler, A.M., Mr. D. M'Donald, to Miss Elizabeth Donnell.

No. 1479 :: Ref. 1847-12-21, 3:1, M.

December 9, at Drumsnatt Church, county of Monaghan, by the Rev. W.H.E. Woodwright, Ralph Dudgeon, Esq., Lieutenant, 76th Regiment, son of the late Captain Dudgeon, of Rosefield, county of Monaghan, to Martha Caroline, second daughter of John Johnson, Esq., of Thornhill.

No. 1480 :: Ref. 1847-12-21, 3:1, M.

On the 14th inst., in St. John's Church, Moira, by the Rev. W.H. Wynne, Rector, Mr. C. Scarlett, Constable, Rathfriland, to Mary, youngest daughter of Mr. Jonathan Rowe, Moira.

No. 1481 :: Ref. 1847-12-21, 3:1, D.

On the 16th inst., in this city, of fever, Leonard, third son of Dr. Robinson of the Infirmary, aged 15 years and 10 months.

No. 1482 :: Ref. 1847-12-21, 3:1, D.

At Fenagh Glebe, Leitrim, Bessie, the beloved wife of the Rev. G.D. Beresford.

No. 1483 :: Ref. 1847-12-21, 3:1, D.

Of fever, on Saturday, Mr. John Call, Master of the Armagh Union Workhouse.

No. 1484 :: Ref. 1847-12-21, 3:1, D.

In Edinburgh, on the 19th ult., Mr. James Morgan, son of the late Jas. Morgan, of Annaclare, near this city, in the 21st year of his age. Mr. Morgan, who early intended to devote himself to the work of the ministry, had completed his second session in the University of Glasgow, and just entered on his theological studies in the Edinburgh Original Secession Hall, where he was taken away in the commencement of his career, and hurried to an early grave. He was a young man who possessed a most amiable and benevolent disposition, an eminent zeal for God and His glory, and a truly pious and religious character. He was much beloved by his fellow-students, and is deeply lamented by a numerous circle of friends.

No. 1485 :: Ref. 1847-12-21, 3:1, D.

On Thursday, 9th instant, at Ballyholly, near Raphoe, aged 32 years, Martha, youngest daughter of Mr. Thomas Blair. Her latter end was peace.

No. 1486 :: Ref. 1847-12-21, 3:1, D.

On the 10th instant, aged 63, Mr. James Foulis, for upwards of 30 years a compositor in the office of the *Belfast Chronicle*.

No. 1487 :: Ref. 1847-12-21, 3:1, D.

At Strabane, on the 11th ult., Mr. Francis O'Brien, aged 70, for upwards of half a century one of the most efficient and successful teachers of youth in this part of Ireland.

No. 1488 :: Ref. 1847-12-21, 3:1, D.

At Valparaiso, South America, on the 7th day of August last, Mr. Wm. John Fenton, son of Mr. Wm. Fenton, Governor of Lifford gaol, aged 29 years.

No. 1489 :: Ref. 1847-12-21, 3:1, D.

At Fivemiletown, on the 27th ultimo, of inflammation in the bowels, Mr. James Stewart of Mullaghmen, much regretted by a large circle of friends.

No. 1490 :: Ref. 1847-12-21, 3:1, D.

On Tuesday last, the infant son of the late Henry Lipsett, Esq., Ballyshannon, aged 8 days.

No. 1491 :: Ref. 1847-12-21, 3:1, D.

December 6, in St. Anne's Cottage, Ventnor, Isle of Wight, George Greer, Esq., Barrister, son of George Greer, Esq., J.P., county Armagh.

No. 1492 :: Ref. 1847-12-28, 3:3, M.

On the 17th inst., in Armaghbreague Church, by the Rev. D. Donaldson, A.M., Incumbent, Mr. Joseph Jenkins, of Peat Hill, to Miss Margaret Duggan, of Muckna, Castleblaney.

No. 1493 :: Ref. 1847-12-28, 3:3, M.

December 23, at Sallaghy Church, county Fermanagh, by the Rev. William Bredin (uncle to the bride), James Mackey, Esq., of this city, to Mary Anne, only daughter of the late William Brittain, Esq., of Bath.

No. 1494 :: Ref. 1847-12-28, 3:3, D.

On Sunday night last, at Melbourne Terrace, James Trueman Bell, Esq., jun., aged 44 years. The deceased was a gentleman universally respected by all who knew him, especially his fellow-citizens by whom he is sincerely and deservedly regretted.

No. 1495 :: Ref. 1847-12-28, 3:3, D.
On the 13th inst., Deborah, eldest daughter of the late John Kinkead, Esq., of Vallenbrook, Newtownhamilton.

No. 1496 :: Ref. 1847-12-28, 3:3, D.
At Culcairn, near Benburb, on the 22d instant, at the advanced age of 86 years, Isabella, relict of the late Moses Wilson, Esq., of same place, and sister of the late Sir Isaac Wilson, Knight, Surgeon in Ordinary to his Royal Highness, the late Duke of Sussex.

No. 1497 :: Ref. 1847-12-28, 3:3, D.
At Fairlawn, near Moy, on the 18th instant, after a short illness, Mr. John Sinclair, aged 37 years.

No. 1498 :: Ref. 1847-12-28, 3:3, D.
At Rosslen, county Fermanagh, on the 11th instant, in the prime of life, Mr. William Temmins, much and deservedly regretted by all who had the pleasure of his acquaintance.

No. 1499 :: Ref. 1847-12-28, 3:3, D.
December 19, at Tonbridge Wells, the Hon. Charles Godfrey Wolff, Baron and Knight Banneret of the late Holy Roman Empire, in the 98th year of his age.

No. 1500 :: Ref. 1847-12-28, 3:3, D.
December 22, at Melbourne Terrace, Armagh, in the 8th year of her age, Lucinda, the beloved child of James T. Bell, jun., Esq.

No. 1501 :: Ref. 1847-12-28, 3:3, D.
On the 22d instant, at her residence, Blessington-street, Dublin, at an advanced age, Lucy Townley Moore, daughter of Ross Moore, Esq., late of Carlingford.

No. 1502 :: Ref. 1848-01-03, 3:5, B.
December 30, on Vicar's Hill, Armagh, Mrs. G. Allen, of a son.

No. 1503 :: Ref. 1848-01-03, 3:5, B.
On the 26th inst., at Tamnamore House, the lady of Richard Lloyd, Esq., high sheriff, county Tyrone, of a son.

No. 1504 :: Ref. 1848-01-03, 3:5, M.
December 27, in Charlemont District Church, by the Rev. J. Disney, Mr. Robert Bewglass, of London and Killyman, county Tyrone, to Anne, seventh daughter of Robt. Corrigan, Esq., of Moss-spring, Charlemont, county Armagh.

No. 1505 :: Ref. 1848-01-03, 3:5, M.
On the 30th ult., in the Second Presbyterian Church, Armagh, by the Rev. Samuel Oliver Edgar, Mr. John Jamison of Ballymurrin, to Eliza, daughter of Mr. Ferguson of Killowen, both near this city.

No. 1506 :: Ref. 1848-01-03, 3:5, M.
On 27th ult., in Stewardstown, at the house of his father, by the Rev. Mooney, C.C., James, eldest son of Mr. Samuel Park, to Miss Mary Anne Collins, niece of Mr. James Corr, both of Stewardstown.

No. 1507 :: Ref. 1848-01-03, 3:5, M.
On the 22nd ult., in Monaghan, John Highland, Esq., Newcastle, to Anne Jane, daughter of the late Wm. Smith, Esq., of Orchard Vale, Monaghan.

No. 1508 :: Ref. 1848-01-03, 3:5, M.
At Ballinamallard, on the 28th ult, by the Rev. Mr. Burke, Ann, eldest daughter of Mr. Christopher Irvine of Cavan, to Mr. David Armstrong of Ballinamallard.

No. 1509 :: Ref. 1848-01-03, 3:5, M.
On the 21st ult., in the Cathedral, Derry, by the Rev. Geo. Smith, Mr. Thomas Duncan, Provision Merchant, Paisley, to Martha, only daughter of Mr. Alexander Bell, of Derry.

No. 1510 :: Ref. 1848-01-03, 3:5, M.
On the 30th ult., in the Parish Church, Newtownlimavady, by the Rev. John Olphert, Valentine Frederick Storey, Captain in her Majesty's 38th Regiment of Foot, to Williamina, youngest daughter of the late Wm. Moody, Esq., of Roe-house, county Londonderry.

No. 1511 :: Ref. 1848-01-03, 3:5, D.
On the 21st ult., at Drummond, near Keady, Co. Armagh, Anne, relict of the late Mr. James M'Crea, aged 75.

No. 1512 :: Ref. 1848-01-03, 3:5, D.
Of typhus fever, on the 19th ult., at Glasgow College, where studying for his degree, Moore Andrew Swan, M.R.C.S.I., aged 21 years, third son of Dr. Swan, Cottage, Donegal. Possessed of a clear intellect, and great firmness of character, he acquired a knowledge of his profession seldom attained at his age. His manner was unassuming; his disposition gentle and mild as a child's; through life his conduct was exemplary, and in death his hopes were fixed on Christ alone for salvation.

No. 1513 :: Ref. 1848-01-03, 3:5, D.
On Christmas night, at the residence of her son, Mr. Richard Hamilton, of Raphoe, Mrs. Maria Hamilton, aged 70 years.

No. 1514 :: Ref. 1848-01-03, 3:5, D.
In Dublin-street, Enniskillen, on the 27th ult., ult., [sic] at the residence of her son-in-law, Mr. Robert Frith, surveyor, Sarah, relict of the late Mr. William Gibson of Swanlinbar, in the 85th year of her age.

No. 1515 :: Ref. 1848-01-03, 3:5, D.
In Ballintra, on the 29th ult., at an advanced age, Mr. Finlay Green.

No. 1516 :: Ref. 1848-01-03, 3:5, D.
At her residence, Merrion-Square, Dublin, on the 24th ult., Lady Catherine, wife of the late Rev. Francis Brownlow.

No. 1517 :: Ref. 1848-01-03, 3:5, D.
On the 22d ult., aged 75 years, Mary, relict of David Finlay, Esq., of Sugarloaf, county Cavan.

No. 1518 :: Ref. 1848-01-03, 3:5, D.
On the 21st ult., at his residence in Douglas, Isle of Man, in the 56th year of his age, Edward Smith Graham, Esq., M.D., late surgeon of 4th Light Dragoons, and third son of Mr. John Graham, formerly of Enniskillen.

No. 1519 :: Ref. 1848-01-10, 2:5, M.
On the 28th ult., at the Scots Church, Gloucester-street, Dublin, by the Rev. William Wilson, James Steen, second son of the Rev. Thomas Millar, of Cookstown, county Tyrone, to Agnes Dawson, second daughter of John Hamilton Reed, Esq., Clonliffe Parade, Dublin.

No. 1520 :: Ref. 1848-01-10, 2:5, M.
At Castle Archdall church, county Fermanagh, 30th December last, by the Rev. George W. Walshe, Mr. Robert Anderson, Brackagh, to Sarah Anne, eldest daughter of Mr. William Graham, Drumall.

No. 1521 :: Ref. 1848-01-10, 2:5, M.
On the 6th inst., at Lisnaskea, by the Rev. John Flanagan, Philip Armstrong, Esq., of Capy, near Enniskillen, to Anne, eldest daughter of James Moore, Esq., of Drumbad, Lisnaskea.

No. 1522 :: Ref. 1848-01-10, 2:5, D.
On the 7th inst., in Scotch-st., Armagh, of inflammation of the bowels, Mr. James Henry, Cabinet-maker, aged 30 years, sincerely and deservedly regretted.

No. 1523 :: Ref. 1848-01-10, 2:5, D.
At his father's residence at Stiloga, near Benburb, on the morning of Tuesday, the 26th ult., after a short illness, John, only son of Mr. Andrew Anderson, aged 34 years.

No. 1524 :: Ref. 1848-01-10, 2.5, D.
At his residence in Fintona, on Saturday, the 1st instant of fever, Andrew Allen Esq.

No. 1525 :: Ref. 1848-01-10, 2:5, D.
At Bellaghy Castle, the residence of his only son John Hill, Esq., on Thursday, the 30th Dec. last, Major John Hill at a very advanced age.

No. 1526 :: Ref. 1848-01-10, 2:5, D.
On 23d December, at Commons, Manorhamilton, Lieutenant P. Armstrong.

No. 1527 :: Ref. 1848-01-10, 2:5, D.
On the 30th December, Mrs. Colhoun, aged 76, relict of the late William Colhoun, Esq., of Green Cottage, Manorcunningham.

No. 1528 :: Ref. 1848-01-17, 3:2, B.
January 2, at the Brewery-house, Bandon, the residence of her mother-in-law, the lady of the Rev. Henry Gillman, of twin sons.

No. 1529 :: Ref. 1848-01-17, 3:2, M.
At Perth, on the 28th Dec., by the Rev. Robert H. Carson, brother to the bride, John Graham, jun., Esq., of Magherafelt, to Charlotte, seventh daughter of the late Rev. Alexander Carson, L.L.D., Tubbermore.

No. 1530 :: Ref. 1848-01-17, 3:2, M.
On the 11th inst., in the Parish Church of Stranorlar, by the Rev. Thomas Fullerton, Mr. William Wisely, eldest son of Mr. John Wisely, Stranorlar, to Jane, only daughter and heiress of Andrew Lepper, Esq., Dunwilley, county Donegal.

No. 1531 :: Ref. 1848-01-17, 3:2, M.
Jan. 12, in St. Thomas's Church, by the Rev. William James Mulloy, M.A., T.C.D., John Thomas Rossborough, Esq., eldest son of the late John Rossborough, Esq., of Mullmagoan House, county Fermanagh, and of Cloncaulfield House, county of Longford, to Mary Grey Wentworth, only surviving child of the late Chief Justice Caesar Colclough, of Duffry Hall, county of Wexford, and next of kin to the late Caesar Colclough, Esq., M.P., of Tintern Abbey, county of Wexford.

No. 1532 :: Ref. 1848-01-17, 3:2, D.
January 11, at her son's residence, Armagh, Matilda, relict of the late James Mulligan, Esq., of Newry.

No. 1533 :: Ref. 1848-01-17, 3:2, D.
On the 3d instant, at Kilmacrie, near Markethill, Mr. Hugh Martin, aged 73 years.

No. 1534 :: Ref. 1848-01-17, 3:2, D.
In Derry, after a lingering illness, aged 19 years, Alexander, forth [sic] son of Mr. James Wilson, of that city.

No. 1535 :: Ref. 1848-01-17, 3:2, D.
At the Lodge, Nn-Limavady, on the 12th inst., of influenza, Robert Conn, Esq., aged 88 years.

No. 1536 :: Ref. 1848-01-17, 3:2, D.
On the 3d inst., at Gortindoragh, near Castlederg, in the 68th year of his age, Mr. Charles Johnston. His illness, a decline of six years' continuance, was borne by him with that calm and holy resignation which a hope of the gospel ever inspires.

No. 1537 :: Ref. 1848-01-17, 3:2, D.
At Stewartstown, on the 9th inst., Henry Mason, Esq., M.D.

No. 1538 :: Ref. 1848-01-17, 3:2, D.
At Cookstown, on the 29th ult., in the 50th year of her age, Margaret, the beloved wife of Mr. John M'Geagh, merchant.

No. 1539 :: Ref. 1848-01-17, 3:2, D.
At the Moor, Donegal, on the 1st inst., Sophia, eldest daughter of the Rev. William Ewing.

No. 1540 :: Ref. 1848-01-17, 3:2, D.
On the 12th inst, at his seat, Woodhill, near Ardara, county of Donegal, Richard Nesbitt, Esq., D.L.

No. 1541 :: Ref. 1848-01-17, 3:2, D.
On Tuesday morning last, at Kinlough House, James Johnston, Esq., Deputy Lieutenant of the county Leitrim, and lately a captain in the 6th carbineers.

No. 1542 :: Ref. 1848-01-17, 3:2, D.
January 11, at her house, 33, North Frederick-street, at the advanced age of ninety years, from suffocation, in consequence of the bed-clothes accidentally taking fire, Alicia, second daughter of the late John Reynell, Esq., of Castle Reynell, county of Westmeath, and aunt to the Countess of Donoughmore.

No. 1543 :: Ref. 1848-01-24, 3:2, M.
On the 21st, in St. Mark's Church, Armagh, by the Rev. B. Wade, Margaret, only daughter of Wm. Barnes, Esq., of Armagh, to Alexander Thomson, Esq., of Gilford, county Down.

No. 1544 :: Ref. 1848-01-24, 3:2, M.
On the 10th instant, by the Rev. H.J. Cavanagh, Eliza, eldest daughter of Mr. S. Drew, Shop-street, Drogheda, to Patrick Marron, Esq., Editor of *The Drogheda Argus*.

No. 1545 :: Ref. 1848-01-24, 3:2, D.
On the 14th inst., at Mount Pleasant, near Clogher, in the 24th year of his age, Wm. Todd, Surgeon, eldest son of the late John Todd, Esq.

No. 1546 :: Ref. 1848-01-24, 3:2, D.
On the 17th inst., at the residence of her niece, Mrs. Harris, Enniskillen, at a very advanced age, Rebecca, relict of the late Rev. Hugh Nevin, D.D., Rector of Derryvoland.

No. 1547 :: Ref. 1848-01-24, 3:2, D.
On the 20th inst., at his residence, Scotchmount, Malone, Mr. Thos. Kennedy, aged 76 years.

No. 1548 :: Ref. 1848-01-24, 3:2, D.
On the 15th inst., in Cadogan-place, London, Elizabeth, wife of Lieutenant-Colonel Verner, and only sister of the Dowager Marchioness of Donegal.

No. 1549 :: Ref. 1848-01-24, 3:2, D.
On Monday the 17th inst., at Dungannon, Mrs. Donaldson, in the 85th year of her age.

No. 1550 :: Ref. 1848-01-24, 3:2, D.
On the 22d inst., in Ogle-street, Mr. Wm. Loughran, aged 41 years.

No. 1551 :: Ref. 1848-01-31, 2:2, B.
January 24, at Glenaghy, near Portadown, the lady of the Rev. Simon Foot, of a son.

No. 1552 :: Ref. 1848-01-31, 2:2, B.
At Cookstown, Mrs. T.A. Vesey, of a son.

No. 1553 :: Ref. 1848-01-31, 2:2, B.
January 23, at Bellamount Forest, Cootehill, the lady of Richard Coote, Esq., of a son.

No. 1554 :: Ref. 1848-01-31, 2:2, M.
In St. Mark's Church, Armagh, on the 27th instant, by the Rev. B. Wade, Mr. William M'Farland, of Cootehill, to Esse Anne, second daughter of Mr. John Douglas, Merchant Tailor, Scotch-street, Armagh.

No. 1555 :: Ref. 1848-01-31, 2:2, M.
On the 25th inst., by the Rev. John Wilson, Joseph Patton, Esq., Trinity College, Dublin, to Anne Alicia, youngest daughter of Alexander Hopkins, Esq., Newtownlimavady.

No. 1556 :: Ref. 1848-01-31, 2:2, M.
At Cullybackey, by the Rev. Hugh Hamilton, Mr. James Getty, Inn-keeper, Mill-street, Ballymena, to Miss Anne Gordon, of Markstown, near Cullybackey.

No. 1557 :: Ref. 1848-01-31, 2:2, M.
On the 26th inst., by the Rev. H. Nugent, C.C., at the residence of the bride's father, Butcher's-street, Derry, Mr. John Galagher, of the firm of Wm. M'Arthur & Co., to Anna, eldest daughter of Mr. M'Lean, merchant.

No. 1558 :: Ref. 1848-01-31, 2:2, D.
On the 14th inst., Mr. James Welsh, Head Miller of the Middletown Mills, of fever, deservedly regretted.

No. 1559 :: Ref. 1848-01-31, 2:2, D.
January 21, at Fintona, aged 26 years, Alexander Eccles, the beloved son of James Buchanan, Esq.

No. 1560 :: Ref. 1848-01-31, 2:2, D.
On Saturday, the 22d inst., of inflammation in the chest, Jane, eldest daughter of Mr. Wm. Kinahan, merchant, Portadown.

No. 1561 :: Ref. 1848-01-31, 2:2, D.
On the 24th inst., at Gardiner's-place, Dublin, Mary, wife of Leonard Dobbin, Esq., and daughter of the Rev. Dr. Miller. Her remains were interred in the Cathedral burying ground of this city, on Friday last.

No. 1562 :: Ref. 1848-01-31, 2:2, D.
On the 19th inst., at the residence of his son-in-law, Wm. Hall, Esq., in the ninety-second year of his age, Hugh Montgomery, Esq., late of Derryscobe, Fermanagh.

No. 1563 :: Ref. 1848-01-31, 2:2, D.
At Lowtherstown, on the 20th instant, in the 70th year of her age, Mrs. Sturdy, relict of the late Mr. Oswald Sturdy, also of that town.

No. 1564 :: Ref. 1848-01-31, 2:2, D.
At the residence of his father, 27, North Cumberland-street, Dublin, on Tuesday last, the 18th instant, the Rev. George Deery, Wesleyan Minister.

No. 1565 :: Ref. 1848-01-31, 2:2, D.
At Carthage-House, Culdaff, county Donegal, the Rev. James Knox, at the advanced age of ninety-two years and nine months.

No. 1566 :: Ref. 1848-02-07, 3:6, B.
On the morning of the 27th ult., in London, the lady of Jas. Bryden, Esq., of a son.

No. 1567 :: Ref. 1848-02-07, 3:6, B.
January 27, at Greek-street, Soho-square, London, (under chloroform), Mrs. Lewis C. Hertslet, of a son.

No. 1568 :: Ref. 1848-02-07, 3:6, M.
On the 25th ult., by the Rev. Oliver Leitch, Letterkenny, Mr. John Tease, Carrick, to Prudence, eldest daughter of Mr. James White, Calhame.

No. 1569 :: Ref. 1848-02-07, 3:6, M.
On Wednesday, the 25th ult., in Aughnacloy, by the Rev. Mr. O'Brien, Mr. Felix O'Dougherty, of Dromerin, to the gay Catherine Conly. The bridegroom is "*rising 82 again May*," and his happy consort "*plump and strapping in her teens*."

No. 1570 :: Ref. 1848-02-07, 3:6, D.
On the 1st inst., of decline, in her 43d year, Anne, wife of Mr. James Burns, Jeweller, of this city.

No. 1571 :: Ref. 1848-02-07, 3:6, D.
January 31, at Strand Hill, county Leitrim, James, only son of James Fawcitt, Esq., aged two years.

No. 1572 :: Ref. 1848-02-07, 3:6, D.
In Strabane, on the 28th ult., Martha, relict of the late Mr. James Cooke, sen., in the 71st year of her age.

No. 1573 :: Ref. 1848-02-07, 3:6, D.
On Saturday, 29th January, at her residence in William-street, Dublin, Mrs. Anne Hull, in the 85th year of her age.

No. 1574 :: Ref. 1848-02-07, 3:6, D.
Of brain fever, at Lowtherstown, on the 1st inst., Jas. Anderson, Esq., Solicitor.

No. 1575 :: Ref. 1848-02-07, 3:6, D.
On Friday, the 28th ult., at the advanced age of 74, at Bella-hill, near Brookborough, the residence of her son, Andrew Armstrong, Esq., Anne, relict of the late John Armstrong, Esq.

No. 1576 :: Ref. 1848-02-07, 3:6, D.
Jan. 25, at his house, in West Derby-street, Liverpool, Alexander M'Creery, Esq., late of Sligo, in the 99th year of his age.

No. 1577 :: Ref. 1848-02-07, 3:6, D.
Jan. 21, at Lackagh, county Donegal, at the residence of Alexander Porter, Esq., Miss Susan Maxwell, sister of the late Hamilton Maxwell, Esq., of Dublin, aged 81 years.

No. 1578 :: Ref. 1848-02-07, 3:6, D.
On the 31st ult., aged 27, Wm. Seney, eldest son of the late Mr. George Hinds, of Enniskillen.

No. 1579 :: Ref. 1848-02-07, 3:6, D.
At Clones, of influenza, on the 24th ult., in the 45th year of his age, Mr. John Burns.

No. 1580 :: Ref. 1848-02-07, 3:6, D.
Suddenly, on the 31st ult., in the 74th year of her age, Jane, wife of Mr. James Browne of Carnagh, near Keady.

No. 1581 :: Ref. 1848-02-07, 3:6, D.
On the 25 ult., at the house of her son-in-law, Mr. Wm. Lecky, Clontarf, Mrs. Rebecca Lecky, relict of the late Oliver Lecky, Esq., of Melmount, Strabane.

No. 1582 :: Ref. 1848-02-07, 3:6, D.
At Bellaghy, on Wednesday, the 2nd inst., at an advanced age, Mr. Pollock.

No. 1583 :: Ref. 1848-02-14, 3:2, M.
At Enniskillen Church, on the 9th inst., by the Rev. H.M. Bradshaw, Hugh Alexander Bradshaw, Esq., of the firm of Bradshaw and Co., Merchants, Donegal and Enniskillen, to Anne Eliza, eldest daughter of John Copeland, Esq., of Hollyhill, Enniskillen.

No. 1584 :: Ref. 1848-02-14, 3:2, M.
On the 3d inst., in Killult Church, John Hurst, Esq., Millmount, to Frances Brown, only daughter, to Mr. Samuel Brown, Crossroads, Donegal.

No. 1585 :: Ref. 1848-02-14, 3:2, D.
Feb. 4, at 61 Mary-street, Dublin, Eliza, the wife of Mr. Jas. Charles, Printer.

No. 1586 :: Ref. 1848-02-14, 3:2, D.
On Monday morning, Mrs. Mary Quinton, (Matron at the county infirmary) relict of the late Mr. Thomas Quinton, of Enniskillen, aged 73.

No. 1587 :: Ref. 1848-02-21, 2:6, B.
On Thursday, the 17th inst., at Madden Rectory, the lady of the Rev. Cosby Stopford Mangan, of a daughter.

No. 1588 :: Ref. 1848-02-21, 2:6, B.
On the 12th inst., at Omagh, the lady of Henry Thompson, M.D., Surgeon, to the Tyrone Infirmary, of a daughter.

No. 1589 :: Ref. 1848-02-21, 2:6, B.
February 13, at the Palace, Kilkenny, the lady of the Lord Bishop of Ossory, and Ferns, of a daughter.

No. 1590 :: Ref. 1848-02-21, 2:6, B.
February 9, at Cork, the lady of Assistant-Commissary General Bishop, of a son.

No. 1591 :: Ref. 1848-02-21, 2:6, M.
On the 8th inst., by the Rev. Matthew Wilson, Ramelton, Mr. David King, Moneygregin, near Newtowncunningham, to Sarah Jane, eldest daughter of Mr. William Patterson, Rubleshaney, near Milford.

No. 1592 :: Ref. 1848-02-21, 2:6, D.
On the 21st of November, at Salem, East Indies, Captain William Wallace Anderson, 25th Madras Infantry, and youngest surviving son of Drummond Anderson, Esq., Belfast, aged 30 years.

No. 1593 :: Ref. 1848-02-21, 2:6, D.
At Admirand, Stranorlar, on the 11th inst., aged 18, Wm. Barr, jun., a youth of most amiable disposition. This family, within the space of 23 months, have been thus obliged to mourn, though not without hope, the death of four excellent members, in the promising prime of life.

No. 1594 :: Ref. 1848-02-28, 3:7, B.
At Belfast, on the 22d inst., the lady of Assistant Commissary General Lister, of a son.

No. 1595 :: Ref. 1848-02-28, 3:7, B.
On the 19th inst., the wife of Robert Wilson, Esq., Benburb, of a daughter.

No. 1596 :: Ref. 1848-02-28, 3:7, B.
At Devonport, Mrs. Mason, of four children, making six in eleven months.

No. 1597 :: Ref. 1848-02-28, 3:7, M.
On the 24th inst., in St. Mark's Church, Armagh, by the Rev. B. Wade, Mary Jane Keys, to Walter Hyatt, Sergeant in the 3d regiment of foot.

No. 1598 :: Ref. 1848-02-28, 3:7, M.
On the 22d inst., at Meigh Church, by the Rev. Charles Seaver, Henry Ribton, Esq., of Newry, to Catherine, second daughter of the late Walter Clarke, Esq., of Egre Lougher, co. Armagh.

No. 1599 :: Ref. 1848-02-28, 3:7, M.
On the 16th inst., in Ballymacormac Church, Thomas A. M'Kee, Esq., of Castleblaney, to Jane Anne, only child of the late Rev. R. Price, of Killashee, county Longford.

No. 1600 :: Ref. 1848-02-28, 3:7, D.
On Saturday, the 26th inst., Margaret, wife of Mr. E. Gardner, of this city, and daughter of the late Rev. Dr. Nelson, of Downpatrick, sincerely and deservedly lamented by a large circle of friends and acquaintances.

No. 1601 :: Ref. 1848-02-28, 3:7, D.
On 26th inst., at Maghery, of influenza, in a few days' illness, Jas., infant son, of Mr. Robert Twinam, and grandson of Mr. Robert Crone, Lakeview, aged 7 months.

No. 1602 :: Ref. 1848-02-28, 3:7, D.
February 19, at Ray, near Manor-Cunningham, county Donegal, Mr. John Montgomery, sen., aged seventy-two years.

No. 1603 :: Ref. 1848-02-28, 3:7, D.
At Convoy, on the 19th inst., Mr. Thomas Warrell, aged 70 years.

No. 1604 :: Ref. 1848-02-28, 3:7, D.
At Strabane, on Monday, the 21st inst., at the house of Mr. John Anderson, Miss Catherine Orr, in the 102d year of her age.

No. 1605 :: Ref. 1848-02-28, 3:7, D.
February 21st, at his residence, Great James's-street, Michael Lipsett, Esq., late of Ballyshannon, aged 38 years.

No. 1606 :: Ref. 1848-02-28, 3:7, D.
On the 14th inst., Mary, second daughter of Mr. Alexander M'Cormick, Commercial Hotel, Derry.

No. 1607 :: Ref. 1848-03-06, 3:6, B.
Feb. 28, at Manston Parsonage, Leeds, the lady of the Rev. Hugh Staples Hamilton, of a son.

No. 1608 :: Ref. 1848-03-06, 3:6, B.
On 1st inst., at Rathfriland, the lady of James Ponsonby Hill, Esq., sub-inspector of constabulary, of a son.

No. 1609 :: Ref. 1848-03-06, 3:6, M.
In the second Presbyterian church, Strabane, on the 1st inst., by the Rev. W.A. Russell, Mr. James Cooke, merchant, to Lilly, youngest daughter of William Murdoch, Esq., of the excise.

No. 1610 :: Ref. 1848-03-06, 3:6, M.
On the 2nd March, Rev. John Foster Moore, A.M., of the Seceding Congregation, Garmany's Grove, Castleblaney, to Anne, eldest daughter, of John Vauce [Vance?], Esq., Gortalowry, Cookstown.

No. 1611 :: Ref. 1848-03-06, 3:6, M.
On the 2nd inst., by the Rev. Mr. O'Loughlin, C.C., Belfast, Ptk. M'Loughlin, Esq., surgeon, Portadown, to Maria, daughter of the late John Keegan, Esq., Ballyhagan, county Armagh.

No. 1612 :: Ref. 1848-03-06, 3:6, D.
Of Hydrocephalus, on the 3d inst., at Pettigo, James, son of Mr. Hugh Maguire, aged 13 years.

No. 1613 :: Ref. 1848-03-13, 3:5, B.
February 7, at Clones, Mrs. Robert Fausset, of a son.

No. 1614 :: Ref. 1848-03-13, 3:5, B.
On the 6th inst., at her father's residence, Waltersland, Stillorgan, the wife of the Rev. T.H. Ball, Curate of Mullabrack, of a son.

No. 1615 :: Ref. 1848-03-13, 3:5, B.
On the 6th instant, at the Palace, near Belfast, the wife of the Rev. Frederick Woods Mant, of a son.

No. 1616 :: Ref. 1848-03-13, 3:5, M.
On the 5th inst., by the Rev. P. Campbell, C.C., Crokstown [Cookstown?], Mr. Felix Keenan, of Ballycumlargy, Moneymore, to Maria Anne, eldest daughter of Chas. Quin, Ballymenagh, Cookstown.

No. 1617 :: Ref. 1848-03-13, 3:5, M.
On the 3d inst., at St. Mark's, Dublin, by the Rev. A. Franklin, a.m., Mr. William Clarke, Solicitor, of Dromore, county Down, to Anne, second daughter of Mr. Edward Bush, of Dublin.

No. 1618 :: Ref. 1848-03-13, 3:5, M.
At St. Anne's Church, Dublin, by the Rev. T.H. Ball, T.S. Galbraith, second son of the late R. Galbraith, of Cappard, Co. [G]alway, Esq., to Mary, daughter of the late Robert Smythe, of Dublin, Esq.

No. 1619 :: Ref. 1848-03-13, 3:5, M.
On the 3d inst., in the Wesleyan church, Frederick street, Belfast, by the Rev. Henry Price, Mr. Henry M. Ashe, merchant, Douglas, Isle of Man, to Martha Jane, daughter of the Rev. Matthew Langtree, Belfast.

No. 1620 :: Ref. 1848-03-13, 3:5, M.
March 2, at Holyrood Church, Southampton, by the Rev. Henry Neville, Joseph Temperant Potts, Esq., of Granite Lodge, county Dublin, to Mary, relict of the Rev. John Henry Potts, diocess of Armagh, and only daughter of the late Rev. John Beresford Hill, county Londonderry.

No. 1621 :: Ref. 1848-03-13, 3:5, M.
On the 4th instant, in the Scots' Church, Tralee, by the Rev. W. Chestnut, Mr. J.W. Yule, Milltown, to Eliza, daughter of the late John Williams, Esq., Callinafercy, county Kerry.

No. 1622 :: Ref. 1848-03-13, 3:5, D.
On the 7th instant, at Leslie-hill, Armagh, in the 29th year of his age, the Rev. Robert A. Irwin, youngest son of the late William Irwin, Esq., Mount Irwin.

No. 1623 :: Ref. 1848-03-13, 3:5, D.
On the 7th instant, at Ballymagirney, near Loughgall, Harriet, the beloved wife of Mr. John Orr, in the 21st year of her age.

No. 1624 :: Ref. 1848-03-13, 3:5, D.
On the 3d inst., at North Great George's-street, Hunt Walsh Chambe, of Hawthorn Hill, in the Co. of Armagh, Esq., in the 61st year of his age.

No. 1625 :: Ref. 1848-03-13, 3:5, D.
March 4, W.F. Carter, Esq., Arnol's Vale, Rostrevor, only son of the Dean of Tuam.

No. 1626 :: Ref. 1848-03-13, 3:5, D.
March 3, at Portsea, Mrs. Acheson, wife of Johnston Hamilton Acheson, Esq., surgeon, R.N.

No. 1627 :: Ref. 1848-03-13, 3:5, D.
On the 6th instant, at Lurgan, Georgiana, wife of John Hazlett, Esq., in the 31st year of her age.

No. 1628 :: Ref. 1848-03-13, 3:5, D.
On the 27th ult., at Lurgan, of apoplexy, Mr. John Cummins, aged 47 years.

No. 1629 :: Ref. 1848-03-20, 3:7, B.
On the 8th instant, at Omagh, the lady of James F. Alexander, Esq., Manager of the Provincial Bank of Ireland, of a son.

No. 1630 :: Ref. 1848-03-20, 3:7, B.
At Dublin, on the 13th instant, the lady of J.M. Greer, Esq., of a daughter.

No. 1631 :: Ref. 1848-03-20, 3:7, M.
On the 8th instant, in the Presbyterian Church of Myroe, by the Rev. Mr. Meharry, Mr. John Cunningham, to Miss Mary Bryson, of Boreva.

No. 1632 :: Ref. 1848-03-20, 3:7, M.
On the 2d instant, in the Presbyterian Church, at Dunfanaghy, by License, by the Rev. David Reid, M.A., Mr. John Wason, son of Mr. James Wason, of Dromore, near Letterkenny, to Miss Eliza Algeo, youngest daughter of the late Mr. Alexander Algeo, of Rashin, near Dunfanaghy.

No. 1633 :: Ref. 1848-03-20, 3:7, M.
On the 2d inst., Rev. John Foster Moore, M.A., of the Seceding Congregation, Germany's Grove, Castleblaney, to Anne, eldest daughter of John Vance, Esq., Gortalowry, Cookstown.

No. 1634 :: Ref. 1848-03-20, 3:7, M.
On the 3d instant, in Castlecaulfield Presbyterian Church, by the Rev. John H. Morell, of Ballybay, the Rev. Charles Lucas Morell, of Dungannon, to Anna, eldest daughter of Henry Brown, Esq., of Donaghmore.

No. 1635 :: Ref. 1848-03-20, 3:7, M.
In the Scots Church, Enniskillen, on the 9th inst., by the Rev. A.C. Maclatchy, Mr. S.I. Stewart, of Kilmelanafy, to Sarah, youngest daughter of Mr. H. Johnston, of Lisnedin, Dromore, county Tyrone.

No. 1636 :: Ref. 1848-03-20, 3:7, M.
On the 15th inst., in Ballinamallard Church by the Rev. Mr. Burke, David Lindsay, Esq., near Fintona, to Ellen, third daughter of Mr. James Johnston, Curren, near Enniskillen.

No. 1637 :: Ref. 1848-03-20, 3:7, D.
At her residence, Ballinahone House, near this city, on the 17th inst, at the advanced age of 71 years, Miss Letitia Lodge, eldest and last surviving daughter of the late Rev. William Lodge, LL.D., formerly Chancellor of the Cathedral of Armagh.

No. 1638 :: Ref. 1848-03-20, 3:7, D.
On Tuesday, the 14th inst., at her residence, Mill-street, Margaret, the wife of Mr. Felix Hughes, of this city. Her maternal affection made her an object of the sweetest love to her family circle—her truly kind and pious disposition commanded the veneration and respect of her numerous friends, all of whom were edified by her exemplary life, and her generous and untiring charity to the poor and destitute will be long and gratefully remembered. She closed her mortal career in the 73d year of her age, in the perfect possession of her mental faculties, and receiving all the consolations of her religion to which through life she was so devotedly attached. The numerous and respectable concourse, of all persuasions, who followed her remains to their resting place, bespoke alike respectful sympathy for the sorrowing relatives and a just tribute of esteem [to] the unobtrusive virtues of the deceased. Requiescant in pace.—*Communicated.*

No. 1639 :: Ref. 1848-03-20, 3:7, D.
At Cootehill, on the 18th inst., Henry Mitchell, Esq., late Lieutenant in the 8th Hussars.

No. 1640 :: Ref. 1848-03-20, 3:7, D.
At 39, William-street, Derry, on the 17th inst., in [the] 27th year of her age, Elizabeth Anne, only daughter of the late Lieut. George W.A. Charleton, of the Royal Artillery.

No. 1641 :: Ref. 1848-03-20, 3:7, D.
On the 7th inst., aged 70 years, Mr. Wm. Hannah, sen., of Warbleshinny, parish of Glendermott.

No. 1642 :: Ref. 1848-03-20, 3:7, D.
Of fever, at Arvagh, county Cavan, George Wiley, Esq., M.D., formerly of Derrygonnelly.

No. 1643 :: Ref. 1848-03-20, 3:7, D.
At Greenmount, county Tyrone, of Consumption, William Parker, of Miltate, near Lisbellaw, aged 27.

No. 1644 :: Ref. 1848-03-20, 3:7, D.
At Rossahilly, near Enniskillen, on Monday, 13th inst., at the advanced age of 110 years, Mr. Thomas Spratt. Up to the last two or three days of his long life, he enjoyed good health, and was even at that advanced age able to stump about his farm and stable.—About seven to ten years ago, he assisted to carry into Enniskillen, a sack of potatoes of 30 stones, off a cart, which had been purchased at market; and no youth could be surer in his step or harder in grip, than he was on that occasion.

No. 1645 :: Ref. 1848-03-20, 3:7, D.
On the 8th instant, at Greenmount, Omagh, Anna Charlotte, the eldest and beloved daughter of the Rev. Samuel G. Rogers.

No. 1646 :: Ref. 1848-03-20, 3:7, D.
Of fever, on the 14th inst., Sarah, the beloved wife of Mr. James Creighton, of Liscall, aged 29 years.

No. 1647 :: Ref. 1848-03-20, 3:7, D.
On the 8th inst., of typhus fever, caught in the discharge of his duty, Rev. Arthur Stevenson, Rector of Ardagh, diocese of Meath, second son of the late James Stevenson, of Fort William, county of Londonderry, Esq.

No. 1648 :: Ref. 1848-03-20, 3:7, D.
At Newtownlimavady, on the 10th inst., after a lingering and painful illness, Mr. John Millar, second son of the late Mr. Charles Millar.

No. 1649 :: Ref. 1848-03-27, 3:6, B.
March 15, in Armagh, the lady of the Rev. R. Quin, of twins—of a son and daughter.

No. 1650 :: Ref. 1848-03-27, 3:6, B.
At Nn-Limavady, on the 12th inst., Mrs. Hugh Lane, of a son.

No. 1651 :: Ref. 1848-03-27, 3:6, B.
On the 21st instant, at Strabane, the lady of David Smyth, Esq., of a son.

No. 1652 :: Ref. 1848-03-27, 3:6, B.
At Oak Park, county Donegal, the residence of her brother, Wm. Wray, Esq., the lady of the Rev. Simon Fausset, of a son.

No. 1653 :: Ref. 1848-03-27, 3:6, B.
March 15, the lady of the Rev. C. Crossle, of a daughter.

No. 1654 :: Ref. 1848-03-27, 3:6, B.
On Saturday, the 18th inst., at Laghey, county Donegal, the lady of the Rev. E. Maturin, of a daughter.

No. 1655 :: Ref. 1848-03-27, 3:6, M.
On the 21st instant, in Killyman Church, by the Rev. Mortimer O'Sullivan, Mr. Thomas Cross, of Myroe, to Jane, only daughter of Mr. Samuel Moses, Sixmilecross.

No. 1656 :: Ref. 1848-03-27, 3:6, M.

On the 16th instant, in Alt Presbyterian Church, by the Rev. S. Stewart, Mr. Samuel Perry, Claudy, to Frances, third daughter of the late Mr. Thomas Barr, of Mullanboy, near Castlefin.

No. 1657 :: Ref. 1848-03-27, 3:6, M.

On the 18th inst., by the Rev. F. Twigg, in St. Thomas's Church, Dungannon, Mr. William Ringland, merchant, Dale Street, Liverpool, to Rachael, daughter of Alex. Frizel, Esq., Dungannon.

No. 1658 :: Ref. 1848-03-27, 3:6, M.

March 22, in St. George's Church, by the Rev. Edward Peppey, A.M., James Corry Lowry, of Rochdale House, in the county of Tyrone and of Mountjoy-square, Dublin, Esq., to Ellen, relict of Frederick Gamble, Esq., and daughter of Charles Johnston, of Mersenden, Berkshire, Esq.

No. 1659 :: Ref. 1848-03-27, 3:6, D.

On the evening of Sunday the 26th March, inst., at his residence, Market-street, Armagh, Mr. Nathaniel Greacen, senior, printer, formerly of Monaghan, aged 75 years. He was a man of the highest character, and truly deserved the name of an "*honest man.*" He died universally respected and beloved.

No. 1660 :: Ref. 1848-03-27, 3:6, D.

On the 17th instant, very suddenly, Mrs. Reid, of Lisferty, near Aughnacloy, aged 56 years.

No. 1661 :: Ref. 1848-03-27, 3:6, D.

March 20, at Newry, Mary, eldest daughter of Constantine Macguire, Esq., J.P., aged 21 years.

No. 1662 :: Ref. 1848-03-27, 3:6, D.

March 21, at the Glebe, Jane Eyre, wife of the Rev. H. Griffin, Ex.-F.T.C.D., Rector of Clonfeacle, and daughter of the late Edward Lysaght, Barrister-at-Law, in the 54th year of her age.

No. 1663 :: Ref. 1848-04-03, 3:4, M.

On the 31st ult., by the Rev. John R. M'Alister, Mr. Patrick M'Lorinan, of Belfast, to Miss Louisa Hughes, daughter of the late Mr. Arthur Hughes, of Armagh.

No. 1664 :: Ref. 1848-04-03, 3:4, M.

On Thursday, the 30th March, in Caledon Church, by the Rev. Mr. Alexander, Mr. Thomas Spencer, Loughgall, to Martha, third daughter of Mr. William Hoey, of Dyan.

No. 1665 :: Ref. 1848-04-03, 3:4, M.

March 28, in the Church of St. Nicholas, Dundalk, by the Rev. J.H. Allpress, Robert Ross Gyles, Esq., of Urker Park, Crossmaglen, eldest son of Robert Ross Gyles, Esq., of Gyles' Castle, Carlingford, to Mary, only daughter of Adam Caldwell, Esq., Dundalk.

No. 1666 :: Ref. 1848-04-03, 3:4, D.

On the 1st inst., at Crossmaglen, suddenly, of "Painter's Colic," John, son of Mr. John Fegan, of the Albert Hotel, Armagh, aged 28 years—his death was so sudded [sic] that an inquest was held on his body, and a verdict returned accordingly.

No. 1667 :: Ref. 1848-04-03, 3:4, D.

On the 30th ult., at Derry Ore, near Verner's Bridge, after a few days' illness, of fever, Mr. Simon Hazelton, third son of the late Mr. William Hazelton, of Anaghbeg, in the county Tyrone, age 56 years. He was an affectionate husband and kind parent, generally beloved and esteemed by a large circle of friends; he has left a widow to deplore his loss.

No. 1668 :: Ref. 1848-04-03, 3:4, D.

March 18, at Springfield, Bundoran, after a short but severe attack of bronchitis, Caroline, the beloved wife of Samuel T. Potter, Esq.

No. 1669 :: Ref. 1848-04-03, 3:4, D.

On the 29th of March, very much lamented, Margaret Martin, daughter of Mr. John Martin, of Ballylane.

No. 1670 :: Ref. 1848-04-10, 2:5, B.

On the 5th inst., Mrs. W. Wann, Markethill, of a daughter.

No. 1671 :: Ref. 1848-04-10, 2:5, B.

On the 7th instant, at Newtownhamilton, the lady of Henry R. Barker, Esq., of a son.

No. 1672 :: Ref. 1848-04-10, 2:5, M.

In St. Mark's Church, Armagh, by the Rev. B. Wade, on the 3d inst., Miss Ann Eliza Walker, youngest daughter of the late Abraham Walker, of Richhill, to Wm. Browne, Esq., Killymaddey, county Tyrone.

No. 1673 :: Ref. 1848-04-10, 2:5, M.

On Thursday, the 30th ult., at Seago Church, by Archdeacon Saurin, David Fox, Esq., of Derryadd, Verner's bridge, to Elizabeth, youngest daughter of Matthew Cooke, Esq., of Sevaghen, near Portadown.

No. 1674 :: Ref. 1848-04-10, 2:5, M.

At Eglish Church, on the 5th inst., by the Rev. Geo. Robinson, John Joseph Johnston, Esq., of Tremount, county Down, to Charlotte, daughter of the late James Johnston, Esq., of Knappa, Co. Armagh.

No. 1675 :: Ref. 1848-04-10, 2:5, M.

April 5, at the Parish Church of St. Anne, by the Rev. T. Hanley Ball, Thomas Mercer Houston, of Heartsfort, Rosstrevor, Esq., to Sarah, daughter of the late Robert Smythe, of Fitzwilliam-square, Esq.

No. 1676 :: Ref. 1848-04-10, 2:5, D.

At Castledawson, on the 26th ult., aged 49 years, Fanny, relict of the late John M'Murray, Esq., R.N., deservedly regretted.

No. 1677 :: Ref. 1848-04-10, 2:5, D.
On the 8th ult., at La Bergerie, Queen's County, Mary Anne, youngest daughter of the late T.D. Clarke, Esq., Q.C., of Merrion-Square, Dublin.

No. 1678 :: Ref. 1848-04-10, 2:5, D.
On the 1st instant, in the 57th year of his age, Mr. Hugh Breen, of the Royal Observatory, Greenwich, and formerly of the city of Armagh.

No. 1679 :: Ref. 1848-04-10, 2:5, D.
April 6, at Killycolp, county Tyrone, the residence of her son-in-law, H.A. Griffith, Esq., Catherine, relict of the Rev. Dr. Buck, at the advanced age of 91 years.

No. 1680 :: Ref. 1848-04-10, 3:1, M.
On the 9th inst., in St. Thomas's Church, Liverpool, by the Rev. J.C. Prince, Mr. William Kirker, Beck, formerly of Keady, in this County, to Mary eldest daughter of Mr. Robert Gurley, Foxleth Park.

No. 1681 :: Ref. 1848-04-10, 3:1, D.
April 12, at Tamlaght Glebe, of fever, aged nineteen years, Marion Collison, third daughter of the Rev. Maxwell Carpendale.

No. 1682 :: Ref. 1848-04-10, 3:1, D.
At Hollybrook, County Fermanagh, in the 59th year of his age, Lieut. Colonel Robert Lowry Dickson, late of the Bengal Army.

No. 1683 :: Ref. 1848-04-24, 3:3, B.
On the 18th inst., at Richmond, county Dublin, the lady of Hugh Harris, Esq., Barrister-at-law, of a daughter.

No. 1684 :: Ref. 1848-04-24, 3:3, M.
In Moy Church, on the 20th inst., by the Rev. Mr. Wrixon, Mr. Thomas Hall, Innkeeper, Copney, to Mirah Jane, eldest daughter of Mr. Joseph Lawson, of Tullyrone, county Armagh.

No. 1685 :: Ref. 1848-04-24, 3:3, M.
April 12, at Healing, by the Rev. Wm. Wright, LL.D., Rector, William Falls, Esq., Milltown House, Dungannon, to Charlotte Jane, only daughter of Rev. D. de Boudry, B.A., Grimsby.

No. 1686 :: Ref. 1848-04-24, 3:3, D.
April 16, at Mountmellick, of rapid pulmonary consumption, in the 22d year of her age, deeply and deservedly regretted, Mary, youngest daughter of the late Rev. John Graham, Rector of Tamlaghtard, in the diocese of Derry.

No. 1687 :: Ref. 1848-05-01, 3:3, B.
At Mount Collyer Park, on the 26th inst., Mrs. J.A. Henderson, of a son.

No. 1688 :: Ref. 1848-05-01, 3:3, M.
In Moy, on Thursday, the 20th ult., by the Rev. Mr. Wrightson, Mr. Thomas Hall, Merchant, Tullyrone, to Mr. John Lawson [sic], Cram Island-House, county Armagh.

No. 1689 :: Ref. 1848-05-01, 3:3, M.
On the 24th inst., at Carrigallen, County Leitrim, by the Rev. John Fisher, Sarah, youngest daughter of the late Robert Elliott, Esq., of Belfast, to James Berry, Esq., of Berrymount, County Cavan.

No. 1690 :: Ref. 1848-05-01, 3:3, M.
On the 23d inst., at Sallaghy church, by the Rev. William Bredin, Mr. James Bryans, of Killard, to Mrs. Hanna Murray, of Derrylee. The gallant bridegroom was only in his 90th year, and it was his third time of presenting himself at the altar of Hymen.

No. 1691 :: Ref. 1848-05-01, 3:3, D.
In this city, on Tuesday last, Mr. Samuel Walker, jun., Printer, aged 18 years. The deceased was a young man of very exemplary conduct, and bore a protracted illness with patience and Christian resignation. On many occasions previous to the final struggle he expressed his anxiety to "*depart and be with Christ.*" His remains were conveyed to their last resting place attended by a respectable concourse of friends and acquaintances.

No. 1692 :: Ref. 1848-05-01, 3:3, D.
In English-street, this day, 1st May, of decline, Mr. Robert Gilmore, regretted by a large circle of friends and acquaintances.

No. 1693 :: Ref. 1848-05-01, 3:3, D.
At Cran, near Fivemiletown, on the 18th inst., John Thomas Galbraith, Esq., (formerly of Enniskillen), aged 73.

No. 1694 :: Ref. 1848-05-01, 3:3, D.
On the 19th inst., in the 22d year of his age, James, second son of Charles Gerrard, Esq., of Bushhill, county Leitrim.

No. 1695 :: Ref. 1848-05-01, 3:3, D.
At Blackpark, Manorhamilton, on Tuesday morning, of fever contracted (it is supposed,) in the discharge of his duty as Poor Law guardian, Mr. Allen Nixon, aged 63.

No. 1696 :: Ref. 1848-05-08, 3:3, B.
At Ellichpoor, Madras, the lady of Andrew W. Mackintyre, of Ballyshannon, Captain of the Madras Horse Artillery, and 3d Regt. Nizam's Light Cavalry, of a son and heir.

No. 1697 :: Ref. 1848-05-08, 3:3, M.
On the 28th ult., in Ballibay Church, by the Rev. H.R. Halahan (uncle to the bride) John S. Dobson, Esq., of Dublin, to Elizabeth Dick, daughter of the Rev. John Dunbar, rector of Ballibay, county Monaghan.

No. 1698 :: Ref. 1848-05-08, 3:3, M.

In Lurgan Presbyterian Meeting House, on Friday the 5th inst., Mr. Robert Moore, of the firm of R. Moore, & Co., Armagh, to Anne, eldest daughter of Mr. Robert Trail, Merchant, Lurgan.

No. 1699 :: Ref. 1848-05-08, 3:3, M.

On the 25th April, in Dromore Church, by the Rev. W. Wearing, William M. Hammersley, Esq., M.D., to Jane, eldest daughter of the late John M'Murray, Esq., R.N., both of Castledawson.

No. 1700 :: Ref. 1848-05-08, 3:3, M.

On the 24th April, Mr. John Milligan, Castledawson, to Isabella Jane, youngest daughter of Stephen Garvin, Esq., Tamnadace, near Castledawson.

No. 1701 :: Ref. 1848-05-08, 3:3, D.

On 29th April, in this city, Miss Catherine Rickard, aged 7 years and 7 months.

No. 1702 :: Ref. 1848-05-08, 3:3, D.

On the 3d inst., Mr. William Vint, of North-street, Belfast, aged fifty-one years.

No. 1703 :: Ref. 1848-05-08, 3:3, D.

At Tempo, on Thursday morning, Mrs. Gamble, relict of the late Joseph Gamble, Esq., M.D., aged 77.

No. 1704 :: Ref. 1848-05-15, 3:3, B.

At Vicar's hill, Armagh, on the 7th instant, Mrs. E. Rogers, of a daughter.

No. 1705 :: Ref. 1848-05-15, 3:3, B.

On the 6th instant, at Bellaghy, the lady of R.H. Gordon, Esq., of a son.

No. 1706 :: Ref. 1848-05-15, 3:3, B.

At Ballyshannon, the lady of the Rev. W. Niblock, of a daughter.

No. 1707 :: Ref. 1848-05-15, 3:3, M.

On the 8th instant, at George's church, Hanover-square, by the Rev. John Brownlow, Robert Peel Dawson, Esq., (late captain in the grenadier guards,) eldest son of the Right Hon. Robert Dawson, of 16, Upper Grosvenor-street, and Castledawson, Ireland, to the Hon. Mary Elizabeth Brownlow, eldest daughter of the late, and sister of the present, Lord Lurgan.

No. 1708 :: Ref. 1848-05-15, 3:3, M.

On Tuesday, the 9th inst., in St. John's Church, Moneymore, by the Hon. and Rev. John P. Hewitt, James William Gregg, Esq., second son of the late James Gregg, Esq., clerk of the peace of the city and county of Londonderry, to Charlotte Janette Finiston, second daughter of the late William Greer Williamson, Esq., royal marines.

No. 1709 :: Ref. 1848-05-15, 3:3, M.

On the 6th instant, in Dundalk, by Dr. Brown, registrar for the district, and afterwards at the house of the bride's father, by the Rev. Mr. Maginnity, C.C., James Raleigh Baxter, Esq., proprietor and editor of the *Dundalk Patriot*, to Rose Mary, youngest daughter of Pierce Murphy, Esq., formerly of Newry.

No. 1710 :: Ref. 1848-05-15, 3:3, M.

On the 9th inst., in Sandholes Presbyterian Church, by the Rev. John Knox Leslie, Cookstown, the Rev. Joseph Geddes, Presbyterian Minister, Sandholes, to Ellen, daughter of Wm. Brown, Esq., Cookstown.

No. 1711 :: Ref. 1848-05-15, 3:3, D.

On the 14th inst., at Black Lion, Co. Cavan, Wm. son of Mr. Wm. Buchanan, merchant, in peaceful hope of resurrection through the merits of Jesus Christ.

No. 1712 :: Ref. 1848-05-15, 3:3, D.

At Kinneary, near Moy, on the 11th inst., Martha, relict of the late Benjamin Hanley, of Loughgall, aged 91 years. Deceased was a member of the Methodist Society for upwards of 70 years, and, "*Through all the changing scenes of life,*" her only hope for salvation (which remained firm to the last) was in the merits of her great Redeemer, Jesus Christ.

No. 1713 :: Ref. 1848-05-15, 3:3, D.

In Moy, on the 13th instant, after a lingering illness, which she bore with Christian fortitude, Sarah, the beloved wife of Mr. Joseph Fulton, aged 43 years.

No. 1714 :: Ref. 1848-05-15, 3:3, D.

In Moy, on the 10th inst., in the seventy eighth year of her age, Beatrice, relict of the late Rev. William Brown, of that place, and mother of the Rev. D.G. Brown, of Newtownhamilton.

No. 1715 :: Ref. 1848-05-15, 3:3, D.

May 6, at his residence, Crosh House, Newtownstewart, aged 50 years, Alexander Wm. Colhoun, Esq., J.P., deeply and deservedly regretted by all his acquaintances. As a kind landlord he could not be excelled, and as a magistrate of the county Tyrone his integrity gave universal satisfaction.

No. 1716 :: Ref. 1848-05-15, 3:3, D.

On Monday, the 8th inst., John Rodgers, Esq., of Cavanaca, aged 88 years. A gentleman highly esteemed by all classes.

No. 1717 :: Ref. 1848-05-15, 3:3, D.

May 8, at Newcomen-terrace, in the 54th year of his age, William Henry Halpin, Esq., second son of the late W.H. Halpin, Esq., of Dublin.

No. 1718 :: Ref. 1848-05-22, 3:4, B.

May 17, at Prospect House, Eyrecourt, the lady of Robert Eyre, Esq., of twin sons.

No. 1719 :: Ref. 1848-05-22, 3:4, B.

May 15, at Fort Johnston, county of Monaghan, the lady of J.B. Tavers, Paymaster 31st Regiment, of a daughter.

No. 1720 :: Ref. 1848-05-22, 3:4, B.

May 11, at Tullynure Lodge, county Tyrone, the lady of the Rev. Michael Kearney, of a son.

No. 1721 :: Ref. 1848-05-22, 3:4, M.

On the 15th inst., in Lisnaskea church, by the Rev. John Flanagan, Mr. R.J. Johnston, Armagh, to Eliza, second daughter of Mr. Robt. Young, Maguiresbridge, county Fermanagh.

No. 1722 :: Ref. 1848-05-22, 3:4, M.

May 16, in St. Anne's, Dublin, by the Venerable Archdeacon Magee, John Alexander Mainley Pinniger, Esq., only son of Broome Pinniger, Esq., of Chippenham, Wilts, to Georgina Catherine, third daughter of the late Nathaniel Garland, Esq., of Michaelstown Hall, Essex, and Woodcote Grove, Surrey, and of Mrs. Garland Cope, of Hyde Park-square, London, and Drumilly, county of Armagh.

No. 1723 :: Ref. 1848-05-22, 3:4, D.

On the 9th inst., in Armagh, Mr. Andrew Wright, aged 38 years.

No. 1724 :: Ref. 1848-05-22, 3:4, D.

Of consumption, on the 12th inst., at the residence of his aunt Miss Magee, in Enniskillen, in the 9th year of his age, Baptist, the only surviving child of the late Andrew Britton.

No. 1725 :: Ref. 1848-05-22, 3:4, D.

On the 14th inst., at Blacklion, William, son of Mr. William Buchanon.

No. 1726 :: Ref. 1848-05-29, 3:1, B.

May 13, at Boulogne-sur-Mer, the lady of Ralph Smith Obre, Esq., Clantilew, county of Armagh, of a daughter.

No. 1727 :: Ref. 1848-05-29, 3:1, B.

May 20, at Tartalaghan Rectory, the lady of the Hon. and Rev. F. Clements, of a daughter.

No. 1728 :: Ref. 1848-05-29, 3:1, M.

On the 24th inst., at Tullylish Church, by the Rev. William Butler Yeats, James Dickson, Esq., Elmfield, Gilford, to Annie, second daughter of Benjamin Haughton, Esq., of Banford House, Gilford.

No. 1729 :: Ref. 1848-05-29, 3:1, D.

On the 24th inst., in Enniskillen, Margaret, wife of Mr. John Frith, aged 69 years.

No. 1730 :: Ref. 1848-05-29, 3:1, D.

On the 19th inst., at his residence, Antrim-place, Belfast, Thos. Druitt, late of Lurgan, Esq.

No. 1731 :: Ref. 1848-05-29, 3:1, D.

May 21, at Killeshandra, in the forty-fourth year of his age, after a long and painful illness, which he bore with Christian fortitude, Jas. Alexander Finlay, Esq., M.D.

No. 1732 :: Ref. 1848-06-05, 3:3, B.

May 27, at Windsor Hill, Newry, the lady of the Rev. W.R. Williams, of a son.

No. 1733 :: Ref. 1848-06-05, 3:3, B.

May 29, at Calry Glebe, Sligo, the lady of the Rev. Dr. Gillmore of a son.

No. 1734 :: Ref. 1848-06-05, 3:3, B.

May 25, at 38, Dawson-street, Dublin, the lady of F.W. Johnston, Esq., 27th Regt., of a son.

No. 1735 :: Ref. 1848-06-05, 3:3, M.

On the 25th ult., in the Presbyterian Meeting-house, Tandragee, by the Rev. James Bell, Mr. James Andrews, of Tandragee, to Miss Hannah Maria M'Namara, of Holywood.

No. 1736 :: Ref. 1848-06-05, 3:3, D.

On Wednesday, the 31st ult., at Lakeview House, county Fermanagh, aged 58 years, Ann, the beloved wife of David Caussen, Esq., after a severe and lingering illness.

No. 1737 :: Ref. 1848-06-05, 3:3, D.

On the 30th ult., Mr. Thomas Davison, of Ardress, aged 72 years.

No. 1738 :: Ref. 1848-06-05, 3:3, D.

On the 19th ult., Sarah, the beloved wife of Mr. Robt. Graham, of Drumardnagross, county Tyrone, aged 74 years. Through life she was distinguished by a disposition peculiarly mild and gentle, which in connexion with experimental religion rendered her a most affectionate mother, a devoted wife, and an ornament to the Wesleyan Methodist society, of which she was more than 40 years a member. During the whole of her affliction her mind was greatly cheered by the prospect of seeing her Redeemer face to face in the heavenly world, and of meeting "*before the throne*" her children who had gone before. Some of the last words she was heard to articulate were, "*Glory to God.*"—(*Communicated.*)

No. 1739 :: Ref. 1848-06-12, 3:3, B.

June 1, at Cavan, the lady of Major Fenwick, 13th Light Infantry, of a son.

No. 1740 :: Ref. 1848-06-12, 3:3, B.

On the 4th inst., at Lurgan, the wife of John Hancock, Esq., J.P., of a daughter.

No. 1741 :: Ref. 1848-06-12, 3:3, M.

In the Presbyterian church, Benburb, on the 9th inst., by the Rev. H. Montgomery, John Porter, Esq., Aughnacavan, Donaghmore, (near Newry,) to Anna, sixth daughter of John Kydd, Esq., Culkeerane House, Moy.

No. 1742 :: Ref. 1848-06-12, 3:3, M.
On the 9th inst., in the Wesleyan Chapel, Wesley-st., Enniskillen, by the Rev. Robert Huston, Mr. John Hilliard, of Tullyavey, to Sarah Bella, secondd aughter [sic] to John Armstrong, Esq., Sydaire, county Fermanagh.

No. 1743 :: Ref. 1848-06-12, 3:3, M.
6th June, in the parish Church, of Ardrahan, county of Galway, by the Rev. William Roe, Rector of Roscrea, and Vicar-General of Clonfert and Kilmacduagh, Robert W.C. Cope, of Loughgall, in the county of Armagh, Esq., to Cecilia Philippa, eldest daughter of Captain Shaw Taylor, of Castle Taylor, and grand-daughter of the late Lieutenant-General Sir John Taylor, K.C.B.

No. 1744 :: Ref. 1848-06-12, 3:3, M.
June 1, in St. Peter's Church, Wm. Newcombe, Esq., of Baggot-street, to Mary Belinda, youngest daughter of the late John Dickson, Esq., of Woodville, county Leitrim.

No. 1745 :: Ref. 1848-06-12, 3:3, M.
June 6, in Eyrecourt Church, by the Rev. R.B. Eyre, Rector, T.L. Gallwey, Esq., Captain Royal Engineers, to Cerise Armit, second daughter of John Eyre, Esq., Eyrecourt Castle.

No. 1746 :: Ref. 1848-06-12, 3:3, M.
June 7, in Donnybrook Church, by the Rev. B.H. Blacker, the Rev. Richard E. Keene, A.M., to Augustine, relict of the late Jas. Johnston, Esq., of Knappa, co. Armagh.

No. 1747 :: Ref. 1848-06-12, 3:3, M.
On the 1st inst., at the church of Drumcree, by the Rev. Mr. Proctor, of Portadown, Mr. James Steele, of Downpatrick, to Barbara, third daughter of the late Mr. James Riddle, of Barn Hill, county Armagh.

No. 1748 :: Ref. 1848-06-12, 3:3, D.
On Saturday, the 10th inst., at the residence of her son, Woodview, near Richhill, Margaret, relict of the late Mr. Wm. Running, at the advanced age of 84 years.

No. 1749 :: Ref. 1848-06-12, 3:3, D.
On the 2d instant, Jane, relict of the late Samuel Parker, Esq., of Jennyfield, near Armagh, aged 64 years.

No. 1750 :: Ref. 1848-06-12, 3:3, D.
June 1, in Kilkenny, Elizabeth Mary, wife of B.M. Prentice, Esq., of Bank of Ireland Office.

No. 1751 :: Ref. 1848-06-12, 3:3, D.
June 2, at Belfast Barracks, after a few days' illness, Ensign G.R. Gray, of the 3d (Buffs) Regiment, aged 20 years and six months.

No. 1752 :: Ref. 1848-06-12, 3:3, D.
June 4, at Lower Mount-st., Dublin, the Rev. M. Echlin, Vicar of Killinagh, in the diocess of Kilmore, eldest son of Daniel Moore Echlin, late of Fitzwilliam-square.

No. 1753 :: Ref. 1848-06-12, 3:3, D.
On 28th May, Mr. John Simpson, watchmaker, Lowtherstown, aged 26 years.

No. 1754 :: Ref. 1848-06-19, 3:2, B.
June 13, in Charles-street, St. James's, London, at the residence of his Grace the Lord Primate of Ireland, the lady of George Dunbar, Esq., of a son and heir.

No. 1755 :: Ref. 1848-06-19, 3:2, M.
On the 13th instant, in Richhill Church, by the Rev. Mr. Hogan, Mr. John Harte, of Tyrella, County Down, to Miss Charlotte Edgar, of Ballybreagh, Co. Armagh.

No. 1756 :: Ref. 1848-06-19, 3:2, M.
June 9, in the Presbyterian Church, Macosquin, the Rev. David Hanson, of Drumkeen, county Monaghan, to Ellen, daughter of the Rev. C. Houston, of Macosquin, Coleraine.

No. 1757 :: Ref. 1848-06-19, 3:2, M.
On Wednesday, the 14th instant, in Aughavea, Fermanagh by the Rev. T. Taylor, John Irvine, Esq., Eagle Mount, Lisnaskea, to Susan Eleanor, second daughter of James Armstrong, Esq., county Coroner, Brookeborough.

No. 1758 :: Ref. 1848-06-19, 3:2, D.
On the 13th inst., at his residence in Cavanagarvin, Mr. William Tecy, at the advanced age of 82 years.

No. 1759 :: Ref. 1848-06-19, 3:2, D.
At Fintona, on the 10th inst., aged 53 years, Amelia, the beloved wife of James Buchanan, Esq., deeply and deservedly regretted by a large circle of friends and acquaintances.

No. 1760 :: Ref. 1848-06-19, 3:2, D.
On the 15th inst., at Ballyshannon, of fever, Mr. John Green, one of the oldest and most respectable merchants of that town. As a tribute of respect his funeral was attended by almost all the clergy and gentry of the surrounding neighbourhood.

No. 1761 :: Ref. 1848-06-19, 3:2, D.
June 12, in Clifford-street, the Right Hon. Lady Montgomerie, daughter of Archibald, eleventh Earl of Eglintoun, and wife of Sir Charles Lamb, Bart.

No. 1762 :: Ref. 1848-06-19, 3:2, D.
At Linfield, near Belfast, on the 16th inst., aged 26 years, Henry Fielding, second son of C.B. Grimshaw, Esq.

No. 1763 :: Ref. 1848-06-19, 3:2, D.
At Belfast, on the 14th instant, Mr. George Stutton, aged 70 years.

No. 1764 :: Ref. 1848-06-19, 3:2, D.
On the 12th inst., at Thenwood-cottage, Norwood, Richard Burges, Esq., late of the 53d Regiment.

No. 1765 :: Ref. 1848-06-26, 2:6, M.
On the 15sh [sic] inst., at Saintfield, by the Rev. T. Blackwood Price, the Rev. Henry M. Archdall, incumbent of Trory, County Fermanagh, to Sarah Elizabeth Blackwood Price, second daughter of J. Price, Esq., of Saintfield House, County Down.

No. 1766 :: Ref. 1848-06-26, 2:6, M.
On the 17th inst., at Camla, county of Monaghan the residence of the Hon. Colonel Henry Westenra, uncle to the bride, William Fitzwilliam Burton, Esq., of Burton Hall, County of Carlow, to Caroline, daughter of Henry Lloyd, Esq., of Farrenrory, county of Tipperary, and granddaughter of the late Sir John Craven Carden, Bart., of The Priory and Templemore.

No. 1767 :: Ref. 1848-06-26, 2:6, M.
On the 9th inst., in St. Ann's Church, by the Rev. Charles Allen, Mr. John Dyer, emigration agent, Belfast, to Ellen, third daughter of the late Mr. Wm. Taylor, of Cork.

No. 1768 :: Ref. 1848-06-26, 2:6, D.
On Wednesday, the 21st inst., in the 14th year of her age, Sarah, second daughter of Mr. Robert Fairley, farmer, Lisdown, County Armagh.

No. 1769 :: Ref. 1848-06-26, 2:6, D.
On 20th inst., at Brookeborough, Rebecca, wife of Mr. Wm. Irwin, of the Constabulary.

No. 1770 :: Ref. 1848-07-03, 3:3, B.
On Sunday morning, in Lisnadill, Mrs. James M'Mahon, of a daughter.

No. 1771 :: Ref. 1848-07-03, 3:3, B.
June 23, at Aughavass Cottage, county Leitrim, the lady of the Rev. John Thomas Warren, of a son and heir.

No. 1772 :: Ref. 1848-07-03, 3:3, B.
At Donegal, on the 24th ult., Mrs. Charles Mulreany, Esq., of a daughter.

No. 1773 :: Ref. 1848-07-03, 3:3, M.
On the 15th inst., in Warrenpoint Church, by the Rev. R. Ellis, John H. Sheppard, Esq., M.D., of Abbeyleix, Queen's County, to Olivia Frances, daughter of the late Samuel Bowker, Esq., Glasslough, county of Monaghan.

No. 1774 :: Ref. 1848-07-03, 3:3, D.
June 24, at his residence, Prehen-House, Derry, in the 56th year of his age, George Knox, Esq.

No. 1775 :: Ref. 1848-07-03, 3:3, D.
On the 24th ult, at his residence, 164, Capel-st., Dublin, Thomas J. M'Dowell, builder, late of Cookstown.

No. 1776 :: Ref. 1848-07-03, 3:3, D.
At Lower Drumney, near Strabane, on the 21st ult., Martha, relict of the late Mr. John Jeffrey, of said place, aged 75.

No. 1777 :: Ref. 1848-07-03, 3:3, D.
On the 22d ult., of consumption, Andrew, fourth son of Mr. Andrew Campbell, merchant, Stewartstown, aged 20 years, late student at the Belfast College.

No. 1778 :: Ref. 1848-07-03, 3:3, D.
On the 21st ult., at Newry, the beloved child of Major Meredith, 13th Light Infantry, aged two years and eleven months.

No. 1779 :: Ref. 1848-07-03, 3:3, D.
On the 23d ult., at the Convent of Mercy, Naas, Miss Margaret Anna, aged 14 years, only child of Patrick Lagan, Esq., of Portadown.

No. 1780 :: Ref. 1848-07-03, 3:3, D.
In Maryborough, Mrs. Crook, wife of the Rev. W. Crook, Wesleyan minister.

No. 1781 :: Ref. 1848-07-10, 3:4, B.
At Leeds, on the 26th of June, the lady of Edward Irwin, Esq., of a son and heir.

No. 1782 :: Ref. 1848-07-10, 3:4, B.
July 5th, at Willoughby-place, Enniskillen, Mrs. Frederick Nixon, of a son.

No. 1783 :: Ref. 1848-07-10, 3:4, M.
In St. Mark's Church in this City, on the 7th inst., by the Rev. Benjamin Wade, A.M., Sinclair Carroll, Architect of Armagh, Esq., to Anne Eliza, eldest daughter of the late William Black, Inspector of Excise, Esq.

No. 1784 :: Ref. 1848-07-10, 3:4, M.
On the 6th inst., in Bar Church, parish of Fintona, by the Rev. Mr. Hudson, John Armstrong, Esq., Tullyreagh, to Elizabeth, youngest daughter of Richard Graham, Esq., of Glengun, County Tyrone.

No. 1785 :: Ref. 1848-07-10, 3:4, M.
In Aughnacloy church, the 6th inst., by the Rev. Mr. M'Master, Mr. Thomas Henry of Pomeroy, to Miss M'Williams of Grenville, Aughnacloy, daughter of the late George M'Williams, Esq.

No. 1786 :: Ref. 1848-07-10, 3:4, M.
On the 27th ult., in Sixmilecross Presbyterian church, by the Rev. T.W. Junk, Mr. William Orr, merchant, Dungannon, to Mary, second daughter of Mr. S. Johnston, of Tyrooney.

No. 1787 :: Ref. 1848-07-10, 3:4, M.
On the 30th June, in Killeshandra Church, by the Rev. Christopher Adamson (brother to the bride), George S. Meares, jun., Esq., to Isabella Ann, third daughter of the late Rev. Arthur Smith Adamson, and grand-daughter to the Hon. Maria Juliana Barry, deceased.

No. 1788 :: Ref. 1848-07-10, 3:4, M.
June 13, at Rye, Westchester County, State of New York, by the Rev. B. Griffin, Mr. Newberry Devenport, Halsted of Rye, to Miss Esther Ann Maria Griffin, of New York.

No. 1789 :: Ref. 1848-07-10, 3:4, M.
In Stirling, N.B., on the 4th inst., by the Rev. Mr. Finlay, John Milling, Esq., of Westport, Ireland, to Jessie, youngest daughter of the late Robert Morrison, Esq., of Alloa.

No. 1790 :: Ref. 1848-07-10, 3:4, M.
At Belfast, on the 7th inst., by the Rev. Robert Knox, in Linenhall-street Presbyterian Church, Mr. Thomas H. Black, of Coleraine, to Hannah, third daughter of the late Mr. John Gilmour, of Lisrone, county Tyrone.

No. 1791 :: Ref. 1848-07-10, 3:4, D.
In Tullyroan, near Loughgall, on Monday last, Mr. Simon Sinclair, aged 47. He was a man universally respected through life, and in death lamented by a large circle of friends and acquaintances.

No. 1792 :: Ref. 1848-07-10, 3:4, D.
On the 2d inst., in St. James's-square, London, the Countess de Grey.

No. 1793 :: Ref. 1848-07-10, 3:4, D.
On the 7th ult., of fever, in New York, Mr. Wm. Parke, jun., late of Stewartstown.

No. 1794 :: Ref. 1848-07-10, 3:4, D.
At his residence, Millfield, Buncrana, on Saturday, the 1st inst., after a protracted illness, Samuel Mitchel, Esq., in the 53d year of his age.

No. 1795 :: Ref. 1848-07-10, 3:4, D.
On the 24th ult., in Ballyjamesduff, Dr. Fitzpatrick, of typhus fever, caught while discharing [sic] the duties of his profession.

No. 1796 :: Ref. 1848-07-10, 3:4, D.
At Ballylin, Ramelton, on Saturday, 1st July, Geo. Bond, second son of Mr. Joseph R. Philson, of Londonderry, aged 3 years.

No. 1797 :: Ref. 1848-07-10, 3:4, D.
On Thursday, the 29th ult., Wm. F. M'Intire, Esq., merchant, of Derry.

No. 1798 :: Ref. 1848-07-10, 3:4, D.
On the 18th ult., at Cootehill, of decline, in the 32d year of her age, Marcella, wife of Mr. Richard Brown, Merchant.

No. 1799 :: Ref. 1848-07-10, 3:4, D.
July 1, at her residence, 8, Fitzgibbon-street, Dublin, Emily, daughter of the late John Patterson, Esq., of Ballyare House, county Donegal.

No. 1800 :: Ref. 1848-07-10, 3:4, D.
At Sharon, near Manorcunningham, of typhus fever, on the 5th inst., in the 34th year of his age, the Rev. William Archer Butler, late Professor of Moral Philosophy in the University of Dublin, and Rector of Raymoghy, in the diocese of Raphoe.

No. 1801 :: Ref. 1848-07-10, 3:4, D.
On the 30th ult. at the house of R. M'Intyre, Esq., Donegall-square, Belfast, Anne Erin, daughter of the late John H. Smith, Esq., Petersburgh, Virginia, America, and niece to Mr. William Kyle, near Newtownlimavady, county Derry.

No. 1802 :: Ref. 1848-07-17, 3:1, B.
July 17, the Lady of the Rev. Benjamin Wade, of a son.

No. 1803 :: Ref. 1848-07-17, 3:1, B.
In Enniskillen, on the 12th instant, Mrs. Rogers, wife of Dr. Rogers, of a daughter.

No. 1804 :: Ref. 1848-07-17, 3:1, B.
On Saturday last, at Killeshandra, the lady of Dr. Kennedy of a son.

No. 1805 :: Ref. 1848-07-17, 3:1, B.
At Hanover-Place, on the 13th inst., the lady of H. Boyde Mackay, Esq., of a daughter.

No. 1806 :: Ref. 1848-07-17, 3:1, M.
On the 13th[?] instant, at the Presbyterian Meeting-house, Armagh, by the Rev. Mr. Flemming, Thomas Wynne, Esq., of Lislea, to Catharine, daughter of Wm. Carroll, Esq., of Russell-street, Armagh.

No. 1807 :: Ref. 1848-07-17, 3:1, M.
On the 2d inst., at the residence of the Rev. Mr. Kelly, C.C., Mr. Felix Donaghy, to Mrs. Ann M'Kenna, eldest daughter of Mr. Charles M'Kenna, near Emyvale.

No. 1808 :: Ref. 1848-07-17, 3:1, M.
On the 8th instant, in Boho Church, by the Rev. Mark Whittaker, Robert, second son, of E. Kerr, Esq., Legg, Churchhill, to Catharine, only daughter of John Faussett, Esq.

No. 1809 :: Ref. 1848-07-17, 3:1, M.
On the 10th instant, at Blackhall-street, Thomas John Ryan, Merchant's-quay, Esq., to Ellen, younger daughter of Peter Chamberlain, Esq.

No. 1810 :: Ref. 1848-07-17, 3:1, M.
On the 6th instant, at St. Leonards-on-Sea, Capt. Wardlaw, Royal Dragoons, eldest son of Lieut.-Gen. Wardlaw, to Mary Jane, only daughter of the late John Hamilton O'Hara, Esq., of Portglenone and Craigbilly, county Antrim.

No. 1811 :: Ref. 1848-07-17, 3:1, D.
July 10, at Carrickmacross, William M'Auly, Esq., formerly of Gloonan Lodge, Ahogil, county of Antrim, in the seventieth year of his age.

No. 1812 :: Ref. 1848-07-17, 3:1, D.
On the 26th ult., in Tullamore, Eliza Isabella Maria, wife of the Rev. Thomas Lougheed, deservedly and sincerely regretted by a numerous circle of friends and acquaintances.

No. 1813 :: Ref. 1848-07-17, 3:1, D.
On the 26th ult., of consumption, William, youngest son of the late Rev. Wm. Ingram, of the Parish of Templemore, county of Donegal, aged 19 years.

No. 1814 :: Ref. 1848-07-17, 3:1, D.
On the 1st inst., in Fitzgibbon-street, Dublin, Emily, daughter of the late John Patterson, Esq., of Ballyare House, county Donegal.

No. 1815 :: Ref. 1848-07-17, 3:1, D.
On the 6th inst., Henry Courtenay, of Harrymount, county Down, Esq., in the 82d year of his age.

No. 1816 :: Ref. 1848-07-17, 3:1, D.
On the 2d instant, at Warrenpoint, William, who was the only surviving son of the late Robert Mollan, Esq., Public Notary, Newry.

No. 1817 :: Ref. 1848-07-17, 3:1, D.
On the 14th of November last, of violent sea sickness, on board the ship *Celin*, of which he was surgeon, while proceeding to Calahar, on the east coast of Africa, John Mitchell, Esq., M.D., aged 29 years, eldest son of the late Henry Mitchell, Esq., of Coothill [sic], late Lieutenant in the 8th Royal Irish Hussars.

No. 1818 :: Ref. 1848-07-24, 3:4, M.
July 13, at St. Pancras' Church, by the Rev. George Pocock, Stewart, youngest son of the late Major James Gibson, formerly of the Irish staff, and many years a magistrate for the city and county of Londonderry, to Eliza, daughter to John Barnes, Esq., of Tavistock-place.

No. 1819 :: Ref. 1848-07-24, 3:4, D.
On the 18th inst., in the 20th year of his age, Robert, third son of Mr. Robert Fairly, farmer, Lisdown, county Armagh.

No. 1820 :: Ref. 1848-07-24, 3:4, D.
On the 12th inst., after a tedious and painful illness, borne with patient resignation to the will of God, Mrs. Happur, at her residence, Crew, Ballygawley, in the 52d year of her age.

No. 1821 :: Ref. 1848-07-24, 3:4, D.
On the 13th inst., at Donaghmore, county Tyrone, Anna, eldest daughter of the Rev. Archibald Hamilton.

No. 1822 :: Ref. 1848-07-24, 3:4, D.
On the 11th inst., at Kilmore, county Fermanagh, in the 82d year of his age, Mr. W. Armstrong, father of the Rev. J. Armstrong, Wesleyan minister. For more than 60 years he was a member of the Wesleyan Methodist Society.

No. 1823 :: Ref. 1848-07-24, 3:4, D.
In Newtownlimavady, on Thursday, the 20th ult., of consumption, Mr. Robert John Given, Watchmaker, aged 23 years.

No. 1824 :: Ref. 1848-07-31, 3:3, B.
On the 4th instant, at the residence of her father, Carr House, Stranton West, Hartlepool, Durham, the lady of George Duffan, Esq., C.E., of a son, who was subsequently named "John Mitchel," in memory of Ireland's illustrious "*Felon*."

No. 1825 :: Ref. 1848-07-31, 3:3, B.
On Sunday, the 23d inst., the lady of M.H. Morphy, Esq., of Enniskillen, of a daughter.

No. 1826 :: Ref. 1848-07-31, 3:3, B.
On Sunday morning, the 23d inst., Mrs. Alexander Flood, of Mullyare, Blacklion, of a son.

No. 1827 :: Ref. 1848-07-31, 3:3, M.
On the 26th instant, in Richhill Church, by the Rev. Mr. Hogan, Mr. Robert Best, to Ruth, only daughter of Mr. John Turtle, both of Richhill.

No. 1828 :: Ref. 1848-07-31, 3:3, M.
At Wexford, on the 27th inst., by the Rev. Mr. White, Mr. Geo., Addey, Loughgall, to Eliza, daughter of the late Jacob Poole, Esq., of Growtown, co. Wexford.

No. 1829 :: Ref. 1848-07-31, 3:3, D.
On the 13th inst., after a protracted illness, Thomas Sinnamon, Esq., of Portadown, aged 71 years.

No. 1830 :: Ref. 1848-07-31, 3:3, D.
At Drumhillary, near Middletown, on the 21st inst., Mr. James Graham, aged 22 years. He was color bearer of the orange society on the 12th, and his remains were conveyed to their resting-place by 26 lodges of his brethren, on Monday, the 24th.

No. 1831 :: Ref. 1848-07-31, 3:3, D.
On Wednesday, the 19th inst., of consumption, after a long and lingering illness, Mrs. Betty, wife of William Betty, Esq., Cappy.

No. 1832 :: Ref. 1848-08-07, 3:3, B.
On the 31st ult., at Dungannon, the lady of Major Cochran, of a son.

No. 1833 :: Ref. 1848-08-07, 3:3, B.
On the 28th ult., at Cadogan Place, the lady of Robert Synnot, Esq., of a son.

No. 1834 :: Ref. 1848-08-07, 3:3, B.
On the 29th ult., at Bellaghy Castle, the residence of her father, John Hill, Esq., the wife of Henry Stewart Bruce, Esq., of a son.

No. 1835 :: Ref. 1848-08-07, 3:3, M.
On the 30th ult., at Dungannon, by the Rev. James Joseph Hughes, R.C.C., Mr. Felix M'Elhone, late of Albany, America, to Catherine, daughter of the late Mr. Patrick M'Gettrick, Ballymote, county Sligo.

No. 1836 :: Ref. 1848-08-07, 3:3, M.
On the 2d instant, in May-st. Presbyterian Church, by the Rev. Dr. Cooke, Mr. Richard Johnston, merchant, of Belfast, to Miss Eliza Ann Armstrong, of Rosevale, near Cromlin.

No. 1837 :: Ref. 1848-08-07, 3:3, D.
On the 9th ult., aged twenty-five years, Marcella, fifth daughter of Mr. Wm. M'Clenahan, Belfast.

No. 1838 :: Ref. 1848-08-07, 3:3, D.
On the 13th ult., at Mullyrodden, near Caledon, Mr. John Reid, aged fifty-nine.

No. 1839 :: Ref. 1848-08-07, 3:3, D.
On the 18th ult., at Lurgan, of disease of the heart, Robert Watson, Esq., in the 72d year of his age.

No. 1840 :: Ref. 1848-08-07, 3:3, D.
In Derry, 29th ult., Robert Louis, the eldest surviving son of the Rev. Robert H. Burgh, Minister of the Chapel of Ease, of that city.

No. 1841 :: Ref. 1848-08-07, 3:3, D.
On 22d ult., at Strabane, Martha, eldest daughter of Samuel Colhoun, Esq.

No. 1842 :: Ref. 1848-08-07, 3:3, D.
At Carrygullon, near Strabane, on Thursday evening, the 27th ult., of putrid fever, Mr. James Morton, son of Mr. Joseph Morton, aged 19, a young man very much beloved.

No. 1843 :: Ref. 1848-08-07, 3:3, D.
At Stewardstown, on the 29th ult., Mr. William Park, in the 62d year of his age.

No. 1844 :: Ref. 1848-08-07, 3:3, D.
Aug. 1, in Sackville-street, Dublin, Mr. Alexander Thompson, aged sixty-nine years, deeply regretted by all who knew him.

No. 1845 :: Ref. 1848-08-14, 3:2, B.
On the 5th instant, at 64, Leeson-street, Dublin, the lady of Chateneufe Tuthill, Esq., of a daughter.

No. 1846 :: Ref. 1848-08-14, 3:2, M.
On the 10th inst., in Drumsallen Church, by Rev. George Hunt, Mr. Joseph Allen, of Aughaterra, to Margaret, youngest daughter of the late Mr. Wm. Greer, of Drumgar, all of this county.

No. 1847 :: Ref. 1848-08-14, 3:2, D.
On Thursday, at Victoria Terrace, Margaret, wife of Robert Buchanan, Esq., of the Royal Engineer Department, after an illness of several months, which she bore with patient resignation and Christian fortitude. Her remains were interred this day (Saturday) in the new Cathedral burying ground, attended by three companies of the local force, in side-arms, under Major Donnellan, and a respectable concourse of citizens, as a mark of esteem for the bereaved husband.

No. 1848 :: Ref. 1848-08-14, 3:2, D.
On the 3d inst., Mr. Henry Garland, of Aughaterra, aged 30 years.

No. 1849 :: Ref. 1848-08-14, 3:2, D.
On the 8th inst., Mr. James M'Sorely, of Tullymore, aged 90 years.

No. 1850 :: Ref. 1848-08-14, 3:2, D.
At Warrenpoint, on Saturday, the 5th instant, Mr. George MacOrmond, of Lifford, for many years connected with the Boundary Survey of Ireland, and latterly in the employment of Mr. Dargan, Railway Contractor, aged 50 years.

No. 1851 :: Ref. 1848-08-14, 3:2, D.
On the 7th instant, at 22, Blessington-street, Dublin, Alexander William Maclean, aged 16 years, only son of Captain Rawdon Maclean, R.N.

No. 1852 :: Ref. 1848-08-14, 3:2, D.
August 7, at his residence, Loughry, in the county of Tyrone, John Lindesay, Esq., J.P. and D.L. of said county.

No. 1853 :: Ref. 1848-08-14, 3:2, D.
August 3, aged 74, Edward Baines, Esq., of Leeds, formerly member of parliament for that borough in three successive parliaments, and senior proprietor of the *Leeds Mercury*, of which he had been proprietor more than 47 years. Mr. Baines was a magistrate of the West Riding and of the borough of Leeds, and was father of Mr. T. Baines, Esq., M.P., for Hull.

No. 1854 :: Ref. 1848-08-21, 2:7, B.
At Boulogne-sur-Mer, on the 8th instant, the lady of Thomas Bond, Esq., Castroneard, county Longford, of a daughter.

No. 1855 :: Ref. 1848-08-21, 2:7, B.
On the 16th inst., in Derry, Mrs. Jackman, of a son.

No. 1856 :: Ref. 1848-08-21, 2:7, B.
August 13, at Ayr Hill, Ramelton, the lady of Benjamin Johnston, Esq., M.D., of a daughter.

No. 1857 :: Ref. 1848-08-21, 2:7, B.
On the 16th inst., Mrs. Robert Leslie Ogilby of a daughter.

No. 1858 :: Ref. 1848-08-21, 2:7, M.
On the 17th inst., in Killinagh Church, county Cavan, by the Rev. James Armstrong, John Thompson, Esq., Proprietor of *The Armagh Guardian*, to Eliza, only daughter of Hugh Brackin, Esq., of Toam, near Black Lion, in said county.

No. 1859 :: Ref. 1848-08-21, 2:7, M.
On the 9th instant, in Lower Clananees Presbyterian Church, by the Rev. James Kinnar, Mr. William Watt, of Bogisland, near Castlecaulfield, to Margaret, relict of the late James Beggs, of same place.

No. 1860 :: Ref. 1848-08-21, 2:7, M.
August 10, at Bideford, North Devon, Thomas Barnard Hart, of Glenalla, county Donegal, Esq., to Elizabeth Anne Smedley, youngest daughter of the late Rev. Edward Smedley, of Dulwich.

No. 1861 :: Ref. 1848-08-21, 2:7, M.
On the 10th inst., in the Second Presbyterian Church, Belfast, John Bowman, Esq., of New Orleans, to Anne, daughter of the late Robert Gamble, Esq., Belfast.

No. 1862 :: Ref. 1848-08-21, 2:7, M.
On the 9th inst., in the Parish Church, Ballymoney, Thomas Keany, Esq., to Miss Rachel M'Loy. The gallant bridegroom, who is one of the few surviving heroes of Waterloo, is nearly four-score, while twenty summers only have passed over the head of the gentle bride.

No. 1863 :: Ref. 1848-08-21, 2:7, D.
On Sunday, the 13th instant, in the 25th year of her age, of a severe bilious attack, attended with spasms, Matilda, youngest daughter of Mr. Patrick Hughes, of the Victoria Hotel, in this city. The deceased was a most estimable young woman, and her premature death is sincerely regretted by all who knew her.

No. 1864 :: Ref. 1848-08-21, 2:7, D.
On the 12th inst., of consumption, at the residence of his brother in Emyvale, Mr. John Charlton Holmes, aged 35 years.

No. 1865 :: Ref. 1848-08-21, 2:7, D.
At Glenavy, on the 4th inst., Mr. Edward Addy, who, for more than 30 years, laboured as a Preacher of the Gospel, in the Primitive Wesleyan Methodist Connexion.

No. 1866 :: Ref. 1848-08-21, 2:7, D.
On the 17th inst., in her 80th year, Mrs. Davison, widow of the late Mr. Samuel Davison, of Derry.

No. 1867 :: Ref. 1848-08-21, 2:7, D.
At Coolafinny, on the 14th inst., the Rev. Marshall Moore, Presbyterian Minister of Faughanvale, in the 50th year of his age, and the 29th of his ministry.

No. 1868 :: Ref. 1848-08-21, 2:7, D.
On the 5th inst., in the 60th year of his age, Finlay Ash, Esq., Ballyconnell, county Donegal, deeply and deservedly regretted.

No. 1869 :: Ref. 1848-08-21, 2:7, D.
At Arva, on the 12th inst., Anne, wife of J.B. Graves, Esq., Resident Magistrate for the county Cavan.

No. 1870 :: Ref. 1848-08-21, 2:7, D.
At her residence, Northgate-street, Chester, Anne, relict of the late John Chamberlaine, Esq., and mother of Mrs. O'Reilly, of Annagh, county Cavan.

No. 1871 :: Ref. 1848-08-21, 2:7, D.
August 14th, at Ballyconnell, Master Joseph Cochrane, aged 16 years.

No. 1872 :: Ref. 1848-08-21, 2:7, D.
At the Glebe House of Aghera, county Meath, the Rev. John Kellett, for many years the esteemed Rector of that parish.

No. 1873 :: Ref. 1848-08-21, 2:7, D.
On the 12th inst., at Broomfield, Ballyhaise, the residence of her son, Rev. Arthur Monypeny, in the 88th year of her age, Letitia, relict of the late Arthur Monypeny, Esq., of Killeshandra.

No. 1874 :: Ref. 1848-08-28, 3:2, B.
On the 22d inst., at Armagh, the wife of Mr. M. M'Neale Johnston, of a son.

No. 1875 :: Ref. 1848-08-28, 3:2, B.
On the 24th instant, at Strabane, Mrs. Edward J. Colgan, of a daughter.

No. 1876 :: Ref. 1848-08-28, 3:2, B.
At Ayr Hill, Ramelton, county Donegal, the lady of Benjamin Johnston, Esq., M.D., of a daughter.

No. 1877 :: Ref. 1848-08-28, 3:2, M.
On Tuesday, the 22d inst., at St. Ann's Church, by the Rev. W. M'Ilwaine, John Patterson, Esq., to Emily, fifth daughter of the late Thomas Welsh, Esq., Belfast.

No. 1878 :: Ref. 1848-08-28, 3:2, M.
On the 22d inst., in St. Ann's Church, Belfast, by the Rev. T.F. Miller, Vicar, Mr. William Burns, Primitive Wesleyan Methodist Preacher, of Banbridge, to Mrs. Sarah Anne Macklin, Belfast.

No. 1879 :: Ref. 1848-08-28, 3:2, M.
August 22, by the Very Rev. the Dean of Armagh, at the parish church of West Twyford, Edmund Burke Roche, M.P., only son of Edmund Roche, Esq., of Trabolgan and Kildinan, county of Cork, to Eliza Caroline, eldest daughter of J.B. Boethby, Esq., of Twyford Abbey, Middlesex.

No. 1880 :: Ref. 1848-08-28, 3:2, M.

August 22, at Loughgall, by the Venerable Archdeacon Magee, James Whitshed, late Captain 74th Highlanders, third son of Lieutenant-General Sir Augustus De Butts, to Anna Eliza, youngest daughter of the late Nathaniel Garland, Esq., of Michaelstown Hall, Essex, and Woodcote Grove, Surrey, and of Mrs. Garland Cope, of Hydepark-square, London, and Drumilly, county Armagh.

No. 1881 :: Ref. 1848-08-28, 3:2, M.

August 17, at the residence of the bride's father, Mr. Henry O'Neil, only son of John O'Neil, Esq., M.D., of Beragh, county Tyrone, to Jane, fourth daughter of Mr. Edward M'Donnell of Mullahead, county Armagh.

No. 1882 :: Ref. 1848-08-28, 3:2, D.

In this city, on Saturday morning last, Anne, the beloved wife of Captain Flack. Deceased was an amiable lady, revered by all who knew her, and her demise is regretted by a respectable circle of sorrowing friends, who fully sympathise with the bereaved husband.

No. 1883 :: Ref. 1848-08-28, 3:2, D.

On the 24th inst., in this city, after a short illness, Mr. Thomas Fitzpatrick, aged 38 years, universally regretted.

No. 1884 :: Ref. 1848-08-28, 3:2, D.

In Cullen-street, on Tuesday last, Mr. Wm. Quin, aged 35 years.

No. 1885 :: Ref. 1848-08-28, 3:2, D.

At Ballybigly, on the 18th instant, Mr. John Watson, at the advanced age of 86 years.

No. 1886 :: Ref. 1848-08-28, 3:2, D.

August 13th, at Philipstown, Margaret Charlotte, Anne, wife of the Rev. Nathaniel Stephens, of Gortin, county Tyrone. During her illness, though young, and leaving two children, she was resigned to the will of her Heavenly Father; and some of her last words were—"*Lord Jesus Christ, save my soul*;" and while her family and friends were at prayer around her, she fell asleep in Jesus her Redeemer.

No. 1887 :: Ref. 1848-08-28, 3:2, D.

On the 22d inst., at Tullybryan, Ballygawley, Mr. John Speer, in the 75th year of his age.

No. 1888 :: Ref. 1848-08-28, 3:2, D.

July 31, in New York, Edward Simon, Esq., Manager of the Park Theatre, and formerly of Crow-street Theatre, Dublin.

No. 1889 :: Ref. 1848-08-28, 3:2, D.

August 20, at Bandon, after a long and painful illness, Henry Baldwin, Esq., of Castle Baldwin, many years a magistrate of the county Cork.

No. 1890 :: Ref. 1848-08-28, 3:2, D.

August 18, at Omagh, Lavinia Eleanor, the beloved wife of Henry Thompson, Esq., M.D.

No. 1891 :: Ref. 1848-09-04, 2:6, B.

On the 14th ult., at Drumheel House, co. Cavan, the lady of Wm. Smith, Esq., of a son.

No. 1892 :: Ref. 1848-09-04, 2:6, B.

On the 29th ult., at the Royal Hotel, Belfast, the lady of Deputy-Assistant-Commissary-General Woodley, of a son.

No. 1893 :: Ref. 1848-09-04, 2:6, M.

On the 21st ult., at Drumsna, county Leitrim, by the Rev. George Geraghty, P.P., John B. Clarke, Esq., Carrick-on-Shannon, to Kate, youngest daughter of the late Michael M'Dermot, Esq., of Drumsna.

No. 1894 :: Ref. 1848-09-04, 2:6, M.

On Friday, 25th ult., at Finner Church, Bundoran, by the Rev. Mr. Potter, Mr. William Armstrong, Enniskillen, to Catherine, youngest daughter of the late Mr. James Armstrong, of Ross, near Enniskillen.

No. 1895 :: Ref. 1848-09-04, 2:6, M.

On the 23d ult., in the Presbyterian Church, Ballyalbany, by the Rev. John Rankin, Mr. Wm. Burns, Monaghan, to Mrs. Scott, formerly of Markethill.

No. 1896 :: Ref. 1848-09-04, 2:6, M.

On the 30th ult., at Bryansford Church, by the Rev. C. Usher, William, eldest son of Thomas A. Pringle, Esq., Tulledon Cottage, county Monaghan, to Esther, only daughter of the late Charles Norris, Esq., Caledon, county Tyrone.

No. 1897 :: Ref. 1848-09-04, 2:6, D.

At Armagh, on the 24th ult., Mr. Anthony Dougan, shoemaker, an old and respectable inhabitant of this city. His remains were attended to his place of worship, the R.C. Chapel, and from thence to their last resting place, the R.C. grave yard, by members of the Benevolent Society of St. Patrick, of which Mr. D. was a member for 44 years; several of the members who attended the funeral were members for 50 and 51 years. We were much pleased with the turn out and appearance of this respectable society, which for so many years has brought into close contact members of every creed and persuasion, and promoted works of charity and Christian benevolence.

No. 1898 :: Ref. 1848-09-04, 2:6, D.

On the 30th August, of malignant fever, Mr. William Riddall, of Richhill, in the 24th year of his age. He departed this life in sure and certain hope of a resurrection to life immortal, through the merits of Christ his Redeemer; he was much respected by all who knew him, and is deeply lamented by a numerous circle of sorrowing friends, who sympathise with his bereaved parent.

No. 1899 :: Ref. 1848-09-04, 2:6, D.
On the 24th ult., at Castleblaney, Mr. John M'Kee, in the sixty-third year of his age.

No. 1900 :: Ref. 1848-09-04, 2:6, D.
At Richhill, on the 25th ult., in the 60th year of her age, Mary Anne, the beloved wife of Mr. Johnston, of Richhill.

No. 1901 :: Ref. 1848-09-04, 2:6, D.
At Ederney, on Saturday, 26th ult., the Rev. Mr. Owens, C.C.

No. 1902 :: Ref. 1848-09-04, 2:6, D.
On the 28th ult., at Sandymount Cottage, Margaret wife of Mr. Robert Williams, of Dublin.

No. 1903 :: Ref. 1848-09-11, 2:6, B.
On 26th ult., at Thornhill, County of Monaghan, the residence of her father, the lady of Ralph Dudgeon, Esq., 3d West India Regiment, of twin sons.

No. 1904 :: Ref. 1848-09-11, 2:6, B.
On the 29th ult., at Harlough, Dungannon, of twins, the lady of the Rev. Alex. G. Stuart, rector of Killincool, county of Louth.

No. 1905 :: Ref. 1848-09-11, 2:6, B.
On the 30th ult., at the Rectory, Louth, the lady of the Rev. John Barclay Scriven, of a daughter.

No. 1906 :: Ref. 1848-09-11, 2:6, M.
September 5, at Monkstown Church, by the Rev. Richard Verschoyle, the Rev. Alexander Rowley Miller, Rector of Heynstown, county of Louth, second son of Rowley Miller, of Moneymore, Esq., D.L., to Maria Elizabeth, second daughter of Marcus Synnot, of Ballymoyer, Esq.

No. 1907 :: Ref. 1848-09-11, 2:6, M.
In Omagh Church, on Thursday, the 31st ult., by the Rev. J.B. Chapman, rector of Drumragh, Robert Johnston, Esq., Cashel-house, in the county of Donegal, to Catherine, eldest daughter of the late George Dick, Esq.

No. 1908 :: Ref. 1848-09-11, 2:6, M.
On the 5th inst., at Drumnakilly, by the Rev. R.G. Dickson, Mr. Irwin Beattie, Doogory House, Omagh, to Miss Jane Anne Johnston, Beragh.

No. 1909 :: Ref. 1848-09-11, 2:6, M.
In Enniskillen, the 5th inst., by the Rev. Mr. Mathias, Mary Jane, only child of Richard Ball, Esq., to George Mahood, Esq., M.D., both of Enniskillen. The happy pair left the same day for Bundoran, where they intend to spend a few days.

No. 1910 :: Ref. 1848-09-11, 2:6, M.
On the 31st ult., at the office of the Registrar of Marriages, Enniskillen, Mr. Robert Macreery, to Miss Jane Rutledge, both of Lisbellaw, in Fermanagh.

No. 1911 :: Ref. 1848-09-11, 2:6, M.
On the 6th ult., at the office of the Registrar of Marriages, Enniskillen, Hugh Ovens Esq., of Fenagh, to Miss Diana Gaddis, of Drumduff, in Fermanagh.

No. 1912 :: Ref. 1848-09-11, 2:6, M.
On the 9th of July, at the Parish Church of Sylvanus, Nashota, U.S., by the father of the bride, the Rev. William Adams, ex-Scholar, T.C.D., eldest son of F. Adams, Esq., of Monaghan, to Elizabeth Marins, only daughter of Bishop Kemble, of the Northeastern Diocese.

No. 1913 :: Ref. 1848-09-11, 2:6, D.
At Charlemont Place, Armagh, on Tuesday last, of inflammation of the bowels, Robert John, third son of Wm. Paton, Esq., J.P., at the early age of 11 years. His remains were interred in St. Mark's Church yard on Friday morning, at 8 o'clock, and were attended by a large number of the inhabitants, and by all his school-fellows, who deeply lament his early removal from them, for he had greatly endeared himself to them by his admirable disposition; but although they lament his sudden separation yet they rejoice in the hope that they shall again rejoin him in a better world. His sorrowing friends and relatives may thus derive consolation under their deep affliction, and trust that although he has ceased to move amongst them he has been transplanted as a fair flower to bloom for ever in the Paradise of God.

No. 1914 :: Ref. 1848-09-11, 2:6, D.
On 9th inst., in this city, Mr. James Birnie, a professor of dancing for upwards of 50 years.

No. 1915 :: Ref. 1848-09-11, 2:6, D.
August 29, at Keynsham, near Bath, Major Edward Stephenson, late of the 3d Regiment, or Buffs.

No. 1916 :: Ref. 1848-09-11, 2:6, D.
August 20, at Hallifax, N.S., Major Carr, 38th Regiment, much regretted by his brother officers. Major Carr was a native of Cork.

No. 1917 :: Ref. 1848-09-11, 2:6, D.
September 3, William Augustus Blakeney, formerly Major in the 87th (or Prince of Wales' Irish) Regiment, in the 77th year of his age.

No. 1918 :: Ref. 1848-09-11, 2:6, D.
August 38 [sic], at his residence, Cloonerar, Captain Robert Powell, Sligo Regiment, aged 74 years.

No. 1919 :: Ref. 1848-09-11, 2:6, D.
September 2, at Dunlewvey House, in the county of Donegal, James Russell, Esq., formerly of Ardglass, in this county (Down.) Mr. Russell, about two years ago, purchased the Dunlewvey property from Sir James Dombraine, since which he had been most indefatigable in his exertions, not only to promote the welfare of his own tenantry, but also to introduce the

habits of industry and enterprise amongst the neighbouring farmers. Mr. Russell was cut off in the midst of his usefulness by typhus fever, leaving a widow and seven daughters to lament his loss.

No. 1920 :: Ref. 1848-09-11, 2:6, D.
Sept. 3, at his residence, the North Gate-street House, Chester, of English cholera, John Edward O'Reilly, Esq., M.B., of Trinity College, Dublin, The O'Reilly of Annagh Abbey, in the county of Cavan.

No. 1921 :: Ref. 1848-09-11, 2:6, D.
On the 31st ult., at Blackrock, Dublin in the 28th year of his age, after a long and painful illness, Thomas Carvill, Esq., late of Dundalk.

No. 1922 :: Ref. 1848-09-11, 2:6, D.
On the 2d instant, Deborah, wife of Mr. Alexander Langton, Warrenpoint.

No. 1923 :: Ref. 1848-09-11, 2:6, D.
On the 1st instant, at Moyrusk, Lisburn, Mrs. Mary Wardwell, relict of the late Mr. John Wardwell, at the advanced aged of 90 years.

No. 1924 :: Ref. 1848-09-11, 2:6, D.
Of fever, on the 20th ult., Mr. Wm. Sharp, of Edensap, near Tempo.

No. 1925 :: Ref. 1848-09-11, 2:6, D.
On Monday last, the 4th inst., in Omagh, Miss Angelina Dick, aged 26 years, second daughter of the late George Dick, Esq., lieutenant of the 57th foot.

No. 1926 :: Ref. 1848-09-11, 2:6, D.
On the 6th inst., in the 33d year of her age, Joanna, the lady of Patrick Moore, Esq., Thistle-House, Dundalk. On Friday her remains were interred in the Chapel of Jonesboro, attended by one of the largest and most respectable funerals that has been in this county for a considerable period.

No. 1927 :: Ref. 1848-09-11, 2:6, D.
On the 2d inst., at Camagh, near Keady, after a protracted illness, Mrs. Campbell, wife of Mr. Alexander Campbell, aged 62 years. In her death the people of that district have lost a kind and generous friend.

No. 1928 :: Ref. 1848-09-18, 2:7, B.
On the 7th September, the lady of John Stanley, Esq., of Armagh, of a daughter.

No. 1929 :: Ref. 1848-09-18, 2:7, B.
September 9 at Easky, Sligo, the lady of George S. Fenton, Esq., of three sons, who with their mother are doing well.

No. 1930 :: Ref. 1848-09-18, 2:7, B.
September 13 at Beechmount, county Tyrone, the lady of John Joyce, Esq., of a son.

No. 1931 :: Ref. 1848-09-18, 2:7, M.
On 12th inst. in Monkstown Church, by the Rev. Henry Stepney, John Calvert Stronge, Esq., son of Sir James Stronge, of Tynan Abbey, county of Armagh, to Zoe Margaret only daughter of the Hon. Henry Caulfeild.

No. 1932 :: Ref. 1848-09-18, 2:7, M.
On the 12th inst. in St. Peter's Church, Wm. Lane, Esq., of Derrylavin, county of Monaghan, to Emily youngest daughter of the late Joshua M'Cormick, Esq., of Dublin.

No. 1933 :: Ref. 1848-09-18, 2:7, M.
On 13th inst., in Strabane Church, by the Rev. Edward Atkinson, Mr. John Kearney, jun., to Miss Clarke formerly of Omagh.

No. 1934 :: Ref. 1848-09-18, 2:7, M.
On the 12th inst., in Strabane Church, by the Rev. Edward Atkinson, Mr. John M'Ashee, of Cavanalee, to Miss M'Crea, of the same place.

No. 1935 :: Ref. 1848-09-18, 2:7, M.
On the 12th inst., at Monkstown Church, by the Rev. St. George Williams, Charles Haydon, Esq., of Ballyshannon, to Charlotte Harriet, youngest daughter of the late John Stanley, Esq., of Gloucester-street, Dublin, and niece of Sir Edward Stanley.

No. 1936 :: Ref. 1848-09-18, 2:7, M.
September 14th, at St. George's Church, Dublin, by the Rev. Henry Baily (brother-in-law to the bride), the Rev. Mark Whittaker, Rector of the parish of Boho, County of Fermanagh, to Rebecca, second daughter of the late Thos. Edwards, Esq., of Dublin.

No. 1937 :: Ref. 1848-09-18, 2:7, M.
In Pettigo Church, Sept. 13th, John Scott, Esq., of Dromore, to Martha, eldest daughter of Hazlett Hamilton, Esq., of Pettigo.

No. 1938 :: Ref. 1848-09-18, 2:7, M.
On 14th inst., in Kilmore Church, by the Rev. J.F. Lloyd, Mr. Archibald Wright, of Bottlehill, to Miss Stothers, of Derryloughan, both in co. Armagh.

No. 1939 :: Ref. 1848-09-18, 2:7, M.
On 12th inst., in Kilmore Church, by the Rev. F.J. Lloyd, Mr. M'Canna, of Belfast, to Grace Bell, second daughter of Mr. John Trotter, of Ballintaggart in this county. The ceremony was afterwards performed by the Roman Catholic priest. The groom was a widower of about 60 years of age, while the bride is yet in her teens.

No. 1940 :: Ref. 1848-09-18, 2:7, M.
On the 16th inst., at Rosstrevor Church, by the Rev. E.J. Evans, Thomas Christmas, Esq., formerly of the 8th Hussars, to Grace, youngest daughter of the late Wm. Clarke Esq., of Rosstrevor.

No. 1941 :: Ref. 1848-09-18, 2:7, D.
In Thomas-st., in this city, on the 12th inst., after a protracted illness, which turned to decline, Anne, third daughter of Mr. Robert Johnston, Bootmaker, aged 22 years. She died rejoicing in the Lord Jesus.

No. 1942 :: Ref. 1848-09-18, 2:7, D.
On the Coast of Africa, of fever, Hugh, son of Robert Pooler, Esq., of Tyross, in this county.

No. 1943 :: Ref. 1848-09-18, 2:7, D.
In Monaghan, on the 16th inst., Miss Sarah Scott, youngest daughter of the late Mr. William Scott, of that town, aged 19 years.

No. 1944 :: Ref. 1848-09-18, 2:7, D.
On 13th inst., at Banagher, near Bellaghy, Mr. G. Godfrey, much regretted.

No. 1945 :: Ref. 1848-09-18, 2:7, D.
On the 12th inst., at Gallina, near Monaghan, in her 69th year, Elizabeth, wife of Alexander Fleming, Esq., of same place.

No. 1946 :: Ref. 1848-09-18, 2:7, D.
At Glasslough, on the 6th inst., Mr. Joseph Purdy, Post Master, Glasslough.

No. 1947 :: Ref. 1848-09-18, 2:7, D.
On the 1st inst., aged 54 years, Isabella, wife of Mr. Hugh Irwin, Skinbuoy, near Douglasbridge, county Tyrone.

No. 1948 :: Ref. 1848-09-25, 3:1, B.
Sept. 10, at Lisnaskea Glebe, the lady of the Rev. John Flanagan, of a child, still born.

No. 1949 :: Ref. 1848-09-25, 3:1, B.
At Belfast, on the 16th inst., Mrs. Charles Howden, of a daughter.

No. 1950 :: Ref. 1848-09-25, 3:1, M.
On the 19th inst., at St. Ann's Church, Belfast, by the Rev. Wm. Reeves, John Dickey, Esq., J.P., of Leighinmore, to Harriet, youngest daughter of Capt. Bowen, of Belturbet, late of the 41st Regiment.

No. 1951 :: Ref. 1848-09-25, 3:1, M.
On the 14th inst., in Killybegs church, by the Rev. Wm. Lodge, Mr. John M'Connell, Coraduffy, to Elizabeth, third daughter of the late Lieutenant John Dodd, Killybegs.

No. 1952 :: Ref. 1848-09-25, 3:1, M.
On the 18th inst., at Stillorgan Church, by the Rev. Wm. Pope, M.A., uncle to the bride, Charles Brent Wale, of Shelford, Cambridgeshire, Esq., second son of the late General Sir Charles Wale, K.C.B., to Henrietta, third daughter of his Grace the Archbishop of Dublin.

No. 1953 :: Ref. 1848-09-25, 3:1, M.
On the 19th inst., in the Presbyterian Church, Mary's-abbey, by the Rev. Wm. M'Caw, of Manchester, Robert Thomas M'Geagh, Esq., of Belfast, merchant, to Maddelene, daughter of the late John Young, Esq., Cookstown, Surgeon, R.N.

No. 1954 :: Ref. 1848-09-25, 3:1, D.
On the 15th inst., at her residence, Whittington-st., Dublin, Anne, relict of the late Thomas Whitsitt, Esq. The gentle tenor of her useful life is best described in the few but emphatic words of the wise man, "*In her tongue was the law of kindness.*"

No. 1955 :: Ref. 1848-09-25, 3:1, D.
In Linen-hall street, Armagh, on Wednesday, Mrs. O'Toole, aged 72 years.

No. 1956 :: Ref. 1848-09-25, 3:1, D.
At his residence, Annaghard, near Clones, after a tedious illness, Thos. Elliot, Esq., aged 48 years.

No. 1957 :: Ref. 1848-09-25, 3:1, D.
At Market-drayton, Shropshire, on the 13th Sept., aged 75, Marcus Corry, Esq.

No. 1958 :: Ref. 1848-09-25, 3:1, D.
Sept. 12, at his residence, Somerhill, Kent, James Alexander Esq., last surviving son of Robert Alexander, Esq., of Boom hall, near Londonderry.

No. 1959 :: Ref. 1848-09-25, 3:1, D.
Sept. 19 at O'Donnell-place, Thornhill, Sligo, in the 71st year of her age, much and deservedly regretted, Elizabeth, relict of Lieutenant-Colonel William Berkeley, of the Hon. East India Company's service.

No. 1960 :: Ref. 1848-09-25, 3:1, D.
On the 7th inst., at Drumnavaddy House, near Banbridge, John Hale, Esq., in the seventieth year of his age.

No. 1961 :: Ref. 1848-10-02, 2:6, B.
On the 24th ult., at Mount Irvin, co. Armagh, the lady of Wm. Geo. Irvin, Esq., of a son.

No. 1962 :: Ref. 1848-10-02, 2:6, B.
On the 24th ult., at Magherafelt, the lady of John Stuart Vesey, Esq., M.D., of a son.

No. 1963 :: Ref. 1848-10-02, 2:6, B.
On the 26th ult., at Drumbunyon House, the wife of Mr. John Devlyn, of a daughter.

No. 1964 :: Ref. 1848-10-02, 2:6, M.
On the 27th ultimo, at Dunsford Church, by the Rev. Robert Casment Greer, brother to the bride, the Rev. James Silcock, Kilmood, to Ellen, eldest daughter of James Greer, Esq., Corbally.

No. 1965 :: Ref. 1848-10-02, 2:6, M.
On the 26th ult., at Newtownbreda, by the Rev. John Kinahan, Matthew Blakiston, Esq., eldest son of Major Blakiston, of Mobberley, Cheshire, to Ann, daughter of Richard B. Blakiston Houston, Esq., of Orangefield, county Down.

No. 1966 :: Ref. 1848-10-02, 2:6, M.
On the 26th ult., by the Rev. Mr. Knox, Mr. Wm. Wilson, to Miss Mary Blair, both of Belfast.

No. 1967 :: Ref. 1848-10-02, 2:6, D.
September 20, at Clifton, near Bristol, aged 72, the Rev. F.L. Gore, lately of Torquay, Devonshire, and for many years Rector of Stewartstown.

No. 1968 :: Ref. 1848-10-02, 2:6, D.
On the 19th ult., at the residence of his father in Ballinderry, Mr. Thos. Haddock, grocer, Ann-street, Belfast.

No. 1969 :: Ref. 1848-10-02, 2:6, D.
At his residence, Castle-lane, Belfast, on the 27th ult., Mr. Garr M'Keown, aged 44 years.

No. 1970 :: Ref. 1848-10-09, 2:7, B.
September 29th, at Middletown, county Armagh, the lady of Francis Clarke, M.D., of a son.

No. 1971 :: Ref. 1848-10-09, 2:7, B.
On the 3d inst., at Newtownhamilton, the lady of Thomas Armstrong, Esq., Sub-Inspector, of twin daughters, still born.

No. 1972 :: Ref. 1848-10-09, 2:7, M.
On the 5th instant, in Moy Church, by the Rev. Richard Wrightson, Mr. William Orr, of Moy, to Sarah, second daughter of Mr. Samuel Corrigan of Derryscollip.

No. 1973 :: Ref. 1848-10-09, 2:7, M.
On the 1st of August, at Badagamo Church, near Galle, Ceylon, by the Rev. Charles Greenwood, John Scott, Esq., M.D., F.R.C.S.I., (formerly of Fivemiletown), to Louisa Burton, daughter of the Rev. John Wattson, D.D., Winford, Northamptonshire, England.

No. 1974 :: Ref. 1848-10-09, 2:7, M.
On the 29th ult., at St. Anne's Church, Dublin, by the Rev. John Wilson, Rector of Derrybrusk, Paul Dane, of Killyhevlin, in the County of Fermanagh, Esq., to Georgina, only surviving child of the late George Sanderson, of Tullylegan, in the County of Tyrone, Esq.

No. 1975 :: Ref. 1848-10-09, 2:7, M.
On 28th ult., in the Second Presbyterian Church, Ramelton, by the Rev. Mathew Wilson, Mr. Andrew Gaily, of Killylastion, Letterkenny, to Mary Jane, eldest daughter of the late Mr. John Gregg, Carrycastle, Ramelton.

No. 1976 :: Ref. 1848-10-09, 2:7, M.
October 4, at Easkey Church, by the venerable the Archdeacon of Achonry, the Rev. John Dawson, Vicar of Eoskey [sic], to Elisabeth Mary, daughter of the late William Bell, Esq., Surgeon of the County Sligo infirmary, &c.

No. 1977 :: Ref. 1848-10-09, 2:7, M.
On 4th inst., in May-street Meeting-house, by the Rev. Edward Breakey, Mr. Wm. Watson, of Monaghan, to Bessy, daughter of the late John M'Dowell, Esq., Maghera, Co. Derry.

No. 1978 :: Ref. 1848-10-09, 2:7, M.
At Kurrachee, on the 15th of July, by the Rev. Thomas Watson, Captain George Stack, of the 24th regiment, [B]ombay, N.I., 5th son of the Rev. Edwd. Stack, Tubrid, Co. Fermanagh, to Elizabeth Esther, second daughter of John Whitehead, Esq., Chelsea; and niece to Major Green, C.B., assistant adjutant-general in Scinde.

No. 1979 :: Ref. 1848-10-09, 2:7, D.
On the 4th inst., at the residence of Mr. Charles Connolly, merchant, Armagh, Constantine Patrick, youngest son of the late Thomas Egan, Esq., Solicitor, Dublin, and grandson of the late Richard Whittington, Esq., of this city, aged 12 years.

No. 1980 :: Ref. 1848-10-09, 2:7, D.
At Rockcorry, on the 30th ult., Mr. Alexander Wilson, merchant, aged 64 years, deservedly regretted.

No. 1981 :: Ref. 1848-10-09, 2:7, D.
On the 2nd inst., at her father's residence, Main-street, Cavan, of pulmonary consumption, Miss Mary Reilly, aged 19 years.

No. 1982 :: Ref. 1848-10-09, 2:7, D.
On the 26th ult., aged 19 years, after a protracted illness, which he bore with great patience and resignation, William, the beloved son of Mr. Guy Beatty, Carnaguiltaugh, near Tempo.

No. 1983 :: Ref. 1848-10-09, 2:7, D.
On the 30th ult., at Ederney, aged 83, Margaret, relict of Mr. Hugh Johnston, formerly of Drumkeen, County Fermanagh.

No. 1984 :: Ref. 1848-10-16, 2:5, B.
On Friday, Mrs. Fitzgerald, 13, College-st., Armagh, of a daughter.

No. 1985 :: Ref. 1848-10-16, 2:5, B.
On the 8th inst., at Seagoe, in the co. Armagh, the lady of the Rev. Capel Wolsley, of a daughter.

No. 1986 :: Ref. 1848-10-16, 2:5, B.
On the 30th ult, at Kinawley Glebe, co. Fermanagh, the lady of Capt. M. Fox, of a son.

No. 1987 :: Ref. 1848-10-16, 2:5, M.
Oct. 5, in St. Mary's Church, Youghal, by the Ven. the Archdeacon of Lismore, Henry Elrington, Esq., 6th Royal Regiment, son of the Rev. Dr. Elrington, Regius Professor of Divinity, Ex-Senior Fellow, T.C.D., and Rector of Armagh, and grandson of the late Lord Bishop of Ferns, to Matilda Rouena, eldest daughter of the late Rev. Pierce William Drew, Rector of Youghal, son of the late John Drew, Esq., of Meanus, county of Kerry, the eldest son of the late Francis Drew, Esq., M.D., of Macollup Castle, co. of Waterford.

No. 1988 :: Ref. 1848-10-16, 2:5, M.
On the 6th inst., at Monkstown, T.W. Hardman, of Talbot-st., Dublin, Solicitor, to Margaret Elizabeth Chambre, daughter of the late H.W. Chambre, of Hawthorn Hill, Armagh, Esq.

No. 1989 :: Ref. 1848-10-16, 2:5, M.
On Thursday last, in Benburb Church, by the Rev. Mr. Kennedy, and subsequently by Rev. Mr. Coyne, Parish Priest, Mr. Simon Ryan, grocer, of this city, to Mary, third daughter of Mr. Wm. Rigg, of Blackwatertown.

No. 1990 :: Ref. 1848-10-16, 2:5, M.
On the 19th ult., by the Rev. Mr. Oulton, at Lurgan, George Johnston, Esq., to Elizabeth, second daughter of Dr. Bell, of Lurgan.

No. 1991 :: Ref. 1848-10-16, 2:5, M.
On the 10th inst., at the office of the Registrar of Marriages, Enniskillen, Mr. Thomas Kerr, of Carrick House, co. Fermanagh, to Miss Mary Johnston, of Enniskillen.

No. 1992 :: Ref. 1848-10-16, 2:5, M.
On the 11th inst., in the Presbyterian Church of Emyvale, by the Rev. Alex. M'Mahon, Rev. Henry Kidd, A.M., Druminis, to Mary A., second daughter of John M'Mahon, Esq., of Tassagh.

No. 1993 :: Ref. 1848-10-16, 2:5, M.
On 11th inst., in St. George's Church, Dublin, by Rev. C. Fleury, Edward Spencer Dix, Esq., of Gardiner's-place, to Isabella Marian, relict of the late T.S. Battersby, Esq., of Ballintoher, Queen's County, and daughter of the late Henry M'Clintock, Esq., Collector of Dundalk.

No. 1994 :: Ref. 1848-10-16, 2:5, D.
On Tuesday last, in Scotch-street, in this city, of consumption, aged 22 years, Catherine Margaret, youngest daughter of Mr. John Henry.

No. 1995 :: Ref. 1848-10-16, 2:5, D.
At Fairview, near Aughnacloy, on the 30th ult., of fever, Mr. Robert M'Camey, aged 33 years. He was much esteemed for his consistent and steady deportment.

No. 1996 :: Ref. 1848-10-16, 2:5, D.
Oct. 6, at Cootehill, Catherine, wife of Wm. Jameson, Esq.

No. 1997 :: Ref. 1848-10-16, 2:5, D.
Oct. 5, at Ballinderry, Arthur, youngest son of Mr. Edward Connor.

No. 1998 :: Ref. 1848-10-16, 2:5, D.
At Tattymacall, near Lisbellaw, on the 8th inst., of rapid decline, Mr. Wm. Ford, teacher of Bailyboro' national school, aged 26 years.

No. 1999 :: Ref. 1848-10-16, 2:5, D.
On 3d inst., at Savilla-place, Warrenpoint, in the 31st year of his age, Wm. Anderson, Esq., youngest son of the Rev. J. Anderson, late of Moygannon, co. Down.

No. 2000 :: Ref. 1848-10-16, 2:5, D.
On 30th Sept., at Solitude, Lurgan, Sarah, the beloved wife of Abraham Bell, Esq.

No. 2001 :: Ref. 1848-10-16, 2:5, D.
October 6, in Belfast, Emma Georgiana Maria, wife of Thomas Frazer, Esq., Surgeon in the Royal Navy, and eldest daughter of James Watt, Esq., Assistant Commissary-General.

No. 2002 :: Ref. 1848-10-16, 2:5, D.
Oct. 7, at Ashbrook, Cullenswood, John Donnelly Wallace, son of William B. Wallace, Esq.

No. 2003 :: Ref. 1848-10-16, 2:5, D.
Oct. 8, in London, aged 85 years, Robert Mayhew Thompson, Esq., formerly Surgeon to the 14th Light Dragoons.

No. 2004 :: Ref. 1848-10-16, 2:5, D.
At Clones, on Tuesday, the 3d inst., Mr. Patrick M'Mahon, at the patriarchal age of 111 years.

No. 2005 :: Ref. 1848-10-16, 2:5, D.
Oct. 7, at Park Cottage, near Wexford, Lieutenant-Colonel Thompson, formerly of the 27th Regiment.

No. 2006 :: Ref. 1848-10-16, 2:5, D.
On the 24th of April, at Sydney, New South Wales, David Chambers, sen., Esq., formerly of Magherafelt, county Londonderry.

No. 2007 :: Ref. 1848-10-23, 3:1, B.
On the 17th inst., at the Rectory, Letterkenny, Mrs. Kingsmill, of a son.

No. 2008 :: Ref. 1848-10-23, 3:1, M.
On 17th inst., at Lifford Church, by the Rev. John King, and afterwards in Murlog Catholic Chapel, by the Very Rev. William Brown, Miss Margaret Gillespie, of Lifford, to Mr. William Loughrey, of same place.

No. 2009 :: Ref. 1848-10-23, 3:1, M.
On the 27th ult., in St. Peter's Episcopal Chapel, Edinburgh, by the Rev. John W. Ferguson, Andrew Green, Esq., of Rathbrogan, Sligo, to Marianne, youngest daughter of Doctor William Thompson, late of Ballyshannon.

No. 2010 :: Ref. 1848-10-23, 3:1, M.
On 10th inst., at Bradfield Church, near Sheffield, by the Rev. S.B. Ward, the Viscount Northland, M.P., eldest son of the Earl of Ranfurly, to Harriet, eldest daughter of the late James Rimington, Esq., of Broomhead Hill, in the county of York.

No. 2011 :: Ref. 1848-10-23, 3:1, M.

On 12th inst. at Donnybrook Church, by the Rev. B.H. Blacker, Chas. Molloy, Esq., M.D., Newry, to Lucy, fourth daughter of the late John Ogle, Esq. Newry.

No. 2012 :: Ref. 1848-10-23, 3:1, M.

On 13th inst., at the Presbyterian Church, Legacurry, by the Rev. Alexander Henderson, Mr. John Robinson, of Keady, to Sarah, daughter of Mr. A. Hill Davidson, of Lisnastrain, near Lisburn.

No. 2013 :: Ref. 1848-10-23, 3:1, D.

In Darling-street, Enniskillen, on Friday last, after a tedious illness, Mrs. Beatty, wife of Mr. R. Beatty, merchant tailor, much regretted.

No. 2014 :: Ref. 1848-10-23, 3:1, D.

On 16th inst., in the 63d year of his age, Mr. Alex. Gwyn, of Waterside, Londonderry.

No. 2015 :: Ref. 1848-10-23, 3:1, D.

Oct. 14, at Drumscambly, near Derrygonnelly, Thomas Rutherford, Esq., aged 33 years.

No. 2016 :: Ref. 1848-10-23, 3:1, D.

Oct. 18, at Brookborough, William Joyce, Esq., aged 41 years.

No. 2017 :: Ref. 1848-10-23, 3:1, D.

On the 16th inst., at Inver House, co. Donegal, the Rev. Alexander Montgomery, rector of Inver.

No. 2018 :: Ref. 1848-10-23, 3:1, D.

On the 15th inst., in Newry, Surgeon Malcolm, of the 9th Regt. of Foot, aged 45.

No. 2019 :: Ref. 1848-10-30, 2:4, B.

On the 22d inst., Mrs. John Gunning, of Enniskillen of a son.

No. 2020 :: Ref. 1848-10-30, 2:4, B.

On the 10th inst., at Londonderry, the wife of Capt. Leach, Royal Engineers, of a son.

No. 2021 :: Ref. 1848-10-30, 2:4, B.

On the 18th inst., at Lisnenan, near Letterkenny, Mrs. Robert Ramsay, jun., of a daughter.

No. 2022 :: Ref. 1848-10-30, 2:4, B.

On the 22d Oct., at New Row, Coleraine, the lady of Dr. T.H. Babington, of a daughter.

No. 2023 :: Ref. 1848-10-30, 2:4, B.

On the 13th inst., at Cherry Hill, the lady of Thos. Ward, Esq., of a daughter.

No. 2024 :: Ref. 1848-10-30, 2:4, B.

October 20, at Killeshar, Florence-Court, the wife of the Rev. Thomas Jebb, of a son.

No. 2025 :: Ref. 1848-10-30, 2:4, M.

At the Cathedral, Derry, on the 24th October, by the Rev. George Smith, George A. O'Driscoll, Esq., to Isabel, widow of the late Rev. William Smith, both of that city.

No. 2026 :: Ref. 1848-10-30, 2:4, M.

On the 24th instant, in Dundalk, by the Rev. Dr. Keeran, Stephen Brown, Esq., to Margaret, third daughter of James Gilmore, Esq., both of that town.

No. 2027 :: Ref. 1848-10-30, 2:4, M.

On the 24th inst., at Holywood Church, by the Rev. J. M'Cormick, Andrew T. Dickey, Esq., of Brookville, Ballymena, to Martha A. Ward, relict of the late Thomas H. Ward, Esq., of Marine, Holywood.

No. 2028 :: Ref. 1848-10-30, 2:4, M.

On the 27th inst., at Clontarf Church, by the Rector, the Rev. James Reid, John Hazleton, Esq., of Lurgan, to Lucinda Jane Vogan, daughter of the late Dr. Vogan, of Armagh.

No. 2029 :: Ref. 1848-10-30, 2:4, M.

October 23, Edward Smith, Esq., youngest son of the late Rev. Nathaniel Smith, Rector of the united parishes of Clonoe and Derrynoose, in the diocese of Armagh, and nephew of the late Captain Sir William Smith, R.H.A., to Sophia, daughter of the late Henry Mitchell, Esq., of Cootehill, late Lieutenant 8th Hussars.

No. 2030 :: Ref. 1848-10-30, 2:4, D.

In Castle-street, on Friday the 27th inst., after long suffering from an attack of gout, Silvester Quin, Esq., aged 83 years.

No. 2031 :: Ref. 1848-10-30, 2:4, D.

In Ballyshannon, on Monday last, at an advanced age, Mr. Thos. Earles, formerly of the Customs department.

No. 2032 :: Ref. 1848-10-30, 2:4, D.

On the 23d inst., at Cronkil, near Verner's-bridge, Mr. John M'Niece, aged 85 years.

No. 2033 :: Ref. 1848-10-30, 2:4, D.

Of fever, on the 23d inst., Mary Jane, eldest daughter of the late Andrew Anderson, Dahliavale, Lurgan, aged fourteen years.

No. 2034 :: Ref. 1848-10-30, 2:4, D.

At Cranaghan Glebe, Ballyconnell, on Friday, the 18th inst., after a long and painful illness, Letitia, the beloved wife of the Rev John Frith.

No. 2035 :: Ref. 1848-10-30, 2:4, D.

On the 19th inst., at the residence of his brother, Clontibret, county Monaghan, Aaron, fifth son of the late Alexander Seed, aged 18 years.

No. 2036 :: Ref. 1848-10-30, 2:4, D.

On the 21st inst., of typhus fever, Mr. John Madden, of the *Anglo Celt* office, Cavan.

No. 2037 :: Ref. 1848-10-30, 2:4, D.

In Montreal, on the 13th Sept., at the advanced age of 89 years, Joseph Workman, sen., Esq., formerly of Ballymacash, near Lisburn, Ireland.

No. 2038 :: Ref. 1848-10-30, 2:4, D.
On the 23d inst., William, aged 16 years, second son of Mr. George Flavel, merchant, Tandragee.

No. 2039 :: Ref. 1848-10-30, 2:4, D.
At Milltown, Strabane, on the 19th instant, Mrs. Snodgrass, relict of Mr. Wm. Snodgrass, of Strabane.

No. 2040 :: Ref. 1848-10-30, 2:4, D.
On the 23d inst., at Strabane, after a few days' illness, Amelia, daughter of the late Edward Joyce, Esq., Beechmount.

No. 2041 :: Ref. 1848-10-30, 2:4, D.
At Strabane, on the 25th instant, Margaret, third daughter of Mr. Joseph Henderson.

No. 2042 :: Ref. 1848-11-06, 3:1, B.
Oct. 30, at John's-place, Parsonstown, the lady of the Rev. William Henry M'Causland, of a son.

No. 2043 :: Ref. 1848-11-06, 3:1, B.
On the 29th ult., at Belnaleck House, county Fermanagh, the lady of W.A. Dane, Esq., of a daughter.

No. 2044 :: Ref. 1848-11-06, 3:1, B.
At Portadown, on the 28th ult., the lady of J.O. Woodhouse, Esq., of a son.

No. 2045 :: Ref. 1848-11-06, 3:1, B.
On the 28th Oct., at Harrybrook, the lady of James Harden, Esq., of a son.

No. 2046 :: Ref. 1848-11-06, 3:1, B.
Nov. 3, the wife of Mr. Robert Bewglass, of St. John's Wood, London, of a daughter.

No. 2047 :: Ref. 1848-11-06, 3:1, B.
October 23, at Falcaragh, Dunfanaghy, Co. Donegal, the wife of Mr. John C. Hurst, of that town, of a daughter.

No. 2048 :: Ref. 1848-11-06, 3:1, M.
Oct. 30, in Belturbet Church, by the Rev. G.D. Beresford, A.M., Rector of Fanagh, the Rev. M.N. Lawder, A.M. Curate of Derrylane, second son of John Lawder, Esq., of Mough House, county of Leitrim, to Anne, eldest daughter of John Gumley, Esq., of Belfast.

No. 2049 :: Ref. 1848-11-06, 3:1, M.
On Monday, the 30th ult., in Drumquin Meetinghouse, by the Rev. J. Davidson, Miss Ann Robb, teacher of Dooish National School, to W.A. Craig, teacher of Burnfoot National School, near Newtownlimivady.

No. 2050 :: Ref. 1848-11-06, 3:1, M.
On the 24th ult., in the Presbyterian Church, Ballycopeland, by the Rev. Robert Black, Mr. Alexander Boyd, of Ballyblack, to Margaret, daughter of Mr. Alexander M'Hinch, of Killaughy, near Donaghadee.

No. 2051 :: Ref. 1848-11-06, 3:1, M.
At Manorhamilton, Winslow Finey, Esq., medical superintendant of the Swanlinbar dispensary, to Isabella, only daughter of the late Charter Armstrong, Esq., of Lakeview, County Leitrim.

No. 2052 :: Ref. 1848-11-06, 3:1, D.
On 27th ult., in Enniskillen, William Henry, infant son of John Morrison.

No. 2053 :: Ref. 1848-11-06, 3:1, D.
On the 28th ult., after a lingering illness, occasioned, it is supposed, by having about two years back swallowed a small copper coin, Eliza, second daughter of Mr. John Forde, of Lisbellaw, in the ninth year of her age.

No. 2054 :: Ref. 1848-11-06, 3:1, D.
October 25, at Rose Hill, near Strabane, Amelia, sister to John Joyce, Esq., Clerk of the Crown, for the County Donegal.

No. 2055 :: Ref. 1848-11-06, 3:1, D.
On the 11th Sept., at Cincinatti, Ohi [sic], U.S. North America, Mr. Thomas Barr, eldest son of Mr. Wm. Barr, Admirand, Stranorlar, a young man of most exemplary Christian character. Consumption has thus entombed, in less than two years and a-half, no fewer than five of Mr. Barr's children.

No. 2056 :: Ref. 1848-11-06, 3:1, D.
At Strabane, the 25th ult., Margaret, third daughter of Mr. Joseph Henderson.

No. 2057 :: Ref. 1848-11-06, 3:1, D.
In the city of Evansville, Indiana, United States of America, on Thursday the 28th of September, Lucia Ann, wife of Mr. James Reilly (formerly of Drummond, near this city) and eldest daughter of Ira French, Esq., of Cincinatti, aged 22 years.

Lucia! thy life's brief history is told;
A daughter, well beloved, and then a bride;
Alas! the bridal robe hid in its fold,
The traitor DEATH—then busy at thy side.

And yet, 'tis beautiful in youth to die—
Lay down each earthly hope with tranquil brow,
Give parting words and sever each soft tie,
And robe in righteousness—as thou has now!

And though thy memory is a bright bequest,
Yet tears will fall—and bitter sighs be given;
FAITH's guiding hand had led thee into rest,
And "sister spirits" welcomed thee to heaven!

No. 2058 :: Ref. 1848-11-13, 2:5, B.
On the 4th inst., at Newry, the lady of Capt. Cubitt, 9th Regiment, of a son.

No. 2059 :: Ref. 1848-11-13, 2:5, B.
Oct. 23, in Cavan, the lady of the Rev. D.W. Preston, of a son.

No. 2060 :: Ref. 1848-11-13, 2:5, B.
On the 8th inst., at Drum Police office, co. Monaghan, the wife of Mr. Francis Gee, constable in that station, of a daughter.

No. 2061 :: Ref. 1848-11-13, 2:5, M.
On the 9th inst., at St. Ann's church, Dungannon, by the Rev. Thomas Twigg, Robert Hood, Esq., solicitor, of Crossdernot-house, to Charlotte, second daughter of the late Thomas Lilburne, Esq., of Dungannon.

No. 2062 :: Ref. 1848-11-13, 2:5, M.
Nov. 5, in Enniskillen, Mr. Anthony Caulfield, to Susan, eldest daughter of Mr. M. Fitzsimon.

No. 2063 :: Ref. 1848-11-13, 2:5, M.
On the 31st ult., at Bellaghy Church, by the Rev. George Ash, Miss Margaret Donaldson, youngest daughter of Mr. John Donaldson, sergeant of the peace police stationed at Bellaghy, to Mr. James Bligh, sub-constable in a revenue force recently located in the same place.

No. 2064 :: Ref. 1848-11-13, 2:5, D.
Nov. 8, in London, Leonard Dobbin, Esq., jun., eldest son of Leonard Dobbin, Esq., in his 24th year. His remains were deposited in the family vault, in the Cathedral Burying-ground of this city yesterday, the 12th inst., attended by a large and most respectable concourse of his friends and citizens.

No. 2065 :: Ref. 1848-11-13, 2:5, D.
Suddenly, in Cavan, on the 9th inst., after only two hours' illness, Lieutenant Broughton, 57th Regiment.

No. 2066 :: Ref. 1848-11-13, 2:5, D.
In Dungarvan, on the 3d inst., at the advanced age of 79 years Neill O'Donnell, Esq., sincerely and deservedly regretted by a large circle of friends. The deceased was lineally descended from the Chiefs of Tyrconnell.

No. 2067 :: Ref. 1848-11-13, 2:5, D.
At Ballinagh, on the 7th inst., of fever, caught in the discharge of his onerous duties, Head-Constable Charles Spinks, aged 37 years. He served for more than fifteen years in the police force, with credit to himself and advantage to his country.

No. 2068 :: Ref. 1848-11-13, 2:5, D.
George Archer, Esq., Clerk of the Peace for the city of Dublin.

No. 2069 :: Ref. 1848-11-13, 2:5, D.
On the 4th instant, of fever, Mr. Joseph Thetford, Master of the Clones Union Workhouse.

No. 2070 :: Ref. 1848-11-13, 2:5, D.
Of apoplexy, at Sligo, on the 2d instant, Samuel Clarke, third son of the late Mr. Samuel Clarke, of Monaghan.

No. 2071 :: Ref. 1848-11-13, 2:5, D.
At Youghal, Robert Laughlen, son of James Gray, Esq., of the Provincial Bank of Ireland.

No. 2072 :: Ref. 1848-11-13, 2:5, D.
November 1, at Ardlogher Cottage, the seat of her uncle, Dr. Brady, Maryanne, eldest daughter of the late Mr. Edward M'Donald, of Enniskillen.

No. 2073 :: Ref. 1848-11-20, 3:2, B.
Oct. 2, in Toronto, Canada West, the wife of Mr. Robert Corrigan, jun., late of Moss-Spring, Charlemont, of a daughter.

No. 2074 :: Ref. 1848-11-20, 3:2, B.
On the 8th inst., at Kilkenny, the lady of Captain Browne, 3d Regiment (the Buffs), of a son.

No. 2075 :: Ref. 1848-11-20, 3:2, B.
In Hull, Mrs. George Cotton, of three fine children, who, with the mother, are doing well.

No. 2076 :: Ref. 1848-11-20, 3:2, B.
Nov. 10, at Downpatrick, the lady of George F. Echlin, Esq., of a daughter.

No. 2077 :: Ref. 1848-11-20, 3:2, B.
On 2d inst., the wife of Mr. James Wilson, Drimnahoagh, Letterkenny, of a son.

No. 2078 :: Ref. 1848-11-20, 3:2, B.
Nov. 5, at Rose Lodge, Magherafelt, the lady of James Thomson Bryan, Esq., of a son.

No. 2079 :: Ref. 1848-11-20, 3:2, M.
On 13th inst., at Ratoath, by the Rev. Henry Johnston, the Rev. Samuel Simson, Rector of Keady, to Eliza, eldest daughter of the late Stuart Crawford, Esq., M.D., Bath.

No. 2080 :: Ref. 1848-11-20, 3:2, M.
On 16th inst., in first Presbyterian Meeting House, Armagh, by Rev. Mr. Fleming, Mr. Andrew Mayne, Thomas-street, Dublin, second son of Mr. George Mayne, Ballygawley, to Jane, eldest daughter of Mr. John Kennedy, Victoria House, Armagh.

No. 2081 :: Ref. 1848-11-20, 3:2, M.
On 14th inst., in Sandys-street Church, Newry, by the Rev. Alexander Henderson, of Lisburn, uncle to the bride, Robert Orr Blacker, Esq., of Belfast, to Anna, eldest daughter of James Henderson, Esq., of Newry.

No. 2082 :: Ref. 1848-11-20, 3:2, M.
On 10th inst., at Antrim, by the Rev. John B. Campbell, D.D., Incumbent, Manchester, Mr. David Browne, Wellbrook, co. Tyrone, formerly of Ballymena, to Margaret, youngest and only surviving daughter of the late John Connor, Esq., Dunmore Cottage.

No. 2083 :: Ref. 1848-11-20, 3:2, M.

At St. John's [sic], N.B., on 17th Oct., by the Very Rev. James Dunphy, V.G., Denis MacGowan, Esq., M.D., of Boston, U.S., son of James MacGowan, Esq., Mercht., Ballyshannon, Ireland, to Louisa, daughter of the late Wm. Doherty, Esq., Merchant, Strabane, Ireland.

No. 2084 :: Ref. 1848-11-20, 3:2, M.

In Tempo Presbyterian Church, on 10th inst., by the Rev. A.T. Holmes, Mr. Hugh Lynch, of Fivemiletown, to Eliza, third daughter of the late Mr. Henry Wood, of same place.

No. 2085 :: Ref. 1848-11-20, 3:2, M.

Nov. 8, in Clonmany Church, by the Rev. H. Young, brother-in-law to the bride, Nicholas John, eldest son of the Rev. N.J. Halpin, of Seville place, Dublin, to Rebecca, youngest daughter of Michael Doherty, Esq., of Glen House, co. Donegal.

No. 2086 :: Ref. 1848-11-20, 3:2, M.

On 13th inst., at Fintona, Margaret, youngest daughter of the late Mr. Francis M'Aree, to Mr. John M'Laughlin, merchant, Moville.

No. 2087 :: Ref. 1848-11-20, 3:2, M.

On the 10th inst., at Kinlough Church, by the Rev. Henry Johnston, the Rev. Archibald St. George, Rector of Rosinvere, to Penelope, youngest daughter of the late Robt. Johnston, Esq., of Kinlough House.

No. 2088 :: Ref. 1848-11-20, 3:2, M.

On 14th inst., at Magherafelt, by the Rev. Mr. Wilson, Mr. James Stewart, of Drumcairn, Stewartstown, to Maria, third daughter of Mr. James Cathcart, of Springlane, Magherafelt.

No. 2089 :: Ref. 1848-11-20, 3:2, M.

On 9th inst., at Rathmullan Church, by the Rev. Horatio Moffat, Mr. James Moore, Coast-guard, to Miss Ann Quigley, second daughter of Mr. W.B. Quigley, Chief Boatman, St. John's Point.

No. 2090 :: Ref. 1848-11-20, 3:2, D.

Nov. 16th, Mary, daughter of the late Rev. Thomas Cuming, of this city.

No. 2091 :: Ref. 1848-11-20, 3:2, D.

On 7th inst., Elizabeth, wife of Mr. Samuel Walker, Turnkey of Armagh Gaol, aged 60 years.

No. 2092 :: Ref. 1848-11-20, 3:2, D.

On 11th instant, at his residence, Cumber-house, County Derry, J.H. Browne, Esq., in the 85th year of his age.

No. 2093 :: Ref. 1848-11-20, 3:2, D.

On 16th inst., at Saint Catherine's, near Churchhill, co. Fermanagh, of inflammation of the chest, George Rogers, Esq., aged 39 years.

No. 2094 :: Ref. 1848-11-20, 3:2, D.

Nov. 7, at the residence of her son, the Venerable the Archdeacon of Ross, in the 78th year of her age, Letitia, relict of the late Alex. Stuart, of Drumreagh, in the co. of Tyrone, Esq., and daughter of the late Rev. William Murray, D.D., many years principal of the Royal School of Dungannon.

No. 2095 :: Ref. 1848-11-20, 3:2, D.

On 16th inst., at the residence of Lieutenant Hamilton, near Strabane, Mr. James Wilson, proprietor of the well known hotel, in Foyle-street, Derry.

No. 2096 :: Ref. 1848-11-20, 3:2, D.

At his residence, Ballymuckle-cur, by an epileptic fit, on the 9th inst., in the 80th year of his age and 45th of his ministry, the Rev. Alex. Mulligan, Pastor of the Seceding Congregation of Culnady.

No. 2097 :: Ref. 1848-11-20, 3:2, D.

At Kilderry, on 1st inst., aged 82, deeply and deservedly regretted, John Baloo, the faithful and attached follower of the late General George Vaughan Hart. He was a member of the Church of England, and for many years past a constant attendant at public worship. He often partook of the Sacrament of the Lord's Supper; and there is every reason to believe, he died in the full assurance of hope, relying only on the merits of the Redeemer.

No. 2098 :: Ref. 1848-11-20, 3:2, D.

Nov. 7, at his residence in Cavan, Samuel Moore, Esq., in the 74th year of his age. He was one of the oldest magistrates of the county.

No. 2099 :: Ref. 1848-11-20, 3:2, D.

On the 14th inst., in the 52d year of her age, Margaret, relict of the late Wm. Logan, of Newry.

No. 2100 :: Ref. 1848-11-20, 3:2, D.

In Trinidad, on the 21st Aug., James Porter, Esq., son of John Porter, Esq., of Lackagh, co. Donegal.

No. 2101 :: Ref. 1848-11-20, 3:2, D.

On the 9th inst., of fever, at Portsmouth, Frederick Wm. Darley, Esq., 77th Regiment, in his 20th year, only son of Capt. Arthur Darley, R.N.

No. 2102 :: Ref. 1848-11-20, 3:2, D.

On 13th inst., at Rostrevor, Henry Hamilton, Esq., of Carpenham, aged 72 years.

No. 2103 :: Ref. 1848-11-20, 3:2, D.

On 5th inst., at Newry, from the effects of a collision on the railway at Crewe, while proceeding with his regiment to Manchester, Major J. Barry Thomas, late of her Majesty's 9th Regt. of Foot, aged 46 years.

No. 2104 :: Ref. 1848-11-27, 3:1, M.

On the 20th inst., in the Presbyterian Church of Clogher, by the Rev. James Malcolmson, the Rev.

Hugh Alexander, Ballyreagh, to Mary, daughter of the Rev. James Phillips, Fivemiletown.

No. 2105 :: Ref. 1848-11-27, 3:1, M.
On the 21st inst., in the Presbyterian Church of Claggin, by the Rev. Henry M'Caw, Stewart Lecky, Esq., Coal Island, to Eliza, daughter of the late John Ramsay, Esq., Claggin.

No. 2106 :: Ref. 1848-11-27, 3:1, M.
On the 22d inst., at St. Ann's Church, Dungannon, by the Rev. Thomas Carpendale, Rector of Donaghmore, the Rev. Robert Hamilton, of Castlecaulfield, to Emily, eldest daughter of Thomas Kinley, Esq., Union Place, Dungannon.

No. 2107 :: Ref. 1848-11-27, 3:1, M.
In Enniskillen Church, on the 22d inst., by the Rev. Mr. Matthias, Mr. William Henry Curry, Organist, of Sligo, to Margaret, youngest daughter of Mr. John Irwin, of that town.

No. 2108 :: Ref. 1848-11-27, 3:1, M.
On the 15th inst., in the Presbyterian Church, Sandholes, by the Rev. Joseph Geddes, Mr. Joseph Gibson, woollendraper, Coagh, to Jane, eldest daughter of Mr. Loftus Wilson, Coalhill, near Dungannon.

No. 2109 :: Ref. 1848-11-27, 3:1, M.
On the 16th inst., in the Presbyterian Church, Sandholes, by the Rev. Joseph Geddes, Mr. James Wolf, Kildress, to Mary, third daughter of Mr. John Reid, of Sheephill.

No. 2110 :: Ref. 1848-11-27, 3:1, M.
Nov. 18, by special license, at 33, Merrion-square North, by the Very Rev. the Dean of the Chapel Royal, Dublin, Francis R. Brooke, Esq., only son of George Brooke, Esq., of Somerton, in the county of Dublin, to the Hon. Henrietta Monck, third daughter of the Viscount Monck.

No. 2111 :: Ref. 1848-11-27, 3:1, M.
Nov. 23, in Mark's Church, Dublin, Robert Little, Esq., of Monaghan, to Angel Ann, only daughter of the late James Wilkinson Slacke, Esq., of Annadale, in the county of Leitrim.

No. 2112 :: Ref. 1848-11-27, 3:1, M
On 17th inst., in the Presbyterian Church, Bushmills, by the Rev. H. Hamill, Mr. John Wilson, of Ballycastle, to Ellen, second daughter of Mr. John Adair, Clogher.

No. 2113 :: Ref. 1848-11-27, 3:1, D.
Friday 17th, at the residence of his father, Kill, near Dunfanaghy, Mr. Samuel Campbell.

No. 2114 :: Ref. 1848-11-27, 3:1, D.
On 24th inst., in Clogher, in the 18th year of her age, Rebecca, second daughter of Mr. John Brown, Bridewell Keeper; and on the 25th, Rebecca, his wife, aged 55, both of fever.

No. 2115 :: Ref. 1848-11-27, 3:1, D.
On 23d inst., at Drummee, Innishmore, co. Fermanagh, at an advanced age, of disease of the heart, Jane, relict of the late William Armstrong, Esq., in sure and certain hope of a glorious resurrection to eternal life through the merits of her Redeemer.

No. 2116 :: Ref. 1848-11-27, 3:1, D.
Nov. 12, at Maguiresbridge, Mr. James M'Neece, son of Thomas M'Neece, Surgeon, R.N., aged 25 years.

No. 2117 :: Ref. 1848-11-27, 3:1, D.
On the 11th inst., at Newtownards, Mrs. M'Cutcheon, aged 60 years.

No. 2118 :: Ref. 1848-11-27, 3:1, D.
On the 18th inst., at Haig Terrace, Kingstown, Miss Emily Maginness, sister to the late Sir John Maginness, Londonderry.

No. 2119 :: Ref. 1848-11-27, 3:1, D.
On 14th inst., at Boulogne-sur-Mer, Mr. Thomas Knox Hannyngton, Esq., the Castle, Dungannon, aged 85 years.

No. 2120 :: Ref. 1848-11-27, 3:1, D.
On 17th inst., at Rostrever, Dr. George G. Simpson, R.N., son of Wm. Simpson, Esq., Newtownards.

No. 2121 :: Ref. 1848-12-01, 3:3, B.
On the 24th ult., at Scarnamallagh Glebe, co. Donegal, the lady of the Rev. Samuel O'Neill Cox, of a son.

No. 2122 :: Ref. 1848-12-01, 3:3, B.
At Anketell Grove, on 27th ult., the lady of Matthew John Anketell, Esq., of a daughter.

No. 2123 :: Ref. 1848-12-01, 3:3, B.
On the 24th of Nov., at Cookstown, the lady of Andrew James Newton, Esq., of a son.

No. 2124 :: Ref. 1848-12-01, 3:3, M.
On the 27th ult., Sir James Murray, of Merrion-square, Dublin, to Mary, daughter of the late Samuel Allen, Esq., M.D., Larne, and niece to Charles M'Garel, Esq., High Sheriff, co. Antrim.

No. 2125 :: Ref. 1848-12-01, 3:3, M.
On the 17th October, at the house of her brother-in-law, William L. Ewing, Esq., Capefield, Gore District, Canada West, by the Rev. J.C. Usher, Thomas Baker, Esq., Lieut. R.N., formerly of Portsea, Hants, England, to Mary Jane, fifth daughter of John M'Ilwaine, Esq., Strabane, Ireland.

No. 2126 :: Ref. 1848-12-01, 3:3, M.
At Killult Church, by the Rev. Mr. Roleston, Mr. Samuel Kyle Hinchey, to Susanna Maria, daughter of Mr. William James, of Bunbeg, Gweedore.

No. 2127 :: Ref. 1848-12-01, 3:3, D.
On the 21st., at Cork Abbey, the seat of her grandfather, the Hon. Edward Wingfield, Cecilia, daughter of Sir William Verner, Bart.

No. 2128 :: Ref. 1848-12-01, 3:3, D.
On the 20th ult., at Tullyhogue, county Tyrone, of consumption, Mary Isabella, eldest daughter of Alex. Crozier, Esq., Lieut. of the Royal North Down Regt. of Militia.

No. 2129 :: Ref. 1848-12-01, 3:3, D.
At Strabane, on Saturday evening last, Mr. John Lennon, music master.

No. 2130 :: Ref. 1848-12-01, 3:3, D.
At Newry, on the 23d ult., Mr. Hugh Fay, for upwards of thirty years guard of the Fair Trader coach, running between Dublin and Belfast.

No. 2131 :: Ref. 1848-12-05, 3:1, B.
On 29th ult., the lady of David White, Esq., of Lisonally House, near Omagh, of a daughter.

No. 2132 :: Ref. 1848-12-05, 3:1, B.
Nov. 29, in Enniskillen, the wife of Wm. Trimble, Esq., proprietor of the *"Impartial Reporter,"* of a daughter.

No. 2133 :: Ref. 1848-12-05, 3:1, B.
Nov. 29, at Retreat, co. Monaghan, the lady of Captain Kirk, Staff Officer, of a daughter.

No. 2134 :: Ref. 1848-12-05, 3:1, M.
Nov. 30, in Strabane Church, by the Rev. James Smyth, William Clarke, Esq., of Maghera, to Jane, daughter of the late Andrew Browne, Esq., Woodbank, near Coleraine.

No. 2135 :: Ref. 1848-12-05, 3:1, M.
Nov. 28, in Camerton Church, Saint Helens, Maryport, by the Rev. Mr. Joyce, Hugh Quin, Esq., P.L.G., Creggan House, Cookstown, county Tyrone, to Elizabeth, youngest daughter of Joseph Cape, Esq., of Saint Helens, Cumberland.

No. 2136 :: Ref. 1848-12-05, 3:1, D.
Nov. 30, at Killycolp, Dungannon, Mary, the beloved wife of H.A. Griffith, Esq., after a long and painful illness.

No. 2137 :: Ref. 1848-12-05, 3:1, D.
Nov. 28, in Peter-street, Drogheda, after a short illness, Thomas Apperson, Esq., proprietor of the *Drogheda Conservative Journal*.

No. 2138 :: Ref. 1848-12-05, 3:1, D.
On Monday, the 27th Nov., at the residence of her Nephew, Mr. James M'William, Keady, Jane, widow of the late Mr. Thomas Cunningham, of Markethill, at the advanced age of 78.

No. 2139 :: Ref. 1848-12-05, 3:1, D.
At Port Robinson, Upper Canada, America, on the 22d October, aged 26 years, Mr. Thomas Blake Thornley, only son of Thomas Thornley, Esq., Sub-Inspector of Constabulary, Coleraine.

No. 2140 :: Ref. 1848-12-05, 3:1, D.
Nov. 28, at Elm Lodge, Sandymount, deeply and deservedly regretted by all who knew her, Mrs. Frances Flood Handcock, granddaughter of the late Sir Frederick Flood, Bart., and relict of the late Rev. John Gustavus Handcock, Rector of the parish of Annaduff, county of Leitrim.

No. 2141 :: Ref. 1848-12-05, 3:1, D.
Nov. 21, at Killilahard, after a few days' illness, Mr. Joseph Coulson, surveyor and engineer, deeply and deservedly regretted. He practised his profession for upwards of forty years to the satisfaction of all parties, which will serve as a monument of his correctness and worth for ages to come. His memory will long remain green in the hearts of all who had the pleasure of knowing him.

No. 2142 :: Ref. 1848-12-11, 2:6, B.
On 1st inst., at the Rectory House, Killyshandra, the lady of Rev. Dr. Martin, of a son.

No. 2143 :: Ref. 1848-12-11, 2:6, B.
On 3d inst., the lady of Richard Hayes, Esq., of Willmount, Ranbridge [sic], of a son.

No. 2144 :: Ref. 1848-12-11, 2:6, B.
On 3d inst., at Benburb, the lady of Mr. Edwin S. Maxwell, Surgeon, of a daughter.

No. 2145 :: Ref. 1848-12-11, 2:6, M.
In Swanlinbar Church, on the 6th inst., by the Rev. John James Egan, Mr. E.B. Drennan, to Letitia, youngest daughter of Andrew Hill, Esq.

No. 2146 :: Ref. 1848-12-11, 2:6, M.
Nov. 30, at Tempo, by the Rev. John Whittaker, Mr. Robert Hunter, merchant, to Sarah, third daughter of John Gibson, Esq., both of Tempo.

No. 2147 :: Ref. 1848-12-11, 2:6, M.
On the 30th ult., at Ewell church, Surrey, Thos. Wallace, Esq., merchant, of Londonderry, to Emma Lincoln, youngest daughter of the late Charles Lane, Esq., surgeon, of London.

No. 2148 :: Ref. 1848-12-11, 2:6, M.
Nov. 30, in the Presbyterian Meeting-house of Tullylish, by the Rev. J. Johnston, James Beck, Esq., of Gilford, merchant, to Mary Ann, eldest daughter of Hamilton Coulter, Esq., of Rosemount Cottage, near Gilford.

No. 2149 :: Ref. 1848-12-11, 2:6, M.
On the 5th inst., at St. Ann's Church, Belfast, by the Rev. T.F. Millar, Vicar, and afterwards by the

Right Rev. the R.C. Bishop of Down and Connor, David Richard Pigot, Esq., second son of the Right Hon. the Lord Chief Baron, to Christina, daughter of Sir Jas. Murray, of Merrion-Square, Dublin.

No. 2150 :: Ref. 1848-12-11, 2:6, M.
Nov. 30, Miss Gore, daughter of Wm. H. Gore, Esq., of Gore Hall, Cheshire, to Edward M. Norris, Esq., youngest son of the late James Norris, Esq., Kieran House, county of Meath.

No. 2151 :: Ref. 1848-12-11, 2:6, M.
On the 4th inst., in the Meeting-house of the Second Congregation, Rosemary-street, by the Rev. John Porter, Mr. Andrew Kirkpatrick, of Belfast, latterly of Antrim, and originally of Castlewellan, to Ann, daughter of Mr. Daniel Drennan, of Drumbeg, near Lisburn.

No. 2152 :: Ref. 1848-12-11, 2:6, M.
On the 6th inst., at Antrim Church, by the Rev. Wm. Greene, Vicar, Wm. Patrick Carr, Esq., Barrister-at-law, fifth son of the Rev. George Carr, of New Ross, county Wexford, to Elizabeth, third daughter of the late John French, Esq., of that town.

No. 2153 :: Ref. 1848-12-11, 2:6, M.
On 5th inst., in the Presbyterian Church, Randalstown, by the Rev. Robert Marr, Mr. Wm. Charleton, of Tamlaght, Coagh, to Miss Sarah Anne Irvine, of Cranfield, county Antrim.

No. 2154 :: Ref. 1848-12-11, 2:6, D.
On 6th inst., of fever, James Simpson, Esq., Aughnacloy.

No. 2155 :: Ref. 1848-12-11, 2:6, D.
On the 2d inst., at Clenavy Glebe, Fanny, wife of the Rev. Ross Jebb.

No. 2156 :: Ref. 1848-12-11, 2:6, D.
On the 3d inst., at his residence, Bessmount, near Dundonald, David Trimble, aged 57 years.

No. 2157 :: Ref. 1848-12-11, 2:6, D.
At his residence, Dominick-street, Galway, after a few days' illness, Counsellor M.J. Burke, Editor and Proprietor of the *Galway Mercury*.

No. 2158 :: Ref. 1848-12-11, 2:6, D.
Suddenly, on the 29th Nov., Mr. Robert Hutcheson, of Mountnorris.

No. 2159 :: Ref. 1848-12-11, 2:6, D.
Dec 4, at Dromarky Cottage, of fever, the Rev. George W. Welsh, Incumbent of Castle Archdall, in the 34th year of his age.

No. 2160 :: Ref. 1848-12-11, 2:6, D.
Nov. 26, of inflammation, Mr. M'Donnell, of 66, Middle Abbey-st., Dublin, at the residence of his Son-in-law, Mr. E. Nolan, Windmill-Hill, Enniskillen.

No. 2161 :: Ref. 1848-12-11, 2:6, D.
On the 5th inst., in London, Mrs. Elizabeth Harvey, second daughter of the late Thomas Harvey, Esq., of Newry, formerly of Greenhill, co. Tyrone.

No. 2162 :: Ref. 1848-12-11, 2:6, D.
On the 1st inst., at her residence in Markethill, in the 80th year of her age, Mrs. Stuart, relict of the late David Stuart, Esq., Rose Hall.

No. 2163 :: Ref. 1848-12-11, 2:6, D.
In Newtownlimavady Workhouse, on the 6th inst., Rebecca Thompson, formerly of the Highlands, aged 100 years.

No. 2164 :: Ref. 1848-12-11, 2:6, D.
On the 5th inst., at Derriaghy, in the 62nd year of her age, Rebecca, wife of Mr. Grainger, and last surviving daughter of the late Mr. W. Roberts of same place.

No. 2165 :: Ref. 1848-12-18, 3:1, B.
Dec. 6, at Edinburgh, the Hon. Mrs. Wm. Maude, of a daughter.

No. 2166 :: Ref. 1848-12-18, 3:1, B.
December 8, at Sprackburn, Letterkenny, the wife of Dr. Little, of a son.

No. 2167 :: Ref. 1848-12-18, 3:1, B.
On the 1st inst., at Killyshandra, the lady of the Rev. Dr. Martin, of a son.

No. 2168 :: Ref. 1848-12-18, 3:1, M.
On the 14th inst., in St. Mark's Church, in this city, by the Rev. Mr. Chamley, Mr. James Matchet, of the Tontine Rooms, to Margaret, daughter of Mr. Simon Armstrong, Durham, England.

No. 2169 :: Ref. 1848-12-18, 3:1, M.
In Tynan Church, on the 7th inst., by the Rev. J. Percival, Mr. Francis Graham, Cornaho, co. Monaghan, to Eliza, second daughter of Mr. Robert Clarke, of Fellowshall, county Armagh.

No. 2170 :: Ref. 1848-12-18, 3:1, M.
On the 5th inst., in Randalstown, by the Rev. Robt. Marr, Mr. W. Charleton, of Tamlaght, Coagh, to Miss Sarah Anne Irvine, Crayfield, co. Armagh.

No. 2171 :: Ref. 1848-12-18, 3:1, M.
In Ardbraccan Church, Richd. Nugent, Esq., son of C.J. Nugent Esq., of Farrenconnel-house, Cavan, to Amelia St. George Stopford, daughter of the Lord Bishop of Meath.

No. 2172 :: Ref. 1848-12-18, 3:1, M.
Dec. 4, in Kilmore Church, by the Rev. J.F. Lloyd, Mr. John Bell, Pensioner, to Mrs. Mary Taplay, both of the county Armagh. The bridegroom, who is 75 years old, has but one tooth and one leg; the bride's age is 65. A youthful couple!

No. 2173 :: Ref. 1848-12-18, 3:1, M.

Dec. 9, at Ballyboy Church, W.J. Dorehill, Esq., Lieut. 3d Regt. of Foot, to Margaret, only daughter of Lieut. Robert Mitchell, half-pay 28th Foot, of Frankford, King's co.

No. 2174 :: Ref. 1848-12-18, 3:1, M.

On the 1st inst., in Banbridge, by the Rev. Robert Anderson, Mr. David Cathcart, woollendraper, to Rachel, eldest daughter of Mr. Joseph Davidson, Banbridge.

No. 2175 :: Ref. 1848-12-18, 3:1, M.

On the 9th inst., at Cork, William Fletcher, Esq., of Limerick, to Madalena, daughter of James Greer, Esq., of Baltimore, U.S., and late of Lissne, Lisburn.

No. 2176 :: Ref. 1848-12-18, 3:1, M.

On the 12th instant, in Magherafelt, by the Rev. James Wilson, George Brown, jun., to Maria, second daughter of Captain Stover, both of Magherafelt.

No. 2177 :: Ref. 1848-12-18, 3:1, M.

On the 11th inst., at Croagh, by the Rev. R. Simpson, Mr. Andrew Alexander, of Bushmills, to Miss Curry, daughter of the late Mr. Wm. Curry, of Magherintendry.

No. 2178 :: Ref. 1848-12-18, 3:1, M.

Dec 8, in Killead, by the Rev. Joseph M'Kee, Mr. Thos. Hunter, Killealy, to Ellen, youngest daughter of the late Mr. Wm. Moore, Crookedstone, and niece of John Moore, Esq., Glendaragh Cottage, Crumlin.

No. 2179 :: Ref. 1848-12-18, 3:1, M.

Dec. 7, in St. Peter's Church, Pimlico, London, by the Rev. Chas. Tower, Robert Tower, Esq., son of the late Rev. Charles Tower, of Shenfield-place, Essex, to Clara, youngest daughter of Lieutenant-Colonel Verner, and niece of the Dowager Marchioness of Donegal.

No. 2180 :: Ref. 1848-12-18, 3:1, M.

Dec. 6, by the Rev. A. Jones, John Ridge, Esq., Cookstown, son of the late Rev. J. Ridge, of Cahir, to Martha Ussher, eldest daughter of Thomas Greer, Esq., Tullylagan, county Tyrone.

No. 2181 :: Ref. 1848-12-18, 3:1, M.

On the 5th inst., by the Rev. George Steen, Mr. Charles Campbell, of Newtownlimavady, to Miss Eliza Taylor, of Fruithill.

No. 2182 :: Ref. 1848-12-18, 3:1, M.

On 6th Dec., in Killogue Church, co. Leitrim, by the Rev. George Hynds, vicar of that parish, Simon Armstrong, jun., Esq., of Manorhamilton, to Eliza, fourth daughter of the late John Palmer, Esq., of Townelea House.

No. 2183 :: Ref. 1848-12-18, 3:1, M.

On the 14th inst., at St. Mark's Church, Portadown, by the Rev. De'L. Willis, John Kiernan, Esq., of Moat House, county Longford, to Emily, second daughter of James Cowan, Esq., Barn Cottage, Carrickfergus.

No. 2184 :: Ref. 1848-12-18, 3:1, D.

On the 13th inst., at the house of her son, Mr. Charles Connolly, merchant, Armagh, after a lingering illness, Ellen, relict of the late Mr. Henry Connolly, aged 74 years.

No. 2185 :: Ref. 1848-12-18, 3:1, D.

On this morning, in English-street, in this city, of water on the brain, James, third son of Mr. John Hall, painter, aged 4 years.

No. 2186 :: Ref. 1848-12-18, 3:1, D.

Dec. 10, at the Barracks, Enniskillen, of fever, Johnston Thompson Richardson, M.D., Surgeon of the 57th Regiment.

No. 2187 :: Ref. 1848-12-18, 3:1, D.

December 9, at Castleblaney, the wife of the Rev. Thomas Boyd of that place.

No. 2188 :: Ref. 1848-12-18, 3:1, D.

In Cavan, on the 3d inst., Eliza Louisa, third daughter of John Hitchcock, Esq., of Dublin.

No. 2189 :: Ref. 1848-12-18, 3:1, D.

Dec. 11, Maria Isabella, infant daughter of G.A. Nixon, M.D., Enniskillen.

No. 2190 :: Ref. 1848-12-18, 3:1, D.

Dec. 10, Michael, infant son of Mr. P. M'Ginn, merchant, Enniskillen.

No. 2191 :: Ref. 1848-12-18, 3:1, D.

On the 9th inst., at her residence, Great George's-street, Dublin, Hannah, relict of the late Joseph Hind, shipbroker, Belfast, aged 57 years.

No. 2192 :: Ref. 1848-12-18, 3:1, D.

On the 28th ult., at Letterkenny, Mr. John Fisher Lyttle, aged 42 years.

No. 2193 :: Ref. 1848-12-18, 3:1, D.

At St. Johnston, at the advanced age of 78 years, Miss Hannah Magill.

No. 2194 :: Ref. 1848-12-18, 3:1, D.

Of typhus fever, on the 9th ult, at Portsmouth, Ensign Darley, of the 77th Regt., grandson of the late William Thornton Todd, Esq., of Buncrana Castle, co. Donegal.

No. 2195 :: Ref. 1848-12-18, 3:1, D.

On the 17th instant, Jane Maria, the daughter of Mr. Bessell, of Belfast.

No. 2196 :: Ref. 1848-12-18, 3:1, D.

On the 14th inst., aged 27 years, Margaret, eldest daughter of Mr. George Patterson, of Belfast.

No. 2197 :: Ref. 1848-12-18, 3:1, D.
On the 11th inst., in Belfast, Mary, the beloved wife of Mr. John Murray, aged 37 years.

No. 2198 :: Ref. 1848-12-18, 3:1, D.
On the 9th inst., at Lisburn, William M'Donald, Surgeon, aged 41 years.

No. 2199 :: Ref. 1848-12-18, 3:1, D.
On the 10th inst., at Woodtown-house, co. Dublin, George Joy, Esq., nephew of the late Lord Chief Baron Joy.

No. 2200 :: Ref. 1848-12-18, 3:1, D.
On the 4th inst., Samuel Gordon, of Downpatrick, Esq., Solicitor.

No. 2201 :: Ref. 1848-12-18, 3:1, D.
At Luney, near Magherafelt, on the 9th instant, of consumption, Mr. James Bell, formerly assistant-master in the Magherafelt Union Workhouse.

No. 2202 :: Ref. 1848-12-25, 2:5, B.
In Swanlinbar, on the 19th inst., the lady of Captain Johnston, of a son.

No. 2203 :: Ref. 1848-12-25, 2:5, B.
On the 18th instant, at Cara House, co. Fermanagh, the lady of Henry Jackson, Esq., of a son.

No. 2204 :: Ref. 1848-12-25, 2:5, M.
Dec. 19, at St. Ann's Church, Belfast, by the Rev. T.F. Miller, Mr. Joseph Daniel Griffith, Officer of Excise, to Mrs. M'Elivee, both of Portadown.

No. 2205 :: Ref. 1848-12-25, 2:5, M.
Dec. 12, the Rev. Henry Herbert Stepney, son of the late Colonel Stepney, of Durrow Abbey, to Thomasine Sophia, relict of Robert Saunderson, of Ravenswood, County of Cavan, Esq., only daughter of the late Colonel Thomas Tenison, of Kilronan Castle, and sister of E.K. Tenison, Esq., M.P.

No. 2206 :: Ref. 1848-12-25, 2:5, M.
On the 14th inst., in Coagh, by the Rev. Robert Holmes, Mr. John Riddle, to Mrs. Sarah Darragh, widow, Aughnacloy, co. Tyrone.

No. 2207 :: Ref. 1848-12-25, 2:5, M.
Nov. 22, at Claggan, co. Tyrone, Stewart Lecky, Esq., of Coalisland, to Jane, daughter of the late John Ramsey, Esq., of Claggan.

No. 2208 :: Ref. 1848-12-25, 2:5, M.
Dec. 19, at Ballynode Church, by the Rev. William H.E. Woodwright, John T. Banks, M.D., of Dublin, to Alice Jane, daughter of the late James Woodwright, Esq., of Gola House, co. Monaghan.

No. 2209 :: Ref. 1848-12-25, 2:5, D.
On the 19th inst., at Lurgangreen, co. Louth, in the 82d year of her age, Elizabeth, relict of the late Wm. Rodgers, Esq.

No. 2210 :: Ref. 1848-12-25, 2:5, D.
At his residence, Moughan, near Markethill, Mr. Archibald Armstrong.

No. 2211 :: Ref. 1848-12-25, 2:5, D.
Dec. 17, at his residence, Cranbrooke, co. Fermanagh, Jas. Taylor, Esq., in the 87th year of his age.

No. 2212 :: Ref. 1848-12-25, 2:5, D.
On the 10th inst., at Caledon, aged 86 years, Miss A. Marshall.

No. 2213 :: Ref. 1848-12-25, 2:5, D.
On the 19th inst., Mr. John Skelton, of Omagh, aged 40 years.

No. 2214 :: Ref. 1848-12-25, 2:5, D.
At Omagh, on the 22d inst., Mr. John Kelly.

No. 2215 :: Ref. 1848-12-25, 2:5, D.
Dec. 15, of apoplexy, John Harris, Esq., M.D., Fellow of the Royal College of Physicians.

No. 2216 :: Ref. 1848-12-25, 2:5, D.
On the 22nd inst., at the Provincial Bank, Monaghan, in his 22nd year, Frederick Malley, Esq., second son of James Malley, Esq., of Castlebar.

No. 2217 :: Ref. 1848-12-25, 2:5, D.
At Yorkville, South Carolina, 3d October last, Capt. John Blair, aged 78 years. He was born in the county Tyrone—spent the early part of his life in Strabane and Donagheady, and emigrated to America in 1796.

No. 2218 :: Ref. 1849-01-01, 2:5, B.
At Bundoran, co. Donegal, the lady of John Allingham, Esq., of a daughter.

No. 2219 :: Ref. 1849-01-01, 2:5, B.
Dec. 22, at Bellaghy Castle, the wife of William Moore, of Moore Fort, Esq., of a son.

No. 2220 :: Ref. 1849-01-01, 2:5, B.
Dec. 25, at Philipstown Rectory, the lady of the Rev. Lord John Beresford, of a son.

No. 2221 :: Ref. 1849-01-01, 2:5, B.
Dec. 18th, at Cara House, co. Fermanagh, the wife of Henry Jackson, Esq., of a son.

No. 2222 :: Ref. 1849-01-01, 2:5, B.
At Cookstown, on the 16th ult., the lady of James Paul, Esq., Ulster Bank, of a son.

No. 2223 :: Ref. 1849-01-01, 2:5, M.
Dec. 27, at St. Mark's Church, Armagh, by the Rev. Alexander Irwin, J.E. Addison, Esq., 70th Regt., to Catherine Annee [sic], eldest daughter of the late George Prentice.

No. 2224 :: Ref. 1849-01-01, 2:5, M.
Dec. 21, at Mellifont Church, by the Rev. W. Beresford, E.W. Jeffreys, Esq., to Letitia Dorothea, daughter of the late Rev. James M'Creight, formerly Rector of Keady.

No. 2225 :: Ref. 1849-01-01, 2:5, M.
Dec. 28, in St. Peter's Church, by the J.H. Armstrong, Edward Benjamin Braddell, Esq., Captain, 70th Regiment, to Elizabeth Malvina, Daughter of William Hopkins, of Fitzwilliam-square, Esq.

No. 2226 :: Ref. 1849-01-01, 2:5, M.
On the 28th ult., at Strabane, by the Rev. Joseph Moreton, rector of Strokestown, Randle Peyton, of Dublin, Esq., solicitor, to Mary, eldest daughter of William Stevenson, Esq., of Strabane.

No. 2227 :: Ref. 1849-01-01, 2:5, M.
At Beragh, on the 24th ult., by the Rev. P. Quinn, P.P., Matthew Rogers, Esq., mercht., to Isabella, third daughter of Edwd. M'Donnell, Esq., of Mullahead House, Tandragee.

No. 2228 :: Ref. 1849-01-01, 2:5, D.
At her residence, Summerhill, Dublin, aged 81 years, Mrs. Johnston, relict of the late — Johnston, Esq., formerly of Knappa.—Her remains passed through this city to-day, for interment at Eglish, the family burying place, attended by a numerous and respectable concourse of sorrowing friends.

No. 2229 :: Ref. 1849-01-01, 2:5, D.
Nov. 21st, in Toronto, Upper Canada, Eleanor, wife of Mr. Robt. Corrigan, jun., late of Moss Spring, Charlemont, Co. Armagh, and daughter of the late Mr. Wm. Bewglass, of Killyman, Moy, county Tyrone.

No. 2230 :: Ref. 1849-01-01, 2:5, D.
On the Morning of 20th ult., at her residence, Woodvill, near Lurgangreen, much respected and lamented, in the 83d year of her age, Elizabeth, relict of the late Mr. Wm. Rogers, for upwards of 40 years post-master of the latter place, and mother of Mr. William Rogers, of Armagh.

No. 2231 :: Ref. 1849-01-01, 2:5, D.
Dec. 18, Edward Alexander, eldest son of the Rev. Francis Hurst, of Errigle Glebe, co. Monaghan, aged 19 years.

No. 2232 :: Ref. 1849-01-01, 2:5, D.
On the 26th ult., Sarah Jane, eldest daughter of the late Mr. John Robinson, printer and bookseller, of Omagh, aged 20 years.

No. 2233 :: Ref. 1849-01-01, 2:5, D.
In Beragh, suddenly, on the 27th ult., Mr. J. M'Farland, merchant.

No. 2234 :: Ref. 1849-01-01, 2:5, D.
Dec. 5, at Malta, W.H. Hotham, Esq., Lieutenant 44th Regiment.

No. 2235 :: Ref. 1849-01-01, 2:5, D.
Dec. 25, Captain Edward D'Arcy, of the Royal Hospital, Kilmainham, and formerly Captain in the 43d Light Infantry. This gallant officer lost both his legs at the siege of New Orleans.

No. 2236 :: Ref. 1849-01-01, 2:5, D.
On the 20th ult., of inflammatory croup, at Corcreevy-house, near Fivemiletown, Robert Acheson T. Burnside, aged 3 years and 2 months. This was an infant of majestic mind, noble form, and of a gracious heart. He breathed his spirit without a murmur into his Saviour's bosom, and is now the first fruits of a numerous and deeply stricken family to God and the Lamb. Amongst many sweet hymns it was his delight to sing, his favourite one was—

O, then to glory run,
See a crown and kingdom won:
Bright, bright, above the sun,
We'll reign for aye.

No. 2237 :: Ref. 1849-01-01, 2:5, D.
On the 26th ult., at Larchfield, Kingscourt, Ellen, the beloved wife of the Rev. Robert Winning, Incumbent of Enniskillen. Her end was perfect peace.

No. 2238 :: Ref. 1849-01-01, 2:5, D.
Of typhus fever, on 21st ult., at Londonderry, where he had been on a visit, the Rev. Anthony Dillon, R.C.C., of Donegal aged 31 years.

No. 2239 :: Ref. 1849-01-08, 3:1, B.
Jan. 1, in Church-st., Enniskillen, Mrs. Wm. Quinton, of a son.

No. 2240 :: Ref. 1849-01-08, 3:1, B.
Dec. 28, at Castle Hamilton, co. Cavan, the lady of Joseph Dickson, Esq., of Drummully House, in the same county, of a son and heir.

No. 2241 :: Ref. 1849-01-08, 3:1, M.
At Plymouth, Lieut. Thomas Parker Wright, 83d Regiment, son of Major Wright, to Mary Macaulay, daughter of Doctor Hamilton, and grand-daughter of the late Rev. Dr. William Hamilton, one of the founders of the Royal Irish Academy.

No. 2242 :: Ref. 1849-01-08, 3:1, M.
On 2d inst., in Donoughmore Church, Thos. Hamilton, Esq., of Dublin, to Margaret Eliza, eldest daughter of the Rev. A. Hamilton, of Donoughmore, co. Tyrone.

No. 2243 :: Ref. 1849-01-08, 3:1, M.
On 2d inst., in Dungannon Church, by the Rev. William Quain, Mr. Samuel W. Cordner, organist, Dungannon, to Mademoiselle Jeane Louise Brenner, late of the Canton de Vaud, Switzerland.

No. 2244 :: Ref. 1849-01-08, 3:1, M.
On 28th ult., at the office of the Registrar of marriages, Enniskillen, Mr. James Armstrong, to Miss Anne Armstrong, both of Trillick.

No. 2245 :: Ref. 1849-01-08, 3:1, M.
January 1st, 1849, in the Presbyterian Church, Middletown, John Sturgeon, Esq., Keady, to Jane Elizabeth, second daughter of the late James Johnston, Esq., Middletown, county Armagh.

No. 2246 :: Ref. 1849-01-08, 3:1, M.

Dec. 27, at Drumlane Church, by the Rev. G.B. Moffatt, James Morton, Esq., to Mary Martha, only daughter of the late James Clarke, Esq., of Belturbet, Civil Engineer, and County Surveyor for Tyrone.

No. 2247 :: Ref. 1849-01-08, 3:1, D.

At Mullabrack, county Armagh, on the 3d of January, 1849, in the 78th year of his age, Rev. Samuel Blacker, L.L.D., for many years Rector of the parish of Mullabrack.

No. 2248 :: Ref. 1849-01-08, 3:1, D.

Mrs. Robt. Corrigan.—(From the *Toronto Christian Guardian*).—In this city, November 21st., Eleanor, wife of Mr. Robert Corrigan, of Yonge-street. Her illness was of a lingering character, which she bore with unwavering Christian fortitude. Mrs. C. was a native of Ireland, of the county Tyrone, near Moy, where she became experimentally acquainted with the gospel of her Lord and Saviour. The Rev. C. Byrne, who was intimately acquainted with her on the Dungannon Circuit, and who has had the opportunity of constantly visiting her during her protracted affliction in this city, states, that her confidence in the adorable Lord was, up to the period of her departure, most satisfactory. Some time before she changed mortality for life, she requested a few friends to sing the 734th hymn of the Wesleyan Collection,

"And let this feeble body fail," &c.

She sweetly joined in the exercise, and while the last stanza was being sung her voice was specially raised, her countenance glowed with heavenly animation, so that all present became deeply persuaded that her spiritual consolations were of a high order. No doubt remained that victory—victory through the blood of the cross, was her joyful possession. By request we make this insertion, in order that her numerous friends may, as far as possible, know that their mourning for a most amiable Christian sister cannot be as that of those who have no hope.

No. 2249 :: Ref. 1849-01-08, 3:1, D.

Dec. 29, at Beechmount, Rathkeale, Jane, second daughter of T. Lloyd, Esq., caused by a sudden hemorrhage, from an accidental gun-shot wound in her foot.

No. 2250 :: Ref. 1849-01-08, 3:1, D.

At his residence, Castletown, Celbridge, on the 4th inst., Lieut.-Colonel Edward Michael Conolly, M.P., for county Donegal.

No. 2251 :: Ref. 1849-01-08, 3:1, D.

On 4th inst., at Fardross, near Clogher, Sophia, wife of Robert Hornidge, Esq.

No. 2252 :: Ref. 1849-01-08, 3:1, D.

On 28th ult., at Mount Pollock, near Dungannon, Mr. James M'Clelland, aged 48 years.

No. 2253 :: Ref. 1849-01-08, 3:1, D.

In Tralee, aged 87 years, George Herbert Chute, Esq., for many years proprietor of the *Western Herald*, and editor of the *Kerry Evening Post*.

No. 2254 :: Ref. 1849-01-08, 3:1, D.

At Flushtown, near Strabane, on 27th ult., Mrs. Mary Bradden, aged upwards of 100 years. The deceased retained her mental and physical faculties until the last, and had a wonderfully retentive memory, which made her conversational relaxations deeply interesting. One of her numerous grandsons was the late Rev. Hugh Monaghan, diocese of Derry.

No. 2255 :: Ref. 1849-01-15, 3:1, B.

Dec. 30, the wife of Robert Anderson, Esq., of Brocka, near Lowtherstown, co. Fermanagh, of a daughter.

No. 2256 :: Ref. 1849-01-15, 3:1, B.

On 9th inst., at Clogher, the wife of Mr. John Bryan of a daughter.

No. 2257 :: Ref. 1849-01-15, 3:1, B.

On 29th ult., the wife of Wm. C. Boyd, Esq., Head Master of Dundalk Endowed School, of a daughter.

No. 2258 :: Ref. 1849-01-15, 3:1, B.

Dec. 7, at Derrybard, co. Tyrone, the seat of her father, the wife of James Lendrum, Esq., of Corkhill, co. Tyrone, of a daughter.

No. 2259 :: Ref. 1849-01-15, 3:1, B.

On 7th inst., in Enniskillen, the wife of Rev. W.H. Bradshaw, of a son.

No. 2260 :: Ref. 1849-01-15, 3:1, B.

On 12th inst., the wife of Mr. Thomas Armstrong, Canal Stores, Caledon, of a daughter.

No. 2261 :: Ref. 1849-01-15, 3:1, B.

On the 8th inst., at Newry, the wife of Mr. W.J. Blackham, of a daughter.

No. 2262 :: Ref. 1849-01-15, 3:1, B.

In Ballyshannon, on the 6th inst., the wife of F.T. Stubbs, Esq., Provincial Bank, of a son.

No. 2263 :: Ref. 1849-01-15, 3:1, B.

On 8th inst., the wife of J. Jones, Esq., Supervisor of Excise, Ballyshannon, of a daughter.

No. 2264 :: Ref. 1849-01-15, 3.1, M.

On Thursday, the 11th inst., at St. Mark's Church, Armagh, by the Rev. James Hardy, brother-in-law to the bride, John George, youngest son of the Late Samuel Woodhouse, Esq., of Norley Hall, Cheshire, to Mary Frances, fourth daughter of the late Robert Harden, of Harrybrook, Esq., J.P., and D.L., co. Armagh.

No. 2265 :: Ref. 1849-01-15, 3:1, M.

In Cavan, by the Right Rev. Dr. Browne, Mr. Cornelius Philips, to Mary Anne, eldest daughter of Mr. John Brady, Merchant.

No. 2266 :: Ref. 1849-01-15, 3:1, M.

On the 11th inst., in Killyman Church, Mr. Thomas Prescott, of Feagey, Parish of Tartaraghan, to Jane, youngest daughter of Mr. Thomas Hays, Canticlay.

No. 2267 :: Ref. 1849-01-15, 3:1, M.

At Killybegs, on 4th Jan. by the Rev. Dr. Mulreany, John Hudson, Esq., of Sligo, to Isabella, second daughter of Capt. Browne, Killybegs.

No. 2268 :: Ref. 1849-01-15, 3:1, M.

On the 8th inst., at Enniskillen, Mr. William Kerr, to Miss Elizabeth Boles, both of Lisdervick, Parish of Killesher, co. Fermanagh.

No. 2269 :: Ref. 1849-01-22, 3:2, B.

In Armagh, on the 17th inst., at the residence of her father, Mr. Wm. Barnes, Margaret, wife of Mr. Alex. Thompson, Gilford, of a son.

No. 2270 :: Ref. 1849-01-22, 3:2, B.

On 14th inst., at Dungannon, the wife of C. Newton, Esq., of a son.

No. 2271 :: Ref. 1849-01-22, 3:2, B.

Jan. 1, at Clones Rectory, the wife of the Rev. T. Hand, of a son.

No. 2272 :: Ref. 1849-01-22, 3:2, B.

Jan. 12, in Enniskillen, Mrs. J. West, of a son.

No. 2273 :: Ref. 1849-01-22, 3:2, M.

In the first Presbyterian Church, Newtownstewart, on the 17th inst., by the Rev. James Alexander, Anthony M'Farland, Esq., of Aldohol, to Miss Catherine Fulton, of Newtownstewart.

No. 2274 :: Ref. 1849-01-22, 3:2, M.

On 10th inst., at 70, Thomas-st., Armagh, by the Rev. J. M'Crystal, C.C., Mr. P. M'Court, bookseller, Armagh, to Miss Catherine Mulligan, late of Dundalk.

No. 2275 :: Ref. 1849-01-22, 3:2, M.

On 16th inst., at Dungannon, Anne Jane, eldest daughter of Mr. John Carnby, Broughshane, Ballymena, to Mr. Alexander Anderson, merchant, Dungannon.

No. 2276 :: Ref. 1849-01-22, 3:2, M.

On 11th inst., at Belfast, by the Rev. T.F. Millar, Henry Dawson, Esq., of the Carbineers, to Harriet Emma, second daughter of Major-General Bainbrigge, C.B., commanding the Belfast District.

No. 2277 :: Ref. 1849-01-22, 3:2, M.

On 10th inst., at Portadown, by the Rev. Henry De La Willis, Mr. John M'Donagh, merchant, of Ballyshannon, to Martha, third daughter of Hugh Matthews, Esq., Annagh House, Portadown.

No. 2278 :: Ref. 1849-01-22, 3:2, M.

Jan. 9, in Clones Church, by the Rev. T. Hand, Wm. Thompson, Esq., of Bourdautian, near Clones, to Martha Jane, eldest daughter of Bernard Armstrong, Esq., of Clinkirk, near Clones.

No. 2279 :: Ref. 1849-01-22, 3:2, M.

Jan. 9, in Liverpool, Morgan O'Connell, Esq., to Elizabeth, daughter of the late Robert Roskell, Esq., of Gateacre.

No. 2280 :: Ref. 1849-01-22, 3:2, D.

At his residence, Ballybay, in the 70th year of his age, Mr. Wm. Gray.

No. 2281 :: Ref. 1849-01-22, 3:2, D.

On 7th inst., aged 82 years, Elizabeth, relict of the late Francis Lucas, Esq., of Dromanagoole, county Armagh.

No. 2282 :: Ref. 1849-01-22, 3:2, D.

Of bilious fever, on 17th inst., Mr. Walker Cockburn, of Ballyshannon.

No. 2283 :: Ref. 1849-01-22, 3:2, D.

Jan. 14, at Florencecourt, of decline, Elizabeth, daughter of Mr. John Ellis, aged 19 years.

No. 2284 :: Ref. 1849-01-22, 3:2, D.

At Fivemiletown, on 13th inst., Wilson, eldest son of the late Dr. Lendrum, aged 17 years.

No. 2285 :: Ref. 1849-01-22, 3:2, D.

Dec. 25, in Clones, of apoplexy, Margaret, wife of Mr. Robert Morgan, aged 56 years.

No. 2286 :: Ref. 1849-01-22, 3:2, D.

Jan. 7, in Clones, aged 61 years, Elizabeth, relict of the late Mr. Martin Connolly.

No. 2287 :: Ref. 1849-01-22, 3:2, D.

Jan. 8, in [the] 68th year of her age, the wife of Mr. Mathew Lough, of Legnakelly, near Clones.

No. 2288 :: Ref. 1849-01-22, 3:2, D.

On 13th inst., at Drumaconnor, aged 89 years, Anne, relict of the late Wm. Moorhead, Esq.

No. 2289 :: Ref. 1849-01-22, 3:2, D.

In Dublin, Eugene O'Cavanagh, the inimitable translator of Moore's *Melodies*.

No. 2290 :: Ref. 1849-01-22, 3:2, D.

Jan. 17, at Hillton, co. Monaghan, aged five years, Sidney Jane, the only daughter of the late Colonel Madden.

No. 2291 :: Ref. 1849-01-22, 3:2, D.

Jan. 12, at Glasgow, aged 59, James Thomson, Esq., L.L.D., Professor of Mathematics in the University of Glasgow, and formerly of the Royal Academical Institution, Belfast.

No. 2292 :: Ref. 1849-01-22, 3:2, D.

Jan. 8, at Rothsaye, of cholera, after a few hours' illness, Mr. Alexander Greer, son-in-law to the late Mr. Rule of Magherafelt, Postmaster.

No. 2293 :: Ref. 1849-01-22, 3:2, D.
On the 10th inst., at Ballymena, Margaret, third daughter of Mr. Joseph M'Kee, formerly of Millview, Keady.

No. 2294 :: Ref. 1849-01-22, 3:2, D.
In Derry, on the 17th instant, the eve of the third anniversary of his consecration, the Right Rev. Dr. Maginn, Roman Catholic coadjutor Bishop of Derry. On his journey from Buncrana to Derry, on the 13th inst., he got a severe wetting, and incautiously set for some time in his damp clothes; during that night, he was seized with shivering, followed by the ordinary symptoms of fever, which, in the course of the succeeding day, assumed the character of typhus. On the Tuesday morning, he complained of pain in the right arm, which, during the night, became intense, and towards morning, the arm swelled to the shoulder, without exhibiting any marks of inflammation, nor was the pain increased by pressure. The swollen part ran rapidly into gangrene: the pulse, for some hours previous to death, could not be felt, and he expired in eighteen hours after the first complaint of severe pain, in the perfect possession of his faculties.

No. 2295 :: Ref. 1849-01-29, 3:1, B.
On 20th inst., at Park View, Tandragee, the lady of the Rev. George Robinson of a daughter.

No. 2296 :: Ref. 1849-01-29, 3:1, B.
Jan. 24, at the Dowager Lady O'Brien's, No. 1, Upper Merrion-st., Dublin, the wife of Wm. Smith O'Brien, Esq., of a son.

No. 2297 :: Ref. 1849-01-29, 3:1, B.
On 20th inst., at Belfast, the wife of John H. Haliday, Esq., M.D., of a son.

No. 2298 :: Ref. 1849-01-29, 3:1, B.
On 22d inst., at Markethill, the lady of the Rev. Charles Seaver, of a son.

No. 2299 :: Ref. 1849-01-29, 3:1, B.
Jan. 18, Mrs. James Armstrong, of Drummainy, Co. Fermanagh, of a son.

No. 2300 :: Ref. 1849-01-29, 3:1, M.
On 23d inst., in the Presbyterian Church, Ballymacarrett, by the Rev. John Meneely, Mr. James Frazer, of the *Banner of Ulster*, to Rosanna, eldest daughter of the late Joseph Agnew, Esq., Redhill.

No. 2301 :: Ref. 1849-01-29, 3:1, M.
Jan. 25, at Donegal Church, Wm. Henry Deane, Esq., C.E., P.L.C. to Annie, daughter of the Rev. Wm. Ewing, Vicar of Donegal.

No. 2302 :: Ref. 1849-01-29, 3:1, D.
On 18th inst., at Markethill, of fever, Margaret, eldest daughter of the late David M'Anally, Esq., Surgeon of the Armagh Militia.

No. 2303 :: Ref. 1849-01-29, 3:1, D.
Jan. 24, at Belfast, in the 75th year of his age, Mr. John Orr, for many years senior clerk in the *News-Letter* Office.

No. 2304 :: Ref. 1849-01-29, 3:1, D.
On 27th inst., of the prevailing epidemic (cholera), Mr. Patrick Toole, a native of Belfast, Ireland, aged about 40 years. The deceased was employed as clerk in this office for the last five months.—*New Orleans Delta*, December 28.

No. 2305 :: Ref. 1849-01-29, 3:1, D.
Jan. 14, at Florencecourt, of decline, Margaret, daughter of Mr. James Ellis, aged 22 years.

No. 2306 :: Ref. 1849-01-29, 3:1, D.
On 20th inst., at Ratho, Edinburgh, Robert Cadell, Esq., the eminent publisher of Sir Walter Scott's works.

No. 2307 :: Ref. 1849-01-29, 3:1, D.
Death of the O'Donel.—At Greyfield House, county of Leitrim, at a very advanced age, The O'Donel, lineal and hereditary descendant of Hugh Roe O'Donel, Chieftain of Tyrconal and hero of 100 battles, son of Hugh, Prince of Tyrconal, by Ina, daughter of Macdonal, Lord of the Isles, and of O'Do Roe O'Donel, Lord Baron of Donegal. By his decease the hereditary title and lineal representation of the O'Donel family, is now vested in his successor and grandson, Constantine O'Donel of George-street, Sligo, who is now the O'Donel.

No. 2308 :: Ref. 1849-02-05, 3:2, B.
On 31st ult., the wife of Robert Burnside, Esq., Stamp Office, Clones, of a daughter.

No. 2309 :: Ref. 1849-02-05, 3:2, B.
Jan. 27, at Levahy, near Enniskillen, Mrs. R. Stone, jun., of a son.

No. 2310 :: Ref. 1849-02-05, 3:2, M.
On 25th ult., at the Office of the Registrar of Marriages, Enniskillen, Mr. John Montgomery, of Gransagh, to Mrs. Humphris, of Trory.

No. 2311 :: Ref. 1849-02-05, 3:2, M.
On 24th ult., in St. Ann's Church, Belfast, by the Rev. Charles Allen, Robert Buchanan, Esq., C.E., to Sarah, relict of the late Lieut. Colonel Cowell, of the 42d Royal Highlanders.

No. 2312 :: Ref. 1849-02-05, 3:2, M.
On 22d ult, in London, Florence Fox, son of W.J. Fox, M.P., to Caroline Phoebe Caulfield, daughter of the late Joseph Caulfield, Esq.

No. 2313 :: Ref. 1849-02-05, 3:2, D.
In this city, this morning, at the residence of the Rev. Dr. Crolly, Roman Catholic Primate, of fever, caught in the discharge of his ministerial duties, the Rev. Patrick Hart, R.C.C., aged 24 years. *(continued...)*

No. 2313, continued: ...The deceased young clergyman had been appointed to this city about eight months ago, and was very faithful in the discharge of his office. To his afflicted father and brothers his early demise is a sore trial, while a large number of his fellow-citizens, although differing widely from him on religious matters, fully sympathise with his sorrowing friends and congregation. He was both kind and tneder [sic] in his ministration to the sick, and possessed eminent literary abilities.

No. 2314 :: Ref. 1849-02-05, 3:2, D.
On Friday, the 26th ult., of consumption, at his residence Cara-street, Clones, in sure and certain hope of a glorious immortality, Mr. David Thompson, in the 46th year of his age. He was long an anxious and zealous member of the Methodist Society, and as an earnest of their cause [sic]. He has left two houses in Clones and two in Newbliss to be sold, and the sum realized (together with any balance that may remain after his relatives have been paid their dividend) to be given to the Methodists of both connexions.

No. 2315 :: Ref. 1849-02-05, 3:2, D.
On 31st ult., of consumption, at the residence of his brother, Marshall Moore, Esq., of Analore Mills, John, youngest son of the late George Moore, Esq., of same place, in the 26th year of his age, much and worthily regretted by a very numerous circle of friends and acquaintances.

No. 2316 :: Ref. 1849-02-05, 3:2, D.
On 1st inst., at Clones, of typhus fever, Arabella, relict of the late Joseph Thetford, Esq., in the 57th year of her age.

No. 2317 :: Ref. 1849-02-05, 3:2, D.
On the 5th November last, in camp, near Mooltan, East Indies, of inflammation on the lungs, (occasioned by a severe cold) Sergeant Robert Stevenson, orderly room clerk of H.M. 32d Regiment of Foot, aged 28 years, eldest son of Mr. Robert Stephenson, of Greenhill, near Ballymena, deeply regretted and highly esteemed by all the officers as well as the non-commissioned, and soldiers of the Regt.—He has left a wife and child to deplore his loss.

No. 2318 :: Ref. 1849-02-05, 3:2, D.
Jan. 27, in Dublin, at an advanced age, Jane, relict of the late Dr. Cupples, of Mullahead, co. Armagh.

No. 2319 :: Ref. 1849-02-05, 3:2, D.
Jan. 25, at Rosefield, near Monaghan, Mary, relict of the late Captain Dudgeon.

No. 2320 :: Ref. 1849-02-05, 3:2, D.
Jan. 20, at Portadown, in her 18th year, after a few days' illness, Elizabeth, daughter of the late Dr. Robinson.

No. 2321 :: Ref. 1849-02-05, 3:2, D.
Jan. 16, in Belfast, of cholera, after an illness of 12 hours, James Moreland, Esq.

No. 2322 :: Ref. 1849-02-12, 3:1, B.
On 31st inst., at Bellaghy, Mrs. Boyd, of a daughter.

No. 2323 :: Ref. 1849-02-12, 3:1, B.
Feb. 8, the wife of Montgomery Armstrong, Esq., of Drummee, Innishmore, Co. Fermanagh, of a son.

No. 2324 :: Ref. 1849-02-12, 3:1, B.
Feb. 5, at Tandragee, the wife of Rev. John Bagley, Wesleyan Minister, of a daughter.

No. 2325 :: Ref. 1849-02-12, 3:1, M.
On 8th inst., in St. Anne's Church, Belfast, by the Rev. E.J. Hartrick, George Dundas, Esq., to Horatia Dora, daughter of the late James Mathias, Esq., R.N., Lowestoft, Suffolk.

No. 2326 :: Ref. 1849-02-12, 3:1, M.
Feb. 5, at St. George's Church, Hanover Square, Louis Maximilian Timmerman, Chevalier de Legion d'Honneur, and late Captain in the Corps de Garde, to Sarah, widow of Sir George Marcus D'Arcy Irvine, Bart., of Castle Irvine, county of Fermanagh.

No. 2327 :: Ref. 1849-02-12, 3:1, M.
In Colebrook church, by the Rev. Mr. Mills, Mr. James Earls of Doone, to Emme Jane, eldest daughter of Mr. Martin Shaw, near Lisnaskea.

No. 2328 :: Ref. 1849-02-12, 3:1, M.
On the 7th inst., in the Office of the Registrar of Marriages, Enniskillen, Mr. John Mathew Wilson, to Miss Eliza Hetherington, both of Enniskillen.

No. 2329 :: Ref. 1849-02-12, 3:1, M.
On 2d inst., at St. Peter's church Dublin, by the Rev. Hamilton Verschoyle, Wm. Graves Esq., J.P., of Gravesend Villa, county Derry, to Kate, relict of the late Hercules John Heyland, Esq., of Gortnamoyagh, and daughter of the late Captain Paterson, of Magherafelt, same county.

No. 2330 :: Ref. 1849-02-12, 3:1, D.
On 2d inst., Elizabeth, relict of the late Mr. Ralph Campbell, of Monaghan, aged 61.

No. 2331 :: Ref. 1849-02-12, 3:1, D.
Feb. 6th, in Cavan, after a short illness, John Brady, Esq., in his 57th year. He was the most extensive tobacco manufacturer in the North.

No. 2332 :: Ref. 1849-02-12, 3:1, D.
On 3d inst., at Lurgan, Mr. John Pentland, in the 83th [sic] year of his age.

No. 2333 :: Ref. 1849-02-12, 3:1, D.
On 3d inst., at Ashton, Newry, Henry Ogle, Esq.

No. 2334 :: Ref. 1849-02-12, 3:1, D.
Jan. 6, at Artgonnell, near Middletown, after a lingering illness, Mary, wife of Mr. Wm. Campbell, aged 56 years.

No. 2335 :: Ref. 1849-02-12, 3:1, D.
Jan. 28, Mrs. John Wilkin, of Carrickreagh, aged 33 years. She is much regretted by those who were acquainted with her.

No. 2336 :: Ref. 1849-02-12, 3:1, D.
On 6th inst., George Langtry, Esq., of Liverpool, son of the late George Langtry, Esq., of Belfast.

No. 2337 :: Ref. 1849-02-12, 3:1, D.
At Cincinnatti, of laringitis, on the 4th Jan., George Scott, jun., son of George Scott, Esq., merchant, Newry, aged 19 years.

No. 2338 :: Ref. 1849-02-12, 3:1, D.
On 2d inst., of scarletina, aged 7 years, Edmund Miles, eldest son of Mr. H.W. Reilly, of Lurgan.

No. 2339 :: Ref. 1849-02-12, 3:1, D.
On 3d inst., at Lurgan, suddenly, of apoplexy, Mr. Joseph Hewitt, schoolmaster.

No. 2340 :: Ref. 1849-02-19, 3:1, B.
On 15th inst., at Campsie House, county Derry, the lady of John Quinn, Esq., of a daughter.

No. 2341 :: Ref. 1849-02-19, 3:1, B.
Jan. 30, at Beragh, county of Tyrone, the lady of Surgeon Perry, of a daughter.

No. 2342 :: Ref. 1849-02-19, 3:1, B.
Feb. 8, at Carlton-terrace, London, the countess of Caledon, of a son.

No. 2343 :: Ref. 1849-02-19, 3:1, B.
On 30th ult., at Dumfries, the wife of Mr. R. Gibson, shoemaker, of a son, he being her twenty first child.

No. 2344 :: Ref. 1849-02-19, 3:1, B.
At Cookstown, 9th Feb. Mrs. Robert Risk, of a son.

No. 2345 :: Ref. 1849-02-19, 3:1, M.
On 5th inst., at Armagh, by the Rev. Mr. Murphy, R.C.C., Miss Mary M'Voy, of the Seven Houses, to Mr. Edward Hurson, merchant, Dungannon.

No. 2346 :: Ref. 1849-02-19, 3:1, M.
On 15th inst., by the Rev. Noble Sheppard, Margaret, second daughter of Mr. James Taylor, Rusheen, to Mr. George James, Head Constable of Police, Coloony.

No. 2347 :: Ref. 1849-02-19, 3:1, M.
In Manorhamilton church, 13th inst., by the Rev. John Hamilton, M.A., Mr. Robert Morrison, merchant, of Ballymote, to Mrs. Irwin, relict of the late Mr. William Irwin, of Dublin.

No. 2348 :: Ref. 1849-02-19, 3:1, M.
On 13th inst., in Moneymore, by the Rev. R. Sinclair, Mr. Hugh Harkness, to Rosanne, eldest daughter of Mr. Robert Harkness, both of Drummond near Moneymore.

No. 2349 :: Ref. 1849-02-19, 3:1, M.
On 8th inst., by the Rev. M. O'Kane, P.P., Omagh, James Brereton, Esq., Toomevara, co. Tipperary, to Miss Bridget O'Kane.

No. 2350 :: Ref. 1849-02-19, 3:1, M.
On 16th inst., in the Independent Chapel, Donaghmore, by the Rev. James Hanson, Mr. James Watt, of Tullyarn, to Mary, eldest daughter of Mr. James M'Naghton, of Mullycrunnett, co. Tyrone.

No. 2351 :: Ref. 1849-02-19, 3:1, M.
On 5th inst., at Monkstown church, co. Dublin, by the Rev. John St. George Williams, John Douglas, Esq, of Mountain Lodge, Keady, to Jemima Kerns, second daughter of Henry Bellhouse, Esq., of Manchester.

No. 2352 :: Ref. 1849-02-19, 3:1, M.
On 7th inst., in Carrickmacross Church, by the Rev. Mr. Thompson, Mr. William Hill, clerk of Dundalk Union, to Miss Elizabeth Hull, niece of the late Mr. Howell, master of the Carrickmacross Workhouse.

No. 2353 :: Ref. 1849-02-19, 3:1, M.
On 12th inst., at 19, Windsor-street, Edinburgh, by the Rev. Wm. Glover, James Syme, Esq., manager of the Provincial Bank of Ireland, Monaghan, to Rebecca, youngest daughter of John Watson, Esq.

No. 2354 :: Ref. 1849-02-19, 3:1, D.
Feb. 14th, at Middletown, co. Armagh, Jonathan David, the infant son of Francis Clarke, Esq., M.D.

No. 2355 :: Ref. 1849-02-19, 3:1, D.
On 13th inst., in Caledon, after a short illness, Jane, second daughter of Mr. James Wilson, aged 16 years and 5 months, very much regretted by all who were acquainted with her.

No. 2356 :: Ref. 1849-02-19, 3:1, D.
At Manorhamilton, 30th Jan., Mr. James Galna, formerly a pupil of the Claremount Deaf and Dumb Institution.

No. 2357 :: Ref. 1849-02-19, 3:1, D.
At Letterkenny, 11th inst., Henry, eldest son of Henry E. Peoples, Esq., aged 22 years.

No. 2358 :: Ref. 1849-02-19, 3:1, D.
On 11th inst., Mr. Jackson Clarke, of Kilmore, near Lurgan, in the 49th year of his age.

No. 2359 :: Ref. 1849-02-19, 3:1, D.
On 6th inst., at Kildress, in the co. Tyrone, in the 57th year of his age, Richard, eldest son of the late Alexander Cluff, Esq., of same place.

No. 2360 :: Ref. 1849-02-19, 3:1, D.

In Donegal, of fever, after a few days' illness, Lieut. Rice, of the Revenue Police, deservedly regretted.

No. 2361 :: Ref. 1849-02-19, 3:1, D.

Jan. 30, near Castlerea, co. Roscommon, of apoplexy, after a few hours' illness, Hugh O'Connor Eccles, Esq., Barrister-at-Law, and late Proprietor of the *Roscommon Messenger*, aged 32.

No. 2362 :: Ref. 1849-02-19, 3:1, D.

Feb. 12, at Mountpleasant, Miss Margaret Moore, aged 25 years, only daughter of Thomas Robert Moore, Esq., of Ballyjamesduff.

No. 2363 :: Ref. 1849-02-19, 3:1, D.

On 15th inst., at Murlog, near Lifford, Jane, the beloved wife of James Houston, Esq.

No. 2364 :: Ref. 1849-02-26, 2:7, B.

Feb. 20, at Knockbawn, co. of Armagh, the lady of George Walter Young, Esq., of a daughter.

No. 2365 :: Ref. 1849-02-26, 2:7, B.

On the 18th inst., at Lurgan, the wife of John Cuppage, Esq., of a daughter.

No. 2366 :: Ref. 1849-02-26, 2:7, B.

February 13, at the Royal Barracks, Dublin, the wife of Captain Jones, K.R. Rifles, of a daughter.

No. 2367 :: Ref. 1849-02-26, 2:7, B.

Feb. 18, at Youghal, the wife of James Gray, Esq., Manager of the Provincial Bank of Ireland, of a son.

No. 2368 :: Ref. 1849-02-26, 2:7, B.

At Wood Lodge, Mountcharles, Donegal, on the 18th inst., the wife of John Fleming, Esq., of a daughter.

No. 2369 :: Ref. 1849-02-26, 2:7, M.

On the 17th inst., in Lea Church, near Portarlington, Mr. John Craig, house-stewart of the Earl of Erne, of Crom Castle, to Elizabeth, eldest daughter of the late Thomas Craig, Esq., architect, Portarlington.

No. 2370 :: Ref. 1849-02-26, 2:7, M.

In the cathedral of Clogher, on the 20th inst., by the Rev. Thomas Taylor, John B. Taylor, Esq., of Liverpool, son of the late Rev. John Taylor, rector of Rossory, co. Fermanagh, to Jane, daughter of the late Robert Ramsay, Esq., of Sligo. The bride was given away by her uncle, Samuel Ramsay, Esq., of Water Hill.

No. 2371 :: Ref. 1849-02-26, 2:7, M.

On the 20th inst., in St. John's Church, Sligo, by the Rev. Samuel Shone, Wm. Jones, Esq., Excise Officer, to Mary, eldest daughter of the late Rev. Josiah Wilson, of Sligo.

No. 2372 :: Ref. 1849-02-26, 2:7, D.

On the 1st of August, 1848, at Decca, East Indies, aged 39 years, Alexander Frederick Donnelly, Esq., of the Bengal Civil Service, youngest son of John and Rebecca Donnelly, of Blackwatertown.—His remains passed through this city on Wednesday last, for interment in Benburb cemetery, according to his special request before death. A large and respectable concourse of sorrowing friends attended, and fully sympathised with his afflicted widow.

No. 2373 :: Ref. 1849-02-26, 2:7, D.

On the 24th inst., at Rosemount, parish of Tartaraghan, Mr. John Dunlop, aged 68 years.

No. 2374 :: Ref. 1849-02-26, 2:7, D.

On the 12th inst., at Strangford, Mr. Wm. Stewart, late of Grange, county Tyrone.

No. 2375 :: Ref. 1849-02-26, 2:7, D.

On the 19th inst., in Enniskillen, after a short illness, Mr. John Canning, merchant, aged 45 years.

No. 2376 :: Ref. 1849-02-26, 2:7, D.

At Madras, Delany Barclay, of the 25th Foot, eldest son of the late Colonel Johnston, of the 8th Lancers, formerly of Bundoran.

No. 2377 :: Ref. 1849-02-26, 2:7, D.

On the 20th inst., Robert J. Weir, Esq., of Dromore, county Fermanagh.

No. 2378 :: Ref. 1849-02-26, 2:7, D.

On the 18th inst., at Dungannon, aged 46, Richard, son of the late Wm. Murray, Esq., of Killymeal, county Tyrone.

No. 2379 :: Ref. 1849-02-26, 2:7, D.

On the 18th inst., Elizabeth, the eldest child of the late Mr. Walker Cockburn, of Ballyshannon, aged 11 years.

No. 2380 :: Ref. 1849-02-26, 2:7, D.

On the 21st inst., of paralysis, William Burrowes, Esq., Cavan.

No. 2381 :: Ref. 1849-02-26, 2:7, D.

At New York, on the 6th inst., Honora MacKeon, aged 36 years, a native of Killeshandra, co. Cavan, Ireland.

No. 2382 :: Ref. 1849-02-26, 2:7, D.

On the 18th inst., William Thomas, aged 25 years, son of Thomas William Barlow, Esq, Ordnance Solicitor, Ireland.

No. 2383 :: Ref. 1849-02-26, 2:7, D.

On the 15th inst., at Manorhamilton, co. Leitrim, of rapid decline after Typhus fever, John Ball, Esq., S.I. of Revenue Police, only son of the late John Ball, Esq., of Dublin, and nephew to the Right Hon. Mr. Justice Ball.

No. 2384 :: Ref. 1849-02-26, 2:7, D.

February 9, in Dublin, after four days' illness, of the effects of virus inhaled in the dissecting-rooms, within a few days of the completion of the twentieth year of his age, and in the third year of his medical studies, Mr. Edward Elsemere M'Causland, second son of the Rev. John C. M'Causland, Armagh. Rarely has it fallen to the lot of the journalist to record an event which has been the subject of more general regret, than the sudden and unexpected death of this very promising and universally esteemed young gentleman, whose purity of mind, integrity of principle, gentlemanlike bearing and conduct, and engaging and unassuming manners, had endeared him to all to whom he was known, while a very considerable measure of talent, coupled with unremitting assiduity and attention to every means of improvement within his reach held out the fairest prospect of success in the useful and honourable profession for which he had destined himself. The esteem in which he was held by his fellow students and the several professors whose classes he had attended has been evinced by their unanimous expressions of sorrow at his early removal, and attendance on his remains to Mount Jerome Cemetery, on Tuesday, the 13th inst. But it was in the domestic circle that he particularly excelled, having been a most attached, dutiful, and affectionate son and brother, who never cost his afflicted parents a tear, save those which they have shed over his untimely grave; but they *"mourn not as others who have no hope,"* for they have the inexpressible consolation of the assurance, that he *"sleeps in Jesus,"* and shall be brought with him *"at his coming"*—with which hope they *"comfort one another."*—*"Even so, come, Lord Jesus!"*

No. 2385 :: Ref. 1849-03-05, 2:6, B.

On the 3d inst., at Toam, near Black Lion, county Cavan, the wife of Mr. Wm. C. Brackin, merchant, of a daughter.

No. 2386 :: Ref. 1849-03-05, 2:6, B.

On the 3d inst., at Ballymacome, near Keady, the wife of Mr. Thomas M'Mahon, of a daughter.

No. 2387 :: Ref. 1849-03-05, 2:6, B.

On the 23d ult., at 16, Upper Grosvenor-street, London, the Honourable Mrs. Robert Peel Dawson, of Castledawson, co. Londonderry, of a daughter.

No. 2388 :: Ref. 1849-03-05, 2:6, B.

On the 25th ult., the wife of Mr. Charles Smyth, leather merchant, Newry Street, Banbridge, of twins, male and female.

No. 2389 :: Ref. 1849-03-05, 2:6, B.

Feb. 19, at Dromore, county Down, the wife of W.E. Clarke, Esq., of a daughter.

No. 2390 :: Ref. 1849-03-05, 2:6, M.

On 24th ult in St. Mark's Church, Armagh, by the Rev. Mr. Wade, Mr. Robert Gourley, Joiner, Calwish [sic] Abbey, Derbyshire, to Rebecca, eldest daughter of the late Mr. John Bell, of this city.

No. 2391 :: Ref. 1849-03-05, 2:6, M.

In Kilmore church, the Rev. John Hamilton, perpetual curate of Tubbercurry, to Isabella Jane, only daughter of William Park, Esq, of Clogher, Drumsna, Co. Leitrim.

No. 2392 :: Ref. 1849-03-05, 2:6, M.

On 27th ult., in Cookstown, by the Rev. Thomas Millar, Mr. John M'Geagh, Stewartstown, to Sarah Jane, second daughter of Mr. Wm. Paul, linen merchant, Cookstown.

No. 2393 :: Ref. 1849-03-05, 2:6, M.

On 20th ult., in Carland, by the Rev. Stewart Carse, Mr. James Bryars, merchant, Dungannon, to to [sic] Mary, eldest daughter of Mr. Thomas Richey, of Creevagh, near Dungannon.

No. 2394 :: Ref. 1849-03-05, 2:6, M.

Feb. 19, in Enniskillen, by the Rev. Mr. Traynor, Mr. John Heyland, to Rose Anne, eldest daughter of Mr. Henry Willoughby.

No. 2395 :: Ref. 1849-03-05, 2:6, M.

Feb. 13, in Dromore Church, by Rev. Henry Lucas St. George, John Conan, Esq., M.D., to Bessie, eldest daughter of James Hamilton, of Lakemount, Esq.

No. 2396 :: Ref. 1849-03-05, 2:6, D.

On 24th ult., at the residence of her son-in-law, Doctor Robinson, Infirmary, Armagh, in her 87th year, Lucy, widow of the late Captain Henry Perry, formerly of the 4th Regiment of Foot.

No. 2397 :: Ref. 1849-03-05, 2:6, D.

Feb. 21, in Armagh, Mr. David Morrison, aged 22 years, youngest son of Mr. John Morrison, of Ardbrin, near Banbridge.

No. 2398 :: Ref. 1849-03-05, 2:6, D.

Feb. 27, at Woodford, near this city, James Cumming, Esq., aged 34 years.

No. 2399 :: Ref. 1849-03-05, 2:6, D.

At Moy, on the 3d inst., Mr. John Lowry, Innkeeper, son of the late Rev. John Lowry, minister of the first congregation of Clenanees.

No. 2400 :: Ref. 1849-03-05, 2:6, D.

Feb. 25, near Richhill, of paralysis, John Carpenter, aged 70 years. He was 46 years a member of the Wesleyan Society, and is sincerely regretted by all with whom he was acquainted.

No. 2401 :: Ref. 1849-03-05, 2:6, D.

Feb. 24, at Mullaghy, near Enniskillen, at the residence of her father, William Robinson, Esq., of decline, Miss Margaret Robinson, aged 36 years.

No. 2402 :: Ref. 1849-03-05, 2:6, D.
At Conyburry, near Lifford, on Monday last, Mr. John Baxter, deputy road surveyor aged 29.

No. 2403 :: Ref. 1849-03-05, 2:6, D.
On 24th ult., the Rev. Samuel Smythe, Vicar of Carnmoney and Ballylinney, and Rector of Ballymartin, in the Diocess of Connor, at the Glebe-house, in the 85th year of his age, and 64th of his Ministry.

No. 2404 :: Ref. 1849-03-05, 2:6, D.
On 22d ult., in Monaghan, of Asiatic cholera, in his 21st year, Thomas Leeper, Esq., second son of the late James George Leeper, Esq., of Monaghan.

No. 2405 :: Ref. 1849-03-05, 2:6, D.
On 20th Feb., at Mullans, near Fintona, aged 40, Dr. Henry West, of Fintona.

No. 2406 :: Ref. 1849-03-05, 2:6, D.
On 1st inst., in the 84th year of his age, at Monaghan, Mr. James Hagan, Superannuated Guard of her Majesty's Mail. He served in the Yeoman Cavalry, in the Cookstown corps, in the Rebellion of 1798, and was generally esteemed and respected by all who knew him.

No. 2407 :: Ref. 1849-03-05, 2:6, D.
In Cootehill, on the 27th ult., Mr. Samuel Macfadden, merchant.

No. 2408 :: Ref. 1849-03-05, 2:6, D.
In Cootehill, on 28th ult., Muns Walsh, Esq., M.D.

No. 2409 :: Ref. 1849-03-05, 2:6, D.
Feb. 24, at Moneyveagh, near Dungannon, Simon Stevenson, Esq., aged 46 years.

No. 2410 :: Ref. 1849-03-12, 2:7, B.
On 2d inst., at Coleraine, the wife of James Jasper Macalden, Esq., M.D., of a daughter.

No. 2411 :: Ref. 1849-03-12, 2:7, M.
In Rossorry church, on the 7th inst., Samuel Gamble of Lenaghan, Esq., to Mary, only daughter of the late James Innis, Esq., of Enniskillen.

No. 2412 :: Ref. 1849-03-12, 2:7, M.
On 1st inst., in Belfast, by the Rev. Charles Allen, Mr. Samuel Henderson, Officer of Customs, to Miss Anna Bell, of Belfast.

No. 2413 :: Ref. 1849-03-12, 2:7, M.
March 7, in St. Anne's Church, John Gage Lecky, Esq., Captain 38th Regiment, to Tamison, third daughter of the late William Edie, Esq., of Thornhill, co. Tyrone.

No. 2414 :: Ref. 1849-03-12, 2:7, M.
Feb. 28, in Magilligan Church, co. of Derry, by the Rev. Robert Gage, Thomas Josiah, eldest son of Thomas Isaac Dimsdale, Esq., of Virgemont, co. Dublin, to Sidney Cust, twin daughter of the late John Cust, Esq., of Magilligan, co. Derry.

No. 2415 :: Ref. 1849-03-12, 2:7, M.
In Calry Church, on 6th inst., by the Rev. A.J. Gilmor, D.D., John Hackett, Esq., to Susan, youngest daughter of Alderman Anderson, J.P., of Sligo.

No. 2416 :: Ref. 1849-03-12, 2:7, M.
On 8th inst., in the Strand Presbyterian Church, by the Rev. James Crawford, Mr. Samuel Dunn, Ardstraw-bridge, to Eliza, eldest daughter of the late Robert Leitch, Esq., Magheracolton.

No. 2417 :: Ref. 1849-03-12, 2:7, D.
March 7, at Melbourne-Terrace, Armagh, after a lingering illness, George Keys, Esq., Student T.C.D., deeply regretted by his sorrowing friends and relatives, who mourn not as those without hope.

No. 2418 :: Ref. 1849-03-12, 2:7, D.
On 6th inst., at Valencia, co. Kerry, the Right Hon. Maurice Fitzgerald, Knight of Kerry, aged 78.

No. 2419 :: Ref. 1849-03-12, 2:7, D.
In Dublin, on 5th inst., Robert Ormsby, Esq., S.I. of constabulary, Brookeboro'. Mr. Ormsby was a man very generally esteemed.

No. 2420 :: Ref. 1849-03-12, 2:7, D.
At Loughgall, on 10th inst., aged 80 years, Mr. William Addy, much esteemed and respected by all who knew him. He was Postmaster of Loughgall for 39 years, since a Post-office was established in the village.

No. 2421 :: Ref. 1849-03-12, 2:7, D.
In Dublin, on 3d inst., of apoplexy, Daniel Auchinaleck, Esq., Clerk of the Peace for the county Tyrone, aged 52.

No. 2422 :: Ref. 1849-03-12, 2:7, D.
On 5th inst., at Brookeborough, Mr. Thomas Johnston, proprietor of the Freemasons' Tavern.

No. 2423 :: Ref. 1849-03-12, 2:7, D.
On Feb. 26, Eliza, second eldest daughter of William Beatty, Esq., of Cappy, co. Fermanagh, from rupture of a blood vessel, aged 12 years.

No. 2424 :: Ref. 1849-03-12, 2:7, D.
Feb. 28th, at Lisbofin, co. Fermanagh, Charles John, the infant son of the Rev. Simon J. Faussett.

No. 2425 :: Ref. 1849-03-12, 2:7, D.
On 8th ult., at Manchester, in the 66th year of her age, Ann Kelso, widow of the late John Kelso, Esq., of Londonderry.

No. 2426 :: Ref. 1849-03-12, 2:7, D.
On 3d inst., after a very short illness, the Rev. Hugh Freel, P.P., Cloghaneely, co. Donegal.

No. 2427 :: Ref. 1849-03-12, 2:7, D.
At Drumads, near Cavan, on 7th inst., Captain Wm. Brady, late of the 60th Foot.

No. 2428 :: Ref. 1849-03-19, 2:7, B.
In Enniskillen, on the 9th inst., the wife of Stephen Callaghan merchant, of a son.

No. 2429 :: Ref. 1849-03-19, 2:7, B.
March 12, at Edenderry, the wife of Robert Saunderson, Esq., M.D., of a son.

No. 2430 :: Ref. 1849-03-19, 2:7, M.
On the 8th inst., in Letterkenny, by the Rev. John Kinnear, Mr. Robert Rankin, of Terhomin, to Miss Margaret Black, of Killaughlig, near Letterkenny.

No. 2431 :: Ref. 1849-03-19, 2:7, M.
On the 7th inst., in Caledon, by the Rev. Andrew M'Cullagh, Samuel Allen, Esq., merchant, Caledon, to Anna, eldest daughter of the late Wm. Stinson, Esq.

No. 2432 :: Ref. 1849-03-19, 2:7, M.
On the 7th inst., in Dromore, by the Rev. J.R. Dill, Mr. George Wadsworth, of Newtownbutler, Fermanagh, to Margaret, daughter of Dr. Stevenson, of Goland, Tyrone.

No. 2433 :: Ref. 1849-03-19, 2:7, M.
On the 6th inst., in Magherafelt, by James Duncan, Esq., Registrar, Mr. Samuel Baird, merchant, Magherafelt, to Sarah, eldest daughter of Mr. Benjamin Donaldson, merchant, same place.

No. 2434 :: Ref. 1849-03-19, 2:7, D.
At Moy, on the 10th inst., in the 59th year of his age, deeply and deservedly regretted, Lieutenant John Caulfeild, late of the 22d foot, and nephew of the late Colonel James Caulfeild, of Drumcairn, Stewartstown.

No. 2435 :: Ref. 1849-03-19, 2:7, D.
On the 15th inst., at Copney, near Loughgall, at the advanced age of 81 years, Sarah, relict of the late Mr. John Gilpin, of said place, and mother of Richard Gilpin, M.D.

No. 2436 :: Ref. 1849-03-19, 2:7, D.
On the 12th inst., in Brookborough, Mrs. Jane Black, aged 87.—By her death a vacancy takes place in Major Sterne's asylum for widows. She was attended to the grave by all the widows in the neighbourhood.

No. 2437 :: Ref. 1849-03-19, 2:7, D.
On the 10th inst., in Monaghan, in her 68th year, Elizabeth, wife of Mr. Joseph Robinson.

No. 2438 :: Ref. 1849-03-19, 2:7, D.
On the 11th inst., of fever, Miss Martha Reed, in the 33d year of her age, matron of the Clones Workhouse.

No. 2439 :: Ref. 1849-03-19, 2:7, D.
On the 2d inst., at Lisburn, Margaret, wife of George Woodhouse, Esq.

No. 2440 :: Ref. 1849-03-19, 2:7, D.
On the 10th inst., James, aged 8 years, and Catherine, aged 11 years, children of Dr. Hannay, of Lurgan.

No. 2441 :: Ref. 1849-03-19, 2:7, D.
On the 7th inst., at Warrenpoint, of cholera, John M. Rutledge, Esq., C.E., aged 27 years.

No. 2442 :: Ref. 1849-03-19, 2:7, D.
On the 11th inst., at Clonmel, John Murphy, Esq., a member of the Society of Friends, and an eminent merchant of Clonmel.

No. 2443 :: Ref. 1849-03-19, 2:7, D.
On the 9th inst., at Tandragee, Elizabeth, fourth daughter of the Very Rev. the Dean of Tuam.

No. 2444 :: Ref. 1849-03-19, 2:7, D.
On the 10th inst., at Belfast, Owen Heaney, aged 102 years.

No. 2445 :: Ref. 1849-03-19, 2:7, D.
At Cookstown, on 10th inst., in the 20th year of her age, Margaret, second daughter of Mr. John Sheppard, merchant.

No. 2446 :: Ref. 1849-03-26, 3:1, B.
In Cavan, on 20th inst., the wife of Mr. William Hague, of Market-square, of a son.

No. 2447 :: Ref. 1849-03-26, 3:1, B.
On 16th inst., the wife of the Rev. M. Leathem, Upper Langfield Glebe, of a son.

No. 2448 :: Ref. 1849-03-26, 3:1, M.
On 23d inst., in the Presbyterian church, Pomeroy, by the Rev. David M'Kinney, Margaret, eldest daughter of James Reed, Esq., of Aughnacloy, to Mr. David Hughes, architect, of same place.

No. 2449 :: Ref. 1849-03-26, 3:1, M.
On 6th inst., in Ballymena, by Rev. Doctor Dobbin, Mr. John Bole of Slat, to Mary Jane, second daughter of Mr. James Fleming, of Bellaghy, co. Derry.

No. 2450 :: Ref. 1849-03-26, 3:1, M.
On 15th inst., at Enniskillen, Mr. George Johnston, of Lisnarrick, to Miss Eliza Irvine, of Tullycreevy, co. Fermanagh.

No. 2451 :: Ref. 1849-03-26, 3:1, M.
March 9, at Hillsborough, Mr. Robert Standfield, to Eliza, daughter of Mr. John Titterington.

No. 2452 :: Ref. 1849-03-26, 3:1, M.
On 22d inst., in the Unitarian Meeting House, Newry, by Rev. Henry Alexander, Hill Irvine, Esq., to Margaret, daughter of the late Rev. John Mitchel, of Newry.

No. 2453 :: Ref. 1849-03-26, 3:1, M.

On 23d March, in the first Presbyterian church, Monaghan, by the Rev. John Bleckley, the Rev. James MacWhinny, to Jemima, third daughter of Alexander King, Esq., of Monaghan.

No. 2454 :: Ref. 1849-03-26, 3:1, M.

On 22d inst., in Sligo, by Rev. James Gulley, Mr. Wm. Poe, of Sligo, to Miss Catherine Crawford, of Scarden.

No. 2455 :: Ref. 1849-03-26, 3:1, M.

On 20th inst., in the first Presbyterian church, Omagh, by the Rev. John Arnold, the Rev. John Black, of Gillygooly, to Anne, eldest daughter of Charles M'Master, Esq., of Omagh.

No. 2456 :: Ref. 1849-03-26, 3:1, D.

At her residence, Abbey-street, Armagh, after a short illness, aged 70 years, Mrs. Jane M'Quin. Through life she was highly esteemed by all who knew her; she was amiable and pious, and contributed to many charitable institutions. As she lived the life of the righteous, so her last end was peace.

No. 2457 :: Ref. 1849-03-26, 3:1, D.

Suddenly at Palnagh, on the 25th instant, Mrs. Lester, aged 68 years, sincerely and deservedly regretted by her numerous family, to whom her social virtues had greatly endeared her.

No. 2458 :: Ref. 1849-03-26, 3:1, D.

On 22d inst., in this city, aged 3 months, Walter Starrett, son of Mr. Robt. J. Johnston, English-street.

No. 2459 :: Ref. 1849-03-26, 3:1, D.

On Thursday last the remains of Mrs. Burnside, relict of the late Matthew James Burnside, Esq., and mother of the Rev. Wm. Burnside, Corcrevey-house, Fivemiletown, who died at the advanced age of 82, was interred in the family vault in the church-yard at that place. She was carried on the shoulders of the tenantry dressed in hat bands at their special request, instead of employing a hearse, the attendants leaving their carriages and walking to the tomb.—A most christian, friendly, and affectionate discourse was delivered from the pulpit by the Rev. John Taylor, L.L.D., of Arvagh, county Cavan, a relative of the deceased, from Psalm xxxvii. 37. He commenced by expressing the awful denunciation which lay on his head provided he spoke any thing but "truth" from the sacred spot in which he stood, and he bore ample testimony to her excellent qualities during her long sojourn in the neighbourhood; every word of which was fully responded to by the assembled congregation, for she was indeed an example of patience, kindness, and charity, under many severe trials in this vale of tears.

No. 2460 :: Ref. 1849-03-26, 3:1, D.

On 14th inst., at Tyrone's ditches, co. Armagh, Mr. David M'Elroy, in the 79th year of his age.

No. 2461 :: Ref. 1849-03-26, 3:1, D.

At Malone, State of New York, on the 18th Feb., of consumption, Mr. Walter Macauley, printer, formerly of Belfast.

No. 2462 :: Ref. 1849-03-26, 3:1, D.

On the 31st Jan., Commodore George C. De Kay, who commanded the United States frigate *Macedonian* on her voyage of aid to the poor of Ireland.

No. 2463 :: Ref. 1849-03-26, 3:1, D.

On the 19th inst., James Augustus, youngest son of Mr. Thomas Wann, aged 16 months.

No. 2464 :: Ref. 1849-03-26, 3:1, D.

In Saintfield, on 5th March, John Stethem Wilson, aged six years; also, on the 17th, Arabella Eliza, aged four years; and on the 18th, Catherine Amelia, aged 14 years; all children of the late Rev. John S. Wilson, Wesleyan Minister.

No. 2465 :: Ref. 1849-03-26, 3:1, D.

On 19th inst., at Graffy, near Strabane, the residence of his father, Surgeon Hugh Kerrigan, late of Castlederg. The deceased and an elder brother, the only sons of their sorrowing and surviving parents, have both died within a few weeks of each other, being previously in the enjoyment of excellent health.

No. 2466 :: Ref. 1849-03-26, 3:1, D.

March 12, at Craig, near Bushmills, Henry Bathurst, Esq., late of the Royal Meath Militia, after a lingering illness; and on the 13th March, Anne, his wife, of inflammation of the chest. Both were interred on the same day, and in one grave.

No. 2467 :: Ref. 1849-03-26, 3:1, D.

March 5, at Arco, in the Italian Tyrol, of fever, Ann Jane, wife of James Henry, Esq., M.D., formerly of Fitzwilliam square, Dublin, and daughter of the late John Patton, Esq., of Castlefin, in the county Donegal.

No. 2468 :: Ref. 1849-04-02, 2:5, D.

Death of the Earl of Gosford, G.C.B.

With feelings of deep regret we have to record the demise of this justly popular nobleman, which took place at his seat, Gosford Castle, in this county, on Tuesday last. A few weeks previously his lordship had been suffering under a severe attack of gout, from which disease he recovered so as to be able to take gentle exercise, and just three weeks ago walked out with Leonard Dobbin, Esq. His lordship, however, was afflicted a second time by inflammation of the lungs and kidneys, which terminated his useful life.

The family was originally of Scottish descent, being settled at Gosford, in the county of Haddington.

—The first Baronet of the family, being Solicitor-General of Scotland, obtained a considerable grant of land, in the County of Armagh, from King James VI. of Scotland and I. of England, in the year 1610.— From him descended Archibald Viscount Gosford, who was born in the year 1718. His son and heir, Arthur first Earl of Gosford, was raised to the Earldom in the year 1806, and expired in the following year. He was succeeded by his eldest son and heir, the late Peer, who was born in the year 1775, and consequently was about 74, at the time of his death. He married, in the year 1805, Mary, daughter of Robert Sparrow, Esq., of Worlingham, in the County of Suffolk, by whom he acquired large estates in that County. At a very early age, his Lordship became Lieutenant-Colonel of the Armagh Militia, of which regiment his father was the Colonel. In this regiment his Lordship served during the eventful year 1798, and some subsequent years; and he succeeded to the Colonelcy, on the death of his father. The Earldom was conferred by the Whigs, during their short tenure of power, in the years 1806-7. In 1830 he was appointed to a situation in the Royal Household, which appointment he held, with a short interval, until he received that of Governor-General of Canada, at a period of great excitement in that colony. In quiet and peaceful times, Lord Gosford would have been just the man for this situation; his mildness and urbanity would have gained golden opinions from all quarters; but he felt his inability to cope with the rebels, and therefore requested to be recalled.

As a landlord, Lord Gosford was a model to that class. Living at home, his constant study was the comfort of his dependents, and the thriving town of Markethill is an evidence of his fostering care and anxiety to make his people happy. To his rural tenantry the deceased Earl was equally indulgent, offering every stimulus to increase their exertions, and affording the best possible opportunities for their improvement in agricultural science.

The deceased Earl is succeeded in his title and estates by his son Archibald, Vicount [sic] Acheson, who is now in Malta. His Lordship was born in 1806; married, in 1832, the only daughter of the 10th Earl of Meath (she was born in 1808); he graduated at Christ Oxford; is a Deputy Lieutenant of Armagh (which County he for many years represented in Parliament), and Colonel of the Militia.

In politics his lordship was a consistent liberal. By his death the situation of Lord Lieutenant and Custos Rotulorum of this county has become vacant. He sat in the Upper House as an Irish representative Peer, and as Baron Worlingham.

The funeral will not take place until the arrival of his son, now Earl of Gosford.

No. 2469 :: Ref. 1849-04-02, 2:7, B.
On 25th ult., in Enniskillen, Mrs. James Jeffers, of a son.

No. 2470 :: Ref. 1849-04-02, 2:7, B.
March 21, at Castleblayney, the wife of Rev. H.M. Archdall, of a daughter.

No. 2471 :: Ref. 1849-04-02, 2:7, M.
In Sligo, by the Rev. Mr. Lupton, Rev. S. Cowdy, to Esther, sister of Rodger Smith, Esq., merchant of that town.

No. 2472 :: Ref. 1849-04-02, 2:7, M.
On 23d ult, in Boyle, by the Rev. J. Maguire, A.M., John Henry Buck, Esq., to Rebecca, eldest daughter of Mr. John Fitzgerald of that town.

No. 2473 :: Ref. 1849-04-02, 2:7, M.
March 20, at Monaghan, the Rev. James Mawhinny, to Jemima, third daughter of Alexander King, Esq., of Monaghan.

No. 2474 :: Ref. 1849-04-02, 2:7, M.
On 27th ult., in Letterkenny, by Rev. John Kinnear, Mr. James Carson, to Miss Jane Mitchell, both of Loughnaginn, near Letterkenny.

No. 2475 :: Ref. 1849-04-02, 2:7, D.
On 28th ult., at the residence of his father, John-street, Sligo, Alex. only son of Lieut. Jones Burrows.

No. 2476 :: Ref. 1849-04-02, 2:7, D.
March 19, at Dungooley, co. Louth, aged 73 years, Mrs. Dawson, of Forkhill Lodge, widow of the late James Dawson, Esq., for many years Assistant-Barrister for co. Armagh.

No. 2477 :: Ref. 1849-04-02, 2:7, D.
At Enniskillen, on 26th ult., Wm. Frith, Esq., late Captain 20th Regt. The Captain had been in delicate health for some time, but his friends had little idea that his death was so near at hand. He was a general favorite with those who knew him.

No. 2478 :: Ref. 1849-04-02, 2:7, D.
On 22d ult., at St. Stephen's-green, Dublin, Miss Anne Doherty sister of the Chief Justice of the Common Pleas.

No. 2479 :: Ref. 1849-04-02, 2:7, D.
At Cootehill, near Dungannon, Mr. Loftus Kitson, at an advanced age.

No. 2480 :: Ref. 1849-04-02, 2:7, D.
On 20th ult., aged 14 years, Caroline Maria, fifth daughter of Jas. Hamilton, Esq., of Fintra House, near Killybegs, co. Donegal.

No. 2481 :: Ref. 1849-04-02, 2:7, D.
On 23rd ult., Francis S. Bell, the youngest child of the late T. Bell, Esq., Armagh.

No. 2482 :: Ref. 1849-04-02, 2:7, D.
On 29th ult., Hanna, relict of the late Mr. William Scott, of Monaghan, aged 49.

No. 2483 :: Ref. 1849-04-02, 2:7, D.
March 21, at Glenbrook, co. Antrim, William Moore, third son of the late Rev. Marshal Moore, of Faughanvale, aged 21 years.

No. 2484 :: Ref. 1849-04-02, 2:7, D.
On 28th ult., Rev. T. O'Reilly, P.P., of Killeshandra, of typhus fever, contracted in the discharge of his clerical duties.

No. 2485 :: Ref. 1849-04-02, 2:7, D.
In Cootehill, 27th ult., Mr. Charles O'Connell, aged 50.

No. 2486 :: Ref. 1849-04-02, 2:7, D.
On 24th ult., of cholera, Mr. William M'Clatchy, officer of Excise, Ennis, co. Clare, eldest son of Mr. Alex. M'Clatchy, Killyberry, Castledawson.

No. 2487 :: Ref. 1849-04-02, 2:7, D.
On 30th ult., at the residence of her brother-in-law, Mr. R. Mountgarrett, Mary Anne, relict of the late Mr. Wm. Hamerton of Derry city, aged 40.

No. 2488 :: Ref. 1849-04-02, 2:7, D.
March 26, at his residence Kiltubrid, near Middletown, Mr. John Morrison at the advanced age of 83 years.

No. 2489 :: Ref. 1849-04-09, 3:3, B.
On the 4th inst., at Carnagh House, the wife of John Robt. Irwin, Esq., of a son.

No. 2490 :: Ref. 1849-04-09, 3:3, B.
At Drumart House, Tandragee, the wife of Henry Hardy, Esq., of a son.

No. 2491 :: Ref. 1849-04-09, 3:3, B.
At Chesterfield House, London, the Marchioness of Abercorn, of a son.

No. 2492 :: Ref. 1849-04-09, 3:3, B.
On the 1st inst., at Townhall-street, Enniskillen, Mrs. W.R. Armstrong, of a son.

No. 2493 :: Ref. 1849-04-09, 3:3, B.
On the 1st inst., at Castle Howard, the wife of Richard Howard Brooke, Esq., of a son.

No. 2494 :: Ref. 1849-04-09, 3:3, M.
On the 22d ult., at Ballindreat, Derry, James Hamilton, Esq., to Mary, daughter of C. Patterson, Esq., of Cloughfin.

No. 2495 :: Ref. 1849-04-09, 3:3, M.
On the 27th ult., in the Presbyterian Church of Finvoy, by the Rev. Andrew Todd, the Rev. Thomas Flavell, Tandragee, to Rosa, daughter of John Keirs, Esq., of Slavney, Finvoy.

No. 2496 :: Ref. 1849-04-09, 3:3, D.
On the 27th ult., at the residence of her son-in-law, Rev. Andrew Maxwell, Castlederg, Isabella, relict of the late Mr. Andrew Baird, Castlefin, aged 81 years.

No. 2497 :: Ref. 1849-04-09, 3:3, D.
On 29th ult., at Daisyhill, co. Armagh, Jane Crawford, daughter of the late Andrew Crawford, Esq., of Castledawson, co. Derry.

No. 2498 :: Ref. 1849-04-09, 3:3, D.
On 27th ult., at Killylea, aged 23 years, Richard Mills, a member of the Wesleyan Society. The burial service as revised by the late Rev. J. Wesley, A.M., was used. His remains were committed to the grave by the Rev. T. Meredith, *"in sure and certain hope of a glorious resurrection."—(Communicated.)*

No. 2499 :: Ref. 1849-04-09, 3:3, D.
On the 31st ult., at Cargan House, Toomebridge, Maryann, daughter of the late Grabriel [sic] Mallon, aged 13 years.

No. 2500 :: Ref. 1849-04-09, 3:3, D.
On the 1st inst., at Portadown, Charles, youngest son of the late Roger Marlay, Esq.

No. 2501 :: Ref. 1849-04-09, 3:3, D.
On the 31st ult., Mrs. Smith, relict of the late Mr. James Smith, of Enniskillen.

No. 2502 :: Ref. 1849-04-09, 3:3, D.
In Enniskillen, on the 1st inst., aged 84, Mrs. Jane Ovens, relict of the late Rev. Wm. Ovens, Rector of Boho.

No. 2503 :: Ref. 1849-04-09, 3:3, D.
On 31st ult., at Ardee, Mr. P. M'Donnell, aged 80 years.

No. 2504 :: Ref. 1849-04-09, 3:3, D.
On 6th inst., in Monaghan, William, eldest son of William Murray, Esq., M.D., aged 18 years.

No. 2505 :: Ref. 1849-04-09, 3:3, D.
On 26th March, at Newtownbutler, Mary Jane, eldest daughter of Mr. Samuel Evans, aged 18 years.

No. 2506 :: Ref. 1849-04-09, 3:3, D.
On the 5th inst., at Waterloo-place, Derry, Mary, third daughter of Mr. John Keys, aged 4 years.

No. 2507 :: Ref. 1849-04-09, 3:3, D.
On 20th ult., at Dsimnacrosh [sic], co. Donegal, Mr. Andrew Elliott, aged 73 years.

No. 2508 :: Ref. 1849-04-09, 3:3, D.
On the 29th ult., at Claggan, near Culdaff, co. Donegal, Mrs. Kirkpatrick, aged 105 years.

No. 2509 :: Ref. 1849-04-09, 3:3, D.
On the 30th ult., at Antrim, of cholera, in her 10th year, Hannah, third daughter of William Crawford, Esq., Manager, Ulster Bank.

No. 2510 :: Ref. 1849-04-09, 3:3, D.
On 27th ult., at Castlewellan, Owen M'Mullen, Esq., in the 62d year of his age.

No. 2511 :: Ref. 1849-04-09, 3:3, D.
On the 21st ult., at Lower Gardiner-street, at an advanced age, Sarah, relict of Charles Jones, Esq., late of Fortland, co. Sligo.

No. 2512 :: Ref. 1849-04-09, 3:3, D.
On the 4th inst., at No. 2, Donegall Pass, Belfast, in the 76th year of his age, John Mitchell, Esq., for many years under-agent to the Earl of Gosford, a situation which he filled to the entire satisfaction of the noble Lord, and in a manner which gained him the respect and esteem of the tenantry, who, on his retirement from office, in May last, presented to him a highly complimentary address, accompanied with a valuable service of plate. Mr. Mitchell resided for a lengthened period at Markethill, where he was greatly esteemed for his upright and honourable character. His remains were removed for interment, in the New Burying-Ground, on the 7th inst., at eight o'clock.

No. 2513 :: Ref. 1849-04-16, 3:2, B.
On 9th April, at Newcastle-on-Tyne, the wife of the Rev. John Clarke Houston, of a son.

No. 2514 :: Ref. 1849-04-16, 3:2, B.
The wife of Rev. Henry Archdall, Trory Glebe, Enniskillen, of a daughter.

No. 2515 :: Ref. 1849-04-16, 3:2, B.
April 7, at Watersland, Stillorgan, the wife of the Rev. Thomas H. Ball, of a son.

No. 2516 :: Ref. 1849-04-16, 3:2, B.
April 8, at Enniksillen, the wife of the Rev. Mr. Matthias, of a daughter.

No. 2517 :: Ref. 1849-04-16, 3:2, B.
On 2nd April, the wife of De Burgh D'Arcy, Esq., of Castletown Cong, of a daughter.

No. 2518 :: Ref. 1849-04-16, 3:2, M.
On 11th April, in Donaghmore, by the Rev. S.J. Moore, Mr. R. Jeffry, Loughorne, to Margaret, second daughter of the late Mr. John M'Cullagh, Aughnacavan, Donaghmore.

No. 2519 :: Ref. 1849-04-16, 3:2, M.
On 10th April, in St. Bride's Church, Dublin, by the Rev. Marcus Rainsford, brother of the bride, Stevenson Cumming Moore, Moorebrook, co. Armagh, Esq., to Elizabeth, eldest daughter of William Ryland Rainsford, Esq., Rainsford Lodge, Newtownbarry, co. Wexford.

No. 2520 :: Ref. 1849-04-16, 3:2, M.
On 10th April, at Enniskillen, by Mr. C. Gamble, Registrar, Mr. Wm. Hamilton, of Derrygonnelly, mercht. to Miss Esther Ovens, of Glenleven.

No. 2521 :: Ref. 1849-04-16, 3:2, D.
On 13th April, near Tynan, Mr. Bernard Hughes, father to Mr. John Hughes, Charlemont Arms Hotel, Armagh, at the advanced age of 76 years.

No. 2522 :: Ref. 1849-04-16, 3:2, D.
Irish Street in this City, on 14th April, Mr. Hugh O'Neill, at the advanced age of 84 years.

No. 2523 :: Ref. 1849-04-16, 3:2, D.
On 8th April, suddenly, the wife of Mr. David Love, of Timikeel, near Portadown.

No. 2524 :: Ref. 1849-04-16, 3:2, D.
At his father's residence, Hermitage, of cholera, after a few hours' illness, Thomas, eldest son of John Tydd, Esq., Sub-Sheriff of Clare.

No. 2525 :: Ref. 1849-04-16, 3:2, D.
On 30th March, at Belfast, Rebecca Doherty, aged 74 years, a native of Springtown, co. Tyrone.

No. 2526 :: Ref. 1849-04-16, 3:2, D.
On 5th March, at Dayton, Ohio, Eliza, daughter of the late Mr. Michael Murphy, of Belfast.

No. 2527 :: Ref. 1849-04-16, 3:2, D.
On 8th April, at Londonderry, Charles Henry, youngest son of the late Thomas Lindsay, Esq., aged 16 years.

No. 2528 :: Ref. 1849-04-16, 3:2, D.
On 8th April, at 48, Burton crescent, London, Thomas Chapman, Esq., late chief proprietor of the *Globe and Traveller* newspaper, in the 86th year of his age.

No. 2529 :: Ref. 1849-04-16, 3:2, D.
On 12th April, at Derry, Miss Catherine Jamieson, aged 20 years.

No. 2530 :: Ref. 1849-04-16, 3:2, D.
Of hooping-cough, on the 10th April, Martha, aged one year and nine months, fourth daughter of Mr. John Keys, Derry.

No. 2531 :: Ref. 1849-04-16, 3:2, D.
On 29th March, Lucinda, relict of the late Mr. Samuel Laird, Ballybofey, aged 80 years.

No. 2532 :: Ref. 1849-04-16, 3:2, D.
At the residence of her brother, No. 66, Fahan-street, Derry, of consumption, Mary Anne, wife of Mr. John Bullard, constabulary, Fivemiletown.

No. 2533 :: Ref. 1849-04-16, 3:2, D.
On 6th April, at Belturbet, Matilda, daughter of Mr. John Fawls, aged 18 years.

No. 2534 :: Ref. 1849-04-16, 3:2, D.
In Dublin, James Molloy, Esq., of Fairview, near Delgany, county Wicklow.

No. 2535 :: Ref. 1849-04-16, 3:2, D.
On 9th April, Mary Butler, aged 12 years, child of W. Elias Handcock, Esq., of Fair House, co. Dublin.

No. 2536 :: Ref. 1849-04-16, 3:2, D.
On 7th April, at Oatlands, near Boyle, Eleanor, aged 18 years, eldest daughter of the late Tobias Peyton, Esq.

No. 2537 :: Ref. 1849-04-16, 3:2, D.
On 27th March, of mortification, the result of a dog's bite, aged 94, Mr. John Eggar, of Bentley, father-in-law to Mr. Jordan, the editor of the *Literary Gazette*.

No. 2538 :: Ref. 1849-04-16, 3:2, D.
In Monaghan, 10th April, Mr. Thomas Henry, Saddler, aged 40 years.

No. 2539 :: Ref. 1849-04-16, 3:2, D.
On 19th April, in South Brooklyn, New York, of typhus fever, Henry, fourth son of Mr. John Breakey, Drumskelt, Ballibay, Ireland.

No. 2540 :: Ref. 1849-04-16, 3:2, D.
At the Castle, Dundrum, Mary, the relict of Joseph Cairns, aged 106 years, surviving her husband 37 years all but two days. This interesting old woman retained her faculties to the last, the hearing and sight only being a little impaired.

No. 2541 :: Ref. 1849-04-16, 3:2, D.
On 10th April, at Laracor Glebe, the Rev. Blayney Irwin, at the advanced age of 84. He was Rector and Vicar of Laracor for 37 years.

No. 2542 :: Ref. 1849-04-16, 3:2, D.
On 10th April, at Glenone Glebe, co. Derry, aged 53, the Rev. Mark Bloxham, A.M. Ex-T.C.D. Chaplain to the Earl of Erroll, and for 23 years Incumbent of the Perpetual Curacy of Lower Tamalaght.

No. 2543 :: Ref. 1849-04-16, 3:2, D.
On 29th March, at Makinson-square, Bolton, in the 66th year of his age, Mr. Samuel Parr. He was in the employ of Messrs. E. and W. Bolling, upwards of 40 years, 28 as manager. He was a noted disciple of Wm. Cobett; he could quote largely from almost any subject that Cobett ever wrote upon. He was never out of a job in his life; for during his leisure hours, as may be seen from his memoranda, he made 578 balloons, 103 pairs of small scales (some of them so small as not to exceed the weight of a fourpenny-piece, and of exquisite workmanship,) he also made 1153 beautiful walking-sticks, and 73 violins.

No. 2544 :: Ref. 1849-04-23, 3:2, B.
On 16th inst., at Mansten Parsonage, Leeds, the wife of the Rev. Hugh S. Hamilton, of a son.

No. 2545 :: Ref. 1849-04-23, 3:2, B.
On 11 instant, at Cary's-fort Lodge, Stillorgan Park, the wife of Thomas Beasley, Esq., of a son.

No. 2546 :: Ref. 1849-04-23, 3:2, B.
On 14 inst., at Balbriggan the wife of the Rev. Hugh Hamilton of a son.

No. 2547 :: Ref. 1849-04-23, 3:2, M.
On 19th inst., by Rev. Alexander Fleming, Mr. Archibald Duff, of Birch-hill, co. Antrim, to Mary, third daughter of the late Mr. Archibald M'Connell, of this city.

No. 2548 :: Ref. 1849-04-23, 3:2, M.
On 13th inst., at Richhill Church, by the Rev. J. Hogan, Thomas Cox, jun., Esq., Cloon-hill, co. Roscommon, to Mary, eldest daughter of Mr. Robert Williamson, Ahory.

No. 2549 :: Ref. 1849-04-23, 3:2, M.
On 12th inst., at Loughgilly Church, by the Rev. Edward M. Hamilton, John James Verschoyle, Esq., Saggart House, co. Dublin, to Catherine Helen Foster, eldest daughter of the Rev. Wm. Foster, of Altameenagh, co. Donegal, and Rector of Loughgilly, co. Armagh.

No. 2550 :: Ref. 1849-04-23, 3:2, M.
April 17, in Castleknock Church, by the Rev. George Stone, the Rev. James Quintin, to Amelia, youngest daughter of the late Jas. Monk, Esq., of Dublin.

No. 2551 :: Ref. 1849-04-23, 3:2, M.
April 17, in St. Peter's Church, Dublin, by the Rev. Thomas W. Roe, Assistant-Minister of St. Mathias, the Rev. Wm. Desney Roe, Curate of St. Michan's, to Anna, second daughter of the late Thos. Grendon, Esq., of Drogheda.

No. 2552 :: Ref. 1849-04-23, 3:2, M.
In Fintona, 19th inst., James Mackay, Esq., of Seskanore, to Margaret, daughter of the late James Hamilton, Esq., of Ecclesgreen.

No. 2553 :: Ref. 1849-04-23, 3:2, M.
On 17th inst., in Belfast, by Rev. Daniel M'Afee, Mr. Joseph Totten, of Woodbine Cottage, Lurgan, to Jane, second daughter of Mr. William M'Collough, of Belfast.

No. 2554 :: Ref. 1849-04-23, 3:2, M.
On 11th inst., in Newry, by Rev. Daniel Bagot, Mr. Joseph Purdy, to Elizabeth, eldest daughter of the late Mr. Henry Magill, both of Newry.

No. 2555 :: Ref. 1849-04-23, 3:2, D.
On 15th inst., at Cappagh, near Omagh, the Rev. Henry H. Harte, of disease of the heart, sincerely and deservedly regretted.

No. 2556 :: Ref. 1849-04-23, 3:2, D.
On 16th inst., at Lisburn, Thomas Hancock, M.D., aged 66 years.

No. 2557 :: Ref. 1849-04-23, 3:2, D.
On 16th inst., at Strabane, Charlotte, relict of Jas. Sproule, Esq.

No. 2558 :: Ref. 1849-04-23, 3:2, D.
On 1st inst., at Manorcunningham, Mr. Stephen Hunter.

No. 2559 :: Ref. 1849-04-23, 3:2, D.
On 11th instant, at Legnathraw, co. Donegal, Hugh Stephenson, Esq., aged 79 years.

No. 2560 :: Ref. 1849-04-23, 3:2, D.
October 22, Thos. Harpur, Esq., of Cecil Hills, New South Wales, formerly of Lime Park, co. Tyrone, and of College-square, Belfast.

No. 2561 :: Ref. 1849-04-23, 3:2, D.
On 16th instant, at Cheltenham, Elizabeth Martha, relict of the Very Rev. Cadogan Keatinge, Dean of Clogher, in the 98th year of her age.

No. 2562 :: Ref. 1849-04-23, 3:2, D.
On 15th inst., of fever, aged 25 years, Richard Mathews Harpur, Student of Trinity college, only son of the late Rev. Mr. Harpur, of [C]astleblayney.

No. 2563 :: Ref. 1849-04-23, 3:2, D.
On the 17th inst., at Hammersmith, Jane Buchanan, second daughter of Richard Turner, of Hammersmith, Dublin, and widow of Wm. Buchanan, of Glasgow.

No. 2564 :: Ref. 1849-04-23, 3:2, D.
On the 17th inst., of cholera, Dr. Lawther, of Ballymena, aged 61 years.

No. 2565 :: Ref. 1849-04-23, 3:2, D.
On the 16th inst., at Ballyworkan House, co. Armagh, after a lingering illness, Grace, relict of the late George Pepper, Esq.

No. 2566 :: Ref. 1849-04-23, 3:2, D.
March 18, in Georgetown, Pennsylvania, in her 80th year, Mrs. Wolfe Tone.

No. 2567 :: Ref. 1849-04-23, 3:2, D.
Of dropsy, after twenty-five years disease of the heart, at Cenchoeur Cottage, Howth, on the 14th inst., aged 55, Miss Mary Isabella Clarke, eldest daughter of the Rev. John Clarke, late of Belfast.

No. 2568 :: Ref. 1849-04-23, 3:2, D.
On the 18th inst., at Enniskillen, Mary, relict of the late Major Stoddart, 45th Regiment, and daughter of the late John Balfour, Esq., of Drumcrew, co. Fermanagh.

No. 2569 :: Ref. 1849-04-23, 3:2, D.
In Enniskillen, on the 13th inst., aged 66, Esther, wife of Mr. Thomas Gallogly.

No. 2570 :: Ref. 1849-04-23, 3:2, D.
On 2d inst., Mary, wife of Mr. James Porter, of Prospect, near Strabane.

No. 2571 :: Ref. 1849-04-23, 3:2, D.
In Toronto, on the 1st ult., of scarlet fever, Frances Margaret, aged 8 years, eldest daughter of Charles William Buchanan, Esq., M.D., and grand daughter of Mr. George Buchanan, of Stranghroy, near Omagh.

No. 2572 :: Ref. 1849-04-23, 3:2, D.
On 16th inst., in Eldon place, Enniskillen, John M'Farland, Esq., aged 88 years, sincerely regretted by a large circle of friends and acquaintances. Mr. M'Farland was through life a very active character, and gave employment to many men, as a carpenter and builder. He was generally respected, and died rejoicing in the sure and certain hope of a blessed immortality.

No. 2573 :: Ref. 1849-04-30, 2:6, B.
On 24th ult., at Clones, the wife of Mr. Thomas Reynolds of a son and heir.

No. 2574 :: Ref. 1849-04-30, 2:6, B.
On 22d inst., the wife of the Rev. W. Sweeny, of Killishandra, of a son.

No. 2575 :: Ref. 1849-04-30, 2:6, B.
April 21, at Victoria Lodge, Donnybrook, the lady of Thomas J. Ryan, Esq., of Merchant's-quay, of a son.

No. 2576 :: Ref. 1849-04-30, 2:6, B.
On 21st inst., at the Under Secretary's Lodge, Phoenix Park, the lady of Thomas N. Redington, Esq., of a daughter.

No. 2577 :: Ref. 1849-04-30, 2:6, M.
On 25th April, in Sandys-street Presbyterian Church, by the Rev. John Moran, Joseph Dickie, Esq., Solicitor, Dundalk, to Kate, youngest daughter of R.G. Wallace, Esq., Solicitor, Newry.

No. 2578 :: Ref. 1849-04-30, 2:6, M.
At Carnmoney Church, on 23rd inst., by the Rev. George Smythe, Major Donald M. Cameron, of the Buffs, son of the late Colonel Allan Cameron, to Susan, youngest daughter of Robert Grimshaw, D.L., Esq., of Longwood, Belfast.

No. 2579 :: Ref. 1849-04-30, 2:6, M.
On 12th inst., in the Presbyterian Church, Ballygawley, by the Rev. William Ferguson, William Beatty, Esq., surgeon, Ballygawley, to Margaret, only daughter of Mr. David Cairns, Drumcullion, near Ballygawley.

No. 2580 :: Ref. 1849-04-30, 2:6, M.
On 11th inst., in Donaghmore, by the Rev. Samuel J. Moore, Robert Jeffrey, Esq., Loughoine, to Margaret second daughter of the late John M'Cullough, Esq., late of Aughnacavan, and niece of the late Hugh M'Cullough, Esq., of Maryvale, co. Down.

No. 2581 :: Ref. 1849-04-30, 2:6, M.
April 17, at St. John's church, Manchester, by the Rev. William Huntington, George Alleyne Rogers, of Killileagh, [C]ork, to Mary Elizabeth, third daughter of the late Thomas Wade Foott, Esq., of Springfort House, Mallow.

No. 2582 :: Ref. 1849-04-30, 2:6, M.
April 25, at Walcut church, Bath, by the Rev. Edward John Evans, M.A. Vicar of Killroney, Rostrevor, the Rev. John Evans, B.A., Minister of Portland chapel, Bath, to Constance, eldest daughter of the late Rev. Arthur Hugh Pearson, Rector of Foxearth, in the co. of Essex.

No. 2583 :: Ref. 1849-04-30, 2:6, M.
April 24, at the residence of the bride's father, Merrion-square, East, by the most Rev. Dr. Murray, John Louis Louis [sic] [C]ronin, Esq., son of Daniel [C]ronin, Esq., of the Park, Killarney, to Maria Elizabeth, daughter of John M'Donnell, Esq., Governor of the Bank.

No. 2584 :: Ref. 1849-04-30, 2:6, M.
At Rosenalis church, Philip Meredith Esq., of Rearyvalley, Queen's county, to Isabella, daugher [sic] of Christopher Bailey, Esq., of [C]appaloughan, in said county.

No. 2585 :: Ref. 1849-04-30, 2:6, M.
On 19th inst., in Dundalk, Richard Verdon, Esq., Dundalk, to Mary Ann, only daughter of the late Edward M'Ardle, Esq., of the same place.

No. 2586 :: Ref. 1849-04-30, 2:6, M.
On 26th inst., by the Rev. Mr. Heron, Sligo, John Alexander, Esq., of Glasgow, to Miss Jenet Sim, of [C]ollooney Abbey.

No. 2587 :: Ref. 1849-04-30, 2:6, M.
April 16, at Drumshambo, by the Rev. Mr. Heslen, P.P., Margaret second daughter of Mr. Thomas O'Rourke and niece to T. Ingoldsby, Esq., of Enniskillen, to George Ford, Esq., Surgeon, Ballinamore, co. Leitrim.

No. 2588 :: Ref. 1849-04-30, 2:6, M.
On 19th, at Enniskillen, by Mr. C. Gamble, Registrar, Mr. Wm. Wilson, Killyvilly, to Miss Jane Elliot, of Garvery.

No. 2589 :: Ref. 1849-04-30, 2:6, D.
On 28th inst., in Thomas-street, Armagh, of cholera, aged 50 years, Mr. Patrick Loughran.

No. 2590 :: Ref. 1849-04-30, 2:6, D.
On 26th inst., at Breen, near Strabane, aged 56 years, Mary, wife of Mr. Wm. Anderson, deeply and deservedly regretted.

No. 2591 :: Ref. 1849-04-30, 2:6, D.
On 21st inst., at his residence, 9, Guildry Court, Glasgow, Mr. Alexander Kerr, in the 62d year of his age. Throughout life he was a man universally esteemed and respected by all who knew him, and left this world rejoicing in hope of a glorious immortality.

No. 2592 :: Ref. 1849-04-30, 2:6, D.
On 8th inst., at Rathkeale, Mr. Twiss, and on 13th, Mrs. Twiss, of cholera.

No. 2593 :: Ref. 1849-04-30, 2:6, D.
On 22d inst., Mr. William M'[C]une, late organist of the cathedral of Downpatrick.

No. 2594 :: Ref. 1849-04-30, 2:6, D.
On 18th inst., at the District Lunatic Asylum, Limerick, John Jackson, Esq., manager of that institution.

No. 2595 :: Ref. 1849-04-30, 2:6, D.
On 19th inst., at Kingstown, Thomas Talbot, Esq., of the Bank of Ireland.

No. 2596 :: Ref. 1849-04-30, 2:6, D.
On 21st inst., of cholera, at Ballymena, in the 28th year of his age, Dr. J.J. M'Ilrath.

No. 2597 :: Ref. 1849-04-30, 2:6, D.
On 25th inst., aged 63 years, Martha, wife of Mr. William Breaky, of Ballidian, near Ballybay.

No. 2598 :: Ref. 1849-04-30, 2:6, D.
On 22d inst., Mrs. Taylor, of Rusheen, near Sligo.

No. 2599 :: Ref. 1849-04-30, 2:6, D.
On 24th inst., in the 75th year of her age, Mrs. Francis Smith, widow of the late Bartin Smith, cutler, of Sligo.

No. 2600 :: Ref. 1849-04-30, 2:6, D.
On 17th inst., of disease in the liver, in the 60th year of his age, John Smyth, Esq., Labby, near Draperstown.

No. 2601 :: Ref. 1849-04-30, 2:6, D.
In Enniskillen, on 20th inst., Mr. John Irwin, gunsmith, aged 70.

No. 2602 :: Ref. 1849-04-30, 2:6, D.
On 21st inst., of inflammation of the bowels, Mrs. Harman, wife of Mr. Patrick Harman, coach maker, Enniskillen.

No. 2603 :: Ref. 1849-04-30, 2:6, D.
On 14th inst., at Lisnarrick, in the 89th year of her age, Mrs. Betty, relict of the late Mr. Andrew Betty.

No. 2604 :: Ref. 1849-04-30, 2:6, D.
On 16th inst., at Cheltenham, in the 93d year of her age, Elizabeth Martha, widow of the late Cardigan Keatinge, Dean of Clogher, and sister of the late James Taylor, Esq., of [C]ranbrooke, co. Fermanagh.

No. 2605 :: Ref. 1849-05-07, 3:2, B.

April 28, at Grange Park, county Tyrone, the lady of Wm. Handy, Esq., of a daughter.

No. 2606 :: Ref. 1849-05-07, 3:2, B.

April 29, in Lower Gardiner-st., the lady of William Overend, Esq., of a daughter.

No. 2607 :: Ref. 1849-05-07, 3:2, B.

May 1, at 25 Arran-quay, the lady of Thomas W. Reeves, Esq., of a daughter.

No. 2608 :: Ref. 1849-05-07, 3:2, M.

On 26th ult., in the Presbyterian church, Raphoe, by the Rev. J. Thomson, Robt. Wilson, Esq., Solicitor, Strabane, to Anne, daughter of the late Samuel Carson, Esq., of Raphoe.

No. 2609 :: Ref. 1849-05-07, 3:2, M.

On 27th ult., at Edinburgh, by the Rev. Thomas Guthrie, D.D., John Given, of [C]oleraine, Esq., to Elizabeth, second daughter of John Boyd, of Dunduan House, Esq., M.P. for [C]oleraine.

No. 2610 :: Ref. 1849-05-07, 3:2, M.

May 3, at Glenan Presbyterian Meeting House, by the Rev. Mr. Field, Mr. William Hoy, of Mulladuff, to Matilda, second daughter of the late Mr. David Woods, of Woodstock, co. Monaghan.

No. 2611 :: Ref. 1849-05-07, 3:2, M.

On 28th ult., by the Rev. David Watson, [C]lough, Mr. John Heron, son of Mr. Robert Heron, to Mary Jane, daughter of Mr. James Heron, both of [C]astlewellan.

No. 2612 :: Ref. 1849-05-07, 3:2, M.

On 26th ult., at Ducie chapel, by the Rev. Dr. Nolan, Mr. Robert Acheson, of Manchester, to Miss M'Intire, of 5, Apsly-place, Waterloo Road, Brighton, in that city.

No. 2613 :: Ref. 1849-05-07, 3:2, M.

May 1, at Tullamore church, by the Rev. James Bredin, Rector of Nurney, uncle to the bride, Edward Flood, Esq., of [C]astletown, Queen's county, to Anne, eldest daughter of the late Edward Bredin, Esq., of Fort Hill, county Fermanagh.

No. 2614 :: Ref. 1849-05-07, 3:2, D

On Thursday last, at Beech's Railway Hotel, Birmingham, the Hon. and Right Rev. Dr. Knox, Lord Bishop of Limerick. He had arrived there from London, about ten days before, on his way to Ireland, but was so unwell he could not proceed farther.

No. 2615 :: Ref. 1849-05-07, 3:2, D.

On the 30th ult., at his residence, Callin-Turlagh, near Charlemont, in the thirty fifth year of his age, of inflammation of the lungs, Mr. Robert Rolston, linen manufacturer, eldest son of Mr. James Rolston of Aghanlig. The large and respectable attendance at his funeral of all classes and denominations, attested the respect and esteem in which he was held. His death is greatly lamented by the working classes, as he kept in constant employment upwards of 600 families in the different branches of the linen trade.

No. 2616 :: Ref. 1849-05-07, 3:2, D.

On 2d inst., in the 56th year of her age, at her residence, Tully, Killeshandra, Margaret, relict of the late [C]harles Magee, Esq.

No. 2617 :: Ref. 1849-05-07, 3:2, D.

In Omagh, on 4th inst., Mrs. Trenar, aged 70 years.

No. 2618 :: Ref. 1849-05-07, 3:2, D.

At Gortin, on 26th ult., of pleurisy, Mr. Wm. H. M'Laughlin, aged 39 years.

No. 2619 :: Ref. 1849-05-07, 3:2, D.

On 22d ult., in the neighbourhood of [C]astlecaulfield, Mr. H. Hagen, aged 110 years.

No. 2620 :: Ref. 1849-05-07, 3:2, D.

At the Glebe, Monaghan, on the 2d inst., Mr. Joseph Nichols, aged 77, late Sergeant of the 49th Regt.

No. 2621 :: Ref. 1849-05-07, 3:2, D.

On 26th ult., at Derry, Mr. James Bradley, in the 17th year of his age.

No. 2622 :: Ref. 1849-05-07, 3:2, D.

April 3, at Drogheda, Francis Forde, Esq., late of [C]arnally, co. Louth, in the 76th year of his age.

No. 2623 :: Ref. 1849-05-07, 3:2, D.

April 23, at Enniskillen, of decline, in the 18th year of his age, Mr. John Moore, second son of Acheson Moore, Esq., [C]oldrum, co. Tyrone.

No. 2624 :: Ref. 1849-05-07, 3:2, D.

April 28, at [C]onvey, in the house of her son, the Rev. John Beatty, Elizabeth, relict of the late Andrew Beatty, aged 64 years.

No. 2625 :: Ref. 1849-05-07, 3:2, D.

At Bridgehill, Lisburn, Susan M'Tear, at the age of 85 years.—She had kept past her for nearly half a century the sheet and shroud in which she was buried.

No. 2626 :: Ref. 1849-05-14, 2:3, B.

May 7th, in Donegal, the wife of Hugh Alexander Bradshaw, Esq., of the firm of Bradshaw & Co., of a son.

No. 2627 :: Ref. 1849-05-14, 2:3, B.

On 7th inst., at Armagh, the lady of Rev. James Hardy, of a son.

No. 2628 :: Ref. 1849-05-14, 2:3, B.

On 8th inst., in Derry, the lady of Thomas Knox, Esq., of a son.

No. 2629 :: Ref. 1849-05-14, 2:3, B.

On 23d ult., at Dungannon, the lady of Wm. James Mines, Esq., of a son and heir.

No. 2630 :: Ref. 1849-05-14, 2:3, B.
At Ballina, county Mayo, the lady of John H. Thompson, Esq., of the Revenue Police, of a daughter.

No. 2631 :: Ref. 1849-05-14, 2:3, M.
May 10, at Fisherwick-Place Church, Belfast, by the Rev. Dr. Morgan, Wm. Forsythe, Esq., of Belfast to Roseanna, daughter of the late Jas. Cochrane, Esq., of Armagh.

No. 2632 :: Ref. 1849-05-14, 2:3, M.
May 13, in Red Rock Presbyterian Church, by Rev. Dr. Harvey, Mr. James Simpson, Colone, near Markethill, to Jane only daughter of Mrs. Taylor, of Daminy.

No. 2633 :: Ref. 1849-05-14, 2:3, M.
May 8, in St. Peter's Church, Dublin, by the Rev. Romney Robinson, D.D., of the Observatory, Armagh, the Rev. William Thompson, of Carrickmacross, to Hannah, second daughter of the Rev. Wm. Pinching, late Rector of the Parish of Carrickmacross.

No. 2634 :: Ref. 1849-05-14, 2:3, M.
May 6, by Rev. Mr. Caulfield, P.P., of Rosslea, Mr. James Graham, mercht., to Bridget, eldest daughter of Mr. Michael M'Phillips, of Ballybreen Cottage, co. Monaghan.

No. 2635 :: Ref. 1849-05-14, 2:3, M.
April 26, at Slavan church, by the Rev. Mr. Dunbar, Edward Hall, Esq., of Portnaclyduff, to Margaret, relict of the late Dr. Wiley, of Arva, and daughter of Robert Robinson, Esq., of Drumbed, (halfway house.)

No. 2636 :: Ref. 1849-05-14, 2:3, M.
April 26, at Enniskillen, by C. Gamble, Esq., Registrar, Mr. Thos. Maguire, Corracloon, parish of Innismacsaint, to Miss Elizabeth Elliott, of Drumcrow. And on 1st May, Mr. Thomas Armstrong, Drummadooran, parish of Boho, to Miss Elizabeth Strong, of Silverhill.

No. 2637 :: Ref. 1849-05-14, 2:3, D.
In Enniskillen, on Wednesday evening, of gout in the heart, Mr. John M'Elroy, generally and deservedly regretted. The deceased was an old and much respected merchant in Enniskillen, and up till within a few weeks since, enjoyed excellent health. He had been ailing with gout in the feet for the last fortnight, but had become convalescent, and on the evening of his decease and during the entire of that day and the day previous looked remarkably well, and enjoyed as good health as ever in his life. About half-past seven he told Mrs. M'Elroy, he felt weak, and while his faithful partner was accompanying him to his bedroom, he dropped on the lobby his limbs became so feeble. Mr. Machan and other friends got him into bed, and medical assistance was sent for, but he died in about ten minutes. His sudden demise has cast a general gloom over a large and extensive circle of sorrowing friends.

No. 2638 :: Ref. 1849-05-14, 2:3, D.
On 8th inst., at Enniskillen, Mr. Hugh M'Iver, tutor.

No. 2639 :: Ref. 1849-05-14, 2:3, D.
On 8th May, at Enniskillen, of inflammation of the bowels, Miss Wilson.

No. 2640 :: Ref. 1849-05-14, 2:3, D.
On 5th May, John Charters, Esq., late of Maguiresbridge.

No. 2641 :: Ref. 1849-05-14, 2:3, D.
May 5, in Fintona, Mr. Michael M'Nesty, aged 72 years.

No. 2642 :: Ref. 1849-05-14, 2:3, D.
On 4th inst., at Glenavy, James, second son of William Sefton, Esq., Ballinderry.

No. 2643 :: Ref. 1849-05-14, 2:3, D.
On 5th inst., Christina, infant daughter of Thomas Ringland, Esq., Ulster Bank, Lurgan.

No. 2644 :: Ref. 1849-05-14, 2:3, D.
On 7th inst., Miss Fleming, of Lurgan, of Asiatic cholera.

No. 2645 :: Ref. 1849-05-14, 2:3, D.
On 11th ult., at Three Springs, Ohio, U.S., Mrs. M. Scott, relict of the late Matthew Scott, of Tullydonnet, near Convoy, aged 74.

No. 2646 :: Ref. 1849-05-21, 3:2, B.
On 8th inst., the lady of the Rev. Charles Crossle, of a daughter.

No. 2647 :: Ref. 1849-05-21, 3:2, B.
May 7, at Convoy House, the lady of James G. Wood, Esq., of a daughter.

No. 2648 :: Ref. 1849-05-21, 3:2, B.
May 14, at Kilcronaghan Glebe, county Derry, the wife of the Rev. Edward J. Hamilton, of a daughter.

No. 2649 :: Ref. 1849-05-21, 3:2, M.
On 8th inst., at Warrenpoint, Mr. Joseph Knox Rutledge, C.E., to Sophia Amelia, daughter of the late John Delamere, of Warrenpoint, Esq.

No. 2650 :: Ref. 1849-05-21, 3:2, M.
On 17th inst., in Hillsborough Presbyterian Church, by the Rev. Alexander Henderson, of Lisburn, James Henderson, Esq., of Newry, to Jane Eliza, relict of the late Henderson Magill, Esq., of Loughaghry, county Down.

No. 2651 :: Ref. 1849-05-21, 3:2, M.
May 17, by the Rev. Charles Fleury, Chaplain of the Mollyneaux Asylum, at St. Peter's Church, Robert

Thomas Bevan, Esq., of Cashel, third son of Humphrey Bevan, Esq., of Dublin, to Matilda, daughter of James Dawes, Esq.

No. 2652 :: Ref. 1849-05-21, 3:2, D.
On 13th inst., of brain fever, Ann, eldest daughter of Mr. Thomas Capper, of Magarity, parish of Tartaraghan, aged 26 years, much and deservedly lamented.

No. 2653 :: Ref. 1849-05-21, 3:2, D.
On 11th inst., at Grange O'Neiland, co. Armagh, Mrs. Patience Dalzall, aged 102 years. She could read without glasses and attended to the affairs of her house to within a few days of her death.

No. 2654 :: Ref. 1849-05-21, 3:2, D.
At Pettigo, on Wednesday, the 16th inst., of decline, in the 30th year of her age, Mary, wife of Mr. John C. Copeland, parish schoolmaster. Deceased was the second daughter of Mr. William Hanley, of Armaghbrague, county Armagh.

No. 2655 :: Ref. 1849-05-21, 3:2, D.
May 15, at Cavan, Mr. Thomas Reilly, aged 32 years.

No. 2656 :: Ref. 1849-05-21, 3:2, D.
May 13, at Castlerahan, Anne M'Manus, widow of the late Bernard M'Manus.

No. 2657 :: Ref. 1849-05-21, 3:2, D.
May 12, at Lisban, Kirkcubbin, the Rev. Walter Kehoe, C.C., of Techmon, co. Wexford.

No. 2658 :: Ref. 1849-05-21, 3:2, D.
May 13, Mr. Thomas Stanley, merchant, Lurgan.

No. 2659 :: Ref. 1849-05-21, 3:2, D.
April 5, at 89, Hester-street, New York, John Markey, late of Belfast, aged 21 years.

No. 2660 :: Ref. 1849-05-21, 3:2, D.
At the residence of his father-in-law, Mr. James M'Intosh, Strabane, on the 16th inst., John Kniting, Esq., of Dublin.

No. 2661 :: Ref. 1849-05-21, 3:2, D.
May 15, in Ballintemple, the Rev. Stuart Smith, aged 42 years.

No. 2662 :: Ref. 1849-05-21, 3:2, D.
May 11, at Bath, aged 73 years, Eliza, relict of the late John H. Houston, Esq., Orangefield, co. Down.

No. 2663 :: Ref. 1849-05-21, 3:2, D.
May 15, Francis Marmion, Esq., of Dublin, Solicitor, late Sessional Crown Prosecutor, co. Louth, aged 37 years.

No. 2664 :: Ref. 1849-05-21, 3:2, D.
May 13, at Newcastle, Miss Waddell, of Rathfriland.

No. 2665 :: Ref. 1849-05-21, 3:2, D.
May 3, at Balbriggan, the Rev. Galbraith Fenton, Minister of Balbriggan Church for upwards of 60 years, and having attained the patriarchal age of 107 years.

No. 2666 :: Ref. 1849-05-21, 3:2, D.
At the residence of his father, on 18th inst., the Rev. John Cunningham. Deceased was for nine years curate of Lurgan, and his death will be deeply lamented by the many who knew him well.

No. 2667 :: Ref. 1849-05-21, 3:2, D.
May 18, Elizabeth, fifth daughter of the late Rev. Robert Butt, of Stranorlar, in the co. Donegal, and sister of Isaac Butt, Esq., Q.C.

No. 2668 :: Ref. 1849-05-21, 3:2, D.
May 7, at the Parsonage, Highwood Writtle, aged 65, Elizabeth, relict of the late Hugh Ovens, Esq., of Artigarvan-lodge, in the co. Tyrone, and daughter of the late Hugh Lyle, Esq., of Jackson-hall, Coleraine.

No. 2669 :: Ref. 1849-05-28, 3:2, B.
On the 22d instant, at the residence of her mother, Mrs. Cope, of Drummilly, county Armagh, the lady of Captain James de Butts, of a daughter.

No. 2670 :: Ref. 1849-05-28, 3:2, B.
On the 21st inst., in Queen Square, Lancaster, the lady of the Rev. Henry de L. Willis, of Portadown, of a son.

No. 2671 :: Ref. 1849-05-28, 3:2, B.
At Buncrana, co. Donegal, the lady of Dr. Percy S. Waddy, of a son.

No. 2672 :: Ref. 1849-05-28, 3:2, B.
In Castlebar, on 15th inst., the lady of Henry Brett, Esq., County Surveyor, of a son.

No. 2673 :: Ref. 1849-05-28, 3:2, B.
May 21, the lady of W.H. Lepper, Esq., Laurel Lodge, of a son.

No. 2674 :: Ref. 1849-05-28, 3:2, B.
May 20, Aghabog, Rectory, co. Monaghan, the lady of the Rev. William Story, of a daughter.

No. 2675 :: Ref. 1849-05-28, 3:2, B.
May 19, at Poplar vale. co. Monaghan, the lady of John Richardson, Esq., of a son.

No. 2676 :: Ref. 1849-05-28, 3:2, B.
On 19th inst., at Colebrooke, the Lady Arabella Brooke, of a son.

No. 2677 :: Ref. 1849-05-28, 3:2, B.
May 23, in Ballycastle, the lady of the Rev. Thomas R. Wrightson, of a son.

No. 2678 :: Ref. 1849-05-28, 3:2, B.
On 22d inst., at Aberystwyth, the lady of Mr. Charles Rhind, Principal of the Cambrian Institution for the Deaf and Dumb, late of Belfast, of a son.

No. 2679 :: Ref. 1849-05-28, 3:2, M.
On the 23d instant, in the Meeting-house of Loughaghny, by the Rev. Dr. Edgar, the bride's uncle, Mr. Hugh Kennedy Stewart, of Drumcann, county Tyrone, to Miss Eliza Jane Edgar, of Annahilt, county Down.

No. 2680 :: Ref. 1849-05-28, 3:2, M.
In this city, on the 24th instant, by the Rev. Henry Martin, Mr. Robert Gordon, of Tassah, near Keady, to Agnes, eldest daughter of the late Mr. John Sloan, druggist, of this city.

No. 2681 :: Ref. 1849-05-28, 3:2, M.
May 22, in Rosemary-street Church, by the Rev. Dr. Barnett, of Moneymore, Mr. Thomas Sloan, second son of Mr. James Sloan, of Lisalbanagh, Magherafelt, to Jane, third daughter of the late Mr. James Ewart, of Belfast.

No. 2682 :: Ref. 1849-05-28, 3:2, M.
May 22, in Tubbermore, by the Rev. W. Brown, M.A., Mr. Thomas Taylor, of Shanetamny, to Mrs. Elizabeth Scott, of Tubbermore.

No. 2683 :: Ref. 1849-05-28, 3:2, M.
May 7, by the Rev. Mr. O'Neal, Mr. John Campbell, Innkeeper, Aughnacloy, to Jane, third daughter of the late Mr. Henry Grant, Newry.

No. 2684 :: Ref. 1849-05-28, 3:2, M.
May 21, at Cookstown, Mr. John Davidson, of Annahavil, to Miss Mary Jane Allen, of Legnacash, co. Tyrone.

No. 2685 :: Ref. 1849-05-28, 3:2, M.
May 18, in Lurgan Church, by the Rev. W.P. Oulton, Mr. George Wilson Beattie, of Lurgan, to Miss Sarah Corner, second daughter of Mr. Thomas Corner, of Hawthorn Lodge, near Lurgan.

No. 2686 :: Ref. 1849-05-28, 3:2, M.
On Thursday last, by the Rev. W. Higginbottom, at Crew Church, parish of Ardstraw, and afterwards by the Rev. Mr. Brown, P.P., Camus, Mr. Wm. M'Gowan, merchant, Newtownstewart, to Alicia, daughter of the late Mr. Michael M'Kinny, Innkeeper, Strabane.

No. 2687 :: Ref. 1849-05-28, 3:2, D.
At Maghera, on the morning of the 22d inst., David Thompson, Esq., aged 50.

No. 2688 :: Ref. 1849-05-28, 3:2, D.
At the residence of Mr. Thompson, of Albany, State of New York, on the 24th of April, 1849, Miss Anne Mulheron, of small pox, formerly of Derry. Only a little over twelve months have elapsed since she emigrated in the bloom and beauty of youth to an only brother in America from Derry.

No. 2689 :: Ref. 1849-05-28, 3:2, D.
On Thursday last, in Newry, at the residence of his father, Robert S. Wallace, Esq., Solicitor, aged 25.

No. 2690 :: Ref. 1849-05-28, 3:2, D.
On the 15th inst., the Rev. Stuart Smith, A.M., Curate of Ballintemple, co. Cavan.

No. 2691 :: Ref. 1849-05-28, 3:2, D.
In Ennis, on 22d inst., after a short illness, Mr. John Leech, aged 69 years.

No. 2692 :: Ref. 1849-05-28, 3:2, D.
May 17, at Ballinakill, near Edenderry, Wm. M'Mullen, Esq., in the 70th year of his age.

No. 2693 :: Ref. 1849-05-28, 3:2, D.
May 19, at the Rev. George Ash's, Bellaghy, Sarah Jane, only daughter of the late Robert Algar, Esq., late collector of customs, at Drogheda.

No. 2694 :: Ref. 1849-05-28, 3:2, D.
At Ballynacross, on the 19th inst., Mr. James Henry, aged 88 years. He was the fourth generation, from his Presbyterian ancestors, who defended civil and religious liberty, under the Walls of Derry, in 1688.

No. 2695 :: Ref. 1849-05-28, 3:2, D.
May 19, at his residence, Curragh, Macosquin, in the 24th year of his age, Mr. Gregory Walker. The health of his body never having been injured by any kind of intemperance, nor that of his mind by violent passions, he retained the use of all his faculties, both bodily and mental, in conjunction with a stock of excellent health, to the last week of his life.

No. 2696 :: Ref. 1849-05-28, 3:2, D.
On the 20th inst., at Athlone, of cholera, after only five hours' illness Isabella Sophia, the beloved and affectionate wife of Major Longworth, 31st Regiment, in her 23d year; and on the following day, of the same disease, at same place, Emily Adelaide Rathborne, sister of Mrs. Longworth, in her 19th year, third daughter of Wm. Rathborne, Esq., of Scripplestown House, co. Dublin.

No. 2697 :: Ref. 1849-05-28, 3:2, D.
On 22d inst., at Stradone House, co. Cavan, Anne, relict of John Garden, Esq., of Barnane, co. Tipperary.

No. 2698 :: Ref. 1849-05-28, 3:2, D.
On 22d inst., at Edgeworthstown, Maria Edgeworth, in the 83d year of her age.

No. 2699 :: Ref. 1849-06-04, 2:7, B.
On the 29th ult., at the Provincial Bank of Ireland, Armagh, Mrs. Bowman, of a son.

No. 2700 :: Ref. 1849-06-04, 2:7, B.
On the 23d ult., on the Ballyjamesduff circuit, the wife of Mr. Abrahnm [sic] Dawson, of a daughter.

No. 2701 :: Ref. 1849-06-04, 2:7, M.

May 24, in Omagh, [C]aptain P. Murray, late of the 36th Regiment, and eldest surviving son of the late Major-General J.P. Murray, to Jane, third daughter of John M'Kenny, Esq., of Omagh.

No. 2702 :: Ref. 1849-06-04, 2:7, D.

On 29th ult., at Mullaloughran, co. Armagh, aged 76 years, Mr. Adam Birch, father of Mr. Robert Birch, Postmaster of this city.

No. 2703 :: Ref. 1849-06-04, 2:7, D.

On the 31st ult., Arthur M'Anally, smith in Messrs. Gardner's foundry, of this city, aged 38 years.

No. 2704 :: Ref. 1849-06-04, 2:7, D.

On 27th ult., at Danesford, Holly Well, co. Fermanagh, of fever, John Tagerty, Esq., M.D., much and deservedly regretted.

No. 2705 :: Ref. 1849-06-04, 2:7, D.

On 23d inst., at Aughnahone, Mary, relict of the late Mr. John Elliot, aged 108 years.

No. 2706 :: Ref. 1849-06-04, 2:7, D.

On 24th ult., at Earl-street, Belfast, Mrs. Garr, relict of the late Edward Garr, Esq.

No. 2707 :: Ref. 1849-06-04, 2:7, D.

On 28th ult., at Kesh, in the house of her brother, Dr. Johnston, Jane, third daughter of the late Rev. W. Johnston, vicar of Inishmagrath, co. Leitrim.

No. 2708 :: Ref. 1849-06-04, 2:7, D.

On the 30th March, at Lucknow, in the 23d year of his age, Robt. Boyle Irwin, Ensign 10th Bengal, N.I., sixth son of the late James Irwin, Esq., Wellbrook, co. Tyrone.

No. 2709 :: Ref. 1849-06-04, 2:7, D.

In Tralee, on the 29th ult., after a few hours' illness of cholera, the Rev. John Byrne, formerly a preacher in the Wesleyan Methodist connexion. In the early part of his life he was a Roman [C]atholic, but became subject to Divine influence, and was savingly converted to God. During a protracted indisposition, which compelled him to retire from the work of the ministry, he was pre-eminent for a steady devotion to his heavenly Father, and died comparatively easy in body, and perfectly resigned and prepared in mind, rejoicing in hope of an abundant entrance being administered to him in the church triumphant.

No. 2710 :: Ref. 1849-06-11, 3:2, B.

At the *"Chronicle"* Office, [C]oleraine, on 3d inst., Mrs. Huey, of a daughter.

No. 2711 :: Ref. 1849-06-11, 3:2, B.

On 8th inst., at Marino cottage, [C]lontarf, the lady of [C]harles [C]. Overend, of a son.

No. 2712 :: Ref. 1849-06-11, 3:2, B.

On 6th inst., at [C]arrickmore, co. Tyrone, the lady of Henry S. St. George, Esq., of a daughter.

No. 2713 :: Ref. 1849-06-11, 3:2, M.

On 1st of June, at Glenelly Presbyterian church, by the Rev. James Alexander, of Douglass, Mr. George Wesley, Moneymore, to Miss Jane Smyth, granddaughter of the late Rev. Robert Reid, of Letterbratt.

No. 2714 :: Ref. 1849-06-11, 3:2, M.

On 6th inst., at Cootehill, Philip O'Donnell, Esq., Provincial Bank of Ireland, Cavan, to Marian, daughter of John Macfadin, Esq., M.D.

No. 2715 :: Ref. 1849-06-11, 3:2, M.

On 30th ult., at the Friends Meeting-house, Grange co. Tyrone, Mr. Benjamin Hobson, Merchant, Belfast, to Elizabeth, youngest daughter of the late James Pillar, Culkerin, Moy, co. Tyrone.

No. 2716 :: Ref. 1849-06-11, 3:2, D.

In Primrose-street, on the 8th instant, after a protracted illness, which he bore with patient resignation to the Divine will, Mr. Peter M'Shane, aged 76, upwards of 50 of which have been spent in this city, with credit to himself and family. He was one of the oldest and most respected inhabitants of Armagh, and the large and respectable concourse of friends who attended his funeral attest how generally he was esteemed by all his fellow-citizens.

No. 2717 :: Ref. 1849-06-11, 3:2, D.

At Enniskillen, on 6th inst., [C]hristiana, second daughter of the late Mr. William Kittson, merchant. Her end was peace.

No. 2718 :: Ref. 1849-06-11, 3:2, D.

On 4th inst., of fever, in the Monaghan Union Workhouse, caught in the discharge of her duties as schoolmistress, Fanny, eldest daughter of Mr. William Thompson, Head constable of constabulary, aged 22 years.

No. 2719 :: Ref. 1849-06-11, 3:2, D.

On 4th inst., Elizabeth, eldest daughter of Mr. William Scott, Monaghan.

No. 2720 :: Ref. 1849-06-11, 3:2, D.

At Downpatrick, 6th inst., Mr. James Miller, aged 84 years. Deceased was one of the oldest methodists of that town, he having heard the venerable Wesley preach in the "Grove" 60 years ago, at which time he was in connexion with that body.

No. 2721 :: Ref. 1849-06-11, 3:2, D.

On 27th inst., at Rosstrevor, Davis George [C]roagan, of Mohill, co. of Leitrim, much regretted.

No. 2722 :: Ref. 1849-06-11, 3:2, D.

June 5, in Charleville, of fever, the Rev. William Hall, Rector of Kilshannick, in the diocese of Cloyne, and lately Rector of Charleville.

No. 2723 :: Ref. 1849-06-11, 3:2, D.

On 2d inst., at Ballygihen Avenue, Kingstown, Walter Molony, Esq., lately Resident Stipendiary Magistrate, Belfast.

No. 2724 :: Ref. 1849-06-18, 3:1, B.

June 13, the wife of Richard Storey, Esq., proprietor of King William III. Arms Hotel, Clones, of a daughter.

No. 2725 :: Ref. 1849-06-18, 3:1, B.

June 10, at Ashford House, Chertsey, Lady Willshire, of a daughter.

No. 2726 :: Ref. 1849-06-18, 3:1, M.

June 12, in the Presbyterian Church, Claggin, by the Rev. H. M'Caw, Mr. Thomas Harkness, Crievagh, to Margaret, second daughter of Mr. James Bell, Dunmore, both of co. Tyrone.

No. 2727 :: Ref. 1849-06-18, 3:1, M.

June 13, at the church of Ardagh, by the Very Rev. the Dean, uncle to the bride, the Rev. Henry Downton, Incumbent of St. John's, Chatham, to Elizabeth, second daughter of the late Alex. M'Kee, Esq., Moneymore.

No. 2728 :: Ref. 1849-06-18, 3:1, M.

June 14, in Monaghan, by the Rev. Henry Maffett, Mr. Wm. Elliott, of Belfast, to Rachel, only surviving daughter of the late Mr. Wm. Scott, of that town.

No. 2729 :: Ref. 1849-06-18, 3:1, M.

June 9, in Dublin, J.G. Strickland, Esq., of Cabragh Parade, to Margaret Hester, eldest daughter of the late Benjamin Friel Foster, Esq., of Drumloo Cottage, Newbliss, co. Monaghan.

No. 2730 :: Ref. 1849-06-18, 3:1, M.

June 7, at Edinburgh, by the Rev. Dr. Candlish, Mr. Alexander Williams, Orangefield, Belfast, to Marion, only daughter of the late Mr. James Douglas, Athol Staneford, New Mains.

No. 2731 :: Ref. 1849-06-18, 3:1, M.

June 12, in Dundalk, by the Rev. Mr. O'Neill, C.C., Richard Downey, Esq., Newry, mercht., to Matilda, fourth daughter of the late Mr. Richard Harcourt.

No. 2732 :: Ref. 1849-06-18, 3:1, M.

May 9, in St. Mary's, Battersea, Robert Culbertson, Esq., of Ballisodare, Sligo, to Agnes, daughter of John Harvey, Esq., of Lavender Hill, Surrey.

No. 2733 :: Ref. 1849-06-18, 3:1, M.

June 11, in Clontarf church by the Rev. Charles Dickinson, Richard Croker Russell, Esq., Royal Navy, to Henrietta Elizabeth, second daughter of the late Francis Dundas, Esq., Captain in her Majesty's 81st Regiment.

No. 2734 :: Ref. 1849-06-18, 3:1, M.

June 12, at Rathmines, by the Rev. N. Roche, C.C., O. Clarke, Esq., of Dundalk, to Kate Anastasia, third daughter of the late W. Ellison, Esq., of Dublin.

No. 2735 :: Ref. 1849-06-18, 3:1, M.

June 12, at the Registrar's office, Enniskillen, Mr. Thomas Ball, Aughaward, to Miss Catherine Earls, of Waughternerry, Enniskillen.

No. 2736 :: Ref. 1849-06-18, 3:1, M.

On the 14th inst., in the Linenhall-street Presbyterian church, Belfast, Matthew M'Clelland, Esq., Derry, to Jane, eldest daughter of Robert Calwell, Esq., Moneymore.

No. 2737 :: Ref. 1849-06-18, 3:1, D.

In the 69th year of his age, on Sunday morning, the 17th inst., Mr. John Turner, Governor of our County Gaol, much and deservedly respected by all who knew him.

No. 2738 :: Ref. 1849-06-18, 3:1, D.

At Drumanan, county of Armagh, on the 6th inst., Mr. William Briggs, aged 88 years. Deceased was a member of the Clantilew Volunteers, commanded by Captain Obre, and afterwards a member of the Crowhill Corps of Yeomanry.

No. 2739 :: Ref. 1849-06-18, 3:1, D.

On the 15th inst., in Camden-street, Dublin, Ellen, relict of the Rev. Philip Ryan, and eldest daughter of the late Rev. Jos. Tenison, of Donoughmore Glebe, Deputy-Governor of the county of Wicklow.

No. 2740 :: Ref. 1849-06-18, 3:1, D.

On the 14th inst., in Fermanagh-street, Clones, of dysentery, Mr. Isaac Edwards, nailor, in the 24th year of his age. He was for many years a consistent member of the Orange institution, and was buried in Clones church-yard, on the 16th inst., borne thither by the respective member[s] of the different lodges in this town, with all the solemnity usual in such cases.

No. 2741 :: Ref. 1849-06-18, 3:1, D.

On the 5th inst., in Nelson-street, Tralee, after a few hours' illness, William Loughlin, Esq., officer of Inland Revenue.

No. 2742 :: Ref. 1849-06-18, 3:1, D.

At Holyhead, on the 12th inst., James Forsythe, Esq., M.D., formerly of Belfast, aged 93 years.

No. 2743 :: Ref. 1849-06-18, 3:1, D.

On 7th inst. at Lakeview, near Newry, Fanny, daughter of the late Adam Bowles, Esq.

No. 2744 :: Ref. 1849-06-18, 3:1, D.

At Lisburn, on the 10th inst., after a few hours' illness, James K. Clarke, Lieut., Royal Artillery.

No. 2745 :: Ref. 1849-06-18, 3:1, D.

On 12th inst., in Dundalk, the wife of Mr. Peter M'Kenny, spirit merchant, aged 26 years.

No. 2746 :: Ref. 1849-06-18, 3:1, D.

At Ardee, on 11th inst., Head-constable M'Quillion.

No. 2747 :: Ref. 1849-06-18, 3:1, D.
On the 2d inst., at South-crescent, Bedford-square, London, Dr. Wm. Wilson, author, of "*Travels in the Holy Land, &c.,*" in the 76th year of his age.

No. 2748 :: Ref. 1849-06-18, 3:1, D.
On 10th inst., in the 16th year of her age, Everina, only surviving daughter of Harvey Nicholson, Esq., River View, Derry.

No. 2749 :: Ref. 1849-06-18, 3:1, D.
On 30th March last, at Calcutta, Thomas Steele, Esq., Barrister-at-Law, in the 27th year of his age, of Asiatic cholera.

No. 2750 :: Ref. 1849-06-18, 3:1, D.
June 7, at Moneltan, co. Donegal, Saml. Delap, Esq., J.P. and D.L.

No. 2751 :: Ref. 1849-06-18, 3:1, D.
On the 9th inst., at the house of her son, Mr. James Fleming of Lurgan, Mrs. Fleming.

No. 2752 :: Ref. 1849-06-18, 3:1, D.
On 11th inst., at the Crescent, Belfast, of inflammation of the lungs, Margaret, wife of Dr. Shannon, of Magherafelt.

No. 2753 :: Ref. 1849-06-18, 3:1, D.
April 23, the Rev. Wm. Farmer of the Church Missionary Society, on his passage home from Shanghae, China.

No. 2754 :: Ref. 1849-06-18, 3:1, D.
June 10th, aged 69, Mr. Thomas M'Collum, who held the situation of master of the Tullyvin Endowed School for the period of 46 years.

No. 2755 :: Ref. 1849-06-18, 3:1, D.
On 9th May, at Conington, Kentucky, aged 30 years, John, eldest son of Mr. Samuel Kennedy, of Quilly, Coleraine, of cholera.

No. 2756 :: Ref. 1849-06-18, 3:1, D.
On 3d inst., after a protracted and painful illness, which he bore with pious resignation to the Divine will, John Patterson, Esq., proprietor of the Ballymagorry Mills, near Strabane, aged 34 years.

No. 2757 :: Ref. 1849 06 18, 3:1, D.
On 11th inst., in Lower Gardiner-ftreet [sic], Dublin, after a short illness, William Murray, Esq., in the 64th year of his age. Mr. Murray was for many years Architect to the Board of Public Works, in which office he succeeded his relative, the late Mr. Francis Johnston. Among Mr. Murrays's works were the College of Surgeons, the District Lunatic Asylums, and several other public buildings, as well as private residences throughout Ireland. He was a member of the Royal Irish Academy, and Treasurer and Fellow of the Royal Hibernian Academy.

No. 2758 :: Ref. 1849-06-18, 3:1, D.
On 22d ult. at Tralee, of cholera, after a few hours' illness, Isabella, wife of John Busteed, Esq., in the prime of life—a life spent in works of love and charity—leaving a young and interesting family to deplore her loss. She became alarmed on hearing that one of her daughters, then ill, had cholera, and was herself seized with the fatal malady. The deceased was daughter to Donald Mackay, Esq., Newry.

No. 2759 :: Ref. 1849-06-25, 3:1, B.
June 22d, in Armagh, the wife of John Thompson, proprietor of *The Armagh Guardian*, of a son.

No. 2760 :: Ref. 1849-06-25, 3:1, B.
June 17, at Ballytrim House, co. Down, the lady of T.K. Lowry, Esq., Barrister-at-Law, of a son.

No. 2761 :: Ref. 1849-06-25, 3:1, M.
June 12, at Jersey, John H.O. Moore, Esq., Major 44th regt. and only son of the late General Sir John Lorenzo Moore, Esq., to Selena Maria, daughter of Wm. W. Childers, Esq., formerly Captain [of] the Royal Highlanders.

No. 2762 :: Ref. 1849-06-25, 3:1, D.
June 18, at Carrickmacross, of cholera, John M'Effer, Esq., A.M., M.B., medical superintendent of the dispensary, aged 49 years.

No. 2763 :: Ref. 1849-06-25, 3:1, D.
June 20, at Donaghmore, in the co. Tyrone, aged 77 years, the Rev. Archibald Hamilton, Incumbent of Derg, in the Diocess of Derry.

No. 2764 :: Ref. 1849-06-25, 3:1, D.
June 16, at 35, Ellis's-quay, Dublin, Mrs. J.A. Sinnott, only daughter of Mr. John Hayes of Cavan.

No. 2765 :: Ref. 1849-06-25, 3:1, D.
June 18, Elizabeth H. Rea, of the County Court-house, Armagh, in her 37th year, beloved and respected by all who knew her.

No. 2766 :: Ref. 1849-06-25, 3:1, D.
June 19, at the residence of her son Mr. William Jebb, Proctor, Monaghan, Mrs. Jane Jebb, aged 49 years, much and deservedly regretted by a large circle of friends and acquaintances, in the full assurance of a blessed immortality.

No. 2767 :: Ref. 1849-06-25, 3:1, D.
June 12, at Clerkhill, near Borrisokane, Mrs. Margaret Kelly, in the 150th year of her age. She had been out walking on Sunday last, and died after a few hours illness, retaining perfect possession of her faculties till the last moment, leaving children to the fifth generation.

No. 2768 :: Ref. 1849-06-25, 3:1, D.
May 23, at Lowtherstown, Mr. Richard Aiken, aged 54 years.

No. 2769 :: Ref. 1849-06-25, 3:1, D.
June 18, at Glencar, near Letterkenny, of disease of the heart, Margaret, eldest daughter of David Hunter, Esq.

No. 2770 :: Ref. 1849-06-25, 3:1, D.
June 16, at Bushmills, Mr. Alexander Hartford, watch and clockmaker, aged 57 years.

No. 2771 :: Ref. 1849-06-25, 3:1, D.
June 19, at Bushmills, after a few days' illness, Mr. Sampson Ingram, aged about 40 years.

No. 2772 :: Ref. 1849-06-25, 3:1, D.
At Barnmeen, on the 9th ult., Catherine, youngest daughter of the late Mr. Thomas Fegan.

No. 2773 :: Ref. 1849-06-25, 3:1, D.
June 15, at his son's residence, Lurgan, aged 63 years, Mr. James Stevenson, Organist of Hillsborough Church for 42 years.

No. 2774 :: Ref. 1849-06-25, 3:1, D.
June 15, in the 41st year of her age, Mrs. Eliza Brennian, wife of Mr. W. Brennian, Teacher, Lurgan.

No. 2775 :: Ref. 1849-06-25, 3:1, D.
In the county of Wicklow, on the 13th inst., Mrs. Sarah Warren, wife of Mr. Thomas Warren, late of Powerscourt, co. of Wicklow, aged 62.

No. 2776 :: Ref. 1849-06-25, 3:1, D.
June 11, at St. David, N.B., Mr. William Gillis, aged 71 years. Mr. Gillis (says the *Halifax Guardian*) was a native of County Armagh, Ireland, and emigrated to this province about 60 years ago; he was universally beloved and respected by all who were acquainted with him, as an honest, upright man. He was a strict adherent to the Presbyterian Church, and his end was peace.

No. 2777 :: Ref. 1849-07-02, 2:6, B.
On Wednesday, in Palace Row, Mrs. Fullarton, of a son.

No. 2778 :: Ref. 1849-07-02, 2:6, B.
On 20th ult., at Thorpe Hesley Glebe, Yorkshire, the lady of the Rev. B.S. Clarke, of a daughter.

No. 2779 :: Ref. 1849-07-02, 2:6, B.
On 20th ult., at Ryde, Isle of Wight, the wife of the Rev. Arthur J. Wade, Incumbent of Trinity Church, Ryde, of a daughter.

No. 2780 :: Ref. 1849-07-02, 2:6, B.
On 23d ult., at 73, Lower Mount street, the lady of Samuel Wauchob, Esq., of a son.

No. 2781 :: Ref. 1849-07-02, 2:6, B.
On 17th ult., at Enniskillen, the wife of R.R. Pringle, Esq., Ordnance Storekeeper and Barrack-master, of a son.

No. 2782 :: Ref. 1849-07-02, 2:6, B.
June 23, at Stewartstown, co. Tyrone, the lady of John Little, Esq., Solicitor, of a son.

No. 2783 :: Ref. 1849-07-02, 2:6, M.
At the Friends' Meeting house, Belfast, John Charles Constable, of Everton, Lancashire, to Elizabeth, daughter of John Lamb, of Belfast.

No. 2784 :: Ref. 1849-07-02, 2:6, M.
At Bruree, John Neville, Esq., of Dundalk, surveyor, for the co. Louth, to Constance, daughter of John Cox, Esq., of Ballyneale, co. Limerick.

No. 2785 :: Ref. 1849-07-02, 2:6, M.
June 26, in St. George's Church, by the Rev. G. Black, Johnston Hamilton Acheson, Esq., Surgeon, R.N., to Frances Anne, second daughter of the late James Armstrong Buchannan, Esq., 4th or King's Own Regiment.

No. 2786 :: Ref. 1849-07-02, 2:6, M.
June 26, in May-Street Church, Belfast, by the Rev. John Lyle, Whiteabbey, Mr. Jonathan Vint, merchant, to Rachel, eldest daughter of Mr. Robt. Gilmore, both of Belfast.

No. 2787 :: Ref. 1849-07-02, 2:6, M.
April 17, by the Rev. William A. Passavant, Pastor of the 1st English Evangelical Lutheran Church, Pittsburg, William Shannon, late of Bushmills, co. Antrim, to Mary Limerick, eldest daughter of Mr. John Scott, of Alleghany City, and late of Church-hill, near Ballykelly, co. Londonderry.

No. 2788 :: Ref. 1849-07-02, 2:6, D.
On Thursday the 28th ult., at his residence, Moss View, near Portadown, in the 63d year of his age, Mr. Arthur Mercer, linen manufacturer. The large and respectable attendance at his funeral, of all classes and denominations, attested the respect and esteem in which he was held. His death is greatly lamented by the working classes, as he kept in constant employment upwards of 500 families in the different branches of the linen trade; and his family and friends cannot but feel deeply grieved for the loss of one whom they respected and loved, yet their sorrow is not without hope.

No. 2789 :: Ref. 1849-07-02, 2:6, D.
In Lisnadill, on Thursday, Mr. Marks, after a few hours' illness.

No. 2790 :: Ref. 1849-07-02, 2:6, D.
In Moneycree, at an advanced age, after a protracted illness, Anne, relict of the late Mr. John Wynne, deservedly regretted by all who knew her.

No. 2791 :: Ref. 1849-07-02, 2:6, D.
June 26, at Brighton, the Right Hon. Lord Louth, of Louth Hall, co. Louth, aged 39 years.

No. 2792 :: Ref. 1849-07-02, 2:6, D.
June 25, at Blackwatertown, Elizabeth, the beloved wife of Alex. Crothers, Esq.

No. 2793 :: Ref. 1849-07-02, 2:6, D.
June 26, at Warrenpoint, Jane, second daughter of the late Robt. Anderson, Esq., of Drumkeen, co. Fermanagh.

No. 2794 :: Ref. 1849-07-02, 2:6, D.
June 7, at his residence, Cootehill, in the 67th year of his age, Richard Philips, Esq., Master of Chancery.

No. 2795 :: Ref. 1849-07-02, 2:6, D.
On 24th ult., at Ballybay, aged 72 years, Sarah, widow of the late James Breaky, of Carmeen, Esq.

No. 2796 :: Ref. 1849-07-02, 2:6, D.
June 26, at an advanced age, the Hon. Frederick Ponsonby, brother of the Bishop of Derry, and of the late General Sir Wm. Ponsonby, who fell at the battle of Waterloo.

No. 2797 :: Ref. 1849-07-02, 2:6, D.
On 17th ult., at her residence, Cortober, of consumption, Mrs. Jane Higinbotham, aged 59.

No. 2798 :: Ref. 1849-07-02, 2:6, D.
June 21, in Tullamore, in her 91st year, Hannah Pim, daughter of the late Joshua Pim, of Tullylast, in the county Kildare.

No. 2799 :: Ref. 1849-07-09, 3:7, B.
On 3d inst., at Cloonlough Cottage, Ballymote, the lady of Andw. Green, Esq., of a son.

No. 2800 :: Ref. 1849-07-09, 3:7, M.
On the 5th inst., at St. Mark's Church, Armagh, by the Rev. C.S. Mangan, Rector of Madden, John Smyth, Esq., 39, Upper Sackville-street, Dublin, to Olivia Henrietta, third daughter of John Cardwell, Esq., Tullyelmer, Armagh.

No. 2801 :: Ref. 1849-07-09, 3:7, M.
On 4th inst. in Belfast, by the Rev. T. Campbell, M.A., the Rev. David Stevenson, B.A., Trinity College, Cambridge, and Curate of St. Thomas's, Lancaster, to Mary, eldest daughter of Thomas H. Higgin, Esq., Belfast.

No. 2802 :: Ref. 1849-07-09, 3:7, M.
June 28, at Dysertegney Church, by the Rev. S. Reed, John, second son of the late Rev. A.G. Carey, of Glendermott, co. Derry, to Fanny, fifth daughter of the Rev. Sir W.J. Macartney, Bart., Rector of Dysertegney, co. Donegal.

No. 2803 :: Ref. 1849-07-09, 3:7, M.
July 4, in St. Peter's Church, Dublin, by the Rev. E. Metcalfe, Paul King Bracken, of Rosemount, Drumcondra, co. Dublin, to Pauline King, fourth daughter of the late Dr. Bracken, of Waterford, and relict of George Beard, Esq., of Mountmellick.

No. 2804 :: Ref. 1849-07-09, 3:7, M.
At St. George's, Hanover square, London, by the Rev. W. Cadman, William Macdonald Macdonald, Esq., of St. Martin's, Perthshire, and Rossie Castle, Forfarshire, to the Honorable Clara Anne Jane Brownlow, second daughter of the late Lord Lurgan.

No. 2805 :: Ref. 1849-07-09, 3:7, M.
June 22, in Liverpool, John Averill Leckey Holland, late Lieutenant in the 86th Regiment, to Susan, daughter of John Coleman, Esq., Portrush.

No. 2806 :: Ref. 1849-07-09, 3:7, M.
At Quebec, Charles Aylwin, Esq., to Hebe Louisa, relict of James Allsopp, Esq., Paymaster of the 44th and 17th Regiments.

No. 2807 :: Ref. 1849-07-09, 3:7, D.
July 4, at Glencrew, near Aughnacloy, after a short illness, Mr. Wm. Corbett, sen., father of Mr. Wm. Corbett, proprietor of the King Wm. Hotel, of that town, aged 68 years.

No. 2808 :: Ref. 1849-07-09, 3:7, D.
June 28, at Clones, the wife of R. Fausset, Esq., of a daughter.

No. 2809 :: Ref. 1849-07-09, 3:7, D.
June 28, at Raveningham, Anna Maria, eldest daughter of Sir Edmund Bacon, Bart., of Raveningham Hall, in the county of Norfolk.

No. 2810 :: Ref. 1849-07-09, 3:7, D.
On 28th ult., suddenly, at Warrington, on his way to London, deeply and most deservedly regretted, Samuel Alexander Kidd, Esq., of Darkley House, eldest son of Samuel Kidd, Esq., Dundrum House, Keady.

No. 2811 :: Ref. 1849-07-09, 3:7, D.
July 2d, in Armagh, suddenly, Mr. Francis Gray, pawnbroker, aged 45 years.

No. 2812 :: Ref. 1849-07-09, 3:7, D.
At Laragh, on 6th July, Mr. James Green, of the firm of Messrs. James Green & Co., of Keady and Laragh Mills. Mr. Green was an active, useful, and enterprising man, and his death will be a public loss in the country, where he promoted works of industry.

No. 2813 :: Ref. 1849-07-09, 3:7, D.
At Rockcorry, on 27th ult., aged 65 years, the relict of the late Rev. Doctor Moore.

No. 2814 :: Ref. 1849-07-09, 3:7, D.
On 27th ult., at Castleblayney, after a few days' illness, Thomas M'Donough, Esq., late Lieutenant in her Majesty's 35th Regiment of Foot.

No. 2815 :: Ref. 1849-07-09, 3:7, D.
At Sallybank, near Enniskillen, on 30th June, Mr. George Greenfield, aged 69.

No. 2816 :: Ref. 1849-07-09, 3:7, D.
On 30th ult., of cholera, Mr. Robert Henderson of Donegal-street, Belfast, aged 26 years.

No. 2817 :: Ref. 1849-07-09, 3:7, D.
On 1st instant, at Ballinahedin, Mr. William Sherard, in the 38th year of his age.

No. 2818 :: Ref. 1849-07-09, 3:7, D.
At Ballytigue at the venerable age of 114 years, Mrs. Carey, mother of the Rev. John Carey, of Killarney, late Parish Priest of Ferriter.

No. 2819 :: Ref. 1849-07-09, 3:7, D.
On 27th ult., at Coach, near Moneymore, Mr. Given Hamilton, jun., aged 25 years.

No. 2820 :: Ref. 1849-07-09, 3:7, D.
At Newry, on 30th ult., Mr. John Small, aged 72 years.

No. 2821 :: Ref. 1849-07-09, 3:7, D.
On the 27th ult., at Hopefield, Belfast, Sarah, wife of Thomas Sinclair, Esq.

No. 2822 :: Ref. 1849-07-09, 3:7, D.
On 23d ult., at Dungannon, Wm. M. Morrow, eldest son of Mr. James Morrow, in the 18th year of his age.

No. 2823 :: Ref. 1849-07-09, 3:7, D.
On the 27th ult., at Dublin, Ronald, son of Sir John Macneill, of Mountpleasant, Dundalk, co. Louth, aged 14 years.

No. 2824 :: Ref. 1849-07-16, 3:7, B.
July 11, at Chelsea, Middlesex, the lady of William Stitt, Esq., of a son.

No. 2825 :: Ref. 1849-07-16, 3:7, B.
July 14, Mrs. Robert Anderson, Lissidian House, of a daughter.

No. 2826 :: Ref. 1849-07-16, 3:7, M.
On the 9th instant, at Knaresborough Church, Yorkshire, by the Rev. George Reid, the Rev. George Hunt, Curate of Drumcree, co. Armagh, son of John Hunt, Esq., Surgeon, Royal County Limerick Regiment, to Caroline, youngest daughter of the late James Johnstone, Esq., of Knappagh, county Armagh.

No. 2827 :: Ref. 1849-07-16, 3:7, M.
On the 19th instant, at Ballyhemlin, by the Rev. Alexander Orr, George Bowden, Esq., M.D., Monaghan, to Ann, daughter of Alex. Allen, Esq., Ballyobican, Ballywalter.

No. 2828 :: Ref. 1849-07-16, 3:7, M.
On the 3d instant, the Rev. Thomas Clugston, of Boardmills, to Anne, eldest daughter of James Quay, Esq., Daisyhill, Mountnorris.

No. 2829 :: Ref. 1849-07-16, 3:7, M.
On the 12th inst., at St. Paul's, Knightsbridge, by the Rev. James Guillemard, vicar of Kirtlington, Oxon, assisted by the Rev. W.J.E. Bennet, the Rev. William Henry Guillemard, B.D., Fellow of Pembroke College, Cambridge, and Head Master of the College, Armagh, to Elizabeth Susanna, eldest daughter of William H. Turner, Esq., of 16, Rutland gate, Hyde Park, London.

No. 2830 :: Ref. 1849-07-16, 3:7, D.
July 11, at her Mother's residence, Mary, eldest daughter of Mr. Andrew Allen, Surgeon, late of Fintona, after a very short but severe illness, which she bore with exemplary fortitude, and christian resignation. She died in the faith of her Redeemer, and a full assurance of a blessed immortality beyond the grave; deeply and deservedly regretted by a numerous circle of friends and companions.

No. 2831 :: Ref. 1849-07-16, 3:7, D.
July 9, near Moneymore, the Rev. William Wylie, in the 70th year of his age.

No. 2832 :: Ref. 1849-07-16, 3:7, D.
July 15, of cholera, Richard Irwine, fourth son of the late Andw. Wallace, Esq., of Belfast.

No. 2833 :: Ref. 1849-07-16, 3:7, D.
July 15, at Holywood, after a few hours' illness, Mary Montgomery, wife of the Rev. J.H. Morell, Ballybay.

No. 2834 :: Ref. 1849-07-16, 3:7, D.
July 8, in Sligo, Mrs. Rebecca Griffin, relict of the late William Griffin, Esq.

No. 2835 :: Ref. 1849-07-16, 3:7, D.
At Caledon, on 3d inst., Mrs. Dorothea Milligan, aged 71 years.

No. 2836 :: Ref. 1849-07-16, 3:7, D.
On 5th inst., Sophia Anne, relict of the late John Knox, Esq., of Maze House, co. Down, and last surviving daughter of the late Rev. George Rogers, Rector of Clonallen, and Chancellor of the diocese of Dromore.

No. 2837 :: Ref. 1849-07-16, 3:7, D.
On 26th May, at Tobago, after a short illness, Assistant-Commissary-General S.J. Towesland, in the 61st year of his age.

No. 2838 :: Ref. 1849-07-16, 3:7, D.
On 3d inst., at Tullyconnaught House, near Banbridge, James Charles Mulligan, Esq.

No. 2839 :: Ref. 1849-07-16, 3:7, D.
June 29th, at Little Island House, county Cork, William Pennefather, Esq., senior, aged 88 years, formerly Surveyor-General in Ireland, and collector of the county Cork, one of the few survivors of the late Irish Parliament, of which he had been a member for 13 years.

No. 2840 :: Ref. 1849-07-16, 3:7, D.
On 3d inst., in Belfast, F.W.H. Charley, second son of the late Hill Charley, Esq., aged 22 years.

No. 2841 :: Ref. 1849-07-23, 3:6, B.
At Vicar's Hill, on Wednesday, 18th July, Mrs. George Allen, of a daughter.

No. 2842 :: Ref. 1849-07-23, 3:6, B.
July 18th, at Newry, the Lady of Henry Nelmes, Esq., of a daughter.

No. 2843 :: Ref. 1849-07-23, 3:6, B.
July 15, at Killea Rectory, Diocese of Raphoe, the lady of Rev. Gage Ball, of a daughter.

No. 2844 :: Ref. 1849-07-23, 3:6, B.
At Castledawson, on the 11th July, Mrs. John Milligan, of a son.

No. 2845 :: Ref. 1849-07-23, 3:6, B.
On 16th inst., at Enniskillen, the wife of the Rev. Mark Whittaker, Rector of Boho, of a son.

No. 2846 :: Ref. 1849-07-23, 3:6, M.
In Lurgan Church, on Sunday, the 15th inst., by the Rev. W.P. Oulton, Mrs. Beatty, to Mr. A. Stanfield, Merchant, both of Lurgan.

No. 2847 :: Ref. 1849-07-23, 3:6, M.
July 17, at Belfast, by the Rev. Mr. Knox, Mr. Joseph Eaton, of Trillic [sic], co. Tyrone, to Ellen, second daughter of the late Samuel Wilson, Esq., of Belfast.

No. 2848 :: Ref. 1849-07-23, 3:6, M.
July 10, at Clough church, by the Rev. V.D. Christian, George Washington Bell, Esq., of Killinure House, county Cavan, to Margaret, second daughter of the late William Syme, Esq., of Perth, Scotland.

No. 2849 :: Ref. 1849-07-23, 3:6, D.
On board the "*Eliza Morrison*," on her passage to Quebec, on the 2d June last, Jemima, the beloved wife of the Rev. James Mawhiney, and daughter of Alexander King, Esq., of Monaghan.

No. 2850 :: Ref. 1849-07-23, 3:6, D.
On 16th inst., Mrs. Lanktree, wife of the Rev. Matthew Lanktree, of cholera. On the morning of her husband's funeral, she was in good health; but when her children returned from his interment, some hours after, she was insensible, and died immediately after.

No. 2851 :: Ref. 1849-07-23, 3:6, D.
July 15, at Byfeld House, Barnes, near London, Anne, the fourth daughter of the late Robert Lindesay, Esq., of Loughry, co. Tyrone.

No. 2852 :: Ref. 1849-07-23, 3:6, D.
July 12, at Ballyconnell, in the 31st year of his age, Dr. James Sturdy, of Belturbet.

No. 2853 :: Ref. 1849-07-23, 3:6, D.
On 11th inst., Mr. James Lowry, of Enniskillen, saddler, aged 26.

No. 2854 :: Ref. 1849-07-23, 3:6, D.
On 16th inst., at Oakfield, near Enniskillen, Mr. James Montgomery.

No. 2855 :: Ref. 1849-07-23, 3:6, D.
On 14th inst., at Drumcaw, near Lisnaskea, Margery, wife of Edward Russell, Esq., aged 48 years.

No. 2856 :: Ref. 1849-07-23, 3:6, D.
At New York, on 27th May last, Fanny, relict of the late Mr. Richard Ellis, Court-house keeper, of Monaghan.

No. 2857 :: Ref. 1849-07-30, 3:1, M.
On 25th inst., at St. Johh's [sic] Chapel, Edinburgh, by the Rev. Berkely Addison, the Rev. Edward William Whatehey, only son of his Grace the Archbishop of Dublin, to Leslie Anne, eldest daughter of the late William James Fraser, Esq., of Ladhope, Roxburghshire.

No. 2858 :: Ref. 1849-07-30, 3:1, M.
July 23, at Rostrevor, Bernard Hughes, Esq., of Belfast, to Margaret Mary Teresa, eldest daughter of the late John Lowry, Esq., of Dublin, and granddaughter of Francis Lowry, Esq., of Killadrown and Mountmellick, in the Queen's county.

No. 2859 :: Ref. 1849-07-30, 3:1, M.
July 24, in Enniskillen church, by the Rev. Mr. Mathias, Mr. J.L. Blackmore, R.E.D., to Miss Mary Anne, third daughter of the late Mr. James Scott, Enniskillen.

No. 2860 :: Ref. 1849-07-30, 3:1, M.
July 19, in Castle Archdall church, the Rev. John Hazelton, Wesleyan Minister, Strabane, to Eliza, daughter of the Rev. William Douglas, Lowtherstown.

No. 2861 :: Ref. 1849-07-30, 3:1, M.
July 17, in Killeter, Mr. James Kerr, of Carndreen, to Anne Jane, daughter of Mr. Robert Thompson, of the same place.

No. 2862 :: Ref. 1849-07-30, 3:1, M.
July 17, in Killeter, Mr. Blythe Harper, of Dreenan, to Margaret, daughter of Mr. Robert Thompson, of [C]arndreen.

No. 2863 :: Ref. 1849-07-30, 3:1, M.
July 18, at Newry, Edmund Byrne Lawless, Esq., of Dublin, to Rose, eldest daughter of Constantine Maguire, Esq., of Newry, J.P.

No. 2864 :: Ref. 1849-07-30, 3:1, M.
July 24, at Monkstown church, by the Rev. Edward Hawkshaw, the Hon. Henry Crichton, brother of the Earl of Erne, to Elizabeth, youngest daughter of the late Colonel Hawkshaw, of Blairs, in the co. Down.

No. 2865 :: Ref. 1849-07-30, 3:1, D.
July 28, at Lurgan, Mrs. Todd, of cholera, much and deservedly regretted by a numerous circle of friends.

No. 2866 :: Ref. 1849-07-30, 3:1, D.
July 26, at Castlebar, Mr. David Milling, aged twenty years.

No. 2867 :: Ref. 1849-07-30, 3:1, D.
July 20, after a few days illness, Drummond Anderson, Esq., senior proprietor of the *Belfast Commercial Chronicle*, in his 73d year.

No. 2868 :: Ref. 1849-07-30, 3:1, D.
July 22, of fever, aged 30 years, the Rev. Edward Breakey, minister of the Presbyterian church, Alfred-place, Belfast.

No. 2869 :: Ref. 1849-07-30, 3:1, D.
July 26, opposite the Ulster Railway Terminus, Belfast, after a severe and tedious illness, Mr. John O'Hanlon, aged 54 years.

No. 2870 :: Ref. 1849-07-30, 3:1, D.
July 19, in the 15th year of her age, Mary Jane, second daughter of Nathaniel Mayne, Esq., of Lake View, Aughnacloy, sincerely and deservedly regretted by all her friends and acquaintances.

No. 2871 :: Ref. 1849-07-30, 3:1, D.
July 16, at Cromac Lodge, Belfast, Margaret C. Blow, wife of Mr. Edwin Blow. On 17th inst., at the same place, her husband, Mr. Edwin Blow. On same day, at the same place, their eldest son, William Blow. On 18th inst., Mr. Arthur K. Miller, brother of Mrs. E. Blow. On 19th inst., at Craigavad, Mr. Franklin B. Shaw, of Dunandry, nephew to the late Mr. Edwin Blow. On 20th inst., at the same place, his sister, Mary B. Shaw.

No. 2872 :: Ref. 1849-08-06, 3:2, B.
At Moy, on 28th ult., Mrs. Crothers of a son.

No. 2873 :: Ref. 1849-08-06, 3:2, B.
July 29, at Enniskillen, the wife of Dr. William Ovenden, of a daughter.

No. 2874 :: Ref. 1849-08-06, 3:2, B.
On the 14th ult., at Portadown, the wife of Alexander Bredin, Esq., M.D., of a son.

No. 2875 :: Ref. 1849-08-06, 3:2, B.
On the 29th ult., at Sanford Terrace, Dublin, the lady of Echlin Molyneux, Esq., of a daughter.

No. 2876 :: Ref. 1849-08-06, 3:2, M.
July 13, at All Souls, Langham Place, London, by special license, William Fox, Esq., of Heath House, Brislington, Somersetshire, to Emma, widow of Sir George Molyneaux, Bart., of Castledillon, co. Armagh.

No. 2877 :: Ref. 1849-08-06, 3:2, M.
On 1st inst., in Keady Church, by the Rev. Mr. Simpson, James Sharpe, Esq., M.D., Cootehill, to Jane, eldest daughter of Alexander M'Combe, Esq., solicitor, Darkly House, Keady, co. Armagh.

No. 2878 :: Ref. 1849-08-06, 3:2, M.
At Clogher Cathedral, on 26th July, Mr. John Brown, bridewell-keeper, to Miss Ellen Durnion, of Ballymagowan.

No. 2879 :: Ref. 1849-08-06, 3:2, D.
On 1st inst., after a painful and long protracted illness, Eliza, wife of Mr. Robert Birch, Postmaster of this city, aged 36 years.

No. 2880 :: Ref. 1849-08-06, 3:2, D.
On 3d inst., Mr. Alexander Stitt, of Glasdrumond, near Markethill, in the 85th year of his age. A pattern through life and an example at death. Blessed are the dead which died in the Lord.

No. 2881 :: Ref. 1849-08-06, 3:2, D.
On 29th ult., at Trillick, Edward Gault, Esq., aged 64.

No. 2882 :: Ref. 1849-08-06, 3:2, D.
On the 28th ult., at his residence, Ballycastle, David Wilson, Esq.

No. 2883 :: Ref. 1849-08-06, 3:2, D.
On the 28th ult., at her house in Lurgan, suddenly, Jane, relict of the late Gabriel Todd, of Ballintagart, county Armagh, Esq.

No. 2884 :: Ref. 1849-08-06, 3:2, D.
On the 31st ult., at his house, Monaghan-street, Newry, Constantine Maguire, Esq., J.P. Counties Down and Armagh, aged 48 years.

No. 2885 :: Ref. 1849-08-06, 3:2, D.
On the 31st ult., at Marcus-square, Newry, Mr. Peacock, son of the late Mr. Peacock, manager of the *Newry Telegraph*, aged 47 years.

No. 2886 :: Ref. 1849-08-13, 3:2, B.
On 5th instant, at Florence Court, the Countess of Enniskillen, of a daughter.

No. 2887 :: Ref. 1849-08-13, 3:2, B.
On Friday, July 27, the lady of Winslow Finlay, Esq., Surgeon to Swanlinbar Dispensary, of a son.

No. 2888 :: Ref. 1849-08-13, 3:2, B.
On 8th instant, at Cargycreevy, the lady of the Rev. R.S. Erwin, of a son.

No. 2889 :: Ref. 1849-08-13, 3:2, B.
On 10th instant, in Main-street, Cavan, the lady of Edward Kennedy, Esq., merchant, of a daughter.

No. 2890 :: Ref. 1849-08-13, 3:2, B.
On 3d, instant, at the Chief Baron's, Guilford-street, London, Lady Pollock, of a daughter, still-born.

No. 2891 :: Ref. 1849-08-13, 3:2, M.
On 9th instant, at Kilmore Church, by the Rev. A. Gilmore, William Cuddy, of Drumnasoo Cottage, Esq, to Frances Elizabeth, youngest daughter of Wm. Jones, Esq., of Mountpleasant.

No. 2892 :: Ref. 1849-08-13, 3:2, M.
On 10th instant, in Killilea Church, by the Rev. Mr. M'Causland, Mr. Lewis Walsh, of Seskanore, to Jane, youngest daughter of the late Mr. Robert Young, of Kilrudden, co. Tyrone.

No. 2893 :: Ref. 1849-08-13, 3:2, M.
On 2d instant, in Dundalk Church, by the Rev. J.H. Allpress, William R. Trotter, of Tandragee, merchant, to Eliza Sarah, youngest daughter of Mr. Thomas Nicholson, Seafield, Kilkeel.

No. 2894 :: Ref. 1849-08-13, 3:2, M.
On 7th instant, in the first Presbyterian Church, Coleraine, by the Rev. William Richey, Robert Remington, Esq., Fort Hill, Banbridge, to Catherine, second daughter of the late John Cochran, Esq., merchant, Coleraine.

No. 2895 :: Ref. 1849-08-13, 3:2, M.
On 6th instant, at the Registrar's office, Enniskillen, by C. Gamble, Registrar, Mr. William Howe, Drumderge, to Miss Elizabeth Pierce, Glencunny, parish of Rossorry.

No. 2896 :: Ref. 1849-08-13, 3:2, D.
On 2d instant, at Ross, near Manorhamilton, Thomas, son of Major Armstrong, aged 24 years, much and deservedly regretted by all who had the pleasure of his acquaintance.

No. 2897 :: Ref. 1849-08-13, 3:2, D.
On 8th instant, of consumption, Maria, eldest daughter of Mr. John Ladley, Solicitor, Joy street, Belfast.

No. 2898 :: Ref. 1849-08-13, 3:2, D.
On 7th instant, suddenly at his residence, in Belfast, Mr. Samuel Sloan, aged 54 years.

No. 2899 :: Ref. 1849-08-13, 3:2, D.
At Dunluce Rectory, on Monday, the 6th instant, aged 67, the Rev. James Morewood, for nearly 23 years Rector of the parish of Dunluce.

No. 2900 :: Ref. 1849-08-13, 3:2, D.
At his residence, Blackrock, near Cork, Lieutenant-Colonel Gerard Quill.

No. 2901 :: Ref. 1849-08-13, 3:2, D.
On 4th instant, of cholera, at Belfast, aged 60 years, Mr. David Bishop, a distinguished botanist, and at one time curator of the Royal Botanic Garden.

No. 2902 :: Ref. 1849-08-13, 3:2, D.
On 5th instant, at Kilcurry, near Ahoghill, Robert Craig, second son of James Craig, Esq., aged 28 years, after a lingering illness of one year.

No. 2903 :: Ref. 1849-08-13, 3:2, D.
On 8th instant, of apoplexy, at his residence in Banbridge, Dr. Robert Kelso, aged 36 years.

No. 2904 :: Ref. 1849-08-20, 2:7, B.
On 28th July, at Madeira, the lady of the Right Hon. Lord Northland, of a son and heir.

No. 2905 :: Ref. 1849-08-20, 2:7, B.
August 13, in Gardiner's-row, the Hon. Mrs. Brooke, of a son.

No. 2906 :: Ref. 1849-08-20, 2:7, B.
On 13th inst., at Eaglemont, Lisnaskea, the wife of John Irvine, Esq., of a son.

No. 2907 :: Ref. 1849-08-20, 2:7, M.
August 14, in Dungannon, by the Rev. Mr. Coyne, P.P., Mr. Thos. Hughes, merchant, to Mary, youngest daughter of the late Mr. James Mallon, Clonfeacle, co. Tyrone.

No. 2908 :: Ref. 1849-08-20, 2:7, M.
August 16, by the Rev. Manasses O'Kane, P.P., of Drumraw, John M'Crossan, of Gortmore, Esq., solicitor, to Margaret, daughter of Mr. Edward Moss, of Omagh, merchant.

No. 2909 :: Ref. 1849-08-20, 2:7, M.
August 7, in Maralin Church, by the Rev. Mr. Mulligan, Miss Anderson, eldest daughter of the late Mr. William Anderson, of Lawnmount, near Lurgan, to Mr. William Gilbert, linen manufacturer, Ballinacor, near Lurgan.

No. 2910 :: Ref. 1849-08-20, 2:7, M.
Aug. 15, at Temple Port Church, by the Rev. Thos. Lanauze, Major Charlton O'Neill, to Catherine, youngest daughter of the late Cosby Wilton, Esq., of Omard, co. Cavan.

No. 2911 :: Ref. 1849-08-20, 2:7, M.
Aug. 14, in St. Paul's Church, by the Rev. W.P.H. Dobbin, Wm. Little, of Limerick, Esq., to Mary, second daughter of George Chadwick, of Cavan, Esq.

No. 2912 :: Ref. 1849-08-20, 2:7, M.
August 1, at Enniskillen, by Rev. A.C. Maclatchy, Mr. Francis Bradford, to Miss Mary Anne Gordon, Enniskillen.

No. 2913 :: Ref. 1849-08-20, 2:7, M.
Aug. 10, at Enniskillen by Rev. A.C. Maclatchy, Mr. Henry Earls, Watternerry, to Mrs. Mary Graham, of Gortmessen, Parish of Enniskillen.

No. 2914 :: Ref. 1849-08-20, 2:7, M.
Aug. 16, at Taney Chuch, county Dublin, by the Rev. Charles Moore, Rector of Monasterevan, Robert Collins, Esq., M.D. of Merrion-square, Dublin, and of Garvary Lodge, co. Fermanagh, to Mary, daughter of the late Rev. John Pitt Kennedy, Rector of Balteagh, co. Derry.

No. 2915 :: Ref. 1849-08-20, 2:7, M.
Aug. 9, at St. Andrew's church, by the Rev. Charles F. Tisdan, A.M., Thomas, youngest son of the late John Walpole, Esq., of Cavan, to Lydia Clibborn, eldest daughter of the late Thos. Greer, Esq., Dungannon.

No. 2916 :: Ref. 1849-08-20, 2:7, M.
Aug. 15, at St. John's church, Sligo, by the Rev. Mr. Christian, Richard Gordon, Esq., to Jessie, daughter of the late David Culberton, Esq., merchant, Sligo.

No. 2917 :: Ref. 1849-08-20, 2:7, M.
Aug. 9, in Carrigart church, by the Rev. G. Prior, Samuel Johnston, Esq., M.D., L.R.C.S.I., only son of Thomas Johnston, Esq., Londonderry, and nephew of the late Dr. Johnston, of Armagh, Surgeon, R.N., to Margaret, youngest daughter of the late Rev. John Wilkinson, Rector of Mevagh.

No. 2918 :: Ref. 1849-08-20, 2:7, D.
On yesterday morning, of apoplexy, Mr. John Fegan, proprietor of the Albert Hotel in this city. He was an old and respectable inhabitant, very generally esteemed.

No. 2919 :: Ref. 1849-08-20, 2:7, D.
On the morning of the 17th inst., of inflammation of the lungs, Ann Jane, the beloved wife of James Crilly, of Armagh.

No. 2920 :: Ref. 1849-08-20, 2:7, D.
At Montreal, Canada East, of Asiatic cholera, on 23d July last, Eliza Johnson, formerly of Armagh.

No. 2921 :: Ref. 1849-08-20, 2:7, D.
On 8th inst., of apoplexy, at Banbridge, Dr. Robert Kelso, aged thirty-six years.

No. 2922 :: Ref. 1849-08-20, 2:7, D.
On the 14th instant, at College Square North, Belfast, George Suffern, Esq.

No. 2923 :: Ref. 1849-08-20, 2:7, D.
On 16th inst., at the residence of her late brother, George Suffern, Esq., Miss Suffern.

No. 2924 :: Ref. 1849-08-20, 2:7, D.
On the 10th inst., of fever, Miss Jardine, Matron of the Banbridge Union Workhouse.

No. 2925 :: Ref. 1849-08-20, 2:7, D.
On the 12th inst., at Monkstown, in his 79th year, Samuel Bell Labatt, Esq., M.D.

No. 2926 :: Ref. 1849-08-20, 2:7, D.
On 3d July, in Philadelphia, Margaret, wife of Mr. Charles Colquhoun, and daughter of M. Andrew Laughlin, formerly of Gortin, co. Trrone [sic].

No. 2927 :: Ref. 1849-08-20, 2:7, D.
August 8, at the Barracks, Dundee, Annesley Charles, third or youngest son of Major De Renzy, barrack-master, aged 14 years.

No. 2928 :: Ref. 1849-08-20, 2:7, D.
On the 11th inst., at Tramore, after a short illness, Amy Irwine, daughter of the late Judge Chamberlain, and affectionate wife of the Archdeacon of Ossory.

No. 2929 :: Ref. 1849-08-20, 2:7, D.
Aug. 8, of cholera, at Waterford, where he was stationed as Staff Officer of Pensioners, in the thirty-fourth year of his age, Captain Thomas R. De Rinzy, on half-pay of the 83d Regiment.

No. 2930 :: Ref. 1849-08-20, 2:7, D.
Aug. 11, at Belfast, of cholera, James O'Neill Falls, Esq.

No. 2931 :: Ref. 1849-08-20, 2:7, D.
Aug. 13, at Kingstown, the Rev. Wm. Jerrard Roper, rector of Monaghan.

No. 2932 :: Ref. 1849-08-20, 2:7, D.
On 10th inst., the Rev. William M'Gowan, of Mountnorris, in the 45th year of his ministry, and the 70th of his age.

No. 2933 :: Ref. 1849-08-20, 2:7, D.
On 5th inst., Robert Fisher Carroll, Esq., medical practitioner, late of Bandon, aged 21 years.

No. 2934 :: Ref. 1849-08-20, 2:7, D.
On 16th of June, at the Island of St. Thomas, West Indies, Robert, son of Mr. Thomas Lipsett, of Ballyshannon.

No. 2935 :: Ref. 1849-08-20, 2:7, D.
Aug. 10, aged 56 years, Anne, wife of James Kerr, Esq., of Dublin, most sincerely and deservedly regretted.

No. 2936 :: Ref. 1849-08-20, 2:7, D.
On 9th inst., at Gortahurk, Holywell, Francis Higgins, aged 101. He was a respectable farmer of the middle class.

No. 2937 :: Ref. 1849-08-20, 2:7, D.
On 14th inst., at Donaghmore, county Tyrone, of disease of the heart, Parnell Neville, second son of the Rev. Michael Kearney, aged six years.

No. 2938 :: Ref. 1849-08-20, 2:7, D.
On 2d inst., at Ballybranagh, near Downpatrick, Widow Roney, in the 107th year of her age. She retained possession of all her faculties up to the period of her death. She was one of three persons living in the townland of Ballybranagh, whose

united ages amount to 290 years; and there are three other persons in the same townland each above 80 years old.

No. 2939 :: Ref. 1849-08-20, 2:7, D.

August 14, at Cahir Barracks, in the fifty-eighth year of her age, after a short but severe illness, Mary, the beloved wife of W.B. Frizell, Esq., Barrack-Master at that station. Mrs. Frizell was a native of Drumcose, near Enniskillen; and her amenity of manners, benevolence of disposition, unostentatious piety, united with many solid and shining virtues, won the affectionate esteem of all who had the rare happiness of her acquaintance.

No. 2940 :: Ref. 1849-08-20, 2:7, D.

We have, this week, to record the demise of Doctor Little, of Sligo, of cholera, on Tuesday last. On Saturday and Sunday he was actively engaged in the country discharging the duties of his profession. On Monday he visited the poorhouse, hospital, and other of our public medical establishments, but complained in the evening of being poorly, that he was very unwell, stating at the same time that he had cholera. Although about 66 years of age, from a natural cheerfulness of manner, accompanied by a kind disposition, by which he studied to make every one happy with whom he associated, he had all the comparative juvenile appearance of a man of 50. As a Physician he stood at the head of his profession, as a Surgeon his character was proverbially eminent—he was frequently called to Dublin and elsewhere to assist in different operations. Dr. Little's death is not only a loss to his own respectable and interesting family, but to the town and county of Sligo and society at large.—*Sligo Guardian*.

No. 2941 :: Ref. 1849-08-27, 3:3, B.

Aug. 19, at Kilcreagh House, co. Dublin, the lady of Francis Hall Tipping, Esq., of a daughter.

No. 2942 :: Ref. 1849-08-27, 3:3, B.

Aug. 23, at the Provincial Bank, Newry, Mrs. William M'Cullough, of a daughter.

No. 2943 :: Ref. 1849-08-27, 3:3, B.

Aug. 23, at 6, Fitzwilliam-square, East, Dublin, the lady of James Hamilton, Esq., of Castle Hamilton, co. Cavan, of a son.

No. 2944 :: Ref. 1849-08-27, 3:3, B.

Aug. 17, at Fairview, co. Kildare, the wife of John S. Maconchy, Esq., of a daughter.

No. 2945 :: Ref. 1849-08-27, 3:3, B.

Aug. 11, at Templebrady Glebe, Carrigallen, the lady of the Rev. Samuel Sandford, of a son.

No. 2946 :: Ref. 1849-08-27, 3:3, M.

On Wednesday last, in St. Mark's Church, by the Rev. Mr. Sharkey, James L. Riggs, Esq., M.D., to Mary, daughter of Samuel Gardner, Esq., both of this city.

No. 2947 :: Ref. 1849-08-27, 3:3, M.

On 21st inst., in St. Peter's Church, by the Rev. Samuel Simpson, Rector of Keady, co. Armagh, John Augustus, fifth son of the late Wm. Foster M'Clintock, of the co. Louth, Esq., to Ellen, youngest daughter of the late Dr. Crawford, of Bath.

No. 2948 :: Ref. 1849-08-27, 3:3, M.

In Seagoe Church, on 23d inst., by the Rev. Capel Woolsely, Mr. Adam Cowser, Farmhill, Keady, to Eliza, eldest daughter of Capt. Williams, Fortwilliam, Portadown.

No. 2949 :: Ref. 1849-08-27, 3:3, M.

Aug. 21, in the Methodist Chapel, Rathdrum, by the Rev. E. Hamilton, Mr. Elias Edge, Drumdangan, to Miss Lucy Carroll, of Rathdrum.

No. 2950 :: Ref. 1849-08-27, 3:3, M.

On 16th inst., at his [sic] father's residence, Coleraine, Margaret Lucy, only daughter of Charles Daly, Esq., to Peter J. Rogers, Esq., of Armagh.

No. 2951 :: Ref. 1849-08-27, 3:3, M.

On 16th inst., at Newtownlimavady, in the co. of Derry, by the Rev. Robert Gage, M.A., Rector of Tamlaghtard, in the same county, Edwyn Henry Vaughan, Esq., Barrister-at-law, of the Inner Temple, and of Byron House, Harrow-on-the-hill, to Henrietta Caroline, third daughter of Marcus M'Causland, Esq., of Fruit-hill, in the county of Derry, and of Lower Berkeley-street, Manchester-square, London.

No. 2952 :: Ref. 1849-08-27, 3:3, M.

Aug. 15, at Killinan Church, by the Rev. John Galbraith, Provost of Tuam, uncle to the bride, Thomas Irvine King, of Dublin, Esq., to Rose, eldest daughter of the late Richard Galbraith, of Cappard, co. of Galway and of Balgair, co. of Stirling, Esq.

No. 2953 :: Ref. 1849-08-27, 3:3, M.

On 5th inst., by the Rev. Dr. Crabbs, Alexander P. M'Kelvey, of Ards, county Donegal, Ireland, to Miss Elizabeth Briscoe, of New York.

No. 2954 :: Ref. 1849-08-27, 3:3, M.

In New York, by the Rev. Mr. M'Clusky, Robert Cohen, of Killybegs, Donegal county, Ireland, to Miss Harriet M'Donald, daughter of James M'Donald, of Dunfanaghy, Donegal county, Ireland.

No. 2955 :: Ref. 1849-08-27, 3:3, D.

On the 20th instant, at Carnteel house, county Tyrone, Mrs. J. M'Williams, aged 35, niece to the late Sir Isaac Wilson, physician to the Duchess of Kent. Her death was rather sudden, caused by inflammation of the bowels; but it is a pleasing reflection to her sorrowing friends to know that she was "*ready for the coming of the son of man.*"

No. 2956 :: Ref. 1849-08-27, 3:3, D.

On 21st inst., at Loughgall, after a very short illness, in the fifty-sixth year of her age, Charlottee [sic], relict of the late Robert Langtry, Esq., of Bellview, near Richhill.

No. 2957 :: Ref. 1849-08-27, 3:3, D.

On 31st ult., at New York, of the prevailing epidemic, Mr. James Carroll, printer, a native of Ireland, in the sixty-second year of his age.

No. 2958 :: Ref. 1849-08-27, 3:3, D.

On 8th inst., at Donaghmore, co. Tyrone, Mrs. Mary Irwin, aged 58 years.

No. 2959 :: Ref. 1849-08-27, 3:3, D.

At Lower Fitzwilliam-street, Dublin, on 25th instant, Arabella, youngest daughter of the late Rev. W. Grattan, of Swanlinbar, co Cavan.

No. 2960 :: Ref. 1849-08-27, 3:3, D.

At Tullybrisland, parish of Faughanvale, at the advanced age of 106, Mary Elly. The deceased retained all her faculties to the last. For several years she had been supported by the bounty of the Major family.

No. 2961 :: Ref. 1849-08-27, 3:3, D.

In Scotland, after a long and tedious illness, John Fforde, Esq., Sub-Inspector of constabulary, and eldest son of the late James Fforde, Esq., of Raughlan, co. Armagh.

No. 2962 :: Ref. 1849-08-27, 3:3, D.

At Mauchiline, on 11th inst., Mr. James Armour, eldest brother of Mrs. Burns, widow of the Bard, in the 84th year of his age.

No. 2963 :: Ref. 1849-08-27, 3:3, D.

In Charlemont-street, Dublin, Miss Marianne Moore, niece of the late Major Jacob, of Harcourt-street, and eldest daughter of Capt. Moore, who was killed by the rebels at Wexford during the eventful year of 1798.

No. 2964 :: Ref. 1849-08-27, 3:3, D.

On 20th inst., Mr. David Fyffe, of Donaghmore, aged 63 years.

No. 2965 :: Ref. 1849-08-27, 3:3, D.

On Sabbath se'nnight, at Dungannon, Edward Lyons, Esq., L.L.D., after a tedious illness.

No. 2966 :: Ref. 1849-08-27, 3:3, D.

On 17th inst., at Greencastle, of internal hemorrhage, Rev. Geo. O'Doherty, P.P. of Moville, in his 43d year of his age.

No. 2967 :: Ref. 1849-08-27, 3:3, D.

On 19th inst., at Glencush, co. Tyrone, Robert M'Crea, Esq., at the advanced age of 92 years.

No. 2968 :: Ref. 1849-08-27, 3:3, D.

On 18th instant, after a few days' illness, Mr. James M'Entire, of Eary, co. Tyrone, in the 36th year of his age.

No. 2969 :: Ref. 1849-08-27, 3:3, D.

On 16th inst, at Cork, of cholera, Alexander O'Driscoll, Esq., of Norton Cottage.

No. 2970 :: Ref. 1849-08-27, 3:3, D.

On the same day [August 16], Miss O'Driscoll, after an attack of the prevailing epidemic, which proved fatal in a few hours.

No. 2971 :: Ref. 1849-08-27, 3:3, D.

On 11th inst., aged 38, Mary Anne, the beloved wife of the Rev. Alexander Caldwell, of Donaghmore.

No. 2972 :: Ref. 1849-08-27, 3:3, D.

Aug. 18, at Eccles-street, after a tedious illness, in the 46th year of his age, Laurence Vernon, Esq., J.P., co. Sligo.

No. 2973 :: Ref. 1849-08-27, 3:3, D.

Aug. 23, in Sligo, of cholera, Archibald Montgomery, Esq., from the Poor Law Commissioners office, Dublin.

No. 2974 :: Ref. 1849-08-27, 3:3, D.

On 21st inst., of cholera, in Sligo, Surgeon White.

No. 2975 :: Ref. 1849-08-27, 3:3, D.

On 22d inst., of cholera, Mrs. Roy, of Castle-street, Sligo.

No. 2976 :: Ref. 1849-08-27, 3:3, D.

On 20th inst., of cholera, Mrs. Maveety, of Holborn-st., Sligo.

No. 2977 :: Ref. 1849-08-27, 3:3, D.

Aug. 20, at Manorhamilton, of cholera, brought on by excessive ball playing, Mr. John M'Donagh, aged 23 years, master of the National School of that town

No. 2978 :: Ref. 1849-08-27, 3:3, D.

Aug. 22, Montgomery Blair, Esq., sub-sheriff for county Sligo, who died in the prime of life, of cholera, at his residence, Ballinode.

No. 2979 :: Ref. 1849-08-27, 3:3, D.

Aug. 21, at Bell's-grove, Mountnugent, Charlotte, the beloved wife of the late Andrew Bell Booth, Esq., aged 44 years.

No. 2980 :: Ref. 1849-08-27, 3:3, D.

Aug. 23, at Downpatrick, Joseph Carson, Esq., aged 80 years.

No. 2981 :: Ref. 1849-08-27, 3:3, D.

Aug. 19, at Downpatrick, after a tedious illness, Miss Saul, in the 79th year of her age.

No. 2982 :: Ref. 1849-08-27, 3:3, D.

Aug. 10, at Drumbane, near Newtownlimavady, in the 75th year of her age, Jane Meldred, relict of Paul Church, Esq., of same place.

No. 2983 :: Ref. 1849-09-03, 3:3, B.
On 24th ult., at Castle Taylor, co. Galway, the lady of Robert Cope, Esq., of Loughgall, co. Armagh, of a daughter.

No. 2984 :: Ref. 1849-09-03, 3:3, B.
At Ramelton, on 23d ult., the wife of Anthony A. Kennedy, Esq., Inland Revenue Officer, of a son.

No. 2985 :: Ref. 1849-09-03, 3:3, M.
On 26th ult., by the Rev. H. O'Loughlin, P.P., Mr. Michael Kerrin, of Enniskillen, to Mary, only daughter of Mr. P. Kerns, Belfast.

No. 2986 :: Ref. 1849-09-03, 3:3, M.
Aug. 28, at Dauntsey, Wilts, by the Rev. Henry P. Elrington, D.D., Janet Fenwick, daughter of the Venerable the Archdeacon of Raphoe, to Joseph Faviere Elrington, Esq., eldest son of the Rev. Charles Richd. Elrington, D.D., Rector of Armagh, and Regius Professor of Divinity in the University of Dublin.

No. 2987 :: Ref. 1849-09-03, 3:3, M.
On 30th ult., in the Cathedral, Lisburn, by the Rev. Hartley Hodson, Mr. John C. Cameron, formerly of Belfast, to Margaret, eldest daughter of Mr. Robert M'Keown, of same place.

No. 2988 :: Ref. 1849-09-03, 3:3, M.
Aug. 23, at Bryansford, co. Down, Alexander, son of the late John Cheyne, Esq., M.D., physician-general to her Majesty's forces in Ireland, to Dora Lynn, daughter of the late Francisco de Jove de Barnardo, of Bilboa.

No. 2989 :: Ref. 1849-09-03, 3:3, M.
On 30th ult., in the office of the Registrar of the Londonderry district, by the Rev. Gibson M'Milen, Joseph Cochrane, Esq., merchant, to Elizabeth, daughter of the late Robert Cowan, Esq., merchant, both of Derry.

No. 2990 :: Ref. 1849-09-03, 3:3, M.
Aug. 24, at Sallaghy church, by the Rev. Wm. Breedin, Mr. James Moore, of Newtownbutler, to Miss Margaret Rennick, of Coragh, near Lisnaskea.

No. 2991 :: Ref. 1849-09-03, 3:3, M.
At St George's, Hanover-square, London, on the 30th ult., Wm. Haig, Esq., second son of the late Robert Haig, Esq., of Dodderbank, co. Dublin, and grandson of Sir Wm. Wolseley, of Wolsely, Staffordshire, Bart., to Harriette Ann Maria Porter, only child of the late Jeremiah Dick, Esq, of North-crescent, Bedford square.

No. 2992 :: Ref. 1849-09-03, 3:3, D.
Aug. 23, in the 24th year of her age, Harriet, daughter of Mr. Wm. Pattison, Newry.

No. 2993 :: Ref. 1849-09-03, 3:3, D.
On 10th ult., at Dundrum, Jane, only daughter of Mr. Mathew Blackwood, of Drumnikelly, co. Down.

No. 2994 :: Ref. 1849-09-03, 3:3, D.
Aug. 29, the Rev. John Studdert, precentor of the diocese of Killaloe, incumbent of St. Dolough's, in the diocese of Dublin, and formerly scholar of Trinity College.

No. 2995 :: Ref. 1849-09-03, 3:3, D.
On 16th ult., after a short illness, Susan Martin, a faithful servant of Mr. John Cameron, Fortview, Clontarf; on 17th, after a few hours' illness, Mr. John Cameron, of the Stamp-office, highly respected and deeply regretted by all who knew him; and on 22d ult., after a brief illness, Henrietta, relict of Mr. John Cameron, of Clontarf, leaving two sons and a daughter entirely unprovided for to deplore their irreparable loss.

No. 2996 :: Ref. 1849-09-03, 3:3, D.
At Ballyshannon, on 17th ult., of fever, Mr. William Stephens, in his 75th year, very much regretted.

No. 2997 :: Ref. 1849-09-03, 3:3, D.
Aug. 23, at Glassthule, co. Dublin, of Asiatic cholera, Mr. John Nesbitt, eldest son of the late Mr. Joseph Nesbitt, of Elmdale, near Newry.

No. 2998 :: Ref. 1849-09-03, 3:3, D.
In Cavan, on 28th ult., Miss Catherine Browne, of Mulrankin, co. Wexford, who resided for the last twenty years with her relative, the Right Rev. James Browne.

No. 2999 :: Ref. 1849-09-03, 3:3, D.
At Belturbet, of decline, on 29th ult., in the 19th year of his age, Master Edward O'Reilly, youngest son of Mr. Luke O'Reilly, Hotel-keeper in that town.

No. 3000 :: Ref. 1849-09-03, 3:3, D.
On 29th July, in Philadelphia, U.S., John Rarnwell, Esq., formerly of Drum, near Omagh.

No. 3001 :: Ref. 1849-09-03, 3:3, D.
On 29th ult., Mr. William Johnston, merchant, Omagh.

No. 3002 :: Ref. 1849-09-03, 3:3, D.
Aug. 28, at Ferbane, after a few hours' illness, Mr. [sic] Sarah Jessop, relict of Wm. Jessop, Esq., of Kincor, King's Co., who also died after a short illness, on the 27th ult.

No. 3003 :: Ref. 1849-09-03, 3:3, D.
Aug. 27, after a protracted and painful illness, Maria, the beloved wife of Henry Kemmis, of Merrion-square, Q.C., and daughter of Arthur Dawson, late of the city of Dublin, and of Castledawson, in the co. Londonderry, Esq., deceased.

No. 3004 :: Ref. 1849-09-03, 3:3, D.
On the morning of the 27th ult., of inflammation of the bowels, aged 23 years, Mr. John   (*continued...*)

No. 3004, continued: ....Johnston Hughes, brother to the Postmaster of Dungannon, and principal of the firm of Messrs. John Hughes & Co., Fire-clay and Brick works, Coalisland.

No. 3005 :: Ref. 1849-09-10, 3:3, B.
On 29th ult., at the Pavilion, Armagh, the lady of D. Crommelin, Esq., of Carrowdore Castle, co. Down, of a daughter.

No. 3006 :: Ref. 1849-09-10, 3:3, B.
Sept. 5, at Abbey-yard, Newry, the lady of Edward Smyth Corry, Esq., Constabulary, of a daughter.

No. 3007 :: Ref. 1849-09-10, 3:3, B.
Sept. 3, in Talbot-street, Dublin, the lady of John Collum, Esq., of a son.

No. 3008 :: Ref. 1849-09-10, 3:3, B.
On 24th ult., at Castle Archdall, the wife of Rev. Michael Burke, of a son, still born.

No. 3009 :: Ref. 1849-09-10, 3:3, B.
On 6th ult., at 10, Mespil Parade, Dublin, the lady of the Rev. Richard Stack, of a son.

No. 3010 :: Ref. 1849-09-10, 3:3, B.
On 4th inst., at Richmond Glebe, co. Tyrone, the lady of the Rev. J.J. Moutray, of a daughter.

No. 3011 :: Ref. 1849-09-10, 3:3, B.
On 24th ult., at Dunkaneely, the wife of Mr. A. M'Neely, of three sons. The mother and children are doing well.

No. 3012 :: Ref. 1849-09-10, 3:3, M.
On 6th Sept., in St. Mark's Church, Armagh, by the Rev. B. Wade, Mr. George Dowling Hughes, to Martha Jane, eldest daughter of Mr. John Douglas, both of this city.

No. 3013 :: Ref. 1849-09-10, 3:3, M.
On 26th ult., at the house of the bride's father, by the Rev. Mr. Hughes, C.C., of Dungannon, Mr. Henry Magee, of Maghery, Verner's Bridge, to Ellen, daughter of Mr. Francis Coleman, of True Hill, near Moy.

No. 3014 :: Ref. 1849-09-10, 3:3, M.
On 21st ult., at Milltown church, near Verner's bridge, co. Armagh, by the Rev. Charles Crosslie, Mr. William Wylie, of Derryfubble, near Benburb, co. Tyrone, to Elizabeth, eldest daughter of Mr. Thomas Verner, Derryane, co. Armagh.

No. 3015 :: Ref. 1849-09-10, 3:3, M.
On 29th ult., in Enniskillen Church, by the Rev. T.A. Mathias, Mr. Joseph Mayers, Aughnacloy, to Sarah, daughter of Mr. Henry Beacom, near Enniskillen.

No. 3016 :: Ref. 1849-09-10, 3:3, M.
On 29th ult., by Rev. Thomas Waugh, Josiah Atwool, Esq., R.E., of Kingstown, to Anna Maria, second daughter of the Rev. William Ferguson, of Dublin.

No. 3017 :: Ref. 1849-09-10, 3:3, M.
At Monkstown Church, the Hon. Henry Crichton, brother to the Earl of Erne, to Elizabeth, daughter of the late Colonel Hawkshaw, of Blaris, co. Down.

No. 3018 :: Ref. 1849-09-10, 3:3, M.
Sept. 3, at Listowel Church, Henry Smith, Esq., S.I., eldest son of David Smith, Esq., J.P., Lakeview, co. Monaghan, to Elizabeth Agnes, eldest daughter of the late J. Sandes, Esq., Listowel.

No. 3019 :: Ref. 1849-09-10, 3:3, M.
Sept. 5, at Seago, by the Rev. Archibald Lawrin, Mr. John Walker, of Seago, to Miss Irwin, of Portadown.

No. 3020 :: Ref. 1849-09-10, 3:3, M.
In Wexford, Edward Boate, Esq., of Waterford, Editor of the *Waterford Guardian*, to Henrietta Bruce O'Neill, of No. 9, Lower Gloucester-street, Dublin, second daughter of the late Edmond O'Neill, Esq., of Ture Castle, co. Donegal.

No. 3021 :: Ref. 1849-09-10, 3:3, D.
Sept. 5, in Sligo, of cholera, C. Reid, Post Master, Sligo.

No. 3022 :: Ref. 1849-09-10, 3:3, D.
Sept. 6, in Sligo, at his residence, Stephen-st., of cholera, William Christian.

No. 3023 :: Ref. 1849-09-10, 3:3, D.
Sept. 2, in Sligo, of cholera, the wife of — Hacket, Esq., Revenue officer.

No. 3024 :: Ref. 1849-09-10, 3:3, D.
Sept. 2, after a few hours' illness, Major Turner, Master of the Horse to his Excellency the Lord Lieutenant.

No. 3025 :: Ref. 1849-09-10, 3:3, D.
Sept. 4, at Mountjoy-Square, South, Ellen, the beloved wife of James Corry Lowry, Esq.

No. 3026 :: Ref. 1849-09-10, 3:3, D.
Sept. 2, at the residence of his son-in-law, J. Charlier, Esq., Bayswater-terrace, Lieutenant-Colonel Richard Cole, in the seventy-seventh year of his age.

No. 3027 :: Ref. 1849-09-10, 3:3, D.
August 7, in New York, of cholera, aged 20 years, Arthur, eldest son of Mr. John Rodgers, of Sixmilecross, co. Tyrone.

No. 3028 :: Ref. 1849-09-10, 3:3, D.
Sept. 7, of cholera, in Stephen-street, Sligo, after a few hours illness, Mr. James Duncan.

No. 3029 :: Ref. 1849-09-10, 3:3, D.
Last week, Jane, infant daughter of Mr. Jacobs, Excise Officer, Sligo.

No. 3030 :: Ref. 1849-09-10, 3:3, D.
At Warrenpoint, in the 14th year of her age, Martha Ross, last surviving child of the late John

Ross, Esq., of Derrylusk, and grand daughter of Alexander Fleming, Esq., of Gallina, co. Monaghan.

No. 3031 :: Ref. 1849-09-10, 3:3, D.
August 31, at Enniskillen, Mr. Henry Busby, smith and farrier, aged 75. His illness (inflammation of the lungs and chest) was only of a few hours' duration. Mr. Busby was an inoffensive, kind neighbour, humble in his manners, yet respected and esteemed by the wealthy and respectable.

No. 3032 :: Ref. 1849-09-10, 3:3, D.
On 4th inst., Mr. Hugh M'Callister, of Ballygawley, aged 77 years.

No. 3033 :: Ref. 1849-09-10, 3:3, D.
On 4th inst., at Marino Crescent, Eliza, the wife of Dr. Walker, late of Dundalk, and eldest daughter of James Thornley, Esq., late of Ballyshannon.

No. 3034 :: Ref. 1849-09-10, 3:3, D.
Sept. 5, at Sandymount, where he was removed for the benefit of his health, John, fourth son of Mr. Thompson of Sandwith-street, late of Maguiresbridge, aged 19.

No. 3035 :: Ref. 1849-09-17, 2:7, B.
On 13th inst., at Belfast, Mrs. R.O. Blackader, of a daughter.

No. 3036 :: Ref. 1849-09-17, 2:7, B.
At Corfu, on the 8th ult., the lady of Assistant-Commissary-General Weir, of a daughter.

No. 3037 :: Ref. 1849-09-17, 2:7, B.
On 12th inst., at Purdysburn, Belfast, the wife of Robert Batt, Esq., of a daughter.

No. 3038 :: Ref. 1849-09-17, 2:7, M.
Sept. 13, in the Presbyterian Meeting House, Richhill, by the Rev. Mr. Mackey, Rev. Mr. Donald, of Newtownstewart, to Miss Running, daughter of Wm. Running, Esq., of Woodview, Richhill.

No. 3039 :: Ref. 1849-09-17, 2:7, M.
In Tassagh Presbyterian Meeting-house, on the 13th inst., by the Rev. Mr. Bennett, Surgeon Finlay, of Rockcorry, to Anne, eldest daughter of George Henry, Esq., of Glenburn, Keady.

No. 3040 :: Ref. 1849-09-17, 2:7, M.
In St. Ann's church, on 12th inst., by the Rev. Wm. Quain, Mr. George Moon, to Sarah Anne, third daughter of Mr. Thos. Agnew, merchant, both of Dungannon.

No. 3041 :: Ref. 1849-09-17, 2:7, M.
On 12th inst., in Fisherwick Place Church, Belfast, by the Rev. Dr. Morgan, the Rev. Dr. John G. Givan, of Hamburg, to Mary Jane, daughter of the Rev. John Brydge, of Brydge Hall, co. Tyrone.

No. 3042 :: Ref. 1849-09-17, 2:7, M.
On 6th inst., by the Rev. James Thomson, Magherally, Mr. Hugh Bell, Merchant, Banbridge, to Margaret, daughter of Mr. Samuel Glass, Merchant, Banbridge.

No. 3043 :: Ref. 1849-09-17, 2:7, M.
On 8th inst., at Ballymena, by the Rev. H.J. Dobbin, D.D., Wm. M'Collough, Esq., Clones, co. Monaghan, to Sarah, relict of James Bell, Esq., late of Ballymena.

No. 3044 :: Ref. 1849-09-17, 2:7, M.
At Ferozepore, on 18th June, by the Rev. Thomas J.C. Fimenger, M.A., Captain Edward Lee, Paymaster, H.M. 10th Regiment, eldest son of the Very Reverend the Dean of Waterford, to Mary Ann, eldest daughter of James Inglis, Esq., Hunly, Aberdeenshire.

No. 3045 :: Ref. 1849-09-17, 2:7, M.
On the 20th ult., at Bridlington, Mr. R. Knowles, hawker, to Miss Catherie Colony. The ceremony was performed by the clergyman in the usual manner, the parties pointing on the book as he proceeded. On coming to the responses they replied in the dumb alphabet. They wrote both their names remarkably well in the register-book.

No. 3046 :: Ref. 1849-09-17, 2:7, M.
On 1th inst., in Enniskillen Church, by the Rev. Mr. Bradshaw, Mr. William Little, to Elizabeth, fourth daughter of Mr. William Armstrong, of Enniskillen.

No. 3047 :: Ref. 1849-09-17, 2:7, M.
On 7th inst., by the Rev. C.K. Irwin, Matilda, eldest daughter of Mr. Wm. Hunter, Magherafelt, to Mr. John Orr, of Tillinkerry, near Magherafelt.

No. 3048 :: Ref. 1849-09-17, 2:7, M.
On 5th inst., in Rostrevor Church, by the Rev. John Evans, Vicar of Kilbroney, John W. Gregg, of Dublin, to Eliza, youngest daughter of the late Mr. Richard Swinerton, of Rostrevor.

No. 3049 :: Ref. 1849-09-17, 2:7, D.
Sept. 12, at 14, Adelaide-road, after a short illness, Master James Johnston, only son of the late James Johnston, Esq., of Knappa, co. Armagh, deeply regretted.

No. 3050 :: Ref. 1849-09-17, 2:7, D.
On 5th Sept., at Sandy Mount, near Richhill, Mr. Gabriel Maclean, aged 78 years, for 50 of which he was a consistant [sic], steady and zealous Member, and for 40 of that period a Deacon of the Independent Society, and intimately connected with the first founders of that body at Richhill. He died in triumphant hope.

No. 3051 :: Ref. 1849-09-17, 2:7, D.
Sept. 4, at Rooskey, co. Monaghan, aged four years and nine months, Hugh, the beloved son of David Hamill, Esq.

No. 3052 :: Ref. 1849-09-17, 2:7, D.
Sept. 12, near Coagh, the beloved wife of Mr. James Smyrl.

No. 3053 :: Ref. 1849-09-17, 2:7, D.
Sept. 8, at Hastings, Richard Byham, secretary to the Ordnance.

No. 3054 :: Ref. 1849-09-17, 2:7, D.
Sept. 3, at Farnham castle, Mrs. Summer, wife of the Lord Bishop of Winchester.

No. 3055 :: Ref. 1849-09-17, 2:7, D.
Sept. 7, at Enniscorthy, the Right Rev. Dr. Keatinge, Roman Catholic Bishop of Ferns, aged 66 years.

No. 3056 :: Ref. 1849-09-17, 2:7, D.
Sept. 7, in London, Patrick Magovern, Esq., late Surgeon in the Royal Navy, formerly of the co. Cavan, and brother of the late Catholic Bishop of Ardagh.

No. 3057 :: Ref. 1849-09-17, 2:7, D.
Sept. 9, at Kingstown, Mary, relict of Captain Edward Hunt, of the 64th Regiment.

No. 3058 :: Ref. 1849-09-17, 2:7, D.
In Bath, the Rev. J.B. Jervois, youngest son of the late S. Jervois, Esq., of Bandon, co. Cork.

No. 3059 :: Ref. 1849-09-17, 2:7, D.
Sept. 10, at Rostrevor, at the advanced age of 86 years, Lydia, relict of the late Wm. Canning, Esq., of Dungannon.

No. 3060 :: Ref. 1849-09-17, 2:7, D.
Sept. 5, at Monomolin Glebe, county Wexford, of fever, caught in the discharge of his duty, the Rev. Wm. Fitzsimon; and on the 10th inst., of the same disease, Jane, his beloved wife.

No. 3061 :: Ref. 1849-09-17, 2:7, D.
At Dungiven, on 7th inst., Margaret, daughter of Mr. Denis M'Closkey, aged 21 years. Her remains were conveyed to the place of interment by young women, 174 of whom attended and marched in procession on the occasion.

No. 3062 :: Ref. 1849-09-17, 2:7, D.
Sept. 10, at Daskey Vicarage, the residence of his brother, the Rev. William Paul Dawson, Rector of Kilmore, Erris, county of Mayo, in the 44th year of his age.

No. 3063 :: Ref. 1849-09-17, 2:7, D.
Sept. 5, at Fintra house, near Killybegs, co. Donegal, James Hamilton, Esq., agd 47 years.

No. 3064 :: Ref. 1849-09-17, 2:7, D.
Sept. 12, at Monreagh, co. Donegall, Mr. David M'Clearn.

No. 3065 :: Ref. 1849-09-17, 2:7, D.
At Greaghnaquinna, in the Bailieborough union, Terence Clarke, aged 62 years. Mr. Clarke was a poor law guardian of the Bailieborough union from 1841 to 1844, when he resigned that office for a more lucrative one, namely, Poor Rate Collector; he has filled the latter office since that time, being a collector for six electoral divisions.

No. 3066 :: Ref. 1849-09-24, 2:6, B.
In Abbey-street, Armagh, on the 21st inst., the lady of Major Farmer, Staff Officer of Pensioners, of a daughter.

No. 3067 :: Ref. 1849-09-24, 2:6, B.
Sept. 24, the lady of the Rev. Benjamin Wade, of a son, stillborn.

No. 3068 :: Ref. 1849-09-24, 2:6, B.
In Charles-street, St. James's Square, at the residence of the Archbishop of Armagh, the lady of George Dunbar, Esq., of a son, stillborn.

No. 3069 :: Ref. 1849-09-24, 2:6, B.
On 17th inst., Mrs. John G. M'Gee, Belfast, of a daughter.

No. 3070 :: Ref. 1849-09-24, 2:6, B.
At Newry, the lady of Edward Smyth Corry, Esq., of the Constabulary, of a daughter.

No. 3071 :: Ref. 1849-09-24, 2:6, B.
On 16th inst., at Tamnamore, the lady of Richard Lloyd, Esq., of a son.

No. 3072 :: Ref. 1849-09-24, 2:6, M.
September 19, in Benburb Church, by the Rev. William Maclean, Rector of Tynan, Walter Hore, Esq., J.P., eldest son of the late Rev. Walter Hore, Rector of Ferns, to Marion Sadleir, youngest daughter of the Rev. Henry Griffin, Rector of Clonfeacle, and ex. F.T.C.D.

No. 3073 :: Ref. 1849-09-24, 2:6, M.
At Hungford, Berks, James Ashwell, Esq., of Tonbridge-wells, Kent, to Mary Hemstead, youngest daughter of the late Richard Barker, Esq.

No. 3074 :: Ref. 1849-09-24, 2:6, M.
On the 19th inst., in the Presbyterian Church, Ballygoney, by the Rev. Wm. Richey, Coleraine, the Rev. H.B. Wilson, Cookstown, to Susan, youngest daughter of the Rev. Thomas Heron, Springbank.

No. 3075 :: Ref. 1849-09-24, 2:6, M.
September 12, at St. Mary's Church, Athlone, by the Rev. J.R. Moffatt, John N. Travers, Esq., son of the late Major-General Sir Robert Travers, K.C.B., to Elizabeth Duffas, eldest daughter of Wm. Hay, Esq., Manager, Provincial Bank of Ireland.

No. 3076 :: Ref. 1849-09-24, 2:6, M.
On the 17th inst., in the First Presbyterian Church, Coleraine, by the Rev. W. Richey, Thomas Waugh, Esq., M.D., Stewartstown, co. Tyrone, to Mary Jane, third daughter of the late Andrew Barry, Esq., Dervock, county Antrim.

No. 3077 :: Ref. 1849-09-24, 2:6, D.
On 21st inst., at Palace Row, in this city, after a long and painful illness, borne with Christian patience and resignation, aged 65 years, Miss Dillon, sister of the Rev. Dr. Dillon, P.P., of Ballymacnab.

No. 3078 :: Ref. 1849-09-24, 2:6, D.
Of congestion of the brain, at New York, on the 26th August last, Charles, second son of Mr. Hugh Maguire, Pettigo, aged 25 years.

No. 3079 :: Ref. 1849-09-24, 2:6, D.
At Tubbercurry, on 19th inst., at the residence of her son, after a short illness of cholera, Jane, relict of the late William Vernon, Esq., of Marino.

No. 3080 :: Ref. 1849-09-24, 2:6, D.
Sept. 15, at De Grey Terrace, Dublin, after a few days' illness, of inflammation of the lungs, Anna Matilda, the beloved wife of John Webb Bradshaw, Esq.

No. 3081 :: Ref. 1849-09-24, 2:6, D.
Of exhaustion on her passage from Ireland, Anne Victoria, widow of the late Major R.J. Jervoise, of the 1st Royal Dragoons, in her 63d year.

No. 3082 :: Ref. 1849-09-24, 2:6, D.
On 18th inst., at Rathgar, Colonel Wm. Persse, late Lieutenant-Colonel of the 16th Lancers.

No. 3083 :: Ref. 1849-09-24, 2:6, D.
At her residence, in Buncrana, on the 18th inst., Amelia, second daughter of the late Captain William Moore, Royal Marines.

No. 3084 :: Ref. 1849-09-24, 2:6, D.
Of cholera, at Cincinatti, on the 24th July, Catherine M'Curdy, daughter of Mr. Robert M'Curdy, (late of Castlefin, Ireland,) but now residing in that place, aged 23 years.

No. 3085 :: Ref. 1849-10-01, 3:2, B.
At Portadown, on the 25th Sept., Mrs. William Langtry, of a son.

No. 3086 :: Ref. 1849-10-01, 3:2, B.
Sept. 14, at Birkenhead, the lady of Wm. Armstrong, C.E., of a son.

No. 3087 :: Ref. 1849-10-01, 3:2, B.
On 25th ult., at Tregeyd Hay, Viscountess Hereford, of a son.

No. 3088 :: Ref. 1849-10-01, 3:2, B.
Sept. 18, at Castledawson, the lady of R.H. Gordon, Esq., of a daughter.

No. 3089 :: Ref. 1849-10-01, 3:2, B.
Sept. 20, in Dundalk, the lady of John Gorges Beresford, Esq., of a son.

No. 3090 :: Ref. 1849-10-01, 3:2, M.
On 25th ult., in the Presbyterian Church, Knappagh, co. Armagh, by the Rev. David Coote, the Rev. James Gilmour, Boveedy, to Dorothea, youngest daughter of the late Thos. Fuller, Esq., Bandon.

No. 3091 :: Ref. 1849-10-01, 3:2, M.
On 26th ult., in Coleraine, by the Rev. J. Wm. M'Kay, Mr. Thos. Gordon, to Harriett, youngest daughter of the late Rev. John Remington.

No. 3092 :: Ref. 1849-10-01, 3:2, M.
At Ballymore Church, by the Rev. Wm. Allmond, Ezekiel Bradshaw Tydd, youngest son of the late Ezekiel Tydd, Esq., of Redmount, county Tipperary, to Barbara, youngest daughter of the late Wm. Wray, Esq., J.P., of Oak Park, co. Donegal.

No. 3093 :: Ref. 1849-10-01, 3:2, M.
On 25th ult., in St. George's Church, by the Rev. Thomas R. Hamilton, Alexander Sinclair Humphreys, Esq., to Anna Sinclair, only child of the late William Gamble, Esq., of Castlefin, county of Donegal.

No. 3094 :: Ref. 1849-10-01, 3:2, M.
On the 27th ult., in Malone Church, Knappagh, by the Rev. J. M'Kenzie, Mr. James Herd, farmer, Malone, to Mary Anne, daughter of the late Mr. J. Rusk, farmer, Malone.

No. 3095 :: Ref. 1849-10-01, 3:2, M.
In St. George's Church, Douglas, Isle of Man, by the Rev. Edward Forbes, Alfred Gossett, Esq., to Marian Catherine, second daughter of the late Rev. William Smyly, Rector of Aghanloo Glebe, county of Londonderry, and grand-daughter of the late John Claudius Beresford, Esq.

No. 3096 :: Ref. 1849-10-01, 3:2, D.
Sept. 2, at Newport, Kentucky, U.S.A., aged 44 years, Alexander, eldest son of the late Mr. Archibald M'Connell, of this city.

No. 3097 :: Ref. 1849-10-01, 3:2, D.
Sept. 21, at Looneystown, near Richhill, aged 30 years, Catherine, youngest daughter of the late Mr. Archibald M'Connell, of this city.

No. 3098 :: Ref. 1849-10-01, 3:2, D.
Sept. 25, of hooping cough, James, youngest son of Mr. Joseph Thompson, of Keady.

No. 3099 :: Ref. 1849-10-01, 3:2, D.
Sept. 15, at Cootehill, Mr. John Higginbotham, in his 50th year.

No. 3100 :: Ref. 1849-10-01, 3:2, D.
Sept. 19, at Maghera, Mr. Henry Rowan, aged 81 years.

No. 3101 :: Ref. 1849-10-01, 3:2, D.
Suddenly, at Letterkenny, on 23d ult., Jane, relict of the late Mr. Martin Laird, aged 72 years.

No. 3102 :: Ref. 1849-10-01, 3:2, D.
Sept. 21, of dysentery, Mrs. Wm. Black, of Belfast, eldest daughter of Mr. Hugh M'Kendrick, late of Belfast.

No. 3103 :: Ref. 1849-10-01, 3:2, D.
Sept. 5, at Liverpool, Eliza, relict of the late Wm. Galt, Esq., Ballysally, co. Derry.

No. 3104 :: Ref. 1849-10-01, 3:2, D.
Sept. 19, at Bath, Maurice Power, Esq., of Lincoln's-inn, second son of the late Tyrone Power, Esq., the Irish comedian.

No. 3105 :: Ref. 1849-10-01, 3:2, D.
Sept. 19, Miss Emily Louisa Kerr, aged 19 years; and on the 23d ult, Mrs. John Anderson, both daughters of the Rev. John Kerr, Rector of Kilkerrin, diocess of Tuam.

No. 3106 :: Ref. 1849-10-01, 3:2, D.
At Montreal, James Gibbon Williams, Esq., of Dublin, merchant.

No. 3107 :: Ref. 1849-10-01, 3:2, D.
Aug. 17, of cholera, at Brooklyn, New York, Mr. James Marshall, son of the late Mr. John Marshall and grandson of the late Rev. Andrew Marshall, Killileagh.

No. 3108 :: Ref. 1849-10-01, 3:2, D.
At Killycarron, co. Armagh, on 21st ult., in the 77th year of his age, Mr. Thomas Acheson. He was a leading member of the Presbyterian Congregation of Tullyallen, for upwards of half a century. The unusually large number of respectable people who attended his remains to the grave, testified the esteem in which this good man was held in the neighbourhood.

No. 3109 :: Ref. 1849-10-08, 3:1, B.
On the 27th ult., at the Bank Lodge, Downpatrick, the lady of the Rev. John R. Echlin, of a son.

No. 3110 :: Ref. 1849-10-08, 3:1, B.
Aug. 29, at New York, the lady of John Henry O'Donnell, Esq., of Ballyshannon, co Donegal, of a daughter.

No. 3111 :: Ref. 1849-10-08, 3:1, B.
At Sydney, New South Wales, on the 6th April, 1849, Mrs. Tom Ray, of a daughter.

No. 3112 :: Ref. 1849-10-08, 3:1, M.
On the 28th ult., at St. Mark's Church, Armagh, by the Rev. B. Wade, Mr. Jas. H. Bourke, Assistant Master of the Armagh Workhouse, to Susanna, second daughter of Mr. Thomas Orr, Armagh.

No. 3113 :: Ref. 1849-10-08, 3:1, M.
On the 30th ult, in Seagoe Church, by the Venerable Archdeacon Saurin, Mr. James Dougan, of Silverwood, to Miss Mary Douglas, youngest daughter of the late George Douglas, of Dougha.

No. 3114 :: Ref. 1849-10-08, 3:1, M.
October 1, in St. Thomas's Church, Dublin, by the Rev. Charles Josiah Hort, Garrison Chaplain, Archibald Collum, Esq., Solicitor, of Enniskillen, to Margaret Elizabeth Bell, of Gloucester-street Terrace, only daughter of Alexander Bell, Esq., Enniskillen, and grand-daughter of the late Rev. Charles Lucas Bell.

No. 3115 :: Ref. 1849-10-08, 3:1, M.
On the 26th ult., by the Rev. J. Mitchell, Omagh, Mary, second daughter of the Rev. A. Johnson, Newbliss, to the Rev. F. Lyttle, Newtownstewart.

No. 3116 :: Ref. 1849-10-08, 3:1, M.
On the 27th ult., at Southill, Bedfordshire, Hon. Mark Kerr, Commander Royal Navy, to Jane Emma Hannah, youngest daughter of the late Major Macan, of Cariff, county Armagh.

No. 3117 :: Ref. 1849-10-08, 3:1, D.
Suddenly at Haddington Cottage, Haddington Road, John Jackson, Esq., his remains were interred in the Cathedral burying ground, Armagh, on 28th ult.

No. 3118 :: Ref. 1849-10-08, 3:1, D.
Sept. 24, at Boyle, in the hope of a glorious resurrection, Abraham Hamilton Rossborough, S.L.C.S. [sic], youngest son of the late John Rossborough, Esq., Mullinagoan House, county Fermanagh, Cloncaulfield, co. Longford, and Nicholson's-court, same co., and youngest grandson of the late Abraham Powell, Esq., Keybrook, co. Sligo, and of Powellsborough House, same co.

No. 3119 :: Ref. 1849-10-08, 3:1, D.
Sept. 29, at Holywood, George, eldest son of Mr. George Harrison, of Belfast.

No. 3120 :: Ref. 1849-10-08, 3:1, D.
August 10, at one o'clock, on board the "*Sarah Sanda*," on his passage home to Quebec, after being at sea only four days, John C. Fisher, D.C.L., twenty-six years Queen's printer, Quebec, to the great grief of his family and friends, in his 55th year.

No. 3121 :: Ref. 1849-10-08, 3:1, D.
At his residence, Breeny Beg, near Bantry, at the advanced age of 82, Jeremiah Daniel O'Sullivan, Esq. For many years Mr. O'Sullivan was connected with the press in London, having been one of the editors of the *Courier*, which has since become amalgamated with the *Globe*.

No. 3122 :: Ref. 1849-10-08, 3:1, D.
Between 1st and 15th of August, at Newcastle, Jamaica, of yellow fever, William Randolph Eppes, Esq., Deputy Commissary-General, aged 53 years, and his two sons, William and Frederick, aged 15 and 7 years.

No. 3123 :: Ref. 1849-10-15, 3:3, B.
Oct. 2, at Levelly Glebe, the lady of the Rev. Loftus Reade, of a daughter.

No. 3124 :: Ref. 1849-10-15, 3:3, B.
Sept. 27, at Hamilton Terrace, Bundoran, the lady of the late Captain Ovens, of a daughter.

No. 3125 :: Ref. 1849-10-15, 3:3, M.
On 4th inst., at Broughshane, by Rev. R. Stewart, D.D., J.C. Hamill, Esq., M.D., of Ballycastle, to Sarah Jane, daughter of the late Samuel Wilson, Esq., of Ballycloughan, near Ballymena.

No. 3126 :: Ref. 1849-10-15, 3:3, M.
On Tuesday, the 9th inst., in Mary-street Presbyterian church, Belfast, by the bride's father, the Rev. J.L. Porter, youngest son of the late Lieutenant William Porter, of Burt, county Donegal, to Margaret Rainey, youngest daughter of the Rev. Henry Cooke, D.D., LL.D., Principal of the Theological College of the Irish General Assembly, and Dean of Residences of Queen's College, Belfast.

No. 3127 :: Ref. 1849-10-15, 3:3, D.
Suddenly, on last night, at Glenaul House, near Benburb, Mr. Bleazeby, agent to Lady Hassard's estate, to which he had been only a few months appointed.

No. 3128 :: Ref. 1849-10-15, 3:3, D.
October 6, universally regretted, at Cecil, county Tyrone, the Rev. Francis Close Gervais, in his 77th year.

No. 3129 :: Ref. 1849-10-15, 3:3, D.
Oct. 4, at Merino crescent, Clontarf, James Thornley, Esq., formerly of Ballyshannon, aged 70 years.

No. 3130 :: Ref. 1849-10-15, 3:3, D.
Sept. 17, at New York, Dr. James Alexander Houston, eldest son of the Rev. Dr. Houston, Ballymena.

No. 3131 :: Ref. 1849-10-15, 3:3, D.
Oct. 15, Jenny, only daughter of the late Mr. James M'Cutcheon, Craigavad, near Holywood.

No. 3132 :: Ref. 1849-10-15, 3:3, D.
At Kilmore, Mrs. Murdoch, aged 70 years.

No. 3133 :: Ref. 1849-10-22, 3:1, B.
At Watt's Bridge, co. Monaghan, the lady of Thomas Irwin, Esq., of a daughter.

No. 3134 :: Ref. 1849-10-22, 3:1, B.
Oct. 12, the lady of Henry Darcus Esq., Great James's-st., Derry, of a son.

No. 3135 :: Ref. 1849-10-22, 3:1, B.
Oct. 14, at Greyabbey, Lady Charlotte Montgomery, of a daughter.

No. 3136 :: Ref. 1849-10-22, 3:1, B.
At Swanmount, co. Donegal, the lady of Hamilton Porter, Esq., of a daughter.

No. 3137 :: Ref. 1849-10-22, 3:1, M.
October 11, in Tralee Church, Richard F. Blennerhassett, Esq., only surviving son of Rowland Blennerhassett, Esq., of Blennerville, co. Kerry, to Honora, youngest daughter of the late Major Ponsonby, of Crotto, same county.

No. 3138 :: Ref. 1849-10-22, 3:1, M.
Oct. 12, in Swanlinbar Church, Robert Brady, Esq., of Monaghan, to Mary, youngest daughter of Andrew Moffitt, Esq., of Clonturkhill, near Swanlinbar.

No. 3139 :: Ref. 1849-10-22, 3:1, M.
Oct. 15, William, third son of Edward Hayes, Esq., of Kingstown, to Kate, second daughter of Valentine Bourke, Esq., of Dublin.

No. 3140 :: Ref. 1849-10-22, 3:1, D.
Oct. 8, James Crawford Ledlie Carson, third son of Dr. Carson, of Coleraine.

No. 3141 :: Ref. 1849-10-22, 3:1, D.
Oct. 16, in Dublin, of scarletina, after a few days' illness, deeply and deservedly regretted, aged 19, John Creagh, third son of the late George Hobbs, Esq., Sub-Inspector of constabulary.

No. 3142 :: Ref. 1849-10-22, 3:1, D.
Oct. 11, aged sixteen, at Cabra, near Cootehill, Master Richard Boyle.

No. 3143 :: Ref. 1849-10-22, 3:1, D.
Oct. 12, at No. 57, Ranelagh-road, Dublin, Mrs. Jane Johnson, relict, of the late Francis Johnson, Esq., of Belfast, in the 78th year of her age.

No. 3144 :: Ref. 1849-10-22, 3:1, D.
Oct. 15, at Rich View, Clonskeagh, co. Dublin, Hellen Fullarton, the infant daughter of Francis Edward James, Esq.

No. 3145 :: Ref. 1849-10-22, 3:1, D.
October 16, at Rathmines, Major-General Munro, K.H., Royal Artillery.

No. 3146 :: Ref. 1849-10-22, 3:1, D.
Oct. 17, after a lingering illness, Captain Nathaniel Low, Paymaster of the Roscommon Regiment of Militia.

No. 3147 :: Ref. 1849-10-22, 3:1, D.
Oct. 14, at Ramsgate, after a severe and lingering illness, Maria Catherine, widow of the late Wm. Pennefather, Esq., of the 85th Regiment, and daughter of the late Thomas Forster, Esq., of the Grove, Bucks, and Elim, in Jamaica.

No. 3148 :: Ref. 1849-10-22, 3:1, D.
At his residence, Eden-place, Derry, on Thursday, the 18th inst., at the advanced age of 77 years, Mr. Wm. Campbell. His death is much and deservedly regretted by a large circle of friends and acquaintances. His strong attachment to the principles of the Revolution of 1688 induced him to join the yeomanry corps of Derry, in which he was promoted to the rank of Sergeant-Major, and as a mark of the esteem in which he was held, the non commissioned   (continued...)

No. 3148 continued: …officers presented him, in 1805, with an elegantly silver-mounted walking stick, [with] an appropriate inscription. He was one of the oldest freemen of the city.

No. 3149 :: Ref. 1849-10-22, 3:1, D.
October 17, at his residence, Carysfort Lodge, Stillorgan Park, county of Dublin, of bronchitis, Thomas Beasley, Esq., formerly an eminent Solicitor.

No. 3150 :: Ref. 1849-10-22, 3:1, D.
On the 14th inst., at Hastings, Elizabeth Mary, wife of the Rev. John Sheal, B.D., rector of Culdaff, Donegal, and curate of Udimore, Sussex.

No. 3151 :: Ref. 1849-10-22, 3:1, D.
On Wednesday morning week, Catherine, the beloved wife of Mr. Wm. Dillon, Bundoran, and sister of the Rev. J. Cassiday, of that place.

No. 3152 :: Ref. 1849-10-22, 3:1, D.
October 13, at Southsea, Portsmouth, after a severe attack of dysentery, Abraham Armstrong, Esq., M.D., universally lamented as he was esteemed and respected.

No. 3153 :: Ref. 1849-10-22, 3:1, D.
October 13, at his residence, 2, Wentworth Terrace, Dublin, Mr. James Daly, printer. He was a man universally known, and his demise is deservedly regretted by his numerous friends and acquaintances.

No. 3154 :: Ref. 1849-10-22, 3:1, D.
On the 19th September, in London, Grace Scott, the beloved child of Mr. and Mrs. G.O. Duncan.

Ah! thou art gone my darling Grace,
We shall be sad and lonely now;
Cold death has changed thy pretty face,
Its chilly damp is on thy brow.

Thy sweet expression, bright blue eyes,
How proud I was to look upon'
Those long-lashed lids no more can rise,
And all their sweetness—is it gone?

Thy wavy curls of golden hair
Now lie unheeded in the grave,
I used to twine with so much care,
One little curl is all I have.

I miss thy merry laugh all day—
Thy prattling tongue at morning-light;
When others like thee are at play
I cannot look—tears dim my sight.

When all is still, and others rest,
I think and dream and wish thee here;
Thine image on my heart's imprest,
And every shadow brings thee near.

Too short with us has been thy stay
For thee to know how thou wert loved,
And only is't one single day—
How sad a day to us it proved.

'Mongst strangers now thy little bed,
But we still guard thy body there,
And plant sweet flowers o'er thy head
To nurse with tenderness and care.

We know, oh sweet reflection 'tis
Where thy pure, sinless soul has gone
To join the angel bands in bliss,
How sweet the thought to dwell upon.

And we who live must hope and pray,
Thy father, mother, brothers, too,
That when from earth we're called away
We may be all prepared to go.

Sweet child farewell! the cold clay lies
Now heavy on thy coffin's lid,
But nought can rend affections ties,
They are strongest with the dead.

Oh, cheering thought, we'll meet again
Where there's no sorrow, sin, nor pain.

M.E.D.

No. 3155 :: Ref. 1849-10-29, 3:2, B.
On the 25th inst., at Coolkeiragh House, the lady of Alexander T. Young, Esq., of a son.

No. 3156 :: Ref. 1849-10-29, 3:2, B.
At Swanmount, county Donegal, the lady of Hamilton Porter, Esq., of a son.

No. 3157 :: Ref. 1849-10-29, 3:2, B.
At Lakeview Cottage, Dungannon, the lady of Mr. John Lilburn, architect and builder, of a daughter.

No. 3158 :: Ref. 1849-10-29, 3:2, M.
Oct. 25, at Benburb Church, Tyrone, by the Rev. Henry Griffin, Rector, and afterwards, conformable to the rites of the Roman Catholic Church, by the Rev. Michael Coyne, P.P., Leonard Henry Dobbin, Esq., of Hackney, near Charlemont, son of Leonard H. Dobbin, Esq., late captain in the Royal Regiment, to Mary Anne, only child of the late Patrick Donnelly, Esq., of Blackwatertown.

No. 3159 :: Ref. 1849-10-29, 3:2, M.
Oct. 24, at the second Presbyterian Meeting House, Dungannon, by the Rev. Thomas Heron, of Springbank, Moneymore, Mary, eldest daughter of the Rev. Andrew Wilson, Elm Lodge, Dungannon, to the Rev. Robert Wallace, Presbyterian Minister, Newry.

No. 3160 :: Ref. 1849-10-29, 3:2, M.
Oct. 17, at Goodmersham, Kent, the Earl of Winchelsea and Nottingham, led to the altar Fanny Margaretta, eldest daughter of E. Rice, Esq., of Dart Court, and M.P., for Dover. The ceremony was performed by the Kev. [sic] Wm. Knight, in the presence of Viscount and Viscountess Maidstone and a select family circle.

No. 3161 :: Ref. 1849-10-29, 3:2, M.
Oct. 22, in the Presbyterian Church, Glenhoy near Augher, by the Rev. James Dales, Mr. Hugh Stokes, second son of the late Rev. H. Stokes, Glenhoy, to Fanny only daughter of Mr. James Stokes, of Belfast.

No. 3162 :: Ref. 1849-10-29, 3:2, M.
Oct. 24, at Belfast, John S. Dickson, Esq., Surgeon, to Sarah, eldest daughter of Thomas Mairs, Esq., Great George's-street, Belfast, and Green Island, Carrickfergus.

No. 3163 :: Ref. 1849-10-29, 3:2, M.
Oct. 24, at Carnmoney Church, Mr. James Archer, Markethill, to Eliza, youngest daughter of Mr. Samuel Hamill, Ballymartin, Templepatrick.

No. 3164 :: Ref. 1849-10-29, 3:2, D.
Oct. 24, suddenly, near Markethill, Mr. James M'Mullin, aged 53 years, much and sincerely regretted by a numerous circle of relations and sorrowing friends—may he rest in peace.

No. 3165 :: Ref. 1849-10-29, 3:2, D.
Suddenly, at Greenisland, on 17th inst., Mrs. Elizabeth Woodhouse, much and deservedly lamented; and on the 19th inst., at same place, Mr. James Woodhouse, her husband, aged 86 years. The respect in which they were held was fully testified by the large and respectable concourse which attended their remains to the family burying ground at Tartaraghan.

No. 3166 :: Ref. 1849-10-29, 3:2, D.
On the 21st inst., at Ardnargle, James Ogilby, Esq., aged 67.

No. 3167 :: Ref. 1849-10-29, 3:2, D.
On the 23d inst., Mr. Wm. Taaffe, master of the Parochial School of Kilkeel, county Down.

No. 3168 :: Ref. 1849-10-29, 3:2, D.
Suddenly, at Strabane, on Friday last, Mr. John Huggins, formerly of Dungannon.

No. 3169 :: Ref. 1849-10-29, 3:2, D.
On Wednesday last, in Strabane, Martha, daughter of Mr. Francis Larmour.

No. 3170 :: Ref. 1849-10-29, 3:2, D.
Oct. 23, at Hilltown Glebe, the Rev. Richard Archer, Vicar of Clonduff, diocese of Dromore.

No. 3171 :: Ref. 1849-10-29, 3:2, D.
On the 22d inst., Miss Mary Hamill, of Catherine-street, Newry, aged thirty-four years.

No. 3172 :: Ref. 1849-10-29, 3:2, D.
On the 24th inst., at Belfast, Mr. Joseph Hindlay, in the 48th year of his age.

No. 3173 :: Ref. 1849-10-29, 3:2, D.
On the 23d inst., at Garden-hill, Belfast, Isaac Thompson, Esq., in the 84th year of his age.

No. 3174 :: Ref. 1849-10-29, 3:2, D.
On the 20th inst., at Lisburn, Annabella, wife of Dr. M'Harg, aged 34 years.

No. 3175 :: Ref. 1849-10-29, 3:2, D.
At Ballycolman, Strabane, on the 15th inst., Mr. John M'Farland, aged 15 years.

No. 3176 :: Ref. 1849-10-29, 3:2, D.
At Cincinatti, of dysentery, Mr. James Mills, formerly of Derry.

No. 3177 :: Ref. 1849-10-29, 3:2, D.
At Cincinatti, U.S., on the 24th of August, in the prime of life, Robert, eldest son of Mr. Robert Love, of Mullaghmena, near Omagh, deeply regretted by his family and friends, both in Ireland and America.

No. 3178 :: Ref. 1849-11-05, 3:1, B.
On 14th inst., at Rockville House, County Monaghan, the lady of John Thomas M'Vittee, Esq., of a son.

No. 3179 :: Ref. 1849-11-05, 3:1, B.
Oct. 19, the wife of John Graham, Esq., solicitor, of a son.

No. 3180 :: Ref. 1849-11-05, 3:1, B.
Oct. 19, at Lakeview Cottage, Blacklion, the lady of Dr. Flood, of a son.

No. 3181 :: Ref. 1849-11-05, 3:1, B.
Oct. 30, at the glebe Lisnaskea, near Enniskillen, the lady of Rev. John Flanagan, of a son.

No. 3182 :: Ref. 1849-11-05, 3:1, M.
Oct. 30, at Kilmore Church, by the Rev. James Jones, David W. Waugh, Esq., of Dublin, to Mary Anne, only daughter of Henry Stanley, Esq., of Derryhale House, Portadown.

No. 3183 :: Ref. 1849-11-05, 3:1, M.
On 1st inst., at the bride's residence, by the Rev. James Ford, P.P., Laurence Gerraghty Esq., officer of Inland Revenue, to Anne, only daughter of the late Mr. Daniel M'Naghten, of Drummuck, co. Monaghan.

No. 3184 :: Ref. 1849-11-05, 3:1, M.
On 26th ult., in Cavan presbyterian meeting-house, by the Rev. Mr. Coote, Mr Wm. M'Kinley, to Prude, eldest daughter of Mr. David Wilson, of Coolkarn.

No. 3185 :: Ref. 1849-11-05, 3:1, M.
Nov. 1, in Grange Church, by the Rev. Henry Cobbe, Mr. James Burns, jeweller, silversmith & watchmaker, Armagh, to Mary Ann, eldest daughter of Mr. Simon Reilly, of Drummond.

No. 3186 :: Ref. 1849-11-05, 3:1, M.
On 31st ult., at Portadown, by the Rev. Henry De L. Willis, Mr Wright Babe, of Ballymagarick, Gilford, to Ann Eliza, eldest daughter of Mr. John Finnegan, of Mullentine, Portadown.

No. 3187 :: Ref. 1849-11-05, 3:1, D.

On 18th ult., Margaret, relict of the late Mr. Hugh Barrett, of Copney, near Verner's Bridge, at the advanced age of 96 years. She retained her faculties to the last moment—was loved and respected by all who knew her, and deeply regretted by a large circle of relatives and friends.

No. 3188 :: Ref. 1849-11-05, 3:1, D.

After a lingering illness, Mrs. Ann Atkinson, of Lisnadill, aged 68(?) years.

No. 3189 :: Ref. 1849-11-12, 3:2, M.

At Belfast, on 1st Nov., by Rev. Dr. Cooke, John Hunter, Esq., of Belfast, to Miss Cordukes, of the Crescent, near that town.

No. 3190 :: Ref. 1849-11-12, 3:2, M.

October 17, at Naples, Commander Thomas Carmichael, Royal Navy, second son of Sir Thomas Gibson Carmichael, of Skirling, Bart., to Frances Marianne, third daughter of the late Rev. Joseph Story, of Bingfield, county Cavan.

No. 3191 :: Ref. 1849-11-12, 3:2, M.

On the 6th inst., at Ballinode Church, by the Rev. J.C. Young, Mr. William West, of Drumrella, Newtownbutler, to Margaret, second daughter of Mr. Robert Wright, of Ballinode Mills, county Monaghan.

No. 3192 :: Ref. 1849-11-12, 3:2, M.

On the 7th inst., in the First Presbyterian Church, Islandmagee, by the Rev. W. Campbell, Mr. William Niblock, Broadisland, to Miss Sarah Wilson, Gransha, Islandmagee.

No. 3193 :: Ref. 1849-11-12, 3:2, M.

On the 2d instant, at Kingstown, James Black, Esq., of Blessington-street, Derry, to Eliza, third daughter of the late James Morrow, Esq., Crevagh, Dungannon.

No. 3194 :: Ref. 1849-11-12, 3:2, M.

In the Cathedral, Derry, on the 4th inst., by the Rev. George Smith, Mr. James Laverty, printer, to Anne Jane, eldest daughter of Mr. Daniel Stewart, both of Derry.

No. 3195 :: Ref. 1849-11-12, 3:2, M.

In St. Peter's Church, Derry, by the Rev. W.C. Magee, Joseph William, son of the Rev. C.H. Minchin, to Lydia Jane, daughter of the late Rev. John Magee, and grand-daughter of the late Archbishop of Dublin.

No. 3196 :: Ref. 1849-11-12, 3:2, M.

Oct. 25, at Poyntzfield House, Cromarty, Major Angus Mackay, of the 21st Royal Fusiliers, to Mary Magdalene Poyntz, eldest daughter of Major Sir George Gun Munro, of Poyntzfield House.

No. 3197 :: Ref. 1849-11-12, 3:2, M.

In Carrickmacross church, by the Rev. J. Thompson, Mr. Francis Kellet, Bailieborough, to Elizabeth, relict of the late Mr. Hooks, of Newry.

No. 3198 :: Ref. 1849-11-12, 3:2, M.

At Pomeroy, on the 8th inst., the lady of the Rev. Alexander F. Hanlon, of a son.

No. 3199 :: Ref. 1849-11-12, 3:2, M.

At Castlecaulfield, on the 5th of Nov., the lady of the Rev. Robt. Hamilton, curate of the parish of Donaghmore, diocese of Armagh, of a son.

No. 3200 :: Ref. 1849-11-12, 3:2, M.

On the 2d inst., at Wellington-street, Ballymena, the lady of Jas. N. Hardy, Esq., of a son.

No. 3201 :: Ref. 1849-11-12, 3:2, M.

At Ballymoyer Glebe, county Armagh, the lady of the Rev. G. Wall, jun., of a son.

No. 3202 :: Ref. 1849-11-12, 3:2, M.

At Beragh, county Tyrone, the wife of Mr. Mathew Rogers, jun., of a daughter.

No. 3203 :: Ref. 1849-11-12, 3:2, D.

At Lisnadill, on the 19th ult., in the 69th year of her age, Mrs. Anne Atkinson, relict of the late Francis Atkinson, Esq. Having found redemption through the atonement of Christ, she was enabled to await the approach of the last enemy with a calm assurance of victory over him; and her sorrowing family are comforted under their painful bereavement by the hope of a reunion in that blessed state, of which the voice of inspiration has declared—"*There shall be no more death, neither sorrow nor crying; neither shall there be any more pain, for the former things are passed away.*"

No. 3204 :: Ref. 1849-11-12, 3:2, D.

On the 9th inst., at his father's residence, of decline, brought on by the rupture of a bloodvessel of the lungs, on the 4th of March, 1844, in Alabama, U.S. America, Philip, eldest son of Mr. Hugh Maguire, of Pettigo, aged 27 years.

No. 3205 :: Ref. 1849-11-12, 3:2, D.

At Lurganboy, county Leitrim, Elizabeth Anne, wife of Henry H. Slade, Esq., resident magistrate, and daughter of the late Hon. Arthur C. Hamilton.

No. 3206 :: Ref. 1849-11-12, 3:2, D.

Nov. 7, in Main-street, Cavan, in the 38th year of her age, Anne, relict of Mr. James Maguire, and sister of the Rev. John Gallagher, C.C., of Ballinamore.

No. 3207 :: Ref. 1849-11-19, 3:1, B.

In Dublin street, Dundalk, on 13th inst., of a son, the wife of Mr. Wm. Hill, clerk of the Dundalk union.

No. 3208 :: Ref. 1849-11-19, 3:1, B.

On 11th inst., at the Rectory, Louth, the lady of the Rev. John Barclay Scriven, of a daughter.

No. 3209 :: Ref. 1849-11-19, 3:1, M.

On 16th inst., in Lurgan Church, by the Rev. Charles Falloon, Mr. W. Paul, to Anna, daughter of Mr. John Gilbert, both of Lurgan.

No. 3210 :: Ref. 1849-11-19, 3:1, M.

On 6th inst., at Clondigad, co. Clare, Robert Gibson Patchell, Esq., second son of John Patchell, Esq., surgeon in the Royal Navy, of Burbuoy Cottage, Moneymore, to Frances, youngest daughter of the late James Heyns, Esq., M.D., of Ennis.

No. 3211 :: Ref. 1849-11-19, 3:1, M.

On 15th inst., by the Rev. John Hamilton, Crossroads, the Rev. James Bell, Presbyterian Minister, Tandragee, to Miss Hamilton, daughter of Dr. Hamilton, of Omagh.

No. 3212 :: Ref. 1849-11-19, 3:1, M.

On 13th inst., in Omagh, by the Rev. Mr. Thompson, Charles Blackham, Esq., to Anne, fourth daughter of John M'Kenny, Esq.

No. 3213 :: Ref. 1849-11-19, 3:1, M.

On 13th inst., in Linenhall-street Presbyterian Church, Belfast, by the Rev. Robert Knox, and afterwards by the Rev. Mr. O'Loughlin, Mr. Thomas Devlin, merchant, of Omagh, to Anna Clarke, second daughter of Samuel Dobbin, Esq., Belfast.

No. 3214 :: Ref. 1849-11-19, 3:1, D.

On 12th inst., rather suddenly, Mr. Wm. Buchanan, of Knockmoyle, near Omagh, aged 82 years.

No. 3215 :: Ref. 1849-11-19, 3:1, D.

On 4th inst., of typhus fever, at Liverpool, on his way to America, Mr. John Lind, late of Dublin, and formerly of Cookstown.

No. 3216 :: Ref. 1849-11-19, 3:1, D.

On 7th instant, at Cushendun, Elizabeth, second daughter of the late Archibald Sinclair, Esq., of Markethill.

No. 3217 :: Ref. 1849-11-19, 3:1, D.

On 12th Nov. in Monaghan, John Walter, the infant son of Mr. William Jebb, Proctor, aged 11 months.

No. 3218 :: Ref. 1849-11-19, 3:1, D.

On 3d inst., in the parish of Templeport, the Rev. Philip M'Gauran, in the 38th year of his age, and tenth of his ministry.

No. 3219 :: Ref. 1849-11-19, 3:1, D.

On 15th inst., of gastric fever, Mary Wilhelmina Knox, aged five years, eldest daughter of the Right Rev. the Lord Bishop of Down and Connor and Dromore.

No. 3220 :: Ref. 1849-11-19, 3:1, D.

On 1st inst., at Lurganboy, Leitrim, Elizabeth Anne, wife of Henry H. Slade, Esq., Resident Magistrate, and daughter of the late Hon. Arthur Cole Hamilton.

No. 3221 :: Ref. 1849-11-19, 3:1, D.

On 8th inst., aged 88 years, Arthur Lepper, Esq., of Three Trees, county Donegal.

No. 3222 :: Ref. 1849-11-19, 3:1, D.

At Strabane, on 8th inst., Isabella, last surviving daughter of the late Claud Hamilton, Esq. Miss Hamilton was the last of her race, in the elder branch, next to that of the present Marquis of Abercorn, in direct descent from Claud Hamilton, first Baron of Paisley; second cousin of the present Sir James John Hamilton, of Woodbrook, county Tyrone, Bart., and nearly related to the noblest blood in this part of Ireland.

No. 3223 :: Ref. 1849-11-26, 2:7, B.

Nov. 18, at Gloucester-crescent, Regent's Park, the Hon. Mrs. Maude, of a daughter.

No. 3224 :: Ref. 1849-11-26, 2:7, B.

Nov. 22, the lady of the Archdeacon of Meath, of a daughter.

No. 3225 :: Ref. 1849-11-26, 2:7, B.

At Swanmount, co. Donegal, the lady of H.P. Molloy, Esq., of a daughter.

No. 3226 :: Ref. 1849-11-26, 2:7, B.

Nov. 16, at Richmond, the lady of Hugh Harris, Esq., of a daughter.

No. 3227 :: Ref. 1849-11-26, 2:7, B.

Nov. 13, at Belfast, the lady of William H. Macartney, Esq., barrister-at-law, of a son.

No. 3228 :: Ref. 1849-11-26, 2:7, B.

Nov. 23, at Terman Rectory, the lady of the Rev. S. Alexander, of a daughter.

No. 3229 :: Ref. 1849-11-26, 2:7, B.

Nov. 17, at Chesham-place, the lady of the Hon. Richard Cavendish, of a son.

No. 3230 :: Ref. 1849-11-26, 2:7, B.

Nov. 19, at Russell-place, Dublin, the lady of Nicholas John Halpin, Esq., of a daughter.

No. 3231 :: Ref. 1849-11-26, 2:7, M.

Nov. 17, in Rostrevor Church, Sandford M'Vittle Lloyd, Esq., M.D., staff surgeon, to Marian, eldest daughter of the late Dr. Curri, of Ballyconnell, co. Cavan.

No. 3232 :: Ref. 1849-11-26, 2:7, M.

Oct. 15, in Philadelphia, by the Rev. Mr. Ogilby, Mr. Edward Knox, of New York, to Eliza, second daughter of Mr. Robert Brown, Rathmullan, county Donegal, Ireland.

No. 3233 :: Ref. 1849-11-26, 2:7, M.

In Scots' Church, Ramelton, 21st inst., by the Rev. Matthew Wilson, Captain Edward Sims, Dunfanaghy, now at Londonderry, to Miss Margaret Henderson, daughter of the late Mr. Henderson, Letterkenny.

No. 3234 :: Ref. 1849-11-26, 2:7, M.
On 20th inst., at the residence of her father, by the Venerable the Archdeacon M'Carron, John Hawkins Dillon, Esq., Donegal, to Eleanor L., daughter of Thos. White, Esq., Waterside, Derry.

No. 3235 :: Ref. 1849-11-26, 2:7, M.
At Philadelphia, 29th ult., by Rev. J.C. Lyons, John Galbraith, Esq., of Mukwonago, Wisconsin, late Consul of Russia and the Netherlands at Belfast, Ireland, to Miss Elizabeth Jones, of Manavunk, Pennsylvania, late of Belfast.

No. 3236 :: Ref. 1849-11-26, 2:7, M.
On 21st inst., Thomas, third son of Joseph Walton, Esq., of Balsall Heath, Warwickshire, to Barbara, eldest daughter of the late Robert Robinson, of Bloomfield, Esq., and step-sister of Captain Porter, 67th Regt.

No. 3237 :: Ref. 1849-11-26, 2:7, M.
Nov. 20, at the church of Mullafary, by the Rev. James Meehan, William Richey, Esq., proprietor of the *Tyrawly Herald*, to Jane, daughter of John Boyde, Esq., of Carrakelly.

No. 3238 :: Ref. 1849-11-26, 2:7, M.
On 20th inst., in St. Ann's church, by the Rev. Charles Allen, Wm. Jolly, Esq., of Stevenston, Lanarkshire, to Margaret, daughter of the late James Fitzgerald, Esq., Clonavilla, co. Monaghan.

No. 3239 :: Ref. 1849-11-26, 2:7, M.
On 15th inst., in Ballymena, by the Rev. J.M. Killen, Comber, Mr. James M. Andrews, Glenwherry, to Sarah, daughter of James Walkingshaw, Esq., Ballykeel, Ballymena.

No. 3240 :: Ref. 1849-11-26, 2:7, M.
On 10th inst., in St. Martin's Church, London, Charles Andrew Poole, Esq., M.D., to Louisa Caroline, youngest daughter of Captain Donovan, of Cardiff, Glamorganshire, South Wales.

No. 3241 :: Ref. 1849-11-26, 2:7, M.
Nov. 16, in the Pettigo Presbyterian Church, by the Rev. John Donaldson, George, eldest son of Mr. George Allingham, Boa Island, to Rebecca, youngest [daughter of] the late Robert Robinson, Esq., Kimid.

No. 3242 :: Ref. 1849-11-26, 2:7, M.
On 15th inst., in the Presbyterian Church, Loughbrickland, by the Rev. R. Anderson, Mr. John S. Jamison, of Banbridge, to Mrs. Main, Roughfort, near Banbridge.

No. 3243 :: Ref. 1849-11-26, 2:7, D.
At Telegraph court, on 17th inst., aged 19, Amelia, second daughter of Mr. James Henderson, Proprietor of *The Telegraph*.

No. 3244 :: Ref. 1849-11-26, 2:7, D.
Nov. 20, in the 83d year of her age, Mrs. Wilson, Clare, near Moira.

No. 3245 :: Ref. 1849-11-26, 2:7, D.
Nov. 15, at Rathfriland, Mr. Atkinson, aged 33 years.

No. 3246 :: Ref. 1849-11-26, 2:7, D.
Nov. 19, at 27, Lowndes square, Lieut.-Colonel Robert La Touche, aged 68.

No. 3247 :: Ref. 1849-11-26, 2:7, D.
Nov. 20, at 8, Upper Pembroke-street, Mary Kate, the infant daughter of William Fetherstonhaugh, Esq., Paymaster 59th Regiment.

No. 3248 :: Ref. 1849-11-26, 2:7, D.
Nov. 3, at Glen Lodge, co. Donegal, William Hume, Esq., J.P.

No. 3249 :: Ref. 1849-11-26, 2:7, D.
Nov. 19, at Liverpool, John, second son of the late James Fisher, Esq., of Londonderry.

No. 3250 :: Ref. 1849-11-26, 2:7, D.
Nov. 14, at Dalkey, co. Dublin, Mrs. Dawson, relict of the late Alexander Dawson, Esq., M.P., for co. Louth.

No. 3251 :: Ref. 1849-11-26, 2:7, D.
Nov. 15, in Drogheda, aged 40 years, Rosetta, wife of Edward Atkinson, Esq., M.D., and daughter of John Shaw M'Cullach.

No. 3252 :: Ref. 1849-11-26, 2:7, D.
June 15, at Port Leopold, Henry Mathias, Esq., late of Dublin, Assistant-Surgeon on board her Majesty's ship *Enterprise*, one of the vessels composing the Arctic Expedition, under the command of Sir James Ross.

No. 3253 :: Ref. 1849-12-03, 3:1, B.
Nov. 19, the lady of Denis Bingham, Esq., Bingham Castle, of a son and heir.

No. 3254 :: Ref. 1849-12-03, 3:1, B.
Nov. 25, at Boulogne-Suer-Mer [sic], the lady of Arthur Ruxton, Esq., of a daughter.

No. 3255 :: Ref. 1849-12-03, 3:1, B.
Nov. 23, the lady of the Rev. S. Alexander, of Termon Rectory, co. Tyrone, of a daughter, being the 58th grand-child of the Rev. Charles Cobb Beresford.

No. 3256 :: Ref. 1849-12-03, 3:1, B.
At 20, Fitzwilliam-place, of a son, the lady of T.R. Browne, Esq., of Aughtentain, co. Tyrone.

No. 3257 :: Ref. 1849-12-03, 3:1, M.
Nov. 22, in the Parish Church of Tullylish, by the Rev. John Stewart, A.B., Mr. Adam Morrison, Two-mile-Flush, Armagh, to Helen Jane, daughter of Mr. Wm. Mills, Waringston.

No. 3258 :: Ref. 1849-12-03, 3:1, M.

Nov. 24, by Hugh S. Homes, Registrar of marriages, Donegal, Mr. Alexander Walker, Trummen, Donegal, to Margaret, daughter of Mr. John Colvin, of same place.

No. 3259 :: Ref. 1849-12-03, 3:1, M.

Nov. 29, in Dundalk, by the Rev. Mr. M'Ginnity, R.C.C., Mary Anne, eldest daughter of Mr. James White, of Dundalk, to Mr. C. Moore, of Dublin.

No. 3260 :: Ref. 1849-12-03, 3:1, M.

Nov. 23, at Newtownstewart Church, by the Rev. Mervyn Wilson, Francis S. Gordon, Esq., to Catherine Matilda, eldest daughter of the late Capt. Saville Speer, 1st Royal Regt. of Foot.

No. 3261 :: Ref. 1849-12-03, 3:1, M.

Nov. 26, in Castleknock Church, by the Rev. Mr. Stone, and afterwards according to the rites of the Roman Catholic Church, Richard Coffy, Esq., eldest son of Christopher Coffy, Esq., of Newcastle, co. Westmeath, to Penelope May, eldest daughter of Wm. Bathbourne, Esq., of Scripplestown House, co. Dublin.

No. 3262 :: Ref. 1849-12-03, 3:1, M.

Nov. 17, John Carey, M.D., second son of John Carey, Esq., officer of law courts, Dublin, to Alicia, fifth daughter of the late Alan Bellingham, Esq., of Castlebellingham, co. Louth.

No. 3263 :: Ref. 1849-12-03, 3:1, M.

On 27th ult., at Strabane, by Rev. W.A. Russell, Mr. James Thompson, jun., Merchant, Strabane, to Eliza, third daughter of Mr. James Dunlop, Cookstown.

No. 3264 :: Ref. 1849-12-03, 3:1, M.

Nov. 27, at St. Mary's Church, Bath, by the Ven. the Archdeacon of Raphoe, the Rev. R.B. Fenwich Elrington, to Louisa, daughter of Robert Orde Fenwick, Esq.

No. 3265 :: Ref. 1849-12-03, 3:1, M.

Nov. 24th, at Killybegs, by the Rev. Wm. Lodge, Louisa, daughter of the late James Hamilton, Esq., Fintra House, Donegal, to Lieut. J.B. Cator, R.N.

No. 3266 :: Ref. 1849-12-03, 3:1, M.

On 27th ult., in St. Ann's Church, by the Rev. Wm. Duffin, Wm. Faren, to Eleanor Duncan, both of Belfast.

No. 3267 :: Ref. 1849-12-03, 3:1, D.

On 30th ult., in Gardner-street, Dublin, of scarlatina, the beloved wife of John Collum, Esq., the eminent solicitor.

No. 3268 :: Ref. 1849-12-03, 3:1, D.

At Axminster, Charles Conrad Brine, of the 27th, or Enniskillen Regiment.

No. 3269 :: Ref. 1849-12-03, 3:1, D.

In Strabane, on 27th ult., very suddenly, Mr. Daniel Cook, aged 59 years.

No. 3270 :: Ref. 1849-12-03, 3:1, D.

Nov. 22, the wife of Mr. Robert John Boyd, Bellaghy.

No. 3271 :: Ref. 1849-12-03, 3:1, D.

At Crevillyvalley, near Ballymena, on 23d Oct., [of] fever, in the 32d year of his age, Mr. Newton Cusack, eldest son of Mr. William Cusack; also, on 19th ult., of fever, in the 22d year of his age, Mr. Wm. Cusack, student of philosophy in the Royal College, Belfast, and third son of Mr. Wm. Cusack.

No. 3272 :: Ref. 1849-12-03, 3:1, D.

On 27th ult., at Thornfield, the seat of his son-in-law, John Mahon, Esq., the Rev. Armstrong Kelly, of Castlekelly, in his 87th year. He was sixth in direct descent from Colonel Colla O'Kelly, who served under the Earl of Clanricarde at Kinsale, temp. Queen Elizabeth, and who was the last acknowledged Chief of Hymaine. He was consequently the 45th representative of the ancient Irish honour of O'Kelly.

No. 3273 :: Ref. 1849-12-03, 3:1, D.

At his residence, near Omagh, on 23[d] ult., in the 84th year of his age, the Rev. James M'Clintock.

No. 3274 :: Ref. 1849-12-03, 3:1, D.

On 27th ult., Thomas, infant son of Mr. Thomas Sands, Donegal.

No. 3275 :: Ref. 1849-12-03, 3:1, D.

On 8th ult., at Curran-hill, Enniskillen, James Johnston, Esq., in the 68th year of his age.

No. 3276 :: Ref. 1849-12-03, 3:1, D.

November 21, at his residence, Tooloobane, county Galway, Wm. Hartly Hodson, Esq., aged 62 years.

No. 3277 :: Ref. 1849-12-03, 3:1, D.

Nov. 20, at Newcomen-place, Dublin, Louise Adelaide, eldest daughter of Henry W. Hardy, Esq., and [sic] member for many years of the Irish parliament, and the biographer of "*The Life of Lord Charlemont.*"

No. 3278 :: Ref. 1849-12-10, 3:1, B.

Dec. 5, at Tandragee, the wife of Edward D. Atkinson, Esq., of a daughter.

No. 3279 :: Ref. 1849-12-10, 3:1, B.

Dec. 3, at Montpelier Parade, Monkstown, the lady of Charles Atkinson, Esq., of a son.

No. 3280 :: Ref. 1849-12-10, 3:1, B.

Nov. 29, the wife of Mr. James Briars, merchant, Dungannon, of a son.

No. 3281 :: Ref. 1849-12-10, 3:1, M.

Nov. 27, at Killaghtee Church, by the Rev. William Welsh, Geo. T.C. Smith, Esq., of Donegal Terrace, Devenport, to Mary Anna, third daughter of the Rev. Joseph Welsh, Rector of Killaghtee, in the co. Donegal.

No. 3282 :: Ref. 1849-12-10, 3:1, D.

Dec. 4, of protracted illness, Margaret, the beloved wife of Mr. Robert Dickie, of No. 2, Albion Court, Glasgow, in the 65th year of her age.

No. 3283 :: Ref. 1849-12-10, 3:1, D.

Dec. 6, of fever in the 50th year of his age, Mr. John Gregg, of Corovahan, near Clones. During life he was deservedly respected by all who knew him, and his death has caused sorrow amongst a numerous circle of friends and mourning relatives.

No. 3284 :: Ref. 1849-12-10, 3:1, D.

Dec. 2, in the 52d year of his age, Mr. Robert Caldwell, merchant, Moneymore.

No. 3285 :: Ref. 1849-12-10, 3:1, D.

Nov. 30, at Castledawson, co. Tyrone, of disease of the heart, Sophia, wife of Edward Litton, Esq., Master in Chancery.

No. 3286 :: Ref. 1849-12-10, 3:1, D.

Dec. 6, at Cairnlough, Glenarm, aged 11 years, John W.C. Lanktree, son of John Lanktree, Esq., J.P.

No. 3287 :: Ref. 1849-12-10, 3:1, D.

Dec. 3, at Belle Villa, Dublin, in his 84th year, Paul Donlevy, Esq.

No. 3288 :: Ref. 1849-12-10, 3:1, D.

At St. Anne's, Neilson, Upper Canada, at an advanced age, Mrs. B Eager, relict of Benjamin Eager, Esq., late of Blesinton, co. Wicklow.

No. 3289 :: Ref. 1849-12-10, 3:1, D.

Nov. 4, at Pittsburgh, Mrs. Robert Kennedy, late of Manorcunningham, in the county Donegal.

No. 3290 :: Ref. 1849-12-10, 3:1, D.

June 30, in Port Philip, Australia, of rapid consumption, Captain Roderick Mackenzie, late of the 96th Regiment, son of the late Sir Kenneth Mackenzie, of Rosshire.

No. 3291 :: Ref. 1849-12-10, 3:1, D.

Dec. 2, at his residence, Grove Hill, county Cork, John Caulfield Irvine, Esq., in his 68th year.

No. 3292 :: Ref. 1849-12-10, 3:1, D.

Nov. 28, at Killencool Rectory, co. Louth, after a few days' illness, Anne, wife of the Rev. Alexander George Stuart, in the 38th year of her age, deeply regretted.

No. 3293 :: Ref. 1849-12-17, 3:1, B.

On the 5th instant, at Dungannon, the wife of Mr. Charles Riley, manager of the gas works, of a daughter.

No. 3294 :: Ref. 1849-12-17, 3:1, B.

Dec. 5, at 9, Upper Fitzwilliam-street, the wife of Richard Mayne, Esq., of Newbliss, Monaghan, of a daughter.

No. 3295 :: Ref. 1849-12-17, 3:1, B.

On 11th inst., the lady of N.M. Montgomery, Esq., Manager of the Ulster Bank, Omagh, of a daughter.

No. 3296 :: Ref. 1849-12-17, 3:1, B.

On the 30th ult., in Drogheda, the lady of James O'Brien, Esq., Barrack-Master of the Drogheda District, of a son.

No. 3297 :: Ref. 1849-12-17, 3:1, B.

On 8th inst., at Laurel Lodge, Monkstown, the wife of J.C. Stronge, Esq., of a son.

No. 3298 :: Ref. 1849-12-17, 3:1, B.

Dec. 8, at Boulogne-Sur-Mer, the lady of Captain Cross (late 68th Light Infantry), of a son.

No. 3299 :: Ref. 1849-12-17, 3:1, B.

Dec. 9, at Plymouth, the wife of Captain Lindsell, 28th Regiment, of a daughter.

No. 3300 :: Ref. 1849-12-17, 3:1, M.

In this city, on Friday last, Mr. Nathaniel Greacen, of Market-Street, to Eleanor, eldest daughter of Mr. John Henry, of Scotch-Street.

No. 3301 :: Ref. 1849-12-17, 3:1, M.

On 13th inst., in the First Presbyterian Meeting-house, Belfast, by the Rev. John Scott Porter, James Aitken, Esq., to Mary Anne, second daughter of John Kennedy, Esq., Belfast.

No. 3302 :: Ref. 1849-12-17, 3:1, M.

Dec. 10, in May-street Presbyterian Church, by the Rev. Dr. Cooke, L.L.D., Hugh Currie Simpson, Ballynafeigh, to Mary, eldest daughter of the late Alexander Graham, Falls. They are both deaf and dumb, and received their education together, under Mr. Martin, in the Ulster Institution for the Deaf and the Dumb and the Blind.

No. 3303 :: Ref. 1849-12-17, 3:1, M.

On 6th inst., in Tassagh Presbyterian Church, by the Rev. Joseph Jenkins, the Rev. Andrew Molyneix, Clontibret, to Mary Ann, daughter of the late Wm. Kidd, Esq., Dundrum, Keady.

No. 3304 :: Ref. 1849-12-17, 3:1, M.

On 9th inst., in Lurgan Church, by the Rev. Wm. P. Oulton, Mr. William Belshaw, to Ann, second daughter of Mr. Wm. Ellis, both of Lurgan.

No. 3305 :: Ref. 1849-12-17, 3:1, M.

Dec. 6, Captain Robert Wale, 33d Regt., son of General Sir Charles Wale, K.C.B., Colonel of the 33d Regiment, to Fanny Ann, only child of the late Sir Edward West, Chief Justice of Bombay.

No. 3306 :: Ref. 1849-12-17, 3:1, M.

On 13th inst., in St. Mark's Church, Dublin, Mr. George A. Kennedy, of Dundalk, to Henrietta Flanigan, third daughter of the late Dr. Flanigan, of the 4th Dragoon Guards.

No. 3307 :: Ref. 1849-12-17, 3:1, M.

Long Courtship.—Married, on the 13th instant, in Drumsallen Church, by the Rev. Chas. Waring after a courtship of 20 years, Mr. Henry Dougan, carpenter, to Miss Margaret Rogers, both of Edenderry, near Benburb. The happy couple's united ages number 107 years.

No. 3308 :: Ref. 1849-12-17, 3:1, D.

Dec. 16, at Maguiresbridge, at the residence of his brother, Mr. Jardine Armstrong, of Innishmore, after a tedious and painful illness, which he bore with christian fortitude and resignation to the Divine Will.

No. 3309 :: Ref. 1849-12-17, 3:1, D.

Dec. 12, of fever, in Ship-street Barracks, Dublin, First Lieut. John Henry Payne, 2d Battalion 60th Rifles, aged 26 years.

No. 3310 :: Ref. 1849-12-17, 3:1, D.

July 22, at Parramatta, in his 67th year, Major George Pitt D'Arcy, formerly of the 39th Regt. of Foot.

No. 3311 :: Ref. 1849-12-17, 3:1, D.

Dec. 6, of scarletina, Hessy Foster, second child of the Rev. S.M. Dill, of Hillsborough.

No. 3312 :: Ref. 1849-12-17, 3:1, D.

Dec. 12, at the residence of his brother, Ballyshannon, Mr. Thos. Wood, Enniskillen, merchant.

No. 3313 :: Ref. 1849-12-17, 3:1, D.

Dec. 7, in Cookstown, of scarletina, Mr. James Paul, of the Ulster Bank.

No. 3314 :: Ref. 1849-12-24, 3:1, B.

On 18th inst., at Lurgan, the lady of James Murray, Esq., of a son and heir.

No. 3315 :: Ref. 1849-12-24, 3:1, M.

On 13th inst., in the Presbyterian Church, Ballymagrame, by the Rev. James Bridge, Mr. John Currans, to Miss Sarah Burns, both of Aughnacloy.

No. 3316 :: Ref. 1849-12-24, 3:1, M.

On 19th inst., in Portadown church, by the Rev. Mr. Willis, Mr. John Orr, of Omagh, to Jane Irwin, eldest daughter of Mr Hugh Mathews, Annagh-house.

No. 3317 :: Ref. 1849-12-24, 3:1, M.

On 18th inst., in George's Church, J.J. Burrowes, Esq., of Gloucester-street, to Henrietta, youngest daughter of the late James Sinclair Moore, of Moorebrook, in the co. Armagh, Esq.

No. 3318 :: Ref. 1849-12-24, 3:1, M.

On 18th inst., in Lurgan Presbyterian Church, by the Rev. Thos. Millar, Richard Bell, son of Abraham Bell, of Bellview, County Armagh, Esq., to Margaret, eldest daughter of George Lockhart, of Lurgan, Esq.

No. 3319 :: Ref. 1849-12-24, 3:1, M.

Nov. 30, in Templepatrick Church, by the Rev. Mr. Adair, Mr. Alexander M'Veigh, Belfast, to Agnes, third daughter of Mrs. May, Templepatrick.

No. 3320 :: Ref. 1849-12-24, 3:1, D.

On 20th inst., aged 67, Sarah, relict of the late Davys Bowman, Esq., Carrickfergus.

No. 3321 :: Ref. 1849-12-24, 3:1, D.

On 13th inst., at Lisburn, in the house of her son-in-law, the Rev. Wm. Hoey, Elizabeth, relict of the late Moses Barnett, of Black Causeway, co. Down, aged 68.

No. 3322 :: Ref. 1849-12-24, 3:1, D.

On 18th inst., in his 55th year, the Rev. Richard Olphert, of Charlestown, County Louth. This esteemed gentleman was on a visit with his son, at Mount Shannon, for the last few months, and by the amiableness of his character secured for friendship and respect of all who knew him. His remains were interred in the family vault in the Cathedral burying-place of this city, on Friday last.

No. 3323 :: Ref. 1849-12-31, 3:1, B.

On the 23d inst., at Portadown, the lady of Mr. Joseph Daunts Griffith, Officer of Ireland Revenue, of a son.

No. 3324 :: Ref. 1849-12-31, 3:1, B.

On the 20th inst., at Anglesey Barracks, Portsmouth, the lady of W.W. Bond, Esq., 4th or Kings Own, of twin daughters.

No. 3325 :: Ref. 1849-12-31, 3:1, B.

On the 25th inst., at Dunfanaghy, county Donegal, Mrs. Meredith, the wife of Wm. Meredith, Esq., Sub-Inspector of Constabulary, of a son.

No. 3326 :: Ref. 1849-12-31, 3:1, M.

Dec. 20, in the Presbyterian Church, Middletown, by the Rev. Samuel Hendren, A.M., Mr. John Wallace, jun., Hillhall, to Miss Margaret Steel, Teravera.

No. 3327 :: Ref. 1849-12-31, 3:1, M.

Dec. 34 [sic], in St. Michael's Church, by the Rev. C.S. Strandford, J. Thompson, Esq., of Belfast, to Kate, daughter of the late Rev. M. Lanktree, of the same place.

No. 3328 :: Ref. 1849-12-31, 3:1, M.

Dec. 25, in Providence Chapel, Lurgan, by the Rev. T. Seymour, Lisburn, Mr. Thomas Nicholson, to Mary, second daughter of the Rev. J. Seymour, minister of the Methodist New Connexion, Lurgan.

No. 3329 :: Ref. 1849-12-31, 3:1, M.

Dec. 21, in the Presbyterian Church, Mountnorris, by the Rev. W.H. M'Ewen, Mr. David Low to Miss Mary Wilson, both of Lisdrumwhor.

No. 3330 :: Ref. 1849-12-31, 3:1, M.
Dec. 21, in the Presbyterian Church, Mountnorris, by the Rev. W.H. M'Ewen, Mr. Archibald Irwin, of Keadymore, to Miss Sleith, of Creigance.

No. 3331 :: Ref. 1849-12-31, 3:1, D.
On 21st inst., of scarletina, at Cookstown, Thomas Francis M'Clelland, son to the late Mr. Thos. F. M'Clelland, of Armagh, and stepson to the deceased Mr. James Paul, of the Ulster Bank, aged 14 years. At his own request, his remains were interred in the same grave with his lamented stepfather.

No. 3332 :: Ref. 1849-12-31, 3:1, D.
On 20th inst., in the 26th year of her age, after a long and painful sickness, Eliza Arabella, second daughter of Mr. Matchett, of Ballymoyer.

No. 3333 :: Ref. 1849-12-31, 3:1, D.
At Ballintra, on 6th inst., Miss Rebecca Corscaden, aged 68 years.

No. 3334 :: Ref. 1849-12-31, 3:1, D.
Dec. 20, in Dublin, of inflammation of the chest, Mr. J. M'Cafferty, Printer, aged 24, formerly of Derry.

No. 3335 :: Ref. 1849-12-31, 3:1, D.
Dec. 22, Sarah, wife of F. Fleming, Esq., Monaghan.

No. 3336 :: Ref. 1849-12-31, 3:1, D.
Dec. 24, at Belturbet, Mrs. Donnelly, wife of Mr. John Donnelly, of that town.

No. 3337 :: Ref. 1850-01-07, 2:5, D.
At Enniskillen, on Thursday, the 2d instant, Mrs. Duff, relict of the late Mr. Peter Duff, aged 60. She was a member of the Primitive Wesleyan Society, for upwards of 30 years.

No. 3338 :: Ref. 1850-01-07, 3:4, B.
On 27th ult., at Pluck Mills, near Eglish, the wife of Mr. Francis Donaghey, of a son and heir.

No. 3339 :: Ref. 1850-01-07, 3:4, B.
Jan. 1, at Dungannon, the wife of Mr. Alexander Anderson, merchant, of a son and heir.

No. 3340 :: Ref. 1850-01-07, 3:4, B.
On 31st ult., the wife of Mr. John Doran, Lurgan, of a son.

No. 3341 :: Ref. 1850-01-07, 3:4, B.
On 3d inst., at Portadown, the wife of James Searight, Esq., Solicitor, of a son.

No. 3342 :: Ref. 1850-01-07, 3:4, B.
On 29th ult., the lady of William Uprichard, Gilford, of a daughter.

No. 3343 :: Ref. 1850-01-07, 3:4, M.
On Christmas Day, in Maguires-bridge Presbyterian Church, by the Rev. Mr. M'Williams, the Rev. James Gibson, Senior Minister of Lislooney, near Tynan, to Margaret, relict of the late William Stitt, Esq., of the city of Dublin, Architect and Builder.

No. 3344 :: Ref. 1850-01-07, 3:4, M.
In Moy Church, on Thursday, the 3d inst., by the brother of the bridegroom, the Rev. Richard Wrightson, Perpetual Curate of Moy, to Harriet, youngest daughter of Arthur Nepeean [sic] Wolesworth, Esq., and grand-daughter of the late Captain Hawkins, R.N.

No. 3345 :: Ref. 1850-01-07, 3:4, M.
On 1st inst., in Lurgan Church, by the Rev. W.P. Oulton, Humphrey Sample, Esq., of Kilkenny, to Miss Sweeny, of the Cottage, Lurgan.

No. 3346 :: Ref. 1850-01-07, 3:4, M.
On 31st ult., at Monkstown Church, by the Rev. Henry Stepney, the Rev. William Willoughby Wynne, Vicar of Dromlease, in the diocess of Kilmore, to Sophia, eldest daughter of Colonel Perceval of Temple House, county Sligo.

No. 3347 :: Ref. 1850-01-07, 3:4, M.
On 27th ult., at St. Peter's Church, Dublin, by the Rev. John T. Whitestone, James, eldest son of John Borton, Esq., of Stone-House, co. Dublin, to Catharine Frances, eldest daughter of George Richard Golding, Esq., of Lyme Park Lodge, co. Tyrone.

No. 3348 :: Ref. 1850-01-07, 3:4, M.
On 29th ult., in St. Mary's Church, Donnybrook, by the Rev. Beaver H. Blacker, brother of the bride, Richard Tipping Hamilton, Esq., Poor Law Inspector, Belmullet, co. Mayo, to Anna, eldest daughter of Latham Blacker, Esq., Solicitor of Customs, London.

No. 3349 :: Ref. 1850-01-07, 3:4, M.
On 2d inst., in Alfred-street Church, by the Rev. George Shaw, Mr. Joseph Anderson, of Belfast, to Amelia, fifth daughter [of] Mr. Samuel Jordan, Derrihore, near Dungannon.

No. 3350 :: Ref. 1850-01-07, 3:4, M.
On 3d inst., in St. Anne's Church, by the Rev. T.F. Miller, Vicar of Belfast, Mr. Roger Davies, chief gardener of Lord Gosford, of Markethill, to Jane, second daughter of the late John Mitchell, Esq., Donegall-pass.

No. 3351 :: Ref. 1850-01-07, 3:4, M.
On 26th ult., by the Rev. Charles Flanagan, P.P., Mr. Thomas Burns, Printer, Ballymena, to Eliza, daughter of Mr. John Loughrey, of Coleraine.

No. 3352 :: Ref. 1850-01-07, 3:4, M.
On 26th ult., in the house of the bride's father, by the Rev. Mr. M'Kenna, C.C., Miss Catherine Campbell, of Belfast, to Mr. John Small, of Armagh.

No. 3353 :: Ref. 1850-01-07, 3:4, M.
On 21st ult., in the Scots Church, Derry, by the Rev. James Denham, D.D., Mr. Joseph Stewart, of Strabane, to Eliza, third daughter of Mr. Charles Lake.

No. 3354 :: Ref. 1850-01-07, 3:4, M.

On 3d inst., at Millifont Church, co. Louth, by the Rev. Francis H. Hall, brother-in-law of the bride, the Rev. John Lyle, of Knockintarn, co. Derry, to Elizabeth Anna, third daughter of the late Rev. James M'Creight, Rector of Keady, co. Armagh.

No. 3355 :: Ref. 1850-01-07, 3:4, D.

On Wednesday, 2d inst., at his residence, in Charlemont, Mr. Thomas Bennett, one of the oldest and most respectable inhabitants of that place.

No. 3356 :: Ref. 1850-01-07, 3:4, D.

On 3d inst. at his residence, in Clones, of consumption, George Moore, Esq., M.D., eldest son of the late George Moore, Esq., of Analore Mills, in the 38th year of his age.

No. 3357 :: Ref. 1850-01-07, 3:4, D.

On 1st inst., suddenly, at Dungannon, of disease of the heart, Catharine, the beloved wife of Mr. James M'Clean, coach builder, of same place.

No. 3358 :: Ref. 1850-01-07, 3:4, D.

On 22d ult., at his residence, Fortwilliam, near Portadown, of apoplexy, Captain Robert Williams, late 50th Foot.

No. 3359 :: Ref. 1850-01-07, 3:4, D.

On 25th ult., Ellen, wife of Mr. Robert Mussen, Lisburn, aged 49 years.

No. 3360 :: Ref. 1850-01-07, 3:4, D.

On 23d ult., at Magherafelt, formerly of Rathfriland, in the 38th year of his age, Mr. Richard P. Fisher.

No. 3361 :: Ref. 1850-01-07, 3:4, D.

On 27th ult., in Dublin, James Fenton Lalor, Esq., who had been one of the principal writers in the *Nation* and *Felon* newspapers.

No. 3362 :: Ref. 1850-01-07, 3:4, D.

On 22d ult., the Rev. James Collins, of Minterburn, in the 55th year of his age, and the 21st of his ministry.

No. 3363 :: Ref. 1850-01-07, 3:4, D.

On 31st ult., Mr. James Kennedy, of Lurgan, famed for his good humour, and an inexhaustible fund of wit.

No. 3364 :: Ref. 1850-01-07, 3:4, D.

On 2d inst., at Seaview Cottage, Belfast, Susan, wife of George Thompson, Esq., Solicitor, Banbridge.

No. 3365 :: Ref. 1850-01-07, 3:4, D.

On the 2d inst., at Enniskillen, of scarletina, aged 10-1/2 years, Samuel Wm. Rogers, youngest son of the late William Cooke Rogers, Esq., Proctor.

No. 3366 :: Ref. 1850-01-07, 3:4, D.

Suddenly, on Christmas Day, at the Glebe-house, Kilteevock, the Rev. Thomas Ramsay, incumbent of that parish, aged 60 years.—Although he had felt indisposed on the morning of that day, and had been affectionately solicited by several of his flock to avoid the risk which they feared he should incur by officiating, he nevertheless stood to his post, and without any apparent difficulty, performed all the services. Shortly, however, after his return he expired without a struggle.

No. 3367 :: Ref. 1850-01-07, 3:4, D.

On 27th ult., Mrs. Murphy, Matron of the Cookstown Union Workhouse.

No. 3368 :: Ref. 1850-01-07, 3:4, D.

On 30th ult., at Belfast, of inflammation of the chest, Sophia, relict of the late Mr. Hugh Byrne, formerly of Banbridge.

No. 3369 :: Ref. 1850-01-07, 3:4, D.

On 28th ult., at Arboe Glebe, of consumption, Sarah Elizabeth, wife of Thomas M'Neece, D.D., Rector of Arboe, and Archbishop King's Lecturer in Divinity in the University of Dublin.

No. 3370 :: Ref. 1850-01-07, 3:4, D.

On 28th ult., at 18, Upper Albany-street, London, Ponsonby Tottenham, Esq., fourth son of Lord Robert Ponsonby Tottenham, Lord Bishop of Clogher.

No. 3371 :: Ref. 1850-01-14, 2:3, M.

On 8th inst., in the First Presbyterian Church, Moneymore, Mr. George Ledlie, Merchant, Newry, to Sarah Jane, second daughter of Mr. James Richey, Rockspring, near Moneymore.

No. 3372 :: Ref. 1850-01-14, 2:3, M.

Jan. 3, in Upper Comber Church, by the Rev. Robert Gage, Elizabeth Harriet Browne, second daughter of the late John H. Browne, Esq., of Comber House, to John Willoughby, only surviving son of the late Henry Cole, Esq., Barrister-at-Law.

No. 3373 :: Ref. 1850-01-14, 2:3, M.

Jan. 1, in Portrush Church, by the Rev. Robert Gage, the Rev. Joseph Seymour Eagar, to Alicia Lecky, only child of Staff Surgeon Kendal.

No. 3374 :: Ref. 1850-01-14, 2:3, M.

Jan. 7, at Groswaith Church, Keswick, by the Rev. Edward Wilson, M.A., William Charles, son of William Burgess, Esq., Architect and Contractor, of Dublin, to Anne, eldest daughter of William Foster, Esq., of the firm of Banks, Foster & Co., Greta Works, and Hadds-house, Keswick.

No. 3375 :: Ref. 1850-01-14, 2:3, M.

Dec. 31, by the Rev. Wm. M'Clure, Mr. Joshua Hatrick, of Donelony, to Margaret, eldest daughter of Mr. David Roulstone, of Muff, co. Derry.

No. 3376 :: Ref. 1850-01-14, 2:3, M.

Jan. 3, in Ramelton, by the Rev. James Reid, Mr. William Stewart, Ramelton, to Elizabeth, youngest daughter of the late Mr. Wm. Black, Ballgreen.

No. 3377 :: Ref. 1850-01-14, 2:3, M.

Jan. 9, at Ardbear house, Clifden, co. Galway, John Geraghty, Esq., of Ballyowen, co. Dublin, son of the late Thomas R. Geraghty, Esq., of Dungannon, to Elizabeth Malone, eldest daughter of Samuel Jones, Esq., and grand-daughter of the late Col. John Campbell, R.A.

No. 3378 :: Ref. 1850-01-14, 2:3, M.

Dec. 15, at Corfu, George de la Poer Beresford, Esq., Aide-de-Camp, son of the late Henry Barre Berresford, of Learmount Castle, Londonderry, Esq., to Anne, daughter of Major-General Conyers, commanding the troops in the Ionian Islands.

No. 3379 :: Ref. 1850-01-14, 2:3, D.

Jan. 1, at Drumhillery, near Keady, Mr. Robert Davidson, in the 74th year of his age, an honest man and a sincere christian.

No. 3380 :: Ref. 1850-01-14, 2:3, D.

Dec. 28, at Legmore, Derriaghy, in the 74th year of his age, Mr. Walter Stewart.

No. 3381 :: Ref. 1850-01-14, 2:3, D.

Dec. 28, in the 64th year of her age, Mrs. A. M'Farlan, Postmistress, Gortin.

No. 3382 :: Ref. 1850-01-14, 2:3, D.

Jan. 3, at Drumcondra, near Dublin, Ann, wife of Thomas Graham, late Lieutenant in the Irish Commissariat.

No. 3383 :: Ref. 1850-01-14, 2:3, D.

Jan. 7, the Rev. James Makeown, minister of the Third Presbyterian Congregation, Ballymena.

No. 3384 :: Ref. 1850-01-14, 2:3, D.

Nov. 15, at Sukkur, Upper Scinde, Francis Roger Barnston Napier, Esq., 3d Bombay N.I., aged 21, eldest son of the Hon. Charles Napier.

No. 3385 :: Ref. 1850-01-14, 2:3, D.

Jan. 4, at Ham Green, England, of consumption, Mary Hall, late of Lowtherstown, co. Fermanagh, in her 23d year.

No. 3386 :: Ref. 1850-01-14, 2:3, D.

Jan. 5, at Lurgan, of consumption, Mr. Patrick Magee, auctioneer.

No. 3387 :: Ref. 1850-01-14, 2:3, D.

Jan. 5, aged 16 years, Sarah Kennedy, eldest child of the Rev. H. Wallace, Derry.

No. 3388 :: Ref. 1850-01-14, 2:3, D.

Dec. 30, at Mountpleasant, Ballyconnel, in the eighty-fourth year of his age, Capt. Joseph Benison, J.P., for the counties of Cavan and Fermanagh.

No. 3389 :: Ref. 1850-01-14, 2:3, D.

Near Omagh, on 28th ult., in the 90th year of her age, Elizabeth, relict of the late Andrew Buchanan, of Killyclogher. She spent the last fifty years of her life in widowhood.

No. 3390 :: Ref. 1850-01-14, 2:3, D.

On 5th inst., Daniel John Harley, youngest son of Mr. John John [sic] Harley, Constable, Lisbellaw, aged 15 months.

No. 3391 :: Ref. 1850-01-21, 2:7, D.

Death of the Rev. Dr. Elrington. When we announced in our paper of Monday last, that Dr. Elrington was rapidly recovering from an attack of gout, from which he had been suffering, we little expected that it would be our melancholy duty to record in this day's publication that he is no more. The progress of his recovery was uninterrupted until the evening of Friday last, and in the early part of that day he appeared to be almost quite restored to his usual health. But about six o'clock, alarming symptoms manifested themselves. Doctors Cuming and Kidd were hastily summoned to attend him every aid which medical skill could afford was promptly rendered; but in vain,—and at half-past nine o'clock on Friday night, this Eminent Divine breathed his last. We shall not attempt to write Dr. Elrington's panagirick. His memory needs not any eulogium from our pen. For the last twenty years he has filled the important situation of Regius Professor of Divinity in the University of Dublin; and in the discharge of its responsible duties he not only gained the highest reputation as a learned and orthodox Divine, but conferred the most valuable services on the Church, by sending forth from his school a numerous body of well-taught students. In the generally diffused learning now to be found amongst the clergy of the Established Church of Ireland is the best memorial of Dr. Elrington's labours as a Theologian. Although, in thus speaking, we are by no means unmindful of the valuable publications which he brought out, and especially his editions of the works of Usher. As a Parochial Clergyman, he was ever on the alert to promote what he judged to be most conducive to the interests of religion, and while strenuous in the maintenance of his own sentiments, he was tolerant and liberal towards those who differed from him. The various public charities connected with Armagh will seriously feel the want of his matured experience in conducting their affairs, as well as of his open purse in assisting their funds—and the tenantry of the glebe lands—and the numerous labourers to whom he gave constant employment at the Deanery, will have reason greatly to lament his loss. But to his own family who looked up to him with most affectionate regard, and whom he loved with the fulness [sic] of a parent's heart, this blow has fallen with a severity that has called forth universal sympathy in their sorrows and bereavement. No day has as yet been named for the interment of his remains.

No. 3392 :: Ref. 1850-01-28, 3:3, B.

On the 24th Inst., Mrs. Wiltshire, Beresford Arms, Armagh, of a daughter.

No. 3393 :: Ref. 1850-01-28, 3:3, B.

On the 25th Inst., the wife [of] Mr. Edward Huson, merchant, Dungannon, of a daughter.

No. 3394 :: Ref. 1850-01-28, 3:3, B.

On 14th Inst., at Heynstown Rectory, Co. Louth, the wife of the Rev. A.R. Miller, of a son.

No. 3395 :: Ref. 1850-01-28, 3:3, M.

On 15th inst., in Lurgan Church, by the Rev. W.P. Oulton, Mr. Charles Wright, to Miss Mary Ellis, eldest daughter of Mr. William Ellis, both of Lurgan.

No. 3396 :: Ref. 1850-01-28, 3:3, M.

On 13th inst., in Lisburn Cathedral, by the Rev. E.L. Fitzgerald, Mr. Robert Gile, Newport, to Sarah, only daughter of Mr. Valentine Ellis, Hillsborough.

No. 3397 :: Ref. 1850-01-28, 3:3, M.

At Halverstown, by the Most Rev. Dr. Murray, Luke M'Donnell, Esq., Barrister, to Isabella, daughter of the late Peter Purcell, Esq.

No. 3398 :: Ref. 1850-01-28, 3:3, M.

On 11th inst., at Terling, Essex, by the Rev. R. Drummond, the Rev. Thomas Owens, of Highwood Vicarage, Writtle, youngest son of the late Hugh Owens, of Artigarvan Lodge, co. Tyrone, Esq., to Lucy Pamella Sophia, only child of the late Captain George Francis Lyon, R.N., grand-daughter of Lord Edward Fitzgerald.

No. 3399 :: Ref. 1850-01-28, 3:3, M.

On 10th inst., at Newry, by the Rev. J. O'Neill, Mr. John Quigley, merchant, Castleblaney, to Miss Elizabeth Jennings, third daughter of the late Mr. Francis Jennings, merchant, Newry.

No. 3400 :: Ref. 1850-01-28, 3:3, M.

On 16th inst., in Hathersage Church, England, by the Rev. H. Cottingham, M.A., Vicar, the Rev. Robert John Clarke, M.A., only son of the Rev. A.S. Clarke, M.A., Enniskillen, Ireland, to Matilda, eldest surviving daughter of the late Major Shuttleworth, of Hathersage Hall, Devonshire.

No. 3401 :: Ref. 1850-01-28, 3:3, M.

On 3d ult., at Cincinatti, U.S.A., by the Rev. Wm. Fisher, Mr. Sam Wann, from Markethill, to Jane, only daughter of the late Wm. Gamble, Esq., formerly of Belfast.

No. 3402 :: Ref. 1850-01-28, 3:3, M.

On 17th inst., in Claggin, by the Rev. Henry M'Caw, the Rev. Robert Sinclair, Rushfield, Moneymore, to Mary, third daughter of James Stanton, Esq., Colreagh, Cookstown.

No. 3403 :: Ref. 1850-01-28, 3:3, M.

On 15th inst., in Desertcreat Church, by the Rev. Thomas H. Porter, D.D., Mr. Hamilton Patterson, assistant county surveyor for Tyrone, to Ellen, youngest daughter of Andrew Wilson, Esq., of Allan Rock, Dungannon.

No. 3404 :: Ref. 1850-01-28, 3:3, D.

On 22d inst., aged 14, Joseph, son of Mr. Wm. Murray, of Tagnavin, near Lurgan.

No. 3405 :: Ref. 1850-01-28, 3:3, D.

At Killybegs, after a few hours' illness, John Nolan, Esq., Sub-inspector of Constabulary. Mr. Nolan was for many years in Enniskillen, and was much respected.

No. 3406 :: Ref. 1850-01-28, 3:3, D.

On 16th inst., at Swanlinbar, at the house of his son-in-law, Mr. Wm. Beatty, Robert Armstrong, Esq., late officer of excise, aged 84.

No. 3407 :: Ref. 1850-01-28, 3:3, D.

Jan. 15, in Omagh, Mr. Charles M'Master, aged 54 years.

No. 3408 :: Ref. 1850-01-28, 3:3, D.

Jan. 9, Mr. James M'Cosh, editor and proprietor of the *Inverness Advertiser*, aged 35 years.

No. 3409 :: Ref. 1850-01-28, 3:3, D.

Jan. 10, the Rev. Thomas Rolleston, Curate of Tullaghobegley, in the diocese of Raphoe, aged 64 years.

No. 3410 :: Ref. 1850-01-28, 3:3, D.

Jan. 14, of scarletina, Alithea Maria, infant daughter of Mr. Leonard Dobbin, Botanic-view, Belfast.

No. 3411 :: Ref. 1850-01-28, 3:3, D.

In Ballyshannon, on 14th inst., Rev. Crozier Irvine, after a lingering illness.

No. 3412 :: Ref. 1850-01-28, 3:3, D.

On 11th inst., at the Royal Mews, Pimlico, Stephen Pearce, Esq., for nearly forty years in the department of the Master of the Horse to the Queen.

No. 3413 :: Ref. 1850-01-28, 3:3, D.

Jan. 16, after a long and painful illness, Grace, relict of the late Rev. Dr. Chambers, D.D., LL.D., of Edinburgh.

No. 3414 :: Ref. 1850-01-28, 3:3, D.

Dec. 27, at Funchal, Madeira, James N. Pike, of Beechgrove, Co. Tyrone, aged 82 [32?] years.

No. 3415 :: Ref. 1850-01-28, 3:3, D.

Jan. 20, in Duelin [sic], Mr. Edward Quin, printer, late of London, and formerly of Cork.

No. 3416 :: Ref. 1850-01-28, 3:3, D.

At Aughnacloy, 22d inst., [–]ursilla, relict of the late Dr. William Frederick Speer, aged 78 years.

No. 3417 :: Ref. 1850-01-28, 3:3, D.

On Wednesday last, at the residence of her brother, the Very Rev. Dean Bellew, M.P., Monaghan, aged 70 years, Alice, relict of the late Mr. Philip M'Manns [sic], and mother of Mr. T.B. M'Manus [sic], one of the state convicts.

No. 3418 :: Ref. 1850-01-28, 3:3, D.

On 21st Dec., Samuel, youngest and last surviving child of Mr. Samuel Keightly, of Ballybofey, aged 18 years.

No. 3419 :: Ref. 1850-02-04, 3:2, B.

Jan. 27, at Elm Grove, Ranelagh, the lady of Charles Gavan Duffy, Esq., of a son.

No. 3420 :: Ref. 1850-02-04, 3:2, B.

Jan. 22, at Belturbet, the lady of Richard White O'Donovan, Esq., of a daughter.

No. 3421 :: Ref. 1850-02-04, 3:2, B.

Nov. 26, at Ahmednuggur, Bombay Presidency, the wife of Lieutenant Cornwallis Oswald Mande, 7th Native Infantry, of a son.

No. 3422 :: Ref. 1850-02-04, 3:2, M.

On 22d ult., at Ardcarne Church, co. Roscommon, by Rev. Geo. Griffith, Wm. Wray, Esq., J.P., Oak Park, Letterkenny. co. Donegal, to Anna, eldest daughter of the late Captain Robert Johnston, formerly of the 67th Regiment, Brook Hill, county Leitrim, D.L. and J.P.

No. 3423 :: Ref. 1850-02-04, 3:2, M.

On 22d ult., in St. Mary's Church, by the Rev. Daniel Mooney, Saint George Williams, Esq., Assistant-Surgeon in the Honourable East India Company's service, to Eliza, second daughter of P.O. Brien, Esq., Proprietor of the *Anglo-Celt*, Cavan.

No. 3424 :: Ref. 1850-02-04, 3:2, M.

On 28th ult., at Killaghtee Church, Killybegs, by the Rev. Joseph Walsh, Mr. John Dodd, merchant, Killybegs, to Jane, second daughter of George Murray, Esq., Milltown.

No. 3425 :: Ref. 1850-02-04, 3:2, M.

At Forkhill, by the Rev. Hugh Mulligan, Mr. Robert O'Hanlon, Mullaghbawn, to Catharine, youngest daughter of the late Mr. James Nugent.

No. 3426 :: Ref. 1850-02-04, 3:2, M.

On 11tn [sic] ult., in Ardstraw, by the Rev. Matthew Clarke, Mr. Samuel Semple, to Jane, third daughter of the late Mr. John Henderson, both of Fyfin, near Castlederg.

No. 3427 :: Ref. 1850-02-04, 3:2, M.

A marriage is to take place shortly in the Duke of Manchester's family, the preliminaries being settled for the marriage of Lord Robert Montagu, second son of his grace, and Miss Cromrie, only daughter and heiress of Mr. John Cromrie, of Cromore, county of Antrim, and grand-daughter of Baron Pennefather. It is said the ceremony is to take place in the course of next month.

No. 3428 :: Ref. 1850-02-04, 3:2, D.

Jan. 28, in Moy, of apoplexy, in the 55th year of her age, Lucinda, the beloved wife of Mr. Thomas Peebles, of that place.

No. 3429 :: Ref. 1850-02-04, 3:2, D.

At Fairview, near Richhill, the relict of the late Rev. William Reid.

No. 3430 :: Ref. 1850-02-04, 3:2, D.

Jan. 24, at Manorhamilton, Simon Armstrong, Esq., aged 73 years.

No. 3431 :: Ref. 1850-02-04, 3:2, D.

Feb. 1, at Lurgan, Mr. Samuel Watts, of the firm of Boyd & Watts, brewers, of Lurgan.

No. 3432 :: Ref. 1850-02-04, 3:2, D.

Jan. 23, in Paris, Miss Croly, sister of the Rev. Dr. Croly, Rector of Stephen's Walbroke.

No. 3433 :: Ref. 1850-02-04, 3:2, D.

Jan. 8, at Drumcrew near Lisnaskea, Thomas William Macartney, Esq., aged 32 years.

No. 3434 :: Ref. 1850-02-04, 3:2, D.

Jan. 23d at Grogy, Mr. Wm. Burnside, at the advanced age of 79.

No. 3435 :: Ref. 1850-02-04, 3:2, D.

Jan. 5, at New York, John Howard Kyan, Esq., the inventor of the process for the preservation of timber.

No. 3436 :: Ref. 1850-02-04, 3:2, D.

On 19th ult., at Dunfanaghy, Mr. Robert Wilkison, for 30 years postmaster of that town.

No. 3437 :: Ref. 1850-02-04, 3:2, D.

On 27th ult., at Funchal, Madeira, James N. Pike, Esq., of Beechgrove, co. Tyrone, aged 32.

No. 3438 :: Ref. 1850-02-04, 3:2, D.

At Ballinamallard, on 26th ult., Mr. William Anderson, aged 75 years. Through all his bodily sufferings to the last moment, he was enabled to rejoice in God his Saviour.

No. 3439 :: Ref. 1850-02-04, 3:2, D.

On 29th ult., Mr. James Keenan, of Enniskillen, inn-keeper, and agent for the Dublin and Enniskillen Royal Mail Coach. Mr. Keenan was the Bianconi of that district; his cars and his cattle on the Bundoran road being very superior. Their punctuality as to time, and the extremely obliging disposition of their owner, were among the comforts which rendered a summer stay at the waters of Bundoran a luxury indeed. He has left a deserving wife and five children to deplore his loss.

No. 3440 :: Ref. 1850-02-11, 3:2, B.
Feb. 1, at Dungannon, the lady of James Hamilton, Esq., surgeon, of a son.

No. 3441 :: Ref. 1850-02-11, 3:2, B.
Feb. 3, at Coalisland, co. Tyrone, the lady of Stewart Lecky, Esq., of a daughter.

No. 3442 :: Ref. 1850-02-11, 3:2, M.
On 31st ult, in Castleblayney Church, by the Rev. Alex. Hurst, Rector of the parish, Parker M'Watty, Esq., to Jane, daughter of the late Robert M'Morran, Esq., both of Castleblayney.

No. 3443 :: Ref. 1850-02-11, 3:2, M.
On 5th inst., in St. George's Church, by the Rev. Gibson Black, James O'Crady, Esq., of Mountjoy-square, Dublin, to Anne, daughter of the late James Sinclair Moore, of Moorebrook, Co. Armagh, Esq.

No. 3444 :: Ref. 1850-02-11, 3:2, M.
On 28th ult., at Athlone, by the Rev. Mr. Askin, Curate of Saint Peter's, and afterwards by the Rev. Mr. Fitzgerald, P.P., Kiltoom, Christopher George Plunkett, Esq., J.P., Co. Roscommon, eldest son of the late George Plunkett, Esq., of Mount Plunkett, to Anne, youngest daughter of the late James Sproule, Esq., of Longfield, same county, cousin to the Countess of Argyle, and great-grand niece to Oliver Goldsmith.

No. 3445 :: Ref. 1850-02-11, 3:2, M.
In Swords Church, on 12th Jan., by the Hon. and Rev. Thomas Howard, Rector, Charles, second son of James Whyte, of Pilton House, Devonshire, Esq., to Mabella, relict of the late Daniel Wilson, of Omagh, Esq.

No. 3446 :: Ref. 1850-02-11, 3:2, M.
On 31st ult., in St. Anne's Church, Belfast, by Rev. Theo. Campbell, William Stewart, Esq., Provincial Bank of Ireland, Belfast, to Cecilia, eldest daughter of the late Lieutenant Thomas Hill, R.N.

No. 3447 :: Ref. 1850-02-11, 3:2, M.
Feb. 7, at St. Anne's Church, Dublin, by Rev. D.A. Doudney, of Bonmahon, Co. Waterford, George Frazey Brady, Esq., M.D., of Gweedore, Co. Donegal, eldest son of Hugh Brady, Esq., Lifford, to Fanny, third daughter of the late James Russell, Esq., J.P., of Dunlewey House, Co. Donegal.

No. 3448 :: Ref. 1850-02-11, 3:2, M.
Feb. 6, in St. Peter's Church, by the Rev. W.H. Krauge, Rev. Charles Hort, Chaplain to the Garrison of Dublin, to Allice Carroll, youngest daughter of the late John Egar, Esq., of Tipperary.

No. 3449 :: Ref. 1850-02-11, 3:2, M.
Feb. 7, in St. Mary's Church, Donnybrook, by Rev. J.H. Todd, Michael King, Esq., of Dungiven, Co. Derry, to Jane Stanley, fifth daughter of the late Charles Hawkes Todd, Professor of Anatomy and Surgery in the Royal College of Surgeons, Ireland.

No. 3450 :: Ref. 1850-02-11, 3:2, M.
Feb. 7, at St. Anne's Church, Dublin, by Rev. D.A. Doudney, of Bonmahon, Co. Waterford, John Russell, Esq., third son of the late Thomas Russell, Esq., of Croydon, Surrey, to Henrietta, eldest daughter of the late James Russell, Esq., J.P., of Dunlewey House, Co. Donegal.

No. 3451 :: Ref. 1850-02-11, 3:2, M.
On 5th inst., by Rev. Henry L. St. George, Mr. Thomas Gray to Miss Isabella Gibson, of Togherdoo.

No. 3452 :: Ref. 1850-02-11, 3:2, M.
Jan. 31, at Queenstown church, by Rev. Henry Woodroffe, Geo. Massey, Esq. of Woodfort, Fermoy, to Maria Rebecca, fourth and only surviving daughter of Alexander Boyle, Esq., of Omagh, late Captain in the Tyrone Militia, and Magistrate of that county.

No. 3453 :: Ref. 1850-02-11, 3:2, M.
On 7th inst., in Cavan church, by Rev. Dr. Carson, George Moore, Esq., of Newtownlimavady, Merchant, to Miss Eliza Lowry, of Cavan.

No. 3454 :: Ref. 1850-02-11, 3:2, M.
On 31st ult., at St. Pancras church, London, by Rev. John E. White, M.A., the Rev. Frederick Cashel, M.A., to Sophia Margaret Henrietta Anne Lyle, youngest daughter of the late Very Rev. T. Carter, Dean of Tuam, and Rector of Ballymore.

No. 3455 :: Ref. 1850-02-11, 3:2, M.
On 29th ult., at Kimbolton castle, the marriage between Lady Olivia Montagu, only daughter of his Grace the Duke of Manchester, and Lord Ossulton, son of the Earl and Countess of Tankerville.

No. 3456 :: Ref. 1850-02-11, 3:2, D.
On 6th inst., at Melton, near Kilmallock, Limerick, in the 30th year of her age, Caroline Louisa, the beloved wife of the Hon. Jas. O'Grant, J.P., son of the Earl Seafield, and second daughter of Eyre Evans, Esq., Ash Hill Towers, in that county.

No. 3457 :: Ref. 1850-02-11, 3:2, D.
At Manorhamilton, 2d inst., after a protracted illness, Jane, the beloved wife of Mr. Ennis, architect.

No. 3458 :: Ref. 1850-02-11, 3:2, D.
On 1st inst., at Greenville, co. Cavan, after a short illness, Ellen Martha, daughter of Perrott Thornton, Esq.

No. 3459 :: Ref. 1850-02-11, 3:2, D.
On 5th inst., at Plush, near Butlersbridge, Mr. John Brady.

No. 3460 :: Ref. 1850-02-11, 3:2, D.
On 6th inst., at Seaview cottage, Belfast, George Thompson, Esq., Solicitor, Banbridge.

No. 3461 :: Ref. 1850-02-11, 3:2, D.

On 1st inst., at Springhill House, co. Tyrone, the residence of his brother, the Rev. A.H. Irvine, William, son of the late Gerrard Irvine, Esq., of Rockfield co. Fermanagh, aged 53.

No. 3462 :: Ref. 1850-02-11, 3:2, D.

On the 30th ult., of apoplexy, Charles, eldest son of the late Wm. Blain, Esq., merchant, Killybegs, aged 24 years.

No. 3463 :: Ref. 1850-02-11, 3:2, D.

On 2d inst., at Markethill, Mrs. M'Kee, relict of the late Barnet M'Kee, Esq.

No. 3464 :: Ref. 1850-02-11, 3:2, D.

On 3d inst., Elizabeth, the beloved wife of Dr. Francis Scott, Dundalk.

No. 3465 :: Ref. 1850-02-11, 3:2, D.

On 26th ult., drowned at sea, John Lowry, a native of Moy. Deceased was grandson to the late Archibald Wm. Houston, Esq., of Crossteely, co. Tyrone, and of the Rev. John Lowry, for many years Minister of the Presbyterian congregation of Upper [C]lenaneese, in said county.

No. 3466 :: Ref. 1850-02-11, 3:2, D.

Sarah, Lady of Wm. Grant Broughton, D.D., Lord Bishop of Sydney, and Metropolitan of Australasia. The deceased had gained the love and respect of all around her, and will be long and deeply regretted. She departed this life at Darlinghuish, near Sydney, on Sunday, the 16th September, 1849, aged 66.

No. 3467 :: Ref. 1850-02-18, 2:2, B.

Feb. 12, in St. John's Wood, London, the wife of Mr. Robert Bewglass, of a daughter.

No. 3468 :: Ref. 1850-02-18, 2:2, B.

At Ballyconnell, the lady of Lieutenant Croker, Revenue Police, of a daughter.

No. 3469 :: Ref. 1850-02-18, 2:2, M.

On Thursday, the 14th instant, at Cappagh Church, by the Rev. James Byrne, Rector, James Evans, Esq., Strabane, to Miss Ann Johnston, Omagh, daughter of John Johnston, Esq., Killybrack.

No. 3470 :: Ref. 1850-02-18, 2:2, M.

Feb. 12th, at the Marriage Registrar Office, Stranorlar, by Henry Alexander Wallen, Esq., F.R.C.S., Mr. James Patton, Lettershambo, to Mary, relict of the late Mr. John Humes, Kiltiferigle, county Donegal.

No. 3471 :: Ref. 1850-02-18, 2:2, M.

On the 7th instant, at Wallasey Church, by the Rev. H. Smythe Cumming, Precentor of Down, and Rector of Seaford, John Bateson, of Liverpool, Esq., to Margaret, fourth daughter of the late Nicholas Maine, of Ballymena, Esq.

No. 3472 :: Ref. 1850-02-18, 2:2, D.

Feb. 16, Mary, third daughter of James Bowman, Esq., Manager of Provincial Bank, Armagh, aged 9 years.

No. 3473 :: Ref. 1850-02-18, 2:2, D.

Feb. 16, Miss Anne Maria Galbraith, of Ranfurly Terrace, Dungannon, deeply regretted by all who had the pleasure of her acquaintance.

No. 3474 :: Ref. 1850-02-18, 2:2, D.

Feb. 8, at Derry, Mrs. Denham, relict of the late Rev. Joseph Denham, of Killeshandra.

No. 3475 :: Ref. 1850-02-18, 2:2, D.

Feb. 11, Mr. Joseph Carson, merchant, Omagh.

No. 3476 :: Ref. 1850-02-18, 2:2, D.

Feb. 7, of typhus fever, Sarah, wife of Mr. W.J. Klophel, master of the Omagh union workhouse, aged 40 years.

No. 3477 :: Ref. 1850-02-18, 2:2, D.

Feb. 9, at Monaghan, aged 13, Edward, eldest son of Mr. Peter M'Quaide, merchant of that town.

No. 3478 :: Ref. 1850-02-18, 2:2, D.

Jan. 23, Myreton, N.B., Jean Park, aged 89, relict of Mr. Andrew Thomson, and only snrving [sic] sister of Mungo Park, the African traveller.

No. 3479 :: Ref. 1850-02-18, 2:2, D.

Feb. 11, at Cashel, near Ballyshannon, Mr. Lewis Lipsett, formerly permanent sergeant of the Ballyshannon yeomanry corpse [sic].

No. 3480 :: Ref. 1850-02-18, 2:2, D.

In Ballyshannon, of Scarletina, Sarah and Estephena Fleming, the interesting children of J.C. Fleming, Esq., solicitor.

No. 3481 :: Ref. 1850-02-18, 2:2, D.

Feb. 5, in Ballyshannon, Mathew Davis, Esq., J.P.

No. 3482 :: Ref. 1850-02-18, 2:2, D.

Feb. 5, at Birkenhead, near Liverpool, Ellen Carr, the wife of Richard Battersby, Esq., of Oakfield, near Carrickfergus.

No. 3483 :: Ref. 1850-02-18, 2:2, D.

Feb. 13, at Banagher Glebe, the Rev. Alexander Ross, aged 63.

No. 3484 :: Ref. 1850-02-18, 2:2, D.

Feb. 10, at Cove House, Kingstown, Major Archibald Robertson, unattached, 62 years, deeply lamented by his family and friends.—He entered the army in April, 1809, as Ensign, in the late 94th Regiment, with which he served in the Peninsula from January, 1810, to the end of the war, including the defence of Caditz, from February to September, 1810, where he was employed as an Assistant-Engineer; lines at Torres Vedras, Pombal, Redinha, Cazal Nova, Foz d'Aronce, and Sabugal; battle of

Fuentet d'Onor, siege and assault of Badajoz, battle of Salamanca, advance upon and capture of Madrid, retreat to Portugal, battle of Neville, the Nive, actions of La Bastide, Sauveterra, Vie Bigorre, and Tarbes, battles of Orthes (severely wounded in the left arm) and Toulouse. For these services he received a medal and eight clasps. He had completed nearly forty-one years of military service, of which thirty-two were in full pay employment. Subsequent to the war, he had served with credit, either regimentally or on the staff, in England, Ireland, and the West Indies.

No. 3485 :: Ref. 1850-02-25, 3:3, B.

Feb. 3, at London, the wife of Thomas Bateson, Esq., M.P., of a daughter.

No. 3486 :: Ref. 1850-02-25, 3:3, B.

Feb. 3, at Learmount, the lady of John Barre Beresford, Esq., of a son.

No. 3487 :: Ref. 1850-02-25, 3:3, B.

On 11th inst., at Ballycastle, the wife of Mr. John Ross, tailor, of a son, her 18th child.

No. 3488 :: Ref. 1850-02-25, 3:3, B.

On 17th inst., at Derryvole, Co. Tyrone, the wife of William Pike, Esq., of Parkfield, Birkenhead, of a son.

No. 3489 :: Ref. 1850-02-25, 3:3, B.

On 1st inst., at Bellaghy, Mrs. Andrew Cullen, jun., of a daughter.

No. 3490 :: Ref. 1850-02-25, 3:3, B.

On 16th inst., at Clones, the wife of Mr. Robert Irwin, of a son.

No. 3491 :: Ref. 1850-02-25, 3:3, M.

On the 14th February, at St. Mark's Church, by the Rev. Mr. Sharkey, Jane, youngest daughter of the late David Whyte Wilson, of Money Carragh, co. Down, to Andrew, eldest son of Robert Oliver, of Wexford.

No. 3492 :: Ref. 1850-02-25, 3:3, M.

By Rev. J. Stephens, Miss Carolina Moondooey, near Raphoe, to Mr. Peoples.

No. 3493 :: Ref. 1850-02-25, 3:3, M.

On 23d inst., in St. Anne's Church, by the Rev. Wm. M'Ilwaine, J.E. Thacker, Esq., Proprietor of the *Sligo Guardian*, to Essy, second daughter of Robert Joynt, Esq., Tide Surveyor of H.M.C., of Belfast.

No. 3494 :: Ref. 1850-02-25, 3:3, M.

On 15th inst., at Castlecaulfield, by Rev. Joseph Acheson, Wm. Irwin, Esq., of Donaghmore, co. Tyrone, to Alicia, only daughter of Thomas Anderson, Esq., Castlecaulfield, merchant.

No. 3495 :: Ref. 1850-02-25, 3:3, M.

On 24th inst., in Dublin, by the Venerable the Archdeacon of Dublin, the Rev. Beaver Henry Blacker, eldest son of Latham Blacker, Esq., Solicitor of Customs, London, to Isabella, eldest daughter of the late Martin Brownley Rutherfoord, Esq., of Merrion-square North.

No. 3496 :: Ref. 1850-02-25, 3:3, M.

On 19th inst., at Riverstown Church, by the Rev. Mr. Percival, Jane Henreitta [sic], third daughter of A.B. Cooper, Esq., of Cooper-hill, to Captain A. M'Kinstry, of the 17th Regiment. Immediately after the ceremony the happy couple started off en route for Armagh.

No. 3497 :: Ref. 1850-02-25, 3:3, M.

On 9th inst., Richard Mayberry, Esq., solicitor, second son of the late A. Mayberry, Esq., of Cleedy Cottage, Kenmare, county Kerry, to Kate Maria, eldest daughter of the late Timothy O'Donovan, Esq., of Ardshill-house, and grand-niece to the late Daniel O'Connell, Esq., M.P.

No. 3498 :: Ref. 1850-02-25, 3:3, M.

On the 18th inst., at Castlecaulfield church, by Rev. Robt. Hamilton, Mr. John Kelly, of Parkenore, to Miss Jane Wood Hardwicke, of same place.

No. 3499 :: Ref. 1850-02-25, 3:3, D.

At Caledon, on Tuesday morning, the 19th inst., aged 34 years, Mr. John M'Crum, formerly of Portadown, deeply and deservedly regretted by a very numerous circle of friends and acquaintances, to whom his many amiable qualities had attached. He was an affectionate and kind hearted son, and has left an aged parent to lament and deplore his loss; his remains were removed on Thursday, to the family burying place, St. Mark's, Armagh.

No. 3500 :: Ref. 1850-02-25, 3:3, D.

On 16th inst., at Drumglass House, Tullycullen, near Dungannon, the beloved wife of — Irwin, Esq., deservedly regretted by a numerous circle of friends and acquaintances.

No. 3501 :: Ref. 1850-02-25, 3:3, D.

At Moate, on the 14th inst., Mr. George Gurd, Postmaster, at an advanced age.

No. 3502 :: Ref. 1850-02-25, 3:3, D.

At Clapham, in the 82d year of her age, Anna Elizabeth, relict of the late Walter Synnot, of Ballymoyer, Co. Armagh.

No. 3503 :: Ref. 1850-02-25, 3:3, D.

On 13th inst., at Hensington House, Oxfordshire, Margaret Mary, wife of George W. Bacon, Esq., daughter and co-heiress of the late Robert Ashworth, Esq., formerly of Shirley House, Twickenham, and Merrion-square, Dublin.

No. 3504 :: Ref. 1850-02-25, 3:3, D.

On 16th inst., at Muff, near Cookstown, of water on the brain, Henry Richard, infant son of Dr. A. Hutchinson.

No. 3505 :: Ref. 1850-02-25, 3:3, D.
On 20th inst., of fever, at Fort Frederick, near Ballibay, co. Monaghan, Frederick Rowley, Esq., Mosserath, Kells, co. Meath.

No. 3506 :: Ref. 1850-02-25, 3:3, D.
On 13th inst., at Westbrook House, county of Wicklow, Lieut.-Colonel John Westlake.

No. 3507 :: Ref. 1850-02-25, 3:3, D.
On 17th inst., at Belfast, of scarlet fever, Henry Bremner, second son of Mr. James Strachan, of the Provincial Bank of Ireland.

No. 3508 :: Ref. 1850-02-25, 3:3, D.
On 17th inst., aged 13 years, Jane, eldest daughter of Robert Hassard, Esq., of Parkmore, co. Antrim.

No. 3509 :: Ref. 1850-02-25, 3:3, D.
February 13, John Armstrong, eldest son of the late John Deering, of Derrybrusk, co. Fermanagh, Esq., Q.C.

No. 3510 :: Ref. 1850-02-25, 3:3, D.
Feb. 16, William Richardson, Esq., surgeon, third surviving son of the Rev. John Richardson, Summerhill House, co. Fermanagh.

No. 3511 :: Ref. 1850-02-25, 3:3, D.
On 23d ult., Mr. John Richey, of Carniheny, near Clogher, brother to the late Rev. W. Richey, Methodist preacher.

No. 3512 :: Ref. 1850-02-25, 3:3, D.
21st February, at Monaghan, in his 38th year, Hugh Barclay, Esq., Solicitor, late Sub-Sheriff of that county.

No. 3513 :: Ref. 1850-03-04, 3:1, B.
On the 26th Feb., at Salt Hill Hotel, near Dublin, Emma, (Lady Molyneux), wife of William Edward Fox, Esq., of a son, prematurely.

No. 3514 :: Ref. 1850-03-04, 3:1, B.
On 25th ult., Mrs. William Armstrong, Church-street, Enniskillen, of a son.

No. 3515 :: Ref. 1850-03-04, 3:1, M.
On 26th ult., in Lisnaskea Church, by Rev. John Flanagan, Mr. George Simpson, watchmaker, Lowtherstown, to Margaret, only daughter of Mr. William Henderson, of same place.

No. 3516 :: Ref. 1850-03-04, 3:1, M.
On 8th ult., by Rev. John Johnston, Tullylish, Mr. Andrew Gracey, to Miss Mary Anderson, Hazelbank, near Banbridge.

No. 3517 :: Ref. 1850-03-04, 3:1, M.
In Clones Church, by the Rev. Thomas Hand, Wm. E., youngest son of the late Rev. William Woolsey, Rector of Castlebellingham, to Charlotte Marian, daughter of John Ross, Esq., Captain and Adjutant of the Monaghan Regiment of Militia.

No. 3518 :: Ref. 1850-03-04, 3:1, M.
Feb. 24, by Rev. James Stephens, P.P., Allsaints and Taughboyne, Jane Rogers Duffy, eldest daughter of the late Mr. Anthony Duffy, Newtowncunningham, co. Donegal, to Cornelius Horgan, Civil Engineer, Ordnance Department, Caherciveen, co. Kerry, Esq.

No. 3519 :: Ref. 1850-03-04, 3:1, M.
Feb. 10, at Castlecaulfield Meeting-house, by the Rev. Joseph Acheson, William Irwin, Esq., of Donaghmore, co. Tyrone, to Alicia, only daughter of Thomas Anderson, Esq., Castlecaulfield, Merchant.

No. 3520 :: Ref. 1850-03-04, 3:1, M.
Feb. 28th, in Strabane, by the Rev. W.A. Russell, Mr. John Kirk, of Mountcharles, to Mary Anne, youngest daughter of Mr. Andrew Blair, of Strabane.

No. 3521 :: Ref. 1850-03-04, 3:1, D.
On the 27th ult., in this city, Fanny, the beloved and affectionate wife of Jacob Barrett, Esq., solicitor. Her remains were interred in the Cathedral burying ground, on Saturday, attended by a large and respectable concourse of friends, and inhabitants of the city, who deeply lament the bereavement of the survivor.

No. 3522 :: Ref. 1850-03-04, 3:1, D.
At Hamilton, Upper Canada, on 1st Jan., in the 21st year of her age, the wife of Mr. Robert Parsons, Primitive Wesleyan Minister, and daughter of Mr. Thomas Kidd, boot-maker, Ballymena.

No. 3523 :: Ref. 1850-03-04, 3:1, D.
Feb. 23, in Stephen's-green, Ellen Georgina, the beloved wife of William Deane Butler, Esq., architect.

No. 3524 :: Ref. 1850-03-04, 3:1, D.
In Sligo, the 22d ult., aged 42 years, Agnes, the beloved wife of Mr. N. Arnold, late of Belfast.

No. 3525 :: Ref. 1850-03-04, 3:1, D.
On 23d ult., Rev. John Leslie, of 28, Summer hill, and of Kincraige, Co. Donegal, aged 89.

No. 3526 :: Ref. 1850-03-04, 3:1, D.
At Cavanreagh, near Draperstown, 13th ult., at the advanced age of 100 years, Martha, relict of the late William Philips, Esq., and mother of Rev. James Philips, Presbyterian Minister, Fivemiletown.

No. 3527 :: Ref. 1850-03-04, 3:1, D.
On 16th ult., in Carlow, Bessie, eldest daughter of the Rev. John Holmes, Wesleyan Minister.

No. 3528 :: Ref. 1850-03-04, 3:1, D.
On the 12th ult., at Rahorran, near Fivemiletown, universally regretted, Mary, wife of Mr. George H. Berney, aged 69 years.

No. 3529 :: Ref. 1850-03-04, 3:1, D.
On Monday night last, after a short illness, in his 63d year, Mr. Mossom Hempton, of Derry, bookseller and printer.

No. 3530 :: Ref. 1850-03-04, 3:1, D.
On 19th ult., at Moyaugh, near Rathmelton, Mr. Joseph Williams, aged 72 years.

No. 3531 :: Ref. 1850-03-04, 3:1, D.
On Friday last, after a short illness, at an advanced age, John O'Hagan, Esq., of Inniskeen.

No. 3532 :: Ref. 1850-03-11, 3:6, B.
March 4, in Enniskillen, the wife of George Mahood, Esq., M.D., of a daughter.

No. 3533 :: Ref. 1850-03-11, 3:6, B.
Feb. 27, at Anketell grove, the lady of Mathew John Anketell, Esq., of a son.

No. 3534 :: Ref. 1850-03-11, 3:6, B.
Feb. 28, at Bentinck Terrace, Regent's Park, the lady of B. Halpin, Esq., of a daughter.

No. 3535 :: Ref. 1850-03-11, 3:6, B.
Feb. 22, Mrs. John West, of Pubble, near Tempo, of a son.

No. 3536 :: Ref. 1850-03-11, 3:6, B.
March 6, the lady of the Rev. Wm. Allman, Dunfanaghy, of a son.

No. 3537 :: Ref. 1850-03-11, 3:6, M.
March 7, in Lisburn Presbyterian Church, by the Rev. A. Henderson, Mr. David Cooper of Clinton, Alleghany county, Pennsylvania, to Mary Jane, daughter of the late Mr. Wm. Newell, Lisburn.

No. 3538 :: Ref. 1850-03-11, 3:6, M.
Feb. 21, in the Presbyterian Church, Tullyallan, by the Rev. J.D. Martin, Mr. Andrew Marshall, Caledon, to Eliza, second daughter of Mr. Alexander Mitchel, Cladybeg, near Markethill.

No. 3539 :: Ref. 1850-03-11, 3:6, D.
March 5, at his residence, Ranfurley Terrace, Dungannon, deeply regretted, John Irving, Esq., late Supervisor of Inland Revenue, of that town.

No. 3540 :: Ref. 1850-03-11, 3:6, D.
March 4, of dysentery, Mr. Robert Sproule, Student of Theology, Belfast.

No. 3541 :: Ref. 1850-03-11, 3:6, D.
March 3, at Portadown, after a long illness, the wife of Doctor M'Glaughlan.

No. 3542 :: Ref. 1850-03-11, 3:6, D.
Feb. 28, of decline, at No. 3, New-row, Dublin, Mr. Samuel Ogle, formerly of Dungannon, county Tyrone, aged 26 years.

No. 3543 :: Ref. 1850-03-11, 3:6, D.
At Drumcullion, near Ballinamallard, at an advanced age, Mrs. Whittaker, relict of the late James Whittaker, Esq.

No. 3544 :: Ref. 1850-03-11, 3:6, D.
March 3, in Enniskillen, Mrs. Stephenson, wife of the Rev. Ephraim Stephenson, minister of the Presbyterian congregation.

No. 3545 :: Ref. 1850-03-11, 3:6, D.
Feb. 25, aged 16 years, Miss Eliza Forsythe, youngest daughter of the late Mr. Wm. Forsythe, of Fintona.

No. 3546 :: Ref. 1850-03-11, 3:6, D.
On the 3d inst., at Stewartstown, aged 89 years, Agnes, relict of Thomas [S]peer, Esq., [S]cran, county Tyrone.

No. 3547 :: Ref. 1850-03-11, 3:6, D.
On Friday se'nnight, at the Deanery House, Leighlin-Bridge, the Hon. and Very Rev. the Dean of Leighlin.

No. 3548 :: Ref. 1850-03-18, 3:2, B.
On 15th inst., at Armagh, the lady of Captain Harvey, 57th Regt., of a daughter.

No. 3549 :: Ref. 1850-03-18, 3:2, B.
On 15th inst., at Belnaleck, near Enniskillen, the lady of W.A. Dane, Esq., under-sheriff of co. Fermanagh, of a son.

No. 3550 :: Ref. 1850-03-18, 3:2, B.
On the 9th inst., in English street, Mrs. James M'Mahon, of a daughter.

No. 3551 :: Ref. 1850-03-18, 3:2, B.
March 8, in London, the wife of John Philpot Curran, Esq., Barrister-at-Law, of a son.

No. 3552 :: Ref. 1850-03-18, 3:2, B.
March 11, at Avilly, co. Leitrim, the lady of W.A. O'Brien, Esq., of a son.

No. 3553 :: Ref. 1850-03-18, 3:2, B.
March 8, at the Parsonage, near Kirkcubbin, Mrs. Brett, of a daughter.

No. 3554 :: Ref. 1850-03-18, 3:2, B.
In Philadelphia, Feb. 1st, Mrs. Cairns, wife of Mr. W. Cairns, Manager of the Emigrants' Friend Society, and Agent for the *American Citizen*, of a son.

No. 3555 :: Ref. 1850-03-18, 3:2, M.
In Armagh, on the 14th inst., by the Rev. A. Fleming, Mr. Wm. Morrison, of Downpatrick, to Mary, youngest daughter of the late Mr. A. Hughes.

No. 3556 :: Ref. 1850-03-18, 3:2, M.
March 12, in St. Thomas's Church, Dublin, by the Rev. Thomas Jervis, Incumbent of Middleton, Arthur Dillon, Esq., J.P., eldest son of the late Bartholomew Dillon, of Ballyquin House, county of Kilkenny, Esq., to Anne, daughter of the late Alexander Cross, of Port-Nelligan, county of Armagh, Esq.

No. 3557 :: Ref. 1850-03-18, 3:2, M.
March, 9, at St. George's, Bloomsbury, by the Hon. and Rev. Montagu Villiers, Matthew, son of the late John Cunningham, Esq., Dunevan, Ballymena, county Antrim, to Caroline, eldest daughter of Wm. Milns, Esq., Oval-road, Regent's-park, London.

No. 3558 :: Ref. 1850-03-18, 3:2, M.

March 7, in Killybegs Church, by the Rev. Edward Labatt, Rector of Kilcar, and Chaplain to the Earl of Enniskillen, James Douglas Gilpin, Esq., R.N., to Hannah, eldest daughter of the late James Hamilton, Esq., Fintra House.

No. 3559 :: Ref. 1850-03-18, 3:2, M.

March 8, by the Rev. T. Blackwood Price, of Newtownards, Mr. John Patterson, of Little Francis-street, Newtownards, to Miss Flora M'Kee, of Ballybofey, near Greyabbey. The bridegroom is aged 77, and the bride is aged 60 years.

No. 3560 :: Ref. 1850-03-18, 3:2, M.

On 5th inst., by the Rev. Mr. White, Wm. B. Ritchie, Esq., Mount-pottinger, Belfast, to Jane, eldest daughter of Thomas Hay, Esq., Milford, co. Donegal.

No. 3561 :: Ref. 1850-03-18, 3:2, M.

On 14th inst., at Kilmore church, co. Cavan, by the Rev. G. M'Donald, Mr. Edward Bennitt, of Crossdoney, late of [A]lbany (America), to Miss Mary Lord of Crossdoney.

No. 3562 :: Ref. 1850-03-18, 3:2, M.

On 8th inst., at Ballinode Church, by the Rev. G. Young, Thos. Connor Sterne, Esq., Ulster Bank, Cootehill, to Attilia Anne, relict of the late Mr. John Hamilton, Newgrove, Monaghan.

No. 3563 :: Ref. 1850-03-18, 3:2, M.

On 6th inst., in Newry, by the Rev. John Moran, Mr. Henry Peel, of Armagh, to Margaret, only daughter of the late Mr. John M'Culla, of Armagh.

No. 3564 :: Ref. 1850-03-18, 3:2, D.

On the 14th inst., in this city, the wife of Mr. Bernard O'Neil, Victualler.

No. 3565 :: Ref. 1850-03-18, 3:2, D.

At Barton-under-Needwood, Mary, sixth daughter of the late Jonathan Peel, Esq., of Accrington House, Lancashire, and cousin of the Right Hon. Sir Robert Peel.

No. 3566 :: Ref. 1850-03-18, 3:2, D.

At Lisburn, John French, Esq., late of the Royal Exchange, London.

No. 3567 :: Ref. 1850-03-18, 3:2, D.

On 12th inst., after a short illness, Mr. Wm. Fox, formerly of Dungannon, salesman of clocks for a number of years in Belfast.

No. 3568 :: Ref. 1850-03-18, 3:2, D.

At Strabane, Ann, the youngest daughter of the late Mr. William Hamilton, merchant.

No. 3569 :: Ref. 1850-03-18, 3:2, D.

On 12th inst., Mr. Thomas Guthridge, sen., of Nursery Park, near Enniskillen, in the 99th year of his age. He was a member of the Wesleyan Methodist Society for nearly 60 years.

No. 3570 :: Ref. 1850-03-18, 3:2, D.

March 6, at Belfast, Helen Elizabeth, eldest daughter of J. Strachan, Esq., of the Provincial Bank of Ireland.

No. 3571 :: Ref. 1850-03-18, 3:2, D.

March 9, of acute inflammation of the lungs, brought on by a neglected cold, Wm. Henry, second son of Charles Scott, Esq., J.P., of Straghery, co. Tyrone, aged 18 years.

No. 3572 :: Ref. 1850-03-18, 3:2, D.

March 9, Wm. Watson, aged 45 years, an active and useful leader in the Wesleyan Methodist Society. The brethren of Orange Lodge 672, of which he was a member, paid the last tribute of respect to the worth of their departed brother, by following his remains to their resting-place.

No. 3573 :: Ref. 1850-03-18, 3:2, D.

At Castleblayney, on 7th inft. [sic], Abigall, the beloved and amiable wife of Doctor M'Birney.

No. 3574 :: Ref. 1850-03-18, 3:2, D.

On 10th inst., at Carne Cottage, co. Cavan, aged 25, Sarah, fourth daughter of the late James Christian, Esq., Sligo.

No. 3575 :: Ref. 1850-03-18, 3:2, D.

On 15th inst., at Botanic-view, of consumption, Margaret, wife of Mr. Wm. M. Barkley, Belfast.

No. 3576 :: Ref. 1850-03-18, 3:2, D.

On 10th inst., Mrs. Mary Ross, daughter of the late Mr. M'Bride, of Sligo.

No. 3577 :: Ref. 1850-03-18, 3:2, D.

March 13th, at Longford Lodge, near Kingstown, Richard Cooper, Esq., of Dunboden Park, brother to E.J. Cooper, Esq., of Markree Castle. He is succeeded in his estate by his son, a Captain in the 7th Hussars.

No. 3578 :: Ref. 1850-03-25, 3:3, B.

March 22, at Loughbawn, co. Monaghan, the Lady of John Harvey Adams, Esq., of a son.

No. 3579 :: Ref. 1850-03-25, 3:3, B.

On 2d inst., in Dublin, the wife of George Hall Stack, Esq., Barrister at Law, of a son.

No. 3580 :: Ref. 1850-03-25, 3:3, M.

March 16, by the Rev. William Bourne, Rector of Rathcormac, J. Florence Murray, Esq., Captain 73d Regiment, son of the late Lieutenant-General John Murray, to Marianne, relict of Lieutenant J.L. Hendley, H.E.I.C.S., and eldest daughter of the Venerable Archdeacon Ryder.

No. 3581 :: Ref. 1850-03-25, 3:3, M.

March 20, in St. Peter's Church, Dublin, by the Rev. William Gabbett, Prebendary of Ballyhooly, Henry R. Crofton, Esq., R.N., to Elizabeth, second daughter of the Rev. Doctor Singer, Regius Professor of Divinity, T.C.D.

No. 3582 :: Ref. 1850-03-25, 3:3, M.
March 20th, at St. John's Church, Sligo, by the Rev. A. Robinson, Marmaduke Richard Eyre, Esq., son of John Eyre, of Eyrecourt Castle, Galway, Esq., to Elizabeth Jane, youngest daughter of the late Andrew Doughlas [sic] Johnston, of Friarstown House, county Leitrim, Esq.

No. 3583 :: Ref. 1850-03-25, 3:3, M.
March 19, in St. Mary's Church, Newry, by the Rev. W.R. Williams, William Fleming, only surviving son of the late Captain Fleming M'Neill, to Mary Ann, daughter of the late Mr. John Frazer, both of Newry.

No. 3584 :: Ref. 1850-03-25, 3:3, M.
March 21, in the Reformed Presbyterian Church, Linen-hall-street, Belfast, by the Rev. Jacob Alexander, of Londonderry, Mr. Alexander M'Vicker, Londonderry, to Miss Sarah Cole, only daughter of the late Mr. William Cole, of Belfast.

No. 3585 :: Ref. 1850-03-25, 3:3, D.
At Davenport, North America, on the 9th February, Hamilton Vance Wallace, Esq., eldest son of the late Alexander Wallace, of Russell-place, Newtownards.

No. 3586 :: Ref. 1850-03-25, 3:3, D.
At Richhill, 24th inst., of fever, Mr. William Hardcourt, aged 30 years.

No. 3587 :: Ref. 1850-03-25, 3:3, D.
On 17th inst., at a very advanced age, at her residence, [C]larendon place, Belfast, Isabella, relict of the late Mr. Andrew Fulton, of Lisburn.

No. 3588 :: Ref. 1850-03-25, 3:3, D.
March 8, at Bath, after a lingering illness, Staff surgeon Griffith Jones, late of the 44th and 58th Regiments.

No. 3589 :: Ref. 1850-03-25, 3:3, D.
March 17, at Westport, Richard Levingston, Esq., at the advanced and unusual age of 100 years.

No. 3590 :: Ref. 1850-03-25, 3:3, D.
On 17th inst., of consumption, after a lingering illness, which she bore with Christian resignation, Eliza Johnston, the beloved wife of Mr. Mountgarrett, Rosville-street [sic], Derry.

No. 3591 :: Ref. 1850-03-25, 3:3, D.
On 13th inst., four days after the birth of her daughter, at Monellan, in the county of Donegall, the seat of the Rev. Robert Delap, the Lady Mary Hewitt, the beloved wife of the Hon. James Hewitt, of Munglas, in the same county, and eldest daughter of the late Earl of Gosford.

No. 3592 :: Ref. 1850-03-25, 3:3, D.
On 18th inst., at Omagh, after a lingering illness, Jane, the beloved wife of Mr. William Skelton.

No. 3593 :: Ref. 1850-03-25, 3:3, D.
March 14, at an advanced age, Dinagh, relict of the late Charles Atkinson, Esq., of Ballintain, co. Sligo.

No. 3594 :: Ref. 1850-03-25, 3:3, D.
On 19th inst., Mr. Benjamin Thompson, of Knocknashane, near Lurgan.

No. 3595 :: Ref. 1850-03-25, 3:3, D.
On the 20th inst., the wife of Mr. Francis O'Hara, of Lurgan.

No. 3596 :: Ref. 1850-03-25, 3:3, D.
March 17, Thomas Taylor, Esq., Cashier of the Hibernian Bank.

No. 3597 :: Ref. 1850-04-01, 3:2, B.
On 29th ult., at Stephen's-green, Dublin, the lady of Robert Burrows, Esq., of Stradone House, co. Cavan, of a daughter.

No. 3598 :: Ref. 1850-04-01, 3:2, B.
On 29th inst., Mrs. James Matchett, of the Albert Hotel, of a daughter.

No. 3599 :: Ref. 1850-04-01, 3:2, B.
On 26th inst., Mrs. Patrick Kearney, of a daughter.

No. 3600 :: Ref. 1850-04-01, 3:2, B.
March 15, at Louth Hall, Lady Louth, relict of Lord Louth, of a daughter.

No. 3601 :: Ref. 1850-04-01, 3:2, B.
March 24, at Killukin Rectory, the lady of the Venerable the Archdeacon of Elphin, of a daughter.

No. 3602 :: Ref. 1850-04-01, 3:2, B.
On 21st inst., the lady of Wm. Keown, Esq., Ballydugan House, co. Down, of a son.

No. 3603 :: Ref. 1850-04-01, 3:2, B.
On 23d ult., Mrs. Bell, wife of Mr. Matthew Bell, of a daughter.

No. 3604 :: Ref. 1850-04-01, 3:2, B.
On 25th ult., at Parkview, near Tandragee, the lady of Rev. R. Johnston of a son.

No. 3605 :: Ref. 1850-04-01, 3:2, M.
At the Officers' quarters, Ayr barracks, on the 18th ult., current by the Rev. John [S]tevenson Colmonell, Mr. James Rankin Alexander, ship-broker, Dublin, to Emma Matilda, youngest daughter of Captain William Buchanan, and Niece of Mr. R. Buchanan, late Ordnance Department, Armagh.

No. 3606 :: Ref. 1850-04-01, 3:2, M.
On 21st ult., in the First Presbyterian Church, Strabane, by the Rev. A.P. Goudy, Mr. Robert M'Kinley, of Lisnabert, to Alice, daughter of Mr. Archibald M'Crea, Strabane.

No. 3607 :: Ref. 1850-04-01, 3:2, M.
March 21, in the Parish Church of Feltwell, by the Rev. John William D'Evelyn, A.M., *(continued...)*

No. 3607, continued: ...Rector of Stanford, John Johnston, Esq., of Weaken Hall, Cambridgeshire, to Mary Sophia, only daughter of James Debenham, Esq., of Manor House, Feltwell, Norfolk.

No. 3608 :: Ref. 1850-04-01, 3:2, M.
In Drogheda, on the 26th inst., Mr. Alexander M'Doughall, proprietor of the *Drogheda Conservative Journal*, to Miss Latimer.

No. 3609 :: Ref. 1850-04-01, 3:2, M.
March 21, at St. Peter's Church, by the Rev. Henry Vere White, Samuel Russell, Esq., of Strawberry Lodge, county Kildare, to Susan Evelina, eldest daughter of Edward Manders, Esq., Manders-Terrace, Ranelagh.

No. 3610 :: Ref. 1850-04-01, 3:2, M.
On 21st ult., in Clogher Presbyterian church, by the Rev. J.R. Dill, Archibald Warnock, Esq., Tullaclena House, parish of Dromore, to Mary Jane, relict of Thomas Gillis, Esq., of Monaghan.

No. 3611 :: Ref. 1850-04-01, 3:2, D.
On 30th inst., Rosanna, eldest daughter of Mrs. Vallely, Armagh, in the 14th year of her age.

No. 3612 :: Ref. 1850-04-01, 3:2, D.
March 24, at Rockhill, Letterkenny, county Donegal, the residence of his brother, Alexander Robert Stewart, Esq., of Ards House, J.P. and D.L., and for many years representative of the county of Londonderry, aged 55 years.

No. 3613 :: Ref. 1850-04-01, 3:2, D.
March 22, at Walsall, Staffordshire, in the 81st year of his age, General Charles Craven, of Richardstown, county Louth, formerly of the 5th Dragoon Guards.

No. 3614 :: Ref. 1850-04-01, 3:2, D.
March 24, in the prime of life, Sophia, lady of John B. Beresford, Esq., of Learmount Castle, co. Derry, daughter of the late Hugh Lyons Montgomery, Esq., of Lawrencetown House, and niece to Col. Blacker, of Carrick.

No. 3615 :: Ref. 1850-04-01, 3:2, D.
March 24, at Birkenhead, James Dwyer, Esq., late of Mountjoy-square, Dublin, Barrister-at-Law, Q.C.

No. 3616 :: Ref. 1850-04-01, 3:2, D.
March 26, at his residence, 34, Aungier-street, after a painful and lingering illness, Doctor Robert Healy, for nearly fifty years a practitioner, in Dublin.

No. 3617 :: Ref. 1850-04-01, 3:2, D.
On 29th ult., at the house of his cousin, Mr. John Baird, Ballymena, Mr. H. Hardy, aged 29 years.

No. 3618 :: Ref. 1850-04-08, 3:1, B.
On 28th ult., at Paradise Cottage, Queen-street, Montrose, the wife of James Strachan, Esq., Inspector of Branches of the Provincial Bank of Ireland.

No. 3619 :: Ref. 1850-04-08, 3:1, M.
On 3d inst., in Cucklehill, Presbyterian Meeting-house, by the Rev. Wm. Henry, Mr. James Rolston, jun., of Ross View Cottage, near Charlemont, to Margaret, third daughter of Mr. W. Brownlee, of Kinnego.

No. 3620 :: Ref. 1850-04-08, 3:1, M.
In Pettigo church, by the Rev. A.V. Watson, A.M., Edmund Atkin, fourth son of Alex. Murray, Esq., Ballinassagart, county Tyrone, to Marrianne, second daughter of Liddle Baxter, Esq., Rock Park, co. Donegall.

No. 3621 :: Ref. 1850-04-08, 3:1, M.
At St. Paul's Chapel, on 2d inst., by the Right Rev. the Bishop of Edinburgh, James Connell, Esq., of Lonninghead, county of Cumberland, to Harriet Elizabeth; and at the same time and place, Thomas Hobbs, Esq., Royal North British Fusiliers, to Mary Alicia, daughters of James Connell, Esq., Longwood, Langholm.

No. 3622 :: Ref. 1850-04-08, 3:1, M.
On 2d. inst., in Limerick, by the Lord Bishop of the diocese, the Rev. Robert Mandeville Rodwell, Esq., Rector of Newcastle, county Limerick, to Mary, third daughter of the Bishop of Limerick.

No. 3623 :: Ref. 1850-04-08, 3:1, M.
March 31, at Dungannon, in the first Presbyterian meeting-house, by the Rev. Charles Lucas Morell, Mr. Alex. Kay, to Catherine, widow of the late Mr. Thomas M'Adam, druggist, of Dungannon.

No. 3624 :: Ref. 1850-04-08, 3:1, D.
On 5th inst., at Ballymena, Sarah, second daughter of Joseph M'Kee, Esq., formerly of Tassagh, co. Armagh.

No. 3625 :: Ref. 1850-04-08, 3:1, D.
On 5th inst., at Cladybeg, near Markethill, Mr. Alex. Mitchell, for many years High Constable in this county.

No. 3626 :: Ref. 1850-04-08, 3:1, D.
On 28th ult., Sarah, the beloved wife of Mr. John Tuft, Edenderry, Loughbrickland.

No. 3627 :: Ref. 1850-04-08, 3:1, D.
On 27th ult., at Magheraglass, near Cookstown, Mr. Wm. Cluff, aged 44 years.

No. 3628 :: Ref. 1850-04-08, 3:1, D.
On 30th ult., at his residence, Ballyho Bridge, near Clones, of effusion of blood on the brain, the Rev. Matthew Clarke, Presbyterian Minister of the above congregation.

No. 3629 :: Ref. 1850-04-08, 3:1, D.
March 12, at St. John's N.B., after a short but severe illness Mr. James Wright, a native of Armagh, Ireland, aged 37 years.

No. 3630 :: Ref. 1850-04-08, 3:1, D.

On 28th ult., at Dungannon, of consumption, Francis, son of Mr. John Hagan, aged nine years.

No. 3631 :: Ref. 1850-04-08, 3:1, D.

Feb. 7, of scarlatina, Elizabeth, aged three years; and on March 31st William Stewart, aged 11 years, the beloved children of John Craig, jun., Esq., of Killygordon, co. Donegal.

No. 3632 :: Ref. 1850-04-08, 3:1, D.

March 30, at Dublin, Bess Jane, relict of John Kirwood, of Newry, aged 56 years.

No. 3633 :: Ref. 1850-04-08, 3:1, D.

The Earl of Macclesfield died on the 31st ult., at Entham-hall, Oxfordshire, in his 87th year.

No. 3634 :: Ref. 1850-04-08, 3:1, D.

March 29, in Lesson-street, Dublin, aged 65 years, Rebecca, eldest daughter of the late Rev. Robert Thompson, formerly of Trillick, co. Tyrone.

No. 3635 :: Ref. 1850-04-15, 3:2, B.

On 7th inst., at Lurgan, the wife of John Cuppage, Esq., of a son.

No. 3636 :: Ref. 1850-04-15, 3:2, B.

On 4th inst., at Fortfield House, Rathfarnham, the lady of Wm. Humphrys, of Ballyhaise House, [co. C]avan, of a daughter.

No. 3637 :: Ref. 1850-04-15, 3:2, B.

On 24th March, at Drumshambo, county of Leitrim, the lady of the Rev. John Bagley, Wesleyan Minister, of a son.

No. 3638 :: Ref. 1850-04-15, 3:2, B.

On 7th inst., at Clara, Mrs. John Armstrong, of a daughter.

No. 3639 :: Ref. 1850-04-15, 3:2, M.

On 9th inst., in the Second Presbyterian Church of Armagh, by the Rev. S. Edgar, D.D., Mr. H. Garmoney, of Naul, to Miss E. Thompson, of Tullnageer.

No. 3640 :: Ref. 1850-04-15, 3:2, M.

On 2d inst., at the house of the lady's brother-in-law, Mr. P. M'Quade, Mr. Matthew Rush, Monaghan, to Alicia, youngest daughter of the late Edward Carolan, Esq., Carrickmacross.

No. 3641 :: Ref. 1850-04-15, 3:2, M.

At Omagh church, on 11th inst., by the Rev. W.N. Thompson, Henry, second son of Mr. John M'Kenny, of Omagh, to Mary Anne, sixth daughter of Mr. John M'Farland, also of Omagh.

No. 3642 :: Ref. 1850-04-15, 3:2, M.

April 8, in St. Mary's, Bryanston-square, London, by the Lord Bishop of Down and Connor, the Very Rev. H.B. Knox, co-Dean of Bockin, and second son of the late Right Hon. George Knox, to Elizabeth Jane, eldest daughter of Rear-Admiral the Hon. E.S.P. Knox, and niece of the Earl of Ranfurly.

No. 3643 :: Ref. 1850-04-15, 3:2, M.

On 4th inst., at the Cathedral, Derry, by the Rev. George Smith, John C. Lepper, Esq., eldest son of Robert Lepper, Esq., Foyle View, county Donegal, to Eliza, second daughter of the late George Bradley, Esq., of Omagh.

No. 3644 :: Ref. 1850-04-15, 3:2, M.

On 5th inst., in St. Thomas's Church, Dublin, by the Rev. James Franks, John Thomas Holland, Esq., of Bellevu, co. Monaghan, to Eliza, eldest daughter of the late John Crawley, Esq., of Raphoe.

No. 3645 :: Ref. 1850-04-15, 3:2, M.

On 11th inst., in the First Presbyterian Church of Londonderry, by the Rev. William Browne, of Buncrana, Thomas Davis, Esq., M.D., Manor-hamilton, to Alice, youngest daughter of the late Samuel Haslett, Esq., Foyle-view, Derry.

No. 3646 :: Ref. 1850-04-15, 3:2, M.

April 9, at Drumbanagher church, by the Very Rev. the [D]ean of Ross, Andrew Borton, Esq., Major in the 9th Regiment, to Caroline Mary Georgina Close, only child of the Rev. J.F. Close, of Morne Rectory, Kilkeel, co. of Down.

No. 3647 :: Ref. 1850-04-15, 3:2, M.

April 8, at St. Peter's, Dublin, by the Rev. Edward Metcalf, Christopher Bagot, Esq., Professor of Civil Engineering, Queen's College, Cork, to Emily Henrietta, eldest daughter of the late Rev. Joshua Story, of Bingfield, county Cavan.

No. 3648 :: Ref. 1850-04-15, 3:2, D.

We regret to record the death of Elizabeth, the beloved wife of Mr. Joseph Porter, of Clones, county Monaghan, which was occasioned by illness she suffered under for many years past, and had borne with christian patience to her last moments. The solemn event took place at the residence of her husband, on the 8th inst., in the 48th year of her age. She was [the] youngest daughter of the late Mr. Alexander Wylie, of Kilwinning, in Ayrshire, Scotland. She came to Clones in the year 1839, and assisted in teaching the system of muslin embroidery (a system almost unknown there at that time,) she was most persevering in her endeavours to have that system enforced; and was then employed as agent by the well known respectable warehouse of Messrs. Hugh Brown & Co., Glasgow, who supplied her with work for the girls so instructed. Mrs. Porter carried on this business ever since, to the entire satisfaction of the company, and paid close on £10,000 for work done in that town and neighbourhood, by females who we doubt not would have been   *(continued...)*

No. 3648, continued: ...otherwise unemployed. There are other agents who have been employed by various houses giving out work in the same town these few years past, so that we may venture to say they have unitedly paid close on a similar sum. She was favoured with religious parents, who instructed her in the great truths of christianity; and through whose instrumentality, together with religious friends and acquaintances, she became pious at a very early period, and persevered steadily in this good path to the end of her life. She died rejoicing in the hope of a glorious immortality. During her life she was respected by all her acquaintances in both countries, and her death has caused sorrow amongst a numerous circle of friends and mourning relatives.—*Communicated.*

No. 3649 :: Ref. 1850-04-15, 3:2, D.
Suddenly, on 6th inst., at his residence, Lurgaboy, Mr. John Scott, aged 64 years, regretted by a numerous circle of friends and acquaintances.

No. 3650 :: Ref. 1850-04-15, 3:2, D.
On 9th inst., at Lifford Common, Jane, wife of Mr. William Cather.

No. 3651 :: Ref. 1850-04-15, 3:2, D.
On 31st., of disease of the heart, Robert Forrester, Esq., late proprietor of Cloverhill, &c. This deeply lamented husband, and father of six surviving children, was long suffering under affliction, by the bereavement of two promising children, the loss of health, and worldly advantages; to which, by the grace of God he became resigned to. Under the spiritual guidance of the Rev. Spenser Knox, he received the cup of salvation. Mr. Forrester's maternal relations are of the highest families in the counties Donegal and Tyrone. At Malross, on the river Tweed or Muris, the Rev. Alexander Forrester possessed an estate of £3,000 a-year. At the time of the persecution of the Clergy in Scotland by the Covenanters, he had to fly from his family estate, being a Clergyman of the Church of England. He came to Ireland, and served as Curate in the Cathedral Church of St. Columbs, in Londonderry, from the Scotch rebellion until after the siege of Derry, in 1688, when he was appointed Rector of Aughdoey. He married in Coleraine, Mary, daughter of Alderman Arthur Church. His son was William Forrester, Alderman of the Corporation of Coleraine, and his son Arthur, a Burgess. Robert Forrester, his second son, was grandfather of the late Robt. Forrester, and the purchaser of Cloverhill, the present family residence. The original records of this ancient Protestant family are to be found in the Cathedral of Londonderry.

No. 3652 :: Ref. 1850-04-15, 3:2, D.
April 7, in Donegal, at an advanced age, Rev. William Guard, Wesleyan Minister.

No. 3653 :: Ref. 1850-04-15, 3:2, D.
On 27th ult., at Magheraglass, near Cookstown, Mr. William Cluff, aged 44 years.

No. 3654 :: Ref. 1850-04-15, 3:2, D.
On 30th of March, in Ballyshannon, Mr. John M'Donagh, sen., merchant, who during his life (75 years), maintained a character worthy of imitation.

No. 3655 :: Ref. 1850-04-15, 3:2, D.
At Dawson Street, Dublin, Bigoe, second son of Gorges Henzell, Esq., late of Drumshallon, in the County of Louth, grandson of the Rev. Doctor Bigoe Henzell, L.L.D., Rector of Dunshaughlin, co. of Meath, and nephew of the late Rev. Dr. Bigoe Henzell, Rector of Kilmanhan, County of Cork, Diocese of Cloyne, Chaplain to the most noble the Marquis of Thormond.

No. 3656 :: Ref. 1850-04-15, 3:2, D.
At Dunboe Rectory, on Easter Day, aged 13, Elizabeth Hayden, daughter of the Venerable the Archdeacon of Derry.

No. 3657 :: Ref. 1850-04-15, 3:2, D.
On 4th inst., in the 86th year of her age, at the house of her son-in-law, Mr. Flanagan, Jane, relict of the late Mr. John Evans of Strabane.

No. 3658 :: Ref. 1850-04-15, 3:2, D.
On 23d March, of consumption, Isabella, aged 14, eldest daughter of John Wilson, Esq., Cavan.

No. 3659 :: Ref. 1850-04-15, 3:2, D.
On 30th ult, in Castleblaney, Mr. John Smith, in the 72d year of his age. He was for many years coach-agent in that town.

No. 3660 :: Ref. 1850-04-15, 3:2, D.
On 4th inst., at the residence of his brother, Ballymoney, John Creer, Esq., eldest son of the late John Creery, Esq., of Orange-hill, Tandragee, in his thirty eighth year.

No. 3661 :: Ref. 1850-04-15, 3:2, D.
On 6th inst., at Derry, Margaret, relict of the late James Loudon, Esq., Purser, Royal Navy.

No. 3662 :: Ref. 1850-04-15, 3:2, D.
On 5th inst., at Ely-place, Emily Kingsbury, relict of the late Venerable Thomas Kingsbury, Archdeacon of Killala, and only daughter of Sir Kildare Dixon Borrowes, of Gilltown, in the co. of Kildare, Bart.

No. 3663 :: Ref. 1850-04-15, 3:2, D.
On 7th inst., in the 32d year of his age, Abraham Walker, of Callan Lodge, Loughgall.

No. 3664 :: Ref. 1850-04-22, 3:2, B.
In English-street, on Wednesday last, Mrs. White, wife of Mr. Samuel White, Bookseller, of a daughter.

No. 3665 :: Ref. 1850-04-22, 3:2, B.
On 14th inst., the wife of Mr. Wm. Mahaffy, of Lurgan, of a son.

No. 3666 :: Ref. 1850-04-22, 3:2, B.

At Dingledycooch Lodge, Bundoran, co. Donegal, the lady of John Allingham, Esq., of a daughter.

No. 3667 :: Ref. 1850-04-22, 3:2, B.

On 15th inst., at Clover Hill, Boyle, county Roscommon, the lady of Thomas Cox, jun., Esq., of a son.

No. 3668 :: Ref. 1850-04-22, 3:2, B.

On 16th inst., at Brandrum House, co. Monaghan, the lady of Thomas Coote, Esq., D.L., of a son.

No. 3669 :: Ref. 1850-04-22, 3:2, B.

At Parsonstown, on 7th inst., the lady of Francis H. Sheilds, Esq., proprietor of the *Kings' County Chronicle*, of a son.

No. 3670 :: Ref. 1850-04-22, 3:2, M.

On 13th inst., at St. Peter's Church, Dublin, by the Very Rev. the Dean of Leighlin, George M'Clintock, Esq., Captain in the 52d Light Infantry, to Catherine, youngest daughter of Sir James M. Stronge, Bart., of Tynan Abbey, county Armagh.

No. 3671 :: Ref. 1850-04-22, 3:2, M.

On 12th inst., in St. Anne Church, Dungannon, by the Rev. Wm. Quain, rector of Drumglass, W.E. Young, Esq., of Belfast, to Elizabeth, second daughter of the late Wm. Dawson, Esq., M.D., of Dungannon.

No. 3672 :: Ref. 1850-04-22, 3:2, M.

On 11th inst., at Newtownlimavady, by the Rev. Robert Gage, M.A., Thomas Tertius, eldest son of Thomas Paget, Esq., of Humstone, co. Leicester, to Katherine Geraldine, fourth daughter of Marcus M'Causland, Esq., of Fruit Hill, co. Derry.

No. 3673 :: Ref. 1850-04-22, 3:2, M.

On 14th inst., by the Rev. James Kelly, C.C., Mr. Patrick M'Ilroy, of Millbrook, to Ann, youngest daughter of Mr. Patrick Kelly, Mossview House, Emyvale, co. Monaghan.

No. 3674 :: Ref. 1850-04-22, 3:2, M.

On 11th inst., in Magheragal Church, by the Very Rev. the Dean of Ross, Jonathan Richardson, Esq., of Glenmore, to Louisa Jane, second daughter of Richard Rollo Houghton, Esq., of Springfield.

No. 3675 :: Ref. 1850-04-22, 3:2, M.

In St. John's Church, Sligo, Neptune Blood Galleway, son of the late Major Galleway, D. Inspector-General of Constabulary, to Alice Anne, daughter of Captain Lawlor, County Inspector.

No. 3676 :: Ref. 1850-04-22, 3:2, M.

April 18, at George's Church, Dublin, by the Rev. Thomas G. Caulfield, Capt. Francis Winter, late of the Bengal Army, son of [the] late John Pratt Winter, Esq., of Agher, co. Meath, to Anna Julia, eldest daughter of Lieutenant-Colonel Caulfield, Bloomfield, co. Westmeath.

No. 3677 :: Ref. 1850-04-22, 3:2, M.

Barclay-street, New York, by special licence, Albert B. Seymour, Esq., Antigua, West Indies, to Fanny, youngest daughter of the late John Rochfort Mayne, Esq., county Cavan, Ireland.

No. 3678 :: Ref. 1850-04-22, 3:2, M.

On 16th inst., by the Rev. Dr. Urwick, Mr. Wm. Robertson, of Sackville-street, Dublin, to Elizabeth Louisa, sixth daughter of Mr. William Kershaw, of Portland-place, Dublin.

No. 3679 :: Ref. 1850-04-22, 3:2, D.

April 15, at 103, Eaton-place, London, the Hon. John Willoughby Michael Viscount Cole, aged five years and four months.

No. 3680 :: Ref. 1850-04-22, 3:2, D.

April 13, in Belfast, Mr. Hugh W. Johnston, merchant.

No. 3681 :: Ref. 1850-04-22, 3:2, D.

On 14th inst., in Cavan workhouse, of typhus fever, Mr. Teriney, schoolmaster of that establishment.

No. 3682 :: Ref. 1850-04-22, 3:2, D.

John Lamb, D.D., 37th master of Corpus Christi College, and Dean of Bristol, expired about half-past twelve o'clock, on the 19th inst., in the 62d year of his age. He was a native of Suffolk, and was admitted of Corpus College in 1807.

No. 3683 :: Ref. 1850-04-22, 3:2, D.

April 19, in College-street, Armagh, Hugh Maculla, Esq. In every relation of life Mr. Maculla was a most eccent[r]ic character; for years he had not left his house, he sat up by night and slept by day, &c.

No. 3684 :: Ref. 1850-04-22, 3:2, D.

On 4th inst., in Benburb, Mr. John Runnett, merchant, aged 36.—A man who was universally beloved and respected.

No. 3685 :: Ref. 1850-04-22, 3:2, D.

At his residence, Turner's Buildings, Rathmines, on 16th inst., the Rev. Wm. Foley, aged 61 years.

No. 3686 :: Ref. 1850-04-22, 3:2, D.

On 14th inst., at Leegan Lodge, co. Galway, deeply regretted by her family and a numerous circle of friends, Harriet, daughter of the late Captain Netterville Blake, of Newborough House, said county.

No. 3687 :: Ref. 1850-04-22, 3:2, D.

On 15th inst., at No. 34, Eccles-street, Dublin, William Weldon Tracy, Esq., at the advanced age of 87 years.

No. 3688 :: Ref. 1850-04-22, 3:2, D.

March 27, at Ballyboe, near Manorcunningham, co. Donegal, aged 25 years, John, youngest son of the late Mr. Samuel Galbraith.

No. 3689 :: Ref. 1850-04-22, 3:2, D.
On 13th inst., at Rathfriland, aged 78, the Rev. Thomas Tate, Minister of the Second Presbyterian Congregation, Rathfriland.

No. 3690 :: Ref. 1850-04-22, 3:2, D.
On 4th inst., at Brussels, Lieut.-Col. Robert Nixon, late of the 1st or Royal Regiment.

No. 3691 :: Ref. 1850-04-22, 3:2, D.
On 15th inst., at Major Waring's Trevor Hill, Daniel Dobbin, aged 48 years,—38 of which he passed in the service of that family.

No. 3692 :: Ref. 1850-04-22, 3:2, D.
In Ballyshannon, on 4th inst., after a protracted illness, William Young, Esq., aged 65.

No. 3693 :: Ref. 1850-04-22, 3:2, D.
On 10th inst. aged 28 years, Robert Bothel M'Cune, captain of the ship "*Mary Stewart*," of Londonderry, only son of Mr. R. M'Cune, organist of the Cathedral, Downpatrick.

No. 3694 :: Ref. 1850-04-22, 3:2, D.
On 12th inst., at his father's residence, in the 22d year of his age, John, son of Mr. Bernard M'Cully, postmaster, Clough, near Rallymena [sic].

No. 3695 :: Ref. 1850-04-22, 3:2, D.
April 15, at Derry, aged 50 years, Capt. James M'Clintock, late of the 88th Regt., and for many years Adjutant of the Londonderry Regiment of Militia.

No. 3696 :: Ref. 1850-04-22, 3:2, D.
On 16th inst., at the house of his brother-in-law, Mr. Wm. White, V.S., Enniskillen, Mr. James Ferguson, of Girvin, Scotland, aged 27.

No. 3697 :: Ref. 1850-04-22, 3:2, D.
April 14, at 3, Stamer-street, Dublin, of bronchitis, in the 64th year of his age, E. Mitchell, Esq.

No. 3698 :: Ref. 1850-04-22, 3:2, D.
April 16, at Fortfield, Rathfarnham, Caroline Jane, infant daughter of Wm. Humphreys, of Ballyhaise House, co. Cavan.

No. 3699 :: Ref. 1850-04-22, 3:2, D.
In Ballina, on 9th inst., of typhus fever, in the 23d year of her age, Margaret, eldest daughter of the Rev. Wm. Hamilton, Baptist Minister.

No. 3700 :: Ref. 1850-04-29, 3:4, B.
On 11th inst., at Dungannon, the wife of Mr. Owen Crofton, Officer of Inland Revenue, of a son.

No. 3701 :: Ref. 1850-04-29, 3:4, B.
On 16th inst., at Coalisland, the wife of Mr. Maynes Campbell, of a son.

No. 3702 :: Ref. 1850-04-29, 3:4, M.
On 24th inst., at Aughnacloy, by the Rev. Mr. Rook, Mr. John Cummins, to Anna Maria, youngest daughter of Lieutenant Banks, H.P., 88th Regt.

No. 3703 :: Ref. 1850-04-29, 3:4, M.
On 18th inst., in the Presbyterian Church, Glascar, by Rev. J. Rogers, Rev. Wm. J. M'Mahon, of Tyrone's-ditches, Poyntzpass, to Jane, second daughter of Mr. James Todd, of Ringclare, Donaghmore.

No. 3704 :: Ref. 1850-04-29, 3:4, M.
On 24th April, at St. Michael's Church, Limerick, William Davis, Esq., of the Provincial Bank, Limerick, to Mary Ann, daughter of the late Thomas W. Monsell, Eq. [sic], Solicitor.

No. 3705 :: Ref. 1850-04-29, 3:4, M.
In the first Presbyterian Meeting House, Dungannon, on the 25th inst., by the Rev. Charles L. Morell, Mr. James Browne, of same place, to Letitia Anne, second daughter of the late Joseph Lee, Esq., of this city.

No. 3706 :: Ref. 1850-04-29, 3:4, M.
On 18th inst., at the residence of the bride's father, by the Rev. P. Hassan, P.P., Roseanne, youngest daughter of Daniel Daly, Esq., Clenone, Portglenone, to John Rickard, Esq., Commercial House, Cookstown.

No. 3707 :: Ref. 1850-04-29, 3:4, D.
On the 3d inst., at his residence, Mullinaveigh, near Caledon, Mr. John Girvin, aged 80 years. Mr. Girvin was through a long life much respected by all who had the pleasure of his acquaintance.

No. 3708 :: Ref. 1850-04-29, 3:4, D.
On 26th inst., in Armagh, Annie Hester, beloved daughter of Mr. James Loudon, aged 3 years.

No. 3709 :: Ref. 1850-04-29, 3:4, D.
On 23d inst., at Dundalk, in the 71st year of his age, Mathew Fortescue, Esq.

No. 3710 :: Ref. 1850-04-29, 3:4, D.
On 24th inst., in Cavan, Miss H. Wilson, aged 66 years. The deceased, who was much respected, was daughter of Dr. Wilson, formerly of that town.

No. 3711 :: Ref. 1850-04-29, 3:4, D.
On 22nd April, Mr. Buchanan, of Aughnacloy, went to bed apparently in good health. Early next morning he was found dead in bed; supposed to have arisen from apoplexy.

No. 3712 :: Ref. 1850-04-29, 3:4, D.
On 21st inst., Martha, eldest daughter of Mr. Robert Robinson, master of the Clogher workhouse.

No. 3713 :: Ref. 1850-04-29, 3:4, D.
In Great Britain street, St. Mary's parish, Dublin, on the 23d inst., Michael David M'Greale, late Assistant Professor of Irish in the Dublin University.

No. 3714 :: Ref. 1850-04-29, 3:4, D.
On 18th of April, at his residence, Shebeg House, Fermanagh, Henry Gresson, Esq., in the 77th year of his age.

No. 3715 :: Ref. 1850-04-29, 3:4, D.
On 16th inst., at Kingstown, Thomas P. Young, upwards of forty years a clerk in the Bank of Ireland, aged 68 years.

No. 3716 :: Ref. 1850-04-29, 3:4, D.
On 24th of Feb., at London, Canada West, after a few days' illness, Charles Poole, M.D., aged 47.

No. 3717 :: Ref. 1850-04-29, 3:4, D.
At Greencastle, co. Donegal, on 11th April, Mary Canning, at the extraordinary age of 117 years. She possessed all her different faculties to the last, and left behind her 110 grandchildren and great grandchildren; she consequently lived in the reigns of five successive Monarchs, viz., Geo. II., III., and IV., and Wm. IV., and Victoria.

No. 3718 :: Ref. 1850-04-29, 3:4, D.
Suddenly, in his Counting-house, South Main-street, Cork, Thos. Lyons, Esq. Mr. Lyons was the first Mayor of Cork, under the *Municipal Corporations Act.* He was one of the most esteemed citizens of Cork.

No. 3719 :: Ref. 1850-04-29, 3:4, D.
On 17th inst., Mr. Daniel Cameron, Ballymoney, aged 66 years. He was descended from a branch of the ancient clan Cameron, of Scotland whom the persecutions conducted by Claverhouse drove out of their native country.

No. 3720 :: Ref. 1850-04-29, 3:4, D.
On the 22d inst., at his residence, Grovesnor-street, Lord F. Beauclerk, uncle to the late Duke of St. Alban's, and also by marriage, to Viscount Dillon.

No. 3721 :: Ref. 1850-05-06, 3:2, B.
May 1, at Caledon Hill, Caledon, the Countess of Caledon, of a daughter.

No. 3722 :: Ref. 1850-05-06, 3:2, B.
On 1st May, the wife of David White, of Lisonally, near Omagh, Esq., J.P., of a son.

No. 3723 :: Ref. 1850-05-06, 3:2, B.
April 21, at 1, Lower Gardiner-street, Dublin, the lady of Doctor Nixon, Enniskillen, of a daughter.

No. 3724 :: Ref. 1850-05-06, 3:2, B.
On 29th ult., at the Glebe, Strangford, the wife of the Rev. John F. Gordon, of a son.

No. 3725 :: Ref. 1850-05-06, 3:2, B.
At Killagan, near Ballymoney, the wife of Robert Huey, Esq., of a son.

No. 3726 :: Ref. 1850-05-06, 3:2, M.
On 3d inst., at the Independent Chapel, Cork, by the Rev. S. Shaw, of Moy, Charolette Allman, only child of [the] late William Clear, Esq., to the Rev. William Shaw, Independent Minister of Cork.

No. 3727 :: Ref. 1850-05-06, 3:2, M.
May 2, in Finglass Church, by Rev. Thomas Thompson, Rev. H. Hudson, of Lisburn, to Hannah, eldest daughter of William Gregory, Esq., Belle Vue.

No. 3728 :: Ref. 1850-05-06, 3:2, M.
On the 25th of April, at St. Mary's Church, by the Rev. Samuel Ferguson, uncle to the bride, Jerome Tisdall, of Charleville, county of Louth, to Frances Catherine, daughter of Joseph Ferguson, Esq., M.D., of Prospect, co. Westmeath.

No. 3729 :: Ref. 1850-05-06, 3:2, M.
On 30th ult., in the Presbyterian Church, Cremore, by the Rev. Alexander Goudy Ross, Mr. Alexander MacDonald, Head Master of the District Model School, Baileboro', co. Cavan, to Susan, third daughter of Daniel C. M'Clure, Esq., Millmount, Portnorris, co. Armagh.

No. 3730 :: Ref. 1850-05-06, 3:2, M.
On 25th ult., at Drumkeeran Church, by the Rev. H.L. Montgomery, Alexander Fraser, Esq., Officer of Inland Revenue, to Anne Maria, eldest daughter of John Buchannan, Esq., of Drumkeeran.

No. 3731 :: Ref. 1850-05-06, 3:2, M.
Same day [25th ult.] at Killarga Church, by the Rev. George Hinds, Henry Trimble, Esq., Sub-Inspector of Constabulary, to Helena, second daughter of John Buchannan, Esq., of said place.

No. 3732 :: Ref. 1850-05-06, 3:2, M.
On 30th ult., in Donegall-square, Wesleyan Church, Belfast, by the Rev. Edward Harpur, Mr. John Whiteside Caldwell, South Frederick-street, Dublin, to Mary, second daughter of John Ladley, Esq., solicitor, Belfast.

No. 3733 :: Ref. 1850-05-06, 3:2, M.
On 25th ult., at the Cathedral, Waterford, by the Rev. E.H. Brien, Alfred Mathias, Esq., only son of the late James Mathias, Esq., R.N., Lowestroft [sic], Suffolk, to Harrietta, eldest daughter of Richard Harris, Esq., Manager of the Provincial Bank of Ireland.

No. 3734 :: Ref. 1850-05-06, 3:2, M.
On 23d ult., at Killeshandra, by Rev. Doctor Martin, F.T.C.D., Charlotte, youngest daughter of the late William Harkness, of Con House, to John Alexander Faris, Esq., of Farrenseer, both of County Cavan.

No. 3735 :: Ref. 1850-05-06, 3:2, M.
On 30th ult., at Carmoney Church, by the Rev. J.C. Smyth, Mr. W.M. Barlow, Gas-works, Belfast, to Anna, eldest daughter of Wm. Stewart, Esq., Silverstream, Whiteabbey.

No. 3736 :: Ref. 1850-05-06, 3:2, M.
On 25th ult., at Lurgan Church, by the Rev. W.P. Oulton, Mr. Thomas Hunter, of Lisburn, to Harriet, youngest daughter of the late Mr. James Stevenson.

No. 3737 :: Ref. 1850-05-06, 3:2, M.

On 1st inst., in Lurgan Church, by the Rev. W.P. Oulton, the Rev. Robert Sewell, Methodist Minister, Cork, to Jane, eldest daughter of the Rev. William Herbert, of Lurgan.

No. 3738 :: Ref. 1850-05-06, 3:2, D.

April 27th at Thornhill, near Black Lion, county Cavan, Jane, youngest daughter of the late Thomas Nixon, Esq.

No. 3739 :: Ref. 1850-05-06, 3:2, D.

In Lower Glentwirth-st., Limerick, William Roche, Esq., late M.P. for the city of Limerick, a Justice of Peace for many years, D.L. &c. since 1835. He was a most excellent public man, and is justly and deeply lamented.

No. 3740 :: Ref. 1850-05-06, 3:2, D.

At Wakefield, Yorkshire, on 26th ult., after a short but painful illness, in the 45th year of his age, Samuel, eldest son of Mr. Andrew Wilson Allan, Dungannon; he held a responsible situation in the Ordinance Survey Department for 24 years. His end was peace.

No. 3741 :: Ref. 1850-05-06, 3:2, D.

April 30, at Cushendall, in the 64th year of his age, Thomas Thornly, Esq., Sub-Inspector of Police.

No. 3742 :: Ref. 1850-05-06, 3:2, D.

April 29, at the Royal School, Cavan, Susanna, relict of the late Rev. John Moore, at the advanced age of 78 years.

No. 3743 :: Ref. 1850-05-06, 3:2, D.

At Rathmines, Dublin, on 2d inst. Henry Maudeley [Mandeley?], Esq., formerly of Cavan, ex-Officer of Excise, aged 78.

No. 3744 :: Ref. 1850-05-06, 3:2, D.

On 15th ult., after a lingering illness, which he bore with great patience and resignation, William John, son of Mr. John Woods, sen., of Banbridge.

No. 3745 :: Ref. 1850-05-06, 3:2, D.

April 27, at Ashfield Lodge, co. Cavan, Louisa, relict of Henry John Clements, Esq., M.P., and daughter of the late James Stewart, Esq., of Killymoon, co. Tyrone, aged 71.

No. 3746 :: Ref. 1850-05-13, 3:4, B.

In Markethill, on 10th inst., the lady of William Wann, Esq., of a son.

No. 3747 :: Ref. 1850-05-13, 3:4, B.

May 4, at Manorhamilton, the lady of John Coleman, Esq., Sub-Inspector of the Revenue Police, of a daughter.

No. 3748 :: Ref. 1850-05-13, 3:4, B.

At the Glebe House, near Waterford, on the 3d inst., the lady of the Rev. Arthur Davis, of a son.

No. 3749 :: Ref. 1850-05-13, 3:4, B.

May 6, at Castlemacadam, the wife of the Rev. T. Hanley Ball, of a daughter.

No. 3750 :: Ref. 1850-05-13, 3:4, M.

On 7th inst., by the Rev. Wm. Quain, Mr. Dickson Patterson, merchant, Dungannon, to Susan, eldest daughter of Mr. Thomas Agnew, same place.

No. 3751 :: Ref. 1850-05-13, 3:4, M.

At Aughnacloy Presbyterian Church, by the Rev. David M'Kee, Mr. James Stevenson, of Kilmacrue-house, to Mrs. Magaffin, widow of the late Mr. Joseph Magaffin, of Ardtrin.

No. 3752 :: Ref. 1850-05-13, 3:4, M.

On 4th ult., at Antigua, in the Cathedral, by the Rev. Edwin O. Roach, Isaac George Glenny, second son of the late George Glenny, Esq., Moore Vale, co. Armagh, Ireland, to Mary Ann Elizabeth, only daughter of Richard H. Mason, Esq., merchant, of that island.

No. 3753 :: Ref. 1850-05-13, 3:4, D.

On Sunday, the 6th inst., at Markethill, William C. Buchannan, the only and beloved son of Mr. Benjamin Browne, Architect, late of Dobbin-street, Armagh.

No. 3754 :: Ref. 1850-05-13, 3:4, D.

On 3d inst., Alice, the infant daughter of James Boyle, Esq., Ulster Bank, Ballymoney.

No. 3755 :: Ref. 1850-05-13, 3:4, D.

On 7th inst., in Belfast, Mr. John M'Connell, of the Hibernian Foundry.

No. 3756 :: Ref. 1850-05-13, 3:4, D.

On 7th inst., at Oak Park, co. Donegal, John, third son of the late Captain Robert Johnston, of Brook Hill, co. Leitrim, aged 18 years.

No. 3757 :: Ref. 1850-05-13, 3:4, D.

May 6, in his 62 year, at Glasslough, Mr. Wm. Johnston. He is much and deservedly regretted by all who knew him.

No. 3758 :: Ref. 1850-05-13, 3:4, D.

At Briansford, co. Down, on the 5th inst., Commander John Bond Morris, aged 75 years. He was universally respected, particularly by the Coast Guard, over whom he was Inspecting Commander, in the Newcastle district.

No. 3759 :: Ref. 1850-05-13, 3:4, D.

On 4th inst., in Ballymena, Joseph M'Kee, Esq., aged 66 years.

No. 3760 :: Ref. 1850-05-13, 3:4, D.

On 2d inst., at the residence of his father, Drumglass House, near Dungannon, Henry Irwin, Esq., aged 37 years.

No. 3761 :: Ref. 1850-05-13, 3:4, D.

May 1, at his residence, Fyfannon, Killybegs, John M'Closkey, aged 64 years. He lived beloved and died lamented.

No. 3762 :: Ref. 1850-05-13, 3:4, D.

May 3, Catherine, for 54 years the beloved wife of Sir Edward Stanley.

No. 3763 :: Ref. 1850-05-13, 3:4, D.

At Tubrid, Kesh, on 8th inst., Tempe Bagot, youngest daughter of the Rev. Edward Stack, aged 22 years.

No. 3764 :: Ref. 1850-05-13, 3:4, D.

On 5th inst., at Cranaghan Glebe, Ballyconnell, Rev. John Frith, Rector of the parish of Tomregan, aged 62.

No. 3765 :: Ref. 1850-05-13, 3:4, D.

On 5th inst., the infant son of Rev. Mr. Bell, Wesleyan Minister.

No. 3766 :: Ref. 1850-05-13, 3:4, D.

On 3d inst., in Londonderry, of jaundice, Mr. Samuel Blackburn.

No. 3767 :: Ref. 1850-05-20, 3:4, B.

On 9th inst., at Nowtownsaville Glebe, the lady of Rev. Charles Maginniss, of a son.

No. 3768 :: Ref. 1850-05-20, 3:4, B.

On 10th inst., at 21, Hatch-street, Dublin, the lady of William Barker, Esq., M.D., of a son.

No. 3769 :: Ref. 1850-05-20, 3:4, B.

On 13th inst., at Glenaghy, Portadown, the lady of Rev. Simon Foot, of a daughter.

No. 3770 :: Ref. 1850-05-20, 3:4, B.

On 13th inst., at Delgany Glebe, the lady of the Rev. W.J. West, of a son.

No. 3771 :: Ref. 1850-05-20, 3:4, B.

On 14th inst., at Farrenconnell House, co. Cavan, the lady of Richard Nugent, Esq., of a daughter.

No. 3772 :: Ref. 1850-05-20, 3:4, B.

May 14, at Moviddy Rectory, the lady of Rev. Hume Babington, of a daughter.

No. 3773 :: Ref. 1850-05-20, 3:4, M.

May 15, in Kilpipe Church, by the Rev. S. Donovan, Rector, Mr. James Robinson, Primitive Wesleyan Methodist Preacher, Armagh, to Miss Anne Hobson, third daughter of the late Abraham Hobson, Esq., Tubberpatrick, co. Wicklow.

No. 3774 :: Ref. 1850-05-20, 3:4, M.

On 2d inst., in the First Presbyterian Church, Glendermott, by Rev. A. Buchanan, Mr. John M'Clelland, of Newtownhamilton, to Miss Eliza Millar, of Drumcorrin.

No. 3775 :: Ref. 1850-05-20, 3:4, M.

April 30, at Providence, Rhode Island, by Rev. Mr. Wylie, Thos. Devin Reilly, Esq., editor of the Boston *Protective Union*, and formerly of the Dublin *Nation*, to Miss Jane Millar, second daughter of the late Mr. Robert Millar, of Enniskillen.

No. 3776 :: Ref. 1850-05-20, 3:4, M.

On 14th inst., in Ardstraw, by Rev. Matthew Clark, Mr. Joseph Kerr, Ardstraw, to Miss Foster, of Newtownstewart.

No. 3777 :: Ref. 1850-05-20, 3:4, M.

On 9th inst., in Buncrana, by Rev. Samuel Reid, Thos. Drakely, Bombardier, Royal Artillery, to Ellen, second daughter of Mr. Abraham Dinsmore, builder, Buncrana.

No. 3778 :: Ref. 1850-05-20, 3:4, M.

On 9th inst., in Ramelton, by Rev. James Kinnear, Lower Clenanees, Dungannon, the Rev. John Kinnear, Letterkenny, to Margaret Fanny, daughter of the late Andrew Alexander, Esq., Kinnycally, co. Donegal.

No. 3779 :: Ref. 1850-05-20, 3:4, D.

Suddenly, on 10th inst., of disease of the heart, at Bondville House, Middletown, co. Armagh, Thomas Bond, Esq., aged 27 years. The assemblage of nobility, clergy, and gentry that attended his remains to their resting-place evinced the general esteem in which he was held. "*In the midst of life we are in death.*"

No. 3780 :: Ref. 1850-05-20, 3:4, D.

At Toronto, on 27th January, of consumption, David Herbert Morphy, Esq., youngest son of the late Captain Morphy, Esq., of Tralee, county Kerry, Ireland.

No. 3781 :: Ref. 1850-05-20, 3:4, D.

On 3d inst. at Beragh, co. Tyrone, the Rev. P. Quinn, P.P., formerly of Tandragee.

No. 3782 :: Ref. 1850-05-20, 3:4, D.

On 16th inst., in Rostrevor, Miss Wallace, of Downpatrick.

No. 3783 :: Ref. 1850-05-20, 3:4, D.

At Brooklyn, New York, after a few days' illness, in the 61st year of his age, Robert Beatty, Esq., eldest son of the late David Beatty, Esq., of the city of Armagh.

No. 3784 :: Ref. 1850-05-20, 3:4, D.

On 13th inst., at Sligo, Anne, wife of James Davidson, Esq.

No. 3785 :: Ref. 1850-05-20, 3:4, D.

On 8th inst., at Drumbannon Cottage, Bailieborough, the residence of his brother, the Rev. William Bell, Richardson Bell, Esq., aged 63 years.

No. 3786 :: Ref. 1850-05-20, 3:4, D.

On 6th inst., Martha, wife of Charles Cochrane, of the Grove, co. Donegal, Esq., and eldest daughter of the late John Patterson, of Ballyare House, co. Donegal, Esq.

No. 3787 :: Ref. 1850-05-20, 3:4, D.

On 11th inst., at the residence of his uncle, John White, Esq., Divernagh, Newry, of water on the brain, Louis Perrin Hancock, fourth son of the late Wm. John Hancock, Esq., Assistant Poor Law Commissioner, aged 17 years.

No. 3788 :: Ref. 1850-05-20, 3:4, D.

On 12th inst., at Richmond, Surrey, of scarletina, Frances Elizabeth, aged 15 years, third daughter of Wm. Beers, Esq., of Newcastle, county Down.

No. 3789 :: Ref. 1850-05-20, 3:4, D.

May 11, at Farrenconnell, county Cavan, in the 64th year of her age, Sophia Maria, the beloved wife of Christopher Edmund John Nugent, Esq., of Farrenconnell.

No. 3790 :: Ref. 1850-05-20, 3:4, D.

Drowned, at sea, Mr. John B. Joint, officer on board the *Dromahaire*, emigrant vessel of Sligo, and eldest son of Robert Joint, Esq., Tide Surveyor of her Majesty's Customs of Belfast. Mr. Joint was swept from on board during a storm encountered by the vessel on her last trip to New York. He was in his 25th year, and beloved and esteemed by all who knew him.

No. 3791 :: Ref. 1850-05-27, 3:4, B.

On 23d inst., at the College, Armagh, the lady of the Rev. W.H. Guillemard, of a daughter.

No. 3792 :: Ref. 1850-05-27, 3:4, B.

On 20th inst., at Grange, Armagh, the lady of James Stanley, Esq., of a son.

No. 3793 :: Ref. 1850-05-27, 3:4, B.

On 20th inst., at Portadown, the lady of John Obins Woodhouse, Esq., of a daughter.

No. 3794 :: Ref. 1850-05-27, 3:4, B.

On 21st inst., at Sligo, the lady of Richard Gordon, Esq., Provincial Bank, of a son.

No. 3795 :: Ref. 1850-05-27, 3:4, M.

On 16th inst., at Monkstown Church, by the Rev. Richard, Radcliffe [sic], Rector of Skryne, Thomas Henry Johnson, Ballymacash, co. Antrim, Esq., to Isabella, youngest daughter of S. Garnett, of Summersea, co. Meath, Esq.

No. 3796 :: Ref. 1850-05-27, 3:4, M.

On 11th inst., at Wenbury Church, John Augustus Hugh Boyd, Lieutenant, R.N., of Ballycastle, co. Antrim, Esq., eldest son of Sir John Boyd, Bart., to Honora Mary, third daughter of Charles B. Calmady, Esq., of Langdon-street.

No. 3797 :: Ref. 1850-05-27, 3:4, M.

On 20th inst., at St. Mary's Church, Clonmel, by the Rev. J.B. Gordon, and afterwards at the residence of the bride's mother, Johnson-street, by the Very Rev. D. Burke, P.P., V.G., Wm. B. Frizelle, Esq., to Alice, only daughter of the late Mr. P. Duggan.

No. 3798 :: Ref. 1850-05-27, 3:4, M.

On 15th inst., in Cootehill, William Alexander, eldest son of Mr. John Sutcliffe, of the Longford Hotel, to Mary, youngest daughter of Mr. J. Gribben, of Coleraine.

No. 3799 :: Ref. 1850-05-27, 3:4, M.

On 21st inst., in Killyshandra, by Rev. Henry Martin, the Rev. C. Adamson, son of the late Rev. A.S. Adamson, Rector of Timahoe, and Incumbent of Grangegorman, and grandson of the Hon. Maria J. Barry, to Elizabeth M.A. Martin, daughter of the Rev. J.C. Martin, D.D., Rector.

No. 3800 :: Ref. 1850-05-27, 3:4, M.

On 26th ult., at Philadelphia, U.S., by the Rev. Dr. Lord, Mr. Wm. L. Brown, formerly of Belfast, to Elizabeth, only daughter of Mr. John Collins, formerly of Cookstown, county Tyrone.

No. 3801 :: Ref. 1850-05-27, 3:4, M.

On 21st inst., at Booterstown Church, by the Rev. J.J. M'Sorley, of St. Peter's, Dublin, George Thomas Macartney, of Manchester, youngest son of the late John Macartney, Esq., of Montgibbon, co. Fermanagh, to Maria Barrett, second daughter of Robert Quale, Esq., Marymount, Blackrock.

No. 3802 :: Ref. 1850-05-27, 3:4, M.

On 24th inst., at the parish Church of Kilskeery, by the Rev. A.H. Irvine, uncle to the bride, James, only son of Audley Caldwell, Esq., of Creeduff House, co. Tyrone, to Catharine, daughter of the late Michael Tuthill, Esq., formerly surgeon of the royal artillery.

No. 3803 :: Ref. 1850-05-27, 3:4, M.

On 23d inst., at the residence of her uncle, W. Babington, Esq., Baggot-street, Dublin, by the Rev. Dr. O'Connell, Thomas, eldest son of John Reilly, Esq., of Derrygarra-House, Butlersbridge, to Sarah, youngest daughter of the late Thomas M'Fadden, M.D., of Cavan.

No. 3804 :: Ref. 1850-05-27, 3:4, D.

At Torquay, England, on Friday, the 24th inst., after a tedious illness, Sophia, youngest daughter of James Jackson, Esq., of Clencorn, co. Monaghan, aged 27 years.

No. 3805 :: Ref. 1850-05-27, 3:4, D.

At Kingscourt, co. Cavan, aged 39 years, Henry Dinning, Esq., medical officer to the fever hospital in that town.

No. 3806 :: Ref. 1850-05-27, 3:4, D.

On 18th inst., at Dunglave, near Swanlinbar, very much regretted, Mr. Andrew Howden, sen., aged 65 years.

No. 3807 :: Ref. 1850-05-27, 3:4, D.

On 15th inst., in London, Major James Palmer, late Inspector-General of Prisons in Ireland, aged 70.

No. 3808 :: Ref. 1850-05-27, 3:4, D.

On 17th inst., near Dungannon, the Rev. John Kerr, for many years Pastor of the Second Presbyterian Congregation of Newry.

No. 3809 :: Ref. 1850-05-27, 3:4, D.

On 19th inst., at Clones, of apoplexy, in 24 hours' illness, aged 54 years, the Rev. John M. Graydon, Rector of Ervatris.

No. 3810 :: Ref. 1850-05-27, 3:4, D.

On 20th inst., aged 41 years, Marcus Babington, Esq., of Derry.

No. 3811 :: Ref. 1850-05-27, 3:4, D.

On 19th inst., aged 34 years, Robert Thomas Blackburne Hearn, Esq., eldest son of the Rev. William Edward Hearn, Kilnaleck, co. Cavan.

No. 3812 :: Ref. 1850-05-27, 3:4, D.

On 19th inst., Rev. James Brown, of Garvagh, in the 88th year of his age, and 56th of his ministry.

No. 3813 :: Ref. 1850-05-27, 3:4, D.

At Bath, on 12th inst., aged 64 years, the Rev. Hamilton Stuart, of Rockfort, co. Donegal.

No. 3814 :: Ref. 1850-05-27, 3:4, D.

On 19th inst., at Carysfort Avenue, Blackrock, John, eldest son of the late Rev. Wm. Armstrong, Curate of Sligo.

No. 3815 :: Ref. 1850-05-27, 3:4, D.

On 20th inst., in her 93d year, Mrs. Watt, of the cottage, relict of the late David Watt, Esq., of Londonderry.

No. 3816 :: Ref. 1850-05-27, 3:4, D.

On 15th inst., at Fitzwilliam Lodge, Blackrock, Dublin, the Earl of Roscommon, in the 52d year of his age.

No. 3817 :: Ref. 1850-05-27, 3:4, D.

On 20th inst., at the Hospital for Incurables, Donnybrook-road, Mary Thompson, aged nearly 100 years, for 75 years an inmate of that institution, during which lengthened period she never transgressed the rules of that benevolent asylum, and to the last hour of her long life expressed her thankfulness to God and gratitude to the governors for the uniform kindness with which she was treated, and for the benefits of the tranquil and happy resting-place she enjoyed for three-quarters of a century. At her dying request the governors insert this notice.

No. 3818 :: Ref. 1850-05-27, 3:4, D.

Death of Sir William Kay, Bart.—This gentleman expired on the 16th inst., at his residence in Pall Mall. The deceased was son of William Kay, Esq., of Montreal, by the daughter of Richard Webber, Esq. He was born in 1777, and succeeded his grand-uncle in the title in 1807.

No. 3819 :: Ref. 1850-06-03, 3:3, B.

May 19, at Lisnacrieve House, the lady of David Lindsay, Esq., of a daughter.

No. 3820 :: Ref. 1850-06-03, 3:3, B.

May 28, at Lismullin Park, co. Meath, the seat of her father, the lady of Major Kelly, 34th Regiment of a daughter.

No. 3821 :: Ref. 1850-06-03, 3:3, B.

May 27, at Darraghmore, co. Tyrone, the lady of Thomas Hamilton, Esq., of a daughter.

No. 3822 :: Ref. 1850-06-03, 3:3, B.

May 26, at Antrim, the lady of George Nixon, Esq., M.D., of a son.

No. 3823 :: Ref. 1850-06-03, 3:3, B.

May 31 the lady of Dr. Armstrong, of Kingscourt, co. Cavan, of a daughter.

No. 3824 :: Ref. 1850-06-03, 3:3, M.

May 26, in the Presbyterian Church, Lower Clenanees, by Rev. James Kinnear, Mr. John Jackson, of Donemony, to Anne, second daughter of Mr. Joseph Black, Drumnafin, near Dungannon.

No. 3825 :: Ref. 1850-06-03, 3:3, M.

May 28, in the Downshire Road Presbyterian Meeting-house, by Rev. John Dodd, Mr. William Brady, Merchant, Clones, to Wilhelmina, daughter of the late Mr. Robert Medill, of Newry.

No. 3826 :: Ref. 1850-06-03, 3:3, M.

Thomas, eldest son of John Reilly, Esq., of Derrygara House, Butler's-bridge, to Sarah, daughter of the late Thomas M'Fadden, M.D., of Cavan.

No. 3827 :: Ref. 1850-06-03, 3:3, M.

May 27, at St. Marylebone Church, London, Captain W.J. Verner, of the 21st R.N.B. Fusiliers, to Mary Anne, youngest daughter of the late John Rogers, Esq., of Langham-place.

No. 3828 :: Ref. 1850-06-03, 3:3, M.

May 26, in Portadown Church, by Rev. Henry de L. Willis, Mr. James M'Cracken, of Ashfield, to Miss Susanna Wright, of Portadown.

No. 3829 :: Ref. 1850-06-03, 3:3, M.

May 29, by Rev. Mr. M'Kenna, Mr. John Loughran, Diamond, Monaghan, to Bridget, only daughter of the late Mr. Laurence Rush, of Dundalk.

No. 3830 :: Ref. 1850-06-03, 3:3, D.

At Fivemiletown, on Saturday, the 25th inst., Mr. Robert Hall, Merchant; respected in the various relations of life, he calmly departed, in the 51st year of his age. The very large and respectable assemblage which followed his remains to the grave, testified that his memory will be long lived in the place he has left to return no more.

No. 3831 :: Ref. 1850-06-03, 3:3, D.

After an illness of thirteen days, caused by dysentery and typhus fever, Mrs. Margaret Rolston, the beloved wife of the Rev. David D. Rolston, formerly of Ballymartrim, co. Armagh; departed this life in full and perfect hope of a joyful resurrection, on the 2d ult., at St. Thomas's [sic], Canada West. She was the eldest daughter of Mr. H. Agnew, late of Stanhope-street, Belfast; and has left her parents, husband, and infant son, to mourn her loss. She finished her pilgrimage in the morning of life. Her end was truly perfect peace and joy, through Christ's sanctifying atonement.

No. 3832 :: Ref. 1850-06-03, 3:3, D.

May 22, in the Castleblayney coach, on his way home to his father's, Mr. Hall Wilson, of the General Post Office, Liverpool, third son to Mr. Andrew Wilson, of Waternerry, co. Fermanagh.

No. 3833 :: Ref. 1850-06-03, 3:3, D.

May 22, Mr. James Gowdy, of Belfast, compositor, aged 45 years.

No. 3834 :: Ref. 1850-06-03, 3:3, D.

May 26, at Magherakellaghan, near Claudy, Strabane, Doctor Charles M'Curdy, aged 21 years.

No. 3835 :: Ref. 1850-06-03, 3:3, D.

May 27, at Lower Fitzwilliam-street, Dublin, Staff Surgeon Copeland Grattan, late of her Majesty's 65th Regiment of Foot, and second son of the late William Grattan, Esq., of Sylvan Park, county Meath.

No. 3836 :: Ref. 1850-06-03, 3:3, D.

May 18, at the residence of his mother, Ballybentra, co. Antrim, of disease of the heart, David Alexander Douglas, M.R.C.S.I., aged 23 years.

No. 3837 :: Ref. 1850-06-03, 3:3, D.

May 25, in [the] 40th year of his age, at Saltport, co. Sligo, after a brief illness, Charles Beatty, Esq. He died esteemed and regretted by all who knew him, and sincerely lamented by a large circle of surviving friends. He was an affectionate brother, a dutiful son, and a faithful friend.

No. 3838 :: Ref. 1850-06-03, 3:3, D.

May 22, at Clones, Miss Jane Wright, aged 53 years.

No. 3839 :: Ref. 1850-06-10, 3:3, B.

On 24th May, at Moneymore, Mrs. David Allen, of that place, of a son.

No. 3840 :: Ref. 1850-06-10, 3:3, B.

June 3, at Bellfield, county of Wicklow, the lady of R.J. Hassard, Esq., of a daughter.

No. 3841 :: Ref. 1850-06-10, 3:3, B.

May 31, at the Main-street, Clonmel, the lady of John Hackett, Esq., *Tipperary Free Press*, of a daughter.

No. 3842 :: Ref. 1850-06-10, 3:3, B.

In Ballyshannon, on 26th May, the lady of T.F. Stubbs, Esq., of the Provincial Bank, of a daughter.

No. 3843 :: Ref. 1850-06-10, 3:3, B.

June 3, at Barford House, near Bridgewater, the Countess of Cavan, of a daughter.

No. 3844 :: Ref. 1850-06-10, 3:3, B.

On 27th May, in Keady, the wife of Mr. Joseph Thompson, of a daughter.

No. 3845 :: Ref. 1850-06-10, 3:3, M.

June 6, in George's Church, by the Rev. George Barton, Charles Stuart Adams, Esq., second son of the Rev. the Dean of Cashel, to Eliza, only daughter of Charles M'Mahon, Esq., of Carrickmacross and Rocksfield, Monaghan.

No. 3846 :: Ref. 1850-06-10, 3:3, M.

May 30, at Holywood Church, by the Rev. John Wrixon, James Wright Connor, Esq., Dungannon to Sarah, eldest daughter of Wm. Hunter, Esq., Belfast.

No. 3847 :: Ref. 1850-06-10, 3:3, M.

In the first Presbyterian Church, Abbey-street, by the Rev. Alex. Fleming, Mr. Henry Crawford, Constabulary, to Elizabeth, youngest daughter of the late Mr. John Turner of this city.

No. 3848 :: Ref. 1850-06-10, 3:3, M.

At the Centenary Chapel, Stephen's-green, Dublin, by the Rev. Robinson Scott, the Rev. Henry M'Beale, to Henrietta Amelia, daughter of the late J.B. Logier, Esq., of Stephen's-green.

No. 3849 :: Ref. 1850-06-10, 3:3, M.

On 5th June, in the First Presbyterian Meetinghouse, Armagh, by the Rev. John Porter, Belfast, Mr. Michael Patton, Dublin, to Hariet Matilda, daughter of Mr. John Ritchie, Moy.

No. 3850 :: Ref. 1850-06-10, 3:3, M.

On 5th inst., in Lurgan Church, by the Rev. W.P. Oulton, W.A. M'Mahon, Esq., of Lurgan, to Jane, youngest daughter of the late Wm. Ferris, of New Park.

No. 3851 :: Ref. 1850-06-10, 3:3, D.

Death of the Rev. Samuel Oliver Edgar, D.D.—It is with sincere regret we announce the death, on Monday night last, in the 67th year of his age, of the Rev. Dr. Edgar, Minister of the Third Presbyterian Church, in this city. The late rev. gentleman was ordained in Armagh in the year 1811, and for the long period of thirty-nine years, discharged the duties of his mission here, with marked ability, exemplary piety, and commendable zeal. Dr. Edgar had the reputation of being profoundly read in Divinity, and extensively conversant with classical literature, ancient and modern. The funeral took place on Thursday. His mortal remains were interred in the burial ground attached to the church, in which he had so long officiated. The pall-bearers were the Rev. Mr. Fleming of the first Presbyterian Church, the Rev. Mr. Sharkey of the established Church, the Rev. Mr. Tracy, Wesleyan Minister, Rev. Dr. Edgar of Belfast (cousin of the deceased), Rev. Mr. Wade of the Established Church, and Dr. Riggs. The mourners were the two brothers of the deceased and his two nephews, one of whom is the Rev. S.O. Edgar of Rathfriland. The funeral was most numerously and respectably attended. Amongst those present were the Rev. Mr. M'Christal, Roman Catholic Church, Thomas Dobbin, Esq., J.P., J. M'Kinstry, J.P., Drs. Colvan, Robinson, &c., the most of the respectable citizens of Armagh. On the melancholy and solemn occasion, a portion of scripture was read by the Rev. Mr. Fleming, and a prayer offered up by the Rev. Dr. Edgar of Belfast. Yesterday, a funeral sermon was preached by the Rev. Mr. Fleming in the Presbyterian Church of the late Rev. gentleman. Next week we hope to give a more detailed obituary of the deceased Rev. Dr.

No. 3852 :: Ref. 1850-06-10, 3:3, D.

On 6th June at Markethill, Ann, eldest daughter of Alexander Pringle, Esq., of Teledon Cottage, Glasslough, aged 26 years; her remains passed through this city on Saturday, to the place of family interment, Caledon.

No. 3853 :: Ref. 1850-06-10, 3:3, D.

On 3d June, at Rose Vale, Dungannon, Jane R., daughter of the Rev. Mr. Bell, Eglish, Dungannon. Deservedly regretted; as her amiableness of disposition secured her the love of all who had the happiness of knowing her.

No. 3854 :: Ref. 1850-06-10, 3:3, D.

At Carnteel House, near Aughnacloy, on 3d June of appoplexy [sic], Mr. John M'Williams, aged 29 years.

No. 3855 :: Ref. 1850-06-10, 3:3, D.

In Trafalgar, Canada, 25th of April, aged 37 years, Jane, wife of David Jarvis, and daughter of the late Mr. James Irwin, of Aughnacloy, County Tyrone, Ireland.

No. 3856 :: Ref. 1850-06-10, 3:3, D.

On 31st May, in the 25th year of his age, Mr. Robt. Walker, Clerk in the stamp-office, Armagh.

No. 3857 :: Ref. 1850-06-10, 3:3, D.

In Ballintra, on June 4, Mr. George Moubray, Woollendraper.

No. 3858 :: Ref. 1850-06-10, 3:3, D.

In Ballintra, on 4th June of Consumption, in the 22d year of her age, Charlotte, youngest daughter of the late Charles Atkinson, Esq.

No. 3859 :: Ref. 1850-06-10, 3:3, D.

At Youngstown, Ohio, on 30th April, Eliza, wife of Dr. M'Curdy aged 36 years, formerly of Castlefin, county Donegal.

No. 3860 :: Ref. 1850-06-10, 3:3, D.

At Mossfield, near Strabane, on 31st May, Mr. James Porter, aged 100 years.

No. 3861 :: Ref. 1850-06-10, 3:3, D.

At Strabane, on June 3, aged 86, Mary, relict of the late Rev. Thomas Anderson, formerly Presbyterian minister of Drumquin.

No. 3862 :: Ref. 1850-06-10, 3:3, D.

On 4th inst., at North Anne-street, Circular-road, aged 34, Mr. Thomas Caine Sharpe, only son of Mr. Charles Sharpe, Anglesea-street, Dublin.

No. 3863 :: Ref. 1850-06-10, 3:3, D.

On 22d May, at Covehill near Letterkenny, in the 69th year of his age, Mr. John O'Donnell, father of the Rev. John O'Donnell, R.C.C. of Donegal, and stepfather of the late Rev. John Martin, Phibsborough, Dublin.

No. 3864 :: Ref. 1850-06-10, 3:3, D.

In Ballyshannon, on June 1, Mr. Robert Edwards, Mathematical Teacher, much regretted.

No. 3865 :: Ref. 1850-06-10, 3:3, D.

Died, at the Parochial House, Dromara, on the 3d inst., in the 60th year of his age, and 37th of his sacred ministry, the Very Reverend Peter Devlin, Vicar-General of the diocese of Dromore, and Priest of Dromara.

No. 3866 :: Ref. 1850-06-10, 3:3, D.

In Bytown (Canada West,) on the 20th, Mr. John Cochran, a native of Magherafelt, County of Derry, Ireland, aged 56 years. The deceased was a worthy member of the Orange Association, and an old and respected inhabitant of Bytown.—His remains were followed to the grave, by a large concourse of his Brethren, together with a great number of those of his friends who were anxious to testify their respect for his worth and character by paying the last sad tribute to his memory.—*Bytown Orange Lily*, May 1.

No. 3867 :: Ref. 1850-06-17, 3:3, D.

The Late Samuel Oliver Edgar, D.D.

In accordance with a previous intimation, we submit a few additional statements relative to the life and character of the above-named Rev. Gentleman. He was the son of Rev. Samuel Edgar, Secession Minister of the Congregation of Loughaghry, in the Parish of Anahilt, (*continued...*)

No. 3867, continued: ...county Down, and was born about the year 1783. He was early distinguished for his studious habits; even in the days of his boyhood he obeyed Paul's injunction to Timothy, and "gave himself to reading." When other lads were absorbed in juvenile sports so attractive to school-boys, young Samuel O. Edgar would quietly retire from his companions to some peaceful spot in a shady grove, and pore over the pages of some favourite theological author. He received his classical education under the able superintendence of the late Dr. Edgar, Professor of Divinity to the Presbyterian Secession Church in Ireland.

His proficiency as a languist [sic] was very respectable. In addition to an accurate knowledge of Hebrew, he was able to read Greek, Latin, and French authorship, with almost as much ease and fluency as English. Before entering upon the discharge of his sacred duties in the office of the holy ministry, he was, in every sense of the words, an able and accomplished theologian. Few men of this or of any other age, ever pursued a more honest, arduous, or patient course of research, in order to ascertain the soundness of his creed, or the scriptural correctness of the religious opinions he embraced and advocated. In the spirite of a genuine Presbyterian, he resolved from the very outset of his course, to "call no man master." He was familiar in a very uncommon degree with all the leading essential features of the evidences of revealed religion, both external and internal. His mind was therefore at all times under the deep immovable conviction, that the Bible contained the unmingled, infallible truth of God. This impression gave all their efficiency to his labours in preaching the Gospel. His views were not only thoroughly Scriptural, but always propounded with that undoubting certainty of their truth and importance, that secures the serious attention of the hearer. He took a clear, accurate, and sound view of every subject that engaged his attention; but in discussion, when the opportunity presented itself, he could indulge in sarcastic irony with damaging effect against an adversary.

His fame, however, rests entirely upon his literary labours. His incessant readings enabled him to accumulate vast treasures of theological and ecclesiastical lore—and like a faithful steward, he felt that they should be employed in his Master's service—accordingly in the "*Variations of Popery*" he accomplished a service of no ordinary magnitude and value to the cause of Protestantism.

In preparing the requisite materials for this work fifteen hours a-day were employed for nearly twenty years of his life, and during this period 1,300 volumes of English, French, Latin, and Greek authorship were carefully perused. The thoroughly Protestant spirit and design of this learned book together with the ability and fidelity of its execution have unquestionably laid every Evangelical Church in Christendom under obligation, and should secure affectionate respect for his memory from every friend of liberty and every foe of Antichrist. His Grace the Lord Primate generously acknowledged the value of his labours by a liberal donation of £50 upon the appearance of each of the first two editions in this country—whilst in America three large editions of the "*Variations*" have lately been printed with a recommendatory notice from 12 of the most learned Divines of the United States, commending it to the notice of every Protestant Minister and layman of Christendom, as a work of pre-eminent value both for learning and ability.

Comparatively unnoticed, therefore, as were the labours, and retired the life of the humble Presbyter of Armagh, the products of his intellectual labour are at this moment doing more to mould the opinions and give a right direction to the efforts of Christians in the noble cities, over the teeming valleys, and even in the thinly peopled woods of the Western Continent, in reference to Popery, than the writings of any British Divine during the present century. As a Pastor, Dr. Edgar was held in affectionate esteem by all the members of the flock committed to his oversight. In the company of strangers, or those with whom he was but little acquainted, he was shy and retiring; but when surrounded by intimate friends, especially his brethren in the ministry, he proved a most instructive and very pleasant companion. Two years ago he had an attack of illness from which he never entirely recovered, and about six months since symptoms of a general break up in his system began to manifest themselves. For about three months before his death he suffered a good deal from indisposition; and Monday the 3d of this month he bid farewell to earth, and died about half-past ten o'clock in the evening. In his every day deportment there was little calculated to attract much public notice, but by the preserving grace of the Master whom he served, he was kept happily free from all that could reflect discredit upon his memory, or dishonour upon the Church to which he belonged.

During the 39 years of his residence in Armagh, the lips of slander never uttered a sentence injurious to his unsullied reputation for the purest morality; yet this formed no part of the foundation that sustained his hope of pardon and acceptance. The perfect righteousness of Christ was his only ground of confidence, and leaning on this immutable and eternal rock—if not in triumph or exultation, at least in the calmness of unshaken trust—he bowed to the appointment of his Father's Sovereign will that summoned him to his rest. "*Blessed are the dead which die in the Lord from henceforth. Yea saith the spirit, that they may rest from their labours; and their works do follow them.*"

No. 3868 :: Ref. 1850-06-17, 3:4, B.
June 7, at Mount Irwin, the lady of Wm. G. Irwin, Esq., of a still-born son.

No. 3869 :: Ref. 1850-06-17, 3:4, B.
June 8, at Montague-square, London, the lady of the Lord Bishop of Down, of a daughter.

No. 3870 :: Ref. 1850-06-17, 3:4, M.
June 6, at St. Mary's Church, Dublin, W.C. Scott, Esq., to Kate E., second daughter of the late Wm. Macfadin, Esq., of Cootehill, co. Cavan.

No. 3871 :: Ref. 1850-06-17, 3:4, M.
June 11, in the Presbyterian Church, Capel street, by the Rev. Wm. B. Kirkpatrick, John Suffern, Esq., of Belfast, to Emily, second daughter of George M'Bride, Esq., of Dublin.

No. 3872 :: Ref. 1850-06-17, 3:4, M.
June 11, in Clabber, near Coleraine, Mr. Wm. Reed, of Ballybay, co. Monaghan, to Elizabeth, eldest daughter of the Rev. Samuel Carlisle.

No. 3873 :: Ref. 1850-06-17, 3:4, M.
June 8, at St. Peter's Church, Dublin, by the Rev. H. White, Thos. White, of Kiltorcan, co. Kilkenny, Esq., to Mary Anne, only daughter of William Watkins, Esq., of Brookview Lodge, Enniskillen.

No. 3874 :: Ref. 1850-06-17, 3:4, M.
At Pettigo Church, on 7th June, by the Rev. C. Mande, Rector of Templecarne, the Rev. Arthur V. Watson, A.M., T.C.D., to Nannie, daughter of Hazlett Hamilton, Esq., of Pettigo and Bundoran.

No. 3875 :: Ref. 1850-06-17, 3:4, M.
June 5, at Gwmgad House, Glasgow, by the Rev. C.P. Miles, Incumbent of St. Jude's, Alexander Mackintosh, Esq., M.D., Physician Superintendent, Royal Lunatic Asylum, Gartnavel, Glasgow, to Elizabeth, daughter of the late James Armour, Esq., M.D., of the same place.

No. 3876 :: Ref. 1850-06-17, 3:4, M.
June 4, at Carrickfergus, by the Rev. Franklin Bewley, Thomas, son of the late Samuel Kennedy, Esq., of Grove-green, Lisburn, to Elizabeth Hancock, only daughter of J. Parker Fletcher, Esq., late of Greenfield, co. Down, and granddaughter of the late Samuel Green, Esq., Lurgan.

No. 3877 :: Ref. 1850-06-17, 3:4, M.
June 4, in the Parish Church, Wakefield, Yorkshire, by the Rev. Henry Jones, Curate, brother-in-law to the bride, the Rev. Matthew Forde Smyth, of Eccles, Manchester, B.A., and Ex-Scholar of Holy Trinity, Dublin, to Henrietta Noble Thompson, youngest daughter of the late Henry Thompson, Esq., Captain in her Majesty's 66th Regt. After the marriage was concluded the bridal party partook of the Holy Sacrament of the Lord's Supper.

No. 3878 :: Ref. 1850-06-17, 3:4, D.
On 8th ult., at Spring-hill, Tynan, in the 69th year of her age, Mrs. Lucinda Carpenter. She has been the subject of a long and severe affliction, the last 23 years confined to her bed; she was an example of christian fortitude, she bore her protracted illness with patience and christian resignation to the divine will; she was blessed with a sound mind and a good understanding, which she possessed in her last moments.

No. 3879 :: Ref. 1850-06-17, 3:4, D.
May 26, at Clogher, aged 48 years, Margaret M'Quade, widow.—She had been suffering from illness of some months standing, and a paralytic attack, of which she died, much regretted by her friends and respectable acquaintances.

No. 3880 :: Ref. 1850-06-17, 3:4, D.
On 17th ult., at his residence, Salisbury Mills, Orange County, John Caldwell, formerly a well-known merchant of New York, and born at Ballymoney, Ireland, in 1769.

No. 3881 :: Ref. 1850-06-17, 3:4, D.
The Right [H]on. Alice Mary, Countess Dowager of Limerick, expired almost suddenly on Thursday evening, at her residence, in Mansfield-st., London.

No. 3882 :: Ref. 1850-06-17, 3:4, D.
June 11, in the 28th year of her age, Miss Mary Jane Wilson, assistant Matron of the Enniskillen Workhouse.

No. 3883 :: Ref. 1850-06-17, 3:4, D.
June 7, aged 17 years, Jane Anne, youngest daughter of the late Mr. Robert Graham, of Ashfield, near Cootehill.

No. 3884 :: Ref. 1850-06-17, 3:4, D.
In Dublin, Miss Parry, for many years governess to the Countess of Clarendon, deeply and sincerely regretted by all who knew her.

No. 3885 :: Ref. 1850-06-17, 3:4, D.
June 3, at Kilkea, co. Clare, Eliza Winkworth, wife of the Rev. Thomas Knox, brother of the Lord Bishop of Down.

No. 3886 :: Ref. 1850-06-17, 3:4, D.
In the month of January last, in California, Samuel, third son of Mr. Joseph Dudgeon, Postmaster of Stewartstown.

No. 3887 :: Ref. 1850-06-17, 3:4, D.
May 30, suddenly, at her residence, Youngstown, Ohio, Eliza, wife of Dr. Robert M'Curdy, and daughter of the late Mr. Wm. Henry, of Castle-street, Sligo, aged 37 years.

No. 3888 :: Ref. 1850-06-17, 3:4, D.
On 7th June, in the 45th year of her age, Jane, wife of Charles Murphy, Esq., of Newgrove, near Cootehill.

No. 3889 :: Ref. 1850-06-24, 3:3, B.

On 12th inst., at Hawthorn Hill, Co. Armagh, the wife of Meredith Chambre, Esq., of a daughter.

No. 3890 :: Ref. 1850-06-24, 3:3, B.

On 12th inst., the lady of M. Singleton, Esq., R.M., Newry, of a son.

No. 3891 :: Ref. 1850-06-24, 3:3, M.

June 20, at Booterstown Church, by the Rev. J.S. Despard, (uncle to the bride,) Francis Cairncross Isdell, Esq., of Rockbrook, co. Westmeath, to Fanny, youngest daughter of the late W. Baker, Esq., of Springfield, Blackrock, and Liseahill, co. Tipperary.

No. 3892 :: Ref. 1850-06-24, 3:3, M.

June 18, in Letterkenny, by the Rev. Dr. Henry, John M'Farland, Esq., Merchant, Omagh, to Margaret Jane, eldest daughter of the Rev. W.H. Henry, D.D., of Letterkenny.

No. 3893 :: Ref. 1850-06-24, 3:3, M.

June 13, in Monreagh, by the Rev. Andrew Long, Mr. Robert M'Clelland, Newtownhamilton, to Miss Margaret Jane Mason, Molenan.

No. 3894 :: Ref. 1850-06-24, 3:3, M.

June 18, in Belfast, by the Rev. James Morgan, D.D., Robert Reid, Esq., of Liverpool, youngest son of the Rev. Edward Reid, of Ramelton, to Mary, daughter of the late Thomas Mackey, Esq., of Glenbank, Belfast.

No. 3895 :: Ref. 1850-06-24, 3:3, M.

May 30, in Holywood Church, Mr. James W. Connor, of Dungannon, to Sarah, eldest daughter of Mr. Wm. Hunter, of Bunker hill House.

No. 3896 :: Ref. 1850-06-24, 3:3, M.

June 13, in Strangford, by the Rev. T. Irvine, Capt. James Higgins, to Miss Elizabeth Ardiss, both of Strangford.

No. 3897 :: Ref. 1850-06-24, 3:3, M.

On 12th inst., in Donoughmore Presbyterian Church, by the Rev. Mr. Moore, George, only son of the late John Bennie, Esq., of Newry, to Jane, youngest daughter of James Parker, of Mount Kearney, Co. Down, Esq.

No. 3898 :: Ref. 1850-06-24, 3:3, M.

June 17, in St. Ann's Church, by the Rev. Mr. Allen, Mr. Robert Martin, of Belfast, merchant, to Margaretta, fourth daughter of G. M'Williams, Esq., Summerview-house, co. Tyrone.

No. 3899 :: Ref. 1850-06-24, 3:3, D.

June 12, at Roslin Villa, Cheshire, Bessie Maria, wife of the Rev. Benedict Asthuse, Incumbent of Trawmese, and daughter of the late B. Dillon, of Ballyquin House, co. Kilkenny, Esq.

No. 3900 :: Ref. 1850-06-24, 3:3, D.

May 25, at Maderia [sic], Lieutenant Colonel MacMahon, half-pay, unattached, aged 76.

No. 3901 :: Ref. 1850-06-24, 3:3, D.

April 14, at Poonamalla, Madras, Lieutenant J.G. Bolton, of H.M. 84th Regt., eldest son of Dr. Bolton, Dungannon.

No. 3902 :: Ref. 1850-06-24, 3:3, D.

June 14, at Dungannon, after a short illness, of consumption, Mr. Thomas Ryan.

No. 3903 :: Ref. 1850-06-24, 3:3, D.

June 18, at his residence, in Rashee, Robert Preston, in the 88th year of his age, who was one of the Irish Volunteers, under the command of Captain Allen, in 1781.

No. 3904 :: Ref. 1850-06-24, 3:3, D.

June 14, in the 78th year of his age, at Castlering, co. Louth, R. Bolton, Esq.

No. 3905 :: Ref. 1850-06-24, 3:3, D.

June 15, at Banbridge, Mary, only daughter, of Mr. William Walker, aged 7 years.

No. 3906 :: Ref. 1850-06-24, 3:3, D.

On 28th April, at Vienna, the Hon. Frances Gabrielle Talbot, sister of Lord Talbot de Malahide.

No. 3907 :: Ref. 1850-07-01, 3:4, B.

June 22, at Tynan, co. Armagh, the wife of the Rev. Stopford J. Ram, of a daughter.

No. 3908 :: Ref. 1850-07-01, 3:4, B.

June 21, at Knockatampul, Virginia, co. Cavan, the lady of the Rev. Hugh O'Neill, of a son.

No. 3909 :: Ref. 1850-07-01, 3:4, M.

In Derryvalley, co. Monaghan, on 26th ult., by the Rev. William Johnston, brother to the bridegroom, John Johnston, Esq., of Belfast, to Mary, eldest daughter of John Jackson, Esq., of Cremorne, county Monaghan.

No. 3910 :: Ref. 1850-07-01, 3:4, M.

On 22d ult., at her aunt's house, Askeston, by the Rev. Mr. Cussen, P.P., Joseph H. M'Mahon, Esq., of Armagh, to Miss C. Lynch, of Sexton-street, Limerick.

No. 3911 :: Ref. 1850-07-01, 3:4, M.

On 17th ult., in St. Ann's Church, Belfast, by the Rev. Mr. Allen, Mr. Robert Martin, of Belfast, merchant, to Margaretta, fourth daughter of George M'Williams, Esq., Summerview, co. Tyrone.

No. 3912 :: Ref. 1850-07-01, 3:4, M.

On 21st ult., in Cork, Rev. Thomas K. Whitaker, Wesleyan minister, to Frances Charlotte, eldest daughter of the late H.K. Reed, Esq., supervisor of Inland revenue at Cork.

No. 3913 :: Ref. 1850-07-01, 3:4, M.

On 25th ult., in St. Thomas's Church, Dublin, by the Rev. Henry M. Archdall, cousin to the bride, William, son of Edward Hardman, Esq., of Upper Mount-street, Dublin, to Harriet Anne, youngest daughter of the late Robert Hamilton, Esq., of Sackville-street, Dublin.

No. 3914 :: Ref. 1850-07-01, 3:4, M.

May 31, in St. Mark's Church, Armagh, by the Rev. Benjamin Wade, Mr. Thomas Galley, Inkeeper [sic], Hillsboro', county Down, to Jessey, eldest daughter of Mr. Hugh Burns, Innkeeper, English-street, Armagh.

No. 3915 :: Ref. 1850-07-01, 3:4, D.

On 23d June, Anna, third daughter of George Lockhart, Esq., Lurgan.

No. 3916 :: Ref. 1850-07-01, 3:4, D.

At Emyvale, at an advanced age, Mr. Samuel Johnston, for 17 years miller at the Emyvale Flour Mills. He was through life a most trustworthy man, and enjoyed the confidence of his employers.

No. 3917 :: Ref. 1850-07-01, 3:4, D.

Feb. 25, at sea, on his passage home from India, in the 21st year of his age, John Gage, Esq., 23d Regiment, M.L.I., youngest son of the Rev. Robert Gage, of Rathlin.

No. 3918 :: Ref. 1850-07-01, 3:4, D.

June 24, at Richmond House, Dundalk, Mrs. Charlotte Bigger, the beloved wife of Lennox Bigger, Esq., and daughter of the late John Eastwood, Esq., of Castletown, aged nearly 90 years.

No. 3919 :: Ref. 1850-07-01, 3:4, D.

June 22, at Aghamarta Castle, co. Cork, Carew S. O'Grady, Esq., aged 64, youngest brother of the First Lord Guillamore, and Registrar of the Court of Exchequer under his lordship, when Chief Baron.

No. 3920 :: Ref. 1850-07-01, 3:4, D.

June 18, in the wreck of the "*Orien*," at Portpatrick, Alexander M'Neill, Esq., of Ardlussa, Jura, and his wife, Anne Elizabeth, fourth daughter of the late John Carstairs, Esq., of Stratford-green, Essex, with Cecil Anne and Hester Mary, their eldest and youngest daughters.

No. 3921 :: Ref. 1850-07-01, 3:4, D.

June 14, at the residence of her son-in-law, Captain Hopkins, Wellington Lodge, near Hillsborough, Anne, relict of the late James Newell, Esq., Castlehill, Rathfriland, aged 76 years.

No. 3922 :: Ref. 1850-07-01, 3:4, D.

June 25, after a very short and painful illness, Viscount Cantilupe, eldest son of the Earl and Countess Delaware, at his father's residence in Upper Grosvenor-street, London.

No. 3923 :: Ref. 1850-07-01, 3:4, D.

June 22, David Todd, of Newry, merchant.

No. 3924 :: Ref. 1850-07-01, 3:4, D.

June 17, at Warrenpoint, aged 30 years, Sarah Anne Elchin, wife of George Vaughan Magenis, Solicitor.

No. 3925 :: Ref. 1850-07-08, 3:2, B.

June 24, Mrs. James Johnston, Main-street, Cavan, of a daughter.

No. 3926 :: Ref. 1850-07-08, 3:2, B.

June 23, the wife of Mr. C. Maguire, pawnbroker, Cavan, of a son.

No. 3927 :: Ref. 1850-07-08, 3:2, B.

June 28, at Drumboe, Lady Hayes, of a son.

No. 3928 :: Ref. 1850-07-08, 3:2, M.

On the 4th inst., in St. Mark's Church, Armagh, by the Rev. B. Wade, Andrew Craig, Esq., Summerhill, to Anna Osborne, daughter of Osborne Kidd, Esq., Tullymore, county Armagh.

No. 3929 :: Ref. 1850-07-08, 3:2, M.

June 24, in Rathdrum Wesleyan Chapel, by the Rev. Robert Hamilton, Mr. Robert Edge, of Rockstown, to Miss Jane Williams, of Ballygannon.

No. 3930 :: Ref. 1850-07-08, 3:2, D.

June 29, at Heathhall, county Armagh, the residence of Thomas Seaver, Esq., of consumption, aged 24 years, Susannah, the eldest daughter of the late Walter Clarke, Esq., of Summer Island, county Armagh.

No. 3931 :: Ref. 1850-07-08, 3:2, D.

June 28, at the residence of his brother-in-law, Carrick Hill, Belfast, Mr. John Kerr, of Rostrevor, aged 64 years.

No. 3932 :: Ref. 1850-07-08, 3:2, D.

June 27, in her 15th year, Lizzie K. Todd, youngest daughter of the late John Todd, of Newry, merchant.

No. 3933 :: Ref. 1850-07-08, 3:2, D.

On 1st inst., at Dungannon, after a few days' illness, of fever, Anne, the beloved wife of the Rev. John R. Darley. Mr. Darley was just about retiring from the position he has so long held of Head Master at the Royal School of Dungannon, and undertaking the duties of the parish of Cootehill, when it pleased the Lord to visit him with this heavy affliction.

No. 3934 :: Ref. 1850-07-15, 3:7, B.

At Cork, on 4th inst., the wife of Archibald Elliott, Esq., Quartermaster, 41st Regt., of a son.

No. 3935 :: Ref. 1850-07-15, 3:7, B.

On 26th ult., at Gortmore, Omagh, the wife of R.D. Coulson Esq., R.M. of a daughter.

No. 3936 :: Ref. 1850-07-15, 3:7, B.

On 2d inst., the wife of J.F. Alexander, Esq., Manager of Provincial Bank, Omagh, of a son.

No. 3937 :: Ref. 1850-07-15, 3:7, M.
On the 13th inst., at Armagh, by the Rev. William Maclean, Rector of Tynan, James Smyth, Esq., 69th Regt., to Olivia M.A., daughter of Joshua P. Barker, of Markethill, Esq.

No. 3938 :: Ref. 1850-07-15, 3:7, M.
On 27th ult., by Very Rev. Dr. Boylan, V.G., Dr. James O'Donnell [sic], M.R.C.S.I., third son of Surgeon O'Donnoll [sic], Ballyshannon, H.P. 77th Regiment, to Mary, niece of the Very Rev. Dr. Boylan, R.C., Rector of Enniskillen.

No. 3939 :: Ref. 1850-07-15, 3:7, M.
On 3d inst., in Monea Church, by the Rev. L.G. Reade, George Gamble, Esq., Lanachran, near Enniskillen, to Anne Jane, second daughter of John Nixon, Esq., Drumanure, Derrygonnelly.

No. 3940 :: Ref. 1850-07-15, 3:7, M.
On 10th inst., in Lurgan, by the Rev. Thomas Millar, Rev. Mr. Shanks, of Saintfield, to Miss Chischolm, of Hoophill-house, Lurgan.

No. 3941 :: Ref. 1850-07-15, 3:7, M.
In Glasslough Church, on 10th inst., by the Rev. W.H. Pratt, A.M., Robert M'Kinstry, Esq., M.D., fourth son of the late Lee M'Kinstry, Esq., of Armagh, to Elizabeth Anne, second daughter of H.G. Johnston of Fortjohnston, co. Monaghan, Esq.

No. 3942 :: Ref. 1850-07-15, 3:7, M.
At Petersham Church, Surrey, Major H.B. Edwardes, C.B., who so greatly distinguishe[d] himself in the late war in the Paujaub [sic] to Emma Sidney, youngest daughter of the late Mr. James Sidney, of Richmond Hill.

No. 3943 :: Ref. 1850-07-15, 3:7, D.
On 1st inst., aged 17 years, Margaret Burgess, fourth daughter of Henry Loftie Rutton, Esq., of Gilford.

No. 3944 :: Ref. 1850-07-15, 3:7, D.
On 12th July, Kate, youngest daughter of Mr. Allen, Vicars' Hill, aged eleven months.

No. 3945 :: Ref. 1850-07-15, 3:7, D.
On 2d inst., at Warrenpoint, Elizabeth Antonia, eldest daughter of the Rev. Mr. M'Kay.

No. 3946 :: Ref. 1850-07-15, 3:7, D.
July 7, at Glassnevin, Henry Maxwell, Esq., formerly known in Louth, aged 88 years.

No. 3947 :: Ref. 1850-07-15, 3:7, D.
On 10th inst., at Warrenpoint, Julia, relict of the late J. Reilly, Esq., J.P.

No. 3948 :: Ref. 1850-07-15, 3:7, D.
At Larah, on 26th ult., of malignant fever caught in the discharge of his sacred duties, in the 53d year of his age and 30th of his ministry, the Rev. Hugh Brady, P.P.

No. 3949 :: Ref. 1850-07-15, 3:7, D.
On 9th inst., in the 8th year of his age, James, son of Mr. John Henderson, Castle-place, Belfast.

No. 3950 :: Ref. 1850-07-15, 3:7, D.
July 1, at Island Cottage, near Clones, aged 72 years, Capt. John Ross, Adjutant, Monaghan Militia.

No. 3951 :: Ref. 1850-07-15, 3:7, D.
On 7th inst., at Cherrymount, Mr. Paul Dane, Clerk of the Enniskillen Union, aged 55.

No. 3952 :: Ref. 1850-07-15, 3:7, D.
At Beechmount, Canada West, Capt. W. Graham, formerly of the 74th Regt., and son of the late Christopher Graham, of Kilmore, co. Fermanagh.

No. 3953 :: Ref. 1850-07-22, 3:2, B.
On 9th inst., in this city, Mrs. Malcolm M'Neale Johnston, of a daughter.

No. 3954 :: Ref. 1850-07-22, 3:2, B.
On 19th inst., at Vicar's Hill, in this city, Mrs. George D. Hughes, of a son.

No. 3955 :: Ref. 1850-07-22, 3:2, M.
On the 19th inst., by the Rev. John West, Mr. Samuel Reid, C.P., of Newtownhamilton, to Emile, only daughter of Mr. Joseph Gleney, of Newtownhamilton.

No. 3956 :: Ref. 1850-07-22, 3:2, M.
On the 17th inst., in the Presbyterian Church, Downshire-road, Newry, by the Rev. J. Dodd, the Rev. C.B. Smith, to Mary Anne, youngest daughter of the late Robert M'Bride, Esq., of Alistragh, county Armagh.

No. 3957 :: Ref. 1850-07-22, 3:2, M.
On 17th inst., in the First Presbyterian Meetinghouse, Newry, by the Rev. Henry Alexander, Mr. Wm. M'Kitterick, to Susan, only daughter of Mr. Thomas Boyd, both of that town.

No. 3958 :: Ref. 1850-07-22, 3:2, M.
On 13th inst., by the Rev. E. Dalton, the Rev. Arthur G. Ryder, A.M., Head Master of Carrickmacross Endowed School, to Anne, eldest daughter of W.H. Gore, Esq., M.D., of Tramore.

No. 3959 :: Ref. 1850-07-22, 3:2, M.
On 3d inst., at Antwerp, by Rev. Henry Daveney, Rev. Maxwell Julius Blacker, second son of the late Lieut.-Colonel V. Blacker, to Emily Georgina, second daughter of Henry Daveney, Esq., Malines, Belgium.

No. 3960 :: Ref. 1850-07-22, 3:2, D.
At Drummilly, co. Armagh, 16th July, Garland Cope, Esq.

No. 3961 :: Ref. 1850-07-22, 3:2, D.
On 15th May, Mrs. Mary Stevenson, of Lanark, Bathurst district, U.C., aged 62 years, eldest daughter of Mr. John Boyd, late of Breakley, near Keady, co. Armagh.

No. 3962 :: Ref. 1850-07-22, 3:2, D.
On 11th inst., in her 75th year, Elizabeth, relict of the late Robt. M'Morran, Esq., of Castleblayney.

No. 3963 :: Ref. 1850-07-22, 3:2, D.
On 12th July, at Balling-house, Banbridge, co. Down, George Crawford, Esq., aged 62.

No. 3964 :: Ref. 1850-07-22, 3:2, D.
On 2d inst., at Strangmore, near Dungannon, the residence of her son-in-law, John P. Barcraft, Ann Malcolmson, relict of the late Thos. Malcolmson, of Lurgan, aged 78 years.

No. 3965 :: Ref. 1850-07-22, 3:2, D.
On 13th inst., Alexander, only son of the late Mr. Alexander Peacock, Printer, of Marcus-square, Newry, aged nine years.

No. 3966 :: Ref. 1850-07-29, 3:2, B.
July 16, at Camla, the residence of Colonel Westenra, the Lady Rossmore, of a daughter.

No. 3967 :: Ref. 1850-07-29, 3:2, B.
On the 5th inst., at Newtownlimavady, Mrs. Hugh Lane, of a son.

No. 3968 :: Ref. 1850-07-29, 3:2, B.
On the night of Wednesday week, the lady of Archibald Collum, Esq., Enniskillen, of a son.

No. 3969 :: Ref. 1850-07-29, 3:2, B.
July 28, at Donegall-place, Belfast, Mrs. B. Hughes, of a daughter.

No. 3970 :: Ref. 1850-07-29, 3:2, B.
July 20, at Dungannon, the lady of Courtenay Newton, Esq., of [a] son.

No. 3971 :: Ref. 1850-07-29, 3:2, B.
July 14, at Omagh, the lady of Mr. M. M'Cann, Inland Revenue, of a son.

No. 3972 :: Ref. 1850-07-29, 3:2, B.
July 4, at Tubrid, the lady of Captain George Stack, of a son.

No. 3973 :: Ref. 1850-07-29, 3:2, B.
July 9, the lady of the Hon. and Rev. Francis Clements, Vicar of Norton, of a daughter.

No. 3974 :: Ref. 1850-07-29, 3:2, B.
July 1, at Portarlington, the lady of Samuel de Vignoles, Esq., of a daughter.

No. 3975 :: Ref. 1850-07-29, 3:2, M.
On 17th inst., in Holywood, by the Rev. Dr. Cooke, Mr. R.G. Mullen, Manchester, to Martha Dugan, daughter of Mr. George Harrison, Belfast.

No. 3976 :: Ref. 1850-07-29, 3:2, M.
On the 9th inst., in the Presbyterian Church, Glascar, by the Rev. James Rogers, Mr. James Law, merchant, Banbridge, to Susanna, third daughter of Mr. James Todd, Ringclave, Donaghmore.

No. 3977 :: Ref. 1850-07-29, 3:2, M.
On 27th ult., at Holywood, co. Down, by the Rev. T. Price, Philip Andrew Armstrong, Esq., M.D. and J.P., of Castletown, Berehaven, co. Cork, to Charlotte Louisa, daughter of the late Major Bailie, of her Majesty's 38th Regiment.

No. 3978 :: Ref. 1850-07-29, 3:2, M.
On the 25th inst., at Phipsborough Church, Dublin, by the Rev. J. Bailie, George Frederick Wales, Esq., Surgeon, of Belfast, to Charlotte, second daughter of the late Thomas Greer, Esq., Tyrone.

No. 3979 :: Ref. 1850-07-29, 3:2, M.
On 10th inst., in Lusk Church, by the Rev. Mr. Potterton, Johnston Wilson, 26, Parliament-street, Dublin, son of John Wilson, Esq., Portadown, to Sarah, third daughter of Thomas Carey, Esq., Rogerstown House, Rush.

No. 3980 :: Ref. 1850-07-29, 3:2, M.
On the 2d inst., at Tullylish Church, near Banbridge, by the Rev. W. M'Ilwaine, Incumbent of St. George's Church, Belfast, Robert Druitt, Esq., London, to Mary, youngest daughter of the late Robert Smyth, Esq., of Strabane.

No. 3981 :: Ref. 1850-07-29, 3:2, M.
July 16, at the Collegiate Church of St. Nicholas, Galway, by the Rev. Edward Eyre Maunsell, the Rev. Joseph Allen Galbraith, F.T.C.D., to Hannah Maria, second surviving daughter of the late Rev. John Bredin, county of Cavan.

No. 3982 :: Ref. 1850-07-29, 3:2, M.
At the same time [July 16, at the Collegiate Church of St. Nicholas, Galway], also by the Rev. Edward Eyre Maunsell, Charles Cheyne, son of the late John Cheyne, M.D., Physician-General to the Forces in Ireland, to Eugenia Eliza, youngest daughter of the late Rev. John Bredin, county of Cavan.

No. 3983 :: Ref. 1850-07-29, 3:2, M.
On the 3d inst., at Wyke Regis, near Weymouth, Dorset, by the Rev. F. Ffolliott, uncle of the bride, assisted by the Rev. E.W. Pears, the Rev. Abraham Hillhouse M'Causland, eldest son of Marcus M'Causland, Esq., of Londonderry, to Barbara Martha, second daughter of Rear-Admiral Payne, R.N., of Weymouth.

No. 3984 :: Ref. 1850-07-29, 3:2, M.
June 4, at St. George's Cathedral, Madras, by the Right Rev. the Lord Bishop, Henry Ambrose Hare, Esq., 17th Regiment, to Charlotte Maria, daughter of Capt. George Hill, of Mountjoy, County Tyrone.

No. 3985 :: Ref. 1850-07-29, 3:2, D.
July 28, at Farmacaffly, near Armagh, Mary, the beloved wife of Mr. George Wilton, formerly of this city.

No. 3986 :: Ref. 1850-07-29, 3:2, D.

On the 23d inst., Jane, relict of Mr. George Frizell, late of Lismulreavey, near Dungannon, aged 84.

No. 3987 :: Ref. 1850-07-29, 3:2, D.

On the 20th inst., at Rathfriland, Susanna, wife of Mr. William Matthews.

No. 3988 :: Ref. 1850-07-29, 3:2, D.

On 23d inst., at the Chapel House, Clogher, Jane Rosetta, the beloved daughter of Mr. William A. Johnston. Her latter end was peace.

No. 3989 :: Ref. 1850-07-29, 3:2, D.

On 18th inst., at Mullaglass, Annabella, the beloved wife of Mr. Wm. Ledlie, aged 35 years, after a protracted illness, which she bore with true Christian fortitude.

No. 3990 :: Ref. 1850-07-29, 3:2, D.

On 14th inst., Mr. James Crawford, of Knockmoyle, aged 78 years.

No. 3991 :: Ref. 1850-07-29, 3:2, D.

On 15th inst., at Dungannon, Surgeon James Cassidy, much regretted.

No. 3992 :: Ref. 1850-07-29, 3:2, D.

On 14th inst., at Braehead, Londonderry, Robert Ramsay, Esq., Lieutenant, R.N., agent of the Board of Emigration at that port.

No. 3993 :: Ref. 1850-07-29, 3:2, D.

On 25th inst., at Magherafelt, after a few hours' illness, Mr. Thos. M'Fall, hotel keeper.

No. 3994 :: Ref. 1850-07-29, 3:2, D.

On 19th inst., in the 14th year of her age, Harriett, youngest daughter of Hutcheson Posnett, Esq., Rose Lodge, Belfast.

No. 3995 :: Ref. 1850-07-29, 3:2, D.

On 21st inst., suddenly, at Vicar's Hall, county of Kildare, shortly after he had returned home from officiating at mid-day service, the Rev. William M'Kenna, Rector of the union of Clare, much and sincerely regretted by a numerous family, and by his parishioners.

No. 3996 :: Ref. 1850-07-29, 3:2, D.

On 25th inst., in Cavan, Mr. Patrick Naulty, Petty Sessions Clerk of that county for a great many years.

No. 3997 :: Ref. 1850-07-29, 3:2, D.

On 15th inst., not more than an hour before the time the veteran actress, Mrs. Glover, breathed her last, Mrs. Manyard, another clever comedian, expired, after a tedious and painful illness.

No. 3998 :: Ref. 1850-07-29, 3:2, D.

On 1st inst., at Taunton, Somersetshire, Charles Vercker, Esq., second son of the late Major John Vercker, of Limerick, and several years Captain in the 27th, or Enniskillen Regiment, in which he served with great distinction throughout the Caffre war, at the Cape of Good Hope.

No. 3999 :: Ref. 1850-07-29, 3:2, D.

On 14th inst., at Ballymena, Catharine, relict of the late Mr. Archibald Cumming, in the 77th year of her age. Her end was peace.

No. 4000 :: Ref. 1850-07-29, 3:2, D.

On 16th July, at Castletown, in the county of Fermanagh, to the inexpressible grief of her family, after a long and painful illness, borne with Christian fortitude and resignation, Charlotte, wife of John Brien, Esq., and daughter of the late Rev. William Dawson, formerly Vicar of Clontibret, in the county of Monaghan.

No. 4001 :: Ref. 1850-07-29, 3:2, D.

On the 20th inst., at Goblusk, William, eldest son of Christopher Graham, Esq., aged 22 years.

No. 4002 :: Ref. 1850-07-29, 3:2, D.

On 17th July, at Waterloo-road, Dublin, Anna Maria, daughter of the late Rev. John Ellison, of Killymard, co. of Donegal.

No. 4003 :: Ref. 1850-07-29, 3:2, D.

Pierce Kenifeck Mahony, Esq., eldest son of P. Mahony, Esq., Clerk of the Crown, Co. Dublin. His death was rather unexpected, for, though he had been ill for a few days, the symptoms did not appear so dangerous as to warrant any impression of so rapidly fatal a result. By his death an office reverts to the Crown, in the Accountant-General's department.

No. 4004 :: Ref. 1850-08-05, 2:3, B.

July 30, at Tartaraghan Glebe, the lady of the Rev. George Robinson, of a daughter.

No. 4005 :: Ref. 1850-08-05, 2:3, M.

July 30, at Killaghtee Church, by the Rev. Mr. Walsh, Hazlitt Betty, Solicitor, of Floraville, Enniskillen, to Anne Jane, eldest daughter of Michael Clark Stephens, Esq., R.N., of Spamount, Dunkaneely.

No. 4006 :: Ref. 1850-08-05, 2:3, D.

July 30, at his residence, Dungannon, Samuel C. Huggins, sen., Esq.

No. 4007 :: Ref. 1850-08-05, 2:3, D.

July 31, aged 15 months, Charles, third son of Mr. R.J. Evans, proprietor of the *Lurgan Chronicle*.

No. 4008 :: Ref. 1850-08-12, 3:1, B.

In Wales, Mrs. Bleasby, widow of the late Arthur Bernard Bleazby, Esq., of Glenaul House, in this county, of a daughter.

No. 4009 :: Ref. 1850-08-12, 3:1, M.

On 6th inst., at Fintona church, by the Rev. Thos. Maunsell, Christopher Buchanan, Esq., Gortatole, Co. Fermanagh, to Eliza, eldest daughter of James Buchanan, Esq., Hardware merchant, Fintona.

No. 4010 :: Ref. 1850-08-12, 3:1, D.
Suddenly, on Wednesday morning last, at Mulvyn, Alexander Auchinleck, Esq., Secretary to the Grand Jury of county Tyrone.

No. 4011 :: Ref. 1850-08-19, 3:1, B.
On 4th inst., at Belfast, the lady of Charles Lanyon, Esq., of a son.

No. 4012 :: Ref. 1850-08-19, 3:1, B.
July 31, at Tullamore, the wife of O.N. Birney, Esq., of a son.

No. 4013 :: Ref. 1850-08-19, 3:1, B.
On 11th inst., the wife of the Rev. James Bell, Tandragee, of a son.

No. 4014 :: Ref. 1850-08-19, 3:1, B.
July 16, at Ballickmoyler, Queen's Co., the wife of James Ponsonby Hill, Esq., Constabulary, of a daughter.

No. 4015 :: Ref. 1850-08-19, 3:1, B.
July 21, the lady of Francis West Connolly, Esq., of Ballinamore, co. Leitrim, of a son.

No. 4016 :: Ref. 1850-08-19, 3:1, B.
On 11th inst., at Benburb, the wife of Walter Hore, Esq., J.P., of a daughter.

No. 4017 :: Ref. 1850-08-19, 3:1, B.
Aug. 8, at the Under-Secretary's Lodge, Phoenix Park, the lady of Thomas N. Redington, Esq., K.C.B., of a daughter.

No. 4018 :: Ref. 1850-08-19, 3:1, B.
On 2d inst., at Sligo, the lady of St. John Purcell, Provincial Bank, of a daughter.

No. 4019 :: Ref. 1850-08-19, 3:1, B.
On 6th inst., at Sligo, the lady of Dr. Homan, of a son.

No. 4020 :: Ref. 1850-08-19, 3:1, B.
On 16th inst., the lady of James Harper, Esq., American Consul, of a daughter.

No. 4021 :: Ref. 1850-08-19, 3:1, B.
On 11th inst., at Ballyshannon, the lady of George Hewison, Esq., I.R. Officer, of a daughter.

No. 4022 :: Ref. 1850-08-19, 3:1, B.
On 1st inst., at Chatham, the lady of Captain Hardy, 58th Regt., of a son.

No. 4023 :: Ref. 1850-08-19, 3:1, B.
On 2d inst., at Bristol, the wife of Frederick S. Hemming, Esq., of Campsie, of a son.

No. 4024 :: Ref. 1850-08-19, 3:1, B.
On 29th ult., at Portarlington, the lady of R.B. Porter, Esq., of a son.

No. 4025 :: Ref. 1850-08-19, 3:1, B.
On 29th ult., at Arvagh, co. Cavan, the lady of Dr. Reynolds, of a daughter.

No. 4026 :: Ref. 1850-08-19, 3:1, M.
On 27th ult., in Derry, by Rev. James Crawford, Mr. Isaac Clements, printer, to Isabella, youngest daughter of the late Mr. Wm. Cunningham, of that city.

No. 4027 :: Ref. 1850-08-19, 3:1, M.
On 1st inst., Viscount Cranley, only son of the Earl of Onslow, to Lady Katherine Anne Cust, youngest daughter of the Earl Brownlow.

No. 4028 :: Ref. 1850-08-19, 3:1, M.
On 8th inst., at Omagh, by the Rev. M.N. Thompson, William Rogar, Esq., M.B., to Elizabeth Gasten, eldest daughter of David Denny, Esq., Omagh.

No. 4029 :: Ref. 1850-08-19, 3:1, M.
July 30, in Donemana, by the Rev. John Monteith, Mr. James Craig, Liscleen, to Lavinia, youngest daughter of Mr. John Walker, Tyrconnelly, co. Tyrone.

No. 4030 :: Ref. 1850-08-19, 3:1, M.
July 31, at Aghavea, by the Rev. Mr. Welsh, Rebecca, eldest daughter of Robert Sharkey, Enniskillen Dragoons, to Mr. Thomas Graham, Family Hotel, Lisnaskea.

No. 4031 :: Ref. 1850-08-19, 3:1, M.
July 18, at Franklinville, United States of America, Richard Millett, Civil Engineer, eldest son of the late Thomas Millett, Esq., Millbrook, county of Tipperary, to Emily, eldest daughter of the late John Mayne, Esq., of Cootehill, co. Cavan.

No. 4032 :: Ref. 1850-08-19, 3:1, M.
July 26, in Sallaghy Church, by the Rev. John Stevenson, uncle to the bride, Mr. John Hicks, of Bunn, co. [F]ermanagh, to Eliza, eldest daughter of Edward Russell, of Corsenchin, near Lisnaskea, Esq.

No. 4033 :: Ref. 1850-08-19, 3:1, M.
At the English Presbyterian Church, Woolwich, Kent by Rev. John Weir, uncle to the bride, Paul Hirsch, Esq., to Mary, eldest daughter of the late Joseph D. Dobbin, Esq., Newtownhamilton, co. Armagh.

No. 4034 :: Ref. 1850-08-19, 3:1, D.
Suddenly, at his residence, at Sandhill, Albion, on Saturday morning, July 6, in consequences of severe injury sustained by a fall from his horse, on the Thursday evening previous, Mr. John Porter, in the 40th year of his age, formerly of Drum, county Monaghan, Ireland; deeply regretted by a numerous circle of friends and relatives.—*Streetsville Weekly Review*, July 13.

No. 4035 :: Ref. 1850-08-19, 3:1, D.
Aug. 12, suddenly, in the Wesleyan Chapel, Bundoran, Mrs. Irwin, from the neighbourhood of Newtownbutler.

No. 4036 :: Ref. 1850-08-19, 3:1, D.
On 6th inst., after a few days illness, aged 28 years, Peter Sheriff, Esq., Denbigh Terrace, Liverpool, deeply lamented by a large circle of friends, by whom he was endeared by many amiable qualities.

No. 4037 :: Ref. 1850-08-19, 3:1, D.
On 18th inst., at Mount Irwin, near Tynan, in this county, Wm. George Irwin, Esq., J.P.

No. 4038 :: Ref. 1850-08-19, 3:1, D.
On 24th ult., at Cahirline, near Castleconnell, Jane, second daughter of the late Wm. Gabbett.

No. 4039 :: Ref. 1850-08-19, 3:1, D.
On 30th ult., at Belfast, Mr. John M'Kindry, in the 71st year of his age.

No. 4040 :: Ref. 1850-08-19, 3:1, D.
On 9th inst., in Enniskillen, Mr. George M'Knight, Printer, aged 38 years.

No. 4041 :: Ref. 1850-08-19, 3:1, D.
On 8th inst., at Monaghan, Mr. James M'Knight, one of the most respected inhabitants of the town.

No. 4042 :: Ref. 1850-08-19, 3:1, D.
On 18th ult., at New York, Mr. John Jennings, late of Saintfield, county Down, Ireland, aged 45.

No. 4043 :: Ref. 1850-08-19, 3:1, D.
On 11th inst., of inveterate bronchitis, aged 37 years, Anne, eldest surviving daughter of the late Rev. John Graham, Rector of Magilligan, co. Derry.

No. 4044 :: Ref. 1850-08-19, 3:1, D.
On 16th ult., after a severe passage from Cuba to Quebec, Capt. John Sim, late of the brig *"Thomas,"* and son of Mr. Andrew Sim, of Warrenpoint.

No. 4045 :: Ref. 1850-08-19, 3:1, D.
On 6th inst., in Dublin, Mrs. Henry, relict of Thomas Henry, Esq., of Anneville, Castleblayney.

No. 4046 :: Ref. 1850-08-19, 3:1, D.
On 30th, at Leeson-street, Dublin, in her 70th year, Anne, wife of the late Peter Burrows, Esq., K.C.

No. 4047 :: Ref. 1850-08-19, 3:1, D.
On 11th inst., Maria Sophia, only daughter of William Smith, Esq., J.P., Drumheel, aged 4 years and 4 months.

No. 4048 :: Ref. 1850-08-19, 3:1, D.
On 14th inst., Hannah, wife of John Cuddy, Esq., merchant, Belfast.

No. 4049 :: Ref. 1850-08-19, 3:1, D.
On 30th ult., at Dublin, Major Harman Jeffares, late of the Royal Newfoundland Corps, aged 63 years.

No. 4050 :: Ref. 1850-08-19, 3:1, D.
On 31st ult., Eliza, only daughter of Thomas Phillips, Esq., J.P., Ahafin, co. Monaghan.

No. 4051 :: Ref. 1850-08-19, 3:1, D.
At Seapoint Terrace, Monkstown, aged 42 years, Frederick Bedford Lang, Esq., Inspector-General of Prisons.

No. 4052 :: Ref. 1850-08-19, 3:1, D.
Mr. John Glen, of Tiverevan, parish of Tamlaghtard, at the advanced age of 105 years.

No. 4053 :: Ref. 1850-08-19, 3:1, D.
On 28th ult., at Prospect House, co. Fermanagh, Alexander Maguire, Esq., J.P., aged 90 years. He was one of the oldest magistrates of the county.

No. 4054 :: Ref. 1850-08-19, 3:1, D.
In Belfast, in the 20th year of his age, William, second son of the late Robert James, M.D., of Balieborough [sic], co. Cavan.

No. 4055 :: Ref. 1850-08-19, 3:1, D.
At his retreat in the Highlands, Inverallort, Major-General Sir Alexander Cameron, K.C.B., Colonel of the 74th Highlanders.

No. 4056 :: Ref. 1850-08-19, 3:1, D.
On 30th ult., at Coalisland House, county Tyrone, Isabella, the beloved wife of George Wilcocks, Esq., in the 68th year of her age.

No. 4057 :: Ref. 1850-08-19, 3:1, D.
On 2d inst., at Clifden Castle, aged 24 years, Richard D'Arcy, Esq., seventh son of the late John D'Arcy, of Clifden Castly [sic], county Galway.

No. 4058 :: Ref. 1850-08-19, 3:1, D.
On 10th inst., at Maryborough, in the 55th year of his age, Wm. Abbott, Esq., Manager of the District Lunatic Asylum.

No. 4059 :: Ref. 1850-08-19, 3:1, D.
On 3d inst., at the Court-house, Clogher, Thomas Francis, eldest son of Mr. M.A. Johnston.

No. 4060 :: Ref. 1850-08-19, 3:1, D.
On 3d inst., at Wallington hall, Norfolk, Eliza, wife of the late Robert Peel, Esq., and aunt of the late Sir R. Peel, Bart.

No. 4061 :: Ref. 1850-08-19, 3:1, D.
At Patena, New South Wales, Major Johnstone, late of the 50th Regiment.

No. 4062 :: Ref. 1850-08-19, 3:1, D.
On 5th inst., at No. 95, Donegall-street, Belfast, Mr. M'Connell, aged 34 years.

No. 4063 :: Ref. 1850-08-19, 3:1, D.
On 28th ult., James Creery, Esq., drowned in Loch Lomond, while bathing.

No. 4064 :: Ref. 1850-08-19, 3:1, D.
On 29th ult., Rev. Wm. Brown, Minister of the Presbyterian Church, Buncrana, aged 42 years.

No. 4065 :: Ref. 1850-08-26, 3:1, B.
On the 20th Inst., at Lislea, county Armagh, the lady of Thomas Wynne, Esq., of a son.

No. 4066 :: Ref. 1850-08-26, 3:1, B.
On 20th Inst., in Dublin, the lady of Rev. Charles Seaver, Assistant Chaplain of Sandford Church, of a daughter.

No. 4067 :: Ref. 1850-08-26, 3:1, B.
On 15th inst., at 27, Richmond-street, Dublin, the lady of C.C. Overend, Esq., of a son.

No. 4068 :: Ref. 1850-08-26, 3:1, M.
Aug. 15th, in the Scots Church, Cork, by Rev. Wm. Magill, L.L.D., Mr. Samuel Nixon, Manchester, (late of Sorrelfield, Manorhamilton) to Mary Eleanor, second daughter of Mr. Wm. Trimble, printer, Enniskillen.

No. 4069 :: Ref. 1850-08-26, 3:1, M.
On 18th inst., at Portadown, by Rev. E. Crolly, P.P., Mr. Patrick Henry, only son of the late Mr. Owen Henry, to Catherine, third daughter of Mr. John Morgan, of Portadown.

No. 4070 :: Ref. 1850-08-26, 3:1, M.
August 20, at Ahamlish Church, by the Rev. William Jeffcott, James Corry Lowry, of Rockdale House, co. Tyrone, and Mountjoy-square, South, Dublin, Esq., to Jane, eldest daughter of Booth Jones, of Streeda, co. Sligo, Esq.

No. 4071 :: Ref. 1850-08-26, 3:1, M.
Aug. 20, in St. Thomas's Church, by the Rev. James S. Franks, John G. Kisby, Esq., to Louisa, relict of Jonathan Smyth, of Urker, co. Armagh, Esq.

No. 4072 :: Ref. 1850-08-26, 3:1, M.
On 20th inst., at Rossorry Church, co. Fermanagh, by Rev. Wm. Welsh, of Ramelton, Albert Smith, Esq., of Tamar Terrace, Devonport, to Jane Eliza, daughter of the late Dr. John Frith.

No. 4073 :: Ref. 1850-08-26, 3:1, M.
Aug. 15, in Ballyrashane Church, J.D. Mitchell, Esq., accountant of the Provincial Bank of Ireland, Ballymena, fourth son of the late George Mitchell, Esq., of Parsonstown, to Margaret, youngest daughter of the late Archibald Dunlop, Esq., of Coleraine.

No. 4074 :: Ref. 1850-08-26, 3:1, D.
On 22d inst., at Woodford, near this city, Ada, the beloved daughter of John Cuming, Esq.

No. 4075 :: Ref. 1850-08-26, 3:1, D.
On 19th inst., Mr. James Mallon, of Thomas-street, Armagh, tailor.

No. 4076 :: Ref. 1850-08-26, 3:1, D.
On 15th inst., at Edinburgh, Mary, relict of the Rev. Richard Olpherts, of Charlestown Glebe, Ardee.

No. 4077 :: Ref. 1850-08-26, 3:1, D.
On 19th inst., at Brighton, after a long and severe illness, in the 81st year of his age, Sir Martin Archer Shee, President of the Royal Academy.

No. 4078 :: Ref. 1850-08-26, 3:1, D.
On 22d inst., in the 73d year of his age, at his residence, 35, North Great George's-street, Richard Farrell, Esq., Q.C., Commissioner of the Court for the Relief of Insolvent Debtors.

No. 4079 :: Ref. 1850-08-26, 3:1, D.
On 16th inst., suddenly, at Curraghtown House, co. Meath, the residence of her son, Martha Jane, relict of the late Mr. Alexander Roberts, formerly of Lislooney, co. Armagh, aged 77 years, having survived her husband only four weeks.

No. 4080 :: Ref. 1850-09-02, 3:2, B.
On 30th ult., the lady of James Foulston, Esq., head master of the National Institute for the Deaf and Dumb, Claremont, of a son.

No. 4081 :: Ref. 1850-09-02, 3:2, B.
On 16th ult., at Bantry, the lady of Redmond Power, Esq., Sub Inspector of Constabulary, of a son.

No. 4082 :: Ref. 1850-09-02, 3:2, B.
On 22d ult., at Killishil Cottage, co. Tyrone, the lady of Rev. Christopher Graham, of a son.

No. 4083 :: Ref. 1850-09-02, 3:2, B.
On 29th ult., at Harold's-cross, the lady of the Rev. Jas. Quinton, of a son.

No. 4084 :: Ref. 1850-09-02, 3:2, B.
On 23d ult., at Carrickmore, the lady of Henry Lucas St. George, Esq., of a son.

No. 4085 :: Ref. 1850-09-02, 3:2, B.
On 23d ult., at Avonview, Rathdrum, county Wicklow, the lady of John Croker, Esq., Sub-Inspector of Constabulary, of a son.

No. 4086 :: Ref. 1850-09-02, 3:2, B.
On 25th ult., in Derry, Mrs. James M'Carter, of a son.

No. 4087 :: Ref. 1850-09-02, 3:2, B.
On 20th ult., at Dungannon, the lady of Charles Coote, Esq., M.D., of a daughter.

No. 4088 :: Ref. 1850-09-02, 3:2, B.
On 27th ult., at Saggart House, the lady of John James Verschoyle, Esq., of a daughter.

No. 4089 :: Ref. 1850-09-02, 3:2, B.
On 27th ult., at Preston, the wife of Mr. Robert Leigh, butcher, of a daughter, the twenty-seventh living child to which she has given birth, all born at single births.

No. 4090 :: Ref. 1850-09-02, 3:2, M.
On 22 ult., in Armaghbrague Church, by the Rev. D. Donaldson, Mr. John Corry, of Roan, to Miss Eliza Hartness, of Rockmount.

No. 4091 :: Ref. 1850-09-02, 3:2, M.

On 20th ult., in Warrenpoint Church, by the Rev. E.J. Evans, Major Wilkinson, 13th (Prince Albert's) Light Infantry, to Elizabeth Mary, eldest daughter of James Jones, Esq., of Mount Edward, co. of Sligo.

No. 4092 :: Ref. 1850-09-02, 3:2, M.

On 18th ult., in St. Peter's Church, Liverpool, Mr. John Kennedy, of Dundalk, to Charlotte Sophia Flanagan, eldest daughter of the late Dr. Flanagan, of the 4th Royal Irish Dragoons.

No. 4093 :: Ref. 1850-09-02, 3:2, M.

On 23d ult., the Rev. Samuel Priestly, Poyntzpass, to Anna, relict of Andrew Craig Ward, Esq., Solicitor, Lisburn, and only daughter of the late Wm. Swiney, Esq., of her Majesty's 90th Regt.

No. 4094 :: Ref. 1850-09-02, 3:2, M.

On 17th ult., in Clontarf Church, by the Rev. Robert G. Atkinson, Rector of Clonmore, Wm. Fenton, Esq., of Kiltegan, co. Wicklow, to Lucinda Sara, sixth daughter of the late Major Frood, of Dundalk.

No. 4095 :: Ref. 1850-09-02, 3:2, M.

On 16th ult., in the Presbyterian Church, Orritor, by Rev. M. M'Murray, Waringstown, co. Down, Mr. David Brown, Wellbrook, co. Tyrone, to Margaret Glasgow, eldest daughter of the Rev. J.G. M'Gowan, Orritor.

No. 4096 :: Ref. 1850-09-02, 3:2, D.

On 29th ult., at Rothsay, Isle of Bute, of dysentery, after a few days' illness, Jane, daughter of the late James Johnston, Esq., of Knappa, co. Armagh. Her remains passed through this city to-day for interment in the family vault, Drumsallan Church-yard. The undertaker was Mr. Alexander Frizzell.

No. 4097 :: Ref. 1850-09-02, 3:2, D.

On 25th ult., aged 20, Mary Jane, eldest daughter of Mr. James Monypenny, merchant, near Portadown. She was greatly beloved by all who knew her; by her death the poor have sustained a great loss, but their loss is her infinite gain.

No. 4098 :: Ref. 1850-09-02, 3:2, D.

On the 23d ult., at Ballinagh, John James Brady, Esq., aged 24 years.

No. 4099 :: Ref. 1850-09-02, 3:2, D.

On 24th ult., at Tunbridge-wells, George Richard Robinson, Esq., M.P., for Poole, and late Chairman of Lloyds, aged 69.

No. 4100 :: Ref. 1850-09-02, 3:2, D.

On 21st ult., James, son of Andrew Campbell, Esq., of Stewartstown, in the 26th year of his age.

No. 4101 :: Ref. 1850-09-02, 3:2, D.

On 24th ult., at Ogle's Grove, Hillsborough, Mr. Henry Davis.

No. 4102 :: Ref. 1850-09-02, 3:2, D.

On 23d ult., at Killycannon, near Markethill, Margaret, fourth daughter of Mr. David Hutcheson.

No. 4103 :: Ref. 1850-09-02, 3:2, D.

On 20th ult., at Sandy-lodge, Ballymena, in the 72d year of her age, Mary, relict of the late Mr. John Davidson, [of] Ballymena.

No. 4104 :: Ref. 1850-09-02, 3:2, D.

On 21st ult., at his residence, No. 4, Richmond-terrace, London, John Henry Ley, Esq., Clerk of the House of Commons, of Trehill, in the county of Devon.

No. 4105 :: Ref. 1850-09-02, 3:2, D.

On 18th ult., at the Duke of Wellington's, Piccadilly, the Right Hon. Charles Arbuthnot.

No. 4106 :: Ref. 1850-09-02, 3:2, D.

On 25th ult., at Westport, Louis [sic] Catharine, eldest daughter of Colonel and Lady Louisa Knox.

No. 4107 :: Ref. 1850-09-02, 3:2, D.

On 22d ult., at Woodview, Blackrock, in his 84th year, Manus O'Keeffe, Esq., much esteemed and regretted.

No. 4108 :: Ref. 1850-09-02, 3:2, D.

On 19th ult., at Stewartstown, the Rev. David Gilkey, Minister of the Second Presbyterian Congregation of Omagh, in the 80th year of his age, and 46th of his ministry.

No. 4109 :: Ref. 1850-09-02, 3:2, D.

On 13th inst., at Beech-hill, aged 62 years, Catherine, wife of Conolly M'Causland Skipton, Esq., and only daughter of the late John Spotswood, Esq., of Bellaghy.

No. 4110 :: Ref. 1850-09-02, 3:2, D.

On 22d ult., aged sixteen months, Moffat, youngest son of Mr. John Arnold, of Belfast.

No. 4111 :: Ref. 1850-09-09, 3:3, B.

On the 4th inst., at Drumnakilly House, the lady of Alex. M'Causland, Esq., of a daughter.

No. 4112 :: Ref. 1850-09-09, 3:3, B.

At Carrickmore, the lady of Henry Lucas St. George, Esq., of a daughter.

No. 4113 :: Ref. 1850-09-09, 3:3, B.

On the 31st ult., at Aghabog Glebe, co. Monaghan, Mrs. William Story, of a son.

No. 4114 :: Ref. 1850-09-09, 3:3, B.

On 29th of August, at Fairview House, near Castledawson, co. Derry, the residence of James Henry, Esq., the lady of John Holland, Esq., Barrister-at-law, Bombay, of a daughter.

No. 4115 :: Ref. 1850-09-09, 3:3, M.

On 2d inst., in Ballymena, by Rev. Dr. Reeves, Mr. George Frederick Stevenson, of Lurgan, to Mary Crawford, youngest daughter of the late Mr. Samuel M'Master, Ballymena.

No. 4116 :: Ref. 1850-09-09, 3:3, M.

John Frederick Pike, Esq., to Dorothea Fisher, of Sibton in the county of Suffolk,—

> For years the Fisher tried with line and hook
> To take the finny tyrant of the brook;
> He nibbled—bit; the bait he seemed to like;
> He bit again and she secured the Pike.

No. 4117 :: Ref. 1850-09-09, 3:3, D.

On 4th inst., at Markethill, Mr. Adam Wann, aged 25 years, esteemed by all who had the pleasure of his acquaintance.

No. 4118 :: Ref. 1850-09-09, 3:3, D.

On 2d Sept., in Enniskillen, Mr. Hugh O'Brien, aged 74.

No. 4119 :: Ref. 1850-09-09, 3:3, D.

On 22d June, at sea, on board the *Lady Consbrook*, from Belfast for New York, Mr. Joseph Maginnis, a native of the county of Down.

No. 4120 :: Ref. 1850-09-09, 3:3, D.

On 29th ult., at Newtownlimavady, aged 75 years, Margaret, relict of the late George Lane, Esq., Armagh.

No. 4121 :: Ref. 1850-09-09, 3:3, D.

On the 1st inst., at Monaghan, Lucy, wife of Mr. James M'Entee.

No. 4122 :: Ref. 1850-09-09, 3:3, D.

On the 3d inst., at Waringstown, the Very Rev. Holt Waring, Dean of Dromore, and Rector of the parish of Shankhill, in the 85th year of his age.

No. 4123 :: Ref. 1850-09-09, 3:3, D.

On 29th ult., Thomas Murphy, Esq., one of the most extensive and respectable merchants of Clonmel.

No. 4124 :: Ref. 1850-09-09, 3:3, D.

On 31st Augt., at Grove Hill, near Strabane, Robert Gordon, Esq., of Stragullen.

No. 4125 :: Ref. 1850-09-09, 3:3, D.

On 4th inst., at Lisinisk, Carrickmacross, after a tedious illness, John James Gibson, Esq., youngest son of the late Adam Gibson, Esq., of same place.

No. 4126 :: Ref. 1850-09-09, 3:3, D.

On 27th ult., at Magherafelt, aged 66 years, Mr. John Duncan.

No. 4127 :: Ref. 1850-09-16, 3:2, B.

On Wednesday, the 11th inst., at Armagh, the lady of Thomas A. Prentice, Esq., of a daughter.

No. 4128 :: Ref. 1850-09-16, 3:2, B.

On Wednesday, the 11th inst., the wife of Mr. James Burns, watchmaker, jeweller, &c., No. 3, Upper English-street, of a daughter.

No. 4129 :: Ref. 1850-09-16, 3:2, B.

On the 14th inst., at Carrickmore, the lady of Henry Cranstown, Esq., of a daughter.

No. 4130 :: Ref. 1850-09-16, 3:2, B.

On the 13th inst., at Pomeroy, Mrs. Villiam [sic] Wallace of a son and heir.

No. 4131 :: Ref. 1850-09-16, 3:2, M.

On 17th ult., at Athens, U. States, Osborne A. Lochrane, Esq., Attorney-at-law, son of Dr. Lochrane, of Middletown, A. and M.R.C.S., Edinburgh, to Victoria Frances, daughter of Colonel H.G. Lamar, ex-Representative in Congress for the city of Athens.

No. 4132 :: Ref. 1850-09-16, 3:2, M.

On 6th inst., in the Presbyterian Church, Minterburn, by the Rev. James Kinnear, of Lower Clenaneese, John Vance, Esq., of the city of New York, to Margaret, eldest daughter of Alex. Pringle, Esq., Bolton's Walls, near Caledon.

No. 4133 :: Ref. 1850-09-16, 3:2, M.

At St. John's Church, Liverpool, by the Rev. Robert Wolsley, Mr. John Kelsey, Mason-street, to Rebecca Jane, third daughter of Mr. Thomas Caldwell, East Langfield, co. Tyrone.

No. 4134 :: Ref. 1850-09-16, 3:2, M.

On 2d inst., in the Presbyterian Church, Tempo, by the Rev. David Clements, Mr. Wm. Rutledge, of Rodeny, to Margaret, eldest daughter of Mr. Edward Funston, Trillick.

No. 4135 :: Ref. 1850-09-16, 3:2, D.

On 9th inst., at Tullyrone, Mr. John Wesley Gilpin, in the 83d year of his age.

No. 4136 :: Ref. 1850-09-16, 3:2, D.

On Wednesday last, at Newry, in the 36th year of his age, Mr. James M'Nally, merchant.

No. 4137 :: Ref. 1850-09-16, 3:2, D.

On Thursday last, at Dundalk, Catherine, wife of Mr. Patrick Moore, for many years organist at Newry Cathedral.

No. 4138 :: Ref. 1850-09-16, 3:2, D.

On 27th ult., of scarletina, Sarah Lydia Nicholson Pike, aged 6 years and 10 months; and on the 7th inst., of same complaint, Hannah Lecky Pike, aged 3 years and 4 months, only daughters of the late James N. Pike, of Derryvale, co. Tyrone.

No. 4139 :: Ref. 1850-09-16, 3:2, D.

On 7th inst., at his residence, in Dungannon, after a protracted illness, occasioned by inflammation of the kidneys, Wm. Robinson, Esq., Superintendent of National Schools.

No. 4140 :: Ref. 1850-09-16, 3:2, D.

On 8th inst., in Dublin, Ellen Mary, eldest daughter and co-heiress of the late Theodore Bailie, of Tirnaskea, county of Tyrone, Esq.

No. 4141 :: Ref. 1850-09-16, 3:2, D.
On 10th inst., John Reynolds Peyton, Esq., J.P. and D.L., of Laheen, county Leitrim, formerly of the 60th Rifles, only son of the late John Peyton, Esq., Colonel of the Leitrim Militia.

No. 4142 :: Ref. 1850-09-16, 3:2, D.
Ronald Macdonald, at Whitebog, near Raddery, died on Friday last, after completing his 105th year and two days.

No. 4143 :: Ref. 1850-09-16, 3:2, D.
On the 4th inst., aged 78, after a short illness, at his lodgings, Trinity College, the Rev. James Ingram, D.D., F.S.A., President of Trinity College, and Rector of Garsington, Oxon.

No. 4144 :: Ref. 1850-09-23, 3:2, B.
On 17th inst., at Acton, the lady of Robert Quinn Alexander, Esq., of a daughter.

No. 4145 :: Ref. 1850-09-23, 3:2, B.
On 16th inst., the wife of Mr. James Henderson, proprietor of the *Newry Telegraph*, of a daughter.

No. 4146 :: Ref. 1850-09-23, 3:2, B.
Sept. 23, the wife of Mr. Robert J. Johnston, Boot and Shoe Depot, 7, English-street, of a son.

No. 4147 :: Ref. 1850-09-23, 3:2, B.
On 18th inst., at the Barbacon Cottage, Bryansford, co. Down, the lady of the Rev. J.A. Beers, of a son.

No. 4148 :: Ref. 1850-09-23, 3:2, B.
On 18th inst., at Willoughby-place, Enniskillen, Mrs. Frederick Nixon, of a son.

No. 4149 :: Ref. 1850-09-23, 3:2, B.
On 14th inst., at Carrickmore, the lady of Henry Cranston, Esq., of a daughter.

No. 4150 :: Ref. 1850-09-23, 3:2, M.
On 6th inst., in Clifden Church, Connemara, by the Rev. W. Brushe, the Rev. R. Ryder, formerly a priest of the Church of Rome in that neighbourhood, but now a missionary in connection with the Irish Church Missions Society of London, to Sarah Maria, only daughter of the late Rev. Robert Bailey, Wesleyan minister.

No. 4151 :: Ref. 1850-09-23, 3:2, M.
On 2d inst., in Dungloe Church, by the Rev. Frederick Corfield, Rector of Templecrone, and Perpetual Curate of Mullaghderg, Ralph Spence Phillips, Esq., of Tarmon House and Meenlecklanore Cottage, county of Donegal, to Bridget, daughter of Patrick O'Donnell, Esq., of Lough Salt. The bridegroom, who is related to the Duke of Hamilton and other members of the peerage, is aged 80; the lady is descended from the great O'Donnell, the late chief of Tyrconnell, and is aged 19.

No. 4152 :: Ref. 1850-09-23, 3:2, M.
On 11th inst., in the Presbyterian Church, Ballygilbert, by the Rev. A. Liggat, Mr. Thomas Anderson, Sligo, to Miss Sarah Coard, Ballygilbert.

No. 4153 :: Ref. 1850-09-23, 3:2, D.
On 18th inst., at his residence in Omagh, of small pox, Joseph Robinson, Esq., surgeon and licentiate apothecary, very deeply regretted.

No. 4154 :: Ref. 1850-09-23, 3:2, D.
On 19th inst., Mr. Edward Moss, merchant, of Omagh.

No. 4155 :: Ref. 1850-09-23, 3:2, D.
On 5th inst., at Rathmines, Mary, relict of Thomas Morgan Mandeville, Esq., assistant commissioner-general, of Carrick-on-Suir.

No. 4156 :: Ref. 1850-09-23, 3:2, D.
On 11th inst., at Dungannon, John Wilson, Esq., aged 84 years.

No. 4157 :: Ref. 1850-09-23, 3:2, D.
On 13th inst., Anne, eldest and last surviving daughter of the late Rev. Wm. Laing, of Newry.

No. 4158 :: Ref. 1850-09-23, 3:2, D.
On 7th inst., Ensign William Sheil, of the 43d Madras Native Infantry, eldest son of the late Simon Sheil, Esq., of Port Nassau, near Ballyshannon, co. Donegal.

No. 4159 :: Ref. 1850-09-30, 3:1, B.
On 23d inst., in English-street, in this city, Mrs. R.J. Johnston, of a son.

No. 4160 :: Ref. 1850-09-30, 3:1, B.
On 22d inst., the lady of the Rev. David Coote, at his residence, near Knappagh, of a son.

No. 4161 :: Ref. 1850-09-30, 3:1, B.
At Upper Ely-place, Dublin, the lady of J. Faviere Elrington, Esq., of a son.

No. 4162 :: Ref. 1850-09-30, 3:1, B.
On 18th inst., at Enniskillen, the wife of John Greham, Esq., Solicitor, of a son.

No. 4163 :: Ref. 1850-09-30, 3:1, B.
On 23d inst., at Enniskillen, the wife of W.H. Morphy, Esq., of a daughter.

No. 4164 :: Ref. 1850-09-30, 3:1, M.
On 26th inst., at Grangegorman Church, by the Rev. Henry R. Bailly, William Griffith, Esq., to Annie Hallam, daughter of the late William George Lanauze, Esq., of Kill, county Cavan.

No. 4165 :: Ref. 1850-09-30, 3:1, M.
On 24th inst., at Monkstown Church, by the Rev. J.T. Whitestone, Rector of Killenan, county Monaghan, Matthew Henry Sankey, Esq., son of the late Matthew Sankey, Esq., of Harcourt-street, to Mary Charlotte, only child of the late Rev. William Lennard Roper, Rector of Monaghan.

No. 4166 :: Ref. 1850-09-30, 3:1, M.
In Aughnamullen Church, the Rev. John Johnston Egan, of Swanlinbar, county Cavan, to Isabella Maria, daughter of the late Rev. James Morell, of Fairview, Ballibay.

No. 4167 :: Ref. 1850-09-30, 3:1, M.
On 19th inst., at Desertmartin, county Derry, by the Rev. J. Spencer Knox, M.A., Rector of Maghera, and Vicar-General of the Diocese of Derry, the Rev. William Arthur Ormsby, M.A., incumbent of St. James's, Norwich, to Helen Adelaide, youngest daughter of the late and Hon. and Right Rev. Wm. Knox, Bishop of Derry.

No. 4168 :: Ref. 1850-09-30, 3:1, M.
On 24th inst., at Crohan, near Killeshandra, county Cavan, by the Rev. Mr. Sweeny, Robert Moore, Esq., merchant, Ballybay, to Anne, youngest daughter of James Berry, Esq., of same place.

No. 4169 :: Ref. 1850-09-30, 3:1, M.
On 20th inst., in the East Wall Wesleyan Chapel, Londonderry, by the Rev. G. M'Millen, William Gilbert, Esq., of Dublin, to Rosanna, daughter of the late Rev. John M'Arthur.

No. 4170 :: Ref. 1850-09-30, 3:1, D.
On 20th inst., Agness, youngest daughter of Wilson Irvine, Esq., of Kearn House, near Portadown. The large and respectable concourse which attended the remains of this young lady to their last earthly resting-place, sufficiently attested the high esteem in which she was held by those who had an opportunity of becoming acquainted with her worth.

No. 4171 :: Ref. 1850-09-30, 3:1, D.
On 19th inst., at 10, Russell-street, Dublin, Martha, youngest daughter of the late James Nixon, Esq., of Prospect, in the county of Fermanagh.

No. 4172 :: Ref. 1850-09-30, 3:1, D.
On 22d inst., at his house, Chichester-street, Belfast, Alex. Turnly, Esq., aged 75 years.

No. 4173 :: Ref. 1850-09-30, 3:1, D.
On 14th inst., at Banbridge, aged 55 years, Mr. Robert M'Clelland, sen., for upwards of thirty years connected with the linen trade of the North of Ireland.

No. 4174 :: **Ref. 1850-09-30, 3:1, D.**
On 23d ult., at Hamilton, Canada West, at the house of her son-in-law, Solomon Brega, Esq., aged 84 years, Mrs. Moore, relict of the late Wm. Henry Moore, Esq., Solicitor, formerly of Grenville-street, Dublin, and Newry, county Down.

No. 4175 :: Ref. 1850-09-30, 3:1, D.
On 13th inst., on board the "*Camillus*," on his passage home from New Orleans, aged 18 years, Arthur Ratcliffe Crossley, Esq., youngest son of the late Captain Crossley, J.P., county inspector of the Londonderry Constabulary.

No. 4176 :: Ref. 1850-09-30, 3:1, D.
On 25th inst., at his residence, Main-street, Cavan, Thos. Bligh, Esq., merchant, after a short illness, of about thirty-six hours.

No. 4177 :: Ref. 1850-10-07, 3:1, B.
Oct. 2, in this city, the lady of John Stanley, Esq., Solicitor, of a son.

No. 4178 :: Ref. 1850-10-07, 3:1, M.
Oct. 1, Wm. Richardson Boyle, Esq., Londonderry, to Catherine, only daughter of John Simpson, Esq., Ballyards, near this city.

No. 4179 :: Ref. 1850-10-07, 3:1, D.
Sept. 12, at Catania, Sicily, of disease of the heart, Francis Charles Hassard, Esq., eldest son of the late Sir Francis Hassard, Knt., of the city of Dublin.

No. 4180 :: Ref. 1850-10-07, 3:1, D.
At Armagh, on Wednesday, Oct. 2, Mr. Joseph Boyd, builder, aged 77 years, a native, and one of the oldest inhabitants of this city—for upwards of 50 years. Mr. Boyd, was a steady and respected member of the Benevolent Society of St. Patrick, the members of which attended his remains to their last resting-place, St. Mark's church yard. He was a good citizen, an honest man, and a sincere christian. His loss is deeply regretted by a large circle of friends.

No. 4181 :: Ref. 1850-10-07, 3:1, D.
Oct. 1, at Enniskillen, Mr. Kilpatrick, an old and respectable inhabitant of that town.

No. 4182 :: Ref. 1850-10-14, 3:2, B.
Oct. 9, at Canal stores, Caledon, Mrs. Thomas Armstrong, of a son.

No. 4183 :: Ref. 1850-10-14, 3:2, B.
Oct. 3d inst., at Killylea, the wife of Dr. John Davidson of a daughter.

No. 4184 :: Ref. 1850-10-14, 3:2, B.
Oct. 1st, at Cootehill, the lady of James Sharpe, Esq., M.D., of a daughter.

No. 4185 :: Ref. 1850-10-14, 3:2, B.
Sept. 25, at Bedale, the wife of H. de la Poer Beresford, Esq., of a son.

No. 4186 :: Ref. 1850-10-14, 3:2, B.
Sept. 20, at the Cottage, Derry, the lady of John Willoughby Cole, Esq., of a daughter.

No. 4187 :: Ref. 1850-10-14, 3:2, B.
On 24th ult., at the Mullins' House, Ballyshannon, the lady of R. Reynolds, Esq., of a daughter.

No. 4188 :: Ref. 1850-10-14, 3:2, B.
On 24th ult., at Anahoe House, Ballygawley, the lady of James Crossle.

No. 4189 :: Ref. 1850-10-14, 3:2, M.
William Blakeman Roberison, Esq., Provincial Bank of Ireland, to Miss Ellen Williams, both of Cork.

No. 4190 :: Ref. 1850-10-14, 3:2, M.

In Dundalk, William M'Master, Esq., to Eliza Anne, daughter of the late Robert Dickie, Esq., of Roachdale, co. Louth.

No. 4191 :: Ref. 1850-10-14, 3:2, M.

On 24th ult., in the Presbyterian Church, Claggin, by the Rev. H. M'Caw, Mr. Robert Hagan, to Miss Mary Anne Clements, both of the county Tyrone.

No. 4192 :: Ref. 1850-10-14, 3:2, M.

On 1st instant, at Lisnadill Church, by the Rev. J. Chamney, William Richardson Boyle, Esq., Londonderry, to Catherine, only daughter of John Simpson, Esq., Ballyards, Armagh.

No. 4193 :: Ref. 1850-10-14, 3:2, M.

On 17th ult., in Philadelphia, U.S., by the Rev. H. Furness, Mr. Moody Maguire, late of Newtownlimivady, Ireland, to Sarah Annie, relict of the late Captain H.S. Straker, of Newcastle-on-Tyne, England.

No. 4194 :: Ref. 1850-10-14, 3:2, M.

In the Island of Achill, by the Rev. W. M'Ilwaine, Incumbent of St. George's Church, Belfast, John Wilson, Esq., Larkhill, county Dublin, to Frances, eldest daughter of the Rev. E. Nangle.

No. 4195 :: Ref. 1850-10-14, 3:2, M.

Sept. 27, in Derry Cathedral, Charles James, Esq., of Raphoe, to Margaret Sophia, second daughter of Lieut. Wm. L. Patterson, late of Mason Lodge, co. Donegal.

No. 4196 :: Ref. 1850-10-14, 3:2, M.

At Dungannon, on 13th ult., by the Very Rev. Dr. Slane, Mr. J. Mullin, merchant, Scotch-street, to Susan, daughter of the late Mr. Arthur Mallon, merchant.

No. 4197 :: Ref. 1850-10-14, 3:2, M.

On 13th ult., in Tullylisk, Mr. John Douglas, merchant, Lurgan, to Arabella, daughter of Mr. William Mills, Clare, Waringstown.

No. 4198 :: Ref. 1850-10-14, 3:2, M.

Andrew Jackson Harrison, Esq., to Anna Jane, eldest daughter of Mr. John Sheill, Castleblayney.

No. 4199 :: Ref. 1850-10-14, 3:2, M.

On 24th ult., Robert Moore, Esq., merchant, Ballibay, to Anna, daughter of James Berry, Esq., of Crohan, Killyshandra.

No. 4200 :: Ref. 1850-10-14, 3:2, M.

On 4th ult., in Dungloe Church, by the Rev. Frederick Corfield, Richard Heard, Esq., Inspecting Officer of Coast Guards, son of Edward Heard, of Kinsale, Esq., to Louisa Caroline, second daughter of Richard C. Chambers, of Lifford, Esq.

No. 4201 :: Ref. 1850-10-14, 3:2, M.

On 3d inst., in the Parish Church of Maghera, by the Rev. J. Spencer Knox, A.M., Vicar General of the diocese of Derry, Mr. David M'Bride, of Keady, Armagh, to Miss Caroline Shannon, of Maghera.

No. 4202 :: Ref. 1850-10-14, 3:2, M.

On 1st inst., at Ballymoney, Thomas Simcock, Esq., V.S., Drogheda, to Margaret, eldest daughter of David Reid, Esq., Ballymoney.

No. 4203 :: Ref. 1850-10-14, 3:2, M.

On the 26th ult., at St. James's church, Dover, by the Rev. John Puckle, Joseph Goff, jun., Esq., eldest son of Joseph Goff, Esq., Hale Park, Hants, to the Lady Adelaide Knox, daughter of the Right Hon. the Earl of Ranfurley.

No. 4204 :: Ref. 1850-10-14, 3:2, M.

On the 5th inst., in St. Mark's Church, Dublin, by the Rev. Eugene O'Meara, Richard Bailie, Esq., of Mounthill, county Armagh, only surviving son of the late John Bailie, Esq., to Anna Sophia, only daughter of the late Edward Carruthers, Esq., of Dublin.

No. 4205 :: Ref. 1850-10-14, 3:2, M.

On 21st ult., by the Rev. Mr. Davidson, Presbyterian Minister, Lough Water, Mr. Robert Sutter, of Klinty, near Ballymena, to Miss Stirling, of said place. The bridegroom is above 80, and the bride upwards of 60; so the united ages of this happy pair are 140.

No. 4206 :: Ref. 1850-10-14, 3:2, M.

On 19th ult., in Scarva, by Rev. W. Reid, Rev. Thomas Kilpatrick, of Cabra Grove, Tandragee, to Miss Margaret Walker, of Ballyloughan, Richhill.

No. 4207 :: Ref. 1850-10-14, 3:2, M.

Oct. 3, in St. Mary's, Shandon, Nathaniel Evans, of Limerick, merchant, son of Samuel Evans, Esq., of Newtownbutler, to Selina, youngest daughter of Josiah Curtis, Esq., Supervisor of Inland Revenue, Cork.

No. 4208 :: Ref. 1850-10-14, 3:2, M.

Oct. 10, in St. George's church, by the Rev. Charles Alexander, Rector of Drumcree, the Rev. Godfrey E. Alexander, Incumbent of Caledon, to Harriett Alexander Shaw, eldest daughter of William J. Alexander Shaw, Esq., of Cruisetown, co. Meath, and Caledon, county Tyrone.

No. 4209 :: Ref. 1850-10-14, 3:2, D.

Oct. 7, at Urney Park, near Strabane, of scarletina, John Wesley, aged 7 years, eldest son of Mr. John Callison, Land steward to A.F. Knox, Esq.

No. 4210 :: Ref. 1850-10-14, 3:2, D.

On 26th ult., of palpitation of the heart, Dr. Samuel Hay Hill, of Ballymena, aged 22 years.

No. 4211 :: Ref. 1850-10-14, 3:2, D.

On 8th inst., at Beragh, Omagh, Mr. Robert Hunter, in the 60th year of his age.

No. 4212 :: Ref. 1850-10-14, 3:2, D.
August 5, at Castletown Delvin, Robert Duke, son of the Rev. Coote C. Mulloy.

No. 4213 :: Ref. 1850-10-14, 3:2, D.
Sept. 27, at Brighton, Lieutenant-Colonel Cross, K.H., aged 63.—The following record of the deceased's services is extracted from Hart's Army List:—Lieutenant-Colonel Cross served in the Peninsula from 1808 to the end of the war, with the exception of a short period in 1809, including the campaign and battle of Corunna, action of Almeida on the Coa, 24th of July, 1810, battle of Busaco, actions at Pombal, Redina (wounded), Mizanda de corvo, Foz d'azouce and Sabugal, battle of Fuentes D'Onor, 3d and 5th of May, 1811, siege of ciudad Rodrigo, actions of San Munos and San Milan, battles of Vittoria, Lesaco Bridge, Bidassoa, Vera, 7th October, Nivelle, Nive (6th, 10th, and 11th December, 1813), Orthes, Tarbes, and Toulouse—received a severe contusion on 18th of June, at Waterloo. [C]olonel Cross served in the light division as a volunteer, with the first battalion of the 52d Light Infantry; when effective in the second battalion, from 31st of December, 1812, to July, 1816. He has received the war medal with ten clasps for [C]orunna, Busaco, Fuentes d'Onor, ciudad Rodgrigo, Vittoria, Pyrenees, Nivelle, Nive, Orthes, and Toulouse.

No. 4214 :: Ref. 1850-10-14, 3:2, D.
October 9, at Rathmines, Jane Louisa, daughter of the late C.R.G.Y. Stephens, of Ballinacargy, county Cavan, Esq., aged 25 years.

No. 4215 :: Ref. 1850-10-14, 3:2, D.
On the 5th inst., at Quivy Lodge, county Cavan, the Countess of Lanesborough.

No. 4216 :: Ref. 1850-10-14, 3:2, D.
Sept. 25, in Cavan, Thos. Bligh, Esq., merchant.

No. 4217 :: Ref. 1850-10-14, 3:2, D.
At 64, Leeson Terrace, Dublin, Anne, the beloved wife of John Cumming, Esq.

No. 4218 :: Ref. 1850-10-14, 3:2, D.
On 3d of April, at Geelong, Port Philip, William, second son of the late Mr Samuel Hamilton, Craig, near Claudy, aged 29 years.

No. 4219 :: Ref. 1850-10-14, 3:2, D.
On 29th ult., at Rosstula, in her 67th year, Sarah, relict of the late Mr. Thomas Hughes, Belfast.

No. 4220 :: Ref. 1850-10-14, 3:2, D.
On 7th inst., at Tullygally, near Lurgan, aged 89 years, Mr. John Cummins.

No. 4221 :: Ref. 1850-10-14, 3:2, D.
Sept. 30, in Pottle, near Bailieboro', after a few days' illness, Mr. James Mahood, in the 60th year of his age.

No. 4222 :: Ref. 1850-10-14, 3:2, D.
The Rev. William Atherton, of the Wesleyan Methodist Society in Wakefield.

No. 4223 :: Ref. 1850-10-14, 3:2, D.
At Buttevant, the Rev. James Laurence Cotter, L.L.D., Vicar of that parish, aged 68.

No. 4224 :: Ref. 1850-10-14, 3:2, D.
Oct. 6, at Lisbofin, co. Fermanagh, in the 32d year of her age, Margaret, youngest daughter of Charles Faussett, Esq.

No. 4225 :: Ref. 1850-10-14, 3:2, D.
Oct. 8, at Ely Lodge, Mrs. Fee, housekeeper.

No. 4226 :: Ref. 1850-10-14, 3:2, D.
At Fintona, on 2d inst., Anna, relict of the late Mr. Thos. Wood, of Enniskillen.

No. 4227 :: Ref. 1850-10-14, 3:2, D.
At Murvagh, Ballintra, on 23d ult., Mrs. Kincaid, relict of the late Surgeon Kincaid, of Raphoe, co. Donegal.

No. 4228 :: Ref. 1850-10-14, 3:2, D.
Aug. 25, at Brooklands, Sydenham, Canada West, Latham Blacker Hamlin [sic], Esq., son of William Blacker [sic], late of Drogheda, Esq., Captain in the Louth Militia.

No. 4229 :: Ref. 1850-10-21, 3:2, B.
On 10th inst., at Enniskillen, the Lady of George Alcock Nixon, Esq., M.D., of a son.

No. 4230 :: Ref. 1850-10-21, 3:2, B.
On 14th inst., at Enniskillen, the wife of Mr. John Molyneux, of a son.

No. 4231 :: Ref. 1850-10-21, 3:2, B.
On 16th inst., at Charlemont, the lady of Wm. Wheeler, Esq., of a daughter.

No. 4232 :: Ref. 1850-10-21, 3:2, B.
On 5th ult., at Figart House, Dunfanaghy, the wife of Mr. David M'Kelvey, jun., of a daughter.

No. 4233 :: Ref. 1850-10-21, 3:2, M.
On 14th inst., by the Very Rev. C. Flannagan, P.P., Mr. Andrew G. Daly, Merchant, Newry, to Eliza, eldest daughter of Mr. Thos. Davock, Coleraine.

No. 4234 :: Ref. 1850-10-21, 3:2, M.
On 15th inst., at Kilbarron parish Church, Ballyshannon, by the Rev. Edward Geo. Dougherty, James Johnston, Esq., of Sligo, and Lowry, county Fermanagh, to Jane, daughter of William Allingham, Esq., Manager Provincial Bank, Ballyshannon.

No. 4235 :: Ref. 1850-10-21, 3:2, M.
In Strabane, 15th inst., by the Lord Bishop of Derry and Raphoe, the Rev. William Alexander, Rector of Termonamongan, Killeter, to Cecilia Frances, second daughter of John Humphreys, Esq., of Miltownhouse, Strabane.

No. 4236 :: Ref. 1850-10-21, 3:2, M.

On 15th inst., at Adelaide-road, Dublin, by the Rev. Joseph Hunter, Henry Cowan, Esq., of Glasgow, to Helena, second daughter of the late John Jephson, Esq., of Northumberland-road.

No. 4237 :: Ref. 1850-10-21, 3:2, M.

In Dromore, on 27th ult., by the Rev. Henry L. St. George, John Caldwell, Esq., Lackagh, to Elizabeth, youngest daughter of John Guy, Esq., of Aughadullagh.

No. 4238 :: Ref. 1850-10-21, 3:2, M.

At Carntall Meeting-house, Clogher, on 15th inst., by the Rev. John Hanna, John Wilson Elliott, Esq., M.D., R.N., to Susan, second daughter of the late Robert Ramsay, of Sligo, Esq.

No. 4239 :: Ref. 1850-10-21, 3:2, M.

On 9th ult, at Symington, Mr. George A. Bell, of New York, to Isabella Elizabeth, youngest daughter of Robert Blakey, Esq., of Belfast.

No. 4240 :: Ref. 1850-10-21, 3:2, D.

On 11th inst., in her 68th year of her age, Jane, the wife of Rev. James Harvey, the venerable minister of the Presbyterian Congregation of Redrock, county Armagh. Her life was marked by gentleness, kindness, and piety, and her latter end was peace.

No. 4241 :: Ref. 1850-10-21, 3:2, D.

On 13th, at Ballyhagan, near Loughgall, of fever, Susanna, beloved wife of Mr. George Hobson.

No. 4242 :: Ref. 1850-10-21, 3:2, D.

On 16th inst., at Bellaghy, near this city, Mr. Samuel Knipe.

No. 4243 :: Ref. 1850-10-21, 3:2, D.

On 13th inst., at Woodville, co. Cavan, Rebecca, eldest daughter of Francis Finlay, Esq.

No. 4244 :: Ref. 1850-10-21, 3:2, D.

On 10th inst., at the Byron Hotel, Sutton, Emily Margaret, wife of William Brooke, Esq., Master in Chancery.

No. 4245 :: Ref. 1850-10-21, 3:2, D.

On 24th ult., in Ballyshannon, Miss Jane Richardson, aged 83.

No. 4246 :: Ref. 1850-10-21, 3:2, D.

On 1st inst., at Donaghadee, Daniel Delacherois, Esq., J.P., D.L., co. Down.

No. 4247 :: Ref. 1850-10-21, 3:2, D.

On 7th of Aug., at Allahabad, aged 20, Ensign W.H. Thompson, 26th Regiment Bengal Native Infantry, eldest son of Lieut.-Col. W.J. Thompson, C.B., Deputy Commissary-General.

No. 4248 :: Ref. 1850-10-21, 3:2, D.

On 1st inst., Rev. J.H. Bouchier, Rector of Ardcanny, Prebend of the Cathedral of Limerick.

No. 4249 :: Ref. 1850-10-21, 3:2, D.

On 26th ult., Thomas Collins, first pupil of the Charlemont [Claremont] Deaf and Dumb Institution, improver of the Manual Alphabet, and inventor of the signs now in general use among the deaf and dumb throughout the kingdom.

No. 4250 :: Ref. 1850-10-21, 3:2, D.

On 13th Oct., at Bundoran after a lingering illness, borne with the most perfect composure and resignation, Mr. Jones Ellis, woollendraper.

No. 4251 :: Ref. 1850-10-21, 3:2, D.

On 12th inst., in No. 3, Cavendish-row, Dublin, at an advanced age, James Denham, Esq., D.L., late of Fair Wood Park, Enniskillen.

No. 4252 :: Ref. 1850-10-21, 3:2, D.

On 11th inst., at Willoughby-place, Enniskillen, Margaret, second daughter of the late John Steel, Esq.

No. 4253 :: Ref. 1850-10-21, 3:2, D.

On 9th inst., at Rathmines, Jane Louisa, daughter of the late C.R.G.Y. Stephens, of Ballinacargy, co. Cavan, Esq., aged 25 years.

No. 4254 :: Ref. 1850-10-21, 3:2, D.

On 12th inst., John Quin, Esq., [of] Cashel-house, co. Tyrone.

No. 4255 :: Ref. 1850-10-21, 3:2, D.

On 12th inst., Eleanor, youngest daughter of Mr. Robt. Cunningham, Dullaghan, Dromore.

No. 4256 :: Ref. 1850-10-21, 3:2, D.

On 17th inst., at Glenan, near Glasslough, aged 72 years, Miss Margaret Johnston, sister of Mr. Thomas Johnston, of Cloncaw.

No. 4257 :: Ref. 1850-10-21, 3:2, D.

On 8th of August, in the East Indies, in the 24th year of his age, [C]harles Burton, eldest son of the late J.B. West, Esq., M.P. for Dublin, and grandson of the late Hon. Judge Burton.

No. 4258 :: Ref. 1850-10-21, 3:2, D.

On 20th ult., at [C]astellamare, near Naples, in consequence of leaping from her carriage when the horses took fright and ran away, Harriet, wife of Dooald Maclean, Esq., and second daughter of the late General Frederick Maitland.

No. 4259 :: Ref. 1850-10-21, 3:2, D.

On 4th inst., at Michael's grove, Bromptom, Elizabeth, wife of Eneas MacDonnell, Esq. This amiable lady never made an enemy and never lost a friend. May she rest in peace.

No. 4260 :: Ref. 1850-10-21, 3:2, D.

On 6th inst., at the residence of Mr. Buchanan, of Straughroy, Nancy Hill, at the advanced age of 104 years. She had the use of all her faculties until the period of her death, and was not known to have been during her long life a day sick. She came to reside in Mr. Buchanan's family as a servant, upwards of fifty years ago, and has lived under four generations in that family. Having been unmarried, her remains were borne to the new graveyard of Cappagh, by the young girls of the neighbourhood.

No. 4261 :: Ref. 1850-10-21, 3:2, D.

Lately, at Kewstoke, near Weston-super-Mare, aged 84, Mr. Hugh Haimans. By his own desire he was buried in his first wife's wedding-gown, which was an old-fashioned light chintz printed cotton; and, by his own request, also, his wife's linsey apron was put in the coffin with him.

No. 4262 :: Ref. 1850-10-28, 3:2, B.

Oct. 18, at Edenderry, the lady of Robert Saunders, Esq., M.D., of a daughter.

No. 4263 :: Ref. 1850-10-28, 3:2, B.

Oct. 16, at 2, Heytesbury Terrace, Dublin, the wife of the Rev. George Labatt, of a son.

No. 4264 :: Ref. 1850-10-28, 3:2, M.

Oct. 22, in Dromore Cathedral, by the Rev. Edward Kent, A.M., Treasurer of the Cathedral, and Rector of Dromore, the Rev. George A.F. Patton, Curate of Dromore, to Catharine, third daughter of the late Henry Magill, Esq., Tullycairne, county Down.

No. 4265 :: Ref. 1850-10-28, 3:2, M.

Oct. 24, in Drumquin, by the Rev. John Davidson, James King, Esq., Cumber, Fintona, to Mary, only daughter of James Davis, Esq., of Laught, near Dungannon.

No. 4266 :: Ref. 1850-10-28, 3:2, M.

Oct. 18, in Seagoe Church, by the Rev. Mr. Woolsey, Mr. Joseph Irwin, Springvale, Gilford, son of William Irwin, Esq., formerly of Armagh, now of New York, to Eliza, eldest daughter of George Ruddell, Esq., Aughacommon, Lurgan.

No. 4267 :: Ref. 1850-10-28, 3:2, D.

On the morning of Thursday, the 24th Oct., instant, at his residence, Rokeby Green, Armagh, in the 56th year of his age, Sinclair Carroll, Esq., Architect,—a man sincerely respected by all, and greatly beloved by his sorrowing family, and all those favored with his intimate acquaintance. He was a good husband, a fond father, and a sincere friend. As a citizen, he contributed to enlarge and adorn the City by the outlay of his capital, and several of its public buildings bear testimony to his taste. He died in sure and certain hope of a blessed resurrection unto eternal life by the sacrifice of a crucified Redeemer. The funeral took place on Saturday morning, and was largely attended, by the respectable inhabitants of the city and neighbourhood. The pall-bearers were John Stanley, Esq., Robert Riddall, Esq., John M'Watters, Esq., William Leathem, Esq., Stevenson Riggs, Esq., and Richard Lindsay, Esq. The usual service was read by the Rev. Alexander Irwin, Rector of St. Marks, in his usual impressive manner. The funeral proceedings were conducted by Mr. Frizell.

No. 4268 :: Ref. 1850-10-28, 3:2, D.

At Frankfort Avenue, Rathmines, Mr. John Hardy, aged 93 years. When twenty years old he invented a machine for doubling and twisting cotton yarn, for which the Dublin Society awarded him a premium of twenty guineas. Four years after he invented a scribbling machine for carding wool, to be worked by horse or water power, for which the same Society awarded him one hundred guineas. He next invented a machine for measuring and sealing linen, and was in consequence appointed by the Linen Board seals-master for all the linen markets in the County of Derry, but the slightest benefit from this he never derived, as the rebellion of '98 broke out about the time he had all his machines completed, and political opponents having represented by memorials to the Board, that by giving so much to one man, hundreds who then were employed would be thrown out of work, the Board changed the seal from the spinning wheel to the harp and Crown, thereby rendering his seals useless, merely giving him £100 by way of remuneration for his loss. About the year 1810, as no doubt many still living will recollect, he demonstrated by an apparatus attached to one of the boats of the Grand Canal Company, at Portobello, the practicability of propelling vessels on the water by paddle wheels; but having placed the paddles on the bow of the boat the action of the backwater on the boat was so great as to prevent its progressing at a greater speed than three miles per hour. This appearing not to answer, without further experiment he broke up the machinery, and allowed others to profit by the ideas he gave on the subject, and to complete on the open sea what he had attempted within the narrow limits of a canal. He also invented a machine for sawing timber; but as it has happened in too many instances to Irishmen the result of all his inventions during a long life has been very considerable loss of time and property, without the slightest recompense from the Government of the country benefitted by his talents.—*Saunders's News-Letter*.

No. 4269 :: Ref. 1850-10-28, 3:2, D.

On Saturday night last, Mr. William Carson, youngest son of the late William Carson, Esq., of Ballyshannon.

No. 4270 :: Ref. 1850-10-28, 3:2, D.

Sept. 15, at Kingston, North America, Mr. John Patterson, sen., formerly of the county Monaghan, Ireland, and father of Mr. John Patterson, of that city.

No. 4271 :: Ref. 1850-10-28, 3:2, D.

At Richhill, Mr. Thomas Clarke. He had formerly been servant, for a lengthened period, in the establishment of Mrs. Cope, of Drummilly, and latterly kept a small public house at the Richhill station of the Ulster Railway. He was much respected in the neighbourhood, and a large number of friends accompanied his remains to Loughgall churchyard, on Friday.

No. 4272 :: Ref. 1850-10-28, 3:2, D.

Oct. 20, at Lisbellaw, Rev. Mr. Martin, minister of the Presbyterian congregation of that place.

No. 4273 :: Ref. 1850-10-28, 3:2, D.

Oct. 20, at Portarlington, aged 70 years, Harriet, relict of the late Rev. Richard Clarke, many years Incumbent of St. Michael's, of that town.

No. 4274 :: Ref. 1850-10-28, 3:2, D.

The Late William Blacker, Esq.

William Blacker, Esq., descended from, and connected with, some of the most ancient families in this county, was one of the younger sons of the late Rev. Dr. St. John Blacker, his mother being a sister of the late Major-General Sir Barry Close, Bart. Engaged in early life largely in mercantile pursuits, he devoted himself, at a maturer period, to the development of the agricultural and economic resources of the country; and, having under his care the management of several most important estates in the north of Ireland, especially those of the Earl of Gosford, Lord Bangor, his relative Colonel Close, &c., &c., he was enabled to see carried into practice, and report, from actual experience, results which others merely theorised upon.

It would be beside the purpose of this brief notice to do more than advert shortly to some of these works; to enlarge at all on them would involve us in a memoir not merely of an individual, but the discussion of most, if not all, the *Vexatlaee Questiones* of the day relative to Agriculture and Economics, Poor law, Corn law, and Currency included.

By his popularly written "*Hints to Small Farmers*;" by his Annual Reports at the Markethill Farming Dinners, of experimental results; by Essays, several of which carried the prizes of the Royal Dublin and Royal Agricultural Societies, he managed to spread not only a spirit of inquiry into matters of such vital importance to this country, but to point out, and urge, into the best and most advantageous course of action, the well-inclined and energetic.

The advancement by Government of capital to landed proprietors, at reasonable and encouraging terms, for the purposes of draining and improving their estates, and at the same time the country.—The employment of practical instructors, to teach the people the management of their land and a proper rotation of crops. The freeing [of] land from from expensive litigation, by granting of easily disposable titles; such were the principal measures that Mr. Blacker pressed again and again on the public and the legislature; and before he died he had the satisfaction to see them all concurred in and carried out, one way or other, though under very depressed circumstances for the country, with regard to the immediate results, from what he had calculated, owing to the concurrent inflictions of famine, poor law, free trade, and open insurrection. Others have carried off with a flourish the merit for each and all of these remedial measures; the long previously published works of Mr. Blacker, however, indelibly record the mine from which the suggestions were originally taken.

On this subject being adverted to, just before his last illness, to Mr. Blacker himself, by a friend solicitous that honour should be given where honour was due, he merely replied, with a calm smile, "*What matter, if the actual good is done, who gets the credit of it. I only wish my advice had been listed to years ago, and the country would have been better prepared for its present disastrous struggle.*"

One of these measures in particular, viz.—the employment of practical instructors—being in some degree in his own power, he did not hesitate to set the experiment a-going, as far as he was able, and succeeded in supplying several well trained and efficient agriculturists, not only to the west and south of Ireland, where Lords Clancarty and Clonbrock especially availed themselves of his assistance—but even to England, where amongst others, Lady Basset, the proprietor of a large and badly cultivated tract in Cornwall, gladly benefitted herself and her district by his recommendations.

At last he had the satisfaction of seeing the measure taken up by the present Lord Lieutenant, the Earl of Clarendon, and carried out with more enlarged means by the Royal Agricultural Society.

Mr. Blacker latterly gave much of his attention to the consideration of the currency question, and not only published several works, but gave very lengthened and important evidence on the subject before the parliamentary committees. He was inclined to the modified support of an inconvertible paper currency.

His last efforts in a literary way were three very cogent and well reasoned "*Pro-Corn-Law tracts,*" published just before his late illness, showing that to the last the vigour and clearness of his intellectual powers were quite unimpaired.

He was a member of most of the literary and industrial societies in this country, and received from them, as well as from those in England and abroad, several honorary distinctions and complimentary resolutions.

Mr. Blacker was unmarried. His loss, as an active, intelligent, and impartial magistrate, and a hospitable and charitable member of the community, will long be felt in the neighbourhood where he resided, and by a numerous circle of friends.

The above sketch has been furnished in the columns of the *Evening Mail*, and may be considered as correct in all its particulars.

The funeral took place on Thursday morning, and was conducted by Mr. Alexander Frizell, the respectable undertaker of this city.—Most of the nobility and gentry, clergy, medical gentlemen, and respectable inhabitants, as well of the city as of the surrounding districts, attended the mournful procession, to Mullabrack churchyard, the place of interment. There were about 25 carriages and other vehicles in attendance, among which were, in addition to that of the family, those of the Earl of Gosford, Col. Blacker, Lady Molyneux, Mrs. Mauleverer, Sir James M. Stronge, Col. Caulfeild, George Robinson, Esq., Capt. St. George, H.L. Prentice, Esq., Wm. Paton, Esq., Dr. Kidd, J.C. M'Kinstry, Esq., J. M'Kinstry, &c., &c. The pall-bearers were the Earl of Gosford, Wm. Paton, Esq., Major Thornton, and Edward Tickell, Esq., Q.C. The following clergymen and medical gentlemen, together with the pall-bearers, wore scarfs:—Rev. A. Irwin, Rector of St. Mark's; the Rev. Messrs. Wade, and Sharkey, of the Established Church; Rev. Messrs. Fleming and M'Alister, Presbyterian Church; Rev. Messrs. Murphy, M'Chrystal, and Troy, Roman Catholic Church; and the Rev. Mr. Martin, of the Independent Church. The medical gentlemen were, Drs. Kidd, Cuming, and Leslie. On arriving at the burial-ground, the funeral service was read, in an impressive and feeling manner, by the Rev. Mr. Frith, curate of Mullabrack, after which the remains of the lamented deceased were committed to their kindred earth, amid the regrets of all who were assembled on the mournful occasion.

No. 4275 :: Ref. 1850-11-04, 3:1, B.
Oct. 26, at Dungannon, the wife of Mr. William Orr, merchant, of a son.

No. 4276 :: Ref. 1850 11 04, 3:1, B.
June 29, at French Rocks, in India, the lady of J. Gason Magrath, Esq., of the 1st Native Bengal Infantry, of a son.

No. 4277 :: Ref. 1850-11-04, 3:1, B.
Oct. 24, at Worcester, the lady of the Rev. D. Melville, of a son.

No. 4278 :: Ref. 1850-11-04, 3:1, B.
Oct. 27, at Crom Castle, Fermanagh, Mrs. Gartside Tipping, of a daughter.

No. 4279 :: Ref. 1850-11-04, 3:1, M.
On 29th ult., in Cavanaleck Meeting-house, by the Rev. James Philips, Mr. J.W. Henry, of Belfast, to Lucinda, fourth daughter of Wm. Alexander, Esq., Fivemiletown.

No. 4280 :: Ref. 1850-11-04, 3:1, M.
On 28th ult., in Philip's Church, Liverpool, by the Rev. P. Hains, Mr. Alexander M'Grew, Omagh, to Miss Elizabeth Davis, Mill-street, Liverpool.

No. 4281 :: Ref. 1850-11-04, 3:1, M.
On 29th Oct., at St. Peter's Church, Dublin, by the Lord Bishop of Ossory, the Earl of Courtown, to Dora, youngest daughter of the late Right Hon. E. Pennefather, Lord Chief Justice.

No. 4282 :: Ref. 1850-11-04, 3:1, M.
On 8th ult., in Cootehill Church, by the Rev. John R. Darley, Mr. Robert Graham, of Cootehill, to Anna Maria, eldest daughter of Mr. John Foy, of Cootehill, Merchant.

No. 4283 :: Ref. 1850-11-04, 3:1, M.
Oct. 20, at Monkstown Church, James Butler Pratt, Esq., youngest son of the late James B. Pratt, of Mullintra, co. Cavan, Esq., to Jane Eleanor, youngest daughter of the late Thomas Maunsell, Esq., of Mount-pleasant square.

No. 4284 :: Ref. 1850-11-04, 3:1, M.
Oct. 24, at St. Mary's, Swansea, by the Hon. and Rev. Sidney Godolphin Osborne, Griffith Llewellen, Esq., of Baglan-hall, Glamorganshire, to Madelina Georgina, eldest daughter of Pascoe St. Leger Grenfell, Esq., of Maesteg-house, near Swansea.

No. 4285 :: Ref. 1850-11-04, 3:1, D.
Oct. 22, at Castleknock, Sarah, wife of Mr. Ralph Stone, late of Enniskillen.

No. 4286 :: Ref. 1850-11-04, 3:1, D.
At Bandon, Margaret, daughter of the late Robert Travers, Esq., J.P.

No. 4287 :: Ref. 1850-11-04, 3:1, D.
On 28th ult., at Rock Ferry, Liverpool, Joseph Kelso, Esq., formerly of Derry.

No. 4288 :: Ref. 1850-11-04, 3:1, D.
Oct. 23, at Lissagoan House, county Cavan, Matilda, wife of James M'Lannahan, Esq., and youngest daughter of the late Dr. Armstrong, of Clones.

No. 4289 :: Ref. 1850-11-04, 3:1, D.
On 24th ult., at Dungannon, Dr. John Hamilton, after a short illness, much and deservedly regretted.

No. 4290 :: Ref. 1850-11-04, 3:1, D.
Oct. 25, at Newtownhamilton, William T. Collyns, M.D., aged 32 years.

No. 4291 :: Ref. 1850-11-04, 3:1, D.
Oct. 26, at 67, Rathmines-road, Dublin, Elizabeth, wife of George Petrie, L.L.D.

No. 4292 :: Ref. 1850-11-04, 3:1, D.

At Clonliffe, on 29th ult., of scarlatina, aged 13, Alicia, third daughter of John Hall, Solicitor.

No. 4293 :: Ref. 1850-11-04, 3:1, D.

Oct. 17, Joshua Wauhop, Esq., of Drumacarrow Lodge, co. Cavan.

No. 4294 :: Ref. 1850-11-04, 3:1, D.

Oct. 29, at his residence in Aughnacloy, county of Tyrone, James Falls, Esq., Solicitor.

No. 4295 :: Ref. 1850-11-11, 3:1, M.

Oct. 31, in Manorhamilton church, by the Rev. Mr. Thompson, William Parke Cullen, Esq., second son of David Cullen, of Castlecar, in the co. Leitrim, Esq., to Rebecca Elizabeth, youngest daughter of the late Hubert Kelly Waldron, of Ashfort House, in the co. Roscommon, Esq. We understand the lady enjoys some considerable land property in her own right.

No. 4296 :: Ref. 1850-11-11, 3:1, M.

Oct. 29, in Cavanaleck Meeting-house, by the Rev. James Philips, Mr. J.W. Henry, of Belfast, to Lucinda, fourth daughter of James Davis, Esq., Fivemiletown.

No. 4297 :: Ref. 1850-11-11, 3:1, D.

Death of Mr. James Riddall.—We have seldom been called on to discharge a more painful duty than that which devolves on us to-day in announcing the decease of our much esteemed friend and fellow townsman, Mr. James Riddall. He departed this life on yesterday morning, at 6 o'clock, after a short illness, at the early age of 33 years, in the sure hope of that reward which awaits the righteous in a world where earthly sorrow is not known, and where the tears of the righteous shall be exchanged for exceeding great joy. In the discharge of his duties, both as a man and a Christian, Mr. Riddall had few equals. For many years his exertions for the moral improvement of those over whom he had influence, were unceasing, and his example had the best effect in promoting that Christian walk and conversation in which he himself so much delighted. Both amidst the ties of relationship, and as a casual acquaintance, his memory will be long cherished, as a kind friend and a sincere promoter of everything connected with religious and moral progress. His remains will be interred to-morrow, at 9 o'clock, in the burying ground of St. Mark's Church.

No. 4298 :: Ref. 1850-11-11, 3:1, D.

Nov. 10, in this city, Anna, aged 27 years, the beloved wife of Rev. Mr. Strangways, one of the Vicars Choral of the Armagh Cathedral. Her remains will be interred in the Cathedral burying place, on Wednesday morning at 9 o'clock.

No. 4299 :: Ref. 1850-11-11, 3:1, D.

On the morning of the 6th Nov., at No. 24, Eden Quay, Dublin, in the 48th year of his age, Mr. John Kent Johnston. Our readers are aware of the enterprising manner in which the Express Newspaper business was carried on by the deceased for many years, having been founded in this country, by the late Capt. Alexander Johnston, his father. Adverse circumstances, however, latterly unfortunately intervening, had no doubt a considerable effect in shortening a life which, since the commencement of Mr. Johnston in business, had been one of great usefulness. His obliging disposition and kindness of heart were well known and fully appreciated by all with whom he had dealings, and no one in the habit of reading the newspapers of the day, whether metropolitan or provincial, could be unaware of how well he deserved the sympathy and encouragement of the public, or, now that he is gone, claims the tribute of its sincerest regret.

No. 4300 :: Ref. 1850-11-11, 3:1, D.

Nov. 2, at Belfast, Catharine, wife of Mr. James Thomson, and daughter of the late Rev. Mathew Lanktree.

No. 4301 :: Ref. 1850-11-11, 3:1, D.

Oct. 29, suddenly, Edward O'Connor, Esq., Barrister-at-Law, and Editor of the *Dublin Evening Packet*.

No. 4302 :: Ref. 1850-11-11, 3:1, D.

Nov. 4, of consumption, near Ballygawley, in the 28th year of his age, Dr. Thomas Devlin, for four years a resident of Dungannon, where he practised in his profession of surgeon.

No. 4303 :: Ref. 1850-11-11, 3:1, D.

On Saturday, the 2d inst., at the residence of her son, Mr. Robert Allen, cabinet-maker, Barrack-street in this city, aged 64 years, Mrs. Allen.

No. 4304 :: Ref. 1850-11-18, 3:1, B.

On 14th inst., the wife of the Rev. Mr. M'Millen, of a son.

No. 4305 :: Ref. 1850-11-18, 3:1, B.

On 10th inst., the wife of Mr. Edward Hughes, Church-street, Portadown, of a son.

No. 4306 :: Ref. 1850-11-18, 3:1, M.

On 8th inst., at Glasslough Church, by Rev. W.H. Pratt, Robert Forde, Esq., M.D., of Downpatrick, to Anne, second daughter of the late Sidney Hamilton Rowan, Esq., of same place.

No. 4307 :: Ref. 1850-11-18, 3:1, M.

On 26th ult., by the Rev. Dr. Dobbin, Ballymena, Mr. William Forsyth, Rosedernot, to Miss Sarah Hood, Tullyrod. It was only after a courtship of thirty-five days that the happy bridegroom succeeded in obtaining the lady's consent.

No. 4308 :: Ref. 1850-11-18, 3:1, M.

Nov. 6, in Coolbanagher Church, Edward Tipping, Esq., of Bellurgan Park, county Louth, to Adelaide

Charlotte Marianne, second daughter of the Rev. Sir Erasmus Dixon Borrowes, Bart.

No. 4309 :: Ref. 1850-11-18, 3:1, D.

Nov. 8, in the Old Men's Asylum, Russell place, North Circular-road, John Medcalf, aged 78 years, after enjoying for many years the blessings afforded in this valued institution, where so many of our aged respected Protestant fellow-citizens have found a retreat in the decline of life.—*Saunders's News-Letter.*

No. 4310 :: Ref. 1850-11-18, 3:1, D.

At Bonehill House, near Tamworth, aged 59 years, Edmund Peel, Esq., brother of the late Sir Robert Peel, Bart.

No. 4311 :: Ref. 1850-11-18, 3:1, D.

On 3d inst., at Clogher, near Ballymena, Mr. William Ross, in the eightieth year of his age. He was for above fifty years a ruling elder in the First Presbyterian Church, Ballymena.

No. 4312 :: Ref. 1850-11-18, 3:1, D.

On the 9th inst., at Leeson Terrace, Dublin, five weeks after the death of his beloved wife, John Cuming, Esq., formerly of Ormond-quay, for many years the most eminent publisher in Ireland. A man of more amiable character, or one more generally esteemed, never breathed.

No. 4313 :: Ref. 1850-11-18, 3:1, D.

In Sienna, the Rev. Henry Hallam, son of the eminent historian of the Middle Ages.

No. 4314 :: Ref. 1850-11-18, 3:1, D.

Nov. 11, Henry Bloomfield Kean, Esq., M.D., formerly Surgeon in H.E.I.C.S., and Surgeon in Ordinary to the Queen in Ireland.

No. 4315 :: Ref. 1850-11-18, 3:1, D.

Oct. 8, in Norwich, America, of consumption, Mary, daughter of the late Mr. Michael Cassidy, of Ballyshannon, aged 18 years.

No. 4316 :: Ref. 1850-11-18, 3:1, D.

Sept. 29, at St. John's, N.B., of jaundice, in the 43d year of his age, Mr. William Armstrong, a native of Quivey, Belturbet, county Cavan, Ireland.

No. 4317 :: Ref. 1850-11-18, 3:1, D.

Nov. 4, at his mother's residence, Glenlcary, Coleraine, Mr. John Harper, aged 40 years, for many years a respected citizen of Philadelphia, U.S., who came to his native land to die. Both in America and here, he was respected and esteemed by all who knew him.

No. 4318 :: Ref. 1850-11-18, 3:1, D.

Nov. 9, at Killymore, near Newtownstewart, Mr. James Stewart, aged 80 years. He left behind him a numerous offspring, consisting of 53 children and grandchildren, all of whom with the exception of one, reside in the same townland. Behind his remains, which were attended by a large nnmber [sic] of respectable persons to Newtownstewart Churchyard, rode seven of his sons, and what is not the least strange part in his obituary, there is a difference in the respective ages of his eldest and his youngest sons of 40 years. They are not, however, the sons of the same mother.

No. 4319 :: Ref. 1850-11-18, 3:1, D.

At Derry, county Kerry, in the 74th year of his age, John Blakeney Kittson, Esq., late of the Constabulary force of Ireland. He was appointed to a lucrative situation in the Constabulary as a remuneration for the meritorious and successful manner in which he defended his house in the county Kerry, when attacked by a party of upwards of 40 armed men; and was also liberally rewarded by the Grand Jury of the County, for his zeal and the loss sustained by the burning of his residence on the occasion. As a private gentleman and landlord he is much to be regretted—not a single tenant having been evicted from his property during the late years of the famine.

No. 4320 :: Ref. 1850-11-18, 3:1, D.

At Milltown, co. Cork, at the age of 96, Richard Eagar, Esq.

No. 4321 :: Ref. 1850-11-18, 3:1, D.

On the 4th inst., at Belfast, Drummond, son of the Rev. J. Scott Porter, aged 6 years.

No. 4322 :: Ref. 1850-11-18, 3:1, D.

We have this week to record the sudden demise of the Rev. Lewis Potter, of Dromard Rectory, Ballisodare, within a few miles of this town. On Sunday last he preached at Montrose, in Scotland, when shortly after his leaving the pulpit he was seized with a spasm in the heart, and was so debilitated on the moment, as to be rendered perfectly helpless; he was carried to his lodgings, where he died the following day at three o'clock.—*Sligo Chronicle.*

No. 4323 :: Ref. 1850-11-18, 3:1, D.

At Middlesborough-on-Tees, Mary Hardy. The deceased was the wife of a labouring man, and for some time past been a member of the religious society denominated "Ranters" or "Primitive Methodists," amongst whom a prominent point of religious belief is the necessity of an immediate and direct revelation of the favour of heaven. For a length of time the unfortunate woman had laboured under the impression that she was rejected by God, and doomed to eternal perdition; and that her terrible destiny was being hastened by the agency of consumptive diseases. Unable any longer to cope with the melancholy produced by these morbid imaginings, she at length, on the 26th ult., cut her throat with a pair of scissors, which act resulted in death two days afterwards.

No. 4324 :: Ref. 1850-11-25, 3:1, M.

Mov. [sic] 14, in St. John's Church, Moneymore, by Rev. J.T. Wright, Jamea [sic] Irwin, Esq., of Carlin House, county Tyrone, to Mary Charlotte, third daughter of the late Samuel Wright, Esq., of Grouse Lodge.

No. 4325 :: Ref. 1850-11-25, 3:1, M.

Nov. 15, in the Richhill Presbyterian Church, by the Rev. A. M'Caldin, Mr. John Cultra, Portadown, to Mrs. Carter, eldest daughter of the late Mr. Archibald M'Connell, Armagh.

No. 4326 :: Ref. 1850-11-25, 3:1, M.

Nov. 17, at Cavan, by Rev. James Browne, D.D., Mr. John M'Cabe, Wesley-street, to Mary, youngest daughter of Mr. Patrick Gallagher, Main-street.

No. 4327 :: Ref. 1850-11-25, 3:1, M.

Nov. 14, at the British Embassy, Paris, by the Rev. Thomas Hale, D.D., Anthony Delacombe Maingay, Esq., East India Company's Civil Service, to Martha, widow of John George Corry, Esq., H.M. 70th Regiment, and county of Monaghan.

No. 4328 :: Ref. 1850-11-25, 3:1, M.

Nov. 14, in St. Paul's Church, Cheltenham, by Rev. Mr. Hull, Dr. J. Collis Browne, H.M.'s 98th Regiment, to Matilda, youngest daughter of the late Lieutenant-Colonel Kersteman, formerly H.M.'s 10th Foot.

No. 4329 :: Ref. 1850-11-25, 3:1, M.

Nov. 20, in Longford Church, by the Very Rev. the Dean of Ardagh, John M. Higginson, Esq., S.I., eldest son of H.T. Higginson, Esq., J.P., of Lisburn, to Susan Arabella, only daughter of the late Captain Conry, J.P., of Lisbrack, county Longford, and cousin to the late Lord Hartland.

No. 4330 :: Ref. 1850-11-25, 3:1, D.

On 15th inst., at Newgrove, Mrs. Elizabeth Wilson, aged 92 years.

No. 4331 :: Ref. 1850-11-25, 3:1, D.

On 11th inst., at Carrickmacross, Thomas Jas. O'Flaherty, Esq., ex-Scholar T.C.D., youngest son of the late Rev. T. O'Flaherty.

No. 4332 :: Ref. 1850-11-25, 3:1, D.

Nov. 13, at the Parade, Kilkenny, Miss Gorman. This benevolent lady, amongst other legacies, bequeathed the munificent sum of £300 to the Protestant Orphan Society.

No. 4333 :: Ref. 1850-11-25, 3:1, D.

Nov. 18, at his residence, Upper Merrion street, Dublin, after a short illness, Jonathan Sisson Cooper, Esq., Comptroller-General of Stamps, aged 73 years.

No. 4334 :: Ref. 1850-11-25, 3:1, D.

Nov. 14, at his residence, Tureen House, Passage West, Jacob Lemon, Esq., in the 83d year of his age. He was one of the last survivors of Lord Rodney's action on the 12th of April, 1782.

No. 4335 :: Ref. 1850-11-25, 3:1, D.

In Dublin, on Sunday morning, after a three days' illness, Peter Blake, Esq., County Inspector of Constabulary for the districts of the County and County of the City of Kilkenny [sic].

No. 4336 :: Ref. 1850-12-02, 3:2, B.

Nov. 26, at Cooper's Hill, co. Sligo, the residence of her father, the lady of Capt. Alexander M'Kinstry, 17th Regiment, of a daughter.

No. 4337 :: Ref. 1850-12-02, 3:2, B.

At Moyne, the lady of John Death, Esq., of a son and heir.

No. 4338 :: Ref. 1850-12-02, 3:2, B.

Oct. 28, at Corfu, the wife of G. de la Poer Beresford, A.D.C., 16th Regt., of a son.

No. 4339 :: Ref. 1850-12-02, 3:2, M.

On 21st ult., in St. Mark's Church, Portadown, by the Rev. H.P. Proctor, Mr. Thomas Macoun, linen manufacturer, to Miss Mary Ann, only daughter of Mr. William Mallagh, merchant, Portadown.

No. 4340 :: Ref. 1850-12-02, 3:2, M.

On 8th ult., in Tralee Church, Andrew Ross, Esq., Manager of the Bank of Ireland, in Galway, to Mary Anne, second daughter of Charles Gerrard, of Bush-hill, co. Leitrim, Esq.

No. 4341 :: Ref. 1850-12-02, 3:2, M.

On 22d ult., in Warrenpoint Church, by the Rev. Dr. M'Kay, Edward Young, eldest son of Edward Kellett, Esq., of Drumroo, co. Monaghan, to Anne Eliza, fourth daughter of Leonard Watson, Esq., of Warrenpoint.

No. 4342 :: Ref. 1850-12-02, 3:2, M.

On 28th ult., in Friends' Meeting-house, Richhill, Joseph Faren, of Belfast, to Elizabeth, daughter of Jacob Allen, Richhill.

No. 4343 :: Ref. 1850-12-02, 3:2, M.

On 14th ult., at Rostrevor, by Rev. Frederick Cashel, Edward Curties, Esq., to Catharine Elizabeth, relict of the late William Frederick Carter, Esq., of Arno's Vale, co. Down, and only daughter of the late Francis Tipping, of Bellurgan Park, county Louth.

No. 4344 :: Ref. 1850-12-02, 3:2, M.

On 17th ult., in Donegal, by Rev. W. Niblock, Rev. J. M'Askie, Clougherney, to Isabella, eldest daughter of the late Thomas Henry, Esq., of Sligo.

No. 4345 :: Ref. 1850-12-02, 3:2, M.

On 20th ult., at the Parish Church, Malahide, near Dublin, by Rev. Francis C. Gosling, of Harkstead,

Suffolk, Richard, eldest son of Richard Gosling, Esq., of Lowndes-square, London, to Mary Shuldham, second daughter of the Rev. Dr. Henry, President of the Queen's College, Belfast.

No. 4346 :: Ref. 1850-12-02, 3:2, D.

On 26th ult., at his residence, in Drummonmore, near Armagh, Mr. Robert Humphries, at the advanced age of 90 years.

No. 4347 :: Ref. 1850-12-02, 3:2, D.

On 16th ult., at Drumconra, Ennis, of fever, aged 23 years, Hugh Ross, second son of the late Right Hon. Sir Michael O'Loghlen, Bart., Master of the Rolls.

No. 4348 :: Ref. 1850-12-02, 3:2, D.

On 24th ult., at Gortmore, Omagh, Charlotte Jane, the infant daughter of R.D. Coulson, Esq., R.M.

No. 4349 :: Ref. 1850-12-02, 3:2, D.

On 22d ult., at Tyrellpass, Thomas Armstrong Lewers, youngest son of Thomas Lewers, Esq., and grandson to the later [sic] Dr. Armstrong, of Clones.

No. 4350 :: Ref. 1850-12-02, 3:2, D.

On 14th ult., at the residence of his son-in-law, Dr. Thompson, Derry, in the 81st year of his age, the Rev. Richard Dill. For more than half a century Mr. Dill ministered in Knowhead, to one of the largest and most respectable congregations in the General Assembly.

No. 4351 :: Ref. 1850-12-02, 3:2, D.

Death of Lord Nugent, M.P.—The Right Hon. Lord Nugent, M.P. for the borough of Aylesbury, expired at his seat, Lillies, on Tuesday afternoon.

No. 4352 :: Ref. 1850-12-09, 3:1, B.

On 2d inst., in Enniskillen, co. Fermanagh, Mrs. Wm. Faulkner, of a son.

No. 4353 :: Ref. 1850-12-09, 3:1, B.

On 26th ult., at Carnagh House, Keady, the lady of John Robert Irwin, Esq., of a daughter.

No. 4354 :: Ref. 1850-12-09, 3:1, B.

On 29th ult., at Ladon-house, Mortlake, the Hon. Mrs. Spring Rice, of a daughter.

No. 4355 :: Ref. 1850-12-09, 3:1, B.

At Richings Park, Bncks [sic], Lady Wiltshire, of a son and daughter.

No. 4356 :: Ref. 1850-12-09, 3:1, B.

On 30th ult., the lady of the Rev. D. Dickinson, Banbridge, of an infant, still-born.

No. 4357 :: Ref. 1850-12-09, 3:1, B.

On 2d inst., in Portadown, the wife of J.F. Wilson, of a daughter.

No. 4358 :: Ref. 1850-12-09, 3:1, M.

Dec. 4, in St. Mark's Church, Armagh, by the Rev. Mr. Sharkey, Mr. Clarke Leckie, of Charleston, South Carolina, U.S., to Julia Anne, only daughter of Mr. B.H. Stewart, Foreman Moulder of Armagh Foundry.

No. 4359 :: Ref. 1850-12-09, 3:1, M.

On 26th ult., at Rossory Church, by the Rev. J. Johnston, the Rev. Henry Geddis, Galway, to Margaret, only daughter of the late Captain Johnston, of Enniskillen.

No. 4360 :: Ref. 1850-12-09, 3:1, M.

On 28th ult., by Rev. Robert Anderson, Mr. David Moore, merchant, Banbridge, to Mary Jane, only surviving daughter of the late Robert M'Clelland, Esq., of Tullyraine.

No. 4361 :: Ref. 1850-12-09, 3:1, M.

On 4th inst., in Cloydagh Church, by the Rev. Hans Caulfield, uncle to the bride, John Barbour, Esq., of Birkenhead, and of Kilbarchan, Renfrewshire, to Alicia, youngest daughter of the late Robert Atkinson, Esq., of Green Hall, co. Armagh.

No. 4362 :: Ref. 1850-12-09, 3:1, M.

On 28th ult., at Mount Pleasant, co. Tyrone, the residence of Francis O'Neill, Esq., uncle of the bride, by the Right Rev. Dr. Kelly, R.C. Bishop of Derry, Barnwall White, Esq., M.D., of Londonderry, to Kate, only surviving child of the late John O'Neill, merchant, Liverpool.

No. 4363 :: Ref. 1850-12-09, 3:1, D.

Death of Major Thornton.—This respected gentleman died on Tuesday morning last, at his residence, Seven Houses, in this city, in the 77th year of his age. Major Thornton formerly served in the 21st Dragoons, but had, for a considerable period, retired from active service, and pursued the occupation of an enlightened and improving agriculturist. He was much respected and esteemed by his fellow citizens, as well as beloved by those whom he employed to carry out his agricultural projects and manage his farm, and his death is very much regretted by all classes. The funeral took place on Thursday morning, and was largely and respectably attended. His remains were conveyed to the family burying place, Grange Church-yard, and deposited in the same grave with those of his mother, which, although she died 50 years ago, were in a state of remarkable preservation. Major T. was never married, and was the last survivor of an ancient and most respectable family.—Robert Innes Thornton was only brother of the late General Sir Wm. Thornton, K.C.B. In 1801 he was appointed Lieutenant in the 46th Regiment of Foot, serving in Limerick, and in 1808 to a Captaincy in the 15th Foot, and afterwards to a Majority in the 21st Light Dragoons. He served as Brigade Major for several years in England, and subsequently on the Staff at the Cape of Good Hope. Major Thornton retired from the service about 30 years ago, and has since resided in this city.

No. 4364 :: Ref. 1850-12-09, 3:1, D.

On Wednesday last, aged 52 years, Matilda, the beloved wife of Mr. John Simpson, of this city. The funeral took place on Friday morning, and was attended by a large number of sorrowing friends and relations, as well as many of the respectable inhabitants of this city.

No. 4365 :: Ref. 1850-12-09, 3:1, D.

Suddenly, at Bristol, Capt. John Frith, 72d Highlanders, aged 48.

No. 4366 :: Ref. 1850-12-09, 3:1, D.

On 20th ult., at his residence, Daisy-hill, Clogher, Andrew Millar, Esq., late Captain and Paymaster in the Royal Tyrone Militia, in the 67th year of his age.

No. 4367 :: Ref. 1850-12-09, 3:1, D.

On 4th inst., Letitia Abigail, the beloved wife of the Rev. Doctor Sadleir, Provost of Trinity College, Dublin.

No. 4368 :: Ref. 1850-12-09, 3:1, D.

At Cheltenham, of scarlatina, Francis, the only and beloved son of John Thompson, of Killibandrick, co. Cavan, aged 10 years.

No. 4369 :: Ref. 1850-12-09, 3:1, D.

On 30th ult., at 18, Lynedoch-place, Edinburgh, Miss Jane Dickson, daughter of the late Dr. William Dickson, formerly Bishop of Down and Connor.

No. 4370 :: Ref. 1850-12-09, 3:1, D.

On 8th ult., at Portland, St. John's, N.B., after a severe illness of inflammation, Mary, wife of Mr. Thomas Middlemore, compositor, of Portland, late of Belfast.

No. 4371 :: Ref. 1850-12-09, 3:1, D.

On 26th ult., Miss Blair, of Strabane, aged 86 years.

No. 4372 :: Ref. 1850-12-09, 3:1, D.

Captain Hutcheson, of the "*Dundalk*" steamer, after a protracted illness, expired on the night of Tuesday last, at the early age of 41. Captain Hutcheson was universally esteemed.

No. 4373 :: Ref. 1850-12-16, 2:7, B.

Dec. 3, at Mooreview House, near Kilmacrenan, the lady of the Rev. F.P. Rogers, of a son.

No. 4374 :: Ref. 1850-12-16, 2:7, B.

Dec. 10, at Enniskillen, the lady of the Rev. Mark Whittaker, of a daughter.

No. 4375 :: Ref. 1850-12-16, 2:7, B.

Dec. 6, at Eagle-mount, Lisnaskea, Mrs. John Irvine, of a son.

No. 4376 :: Ref. 1850-12-16, 2:7, B.

Dec. 5, at 11, Pembroke-street, Dublin, the lady of Rev. Beaver H. Blacker, of a son.

No. 4377 :: Ref. 1850-12-16, 2:7, M.

On Thursday, the 12th inst., by the Rev. Mr. M'Naughtan, at the Presbyterian Church of Ballysillan, Archibald Campbell Colvil, Esq., of Belfast, to Charlotte, sixth daughter of the late Andrew M'Clelland, Esq., of Banbridge.

No. 4378 :: Ref. 1850-12-16, 2:7, M.

Dec. 5, in Monaghan, by the Rev. Henry Maffit, James Wright, Esq., Emyvale, to Mary, relict of the late Matthew Logan, Esq., Merchant, Monaghan.

No. 4379 :: Ref. 1850-12-16, 2:7, M.

Mr. William Johnston, of Dungannon, to Miss Adelaide Boardman.

No. 4380 :: Ref. 1850-12-16, 2:7, M.

Dec. 11, in Belfast, by Rev. David Hamilton, Mr. James Wilson, merchant, Belfast, to Maryann, relict of Mr. James Ireland, of same place.

No. 4381 :: Ref. 1850-12-16, 2:7, M.

Dec. 3, in Walcot Church, Bath, by the Rev. S.H. Waddrington, M.A., Rector, the Rev. Hans Atkinson, A.M., Vicar of Cloydagh, co. Carlow, and domestic chaplain to the Earl of Charlemont, to Louisa Lavinia, youngest daughter of Edwin T. Caulfeild, Raheenduff, Queen's County, and of Lansdown crescent, Bath.

No. 4382 :: Ref. 1850-12-16, 2:7, D.

Lines suggested by the early and happy death of Miss Sinclair, Tullyroan.

Oh happy day when first she knew
The Saviour's pardoning love,
For now among the blessed throng
She praises God above.

No more on earth she'll worship now
The God she loved so well.
But in a far more lovely land
His endless mercies tell.

When first she felt religious power
Dawn on her youthful soul,
No idol in her heart she kept,
But gave to God the whole.

And now a diadem she wears,
And garments pure and white,
In the Jerusalem above,
Where dwell the saints of light.

Let not a tear of sorrow fall—
Let no vain grief be shown,—
A union shortly will take place
Where sorrow is unknown.

Rather rejoice; and while we stop
In this sad vale of tears,
Oh, may our love to God approach
The fervency of her's [sic].

W. M'C.

No. 4383 :: Ref. 1850-12-16, 2:7, D.

Dec. 9, at Mullaghbawn, Black Lion, after a protracted and painful illness, which she bore with Christian resignation to the Divine will, Mary, the affectionate wife of Mr. Thomas Elliott, very sincerely regretted by a numerous circle of friends and acquaintances.—Amongst those who paid the last tribute of respect to her memory, and attended her remains to the place of interment, Florencecourt Church-yard, where they were deposited between those of her father and mother, was the Earl of Enniskillen.

No. 4384 :: Ref. 1850-12-16, 2:7, D.

Dec. 13, in Armagh, at the residence of her son, William Barker, Esq., Elizabeth, relict of the late Rev. William Barker, Rector of Newtownhamilton. Her remains were interred in Mullabrack Church yard, this day, attended by a large and respectable concourse of the inhabitants of this city and surrounding neighbourhood, there were upwards of 30 vehicles, Rev. Mr. Wright officiated, and read the service in a very solemn and impressive manner. Mr. Alexander Frizell, conducted the funeral.

No. 4385 :: Ref. 1850-12-16, 2:7, D.

Dec. 13, at Termon Rectory, at an advanced age, the Rev. Charles Cobb Berresford. The interment of his remains takes place to-morrow—Tuesday, 17th inst.

No. 4386 :: Ref. 1850-12-16, 2:7, D.

Dec. 10, at Tullyrone, near Loughgall, Isabella, second daughter of the late Mr. Simon Sinclair, aged 21 years.

No. 4387 :: Ref. 1850-12-16, 2:7, D.

Dec. 9, at Port Nassau, near Ballyshannon, Mr. James Stewart, aged 95 years.

No. 4388 :: Ref. 1850-12-16, 2:7, D.

Dec. 8, at Cormeen, co. Monaghan, Mr. Thomas Faulkner, in the 60th year of his age, for several years past a member of the Aughnamullen Orange Lodge.

No. 4389 :: Ref. 1850-12-16, 2:7, D.

Dec. 7, in the 87th year of her age, Isabella, relict of the late Mr. Wm. Dudgeon, of Mullaghmore, near Omagh.

No. 4390 :: Ref. 1850-12-16, 2:7, D.

Dec. 7, at Monkstown, of brain fever, aged twelve years and nine months, Alan Beckford Long, third son of the late Frederick Beckford Long, Esq., Inspector-General of Prisons.

No. 4391 :: Ref. 1850-12-16, 2:7, D.

Mary Catharine, wife of William Crosbie, Esq., Provincial Bank, Dungarvan.

No. 4392 :: Ref. 1850-12-16, 2:7, D.

Dec. 5, Gowan Gilmor, Esq., of Ballyglass, one of the oldest grand jurors of the county Sligo.

No. 4393 :: Ref. 1850-12-16, 2:7, D.

Nov. 27, aged 57 years, Catherine, wife of Mr. Charles Sheals, Mount Vernon Road, Liverpool, and daughter of the late Andrew Newton, Esq., of Coagh, county Tyrone.

No. 4394 :: Ref. 1850-12-16, 2:7, D.

Dec. 5, of scarletina, Thos. James, only son of Mr. John M'Adam, merchant, Omagh, aged 5 years.

No. 4395 :: Ref. 1850-12-16, 2:7, D.

At Waterford, Miss Martha Parker, daughter of the late Mr. John Parker, for 50 years connected with the Cathedral.

No. 4396 :: Ref. 1850-12-16, 2:7, D.

Nov. 22, Mrs. Kieran, wife of Mr. James Kieran, of Omagh.

No. 4397 :: Ref. 1850-12-16, 2:7, D.

Dec. 8, at Manchester-terrace, Portadown, in the 76th year of his age, Mr. John Atkinson.

No. 4398 :: Ref. 1850-12-16, 2:7, D.

Dec. 10, at Brookeborough, Mr. Edward Noble, formerly of Coolcaughal, at the advanced age of 97 years.

No. 4399 :: Ref. 1850-12-23, 3:1, M.

Dec. 17, at Lisnaskea Church, by the Rev. J. Flanagan, John Moore, Esq., Ballymacrue House, co. Cavan, to Miss Graham, eldest daughter of William Graham, Esq., Drumack, co. Fermanagh.

No. 4400 :: Ref. 1850-12-23, 3:1, M.

Dec. 10, at St. James's Church, Dover, Thomas Beevor, Esq., eldest son of Sir T.B. Beevor, at Hargham-hall, Norfolk, to Sophia Jane, widow of the late Isaac Jermy, Esq., of Stanfield-hall, in the same co., who, with his father, was assassinated by Rush.

No. 4401 :: Ref. 1850-12-23, 3:1, M.

Dec. 17, at St. Peter's Church, by the Rev. M.F. Day, the Rev. W. Lett, Ex-F.T.C.D., Rector of Derryvullen, co. of Fermanagh, to Mary, eldest daughter of Jonathan Stackhouse, Esq.

No. 4402 :: Ref. 1850-12-23, 3:1, D.

Anne, sister of Lieut.-Colonel Huey, 68th Regt.

No. 4403 :: Ref. 1850-12-23, 3:1, D.

Dec. 10, aged 27, Mary Irwin, wife of Mr. William Campbell, of Artgonnell. She died beloved and respected by all who had the pleasure of her acquaintance. Also, her infant daughter, aged four months.

No. 4404 :: Ref. 1850-12-23, 3:1, D.

Dec. 13, at the rock, Dunamace, Wm. Lalor, at the advanced age of 106 years, having lived to see his great-grandchildren married. His wife, who is over 100, accompanied the funeral, and is still in excellent health.

No. 4405 :: Ref. 1850-12-23, 3:1, D.

Dec. 10, the Parish Priest of Stradbally, Queen's County.

No. 4406 :: Ref. 1850-12-23, 3:1, D.
At Lungy, at an advanced age, Charles Martin, Esq., Magistrate of co. Sligo and Commissioner for the town. Deceased was brother to Abraham Martin, Esq.

No. 4407 :: Ref. 1850-12-23, 3:1, D.
Dec. 21, at Lurgan, near Blacklion, of fever, Mr. Johnston Caldwell; he was a young man in the prime of life, health, and strength.

No. 4408 :: Ref. 1850-12-23, 3:1, D.
Dec. 1, in Harrisburgh, Pennsylvania, from injury surtained [sic] by the upset of a stage coach, aged 37 years, Rev. James Power, brother to Rev. John Power, C.C., Clonmel, Rev. Patrick Power, C.C. Carrick-on-Suir, and Rev. Roger Power, C.C. Waterford.

No. 4409 :: Ref. 1850-12-23, 3:1, D.
On 18th inst., at Landaff Lodge, Thurles, John Cahill, Esq., Crown Solicitor for co. Tipperary.

No. 4410 :: Ref. 1850-12-30, 2:7, B.
On 23d instant, the lady of the Rev. Benjamin Wade, of twins, a son and daughter, the former of whom was still born.

No. 4411 :: Ref. 1850-12-30, 2:7, D.
On 29th instant, at Mulleoghran, Lydia, widow of the late Mr. William Albin, aged 97 years. Although but 4 years old when the French landed in Carrickfergus, she perfectly recollected to have seen them marched through Armagh, prisoners.

No. 4412 :: Ref. 1850-12-30, 2:7, D.
On 10th instant, aged 27 years, Mary, wife of Mr. Richard Irwin, nnd [sic] 6th daughter of Mr. Wm. Campbell, of Artgonnell. Also, her infant daughter, aged 4 months.

No. 4413 :: Ref. 1850-12-30, 2:7, D.
On 25th instant, aged 21 years, William, eldest son of Mr. David Griffin, of this city.

No. 4414 :: Ref. 1851-01-06, 2:7, M.
On 5th inst., in this City, by the Rev. Mr. Rogers, P.P., Mr. John W.C. Sinnamon, Printer, to Miss Catherine Hughes.

No. 4415 :: Ref. 1851-01-06, 2:7, D.
On 3d inst., of consumption, at the residence of his brother, Mr. James Wilkin, Mullingar, William Henry Wilkin, of Dobbin-st., in this city, aged 29 years.

No. 4416 :: Ref. 1851-01-06, 2:7, D.
On 29th ult., aged 82, Mr. Daniel M'Carten, of Ogle-street, formerly schoolmaster, an old and respected inhabitant of this city.

No. 4417 :: Ref. 1851-01-13, 3:1, B.
At Donamoine Glebe, Mrs. Loftus Tottenham, of a daughter.

No. 4418 :: Ref. 1851-01-13, 3:1, B.
In Ballinasloe, the wife of Rev. Mr. Hickey, Wesleyan Methodist minister, of a son.

No. 4419 :: Ref. 1851-01-13, 3:1, B.
Jan. 6, at Longwood-avenue, [the wife of] Mr. Paul K. Bracken, of a son.

No. 4420 :: Ref. 1851-01-13, 3:1, B.
On 5th inst., the wife of Mr. David Anderson, merchant, Cookstown, of a son.

No. 4421 :: Ref. 1851-01-13, 3:1, B.
On 12th ult., the lady of John Stephens, Esq., of Ballyshannon, of a son.

No. 4422 :: Ref. 1851-01-13, 3:1, B.
On 2d inst., at Castle-Taylor, co. Galway, the lady of Robert Wright Cope Cope [sic], Esq., of Loughgall, of a daughter.

No. 4423 :: Ref. 1851-01-13, 3:1, B.
Jan. 7, at Glenageary, the lady of George A. Grierson, Esq., of a son.

No. 4424 :: Ref. 1851-01-13, 3:1, B.
On 29th ult., at Aughalane House, Pettigo, the lady of William St. George, Esq., of a son.

No. 4425 :: Ref. 1851-01-13, 3:1, B.
On 22d ult., at Colebroke [sic], the Hon. Lady Brooke, of a daughter.

No. 4426 :: Ref. 1851-01-13, 3:1, B.
On 17th ult., at Chesterfield-house, the Marchioness of Abercorn, of a daughter.

No. 4427 :: Ref. 1851-01-13, 3:1, B.
On 18th ult., the lady of Wm. Overend, Esq., Barrister-at-Law, of a daughter.

No. 4428 :: Ref. 1851-01-13, 3:1, M.
Jan. 7, in the Presbyterian Church, Middletown, by the Rev. Samuel Hendren, Mr. George Parks, Crossdall, to Miss Esther Short, of Drumnail.

No. 4429 :: Ref. 1851-01-13, 3:1, M.
On 20th ult., at Seagoe Church, Portadown, by Archdeacon Saurin, Mr. Ebenezer Cavins, of Ballynagarrick, to Margaret, second daughter of Mr. John Maginess, of Ballydonaghy.

No. 4430 :: Ref. 1851-01-13, 3:1, M.
Jan. 4, in St. Thomas's Church, M.C. Howe, Esq., ex-scholar of T.C.D., to Hester Jane, eldest daughter of the late James Charles Prentice, Esq., M.D., of Rathdrum, co. Wicklow.

No. 4431 :: Ref. 1851-01-13, 3:1, M.
Jan. 9, at the Tabernacle, City Road, London, by the Rev. James Carlile, D.D., of Woolwich, James Hay Dobbin, Esq., fifth son of Capt. Leonard Dobbin, late of the Royal Regt., to Elizabeth, daughter of the late Hugh Hall, Esq.

No. 4432 :: Ref. 1851-01-13, 3:1, M.
On 7th inst., in the Presbyterian Church, Pettigo, by Rev. John Davidson, Rev. John Donaldson, to Laura Matilda, third daughter of John Given, Esq., Tullyhommon House, Pettigo.

No. 4433 :: Ref. 1851-01-13, 3:1, M.

On 20th ult., at Cooltrain Church, by the Rev. W. Pakenham Walsh, Robert P. Welsh, Esq., L.R.C.S.I., Brookeborough, to Elizabeth Wilson, only child of John Edward Taylor, Esq., J.P., Cranbrook, county Fermanagh.

No. 4434 :: Ref. 1851-01-13, 3:1, M.

On 18th ult., in Clogherney Church, by the Rev. A. Young, James M'Farland, Esq., Cammowen Green, to Lydia, relict of the late Mr. James Clarke, Curr, near Beragh. The bridegroom, it is said, is on the wrong side of 80, and his better half is only 71.

No. 4435 :: Ref. 1851-01-13, 3:1, M.

In the Presbyterian Church, Drumhillery, near Keady, by Rev. James M'Cauley, on 2d inst., Mr. Mawhinny, of Carnagh, to Anne, relict of the late Mr. Robert Davidson. Strange to say, the interesting bride has previously had six husbands, and is now above ninety years of age.

No. 4436 :: Ref. 1851-01-13, 3:1, M.

In the same church [Presbyterian Church, Drumhillery, near Keady,] also by Rev. James M'Cauley, on 7th inst., Mr. Wm. Giland, of Curryhews, to Anne, only daughter of Mr. Robert Murray, of Drumhillery.

No. 4437 :: Ref. 1851-01-13, 3:1, M.

On 19th ult., by Rev. Mr. Molyneaux, Mr. Thomas Campbell, of Brackley, Keady, to Anne, eldest daughter of the late Mr. Alexander Reed, Clontibret, Monaghan.

No. 4438 :: Ref. 1851-01-13, 3:1, M.

Dec. 18, in Edinburgh, Gore Gregory Cochrane, Esq., of Cootehill, co. Cavan, to Elizabeth Matilda, youngest daughter of the late Richard Darley, Esq., and sister to the Rev. John R. Darley, late Principal of the Royal School, Dungannon.

No. 4439 :: Ref. 1851-01-13, 3:1, D.

Jan. 9, at the residence of her brother, Dr. Leslie, of disease of the heart, under which she laboured for many years, Henrietta, youngest daughter of the late Doctor John Leslie, of this city, aged 16 years, in sure hope of a glorious resurrection.

No. 4440 :: Ref. 1851-01-13, 3:1, D.

Jan. 7, at Derrydaragh, Mary, wife of Wm. Wilson, Esq., aged 67 years.

No. 4441 :: Ref. 1851-01-13, 3:1, D.

Jan. 9, at the residence of his son, Rev. E.O. Disney, Newtownhamilton, Thomas Disney, Esq., aged 85 years.

No. 4442 :: Ref. 1851-01-13, 3:1, D.

On Saturday, Mr. Bernard Branagan, of Castle-street, hotel-keeper, aged 37 years.

No. 4443 :: Ref. 1851-01-13, 3:1, D.

At Sydney, N.S. Wales, Thomas Walker, Esq., Assistant Commissary-General.

No. 4444 :: Ref. 1851-01-13, 3:1, D.

Dec. 28, at Ramsgate, aged 70 years, William W. Algeo, Esq., of Armagh.

No. 4445 :: Ref. 1851-01-13, 3:1, D.

On 30th ult., Mr. George Morrow, of Magherafelt, painter and glazier, aged 73 years.

No. 4446 :: Ref. 1851-01-13, 3:1, D.

On 7th inst., at Kingston, Mrs. Archdall, relict of the late General Archdall.

No. 4447 :: Ref. 1851-01-13, 3:1, D.

At Aughalane, near Pettigo, on 6th inst., Emily, the wife of Wm. St. George, Esq.

No. 4448 :: Ref. 1851-01-13, 3:1, D.

On 11th ult., at Berwick Hall, Susan, the beloved wife of the Rev. J. Thompson, Presbyterian Minister of Raphoe.

No. 4449 :: Ref. 1851-01-13, 3:1, D.

Jan. 7, at Poplar Vale, co. Monaghan, Frances Dorothy, wife of John Richardson, Esq.

No. 4450 :: Ref. 1851-01-13, 3:1, D.

At Mountjoy-square, Dublin, Charlotte, wife of James Major, Esq., Q.C., Assistant-Barrister for co. Monaghan.

No. 4451 :: Ref. 1851-01-13, 3:1, D.

On 29th Dec., at Sligo, Robert Christian, Esq., Stamp Distributor, and Secretary to the Grand Jury of that County for the last 33 years.

No. 4452 :: Ref. 1851-01-13, 3:1, D.

On 17th ult., in the 29th year of his age, after a few days' sickness, Mr. William Stewart, elder son of Mr. Hugh Stewart, of Creeve, in this County.

No. 4453 :: Ref. 1851-01-13, 3:1, D.

On 19th ult., in Enniskillen, Mary, wife of Mr. Jas. Coulter, aged 30.

No. 4454 :: Ref. 1851-01-13, 3:1, D.

On 3d inst., aged 60, Jane, wife of Robert Morrow, Esq., Rockville, Ballyjamesduff.

No. 4455 :: Ref. 1851-01-13, 3:1, D.

At Killeshandra, on the 20th ult., in the 22d year of his age, James Whelan.

No. 4456 :: Ref. 1851-01-13, 3:1, D.

On 21st ult., suddenly, of apoplexy, Andrew Armstrong, Esq., A.M., one of the resident masters of Trinity College, Dublin.

No. 4457 :: Ref. 1851-01-13, 3:1, D.

On 21st ult., at Lurgan, Thomas Mathews, Esq., Solicitor, aged 84 years.

No. 4458 :: Ref. 1851-01-13, 3:1, D.

On 8th inst., of lockjaw, at Donaghmore, Surgeon Daniel M'Mullen, attended to his last moments by Dr. Henry, of Pomeroy, who exhausted every resource of medical skill in, alas! a vain attempt to restore him to his sorrowing family and friends.

No. 4459 :: Ref. 1851-01-13, 3:1, D.

At Fareagh, near Omagh, on 1st inst., Miss Nancy Patton. She retained her memory to the last, and related incidents in the neighbourhood now beyond the memory of every other person in it. She was very much respected throughout her long life, and died in the 100th year of her age.

No. 4460 :: Ref. 1851-01-13, 3:1, D.

At Sacramento City, California, Oct. 22, Patrick Evans; 25th, W.H. Thomson and James Clark; 27th, John Haffarman; 29th, all of cholera [sic]; Mrs. Allen O'Brien, Daniel Crone, Nov. 6th, both all of [sic] diarrhoea, Mrs. Lawless; John Fox. At San Francisco, California, Nov. 2, aged 46, Richard Nagle; 13th, also of cholera, 32, John Kennely; and John Donninem, all from Ireland.

No. 4461 :: Ref. 1851-01-20, 3:1, M.

On the 15th instant, in the First Presbyterian Church, in this city, by the Rev. A. Fleming, the Rev. William Craig, Presbyterian Minister of Dromara, to Charlotte, youngest daughter of the late Alexander Prentice, Esq., of Armagh.

No. 4462 :: Ref. 1851-01-20, 3:1, M.

On Thursday last, in Richhill Church, by the Rev. Mr. Hogan, Mr. John Bradley, late of Liverpool, and head groom to Mr. W. Beck, to Celia, daughter to the late John Cunningham, of Ardrea, parish of Loughgall.

No. 4463 :: Ref. 1851-01-20, 3:1, M.

January 9, in Newmarket Church, Samuel Gordon, Esq., accountant of the Provincial Bank of Ireland at Cork, to Cecilia, second daughter of the late Lieutenant Philip Purdon.

No. 4464 :: Ref. 1851-01-20, 3:1, M.

On 11th instant, in London, George Craigie Balfour, Esq., of Hescombe, Orkney, and Ashburn House, Bute, to Sarah, youngest daughter of the late Clement M'Coan, Esq., of Dunlow, county Tyrone.

No. 4465 :: Ref. 1851-01-20, 3:1, D.

On Wednesday last, in Palace-row, aged 50 years, Mr. William Murray, one of the oldest Orangemen in this city.

No. 4466 :: Ref. 1851-01-20, 3:1, D.

January 9, at the Rectory, Newtownhamilton, after a few days' illness, in his 85th year, Thomas Disney, Esq., of Adamstown, county Meath.

No. 4467 :: Ref. 1851-01-20, 3:1, D.

January 7, at Kingstown, Jane, relict of General Archdall, of Castle Archdall, late M.P. for Fermanagh, and daughter of Gustavus Rochfort, Esq., of Rochfort, formerly M.P. for county Westmeath.

No. 4468 :: Ref. 1851-01-20, 3:1, D.

On the 10th November, at Simla, East Indies, Captain John Bracken, Deputy Adjutant Assistant-General of the Bengal army.

No. 4469 :: Ref. 1851-01-20, 3:1, D.

On 25th ult., at Rome, M. Frederic Bastiat, the great political economist of France.

No. 4470 :: Ref. 1851-01-27, 3:4, B.

Jan. 19, at Black Lion, co. Cavan, Mrs. Brackin, wife of Mr. Wm. Copeland Brackin, merchant, of a son and heir.

No. 4471 :: Ref. 1851-01-27, 3:4, B.

Jan. 20, at Lisnaskea Glebe, the wife of the Rev. John Flanagan, of a son.

No. 4472 :: Ref. 1851-01-27, 3:4, B.

On 15th inst., Mrs. James Evans, Strabane, of a son.

No. 4473 :: Ref. 1851-01-27, 3:4, B.

Jan. 15, at the Crescent, Londonderry, the wife of George A. O'Driscoll, Esq., of a son.

No. 4474 :: Ref. 1851-01-27, 3:4, B.

Jan. 14, the lady of Andrew Green, Esq., Cloonlurg Cottage, Ballymote, of a son.

No. 4475 :: Ref. 1851-01-27, 3:4, M.

On 21st inst., at the residence of her brother, 189, Great Brunswick-street, Dublin, by the Rev. J.T. Laphan, D.D., P.P., Charles C. Farrell, Esq., 19 Lower Ormond Quay, Dublin, and Legavoreen, Drogheda, to Margaret Eleanor, youngest daughter of the late John Carolan, Esq., 15, Grenville-st., Dublin.

No. 4476 :: Ref. 1851-01-27, 3:4, D.

Jan. 9, John Maguire, of Enniskillen, at the residence of his brothe[r], Rev. P. Maguire, P.P., Aughalurcher, co. Fermanagh.

No. 4477 :: Ref. 1851-01-27, 3:4, D.

Jan. 13, at Tullyroan, near Loughgall, Mr. John Wesley Gilpin, aged 44 years.

No. 4478 :: Ref. 1851-01-27, 3:4, D.

On 16th inst., at 4, Lower Rutland-street, Dublin, Eliza, only child of the late William Donaldson, of Freeduff, co. Armagh.

No. 4479 :: Ref. 1851-01-27, 3:4, D.

Elizabeth, wife of James Crosbie, Esq., manager of the Provincial Bank, Strabane.

No. 4480 :: Ref. 1851-02-03, 2:7, D.

We regret to announce the death of Alexander Russell, Esq., late Manager of the Provincial Bank, Dungannon. This gentleman held the principal office in that extensive Bank upwards of 16 years, and was highly respected by rich and poor. He departed this life on the 21st January, 1851, at Grange Bank, Morning side, near Edinburgh.

No. 4481 :: Ref. 1851-02-03, 2:7, D.

Jan. 12, at Levaghy, near Portadown, Mr. Jacob Roney, aged 90 years.

No. 4482 :: Ref. 1851-02-03, 2:7, D.

At the residence of her son, Richard Coulter, Esq., Carnmeen, county Down, on Sunday, January 26th, Deborah, relict of the late John Coulter, Esq., aged 85 years. Mrs. Coulter was an humble, pious, resigned Christian; meek, unobtrusive, and charitable. She was highly esteemed by all who knew her. Being full of years, she resigned her breath placidly, and almost without a struggle, to Him who gave it, dying, as she had lived, in the bosom of her family, and in firm reliance, through the blood of the Covenant, on the great Captain of our salvation, the Lord Jesus Christ, who hath said, *"Come, ye blessed of my Father, inherit the Kingdom prepared for you from the foundation of the world."* Amen.

No. 4483 :: Ref. 1851-02-03, 2:7, D.

Jan. 24, at the house of her son, Rev. Mr. Rooney, P.P., of Ballymacnab, Mrs. Rooney, relict of Mr. Peter Rooney, at the advanced aged of 82 years.

No. 4484 :: Ref. 1851-02-10, 3:2, B.

On 28th ult., at Abbey-street, Armagh, the lady of the Rev. Alex. Fleming, of a son.

No. 4485 :: Ref. 1851-02-10, 3:2, B.

On the 2d inst., at Norley Hall, Cheshire, the lady of John G. Woodhouse, Esq., of a daughter.

No. 4486 :: Ref. 1851-02-10, 3:2, B.

On 3d inst., at Strabane, Mrs. William Wright, of a daughter.

No. 4487 :: Ref. 1851-02-10, 3:2, B.

On 25th ult., at No. 33, Blessington-street, Dublin, Mrs. Henry Richardson, of a son.

No. 4488 :: Ref. 1851-02-10, 3:2, B.

On 12th ult., at Ramelton, the wife of Mr. A.A. Kennedy, officer of Inland Revenue, of a daughter.

No. 4489 :: Ref. 1851-02-10, 3:2, B.

On 24th ult., in Dublin, the lady of Rev. Sidney Smith, D.D., rector of Aghalurcher, Fermanagh, of a son.

No. 4490 :: Ref. 1851-02-10, 3:2, M.

On 4th inst., at Mullabrack Church, by the Rev. J.B. Frith, John Corr, Esq., Monaghan, to Elizabeth, second daughter of the late Mr. R. Woodhouse, of Markethill.

No. 4491 :: Ref. 1851-02-10, 3:2, M.

On 30th ult., in St. Mark's Church, Armagh, by Rev. Benjamin Wade, Mr. William Thornberry, turnkey in the county prison, to Mary, eldest daughter of Mr. William Hughes, Armagh.

No. 4492 :: Ref. 1851-02-10, 3:2, M.

On 30th ult., at Glenhoy, Mr. James Hooks, of Tyrhanny, to Miss Ellen Wilson, of the Raws, county Armagh.

No. 4493 :: Ref. 1851-02-10, 3:2, M.

On 5th inst., in Dublin, Capt. R. Willington Kyffin, 12th Regt., to Mary Anne, youngest daughter of the late John Sinclair, Esq., of Dungannon, and Surgeon of the Royal Tyrone Militia.

No. 4494 :: Ref. 1851-02-10, 3:2, M.

In Ballinamallard Church, by the Rev. Henry A. Burke, A.M., Henry John Clements Wallace, Esq., Manorhamilton, to Margaret, third daughter of the late James Johnston, of Curran-hill, county Fermanagh.

No. 4495 :: Ref. 1851-02-10, 3:2, M.

Jan. 23, Mr. Thomas Johnston, of Glenan, co. Monaghan, to Anne, only daughter of the late Mr. J. Bryans, of Killaneel.

No. 4496 :: Ref. 1851-02-10, 3:2, M.

On 29th ult., in Sixmilecross, Rev. David M'Kinny, Pomeroy, to Eliza, third daughter of Mr. Samuel Johnston, Tyrooney, Sixmilecross.

No. 4497 :: Ref. 1851-02-10, 3:2, M.

On 6th inst., at Keady, by the Rev. Francis Kelly, P.P., Mr. P. Woods, to Mary, eldest daughter of Mr. Thomas Raverty.

No. 4498 :: Ref. 1851-02-10, 3:2, M.

On 28th ult., Henry Russell, Esq., of Belfast, to Mary, eldest daughter of the late Thomas Bligh, Esq., of Cavan.

No. 4499 :: Ref. 1851-02-10, 3:2, M.

On 19th ult., by Rev. W. M'Conville, P.P., Cookstown, Mr. Chas. M'Kernan, of Drumcraw, to Eliza, second daughter of Mr. Charles Quinn, Ballymenagh, Cookstown.

No. 4500 :: Ref. 1851-02-10, 3:2, M.

On 12th ult., in Strabane Church, by Rev. James Smith, Mr. John Alexander, to Mary, second daughter of Mr. Joseph Mehaffy, of Strabane.

No. 4501 :: Ref. 1851-02-10, 3:2, M.

In the Cathedral, Derry, by Rev. George Smyth, Jabez Shelton, Esq., London, to Sarah Anne, eldest daughter of Alex. M'Cormick, Esq., of the Commercial Hotel, Londonderry.

No. 4502 :: Ref. 1851-02-10, 3:2, D.

On 2d inst., Annabella, the beloved wife of James Harden of Hrrrybrook [sic], Esq., J.P., D.L., County of Armagh.

No. 4503 :: Ref. 1851-02-10, 3:2, D.

At Waterford, Joshua Jacob, Esq., of the Society of Friends, aged 78 years.

No. 4504 :: Ref. 1851-02-10, 3:2, D.
On 11th ult., at Connaught-place, Kingstown, the residence of his mother, William Stewart, Esq., M.D., third son of the late William Stewart, of Hornhead, Esq.

No. 4505 :: Ref. 1851-02-10, 3:2, D.
On 7th inst., after a long and painful illness, which she bore with Christian resignation and patience, Susan, the dearly beloved wife of Mr. Joseph Patterson, of Moy, aged 26 years. She resigned her soul into the hands of her Redeemer, choosing to depart and be with Christ, which is far better.

No. 4506 :: Ref. 1851-02-10, 3:2, D.
In Dublin, Wm. Gardner, Esq., Surgeon of the 4th Dragoons, of Tower Hill, county Sligo.

No. 4507 :: Ref. 1851-02-10, 3:2, D.
On 25th ult., Margaret Helen, wife of the Rev. Dr. Croly, rector of St. Stephen's, and St. Benet's, London.

No. 4508 :: Ref. 1851-02-10, 3:2, D.
On 13th ult., at Ramelton, aged 20 years, Lizzie, the beloved wife of Mr. A.A. Kennedy, officer of Inland Revenue, of consumption.

No. 4509 :: Ref. 1851-02-10, 3:2, D.
Suddenly, at Strabane, on 31st ult., Mr. Neal Doherty, Innkeeper.

No. 4510 :: Ref. 1851-02-10, 3:2, D.
On 5th inst., Jane, the beloved wife of Samuel Law, Esq., Hazel-bank, county Down.

No. 4511 :: Ref. 1851-02-10, 3:2, D.
On 5th inst., at Monaghan, at an advanced age, the Very Rev. Patrick Bellew, Roman Catholic Dean of Clogher, and Parish Priest of Monaghan.

No. 4512 :: Ref. 1851-02-10, 3:2, D.
At Londonderry, W. M'Carter, sen., Esq., in the 84th year of his age.

No. 4513 :: Ref. 1851-02-10, 3:2, D.
On 1st inst., Mrs. O'Brien, relict of the late Mr. Patrick O'Brien, victualler, Ballyshannon.

No. 4514 :: Ref. 1851-02-10, 3:2, D.
On 31th [sic] ult., at Newry, aged 60 years, Warren Mountgarret, youngest son of the late Rev. John Mountgarret, Rector of the parish of Donoughmore, and senior Captain in the Armagh Militia.

No. 4515 :: Ref. 1851-02-17, 3:1, B.
Feb. 15, the lady of Hugh Boyle, Esq., Mall, Armagh, of a son.

No. 4516 :: Ref. 1851-02-17, 3:1, B.
On 10th inst., at Magheralin, the lady of Robert H. Dolling, Esq., of a son and heir.

No. 4517 :: Ref. 1851-02-17, 3:1, B.
On 12th inst., the wife of Mr. James Burke, master of the Dungannon Workhouse, of a daughter.

No. 4518 :: Ref. 1851-02-17, 3:1, M.
On 13th inst., at Cremore Meetinghouse, Mountnorris, by the Rev. Mr. M'Ewing, Mr. Samuel Girvin, to Ann, second daughter of the late Mr. Gilbert Marshall, Glasdrummond.

No. 4519 :: Ref. 1851-02-17, 3:1, M.
Feb. 12, by the Rev. A. M'Creaght, John Armstrong, Esq., Solicitor, of Belturbet, to Sarah, eldest daughter of the Rev. George B. Moffatt, rector of Drumlane, co. Cavan.

No. 4520 :: Ref. 1851-02-17, 3:1, M.
Feb. 5, at St. Peter's Church, by the Rev. Edward Metcalf, Capt. R. Willington Kyffin, 12th Regiment, to Mary Ann, youngest daughter of the late John Sinclair, Esq., Dungannon, and Surgeon of the Royal Tyrone Militia.

No. 4521 :: Ref. 1851-02-24, 3:1, B.
February 20, on Vicars'-hill, Mrs. Rogers, wife of Mr. Edward Rogers, Vicar Choral of the Armagh Cathedral, of a son.

No. 4522 :: Ref. 1851-02-24, 3:1, B.
February 20, at Donegal, Mrs. Bradshaw, wife of Hugh Alexander Bradshaw, Esq., of the firm of Bradshaw and co., coal, timber, slate, and general merchants, of Donegal and Enniskillen, of a son.

No. 4523 :: Ref. 1851-02-24, 3:1, B.
February 16, at Killesher, Florencecourt, the wife of the Rev Thomas Jebb, of a son.

No. 4524 :: Ref. 1851-02-24, 3:1, B.
At Enniskillen, on 12th inst., the lady of David Webster, junior, Esq., of a daughter.

No. 4525 :: Ref. 1851-02-24, 3:1, B.
On 13th inst., at Arney Lodge, county Fermanagh, the lady of Edward Dunsterville, Esq, S I, of Constabulary, of a son.

No. 4526 :: Ref. 1851-02-24, 3:1, M.
January 15, in Allegheny city, Pennsylvania, U.S.A., by Rev. Mr. Quick, Mr. John M'Cord, to Jane, third daughter of the late Mr. Hugh Copeland, of Enniskillen, Ireland.

No. 4527 :: Ref. 1851-02-24, 3:1, M.
On 4th instant, in Killult Church, by Rev. Alexander Stewart, Mr. William Kerr, (formerly of Derry,) landsteward to Wybrant Olpherts, Esq, to Mary, youngest daughter of Mr Thomas Robinson, merchant, Falcaragh.

No. 4528 :: Ref. 1851-02-24, 3:1, M.
Feb. 18, in Monkstown Church, the Rev. Joseph Wright, of Brohatua, county of Louth, to Catherine, daughter of Alexander Hamilton, Esq., Q.C., LL.D., Rutland-Square, Dublin.

No. 4529 :: Ref. 1851-02-24, 3:1, M.

On 12th inst., in Clontarf Church, John Busteed, Esq., of Tralee, County Kerry, to Mary, daughter of the late John Fitzgerald, Esq., of Armagh.

No. 4530 :: Ref. 1851-02-24, 3:1, M.

At Liverpool, on 11th inst., Edward Comyn Griffith, Esq., to Anna Maria, eldest daughter of the late Mr. Robert Hume, formerly of the county Tyrone.

No. 4531 :: Ref. 1851-02-24, 3:1, M.

On 18th inst., by Rev. D.E. Coyle, James Sheil Dougherty, Esq., of Red Castle, Co. Donegal, to Louisa Augusta, daughter of the late Simon Sheil, Esq., M.D., of Ballyshannon.

No. 4532 :: Ref. 1851-02-24, 3:1, D.

On the 16th inst., in the 18th year of his age, Chas. Graham, eldest son of Charles Foster, Esq., Armagh.

No. 4533 :: Ref. 1851-02-24, 3:1, D.

On 4th inst., at 13, Church-lane, Belfast, Mr. John M'Veigh.

No. 4534 :: Ref. 1851-02-24, 3:1, D.

In Stranorlar, Feb. 18, Andrew Doherty, aged 95, one of the few remaining members of the old Irish Volunteers.

No. 4535 :: Ref. 1851-02-24, 3:1, D.

On 17th inst., in Derry, John Austin, late of Grange Foyle, co. Tyrone, Esq., at the advanced age of 86.

No. 4536 :: Ref. 1851-03-02, 2:7, D.

On the 28th Feb., at Loughgall, John Hanly, Esq., J.P.

No. 4537 :: Ref. 1851-03-02, 2:7, D.

March 1, in Thomas-street, Armagh, Mr. William Hodgens, aged 82 years.

No. 4538 :: Ref. 1851-03-02, 2:7, D.

On 19th Feb, at Clonfeacle Glebe, Sophia Elizabeth, eldest daughter of the Rev. Henry Griffin, Ex-FTCD.

No. 4539 :: Ref. 1851-03-02, 2:7, D.

On 21st Feb, at Naul, near Killyleagh, county Armagh, Sarah, wife of Mr John Steel, and eldest daughter of Mr Edward Archer, of Culligan, near Caledon, aged 35 years.

No. 4540 :: Ref. 1851-03-02, 2:7, D.

On 22d Feb, at Camla Vale, Monaghan, the Hon Mary Augusta Westenra, eldest child of Lord and Lady Rossmore, in the fourth year of her age.

No. 4541 :: Ref. 1851-03-10, 2:1, B.

Feb. 12, at Charlemont Fort, the wife of Captain Henry B. Savile, R.A., of a son.

No. 4542 :: Ref. 1851-03-10, 2:1, B.

Feb. 12, at Fort Royal, co. Donegal, the lady of Caesar G. Otway, Esq., of a son.

No. 4543 :: Ref. 1851-03-10, 2:1, B.

March 2, the wife of Robert Orr Blackader, Esq., Manager of the Belfast Banking Company's Branch, Dundalk, of a daughter.

No. 4544 :: Ref. 1851-03-10, 2:1, B.

Feb. 25, at Tully O'Donnell, Dungannon, the lady of Thomas Staples Irwin, Esq., of a son.

No. 4545 :: Ref. 1851-03-10, 2:1, B.

Feb. 25, at Ballyconnell House, co. Cavan, the lady of J. Haverfield, Esq., of a daughter.

No. 4546 :: Ref. 1851-03-10, 2:1, B.

Feb. 28, at No. 10, Lower Hartstronge-street, Limerick, the lady of William Davis, Esq., Provincial Bank, of a son.

No. 4547 :: Ref. 1851-03-10, 2:1, B.

Feb. 27, at Sydney-avenue, Blackrock, the lady of the Rev. Robt. J.L. M'Ghee, of a son.

No. 4548 :: Ref. 1851-03-10, 2:1, M.

On 2d inst., at Ballyshannon, by the Registrar of Marriages for that district, Mr. Dobbs of Beleek, to Miss M'Goldrick, of same place.

No. 4549 :: Ref. 1851-03-10, 2:1, M.

Jan. 28, at St. George's Church, Dublin, by the Rev. Richard Barton, Mary, eldest daughter of the late Thomas Bligh, Esq., of Cavan, to Henry Russell, Esq., Belturbet.

No. 4550 :: Ref. 1851-03-10, 2:1, M.

Feb. 25, in St. George's Church, by the Rev. W.H. Krause, the Rev. Baptist Barton Crozier, seventh son of the late John Crozier, of Gortra, co. Fermanagh, Esq., to Kate Mary, only daughter of the late John Bolland, of Blessington-street, Esq.

No. 4551 :: Ref. 1851-03-10, 2:1, M.

Feb. 26, at Derriaghy, near Lisburn, by the Rev. John N. Griffin, Minister of Harold's-cross Church, Dublin, Charles William Thompson, Esq., A.M., Captain 58th Regiment, eldest son of the late Lieut-Colonel Thompson, formerly of the 27th Regiment, to Emily, daughter of William Caldbeck, Esq., Lisburn, and Cloragh, county Dublin.

No. 4552 :: Ref. 1851-03-10, 2:1, M.

March 3, by Rev. Henry Harbison, Dungannon, Andrew Harbison, Esq., merchant, Belfast, to Mary, eldest daughter of Fergus O'Farrell, Esq., merchant, Belfast.

No. 4553 :: Ref. 1851-03-10, 2:1, M.

Feb. 27, in Omeath Church, by the Rev. Dr. Hogg, Mr. Joseph Bell, Master of Newry Workhouse, to Sarah Lumley, daughter of Edmund Agnew, Esq., late of Belfast.

No. 4554 :: Ref. 1851-03-10, 2:1, M.

Feb. 13, in Cookstown, by Rev. T. Miller, Lurgan, Joseph, son of John M'Cormick, Esq., to Sarah, daughter of the Rev. Thomas Millar, Cookstown.

No. 4555 :: Ref. 1851-03-10, 2:1, M.

March 4, at Keady, by Rev. Mr. Jennings, Mr. H.M. Oliver, of Lancingburg, New York, to Sarah Anne, eldest daughter of Samuel Gibson, Esq., Keady.

No. 4556 :: Ref. 1851-03-10, 2:1, D.

March 3, in Scotch-street, Armagh, Mr. James Donelly, aged 53—an old and respectable inhabitant.

No. 4557 :: Ref. 1851-03-10, 2:1, D.

On the 4th inst., in his eighty-second year, the Rev. Charles Atkinson, L.L.D., for thirty-nine years Incumbent of the parish of Creggan, County of Armagh.

No. 4558 :: Ref. 1851-03-10, 2:1, D.

March 1, at 2, Longford Terrace, Dublin, Robert Macartney, Esq., late of Moybane, near Enniskillen.

No. 4559 :: Ref. 1851-03-10, 2:1, D.

Feb. 21, at 44, Mill street, Belfast, Mr Francis Weldon, formerly of Lisburn, in the 45th year of his age.

No. 4560 :: Ref. 1851-03-10, 2:1, D.

At Rockfield, co. Cavan, Thomas Berry, one of the coroners of the county.

No. 4561 :: Ref. 1851-03-10, 2:1, D.

Feb. 21, at Rathmines, Rev. Richard Stack, Curate of St. Peter's, Dublin, aged 35 years.

No. 4562 :: Ref. 1851-03-10, 2:1, D.

Feb. 17, at the residence of her brother, the Rev. Thomas Stack, Omagh, Miss Mary Lindsay, aged 78 years.

No. 4563 :: Ref. 1851-03-10, 2:1, D.

Jun. 12, at Pittsburg, U.S., Mr. William Marshall, formerly of Dunadry, co. Antrim.

No. 4564 :: Ref. 1851-03-10, 2:1, D.

At Leith-links, on 18th ult., George Thompson, Esq., late principal clerk to the Hon. Board of Trustees, Edinburgh.

No. 4565 :: Ref. 1851-03-17, 3:1, B.

March 6, at Ardress Glebe, county Fermanagh, the Lady Adam Loftus, of a son.

No. 4566 :: Ref. 1851-03-17, 3:1, B.

March 9, at 103, Eaton-place, London, the Countess of Enniskillen, of a son.

No. 4567 :: Ref. 1851-03-17, 3:1, B.

Feb. 25, at Carndonagh, the wife of the Rev. Simon J. Fausset, of twin sons.

No. 4568 :: Ref. 1851-03-17, 3:1, M.

March 2, by Rev. Mr. Gartland, Mr. James Fitzsimmons, to Jane, eldest daughter of Mr. E. Willoughby, both of Enniskillen.

No. 4569 :: Ref. 1851-03-17, 3:1, M.

Feb. 25, Arthur Lowry Galbraith, Esq., of Beragh, to Miss Isabella Warnock, of Tullaclena House, Dromore, county Tyrone.

No. 4570 :: Ref. 1851-03-17, 3:1, M.

March 7, in the Presbyterian Church, Carrickfergus, by the Rev. James White, George Quarry, Woodbine-cottage, Tandragee, to Ann, youngest daughter of Mr. James Woodside, merchant, Carrickfergus.

No. 4571 :: Ref. 1851-03-17, 3:1, M.

Feb. 16, at Tunnyinn, co. Cavan, by Rev. Mr. Smith, P.P., Kill, Edward M'Nulty, Esq., woollen merchant, Cootehill, to Susan, youngest daughter of Terence M'Entee, Esq.

No. 4572 :: Ref. 1851-03-17, 3:1, M.

1st inst., at Mountrath church, by the Very Rev. the Dean of Ferns, Rev. Thomas Kennedy, Incumbent of Shanoho, co. Monaghan, to Georgina Hester, third daughter of James Smith, Esq., New Park, Queen's county.

No. 4573 :: Ref. 1851-03-17, 3:1, M.

On 3d inst., at St. Mary's, Cheltenham, by Rev. George Adlington, Loftus Algernon Abraham Tottenham, Esq., nephew of the Earl of Erne, to Constance Marian, second daughter of the late Newton Wigney, Esq., M.P. for Brighton.

No. 4574 :: Ref. 1851-03-17, 3:1, M.

On 27th January, at Niagara, Canada West, by the Rev. Charles W. Chester, G.G. Granville Munro, Esq., Lieutenant Royal Canadian Rifle Regiment, to Annie, third daughter of Captain George Vallancey Hamilton, of the same regiment. (It will be remarkable in the recollection of newspaper readers, that a very remarkable and painful paragraph, involving the relatives of the parties whose union is here noticed, went the rounds of the entire press, a few months since.)

No. 4575 :: Ref. 1851-03-17, 3:1, D.

On Monday, February 10th, 1851, at Louisville, in America, deeply lamented, Miss Mary Mills, daughter of the late Mr. James Mills, master of the Drelincourt School, in this city.

No. 4576 :: Ref. 1851-03-17, 3:1, D.

March 12, at Lislea Bleach Works, near this city, Mr. John Kirk, in the 77th year of his age, for upwards of 60 of which he had been in the employment of Mr. Wynne's family, having served the grandfather and father of the present proprietor, and after the death of the present proprietor's father, for about 16 years, had had the entire management of the business, which he conducted with the utmost fidelity.

No. 4577 :: Ref. 1851-03-17, 3:1, D.

In Bishop-street, on Sunday, the 9th inst., at the house of her son-in-law (Mr. Robert Young, of the *Derry Standard*), Elizabeth, relict of the late Mr. Alexander M'Nicholl, of the Deerpark, near Omagh, and only daughter of the late Rogers Clarke, Esq., of

Lammy, formerly Adjutant of the Omagh and Fintona Corps of Volunteers, in the 70th year of her age. Her end was peace.

No. 4578 :: Ref. 1851-03-17, 3:1, D.
March 13, at Cloughjordan, Mr. James Armitage, aged 109 years. For 89 years he was in Church membership with the Baptist Society, and for upwards of 90 years he enjoyed an evidence of acceptance with his God. "*His end was peace.*"

No. 4579 :: Ref. 1851-03-24, 2:7, B.
March 14, in Tralee, the lady of Wm. Beveridge, Esq., Provincial Bank, of a son.

No. 4580 :: Ref. 1851-03-24, 2:7, B.
March 10, at Castledillon, Armagh, Lady Molyneux, of a son.

No. 4581 :: Ref. 1851-03-24, 2:7, B.
March 11, at Ontario Terrace, Rathmines, the lady of Henry Maxwell, Esq., Lieutenant, Revenue Police, Blacklion, of a daughter.

No. 4582 :: Ref. 1851-03-24, 2:7, B.
March 16, at Anketell-grove, the lady of Matthew John Anketell, Esq., of a son.

No. 4583 :: Ref. 1851-03-24, 2:7, M.
On the 13th inst., in the Parish Church of Tartaraghan, by the Rev. — Robinson, Rector, Mr. James Elden, of Clonmacash, to Esther, eldest daughter of Mr. Henry M'Cadim, of Cloncore. The splendid turnout of the wedding party brought to the recollection of the inhabitants of the parish the prosperous days of bygone times, and was considered by them a certain indication of returning prosperity to the country.

No. 4584 :: Ref. 1851-03-24, 2:7, M.
March 18, in Fisherwick Place Church, Belfast by the Rev. James Morgan, D.D., the Rev. William Oliver, of Dunluce, to Rebecca Jane, daughter of John Montgomery, Esq., Elm Grove, Belfast.

No. 4585 :: Ref. 1851-03-24, 2:7, M.
March 13, in the Presbyterian Church, Portadown, by the Rev. James Bell, George Acheson, Esq., Tandragee, to Jane, youngest daughter of the late William Hutcheson, Esq., Portadown.

No. 4586 :: Ref. 1851-03-24, 2:7, M.
March 15, in Limerick, James, son of Henry Clendinning, Esq., of Wheatfield, Richhill, co. Armagh, to Margaret, youngest daughter of the late T.K. Kidd, Esq.

No. 4587 :: Ref. 1851-03-24, 2:7, D.
Of fever, at Enniskillen, Mr. Montague Talbot, formerly manager of the Theatre Royal, Limerick.

No. 4588 :: Ref. 1851-03-24, 2:7, D.
March 18, at Ballyougry, Mr. Andrew Mills, formerly of Strabane.

No. 4589 :: Ref. 1851-03-24, 2:7, D.
March 22, suddenly, at Stewartstown, Rev. Mr. O'Toole, C.C., his remains passed through this city to-day, for interment at Ballymacnab.

No. 4590 :: Ref. 1851-03-24, 2:7, D.
March 18, at the Glebe, Dundonald, in the eighty-second year of his age, the Rev. R.M. Dillon, for forty-one years rector of the parish.

No. 4591 :: Ref. 1851-03-24, 2:7, D.
March 18, at Newry, Jane, relict of the late John Henry, Esq., of Frankford Cottage, Castleblayney, in the fifty-second year of her age.

No. 4592 :: Ref. 1851-03-24, 2:7, D.
March 9, in London, Trevor Corry, youngest son of the late Trevor Corry, Esq., of Newry.

No. 4593 :: Ref. 1851-03-24, 2:7, D.
March 9, at Castle-street, Sligo, after a long and painful illness, which she bore with meek resignation to the Divine will, Fanny, the beloved daughter of George Leech, Esq., in her thirteenth year.

No. 4594 :: Ref. 1851-03-24, 2:7, D.
March 19, at her residence in Lower Baggot-street, Dublin, after a protracted illness, which terminated suddenly in water on the chest, Elizabeth, relict of the Most Rev. Charles Dickenson, D.D., Bishop of Meath.

No. 4595 :: Ref. 1851-03-31, 3:1, B.
March 29, Mrs. Matchett, wife of Mr. James Matchett, of the Albert Hotel, Armagh, of a son.

No. 4596 :: Ref. 1851-03-31, 3:1, B.
March 22, at Marlow Lodge, near Ludlow, Shropshire, the wife of Captain W.J. Verner, of the 21st Fusiliers, of a daughter.

No. 4597 :: Ref. 1851-03-31, 3:1, M.
March 18, in the First Presbyterian Church, Ahoghill, by the Rev. D. Adams, Mr. John M'Clure, Churchville, Canada West, to Jane, eldest daughter of Mr. J. M'Clure, Castletown, co. Armagh.

No. 4598 :: Ref. 1851-03-31, 3:1, M.
On 25th inst., in Clones Church, by the Rev. Charles Welsh, Mr. William Humphreys, Monaghan, to Olivia, eldest daughter of Thos. Welsh, Esq., Clones, late Lieutenant of the Leitrim Regiment of Militia.

No. 4599 :: Ref. 1851-03-31, 3:1, M.
On 21st inst., in the First Presbyterian Church, Dungannon, by the Rev. Charles L. Morell, Mr. John Wilson, C.E., of Benburb, to Miss Eliza Cowan, of Dungannon.

No. 4600 :: Ref. 1851-03-31, 3:1, D.
On the 20th inst., at his father's residence, Barrack-street, after a protracted illness, John Allen, aged 22 years, much regretted by those who knew him on account of the many estimable qualities both of heart and head with which he was gifted.

No. 4601 :: Ref. 1851-03-31, 3:1, D.
March 28, in Ballynahone, near Armagh, of decline, Anne Jane, the beloved wife of Mr. Wm. Croft, aged 29 years, deeply lamented by all who knew her.

No. 4602 :: Ref. 1851-03-31, 3:1, D.
On 26th inst., at Lakeview, Rev. Robert Fleming, for more than 14 years minister of the Presbyterian Cavan congregation.

No. 4603 :: Ref. 1851-03-31, 3:1, D.
On 26th inst., at Glenfarm-Hall, Blacklion, Nicholas Loftus Tottenham, Esq., D.L. and J.P.

No. 4604 :: Ref. 1851-03-31, 3:1, D.
On 20th inst., at Crossmaglen, aged 6 years, Louis Anderson, son of Gordon Holmes, Esq., sub-inspector of constabulary.

No. 4605 :: Ref. 1851-04-07, 3:1, B.
April 3, at Keady, the wife of John Sturgeon, Esq., of a son.

No. 4606 :: Ref. 1851-04-07, 3:1, B.
April 2, at Ballyconnell House, county Donegal, the lady of Wybrants Olpherts, Esq., of a son.

No. 4607 :: Ref. 1851-04-07, 3:1, M.
April 2, in the Second Presbyterian Church, Armagh, by the Rev. Wm. Henderson, Mr. Thomas White, Cullintra, to Sarah Jane, daughter of Mr. A. Jameson, Ballymorrin, County Armagh.

No. 4608 :: Ref. 1851-04-07, 3:1, M.
April 3, in Grange Church, near this city, by the Rev. Mr. Kilpatrick, Mr. Henry Clogher, jun., of Drummonbeg, to Isabella, eldest daughter of Mr. Arthur Saunders, of Greenman, Loughgall.

No. 4609 :: Ref. 1851-04-07, 3:1, M.
April 2, in St. Mary's Church, Dublin, by the Rev. Mr. Mooney, James Lindsay, Esq., merchant, Belfast, to Eliza, youngest daughter of the late John Armstrong, Esq., Bella Hill, co. Fermanagh.

No. 4610 :: Ref. 1851-04-07, 3:1, D.
March 17, at Kilburn House, near London, Mary Ann, wife of Mr. W.H. Smith, of London, and Eden-quay, Dublin.

No. 4611 :: Ref. 1851-04-14, 2:7, B.
The lady of William O'Brien, Esq., *Freeman's Journal*, Dublin, of a son.

No. 4612 :: Ref. 1851-04-14, 2:7, B.
March 26, at 19, Upper Merrion-street, the wife of John Madden, Esq., of Roslea Manor, of a son and heir.

No. 4613 :: Ref. 1851-04-14, 2:7, B.
March 15, at Hibernian Lodge, the residence of her father, Thos. Williams, Esq., the lady of the late Thomas E. Wilson, Esq., of a posthumous son.

No. 4614 :: Ref. 1851-04-14, 2:7, M.
March 27, at Dromore Cathedral, Adam Johnston, Esq., of Glenalina, Belfast, to Margaret, eldest daughter of John Harrison, Esq., of Dromore.

No. 4615 :: Ref. 1851-04-14, 2:7, M.
April 1, by Rev. Doctor Cooke, Charles Hurst, Esq., M.D., Belfast, to Mrs. M. Frazer, of Locust Lodge, co. Down.

No. 4616 :: Ref. 1851-04-14, 2:7, M.
At Ballinamore, county Leitrim, on 20th March, by Rev. Richard S. Clifford, James E. Flynne, Esq., to Mary, Isabella, [sic] eldest daughter of the late William MacFaden, merchant, Cootehill, co. Cavan.

No. 4617 :: Ref. 1851-04-14, 2:7, D.
April 8, after a lengthened illness, Mr. Robert Anderson, of Palnagh, near Killilea, in this county, aged 69 years.

No. 4618 :: Ref. 1851-04-14, 2:7, D.
April 11, at Corr, near Benburb, Mr. Toal Mallen.

No. 4619 :: Ref. 1851-04-14, 2:7, D.
April 6, at Newry, after a short illness, Mr. Alexander Warner, of Monaghan, aged 30 years.

No. 4620 :: Ref. 1851-04-14, 2:7, D.
In the 53d year of his age, James Kelly, Esq., of Annahean, co. Monaghan.

No. 4621 :: Ref. 1851-04-14, 2:7, D.
On 3d inst., aged 26, at Funchal, Madeira, Esther, wife of William Pringle, jun., Esq., formerly of Tyledon Cottage, co. Monaghan.

No. 4622 :: Ref. 1851-04-14, 2:7, D.
On 25th inst., at Carlow, Alexander Harrison, Esq., C.E., formerly County Surveyor of Monaghan.

No. 4623 :: Ref. 1851-04-14, 2:7, D.
Feb. 28, in New York, Mr. John Armstrong, formerly of Monaghan.

No. 4624 :: Ref. 1851-04-14, 2:7, D.
At New Ross, Mr. George H. Irwin, Primitive Wesleyan Methodist Preacher.

No. 4625 :: Ref. 1851-04-14, 2:7, D.
Jan. 30, at Cambridge-square, Hyde-park, London, Anna Maria, second daughter of Lieutenant-General Sir Augustus De Butts, K.C.H., R.E.

No. 4626 :: Ref. 1851-04-14, 2:7, D.
March 23, after a few days' illness, the Rev. James Donaldson, minister of the Presbyterian Church, Castlewellan.

No. 4627 :: Ref. 1851-04-14, 2:7, D.
March 29, at Savilla-place, Warrenpoint, Francis Forde, Esq., of decline—deeply regretted by all who knew him.

No. 4628 :: Ref. 1851-04-14, 2:7, D.

March 30, at 14, Dawson-street, Dublin, aged 70, the Rev. George Brabazon, Rector of the parish of Painstown, co. Meath, for 47 years Register of that diocese.

No. 4629 :: Ref. 1851-04-14, 2:7, D.

March 7, suddenly, off the coast of Sicily, on his passage from India, John Anderson, Esq., M.D., youngest son of the late Dr. Anderson, Selkirk, Assistant-Surgeon H.M. 22nd Regiment, and medical attendant of Sir Charles Napier.

No. 4630 :: Ref. 1851-04-14, 2:7, D.

April 8, at his residence, Rosetta Cottage, Bushfield Avenue, deeply and deservedly regretted by a numerous circle of acquaintances, Edward Bull, Esq., of the *Warder* newspaper. A good husband, an affectionate father, and a faithful friend.

No. 4631 :: Ref. 1851-04-14, 2:7, D.

March 26, at the Rectory, Castleblakeney, the Rev. Mr. Doyle, incumbent of that parish. He lived to an advanced age, and was brother to General Sir John Milley Doyle.

No. 4632 :: Ref. 1851-04-21, 2:3, B.

On the 12th inst., at No. 1, Market-street, Mrs. Robert Moore, of a son.

No. 4633 :: Ref. 1851-04-21, 2:3, B.

April 14, at Newry Barracks, Mrs. Henry William Nelmes, of a daughter.

No. 4634 :: Ref. 1851-04-21, 2:3, B.

On the 15th inst., at Enniskillen, the wife of R.R. Pringle, Esq., Ordnance Storekeeper and Barrack Master, of a son.

No. 4635 :: Ref. 1851-04-21, 2:3, B.

April 12 at Enniskillen, the wife of Doctor Mahood, of a son.

No. 4636 :: Ref. 1851-04-21, 2:3, M.

On the 4th inst., in Mullabrack Church, by the Rev. J.B. Frith, Mr. Charles M'Clelland, jun., of Ballynewry, to Matilda, youngest daughter of Mr. Henry Spence, of Drumatee.

No. 4637 :: Ref. 1851-04-21, 2:3, M.

At Derryvoland church, co. Fermanagh, by the Rev. Gorges Irvine, Mr. Thomas Wilson, Killgrania, to Ann Jane, daughter of the late Mr. John Wilson, Derryhillagh.

No. 4638 :: Ref. 1851-04-21, 2:3, M.

On the 10th inst., in the Cathedral of Connor, by the Rev. Thomas Thompson, Vicar of Derriaghy, Thomas F. Caldbeck, Esq., youngest son of William Caldbeck, of Lisburn, to Charlotte, youngest daughter of the late William Stewart, Esq., M.D., of Lisburn.

No. 4639 :: Ref. 1851-04-21, 2:3, D.

On Tuesday, the 15th inst., in the 22d year of his age, Thomas, fifth son of Mr. James Close, merchant, Armagh. The affliction which the death of this most amiable young man has caused in his family will not easily be obliterated; the numerous and respectable assemblage that accompanied his remains to the grave, bear ample testimony to the high esteem in which he was held by all who knew him, and the marks of sorrow evident on the countenances of his companions, proved how sincerely they regretted his loss.

No. 4640 :: Ref. 1851-04-21, 2:3, D.

At Moira, of paralyism, April 17, aged 70, John Richardson, formerly of Tullygoney near Benburb, co. Tyrone.

No. 4641 :: Ref. 1851-04-21, 2:3, D.

April 9, at Dungannon, Mr. Thomas H. Harvey, officer of inland revenue, aged 24 years.

No. 4642 :: Ref. 1851-04-21, 2:3, D.

April 10, suddenly, of disease of the heart, Mr. James M'William, proprietor of the Victoria Hotel, Banbridge, in the 57th year of his age.

No. 4643 :: Ref. 1851-04-21, 2:3, D.

April 5, Matilda, youngest daughter of Edward Archdall, Esq., of Riversdale, in Fermanagh.

No. 4644 :: Ref. 1851-04-21, 2:3, D.

April 14, in the 70th year of her age Mary, wife of Mr. Thomas Graham, of Knockmanowl, co. Fermanagh.

No. 4645 :: Ref. 1851-04-28, 2:7, B.

On 20th inst., the wife of Mr. Robert Bewglass, of Rectory Place, Woolwich, Kent, of a daughter.

No. 4646 :: Ref. 1851-04-28, 2:7, B.

On 19th inst., at Edenderry, Portadown, the wife of John Watson, hotel keeper, of a daughter.

No. 4647 :: Ref. 1851-04-28, 2:7, B.

At Sligo, the lady of John G. Jones, Esq., Barrister-at-Law, of a daughter.

No. 4648 :: Ref. 1851-04-28, 2:7, B.

April 23, in Ballyshannon, the wife of the Rev. Mr. Bell, Wesleyan Minister, of a son.

No. 4649 :: Ref. 1851-04-28, 2:7, M.

On 24th inst., in Tandragee Church, by the Rev. Mr. Johnston, Mr. James Woods, Mountain Lodge, near Belfast, to Eleanor, only daughter of the late Mr. James Acheson, of Tandragee.

No. 4650 :: Ref. 1851-04-28, 2:7, M.

April 16, in Lurgan Church, by Rev. Charles Falloon, A.M., Hannah, eldest daughter of Mr. James Thompson, Lurgan, to Morgan Maguire, Esq., of Dublin.

No. 4651 :: Ref. 1851-04-28, 2:7, M.

April 23, in Lurgan Church, by the Rev. W.P. Oulton, Mr. Edward Johnston, to Lucinda, eldest daughter of the late Thomas West, both of Lurgan.

No. 4652 :: Ref. 1851-04-28, 2:7, M.
April 10, at Edgeworthstown Church, by Rev. J.H. Powell, Mr. Matthew T. King, son of Mr. Alexander King, of Monaghan, to Florence, daughter of Mr. George Cowen, of Edgeworthstown.

No. 4653 :: Ref. 1851-04-28, 2:7, M.
April 12, at Abbeylara Church, Thomas Porter, Esq., C.I. of Constabulary, Longford, to Eliza, daughter of the late R. Adams, Esq., of Mullingar, co. Westmeath.

No. 4654 :: Ref. 1851-04-28, 2:7, M.
April 27, at Liverpool, Richard, son of John Hilton, Esq., timber merchant, Liverpool, to Jane Gardner, youngest daughter of the late Mr. Robert Hume, formerly of the County Tyrone.

No. 4655 :: Ref. 1851-04-28, 2:7, D.
On 13th inst., at Billis, co. Monaghan, in the 26th year of his age, Mr. Alexander Bell.

No. 4656 :: Ref. 1851-04-28, 2:7, D.
On 16th inst., in the 66th year of his age, Mr. John M'Coy, of Drumnoland, county Monaghan, greatly lamented.

No. 4657 :: Ref. 1851-04-28, 2:7, D.
April 19, at Curlough, near Caledon, Mary Jane, youngest daughter of Thomas Swan, Esq., aged 16 years.

No. 4658 :: Ref. 1851-04-28, 2:7, D.
On 21st inst., at Ballymoney, aged twenty years, Anna Maria, the beloved daughter of James Boyle, Esq., Manager, Ulster Bank.

No. 4659 :: Ref. 1851-04-28, 2:7, D.
On 23d inst., at Errigle Glebe, Aughnacloy, Sophia, the second daughter of Rev. Francis Hurst, aged 18.

No. 4660 :: Ref. 1851-04-28, 2:7, D.
April 21, at Bungalo, Lowtherstown, the residence of her son, Isabella, wife of Mr. Robert Armstrong, hotel, Trillick.

No. 4661 :: Ref. 1851-04-28, 2:7, D.
April 24, at his residence, Orchard-street, Derry, Edward Hyslop, Esq., for many years Proprietor and Editor of the *Londonderry Journal*, aged 58 years.

No. 4662 :: Ref. 1851-04-28, 2:7, D.
April 17, in Enniskillen, Mr. Charles Little.

No. 4663 :: Ref. 1851-04-28, 2:7, D.
April 23, at Lisbellaw, in the 82d year of his age, Mr. William Taylor.

No. 4664 :: Ref. 1851-04-28, 2:7, D.
April 20, at his residence, Lower Gardiner-street, Dublin, Mr. Wm. Dobbin, aged 66 years.

No. 4665 :: Ref. 1851-04-28, 2:7, D.
Feb. 3, at Buenos Ayres, after a residence of more than 30 years in that city, James Lepper, Esq., of Strabane, in the county of Tyrone, retired Surgeon in the Royal Navy.

No. 4666 :: Ref. 1851-04-28, 2:7, D.
April 23, at Anketell Grove, in the 61st year of his age, William Anketell, Esq.

No. 4667 :: Ref. 1851-04-28, 2:7, D.
April 17, at the Cove of Cork, Jane, wife of Charles Maturin, Esq., eldest daughter of Daniel Baird, Esq., of Derry.

No. 4668 :: Ref. 1851-04-28, 2:7, D.
April 20, at the house of his sister, near Drumshambo, Mr. Terence Fergus—steadfast in the faith of the Gospel. He abjured the errors of Popery in St. Audeon's Church, on the 3d of May, 1846; and since that time, amid much persecution, lived a faithful Protestant.

No. 4669 :: Ref. 1851-04-28, 2:7, D.
Recently, at St. Louis, Missouri, U.S.A., Lucas Babington, Esq., late of Newry, brother in law of R. Lawrenson, Esq., Mount Drummond, and son-in-law of the late Charles Pasley, Esq., of Gardiner's-place. He arrived in St. Louis, as an emigrant, in the month of January last, with a large family, to become a proprietor in the west; but in little more than one month afterwards he fell a victim to typhus fever.

No. 4670 :: Ref. 1851-05-05, 2:5, B.
On 29th ult., the wife of Mr. John Lonsdale, Loughgall, of a son.

No. 4671 :: Ref. 1851-05-05, 2:5, B.
On 23d ult., at Farren Connell House, co. Cavan, the lady of Richard Nugent, Esq., of a son and heir.

No. 4672 :: Ref. 1851-05-05, 2:5, M.
Feb. 19, at Natches, U.S., Francis Scott, Esq., of Alexandria, Barrister-at-Law, and son of the late Judge Scott, U.S., to Eliza Maria Elgee, daughter of John Kingsbury Elgee, Esq., of Alexandria, Barrister-at-Law, and granddaughter of the late John Duff, Esq., J.P., of Mountcaulfield, in the County of Armagh.

No. 4673 :: Ref. 1851-05-05, 2:5, M.
On 29th ult., at St. George's Church, Dublin, by the Rev. Jonathan Chamley, Arthur Henry Montgomery, Esq., of Crieve House, Co. Monaghan, second son of the late Alexander Nixon Montgomery, Esq., of Bessmont Park, in the same county, to Henrietta Frances, eldest daughter of the late Rev. Frances Chamley, Vicar of Wicklow.

No. 4674 :: Ref. 1851-05-05, 2:5, M.
By special license, at the Office of the Registrar of Marriages, Belfast, Mr. J.W. Freiland, of Glasgow, to Anne, only daughter of William Gibson, Esq., Woodlawn House, Richhill, County Armagh.

No. 4675 :: Ref. 1851-05-05, 2:5, M.
On 15th ult., in Killead Presbyterian Church, by the Rev. H.R. Macredy, Mr. James Meeke, of the Ulster Bank, Banbridge, to Mary, third daughter of Mr. Wm. M'Elrath, Millform, Killead.

No. 4676 :: Ref. 1851-05-05, 2:5, M.
April 30, in Killester Church, county of Fermanagh, by the Rev. William Sheppard, Mr. William R. Strawhorne, to Miss H. Wilson, of Rossoy.

No. 4677 :: Ref. 1851-05-05, 2:5, M.
April 26, in St. Paul's Church, by the Rev. W. Le Fanu, John Dwyer, jun., of Longford, to Joanna, fifth daughter of Mr. George Chadwick, of Cavan.

No. 4678 :: Ref. 1851-05-05, 2:5, M.
In Aghavea church, John Clarke, Esq., of Aghavea, county Fermanagh, to Eliza, youngest daughter of George Harrison, Esq., Dairy Hill, Queen's County.

No. 4679 :: Ref. 1851-05-05, 2:5, D.
On 20th ult., of scarletina, in the 10th year of her age, Elizabeth, eldest daughter of the Rev. Thomas M'William, of Creggan.

No. 4680 :: Ref. 1851-05-05, 2:5, D.
On 21st ult., of fever, Margaret, third daughter of James M'Gowan, Esq., of Ballyshannon, universally regretted.

No. 4681 :: Ref. 1851-05-05, 2:5, D.
On 29th inst., at the residence of her brother, Kilmore, near Lurgan, Miss Sarah Macoun, aged 81 years.

No. 4682 :: Ref. 1851-05-05, 2:5, D.
April 27, at Lurgan, Ann, relict of the late Dr. Miller, in her 81st year.

No. 4683 :: Ref. 1851-05-05, 2:5, D.
On 23d ult., at the Grange, Emily, eldest daughter of Joseph Greer, Esq., and relict of the late James Lowry, Esq., Rockdale, county Tyrone.

No. 4684 :: Ref. 1851-05-05, 2:5, D.
On 25th ult., in Omagh, the Rev. James M'Cutchan, retired Wesleyad [sic] Minister, aged 76 years—forty of which were spent in the active duties of his calling.

No. 4685 :: Ref. 1851-05-05, 2:5, D.
On 26th ult., at Aughnacloy, after a few week's [sic] illness, the Rev. James Bridge, A.M., in the 65th year of his age, and 43d of his ministry. He was for more than 40 years minister of the Presbyterian Congregation of Ballymagrane, formerly in connexion with Secession Synod.

No. 4686 :: Ref. 1851-05-05, 2:5, D.
On 27th ult., at Ballymullen, near Newtownbutler, at the age of 106 years, John Kettyle. Up to a few days before his death he was able to walk 7 or 8 miles in a day, which he frequently did.

No. 4687 :: Ref. 1851-05-05, 2:5, D.
On 26th ult., at Aghamore, county Fermanagh, in the 41st year of her age, Sarah Jane, the beloved wife of the Rev. Wm. Bredin, curate of Salaghey, parish of Galoon, leaving a large infant family of 12 children to lament the loss.

No. 4688 :: Ref. 1851-05-05, 2:5, D.
At Pettigo, on 22d ult., in his 38th year, John Caldwell Given, Esq.

No. 4689 :: Ref. 1851-05-10, 2:4, B.
On 29th ult., in Enniskillen, the wife of Mr. John Gunning, Druggist, of a son.

No. 4690 :: Ref. 1851-05-10, 2:4, B.
On 4th inst., at Miltown Park, Donnybrook, the lady of J.C. Stronge, Esq., of a daughter.

No. 4691 :: Ref. 1851-05-10, 2:4, B.
On 2d inst., Mrs. A. Grahan, of Beech-hill, near Omagh, of a daughter.

No. 4692 :: Ref. 1851-05-10, 2:4, B.
At 31, Hill-street, Berkeley-square, London, the Viscountess Lewisham, of a son and heir.

No. 4693 :: Ref. 1851-05-10, 2:4, B.
March 23, at Mangalore, the wife of Lieutenant E.O. Leggatt, 35th Regt., M.N.I., of a son.

No. 4694 :: Ref. 1851-05-10, 2:4, M.
In Mullabrack Church, on Wednesday, the 7th inst., by the Rev. John Frith, Mr. John Hamilton, to Sarah, daughter of Mr. Black, Cabra, near Markethill.

No. 4695 :: Ref. 1851-05-10, 2:4, M.
Miss Edwards, daughter of Robert Edwards, Esq., of Bandon, to the Rev. Frederick Stephens, Wesleyan Minister.

No. 4696 :: Ref. 1851-05-10, 2:4, M.
On 5th inst., at Omagh, by Rev. Mr. O'Kane, P.P., Alexander Harkin, M.R.C.S.E., Esq., of Belfast, to Theresa, daughter of the late James Quin Esq., Solicitor, Omagh.

No. 4697 :: Ref. 1851-05-10, 2:4, D.
At Nenagh, after a long and painful illness, the Rev. James Sullivan, Wesleyan Minister.

No. 4698 :: Ref. 1851-05-10, 2:4, D.
On 3d inst., Bessie, wife of Mr. John Sinnamon, Ballintegart, Portadown.

No. 4699 :: Ref. 1851-05-10, 2:4, D.
At Cookstown, on 4th inst., aged 49 years, Mr. John Glasgow, merchant, after an illness of nearly nine months, which he bore with Christian resignation and patience.

No. 4700 :: Ref. 1851-05-10, 2:4, D.
May 6, at Charlemont-place, Dublin, aged 46 years, Isabella, wife of the Rev. Thomas B. Armstrong, of Kilmuckridge, in the county of Wexford.

No. 4701 :: Ref. 1851-05-10, 2:4, D.
On 3d inst., suddenly, at Burlington place, Dublin, Anne, relict of George Buchanan, Esq., M.D., Surgeon of the county of Down Infirmary, and eldest daughter of Richard Wright, Esq., of Pembroke-place.

No. 4702 :: Ref. 1851-05-10, 2:4, D.
On 8th inst., at the residence of Hugh Wallace, Esq., Clady Cottage, Dunadry, John Collins, Esq., Solicitor, Belfast, in the thirty-sixth year of his age.

No. 4703 :: Ref. 1851-05-17, 3:2, B.
On the 12th inst., at Mountain Lodge, County Armagh, the lady of John Douglas, Esq., of a daughter.

No. 4704 :: Ref. 1851-05-17, 3:2, B.
At Carrickfergus, the lady of Captain Rowan, R.N., of a daughter.

No. 4705 :: Ref. 1851-05-17, 3:2, B.
In Enniskillen, the wife of Mr. Wm. Armstrong, of a daughter.

No. 4706 :: Ref. 1851-05-17, 3:2, B.
At Willoughby-place, Enniskillen, the lady of the Rev. J.A. Mathias, of a daughter.

No. 4707 :: Ref. 1851-05-17, 3:2, M.
In St. Peter's Church, Dublin, by the Rev. Mr. M'Sorley, John Keys, Esq., of the Provincial Bank, Cork, to Sarah, youngest daughter of the late Mr. John Irvine, of Enniskillen.

No. 4708 :: Ref. 1851-05-17, 3:2, M.
At Castleblayney, Mr. William A. M'Kenzie, of Great Brunswick-street, Dublin, to Olivia, second daughter of John Sheil, Esq., Castleblayney.

No. 4709 :: Ref. 1851-05-17, 3:2, M.
On the 15th inst., in the Parish Church, by the Rev. T.F. Miller, Vicar, Mr. John H. Atkinson, to Mary Kennedy, eldest daughter of Mr. John Willis, both of Belfast.

No. 4710 :: Ref. 1851-05-17, 3:2, M.
On the 9th inst., in the Presbyterian Church, Warrenpoint, by the Rev. John Dodd, Mr. James Lang, to Eliza, eldest daughter of Mr. James Craig, of Newry.

No. 4711 :: Ref. 1851-05-17, 3:2, M.
In Lisnaskea church, county Fermanagh, by the Rev. John Flanagan, Mr. Edward Gowan, woollen-draper, &c., Lisnaskea, to Margaret, daughter of Wm. Hall, Esq., Drumlught.

No. 4712 :: Ref. 1851-05-17, 3:2, D.
At her residence, in English-street, on Wednesday last, Eliza Jane, the beloved wife of Mr. John M'Watters, aged 42 years. She discharged the various duties of life faithfully and affectionately, and is sincerely regretted by a large circle of friends.

No. 4713 :: Ref. 1851-05-17, 3:2, D.
On Saturday, the 11th inst., at the residence of her father, 11, Fitzwilliam-square west, Harriet Catherine, the eldest daughter of John Collum, Esq., Solicitor.

No. 4714 :: Ref. 1851-05-17, 3:2, D.
Of gastric fever, at the Constabulary Barrack, Phoenix Park, aged 13 years, Herbert W. Cramer Roberts, third son of Captain Cramer Roberts, Commandant.

No. 4715 :: Ref. 1851-05-17, 3:2, D.
At Cottage Park, Avenue, [sic] Sandymount, Wm. West, Esq., late of Cloone, in the County of Leitrim, and brother of the late John Beatty West, Esq., formerly M.P. for Dublin.

No. 4716 :: Ref. 1851-05-17, 3:2, D.
In London, Alexander M'Kee, surgeon, eldest son of the late Alexander M'Kee, Esq., of Moneymore, County Derry.

No. 4717 :: Ref. 1851-05-17, 3:2, D.
On the 9th inst., at his residence, near Low Mills, Lurgan, Mr. Joseph Gaskin.

No. 4718 :: Ref. 1851-05-17, 3:2, D.
At Athlone, Anne, second daughter of William Joyce, Esq.

No. 4719 :: Ref. 1851-05-17, 3:2, D.
May 8, at Bergin place, Grand Canal, of disease of the aorta and heart, Francis Hely Hutchinson Johnstone, Esq., late of the 89th Regt., and Royal West India Rangers, son of the late Francis H. Johnstone, Esq., of Blackpool House and Rathpeacon, county Cork, J.P., Q.C., and grandson of the late James Alexander Hope Johnstone, Esq., of Annan, Dumfriesshire. Deceased was an old officer, having entered the 89th Regt. as Ensign, in 1811.

No. 4720 :: Ref. 1851-05-24, 3:1, B.
At Donegal, on the 15th inst., the wife of Mr. William Wallace, of a daughter.

No. 4721 :: Ref. 1851-05-24, 3:1, B.
On the 21st inst., Mrs. William Smyth, of Townsend-street, Belfast, of a daughter.

No. 4722 :: Ref. 1851-05-24, 3:1, M.
On Thursday, in the second Presbyterian meeting-house, in this city, by the Rev. Mr. Henderson, Miss Margaret Cole, daughter of Mr. Robert Cole, merchant, Barrack-street, to James Mackie, Esq., Kilberney, Scotland.

No. 4723 :: Ref. 1851-05-24, 3:1, M.
On the 15th inst., in the Meeting House of the Second Presbyterian Congregation, Belfast, by the Rev. John Porter, William Dobbin, Esq., Belfast, to Catherine, third daughter; and, at the same time and place, William Douglas, Esq., Camperdown, Comber, to Jane, fourth daughter, of the late James Greenfield, Esq., merchant, Belfast.

No. 4724 :: Ref. 1851-05-24, 3:1, M.

On the 14th inst., in the Presbyterian Church, Glascar, by the Rev. J. Rogers, A.M., Mr. Isaac Kydd, Glascar, son of John Kydd, Esq., Moy, to Jane, daughter of Isaac Bradford, Esq., Donaghmore, Newry.

No. 4725 :: Ref. 1851-05-24, 3:1, M.

Mr. Alexander M'Cormick, Commercial Hotel, Derry, to Mary Anne, daughter of Mr. John M'Grotty, Coleraine.

No. 4726 :: Ref. 1851-05-24, 3:1, M.

The Rev. Henry Johnston, son of the late Robt. Johnston, Esq., of Kinlough House, county Leitrim, to Letitia Jemima, eldest daughter of the late Joseph Meredith, Esq., of Cloonamahon, county Sligo.

No. 4727 :: Ref. 1851-05-24, 3:1, M.

Francis George Joynt, Esq., Assistant-Surgeon in the East India Company's Service, son of Anthony Joynt, Esq., Ballina, to Jane, daughter of the late John Douglas Porter, Esq.

No. 4728 :: Ref. 1851-05-24, 3:1, M.

On 21st inst., at Seagoe Church, by the Rev. Capel Wolsley, David May, Esq., watchmaker and jeweller, of Portadown, to Harriet, third daughter of the late Captain Williams, of Fortwilliam, near Portadown.

No. 4729 :: Ref. 1851-05-24, 3:1, D.

On the 31st ult., of inflammation, in three days' illness, John Carpenter, aged 15 years, at the residence of his uncle, Wm. A. Carpenter, of Lebawn Cottage, Tynan, and eldest son of Richard Carpenter, of Tynan Abbey.

No. 4730 :: Ref. 1851-05-24, 3:1, D.

On the 13th April, in New York, of malignant scarletina, Selina Elizabeth, aged ten years; on the 15th, Samuel Magee, aged four years; and on the 26th, Emily Margaret, aged 6 years, the beloved children of Mr. Watson Kidd, late of Keady, county Armagh.

No. 4731 :: Ref. 1851-05-24, 3:1, D.

May 21, at the Retreat, near this city, Mr. Arthur Graham, merchant, of Aughnacloy, aged 50 years.

No. 4732 :: Ref. 1851-05-24, 3:1, D.

On the 18th inst., at Weedon, of hooping cough, Emily Rosetta Binsteed, twin daughter of W.W. Bond, Esq., Paymaster 4th (King's Own Regiment), aged sixteen months and twenty eight days.

No. 4733 :: Ref. 1851-05-24, 3:1, D.

On the 17th inst., at Monaghan, John Johnston, Esq., Manager of the Belfast Bank there.

No. 4734 :: Ref. 1851-05-24, 3:1, D.

At Crawfordsburn, on 18th inst., Frederick Sharman Crawford, Esq., aged 36 years.

No. 4735 :: Ref. 1851-05-24, 3:1, D.

In Montreal, Mrs. Eliza Lingard, a native of the county Fermanagh, Ireland.

No. 4736 :: Ref. 1851-05-24, 3:1, D.

On the 16th inst., at the house of Francis Forster, Esq., Roshine Lodge, Donegal, Margaret Young, daughter of the late Thomas Young, Esq., of Lough Eske, Donegal.

No. 4737 :: Ref. 1851-05-24, 3:1, D.

On yesterday evening, of influenza, which had latterly turned to decline, Mrs. James Close, of Scotch-street, in this city. It has seldom fallen to our lot to record the death of an individual which our fellow-citizens of all classes seem to unite in regretting so sincerely. She was a kind and sympathizing neighbour, ever ready to feel and console the afflictions of others; a generous and unobtrusive benefactor to the poor, who will seriously feel her loss. In all the relations of life, as a wife, a mother, and a friend, she has left an example well worthy of imitation; and her pious and unhesitating resignation to the inevitable decree of our mortality when announced to her by her physicians, is a consoling proof that while she felt the separation from those she loved, her mind was regulated to meet the stroke, in the sure and certain hope of joining them again in a happy eternity, where there shall be no more sorrow, and where we trust she will receive the reward of a well-spent life. *Requiescat in pace.—(Communicated.)*

No. 4738 :: Ref. 1851-05-24, 3:1, D.

May 7, in Palnagh, in this county, Mr. William Lester, at the advanced age of 80 years. More than 50 years since, while on business in Manchester he was, through the instrumentality of methodism, brought to seek for, and by faith enabled to experience *"redemption through His (Christ's) blood, the forgiveness of sins, according to the riches of his grace."* For half a century he knew the blessedness of those *"whose iniquities are forgiven, and whose sins are covered."* Shortly after his conversion he felt the love of Christ constraining him to call sinners to repentance, in which important but delightful work he frequently and acceptably engaged as a local preacher, in connection with the Primitive Methodist Society, til the infirmities of old age compelled him to retire. Though Mr. Lester was strongly attached to Primitive Wesleyan Methodism, and a steady member of the Established Church, he was no bigot, he loved all who he believed loved the Lord Jesus in sincerity and in truth,—he heartily rejoiced if sinners were turned from darkness to light, by the efforts of any Christian denomination. As in his life his object was to glorify God—in his death, like good old Simeon, he was prepared to say, *"Lord lettest thou thy servant depart in peace, for mine eyes have seen thy salvation."*

No. 4739 :: Ref. 1851-05-24, 3:1, D.
Death of the Rev. James Hodgens.
We regret to announce the death of the Rev. James Hodgens, for some years minister of the Independent Chapel, Belfast. The melancholy event took place on Tuesday, 13th inst., at his residence, Antrim Place. Mr. Hodgens had attained on the 42d year of his age, and the eleventh of his Ministry, when a wise but mysterious Providence removed him from the sphere of his labours. During the period of his residence in Belfast, he was distinguished by an humble and unostentatious piety, united with a good understanding and great zeal in his Master's service. While health permitted him he preached frequently in the open air and was truly instant in season and out of season;—while he was invariably devoted to the interests of evangelical truth, he was yet a lover of all good men; and wherever he found the love of Christ, there was his heart poured out, whatever might be the religious denomination under which it appeared. This spirit was very appropriately exercised in the services observed at his funeral, which were conducted by the Rev. Mr. Eccles, Baptist Minister, the Rev. Mr. O'Hanlon (Mr. Hodgen's [sic] successor), and the Rev. Dr. Morgan, Presbyterian Minister. Mr. Hodgens was a native of Richhill, near Armagh, and received his education in the Dublin Theological Institution, under the Rev. Dr. Urwick and the late Rev. Mr. F. Cooper. In the beginnning of his ministry he served as a missionary in the South and West of Ireland, but the last nine years of his labours were spent in Belfast, where he acquired an honourable place and died universally beloved and lamented.

No. 4740 :: Ref. 1851-05-31, 3:1, B.
On 24th inst., the lady of R.H. Gordon, Esq., of Castledawson, of a son.

No. 4741 :: Ref. 1851-05-31, 3:1, B.
At Castletown, Berehaven, county Cork, the lady of Philip A. Armstrong, Esq., M.D., of a son.

No. 4742 :: Ref. 1851-05-31, 3:1, B.
May 27, in this city, Mrs Maxwell, of a son.

No. 4743 :: Ref. 1851-05-31, 3:1, B.
On 22d inst., the lady of Rev. Thomas Davis Bain, Banbridge, of a son.

No. 4744 :: Ref. 1851-05-31, 3:1, B.
At Glengarro, county Cork, the lady of Robert H. Disney, Esq., of a son.

No. 4745 :: Ref. 1851-05-31, 3:1, B.
At 127, Lower Baggot-street, Dublin, the wife of the Rev. W.C. Maude, of a son.

No. 4746 :: Ref. 1851-05-31, 3:1, M.
In Clones Church, on 27th inst., by the Rev. Thomas Hand, Mr. Francis Graham, of that town, to Eliza, eldest daughter of Sergeant Major Purcell, 47th regt., Corfu.

No. 4747 :: Ref. 1851-05-31, 3:1, M.
May 23, at Kildallen Church, by the Rev. W.F. Sanders, George Rea, Esq., of Reville Lodge, Ballyhaise, to Marianne Huggins, daughter of the late John Huggins, Esq., Kildallen.

No. 4748 :: Ref. 1851-05-31, 3:1, M.
At Kilskerry Glebe, Fermanagh, John W. Ellison, Esq., Barrister-at-Law, led to the hymenal altar the eldest daughter of the Rev. John Grey Porter.

No. 4749 :: Ref. 1851-05-31, 3:1, M.
In Derryvullen church, by the Rev. G. Irwin, Mr. John Wallace, of Blacklion, to Margaret, daughter of Mr. George Stewart, of Lowtherstown.

No. 4750 :: Ref. 1851-05-31, 3:1, M.
On 21st inst., in Clontarf Church, William Perrin, Esq., fourth son of the Right Hon. Louis Perrin, one of the Justices of the Court of Queen's Bench, to Isabella Ann, daughter of the late Wm. Allman, Esq., M.D., Professor of Botany in the University of Dublin.

No. 4751 :: Ref. 1851-05-31, 3:1, M.
At Plymouth, Wm. P. Reed, Esq., son of the late Lieutenant-Col. John Reed, K.H., to Katherine, daughter of John Humphreys, Esq., of Miltown House, county Tyrone.

No. 4752 :: Ref. 1851-05-31, 3:1, M.
In St. Peter's Church, Dublin, by the Rev. Richard Keane, Benjamin Reeves, Esq., son of Benjamin Reeves, Esq., of Ballinasloe, to Helena, fourth daughter of the late Henry Coulston Heacock, Esq., of Ballynacourty, county of Limerick.

No. 4753 :: Ref. 1851-05-31, 3:1, M.
May 28, in the Church of St. Nicholas Without, Dublin, by the bride's uncle, the Rev. E.H. Halahan, the Rev. Wm. D. Murray, to Mary Sophy, eldest daughter of the late Lieutenant Halahan, 44th Regiment.

No. 4754 :: Ref. 1851-05-31, 3:1, M.
In May-street church, by the Rev. Dr. Cooke, Mr. Hugh Hamilton, to Arabella, daughter of Mr. Richard Robinson, of Belfast.

No. 4755 :: Ref. 1851-05-31, 3:1, M.
On 21st inst., in St. Mark's Church, by the Dean of Cashel, uncle to the bride, E.R. Bredin, Esq., of Rice Hill, county Cavan, to Caroline Martha, third daughter of Charles J. Adams, Esq., of Shinan House, county Cavan.

No. 4756 :: Ref. 1851-05-31, 3:1, D.
At Summerhill, Fermanagh, in the thirty-third year of his age, Robert Richardson, Esq., fourth son of the Rev. John Richardson.

No. 4757 :: Ref. 1851-05-31, 3:1, D.
At Carricknahorna, near Ballyshannon, Mrs. Elliott, wife of Mr. Andrew Elliott.

No. 4758 :: Ref. 1851-05-31, 3:1, D.
At Auburn, in Westmeath, Elenor, the beloved wife of Lorenzo Dundas, Esq.

No. 4759 :: Ref. 1851-05-31, 3:1, D.
On 26th inst., at his residence, in Dublin, at the advanced age of ninety-eight years, Cornelius M'Laughlin, Esq.

No. 4760 :: Ref. 1851-05-31, 3:1, D.
On 20th March, at Agra, East Indies, Veronica Scott, wife of James Anderson, Esq., M.D., 2d Fusiliers.

No. 4761 :: Ref. 1851-05-31, 3:1, D.
At her residence, Smithfield, after a short illness, Ann Jane, wife of Mr. Wm. Todd.

No. 4762 :: Ref. 1851-05-31, 3:1, D.
In Derry, Mr. James Scott, at the advanced age of 92 years.

No. 4763 :: Ref. 1851-05-31, 3:1, D.
On 28th February last, at Foo-chou-foo, China, in the 33d year of his age, Wm. Connor, Esq., H.B.M., [sic] Vice-Consul at that place, and late of Derry.

No. 4764 :: Ref. 1851-05-31, 3:1, D.
At New York, John Barclay Sheil, Esq., M.D., late of Ballyshannon, in the 53d year of his age.

No. 4765 :: Ref. 1851-06-07, 2:7, B.
On the 27th ult., at Edinburgh, Lady Claud Hamilton, of a daughter.

No. 4766 :: Ref. 1851-06-07, 2:7, B.
On the 27th ult., the wife of the Rev. T. Hanley Bell, of a daughter.

No. 4767 :: Ref. 1851-06-07, 2:7, B.
At Bridge-st., Coleraine, the wife of Mr. Wm. Ellis, grocer, wine, and spirit merchant, of a daughter.

No. 4768 :: Ref. 1851-06-07, 2:7, B.
At Drogheda, the lady of Thomas Watts, Esq., Supervisor of Inland Revenue, of a daughter.

No. 4769 :: Ref. 1851-06-07, 2:7, B.
At Aughafadd, near Clogher, county Tyrone, on 31st ult., the lady of James Graham, Esq., of a son.

No. 4770 :: Ref. 1851-06-07, 2:7, M.
On the 3d inst., by the Rev. Thomas Watters, Newtownards, William Simpson, Esq., Surgeon, R.N., to Anna, daughter of the late Michael Henry Rankin, Esq., Newtownards.

No. 4771 :: Ref. 1851-06-07, 2:7, M.
At Aberdeen, by the Rev. J. Bryce, of Gilcomston Free Church, the Rev. Wm. M'Clure, of Londonderry, to Barbara, eldest daughter of John Dickie, Esq.

No. 4772 :: Ref. 1851-06-07, 2:7, M.
In Rosemary-street Church, Belfast, by the Rev. Mr. Knox, Mr. Wm. J. Robinson, to Miss Euphemia Anderson, both of Belfast.

No. 4773 :: Ref. 1851-06-07, 2:7, M.
On the 3d inst., by the Rev. S. Simpson, in the Presbyterian Church, Ormond Quay, Dublin, the Rev. John Dougan, Loughmorne, to Sarah Jane, eldest daughter of Thomas Wilson, Esq., Aughakist, county Monaghan, and niece of the late Rev. Josias Wilson.

No. 4774 :: Ref. 1851-06-07, 2:7, M.
In Sandys-street Presbyterian Church, Newry, by the Rev. John Moran, John Warnock, Esq., M.D., Fintona, to Eliza Ellen, daughter of Mr. James Sherrard, merchant, Fintona.

No. 4775 :: Ref. 1851-06-07, 2:7, D.
On the 6th inst., at Wood Park, county Armagh, Alicia Maria, relict of the late Rev. Silver Oliver, Rector of Loughgall, diocese of Armagh, aged 60 years.

No. 4776 :: Ref. 1851-06-07, 2:7, D.
June 1, at Gosford Castle, Jonathan Steed, Esq., Landscape Gardener to the Earl of Gosford.

No. 4777 :: Ref. 1851-06-07, 2:7, D.
In Belfast, at the house of her son-in-law, the Rev. Thomas Toye, Mrs. Charlotte Shaw, relict of the late Wm. Shaw, Esq., city of Cork.

No. 4778 :: Ref. 1851-06-07, 2:7, D.
At Milltown, near Ballyclare, after a long and severe illness, Mrs. Archer, wife of Samuel Archer, aged 68 years.

No. 4779 :: Ref. 1851-06-07, 2:7, D.
At Cheltenham, the lady Louisa Anne Bernard, sister of the Earl of Bandon.

No. 4780 :: Ref. 1851-06-07, 2:7, D.
At Islington, Charles Hill, Esq., aged 52, Secretary to the Board of Green Cloth, and 36 years in the Lord Steward's Department of the Royal Household.

No. 4781 :: Ref. 1851-06-07, 2:7, D.
At 22, Stephen's-green, North, Mary, wife of Robert Adams, Esq., M.D.

No. 4782 :: Ref. 1851-06-07, 2:7, D.
Brice Smith, Esq., Brookfield, Banbridge, one of the most extensive manufacturers connected with the linen trade.

No. 4783 :: Ref. 1851-06-07, 2:7, D.
At the Lodge, Navan, Mrs. Eleanor Wade, in her 74th year.

No. 4784 :: Ref. 1851-06-07, 2:7, D.
The Rev. John M. Duncan, one of the most eminent of Presbyterian ministers, in Baltimore, U.S.

No. 4785 :: Ref. 1851-06-07, 2:7, D.

Of dysentery, together with a pneumonic infection, Mary Anne, the beloved wife of Mr. Samuel Lindsay, of Tattykeeran, Beragh, Dungannon.

No. 4786 :: Ref. 1851-06-07, 2:7, D.

At Drumgole, after an illness of some weeks, borne with patience and Christian resignation, Mr. John Crawford, for many years ruling elder in the Presbyterian Church at Drum.

No. 4787 :: Ref. 1851-06-07, 2:7, D.

At his residence, Rosehill, Fahan, Mr. Joseph Alexander, formerly of Derry, aged 42 years.

No. 4788 :: Ref. 1851-06-07, 2:7, D.

In Muff, county Donegal, in the 25th year of his age, Mr. Patrick Dougherty, only son of Mrs. Dougherty, and nephew to the late T. Dougherty, Esq., of Redcastle.

No. 4789 :: Ref. 1851-06-07, 2:7, D.

At Dungannon, on 28th ult., after a lingering illness, Susan, daughter of Mr. Thomas Monaghan, aged 16 years.

No. 4790 :: Ref. 1851-06-07, 2:7, D.

At Pettigo, county Donegal, Mrs. J. Campbell, aged 81 years.

No. 4791 :: Ref. 1851-06-07, 2:7, D.

May 30, at Woodville, county of Cavan, Anne, the beloved wife of Francis Finlay, Esq.

No. 4792 :: Ref. 1851-06-14, 3:2, B.

On 6th inst., the wife of the Rev. Henry Martin, Congregational Minister, of this city, of a daughter.

No. 4793 :: Ref. 1851-06-14, 3:2, B.

At Dromore, County Down, the lady of Waldron Burrowes, Esq., of a son.

No. 4794 :: Ref. 1851-06-14, 3:2, B.

At Home Ville, Rathmines, the lady of A.L. Fleming, Esq., of a son.

No. 4795 :: Ref. 1851-06-14, 3:2, M.

June 10, by special license, in Drumeena Church, by the Rev. Wm. Ashe, Mr. Joseph Porter, of Clones, county Monaghan, to Margaret, youngest daughter of Mr. George Henderson, of Cloverhill, co. Cavan.

No. 4796 :: Ref. 1851-06-14, 3:2, M.

Richard Graves, second son of Wm. Graves, Esq., of the Bank of Ireland, to Jane, second daughter of the late George Furey, Esq., of Mount-street.

No. 4797 :: Ref. 1851-06-14, 3:2, M.

June 11, in the Presbyterian Church, Tempo, the Rev. James Malcomson, Aughentain, to Mary Ann, eldest daughter of James Johnston, Esq., Corrylongford, near Fivemiletown.

No. 4798 :: Ref. 1851-06-14, 3:2, M.

June 10, at the residence of the bride's father, Dungannon, by the Rev. Mr. Hughes, Mr. Henry M'Glade, spirit merchant, Belfast, to Bridget, only daughter of Mr. James M'Guskian.

No. 4799 :: Ref. 1851-06-14, 3:2, M.

June 10, at Mullabrack, by the Rev. J.B. Frith, James Wann, Esq., of Cavan, to Amanda Wilhelmina Antoinette, second daughter of Augustus Selss [sic], Esq., of Coasfeld, Westphalia.

No. 4800 :: Ref. 1851-06-14, 3:2, D.

In English-street, Mr. Edward Corvan, aged 88 years.

No. 4801 :: Ref. 1851-06-14, 3:2, D.

June 10, at Magherafelt, Mr. David Graham, aged 67 years.

No. 4802 :: Ref. 1851-06-14, 3:2, D.

On 30th ult., at Clarlemont-terrace [sic], Kingstown, Thomas Stewart, Esq., youngest brother of the late William Stewart, Esq., Horn Head, co. Donegal, aged 69.

No. 4803 :: Ref. 1851-06-14, 3:2, D.

At Warrenpoint, on 8th inst., Margaret, third daughter of the late Robert Anderson, Esq., of Drumkeen, county Fermanagh.

No. 4804 :: Ref. 1851-06-14, 3:2, D.

June 11, at 15, North Richmond-street, Dublin, Thomas, eldest son of Barry Collins, Esq.

No. 4805 :: Ref. 1851-06-14, 3:2, D.

May 30, at Heidelberg, Anne, the beloved wife of Edward Thomas Litton, Esq., of Altmore, county of Tyrone.

No. 4806 :: Ref. 1851-06-14, 3:2, D.

June 9, at Narraghmore Rectory, county Kildare, in his 83d year, the Venerable John Torrens, D.D., for thirty-two years Archdeacon of Dublin, and for thirty-seven years Rector of the Parish of Narraghmore.

No. 4807 :: Ref. 1851-06-14, 3:2, D.

At Pettigo, county Donegal, Mrs. J. Campbell, aged 81 years.

No. 4808 :: Ref. 1851-06-14, 3:2, D.

At Nn. Cunningham, Mr. George Dugall, in the 57th year of his age.

No. 4809 :: Ref. 1851-06-14, 3:2, D.

At sea, on the 16th April last, on her voyage home from India, Marianne, wife of Edward M. Wylly, Bengal Civil Service, and daughter of the late Robert Maginniss, Esq., of Derry.

No. 4810 :: Ref. 1851-06-21, 3:1, B.

June 16, the wife of Mr. Wm. M'Clelland, Moy, of a son.

No. 4811 :: Ref. 1851-06-21, 3:1, B.
In Eaton-square, the wife of Captain the Hon. Francis Maude, R.N., of a son.

No. 4812 :: Ref. 1851-06-21, 3:1, B.
June 13, at Monkstown, County Dublin, Lady Murray, of a son.

No. 4813 :: Ref. 1851-06-21, 3:1, M.
June 12, in Tallaght Church, by the Rev. S.G. Cotton, brother to the bride, John C. Irvine, Esq., third son of the late Wm. Irvine, Prospect Hill, Esq., Clerk of the Crown for the county Fermanagh, to Ellen, third daughter of Francis R. Cotton, of Allerton, county Dublin, Esq.

No. 4814 :: Ref. 1851-06-21, 3:1, M.
June 10, in Monkstown Church, by the Rev. Thomas Rook, Isaac Bracken, F.R.C.S.I., eldest son of the late John King Bracken, Esq., M.B., of the city of Waterford, to Alicia Caroline, fourth daughter of the late Robert Smyth, Esq., of Portlick Castle, county of Westmeath.

No. 4815 :: Ref. 1851-06-21, 3:1, D.
On Wednesday, 18th inst., at Carnteel House, county Tyrone, Mary, widow of the late John M'Williams, Esq. She died in the full assurance of faith.

No. 4816 :: Ref. 1851-06-21, 3:1, D.
On the 14th inst., of brain fever, Mrs. Maxwell, wife of Mr. Maxwell, painter, Mall, Armagh.

No. 4817 :: Ref. 1851-06-21, 3:1, D.
On the 16th inst., Mr. James Dickson, student of medicine, second son of the late Wm. Dickson, surgeon, Belfast.

No. 4818 :: Ref. 1851-06-21, 3:1, D.
On the 16th inst., at Glenarm, Emily, daughter of J.B. Bankhouse, Esq.

No. 4819 :: Ref. 1851-06-21, 3:1, D.
June 11, in Armagh, Henry John, third son of the late Robert James, Esq., M.D., of Bailieborough, aged 10 years.

No. 4820 :: Ref. 1851-06-21, 3:1, D.
June 14, Margaret, wife of Mr. George Eccles, of Enniskillen, saddler, aged 35.

No. 4821 :: Ref. 1851-06-21, 3:1, D.
June 15, Elizabeth, relict of the late Henry Porter, formerly of Lurgan, aged 81 years.

No. 4822 :: Ref. 1851-06-28, 3:1, B.
On 27th inst., in Thomas-street, the wife of Mr. Owen O'Callaghan, merchant, of a son.

No. 4823 :: Ref. 1851-06-28, 3:1, B.
At Ballyhenry, county Wicklow, the lady of Livingstone Thompson, Esq., of a son.

No. 4824 :: Ref. 1851-06-28, 3:1, B.
On 22d inst., the lady of the Rev. Robert Hamilton, Castlecaulfield, of a daughter.

No. 4825 :: Ref. 1851-06-28, 3:1, B.
On 21st inst., the wife of John Cuppage, Esq., Lurgan, of a son.

No. 4826 :: Ref. 1851-06-28, 3:1, B.
At Desart Glebe, the lady of Rev. Redmond M'Causland, of a son.

No. 4827 :: Ref. 1851-06-28, 3:1, B.
On 21 inst., at 20, Lowndes-square, the Countess of March, of a daughter.

No. 4828 :: Ref. 1851-06-28, 3:1, B.
On 23d inst., in Guildford-street, Lady Pollock, of a son.

No. 4829 :: Ref. 1851-06-28, 3:1, B.
At Dunfanaghy, county Donegal, the lady of the Rev. William Allman, of a daughter.

No. 4830 :: Ref. 1851-06-28, 3:1, M.
On 26th inst., in Tandragee Church, by Rev. Richard Johnson, Adam Fulton, Esq., Cookstown, to Margaret, youngest daughter of the late James Seawright, Esq., Newry.

No. 4831 :: Ref. 1851-06-28, 3:1, M.
On 17th inst., in Limerick, Stephen Meade, jun., Esq., son of Stephen Meade, Esq., Rathmines, county Dublin, to Eliza, youngest daughter of the late John Hogan, Esq., M.D., of Limerick.

No. 4832 :: Ref. 1851-06-28, 3:1, M.
On 20th inst., in the Church of Dromore, by Rev. H.L. St. George, William K. Irwine, Esq., son of Captain Irwine, Drumglass House, near Dungannon, to Anne, second daughter of James Hamilton, Esq., of Lakemount.

No. 4833 :: Ref. 1851-06-28, 3:1, M.
On 12th inst., by Rev. Mr. Farrell, Mr. David Connor, to Elizabeth, daughter of William Hunter, Esq., of Belfast.

No. 4834 :: Ref. 1851-06-28, 3:1, M.
On 26th ult., at New York, by Rev. Dr. Cone, Mr. John Mullen, late master printer in Belfast, to Anna, third daughter of the late Mr. Benjamin Neely, of same place.

No. 4835 :: Ref. 1851-06-28, 3:1, M.
On 10th inst., at the residence of the bride's father, by Rev. D.E. Coyle, P.P., Stranorlar, Mr. Francis M'Closkey, Fyfannan house, Killybegs, to Susannah, eldest daughter of Mr. Patrick Kerrigan, Curraughmoan, Stranorlar.

No. 4836 :: Ref. 1851-06-28, 3:1, M.
On 25th inst., in the house of the bride's aunt, 75, Harcourt-st., by special license from   (*continued...*)

No. 4836, continued: ...his Grace the Lord Primate of all Ireland, Frederic [sic] Percy Lea, Lieutenant in her Majesty's 57th Regiment of Foot, youngest son of J. Lea, of Donnybrook, to Elizabeth Anne Louisa, only daughter of Sir Edward Newenham Meredyth, Bart., county of Kilkenny, and cousin to the Countess of Miltown.

No. 4837 :: Ref. 1851-06-28, 3:1, M.
On 20th inst., in the First Presbyterian Church, Saintfield, by Rev. Wm. Davidson, brother-in-law to the bride, the Rev. Robert M'Ewan, minister of Saintfield, to Eliza, youngest daughter of James Cleland, Esq., Woodside, county Down.

No. 4838 :: Ref. 1851-06-28, 3:1, D.
On 22d inst., at Rokeby Green, in this city, Mary Margaret, youngest daughter of Mr. John M'Connell.

No. 4839 :: Ref. 1851-06-28, 3:1, D.
On 18th inst., at Foxpark, Mr. John Woodhouse, in the 74th year of his age. He was much esteemed and is deeply regretted.

No. 4840 :: Ref. 1851-06-28, 3:1, D.
On 26th inst., Grace, only daughter of Mr. Wm. M. Barkley, Queen's-square, Belfast, aged 16 years.

No. 4841 :: Ref. 1851-06-28, 3:1, D.
On 12th inst., at Lismacarrol, Mr. John M'Causland, jun., aged 30 years.

No. 4842 :: Ref. 1851-06-28, 3:1, D.
On 13th inst., at Hervey Hill, aged 36 years, Anne, second daughter of Rev. William Napper, Rector of Tamlaghtocrilly.

No. 4843 :: Ref. 1851-06-28, 3:1, D.
On 17th inst., at Bungola, Lowtherstown, the residence of her brother, in the 25th year of her age, Ellen, eldest daughter of Mr. Robert Armstrong, Hotel, Trillick, after a lingering illness which she bore with great patience and Christian fortitude.

No. 4844 :: Ref. 1851-06-28, 3:1, D.
On 6th inst., at Seskanore Mills, of inflammation on the lungs, aged 26 years, Jane, the beloved wife of Mr. Louis Walsh.

No. 4845 :: Ref. 1851-07-05, 3:1, B.
June 29, at Glasslough, the lady of Robert M'Kinstry, Esq., M.D., of a son.

No. 4846 :: Ref. 1851-07-05, 3:1, B.
On 24th ult., the lady of James Lendrum, Esq., of Corkhill, of a son.

No. 4847 :: Ref. 1851-07-05, 3:1, M.
At Newark, John, son of Edward Gilling Hallewell, Esq., M.P., of the Royal Crescent, Cheltenham, to Eliza Catherine, daughter of Wm. Brodhurst, of the Friary, Newark.

No. 4848 :: Ref. 1851-07-05, 3:1, M.
On 24th ult., at the residence of the bride's father, by Right Rev. Dr. Cullen, Hugh Cullen of Croan, county of Carlow, to Ellen, second daughter of Thomas Moamberlaine, Esq., of Crowhill, county Kildare.

No. 4849 :: Ref. 1851-07-05, 3:1, M.
On 28th May, at Quebec, Edward D. Ashe, Esq., Lieutenant, Royal Navy, in charge of Observatory, to Marcella, eldest daughter of the Rev. Gilbert Percey, Incumbent of St. Peter's, Quebec, and formerly of Ballymoyer, co. Armagh.

No. 4850 :: Ref. 1851-07-05, 3:1, D.
June 29, in this city, Lucy Frances, aged 20, eldest daughter of Dr. Robinson, Surgeon of the Armagh County Infirmary.

No. 4851 :: Ref. 1851-07-05, 3:1, D.
June 30, in this city, aged 46 years, Mr. Robert Calwell, much regretted by all who knew him.

No. 4852 :: Ref. 1851-07-05, 3:1, D.
June 20, at Strabane, Mr. Robert Hannah.

No. 4853 :: Ref. 1851-07-05, 3:1, D.
June 27th at Castleblaney, Jane, wife of Mr. James Birch.

No. 4854 :: Ref. 1851-07-05, 3:1, D.
In Sligo, in consequence of injury sustained by a fall from his horse, Lieut. Hamilton, R.N., of the Coast Guards.

No. 4855 :: Ref. 1851-07-12, 3:2, B.
July 8, at Brookborough, the lady of Matthew H. Shankey, Esq., of a son.

No. 4856 :: Ref. 1851-07-12, 3:2, B.
On 29th ult., in this city, the wife of Mr. John Small, flax merchant, of a daughter.

No. 4857 :: Ref. 1851-07-12, 3:2, B.
At Ballyoonan, county Louth, the lady of Robert Walker Greer, Esq., of a daughter.

No. 4858 :: Ref. 1851-07-12, 3:2, M.
On 2d inst., by the Rev. Alexander Henderson, Lisburn, Mr. Edward Higginson, merchant, to Margaret Lindsay, daughter of Captain Joseph Crawford, of Lisburn.

No. 4859 :: Ref. 1851-07-12, 3:2, M.
July 1, in London, by Rev. John Sheil, B.D., the Rev. W.J.M. Young, A.B., Curate of Culdaff, county Donegal, to Georgina Caroline, youngest daughter of the late Thomas Johnston, Esq., of Harrington-street, Dublin.

No. 4860 :: Ref. 1851-07-12, 3:2, D.
On 1st inst., Mr. Andrew Jelly, of Portadown.

No. 4861 :: Ref. 1851-07-12, 3:2, D.
On 3d inst., in the 27th year of his age, William, son of Mr. Alex. Armstrong, Cragheen Cottage, near Ballinamallard.

No. 4862 :: Ref. 1851-07-12, 3:2, D.
On 30th ult., at Castleblayney, after a short illness, George Shegog, Esq., M.D., in his 80th year.

No. 4863 :: Ref. 1851-07-12, 3:2, D.
June 28, Joseph Ringland Anderson, aged seventeen years, son of Mr. John Anderson, of Killilea, county Armagh.

No. 4864 :: Ref. 1851-07-12, 3:2, D.
June 30, at Waterloo Cottage, Cookstown, Captain R. Lind, in the 71st year of his age.

No. 4865 :: Ref. 1851-07-12, 3:2, D.
July 6, at Emyvale, Newry, Isabella Barclay, wife of George Henderson, Esq., Editor of the *Newry Telegraph*, and daughter of the late Alexander Williamson, Esq., Lambeg.

No. 4866 :: Ref. 1851-07-19, 2:5, B.
On 10th inst., at Cavan, the lady of Rev. W.P. Moore, of a daughter.

No. 4867 :: Ref. 1851-07-19, 2:5, B.
On the 10th inst., at Upper Gardiner-street, Dublin, the lady of Ambrose Nugent, Esq., of a son.

No. 4868 :: Ref. 1851-07-19, 2:5, M.
July 17, at Ballymoyer Church, by Rev. Samuel Butcher, D.D., F.T.C.D., assisted by Rev. Garret Wall, the Rev. Francis Crawford, Incumbent of Portadown, to Janet Agnes, third daughter of Marcus Synnot, Esq., Ballymoyer, co. Armagh.

No. 4869 :: Ref. 1851-07-19, 2:5, M.
On 9th inst., in the Cathedral, Derry, by Rev. George Smith, William Betty, Esq., of Cappy House, Enniskillen, to Jemima Harriet, youngest daughter of the late Mr. Gaston, Buncrana.

No. 4870 :: Ref. 1851-07-19, 2:5, M.
July 12, at St. Peter's Church, by Rev. Henry Jellett, A.M., the Rev. Hewitt R. Poole, Fellow of Trinity College, Dublin, to Harriet Dorothea, only daughter of the late Rev. Morgan Jellett, Rector of Tullycorbet, county Monaghan.

No. 4871 :: Ref. 1851-07-19, 2:5, M.
On 15th inst., in the Presbyterian Church of Richhill, by Rev. Andrew M'Calden, Mr. James Caird, of Banbridge, merchant, to Elizabeth, daughter of Mr. Thomas Greer, Mullalelish.

No. 4872 :: Ref. 1851-07-19, 2:5, D.
On 14th inst., at Markethill, Emily Wingfield Barker, eldest daughter of the late Joshua David Barker, Esq.

No. 4873 :: Ref. 1851-07-19, 2:5, D.
July 10, at the Glebe, Glenavy, the Rev. Ross Jebb, aged seventy years.

No. 4874 :: Ref. 1851-07-19, 2:5, D.
July 13, at his residence in Monaghan, Mr. Holmes, at a comparatively early age.

No. 4875 :: Ref. 1851-07-19, 2:5, D.
June 17, at Bayou Sara, Louisiana, U.S.A., in the fifty-third year of his age, Mr. Robert Wilson, Printer, of Dublin.

No. 4876 :: Ref. 1851-07-19, 2:5, D.
June 29, at Donegal, Miss Elizabeth Brigham, aged 59 years.

No. 4877 :: Ref. 1851-07-19, 2:5, D.
July 6, in Ballina, at the residence of his brother-in-law, Mr. A. Little, R.J. King, aged 26, fifth son of Samuel King, Esq., of Coal Island Mills, Dungannon.

No. 4878 :: Ref. 1851-07-19, 2:5, D.
July 9, at Ballybay, George Hayes, Esq., second son of the late Wm. Hayes, Esq., of Millmount, Banbridge.

No. 4879 :: Ref. 1851-07-19, 2:5, D.
July 10, at 32, Bryanstone-square, London, Marianne, relict of the late John Henry Burges, Esq., of Parkanour, county Tyrone, and sister of the late Sir Wm. Johnstone, Bart., of Gilford, co. Down.

No. 4880 :: Ref. 1851-07-19, 2:5, D.
July 10, at Rusky, of brain fever, the Rev. James Newell, Minister of the Presbyterian Church, Scotland, in the 26th year of his age.

No. 4881 :: Ref. 1851-07-19, 2:5, D.
July 12, at Corkill Lodge, Enniskillen, Henry, infant son of James Lendrum, Esq.

No. 4882 :: Ref. 1851-07-19, 2:5, D.
July 13, one mile south of Enniskillen, at the very advanced age of 107 years, Peggy Kavanagh. The youngest of her family, an orphan lad of seventy, still survives her, and is yet unprovided for.

No. 4883 :: Ref. 1851-07-26, 2:3, B.
At Dungannon, the lady of R. Leslie Ogilby, Esq., of a daughter.

No. 4884 :: Ref. 1851-07-26, 2:3, B.
On 21st inst., the wife of Mr. Edward Coyle, merchant, Portadown, of a son.

No. 4885 :: Ref. 1851-07-26, 2:3, B.
July 6, at Drumheel, co. Cavan, the lady of William Smith, Esq., of a son.

No. 4886 :: Ref. 1851-07-26, 2:3, B.
July 14, at Magheramena, co. Fermanagh, the lady of Jas. Johnston, Esq., of a daughter.

No. 4887 :: Ref. 1851-07-26, 2:3, M.

July the 26, in the Cathedral, Armagh, by the Rev. Mr. Mangan of Madden, Dr. Wyse, of 2, Sackville-street, Dublin, to Elizabeth, daughter of John Cardwell, Esq., Tullyelmer, Armagh.

No. 4888 :: Ref. 1851-07-26, 2:3, M.

At New York, Annie, eldest daughter of John Henry, Esq., Laurel Hill, co. Monaghan, to Mr. John Steele, formerly of same town.

No. 4889 :: Ref. 1851-07-26, 2:3, M.

On 22d inst., by Rev. James Hume, in the Presbyterian Church, Scarva, Mr. Joseph Geddis, to Miss Elizabeth Martin, both of Gilford.

No. 4890 :: Ref. 1851-07-26, 2:3, D.

At Rus in Urbe, Kingstown, on the 20th inst., James Wentwith Kearney, Esq., late Barrack Master, at Armagh.

No. 4891 :: Ref. 1851-07-26, 2:3, D.

At Maderia, India, on the 23d May last, C. Carleton, Esq., 44th Regt., Madras Native Infantry.

No. 4892 :: Ref. 1851-07-26, 2:3, D.

At Cavan, at the home of his brother, on his way home to Enniskillen, Arthur Richard (Ensign in the 3d West India Regiment) son of Arthur Thompson, Esq., Willoughby-place, Enniskillen. This young gentleman on entering upon service, was taken ill of the fever peculiar to the West Indies, from the effects of which he never rallied.

No. 4893 :: Ref. 1851-07-26, 2:3, D.

On 17th instant at Cookstown, Samuel L. Porter, M.D., aged 50 years.

No. 4894 :: Ref. 1851-08-02, 3:3, B.

July 28, at Mount Collyer Park, Mrs. J.A. Henderson, of a daughter.

No. 4895 :: Ref. 1851-08-02, 3:3, B.

July 16, at Clune's-vennal, Newtown, the wife of Mr. A. Johnston, sawyer, of twin sons. Sixteen months ago Mrs. Johnston presented her husband with twin daughters. The whole are alive and doing well.

No. 4896 :: Ref. 1851-08-02, 3:3, M.

July 30, at St. Mark's Church, Armagh, by the Rev. William Maclean, Rector of Tynan, and Prebendary of Armagh Cathedral, Stewart Maxwell, Esq., son of the Rev. P.B. Maxwell, Birdstown, County Donegal, to Annie, third daughter of William Paton, Esq., of Armagh.

No. 4897 :: Ref. 1851-08-02, 3:3, M.

July 27, in this city, by Rev. Mr. M'Chrystall, Mr. John Thompson, Ulster Railway, Armagh, to Mary Jane Frances, daughter of the late Mr. Milligan, Enniskillen, and niece to Surgeon Milligan, late of the Enniskillen Dragoons.

No. 4898 :: Ref. 1851-08-02, 3:3, M.

July 17, by the Most Rev. Dr. M'Gettigan, Daniel Quinn, Esq., merchant, Longford, to Madge, youngest daughter of the late Hugh Mulreany, Esq., Mountcharles, Donegal.

No. 4899 :: Ref. 1851-08-02, 3:3, M.

July 22, at St. Anne's Church, Belfast, and afterwards by the Rev. Mr. Gallogly, C.C., Mr. William Penton, merchant, to Catherine, eldest daughter of the late Mr. Francis Magee, of North street, Belfast.

No. 4900 :: Ref. 1851-08-02, 3:3, M.

At Huddersfield, Thomas Hastings Irwin, Esq., son of the late Wm. Irwin, Esq., of Mount Irwin, county Armagh, to Frances, relict of Wm. Irlam, Esq., of Rudy, Cheshire.

No. 4901 :: Ref. 1851-08-02, 3:3, M.

July 24, at Bryansford, by the Rev. C. Ussher, Mr. Robert Reynolds, of Manorwater House, co. Fermanagh, to Louisa Jane, youngest daughter of Henry Francis Atkinson, Esq., of Newcastle, co. Down.

No. 4902 :: Ref. 1851-08-02, 3:3, M.

June 19, at Nachetoehes, United States of America, at the residence of the bride's uncle, J.W. Hanna, Esq., M.D., Thomas Browne, Esq., Texas, U.S., to Jane, second daughter of the late Mr. Robert Hanna, Strabane.

No. 4903 :: Ref. 1851-08-02, 3:3, D.

July 22, at the house of her brother-in-law, Mr. Simon Sinclair, Kinneary, in the 19th year of her age, Elizabeth, youngest daughter of Mr. Wm. Jackson, of Ballymagerny, near Loughgall. Although delicate for some time past, she left her father's house on that evening seemingly in good health. To the young as well as the aged it may be said, "*Be ye also ready*," for surely "*In the midst of life we are in death.*"

No. 4904 :: Ref. 1851-08-02, 3:3, D.

July 18, at his residence, Mullentine, near Portadown, Mr. Thos. Cregan, much and deservedly regretted by his family and numerous acquaintances.

No. 4905 :: Ref. 1851-08-02, 3:3, D.

July 24, in Hibernia-place, Holywood, Joseph Sherrard, late of New York, fifth son of Mr. James Sherrard, Fintona, co. Tyrone.

No. 4906 :: Ref. 1851-08-02, 3:3, D.

July 25, after 56 years' service in the General Post Office, Wm. Milliken, Esq., aged 71 years.

No. 4907 :: Ref. 1851-08-02, 3:3, D.

July 27, at Rockdale House, county Tyrone, of malignant measles, Hercules Lowry, Esq., third son of the late James Lowry, Esq., aged thirty-two years.

No. 4908 :: Ref. 1851-08-02, 3:3, D.

July 28, at Portarlington, Charles de Bacquencourt, twin son of Thomas Desvoeux, Esq.

No. 4909 :: Ref. 1851-08-02, 3:3, D.

Lately, at Aire, in the Pas de Calais, aged 91 years, one of the most remarkable beer-bibbers upon record. From the age of 18 to 60 his daily dose of beer averaged ten litres, or nearly a gallon and a half per diem.

No. 4910 :: Ref. 1851-08-09, 2:6, M.

July 26, at Brussels, by the Rev. M.J. Blacker, Murray Macgregor, youngest son of the late Lieutenant-Colonel Valentine Blacker, C.B., Surveyor-General of India, to Frances Elizabeth, daughter of the late Samuel Blacker, L.L.D., Rector of Mullabrack, Armagh.

No. 4911 :: Ref. 1851-08-09, 2:6, M.

On 1st inst., at St. Ann's Church, Dungannon, by the Rev. Wm. Quin, Hamilton Acheson Baxter, Esq., of Rock Park, Co. Donegal, to Frances, daughter of Mr. Thomas Hancock, Dungannon.

No. 4912 :: Ref. 1851-08-09, 2:6, M.

On 1st inst., in the Presbyterian Church, Claggin, by the Rev. Henry M'Caw, Mr. John Wilson Greenville, Cookstown, to Miss Getty, of same place.

No. 4913 :: Ref. 1851-08-09, 2:6, M.

At St. George's Church, Hanover-square, Captain the Hon. Strange Jocelyn, second son of the Earl of Roden, to the Hon. Miss Hobhouse, daughter of Lord Broughton.

No. 4914 :: Ref. 1851-08-09, 2:6, M.

July 17, Daniel Quinn, Esq., merchant, Longford, to Madge, youngest daughter of the late Hugh Mulreany, Esq., Mountcharles, Donegal.

No. 4915 :: Ref. 1851-08-09, 2:6, M.

August 5, at Muff Church, county Donegal, by the Rev. George Smyth, Wm. Thompson, Esq., merchant, of Derry, to Isabella youngest daughter of the late John Wood, Esq., Enniskillen.

No. 4916 :: Ref. 1851-08-09, 2:6, D.

At Newtownstewart, on 30th ult., Mr. William M'Gowan, Innkeeper, aged 26 years.

No. 4917 :: Ref. 1851-08-09, 2:6, D.

The Rev. Dr. O'Neill, P.P., Arboe, at the age of 100 years.

No. 4918 :: Ref. 1851-08-09, 2:6, D.

August 1, in Vyvian terrace, Clifton, Mrs. Lee, author of the "*Canterbury Tales*," and other literary works, aged 95 years.

No. 4919 :: Ref. 1851-08-09, 2:6, D.

On 1st inst., at Castleblayney, Eliza, the beloved wife of William N. Irwin, Esq., M.D.

No. 4920 :: Ref. 1851-08-09, 2:6, D.

On 3d inst., at Rathbeg, co. Tipperary, the residence of her son, Maria Susanna Lemon Reade, relict of the late Henry Loftus Reade, Esq., late of Moreton, Wexford.

No. 4921 :: Ref. 1851-08-09, 2:6, D.

At New York, the Rev. A. Denham, D.D., and M.D., formerly of Banbridge, county Down, brother of Mrs. Davis, of Belfast, and cousin of the late Mr. Denham, of Enniskillen.

No. 4922 :: Ref. 1851-08-09, 2:6, D.

July 21, at Corcrain House, Portadown, the residence of her son-in-law, Joseph Druitt, Esq., in her 76th year, Mrs. Henning, late of Lurgan.

No. 4923 :: Ref. 1851-08-09, 2:6, D.

Mary, eldest daughter of the late Roger Trumble, Esq., Oldrock, county Sligo.

No. 4924 :: Ref. 1851-08-09, 2:6, D.

July 27, at Abbeyview, county Sligo, in her 85th year, after a few days' illness, Elizabeth, relict of Wm. Phillips, Esq., and daughter of Robert Johnston, Esq., for many years Clerk of the Crown for the Province of Ulster.

No. 4925 :: Ref. 1851-08-09, 2:6, D.

On 3d inst., at Bangor, Mr. A. Smith, of Cookhill, near Dungannon, in advanced life.

No. 4926 :: Ref. 1851-08-09, 2:6, D.

On 3d inst., at Deer Park, Charleville, of malignant typhus fever, William B. Sanders, Esq., Chairman of the Kilmallock Board of Guardians. It is only about six months since the death of his worthy predecessor, Mr. Gubbins, of Kilrush. Both valuable lives have been lost by constant attention to their duties at the board of guardians.

No. 4927 :: Ref. 1851-08-16, 3:2, B.

August 14, in Armagh, Mrs. Thompson, wife of John Thompson, Proprietor of *The Armagh Guardian*, of a daughter.

No. 4928 :: Ref. 1851-08-16, 3:2, B.

In Armagh, August 10, Mrs. Adams, wife of Mr. John Clarke Adams, of a daughter.

No. 4929 :: Ref. 1851-08-16, 3:2, B.

On 7th inst., at Banbridge, the lady of the Rev. William Metge, of a son.

No. 4930 :: Ref. 1851-08-16, 3:2, B.

July 31, at Belturbet, the lady of Doctor Sothergill, of a son.

No. 4931 :: Ref. 1851-08-16, 3:2, B.

On 6th August, at Lifford, the lady of Doctor Little, of a son.

No. 4932 :: Ref. 1851-08-16, 3:2, M.

On 14th inst., at St. Thomas's Church, Dublin, by the Rev. Edward Hardy, William Hardy, Esq., of Loughgall, county Armagh, to Elizabeth, daughter of the late Lieutenant-Colonel Hearn, 43d Regiment, of Correa, in the county of Westmeath.

No. 4933 :: Ref. 1851-08-16, 3:2, M.
On 12th inst., in Dungannon, by Rev. Charles L. Morell, Mr. John M'Geagh, of Cookstown, to Margaret, daughter of Mr. James Dickson, of Dungannon.

No. 4934 :: Ref. 1851-08-16, 3:2, M.
On 8th inst., in Clontibret, by the Rev. A. Molyneux, David Dickson, Esq., Castleblayney, to Matilda Jane, second daughter of Ross Lewers, Esq., Brookmount, Monaghan.

No. 4935 :: Ref. 1851-08-16, 3:2, M.
On 9th inst., in St. Peter's Church, Dublin, by the Rev. Mr. M'Sorley, Robert Stone, Esq., of Carnew, county Wicklow, to Julia Rebecca, daughter of Corry Fowler, Esq., of Dublin.

No. 4936 :: Ref. 1851-08-16, 3:2, D.
On 10th inst., rejoicing in prospect of entering on the glories of an eternal Sabbath, Marianne, fourth daughter of William Armstrong, Esq., Brookboro'.

No. 4937 :: Ref. 1851-08-16, 3:2, D.
On 7th inst., at Emyville, Newry, aged 11 years, Emily, eldest child of Geo. Henderson, Esq., Editor of the *Newry Telegraph*.

No. 4938 :: Ref. 1851-08-16, 3:2, D.
In Belfast, Mr. William Thompson, late of Lurgan, in the 64th year of his age.

No. 4939 :: Ref. 1851-08-16, 3:2, D.
On 22d ult., aged 102 years, Mr. William Forde, of Mullantine, near Portadown, farmer. He was most temperate in his habits, and retained his faculties to the last.

No. 4940 :: Ref. 1851-08-16, 3:2, D.
On 3d inst., at his residence, Portsalon, county Donegal, Baptist J. Barton, Esq., J.P., aged 34.

No. 4941 :: Ref. 1851-08-16, 3:2, D.
July 18, at New York, the Rev. Mr. Mulligan, a native of Tullyconnaught, county Down.

No. 4942 :: Ref. 1851-08-16, 3:2, D.
On 9th inst., at Strabane, David, youngest son of Mr. John Crosbie, aged five years.

No. 4943 :: Ref. 1851-08-16, 3:2, D.
On 10th inst., at Kingstown, aged 55 years, Hannah, daughter of the late Wm. Kent, formerly of Aungier-street, Dublin.

No. 4944 :: Ref. 1851-08-16, 3:2, D.
On 12th inst., Mr. John Edgar, of Anahilt, aged seventy-three years.

No. 4945 :: Ref. 1851-08-16, 3:2, D.
On 12th inst., at Nenagh, in the sixty-second year of his age, John Kempston, Esq., Editor and Proprietor of the *Nenagh Guardian*.

No. 4946 :: Ref. 1851-08-16, 3:2, D.
On 1st inst., at Clifton, Miss Harriett Lee, the patriarch of English authoresses, at the age of 95. To most of the generation now busied with fiction, drama, and poetry, this announcement will be a surprise; so long protracted was Miss Lee's life, and so many years have elapsed since her last appearance in the world of imaginative creation took place.

No. 4947 :: Ref. 1851-08-23, 2:7, B.
At Lisnacrieve House, the wife of D. Lindsay, Esq., of a daughter.

No. 4948 :: Ref. 1851-08-23, 2:7, B.
At Waterhill House, the lady of J.W. Elliott, Esq., Surgeon, R.N., of a son.

No. 4949 :: Ref. 1851-08-23, 2:7, B.
On 8th inst., at the Brewery, Monaghan, the lady of Jas. Warren, Esq., of a son.

No. 4950 :: Ref. 1851-08-23, 2:7, B.
August 13, the lady of the Rev. W.J. West, of Delgany Glebe, co. Wicklow, of a son.

No. 4951 :: Ref. 1851-08-23, 2:7, B.
On 17th inst., at Warrenpoint, the wife of J. Walker, Esq., C.E., of a daughter.

No. 4952 :: Ref. 1851-08-23, 2:7, B.
On 17th inst., at Hackney, near Charlemont, the wife of Leonard Dobbin, jun., Esq., of a son.

No. 4953 :: Ref. 1851-08-23, 2:7, M.
On Friday, the 15th inst., in St. John's Church, Middletown, by the Rev. Thomas Jervis Whitel, Casey, 9th daughter of Mr. William Campbell, of Artgonnell, to Mr. Robert Mackey, of Monaghan.

No. 4954 :: Ref. 1851-08-23, 2:7, M.
On 12th inst., in London, James, eldest son of F. Blake, Esq., of Gregg Castle, co. Galway, to Helena Charlotte, eldest daughter of the late Arthur French, Esq., of Ballibay, co. Monaghan.

No. 4955 :: Ref. 1851-08-23, 2:7, M.
On 14th inst., in Warrenpoint, by Rev. Isaac Patterson, Mr. John Smith, of the same place, to Mary Anne, youngest daughter of the late Mr. Robert Mollan, of Newry.

No. 4956 :: Ref. 1851-08-23, 2:7, M.
On 14th inst., at Dungarvan Church, by the Rev. William Galley Giles, Wm. Crosbie, Esq., Manager of the Provincial Bank of Ireland, Dungarvan, to Rosetta Hawksly, third daughter of the late St. Leger John Watkins, Captain 88th Regiment, and grand-daughter of the Hon. Wm. St. Leger Watkins.

No. 4957 :: Ref. 1851-08-23, 2:7, M.
On 16th inst., at St. James's Church, Westminster, by the Rev. A.F. Heber Scholefield, Charles Keeling, third son of the late Rev. J. Scholefield, F.T.C.,

Oxford, and rector of Barton-on-the-Health [sic], Warwickshire, to Sarah Maria, youngest daughter of the Rev. George Evans, of Cheltenham, and grand daughter of Edward Evans, Esq., J.P., of Gortmerron-house, co. Tyrone.

No. 4958 :: Ref. 1851-08-23, 2:7, M.
Tuesday, at St. Michael's Church, by the Baron Riversdale, Lord Bishop of Killaloe, the Rev. William Edwards, Precentor of Killaloe, to Annabella, youngest daughter of the Lord Bishop of Limerick.

No. 4959 :: Ref. 1851-08-23, 2:7, D.
On 14th inst., at Glenville, co. Cork, the Very Rev. Edward Gustavus Hudson, Dean of Armagh, aged 61 years.

No. 4960 :: Ref. 1851-08-23, 2:7, D.
At Toronto, on 14th July, Mr. George Givan, late of Omagh, co. Tyrone, Ireland, aged 36 years.

No. 4961 :: Ref. 1851-08-23, 2:7, D.
On 17th inst., at Tandragee School House, Hariet Anna, youngest daughter of Mr. Jerome Cuthbert, aged 2 years 3 months.

No. 4962 :: Ref. 1851-08-23, 2:7, D.
Aug. 19, at Coolkeiragh House, Londonderry, Alexander Thomas, the beloved son of Richard Young, Esq.

No. 4963 :: Ref. 1851-08-23, 2:7, D.
On 20th inst., at Moy, Mary Jane, daughter of Mr. John Ritchie. Her remains will be removed for interment, in Tullynakill, on Saturday, 23d inst., leaving the terminus of the Ulster Railway, Belfast, at a quarter past eleven, a.m.

No. 4964 :: Ref. 1851-08-30, 3:2, B.
August 13, at Athlone, Mrs. Dawson, the wife of Rev. A. Dawson, Primitive Wesleyan Minister, of a daughter.

No. 4965 :: Ref. 1851-08-30, 3:2, B.
At Haddington Terrace, Kingstown, the lady of Michael D. Hassard, Esq., of a daughter.

No. 4966 :: Ref. 1851-08-30, 3:2, B.
August 21, at Camden Town, London, the wife of Mr. Charles Francis Cumming, of Carrickmacross, of a son.

No. 4967 :: Ref. 1851-08-30, 3:2, M.
August 26, in the Wesleyan Chapel, Cootehill, by the Rev. Robt. Hamilton, Mr. Edward Ranson of Ashfield, to Miss Anne Young, Gortnaneau.

No. 4968 :: Ref. 1851-08-30, 3:2, M.
On 19th inst., in St. Peter's Church, Dublin, Thomas Pentland, Esq., of Lurgan, to Anne Jane, third daughter of the late Thomas Carroll, Esq., Waterloo Road, Dublin.

No. 4969 :: Ref. 1851-08-30, 3:2, M.
On 21st inst., at Richhill Church, by Rev. James Jones, jun., Harriet, third daughter of Mr. Robert Williamson, of Ahory, to Mr. John Tuft of Edenderry, Scarva, co. Down.

No. 4970 :: Ref. 1851-08-30, 3:2, M.
August 23, by Rev. J.W. Chartres, L.L.D., Anderson Cooper, Esq., of the Provincial Bank of Ireland, to Rachel, eldest daughter of Thomas Pounder, Esq., Mill-park House, Enniscorthy.

No. 4971 :: Ref. 1851-08-30, 3:2, M.
August 26, in Tamlaghtard Church, county Londonderry, by the Rev. Robert Gage, Sir Frederick William Heygate, Bart., of South-end, Essex, and of Roecliffee [sic], Leicestershire, to Marianne, only daughter of the late Conolly Gage, Esq., of Bellarena, co. Londonderry.

No. 4972 :: Ref. 1851-08-30, 3:2, M.
Mr. David Ritchie, grocer, Claudy, to Jane, daughter of Mr. Thos. M'Candless, Cumber Mills.

No. 4973 :: Ref. 1851-08-30, 3:2, D.
In Scotch-street, this day, Mr. John Henry, Cabinet-maker, aged 78 years, an old and respected inhabitant of this city.

No. 4974 :: Ref. 1851-08-30, 3:2, D.
August 18, in the third year of her age, Mary, daughter of Mr. Matthew R. Bell, Russell-street, Armagh.

No. 4975 :: Ref. 1851-08-30, 3:2, D.
At his residence, Mall, Armagh, on 24th inst., Mr. James M'Cune, aged 80 years, for the entire of which he was a respected resident of the city.

No. 4976 :: Ref. 1851-08-30, 3:2, D.
August 26, in Lower English-street, Mr. James Warnell, aged 50.

No. 4977 :: Ref. 1851-08-30, 3:2, D.
August 4, at Springfield, Massachusetts, Michael, third son of the late Mr. Michael Murphy, of Belfast.

No. 4978 :: Ref. 1851-08-30, 3:2, D.
August 18, at Bridge Cottage, Carndonagh, Gawin, Wm. Hamilton Rowan, Esq., of consumption, Sub-Inspector of Constabulary, in his 28th year.

No. 4979 :: Ref. 1851-08-30, 3:2, D.
August 21, at her lodgings, Passage, Catherine M'Mullen, widow of the late Rev. Daniel M'Mullen, Wesleyan Minister.

No. 4980 :: Ref. 1851-08-30, 3:2, D.
At his residence, Denmark-street, Dublin, Mr. John Turney, at the age of 112 years.

No. 4981 :: Ref. 1851-08-30, 3:2, D.
At Ballyshannon, Robert M'Donagh, Esq., who had only recently arrived from Jamaica on a visit to his brother, Mr. John M'Donagh, merchant, for the benefit of his health.

No. 4982 :: Ref. 1851-08-30, 3:2, D.
August 25, Margaret, eldest daughter of the late Mr. John Irvine, Enniskillen.

No. 4983 :: Ref. 1851-08-30, 3:2, D.
August 19, of fever, caught in the discharge of his duty, Mr. James Williams, Master of the Monaghan Union Workhouse. Mr. W. entered on the onerous duties of Master of this Workhouse, at its opening in the year 1842, and from the faithful and honest discharge of his most important duties earned the confidence and respect of both the Guardians, rate-payers, and of all that knew him. The Guardians have unanimously expressed their regret at the loss sustained by the Union.

No. 4984 :: Ref. 1851-08-30, 3:2, D.
August 19, at Portarlington, in her 88th year, Caroline, relict of Thomas Stannus, Esq. Her husband was a member of the Irish Parliament, and her brother, Hans Hamilton, Esq., of Sheep Hill, sat for years in the Legislature, as representative for the county Dublin; another brother was the late Major-General Christopher Hamilton, formerly of the 97th Regiment. The Very Rev. James Stannus, of Lisburn, Dean of Ross, the highly-respected agent of the Marquis of Hertford, is the only son who has outlived his venerable mother. Her removal is mourned with regret as keen and sorrow as general, as would the premature shortening of some young and promising life.

No. 4985 :: Ref. 1851-09-06, 3:2, B.
At Oxmantown-place, Parsonstown, the lady of John Waters, Esq., M.D., of a son.

No. 4986 :: Ref. 1851-09-06, 3:2, B.
Aug. 25, the lady of the Hon. and Rev. Francis Clements, Vicar of Norton, of a still-born child.

No. 4987 :: Ref. 1851-09-06, 3:2, B.
Aug. 25, at Swanlinbar, the lady of the Rev. John J. Egan, of a daughter.

No. 4988 :: Ref. 1851-09-06, 3:2, B.
Aug. 26, at 14, Bernard-street, Russell-square, London, Mrs. G. Godolphin Osborn, of a son.

No. 4989 :: Ref. 1851-09-06, 3:2, B.
Aug. 30, Lady Arabella Brooke, of a son.

No. 4990 :: Ref. 1851-09-06, 3:2, B.
Sept. 2, at Gosford Place, Armagh, the lady of Henry Davison, Esq., of a son.

No. 4991 :: Ref. 1851-09-06, 3:2, M.
Aug. 21, in Clogher [C]athedral, by Hon. and Very Rev. Dean Maude, Dean of Clogher, Mr. Alexander Steen, Clogher, to Jane, eldest daughter of Mr. Matthew Law, Letbeg.

No. 4992 :: Ref. 1851-09-06, 3:2, M.
Aug. 27, at Kilskeery, by Rev. W. Crawford, George Roberts Crowe, Esq., of Longford, to Magdalene, third daughter of Andrew Crawford, Esq., of Trillic.

No. 4993 :: Ref. 1851-09-06, 3:2, M.
Aug. 27, in Mount Temple church, co. Westmeath, by Rev. W. Peacocke, Robert W., son of Mr. John Lynch, merchant, Longford, to Hannah, daughter of the late Mr. Joseph Whitley, Enniskillen.

No. 4994 :: Ref. 1851-09-06, 3:2, M.
Aug. 28, William Alfred Tredennick Hamilton, Esq., of Sea-view, Donegal, to Jane, daughter of Anthony Brownless, Esq., Thornhill-park, Islington.

No. 4995 :: Ref. 1851-09-06, 3:2, M.
Aug. 29, in the Presbyterian church of Minterburn, by Rev. Alex. Gray, A.M., Mr. James Milnes, of Tullyblerty, Aughnacloy, to Mary Jane, daughter of the late Mr. James M'Cleery, Mullicarnon, Caledon.

No. 4996 :: Ref. 1851-09-06, 3:2, M.
Sept. 2, John, second son of William Allingham, Esq., of Ballyshannon, to Eliza, youngest daughter of the late William Christian, Esq., of Rathbraghan, county Sligo.

No. 4997 :: Ref. 1851-09-06, 3:2, M.
Sept. 2, in the Wesleyan Chapel, Armagh, by the Rev. Robert H. Lindsay, Wesleyan minister, Mr. Thomas C. Bowers, of Dublin, to Mary, daughter of the late Mr. W. Davis, of Tandragee.

No. 4998 :: Ref. 1851-09-06, 3:2, M.
Sept. 6, at Clarlemont [sic], Townshend Dobbin, Esq., of the Adjutant General Department, fourth son of Captain Leonard Dobbin, late of "*the Royal*," to Emily Anne, sole surviving daughter of the late James Lawson, Esq., of Charlemont.

No. 4999 :: Ref. 1851-09-06, 3:2, M.
At Westbury-upon-Tyne, E.A. Hardy, Esq., Lieutenant 1st Bombay Lancers, eldest son of the late Colonel E. Hardy, Bombay Artillery, to Grace Maxwell, daughter of P.F. Aiken, Esq., Grove House, Durdham, Down.

No. 5000 :: Ref. 1851-09-06, 3:2, D.
July 19, the Rev. David Shields, of Salem Church, Philadelphia, aged 38 years, son to Mr. Thomas Shields, of Omagh, co. Tyrone.

No. 5001 :: Ref. 1851-09-06, 3:2, D.
At Galena, Illinois, George Cottnam Giles, aged 25 years, eldest son of the late Richard Giles, Esq., of Cootehill, co. Cavan.

No. 5002 :: Ref. 1851-09-06, 3:2, D.
After severe suffering, the Rev. James Mockler, one of the Vicars Choral of the Cathedral of Lismore, and Rector of Kilcronan, county Waterford.

No. 5003 :: Ref. 1851-09-06, 3:2, D.
Aug. 16, at her father's residence, Stephen's green, aged 15 years, Sarah Elizabeth, daughter of the Rev.

Daniel M'Afee. Her death was caused by being precipitated from a car, the horse having run away; she was taken up senseless, and expired after a few hours.—She was distinguished by great amiability of disposition, and was decidedly pious.

No. 5004 :: Ref. 1851-09-06, 3:2, D.
Aug. 18, aged 75 years, Mr. John M'Causland, Lismacaroll, county Derry.

No. 5005 :: Ref. 1851-09-06, 3:2, D.
Aug. 24, at 10, Coates Crescent, General Sir Alexander Halkett, K.C.H., fifth son of Sir John Wedderburne Halkett, Bart., of Pitfirrane.

No. 5006 :: Ref. 1851-09-06, 3:2, D.
Aug. 26, at the Grove, Watford, the infant daughter of the Earl and Countess of Clarendon.

No. 5007 :: Ref. 1851-09-06, 3:2, D.
Aug. 27, at Wellington-place, Grand Canal, Dublin, aged 88 years, Joseph Fenton, Esq., only surviving friend of the venerable John Wesley, in Dublin, and accompanied him on his departure at his last visit to Ireland.

No. 5008 :: Ref. 1851-09-06, 3:2, D.
Aug. 28, at 4, Lower Glocester-street [sic], Dublin, Frances, relict of Thomas J. White, aged 76 years.

No. 5009 :: Ref. 1851-09-06, 3:2, D.
Aug. 29, at Drayton Lodge, Monkstown, Evans Kettlewell, Esq., of Thomastown, co. Meath, formerly of the 96th Regt.

No. 5010 :: Ref. 1851-09-06, 3:2, D.
Aug. 29, at Tattymacall, near Lisbellaw, Mr. John Ford, aged 57 years.

No. 5011 :: Ref. 1851-09-13, 3:2, B.
Sept. 5, in Charles-street, St. James's Square, London, at the residence of his Grace the Archbishop of Armagh, the lady of George Dunbar, Esq., of a son.

No. 5012 :: Ref. 1851-09-13, 3:2, M.
Sept. 2, by Rev. James Colhoun, Mr. Terence Fitzpatrick, merchant, Ballygawley, to Anne, third daughter of the late Mr. Peter Fox, merchant, of Omagh, Co. Tyrone.

No. 5013 :: Ref. 1851-09-13, 3:2, M.
Sept. 3, at Portsea, by Rev. George Tottenham, Curate of Tynan, Lieutenant John Francis Tottenham, R.N., to Laura Ellen Dodd, daughter of Edward Taylor Jauvenir, Esq., of the Great Salterns, Portsmouth.

No. 5014 :: Ref. 1851-09-13, 3:2, M.
Sept. 11, by Rev. Andrew M'Cullagh, Presbyterian Minister, Caledon, William Scott Hay, Esq., Bankhead, Aberdeenshire, Scotland, to Margaret Jane, only daughter of Wm. Tassey, Esq., sen., Caledon. Immediately after the ceremony the happy couple set out for Pittsburgh, U.S.A.

No. 5015 :: Ref. 1851-09-13, 3:2, D.
At New Orleans, of Asiatic cholera, William Ruddy, Esq., late of Clones, co. Monaghan.

No. 5016 :: Ref. 1851-09-13, 3:2, D.
Aug. 10, at Clifton, Staten Island, Rose Jane, wife of Mr. James Farquhar, watchmaker, New York, formerly of Newry, Armagh, and Belfast.

No. 5017 :: Ref. 1851-09-13, 3:2, D.
Aug. 31, at Waterford, after two hours' illness, Miss Eliza Shiel, sister of the late Right Hon. Richard Lalor Shiel.

No. 5018 :: Ref. 1851-09-13, 3:2, D.
Sept. 3, Lydia, relict of the late John Fforde, Esq., of Reughlin, co. Armagh.

No. 5019 :: Ref. 1851-09-13, 3:2, D.
Sept. 4, at Trevor Hill, Newry, Letitia, the beloved wife of Capt. William Boyle.

No. 5020 :: Ref. 1851-09-13, 3:2, D.
Sept. 4, James Haverty, Esq., aged 36 years, for many years an eminent reporter on the *Freeman's Journal*, and *London Morning Chronicle*.

No. 5021 :: Ref. 1851-09-13, 3:2, D.
Sept. 5, at Canonmills, Edinburgh, aged 75 years, Dr. Patrick Neill, the distinguished naturalist.

No. 5022 :: Ref. 1851-09-13, 3:2, D.
Sept. 6, at the residence of her brother, Clare, near Lurgan, Miss Catherine Mills, in her 17th year.

No. 5023 :: Ref. 1851-09-13, 3:2, D.
At Flower Hill, co. Galway, Sept. 6, Lord Riverston. This peerage was granted by James II., when he was fighting in Ireland for his crown, but was not acknowledged by the English Government. Lord Riverston was heir presumptive to the Earldom of Westmeath. He leaves two sons.

No. 5024 :: Ref. 1851-09-20, 2:6, B.
Betsy, wife of Abraham Overstoke, of Highland county, Ohio, aged 71 years, gave birth to a child a [few?] weeks since.

No. 5025 :: Ref. 1851-09-20, 2:6, B.
Sepr. 8, at Marblehill House, co. Donegal, the lady of John Wm. Seymour, Esq., of a son.

No. 5026 :: Ref. 1851-09-20, 2:6, B.
Sepr. 8, at Cookstown, the wife of Rev. John Knox Leslie, of a son.

No. 5027 :: Ref. 1851-09-20, 2:6, B.
Sepr. 10, at Brandrum house, co. Monaghan, the lady of Thomas Coote, Esq., D.L., of a son.

No. 5028 :: Ref. 1851-09-20, 2:6, B.
Sepr. 14, in Derry, the lady of Joseph Maxwell, Esq., M.D., (late Physician and Surgeon to the Tyrone Infirmary), of a son.

No. 5029 :: Ref. 1851-09-20, 2:6, M.
Sepr. 10, Giles William Cullen, Esq., S.I. of Constabulary, second son of the late Colonel Cullen, of Skreeny, co. Leitrim, to Henrietta Catherine, youngest daughter of Thomas Cannon, Esq., of Portrane, Queen's County.

No. 5030 :: Ref. 1851-09-20, 2:6, M.
Sepr. 16, in Fintona Church, by Rev. Henry L. Tottenham, Rector of Donacavey, John Nelis, of Omagh, Esq., Proprietor of the *Tyrone Constitution*, to Margaret Georgina, third daughter of James Buchanan, of Fintona, Esq.

No. 5031 :: Ref. 1851-09-20, 2:6, D.
Augt. 28, at the Royal Navy Hospital, Stone-house, Plymouth, Dr. John Coulter, surgeon H.M.S. *Bellerophon*, eldest son of Daniel Coulter, Esq., Drumconnis House, Omagh, aged 47 years.

No. 5032 :: Ref. 1851-09-20, 2:6, D.
Sepr. 5, at Dungannon, in the 89th year of his age, Mr. Owen M'Shane, merchant tailor.

No. 5033 :: Ref. 1851-09-20, 2:6, D.
Sepr. 9, Elizabeth, wife of George Law, Esq., of Gilford.

No. 5034 :: Ref. 1851-09-20, 2:6, D.
Sepr. 9, at Homberg, Germany, the Rev. Joseph John Freeman, one of the Secretaries of the London Missionary Society, aged 57 years.

No. 5035 :: Ref. 1851-09-20, 2:6, D.
Sepr. 10, aged 22 years, Mrs. Flynn, Matron of the Downpatrick Union Workhouse.

No. 5036 :: Ref. 1851-09-20, 2:6, D.
Sepr. 10, aged sixteen months, Louisa, daughter of Mr. Samuel W. Cordner, organist, of Tandragee.

No. 5037 :: Ref. 1851-09-20, 2:6, D.
Sepr. 10, at Cloghan, co. Fermanagh, J.W.B. Latimer, Esq., aged 58 years.

No. 5038 :: Ref. 1851-09-20, 2:6, D.
Sepr. 12, at his seat, Palmerston, near Dublin, John, Earl of Donoughmore, in the 64th year of his age. He has left two sons (the eldest of whom, Lord Suirdale, succeeds to the title and estates,) three daughters, an amiable widow. The late Earl was John Hely Hutchinson, Earl of Donoughmore, Viscount Suirdale, of Knocklofty, county Tipperary, Privy Councillor for Ireland, and Lieutenant of the county Tipperary.

No. 5039 :: Ref. 1851-09-20, 2:6, D.
Sepr. 13, Mr. John Burrell, for many years flour miller to Osborne Kidd, Armagh, Esq., and much respected for attention and fidelity in his employment. A few days previous to his death he fell through a trap door, and sustained severe injuries, of which he died.

No. 5040 :: Ref. 1851-09-20, 2:6, D.
Sepr. 13, Mr. Samuel Tucker, late of Manchester, son of Mr. Edward Tucker, of Belfast.

No. 5041 :: Ref. 1851-09-20, 2:6, D.
Sepr. 14, Catherine, daughter of the late James King, Esq., of Knockballymore, county Fermanagh, and first cousin to the Earl of Erne.

No. 5042 :: Ref. 1851-09-20, 2:6, D.
Sepr. 15, suddenly, Joseph Bewley, Esq., one of the purest philanthropists in Dublin; and during the Irish famine this worthy good man exerted himself night and day in the cause of humanity, and his health never recovered from the personal sacrifices he then made.

No. 5043 :: Ref. 1851-09-20, 2:6, D.
Sepr. 15, at Ballycassidy, Lowtherstown, Mrs. Ball, relict of the late John Ball, Esq., Levaghy House.

No. 5044 :: Ref. 1851-09-20, 2:6, D.
Sepr. 15, at 25, Eliza Place, Belfast, Alexander Claudius Colhoun, Esq., late of Donoughmore, county Tyrone, aged 51 years.

No. 5045 :: Ref. 1851-09-27, 3:2, B.
Sepr. 17, at Markethill, the lady of Wm. Wann, Esq., of a daughter.

No. 5046 :: Ref. 1851-09-27, 3:2, B.
Sepr. 18, at Kingstown, the wife of the Rev. William Stacpoole, L.L.D., of a daughter.

No. 5047 :: Ref. 1851-09-27, 3:2, B.
Sepr. 19, in Market-street, Monaghan, the lady of John Mitchell, Esq., of a son.

No. 5048 :: Ref. 1851-09-27, 3:2, B.
Sepr. 20, at Avon Lodge, Armagh, the lady of W.H. Davis, Esq., of a daughter.

No. 5049 :: Ref. 1851-09-27, 3:2, B.
Sepr. 24, at Dundrum, the lady of the Rev. T.D. Gregg, of a son.

No. 5050 :: Ref. 1851-09-27, 3:2, B.
Sepr. 25, at Ecclesgreen, Fintona, Mrs. Hamilton, of a daughter.

No. 5051 :: Ref. 1851-09-27, 3:2, M.
Sepr. 16, in All Saints Church, Belfast, Mr. John Atkinson, of Fairview House, Ballytrue, co. Armagh, to Elizabeth, eldest daughter of Mr. Richard Atkinson, of Belfast.

No. 5052 :: Ref. 1851-09-27, 3:2, M.
Sepr. 18, in Tynan Church, by Rev. Wm. Maclean, Mr. J.R. Hayes, son of the late Mr. James Hayes, of Maghery, to Sarah Jane, daughter of Mr. John Gamble, of Belteagh.

No. 5053 :: Ref. 1851-09-27, 3:2, M.
Sepr. 19, at Kilkeel Church, co. Down, by the Rev. R.A. Hull, Mr. James Hanna, merchant, Kilkeel, to Miss Isabella Munn, of same place.

No. 5054 :: Ref. 1851-09-27, 3:2, M.
Sepr. 23, in Monkstown, by the Rev. Mr. Rooke, and afterwards by the Rev. B. Sheridan, P.P., Kingstown, George, eldest son of Professor Smith, Mus. Doc. T.C.D., to Hannah, youngest daughter of the late Bernard Daly, Esq., of Athlone.

No. 5055 :: Ref. 1851-09-27, 3:2, M.
Sepr. 23, in St. Anne's Church, Belfast, by the Rev. W. M'Ilwaine, Richard Stack, Esq., of Omagh, to Scholina Eliza, eldest daughter of C. Bessel, Esq., of Belfast.

No. 5056 :: Ref. 1851-09-27, 3:2, M.
At St. Mary's Church, Scarborough, by Hon. and Very Rev. the Dean of Ripon, John Whittaw Allen, Esq., son of the late Benjamin Haig Allen, Esq., of Huddersfield, to Eliza, daughter of the Rev. Dr. Whiteside, Vicar of Scarborough, and niece of James Whiteside, Esq., M.P. for Enniskillen.

No. 5057 :: Ref. 1851-09-27, 3:2, D.
Sepr. 17, in Macknagh, near Lisnaskea, Patrick M'Caherry, at the advanced age of 103.

No. 5058 :: Ref. 1851-09-27, 3:2, D.
Sepr. 18, of consumption, at the gardener's house, on the Palace grounds, Armagh, Mrs. Yeoman, wife of Mr. Yeoman, gardener to the Lord Primate.

No. 5059 :: Ref. 1851-09-27, 3:2, D.
Sepr. 20, in Armagh, of fever, Mrs. Barnett, wife of Mr. Barnett, house steward to the Lord Primate.

No. 5060 :: Ref. 1851-09-27, 3:2, D.
Sepr. 23, at Ballybreagh House, Richhill, after a lingering illness, and in the prime of life, Mr. Joseph C. Atkinson, of Belfast.

No. 5061 :: Ref. 1851-09-27, 3:2, D.
Sepr. 23, suddenly, at Rossfad, co. Fermanagh, aged 57 years, Mr. Henry Beggs, land stewart [sic] to H.M. Richardson, Esq. He had acted in the above capacity under the late Major Richardson, and served his employers with the strictest honesty, integrity, and devotion to their interests for nearly 44 years.

No. 5062 :: Ref. 1851-10-04, 3:2, B.
Sepr. 26, in London, the wife of Mr. James Hay Dobbin, of the *Wesleyan Times* office, of a son.

No. 5063 :: Ref. 1851-10-04, 3:2, B.
[Sepr.] 28th, at Ballymoyer Glebe, the lady of Rev. Garrett, Wall, jun. [sic], of a son.

No. 5064 :: Ref. 1851-10-04, 3:2, B.
[Sepr.] 28th, at Killishill Cottage, co. Tyrone, the wife of the Rev. Christopher Graham, of a son.

No. 5065 :: Ref. 1851-10-04, 3:2, B.
[Sepr.] 29th, at Lough Bawn, co. Monaghan, the lady of John Hervey Adams, Esq., of a daughter.

No. 5066 :: Ref. 1851-10-04, 3:2, M.
Sepr. 23, Simeon Ussher, Esq., son of Captain R.B. Ussher, of Harcourt-street, Dublin, to Mary Jane, eldest daughter of Robert Morris, of Lurgan.

No. 5067 :: Ref. 1851-10-04, 3:2, M.
[Sepr.] 24th, Mr. Thomas Orr, Station Master, Belfast and Ballymena Railway, Carrickfergus, to Miss Loughlin.

No. 5068 :: Ref. 1851-10-04, 3:2, M.
[Sepr.] 24th, Mr. John King, of Manchester, only surviving son of the late Samuel King, Esq., of Coal-island Mills, to Lizzy, youngest daughter of George Hildebrand, Esq., of Cherry Cottage, Westport.

No. 5069 :: Ref. 1851-10-04, 3:2, M.
[Sepr.] 24th, Robert Johnston, Esq., of Omagh, to Susanna Elizabeth, eldest daughter of the late Charles Sidley, Esq., Carrick-on-Shannon.

No. 5070 :: Ref. 1851-10-04, 3:2, M.
[Sepr.] 25th, Mr. Thomas T. Greer, Belfast to Eliza Jane, only daughter of Mr. Alexander Stewart, Carrickmore, Tyrone.

No. 5071 :: Ref. 1851-10-04, 3:2, M.
[Sepr.] 27th, John Hazlette, Esq., of Lurgan, to Caroline, daughter of Thomas Osborn, Esq., of Greenwich, Deputy Commissary General.

No. 5072 :: Ref. 1851-10-04, 3:2, M.
Oct. 3, in Armagh Cathedral, by Rev. Richard Oulton, Mr. Robert Armstrong, of Lurgan, to Eleanor, daughter of the late Thos. Wynne, of Lislea House, county Armagh, Esq.

No. 5073 :: Ref. 1851-10-04, 3:2, D.
Sepr. 12 and 24, respectively, Edward, aged 6, and John, aged 3 years, sons of Dr. M'Mullen, of Downpatrick.

No. 5074 :: Ref. 1851-10-04, 3:2, D.
[Sepr.] 13th, at the residence of her husband, (Thomas Shekeleton, Esq., Banbridge), Eliza Winning, daughter of the Rev. Henry Hunter, of Hillhall.

No. 5075 :: Ref. 1851-10-04, 3:2, D.
[Sepr.] 14th, James Fennimore Cooper, the great American novelist.

No. 5076 :: Ref. 1851-10-04, 3:2, D.
[Sepr.] 19th, at Kirkcubbin, Mr. Charles Hanna, Clerk of Petty Sessions, in the 81st year of his age. He was the last officer of the Ards Yeomen Infantry, under the command of the Hon. R. Ward. He received his commission as lieutenant in the year 1803.

No. 5077 :: Ref. 1851-10-04, 3:2, D.
[Sepr.] 20th, at Springfield, co. Antrim, aged 82 years, Morgan Jellett, Esq., one of the last surviving officers of the old Irish Volunteers.

No. 5078 :: Ref. 1851-10-04, 3:2, D.
[Sepr.] 21st, Christiana Mary, daughter of the Rev. William Fausset.

No. 5079 :: Ref. 1851-10-04, 3:2, D.
[Sepr.] 26th, Mr. Joseph Godber, of Tully, near Florencecourt, in the 89th year of his age.

No. 5080 :: Ref. 1851-10-04, 3:2, D.
[Sepr.] 27th, aged 40, Anna, wife of Mr. John Kyle, Strabane.

No. 5081 :: Ref. 1851-10-04, 3:2, D.
[Sepr.] 29th, at Seaview, near Rostrevor, Robert Samuel Torrens, Esq., late a Captain in the 47th Regiment of Foot, and last surviving son of the Hon. Judge Torrens, in his thirty-third year.

No. 5082 :: Ref. 1851-10-04, 3:2, D.
[Sepr.] 29th, in Dungannon, of consumption, aged 27 years, Mr. William Douglas, eldest son of Mr. Douglas, bookseller, Market-square.

No. 5083 :: Ref. 1851-10-04, 3:2, D.
[Sepr.] 29th, at Annagh House, Clogher, Francis Ramsay, Esq., much regretted by his intimate friends and acquaintances.

No. 5084 :: Ref. 1851-10-04, 3:2, D.
[Sepr.] 29th, in Abbey-street, Armagh, Mr. James Smyth, in the 90th year of his age. Mr. Smyth was a man of simple, unassuming manners, true and just in his dealings with the world, unaffected and decided in sterling piety. During an illness of six weeks he manifested perfect resignation to the divine will, arising from a consciousness of his acceptance with God, and a well-grounded hope of glory, honour, immortality, and eternal life. His end was truly peaceful, and triumphant.

No. 5085 :: Ref. 1851-10-11, 2:7, B.
Sept. 28, at Cloughjordan, Co. Tipperary, Mrs. Waugh, wife of John T. Waugh, Esq., Excise, of a daughter.

No. 5086 :: Ref. 1851-10-11, 2:7, B.
Oct. 1, at the Provincial Bank of Ireland, Monaghan, Mrs. Syms, of a daughter.

No. 5087 :: Ref. 1851-10-11, 2:7, B.
Oct. 1, at Victoria-street, Belfast, Mrs. John Wilson, of a son.

No. 5088 :: Ref. 1851-10-11, 2:7, B.
Oct. 1, at Learmount, Co. Derry, the wife of George de la Poer Beresford, 16th Regt., A.D.C., of a son.

No. 5089 :: Ref. 1851-10-11, 2:7, M.
July 28, at Kamptee, E.I., Major C. Pooley, 38th Regiment, N.I., to Eliza, youngest daughter of the late Rev. N. Smith, Rector of the parishes of Derrynoose and Clonoe, Archdiocese of Armagh.

No. 5090 :: Ref. 1851-10-11, 2:7, M.
Sept. 27, at Elympton, Harriett Elizabeth Nucella, to C.B. Mitchell, Esq., surgeon, Deddington, son of the late Richd Mitchell, Esq., Monaghan.

No. 5091 :: Ref. 1851-10-11, 2:7, M.
Oct. 1, in Dublin, by Rev. T.H. Porter, D.D., Rector of Desertcreight, Co. Tyrone, assisted by Rev. A.G. Stuart, rector of Killincool, H.L. Tottenham, Esq., Barrister-at-Law, eldest son of the late Henry Tottenham, Esq., M.P., to Joice, relict of E.L. Colvill, Esq., and daughter of the late James Lowry, of Rockdale House, Co. Tyrone, Esq.

No. 5092 :: Ref. 1851-10-11, 2:7, M.
Oct. 1, in Dublin, by Rev. Franklin Bewley, brother to the bride, Robert Thacker, Esq., of Charlemont-mall, to Sarah Caroline, youngest daughter of the late Thomas Bewley, Esq., of Palmyra, Co. Dublin.

No. 5093 :: Ref. 1851-10-11, 2:7, M.
Oct. 1, at Glenferness House, Captain Richard Roney, 96th Regt., to Rose Anne, second daughter to John Dougal, Esq., of Glenferness, Nairnshire.

No. 5094 :: Ref. 1851-10-11, 2:7, M.
Oct. 8, at Warrenpoint Church, by the Rev. Dr. M'Kay, William, eldest son of John Macoun, Esq. Kilmore, near Lurgan, to Anna Jane, eldest daughter of Thomas Stevenson, Esq., Clanrolla, near Lurgan.

No. 5095 :: Ref. 1851-10-11, 2:7, M.
Oct. 4, at Booterstown Church, by Rev Benjamin Wade, cousin to the bride, John Joseph, eldest son of the late Joshua Pim, of Dublin, and Tyrrellspass, Co. Westmeath, Esq., to Elizabeth Maria, second daughter of the late George Booker, Esq., of Sidney Lodge, county Dublin.

No. 5096 :: Ref. 1851-10-11, 2:7, M.
Oct. 5, at the Parochial House, Beragh, by Rev. H. Murphy, P.P., Mr. James Mullin, jun., Dungannon, to Mary, eldest daughter of Mr. Charles M'Aleer, Pomeroy.

No. 5097 :: Ref. 1851-10-11, 2:7, D.
Aug. 30, at New York, aged 6 months, John Mitchell, son of Thos. Devin Reilly.

No. 5098 :: Ref. 1851-10-11, 2:7, D.
Sept. 17, Anne Maria, eldest daughter of Mr. Henry A. Burke, Rector of Magheracross, county Fermanagh.

No. 5099 :: Ref. 1851-10-11, 2:7, D.
Oct. 1, in Tralee, in the 65th year of his age, Jeffrey Eager, Esq., late of the Royal York Rangers,

Registrar of the diocese of Ardfert and Aghadoe, and one of the proprietors of the *Kerry Evening Post*.

No. 5100 :: Ref. 1851-10-11, 2:7, D.
Oct. 2, in the 80th year of her age, the wife of William Fleming, Esq., of Bundoran, and daughter of the late Daniel Bradshaw, Esq., of Florencecourt, at whose house the founder of [M]ethodism, Rev. J. Wesley stopped when he came to that part of the country, and of whom she retained a perfect recollection.

No. 5101 :: Ref. 1851-10-11, 2:7, D.
Oct. 3, at Bunker's-hall, Belfast, aged 53 years, Mary, wife of John Wallace, Esq., solicitor, Belfast.

No. 5102 :: Ref. 1851-10-11, 2:7, D.
Oct. 4, at Newtownlimavady, Matthew Patterson, aged 97. He was the last in this neighbourhood of the old Volunteers of 1782.

No. 5103 :: Ref. 1851-10-11, 2:7, D.
Oct. 5, at his residence, Nootka, Carlingford, Hugh Moore, Esq., J.P. for county Louth.

No. 5104 :: Ref. 1851-10-11, 2:7, D.
Oct. 5, in this city, Mrs. Rickard, relict of the late Mr. James Rickard.

No. 5105 :: Ref. 1851-10-11, 2:7, D.
Oct. 7, at Killiney, Co. Dublin, Mary, wife of Matt H. Shankey, Esq., Brookeborough, and only child of late Rev. W.m. [sic] L. Roper, of Monaghan, in her 26th year.

No. 5106 :: Ref. 1851-10-18, 2:2, B.
June 22, in lat. 27 S., long. 107 W., 14,520 miles from Belfast, on board the ship *Alceste*, bound for San Francisco, the wife of David Brown, formerly of Cookstown, of a son.

No. 5107 :: Ref. 1851-10-18, 2:2, B.
Oct. 3, at Newtownhamilton, the lady of Henry R. Barker, Esq., solicitor, of a son.

No. 5108 :: Ref. 1851-10-18, 2:2, B.
Oct. 11, in Armagh, Mrs. James M'Mahon, of a son.

No. 5109 :: Ref. 1851-10-18, 2:2, B.
Oct. 14, at Tandragee Castle, the Duchess of Manchester of a daughter.

No. 5110 :: Ref. 1851-10-18, 2.2, B.
Oct. 15, the lady of George Eccles Nixon, Esq., late of the 1st Bombay Lancers, H.E.I.C. service, of a daughter.

No. 5111 :: Ref. 1851-10-18, 2:2, B.
Oct. 16, in this city the lady of Thos. A. Prentice, Esq., Stamp Distributor, of a son.

No. 5112 :: Ref. 1851-10-18, 2:2, M.
Oct. 6, in Strabane church, by Rev. John King, Mr. James Kinch, of Strabane, to Catherine, only child of Mr. John Orr, of same place.

No. 5113 :: Ref. 1851-10-18, 2:2, M.
Oct. 9, by Rev. H.R. Macready, Mr. William Eakin, Glasslough, to Helen M'Alister, daughter of the late John Molyneux, Esq., Beechfield, Antrim.

No. 5114 :: Ref. 1851-10-18, 2:2, M.
Oct. 10, at Clones church, by Rev. Thomas Hand, Marshall Moore, Esq., of Analore, to Sarah Elizabeth, daughter of the late Robert M'Kean, Esq., co. Armagh.

No. 5115 :: Ref. 1851-10-18, 2:2, M.
Oct. 15, in the Parish church, Drumcree, by the Venerable the Archdeacon of Dromore, David Wilson Irwin, Esq., merchant, Portadown, to Fanny, eldest daughter of the late William Robb, Esq., Derrybroughas House, near Portadown.

No. 5116 :: Ref. 1851-10-18, 2:2, M.
Oct. 15, in Moy church, by Rev. Richard Wrightson, Mr. John Neill, Belfast, to Elizabeth Harriett, youngest daughter of the late Rev. John Mallin, Primitive Wesleyan Minister.

No. 5117 :: Ref. 1851-10-18, 2:2, M.
Oct. 15, in St. Mary's church, Donnybrook, by Rev. J. Moffatt, the Rev. Ralph Dawson Welsh, of Brookborough, co. Fermanagh, to Olivia Mary, second daughter of John West Welsh, Esq., of Sandymount.

No. 5118 :: Ref. 1851-10-18, 2:2, M.
John C.W. Lever, Esq., M.D., of Wellington-street, London-bridge, to Mary Ann, daughter of Charles Farebrother, Esq., of Most House, Stockwell, and Alder-man of London.

No. 5119 :: Ref. 1851-10-18, 2:2, M.
In Kilmore church by the Very Rev. Lord Fitzgerald and Vesci, Mr. Christopher Moffatt, of Prospect, to Sidney, eldest daughter of Noble Paget, Esq., of Farragh House, co. Cavan.

No. 5120 :: Ref. 1851-10-18, 2:2, D.
Oct. 8, suddenly at Foxhall, Letterkenny, Daniel Chambers, Esq., J.P., in the 62d year of his age.

No. 5121 :: Ref. 1851-10-18, 2:2, D.
Oct. 10, at Donagh Glebe, diocese of Derry, Rev. George Marshall, M.A., rector of that parish, aged 84. He was the senior clergyman of that diocese, having been a rector in it during 57 years.

No. 5122 :: Ref. 1851-10-18, 2:2, D.
Oct. 10, at 12, Queen-street, Enniskillen, of bilious attack, Mrs. Susan Gibson, aged 54 years.

No. 5123 :: Ref. 1851-10-18, 2:2, D.
Oct. 10, at Brookeborough, aged 19, Miss Margaret M'Elroy; regretted by all who knew her.

No. 5124 :: Ref. 1851-10-18, 2:2, D.
Oct. 11, at Holywood, in the 52d year of her age, Sarah, wife of the Rev. Wm. Hart, late Professor of Hebrew and Oriental Literature to the General Assembly.

No. 5125 :: Ref. 1851-10-18, 2:2, D.
Oct. 13, Mr. Hugh Shields, Clones, aged 58 years.

No. 5126 :: Ref. 1851-10-18, 2:2, D.
At Redhills, co. Cavan, John Ingham, Esq., Solicitor, aged 76 years.

No. 5127 :: Ref. 1851-10-25, 3:1, B.
Oct. 2, at Swanlinbar, the wife of Captain Johnston, J.P., of a daughter.

No. 5128 :: Ref. 1851-10-25, 3:1, B.
Oct. 13, in Cavan, Mrs. Richard Armstrong, of a son.

No. 5129 :: Ref. 1851-10-25, 3:1, B.
Oct. 22, at Enniskillen, the wife of Mr. John M'Mahon, Royal Engineer Department, of a daughter.

No. 5130 :: Ref. 1851-10-25, 3:1, M.
Oct. 21, at the Wesleyan Chapel, Limerick, by Rev. T. Meredith, Captain D.J. Jenkins, of the *European* screw steamer, to Eliza, daughter of the late Rev. John Howe, Wesleyan Minister.

No. 5131 :: Ref. 1851-10-25, 3:1, D.
At Rahara House, near Athlone, aged 96, Francis Sproule, Esq., one of the Volunteers of 1782.

No. 5132 :: Ref. 1851-10-25, 3:1, D.
Oct. 12, at Clontarf, Moutray Erskine, Esq., Solicitor, Cavan, in the 38th year of his age.

No. 5133 :: Ref. 1851-10-25, 3:1, D.
Oct. 13, at Ostend, on his return from Hamburgh, Andrew Gray, Esq., of New York, youngest son of the late George Gray, of Graymount, Esq., co. Armagh.

No. 5134 :: Ref. 1851-10-25, 3:1, D.
Oct. 15, at Dungannon, Mrs. Dickson, relict of Wm. Dickson, Esq., late of Dungannon.

No. 5135 :: Ref. 1851-10-25, 3:1, D.
Oct. 18, in Moy, in the 58th year of his age, Galbraith Johnston, Esq., (half-pay) Lieutenant, Royal West Middlesex Militia. Deceased was a useful citizen, and as superintendent of the Sunday School took a great interest in the education of youth. He was chairman of the town-commissioners, and his general character endeared him to all with whom he was acquainted. His remains were accompanied by a large concourse of friends.

No. 5136 :: Ref. 1851-10-25, 3:1, D.
Oct. 19, at Roxboro' in the County Armagh, (where she had been some time since removed for the benefit of her health) Elizabeth, the dearly beloved and affectionate wife of William Armstrong, of the city of Dublin, Esq., in the 69th year of her age, having borne with christian fortitude and resignation to the divine will, a long and painful illnesss. To her family her many virtues had most deeply endeared her; but in deploring her irreparable loss, they enjoy the happy consolation of knowing, that her's [sic] has been indeed a passage from death unto life. She died as she lived in the faith of Jesus, and the sure and certain hope of a joyful resurrection.

No. 5137 :: Ref. 1851-10-25, 3:1, D.
Oct. 19, at the residence of his son, the Rev. Dr. Dobbin, of Ballymena, the Rev. Hamilton Dobbin, of Lurgan, in the 73d year of his age, and the 52d of his Ministry. His remains were removed for interment, in Lurgan, on Wednesday.

No. 5138 :: Ref. 1851-10-25, 3:1, D.
Oct. 20, in Armagh, Isaac, son of Mr. John Simpson, merchant, aged 10 years.

No. 5139 :: Ref. 1851-10-25, 3:1, D.
Oct. 22, near this city, Miss Elizabeth Moore, age 48 years.

No. 5140 :: Ref. 1851-11-01, 2:7, M.
Oct. 22, by Rev. N.J. Raven, M.A., vicar of Tharnham-curra-Holme, brother of the bride, Rev. David M'Anally, of Blymhill, Staffordshire, second son of Charles M'Anally, Esq., of Markethill, co. Armagh, to Anne, eldest daughter of the late John Raven, Esq., of Summerfield, also of Harpley, in the county of Norfolk.

No. 5141 :: Ref. 1851-11-01, 2:7, M.
Oct. 23, at St Peter's Church, Dublin, John Richardson, Esq., Barrister-at-Law, eldest son of the Rev. John Richardson, of Summerhill, co. Fermanagh, to Mary Ann, eldest daughter of William Trench, Esq., of Cloonequin, co. Roscommon.

No. 5142 :: Ref. 1851-11-01, 2:7, M.
Oct. 29, in Strabane, by Rev. David Maginnis, Belfast, the Rev. John Orr, Comber, co. Down, to Sarah Jane, eldest daughter of Mr. James Porter, Strabane.

No. 5143 :: Ref. 1851-11-01, 2:7, M.
At St. Peter's Church, Dublin, by Rev. Henry Wolfenden, brother to the bride, Mr. James Brierly, Dublin, to Georgina Susanna, third daughter of the late Wm. Wolfenden, Esq., Salisbury-terrace, Rathgar, co. Dublin.

No. 5144 :: Ref. 1851-11-01, 2:7, D.
Oct. 6, at Sandymount, near Dublin, [the] wife of Mr. Richard Tener, merchant, Dungannon, and daughter of the late Mr. David Brown, of Donaghmore, co. Tyrone.

No. 5145 :: Ref. 1851-11-01, 2:7, D.
Oct. 10, at Letterkenny, Miss Susanna Laird, aged 60 years.

No. 5146 :: Ref. 1851-11-01, 2:7, D.
Oct. 19, in this city, aged five years, of scarletina, Elizabeth M. Sim, eldest daughter of Mr. C. Sim, of Manchester, and grand-daughter of Mr. James Rea, of this city.

No. 5147 :: Ref. 1851-11-01, 2:7, D.

Oct. 20, at Chesterfield, George Webster, 28 years of age, little more than four feet in height, and weighing the extraordinary weight of between eighteen and nineteen stones. Three days prior to his death, he had occasion to dress his toe-nails, and in doing so cut one of them to the quick, which bled profusely. He regarded it as only a trivial matter, and took no further notice till acute pain in his foot, along with other symptoms, indicated that it was "gathering." Mortification ensued, and he died on the day above named.

No. 5148 :: Ref. 1851-11-01, 2:7, D.

Suddenly, at his residence, Hermitage, R.B. Wynne, Esq. Clerk of the Peace of the co. Sligo.

No. 5149 :: Ref. 1851-11-01, 2:7, D.

Oct. 22, at Nursery Park, Enniskillen, Sarah, wife of Mr. Thomas Guttridge, in the full triumph of saving faith.

No. 5150 :: Ref. 1851-11-01, 2:7, D.

Oct. 24, in Dublin, William Henry, only son of the late William Johnston, Esq., of Brookvale, co. Monaghan.

No. 5151 :: Ref. 1851-11-01, 2:7, D.

Oct. 27, in this city, after a protracted illness, the lady of Alexander Robinson, Esq., M.D., Surgeon to the County Infirmary. The deceased was greatly and most deservedly esteemed by a large circle of friends. Her loss will be much felt by the poor, to whom she was a generous and unostentatious benefactress.

No. 5152 :: Ref. 1851-11-01, 2:7, D.

Oct. 24, Vice Admiral James Noble at a ripe old age, after having been in the service no less than 64 years. Of this time, however, he served afloat only thirteen years, but it was during the most active period of the war. The veteran officer was one of Nelson's lieutenants, and was desperately wounded when serving with the immortal hero. He was the "Noble" spoken of by Nelson when in his dispatches he refers to "those fine fellows, Hardy, Gage, and Noble," and yet he has died plain "James Noble" of the "reserved half-pay list."

No. 5153 :: Ref. 1851-11-01, 2:7, D.

Lately, at Greet, near Winchcombe, Gloucestershire, aged 78, Mr. Thomas Hale, farmer. The deceased was formerly in poor circumstances, but a considerable sum having been left him by some maiden ladies, his prospects underwent a change for the better, and by his industrious and careful habits he managed to accumulate a large fortune, worth more than £100,000.

No. 5154 :: Ref. 1851-11-08, 2:6, B.

Oct. 23, the lady of Charles Jones, Esq., Russian, Enniskillen, of a son.

No. 5155 :: Ref. 1851-11-08, 2:6, B.

Oct. 25, at Beragh, Mrs. Matthew Rodgers, jun., of a son.

No. 5156 :: Ref. 1851-11-08, 2:6, B.

Oct. 25, at Dundas, Canada West, Mrs. Thomas Howe, formerly of Cavan, of a daughter.

No. 5157 :: Ref. 1851-11-08, 2:6, B.

Oct. 28, at Abbeyview, Sligo, the lady of Alexander Philips, Esq., of a daughter.

No. 5158 :: Ref. 1851-11-08, 2:6, B.

Oct. 31, the wife of John Hassett, a small farmer, was happily delivered of three sons, at Birdhill, all of whom with their mother are doing well.

No. 5159 :: Ref. 1851-11-08, 2:6, M.

Oct. 23, at Greenock, by Rev. John Macnaghtan, of Belfast, Wm. Macnaghtan, Esq., merchant, San Fernando, Trinidad, to Agnes Allan, eldest daughter of Robert Blair, Esq., Greenock.

No. 5160 :: Ref. 1851-11-08, 2:6, M.

Oct. 29, in Garvagh, by the bride's uncle, Rev. Dr. Huston, Macosquin, Mr. Samuel Allen, Planting Lodge, Cookstown, to Elizabeth, eldest daughter of Mr. Matthew Huston, Churchhill.

No. 5161 :: Ref. 1851-11-08, 2:6, M.

Oct. 30, in Belfast, by Rev. T.F. Miller, and afterwards by the Rev. Henry O'Loughlin, Waring Curran, Esq., merchant, Belfast, to Mary, daughter of the late Mr. Abraham Walker, Crossan House, near Lisburn.

No. 5162 :: Ref. 1851-11-08, 2:6, M.

Oct. 30, at Belfast by Rev. James MacIvor, of Moyle Rectory, co. Tyrone, Henry O. Johnston, Esq., of Liverpool, to Emily, daughter of the late Francis Murray, Esq., Belfast.

No. 5163 :: Ref. 1851-11-08, 2:6, M.

Nov. 6, at St. Mark's Church, by the Rev. Edward Ogle Disney, Rector of Newtownhamilton, the Rev. James Disney, Rector of Killyman, to Susan, eldest daughter of William Paton, Esq.

No. 5164 :: Ref. 1851-11-08, 2:6, D.

Oct. 10, at Montreal, in his 82d year, James Buchanan, Esq., for nearly 25 years an active magistrate of co. Tyrone, and many years her Majesty's Consul at New York.

No. 5165 :: Ref. 1851-11-08, 2:6, D.

Oct. 19, at Edenderry, King's County, Jane, the beloved wife of Captain Murray, S.I. of Constabulary, and third daughter of the late Mr. John M'Kenny, of Omagh.

No. 5166 :: Ref. 1851-11-08, 2:6, D.

Oct. 24, at Tandragee, of consumption, aged 20 years, Eliza Sarah, wife of Mr. R. Trotter, merchant.

No. 5167 :: Ref. 1851-11-08, 2:6, D.

Oct. 24, at Belfast, in the 85th year of her age, Jane, wife of Mr. Wm. Anderson, formerly of Newtownstewart, co. Tyrone.

No. 5168 :: Ref. 1851-11-08, 2:6, D.

Oct. 28, suddenly, Eliza, wife of Mr. James M'Callen, Glasslough.

No. 5169 :: Ref. 1851-11-08, 2:6, D.

Oct. 28, at Dunfane, near Ballymena, aged 81 years, Mr. Robert Aickin. On the 27th of June, 1798, he saved the life of William M'Claverty, Esq., a magistrate of Ballymena, who was nearly being killed by a body of United Irishmen.

No. 5170 :: Ref. 1851-11-08, 2:6, D.

Oct. 29, at Brighton, William Wyon, R.A., chief engraver of her Majesty's Mint.

No. 5171 :: Ref. 1851-11-08, 2:6, D.

Ot. [sic] 29, in Derry, Mr. James M'Williams, for twenty years guard of one of Her Majesty's mails.

No. 5172 :: Ref. 1851-11-08, 2:6, D.

Oct. 31, at Moorview, Letterkenny, in the second year of her marriage, the youthful wife of the Rev. N.P. Rogers.

No. 5173 :: Ref. 1851-11-08, 2:6, D.

Nov. 1, in Newry, at the residence of her son-in-law, Sarah, relict of the late Mr. William Patterson, of Armagh, aged 58 years.

No. 5174 :: Ref. 1851-11-08, 2:6, D.

Nov. 2, in London, Edith, second daughter of Sir James and Lady Emerson Tennent.

No. 5175 :: Ref. 1851-11-08, 2:6, D.

Nov. 4, at Augher Castle, co. Tyrone, Sir James Richardson Bunburry, Bart., D.L.

No. 5176 :: Ref. 1851-11-08, 2:6, D.

Nov. 4, aged 77 years, Agnes, relict of the late James Todd, Esq., of Ballynaskea, co. Down, and daughter of the late David Ross, Esq., of Liscarney, co. Monaghan.

No. 5177 :: Ref. 1851-11-08, 2:6, D.

Nov. 1, in the 33d year of her age, at the residence of her brother-in-law, Mr. Thompson, Barrack-hill, in this city, Mrs. M'Coy, third daughter of Mr. John Kitson, of same place, much regretted by her relatives and friends.

No. 5178 :: Ref. 1851-11-08, 2:6, D.

Nov. 1, in the third year of his age, at the residence of Mr. Wm. Barnes, Scotch-street, Armagh, Wm. Barnes, son of Mr. Alexander Thompson, of Gilford.

No. 5179 :: Ref. 1851-11-15, 2:6, B.

Oct. 29, the wife of Mr. Jos. Hurst, silk-dresser, Todmorden, of two boys and a girl.

No. 5180 :: Ref. 1851-11-15, 2:6, B.

Oct. 31, at Birdhill, near Killaloe, the wife of John Hassett, a small farmer, of three sons, all of whom with their mother are doing well.

No. 5181 :: Ref. 1851-11-15, 2:6, B.

Nov. 8, at Trillick, Mrs. Robert Bouker, of a son.

No. 5182 :: Ref. 1851-11-15, 2:6, B.

Nov. 8, at the Rectory, Tralee, the lady of the Rev. Anthony Denny, of a son.

No. 5183 :: Ref. 1851-11-15, 2:6, B.

Nov. 10, at Edinburgh, the lady Blanche Balfour, of a son.

No. 5184 :: Ref. 1851-11-15, 2:6, M.

March 27, at North Adelaide, South Australia, by the Rev. Mr. Hull, Charles Goldsmith, Esq., of Port Adelaide, to Anna, youngest daughter of the late Robert D. Mathews, Esq., of Kilkenny.

No. 5185 :: Ref. 1851-11-15, 2:6, M.

Nov. 6, in Caledon, by Rev. H.T. Fleming, Mr. Vaughan Montgomery, Belfast, to Margaret, eldest daughter of the late Mr. Pettigrew, Esq., Crilly-house, co. Tyrone.

No. 5186 :: Ref. 1851-11-15, 2:6, M.

Nov. 6, in Moneymore, by Rev. Dr. Barnett, David, son to the late Mr. Samuel Stewart, of Carndaisay, to Nancy, eldest daughter of Mr. Henry Kennedy, of Knockadoo.

No. 5187 :: Ref. 1851-11-15, 2:6, D.

Oct. 28, at Tullynure, near Omagh, Mr. James M'Connell, aged 61.

No. 5188 :: Ref. 1851-11-15, 2:6, D.

Oct. 28, at Gortnagross, near Killeter, aged 39 years, Mr. Samuel Sproule.

No. 5189 :: Ref. 1851-11-15, 2:6, D.

Nov. 4, at Augher Castle, co. Tyrone, Sir James Mervyn Richardson Bunbury, Bart. The deceased was born in 1781. In 1810 he married the daughter of John Cary Moubray, Esq., of Favour Royal, co. Tyrone. He succeeded his father in 1839, having, in 1822, assumed the name of Richardson. Sir James leaves issue 10 children, the eldest of whom John, born in 1813, succeeds to the title and estates.

No. 5190 :: Ref. 1851-11-15, 2:6, D.

Nov. 4, at The Pradoe, Shropshire, aged 71 years, the Hon. Thos. Kenyon.

No. 5191 :: Ref. 1851-11-15, 2:6, D.

Nov. 7, Charles, eldest son of the late Alexander C. Colhoun, Esq., aged 18 years.

No. 5192 :: Ref. 1851-11-15, 2:6, D.

Nov. 8, near Omagh, Mrs. Hawkins, aged 75 years.

No. 5193 :: Ref. 1851-11-15, 2:6, D.
Nov. 8, at 20, Rutland-square North, Dublin, aged 3 years and 10 days, Elizabeth, eldest daughter of William Auchinleck Dane, Esq.

No. 5194 :: Ref. 1851-11-15, 2:6, D.
Nov. 10, at Kingstown, Robert, eldest son of the late Captain Robert Denny, of the 3d Buffs.

No. 5195 :: Ref. 1851-11-15, 2:6, D.
Nov. 10, at Enniskillen, Mr. William Gibbins, aged 76.

No. 5196 :: Ref. 1851-11-15, 2:6, D.
Nov. 12, at Middletown, of decline, Mary Anne, second daughter of Mr. Matthew Johnston, aged 15 years.

No. 5197 :: Ref. 1851-11-22, 3:1, B.
Nov. 5, at Benburb, the lady of Walter Hore, Esq., of a daughter.

No. 5198 :: Ref. 1851-11-22, 3:1, B.
Nov. 11, at Tandragee, the lady of Rev. R. Johnston, of a son.

No. 5199 :: Ref. 1851-11-22, 3:1, B.
Nov. 13, Mrs. C. Howden, Malone, Belfast, of a son.

No. 5200 :: Ref. 1851-11-22, 3:1, M.
Nov. 12, at Stoke-next-Guildford, James D'Arcy, Esq., to Mary Andrews.

No. 5201 :: Ref. 1851-11-22, 3:1, M.
Nov. 13, in St. Anne's Church, Belfast, Mr. G.L. Archer, Markethill, to Marianne, eldest daughter of the late Mr. Edward M'Seveney, of same place.

No. 5202 :: Ref. 1851-11-22, 3:1, M.
Nov. 14, in Glastry, by Rev. W. M'Mullan, Coleraine, Mr. James Wallace, eldest son of Mr. John Wallace, Edenderry, to Margaret, youngest daughter of the late Hugh Brown, Esq., Ballylimp.

No. 5203 :: Ref. 1851-11-22, 3:1, M.
Nov. 17, at Dungannon, by Rev. Wm. Quain, John Holland, Esq., Officer of Inland Revenue, to Eliza, second daughter of Mr. James Wilson, Dungannon, merchant.

No. 5204 :: Ref. 1851-11-22, 3:1, M.
Nov. 18, in St. Peter's Church, Dublin, the Rev. John A. Darley, Cootehill, to Anna, eldest daughter of the Hon. John Plunkett.

No. 5205 :: Ref. 1851-11-22, 3:1, D.
Sept. 17, Mr. M. M'Sweeny, Compositor, of Mr. Hansard's office, London. Deceased was a free member of the Widow and Orphan's fund.

No. 5206 :: Ref. 1851-11-22, 3:1, D.
In Louisville, State of Ky., U.S., Mrs. E.A. Johnson, aged 22 years, a native of Killead, county Antrim.

No. 5207 :: Ref. 1851-11-22, 3:1, D.
Thomas Conway, butter buyer, of Limerick.

No. 5208 :: Ref. 1851-11-22, 3:1, D.
At Brussels, T. Oldham, Esq., late engineer of the Bank of England, in his 50th year.

No. 5209 :: Ref. 1851-11-22, 3:1, D.
Oct. 30, in the 83d year of her age, Charlotte, relict of J. Carey, of Silverbrook, county Tyrone.

No. 5210 :: Ref. 1851-11-22, 3:1, D.
Nov. 5, at Burt, near Derry, Anna Eliza, youngest daughter of Mr. Alexander Leathem.

No. 5211 :: Ref. 1851-11-22, 3:1, D.
Nov. 5, at Marseilles, M.F. Grenier, a retired manufacturer, aged 104 years seven months.

No. 5212 :: Ref. 1851-11-22, 3:1, D.
Nov. 9, of inflammation, at Ardagarvan, in the parish of Leckpatrick, co. Tyrone, Mr. Robert Porter, in the 105th year of his age. He was born near Castlefin, in Donegal, and lived the last 76 years of his life in the neighbourhood in which he breathed his last—30 in one house and 40 in another. His memory of the events of early life was very strong, and the melancholy death of Miss Knox, who was shot by her lover, when her father was aimed at, seemed to have taken a strong hold in his imagination. From that event he reckoned his age being then 14 years old.

No. 5213 :: Ref. 1851-11-22, 3:1, D.
Nov. 10, at Omagh, Mrs. Thomas Shields, aged 79 years.

No. 5214 :: Ref. 1851-11-22, 3:1, D.
Nov. 11, the Hon. Anne Douglas Challinor Westenra, daughter of the Right Hon. Lord Rossmore. Born on the 13th April, 1848.

No. 5215 :: Ref. 1851-11-22, 3:1, D.
Nov. 11, at Adelaide-place, [C]ork, T. Gelston, Esq., A.C. General to her Majesty's forces.

No. 5216 :: Ref. 1851-11-22, 3:1, D.
Nov. 11, at Mountcharles, Donegal, after a short illness, M.F. Dornin, Esq., late of the Excise Department, aged 70 years.

No. 5217 :: Ref. 1851-11-22, 3:1, D.
Nov. 13, at Whitehall, Crumlin, Mr. Goodwin, printer, of Dublin, in the 75th year of his age.

No. 5218 :: Ref. 1851-11-22, 3:1, D.
Nov. 16, in Dublin, Alice second daghter [sic] of the late Rev. G.L. Gresson.

No. 5219 :: Ref. 1851-11-22, 3:1, D.
Nov. 16, in Armagh, Margaret, third daughter of Mr. C. Sim, of Manchester.

No. 5220 :: Ref. 1851-11-22, 3:1, D.
Nov. 17, in Dublin, Alderman Keshan: In 1846 he filled the office of Lord Mayor.

No. 5221 :: Ref. 1851-11-22, 3:1, D.
Nov. 18, Anna Maria, wife of James Greer Bell, of Tullylish-house, Gilford.

No. 5222 :: Ref. 1851-11-29, 3:1, B.
Nov. 6, at Dungannon, the wife of Mr. Edward Hueston, of a daughter.

No. 5223 :: Ref. 1851-11-29, 3:1, B.
Nov. 18, at Ballyshannon, the wife of Mr. John Andrews, of a son.

No. 5224 :: Ref. 1851-11-29, 3:1, B.
Nov. 19, at Grosvenor Crescent, the wife of Colonel Thos. Wood, of a daughter.

No. 5225 :: Ref. 1851-11-29, 3:1, B.
Nov. 21, at 10, Upper Cumberland-street, Dublin, the wife of Mr. John M. Scully, of two boys and a girl—mother and children are doing well.

No. 5226 :: Ref. 1851-11-29, 3:1, B.
Nov. 22, at Termon Rectory, Dungannon, the lady of the Rev. B. Alexander, of a daughter.

No. 5227 :: Ref. 1851-11-29, 3:1, B.
Nov. 24, at Newpark, Cashel, the lady of the Rev. John Hare, Rector of Tullycorbet, co. Monaghan, of a daughter.

No. 5228 :: Ref. 1851-11-29, 3:1, M.
Nov. 18, at the Parish Church of Drumachose, by the Rev. Robert Gage, Captain James Roy Norton, Hants Light Infantry, to Julia, youngest daughter of Marcus Gage, Esq., of Strieve-hill, co. Londonderry.

No. 5229 :: Ref. 1851-11-29, 3:1, M.
Nov. 20, in St. Anne's Church, Belfast, by Rev. Theophilus Campbell, M.A., Incumbent of Trinity Church, John Praeger, Esq., to Mary, daughter of the late Hill Charley, Esq.

No. 5230 :: Ref. 1851-11-29, 3:1, M.
Nov. 20, in St. Mary's Church, by Rev. A. Leeper, Dr. Wilson, of Swords, co. Dublin, to Sarah Jane, only daughter of the late Gervas Murray, of 63, Great Britain-street, and Mount Vernon, Dollymount, and grandchild of the late Francis Collins, Esq., Drogheda.

No. 5231 :: Ref. 1851-11-29, 3:1, M.
Nov. 27, in the Third Presbyterian Church, Armagh, by Rev. J.R. M'Alister, Mr. John Love, of Timakeel, to Mary, daughter of Mr. Robert Calvert, of Breagh, Parish of Seaford [sic].

No. 5232 :: Ref. 1851-11-29, 3:1, M.
In St. James's Chapel, London, Henry R. Percy, Esq., M.D., eldest son of the Rev. Wm. A. Percy, of Carrick-on-Shannon Rectory, to Emma, third and youngest daughter of Major John B. Orde, late of the Dragoon Guards, of Westwood Hall, Northumberland.

No. 5233 :: Ref. 1851-11-29, 3:1, D.
At Greenville, Tennessee, U.S.A., in the 64th year of his age, William Galway Dickson, Esq., son of the late Rev. Dr. Dickson, of Keady.

No. 5234 :: Ref. 1851-11-29, 3:1, D.
Oct. 24, of fever, at St. Louis, Missouri, United States, in the 22d year of his age, Joseph Henderson Singer, second son of the Venerable Archdeacon Singer, Regius Professor of Divinity in the University of Dublin.

No. 5235 :: Ref. 1851-11-29, 3:1, D.
Nov. 14, at his residence, 81, Amien's-street, the Rev. Henry Deery, Wesleyan Minister, aged 74 years. He died triumphing in that faith of which he was for 53 years a zealous and most efficient teacher.

No. 5236 :: Ref. 1851-11-29, 3:1, D.
Nov. 16, at Cheltenham, Jane, relict of John Chambers, Esq., Barrister-at-law, and daughter of the late Thomas Young, Esq., of Lough Eske, co. Donegal.

No. 5237 :: Ref. 1851-11-29, 3:1, D.
Nov. 16, the Rev. James Tisdale, Rector of Ballinderry, co. Derry, aged 67.

No. 5238 :: Ref. 1851-11-29, 3:1, D.
Nov. 17, in Ballyshannon, at the advanced age of 95 years, Mrs. M'Gowan, relict of the late Mr. Denis M'Gowan.

No. 5239 :: Ref. 1851-11-29, 3:1, D.
Nov. 18, at Bristol, Clara, aged 18, only child of Mrs. Rennolds, relict of Samuel Rennolds, Esq., and sister to Major Sterne, of Gola castle. She was attacked with fever in the brain and only survived a few days.

No. 5240 :: Ref. 1851-11-29, 3:1, D.
Nov. 19, at Celbridge, Sarah, daughter of Mr. William Clemenger, Kilmore, Cavan.

No. 5241 :: Ref. 1851-11-29, 3:1, D.
Nov. 19, in Ballyshannon, after a severe and tedious illness, borne with the most extraordinary resignation (for one of her tender age) to the will of the Redeemer, Jane, the beloved child of Mr. Hugh Chittick, in the 11th year of her age.

No. 5242 :: Ref. 1851-11-29, 3:1, D.
Nov. 21, at the residence of his father, Market-street, Monaghan, William Williamson, aged 21 years.

No. 5243 :: Ref. 1851-11-29, 3:1, D.
Nov. 21, at Clifton, Richard B. Blackwood, Esq., of Clonervy, co. Cavan, aged 72 years.

No. 5244 :: Ref. 1851-11-29, 3:1, D.
Fov. [sic] 22, at his residence, 13, Eustace-st., William Flavelle, Esq., deeply and sincerely regretted by a numerous circle of friends and relatives. He died as he lived a true christian, in the 70th year of his age.

No. 5245 :: Ref. 1851-11-29, 3:1, D.

Nov. 26, in Linnen Hall-street, Mr. John Donnelly, proprietor of the Linnen Hall Hotel, aged 52 years. Mr. Donnelly was a respectable upright man and the architect of his own fortune.

No. 5246 :: Ref. 1851-11-29, 3:1, D.

Nov. 26, at Brookborough, aged 96, Sergeant Thomas Murphy, a brave and distinguished soldier of Major Sterne's regiment the 82d. His gallant conduct was frequently noticed by his officers, but particularly at Niagara, in North America, when under the command of Major General Proctor. The Major attended his funeral and offered his bereaved and aged widow a room in his asylum in Brookborough, during the remainder of her life.

No. 5247 :: Ref. 1851-11-29, 3:1, D.

Nov. 26, at Corkhill Lodge, Enniskillen, aged 71 years, Mary Jane, the beloved wife of George Lendrum, Esq., of Jamestown, who was taken to her everlasting rest in the most perfect reliance on the merits of her Saviour.

No. 5248 :: Ref. 1851-11-29, 3:1, D.

At his residence, Lower Baggot street, Dublin, aged 66 years, William Farrell, Esq., architect, deservedly regretted by a numerous circle of friends.

No. 5249 :: Ref. 1851-11-29, 3:1, D.

At Barnstaple, Mr. John Avery, aged 77, proprietor of the *North Devon Journal*.

No. 5250 :: Ref. 1851-12-06, 3:1, B.

Nov. 24, in Ballyshannon, the lady of the late Robert M'Donagh, Esq., formerly of Jamaica, of a son.

No. 5251 :: Ref. 1851-12-06, 3:1, B.

Nov. 29, at Upper Parnell-place, the wife of the Rev. J. Quintin, of a daughter.

No. 5252 :: Ref. 1851-12-06, 3:1, M.

July 16, at Adelaide, South Australia, Luke M. Cullen, Esq., Solicitor, Adelaide, to Susanna Draper, eldest daughter of Mr. Joseph M'Minn, North Adelaide, formerly of Newry.

No. 5253 :: Ref. 1851-12-06, 3:1, M.

Nov. 18, at St. Andrew's Church, Plymouth, Rev. Wm. Rose, vicar of Dungiven, co. Londonderry, to Caroline Matilda, second daughter of the late Arthur Luce Trelawny Collins, Esq., of the Royal Artillery, and of Ham, co. Devon.

No. 5254 :: Ref. 1851-12-06, 3:1, M.

Nov. 23, the marriage of the Earl of Lanesborough with Frederic Emma, relict of Sir Richard Hunter, of Dulany House, Sussex, was solemnized at St. George's Church, Hanover-square, London.

No. 5255 :: Ref. 1851-12-06, 3:1, M.

Nov. 26, in the First Presbyterian Church, Keady, by Rev. Joseph Jenkins, Mr. Hugh Eccles, merchant, Keady, to Anne, second daughter of Mr. James Scott, superintendent of the bleachworks, Annvale, Keady.

No. 5256 :: Ref. 1851-12-06, 3:1, M.

Nov. 27, in St. Mary's Church, Newry, by Very Rev. the Dean of Dromore, Mr. Richard Sergeant, to Eliza, youngest daughter of the late Thomas Radcliffe, both of Newry.

No. 5257 :: Ref. 1851-12-06, 3:1, M.

Nov. 27, by Rev. Mr. Lennon, P.P., Stewartstown, Surgeon Mooney, of Dungannon, late of Glasgow, to Miss Ellen M'Mahon of Coalisland.

No. 5258 :: Ref. 1851-12-06, 3:1, M.

Nov. 27, at Thurles Church, Mr. Samuel Shaw, of Waterford, to Lydia Love, daughter of Joshua Lester, Esq., of Thurles.

No. 5259 :: Ref. 1851-12-06, 3:1, M.

Dec. 1, at Kilskeery, co. Tyrone, by Rev. Wm. Crawford, brother to the bride, Rev. Stewart Smyth, of Selby, England, to Elizabeth, fourth daughter of Andrew Crawford, Esq., Trillick.

No. 5260 :: Ref. 1851-12-06, 3:1, M.

Dec. 4, in Benburb Church, by Rev. Mr. Maunsell, Mr. Joseph Fraser, to Sarah, second daughter of Mr. James Rolston, Callan-bridge.

No. 5261 :: Ref. 1851-12-06, 3:1, M.

At St. James's Church, London, the Hon. Frederick, youngest son of the Earl Codogan [sic], to Lady Adelaide Paget, youngest daughter of the Marquis of Anglesey.

No. 5262 :: Ref. 1851-12-06, 3:1, M.

Robert William Rickart, Hepburn [sic], Esq., of Rickarton, N.B., to Helen Maria, daughter of Lieut.-Col. James J. Forbes Leith, of Whitehaugh, N.B., and grand daughter of the late Lieut.-Col. James Stewart, of the 42d.

No. 5263 :: Ref. 1851-12-06, 3:1, M.

In Jersey, Lt. Tanchell, to the daughter of the late Major Blake.

No. 5264 :: Ref. 1851-12-06, 3:1, M.

At Heddon-on-the-Wall, Hill Wallace, Esq., Bombay Horse Artillery, to Harriet Sophia, daughter of the late Captain Frederick W. Burgoyne, Royal Artillery.

No. 5265 :: Ref. 1851-12-06, 3:1, M.

At Simla, Edward James Simpson, Esq., Captain 69th Bengal Infantry, and A.C. General to Sir Wm. Gomm, Commander-in-Chief in India, to Ellen Theophila, daughter of Colonel George Denniss, C.B., late of the Bengal Horse Artillery.

No. 5266 :: Ref. 1851-12-06, 3:1, M.

At the Mauritius, Captain Bowers, 97th Regt., to Frances, daughter of Lieut. H. Hunter, R.N.

No. 5267 :: Ref. 1851-12-06, 3:1, D.

Sept. 12, at New York, John, youngest son of the late Hugh Boyle, Esq., Rush-hall, county Londonderry.

No. 5268 :: Ref. 1851-12-06, 3:1, D.

Oct. 5, at Saint Clare, Quebec, Robt. Crawford, Esq., aged 38 years, only son of the late John Crawford, Esq., of Tatnagole, co. Tyrone.

No. 5269 :: Ref. 1851-12-06, 3:1, D.

Nov. 9, at Charleston, South Carolina, aged 28 years, Sarah Annie, wife of Moody Maguire, Esq., formerly of Nn.-Limavady, and second daughter of the late Robert M'Naul, Esq., Bushmills.

No. 5270 :: Ref. 1851-12-06, 3:1, D.

Nov. 17, at Clones, of disease of the heart, Mr. Michael M'Elroy, merchant, aged 52.

No. 5271 :: Ref. 1851-12-06, 3:1, D.

Nov. 19, in Doonin, co. Fermanagh, Mr. John Hamilton, in the 70th year of his age.

No. 5272 :: Ref. 1851-12-06, 3:1, D.

Nov. 21, in Clifton, B.B. Blackwood, Esq., of Clonervy, co. Cavan, aged 72 years.

No. 5273 :: Ref. 1851-12-06, 3:1, D.

Nov. 21, in Cabra Lodge, co. Cavan, of inflammation of the lungs, Mr. Henry Williams, late Head-Constable of Constabulary, and stewart to Colonel Pratt.

No. 5274 :: Ref. 1851-12-06, 3:1, D.

Nov. 23, in the 73d year of her age, Elizabeth, relict of the late Edward M'Conkey, Esq., of Sion Hill, Hillsborough.

No. 5275 :: Ref. 1851-12-06, 3:1, D.

Nov. 26, at Holywood, Hugh G. Marshall, aged 28 years, late Sergeant-Major of the 6th Inniskilling Dragoons.

No. 5276 :: Ref. 1851-12-06, 3:1, D.

Nov. 27, at Muff Glebe, Cookstown, Jane, relict of the late Capt. Wm. Boyes, H.M. 76th Foot, aged 83 years.

No. 5277 :: Ref. 1851-12-06, 3:1, D.

Nov. 28, at the residence of his father, in Wexford, Caesar Augustus Kidd, Esq., aged 37 years.

No. 5278 :: Ref. 1851-12-06, 3:1, D.

Nov. 28, at Enniskillen, John, second son of Mr. Molyneux, aged 5 years.

No. 5279 :: Ref. 1851-12-06, 3:1, D.

Nov. 28, at Enniskillen, Mr. John (Jack) Collum.

No. 5280 :: Ref. 1851-12-06, 3:1, D.

Nov. 29, at Stewartstown, Mr. Andrew Campbell, merchant, aged 65 years.

No. 5281 :: Ref. 1851-12-06, 3:1, D.

Decr. 1, at 25, Eliza Place, Belfast, Margaret, the beloved wife of Mr. John M'Donnell, and daughter of John Adams, Esq., formerly of this city, aged 24 years. Her remains were interred in St. Mark's Church burying ground, Armagh, on Thursday.

No. 5282 :: Ref. 1851-12-06, 3:1, D.

Dec. 1, at Benoan, co. Tyrone, Andrew, son of Mr. Jas. Roddy, aged 17 years.

No. 5283 :: Ref. 1851-12-06, 3:1, D.

Dec. 5, at Balloo House, co. Down, in his 10th year, Hugh, eldest son of Robert Steele Nicholson, Esq., J.P.

No. 5284 :: Ref. 1851-12-06, 3:1, D.

At an advanced age, at Altavilla, Queen's County, Mrs. Luther, relict of Anthony Guy Luther, Esq., late of Clonmel.

No. 5285 :: Ref. 1851-12-13, 2:2, D.

Death of Mrs. Kidd.

It is our painful duty to record the demise of an amiable person, the lady of Thomas Kidd, Esq., J.P., and Chairman of the Town Commissioners, which took place at her residence in English-street, on the morning of the 9th inst., in the 45th year of her age. The deceased had been only suffering a few days, and bore her affliction with truly Christian patience and resignation to the Divine will.—The news of her departure caused universal sorrow in this city, as evidenced in the shops generally being closed, the only outward form of sympathy that could be shown for her worthy and affectionate partner and his bereaved family and friends. Very respectably descended, she was indeed an ornament to her sex—faithful in the discharge of every social duty, and jealous of the performance of every Christian obligation. Unassuming among those with whom she associated in friendly intercourse—unostentatious in the distribution of her charity to the poor; her loss is felt by all classes, but chiefly by her affectionate husband and children whom she loved with unexampled parental attachment. While in life few ladies were more generally respected—now in death none could be more universally lamented by high and low, rich and poor.

The Funeral took place yesterday morning, at 10 o'clock, and was attended by a large and respectable concourse of the gentry, clergy, and merchants of this city and immediate neighbourhood besides those of her personal relatives. In the mournful cortege was noticed wearing scarfs and headbands:

Clergymen—Rev. Messrs. Irwin, Wade, and Sharkey.

Pall-Bearers—George Robinson, Esq., D.L., High-sheriff, Wm. Paton, Esq., Thomas Dobbin, Esq., George Scott, Esq., John Stanley, Esq., John M'Kinstry, Esq.

Chief Mourners—Counsellor Kidd, Mr. Johnston, brother of deceased, Mr. Osborne Kidd, Mr. Benjamin

Kidd, Messrs. E. and A. Kidd, Mr. T.A. Shillington, Mr. Hugh Boyle.

Doctors—Cumming, Robinson, and Brice.

On arriving at St. Mark's churchyard, the procession was met by the Rev. Mr. Irwin, rector of this parish, by whom the funeral service was read in an impressive manner, and the body, (enclosed in a stuff shell coffin, covered by one of lead, and one of oak, weighing about 7 cwt.) was deposited in the vault. The whole funeral arrangements were under the superintendence of the Messrs. Frizell, of this city.

No. 5286 :: Ref. 1851-12-13, 2:7, B.

Nov. 28, at the Parsonage, Belfast, the lady of Rev. Edward J. Hartrick, of a son.

No. 5287 :: Ref. 1851-12-13, 2:7, B.

Dec. 1, at Minterburn, near Caledon, the wife of Mr. Alexander Spence, teacher of Brantry Parochial School, of a son.

No. 5288 :: Ref. 1851-12-13, 2:7, B.

Dec. 4, at Tullycleagh Glebe, co. Fermanagh, the wife of the Rev. Wm. T. Lett, of a son.

No. 5289 :: Ref. 1851-12-13, 2:7, B.

Dec. 5, the lady of Edward Tipping, Esq., of Bellurgan, of a daughter.

No. 5290 :: Ref. 1851-12-13, 2:7, B.

Dec. 5, at Hollyfort Cottage, Gorey, the lady of the Rev. J. Meade Hobson, of a son.

No. 5291 :: Ref. 1851-12-13, 2:7, B.

Dec. 9, at Drumcondra, the lady of Charles C. Overend, Esq., of a son.

No. 5292 :: Ref. 1851-12-13, 2:7, B.

At Fortwilliam, Mrs. William Tredennick, of a daughter, her 12th child.

No. 5293 :: Ref. 1851-12-13, 2:7, B.

At the Provincial Bank, Kilkenny, the lady of Andrew M'Kean, Esq., Manager, of a daughter.

No. 5294 :: Ref. 1851-12-13, 2:7, B.

At Ballymena, the wife of Rev. W. Cambell, of a son.

No. 5295 :: Ref. 1851-12-13, 2:7, M.

Dec. 3, at Carrickmacross, Rev. James F. M'Cormick, to Ellen, second daughter of the late Captain Gibson, of Lisaniske, co. Monaghan.

No. 5296 :: Ref. 1851-12-13, 2:7, M.

Dec. 4, at Kilbannon Church, Robert Murray, Esq., M.R.C.S.I., of Lough Dona, co. Monaghan, to Annie, second daughter of Charles Gamble, Esq., of Castletown Cambie, Tipperary.

No. 5297 :: Ref. 1851-12-13, 2:7, M.

Dec. 4, in Galway, John James Moutray, Esq., of the Custom-house, Galway, son of Alexander Moutray, Esq., of Ballinsaggart, co. Tyrone, to Mary, only daughter of the late William Edward Armstrong, Esq., of Fortland, co. Roscommon, Solicitor.

No. 5298 :: Ref. 1851-12-13, 2:7, M.

Dec. 8, in St. Mark's Church, Portadown, by Rev. Henry Paine, Proctor, Mr. William Wilson, to Jane, only daughter of the late George Annesley, Esq., Portadown.

No. 5299 :: Ref. 1851-12-13, 2:7, D.

Sept. 9, at the Gambia, of fever, John Hardy, Esq., Lieutenant in the 3rd West India Regiment, son of Charles Hardy, Esq., late of Coalisland, co. Tyrone.

No. 5300 :: Ref. 1851-12-13, 2:7, D.

Dec. 1, Hannah, widow of the late Doctor John Murray, M.D., of Ford Lodge House, co. Cavan.

No. 5301 :: Ref. 1851-12-13, 2:7, D.

At her residence, Eary, in co. Tyrone, Anne, relict of the late James M'Entire, Esq., aged 78 years.

No. 5302 :: Ref. 1851-12-13, 2:7, D.

Dec. 4, at Fortwilliam, co. Donegal, Maria, the beloved wife of William Tredennick, Esq., and daughter of the late Archbishop Magee, leaving eleven children to deplore her irreparable loss.

No. 5303 :: Ref. 1851-12-13, 2:7, D.

Dec. 4, at Strabane, Elizabeth Janet, eldest daughter of James Crosbie, Esq.

No. 5304 :: Ref. 1851-12-13, 2:7, D.

Dec. 4, at Churchhill, Morningside, Grace Pratt, third daughter of the late Rev. Dr. Chalmers.

No. 5305 :: Ref. 1851-12-13, 2:7, D.

Dec. 5, died suddenly, Edward Moore, of Seymour-place, London, late of O'Connor and Moore, of Dublin. He has left £10,000 to the churches of Dublin.

No. 5306 :: Ref. 1851-12-13, 2:7, D.

Dec. 5, in Dundalk, Mrs. Shekleton, relict of Alexander Shekleton, Esq.

No. 5307 :: Ref. 1851-12-13, 2:7, D.

Dec. 6, at The Bush, Killyman, near Dungannon, Susan, relict of the late Lieutenant Alexander M'Clean, in the sixty-ninth year of her age.

No. 5308 :: Ref. 1851-12-13, 2:7, D.

Dec. 6, Mr. Francis Buckley, for many years Superintendent of the Royal Zoological Gardens, Phoenix Park.

No. 5309 :: Ref. 1851-12-13, 2:7, D.

Mr. David Smith, aged 75 years. He served through the Peninsular wars, and at Waterloo, after which he filled the situation of schoolmaster and vestry clerk for 32 years.

No. 5310 :: Ref. 1851-12-13, 2:7, D.

Dec. 9, at Tullylegan, Cookstown, in the 21st year of his age, Usher Greer, Esq.

No. 5311 :: Ref. 1851-12-20, 3:1, B.
In Kilkenny, the lady of Andrew M'Kean, Esq., manager of the Provincial Bank, of a daughter.

No. 5312 :: Ref. 1851-12-20, 3:1, B.
Decr. 8, in Lynn's Place, Sligo, the lady of James Harper, Esq., of a son.

No. 5313 :: Ref. 1851-12-20, 3:1, B.
Decr. 13, at 6, Donegall Square South, Belfast, Mrs. E. Tucker, of a son.

No. 5314 :: Ref. 1851-12-20, 3:1, B.
Decr. 15, at the Glebe, Strangford, the wife of the Rev. John F. Gordon, of a son.

No. 5315 :: Ref. 1851-12-20, 3:1, M.
In Clonmel, John Cowell, Esq., quartermaster of the 12th Regt., to Frances, eldest daughter of the late Wellington Kyffin, Esq., captain in the Royal Tyrone Militia.

No. 5316 :: Ref. 1851-12-20, 3:1, M.
Decr. 2, in the Presbyterian Church at Draperstown, by the Rev. Samuel Smyth, Robert M'Geagh, Esq., merchant, Cookstown, to Isabella M. Smyth, eldest daughter of the late John Smyth, Esq., of Labbyvale, near Draperstown.

No. 5317 :: Ref. 1851-12-20, 3:1, M.
Decr. 13, by Rev. Henry Eaton, in St. Audeon's church, Dublin, John Duggan Timmons, Esq., of Baltimore, America, to Rebecca, daughter of Mr. James Copeland, of Lisbellaw, Co. Fermanagh.

No. 5318 :: Ref. 1851-12-20, 3:1, M.
Decr. 18, by the Rev. John R. M'Alister in the First Presbyterian Church, Armagh, William Carroll, jun., Esq., of Drumadd, to Miss Mary Ann Lewers, of Milford near this city, daughter of the late Samuel Lewers, Esq.

No. 5319 :: Ref. 1851-12-20, 3:1, D.
Nov. 30th, at Cleggean near Blacklion, of inflammation, Elizabeth, wife of Mr. John Hamilton, aged 24.

No. 5320 :: Ref. 1851-12-20, 3:1, D.
Decr. 5, at Magir near Strabane, John M'Elwain, Esq., aged 86. Through life he was a man of active habits, and sustained a character for strict integrity, and unostentatious piety.

No. 5321 :: Ref. 1851-12-20, 3:1, D.
Decr. 7, at Cobham, Surrey, Mr. William Watts, aged 100.

No. 5322 :: Ref. 1851-12-20, 3:1, D.
Decr. 8th, drowned in the wreck of the Barque, *Robert Bradford*, on her passage from Calcutta and the Cape, to Liverpool, at Peurhos [Penrhos] Point, near Holyhead, Charles, aged 19 years, 4th son of Mr. Christr Craham, of Goblusk, county Fermanagh, sincerely and deeply regretted.

No. 5323 :: Ref. 1851-12-20, 3:1, D.
Decr. 9, at Mass Lane, Sligo, Mr. Patrick Flanagan.

No. 5324 :: Ref. 1851-12-20, 3:1, D.
Decr. 10, in Limerick, Rebecca, eldest daughter of Mr. John Ramsay, Wesleyan minister.

No. 5325 :: Ref. 1851-12-20, 3:1, D.
Decr. 11, at 18, Elliott's-Square, Saint Sepulchre, London, Mr. J. Jackson, late merchant of Charlemont, county Armagh.

No. 5326 :: Ref. 1851-12-20, 3:1, D.
Decr. 11, Robert Cary, Esq., S.I. of Constabulary, youngest and last surviving son of the late Rev. Edward Cary, rector of Newtownbarry, co. Wexford.

No. 5327 :: Ref. 1851-12-20, 3:1, D.
Decr. 11, aged 62, James E. Woods, Esq., of the Middle Temple, for upwards of 30 years one of the reporters of *The Times*.

No. 5328 :: Ref. 1851-12-20, 3:1, D.
Decr. 11, at his residence in Harcourt Street, Dublin, Thomas Thompson, Esq., late Solicitor to the General Post-office in Ireland, aged 73 years.

No. 5329 :: Ref. 1851-12-20, 3:1, D.
Decr. 13, at Hermitage, co. Leitrim, Frances Young, youngest daughter of Andrew Carleton, Esq.

No. 5330 :: Ref. 1851-12-20, 3:1, D.
Decr. 14, at Fivemiletown, Jane, relict of the late Mr. Robert Hall of that town, aged 42 years.

No. 5331 :: Ref. 1851-12-20, 3:1, D.
Decr. 15, Mr. John Creden, of Enniskillen, merchant, of inflammation in the bowels. He was about on Friday. We deplore the vacuum created by the loss of so good, so useuf [sic], and so upright a citizen.—As a politician, he possessed strong notions of justice and fair play, and was conscientious in his opinions. As a merchant he was industrious and honourable—confiding in all his dealings. Warm in his friendship, he possessed all the more virtuous characteristics of the Celt, as husband, father, friend.

No. 5332 :: Ref. 1851-12-20, 3:1, D.
Decr. 16, at his residence, Bessmount, Monaghan, John Hatchell, Esq., universally regretted.

No. 5333 :: Ref. 1851-12-20, 3:1, D.
Decr. 18, at Caledon, Walter T. Knox, Esq., much esteemed and regretted.

No. 5334 :: Ref. 1851-12-27, 2:5, B.
On the 22d inst., in Dublin, the lady of Colonel J. Bloomfield Gough, of a son.

No. 5335 :: Ref. 1851-12-27, 2:5, M.
On the 22d inst., in Belfast, Mr. Patrick Coleman, spirit merchant, to Eliza Jane, eldest daughter of the late John Allen, Esq., Kilcarron, county Armagh.

No. 5336 :: Ref. 1851-12-27, 2:5, M.
On the 17th inst., at No. 4, Minor-place, Edinburgh, Samuel Wright Knox, of Coleraine, Esq., to Elizabeth, eldest daughter of the late Wm. Gordon Mack, Esq., Glasgow.

No. 5337 :: Ref. 1851-12-27, 2:5, M.
At Thorald, Canada West, Frederick F. Ball, Esq., to Eliza, only daughter of the late George L. Johnstone, Esq., of Lesize-house, in the county Down.

No. 5338 :: Ref. 1851-12-27, 2:5, M.
On the 18th inst., by the Rev. John R. M'Alister, in the First Presbyterian Church, in this city, Wm. Carroll, jun., of Drumadd, to Mary Ann, daughter of the late Samuel Lewers, Esq.

No. 5339 :: Ref. 1851-12-27, 2:5, D.
On his passage home from Hong Kong to Singapore, Mr. Chas. Coffey, surgeon of her Majesty's ship *Pilot*, son of the late Dr. Coffey, of Belfast.

No. 5340 :: Ref. 1851-12-27, 2:5, D.
On the 18th inst., at Warrenpoint, after a tedious illness, Richard Hale, aged 40, son of the late Mr. Francis Hale, of Banbridge.

No. 5341 :: Ref. 1851-12-27, 2:5, D.
On the 20th inst., in Eaton-square, Sir Bruce Chichester, Bart., of Arlington-court, Devon, aged 57.

No. 5342 :: Ref. 1851-12-27, 2:5, D.
At Abbey-yard in Newry, on the 21st inst., Zara, second daughter of the late Isaac Corry, sen.

No. 5343 :: Ref. 1851-12-27, 2:5, D.
On the 21st inst., at Anahoe House, aged 74, Letitia, the beloved wife of Henry Crossle, Esq.

No. 5344 :: Ref. 1851-12-27, 2:5, D.
On the 16th inst., in the 34th year of his age, and tenth of his ministry, the Rev. Abraham Liggat, of Ballygilbert.

No. 5345 :: Ref. 1851-12-27, 2:5, D.
On the 18th inst., at Kescum, in the 32d year of her age, Anne, wife of the Rev. James Rogers, of Glascar.

No. 5346 :: Ref. 1851-12-27, 2:5, D.
On the 15th October, of a wound received in action with the Caffres, near Waterkloof, Lieutenant R.P. Norris, of the 6th Royal Regiment, eldest son of the Rev. D.G. Norris, of the Vicarage, Kensingham, Suffolk.

No. 5347 :: Ref. 1852-01-03, 2:6, B.
At Bar, Parsonage, Fintona, on Monday, 22d ult., the lady of the Rev. John C. Hudson, of a son.

No. 5348 :: Ref. 1852-01-03, 2:6, M.
Jan. 1, in the First Presbyterian Church, Armagh, by the Rev. Mr. Carson, Mr. Robert Temple, of this city, to Matilda, second daughter of the late Mr. Wm. M'Cullough, of this city.

No. 5349 :: Ref. 1852-01-03, 2:6, D.
On 28th ult., at Enniskillen, Mr. Nathaniel Bradford, watchmaker.

No. 5350 :: Ref. 1852-01-03, 2:6, D.
At Ballyshannon, Mrs. Cockburn, relict of the late Mr. Cockburn, hotel keeper.

No. 5351 :: Ref. 1852-01-03, 2:6, D.
In Cavan, on the 26th ult., Mr. Thomas Hinds, victualler and chandler, aged 53.

No. 5352 :: Ref. 1852-01-03, 2:6, D.
At Newry, Robert Thompson, Esq., brother of Mrs. Sterne, of Gola Castle.

No. 5353 :: Ref. 1852-01-10, 2:6, B.
At Tartaraghan glebe, on Wednesday, the 7th inst., the lady of the Rev. G. Robinson, of twins—a boy and a girl.

No. 5354 :: Ref. 1852-01-10, 2:6, B.
Dec. 27, at Eyrecourt castle, the lady of John Eyre, jun., Esq, of a son.

No. 5355 :: Ref. 1852-01-10, 2:6, B.
Dec. 28, at Enniskillen, the lady of Major Kelly, 31st regt, of a daughter.

No. 5356 :: Ref. 1852-01-10, 2:6, B.
Dec. 29, at Dundalk, of fever, the Rev James Beatty, Presbyterian minister.

No. 5357 :: Ref. 1852-01-10, 2:6, B.
Jan 3, the lady of the Rev Benjamin Wade, Victoria-terrace, Armagh, of a daughter.

No. 5358 :: Ref. 1852-01-10, 2:6, B.
Jan 3, the lady of Robert W Newton, Esq, Gorton House, Dungannon, of a daughter.

No. 5359 :: Ref. 1852-01-10, 2:6, B.
Jan 4, at Sligo, the lady of James Walker, Esq, solicitor, of a son.

No. 5360 :: Ref. 1852-01-10, 2:6, M.
Dec 26, at New Shoreham, Sussex, Edward R. Disney, A.M., T.C.D., Kilkenny, to Mary Emma, eldest daughter of the late Rear-Admiral Ryves, of Shroton House, Dorsetshire.

No. 5361 :: Ref. 1852-01-10, 2:6, D.
Dec 7, in New York, John, third son of James Buchanan, of Fintona, Esq., aged 23 years.

No. 5362 :: Ref. 1852-01-10, 2:6, D.
Jan 1, at Pleasant Ville, Rathgar, Robert Prescott, late secretary, Dundalk and Enniskillen railway company.

No. 5363 :: Ref. 1852-01-10, 2:6, D.
Jan 1, at Lurgan, Henry, son of the late Mr. John Nettleton, of that town.

No. 5364 :: Ref. 1852-01-10, 2:6, D.
Jan 6, at the Bush, Killyman, near Dungannon, Susan, relict, of the late Lieutenant Alexander M'Clean, in the sixty-ninth year of her age.

No. 5365 :: Ref. 1852-01-17, 2:6, M.
Dec. 13, in Benmore church, Mr. Wm. H. Robinson, Lisnaskea, to Margaret, eldest daughter to Mr. James Robinson, Cosbystown.

No. 5366 :: Ref. 1852-01-17, 2:6, M.
Dec. 14, at Rossorry church, Mr. Thomas Elliott, Blacklion, to Mary Anne, daughter of the late John Gamble, Esq., of Lenaghan.

No. 5367 :: Ref. 1852-01-17, 2:6, M.
At Armagh, on the 14th inst., by the Rev. Dr. Rogers, Miss Carpenter, daughter of the late William Carpenter, Esq., Dobbin-street, to James Moore, Esq., Customs, Belfast.

No. 5368 :: Ref. 1852-01-17, 2:6, D.
Sep. 10, at Hollydaysburgh, Pennsylvania, America, Mr. George Mulholland, youngest and only son of George Mulholland, Esq., formerly of Tullyconnaught, co. Down.

No. 5369 :: Ref. 1852-01-17, 2:6, D.
Jan. 2, Sophia, wife of Vesey Daly, Esq., clerk crown, co. Fermanagh.

No. 5370 :: Ref. 1852-01-17, 2:6, D.
Jan. 3, at Dungannon, Mr Hugh Adams.

No. 5371 :: Ref. 1852-01-17, 2:6, D.
Jan. 4, aged 3 months, John Robert, the infant son of Mr. Robert Graham of Cootehill.

No. 5372 :: Ref. 1852-01-17, 2:6, D.
Jan. 5, Dublin, Mr. Francis Ball, aged 32 years.

No. 5373 :: Ref. 1852-01-17, 2:6, D.
Jan. 7, Mr. John Shaw M'Mullan, of Clogher, aged 29 years.

No. 5374 :: Ref. 1852-01-17, 2:6, D.
Jan. 8, in Armagh, Mr. John Henry, aged 62 years.

No. 5375 :: Ref. 1852-01-17, 2:6, D.
Jan. 9, Stewart Whittaker, Esq., for many years stamp distributor for the counties of Fermanagh and Cavan.

No. 5376 :: Ref. 1852-01-17, 2:6, D.
Jan. 10, Mr. Wilson of Derryhillagh.

No. 5377 :: Ref. 1852-01-17, 2:6, D.
Jan. 12, Mr. Thomas Stevenson, in Enniskillen at the advanced age of 102 years.

No. 5378 :: Ref. 1852-01-17, 2:6, D.
Jan. 8, the Rev. Michael Minnitt Raynes, vicar of Newton-on-Trent, aged 50 years.

No. 5379 :: Ref. 1852-01-17, 2:6, D.
Jan. 16, in this city after an illness of a few days, Sergt. Major Nevill of the local force here, aged 57 years—For many of which he was an inhabitant of this city, and was highly respected in his calling. His remains will be interred in St. Marks church burying ground this day at 4 o'clock, p.m., attended by Major Farmer and the local force.

No. 5380 :: Ref. 1852-01-24, 3:1, M.
Jan. 19, in the Glen Chapel, by the Rev. John M'Donnell, P.P., Donaghmore, Marc Antony Savage, Esq., surgeon, of this city, to Mary, second daughter of the late Bernard Rice, Esq., of Derrycraw, near Newry.

No. 5381 :: Ref. 1852-01-24, 3:1, D.
Jan. 1, in Brooklyn, New York, of consumption, Mr. James Johnston, aged 22 years and 8 months, son of Matthew Johnston, Middletown, county Armagh, Ireland.

No. 5382 :: Ref. 1852-01-24, 3:1, D.
Jan. 7, at Storm-hill, co. Armagh, after a short but most painful illness, borne with christian resignation, Abraham Kidd, Esq. He died in perfect peace.

No. 5383 :: Ref. 1852-01-24, 3:1, D.
Jan. 9, at Cootehill, Elizabeth, wife to Charles M'Dermott, solicitor, aged 75 years. Mrs. M'Dermott was mother-in-law to the late Captain Jasan Hassard, of Bawnboy, and aunt to Charles M'Mahon, of Carrickmacross, co. Monaghan, solicitor.

No. 5384 :: Ref. 1852-01-24, 3:1, D.
Jan. 13, at the residence of her brother, Dr. Osborne, Castletown Lodge, Fintona, Isabella Osborne, aged seventy years.

No. 5385 :: Ref. 1852-01-24, 3:1, D.
At Moat, the residence of her son-in-law, Thomas Edwards, Esq., Mary, relict of the late William Reynolds, Esq., of Feduff, in the county Armagh, in the seventy-third year of her age.

No. 5386 :: Ref. 1852-01-24, 3:1, D.
Jan. 14, at Carlton-villas, James Marshall, Esq., late Secretary of the Provincial Bank of Ireland.

No. 5387 :: Ref. 1852-01-24, 3:1, D.
Jan. 20, at Belfast, Mr. Edward Hennesey, Principal Accountant in the Ulster Bank since its commencement.

No. 5388 :: Ref. 1852-01-24, 3:1, D.
In Thomas-street, in this city, on Thursday, Mr. Arthur Conry, grocer and chandler.

No. 5389 :: Ref. 1852-01-24, 3:1, D.
Jan. 8, the Rev. Michael Minnet Raynes, vicar of Newton-on-Trent, aged 80 years.

No. 5390 :: Ref. 1852-01-31, 3:1, B.
Jan. 20, in Thomas-street, Armagh, Mrs. Samuel Magowan, of a son.

No. 5391 :: Ref. 1852-01-31, 3:1, B.
Jan. 23, at the *Coleraine Chronicle* Office, Mrs. Huey, of a son.

No. 5392 :: Ref. 1852-01-31, 3:1, B.
Jan. 25, at Chelsea, London, the lady of Wm. Stitt, Esq., of a son.

No. 5393 :: Ref. 1852-01-31, 3:1, B.
Jan. 26, in Enniskillen, the wife of Dr. Wm. Ovenden, of a son.

No. 5394 :: Ref. 1852-01-31, 3:1, M.
Jan. 27, at Kilskery Church, by Rev. J.G. Porter, father of the bride, Nicholas Montgomery Archdall, Esq., fifth son of Edward Archdall, Esq., of Riversdale, to Adelaide Mary Jane, the lovely and accomplished daughter of Rev. J.G. Porter, Kilskery and Belleisle, county Fermanagh.

No. 5395 :: Ref. 1852-01-31, 3:1, D.
Jan. 20, at Stephen-street, Sligo, after a short illness, Anthony C. Sidley, in his 60th year.

No. 5396 :: Ref. 1852-01-31, 3:1, D.
Jan. 21, at 2, Adelaide-road, Dublin, Thomas Bell, Esq., after a short illness (arising from an accident). He was for many years superintendent of the cancel note office in the Bank of Ireland.

No. 5397 :: Ref. 1852-01-31, 3:1, D.
At Cavan, near Ballinamallard, Mr. Christopher Irvine, aged 73 years, 52 of which he was a Wesleyan Class Leader.

No. 5398 :: Ref. 1852-02-07, 2:4, B.
On 4th inst., at Lurgan, the wife of John Hancock, Esq., J.P., of a daughter.

No. 5399 :: Ref. 1852-02-07, 2:4, M.
Feb. 4, in Lisbellaw church, by Rev. Walter Young, James Brackin, Esq., of Tome, Black Lion, Co. Cavan, to Rebecca, daughter of Archibald Collum, Esq., Tullyharney, Lisbellaw.

No. 5400 :: Ref. 1852-02-07, 2:4, M.
On the 18th of July, by the Rev. John Watt, Wm. George, fourth son of Richard Blackham, Esq., of Adelaide, South Australia, to Anna Maria, eldest daughter of the late Wm. Blackham, Esq., of Newry, Ireland.

No. 5401 :: Ref. 1852-02-07, 2:4, M.
Feb. 1, by the Rev. John West, in the first Presbyterian Meeting House, Newtownhamilton, John, eldest son of Mr. William Maclean, Merchant, to Mary, second daughter to Mr. M. Shaw, both of Newtownhamilton.

No. 5402 :: Ref. 1852-02-07, 2:4, D.
Feb. 1, at his residence, Bellamont Forest, Cootehill, Richard Coote, Esq., aged 49 years, deeply regretted.

No. 5403 :: Ref. 1852-02-07, 2:4, D.
Jan. 28, at his residence, Newcastle, co. Mayo, after a prolonged illness, Captain Andrew C. O'Malley, the last surviving brother of the late gallant Major-General George O'Malley, and of Major Owen O'Malley.

No. 5404 :: Ref. 1852-02-07, 2:4, D.
Jan. 25, at No. 19, Talbot-street, Dublin, Margaret, the beloved wife of Thomas Moore, Esq., aged 36 years.

No. 5405 :: Ref. 1852-02-07, 2:4, D.
Feb. 2, at Ramoan Rectory, in her 81st year, Jane, relict of the late venerable Thomas B. Monsell, Archdeacon of Derry, and Precentor of Christ Church.

No. 5406 :: Ref. 1852-02-07, 2:4, D.
Jan. 3, at the advanced age of 91, Mr. Arthur Fegan, who has been a resident of this city for the last 60 years.

No. 5407 :: Ref. 1852-02-14, 3:1, B.
Feb. 11, at 47, Grafton-street, Dublin, the wife of George Addey, of a son.

No. 5408 :: Ref. 1852-02-14, 3:1, M.
On Monday the 9th in St. Patrick's Chapel, by the Rev. Mr. Rodgers, Mr. R. Feeney, of Dungannon, to Mary Anne, eldest daughter of Mr. Patrick Devlin of this city.

No. 5409 :: Ref. 1852-02-14, 3:1, D.
In Armagh, on the 11th inst., in the 30th year of her age, Mary, daughter of Patrick Hughes, Esq., Victoria Hotel, and relict of Mr. Hugh Fitzpatrick, merchant, formerly of this city.

No. 5410 :: Ref. 1852-02-14, 3:1, D.
Feb. 2, at his residence, Rathrowel, Dundalk, the Rev. Richard Woods, Rector of Derver, county of Louth, diocese of Armagh. Upright and honourable in life, his death will be sincerely regretted.

No. 5411 :: Ref. 1852-02-14, 3:1, D.
At San Francisco, Dec. 5, of disease of the lungs, Thomas Kernaghan, Esq., jun., formerly of Enniskillen, county Fermanagh.

No. 5412 :: Ref. 1852-02-21, 3:1, B.
Feb. 12, at Woodford Cottage, Armagh, the lady of John Cuming, Esq., of a son.

No. 5413 :: Ref. 1852-02-21, 3:1, B.
Feb. 14, Mrs. Hughes, wife of Mr. George D. Hughes, Vicars'-hill, Armagh, of a daughter.

No. 5414 :: Ref. 1852-02-21, 3:1, B.
Feb. 16, in Enniskillen, the lady of George A. Nixon, Esq., M.D., of a son.

No. 5415 :: Ref. 1852-02-21, 3:1, B.
Feb. 18, at Upper Gloucester-street, Dublin, the wife of Charles Stanley, Esq., of Roughan House, co. Tyrone, of a daughter.

No. 5416 :: Ref. 1852-02-21, 3:1, M.
Feb. 15, in Armagh, by Rev. Mr. Rodgers, P.P., Mr. Peter M'Shane, Victualler, to Sarah, daughter of Mr. Laurence Sherry, Pawnbroker, Ogle-street.

No. 5417 :: Ref. 1852-02-21, 3:1, M.
Feb. 19, in Armagh, by Rev. Mr. Rodgers, P.P., Mr. Hans Moncks, clerk to Mr. Samuel Morrow, Victualler, Armagh, to Mary, daughter of the late Mr. Thomas Mullen, of Blackwatertown. (This was nearly being one of those cases of disappointment which illustrate the truth of the adage "*the course of true love seldom runs smoot*h." The groom had drawn £1, for nuptial expenses, when meeting with a friend they sat down to moisten their affections, leaving the bride a long time in suspense for the performance of the marriage ceremony. Meantime, the cash was gone, and the groom's friend having been placed in "durance" on suspicion, the ceremony was got on with as if no mishap had occurred.)

No. 5418 :: Ref. 1852-02-21, 3:1, D.
Feb. 2, Elizabeth, wife of William Moore, of Molenan, co. Derry, Esq., and daughter of the late Samuel Maxwell of Armagh, Esq.

No. 5419 :: Ref. 1852-02-21, 3:1, D.
Dec. 12, at Lahore, in the Punjaub, aged 26 years, Edward Oliver Barker, Lieutenant H.M. 96th Regt., fourth son of Richard Barker, Esq., of Gardiners-row, Dublin.

No. 5420 :: Ref. 1852-02-21, 3:1, D.
Feb. 3, John M'Waters, Esq., of Rasharkin, near Ballymena, at the advanced age of 81.

No. 5421 :: Ref. 1852-02-21, 3:1, D.
Feb. 5, at Burt, Derry, Alexander Leathem Esq., in the 77th year of his age.

No. 5422 :: Ref. 1852-02-21, 3:1, D.
Feb. 10, at Paris, aged 18, Lieut. St. John Maxwell Blacker, 21st Fusileers, eldest son of the late Lieut. Colonel St. John Blacker.

No. 5423 :: Ref. 1852-02-21, 3:1, D.
Feb. 12, [a]t Doon, near Tempo, John Bell, Esq., Solicitor, aged 44.

No. 5424 :: Ref. 1852-02-21, 3:1, D.
Feb. 4, Robert Blackwood, Esq., of the firm of Messrs. Blackwood and Sons, the eminent publishers of Edinburgh.

No. 5425 :: Ref. 1852-02-21, 3:1, D.
Feb. 15, in Newry, Mr. Arthur Maphett, in his 75th year, during 38 of which he was book-keeper in the *Telegraph* establishment.

No. 5426 :: Ref. 1852-02-21, 3:1, D.
Feb. 15, in Enniskillen, Mr. Thomas Gallogly, aged 76 years.

No. 5427 :: Ref. 1852-02-28, 3:2, B.
Feb. 17, at Rock-view, co. Cavan, the lady of the Rev. Baptist B. Crozier, of a daughter.

No. 5428 :: Ref. 1852-02-28, 3:2, B.
Feb. 22, the wife of Mr. William Quinton, Enniskillen, of a daughter.

No. 5429 :: Ref. 1852-02-28, 3:2, B.
Feb. 26, in English-street, Mrs. M'Nally of a daughter.

No. 5430 :: Ref. 1852-02-28, 3:2, B.
Feb. 17 the wife of Mr. Thomas M'Alister, Cookstown, of a daughter.

No. 5431 :: Ref. 1852-02-28, 3:2, M.
Dec. 30, at St. Paul's Cathedral, Calcutta, Rev. Geo. G. Cuthbert, Secretary to the Calcutta Committee of the Church Missionary Society, to Eliza, eldest daughter of the late George Cuppadge, Esq., of Galway.

No. 5432 :: Ref. 1852-02-28, 3:2, M.
Jan. 26, at Lisburn, Mr. John M'Creary, of Edentrillie, to Mary, relict of the late Mr. Asa Archer, of Backnamulough. The charming bride is in her 77th year, while her successful lover is just 23.

No. 5433 :: Ref. 1852-02-28, 3:2, M.
Feb. 5, at Boston, Otto Goldshmidt, the pianist, of Hamburg, to Maddle. Jenny Lind, of Stockholm, Sweden.

No. 5434 :: Ref. 1852-02-28, 3:2, M.
Feb. 7, at Holywood by Rev. R. Oulton, Mr. Henry Douglas, of Leeds, to Sarah, youngest daughter of the late James Shaw, Esq., Dublin.

No. 5435 :: Ref. 1852-02-28, 3:2, M.
Feb. 19, in Horetown Church, by Rev. J.C. Martin, D.D., uncle of the bride, the Rev. Gerald Fitzgerald, Incumbent of Bantry, Co. Tyrone, to Mary, eldest daughter of David Beatty, Esq., Raheenduff, County Wexford.

No. 5436 :: Ref. 1852-02-28, 3:2, M.
Feb. 19, at Riverstown, Christopher L'Estrange, Esq., of Somertown, co. Sligo, to Charlote [sic] Anne, youngest daughter of A.B. Cooper, Esq., Cooper's-hill.

No. 5437 :: Ref. 1852-02-28, 3:2, M.
Feb. 22, by Rev. Hugh Mulligan, Mr. Thomas Marron, mercht., Newry, to Rose, second daughter of Mr. John M'Cormick, of Forkhill.

No. 5438 :: Ref. 1852-02-28, 3:2, M.
Feb. 24, in the New Church of Magheralin, near Lurgan, Charles Pelling, Esq., Belfast, to Sarah, youngest daughter of the late Thomas Richardson, Esq., of Dublin.

No. 5439 :: Ref. 1852-02-28, 3:2, M.

Feb. 24, in Delgany Church, by the Hon. and Rev. Charles Maude, the Rev. James Godley, of Ashfield, co. Cavan, to Eliza Frances, fourth daughter of the late Peter La Touche, Esq., of Belview.

No. 5440 :: Ref. 1852-02-28, 3:2, M.

Feb. 24, John Hamilton, Esq., of Braehead, Lanarkshire, and Worsley, Lancashire, to Barbara Elizabeth, eldest daughter of the late Hubert Kelly Waldron, Esq., of Ashfort House, co. Roscommon.

No. 5441 :: Ref. 1852-02-28, 3:2, M.

Feb. 12, James M'Whinny, Esq., Lakeview, Castledawson, to Isabella Jane Charles, eldest daughter of W. Charles, Esq., Cookstown.

No. 5442 :: Ref. 1852-02-28, 3:2, D.

In New York, Feb. 9, Andrew Bracken, aged 84 years, native of the county Longford, parish of Edgeworthstown.

No. 5443 :: Ref. 1852-02-28, 3:2, D.

Feb. 9, at Donahendry Rectory, co. Tyrone, Margaretta, second daughter of the Rev. J. Gerahty.

No. 5444 :: Ref. 1852-02-28, 3:2, D.

Feb. 10, Miss Georgiana Bingham, of disease of the chest. She was cut off in the bloom of her youth, and after three years' painful suffering, she perfectly reconciled [sic], resigned her spirit to Him who gave it, convinced that one hour in Heaven would more than compensate for all her sufferings. Miss Bingham, was the only surviving daughter of Mr. G.E. Bingham, of this city, and of the House of Castlebar, in the co. Mayo.

No. 5445 :: Ref. 1852-02-28, 3:2, D.

Feb. 12, at Knockinkerragh, near Coleraine, Susan Black, in her 100th year of her age.

No. 5446 :: Ref. 1852-02-28, 3:2, D.

Feb. 13, at Rosebrooke, Carrickfergus, the Rev. John Gwynn, aged eighty-nine years, in the sixty-eighth year of his Ministry, and the fifty-second of his incumbency, as Prebendary of Kilroot, and Rector of Ballynure.

No. 5447 :: Ref. 1852-02-28, 3:2, D.

Feb. 13, at Beachmount, co. Tyrone, John Joyce, Esq., Clerk of the Crown for Donegal.

No. 5448 :: Ref. 1852-02-28, 3:2, D.

Feb. 15, Mr. John Scott, of Omagh, very generally and deservedly regretted.

No. 5449 :: Ref. 1852-02-28, 3:2, D.

Feb. 15, Mr. Robert Cochran, Postmaster of Gilford, aged 53 years.

No. 5450 :: Ref. 1852-02-28, 3:2, D.

Feb. 17, in London, William Thompson, Esq., President of the Belfast Natural History and Philosophical Society, in the 45th year of his age.

No. 5451 :: Ref. 1852-02-28, 3:2, D.

Feb. 18, at Edinburgh, the Rev. Christopher Anderson, aged 70 years. Mr. Anderson was long distinguished as an eminent minister, and his "*Historical Sketches of the Native Irish*" is a standard book.

No. 5452 :: Ref. 1852-02-28, 3:2, D.

Feb. 19, Cecilia Mary, the infant daughter of James Johnston, Esq., of Maghermena.

No. 5453 :: Ref. 1852-02-28, 3:2, D.

Feb. 20, in Enniskillen, of dropsy, Mr. John Kelso, aged 56 years.

No. 5454 :: Ref. 1852-02-28, 3:2, D.

Feb. 20, the lady of R.M. Miller, Esq., R.M., Portadown.

No. 5455 :: Ref. 1852-02-28, 3:2, D.

Feb. 20, the Right Hon. Sir Herbert Jenner Fust, in the 75th year of his age.

No. 5456 :: Ref. 1852-02-28, 3:2, D.

Lately, at Prague, aged 100, Kurleander, the oldest of pianists, and, no doubt, of all musicians.

No. 5457 :: Ref. 1852-02-28, 3:2, D.

Feb. 26, in this city, the Rev. Eugene Troy, C.C., for the last five years. He had officiated in the chapel the day previous, and altho' latterly in a delicate state of health his demise was sudden and unexpected. In general he was esteemed by the inhabitants of this city, as an unobtrusive man, faithfully discharging what he believed his religious duties.

No. 5458 :: Ref. 1852-03-06, 2:6, M.

Feb. 26, by Rev. Richard Wrightson, Mr. William Rolston, of Aughanlig, near Moy, to Mary Anne, eldest daughter of Mr. Samuel Corrigan, of Derryscollop.

No. 5459 :: Ref. 1852-03-06, 2:6, D.

Jan. 4, at San Francisco, Mr. Hugh Kelly, aged 35, native of Ireland.

No. 5460 :: Ref. 1852-03-06, 2:6, D.

Feb. 11, at Mullaletragh, near Richhill, Mr. Jacob Bell, aged 71 years.

No. 5461 :: Ref. 1852-03-06, 2:6, D.

Feb. 20, in Tullyharm, co. Tyrone, at the advanced age of 92 years, Mr. Hugh Young.

No. 5462 :: Ref. 1852-03-06, 2:6, D.

Feb. 22, at Bunbury Lodge, Carlow, Thomas Charles Bunbury, Esq.

No. 5463 :: Ref. 1852-03-06, 2:6, D.

Feb. 24, Jane, relict of Mr. Joseph Shillington of Crew Bridge, aged 63 years.

No. 5464 :: Ref. 1852-03-06, 2:6, D.

Feb. 24, at Castleblaney, Anne, relict of the late Wm. Hamilton, Esq.

No. 5465 :: Ref. 1852-03-06, 2:6, D.
Feb. 25, William Pringle, Esq., of Glasslough, in the seventy-fourth year of his age.

No. 5466 :: Ref. 1852-03-06, 2:6, D.
Feb. 26, of scarlatina, in the 6th year of his age, John, eldest son of John Hancock, Esq., J.P., Lurgan.

No. 5467 :: Ref. 1852-03-06, 2:6, D.
Feb. 27, at Hardwicke-street, Elizabeth relict of the late Major James Palmer, formerly Inspector-General of Prisons in Ireland.

No. 5468 :: Ref. 1852-03-06, 2:6, D.
Feb. 28, aged sixty-five years, Margaret wife of Abraham Denroche, Esq., proprietor of the *Kilkenny Moderator*.

No. 5469 :: Ref. 1852-03-06, 2:6, D.
Feb. 20, at 41, Lower Mount-street, Dublin, Sarah, second daughter of Mr. William Armstrong, of Brookboro', aged 24 years. She died rejoicing in God her Saviour.

No. 5470 :: Ref. 1852-03-06, 2:6, D.
Feb. 20, Mr. John Fleming, Land Surveyor, Monaghan.

No. 5471 :: Ref. 1852-03-06, 2:6, D.
Feb. 20, of inflammation of the chest, at the Manse, Abbey-street, John Alexander, son of the late Rev. Alex. Fleming, aged 13 months.

No. 5472 :: Ref. 1852-03-06, 2:6, D.
March 1, at Glengall-street, Belfast, the Rev. Thomas Ridgway, in his 95th year.

No. 5473 :: Ref. 1852-03-06, 2:6, D.
March 4, Mr. John James Williams, of Church-square, Monaghan, aged 18 years.

No. 5474 :: Ref. 1852-03-13, 3:3, B.
Feb. 28, the wife of Blayney Leslie, Esq., of Nutfield, Lisnaskea, of a son.

No. 5475 :: Ref. 1852-03-13, 3:3, B.
March 4, at Donaghmore, co. Tyrone, the wife of Thos. Hamilton, Esq., of a son.

No. 5476 :: Ref. 1852-03-13, 3:3, B.
March 6, at the Palace, Cashel, the lady of the Rev. Newport B. White, of a daughter.

No. 5477 :: Ref. 1852-03-13, 3:3, B.
March 8, at Armagh, the wife of Captain Cary, 31st Regt., of a daughter.

No. 5478 :: Ref. 1852-03-13, 3:3, B.
March 9, the wife of Mr. Wm. R. Armstrong, [I]mperial Hotel, Enniskillen, of a son.

No. 5479 :: Ref. 1852-03-13, 3:3, B.
March 10, at Armagh, the lady of John Stanley, Esq., of a son.

No. 5480 :: Ref. 1852-03-13, 3:3, M.
March 12, in Clones Church, by the Rev. Thomas Hand, Rector, George Glass, Esq., Templemore, co. Tipperary, to Marianne, eldest daughter of Mr. James Courtney, Clones, county Monaghan.

No. 5481 :: Ref. 1852-03-13, 3:3, D.
Feb. 24, of paralysis, aged 66 years, Mr. James Ellis, of Croughrim, near Florencecourt.

No. 5482 :: Ref. 1852-03-13, 3:3, D.
Feb. 24, at 18, Windsor Grove, Old Kent Road, London, Henry Atkinson, formerly of Brookfield, Moy, and eldest son of the late Henry Atkinson, Ballyreagh-house, co. Armagh.

No. 5483 :: Ref. 1852-03-13, 3:3, D.
March 2, at Birkenhead, William, eldest son of the late Rev. William Smith, rector, of Ballycloy, co. Tyrone.

No. 5484 :: Ref. 1852-03-13, 3:3, D.
March 2, aged 64 years, at Booterstown-avenue, John Barry, Esq., for many years an officer of the Bank of Ireland.

No. 5485 :: Ref. 1852-03-13, 3:3, D.
March 4, at Prospect, Belfast, Letitia, eldest daughter of James Bristow, Esq.

No. 5486 :: Ref. 1852-03-13, 3:3, D.
March 5, at Cavan, Eliza, wife of Bernard Coyne, Esq. M.D.

No. 5487 :: Ref. 1852-03-13, 3:3, D.
March 7, in the nineteenth year of her age, Jane, third daughter of the late Mr. John Cargill, of Mulladuff, near Glasslough, co. Monaghan.

No. 5488 :: Ref. 1852-03-13, 3:3, D.
March 11, at Armagh, in giving birth to still born twins, Mary Jane, wife of Mr. John Armstrong, first turnkey in our county prison.

No. 5489 :: Ref. 1852-03-20, 8:5, B.
March 19, at the Mall, the lady of Major Parmer, Staff Officer, of a daughter.

No. 5490 :: Ref. 1852-03-20, 8:5, B.
On Patrick's Day, Mrs. Hughes, Charlemont Arms Hotel, Armagh, of a son.

No. 5491 :: Ref. 1852-03-20, 8:5, B.
Mar. 12, at Parkhurst, Isle of Wight, the wife of Major King, 36th Regiment, of a son.

No. 5492 :: Ref. 1852-03-20, 8:5, M.
Jan. 13, at Calcutta, by Rev. J. Gawen, M.A., Robert, son of Major Doran, late of the 18th Royal Irish, to Mary Rebecca, daughter of the late Thomas Bracken, Esq., of Belcamp, St. Paul's, Essex.

No. 5493 :: Ref. 1852-03-20, 8:5, M.
Mar. 2, in Belmullet, by Rev. Daniel Foley, Erris, Rev. Thomas W. Baker, Wesleyen [sic] Missionary,

Erris, to Anne, eldest daughter of Samuel Bourns, Esq., of Rossport House, Erris, co. Mayo.

No. 5494 :: Ref. 1852-03-20, 8:5, M.

Mar. 3, at Cabry Church, by Rev. Doctor Gilmore, Abraham Dobbin, Esq., merchant, Sligo, to Magdalene, eldest daughter of the late Jerrald Irvine, Esq., merchant, Strabane.

No. 5495 :: Ref. 1852-03-20, 8:5, M.

Mar. 11, in the First Presbyterian Church, at Markethill, by Rev. A.G. Ross, brother-in-law, to the bride, John Cornier, eldest son of the late Robert S.W. M'Clure, Esq., of Lisburn, to Jane, fourth daughter of Daniel M'Clure, Esq., of Millmount, Markethill.

No. 5496 :: Ref. 1852-03-20, 8:5, M.

Mar. 11, at Kilcullen Church, by Rev. William N. Sherrard, Mr. Thomas Elliot, son of John Elliott, Esq., of Marlbank, near Enniskillen, to Jane Turner, youngest daughter of the late Matthew Turner, Esq., of Miltown, co. Wicklow.

No. 5497 :: Ref. 1852-03-20, 8:5, M.

Mar. 12, at Clones Church, by Rev. Thomas Hand, Rector, George Glass, Esq., Templemore, co. Tipperary, to Marianne, eldest daughter of James Courtney, Esq., Clones, co. Monaghan.

No. 5498 :: Ref. 1852-03-20, 8:5, M.

In Knappa Meeting House, by the Rev. David Coote, Mr. Hugh Garmony, of Nall, near Killylea, to Eleanor, only daughter of Mr. Alexander Menary, of Cavan, Belaghyl, both of co. Armagh.

No. 5499 :: Ref. 1852-03-20, 8:5, M.

Dec. 29, at Gwalior, Lieut. William Boyd Irwin, Adjutant, Grenadier Regiment, Scinde Contingency, son of the late James Irwin, Esq., Wellbrook, co. Tyrone, to Mary Eliza, only daughter of Captain J. Hennesey, commanding 1st Grenadier Regiment, S.C.

No. 5500 :: Ref. 1852-03-20, 8:5, D.

Mar. 7, in the 19th year of her age, Jane, third daughter of the late Mr. John Cargill, Mulladuff, near Glasslough, co. Monaghan.

No. 5501 :: Ref. 1852-03-20, 8:5, D.

Mar. 9, at Coleman's Hotel, Portrush, suddenly, Caroline, the beloved wife of Charles Knight, Esq., M.D. She breadfasted [sic] in her usual health, and in less than an hour after had passed from time to eternity.

No. 5502 :: Ref. 1852-03-20, 8:5, D.

Mar. 13, at Hockley, near Charlemont, co. Armagh, L.H. Dobbin, Esq., late Captain 1st or Royal Regiment, aged 71.

No. 5503 :: Ref. 1852-03-20, 8:5, D.

At Willymaddy, of Scarlatina, Thomas Henry, second son of Mr. John Frazer, aged 3 years and 3 months.

No. 5504 :: Ref. 1852-03-20, 8:5, D.

Mar. 18, Robert James, infant son of Mr. Robert Moore, of the firm of Messrs. Robert Moore and Co., Armagh.

No. 5505 :: Ref. 1852-03-27, 5:5, B.

At Cloonlurg Cottage, Ballymote, the lady of Andrew Green, Esq., of a daughter.

No. 5506 :: Ref. 1852-03-27, 5:5, B.

March 9, at Lurgan, Mrs. John Armstrong, of a daughter.

No. 5507 :: Ref. 1852-03-27, 5:5, B.

March 16, in Cavan, the lady of William Thompson, Esq., of the Ulster Bank, of a son.

No. 5508 :: Ref. 1852-03-27, 5:5, M.

March 19, in the Presbyterian Church Minterburn, by Rev. Alexander Gray, A.M., Mr. Joseph Marshall, to Miss Agnes Hopps, both of Minterburn.

No. 5509 :: Ref. 1852-03-27, 5:5, D.

March 18, in this City, after a few days' illness, Sarah Anne, the faithful, affectionate, and very dearly-beloved wife of the Rev. John C. M'Causland, (Incumbent of Killylea) and only daughter of the late Edwd. Elsmere Esq.;—leaving an attached husband, and six surviving children, to mourn for "a little while," ("*not as those who have no hope,*") their temporary separation from one of the best of wives and mothers. She "*sleeps in Jesus*," in whose merits and atonement was reposed all her confidence for Eternity; and "shall be satisfied, when she awakes with His likeness." "*Even, so, come, Lord Jesus!*"

No. 5510 :: Ref. 1852-03-27, 5:5, D.

March 20, in Dublin, aged seventy-two years, Elizabeth Maria St. Clair, youngest and last surviving daughter of the late Colonel Alexander Gordon, of Belview, co. Fermanagh, and Feltrim, co. Dublin, relict of William Stirling St. Clair, Esq., late Major, Co. Dublin Regiment of Militia, and J.P. for the counties of Wicklow and Dublin.

No. 5511 :: Ref. 1852-03-27, 5:5, D.

March 21 at Abbey-Street in this City, of bronchitis, Issabella Jane, third daughter of Mr. Charles B. Reynolds, aged 4 years.

No. 5512 :: Ref. 1852-03-27, 5:5, D.

March 21, in Belfast, Mr. John Small, aged 40 years.

No. 5513 :: Ref. 1852-04-03, 8:4, B.

Mar. 22, at Kircubbin, co. Down, the lady of the Rev. W.H. Brett, of a son.

No. 5514 :: Ref. 1852-04-03, 8:4, M.

March 25, in Ballymoney, Mr. Henry Rowan, mercht. Clones, to Catherine, daughter of Wm. M'Intyre, Esq.

No. 5515 :: Ref. 1852-04-03, 8:4, M.

March 30, in St. Thomas's Church, Dublin, by Rev. H.W. Young, Robert Crookshank, of Gardiner-street, Esq., Solicitor, son of the late Rev. C.H. Crookshank, Rector of Tyhollan, co. Monaghan, and grandson of the late Right Hon. Judge Crookshank, Newtown Park, co. Dublin, to Olivia Henrietta Agnes, daughter of the late Hunt Walsh Chambre, of Hawthorn Hill, co. Armagh, Esq.

No. 5516 :: Ref. 1852-04-03, 8:4, D.

Mar. 19, at Raphoe, Esther, relict of the late Rev. John Wilkinson, rector of Mevagh, co. Donegal.

No. 5517 :: Ref. 1852-04-03, 8:4, D.

Mar. 20, at Queenstown, in the nineteenth year of his age, Edward Owen, only son of James O'Callaghan, Esq., J.P., Dundalk.

No. 5518 :: Ref. 1852-04-03, 8:4, D.

Mar. 26, at Peter's Place, Dublin, aged 82 years, Miss Catherine Archdall, daughter of the late Col. Mervyn Archdall, of Castle Archdall, Fermanagh, M.P.

No. 5519 :: Ref. 1852-04-03, 8:4, D.

Mar. 27, at Newcastle, co. Down, aged 62, Henry Francis Atkinson, Esq., third son of the late Edward Atkinson, Esq., of Drumcree, co. Armagh.

No. 5520 :: Ref. 1852-04-03, 8:4, D.

Mar. 27, in Newry, Cornelius Denvir, Esq., aged 29 years.

No. 5521 :: Ref. 1852-04-03, 8:4, D.

Mar. 27, at Doon, near Tempo, Mr. William Little, aged 77 years.

No. 5522 :: Ref. 1852-04-03, 8:4, D.

Mar. 28, at Birmingham, the Lady Olivia Acheson.

No. 5523 :: Ref. 1852-04-03, 8:4, D.

Mar. 28, in Enniskillen, Mr. John Ferguson, Coach builder, aged 54 years.

No. 5524 :: Ref. 1852-04-03, 8:4, D.

In Enniskillen, at the advanced age of 93 years, Mrs. Anne Frith, relict of the late Mr. James Frith, of Derryinch.

No. 5525 :: Ref. 1852-04-03, 8:4, D.

— [sic], at Sweet Springs, on Friday, the 27th of Feb., Thomas J. Barnett, in the 28th year of [his] age. Mr. Barnett was a native of the Townland of Ballagh, Parish of Clogher, Co. of Tyrone, Ireland, and son of Thomas Barnett, Esq. He emigrated to this country (U.S.A.) in the spring of the year 1841, and resided for a few months after his arrival in or near Pittsburg Pa., whence he removed in the month of June to Fincastle Va., to except [sic] a situation offered to him by James McDowell, Esq.—with whom he lived as confidential clerk and salesman until January 1848, when Mr. McDowell ceased mercantile operations, and since that time, excepting the year 1850, Mr. Barnett has occupied the highly responsible position of chief manager of the Sweet Springs, discharging its onerous duties to the entire satisfaction of the Proprietors and all others interested. It can truly be said that no young gentleman has ever resided in Fincastle, who was more distinguished than Mr. Barnett for business talents, untiring devotion to the interests of his employer, for high and honourable conduct, and nobleness and generosity of soul. The writer of this humble testimony although unconnected with the deceased, is well informed that no young gentleman has ever left Ireland who had enjoyed in early life better advantages than he, and his fine education and pure and polished bearing when he first became an inhabitant of our village, was grateful evidence of his highly respectable parentage, and he preserved unsullied his noble character for truth, honesty, candour, disenterestedness [sic] and generosity. He has died universally lamented. He was interred on Sunday afternoon, the 20th inst., with regret and his remains were attended to the grave by one of the largest concourse of citizens that has been witnessed for many years.—The funeral services were performed, and his funeral sermon pronounced by Rev. Mr. McElroy.—*American paper*.

No. 5526 :: Ref. 1852-04-10, 8:5, B.

Mar. 27, at Glanmire, the lady of George Wade, Esq., S.I., of a daughter.

No. 5527 :: Ref. 1852-04-10, 8:5, B.

Mar. 30, at Roxboro, co. Armagh, Mrs. William Palmer, of a son.

No. 5528 :: Ref. 1852-04-10, 8:5, M.

Feb. 21, at Georgetown, District of Columbia, United States, Mr. J.T. Graham, Secretary, Baltimore, Emigrants' Friend Society, formerly of Maguiresbridge, to Rebecca H., daughter of David S. Campbell, Esq., Fairfax, Virginia.

No. 5529 :: Ref. 1852-04-10, 8:5, M.

Mar. 24, in Ballinode Church, by Rev. J.R. Young, Mr. Robert Spratt, Fivemiletown, to Elizabeth, third daughter of Mr. R. Wright, Ballinode Mills, Monaghan.

No. 5530 :: Ref. 1852-04-10, 8:5, M.

Mar. 25, at the Cathedral, Killaloe, Captain Charles Higginbotham, 63d Regiment, to Augusta Mary, eldest daughter of Charles P. Dawson, Esq., Inspector of Revenue Police.

No. 5531 :: Ref. 1852-04-10, 8:5, M.

Mar. 25, in Belfast, Walker Thomas G. Lindsay, Esq., of Belfast, to Catherine, second daughter of Cuthbert Hunter, Esq., Walker cottage, Newcastle-on-Tyne.

No. 5532 :: Ref. 1852-04-10, 8:5, M.
Mar. 31, in the Presbyterian Church, Lurgan, Mr. William Brown, Ulster Bank, Lurgan, to Jane Eliza, second daughter of the late Mr. Wm. Lockhart, of same place.

No. 5533 :: Ref. 1852-04-10, 8:5, M.
April 4, in St. Mary's Church, Z. Wallace, Esq., Cavan, to Miss N. Bourns, daughter of Matthew Bourns, Esq., M.D., Belmullet.

No. 5534 :: Ref. 1852-04-10, 8:5, D.
Mar. 14, at Cincinatti, Ohio, U.S., after a protracted illness, Mr. William James Laird, eldest son of Doctor Laird, of Ballybofey, co. Donegal.

No. 5535 :: Ref. 1852-04-10, 8:5, D.
Mar. 21, at Rockville, Ballyshannon, Charles O'Neill, Esq., formerly Captain in the 70th regiment.

No. 5536 :: Ref. 1852-04-10, 8:5, D.
Mar. 22, Simon, second son of the late Simon Shiel, Esq., M.D., of Portnassau, Ballyshannon.

No. 5537 :: Ref. 1852-04-10, 8:5, D.
Mar. 28, aged 52 years, Mr. James Greer, merchant, Newry.

No. 5538 :: Ref. 1852-04-10, 8:5, D.
Mar. 29, Mary, relict of the late James M'Creight, Esq., of Watkinshaw's Grove, co. Armagh, in the 88th year of her age.

No. 5539 :: Ref. 1852-04-10, 8:5, D.
On the first inst., at the house of his father at Glasmullagh, near Omagh, of consumption, Mr. Archibald Rodgers, aged 25 years.

No. 5540 :: Ref. 1852-04-10, 8:5, D.
April 2, at Keady, Mr. James Bradley, aged 68 years. He was one of the oldest merchants in this city, and is deservedly regretted by all who knew him.

No. 5541 :: Ref. 1852-04-10, 8:5, D.
April 4, at Belmont, Kilbeggan, John Thompson, Esq., late of Clara, King's County, aged 75 years.

No. 5542 :: Ref. 1852-04-10, 8:5, D.
At Derrylin, Mr. Archibald Gardiner, of paralysis, which resulted in fever, aged 45 years.

No. 5543 :: Ref. 1852-04-10, 8:5, D.
At Monbrief, near Lurgan, aged 45 years, Anne, the beloved wife of Alexander M'Laughlin.

No. 5544 :: Ref. 1852-04-17, 5:6, B.
At Higginstown House, Ballyshannon, the lady of Henry Coane, Esq. of a son.

No. 5545 :: Ref. 1852-04-17, 5:6, B.
At the Provincial Bank, Newry, April 10, Mrs. Wm. M'Cullough, of a daughter.

No. 5546 :: Ref. 1852-04-17, 5:6, B.
April 11, at 41, Dawson street, Dublin, the Hon. Mrs. F.R. Handcock, of a son.

No. 5547 :: Ref. 1852-04-17, 5:6, M.
April 3, in Newry, Samuel Glenny, Esq., of Liverpool, to Harriet, youngest daughter of the late John Maxwell, Esq., of Dundalk.

No. 5548 :: Ref. 1852-04-17, 5:6, M.
Mar. 16, at Boston, James, eldest son of the Hon. Abbot Lawrence, Minister at this Court, to Elizabeth, only daughter of the historian, W.H. Prescott, Esq.

No. 5549 :: Ref. 1852-04-17, 5:6, D.
April 5, Mr. James Jenkins of Altinamoichan, Co. Armagh in the 73d year of his age, after a tedious illness, which he bore with patience and resignation.

No. 5550 :: Ref. 1852-04-17, 5:6, D.
April 5, at Drumyarkin, near Cootehill, Mr. Edward Mayne, Relieving Officer, Cootehill Union, aged 56.

No. 5551 :: Ref. 1852-04-17, 5:6, D.
April 8, in Enniskillen, of water on the brain, James Charles, aged 7 years, only child of the late Mr. James Innes, junior.

No. 5552 :: Ref. 1852-04-17, 5:6, D.
April 12, in Dawson-street, Dublin, in the sixteenth year of her age, of rapid consumption, after measles, Jeanie, youngest beloved daughter of the late Rev. Charles Atkinson, L.L.D., Rector of Creggan, Armagh.

No. 5553 :: Ref. 1852-04-17, 5:6, D.
April 14, in this City, John Patrick, the infant son of Mr. Hughes, Charlemont Arms, Hotel.

No. 5554 :: Ref. 1852-04-17, 5:6, D.
April 16, in this city, Mr. Felix Hughes, aged 75 years. He was an upright citizen, of strict integrity in his dealings, and one of the very few who are entitled to the respect and confidence of all parties, a mark of public esteem which he enjoyed for many years past. His remains will be interred in Madden chapel yard on Sunday next.

No. 5555 :: Ref. 1852-04-24, 8:6, B.
Apl. 20, in Armagh, the wife of Mr. Richard Graves, Solicitor, of a daughter.

No. 5556 :: Ref. 1852-04-24, 8:6, B.
Apl. 22, in Armagh, Mrs. James Gardner, of a son.

No. 5557 :: Ref. 1852-04-24, 8:6, M.
Apl. 3, Mr. J.W. Magrath, to Mary, eldest daughter of Robert Fivey, Charlemont-mall, and Rostrevor, co. Down, Esq.

No. 5558 :: Ref. 1852-04-24, 8:6, M.
Apl. 13, Rev. Thomas MacNeece, D.D., to Frances, relict of George Digges Latouche, Esq., and daughter of the late Rev. Caesar Otway.

No. 5559 :: Ref. 1852-04-24, 8:6, M.
Apl. 14, Rev. William H.E. Wood Wright, of Gola House, co. Monaghan, to Jane Elizabeth, only daughter of Nathaniel Stewart, Esq., of Shellfield, co. Donegal.

No. 5560 :: Ref. 1852-04-24, 8:6, D.
Apl. 3, William John, only son of Mr. James Evans, Strabane, aged 14 months.

No. 5561 :: Ref. 1852-04-24, 8:6, D.
Apl. 3, at Newry, John, aged 30 years, second son to Edward Brown, Esq., Cootehill.

No. 5562 :: Ref. 1852-04-24, 8:6, D.
Apl. 6, in Fintona, the Rev. John Moore, R.N., aged 52 years.

No. 5563 :: Ref. 1852-04-24, 8:6, D.
Apl. 7, at Bridgeton, Mr. William Hill.

No. 5564 :: Ref. 1852-04-24, 8:6, D.
Apl. 11, at Donegal, Sarah Martha, wife of Mr. John M'Meehan, aged 25 years.

No. 5565 :: Ref. 1852-04-24, 8:6, D.
Apl. 13, at Omagh, aged 27 years, James Blacker Buchannan, Esq.

No. 5566 :: Ref. 1852-04-24, 8:6, D.
Apl. 13, Mr. James Copeland, Schoolmaster and Purveyor of Down Gaol, aged 50 years.

No. 5567 :: Ref. 1852-04-24, 8:6, D.
Aprl. 14, at Thonock Hall, Lincolnshire, Edward Bacon, Esq., D.L., J.P., county Armagh, only surviving son of Sir Edmund Bacon, Bart., of Raveningham Hall, co. Norfolk.

No. 5568 :: Ref. 1852-04-24, 8:6, D.
April 14, at Mauchline, Ayrshire, Miss Hamilton, youngest daughter of the late Gavin Hamilton, Esq., the friend and patron of Robert Burns, the poet.

No. 5569 :: Ref. 1852-04-24, 8:6, D.
April 15, aged ten months, William Allan Murray, son of Sir James Murray, Waterloo-road, Dublin.

No. 5570 :: Ref. 1852-04-24, 8:6, D.
April 16, at Rectory, Ahabog, co. Monaghan, Elizabeth Jane, daughter of the Rev. Wm. Story, aged nearly eight years.

No. 5571 :: Ref. 1852-04-24, 8:6, D.
April 16, Theophilus Edward Lucas Clements, Esq., of Rakenny, co. Cavan, aged 49.

No. 5572 :: Ref. 1852-04-24, 8:6, D.
April 20, Anne Constantia, the youngest daughter of the Rev. W.B. Yeats, Rector of Tullylish, co. Down.

No. 5573 :: Ref. 1852-05-01, 5:6, B.
April 22, at the Endowed School, Dundalk, the lady of the Rev. E.M. Goslett, of a son.

No. 5574 :: Ref. 1852-05-01, 5:6, M.
April 13, in the Roman Catholic Chapel, Moneymore, by the Rev. James Quin, R.C.C., brother to the bride, P. M'Loughlin, Esq., surgeon, Portadown, to Ellen, second daughter of the late Charles Quin, Esq., Moneyhaw house, Moneymore.

No. 5575 :: Ref. 1852-05-01, 5:6, M.
April 15, at Killevan Church, co. Monaghan, by Rev. Hamilton Haire, Edward Golding, Esq., of Castleblayney, to Mary, second daughter of the late Brabazon Noble, Esq., of Dundalk.

No. 5576 :: Ref. 1852-05-01, 5:6, D.
Feb. 27, at St. John's [sic] New Brunswick, after a lingering illness, Mr. John Fawcett, a native of co. Sligo, Ireland, in the 69th year of his age.

No. 5577 :: Ref. 1852-05-01, 5:6, D.
April 16, at Dartey, near Cootehill, in the 23rd year of his [sic] age, Miss Isabella Pringle Lyttle, eldest daughter of James Lyttle, Esq.

No. 5578 :: Ref. 1852-05-01, 5:6, D.
April 19, at Ballymena, Mr. John Brangin, in the 72nd year of his age.

No. 5579 :: Ref. 1852-05-01, 5:6, D.
April 10, at Crow hill, Lurgan, in the 10th year of his age, Adam Weir, second son of the late James Morrison, Esq., Lurgan.

No. 5580 :: Ref. 1852-05-01, 5:6, D.
April 20, at Newbliss House, co. Monaghan, Mrs. Mary Foster, relict of the Rev. Richard Foster, aged 75 years.

No. 5581 :: Ref. 1852-05-01, 5:6, D.
April 20, aged 60, Susanna, relict of the late Francis Saunderson, of Prospect House, Tandragee.

No. 5582 :: Ref. 1852-05-01, 5:6, D.
April 21, at Grange, co. Westmeath, aged 32 years, wife of Gorges Graham, of Summerhill, co. Cavan, Esq., and youngest daughter of the late Edward Tisdall, of Rathcoole House, co. Louth, Esq.

No. 5583 :: Ref. 1852-05-01, 5:6, D.
April 23, at the residence of his son-in-law, Dr. Denham, of Derry, the Rev. Samuel Hanna, D.D., Senior Pastor of Rosemary-street Church, Belfast, and Senior Professor of Theology for the General Assembly.

No. 5584 :: Ref. 1852-05-01, 5:6, D.
April 25, at his residence, Tilledon Cottage, Glasslough, co. Monaghan, Thomas Alexander Pringle, Esq., aged 64.

No. 5585 :: Ref. 1852-05-01, 5:6, D.
April 25, at an advanced age, at her residence, Palace-row, Armagh, Mrs. Carson.

No. 5586 :: Ref. 1852-05-01, 5:6, D.
April 25, at Lisnagannon, near Loughbrickland, Michael Strain, at the advanced age of 99 years. He enjoyed good health up to within a few weeks of his decease.

No. 5587 :: Ref. 1852-05-01, 5:6, D.
April 27, at Millvale, Rostrevor, Milliam [sic] Moffat, Esq., M.D., in the 39th year of his age.

No. 5588 :: Ref. 1852-05-01, 5:6, D.

April 28, at No. 8, Waring-street, Belfast, in the 83d year of his [sic] age, Jane, relict of the late Rev. Matthew Tobias, Wesleyan minister.

No. 5589 :: Ref. 1852-05-01, 5:6, D.

April 28, at Beechmount, Belfast, Lewis Reford, Esq., aged 63 years. He was one of the oldest merchants in Belfast.

No. 5590 :: Ref. 1852-05-01, 5:6, D.

Lately, at Lewisham, Kent, aged 103, Ann Kelly.—From early youth she was a member of the theatrical profession, and acted at various theatres in England, Ireland, and Scotland. She was in the same company with the late Edmund Keane, and also with James Sheridan Knowles, during his brief career as an actor, and it was her proudest boast that she had often played Alicia to the Jane Shore of Mrs. Siddons. It was somewhat singular that, though she was twice married, she never had occasion to change her maiden name, both husbands bearing the name of Kelly.

No. 5591 :: Ref. 1852-05-08, 5:6, B.

In Enniskillen, the lady of Archibald Collum, Esq., of a son.

No. 5592 :: Ref. 1852-05-08, 5:6, M.

April 20, John Kelly, Esq., of Black Rock, Dundalk, to Mary, youngest daughter of George Gartlan, Esq., of Lannatt.

No. 5593 :: Ref. 1852-05-08, 5:6, M.

April 28, in St. George's Church, Henry Murray, second son of Frederick Campbell, Esq., of Brittas, co. Meath, to Sarah Elizabeth, only daughter of Charles C. Irvine, Esq., of Cowley-place, and Johnstown House, co. Fermanagh.

No. 5594 :: Ref. 1852-05-08, 5:6, M.

April 29, in Omagh Church, by Rev. M.N. Thompson, George Molony, Esq., son of the late Walter Molony, Esq., R.M., Belfast, to Susan Anabella, daughter of G. Wade, Esq., late co. Inspector of Tyrone.

No. 5595 :: Ref. 1852-05-08, 5:6, M.

May 5, in Solderstown [sic] Church, parish of Aughalea, by Rev. Robert Hill, Mr. James Gilbert, merchant, Portadown, to Eliza Jane, youngest daughter of the late Mr. Stephen Gilbert, Aughagallon, near Lurgan.

No. 5596 :: Ref. 1852-05-08, 5:6, D.

April 1, at Brooklyn, New York, from decay of nature, aged 145 years, Mrs. Elizabeth Fitzpatrick. The venerable deceased was a native of Scotland, and had led to the altar no less than eight members of the male sex, four in Scotland and four in America. She was wonderfully active, and her eyesight was so good that she nearly [neatly?] back-stitched a shirt front the day before her death. Thirty children survive her.

No. 5597 :: Ref. 1852-05-08, 5:6, D.

April 26, at Mauchline, Janet Armour, relict of Mr. William Lees, of Mauchline, and sister of the late Jean Armour, wife of the bard, Robert Burns. Mrs. Lees was the last branch of the Armour family.

No. 5598 :: Ref. 1852-05-08, 5:6, D.

April 29, at Enniskillen, of inflammation of the lungs, Rev. Ephraim Stephenson. He had attained the patriarchal age of 87 years, during 48 of which he was the Presbyterian Minister of Enniskillen; and after a brief illness he calmly fell asleep in Jesus.

No. 5599 :: Ref. 1852-05-08, 5:6, D.

May 2, in Ballyshannon, Mr. James Nolan, Sub-Inspector of Constabulary, after a short but severe illness, very generally esteemed both by the inhabitants and the force over which he presided.

No. 5600 :: Ref. 1852-05-08, 5:6, D.

May 5, in Ballintra, Mr. Henry Dunsmore. He was found dead in his bed.

No. 5601 :: Ref. 1852-05-15, 5:4, B.

May 7, in Armagh, Mrs. Malcolm M'Neal Johnston, of a son.

No. 5602 :: Ref. 1852-05-15, 5:4, B.

May 11, at No. 40, Grosvenor-square, London, the Countess of Verulam, of a son and heir.

No. 5603 :: Ref. 1852-05-15, 5:4, M.

March 3, in Philadelphia, Mr. Andrew Gordon, merchant, to Mary, third daughter of Mr. Charles Caldwell, of Drumrawn, near Drumquin, co. Tyrone.

No. 5604 :: Ref. 1852-05-15, 5:4, M.

April 29, in Bray Church, Rev. T.P. Ball, third son of late Rev. John Ball, of co. Wicklow, to Henrietta, only daughter of the late Henry Walsh, Esq., and niece of Sir William Crosbie, Bart.

No. 5605 :: Ref. 1852-05-15, 5:4, M.

May 6, by Rev. Thomas Millar, Lurgan, Andrew Mercer, Esq., Belfast, to Catherine, niece of James Fleming, Esq., of Lurgan.

No. 5606 :: Ref. 1852-05-15, 5:4, M.

May 6, at Loughgall Church, by Rev. Edward C. Hardy, brother to the bride, David Galbraith, of Lower Gardiner-street, Esq., second son of the late Rev. John Galbraith, vicar of Tuam, co. Galway, to Emma Elizabeth Cope, youngest daughter of the late John Hardy, of Loughgall, Esq.

No. 5607 :: Ref. 1852-05-15, 5:4, M.

May 6, at St. Andrew's Church, Montpellier, Bristol, by Rev. Arthur Molony, Rector of Derryloran, county Tyrone, uncle to the bridegroom, William George Molony, Esq., to Mary Eliza, eldest daughter of William Player, Esq., of Ashley Court, Bristol.

No. 5608 :: Ref. 1852-05-15, 5:4, M.
May 10, in Kilmore Church, by Rev. John Finlay, Mr. James Loney, Tynan, to Eliza, fourth daughter of Mr. Richardson Greer, Kilmore.

No. 5609 :: Ref. 1852-05-15, 5:4, M.
May 11, in the Cathedral of Derry, by Very Rev. the Dean of Derry, the Rev. Charleton Maxwell, Rector of Lower Badony, son of the Rev. P.B. Maxwell, of Birdstown, co. Donegal, to Emily Augusta Grace Ponsonby, youngest daughter of the Hon. and Right Rev. the Lord Bishop of Derry and Raphoe.

No. 5610 :: Ref. 1852-05-15, 5:4, D.
April 30, at Beechmount, co. Tyrone, Eliza Anne, widow of the late John Joyce, Esq., aged 32 years.

No. 5611 :: Ref. 1852-05-15, 5:4, D.
April 30, at Mountcharles, Mr. George Kirk, aged 88 years.

No. 5612 :: Ref. 1852-05-15, 5:4, D.
May 5, at Strabane, Mr. Thomas M'Neilance, inn-keeper.

No. 5613 :: Ref. 1852-05-15, 5:4, D.
May 8, at Castleview, Carlingford, in the 95th year of his age, William Moore, Esq.

No. 5614 :: Ref. 1852-05-15, 5:4, D.
May 9, in Newry, at the advanced age of 84 years, Mrs. Maguire, sister of the late Denis Caulfield, Esq.

No. 5615 :: Ref. 1852-05-15, 5:4, D.
May 8, at No. 15, Merrion-square North, Dublin, Lady Fitzgerald, aged 88 years, relict of the late Lieutenant-General Sir Augustine Fitzgerald, Bart., of Carrigorae, co. of Clare. Mr. Edward Barton, brother to Folliott Barton, Esq., of Clonelly, is one of her residuary Legatees.

No. 5616 :: Ref. 1852-05-15, 5:4, D.
May 9, in Enniskillen, co. Fermanagh, Mrs. Cunningham, relict of the late Mr. Anthony Cunningham, merchant.

No. 5617 :: Ref. 1852-05-15, 5:4, D.
May 14, at Rokeby-green, Armagh, aged 40 years, Mr. John M'Connell, farming implement manufacturer. He was a quiet, unassuming citizen, respected by all who knew him—a man of the highest character for integrity in his dealing.

No. 5618 :: Ref. 1852-05-15, 5:4, D.
In Irish-street, Armagh, Mrs. Jane Hart, relict of Mr. Hart, aged 65 years, very generally esteemed and sincerely regretted.

No. 5619 :: Ref. 1852-05-22, 5:6, B.
May 9, at Portadown, co. Armagh, the lady of the Rev. Francis Crawford, of a still-born daughter.

No. 5620 :: Ref. 1852-05-22, 5:6, B.
May 9, at Castleblayney, Mrs. S. M'Birney of a daughter.

No. 5621 :: Ref. 1852-05-22, 5:6, B.
May 12, Mrs. James Burns, 3, Upper English-street, of a son.

No. 5622 :: Ref. 1852-05-22, 5:6, B.
May 12, at Brookborough, the wife of Captain J.S. Howard, 44th Regiment, of a daughter.

No. 5623 :: Ref. 1852-05-22, 5:6, B.
May 18, in Enniskillen, the lady of John Graham, Esq., Solicitor, of a son.

No. 5624 :: Ref. 1852-05-22, 5:6, M.
May 1, at Stoke Church, Rev. C.B. Fenwick, of Mountcharles, co. Donegal, to Sophia Anne, third daughter of Philip M. Little, Esq., of St. Michael's terrace, Stoke, Devonport.

No. 5625 :: Ref. 1852-05-22, 5:6, M.
May 13, in Armaghbreague Church, by Rev. D. Donaldson, Mr. Wm. Smith, son of Mr. John Smith, of Lake View cottage, to Miss Ann M'Cullagh of Church Hill.

No. 5626 :: Ref. 1852-05-22, 5:6, M.
May 14, in the Parish Church of Bangor, by Rev. J.W. Devlin, Mr. Samuel Allen Thompson, of Belfast, to Miss Prudence M'Math, Bangor.

No. 5627 :: Ref. 1852-05-22, 5:6, M.
April 15, at Floyd's Fork, Jefferson County, U.S.A., Mr. Thomas Stafford to Polly Goben. The bride is 19 years old, and the bridegroom 77; he weighs some 300 pounds, and is so fat as scarcely to be able to walk, and, when in bed, raises himself or turns over by means of pullies fastened to the ceiling. He went to the city in a waggon to procure the licence, and on his return was met by the young bride at the forks of the road, where the parson joined them in wedlock, the ceremony being performed in the waggon.

No. 5628 :: Ref. 1852-05-22, 5:6, D.
May 10, at Finnis, Dromara, Jane, relict of Mr. James Bailie, Artanna, Seaforde. She was in her 93d year, and had, at her death, four children, twenty-six grand-children, and forty-four great grandchildren—in all seventy-four descendants.

No. 5629 :: Ref. 1852-05-22, 5:6, D.
May 14, very sincerely regretted, Mrs. Mathews, wife of Sub Inspector Mathews, Dungannon, and daughter of the late W. Lodge Kidd, Esq., M.D., of Armagh.

No. 5630 :: Ref. 1852-05-22, 5:6, D.
May 16, in Belfast, aged 40 years, Sarah, relict of the late John Small.

No. 5631 :: Ref. 1852-05-22, 5:6, D.
May 17, at Glasnevin House, Dublin, in her 92d year, the Hon. Catherine Eliza Lindsay, relict of the late Hon. Charles Lindsay, D.D., Lord Bishop of Kildare.

No. 5632 :: Ref. 1852-05-29, 5:2, B.
May 20, at Drumglas House, Dungannon, the wife of Wm. Hamilton Irwin, Esq., of a son.

No. 5633 :: Ref. 1852-05-29, 5:2, B.
May 20, Mrs. P. Maginn, Esq. [sic], Enniskillen, of a daughter.

No. 5634 :: Ref. 1852-05-29, 5:2, B.
May 26, at Trory Glebe, co. Fermanagh, the lady of the Rev. Henry Mervyn Archdall, of a daughter.

No. 5635 :: Ref. 1852-05-29, 5:2, M.
May 25, at Newry, by Rev. Mr. Irwin, P.P., J. Monahan, Esq., Willowbrook, Scarva, Inspector of the Newry Navigation, to Ann Eliza, youngest daughter of E. M'Donnell, Esq., Mullahead House, Tandragee. After the conclusion of the ceremony, the happy pair immediately went off for the Continent, where they [will] pass the honeymoon.

No. 5636 :: Ref. 1852-05-29, 5:2, M.
May 17, in the Presbyterian Church, Coagh, by Rev. Robert Holmes, David Brown, Esq., merchant, Dungannon, to Annie, second daughter of John Aiken, Esq., of Coagh.

No. 5637 :: Ref. 1852-05-29, 5:2, M.
May 17, at Campbell field, near Ayr, Scotland, Mr. Andrew Mair, Lisnaskea, Co. Fermanagh, Ireland, to Mannon, fourth daughter of Alexander Patterson, Esq.

No. 5638 :: Ref. 1852-05-29, 5:2, M.
May 20, at Myroe, co. Londonderry, Rev. Thomas Meharry, to Georgina, second daughter of the late Andrew Nixon, of Lurgan Lodge, co. Cavan, Esq., Barrister-at-Law.

No. 5639 :: Ref. 1852-05-29, 5:2, D.
May 20, in Enniskillen, of small pock, the infant child of Archibald Collum, Esq., Solicitor.

No. 5640 :: Ref. 1852-05-29, 5:2, D.
May 25, at Kildarton, Armagh, Mr. William Dobbin, deeply and deservedly regretted.

No. 5641 :: Ref. 1852-05-29, 5:2, D.
May 25, at Portadown, at the advanced age of ninety-four years, Mrs. Margaret Hamilton, relict of the late Robert Hamilton, co. Down.

No. 5642 :: Ref. 1852-06-05, 8:5, M.
May 27, at Hornsey Church, by Hon. and Rev. Francis T. Noel, Hon. Henry Noel, to Emily Elizabeth, second daughter of Hon. and Rev. Baptist Noel.

No. 5643 :: Ref. 1852-06-05, 8:5, M.
June 1, in Lavey Church, by the father of the bride, the Rev. John H. Morell, of Cumry Lodge, Ballibay, to Hester Frances Elizabeth Wilhelmina, youngest daughter of the Rev. James Lowry Dickson, Rector of the Parish of Lavey, County Cavan.

No. 5644 :: Ref. 1852-06-05, 8:5, M.
June 1, at St. Malachi's Roman Catholic Church, by the Right Rev. Dr. Denvir, Cornelius M. Hughes, Esq., Longfield-house, Forkhill, co. Armagh, to Eliza, eldest daughter of Mr. John M'Kenna, Bridge-street, Belfast.

No. 5645 :: Ref. 1852-06-05, 8:5, D.
Dec. 31, 1851, at Launceston, Van Dieman's Land, aged 68, Capt. Walter Synnot, son of the late Sir Walter Synnot, of Ballymoyer, county Armagh.

No. 5646 :: Ref. 1852-06-05, 8:5, D.
May 3, at New York, Mr. Richard M'Donagh, formerly of Donegal, aged 25 years.

No. 5647 :: Ref. 1852-06-05, 8:5, D.
May 18, at Grove-hill, near Omagh, Margaret, the beloved wife of William M'Kelvey, Esq.

No. 5648 :: Ref. 1852-06-05, 8:5, D.
May 21, at Dungannon, of consumption, aged 17 years, Edward, eldest son of the late Edward Lyons, Esq., L.L.D., of Newry.

No. 5649 :: Ref. 1852-06-05, 8:5, D.
May 25, at Killinchy, co. Down, John Potter M'Connell, Esq., aged 44 years, last surviving son of John M'Connell, Esq., late of Donegall place, Belfast, claimant of the dormant title of Monteith, in Scotland, now in abeyance.

No. 5650 :: Ref. 1852-06-05, 8:5, D.
May 26, in the 34th year of her age, after a prolonged illness, ensuing on measles, the lady of Sir Lucius O'Brien, Bart., M.P.

No. 5651 :: Ref. 1852-06-05, 8:5, D.
At Christiantown, Co. Louth, formerly of Caledon, in the Co. Tyrone, where he was highly esteemed and respected, Henderson Crozier, Esq., half-pay officer of the 22d Regiment of Foot.

No. 5652 :: Ref. 1852-06-12, 8:5, B.
May 29, at the residence of her father, Mr. Cole, Armagh, the lady of James Mackie, Esq., Kilberney, Scotland, of a son.

No. 5653 :: Ref. 1852-06-12, 8:5, B.
May 31, the wife of Mr. James M. Ross, Monaghan, of a son.

No. 5654 :: Ref. 1852-06-12, 8:5, B.
May 31, at the Constabulary Barracks, Phoenix-park, the lady of George W. Hatchell, Esq., M.D., of a son.

No. 5655 :: Ref. 1852-06-12, 8:5, B.
June 1, at Manorwater-house, County Fermanagh, Mrs. Robert Reynolds, of a son.

No. 5656 :: Ref. 1852-06-12, 8:5, B.
June 4, at Levahy [Lovahy?], the wife of Mr. Ralph Stone, of a son.

No. 5657 :: Ref. 1852-06-12, 8:5, B.
June 5, at Anketell Grove, the lady of Matthew John Anketell, Esq., of a daughter.

No. 5658 :: Ref. 1852-06-12, 8:5, M.
May 24, at the British Consulate, Bayonne, Fizherbert Darce Lucas, second son of the Right Hon. Edwd. Lucas, of Castleshane, Monaghan, to Laura Adelaide Scudamore, only child of Lieutenant-Colonel Scudamore, of Kent-church-court, Herefordshire.

No. 5659 :: Ref. 1852-06-12, 8:5, D.
May 23, Elizabeth, relict of the late Mr. John Wallace, of Omagh, aged 87.

No. 5660 :: Ref. 1852-06-12, 8:5, D.
May 27, Jane Maria, (fifth) daughter of the Rev. Henry A. Burke, Rector of Ballinamallard.

No. 5661 :: Ref. 1852-06-12, 8:5, D.
May 29, at Garvey, Aughnacloy, James Montgomery, Esq., aged 66 years.

No. 5662 :: Ref. 1852-06-12, 8:5, D.
May 29, at Sedan, France, Major Hill, late 45th Regiment, eldest son of the late Major Hill, of Bellaghy Castle, co. Londonderry.

No. 5663 :: Ref. 1852-06-12, 8:5, D.
May 29, at Greenfort, co. Donegal, aged 27, W.G.F. Copland, Esq., eldest son of the late William Copland, Esq., of Clapham, Surrey.

No. 5664 :: Ref. 1852-06-12, 8:5, D.
June 2, at Aughamore, in the 18th year of her age, Maria, eldest daughter of the Rev. Wm. Bredin, of Sallaghy.

No. 5665 :: Ref. 1852-06-12, 8:5, D.
June 2, at Dundalk-street, Newtownhamilton, of disease of the heart, Mr. Samuel Reid.

No. 5666 :: Ref. 1852-06-12, 8:5, D.
June 3, at Omagh, by disease of the heart, George Wade, Esq., late County Inspector of Constabulary, aged 65 years.

No. 5667 :: Ref. 1852-06-12, 8:5, D.
June 3, Jane Armstrong, aged 15 years, eldest daughter of C. Gamble, Esq., Enniskillen.

No. 5668 :: Ref. 1852-06-12, 8:5, D.
June 4, Miss Jane Quinton, aged 80, better known as 'Orange Jenny.' She was ardently attached to the orange cause, throughout her long life, and she invariably insisted upon 'hats off' when crossing the Boyne, on the Dublin coach.—*Enniskillen paper.*

No. 5669 :: Ref. 1852-06-12, 8:5, D.
June 5, at Markethill, Margaret, relict of [the] late John Mitchell, Esq., aged 76 years.

No. 5670 :: Ref. 1852-06-12, 8:5, D.
June 5, at Pembroke place, Dublin, aged thirteen years and nine months, Eliza, second daughter of Richard Mayne, Esq., of Newbliss, co. Monaghan.

No. 5671 :: Ref. 1852-06-12, 8:5, D.
June 6, at Kircubbin, James, son of the late Mr. John Boyd.

No. 5672 :: Ref. 1852-06-12, 8:5, D.
June 7, at Charlemont-place, Maria, relict of the late Richare [sic] Mollan, Esq., M.D., formerly of Newry.

No. 5673 :: Ref. 1852-06-12, 8:5, D.
June 8, in the prime of life, Kitty, youngest daughter of Wm. Armstrong, pawnbroker, Enniskillen.

No. 5674 :: Ref. 1852-06-19, 8:4, B.
June 8, at the Brewery House, Kinsale, Mr. John H. Williams, of a son.

No. 5675 :: Ref. 1852-06-19, 8:4, B.
June 10, at Ipswich, the wife of the Rev. D.H. Elrington, of a daughter.

No. 5676 :: Ref. 1852-06-19, 8:4, B.
June 12, at Abbey-yard, Newry, the lady of Isaac Corry, Esq., D.L., J.P., of a daughter.

No. 5677 :: Ref. 1852-06-19, 8:4, B.
On the 16th inst., at Dungannon, the lady of the Rev. F.H. Ringwood, of a daughter.

No. 5678 :: Ref. 1852-06-19, 8:4, M.
May 27, at Clare, Presbyterian Church, by the bride's Father, the Rev. Andrew M'Caldin, Presbyterian Minister, Richhill, to Margaret, second daughter of Rev. J. Bell, Broomfield.

No. 5679 :: Ref. 1852-06-19, 8:4, M.
June 4, at Frankfort, Rev. J.F. Close, of Morne Rectory, Kilkeel, Ireland, to Maria Esther, relict of the late Col. Steinhelt, and daughter of the Rev. J. Fullagar.

No. 5680 :: Ref. 1852-06-19, 8:4, M.
June 9, in Clones Church, by the cousin of the Bride-groom, the Rev. Thomas Howe, Mr. John Bell, of Killifargy, parish of Currin, to Miss Isabella Blakely of Granshaw, Clones.

No. 5681 :: Ref. 1852-06-19, 8:4, M.
June 9, at Monkstown Church, by Rev. S. Ferguson, uncle to the bride, the Rev. William Edward Mulgan, Curate of Magheralin, County Down, to Arabella Maria, second daughter of the late Captain Stringer, of Tassah, County Armagh.

No. 5682 :: Ref. 1852-06-19, 8:4, M.
June 10, at the Cathedral, Londonderry, by Rev. R. Hinginbotham, William George Smart, Esq., son of the late Wm. Smart, Esq., to Edith, youngest daughter of David Webster, Esq., Manager of the Provincial Bank of Ireland, Londonderry.

No. 5683 :: Ref. 1852-06-19, 8:4, D.
Mr. Charles Boucher, of Berthier, district of Montreal, at the advanced age of 106. He was married to three wives, with whom he had sixty children! He

leaves forty-three children, sixty-six grand children, thirteen great grand-children, twenty-eight nephews, seventy grand-nephews, and eighteen great grand-nephews.—*Canadian paper*.

No. 5684 :: Ref. 1852-06-19, 8:4, D.
May 24, at Paris, Tennessee, U.S.A., of fever, in the 26th year of his age, John, eldest son of [the] late John Kane, Esq., of Summerhill, County Armagh.

No. 5685 :: Ref. 1852-06-19, 8:4, D.
June 1, at Conisbrough, Lady Emma Francis, widow of Sir Philip Francis, G.C.B., the reputed author of the "*Letters of Junius*," and daughter of the late Rev. H. Watkins, prebendary, of York, and Southwell.

No. 5686 :: Ref. 1852-06-19, 8:4, D.
June 2, in London, Robert Ponsonby Staples, Esq., youngest son of the late Right Hon. John Staples, of Lissane, co. Tyrone, brother of the Dowager Marchioness of Ormonde, in the 68th year of his age.

No. 5687 :: Ref. 1852-06-19, 8:4, D.
June 7, aged 16 years, Diana, second daughter of the late Mr. Johnston M'Caw, of Tegnavin, near Lurgan.

No. 5688 :: Ref. 1852-06-19, 8:4, D.
June 8, at Florence-court, Mrs. Godbert, wife of Mr. Joseph Godbert, of apoplexy.

No. 5689 :: Ref. 1852-06-19, 8:4, D.
June 10, at London, from the bursting of a blood-vessel, Mr. Andrew Thomson, jun., tutor to the Royal family.

No. 5690 :: Ref. 1852-06-19, 8:4, D.
June 10, at Grange near this city, of fever, James, third son of Mr. James Taylor, aged 22 years, deeply lamented by his sorrowing parents, and friends, and in sure and certain hope of a resurrection to life eternal.

No. 5691 :: Ref. 1852-06-19, 8:4, D.
June 11, at Glenview, Carrickfergus, aged 23 years, John, second son of John Coates, Esq., Secretary to the co. Antrim Grand Jury.

No. 5692 :: Ref. 1852-06-19, 8:4, D.
June 11, at Inch, near Derry, Rev. Samuel Armour, Presbyterian Minister, in the 19th year of his Ministry, aged 59 years.

No. 5693 :: Ref. 1852-06-19, 8:4, D.
June 12, at Newry, Mr. Samuel Hall, Licenciate, of the Ahoghill Presbytery, General Assembly, and Principal of the Newry Academy.

No. 5694 :: Ref. 1852-06-19, 8:4, D.
June 13, the infant child of Mr. Coutts, of Enniskillen, aged two years and three months.

No. 5695 :: Ref. 1852-06-19, 8:4, D.
June 15, at Enniskillen, Miss Hall; her illness was painful and tedious, but her examplary [sic] life prepared her to bear the dispensations of her heavenly Master without complaining.—Her end was peace.

No. 5696 :: Ref. 1852-06-26, 8:5, B.
June 11, at Cavan, the wife of W.W. Bond, Paymaster of the 4th (King's Own Regiment), of a daughter.

No. 5697 :: Ref. 1852-06-26, 8:5, B.
June 16, at 24, Upper Fitzwilliam-street, Dublin, the lady of J. Faviere Elrington, Esq., of a daughter.

No. 5698 :: Ref. 1852-06-26, 8:5, B.
June 18, at Dungannon, the lady of Rev. F.H. Ringwood, of a daughter.

No. 5699 :: Ref. 1852-06-26, 8:5, B.
June 18, at 21, Rutland-square, North, Dublin, the lady of William Humphrys, Esq., of Ballyhaise House, co. Cavan, of a daughter.

No. 5700 :: Ref. 1852-06-26, 8:5, B.
June 19, at Upper Sackville street, Dublin, Mrs. R.F. Mulvany, of a dughter [sic].

No. 5701 :: Ref. 1852-06-26, 8:5, B.
June 21, at No. 3, Great Stanhope-street, the Hon. Mrs. Vesey Dawson, of a son, still born.

No. 5702 :: Ref. 1852-06-26, 8:5, M.
June 7, by Rev. Mr. Jones, Mr. William Ross of New York, son of Mr. Thomas Ross, of Armagh, Ireland to Miss Florida L. Ellison, of Bridgeport, Connecticut, U.S.A.

No. 5703 :: Ref. 1852-06-26, 8:5, M.
June 10, in Armaghbrague church, by Rev. D. Donaldson, Mr. William M'Murdy, to Miss Agnes Monaghan, both of that parish.

No. 5704 :: Ref. 1852-06-26, 8:5, M.
June 11, at Monkstown Church, Hugh Fraser, Esq., of Balloch, Culloden, Inverness, to Augusta Mary, eldest daughter of Professor Smith, Mus.D., T.C.D.

No. 5705 :: Ref. 1852-06-26, 8:5, M.
June 13, at Portrush, at Chichester [sic; should read, 'by the Rev. Mr. Chichester'?], William H. Willcocks, Esq., of Dungannon, to Marianne, second daughter of the late James Gray, Esq., of Coalisland.

No. 5706 :: Ref. 1852-06-26, 8:5, M.
June 14, at Lowtherstown, Mr. John Gibson, of Tempo, to Mary, daughter of S. Rutledge, Esq., of Badoney Cottage.

No. 5707 :: Ref. 1852-06-26, 8:5, M.
June 14, in Ballycastle, by Rev. Wallace M'Mullan, Rev. James C. Bass, to Mary Leedor, youngest daughter of Thomas Tippett, Esq., Ballycastle, co. Antrim.

No. 5708 :: Ref. 1852-06-26, 8:5, M.
June 15, in the Scots Church, Kingston, by Rev. Dr. Kirkpatrick, the Rev. J. Hall, Minister First Presbyterian Congregation, Armagh, to   (*continued...*)

No. 5708, continued: ...Emily, relict of the late John Irwin, Esq., and youngest daughter of the late Lyndon Bolton, Esq.

No. 5709 :: Ref. 1852-06-26, 8:5, M.
June 15, in Fintona Church, by Rev. Thos. Maunsell, John Eccles Hamilton, Esq., Surgeon, R.N., to Emily, second daughter of James Buchanan, Esq., Fintona.

No. 5710 :: Ref. 1852-06-26, 8:5, M.
June 16, in Dublin, by Rev. Richard Dill, William Maxwell, Esq., merchant, Cootehill, to Elizabeth, daughter of Robert Small, Esq., Ballieborough.

No. 5711 :: Ref. 1852-06-26, 8:5, M.
June 17, at St. Peter's Church, by Rev. Edw. Pepper, uncle to the bridegroom, assisted by Rev. Alexander Braddell, brother to the bride, Robert Lowry, Esq., of Cormeen, county Monaghan, son of the late James Lowry, Esq., of Rockdale, co. Tyrone, to Louisa, daughter of the late George Braddell, Esq., of Prospect, co. Wexford, and 41, Upper Fitzwilliam-street, Dublin.

No. 5712 :: Ref. 1852-06-26, 8:5, M.
June 17, in Ballintra Church, by the Rev. John Kinkade, Mr. Nicholas Sims, of Castlefin, to Eliza, only daughter of the late Thomas Graham, Esq., Strabane.

No. 5713 :: Ref. 1852-06-26, 8:5, M.
June 23, in St. Peter's Church, Dublin, by the Rev. Thomas M'Neece, D.D., Rev. Thomas Twigg, jun., eldest son of Rev. Thomas Twigg, of Thorehill, co. Tyrone, to Margaret, only daughter of Robert Henry Bolton, Esq., M.D., of Dungannon.

No. 5714 :: Ref. 1852-06-26, 8:5, D.
June 3, in New York, of consumption, Daniel Corr, aged 21 years, son of James Corr, of the parish of Loughgall, co. Armagh, Ireland.

No. 5715 :: Ref. 1852-06-26, 8:5, D.
June 9, at Arthurstown, co. Wexford, J.H. Clarke, Esq., Sub-Inspector of Constabulary.

No. 5716 :: Ref. 1852-06-26, 8:5, D.
June 12, at Ballygawley, in the 70th year of his age, Robert Armstrong, Esq., brother of Adam Armstrong, Esq., distiller.

No. 5717 :: Ref. 1852-06-26, 8:5, D.
June 13, at the residence of his brother-in-law, Mr. John Anderson, Sion, Strabane, Mr. James Plunket, late of Belfast, aged 33 years.

No. 5718 :: Ref. 1852-06-26, 8:5, D.
June 16, in Belnaclogh, John, son of the late Rev. Hugh Stokes, of Glenhoy, co. Tyrone.

No. 5719 :: Ref. 1852-06-26, 8:5, D.
June 19, at Carrickfad, co. Leitrim, aged 74, Jane, relict of the late Mr. Wm. Graham.

No. 5720 :: Ref. 1852-06-26, 8:5, D.
June 22, of apoplexy, Catherine, daughter of Mr. Jas. Rafferty, of Omagh, aged 17 years.

No. 5721 :: Ref. 1852-06-26, 8:5, D.
June 23, Margaret, daughter, of Mr. Richard Kernan, Seedsman, Enniskillen.

No. 5722 :: Ref. 1852-07-03, 8:5, B.
At Paris, the lady of Colonel B.S. Rotch, (daughter of Hon. Abbot Lawrence) of a daughter.

No. 5723 :: Ref. 1852-07-03, 8:5, B.
June 20, at Kirkcubbin, the wife of the late Mr. John M. Shaw, of a son.

No. 5724 :: Ref. 1852-07-03, 8:5, B.
June 24, the lady of John C. Irvine, Esq., Lieutenant of Revenue Police, Borrisoleigh, of a daughter.

No. 5725 :: Ref. 1852-07-03, 8:5, B.
June 24, at Dublin, the wife of W.G. Chamney, Esq., Barrister-at-Law, of a son.

No. 5726 :: Ref. 1852-07-03, 8:5, B.
June 26, at London, the Lady Louisa Alexander, wife of Henry Alexander, Esq., of Forkhill, of a son and heir.

No. 5727 :: Ref. 1852-07-03, 8:5, B.
June 26, at Edgeworthstown, the wife of Mathew Trimble King, Esq., Monaghan, of a daughter.

No. 5728 :: Ref. 1852-07-03, 8:5, B.
June 27, at 52, Eaton-square, London, the wife of Captain the Hon. Francis Maude, R.N., of a son.

No. 5729 :: Ref. 1852-07-03, 8:5, B.
June 28, at Loughgall, the lady of William Hardy, Esq., of a daughter.

No. 5730 :: Ref. 1852-07-03, 8:5, M.
June 7, by Rev. Mr. Janes, Mr. William Ross of New York, son of Mr. Thomas Ross, of Armagh, Ireland, to Miss Florinda L. Ellison, of Bridgeport, Connecticut, U.S.A.

No. 5731 :: Ref. 1852-07-03, 8:5, M.
June 23, at Lurgan Church, Mr. Delway Walkington, of Mobile, U.S., to Anna Maria Bell, youngest daughter of Dr. Bell, Lurgan.

No. 5732 :: Ref. 1852-07-03, 8:5, M.
June 24, in Kinnitty, King's County, Augustus Sheil, of Castledawson, co. Derry, Esq., to Hanna Revelina, third daughter of the Rev. John Exshaw, rector of Kinnitty.

No. 5733 :: Ref. 1852-07-03, 8:5, M.
June 24, at Limerick, Edward Probyn, Esq., of Pontypool, Monmouthshire, and of Tandragee, co. Armagh, to Ruth Louisa, eldest daughter of John Wiglesworth, Esq., Collector of Inland Revenue, Limerick.

No. 5734 :: Ref. 1852-07-03, 8:5, M.
June 25, in St. Mary's Church, Newry, by the Very Rev. Daniel Bagot, Dean of Newry, Rev. A.L. Ford, to Eliza Charlotte Harrison, only daughter of Rev. A.L. Dobbin.

No. 5735 :: Ref. 1852-07-03, 8:5, M.
June 25, in Glascar, Mr. John Hanna, Ballydougherty, co. Armagh, to Isabella, daughter of Mr. A. Arbuthnot, Renshaw.

No. 5736 :: Ref. 1852-07-03, 8:5, M.
At Jersey, Rev. John Paterson, to Anna Brogden, eldest daughter of the late Edward Labarte, Esq., of Springfield, Clonmel.

No. 5737 :: Ref. 1852-07-03, 8:5, M.
At St. George's, Hanover-square, P.M. Murphy, Esq., Q.C., and Assistant Barrister for co. Cavan, to Jane, widow of the late Thomas Tench Vigors, Esq., of Erindale, D.L. of co. Carlow.

No. 5738 :: Ref. 1852-07-03, 8:5, D.
June 19, at Modubawn, near Cootehill, of malignant typhus fever, caught in the discharge of his clerical duties, the Rev. Thomas Brady, C.C., in the 35th year of his age, and the eighth of his ministry.

No. 5739 :: Ref. 1852-07-03, 8:5, D.
June 20, at Kirkcubbin, Mr. John M. Shaw, postmaster, aged 38 years.

No. 5740 :: Ref. 1852-07-03, 8:5, D.
June 20, at his residence Commercial Hotel, Stewartstown, of paralysis, Mr. William Brown, aged 61 years.

No. 5741 :: Ref. 1852-07-03, 8:5, D.
June 21, at Crossmaglen, aged 9 years, Matilda, fifth daughter of Gordon Holmes, Esq., Sub-Inspector of Constabulary.

No. 5742 :: Ref. 1852-07-03, 8:5, D.
June 21, at Leeson-Street, Geo. Christian, Esq., formerly of Carrick-on-Suir.

No. 5743 :: Ref. 1852-07-03, 8:5, D.
June 22, at Portstewart, Mrs. Mary Moore, relict of John Moore, Esq., late of Drumbanagher, in the county of Armagh, and daughter of the late Sir Annesley Stewart, Bart., of Fortstewart, County Donegal.

No. 5744 :: Ref. 1852-07-03, 8:5, D.
June 27, after a protracted illness, borne with Christian patience, aged 36 years, in the conscious enjoyment of a living hope of eternal blessedness, Mary Jane, the beloved wife of Mr. Thomas George M'Bride, C.E., Armagh, leaving a bereaved husband and two children to deplore her loss; and, also, deeply regretted by a numerous circle of friends.

No. 5745 :: Ref. 1852-07-03, 8:5, D.
At Serpentine-avenue, county Dublin, Mr. John Butcher, aged 76. He served in the navy from an early age, and was in all the principal actions of the late war, under Hoare, Collingwood, Hood and Nelson, at Trafalgar, and the Nile, and in the *Mars*, 74, under the late Admiral Oliver, when engaged with three French frigates, when the *Mars* took one (the *Le Rhin*). He remained in the navy up to the peace of 1815, and since that time he chiefly resided in Ireland.

No. 5746 :: Ref. 1852-07-10, 8:5, B.
June 24, at Sandymount, the lady of Christopher John Cottenham, Esq., of a son.

No. 5747 :: Ref. 1852-07-10, 8:5, B.
June 30, at Omagh, the lady of Richard Stack, Esq., Solicitor, of a daughter.

No. 5748 :: Ref. 1852-07-10, 8:5, B.
July 3, in Lower Baggot-street, Dublin, the lady of Henry Loftus Tottenham, Esq., Barrister-at-Law, of a son.

No. 5749 :: Ref. 1852-07-10, 8:5, B.
July 3, at Cliftonville, the wife of Robert Lindsay, Esq., of a son.

No. 5750 :: Ref. 1852-07-10, 8:5, M.
January 9, at Melbourne, by the Rev. Townsend Somerville, late of Drishane, County Cork, to Mary, third daughter of the late Roger Anketell, Esq., Ivy-hill, co. Monaghan, Ireland.

No. 5751 :: Ref. 1852-07-10, 8:5, M.
In St. Andrew's Church, Dublin, Mr. George Patton, Printer, to Rebecca, daughter of the late Mr. John Elliott, of Lisnaskea, co. Fermanagh.

No. 5752 :: Ref. 1852-07-10, 8:5, M.
June 24, in Portstewart, Mr. John M'Munn, printer, Paisley, to Eliza Ann, only daughter of the late Mr. John Parker, and sister to Mr. John Parker, postmaster, Portstewart.

No. 5753 :: Ref. 1852-07-10, 8:5, M.
June 29, at Burt Church, Mr. Samuel Leathem, jun., to Elizabeth, youngest daughter of Mr. Wm. Leathem, of Burt.

No. 5754 :: Ref. 1852-07-10, 8:5, M.
July 5, in the Wesleyan Church, Donegall-square, East, Belfast, by Rev. Dr. Newton, of Liverpool, Rev. Edward Best, of Armagh, to Anna Woods, third daughter of Rev. Thomas Ballard, Wesleyan Minister.

No. 5755 :: Ref. 1852-07-10, 8:5, M.
July 7, in St. Peter's Church, Dublin, by Rev. Sir John Bunbury, Bart., Robert William Lowry, Esq., Barrister-at-Law, and J.P., co. Tyrone, eldest son of Robert William Lowry, Esq., of Pomeroy House, in the same county, D.L., and J.P., and of Belmore place, co. Westmeath, to Frances Elizabeth, youngest daughter of Benjamin Geale Brady, Esq., Mount Geale, co. Kilkenny.

No. 5756 :: Ref. 1852-07-10, 8:5, D.
Feb. 1, at Melbourne, Dr. John Kidd, Royal Navy, F.R.C.S., and uncle of Abraham Kidd, M.D., of Ballymena, in the 48th year of his age.

No. 5757 :: Ref. 1852-07-10, 8:5, D.
June 25, suddenly, in Cavan, Mrs. James O'Brien, of disease of the heart.

No. 5758 :: Ref. 1852-07-10, 8:5, D.
June 25, aged 24 years, Mr. James Coyle, printer, and proprietor of the Coleraine News Room.

No. 5759 :: Ref. 1852-07-10, 8:5, D.
June 26, at Pettigo, Robert, only son of Mrs. M'Cutcheon, in the 19th year of his age, after a few days' illness, caused by inflammation of the brain, brought on by a slight cold.

No. 5760 :: Ref. 1852-07-10, 8:5, D.
June 27, in Ballyshannon, Anne, widow of James Lipsett, Esq., aged 68 years.

No. 5761 :: Ref. 1852-07-10, 8:5, D.
June 28, at the Close, Raphoe, at the advanced age of 91 years, Mrs. Ramsay, widow of the late Rev. Wm. Ramsay.

No. 5762 :: Ref. 1852-07-10, 8:5, D.
July 2, at Urney, co. Tyrone, Hugh Knox, Esq., at the advanced age of 85 years, father of the Rev. Robt. Knox, of Belfast.

No. 5763 :: Ref. 1852-07-10, 8:5, D.
July 3, at Mowhan, near Markethill, of gastric fever, Mrs. Agnes Armstrong, aged 61 years.

No. 5764 :: Ref. 1852-07-10, 8:5, D.
July 3, at Belfast, Mrs. Fleming, widow of the late Rev. A. Fleming, of Armagh, and youngest daughter of the late William Weir, Esq., of Cookstown, in the 40th year of her age. Her remains having been conveyed here by the Ulster Railway on Tuesday morning, were attended to the place of interment by the members of the General Assembly, where the funeral service was conducted by the Rev. Drs. Cooke and Morgan. They were deposited in the same vault with those of her deceased husband and child.

No. 5765 :: Ref. 1852-07-10, 8:5, D.
July 3, James, son of the late Mr. Andrew Kidney, of Enniskillen, baker, aged 15 years.

No. 5766 :: Ref. 1852-07-10, 8:5, D.
In Scotland, Mr. James Coutts, of Enniskillen, merchant.

No. 5767 :: Ref. 1852-07-10, 8:5, D.
July 4, at Moy, Kate, the beloved wife of the Rev. A.A. Nixon, Incumbent of Charlemont.

No. 5768 :: Ref. 1852-07-10, 8:5, D.
July 4, in Dover, Widow Staples, in the 100th year of her age, having lived in the reign of four kings, and during fourteen years of that of Queen Victoria. She remembered the sensation caused by the death of the celebrated General Wolfe, on his taking Quebec, in 1759, also the death of George II. Her children are all advanced in life, the eldest being between 70 and 80 years of age.

No. 5769 :: Ref. 1852-07-10, 8:5, D.
July 5, at Newry, Marianne, relict of the late Rev. Josias Erskine.

No. 5770 :: Ref. 1852-07-10, 8:5, D.
July 5, Mr. Samuel Milligan, master printer, of Derry, aged 35 years.

No. 5771 :: Ref. 1852-07-10, 8:5, D.
July 6, at Dalymount, North Circular-road, Phibsborough, George, the only son of Mr. Valentine Delany, Library, Four Courts.

No. 5772 :: Ref. 1852-07-10, 8:5, D.
The oldest inhabitant of the borough of Monmouth is at last dead, after attaining the patriarchal age of 104.

No. 5773 :: Ref. 1852-07-17, 8:5, B.
July 2, at Cootehill, the wife of James Sharpe, Esq., M.D., of a son.

No. 5774 :: Ref. 1852-07-17, 8:5, B.
July 5, in Lurgan, the wife of Thomas Pentland, Esq., of a son.

No. 5775 :: Ref. 1852-07-17, 8:5, B.
July 8, at Williamstown, Clones, the lady of Francis Johnston, Esq., of a daughter.

No. 5776 :: Ref. 1852-07-17, 8:5, B.
July 9, at Dalston, London, the wife of the Rev. John Flannagan, of a daughter.

No. 5777 :: Ref. 1852-07-17, 8:5, B.
July 12, the wife of Mr. Robert Bewglass, of Woolwich, Kent, of a daughter.

No. 5778 :: Ref. 1852-07-17, 8:5, M.
In the Friends' Meeting-house, Lurgan, Thomas Fawcett, Laurel Hill, near Lisburn, to Sarah, daughter of the late Benjamin Thompson, of Spring Hill near Waringstown.

No. 5779 :: Ref. 1852-07-17, 8:5, M.
July 6, at Holywood Church, Thomas, only son of Thomas Batt, Esq., of Rathmullen House, co. Donegal, to Charlotte, eldest daughter of the Venerable Dalrymple Hesketh Knox, Archdeacon of Killaloe.

No. 5780 :: Ref. 1852-07-17, 8:5, M.
July 13, at St. Peter's Church, Dublin, by the Rev. John Blair Chapman, ex-F.T.C.D., Rector of Drumragh, co. Tyrone, uncle to the bride, Robert John Turnley Macrory, of Rutland-square, Dublin, Esq., eldest son of Adam John Macrory, of Duncairn, co. Antrim, Esq., to Sarah Elizabeth Hutchison, daughter of the late Edward Bunting, Esq., of Dublin.

No. 5781 :: Ref. 1852-07-17, 8:5, D.

At Poekataroo, Australia, in January last, John, youngest son of the late Charles Lewis, Esq., J.P., Kilkeel, Ireland.

No. 5782 :: Ref. 1852-07-17, 8:5, D.

July 2, at Kilmun, Argyleshire, Thomas Thompson, M.D., F.R.S.L. and E., &c., Regius Professor of Chemistry in the University of Glasgow, in his 80th year.

No. 5783 :: Ref. 1852-07-17, 8:5, D.

July 5, at Paris, of a cerebral fever, George Nugent, the only son of the Marquis of Westmeath, aged eight years.

No. 5784 :: Ref. 1852-07-17, 8:5, D.

July 7, at Dover, in the 55th year of his age, Captain Molyneux, late of the 37th Regiment, second son of the late General Sir Thomas Molyneux, Bart., of Castle Dillon, co. Armagh.

No. 5785 :: Ref. 1852-07-17, 8:5, D.

July 7, at Seville-place, Dublin, Mr. James Waddell, connected with the reporting department of the *Daily Express*, whose columns have daily borne evidence of his professional ability; having only entered on his 20th year.

No. 5786 :: Ref. 1852-07-17, 8:5, D.

July 9, at the residence of his grandfather, the Rev. William Douglas, Lowtherstown, of water in the head, William Nesbitt, aged 9 years, only son of Robert Nesbitt, Esq., of Derry.

No. 5787 :: Ref. 1852-07-17, 8:5, D.

July 13, of consumption, at Gartinardress, in the county of Cavan, in the 28th year of her age, Mary Clemina, the beloved wife of Wm. Young, Esq., Solicitor and Clerk of the Crown for the county of Roscommon.

No. 5788 :: Ref. 1852-07-17, 8:5, D.

Feb. 1, at Melbourne, Dr. John Kidd, R.N., F.R.C.S., and uncle of Abraham Kidd, M.D., of Ballymena, in the forty-eighth year of his age, much respected and liked by his friends and brother officers. He received his medical education at Dublin and Edinburgh, and entered as an assistant surgeon in the royal navy at an early age. He was soon promoted to the rank of surgeon, and had the honour of serving his country about twenty years. He was distinguished as a cool and steady operator, prompt in the treatment of disease, and skilful in his diagnostics. He saw much service, and his name is honourably mentioned in an Auckland paper, dated 17th January, 1846, by Colonel H. Despard, to his Excellency Governor Grey. He was then surgeon on board H.M.S. *Castor*. On this occasion (an engagement with the rebel chiefs Kawii and Heke) he and Dr. Pine were the senior medical officers among both naval and military, when a large number of officers and men were either killed or wounded.—*Lancet*.

No. 5789 :: Ref. 1852-07-24, 5:6, B.

July 11, the Viscountess Jocelyn, of a son.

No. 5790 :: Ref. 1852-07-24, 5:6, B.

July 16, Mrs. Thomas Donnelly, Enniskillen, of a son.

No. 5791 :: Ref. 1852-07-24, 5:6, B.

July 20, at Carrickmore, Termon, the lady of Henry St. George, Esq., of a son.

No. 5792 :: Ref. 1852-07-24, 5:6, M.

June 26, in St. John's Church, Buffalo, N.Y., America, George Frederick Allman, Esq., son of the late Capt. Allman, 48th regiment, Earcourt, co. Galway, to Nicholina, only daughter of Joseph Seaver, Esq., formerly Lieutenant in the 21st regiment, and grand-daughter of the late Captain Seaver, J.P., of Heath Hall, Newry.

No. 5793 :: Ref. 1852-07-24, 5:6, M.

July 7, in the Church of Ballybay, J.H. Ranson, Esq., Dundalk, to Eliza, eldest daughter of the late John Thomas Roberts, Esq., of Ballybay.

No. 5794 :: Ref. 1852-07-24, 5:6, M.

July 7, in St. Peter's Church, Dublin, R.W. Lowry, Esq., eldest son of R.W. Lowry, Esq., of Pomeroy House, co. Tyrone, to Frances Elizabeth, daughter of B.G. Brady, Esq., Mount Geale, co. Kilkenny.

No. 5795 :: Ref. 1852-07-24, 5:6, M.

July 13, in St. James's church, Paddington, Joseph Story, Esq., Bingfield, co. Cavan, to Caroline Sophia Kenneth, second daughter of the late Neville Reid, Esq., of Runnymede, Berks.

No. 5796 :: Ref. 1852-07-24, 5:6, M.

July 15, in St. Anne's Church, William Holland Furlonge, Esq., to Hester Elizabeth, eldest daughter of Robert Shekleton, Esq., M.D.

No. 5797 :: Ref. 1852-07-24, 5:6, M.

July 20, in St. Andrew's Church, Dublin, George Hugh Kidd, Esq., M.D., Great Brunswick street, Dublin, to Frances, second daughter of Wm. Rigby, Esq., Suffolk street.

No. 5798 :: Ref. 1852-07-24, 5:6, M.

In St. Mark's Church, Portadown, by Rev. F. Crawford, Incumbent, Mr. John Williamson, Portadown, to Rachel, eldest daughter of Mr. Wm. Totten, of Anagh, near Portadown.

No. 5799 :: Ref. 1852-07-24, 5:6, D.

July 2, at Greenwich, aged 63, George Hamilton, Barrack-master, 1st Class, and formerly Brevet Captain, 16th Lancers. He was the youngest and last surviving son of the late Major James Hamilton, of Grange, co. Tyrone.

No. 5800 :: Ref. 1852-07-24, 5:6, D.
July 17, at Farm Lodge, Lurgan, James M. Mercer, aged 27 years.

No. 5801 :: Ref. 1852-07-24, 5:6, D.
July 19, of hooping-cough, Tereza Elizabeth Clarke, daughter of Mr. John Clarke Adams, Armagh, aged 11 months.

No. 5802 :: Ref. 1852-07-24, 5:6, D.
July 20, Miss Corry, of Newtownbutler, last surviving sister of Capt. Corry, J.P., Enniskillen.

No. 5803 :: Ref. 1852-07-24, 5:6, D.
July 21, at the residence of her son-in-law, Major Farmar, Staff-officer of pensioners in this city, Mrs. Unity Cunningham, widow of the late James Cunningham, Esq., R.N., of Batramsley Lodge, Lymington, Hants, deeply and sincerely lamented.

No. 5804 :: Ref. 1852-07-24, 5:6, D.
Lately, at Munich, aged 78 years, M. Gruithusion, one of the most distinguished astronomers of Germany.

No. 5805 :: Ref. 1852-07-31, 8:5, B.
July 15, at St. Alben's Villas, Kentish Town, the wife of Captain C.W. Thompson, 58th Regiment, of a daughter.

No. 5806 :: Ref. 1852-07-31, 8:5, B.
July 15, at Charlemont, co. Armagh, the wife of T.R. Dobbin, Esq., of the Adjutant-General's Department, Dublin, of a daughter.

No. 5807 :: Ref. 1852-07-31, 8:5, B.
July 20, at Omagh, the lady of Doctor Hamilton, jun., of a daughter, still-born.

No. 5808 :: Ref. 1852-07-31, 8:5, B.
July 21, at Farren Connell House, co. Cavan, the lady of Richard Nugent, Esq., of a son.

No. 5809 :: Ref. 1852-07-31, 8:5, B.
July 21, at Carrick-on-Suir, the lady of F.J. Heath, Esq., Sub-Inspector of Constabulary, of a son.

No. 5810 :: Ref. 1852-07-31, 8:5, B.
July 23, at Edgbaston, the wife of Rev. Wm. Seaton, Association Secretary to the London Society for Promoting Christianity among the Jews, of a son.

No. 5811 :: Ref. 1852-07-31, 8:5, B.
July 26, the lady of George Wyse, Esq., M.D., Upper Sackville-street, Dublin, of a son.

No. 5812 :: Ref. 1852-07-31, 8:5, M.
July 15, in Newry, William Irwin, Esq., son of the late Rev. B. Irwin, rector of Laracoe, co. Meath, to Bithia, daughter of the late G. Glenny, Esq., of Moorevale, co. Armagh.

No. 5813 :: Ref. 1852-07-31, 8:5, M.
July 15, at the Roman Catholic Chapel, Cadogan-st., London, and also at the old parish church of Brompton, Antoine Marie Dieu Donne Chable, to Isabella Jane, daughter of the late Charles Silver Oliver, Esq., of Sun lodge, co. Cork.

No. 5814 :: Ref. 1852-07-31, 8:5, M.
July 26, at St. Ann's Church, Belfast, by the Rev. Edward Maguire, cousin to the bride, Mr. Anthony Lester, of Corn Market, Belfast (late of this city), to Rosetta, second daughter of James Ewart, Esq., of Great George's-street, Belfast.

No. 5815 :: Ref. 1852-07-31, 8:5, M.
July 27, at St. Peter's Church, Dublin, by Lord Bishop of Tuam, uncle to the bride, Richard, second son of the Right Hon. Baron Greene, to Louisa Lelias, fourth daughter of the Hon. John Plunket, and granddaughter of Lord Plunket, and the Right Hon. Charles Kendal Bushe, late Chief-Justice of the Queen's Bench.

No. 5816 :: Ref. 1852-07-31, 8:5, M.
On 28th inst., in St. Mark's Church, in this city, by the Rev. Benjamin Wade, Mr. George Beatty, Printer, to Grace, second daughter of the late Mr. James Barber, Gortmarron, county Tyrone.

No. 5817 :: Ref. 1852-07-31, 8:5, M.
Spencer Geo. Augustus, Lieut. 1st Royals, third son of T.H. Thursby, Esq., of Leamington Hastings, near Southam, to Kate Dorcas, second daughter of Sir Geo. Forster, Bart., of Coolderry, co. Monaghan.

No. 5818 :: Ref. 1852-07-31, 8:5, D.
June 25, at Carnaby, near Bridlington, Yorkshire, George Robinson, Esq., in his eighty-first year. He was one of the celebrated agriculturists of the East Riding, and distinguished as a most successful breeder of Leicestershire sheep, short-horns, and blood stock. He was the breeder of Carnaby, Bolivar, Bounce, Logic, Cato, Jerry, Morpeth, Melbourne, &c., and never trained a horse that was not a winner during the last 50 years. The Carnaby stud are well known.

No. 5819 :: Ref. 1852-07-31, 8:5, D.
July 12, Rev. F. O'Reilly, parish priest of Glenade, in the county Leitrim.

No. 5820 :: Ref. 1852-07-31, 8:5, D.
July 14, Ann, wife of the Rev. Edward Stuart, Presbyterian Minister, Clough, aged 27 years, and second daughter of Samuel Floyd, Esq., Kilkeel.

No. 5821 :: Ref. 1852-07-31, 8:5, D.
July 14, in Cork, Ellen, relict of Patrick Armstrong, Esq.

No. 5822 :: Ref. 1852-07-31, 8:5, D.
July 14, Mr. William Stephens, of Ballyshannon, aged 40 years.

No. 5823 :: Ref. 1852-07-31, 8:5, D.
July 16, at Ballyshannon, Donegal, Margaret, relict of John Irwin Eeles, Esq., late Lieut. in the 49th

regiment, and eldest daughter of the late Major Bunbury, of Johnstown, county Carlow.

No. 5824 :: Ref. 1852-07-31, 8:5, D.
July 17, at Castleblayney, Quartermaster John Maudsley, a native of Belturbet, and one of the old India heroes of the 8th Hussars. His name is honourably mentioned in the published records of his regiment, in which he had served 37 years. He was one of the hundred dismounted dragoons of his regiment at the assault of the fortress of Kalunga, where his gallant chief, the late General Sir Robert Rollo Gillespie, fell by his side, and—as poor Mr. Maudsley, excited by heroic reminiscences and generous feeling, used to tell—breathed his last gasp in his arms.

No. 5825 :: Ref. 1852-07-31, 8:5, D.
July 21, in his 26th year, looking to Jesus and washed in His most precious blood, Henry Michael, son of the late Captain John Murray Browne, 75th Regiment, and nephew of Charlotte Elizabeth.

No. 5826 :: Ref. 1852-07-31, 8:5, D.
July 22, at Ballygallon, Coleraine, Mr. Joseph Wilson, jun.

No. 5827 :: Ref. 1852-07-31, 8:5, D.
July 22, at Willmount, near Markethill, Wm. Morrison, aged 82 years. He was a member of the Society of Friends.

No. 5828 :: Ref. 1852-07-31, 8:5, D.
July 24, at Kew, in the twenty-seventh year of her age, Sarah, the beloved wife of Mr. Alexander Johnston, jun., of 324, Strand, London.

No. 5829 :: Ref. 1852-07-31, 8:5, D.
July 26, in the faith of Christ, John M'Mahon, Tassagh, in the 83d year of his age.

No. 5830 :: Ref. 1852-07-31, 8:5, D.
July 27, Miss Susanna Kittson, for many years Postmistress of Derrygonnelly, county Fermanagh.

No. 5831 :: Ref. 1852-07-31, 8:5, D.
July 27, Foster, youngest son of the Rev. John Elliott, of Smithborough, Co. Monaghan, aged 17 years.

No. 5832 :: Ref. 1852-07-31, 8:5, D.
July 29, at Belfast, by drowning, Mr. Edward Vincent, an old and respected letter-carrier. Mr. Vincent was that evening bathing in the river, almost opposite his owen [sic] residence, in Ballymacarrett, and having, it is believed, been seized with cramp, was submerged and drowned before assistance could reach him. The deceased has left a wife and family to deplore his premature and mournful death.

No. 5833 :: Ref. 1852-08-07, 4:3, B.
January 18, at Adelaide, South Australia, the lady of R.T. Tracy, Esq., M.D., late of Limerick, of a daughter.

No. 5834 :: Ref. 1852-08-07, 4:3, B.
June 28, at Malta, the lady of Major Fenwick, of H.M. 76th regt., of a daughter.

No. 5835 :: Ref. 1852-08-07, 4:3, B.
July 22, at Springfield, Mohill, the lady of Rev. S.E. Hoops, of a son.

No. 5836 :: Ref. 1852-08-07, 4:3, B.
July 26, at [R]etreat, co. Cavan, the wife of E.R. Bredin, Esq., J.P., of a son and heir.

No. 5837 :: Ref. 1852-08-07, 4:3, B.
July 29, under the influence of chloroform (fourth occasion), Mrs. John Oliver Smith, Richmond-villa, Brighton, of a daughter.

No. 5838 :: Ref. 1852-08-07, 4:3, B.
July 30, at Aghadown Glebe, the lady of the Archdeacon of Ross, of a daughter.

No. 5839 :: Ref. 1852-08-07, 4:3, B.
July 31, at Drumnakilly parsonage, Omagh, the lady of the Rev. Edward Moore, of a son.

No. 5840 :: Ref. 1852-08-07, 4:3, B.
Aug. 1, at Carnagh House, Keady, the wife of John Robert Irwin, Esq., of a daughter.

No. 5841 :: Ref. 1852-08-07, 4:3, B.
Aug. 1, at No. 6, Harcourt-street, Dublin, the wife of Captain G.A. Maude, Royal Horse Artillery, of a son.

No. 5842 :: Ref. 1852-08-07, 4:3, M.
June 22, at Rodney, Mississippi, by Rev. Dr. R.A. New, Mr. James Stewart, to Miss Mary Murdock, formerly of Tullaree, Glasslough.

No. 5843 :: Ref. 1852-08-07, 4:3, M.
June 29, at Biloxi, Mississippi, by Rev. C.H. Williamson, of New Orleans, Thomas Seller, Esq., of New Orleans, to Adele Leonide, fourth daughter of the late John Bligh Byrne, Esq., Lurgan, co. Armagh.

No. 5844 :: Ref. 1852-08-07, 4:3, M.
July 18, in St. Bridget's Church, Dublin, by Rev. John Drury, Mr. Benjamin Collins, South Great George's-street, to Maria Eliza, youngest daughter of Mr. Henry Godkin, Gorey, co. Wexford.

No. 5845 :: Ref. 1852-08-07, 4:3, M.
July 22, in St. Anne's Church, Dublin, by Rev. H. Vereker, brother to the bride, John Henry, son of Joshua Nunn, Esq., of Dawson-street, Dublin, to Catherine Elizabeth, eldest daughter of H. Vereker, of Wellington-road, Esq.

No. 5846 :: Ref. 1852-08-07, 4:3, M.
July 29, at St. Mary's Bryanston-square, London, by Right Rev. the Lord Bishop of London, assisted by the Rev. Anthony Cotterell Lefroy, the Rev. Ernest Hawkins, M.A., minister of Curzon-street Chapel, and secretary to the Society for the   (*continued...*)

No. 5486, continued: ...Propagation of the Gospel in Foreign Parts, to Sophia Anna, third daughter of the late Rev. John Henry George Lefroy, of Ewshot-house, Hants, and rector of Ashe, Hants, and of Compton, Surrey.

No. 5847 :: Ref. 1852-08-07, 4:3, M.
July 29, at St. John's Chapel, Edinburgh, by Rev. Francis Flavell, Rector of Loughgall and Prebendary of Armagh, Colonel William Cox, K.H., Assistant-Quartermaster-General, Limerick District, to Matilda, daughter of the late James Hay, Esq., writer to the *Signet*.

No. 5848 :: Ref. 1852-08-07, 4:3, M.
July 29, at Bray Church, by the Venerable Archdeacon Singer, Regius Professor of Divinity, T.C.D., the Rev. Maurice F. Day, Incumbent of St. Matthias, Dublin, to Jane, second daughter of Joseph Gabbett, Esq., of 17, Lower Mount-street, Dublin.

No. 5849 :: Ref. 1852-08-07, 4:3, M.
July 29, at Knockbreda, by Rev. Ed. Hartrick, O'Neill Bayly, Esq., Madison, United States, to Caroline Ann, youngest daughter of the late James Irwin, Esq., Willbrooke, Co. Tyrone.

No. 5850 :: Ref. 1852-08-07, 4:3, M.
July 29, in the Cathedral, Derry, by Rev. Robert Higinbotham, James, only son of the late Mr. John Hamilton, of Doonin Cottage, co. Fermanagh, to Miss Magee, daughter to Mr. Henry Magee, late Head Constable of Constabulary, Derry.

No. 5851 :: Ref. 1852-08-07, 4:3, M.
July 29, at Gowran Church, George Vandeleur Steele, Esq., younger son of the late George Steele, Esq., of Harristown, Queen's County, to Susan, eldest daughter of the Rev. Alexander Staples, D.D., Rector of Gowran, co. Kilkenny.

No. 5852 :: Ref. 1852-08-07, 4:3, M.
July 30, in the Wesleyan Chapel, Dungannon, by Rev. John Armstrong, Rev. John Dwyer, to Frances Maria, youngest daughter of the late Mr. John M'Kells, of Moy, Co. Tyrone. They were presented with a very handsome Bible and hymn-book, by the young men of the Congregation.

No. 5853 :: Ref. 1852-08-07, 4:3, M.
July 30, in the Presbyterian Church, Downshire Road, Newry, by the Rev. William Henderson, of Armagh, Mr. James Woods, wine and spirit merchant, to Maria, youngest daughter of the late Mr. Alexander Peacock, sen., both of Newry.

No. 5854 :: Ref. 1852-08-07, 4:3, M.
July 31, the marriage was solemnised between Captain Lowther, M.P., First Life Guards, and Miss Caulfield, eldest daughter of St. George Caulfield, Esq., and the Hon. Mrs. Caulfield. The ceremony took place at St. Paul's Church, Knightsbridge.

No. 5855 :: Ref. 1852-08-07, 4:3, M.
Aug. 3, at Carrickfergus, by Very Rev. the Dean of Connor, William Edward Batwell, Esq., Solicitor, Belfast, to Jane Sloane, eldest daughter of Richard Thompson, Esq., Woodburn Cottage, Carrickfergus.

No. 5856 :: Ref. 1852-08-07, 4:3, D.
July 9, at Philadelphia, in the 25th year of his age, in full hope of a blessed immortality, through the merits of his Redeemer, William S. West, eldest son of the Rev. John West, of Newtownhamilton.

No. 5857 :: Ref. 1852-08-07, 4:3, D.
July 19, at his residence, Liskey, near Strabane, Mr. Hugh Stewart, aged 61 years.

No. 5858 :: Ref. 1852-08-07, 4:3, D.
July 20, at Mullerton House, near Kilkeel, Susanna, wife of Henry Atkinson, Esq.

No. 5859 :: Ref. 1852-08-07, 4:3, D.
July 21, James, son of Mr. Richard Gwynn, Strabane, aged 27 years.

No. 5860 :: Ref. 1852-08-07, 4:3, D.
July 29, at Kingstown, Miss Catherine Wentworth, of Portadown.

No. 5861 :: Ref. 1852-08-07, 4:3, D.
July 30, Eliza, second daughter of Walter Scott, Esq., of Strabane, merchant, aged six years.

No. 5862 :: Ref. 1852-08-07, 4:3, D.
July 31, at Rockdale House, Co. Tyrone, Thomas William, second son of the late James Lowry, Esq., of Rockdale.

No. 5863 :: Ref. 1852-08-07, 4:3, D.
Aug. 1, of apoplexy, aged seventy four, Mr. John Lewis, of Belfast.

No. 5864 :: Ref. 1852-08-07, 4:3, D.
Aug. 1, at Sandy-row, Belfast, Robert, sixth son of Wm. Baird, aged eleven.

No. 5865 :: Ref. 1852-08-07, 4:3, D.
Aug. 1, at 19, Graeme Street, Glasgow, Mrs. Graham, third daughter of H.S. Nixon, Esq. late of Nixon Lodge, co. Cavan.

No. 5866 :: Ref. 1852-08-07, 4:3, D.
Aug. 2, William Thomas, infant son of Mr. Thomas Gilmore.

No. 5867 :: Ref. 1852-08-07, 4:3, D.
Aug. 2, at 103, North Queen Street, Belfast, Alicia, daughter of the late Jacob Hancock, of Lisburn, Esq.

No. 5868 :: Ref. 1852-08-07, 4:3, D.
Aug. 3, at the Royal Hotel, Holyhead, on her way to Ireland, Louisa, relict of the late John Lushington Reilly, Esq., of Scarva.

No. 5869 :: Ref. 1852-08-07, 4:3, D.
Aug. 4, Mr. William Davidson, of Ballymena, aged 38 years. His remains were interred in Armagh 6th August.

No. 5870 :: Ref. 1852-08-14, 5:5, B.
July 27, at Broomfield, co. Cavan, the lady of Rev. A. Monypenny, of a daughter.

No. 5871 :: Ref. 1852-08-14, 5:5, B.
July 28, at Lupta, near Ballyshannon, co. Donegal, the wife of J. King, Esq., of a son.

No. 5872 :: Ref. 1852-08-14, 5:5, B.
July 30, the wife of James F. Alexander, Esq., Provincial Bank of Ireland, Omagh, of a son.

No. 5873 :: Ref. 1852-08-14, 5:5, B.
Aug. 1, at Miltown-house, co. Tyrone, the wife of J.J. Hamilton Humphreys, Esq., Barrister-at-law, of a daughter.

No. 5874 :: Ref. 1852-08-14, 5:5, B.
Aug. 5, at Newtownlimavady, Mrs. Hugh Lane, of a son.

No. 5875 :: Ref. 1852-08-14, 5:5, B.
On the 7th instant, at Gilford, the wife of the Rev. J. Stewart, of a son.

No. 5876 :: Ref. 1852-08-14, 5:5, B.
Aug. 9, at Waterford, the lady of John Allingham, Esq., Provincial Bank, of a son.

No. 5877 :: Ref. 1852-08-14, 5:5, B.
On the 10th instant, at the Castle, Dublin, the Lady Fanny Lambert, of a daughter.

No. 5878 :: Ref. 1852-08-14, 5:5, M.
July 22, Viscount Mandeville, eldest son of the Duke of Manchester, to the Comtesse Louise Fredericke Auguste D'Alten, in the Palace Chapel in Hanover, in the presence of her Majesty the Queen of Hanover, the Royal Princess, and a distinguished assembly of friends.

No. 5879 :: Ref. 1852-08-14, 5:5, M.
Aug. 3, in Rathclarin Church, William A. Treacy, Esq., Surveyor for the West Riding of Cork, to Agnes Johnston, second daughter of John J. Thompson, Esq., Manager of the Provincial Bank of Ireland, Bandon.

No. 5880 :: Ref. 1852-08-14, 5:5, M.
Aug. 5, at Heston, Middlesex, Alfred Williams, Esq., C.E., of Newport, Monmouthshire, to Anna Matilda, fourth daughter of the late Hon. James Hook, H.M. Judge of the Mixed Commission Courts at Sierra Leone, and granddaughter of the late Dr. Adam Clarke.

No. 5881 :: Ref. 1852-08-14, 5:5, M.
Aug. 5, at St. Mary's Clapham, Surrey, Michael B. Lane, Esq., of Londonderry, Solicitor, to Mary Isabel, eldest daughter of the late Robert Hills, Esq., Commander in the Royal Navy of Portugal, and formerly of South-hill, Henley-on-Thames.

No. 5882 :: Ref. 1852-08-14, 5:5, M.
Aug. 5, at Ballyjamesduff, the Rev. Mr. Hogg, of Drumkilroosk, to Elizabeth, daughter of Robert Morrow, Esq., of Rockville.

No. 5883 :: Ref. 1852-08-14, 5:5, M.
Aug. 5, at Cockayne Hatley, Bedfordshire, by the Hon. and Rev. Ricard [sic] Cust, Captain Henry Francis Cust, Private Secretary to the Lord Lieutenant of Ireland, to Sarah Jane, widow of Major Sidney Streatfield, and daughter of I. Cookson, Esq., of Meldonpark, Northumberland.

No. 5884 :: Ref. 1852-08-14, 5:5, M.
Aug. 5, a couple were married, by license, at the parish church, Blackburn, and it was afterwards discovered that the woman was the man's step-daughter—the daughter of his first wife.

No. 5885 :: Ref. 1852-08-14, 5:5, M.
Aug. 6, at Dungannon, by Rev. C.L. Morell, James Robert Girvin, Esq., Roan Mills, Armagh, to Jane, youngest daughter of John M'Clelland, Esq., Dungannon.

No. 5886 :: Ref. 1852-08-14, 5:5, M.
Aug. 6, in the Ballinderry Presbyterian Church, by the Rev. Henry Leebody, Mr. John M'Neight, to Miss Anne Jane Wright, both of Magheragall.

No. 5887 :: Ref. 1852-08-14, 5:5, M.
Aug. 11, in the Presbyterian Church, Lisburn, by Rev. Alexander Henderson, Captain Henry Maxwell, of the ship *Asia*, son of the late Mr. James Maxwell, Portaferry, to Eleanor Georgina, second daughter of Wm. Kelsey, Esq., Plantation, Lisburn.

No. 5888 :: Ref. 1852-08-14, 5:5, D.
June 16, at Philadelphia, U.S., Mary Anne, daughter of the late Thomas Howe, Esq., of Redhills, and relict of Lieut. John Francis, late of Redhills, co. Cavan, Ireland.

No. 5889 :: Ref. 1852-08-14, 5:5, D.
Augt. 1, at Kilwendeage, South Wales, William Loftus Saurin, the beloved child of Mark Saurin, Esq., and grandson of the late Right Hon. and Right Rev. Lord Bishop of Dromore, aged four years and seven months.

No. 5890 :: Ref. 1852-08-14, 5:5, D.
Augt. 3, at Letterkenny, Mrs. Elliott, aged 83 years.

No. 5891 :: Ref. 1852-08-14, 5:5, D.
Augt. 4, at Bushey, Hertfordshire, on his birth-day, aged 97, John Smith, formerly a soldier in the British army, and as such present at the battle of Bunker's Hill, June 17, 1775.

No. 5892 :: Ref. 1852-08-14, 5:5, D.
Augt. 5, at Inverness-terrace, Bayswater, aged 49, the Rev. John Parry, rector of St. John's, Wapping, and late Fellow of Brasenose College, Oxford, of confluent smallpox, after 11 days' illness.

No. 5893 :: Ref. 1852-08-14, 5:5, D.
Augt. 6, Mrs. C.H. Courtenay, widow of the late Charles Henry Courtenay, Esq., Southwark, Newry.

No. 5894 :: Ref. 1852-08-14, 5:5, D.
Augt. 6, at Cloghaneely, co. Donegal, Commander John M'Gladery, R.N., aged 77 years. In the early part of his life he was actively engaged in the service of his country, having been present at the principal naval engagements which occurred towards the close of the last, and the beginning of the present century, and also in several minor actions. While midshipman on board the *Culloden*, he took part in the following battles—Hothian's, 1795; Cape St. Vincent; the attack on Teneriffe; and the Nile; while in the *Foudroyant* he was present at the capture of the *Moringo*, and the *Belle Poule*; he also served in the *Leopard* and *Otter*, and during that time took part in the reduction of the Isle of France, and the capture of the *Venus*, and the recapture of the *African* and *Ceylon*. The last thirty years of his life was spent in the coast-guard service.

No. 5895 :: Ref. 1852-08-14, 5:5, D.
Augt. 7, at Ballaghmore, co. Fermanagh, Jane, relict of the late James Quinton, Esq., and mother of Wm. Quinton, Esq., Enniskillen.

No. 5896 :: Ref. 1852-08-14, 5:5, D.
Augt. 7, in Letterkenny, the Rev. William Henry, D.D., in the sixty-fourth year of his age, and the fortieth year of his ministry. The late Dr. Henry was a man of first-rate talents, and of the most varied learning and accurate scholarship. He was a most faithful and devoted gospel minister, and a very popular public speaker.

No. 5897 :: Ref. 1852-08-14, 5:5, D.
A man named Magilligan, who had a wife and five children, was, on August 8, near Strabane, killed by lightning. He was at the time engaged in saving a stack of turf.

No. 5898 :: Ref. 1852-08-14, 5:5, D.
Aug. 8, at Dundalk, James O'Callaghan, Esq., for many years a magistrate of the County Louth.

No. 5899 :: Ref. 1852-08-14, 5:5, D.
Aug. 8, at Lurgan, Thomas Howard, the infant son of Mr. Thomas Pentland.

No. 5900 :: Ref. 1852-08-14, 5:5, D.
Aug. 8, at Dawson-street, Dublin, Jane, the beloved wife of Joshua Nunn, Esq.

No. 5901 :: Ref. 1852-08-14, 5:5, D.
Aug. 10, Lieut. Gen. Sir Thomas Downman.—The death of this most distinguished officer, took place in a sudden manner at Woolwich, where he was commandant.

No. 5902 :: Ref. 1852-08-14, 5:5, D.
Aug. 10, in the forty-third year of his age, at Stewartstown, the Rev. James Lennon, P.P.

No. 5903 :: Ref. 1852-08-14, 5:5, D.
Aug. 11, at 48, Waring-street, Belfast, of consumption, Samuel, son of John Hoy, aged 17 years.

No. 5904 :: Ref. 1852-08-14, 5:5, D.
At her residence in Tralee, Mrs. Morphy, relict of Richard Morphy, Esq.

No. 5905 :: Ref. 1852-08-14, 5:5, D.
Mr. John Thompson, of Derrycrew, near Loughgall, after a long confinement, aged 76 years. He was much regretted by those who knew him.

No. 5906 :: Ref. 1852-08-21, 4:3, B.
Aug. 9, at Derry, the wife of Mr. M'Murray, Auctioneer, of a son, her eighteenth child.

No. 5907 :: Ref. 1852-08-21, 4:3, B.
Aug. 9, at Barondown, Co. Wexford, the lady of Robert Dowse, Esq., of a son.

No. 5908 :: Ref. 1852-08-21, 4:3, B.
Aug. 10, at the Castle, Dublin, the Lady Fanny Lambart, of a daughter.

No. 5909 :: Ref. 1852-08-21, 4:3, B.
Aug. 12, Mrs. Lever, the wife of Dr. Lever, M.D., of a daughter.

No. 5910 :: Ref. 1852-08-21, 4:3, B.
Aug. 13, the Countess of Clarendon, of a son.

No. 5911 :: Ref. 1852-08-21, 4:3, B.
At the Legation of the United States, at Lima, the lady of the Hon. J. Randolph Clay, Charge d'Affaires of the United States, of a son.

No. 5912 :: Ref. 1852-08-21, 4:3, B.
Aug. 17, at Crilly-house, co. Tyrone, the wife of Vaughan Montgomery, Esq., of a son.

No. 5913 :: Ref. 1852-08-21, 4:3, M.
Aug. 5, at Donnybrook Church, Rev. A.W. Edwards, Prebendary of Donaghmore, to Caroline Stanley, youngest daughter of the late C.H. Todd, Esq., Professor of Anatomy R.C.S., Ireland.

No. 5914 :: Ref. 1852-08-21, 4:3, M.
Aug. 11, at Thames Ditton, Surrey, John Turner, Esq., Captain, Royal Horse Artillery, to Caroline, daughter of the Lord Chancellor.

No. 5915 :: Ref. 1852-08-21, 4:3, M.
Aug. 11, at St. Andrew's church, John Armstrong Fairs, M.D., Dublin, to Matilda Susanna, second daughter of Rev. J.H. Mason, Chancellor of St. Patrick's Cathedral, Dublin.

No. 5916 :: Ref. 1852-08-21, 4:3, M.
Aug. 12, at Benmore church, co. Fermanagh, William M. Burke, Esq., M.D., Ballydugan, co. Galway, to Harriet Isabella, only daughter of the Rev. Hugh Hamilton, rector of Innismacsaint.

No. 5917 :: Ref. 1852-08-21, 4:3, M.
Aug. 12, at Lurgan, Richard G. Bushby, Esq., of Kirkkale [sic], Liverpool, to Annie Julia, only child of F. Usher, Esq.

No. 5918 :: Ref. 1852-08-21, 4:3, M.
Aug. 12, in Coleraine, James Clarke, Esq., of Porthall, Strabane, to Anne, daughter of the late D. Taylor, Esq.

No. 5919 :: Ref. 1852-08-21, 4:3, M.
Aug. 13th, in Brantry Church, by Rev. G.E. Alexander, Mr. Jno. Baker, Armagh, to Isabella, only daughter of Mr. Thomas Cadoo, Mullin, Co. Tyrone.

No. 5920 :: Ref. 1852-08-21, 4:3, M.
Aug. 14th, in Mark's Church, Dublin, Alexander M'Donald, Esq., of Hillsboro', Co. Down, to Eliza, youngest daughter of the late John Falkner, Esq., of Belfast.

No. 5921 :: Ref. 1852-08-21, 4:3, M.
Aug. 17, in St. Anne's Church, Belfast, Mr. James Jenkins, of Belfast, to Elizabeth, third daughter of Mr. Alexander Crawford, Mount Charles.

No. 5922 :: Ref. 1852-08-21, 4:3, M.
In Ballymoney, by Rev. Robert Park, A.M., John Maddison, Esq., Officer Inland Revenue, Leith, to Mary Jane, daughter of the late Joseph Anderson, Esq., Ballymoney.

No. 5923 :: Ref. 1852-08-21, 4:3, M.
Aug. 5, in Fahan Church, Minchin Lloyd, Esq., of Summerhill, co. Derry, to Elizabeth, relict of the Rev. James Graham.

No. 5924 :: Ref. 1852-08-21, 4:3, M.
Aug. 11, in Donnybrook Church, R. Burrowes Brunker, Esq., of York-street, to Sarah, relict of William Rutherford, Esq., J.P., of Drum, co. Monaghan.

No. 5925 :: Ref. 1852-08-21, 4:3, D.
June 29th, at Georgetown, Demerara, in the 72d year of his age, Jeffrey Hart Bent, Chief Justice of British Guiana. He held the commission of Judge under four Sovereigns, his first appointment to the Bench of New South Wales bearing date in 1814. He was subsequently, in succession, Chief Justice of Grenada, of St. Lucia, first puisne Judge of Trinidad, and for the last 16 years Chief Justice of British Guiana, served in the West Indies (with but one leave of absence) for 32 years. So long a career of service, unrewarded by any mark of distinction from the Sovereign, is totally unprecedented.

No. 5926 :: Ref. 1852-08-21, 4:3, D.
July 30, at Strasbourg, William M'Cann, Esq., of Herbert House, Booterstown, brother of James M'Cann, Esq., M.P., for Drogheda.

No. 5927 :: Ref. 1852-08-21, 4:3, D.
Aug. 8, at Drumnabuoy, near Strabane, Mary Anne, relict of the late Robert Smylie, Esq., Camus.

No. 5928 :: Ref. 1852-08-21, 4:3, D.
Aug. 9, at Ballinagh, co. Cavan, Anne Eliza, wife of T.S. O'Reilly, Esq., M.D.

No. 5929 :: Ref. 1852-08-21, 4:3, D.
Aug. 9, at Millvale, Rostrevor, Eliza Smith, eldest daughter of the late Mr. Samuel Walker, Tandragee.

No. 5930 :: Ref. 1852-08-21, 4:3, D.
Aug. 9, at Rossvoyland Lodge, near Donegal, Miss Hamilton, daughter of the late Captain Hamilton, of the Coast Guard Service.

No. 5931 :: Ref. 1852-08-21, 4:3, D.
Aug. 10, at Plymouth, John Carley, Esq., Belfast, Barrister-at-Law.

No. 5932 :: Ref. 1852-08-21, 4:3, D.
Aug. 12, at 39, Harwicke-street, Dublin, Miss Waller, daughter of the late Richard Waller, Esq., of Dawson-street, at a very advanced age.

No. 5933 :: Ref. 1852-08-21, 4:3, D.
Aug. 13, in Lisnaskea, at the house of her son-in-law, Mr. James Haire, Alicia Graham, aged 78 years.

No. 5934 :: Ref. 1852-08-21, 4:3, D.
Aug. 14, at his residence, Willoughby place, Enniskillen, A. Thompson, Esq., aged 56. In 1830, Mr. Thompson was an extensive tobacco manufacturer, but having served as a juror after the Macken fight, in which a conviction was obtained, exclusive dealing induced him to give up business and retire into private life.

No. 5935 :: Ref. 1852-08-21, 4:3, D.
Aug. 14, at Rathmines, Walter Glascock, Esq., late Assistant Registrar of Deeds, Dublin.

No. 5936 :: Ref. 1852-08-21, 4:3, D.
Aug. 14, at Belnaleck, co. Fermanagh, aged 80 years, Mr. Christopher Betty.

No. 5937 :: Ref. 1852-08-21, 4:3, D.
Aug. 15, in Enniskillen, Mrs. Mary M'Aloon, aged 63.

No. 5938 :: Ref. 1852-08-21, 4:3, D.
Aug. 16, John, eldest son of George Beatty, of Killikeran, Brookboro', of fever.

No. 5939 :: Ref. 1852-08-21, 4:3, D.
Aug. 16, at Newry, in his sixty-first year, George Guy, Esq., shipowner.

No. 5940 :: Ref. 1852-08-21, 4:3, D.
Aug. 16, at Killishill Rectory, co. Tyrone, after an illness of many months, Frances Nugent, daughter of the Rev. R.H. Horner.

No. 5941 :: Ref. 1852-08-21, 4:3, D.
Aug. 16, at her mother's house, Gledstown, Maguiresbridge, Mary Finlay, widow of the Rev. Joseph O'Reilly, late Minister of Lisbellaw.

No. 5942 :: Ref. 1852-08-21, 4:3, D.
Aug. 16, John Crozier, Esq., Gortra, Newtownbutler, J.P., for the county of Fermanagh, and senior magistrate of the district, in consequence of a fall from his horse.

No. 5943 :: Ref. 1852-08-21, 4:3, D.
Aug. 17, at Lower Gardiner-street, Dublin, Catherine, daughter of Thomas Kernaghan, Esq., of Enniskillen.

No. 5944 :: Ref. 1852-08-28, 5:6, B.
Aug. 17, at Armagh, the wife of Mr. Wm. Campbell, of a daughter.

No. 5945 :: Ref. 1852-08-28, 5:6, B.
Aug. 17, the lady of Francis West Connolly, Esq., of Ballinamore, co. Leitrim, of a daughter.

No. 5946 :: Ref. 1852-08-28, 5:6, B.
Aug. 20, at Inistioge, co. Kilkenny, the lady of Alex. Hamilton, Esq., of a son.

No. 5947 :: Ref. 1852-08-28, 5:6, B.
Aug. 20, at Grenville-place, Cork, the wife of John Francis Maguire, M.P., of a daughter.

No. 5948 :: Ref. 1852-08-28, 5:6, B.
At Elizabeth Town, New Jersey, U.S.A., the Lady of Bernard Falls Henry, Esq., late of Portrush, of a son.

No. 5949 :: Ref. 1852-08-28, 5:6, M.
Aug. 3, at New York, Mr. Robert Nugent, formerly of Dundalk, to Prudentia, daughter of the late George Foyle, Esq., New Orleans.

No. 5950 :: Ref. 1852-08-28, 5:6, M.
Aug. 13, in Tullylish, Mr. Robert Dobson, Turleenan, Moy, to Anne, sixth daughter of Mr. Wm. Mills, Clare, Waringstown.

No. 5951 :: Ref. 1852-08-28, 5:6, M.
Aug. 19, in Glenavy Church, Mr. Henry Thompson, of Gilford, to Sarah Anne, eldest daughter of the late John M. Johnston, Esq., Glenavy.

No. 5952 :: Ref. 1852-08-28, 5:6, M.
Aug. 19, in the Independent Meeting-house, Donegall-place, Belfast, by the Rev. Dr. Bryce, Mr. Francis Smyth, to Elizabeth, eldest daughter of Mr. John M'Blain, Belfast.

No. 5953 :: Ref. 1852-08-28, 5:6, M.
Aug. 19, in St. Mary's, Cheltenham, Captain Robert Hedley, 62d Regt., to Charlotte Emma, youngest daughter of the late Charles Coote, Esq., of Bellamont Forest, co. Cavan, and niece of the late Lord Baron Cremorne.

No. 5954 :: Ref. 1852-08-28, 5:6, M.
Aug. 21, at Swanscombe, Kent, Francis Nethersole, eldest son of George Cates, Esq., of Darenth, to Anna Georgiana, second daughter of General and Lady Charlotte Bacon.

No. 5955 :: Ref. 1852-08-28, 5:6, M.
Aug. 24, in Monkstown Church, by the Very Rev. the Dean of Dromore, assisted by the Rev. Charles Seaver, Thomas Seaver, of Heath Hall, co. Armagh, Esq., to Maria Nicholina, only child of the late Stephenson Seaver, Esq.

No. 5956 :: Ref. 1852-08-28, 5:6, M.
Aug. 26, in St. Ann's Church, Belfast, James Hewetson, Esq., to Lizzie, daughter of the late Geo. Gardner, Esq., both of Belfast.

No. 5957 :: Ref. 1852-08-28, 5:6, M.
At Wenlock, Shropshire [sic], Robert Gore, of Clogher, Esq., son of the Hon. and Very Rev. the late Dean of Killala, to Elizabeth, daughter of H.G. Edwards, of Ravengh [sic], co. Tyrone.

No. 5958 :: Ref. 1852-08-28, 5:6, D.
June 23, a man died in the district of Benjoemas, Batavia, in the 116th year of his age. An unusual case of longevity in that country; he was a labouring man, had four wives, and has left eight children, the eldest of whom is 72, and the youngest 16.

No. 5959 :: Ref. 1852-08-28, 5:6, D.
June 23, at Chillakall, Zillah Rungpore, Bengal, Mrs. Sarah Sankey, late of London, aged 59, from dysentery.

No. 5960 :: Ref. 1852-08-28, 5:6, D.
June 28, at Stellingsbosch, Cape of Good Hope, Daniel O'Flinn, Esq., M.D., and resident magistrate, son of the late William O'Flinn, Esq., M.D., of Flynnville, near Cloyne, Co. Cork.

No. 5961 :: Ref. 1852-08-28, 5:6, D.
Aug. 8, at Cirencester, Miss Sarah Lediard, aged 70, only surviving issue of William Lediard, late of Cirencester, a Lieutenant in the Plymouth division of the Royal Marines, who served under Sir George Bridges, afterwards Lord Rodney, on board the *Anson*, April 12, 1782, obtaining a decisive victory over the French fleet under De Grasse; and on Lieutenant Lediard returning to England in the *Ville de Paris*, the vessel sank, and all on board perished.

No. 5962 :: Ref. 1852-08-28, 5:6, D.
Aug. 11, at Sudbury, Suffolk, Miss Gainsborough, aged 66. Her time and property were exclusively devoted to the cause of God and the temporal and eternal interests of the poor around her, by whom, as

well as by a large circle of Christian friends, her memory will ever be held in affectionate remembrance.

No. 5963 :: Ref. 1852-08-28, 5:6, D.

Aug. 14, at Parkhurst, Isle of Wight, Emma Catherine, relict of Robert Langford Besnard, Esq., of Cork.

No. 5964 :: Ref. 1852-08-28, 5:6, D.

Aug. 17, at the Gate Cottage, Deanery, Armagh, aged 63, Mr. John Raubb, for more than thirty years a favoured and faithful servant in the family of the late Rev. Dr. Elrington.

No. 5965 :: Ref. 1852-08-28, 5:6, D.

Aug. 18, George Spear, Esq., Treasurer of the County of the Town of Carrickfergus.

No. 5966 :: Ref. 1852-08-28, 5:6, D.

Aug. 19, Rev. J.C. Ledlie, D.D., minister of the congregation of Eustace-street, Dublin. He preached in his own pulpit on Sunday, though labouring under sickness at the time. He afterwards grew rapidly worse, and finally sank to rest on Thursday morning, about eleven o'clock. He had been 24 years minister of Eustace street, having for twenty-four years previously been the pastor of the first Presbyterian congregation in Larne, in which he succeeded the Rev. Dr. Worral. He had been educated in Calvinistic priniciples, which he renounced during his first ministry in Donegal. He was a man of great ability—of sound principles, and of strong feelings.

No. 5967 :: Ref. 1852-08-28, 5:6, D.

Aug. 20, at Rathgar, Thomas Torrens Rowley Miller, Esq., of Marlborough-street, Dublin, in his forty-first year.

No. 5968 :: Ref. 1852-08-28, 5:6, D.

Aug. 21, [a]t Rathmines, Sarah, the beloved wife of the Rev. Dr. Urwick.

No. 5969 :: Ref. 1852-08-28, 5:6, D.

Aug. 21, at Bundoran, Martha Hawley, wife of Col. Archdall, of Castle Archdall, co. Fermanagh.

No. 5970 :: Ref. 1852-08-28, 5:6, D.

Aug. 21, at Sedennan, near Omagh, Mr. Jas. Greer, upwards of 80 years of age.

No. 5971 :: Ref. 1852-08-28, 5:6, D.

Aug. 22, Rev. Dr. Alexander, of Belfast, in the 80th year of his age, and the forty-ninth of his ministry. The leading public events of his life are easily told. He was licensed to preach the everlasting Gospel in 1803, and in the same year he was invited to become the pastor of the Covenanting Congregation in the neighbourhood of Derry, and ordained to that charge. There he spent twenty-two years of his life, and was exceedingly popular and much beloved. The Rev. Josias Alexander, of Belfast, died in 1823, and in 1825, Dr. Alexander was invited to accept the charge of the Belfast Reformed Presbyterian Church, which had been raised entirely through the singularly popular talents and extraordinary labours of his deceased brother. In 1826 he was installed to this pastorate, and with great ability, as well as with much acceptance to the congregation, he continued to discharge the onerous duties, both public and private, connected with that office, until 1850, when, through age and increasing infirmities, he was compelled to resign active service in Church, and the Rev. Robert M. Henry, a most excellent young minister, of decided talents and great eloquence, was, with the Doctor's most cordial approval, ordained as his assistant and successor.

No. 5972 :: Ref. 1852-08-28, 5:6, D.

At Ramridge cottage, Andover Hants, Mr. Gawlers, aged 87 years.

No. 5973 :: Ref. 1852-08-28, 5:6, D.

At Portlehew, Scotland, Helen, alias "Auld Nelly," Main, in the 102d year of her age.

No. 5974 :: Ref. 1852-08-28, 5:6, D.

Of yellow fever, a month after his arrival at Port-au-Prince, Mr. W.K. Gretton, vice-consul of England.—His young wife had preceded her husband to the grave but twenty-four hours, leaving alone their young child. Mr. Gretton was of a distinguished family in England, and had been a captain in the 5th Carbineers. Mrs. Gretton was a daughter of Lieutenant-General Sir John Burgoyne.

No. 5975 :: Ref. 1852-09-04, 8:2, B.

June 28, at the Bishop's Palace, Calcutta, the wife of the Rev. John Bloomfield, of a daughter.

No. 5976 :: Ref. 1852-09-04, 8:2, B.

Aug. 27, at Great Yarmouth, the wife of the Rev. Edward Whately, of a daughter.

No. 5977 :: Ref. 1852-09-04, 8:2, B.

Aug. 29, at Ballymore-house, Tandragee, the wife of the Rev. James Bell, of a daughter.

No. 5978 :: Ref. 1852-09-04, 8:2, M.

Aug. 19, in Bryansford Church, the Rev. Andrew Creery, incumbent of Dunseverick, Cavan, to Alice, daughter of the late John Tate, Esq.

No. 5979 :: Ref. 1852-09-04, 8:2, M.

Aug. 20, in the Parish Church, Knockcloghrim, Mr. John M'Kenna, land steward, Knockcloghrim, to Sarah, eldest daughter of Mr. Wm. Palmer, Aughentain Mills, Co. Tyrone.

No. 5980 :: Ref. 1852-09-04, 8:2, M.

Aug. 25, at Bishopwearmouth, Wm. Lewers, Esq., of the Middle Temple, Barrister-at-Law, to Sarah Elizabeth, youngest daughter of Wm. Nicholson, Esq., Nicholson House.

No. 5981 :: Ref. 1852-09-04, 8:2, M.
Aug. 26, at St. Peter's, Eaton-square, London, Edward Copleston Buckland, Esq., second son of the Very Rev. Dean of Westminster, to Rose Mary, daughter of the late John Walter, Esq.

No. 5982 :: Ref. 1852-09-04, 8:2, M.
Aug. 27, in Sandholes Presbyterian Church, near Cookstown, William, son of Mr. Hugh Treanor, of Glencan, to Eliza Jane, daughter of Mr. Thomas M'Manus, of Lamy, near Dungannon.

No. 5983 :: Ref. 1852-09-04, 8:2, M.
Aug. 28, at St. Peter's Church, Dublin, Henry Lowry, Esq., youngest son of the late Charles Frederick Barnwell, of Woburn-place, London, to Henrietta Martha, eldest daughter of the late James Lowry, Esq., of Rochdale [sic] House, Co. Tyrone.

No. 5984 :: Ref. 1852-09-04, 8:2, M.
Aug. 30, in Stranorlar, Samuel Laird, of Ballybofey, Esq., to Eliza Jane, daughter of Mr. William Barr, Admirand.

No. 5985 :: Ref. 1852-09-04, 8:2, M.
Aug. 31, in Carlisle, Rev. Samuel Stewart, A.M., curate of St. Stephen's, South Shields, to Sarah, eldest daughter of the Rev. John Elliott, Smithborough.

No. 5986 :: Ref. 1852-09-04, 8:2, D.
Aug. 13, at Frankfort on the Maine, after a few days illness, Hester Emily, wife of the Rev. P.B. Maxwell, of Birdstown, co. Donegal.

No. 5987 :: Ref. 1852-09-04, 8:2, D.
Aug. 15, at Portnassua [sic], Ballyshannon, Anne Olivia, youngest daughter of the late Simon Sheil, Esq., J.P.

No. 5988 :: Ref. 1852-09-04, 8:2, D.
Aug. 16, at Cleen cottage, Dromahair, Mr. James Stewart, of paralysis.

No. 5989 :: Ref. 1852-09-04, 8:2, D.
Aug. 20, at Grove hill, near Omagh, Emily, youngest daughter of William M'Kelvey, Esq.

No. 5990 :: Ref. 1852-09-04, 8:2, D.
Aug. 22, at Downpatrick, Mrs. Robert M'Cune.

No. 5991 :: Ref. 1852-09-04, 8:2, D.
Aug. 25, after a protracted illness, at his residence, Cork District Lunatic Asylum, Eugene O'Neil, Esq., M.D., moral governor of that institution.

No. 5992 :: Ref. 1852-09-04, 8:2, D.
Aug. 26, at Carpenter's-hall, after a lingering illness, but terminating most suddenly, Richard Webb Jupp, Esq., aged 85, senior member of the corporation of London, and for 54 years clerk of the Worshipful Company of Carpenters.

No. 5993 :: Ref. 1852-09-04, 8:2, D.
Aug. 27, at Knocknacarry, Courtenay, youngest child of Courtenay Newton, Esq., of Dungannon.

No. 5994 :: Ref. 1852-09-04, 8:2, D.
Aug. 29, at the Rectory, Lurgan, of English cholera, the Hon. Mrs. C. Knox, aged 75, widow of the late Archdeacon of Armagh, and aunt to the present Earl of Ranfurley. She has left four sons, including the Bishop of the Diocese and the Vicar-General of Down and Connor, to lament her loss; her mortal remains were interred in the Bishop's vault, Holywood.

No. 5995 :: Ref. 1852-09-04, 8:2, D.
Aug. 29, in Lowtherstown, Johnston Anderson, Esq., aged 42 years. His remains were deposited at Ballinamallard, on Tuesday, and such a large and respectable funeral was seldom witnessed, which showed the esteem which he was held in.

No. 5996 :: Ref. 1852-09-04, 8:2, D.
Aug. 30, at Waltham terrace, Merrion-avenue, Margaret Jane Mary, eldest daughter of John O'Dwyer, Esq., Taxing Master in Chancery.

No. 5997 :: Ref. 1852-09-04, 8:2, D.
At Cheltenham, in the ninety-fourth year of her age, Jane, relict of Edward Johnston, Esq., of Dromin, co. Wicklow, and Woodpark, co. Armagh. She was the daughter of George Paul Monck, Esq., by Lady Aramenta Beresford, sister of George de La Poer, first Marquess of Waterford.

No. 5998 :: Ref. 1852-09-11, 8:3, B.
Aug. 30, at Finaghy house, co. Antrim, the wife of W.M. Makenzie, Esq., Dungloe, co. Donegal, of a daughter.

No. 5999 :: Ref. 1852-09-11, 8:3, B.
Sept. 1, in Newtonhamilton, at the residence of her brother, the wife of Mr. Robert Barr, of Sydney, of a son.

No. 6000 :: Ref. 1852-09-11, 8:3, B.
Sept. 2, at Omagh, the wife of Henry Thompson, Esq., M.D., of a daughter.

No. 6001 :: Ref. 1852-09-11, 8:3, B.
Sept. 3, at Brunswick-square, Brighton, the wife of the Rev. William Montgomery Beresford, of Mellifont Glebe, co. Louth, Ireland, of a daughter.

No. 6002 :: Ref. 1852-09-11, 8:3, B.
Sept. 4, at 7, Clanbrassil Terrace, Dublin, the wife of Christopher Mulveny, Esq., C.E., Engineer to the Grand Canal Company, of a son.

No. 6003 :: Ref. 1852-09-11, 8:3, B.
Sept. 4, at Derby, the wife of Mr. A.J. Henley, of a son.

No. 6004 :: Ref. 1852-09-11, 8:3, M.
Aug. 26, at Ballymore, co. Donegal, Mr. Thomas Brown, to Harriet, fourth daughter of Mr. John Mitchell, Inspecting Chief Officer, Coast Guard district of Sheephaven.

No. 6005 :: Ref. 1852-09-11, 8:3, M.
Aug. 31, at St. Anne's Church, Belfast, Henry, eldest son of Henry Mitchell, Esq., of Drunreaske, Monaghan, to Mary, eldest daughter of the late Richard Ashmore, Esq., of Belfast.

No. 6006 :: Ref. 1852-09-11, 8:3, M.
Sept. 7, in St. Anne's Church, Belfast, Alexander John, Esq., Solicitor, Dublin, to Anne, eldest daughter of John Bates, Esq., Belfast.

No. 6007 :: Ref. 1852-09-11, 8:3, M.
Aug. 12, at the Spanish Legation, Washington, U.S., by proxy, Aggrapina Zaggrewskey MacLeod, daughter of Alexander N. MacLeod, of Harris, to Jose Maria Magallon, second son of the Marquis de San Adrien. His Excellency Don Angel, Calderon, de la Barca, her Catholic Majesty's Minister to the United States, stood as proxy.

No. 6008 :: Ref. 1852-09-11, 8:3, D.
Sept. 1, in the 34th year of her age, Margaret Georgina, wife of Thomas L. Mayne, Esq., Monaghan.

No. 6009 :: Ref. 1852-09-11, 8:3, D.
Aug. 6, at Boston, U.S. in the 40th year of his age, universally regretted by his friends and acquaintances, Mr. Patrick Gallagher, formerly of Letterkenny, and son to the late James Gallagher, of Swilly View, Esq., near Letterkenny, co. Donegal.

No. 6010 :: Ref. 1852-09-11, 8:3, D.
Aug. 18, at New York, of pulmonary consumption, in the 24th year of his age, Dr. Edward Fitzgerald, of Donoughmore, co. Cork, Ireland.

No. 6011 :: Ref. 1852-09-11, 8:3, D.
Aug. 19, at New York, Constantine Corr, aged twenty-nine years, son of James Corr, of Mullaghmore, Co. Armagh, Ireland.

No. 6012 :: Ref. 1852-09-11, 8:3, D.
Aug. 19, at New York, Patrick Sheridan, aged fifty-two years, a native of Co. Cavan, Ireland.

No. 6013 :: Ref. 1852-09-11, 8:3, D.
Aug. 22, at New York, John Mulligan, aged thirty-eight years, a native of Carrickadurhis, co. Longford, Ireland.

No. 6014 :: Ref. 1852-09-11, 8:3, D.
Aug. 23, at New York, Elizabeth M'Cafferey, in the thirteenth year of her age, daughter of Thomas M'Cafferey, Co. Cavan, Ireland.

No. 6015 :: Ref. 1852-09-11, 8:3, D.
At New York, of Consumption, Bridget Bradley, wife of Patrick Hegarty, Native of Killred, Co. Derry, Ireland, aged 27 years.

No. 6016 :: Ref. 1852-09-11, 8:3, D.
Aug. 26, at Dunadry, Mr. George Gordon George.—Officer of Inland Revenue, aged 32 years.

No. 6017 :: Ref. 1852-09-11, 8:3, D.
Aug. 30, the Rev. Edward Blackstock, of Camden town, in his sixty-second year.

No. 6018 :: Ref. 1852-09-11, 8:3, D.
Aug. 30, in Belfast, aged twenty-three years, John Campbell, of Crumlin, Student of Divinity, under the care of the Remonstrant Synod of Ulster.

No. 6019 :: Ref. 1852-09-11, 8:3, D.
Aug. 30, at Castle-street, Reading, T. Ord, Esq., late of the Bank of England, in his 91st year.

No. 6020 :: Ref. 1852-09-11, 8:3, D.
Aug. 31, at Beragh, near Dungannon, Mr. Thomas Greeves, aged 59 years.

No. 6021 :: Ref. 1852-09-11, 8:3, D.
Sep. 3, at Tunbridge Wells, George R. Porter, Esq., Joint Secretary to the Board of Trade.

No. 6022 :: Ref. 1852-09-11, 8:3, D.
Sept. 4, at Armagh, John, youngest son of James Bowman, Esq., Manager of the Provincial Bank, Ireland, aged 3 years.

No. 6023 :: Ref. 1852-09-11, 8:3, D.
Sept. 4, at Glasgow, of consumption, Mr. Felix O'Neill, compositor.

No. 6024 :: Ref. 1852-09-11, 8:3, D.
Sep. 6, at the house of her uncle, Dr. Copland, F.R.S., Old Burlington Street, London, Jemima Scott, aged 18, youngest daughter of the late Captain James Scott.

No. 6025 :: Ref. 1852-09-11, 8:3, D.
Sept. 7, at Huntley, the residence of her sisters, the Misses Dunbar, Elizabeth, wife of Henry Herron, Esq., Gilford. Her remains will be removed from Huntley, for interment, to the family burying-ground, Banbridge, on Saturday morning, the 11th instant, at half-past eleven o'clock.

No. 6026 :: Ref. 1852-09-11, 8:3, D.
Sept. 7, at the residence of her brother, 5, Mill-street, Belfast, Miss Mary Ann Murray, daughter of the late Dr. Murray.

No. 6027 :: Ref. 1852-09-11, 8:3, D.
Sept. 9, at 5, Royal Terrace, Belfast, Jane, relict of the late George Hamilton Smith, Esq., Lieutenant R N, and Comptroller of Customs, St John's [sic] New Brunswick.

No. 6028 :: Ref. 1852-09-11, 8:3, D.
Aug. 10, in his twentieth year, on board the American packet-ship *Garrick*, from New York, Wm. Samuel, fourth son of the late Mr. John Todd, merchant, Newry.

No. 6029 :: Ref. 1852-09-11, 8:3, D.
John Kemble Charman, Esq.—We regret to announce the death of this gentleman, which took place on Thursday evening, at half-past six o'clock.

No. 6030 :: Ref. 1852-09-18, 8:3, B.
Sep. 6, at Mountjoy, the wife of D. White, Esq., J.P., of a son.

No. 6031 :: Ref. 1852-09-18, 8:3, B.
Sep. 7, at Skreen, co. Sligo, the lady of Henry Maxwell, Esq., of a son.

No. 6032 :: Ref. 1852-09-18, 8:3, B.
Sep. 7, at Templeport Rectory, the wife of the Rev. Thomas La Nauze, of a son.

No. 6033 :: Ref. 1852-09-18, 8:3, B.
Sep. 8, at Hackwood, Killeshandra, the wife of F.H.B. Phillips, Esq., Royal Artillery, of a daughter.

No. 6034 :: Ref. 1852-09-18, 8:3, B.
Sep. 8, at the Archdeaconry, Clontibret, the lady of [the] Archdeacon of Clogher, of a daughter.

No. 6035 :: Ref. 1852-09-18, 8:3, B.
Sep. 13, the wife of Mr. James Crow, Queen's Arms, Portadown, of a daughter.

No. 6036 :: Ref. 1852-09-18, 8:3, B.
At Salthill, Galway, the wife of L.S. Mangan, Esq., of a daughter.

No. 6037 :: Ref. 1852-09-18, 8:3, M.
Sep. 2, at Newtownstewart Church, by Rev. James Smyth, Rector of Strabane, father of the bridegroom, Oswald Smyth, Esq., Lieut. 33d Madras N.I., to Mary, eldest daughter of the late Alexander Auchinleck, Esq., of Mulvin, co. Tyrone, and granddaughter of the late Sir John James Burgoyne.

No. 6038 :: Ref. 1852-09-18, 8:3, M.
Sep. 7, in Coleraine Church, Mr. Wm. John Totten, of Lurgan, to Charlotte, daughter of the late Mr. Richard Wright, of Castlecomer, co. Kilkenny.

No. 6039 :: Ref. 1852-09-18, 8:3, M.
Sep. 7, at Portrush, Smith Bryan, of Belfast, Esq., to Barbara Susan, daughter of the late Capt. Richardson, of Portrush, and grand-daughter of the late Rev. Wm. Richardson, D.D., Rector of Clonfeacle, co. Tyrone.

No. 6040 :: Ref. 1852-09-18, 8:3, M.
Sep. 9, at Glasslough Church, by Rev. W.S. Evans, Mr. John Woods, Merchant, to Mary Jane, the only daughter of Mr. Joseph Wright, Merchant, both of Emyvale.

No. 6041 :: Ref. 1852-09-18, 8:3, M.
Sep. 10, in St. Mary's Church, Manchester, by Rev. E. Lane, Mr. J. Addey, merchant, to Mary Augusta, daughter of the late John Greer, Esq., of Lurgan.

No. 6042 :: Ref. 1852-09-18, 8:3, M.
Sep. 13, at Hill-hall Presbyterian Church, by Rev. Alexander Henderson, Robert Ardill, Esq., Leeds, to Catherine Jane, daughter of William Barbour, Esq., Hilden, Lisburn.

No. 6043 :: Ref. 1852-09-18, 8:3, M.
Sep. 14, in St. Peter's Church, Dublin, Baptist Kernaghan, Esq., Solicitor, Lower Gardiner-street, to Mary, third daughter of Thomas Saunders, Esq., Hilton Lodge, Rathmines.

No. 6044 :: Ref. 1852-09-18, 8:3, D.
Sep. 1, at Cloone Glebe, co. Leitrim, Jane, the beloved wife of the Rev. Andrew Hogg.

No. 6045 :: Ref. 1852-09-18, 8:3, D.
Sep. 7, at his lodgings, in Gortin, in the 27th year of his age, of a few days' illness, Mr. Alexander Patton, Ordnance Surveyor, second son of Dr. Patton, of Kilmacrenan.

No. 6046 :: Ref. 1852-09-18, 8:3, D.
Sep. 9, at Farrenconnell House, co. Cavan, Richard Oliver William Beresford, the beloved infant son of Mr. and Mrs. Richard Nugent.

No. 6047 :: Ref. 1852-09-18, 8:3, D.
Sep. 11, at Archdall Lodge, Bundoran, Frances, relict of Captain Skene, Royal Navy, Companion of the Bath, of Lethenty, Aberdeenshire.

No. 6048 :: Ref. 1852-09-18, 8:3, D.
Sep. 12, Sophie Frances, eldest daughter of the Venerable M.G. Beresford, Archdeacon of Ardagh.

No. 6049 :: Ref. 1852-09-18, 8:3, D.
At Tullyallen, co. Tyrone, the Rev. John Kelly, P.P., aged forty-four years.

No. 6050 :: Ref. 1852-09-18, 8:3, D.
At Blackrock, co. Louth, aged fourteen months, Jos., the beloved child of James R. Baxter, Esq., Dundalk.

No. 6051 :: Ref. 1852-09-25, 8:2, B.
Sep. 13, at the Crescent, Derry, the wife of George A. O'Driscoll, Esq., of a son.

No. 6052 :: Ref. 1852-09-25, 8:2, B.
Sep. 19, at Newry, the wife of James Henderson, Esq., proprietor of the *Newry Telegraph*, of a son.

No. 6053 :: Ref. 1852-09-25, 8:2, B.
At Flush House, Augher, co. Tyrone, the lady of Joseph Weld, Esq., of a daughter.

No. 6054 :: Ref. 1852-09-25, 8:2, M.
Sep. 9, at Carrick-on-Shannon by Rev. William Percy, John Sullivan, Esq., of Anne Vale, Golden Bridge, to Margaret Dorethea, eldest daughter of Wm. Johnston Peyton, Esq., of Summerhill, co. Leitrim.

No. 6055 :: Ref. 1852-09-25, 8:2, M.
Sep. 16, at Monkstown church, Joseph Robinson, Esq., of Hereford, solicitor, to Georgiana Buchanan, daughter of the late James Buchanan, Esq., many years her Majesty's Consul at New York.

No. 6056 :: Ref. 1852-09-25, 8:2, M.

Sep. 16, in the Presbyterian Church, Middletown, by Rev. Samuel Hendren, A.M., Mr. John Wilson jun., Legacorry, to Jane, daughter of the late Mr. George Johnston, Shelvins.

No. 6057 :: Ref. 1852-09-25, 8:2, M.

Sep. 16, in Carlan [sic] Presbyterian Church by the Rev. Hugh Alexander, Ballyreagh, Rev. Alexander Gray, A.M., Minterburn, to Mary Elizabeth, youngest daughter of the late Doctor Thomas Dunn, Surgeon, Royal Navy, Jamaica.

No. 6058 :: Ref. 1852-09-25, 8:2, M.

Sep. 22, in the Presbyterian Church, Downshire-road, Newry, by Rev. John Dodd, Robert Johnston, M.D., Newry, to Matilda, eldest daughter of the late Mr. D. Todd, Merchant, Newry.

No. 6059 :: Ref. 1852-09-25, 8:2, D.

Aug. 20, at Philadelphia, Dr. George Stewart, in the 37th year of his age. Dr. Stewart was born in the North of Ireland; and in early life he left the land of his fathers to join an elder brother, who was practising as a physician in Philadelphia.

No. 6060 :: Ref. 1852-09-25, 8:2, D.

Sep. 12, at Kingstown, Isabella Jemima, youngest daughter of Henry Carey, Esq.

No. 6061 :: Ref. 1852-09-25, 8:2, D.

Sep. 12, William Bigger, of Harcourt-street, Esq., Ballast Master to the Corporation for preserving and improving the Port of Dublin, aged 75.

No. 6062 :: Ref. 1852-09-25, 8:2, D.

Sep. 12, at Rutland, near Carlow, Mrs. Mary Gray, at the advanced age of 102 years; she died after a few moments' illness, being on the same day engaged in the discharge of her domestic duties.

No. 6063 :: Ref. 1852-09-25, 8:2, D.

Sep. 14, at Ramsgate, Mr. Pugin, the distinguished architect. For some time past he had resided at Hammersmith, under the care of a particular friend, and was fast recovering from the state into which, unhappily, the pressure of arduous professional duties had reduced him. On Saturday his medical attendant advised his removal to Ramsgate, the air of that place being considered milder, and more calculated still further to improve his health. Mr. Pugin accordingly went, but on Monday evening he was seized with an epileptic fit, from which, we believe, he never recovered, and his death took place the following day at three o'clock.

No. 6064 :: Ref. 1852-09-25, 8:2, D.

Sep. 15, at the residence of his father, Narrowater, at an early age, Dr. Hugh M'Cann, of Dundalk, much and deservedly regretted by all who knew him.

No. 6065 :: Ref. 1852-09-25, 8:2, D.

Sep. 15, at 2, Rathmines Road, Dublin, Alexander Dixon, Esq., Distiller, of Riversdale House, Belturbet, aged 55. Deceased was interred in Belturbet on Saturday last, and the large assemblage, of all classes, which followed his remains to their last earthly resting place, testified how universally he was esteemed, and his great public loss deplored. He was a man of uncommon energy and talent, of remarkable forethought, enterprise, and perseverance, and Belturbet has sustained a loss by his demise, the vacuum of which will not readily be filled up.

No. 6066 :: Ref. 1852-09-25, 8:2, D.

Sep. 16, James O'Neil, in Salford, Manchester, at the advanced age of 107 years. He was born on the 2d of March, 1745, entered the army in 1774, served 38 years and was discharged in 1812. He has, therefore, been 40 years a pensioner.

No. 6067 :: Ref. 1852-09-25, 8:2, D.

Sep. 17, aged 27 years, at Haslar Hospital, Gosport, of rapid inflammation of the lungs, the effect of long immersion in the water by the upsetting in a squall of the Pinnace of her Majesty's ship *Neptune*, Lieutenant Samuel Lewin Wilson, Royal Marines, youngest son of Captain P.T. Wilson, of that corps.

No. 6068 :: Ref. 1852-09-25, 8:2, D.

Sep. 18, at Rosevale, near Lisburn, in the 96th year of his age, Mr. Wm. Hodgens, one of the old Irish Volunteers.

No. 6069 :: Ref. 1852-09-25, 8:2, D.

Sep. 8, at Ballyconnell, co. Cavan, Jane, youngest daughter of the late Mr. George Gallogly, aged forty-four years.

No. 6070 :: Ref. 1852-09-25, 8:2, D.

Sep. 18, at Woodley, co. Dublin, Laura, the infant daughter of Samuel Smylie, Esq.

No. 6071 :: Ref. 1852-09-25, 8:2, D.

Sep. 18, at Plymouth, Catherine Frances, wife of Wm. Charles Macready.

No. 6072 :: Ref. 1852-09-25, 8:2, D.

Sep. 19, at Woodhouse, Dulwich, Philip Novelli, Esq., in his 73d year.

No. 6073 :: Ref. 1852-09-25, 8:2, D.

Sep. 21, at Enniskillen, Catherine Margaret, eldest daughter of the late Major Stoddart, 45th Regiment, and niece to the late Admiral Stoddart, of her Majesty's Navy.

No. 6074 :: Ref. 1852-09-25, 8:2, D.

Sep. 21, at the residence of her father, in North-street, Newry, Anne, only child of Mr. James Savage, in her 21st year, to the inexpressible grief of her afflicted family and the sorrow of a numerous circle of friends.

No. 6075 :: Ref. 1852-10-02, 8:3, B.
Sep. 17, at Cookstown, the wife of Mr. R. M'Geagh, merchant, of a daughter.

No. 6076 :: Ref. 1852-10-02, 8:3, B.
Sep. 17, at Dungiven, the wife of the Rev. Wm. Ross, of a son.

No. 6077 :: Ref. 1852-10-02, 8:3, B.
Sep. 27, at Lurgan, the wife of John Cuppage, Esq., of a son.

No. 6078 :: Ref. 1852-10-02, 8:3, M.
Sep. 30, at the Cathedral, Armagh, by Rev. George Robinson, Rector of Tartaraghan, and brother of the bride, Rev. John Sharkey, Chaplain H.E.I.C.S., and late curate of Armagh, to Mary, second daughter of George Robinson, Esq., D.L., Armagh.

No. 6079 :: Ref. 1852-10-02, 8:3, M.
Sep. 21, at South Hackney Church, London, Anthony Denny, Esq., of Derryvulland, co. Fermanagh, to Sarah Jane, eldest daughter of Rev. G.P. Lockwood, M.A., Rector of South Hackney.

No. 6080 :: Ref. 1852-10-02, 8:3, M.
Sep. 21, in Randalstown, by Rev. Robert Marr, Mr. Thomas Hill, of Tullinamullin, to Miss Rachel Bell, Lenagh.

No. 6081 :: Ref. 1852-10-02, 8:3, M.
Sep. 23, in Belfast, by Rev. Dr. Morgan, Mr. Wm. Massey, to Miss Ann Jane Watson, both of Belfast.

No. 6082 :: Ref. 1852-10-02, 8:3, M.
Sep. 27, at the British Embassy, Paris, Fitzherbert Filgate, of Hillsborough, co. Down, Esq., to Catherine, eldest daughter of the Right Hon. Edward Lucas, of Castleshane, co. Monaghan.

No. 6083 :: Ref. 1852-10-02, 8:3, M.
Sep. 29, in Tempo Church, by Rev. W.H. Bradshaw, Mr. John Gallogly, of Enniskillen, to Mary, eldest daughter of the late Mr. John Ferguson of Enniskillen.

No. 6084 :: Ref. 1852-10-02, 8:3, D.
Sep. 16, in almost the prime of life, the Right Rev. Thomas Stewart Townsend, D.D., Bishop of Meath. He was consecrated bishop on All Saints Day, 1850, in the room of the venerated Bishop Stopford, who died on the 17th of Sep., 1850. He has left a young and numerous family to lament his irreparable loss to them. The Bishop had been, for a considerable time, suffering from a pulmonary affection, and died at Malaga, whither he had proceeded for the benefit of his health, and where he had only arrived the day previous to his decease.

No. 6085 :: Ref. 1852-10-02, 8:3, D.
Sep. 16, at Grange Oneiland, Mr. Richard Taylor, aged 66 years. His funeral was large and respectable, the largest that for years occurred at Kilmore, and testified the regard his neighbours entertained for his memory.

No. 6086 :: Ref. 1852-10-02, 8:3, D.
Sep. 17, at St. Martin's-in-the-Fields, London, in full possession of his faculties, having attained the age of 102 years and 7 months, Mr. James Coleman. Throughout his whole life he preserved such careful habits that he was enabled to pursue his calling until after his 100th year.

No. 6087 :: Ref. 1852-10-02, 8:3, D.
Sep. 19, at Sandford-terrace, Sarah Jane, daughter of the Rev. G. De Butts.

No. 6088 :: Ref. 1852-10-02, 8:3, D.
Sep. 20, at Whitehall, co. Fermanagh, Hannah, eldest daughter of Captain A. Nixon, J.P.

No. 6089 :: Ref. 1852-10-02, 8:3, D.
Sep. 20, at Tamlaght, Nowtownlimavady [sic], after a few hours' illness, Miss Jenny Gault.

No. 6090 :: Ref. 1852-10-02, 8:3, D.
Sep. 20, at Dunbrock, Newtownlimavady, Mr. Wm. M'Closkey, teacher, after a brief suffering.

No. 6091 :: Ref. 1852-10-02, 8:3, D.
Sep. 21, at Redcar, in her 89th year, Mrs. Hannah Greame, sister of the late Mrs. Sadlier, of Leeds, and Aunt of Samuel Greame Fenton, Esq.

No. 6092 :: Ref. 1852-10-02, 8:3, D.
Sep. 21, James Alexander, eldest son of James Henry, Esq., Curlust, near Tandragee, aged 18.

No. 6093 :: Ref. 1852-10-02, 8:3, D.
Sep. 21, at an advanced age, Jane, relict of the late Mr. John Campbell, of Scotch-street, Armagh. The large and respectable concourse of citizens, who attended her remains to their last resting place, in the Cathedral burying ground, of this city, testified the respect entertained for her by the inhabitants. Her latter end was peace.

No. 6094 :: Ref. 1852-10-02, 8:3, D.
Sep. 23, at his residence, Ahory, near Richhill, Mr. Robert Williamson, aged 86 years, much and deservedly regretted, by a large circle of friends who mourn his loss. His end was peace. On the following day at the same place, his grandchild, John Thomas, infant son of Mr. John Tuft, Edenderry, Scarva, co. Down.

No. 6095 :: Ref. 1852-10-02, 8:3, D.
Sep. 23, Mary, wife of Mr. P. M'Guiness, Market-street, Monaghan.

No. 6096 :: Ref. 1852-10-02, 8:3, D.
Sep. 23, Alexander Fleming, Esq., of Galina, Monaghan, in the 76th year of his age.

No. 6097 :: Ref. 1852-10-02, 8:3, D.
Sep. 28, John Ure, Esq., of Dundalk.

No. 6098 :: Ref. 1852-10-02, 8:3, D.
Sep. 23, at Glen Uske, Colonel Sir Digby Macworth, Bart., aged sixty-four.

No. 6099 :: Ref. 1852-10-02, 8:3, D.
Sep. 23, at Granby-row, aged seventy years, Arabella Meares, relict of Thomas Watkins, Esq., of Johnstown, co. Tipperary, and eldest daughter of the late Francis Waldron, Esq., of Drumsna.

No. 6100 :: Ref. 1852-10-02, 8:3, D.
Sep. 24, at the residence of her brother, Derryloran Rectory, Cookstown, Miss Anne Molony.

No. 6101 :: Ref. 1852-10-02, 8:3, D.
Sep. 25, aged nineteen years, Jane Eliza, eldest daughter of Patrick Denvir, Esq., Dundalk.

No. 6102 :: Ref. 1852-10-02, 8:3, D.
Sep. 25, Mrs. Watt, wife of Mr. William Watt of Enniskillen.

No. 6103 :: Ref. 1852-10-02, 8:3, D.
Sep. 26, at Bushyfield, Rev. Robert Stewart, D.D., aged 69.

No. 6104 :: Ref. 1852-10-02, 8:3, D.
Joseph Ady.—We must not omit a passing record of the death of one who, in a sense, might be called "a man of letters," the too famous Joseph Ady. Although always ready to inform others of "something to their advantage," he was unable to do much good for himself; and after a long life, chiefly spent in his unprincipled yet amusing system of swindling, he died lately in distress and debt.

No. 6105 :: Ref. 1852-10-09, 8:3, B.
Sep. 18, at Yorkville, county Wexford, the lady of the Rev. Stewart Hickey, of a son.

No. 6106 :: Ref. 1852-10-09, 8:3, B.
Sep. 23, at Darley-house, Sunbury, Middlesex, the wife of Captain Hayes, 46th Regt., of a daughter.

No. 6107 :: Ref. 1852-10-09, 8:3, B.
Oct. 3, at Stratford House, Stroud, Gloucestershire, the lady of Captain Hallewell, 28th Regiment, of a son.

No. 6108 :: Ref. 1852-10-09, 8:3, M.
Sep. 23, in Killinkere Church, Robert Taylor, Esq., of Lishall, co. Cavan, to Marianne, second daughter of the late Bernard Parr, Esq., of Carnavica, same county.

No. 6109 :: Ref. 1852-10-09, 8:3, M.
Sep. 30, at Castlenock church, Wm. John Beasley, Esq., of Torquay, Devonshire, to Mary Clarke, daughter of Alex. Ferrier, Esq., of Knockmaroon, co. Dublin.

No. 6110 :: Ref. 1852-10-09, 8:3, M.
Oct. 5, at Tullyherron Chapel, by the Rev. Mr. M'Parland, C.C., Newtownhamilton, brother to the bride, Mr. John M'Quade, merchant, Markethill, to Mary Anne, only daughter of Mr. John M'Parlan [sic], Carrickgollaghy.

No. 6111 :: Ref. 1852-10-09, 8:3, M.
In Newtown-Stewart Church, Oswald Smith, Esq., of the 33d Madras Native Infantry, eldest son of the Rev. J. Smith, rector of Camus Juxta Mourne, county Tyrone, to Mary, eldest daughter of the late Alex. Auchinleck, Esq., of Liscreevaghan, Strabane.

No. 6112 :: Ref. 1852-10-09, 8:3, D.
Aug. 24, at York, on the Grand River, Canada, Mr. James Davis, aged 76 years, at the residence of his son, where he arrived from Enniskillen only two days before his death. He had been an old inhabitant of Enniskillen, was one of the Enniskillen Yeomanry who was at the Battle of Ballinamuck in 1798, and used to boast that he put the first Orange flag on the old steeple of the Enniskillen Church.

No. 6113 :: Ref. 1852-10-09, 8:3, D.
Aug. 30, at Caynga [Cayuga?], County of Haldimand, Canada West, Isabella, sister of the late Sinclair Carroll, Esq., of Armagh, and daughter of the late John Carroll, Esq., of Moy.

No. 6114 :: Ref. 1852-10-09, 8:3, D.
Sep. 13, in Tuam, at the advanced age of 110 years, Mrs. Patrick Griffin, mother of John Griffin, Esq.

No. 6115 :: Ref. 1852-10-09, 8:3, D.
Sep. 24, at Christiana, Prince Gustavus, Duke of Upland, and second son of the King of Sweden. He landed there on the 16th ult., with their Majesties, and complained of indisposition. On the following day he was seized with violent fever, which ended fatally.

No. 6116 :: Ref. 1852-10-09, 8:3, D.
Sep. 28, Charles M'Farland, Esq., of Gortin, aged 61 years.

No. 6117 :: Ref. 1852-10-09, 8:3, D.
Sep. 28, at Kingstown, Anne, relict of the Right Rev. Samuel Kyle, D.D., late Lord Bishop of Cork, Cloyne and Ross.

No. 6118 :: Ref. 1852-10-09, 8:3, D.
Sep. 28, at Ballymena, Mary, wife of Mr. Alexander M'Clung, formerly of Keady, co. Armagh, aged eighty years.

No. 6119 :: Ref. 1852-10-09, 8:3, D.
Captain D. M'Kinlay, of the *Oscar* screw steamer, plying between Belfast and London. The *Oscar* left Belfast Oct. 2d, on her passage to London, and the deceased, who commanded her, when off Beachy Head, was caught by a very heavy sea and swept overboard. The night was very dark, and the rain at the time was falling in torrents, so that, though every exertion was made by the engineer in turning the vessel, and all hands on board did everything that human ingenuity could suggest under the circumstances, the unfortunate man was not discovered.

No. 6120 :: Ref. 1852-10-09, 8:3, D.
Oct. 2, Mr. Mathew Grinless, Portadown.

No. 6121 :: Ref. 1852-10-09, 8:3, D.
Oct. 2, at Carrickmacross, Mary Barbara, eldest daughter of George and Lydia Morant.

No. 6122 :: Ref. 1852-10-09, 8:3, D.
Oct. 2, at Cookstown, Enniskerry, in the county of Wicklow, Willis Hill Mecredy, Solicitor, aged 75 years. Mr. Mecredy was one of the most eminent solicitors in Ireland, and had long enjoyed the respect of numbers of his own profession and of the public.

No. 6123 :: Ref. 1852-10-09, 8:3, D.
Oct. 2, in Edinburgh, Mr. Thomas Thomson, the coadjutor of Lord Jeffrey, Sydney Smith, and Lord Brougham, in the establishment of *The Edinburgh Review*. Mr. Thomas was principal clerk of Session.

No. 6124 :: Ref. 1852-10-09, 8:3, D.
Oct. 3, at Woolwich, Anne, wife of Lieutenant Col. Wilford, of the Royal Regiment of Artillery.

No. 6125 :: Ref. 1852-10-09, 8:3, D.
Oct. 4, Mr. James Robinson, Edenderry, Portadown.

No. 6126 :: Ref. 1852-10-09, 8:3, D.
Oct. 4, at Monkstown, in her seventeenth year, Ellen, third daughter of Jeremiah John Murphy, Esq., Master in Chancery.

No. 6127 :: Ref. 1852-10-09, 8:3, D.
At the residence of Robert M'Clelland, Esq., Bellmount, Banbridge, Anna Gage, relict of the late Alex. Stewart, Esq., Ligoneil, Belfast.

No. 6128 :: Ref. 1852-10-09, 8:3, D.
An old woman died at Sheffield a few days since, who had been receiving parochial relief for many years. At her decease it was found she had property by her to the amount of nearly £1,000.

No. 6129 :: Ref. 1852-10-09, 8:3, D.
Oct. 3, at the Wesleyan Chapel, Norton, near Askern, Mr. James Calvert, of Heslington, near York, whilst reading the beautiful parable given in the 15th chapter of St. Luke's Gospel. The congregation were listening with the deepest attention, when all in a sudden, after uttering the words, "*I will arise and go to my—,*" the preacher exclaimed, "*Oh! my dear friends!*" and fell down in the pulpit and almost immediately expired.

No. 6130 :: Ref. 1852-10-09, 8:3, D.
Oct. 5, a woman named Esther Gracey, wife of a carpenter residing in Newry, went into a shop to purchase some candles, and while standing at the counter, apparently in good health, she exclaimed, "Lord bless me, I don't know what's come over me—there's a great lightness in my head," fell down, and expired. The deceased, who was about fifty years of age, has left a family to deplore her sudden removal from among them.

No. 6131 :: Ref. 1852-10-09, 8:3, D.
Oct. 2, the Rev. Mr. Grace, P.P., suddenly dropped dead in Thurles.

No. 6132 :: Ref. 1852-10-09, 8:3, D.
Oct. 3, a woman, named Margaret Halligan, was burned to death in Dublin, her garments having caught the fire as she was putting on a kettle.

No. 6133 :: Ref. 1852-10-16, 8:2, B.
Sep. 30, at Bath, Lady Wade, of a daughter.

No. 6134 :: Ref. 1852-10-16, 8:2, B.
Oct. 3, at Coleraine, the wife of Mr. J. M'Combie, Proprietor of the *Coleraine Chronicle*, of a daughter.

No. 6135 :: Ref. 1852-10-16, 8:2, B.
Oct. 5, at Crieve House, co. Monaghan, the lady of A.H. Montgomery, Esq., of a son.

No. 6136 :: Ref. 1852-10-16, 8:2, B.
Oct. 7, at Aughnacloy, co. Tyrone, the wife of Charles Blackham, Esq., of a son.

No. 6137 :: Ref. 1852-10-16, 8:2, B.
Oct. 9, the wife of R.O. Blackader, Esq., Dundalk, of a daughter.

No. 6138 :: Ref. 1852-10-16, 8:2, B.
Oct. 10, in Scotch-street, Armagh, the wife of Mr. Andrew P. Sheppard, of a son.

No. 6139 :: Ref. 1852-10-16, 8:2, B.
Oct. 4, at 5, Clifford-Street, London, the Wife of Wm. Bowman, Esq., of a daughter, who survived only four days.

No. 6140 :: Ref. 1852-10-16, 8:2, M.
Oct. 6, in Magherafelt, by Rev. C.K. Irwin, Rev. A. Staples Irwin, of Marlacco [sic], co. Armagh, to Mary Olivia, eldest daughter of William Augustus Hardcastle, Esq., late of her Majesty's 31st Reg.

No. 6141 :: Ref. 1852-10-16, 8:2, M.
Oct. 6, at Tullylish, by Rev. Drummond Anderson of St. Stephen's, Liverpool, Francis Anderson, Esq., M.D., H.E.I. Co.'s Service, to Helen, eldest daughter of Rawdon Nicholson, Esq., Stramore House, co. Down.

No. 6142 :: Ref. 1852-10-16, 8:2, M.
Oct. 7, in Ballymascanlon church, Mr. John Henry Barrett, of Jonesborough, to Miss Martha Perkins.

No. 6143 :: Ref. 1852-10-16, 8:2, M.
Oct. 7, at Bridge of Crin chapel, Mr. Patrick Kelly, of Bath Hill, co. Monaghan, to Rose, youngest daughter of the late Mr. Bernard M'Ardle, Shortstone.

No. 6144 :: Ref. 1852-10-16, 8:2, D.
June 15, 1851, at the North Ford, Sacramento, California, in the 25th year of his age, John, third son of the late John Todd of Newry, Merchant.

No. 6145 :: Ref. 1852-10-16, 8:2, D.
Sept. 18, drowned, while bathing in the Scioto river, Columbus, Ohio, U.S.A., in the 17th year of his age, John George, Second [sic] son of John Geary, Esq., Proprietor of the *"Capital City Fact"* newspaper, late of Dublin.

No. 6146 :: Ref. 1852-10-16, 8:2, D.
Sep. 24, at Strabane, Miss Eliza Martin, second daughter of the late Mr. Samuel Martin, of Strabane.

No. 6147 :: Ref. 1852-10-16, 8:2, D.
Sep. 26, at Clohog, near Omagh, Mr. John Gibson, aged 33.

No. 6148 :: Ref. 1852-10-16, 8:2, D.
Sep. 28, at Thornhill, in the 77th year of his age, John Johnson, Esq., the father of the Monaghan Grand Jury, and one of the eldest, most efficient, and venerated Magistrates of that county. By him the scales of justice were firmly, yet kindly upheld.

No. 6149 :: Ref. 1852-10-16, 8:2, D.
Sep. 27, at Ballymackney, near Carrickmacross, the residence of her mother, Jane, eldest daughter of the late Wm. Daniell, Esq., aged 20 years.

No. 6150 :: Ref. 1852-10-16, 8:2, D.
Sep. 28, at Gortin, co. Tyrone, aged 60 years, after a long and lingering illness, which he bore with Christian resignation and submission to the will of his heavenly Father, Mr. Charles M'Farland.

No. 6151 :: Ref. 1852-10-16, 8:2, D.
Sep. 28, at Dunseverick, near Bushmills, William M'Kenzie, aged 70 years, for many years merchant in Coleraine.

No. 6152 :: Ref. 1852-10-16, 8:2, D.
Sep. 30, at Hounslow, of epilepsy, Rev. Robert Andrews (youngest son of the late Edward Andrews, Esq., of Leyton, Essex), late tutor and Fellow of Queen's College, Cambridge, aged 32.

No. 6153 :: Ref. 1852-10-16, 8:2, D.
Sep. 30, at Kilvin, near Omagh, Catherine, second daughter of the late Mr. John Campbell, aged 55 years.

No. 6154 :: Ref. 1852-10-16, 8:2, D.
Oct. 3, at an advanced age, Mr. James Hamilton, postmaster, Verners Bridge. He was highly esteemed by all who knew him.

No. 6155 :: Ref. 1852-10-16, 8:2, D.
Oct. 4, at Barrack-street, Armagh, of bronchitis, Mr. Owen Caffrey, aged 66 years. Mr. Caffry [sic] conducted a school in Armagh for 43 years.

No. 6156 :: Ref. 1852-10-16, 8:2, D.
Oct. 4, at Markethill, John T. Moneypenny, Esq., M.D., for thirteen years the humane and efficient surgeon of the Newtownhamilton Dispensary.

No. 6157 :: Ref. 1852-10-16, 8:2, D.
Death of Lord Dinorben.—This young nobleman breathed his last at his ancestral mansion, Kinmel-park, this evening, (Oct. 6). He had long suffered severely from epileptic fits, and was attacked in an alarming manner on the Sunday previous, from which attack his lordship never rallied. It will be remembered that since the death of the late venerable and respected Lord Dinorben, father of the present deceased nobleman, much litigation has been caused, owing to the mental infirmity of his successor. The new proprietor of Kinmel is Mr. Hughes, son of the late Mr. J. Hughes, of the Beach Rhyl, North Wales.

No. 6158 :: Ref. 1852-10-16, 8:2, D.
Oct. 6, at Belfast, Anne Auchinleck, relict of the late Rev. Claude Morrison, of Sligo.

No. 6159 :: Ref. 1852-10-16, 8:2, D.
Oct. 8, in Eccles-street, James Eccles Auchinleck, Esq., aged 22 years, eldest son of the Rev. John Auchinleck, of Dunboyne.

No. 6160 :: Ref. 1852-10-16, 8:2, D.
Oct. 9, Mr. John May, near Portadown.

No. 6161 :: Ref. 1852-10-16, 8:2, D.
Oct. 9, at the residence of his son, in Dalymount Terrace, Phibsborough, Mr. Richard Quigly, in the 74th year of his age, for many years Assistant to the Secretary of the O'Connell Tribute.

No. 6162 :: Ref. 1852-10-16, 8:2, D.
Oct. 12, William B. Wallace, Solicitor, Dublin.

No. 6163 :: Ref. 1852-10-16, 8:2, D.
At Downing's House, co. Kildare, James Crawford, Esq., late C.I., of Constabulary for the county.

No. 6164 :: Ref. 1852-10-16, 8:2, D.
The Galway papers, last week, mention the death, in that city of a venerable French lady, at the age of 86. Madame Blumeberg had resided in Ireland for sixty years—having fled from her native country during the convulsions of the first great revolution which, at the close of the last century, filled Europe with consternation. In that tragic time Madame Blumeberg was sentenced to the guillotine, and sent, after condemnation, to a prison in Paris, from which she was unexpectedly released by one of those sudden changes of Government which, in those days, shifted authority from party to party.

No. 6165 :: Ref. 1852-10-23, 8:3, B.
Oct. 4, at Ballyshannon, the wife of Thomas Watts, Esq., Supervisor of Inland Revenue, of a daughter.

No. 6166 :: Ref. 1852-10-23, 8:3, B.
Oct. 13, at Cavenacaw, near Armagh, the wife of Mr. Robert Temple, (firm of Messrs. Wm. Boyd & Co., Armagh), of a son.

No. 6167 :: Ref. 1852-10-23, 8:3, B.

Oct. 16, at Lee-place, Upper Clapton, the wife of Alexander C. Brice, Esq., of a son.

No. 6168 :: Ref. 1852-10-23, 8:3, B.

At Cloghjordan, the lady of John Glass, Esq., officer of Inland Revenue, of a daughter.

No. 6169 :: Ref. 1852-10-23, 8:3, B.

In Belturbet, the lady of Dr. O'Donovan, of a daughter.

No. 6170 :: Ref. 1852-10-23, 8:3, B.

A Belgian paper states, that a woman, thirty-three years of age, is now living at Liege, who affords an astonishing example of fertility. She was lately confined of triplets, who are respectively her 22d, 23d, and 24th children. She has thus had, during nine years of married life, twenty-four children, all in good health, and of the female sex.

No. 6171 :: Ref. 1852-10-23, 8:3, M.

Oct. 1, in Minterburn, by Rev. Alex. Gray, A.M., Mr. David Dickson, Benburb, to Miss Agnes Leslie, Minterburn.

No. 6172 :: Ref. 1852-10-23, 8:3, M.

Oct. 6, at Cooltrain Church, by Rev. Sidney Smith, D.D., F.T.C.D., J. Fawcett, Esq., J.P., of Drumma-connor, to Margaret, Widow of the late Thomas W. Macarthey, Esq., and second daughter of Charles Moorhead, Esq., Lieutenant, H.P., 71st Highland Light Infantry.

No. 6173 :: Ref. 1852-10-23, 8:3, M.

Oct. 11, at Doncaster, Charles C. Beardshaw, Esq., third son of W. Beardshaw, Esq., Sheffield, and of West Bank, Yorkshire, to Letitia, eldest daughter of Henry E. Peoples, Esq., Distributor of Stamps, county Donegal.

No. 6174 :: Ref. 1852-10-23, 8:3, M.

Oct. 11, at Blanchardstown, Thomas Macken, Esq., to Miss Anne Miller, step-daughter of Bernard M'Garry, Esq., of Ashtown, co. Dublin.

No. 6175 :: Ref. 1852-10-23, 8:3, M.

Oct. 13, in St. Peter's Church, Dublin, R.A. Adams, Esq., second son of Francis Adams, Esq., of Ballyhaise and Monaghan, to Elizabeth, daughter of the late John Morrow, Esq., Lower Ormond-Quay, Dublin.

No. 6176 :: Ref. 1852-10-23, 8:3, M.

Oct. 13, in Castlecaulfield, James Rooney, of Mullaghriffy, eldest son of William Rooney, of Killy-morgan, Ballygawley, to Matilda, eldest daughter of James Young, Esq., of Killymaddy, Castlecaulfield.

No. 6177 :: Ref. 1852-10-23, 8:3, M.

Oct. 13, at St. Thomas's Church, Dublin, by Rev. James Campbell, L.L.D., Incumbent of Forkhill, the Rev. Henry Wray Young, to Jane Hunt, youngest daughter of the late Hunt Walsh Chambre, Esq., of Hawthorn-hill, co. Armagh.

No. 6178 :: Ref. 1852-10-23, 8:3, M.

Oct. 14, at Loughcrew Church, Co. Meath, by the uncle of the bride, the Rev. Edward Wade, Captain Blackwood Price, Royal Artillery, son of James Price, Esq., Saintfield, Co. Down, to Ann Maria, daughter of the late Colonel Wade, C.B.

No. 6179 :: Ref. 1852-10-23, 8:3, M.

Oct. 14, at Tullylish, Mr. John Morton, eldest son of Mr. Andrew Morton, of Orange-hill, Banbridge, to Sarah, second daughter of Mr. Hamilton Coulter, of Loughans, Gilford.

No. 6180 :: Ref. 1852-10-23, 8:3, M.

Oct. 18, at the house of the father of the bride, by the Rev. the Chief Rabbi, Rudolph Auerbach, Esq., of Frankfort-on-the-Main, to Fanny, third daughter, of Mr. H.N. Solomon, Edmonton.

No. 6181 :: Ref. 1852-10-23, 8:3, M.

In the Church of Annaduff, co. Leitrim, by Rev. Thomas Bolton Jones, William Jones, Esq., Drumard, to Eliza, daughter of the late Thomas Duke, Esq., and niece to Doctor John Duke, formerly of the Leitrim Militia.

No. 6182 :: Ref. 1852-10-23, 8:3, D.

Oct. 1, at Gorey, at the house of his daughter, Mrs. Martha Earl, Mr. John Webster, of Ballyrahan, diocese of Ferns, at the advanced age of 100.

No. 6183 :: Ref. 1852-10-23, 8:3, D.

Oct. 7, at Gayfield, Muff, co. Derry, Elizabeth, wife of Mr. William Smith, and daughter of Mr. William Campbell, formerly of Sandymount; also, two of her daughters, Catherine, aged 14 years; and Elizabeth, aged 4 years.

No. 6184 :: Ref. 1852-10-23, 8:3, D.

Oct. 10, at Annaquinea [sic], Dungannon, of con-sumption, after a protracted illness, Anne, eldest daughter of Jas. Young, Esq., aged 29 years.

No. 6185 :: Ref. 1852-10-23, 8:3, D.

Oct. 10, at Lauriston Castle, Sophia Frances, wife of the Right Hon. Lord Rutherford, and youngest daughter of the late Sir James Stewart, of Ramelton, and Port Stewart, Baronet.

No. 6186 :: Ref. 1852-10-23, 8:3, D.

Oct. 12, at the Governesses' Home, Camden-street, Madame Maria De Latour, for many years governess in the family of Her Excellency the Countess of Eglinton.

No. 6187 :: Ref. 1852-10-23, 8:3, D.

Oct. 12, in Monaghan, Sergeant M'Elles, of the Monaghan Militia, and formerly of the 8th Light Dragoons.

No. 6188 :: Ref. 1852-10-23, 8:3, D.

Oct. 13, after a protracted illness, which he bore with Christian resignation, David, only son of the late Mr. John Wiles, of Newtownhamilton, aged 20 years.

No. 6189 :: Ref. 1852-10-23, 8:3, D.

Oct. 14, suddenly, at the Glebe House, Bangor, aged 12 years, Richard Edward, son of the Rev. Richard Binney, Incumbent of that parish.

No. 6190 :: Ref. 1852-10-23, 8:3, D.

Oct. 14, at Old Park, Mary, the beloved wife of Mr. William Herd, aged 32 years.

No. 6191 :: Ref. 1852-10-23, 8:3, D.

Oct. 14, at his residence in Mullaghmore, the Rev. W.S. Cuthbert, perpetual curate of Cappagh.

No. 6192 :: Ref. 1852-10-23, 8:3, D.

Oct. 15, at Victoria-place, Belfast, Isabella, daughter of the Rev. Thomas Drew, D.D.

No. 6193 :: Ref. 1852-10-23, 8:3, D.

Oct. 16, at the Rectory, Templetuohy, in his seventy-eighth year, the Rev. Mungo Noble Thompson, Rector of the united parishes of Templetuohy and Loughmore, and Prebendary of Kilbragh, in the diocese of Cashel.

No. 6194 :: Ref. 1852-10-23, 8:3, D.

Oct. 17, at Bath, Rev. Edward Mangin, M.A., aged 80, Prebendary of Bath [Rath], in the diocese of Killaloe, Ireland.

No. 6195 :: Ref. 1852-10-23, 8:3, D.

Oct. 18, at Eltham, Kent, after a very short illness, Isaac Guillemard, M.D., aged 41.

No. 6196 :: Ref. 1852-10-23, 8:3, D.

Oct. 18, at Blackrock, in the 79th year of his age, Alexander Hamilton, Esq., Q.C., formerly of Rutland-square, Dublin, and of Newtownhamilton, co. Armagh.

No. 6197 :: Ref. 1852-10-23, 8:3, D.

Oct. 18, at Newry, Mr. Robert M'Gowan, Scholar, Queen's College, Galway.

No. 6198 :: Ref. 1852-10-23, 8:3, D.

Oct. 19, Mr. Nathaniel Kronheim, Agent for the Society for Promoting Christianity among the Jews.

No. 6199 :: Ref. 1852-10-23, 8:3, D.

At an advanced age, at the residence of her son-in-law, Mr. Robert Eakin, Ballyhenny, Ramelton, Sarah, relict of the late Mr. Robert Stevenson, Dromore, Letterkenny.

No. 6200 :: Ref. 1852-10-23, 8:3, D.

Suddenly, Mr. James Gallagher, innkeeper, Bundoran.

No. 6201 :: Ref. 1852-10-30, 5:6, B.

Oct. 3, at Paignton, the wife of Thomas Mills, Esq., of a daughter.

No. 6202 :: Ref. 1852-10-30, 5:6, B.

Oct. 10, at Tullaker, the lady of S. Stackpoole, Esq., of a daughter.

No. 6203 :: Ref. 1852-10-30, 5:6, B.

Oct. 13, at Greenhithe, Kent, Mrs. Randal G. Vogan, of a son.

No. 6204 :: Ref. 1852-10-30, 5:6, B.

Oct. 20, at 26, Gardiner's-place, Dublin, the lady of Henry B. Gresson, Esq., of a daughter.

No. 6205 :: Ref. 1852-10-30, 5:6, B.

Oct. 22, in London, the Hon. Mrs. Maude, of a son and heir.

No. 6206 :: Ref. 1852-10-30, 5:6, M.

Oct. 13, in Inver Church, James Hamilton, Esq., of Dountinny, co. Donegal, only surviving son of the late Benedict Hamilton, Esq., of Font Hill, co. Carlow, to Alicia Spenser, fourth daughter of Andrew M'Munn, Esq., of Inver, Donegal.

No. 6207 :: Ref. 1852-10-30, 5:6, M.

Oct. 13, in Belfast, R.W. Pring, Esq., son of Elijah Pring, Esq., of Westmoreland-street, Dublin, to Eliza, eldest daughter of J. Grattan, Esq., of Belfast.

No. 6208 :: Ref. 1852-10-30, 5:6, M.

Oct. 14, in Strabane, Mr. Alexander M'Clelland, to Catherine, youngest daughter of Mr. Hugh Hamilton, both of Strabane.

No. 6209 :: Ref. 1852-10-30, 5:6, M.

Oct. 18, at Charlton, near Dover, C.W. Maude, Esq., late H.E.I.C.S., to Emily, daughter of the late Samuel Brooke, Esq., of Finchley, Middlesex.

No. 6210 :: Ref. 1852-10-30, 5:6, M.

Oct. 19, at Ballylesson Church, John Strean Armstrong, Esq., M.D., to Margaret, fourth daughter of the late John Thomson, Esq., of Belfast.

No. 6211 :: Ref. 1852-10-30, 5:6, M.

Oct. 21, at Sutton-on-Hone, Arthur Z. Button, Esq., of Muckinge, to Julienne Emily, second daughter of Richard Saunders, Esq., of Hawley house, in the county of Kent, and of Largay, co. Cavan, Ireland.

No. 6212 :: Ref. 1852-10-30, 5:6, M.

Oct. 23, at Hampstead, by Rev. W. Shepherd, M.A., rector of Margaret Roding, and rural dean, father of the bridegroom, assisted by Rev. John Ayre, M.A., of Hampstead, and domestic chaplain to the Earl of Roden, Sarah, eldest daughter of Anthony Highmore, Esq., to William Ashton Shepherd, Esq., Assistant-surgeon, H.E.I.C.S., Bombay.

No. 6213 :: Ref. 1852-10-30, 5:6, M.

Oct. 25, in Derrymacash Chapel, by the brother of the bride, Mr. John Morgan, jun., merchant, Portadown, to Mary, youngest sister of Rev. L.L. Morgan, P.P., Seago, co. Armagh.

No. 6214 :: Ref. 1852-10-30, 5:6, M.

Oct. 26, at Newmills, co. Tyrone, by the Venerable the Archdeacon of Armagh, John Thomas Bell, Esq., L.L.D., to Catherine, daughter of the late Rev. Charles Richard Elrington, D.D., Regius Professor of Divinity in the University of Dublin.

No. 6215 :: Ref. 1852-10-30, 5:6, M.

Oct. 27, in St. Mark's Church, Portadown, by Rev. H.P. Proctor, Hamilton Robb, Esq., Linen Manufacturer, to Elizabeth, second daughter of Hartford Montgomery, Esq., Merchant, Portadown.

No. 6216 :: Ref. 1852-10-30, 5:6, D.

Aug. 16, at Calcutta, aged 44, Henry Whitelock Torrens, Esq., of the Bengal Civil Service, Resident at the Court of his Highness the Newaub Nazim of Bengal, eldest son of the late Major-General Sir H. Torrens, K.C.B., K.T.S., Adjutant-General to the Forces.

No. 6217 :: Ref. 1852-10-30, 5:6, D.

Oct. 2, at Rome, Count Jerome Sebastiani, aged 83.

No. 6218 :: Ref. 1852-10-30, 5:6, D.

Oct. 5, at the Manse, Ballymena, Annie, daughter of the Rev. Dr. Dobbin, aged 3 years and 2 months.

No. 6219 :: Ref. 1852-10-30, 5:6, D.

Oct. 5, at New York, Peter Hughes, aged thirty-four years, formerly of Parish of Clonfeacle, co. Tyrone, Ireland.

No. 6220 :: Ref. 1852-10-30, 5:6, D.

Oct. 8, at Murray-street, Oldham-road, Manchester, aged 72, Mr. Joseph Harper, Letterpress Printer. The deceased had followed the profession for a period of sixty-one years, commencing in 1791. He attended his employment until within a fortnight of his death, and retained his mental faculties to the last.

No. 6221 :: Ref. 1852-10-30, 5:6, D.

Oct. 13, at the Grange, aged 92 years, Mary, widow of the late Sir R. Brooke, Bart., of Norton Priory, Cheshire.

No. 6222 :: Ref. 1852-10-30, 5:6, D.

Oct. 14, Rear-Admiral Henry Bourchier (1846 on the retired list). This officer served as lieutenant of the *Unicorn*, and commanded one of her boats at the capture of the French Privateer *Tape-a bord*, of four guns and 46 men, off St. Domingo, in 1805. As commander of the *Hawk*, in 1811, he was present at the capture of the French 14-gun privateer *Furet*; also at the destruction of the French frigate *Amazon*, and engaged, under Cape Barfleur, three French gunbrigs, two luggers, and convoy. Two of the brigs and a great part of the convoy, being driven on shore, were destroyed or brought off by the boats belonging to the *Hawk*. For these services he was gazetted in 1805 and in 1811.

No. 6223 :: Ref. 1852-10-30, 5:6, D.

Oct. 16, of rheumatism in the heart, aged 71 years, Miss Anne Graham, only daughter of the late James Graham, Esq., of Clones, co. Monaghan, and of Ballymahon, co. Longford.

No. 6224 :: Ref. 1852-10-30, 5:6, D.

Oct. 17, at his residence, in Glennan, Mr. James Johnston, one of the oldest Freemasons in the County Monaghan.

No. 6225 :: Ref. 1852-10-30, 5:6, D.

Oct. 18, at Bourney Glebe, co. Tipperary, John H., the eldest son of the Rev. H.C. Tuthill.

No. 6226 :: Ref. 1852-10-30, 5:6, D.

Oct. 19, at the rectory, Templeport, the Rev. Thomas La Nauze.

No. 6227 :: Ref. 1852-10-30, 5:6, D.

Oct. 21, aged thirty-six, Mrs. Tracy, Superioress of St. Clare's Convent, Newry.

No. 6228 :: Ref. 1852-10-30, 5:6, D.

Oct. 23, at Dumcairn, near Armagh, after a few days' illness, Mr. Edward Downey, aged 59 years, much regretted by all who knew him.

No. 6229 :: Ref. 1852-10-30, 5:6, D.

Oct. 23, at Ballybofey, co. Donegal, Mr. John Toner, merchant, after an illness of two days.

No. 6230 :: Ref. 1852-10-30, 5:6, D.

Oct. 23, at Victoria-place, Belfast, Francis William, son of the Rev. Thomas Drew, D.D.

No. 6231 :: Ref. 1852-10-30, 5:6, D.

Oct. 26, after a short illness, at the Glebe, Kilkeedy, Rev. John Lucas, Rector of Kilkeedy and Inchicronan, diocese of Killaloe.

No. 6232 :: Ref. 1852-10-30, 5:6, D.

Oct. 27, at Tartaraghan Glebe, Isabelle Olivia, the infant and twin daughter of the Rev. Geo. Robinson.

No. 6233 :: Ref. 1852-10-30, 5:6, D.

At St. Omer's, France, Captain Robert Parkinson, brother to Mr. John Parkinson, of Arran-quay, Dublin, and Mr. Hill Parkinson, Enniskillen.

No. 6234 :: Ref. 1852-10-30, 5:6, D.

At his residence, near Blackrock, Alexander Hamilton, Esq., L.L.D, Q.C., of Rutland-square, Dublin, and of Newtownhamilton, County Armagh, eldest son of the late Dr. Hugh Hamilton, Lord Bishop of Ossory.

No. 6235 :: Ref. 1852-11-06, 8:2, B.

Oct. 15, at Donegal, the wife of William Harte, Esq., County Surveyor, of a son.

No. 6236 :: Ref. 1852-11-06, 8:2, B.

Oct. 21, in Albany-street, London, the wife of M. Turner, solicitor, was safely delivered of three children—two boys and a girl. The mother and children are doing well.

No. 6237 :: Ref. 1852-11-06, 8:2, B.
Oct. 29, at Ealing, Middlesex, the wife of Samuel Lover, Esq., of a daughter, still-born.

No. 6238 :: Ref. 1852-11-06, 8:2, B.
Oct. 31, at Diswellstown, co. Dublin, the wife of the Hon. Henry Sugden, of a daughter.

No. 6239 :: Ref. 1852-11-06, 8:2, B.
In Ballina, the lady of the Rev. Robert Bell, Wesleyan minister, of a daughter.

No. 6240 :: Ref. 1852-11-06, 8:2, M.
Oct. 26, in the Cathedral, Derry, Mr. Alexander Shannon, of Derry, painter, to Anne, second daughter of the late Mr. Andrew Fullerton, Canary, co. Armagh.

No. 6241 :: Ref. 1852-11-06, 8:2, M.
Oct. 28, in St. Peter's Church, Dublin, Rev. Benjamin A. Newcombe, to Eliza, youngest daughter of the late John D. Eccles, of Ecclesville, co. Tyrone.

No. 6242 :: Ref. 1852-11-06, 8:2, D.
July 29, Mr. G. Sullivan, Consul at Amoy. The situation of consul seems to be the most fatal one in the diplomatic service in China, as, during the short period which has elapsed since the opening of the five ports, no less than five consuls have died, viz., Messrs. Thom, Lay, Layton, Connor, and Sullivan.

No. 6243 :: Ref. 1852-11-06, 8:2, D.
Sept. 22, at New York, after a short but painful illness, which she bore with Christian patience, Phoebe Holmes, late of the town of Donegal.

No. 6244 :: Ref. 1852-11-06, 8:2, D.
Sept. 30, at Oporto, William, son of the late Thomas Harvey, Esq., of Londonderry.

No. 6245 :: Ref. 1852-11-06, 8:2, D.
Oct. 18, at Tunnylummon, co. Fermanagh, Mr. John Price, aged 80 years. He was discharged from the Royal Irish Artillery on the 31st December, 1801, and has been in receipt of a pension for 51 years. Four of his sons entered the British army, two of whom are in the receipt of pensions, after having served the full term of years.

No. 6246 :: Ref. 1852-11-06, 8:2, D.
Oct. 19, in Ballyshannon, Mrs. Flanagan, wife of Mr. John Flanagan, of Back-street.

No. 6247 :: Ref. 1852-11-06, 8:2, D.
Oct. 21, Robert Francis Boyd, eldest son of William Boyd, of Capel-street.

No. 6248 :: Ref. 1852-11-06, 8:2, D.
Oct. 22, in Trillick, Mr. Robert Armstrong, deeply regretted by his numerous friends and relatives.

No. 6249 :: Ref. 1852-11-06, 8:2, D.
Oct. 24, of fever, at 21, Charlemont-street, Dublin, Alexander, third son of Liddle Baxter, Esq., late of Enniskillen.

No. 6250 :: Ref. 1852-11-06, 8:2, D.
Oct. 24, at Macroom, Edward Ledger, Esq., Sub Inspector of Police, aged 52 years.

No. 6251 :: Ref. 1852-11-06, 8:2, D.
Oct. 25, At [sic] Maguire's Bridge, Mr. James Palmer, in the 76th year of his age, for more than 52 years a member of the Primitive Wesleyan Methodist Society.

No. 6252 :: Ref. 1852-11-06, 8:2, D.
Oct. 27, at his residence, Great Brunswick-street, aged 83 years, Sir Edward Stanley.

No. 6253 :: Ref. 1852-11-06, 8:2, D.
Oct. 28, in Temple-street, Dublin, the Rev. George Hamilton Ash, Rector of Lower Cumber, in the diocese of Derry, in the fifieth year of his age.

No. 6254 :: Ref. 1852-11-06, 8:2, D.
Oct. 28, at 17, Opera-arcade, London, Mr. John Morris, aged 60, for nearly 30 years the faithful servant of the late firm of Green and Ward, 20, Cockspur-street.

No. 6255 :: Ref. 1852-11-06, 8:2, D.
Oct. 30, aged twenty-eight years, Rev. John Clarke Huston, son of the Rev. Clarke Huston, D.D., of Ballymena, and late Minister of Clavering-place Congregation, Newcastle on-Tyne.

No. 6256 :: Ref. 1852-11-06, 8:2, D.
Oct. 31, at Kensington, in his twenty-ninth year, beloved by all who knew him, Vincent, youngest son of Mr. Leigh Hunt.

No. 6257 :: Ref. 1852-11-06, 8:2, D.
Oct. 31, at Brookley, Armagh, James Oliver, Esq., aged 83, the last member of the Armagh Company of Volunteers.

No. 6258 :: Ref. 1852-11-06, 8:2, D.
Nov. 2, in Dungiven, Mr. E. Wray, of Philadelphia, U.S.

No. 6259 :: Ref. 1852-11-13, 8:3, B.
Oct. 26, at Portadown, the wife of Samuel M'Ilveen, of a son.

No. 6260 :: Ref. 1852-11-13, 8:3, B.
Nov 1, at Belfast, Mrs. John Seed, of a daughter.

No. 6261 :: Ref. 1852-11-13, 8:3, B.
Nov. 2, at Barkhall, Letterkenny, the wife of the Rev. Oliver Leitch, of a daughter.

No. 6262 :: Ref. 1852-11-13, 8:3, B.
Nov. 4, at Portadown, the wife of James Searight, Esq., solicitor, of a daughter.

No. 6263 :: Ref. 1852-11-13, 8:3, B.
Nov. 8, at Tome, near Black Lion, co. Cavan, Mrs. Brackin, wife of James Brackin, Esq., of a daughter.

No. 6264 :: Ref. 1852-11-13, 8:3, B.
Nov. 11, at Portadown, the Lady of J.O. Woodhouse, Esq., of a daughter.

No. 6265 :: Ref. 1852-11-13, 8:3, M.
Oct. 26, in Killemard Church, T. Ross, Esq., S.I., Constabularly [sic], of Kesh, co. Fermanagh, to Jane West, eldest daughter of Robert Ball Steele Esq., late of the 27th Foot.

No. 6266 :: Ref. 1852-11-13, 8:3, M.
Nov. 1, in Tandragee, Mr. James Moody, Poyntzpass, to the eldest daughter of Mr. John Sifton, Commercial Hotel, Tandragee.

No. 6267 :: Ref. 1852-11-13, 8:3, M.
Nov. 2, in Mary's Church, Dublin, Mr. Samuel M'Quilkin, Principal of the Boarding and Day-school, No. 7, Mall-Wall, Derry, to Kate, youngest daughter of Mr. John Crawford, late of Boyle, co. Roscommon.

No. 6268 :: Ref. 1852-11-13, 8:3, M.
Nov. 2, at St. Augustine's Church, Liverpool, J.H. Chambers, Lieutenant in the 46th Regiment, to Mary Elizabeth, daughter of the late Rev. S.W. Perkins, M.A.

No. 6269 :: Ref. 1852-11-13, 8:3, M.
Nov. 3, in the Wesleyan church, Donegal-square, Belfast, William M'Carter, Esq., Belfast, to Catherine, daughter of the late Gilbert Shanks, Esq., Mountgilbert, co. Antrim.

No. 6270 :: Ref. 1852-11-13, 8:3, M.
Nov. 4, at Churchhill, Edinburgh, William Wood, Esq., accountant, to Margaret Parker, fourth daughter of the late Rev. Thomas Chalmers, D.D., L.L.D.

No. 6271 :: Ref. 1852-11-13, 8:3, M.
Nov. 5, in Tempo, Mr. Robert Patterson, Effernen, to Miss Catherine Leard, of Badoney, near Trillick.

No. 6272 :: Ref. 1852-11-13, 8:3, M.
Nov. 5, in Gilford, Mr. James Corbitt, to Miss Ann Jane Hughes, both of Gilford.

No. 6273 :: Ref. 1852-11-13, 8:3, M.
Nov. 6, at St. Peter's church, Dublin, the Rev. Thos. Atkinson, Rector of Doon, co. Limerick, to Elizabeth, daughter of the Ven. Henry Irwin, Archdeacon of Emly, and Minister of Sanford church.

No. 6274 :: Ref. 1852-11-13, 8:3, M.
Nov. 9, at Newry, Mr. Michael Kelly, Dundalk, to Catherine, second daughter of Mr. Bernard Coleman, Newry.

No. 6275 :: Ref. 1852-11-13, 8:3, M.
Nov. 11, at St. Mark's Church, Armagh, by Rev. B. Wade, William Bertram Ochiltree, Esq., of Richhill, to Anna, eldest daughter of the late Mr. James Graham, this City.

No. 6276 :: Ref. 1852-11-13, 8:3, M.
Nov. 11, in Middletown, by Rev. J. White, Mr. Thomas W. Menagh, Caledon, to Hariet Elizabeth, second daughter of Mr. Wm. Lyndon, Middletown.

No. 6277 :: Ref. 1852-11-13, 8:3, M.
On the 11th inst., in St. Patrick's Chapel, in this city, Miss Catherine M'Cann, to Nicholas Carolan, Esq., Dundalk.

No. 6278 :: Ref. 1852-11-13, 8:3, D.
May 26, at Morpeth, Australia, Andrew, youngest son of the late Rev. John M'Ilwaine, Morne, co. Down.

No. 6279 :: Ref. 1852-11-13, 8:3, D.
June 8, at Stanfield, New Norfolk, Henry Emmet Fitzgerald, the infant son of Thomas Francis Meagher, Esq., aged four months.

No. 6280 :: Ref. 1852-11-13, 8:3, D.
Oct. 18, by falling from a building in Hamilton Avenue, Brooklin, U.S., James M'Murn, aged 25 years, a native of co. Cavan, Ireland.

No. 6281 :: Ref. 1852-11-13, 8:3, D.
Oct. 27, the Rev. Wm. Seaton, minister in the Methodist Connection, Rochdale, aged fifty-six years. He was the last male descendant of the Earl of Wintoun, whose titles, honours, and estates, were forfeited for his share in the Scottish Rebellion in 1715.

No. 6282 :: Ref. 1852-11-13, 8:3, D.
Nov. 27 [sic], at his hotel, in the avenue, St. Cloud, Paris, Le Colonel Marquis Bouffet de Montanban, the intimate and tried-friend of Prince Louis Napoleon in his life and captivity, in his fifty-eighth year.

No. 6283 :: Ref. 1852-11-13, 8:3, D.
Oct. 30, at Ballina, co. Mayo, Julia Fowler, widow of the Rev. R. Bell, Wesleyan minister.

No. 6284 :: Ref. 1852-11-13, 8:3, D.
Oct. 30, at Coleraine, Margaret, relict of the late James Galt, Esq., Coleraine.

No. 6285 :: Ref. 1852-11-13, 8:3, D.
At Hastings, Elizabeth, eldest daughter of the late Christopher James Campbell, Esq., assistant-secretary to the General Post-office.

No. 6286 :: Ref. 1852-11-13, 8:3, D.
Nov. 1, at Needham-place, Newry, Margaret, wife of Frederick William Kidd, Esq.

No. 6287 :: Ref. 1852-11-13, 8:3, D.
Nov. 1, at Streatham, in the 79th year of his age, John Henry Capper, Esq., formerly of the Secretary of State's-office, Whitehall, having been in the Home Department 53 years. He served under 17 successive Secretaries of State, and held the appointment of Superintendent of Convicts for 30 years.

No. 6288 :: Ref. 1852-11-13, 8:3, D.
Nov. 1, at Slane, in the 50th year of his age, Mr. W. Mills.

No. 6289 :: Ref. 1852-11-13, 8:3, D.
Nov. 2, Mrs. Mary Somers, relict of Patrick Somers, Esq., of Chaffpool, co. Sligo, and mother of John Patrick Somers, Esq., late M.P. for the borough of Sligo.

No. 6290 :: Ref. 1852-11-13, 8:3, D.
Nov. 2, M. Ernest Corr, of Brussels—a student of law—scarcely 21 years, whose first successes afforded grounds for the most brilliant hopes. The family of Corr, is Irish, long settled in Belgium, enjoying high consideration by their worth, position, and genius.

No. 6291 :: Ref. 1852-11-13, 8:3, D.
Nov. 3, at his residence, Drumkeen House, co. Cavan, Henry Theophilus Kilbee, J.P.

No. 6292 :: Ref. 1852-11-13, 8:3, D.
Nov. 3, Patrick Lowe, a pensioner from the 52d Regiment of Light Infantry, aged 84. He was present at every battle and siege during the late war, under the Duke of Wellington. He formed one of the "forlorn hope" at Badajoz, where he personally captured the governor of that fortress, and for which he obtained a large reward; he was also present at Waterloo, and had a medal with 13 clasps, which he never wore, as he considered himself wronged in not getting a 14th.

No. 6293 :: Ref. 1852-11-13, 8:3, D.
Nov. 5, Mr. Edward M'Kendry, of Grange, near Toome Bridge, aged 29.

No. 6294 :: Ref. 1852-11-13, 8:3, D.
Nov. 6, at Leatherhead, Surrey, Mary, relict of the late Thomas Tegg, Esq., of Cheapside, London, publisher, aged 71.

No. 6295 :: Ref. 1852-11-13, 8:3, D.
Nov. 6, after a painful illness which she bore with Christian resignation and submission to the will of her heavenly father, and with a full assumption of a blessed immortality beyond the grave, aged 84 years, Fanny, relict of the late Mrs. [sic] Hugh M'Clean, Crunsaught, near Mountnorris.

No. 6296 :: Ref. 1852-11-13, 8:3, D.
Nov. 7, at No. 27, Euston-place, New-road, London, Mr. John E. Moody, the eminent comic vocalist, in the 38th year of his age.

No. 6297 :: Ref. 1852-11-13, 8:3, D.
Nov. 7, at Randalstown, Mr. Henry Anderson, aged 86 years—one of the oldest Freemasons and Yeomen in that place.

No. 6298 :: Ref. 1852-11-13, 8:3, D.
Nov. 7, in Clonkee, near Clones, James, son to Mr. William Moore, aged 15 years.

No. 6299 :: Ref. 1852-11-13, 8:3, D.
Nov. 8, at Lisburn, Mr. Edward Cupples Mussen, in the 39th year of his age.

No. 6300 :: Ref. 1852-11-13, 8:3, D.
Nov. 8, at 33, Lower Gardiner-street, Dublin, in the 74th year of his age, John Fottrell, Esq., Secretary of the Hibernian Bank.

No. 6301 :: Ref. 1852-11-13, 8:3, D.
Baron Billing, formerly Minister Plenipotentiary, Frankfort, has died of apoplexy. He was only 50 years of age.

No. 6302 :: Ref. 1852-11-13, 8:3, D.
Mr. Sparks, jun., of Liverpool, the gentleman whose legs were shattered by a railway carriage at the Huyton station in the London and North-Western Railway, died on Friday night week.

No. 6303 :: Ref. 1852-11-13, 8:3, D.
Killed at Matamoras, Alexander Finlay, late of Jersey City, eldest son of the late Robert Finlay, Castleblaney, Co. Monaghan, Ireland.

No. 6304 :: Ref. 1852-11-13, 8:3, D.
The remains of the late lamented Dr. Townsend, Lord Bishop of Meath, were on 3d Nov. interred, at Ardbraccan. The funeral was strictly private.

No. 6305 :: Ref. 1852-11-20, 8:2, B.
Nov. 11, at Omagh, the lady of Captain Stack, of the East India Company's service, of a son.

No. 6306 :: Ref. 1852-11-20, 8:2, M.
Oct. 20, at the King's Chapel, Boston, U.S., Rev. John Cordner, of Montreal, Canada, to Miss Caroline Hall, daughter of Rev. Francis Parkman, D.D., Boston.

No. 6307 :: Ref. 1852-11-20, 8:2, M.
Oct. 25, at St. Malachi's Church, St. John's [sic], New Brunswick, Thomas Robert Owens, Esq., M.D., Boston, U.S., to Elizabeth, daughter of the late Wm. Doherty, Esq., merchant, of St. John's, N.B., and formerly of Strabane, Ireland.

No. 6308 :: Ref. 1852-11-20, 8:2, M.
Nov. 3, at St. Peter's Church, London, Samuel Denny, Esq., M.D., R.N., son of David Denny, Esq., Omagh, to Eliza, daughter of the late Lieutenant-Colonel Renwick.

No. 6309 :: Ref. 1852-11-20, 8:2, M.
Nov. 10, in St. George's Presbyterian Church, Liverpool, by Rev. S.G. Morrison, of Dublin, Mr. Samuel D. Brain, of London, to Elizabeth, daughter of Mr. Benjamin Morrison, of Portadown.

No. 6310 :: Ref. 1852-11-20, 8:2, D.
Oct. 21, at Calton, John Campbell, late 42nd Foot, at the advanced age of 91 years. John enlisted at Glasgow in the year 1793. In 1794 he commenced his first campaign under the command of *(continued...)*

No. 6310, continued: ...the Duke of York, in Holland. He served in Egypt, under Sir Ralph Abercrombie, and after the French abandoned that country, he joined the army in the Peninsula; was at the retreat from Coranna, and was within ten yards of Sir John Moore when he fell from his horse. Under the Duke of Wellington he was present at the battles of Salamanca, Pyrenees, Vittoria, Orthes, and Toulouse, was wounded at the battle of Toulouse, and received his discharge in 1814, with 1s. per day pension.

No. 6311 :: Ref. 1852-11-20, 8:2, D.
Oct. 31, at Coleraine, Annie Georgiana, infant daughter of Mr. J. M'Combie.

No. 6312 :: Ref. 1852-11-20, 8:2, D.
Nov. 5, at Ballygawley, Adam Armstrong Esq., brewer.

No. 6313 :: Ref. 1852-11-20, 8:2, D.
Nov. 5, Francis Huddleston, Esq., formerly captain in the Cambridge Militia, and 46th Foot.

No. 6314 :: Ref. 1852-11-20, 8:2, D.
Nov. 8, Charlotte, youngest daughter of the late Lieutenant James Westwater, of the 3d Garrison Battalion, and grand-daughter of the late Rev. John M'Clelland, co. Tyrone.

No. 6315 :: Ref. 1852-11-20, 8:2, D.
Nov. 10, the Right Rev. Father Bernard Palmer, in the 71st year of his age; he was the first person exalted to the rank of mitred abbott in England since the Reformation. He served his novitiate at Lullworth, but lived for some years in the chief house of the Cistercian order in France.

No. 6316 :: Ref. 1852-11-20, 8:2, D.
Nov. 10, at Chester-square, London, Gideon Algernon Mantell, Esq., LL.D., F.R.S., author of the "*Wonders of Geology*," "*Medals of Creation*," and other works.

No. 6317 :: Ref. 1852-11-20, 8:2, D.
Nov. 10, at Cabin-hill, near Dervock, the residence of her daughter, Mrs. Thompson, at an advanced age, Jane, relict of the late Rev. Thomas Bell, for forty-seven years Minister of the Presbyterian Church, Mosside.

No. 6318 :: Ref. 1852-11-20, 8:2, D.
Nov. 11, at the Hotel, Crewe Railway Station, on his way to Ventnor, Edward William, eldest son of the Rev. Edward M. Hamilton, of Brown-hall, co. Donegal, aged 22 [years].

No. 6319 :: Ref. 1852-11-20, 8:2, D.
Nov. 11, at Great Britain-street, Dublin, Mr. John Ferguson, for many years guard of the Enniskillen shareholder coach.

No. 6320 :: Ref. 1852-11-20, 8:2, D.
Nov. 12, at Dundalk, Mr. Anthony M'Court, aged 62, a much respected inhabitant of the town.

No. 6321 :: Ref. 1852-11-20, 8:2, D.
Nov. 13, at the Priory, Newcastle-on-Tyne, Rev. Clarke Houston, D.D., of Ballymena, father of the late Rev. John Clarke Houston, whose death took place on the 28th ult.

No. 6322 :: Ref. 1852-11-20, 8:2, D.
Nov. 14, at his father's residence, Crawfordsburn, Richard Minnis, aged twenty-seven years.

No. 6323 :: Ref. 1852-11-20, 8:2, D.
Nov. 16, at No. 1, Adelaide-place, Belfast, aged ten years, Georgina, youngest child of Mr. F.D. Finlay, Belfast.

No. 6324 :: Ref. 1852-11-27, 8:6, B.
At Anglesboro' House, Mitchelstown, the wife of the Rev. William Rowley Archdall, A.M., of a daughter.

No. 6325 :: Ref. 1852-11-27, 8:6, B.
At Galway, the wife of James J. Flynn, Esq., of a son.

No. 6326 :: Ref. 1852-11-27, 8:6, B.
At Crocknacrieve, co. Fermanagh, the wife of F.G. Bloomfield, Esq., of a daughter.

No. 6327 :: Ref. 1852-11-27, 8:6, B.
Last week, at Ballytera, near Dungarvan, a woman, named Bridget Dohera, gave birth to four male children.—*Waterford Paper*.

No. 6328 :: Ref. 1852-11-27, 8:6, M.
Nov. 15, in Edinburgh, William Bredin, Esq., Sub-Agent of the Bank of Ireland, Limerick, formerly in the same capacity at Armagh, son of the late Major-General Bredin, Royal Artillery, to Kate, eldest daughter of the late John Gabbett, Esq., of the city of Limerick, and Redmonstown, co. Tipperary.

No. 6329 :: Ref. 1852-11-27, 8:6, M.
Nov. 16, at Banbridge, Alfred Leighten Sadlier, Esq., to Miss Kate Evelina St. Leger.

No. 6330 :: Ref. 1852-11-27, 8:6, M.
Nov. 20, in St. Peter's Church, Dublin, Robt. Chartres Wilson, youngest son of William Augustus Hunt, Esq., Charleville Mall, and nephew of General Arthur Hunt, Royal Artillery, to Eliza Rebecca, eldest daughter of Rev. Dawson Deane Heather, Eagle-terrace, Upper Leeson-street, Dublin.

No. 6331 :: Ref. 1852-11-27, 8:6, M.
Nov. 23, at Monkstown Church, by the Venerable the Archdeacon of Dublin, Maxwell, eldest son of Colonel Close, of Drumbanagher, co. Armagh, to Catherine, daughter of Henry Close, Newtown-park, co. Dublin, Esq.

No. 6332 :: Ref. 1852-11-27, 8:6, D.
Aug. 28, at Archangel, Russia, by the rupture of a blood vessel, while discharging his duty as master of the *Matthew King*, Captain John Wilson Martin, late of Ringford, near Ardglass, co. Down.

No. 6333 :: Ref. 1852-11-27, 8:6, D.
Sept. 18, at Free-Town, Sierra Leone, Mr. Edward Ritchie, of the country fever, after a residence of 16 years in the colony.

No. 6334 :: Ref. 1852-11-27, 8:6, D.
Nov. 11, at Strabane, Jane, wife of Mr. Peter M'Cullow, Innkeeper.

No. 6335 :: Ref. 1852-11-27, 8:6, D.
Nov. 12, at Muckrim, Mr. John Griffin, in the 80th year of his age. He was a marine, and served with Lord Nelson at the battle of the Nile, at Copenhagan, and Trafalgar.

No. 6336 :: Ref. 1852-11-27, 8:6, D.
Nov. 14, at Passage, Johanna Walsh, in the 105th year of her age. Previous to her death she had been only one week confined to her bed. She has left a daughter, who is at present upwards of eighty years old.—*Waterford Mail*.

No. 6337 :: Ref. 1852-11-27, 8:6, D.
Nov. 15, in Cookstown, Mr. James M'Geagh, aged 68 years.

No. 6338 :: Ref. 1852-11-27, 8:6, D.
Nov. 19, at The Abbey, Jane, youngest daughter of Richard Davison, Esq., M.P.

No. 6339 :: Ref. 1852-11-27, 8:6, D.
Nov. 21, in Dublin, after a short illness, Louisa, relict of the late Rev. Joseph Storey, of Bingfield, co. Cavan.

No. 6340 :: Ref. 1852-11-27, 8:6, D.
Nov. 28 [sic], Robert, son of Doctor Taylor, of Bailieborough.

No. 6341 :: Ref. 1852-11-27, 8:6, D.
At Rathdonnell, near Collon, co. Louth, Mrs. Doherty, at the advanced age of 105 years. During the last harvest she superintended her reapers. Up to a short time before her death she retained all her faculties unimpaired.

No. 6342 :: Ref. 1852-11-27, 8:6, D.
At Roscommon, Peter M'Keogh, Esq., of No. 5, Belvidere-place, Dublin. Mr. M'Keogh was Crown-Solicitor for Roscommon, Leitrim, and Sligo.

No. 6343 :: Ref. 1852-11-27, 8:6, D.
Nov. 16, in Lurgan, Mr. Youngstown Brown, jun., aged 43 years.

No. 6344 :: Ref. 1852-11-27, 8:6, D.
Nov. 16, at New Ground, Guernsey, aged 62 years, Major Jas. Johnston, late of the 44th Regiment, eldest son of the late Captain Alex. Johnston, of the 25th Regiment (The King's Own Borderers,) and late of Dublin.

No. 6345 :: Ref. 1852-11-27, 8:6, D.
Nov. 16, Miss Mary Hall, of Blesinton, aged seventy-two years.

No. 6346 :: Ref. 1852-11-27, 8:6, D.
Nov. 17, after a short illness, of inflammation of the lungs, aged 53, William John H. Skiffington, of Dungannon.

No. 6347 :: Ref. 1852-11-27, 8:6, D.
Nov. 18, in Dumfries, John M'Diarmid, Esq., of the *Dumfries Courier*.

No. 6348 :: Ref. 1852-11-27, 8:6, D.
Nov. 18, at Shirley Park, Surrey, after a short illness, the Countes[s] of Eldon.

No. 6349 :: Ref. 1852-12-04, 8:4, B.
Nov. 21, the lady of the Rev. William Allman, of Dunfanaghy, of a daughter.

No. 6350 :: Ref. 1852-12-04, 8:4, B.
Nov. 24, at Kildeney Glebe, near Ballyshannon, the wife of Captain R.A. Logan, H.M. 57th Regiment of a son.

No. 6351 :: Ref. 1852-12-04, 8:4, B.
Nov. 25, at Glengeary, Kingstown, the wife of George A. Grierson, Esq., of a daughter.

No. 6352 :: Ref. 1852-12-04, 8:4, B.
Nov. 25, at Rockcorry, Mrs. Robert Murray, of a son.

No. 6353 :: Ref. 1852-12-04, 8:4, B.
Nov. 27, at Portadown, the wife of David Irwin, Esq., of a daughter.

No. 6354 :: Ref. 1852-12-04, 8:4, B.
Nov. 28, at Armagh, the lady of Stewart Maxwell, Esq., of a son.

No. 6355 :: Ref. 1852-12-04, 8:4, M.
Nov. 22, at Portrush, by the Rev. Mr. Chichester, Mr. Jeremiah Ellis, Printer, Coleraine, to Sarah Anne, second daughter of Mr. Alexander M'Donnell, near Ballymoney.

No. 6356 :: Ref. 1852-12-04, 8:4, M.
Nov. 23, W.J. M'Guckin, Esq., of Castle-dawson, [to] Fanny Julia, second daughter of the late Robert Costelloe, Esq., Inspector of Revenue Police, co. Donegal.

No. 6357 :: Ref. 1852-12-04, 8:4, M.
Nov. 24, at Shropshire, Rev. J.W. Irwin, curate of Raymocky, co. Donegal, to Florine, only daughter of the late Rev. John Griffiths Lloyd, of Trowscoed Hall, Montgomeryshire.

No. 6358 :: Ref. 1852-12-04, 8:4, M.
Nov. 25, at Clough, John Williams, Officer of Inland Revenue, to Isabella, daughter of the late Rev. Francis Dill, of Clough.

No. 6359 :: Ref. 1852-12-04, 8:4, M.
Nov. 25, in Armaghbreague Church, by Rev. D. Donaldson, Mr. J. Overend, to Miss Martha M'Creery, of Rock-cottage, Aughnagurgan.

No. 6360 :: Ref. 1852-12-04, 8:4, M.
In London, Samuel Denny, Esq., M.D., of the Royal Navy, son of David Denny, Esq., of Omagh, co. Tyrone, to Eliza, daughter of late Lieut. Col. Renwick.

No. 6361 :: Ref. 1852-12-04, 8:4, D.
Oct. [—], at Peterborough, U.C., George, second son of George Crozier, Esq. late of Banbridge, Co. Down.

No. 6362 :: Ref. 1852-12-04, 8:4, D.
Oct. 23, at New Orleans, aged 32 years, Thomas, fourth son of the late Thomas M'Fall, Esq., of Magherafelt.

No. 6363 :: Ref. 1852-12-04, 8:4, D.
Nov. 16, in Armagh, Mrs. Edmonson, wife of N. M'N. Edmonson, Esq., assistant-astronomer in the Armagh Observatory.

No. 6364 :: Ref. 1852-12-04, 8:4, D.
Nov. 19, at Clifton, Percy S.E. Walmisley, Esq., clerk of the Journals of the House of Lords.

No. 6365 :: Ref. 1852-12-04, 8:4, D.
Nov. 20, the Rev. James Lecky, A.B., incumbent of Willenhall, England, a native of Kilkenny.

No. 6366 :: Ref. 1852-12-04, 8:4, D.
Nov. 22, at Gortree, William Archibald, second son of Dr. Wm. Semple, aged two years.

No. 6367 :: Ref. 1852-12-04, 8:4, D.
Nov. 23, at Westport House, after a lingering illness, the Marchioness of Sligo.

No. 6368 :: Ref. 1852-12-04, 8:4, D.
Nov. 23, at Derry, of paralysis, Mr. Wm. Thompson, aged sixty-one years.

No. 6369 :: Ref. 1852-12-04, 8:4, D.
Nov. 24, at Eastbourne, Sussex, Henrietta Frances, relict of the late Colonel Rawdon, and daughter of the late Richard Dawson, Esq., of Ardee, co. Louth.

No. 6370 :: Ref. 1852-12-04, 8:4, D.
Nov. 26, at Ballykelly, near Bandbridge [sic], John, youngest son of Mr. James Hill Dickson, aged twenty-two years.

No. 6371 :: Ref. 1852-12-04, 8:4, D.
Nov. 27, at No. 6, Great Cumberland-place, London, in the thirty-seventh year of her age, Augusta Ada, wife of William, Earl of Lovelace, and only daughter of George Gordon Noel Lord Byron.

No. 6372 :: Ref. 1852-12-04, 8:4, D.
Nov. 28, at Marleborough, Rev. Thomas Meyler, M.A., Pembroke College, Oxford, master of the Royal Free Grammar School, and vicar of Baydon, aged 53.

No. 6373 :: Ref. 1852-12-04, 8:4, D.
Nov. 28, at Edinburgh, Alexander, aged nine years, youngest son of Captain Blackwood.

No. 6374 :: Ref. 1852-12-04, 8:4, D.
Nov. 30, at Parsonstown, Mrs. Carlile, wife of the Rev. Dr. Carlile, of the Scots Church, Mary's Abbey, Dublin, now residing at Parsonstown.

No. 6375 :: Ref. 1852-12-04, 8:4, D.
In Sligo, Eleanor, relict of Captain Ormsby, of the 52nd Light Infantry.

No. 6376 :: Ref. 1852-12-04, 8:4, D.
At Cherry-street, New York, Joseph Toel, carpet manufacturer, a native of Newry.

No. 6377 :: Ref. 1852-12-04, 8:4, D.
Dec. 3, in Charter School Street, Armagh, Margaret, wife of Mr. John Clarke, in the 85th year of her age—for upwards of 55 years she and her surviving husband were partners.

No. 6378 :: Ref. 1852-12-11, 8:3, B.
Nov. 19, at Burnley, Lancashire, the wife of Mr. W. Duckett, architect, of three children (two girls and a boy)—all of whom, with their mother, are doing well.

No. 6379 :: Ref. 1852-12-11, 8:3, B.
Nov. 28, at Glasslough, the wife of Robt. M'Kinstry, Esq., M.D., of a daughter.

No. 6380 :: Ref. 1852-12-11, 8:3, B.
Nov. 29, at Bishops-street, Dublin, the wife of Mr. Thomas Henderson, late of Armagh, of a daughter.

No. 6381 :: Ref. 1852-12-11, 8:3, B.
Dec. 7, at Ballinahone House, Armagh, the wife of Francis C. Isdell, Esq., of a daughter.

No. 6382 :: Ref. 1852-12-11, 8:3, B.
Dec. 2, the wife of — Huffman, Esq., of Doctors' Commons, London, of a daughter.

No. 6383 :: Ref. 1852-12-11, 8:3, B.
Dec. 6, at Edenderry, Portadown, the wife of David Bright, Esq., of a daughter.

No. 6384 :: Ref. 1852-12-11, 8:3, M.
Nov. 17, at St. John's Church, New York, Mr. Robert Irwin, of Jenet's-pass, to Rachel, third daughter of the late Mr. John Rogers, of Newry.

No. 6385 :: Ref. 1852-12-11, 8:3, M.
Nov. 27, in Drumholme, Mr. Edward Mulheron, of Pettigo, to Mary, daughter of Mr. James Mulloy, of Laghey.

No. 6386 :: Ref. 1852-12-11, 8:3, M.
Dec. 1, William, second son of Charles Clarke, Esq., late surgeon in the 21st Fusiliers, of Rathdrum, county Wicklow, to Harriet Wilhelmina M'Clintock, fourth daughter of the late William Milligan, Esq., surgeon in the Inniskilling Dragoons.

No. 6387 :: Ref. 1852-12-11, 8:3, M.
On same day [Dec. 1], Edward, third son of Charles Clarke, Esq., late surgeon in the 21st Fusiliers,

to Anna Jane, eldest daughter of [the] late William Milligan, Esq., surgeon in the Inniskilling Dragoons.

No. 6388 :: Ref. 1852-12-11, 8:3, M.
Dec. 2, in St. Thomas-street, Dublin, William Woods, Esq., of Trinity College, Dublin, to Susan, relict of Wm. Montgomery, Esq., of Lisbellaw, co. Fermanagh.

No. 6389 :: Ref. 1852-12-11, 8:3, M.
Dec. 3, Mr. John Sloan, to Eliza, fifth daughter of the late Mr. Wm. M'Cully, both of Aughnacloy.

No. 6390 :: Ref. 1852-12-11, 8:3, M.
Dec. 4, R.R.W. Lingen, Esq., assistant-secretary to the Committee of Privy Council on Education, to Emma, second daughter of Robert Hutton, Esq., of Putney-park.

No. 6391 :: Ref. 1852-12-11, 8:3, M.
Dec. 6, in Banbridge, Mr. William Coulter, Drumnagally, to Miss Violet Wright, Banbridge.

No. 6392 :: Ref. 1852-12-11, 8:3, M.
Dec. 8, in Derry, Captain Maxwell, 34th Regt., to Margaret M'Lean, daughter of Patrick Gilmore, Esq., the Grove, Londonderry.

No. 6393 :: Ref. 1852-12-11, 8:3, D.
At Bantry, Helen, the wife of Redmond Power, Esq., Sub-Inspector of Constabulary.

No. 6394 :: Ref. 1852-12-11, 8:3, D.
In Sligo, Anne, daughter of the late Rev. J. Wilson.

No. 6395 :: Ref. 1852-12-11, 8:3, D.
Nov. 15, at Maguiresbridge, James Elliott, Esq.

No. 6396 :: Ref. 1852-12-11, 8:3, D.
Nov. 22, at Aughagallon, near Lurgan, Mary, wife of Jonathan Gilbert, Esq., in her 68th year.

No. 6397 :: Ref. 1852-12-11, 8:3, D.
Nov. 30, at Cambridge, suddenly, by a fall from his horse, the Rev. George Howson, M.A., Fellow and Assistant-tutor of Christ's College, Cambridge, and late Vice-principal of the Collegiate Institution, Liverpool, in the 28th year of his age.

No. 6398 :: Ref. 1852-12-11, 8:3, D.
Nov. 30, at a very advanced age, in Cavan, Araminta Erskine.

No. 6399 :: Ref. 1852-12-11, 8:3, D.
Nov. 30, A.P. Gibson, Esq., of London, late Consul General at St. Petersburg for the United States of America.

No. 6400 :: Ref. 1852-12-11, 8:3, D.
Dec. 1, Georgina, the infant daughter of Mr. George M'Carter, Strabane.

No. 6401 :: Ref. 1852-12-11, 8:3, D.
Dec. 2, Stephen William Creaghe, Esq., president of the Money Order Office, General Post Office.

No. 6402 :: Ref. 1852-12-11, 8:3, D.
Dec. 3, at Portadown, Doctor Wm. Leebody, deservedly lamented by all who knew him. His remains were removed to Armagh, for interment, on Monday morning last.

No. 6403 :: Ref. 1852-12-11, 8:3, D.
Dec. 4, in Kilkenny, in the fifty-eighth year of her age, of disease of the heart, Miss Ellen Bracken, sister of the late recorder of that city.

No. 6404 :: Ref. 1852-12-11, 8:3, D.
Dec. 4, at Toughblane, near Hilsborough [sic], Mr. James Mahood.

No. 6405 :: Ref. 1852-12-11, 8:3, D.
Mr. Thomas Farrell, of Marlborough-street, suddenly, while hunting.

No. 6406 :: Ref. 1852-12-11, 8:3, D.
Dec. 6, at Tullydoey near Blackwatertown in the 92nd year of her age, Lydia, relict of Thomas Jackson Esq of same place.

No. 6407 :: Ref. 1852-12-11, 8:3, D.
The numerous friends of Mr. William Kernaghan, formerly of Sligo, whose death was announced some time since, will be glad to learn that he is well. His brother, Mr. B. Kernaghan, has just received a letter from him, written in October, from San Juan del Sur.

No. 6408 :: Ref. 1852-12-18, 8:2, B.
Dec. 4, at Rutland-square, North, Dublin, the wife of W.A. Dane, Esq., of a son.

No. 6409 :: Ref. 1852-12-18, 8:2, B.
Dec. 7, the lady of Hugh Boyle, Esq., Mall, Armagh, of a son.

No. 6410 :: Ref. 1852-12-18, 8:2, B.
Dec. 14, at Vicars Hill, the wife of George B. Allen, Esq., Mus. Bac. Oxon., of a daughter.

No. 6411 :: Ref. 1852-12-18, 8:2, B.
Dec. 14, at Tempo, co. Fermanagh, the wife of Rev. D. Clements, P.M., of a son.

No. 6412 :: Ref. 1852-12-18, 8:2, M.
Nov. 15, in Philadelphia, E.I. Sears, Esq., of Baltimore, to Catherine, eldest daughter of Gorges Irvine, Esq., of Enniskillen.

No. 6413 :: Ref. 1852-12-18, 8:2, M.
Dec. 3, in Tullylish Church, Mr. William Gough to Margaret, youngest daughter of Mr. John Emerson, both of Laurencetown, Banbridge.

No. 6414 :: Ref. 1852-12-18, 8:2, M.
Dec. 9, in the Cathedral, Armagh, by Rev. Mr. Wade, and afterwards in the Roman [C]atholic Chapel, by Rev. Mr. Gallogly, R.C.C., Mr. Peter Smallon, baker, Belfast, to Deborah, second daughter of the late Mr. C. Wilson, Caledon.

No. 6415 :: Ref. 1852-12-18, 8:2, M.

Dec. 9, in Clarke's-bride [sic], Mr. George Graham of Tullyvallen, to Susanna, daughter of Mr. Andw. Clarke, Cortamlet.

No. 6416 :: Ref. 1852-12-18, 8:2, M.

Dec. 16, in Kilskerry Church, by Rev. A.H. Irvine, Mr. Thomas G. M'Bride, C.E., Armagh, to Margaret, fourth daughter of Guy Bleakley, Garvaughey House, co. Tyrone, Esq.

No. 6417 :: Ref. 1852-12-18, 8:2, M.

In the Church at Benburb, by the Rev. Mr. Maunsel, Constable Wm. Armstrong, in charge of the Derrycorry Police Party, to S. Anne, eldest daughter of Mr. Nathaniel Holmes of Tullygoney, co. Tyrone.

No. 6418 :: Ref. 1852-12-18, 8:2, M.

Dec. 17, in the Presbyterian Meeting House, Mall, by the Rev. Mr. M'Alister, Color Sergeant Gully, 46th Regt., to Miss Matilda Girvan.

No. 6419 :: Ref. 1852-12-18, 8:2, D.

Nov. 27, aged 5 years and 3 months, Georgina, and on Nov. 30, aged 10 months, Victoria—two youngest children of Mr. George Paton, Belfast.

No. 6420 :: Ref. 1852-12-18, 8:2, D.

Dec. 2, at Dungarvan, aged 101 years, Mrs. Eleanor Higgins, late of Galway.

No. 6421 :: Ref. 1852-12-18, 8:2, D.

Dec. 4, at Lowtherstown, aged 46, Catherine, wife of Mr. Gerard Irvine.

No. 6422 :: Ref. 1852-12-18, 8:2, D.

Dec. 4, at Newry, in the 43rd year of her age, Marianne, wife of Charles O'Hagan, Esq., Courtenay-hill.

No. 6423 :: Ref. 1852-12-18, 8:2, D.

Dec. 4, after a short illness, in the 16th [sic] year of his age, John Smyth, Esq., M.D., of Belmont House, Stillorgan.

No. 6424 :: Ref. 1852-12-18, 8:2, D.

Dec. 5, at Camla Vale, Monaghan, aged 83 years, Colonel Henry Westenra. Deceased was brother to the late Lord Rossmore, and uncle to the present peer.

No. 6425 :: Ref. 1852-12-18, 8:2, D.

Dec. 7, at Rutland House, Grand Canal, Dublin, aged 91 years, Thomas Barnes, Esq., barrister-at-law.

No. 6426 :: Ref. 1852-12-18, 8:2, D.

Dec. 7, at Preston, Lancashire, of fever, Mr. Hargraeves Cockshot, late of Dundalk, corn merchant.

No. 6427 :: Ref. 1852-12-18, 8:2, D.

Dec. 9, at Dundalk, Rose, relict of the late Mr. Wm. Ryan.

No. 6428 :: Ref. 1852-12-18, 8:2, D.

Dec. 10, at Navan, Very Rev. Eugene O'Reilly, P.P., Navan, V.G. and Archdeacon of the diocese of Meath, in the 84th year of his age, and 60th of his ministry.

No. 6429 :: Ref. 1852-12-18, 8:2, D.

Dec. 10, at his residence, Dungannon, Mr. James Dickson, merchant, aged 60 years.

No. 6430 :: Ref. 1852-12-18, 8:2, D.

On the 12th inst., in Thomas-street, Armagh, of inflammation of the bowels, Miss Margaret Johnston, youngest daughter of Mr. Robert Johnson, in the 20th year of her age, seriously and deservedly regretted by numerous friends and acquaintances. She bore her sufferings with Christian fortitude, and died in hope of a glorious resurrection.

No. 6431 :: Ref. 1852-12-18, 8:2, D.

Dec. 12, at Eddnaharnon Cottage, Letterkenny, of influenza, Eliza Jane, daughter of Mr. Thomas Roulston, aged 5 years and 10 months.

No. 6432 :: Ref. 1852-12-18, 8:2, D.

Dec. 12, at Holywood, William, third son of the late Mr. William Paton, Holywood Mills.

No. 6433 :: Ref. 1852-12-18, 8:2, D.

Dec. 12, Rev. Dr. Doyle, in the 70th year of his age.

No. 6434 :: Ref. 1852-12-25, 8:2, B.

Dec. 14, at Anketell Lodge, Stewartstown, the wife of M'Crea Blair, Esq., of a son.

No. 6435 :: Ref. 1852-12-25, 8:2, B.

Dec. 21, at the Royal Hospital, Kilmainham, the wife of Colonel Eden, of a daughter.

No. 6436 :: Ref. 1852-12-25, 8:2, M.

Dec. 8, at St. George's Church, Dublin, by Very Rev. Dean of Killaloe, uncle to the bride, T.S. Blacker, Esq., of Armagh, to Frances Mary Anne, daughter of the late Thomas Arthur Forde, Esq., of Mountjoy-square, Dublin.

No. 6437 :: Ref. 1852-12-25, 8:2, M.

Dec. 16, in the Church of Tydavnet, by Rev. G.R. Young, Vicar of Errigle, Francis John Gervais, Esq., of Cecil, Co. Tyrone, to Annie Catherine, eldest daughter of the Rev. R.G. Young, Rector of Tydavnet.

No. 6438 :: Ref. 1852-12-25, 8:2, M.

Dec. 18, at the parish church, Mountnessing, Essex, by the Rev. T.M. Ready, Alfred Bingham, Esq., of the Stock-Exchange, London, to Mary Anne, eldest daughter of G. Fulcher, Esq., of Mark-lane.

No. 6439 :: Ref. 1852-12-25, 8:2, M.

Dec. 20, in the Wesleyan Chapel, Abbey-street, Armagh, by the Rev. Mr. Ballard, superintendent of this circuit, Mr. Joseph Turner Smyth, of Dublin, to Miss Rebecca Gardner Duncan, of Armagh.

No. 6440 :: Ref. 1852-12-25, 8:2, M.

Dec. 21, in Derry, by Rev. Wm. M'Clure, Rev. William James M'Connell, of Gortnessey, to Jane, youngest daughter of the late John Brigham, Esq., merchant, of Derry.

No. 6441 :: Ref. 1852-12-25, 8:2, M.

Dec. 22, in Saint Peter's Church, Dublin, by Rev. Cadwallader Woolsley, Robert B. Woolsley, Esq., eldest son of John Woolsley, Esq., M.D., to Lalla Marcella, daughter of the late Captain George Bingham.

No. 6442 :: Ref. 1852-12-25, 8:2, M.

Dec. 23, Mr. Matthew Holland, linen manufacturer, Ballyknock, Tandragee, to Sarah, second daughter of Samuel Byers, Esq., Mowhan, Mountnorris.

No. 6443 :: Ref. 1852-12-25, 8:2, D.

Dec. 8, at Rue de Castiglione, Paris, Henrietta, eldest daughter of the late Thomas Whealan, Esq., of Ballyconnell, co. Carlow.

No. 6444 :: Ref. 1852-12-25, 8:2, D.

Dec. 9, at Lara, Margaret, relict of the late Mr. John Beggs, merchant of Aughnacloy, aged eighty-eight.

No. 6445 :: Ref. 1852-12-25, 8:2, D.

Dec. 13, Samuel M'Clintock, of Seskinore Lodge, co. Tyrone, and Newton House, co. Louth, aged sixty-two, long a magistrate of both counties.

No. 6446 :: Ref. 1852-12-25, 8:2, D.

Dec. 13, at her house in Lerwick, Zetland, aged 88, Mrs. Copland, widow of the late James Copland, Esq., of Lerwick, formerly of the Island of Noss, and the revered mother of Dr. James Copland, F.R.S., &c., of Old Burlington-street, London. Her loss will be regretted by all classes in the Zetland and Orkney Isles.

No. 6447 :: Ref. 1852-12-25, 8:2, D.

Dec. 14, at Springhill, Strabane, Rebecca, the beloved wife of Mr. Wm. Blair.

No. 6448 :: Ref. 1852-12-25, 8:2, D.

Dec. 14, of a few days' illness, aged twenty-five years, at Marino Crescent, Clontarf, John, only surviving child of Mr. John Singleton, late of Lisburn, co. Antrim, and for the last few months a resident of Armagh.

No. 6449 :: Ref. 1852-12-25, 8:2, D.

Dec. 16, at Nelson lodge, Chelsea, Lady Stronge, relict of William Holmes, Esq., of Grafton-street, Bond-street, London, and mother of Sir James Matthew Stronge, Bart., of Tynan Abbey in this county.

No. 6450 :: Ref. 1852-12-25, 8:2, D.

Dec. 17, at North Frederick-street, Dublin, James Doherty, Esq., Q.C., Father of the North Western Bar.

No. 6451 :: Ref. 1852-12-25, 8:2, D.

Dec. 20, in Clones, Mr. Thomas Maguiniss, in the 49th year of his age.

No. 6452 :: Ref. 1852-12-25, 8:2, D.

At Toronto, Canada, John Dunbar, Esq., formerly of Cavan, aged fifty-five years.

No. 6453 :: Ref. 1852-12-25, 8:2, D.

At Balbirnie, N.B., Harry, infant son of Mr. and Lady Georgiana Balfour, aged 15 days.

:: :: ::

Transcript of Mr. John Thompson's editorial article, from the inaugural edition of *The Armagh Guardian* published December 3, 1844.

To Our Readers.

Kind Friends,—In presenting to you the first number of the Armagh Guardian, we are led to make a few observations, by way of introduction; not so much from custom as necessity.

The difficulties attending a beginning, though proverbially great in the verse of a poet, are nothing less in the prose of a prospectus, too generally the most complacent of moral fictions, but frequently the herald of truth. In addressing you we cannot appeal to the past for a recommendation; and are, therefore, thrown upon the future, which brings us in contact with *promise*—the parent of hope. But, notwithstanding the disadvantages under which we labour with respect to the *past*, a field so limitless as that upon which we have entered would afford ample room for discursive declamation, were it not so obscure a region; and that brevity is allowed to be the soul of wit.

It has been said that the empire of letters, by which the mind is governed, constitutes a republic, and accordingly its benefits ought not to be exclusive. It is necessary that its workings and progress be manifest to every one, and such instruction and amusement as it furnishes be placed within the reach of all; which can alone be effected by an intimate acquaintance with the history of the existing period, to be obtained only through the medium of the Press. *Our* object, then, is to assist in spreading that knowledge we have just alluded to, and which is admitted to be essential for the better understanding of the relative position of each individual in the present well-ordered arrangements of society. Whilst, therefore, we declare the GUARDIAN the advocate of the just and inalienable rights of the landlord, we shall never join any who would oppress the tenant; but reminding the former that property has *duties* as well as rights, we shall impress upon the latter what is imperative on *him*, that mutual co-operation for general good may more and more obtain. Holding the opinion that

> An empire built on Agriculture's race
> Is firm as the rocky mountain's solid base,

the reader will not be surprised at our determination to strengthen and uphold so great a bulwark of British glory. Happy would it be for Ireland were her sons to devote themselves to that employment for which nature has so peculiarly adapted them, rather than following the phantoms of independence, originated in the wildest imagination of infantine old men.

The Agriculturist will find in us a steady friend, while the mercantile and manufacturing interests will be carefully attended to.

Another and more important trait of the character of this Journal is its *religious* sentiments. They are strictly PROTESTANT, to assist in the diffusion of which our best exertions shall be employed; that in some measure we may answer the end of existence, by spreading the glory of God.

The present has been called an age of utilitarianism, and judging of things as they appear daily in the political world we would be almost forced to sign the sentiment; for among those who clamour *most* how few are there regarding themselves *least*—expediency, not principle, is the divinity more frequently worshipped by our modern politicians—it is too palpable to be misunderstood, and too glaring to deceive scrutiny. Yet, notwithstanding the absurdities proposed by the greatest hunters after popularity, that more than Athenian rage for novelty that predominates in our national character, permits these efforts to "*fashion and refine the race*" to make more or less impression; yea, the greater the absurdity, the stronger the claim, as the epilepsy of MAHOMET confirmed his inspiration. To assist in exposing this character on the one hand, and guiding aright that passion on the other we shall labour zealously and independently, though they be found in the wake of those whose path is dazzled by the glare of the meteor, or "the lawless sweep of the comet." We are Conservative—the cause is good—and as such we enter the political arena.

Nevertheless, we shall endeavour to discuss every subject calmly and dispassionately, in order to bring before our readers the TRUTH, and present them with a real picture of the state of affairs locally and generally; depending rather upon the force than the number of our arguments. It is our desire to be the friend of all, and as such, though we differ in opinion with many, to treat ALL courteously. If then, while we *guard* the principles of Conservatism, we can in any the least degree soften the asperities of manner—strengthen the gentler sympathies of human nature—improve the conduct of every grade of social existence, by instilling right sentiments into the mind—furnish those who may patronise us with materials for thinking, so that the present level of knowledge may be elevated. If we can do these things our object will be gained. We want not to increase the stock of prejudices by creating artificial grievances and dressing them in giant form—we want not to fan the flame of political dissension. Far otherwise; we desire such a state of society—if it can be effected—

When Sidney shall with Cato rest,
And Russel move the patriot's breast,
No more than Brutus now.

We know that there are many able journals carrying on this good work, and we feel that at most we are a mere atom in the great world of literature; but in a system composed of such atoms *one* is still something. A promise of a wide field for developing the great agricultural and other resources of this county seems just now to present itself by the introduction of railways; at which time we make our appearance in a Journal that we hope to make in some measure useful to a people who, for intelligence and respectability, stand second to none in the kingdom. It is thus especially we would call attention to the present publication. But, whilst we lay claim to patronage upon this consideration, we are not to be supposed to build upon *it* exclusively. "*It is not* (said BURKE,) *a predilection to mean, sordid, and home-bred cares that will avert the consequences of a false estimation of our interest.*" What this great philosopher said of a nation, is applicable to a county or city; therefore, we must expand our minds to the compass of their object—the sphere of duty must be enlarged—the importance of this county, both as a nucleus of agriculture, and the focus of trade for a great tract of country, may not any longer be kept secret, lest the fatal consequences of our concerns shrinking to the circumscribed dimensions of our minds be the result. These are things which we shall steadily keep before the public in their true bearings and relations locally and generally.

We trust our readers will excuse the length to which these observations have extended; less would not explain our intentions. We thank those who have given us such a hearty welcome. From all we crave a fair trial, confident that further acquaintance will obtain for us more extensive support; finally pledging ourselves to be found aiding the march of mind, till the majesty of understanding shall subdue the feuds of party, and TRUTH can be greeted with an universal song of triumph.

3. INDEX OF SURNAMES

A poor traveller, 1046
Abbott, 4058
Abercorn, 424, 2491, 3222, 4426
Abercrombie, 6310
Acheson, 137, 1626, 2468, 2612, 2785, 3108, 3494, 3519, 4585, 4649, 5522
Achonry, 1976
Adair, 2112, 3319
Adams, 331, 363, 435, 439, 774, 820, 1349, 1912, 3578, 3845, 4597, 4653, 4755, 4781, 4928, 5065, 5281, 5370, 5801, 6175
Adamson, 1787, 3799
Addey, 1828, 5407, 6041
Addison, 2223, 2857
Addy, 249, 1865, 2420. *See also* Ady.
Adlington, 4573
Adshead, 1089
Ady, 6104. *See also* Addy.
Agnew, 2300, 3040, 3750, 3831, 4553
Aickin, 5169
Aiken, 2768, 4999, 5636
Aitken, 3301
Albin, 4411
Alcorn, 335
Aldridge, 602
Alexander, 63, 272, 421, 437, 893, 906, 935, 1203, 1251, 1304, 1419, 1629, 1664, 1958, 2104, 2177, 2273, 2452, 2586, 2713, 3228, 3255, 3584, 3605, 3778, 3936, 3957, 4144, 4208, 4235, 4279, 4500, 4787, 5226, 5726, 5872, 5919, 5971, 6057
Algar, 2693
Algeo, 121, 701, 1355, 1632, 4444
Allan, 107, 590, 3740. *See also* M'Allen.
Allen, 20, 472, 516, 638, 976, 1116, 1423, 1502, 1524, 1767, 1846, 2124, 2311, 2412, 2431, 2684, 2827, 2830, 2841, 3238, 3839, 3898, 3903, 3911, 3944, 4303, 4342, 4600, 5056, 5160, 5335, 6410. *See also* M'Allen.
Allingham, 221, 2218, 3241, 3666, 4234, 4996, 5876
Allman, 3536, 4750, 4829, 5792, 6349
Allmond, 3092

Allott, 919
Allpress, 1665, 2893
Allsopp, 2806
Anderson, 428, 712, 756, 1125, 1137, 1237, 1261, 1520, 1523, 1574, 1592, 1604, 1999, 2033, 2174, 2255, 2275, 2415, 2590, 2793, 2825, 2867, 2909, 3105, 3242, 33839, 3349, 3438, 3494, 3516, 3519, 3861, 4152, 4360, 4420, 4617, 4629, 4760, 4772, 4803, 4863, 5167, 5451, 5717, 5922, 5995, 6141, 6297
Andrews, 367, 1735, 3239, 5200, 5223, 6152
Anglesey, 5261
Anketell, 287, 338, 1086, 2122, 3533, 4582, 4666, 5657, 5750
Annesley, 795, 5298
Appelbe, 404
Apperson, 2137
Apsley, 393
Arbuthnot, 1000, 4105, 5735
Archdall, 434, 822, 1765, 2470, 2514, 3913, 4446, 4467, 4643, 5394, 5518, 5634, 5969, 6324
Archer, 52, 2068, 3163, 3170, 4539, 4778, 5201, 5432
Ardagh, 735, 1204, 2727, 3056, 4329, 6048
Ardill, 6042
Ardiss, 3896
Argyle, 3444
Armagh, 427, 1879, 3068, 4959, 5011, 5994, 6214
Armitage, 4578
Armour, 2962, 3875, 5692
Armstrong, 75, 115, 148, 152, 176, 182, 336, 406, 428, 473, 492, 525, 678, 769, 787, 1028, 1075, 1309, 1508, 1521, 1526, 1575, 1742, 1757, 1784, 1822, 1836, 1858, 1894, 1971, 2051, 2115, 2168, 2182, 2210, 2225, 2244, 2260, 2278, 2299, 2323, 2492, 2636, 2896, 3046, 3086, 3152, 3308, 3406, 3430, 3514, 3638, 3814, 3823, 3977, 4182, 4288, 4316, 4349, 4456, 4519, 4609, 4623, 4660, 4700, 4741, 4843, 4861, 4936, 5072, 5128, 5136, 5297, 5469, 5478, 5488, 5506, 5673, 5716, 5763, 5821, 5852, 6210, 6248, 6312, 6417
Arnold, 2455, 3524, 4110

Arthure, 117
Ash, 297, 437, 1868, 2063, 2693, 6253
Ashe, 1135, 1369, 1619, 4795, 4849
Ashmore, 6005
Ashton, 666
Ashwell, 3073
Ashworth, 3503
Askin, 3444
Asthuse, 3899
Atherton, 4222
Atkinson, 284, 314, 390, 488, 517, 791, 1088, 1217, 1933, 1934, 3188, 3203, 3245, 3251, 3278, 3279, 3593, 3858, 4094, 4361, 4381, 4397, 4557, 4709, 4901, 5051, 5060, 5482, 5519, 5552, 5858, 6273
Atthill, 1381
Atwool, 3016
Auchinaleck, 2421
Auchinleck, 33, 4010, 6037, 6111, 6159
Auerbach, 6180
Austin, 732
Australasia, 3466
Australia, 1429
Aveo, 470
Averell, 894
Avery, 5249
Avil, 451
Aylwin, 2806
Ayre, 6212
Babe, 3186
Babington, 863, 1102, 2022, 3772, 3803, 3810, 4669
Bacon, 2809, 3503, 5567, 5954
Bagley, 2324, 3637
Bagot, 864, 945, 2554, 3647, 5734
Bailey, 2584, 4150. *See also* Bailie, Baille, Bailly, Baily, *and* Bayly.
Bailie, 3977, 3978, 4140, 4204, 5628
Baille, 1209
Bailly, 4164
Baily, 1936
Bain, 4743
Bainbrigge, 2276
Baines, 1173, 1853
Baird, 59, 843, 1474, 2433, 2496, 3617, 4667, 5864

Baker, 295, 1309, 2125, 3891, 5493, 5919
Baldwin, 1889
Balfour, 2568, 4464, 5183, 6453
Ball, 524, 1614, 1618, 1675, 1909, 2383, 2515, 2735, 2843, 5043, 5337, 5372, 5604
Ballantine, 1122
Ballard, 5754, 6439
Baloo, 2097
Bampfield, 127
Bampton, 161
Bandon, 4779
Bangor, 4274
Bankhouse, 4818
Banks, 2208, 3702
Bannon, 42
Barber, 81, 5816
Barbour, 4361, 6042
Barclay, 17, 3512
Barcraft, 3964. *See also* Barkley, Barklie, *and* Berkeley.
Barker, 317, 1011, 1671, 3073, 3768, 3937, 4384, 4872, 5107, 5419
Barkley, 3575, 4840
Barklie, 927
Barlow, 2382, 3735
Barnes, 166, 1543, 1818, 1828, 2269, 5178, 6425
Barnett, 489, 2681, 3321, 5059, 5186, 5525
Barnette, 737
Barnsley, 1105
Barnwell, 5983
Barr, 874, 1243, 1471, 1593, 1656, 2055, 5984, 5999
Barret, 273, 627
Barrett, 363, 3187, 3521, 6142
Barry, 649, 735, 1189, 1384, 1787, 3076, 3799, 5484. *See also* Berry.
Barton, 301, 460, 1416, 3845, 4549, 4940, 5615
Bass, 298, 5707
Basset, 4274
Bastiast, 4469
Bates, 470, 1343, 6006
Bateson, 3471, 3485
Bathbourne, 3261
Bathurst, 2466
Batt, 3037, 5779

Battersby, 1993, 3482

Batwell, 5855

Baxter, 522, 1709, 2402, 3620, 4911, 6050, 6249

Baylis, 213

Bayly, 5849. *See also* Bailey, Bailie, Baille, Bailly, *and* Baily.

Beacom, 3015

Beard, 2803

Beardshaw, 6173

Beasley, 504, 2545, 3149, 6109

Beattie, 293, 1908, 2685

Beatty, 8, 49, 159, 631, 1075, 1221, 1313, 1421, 1442, 1982, 2013, 2423, 2579, 2624, 2846, 3406, 3783, 3837, 5356, 5435, 5816, 5938

Beaty, 724

Beauclerk, 3720

Beck, 1680, 2148

Beers, 3788, 4147

Beevor, 4400

Beggs, 361, 1859, 5061, 6444

Begley, 453

Bell, 285, 448, 527, 569, 723, 788, 926, 935, 1041, 1099, 1213, 1230, 1341, 1360, 1406, 1409, 1494, 1500, 1509, 1735, 1976, 1990, 2000, 2172, 2201, 2390, 2412, 2481, 2726, 2848, 3042, 3043, 3114, 3211, 3318, 3603, 3765, 3785, 3853, 4013, 4239, 4553, 4585, 4648, 4655, 4766, 4974, 5221, 5396, 5423, 5460, 5678, 5680, 5731, 5977, 6080, 6214, 6239, 6283

Bellew, 3417, 4511

Bellhouse, 2351

Bellingham, 707, 1251, 3262

Belmore, 232

Belshaw, 3304

Benison, 477, 3388

Bennet, 882, 2829

Bennett, 322, 757, 979, 1236, 3039, 3355

Bennie, 1194, 3897

Bennitt, 3561

Benson, 177, 266, 429, 656, 838, 1271

Bent, 5925

Beresford, 1468, 1482, 2048, 2220, 2224, 3089, 3095, 3255, 3378, 3486, 3614, 4185, 4338, 5088, 5997, 6001, 6046, 6048. *See also* Berresford.

Berkeley, 1959. *See also* Barclay, Barkley, *and* Barklie.

Bernard, 4779

Berney, 3528. *See also* Birney, Birnie, M'Birney, *and* M'Burney.

Berresford, 3378, 4385. *See also* Beresford.

Berry, 394, 1277, 1689, 4168, 4199, 4560. *See also* Barry.

Besnard, 5963

Bessel, 5055

Bessell, 2195

Best, 1827, 5754

Bestall, 1424

Betty, 264, 1068, 1831, 2603, 4005, 4869, 5936

Bevan, 2651

Beveridge, 4579

Bewglass, 1232, 1504, 2046, 2229, 3467, 4645, 5777

Bewley, 1070, 1432, 3876, 5042, 5092

Bicknell, 915

Bigger, 3918, 6061

Billing, 6301

Bingham, 3253, 5444, 6438, 6441

Binney, 6189

Birch, 1153, 1240, 2702, 2879, 4853

Birney, 1284, 4012

Birnie, 1914

Birrill, 409

Bishop, 1590, 2901

Black, 19, 69, 86, 285, 333, 370, 475, 1008, 1404, 1783, 1790, 2050, 2430, 2436, 2455, 2785, 3102, 3193, 3376, 3443, 3824, 4694, 5445

Blackader, 3035, 4543, 6137

Blackburn, 3766

Blacker, 583, 1746, 2011, 2081, 2247, 3348, 3495, 3614, 3959, 4228, 4274, 4376, 4910, 5422, 6436

Blackham, 2261, 3212, 5400, 6136

Blackmore, 2859

Blackstock, 6017

Blackwell, 327

Blackwood, 712, 895, 2993, 5243, 5272, 5424, 6373

Blain, 3462. *See also* M'Blain.

Blair, 1485, 1966, 2217, 2978, 3520, 4371, 5159, 6434, 6447

Blake, 3686, 4335, 4954, 5263

Blakely, 5680. *See also* Blakely, Bleackey, Bleakley, *and* Bleckley.

Blakeney, 1917

Blakey, 4239

Blakiston, 1965

Bleackey, 1404

Bleakley, 6416

Bleasby, 4008

Bleazby, 680, 4008

Bleazeby, 3127

Bleckley, 444, 2453

Bleeks, 461

Blennerhassett, 3137

Bligh, 2063, 4176, 4216, 4498, 4549

Bloomfield, 591, 5975, 6326

Blow, 2871

Bloxham, 2542

Blumeberg, 6164

Boardman, 4379

Boate, 3020

Boethby, 1879

Boland, 600

Bole, 2449

Boles, 2268

Bolland, 4550

Bolling, 2543

Bolton, 3901, 3904, 5708, 5713

Bond, 99, 238, 661, 1083, 1315, 1854, 3324, 3779, 4732, 5696

Booker, 286, 5095

Booth, 742, 2979

Borland, 866, 1417, 1452

Borrowes, 3662, 4308

Borton, 3347, 3646

Boswell, 944

Bosworth, 1409

Boucher, 5683

Bouchier, 4248

Boughton, 2065

Bouker, 5181

Bourchier, 6222

Bourke, 3112, 3139. *See also* Burke.

Bourne, 3580

Bourns, 5493, 5533. *See also* Burns.

Bowden, 2827

Bowen, 1950

Bowers, 4997, 5266

Bowker, 1773

Bowles, 2743

Bowman, 968, 1861, 2699, 3320, 3472, 6022, 6139

Boyd, 157, 261, 348, 641, 1119, 1395, 1459, 2050, 2187, 2257, 2322, 2609, 3270, 3796, 3957, 3961, 4180, 5671, 6247

Boyde, 588, 3237

Boyes, 5276

Boylan, 3938

Boyle, 58, 3142, 3452, 3754, 4178, 4192, 4515, 4658, 5019, 5267, 5285, 6409

Brabazon, 398, 4628

Bracken, 787, 2803, 4419, 4468, 4814, 5442, 5492, 6403

Brackenridge, 608

Brackin, 1269, 1858, 2385, 4470, 5399, 6263

Braddell, 2225, 5711

Bradden, 2254

Bradford, 2912, 4724, 5349

Bradley, 2621, 3643, 4462, 5540, 6015

Bradshaw, 787, 1583, 2259, 2626, 3046, 3080, 4522, 5100, 6083

Brady, 2072, 2265, 2331, 2427, 3138, 3447, 3459, 3825, 3948, 4098, 5738, 5755, 5794

Bragan, 990

Brain, 6309

Branagan, 4442

Brangan, 355

Brangin, 5578

Branigan, 60

Breaden, 1421

Breakey, 1977, 2539, 2868

Breaky, 2597, 2795

Bredin, 38, 438, 1493, 1690, 2613, 2874, 3981, 3982, 4687, 4755, 5664, 5836, 6328

Breedin, 2990

Breedon, 131

Breen, 1334, 1678

Brega, 4174

Brenner, 2243

Brennian, 2774

Brereton, 2349

Brett, 500, 2672, 3553, 5513
Briars, 3280. *See also* Bryars.
Brice, 5285, 6167. *See also* Bryce.
Brickley, 205
Bridge, 3315, 4685. *See also* Bridges, *and* Brydge.
Bridges, 5961
Brien, 1381, 3423, 3733, 4000, 4513. *See also* Bryan, O'Brian, *and* O'Brien.
Brierly, 5143
Briggs, 2738
Brigham, 4876, 6440
Bright, 6383
Brine, 3268
Briscoe, 1426, 2953
Bristol, 3682
Bristow, 5485
Brittain, 1493
Britton, 1724
Brockey, 224
Brodhurst, 4847
Brooke, 47, 318, 591, 2110, 2493, 2676, 2905, 4244, 4425, 4989, 6209, 6221
Brooks, 116
Brougham, 6123
Broughton, 3466, 4913
Brown, 206, 208, 306, 407, 483, 597, 687, 702, 837, 864, 1039, 1214, 1239, 1472, 1584, 1634, 1709, 1710, 1714, 1798, 2008, 2026, 2114, 2176, 2682, 2686, 2878, 3232, 3648, 3800, 3812, 4064, 4095, 5106, 5144, 5202, 5532, 5561, 5636, 5740, 6004, 6343
Browne, 1159, 1580, 1672, 2074, 2082, 2092, 2134, 2265, 2267, 2998, 3256, 3372, 3645, 3705, 3753, 4326, 4328, 4902, 5825
Brownlee, 3619
Brownless, 4994
Brownlow, 1516, 1707, 2804, 4027
Bruce, 53, 718, 1834
Brunker, 5924
Brushe, 4150
Bryan, 1168, 2078, 2256, 6039. *See also* Brien, O'Brian, *and* O'Brien.
Bryans, 1690, 4495
Bryars, 2393. *See also* Briars.
Bryce, 4771, 5952. *See also* Brice.

Bryden, 290, 823, 1566
Brydge, 250, 3041. *See also* Bridge *and* Bridges.
Bryson, 390, 714, 1631
Buchanan, 75, 1559, 1711, 1759, 1847, 2311, 2563, 2571, 3214, 3389, 3605, 3711, 3774, 4009, 4260, 4701, 5030, 5164, 5361, 5709, 6055
Buchannan, 1343, 2785, 3730, 3731, 5565
Buchanon, 1725
Buck, 1679, 2472
Buckland, 5981
Buckley, 5308
Bugloss, 1117
Bull, 685, 4630
Bullard, 2532
Bunburry, 5175
Bunbury, 5189, 5462, 5755, 5823
Bunting, 5780
Burdett, 704, 828
Burges, 1764, 4879
Burgess, 3374
Burgh, 1840
Burgoyne, 5264, 5974, 6037
Burke, 106, 554, 556, 1442, 1508, 1636, 2157, 3008, 3797, 4494, 4517, 5098, 5660, 5916. *See also* Bourke.
Burnett, 764
Burningham, 1442
Burns, 662, 733, 1224, 1570, 1579, 1878, 1895, 2962, 3185, 3315, 3351, 3914, 4128, 5568, 5597, 5621. *See also* Bourns.
Burnside, 133, 778, 2236, 2308, 2459, 3434
Burrell, 5039
Burrowes, 409, 780, 2380, 3317, 4793
Burrows, 2475, 3597, 4046
Burton, 1367, 1426, 1766, 4257
Busby, 3031
Bush, 1617
Bushby, 5917
Bushe, 5815
Busteed, 2758, 4529
Butcher, 4868, 5745
Butler, 799, 1478, 1800, 3523
Butt, 765, 2667
Button, 6211
Byers, 6442

Byham, 3053
Byrne, 12, 859, 2248, 2709, 3368, 3469, 5843
Byron, 6371
Cadell, 2306
Cadman, 2804
Cadogan, 5261
Cadoo, 5919
Caffrey, 6155. *See also* M'Cafferey.
Caher, 799
Cahill, 4409
Caird, 4871
Cairnes, 1227
Cairns, 2540, 2579, 3554
Caldbeck, 4551, 4638
Caldwell, 162, 591, 777, 1440, 1665, 2971, 3284, 3732, 3802, 3880, 4133, 4237, 4407, 5603
Caledon, 658, 934, 2342, 3721
Calhoun, 150. *See also* Colhoun, *and* Colquhoun.
Call, 1483
Callaghan, 2428. *See also* O'Callaghan.
Callison, 490, 4209
Calmady, 3796
Calvert, 5231, 6129
Calwell, 2736, 4851
Cambell, 5294. *See also* Campbell.
Cameron, 2578, 2987, 2995, 3719, 4055
Campbell, 13, 76, 226, 401, 443, 683, 913, 919, 973, 1006, 1250, 1410, 1616, 1777, 1927, 2082, 2113, 2181, 2330, 2334, 2683, 2801, 3148, 3192, 3352, 3377, 3446, 3701, 4100, 4403, 4412, 4437, 4790, 4807, 4953, 5229, 5280, 5528, 5593, 5944, 6018, 6093, 6153, 6177, 6183, 6285, 6310. *See also* Cambell.
Candlish, 2730
Canning, 790, 2375, 3059, 3717
Cannon, 5029
Cantilupe, 3922
Cape, 2135
Capper, 2652, 6287
Caraher, 1043
Carden, 1766
Cardwell, 115, 1079, 2800, 4887
Carey, 164, 2802, 2818, 3262, 3979, 5209, 6060
Cargill, 5487, 5500
Carleton, 4891, 5329
Carley, 5931

Carlile, 992, 4431, 6374
Carlisle, 3872
Carlow, 244, 1209
Carmichael, 642, 3190
Carnby, 2275
Carolan, 3640, 4475, 6277
Carpendale, 854, 1014, 1681, 2106
Carpenter, 267, 372, 633, 2400, 3878, 4729, 5367
Carr, 957, 1916, 2152
Carrell, 2949
Carroll, 725, 974, 1043, 1783, 1806, 2933, 2957, 4267, 4968, 5318, 5338, 6113
Carruthers, 1407, 4204. *See also* Caruthers, *and* Crothers.
Carse, 996, 2393
Carson, 601, 1158, 1200, 1430, 1529, 2474, 2608, 2980, 3140, 3453, 3475, 4269, 5585
Carstairs, 3920
Carter, 1625, 2443, 3454, 4325, 4343. *See also* M'Carter.
Caruthers, 1383
Carvill, 88, 1921
Cary, 5326, 5477
Casebourne, 903
Casey, 226
Cashel, 1091, 3454, 3845, 4343, 4755
Cassiday, 3151
Cassidy, 1359, 3991, 4315
Castle-Stuart, 943
Castlestuart, 312
Cates, 5954
Cathcart, 19, 400, 2088, 2174
Cather, 3650
Cator, 3265
Caulfeild, 1931, 2434, 4274, 4381
Caulfield, 757, 833, 2062, 2312, 2634, 3676, 4361, 5614, 5854
Caussen, 1736
Cavan, 207, 1356, 3843
Cavanagh, 1544. *See also* Kavanagh, *and* O'Cavanagh.
Cavendish, 661, 3229
Cavins, 4429
Chable, 5813
Chadwick, 2911, 4677
Chalmers, 5304, 6270

Chambe, 1624
Chamberlain, 1809, 2928
Chamberlaine, 1870
Chambers, 66, 157, 881, 1429, 2006, 3413, 4200, 5120, 5236, 6268
Chambre, 767, 1988, 3889, 5515, 6177
Chamley, 161, 2168, 4673
Chamly, 934
Chamney, 4192, 5725
Chancellor, 5914
Chapel Royal, 2110
Chapman, 281, 1907, 2528, 5780
Charlemont, 3277, 4381
Charles, 1585, 5441
Charleton, 1640, 2153, 2170
Charley, 2840, 5229
Charlier, 3026
Charman, 6029
Charters, 2640
Chartres, 4970
Cheetham, 391
Cherry, 805
Chester, 4574
Chestnut, 1621
Cheyne, 2988, 3982
Chichester, 1104, 1283, 5341, 6355
Chief Baron, 2149, 2890. *See also* Lord Guillamore.
Chief of Hymaine: *See* Clanricarde.
Childers, 2761
Chischolm, 3940
Chisholm, 313
Chittick, 5241
Christian, 4, 2848, 2916, 3022, 3574, 4451, 4996, 5742
Christmas, 1940
Church, 445, 1132, 2982, 3651
Chute, 2253
Clancarty, 4274
Clanricarde, 3272
Clarendon, 3884, 4274, 5006, 5910
Clark, 3776, 4460
Clarke, 255, 286, 462, 506, 540, 921, 1031, 1053, 1167, 1258, 1408, 1598, 1617, 1677, 1893, 1933, 1940, 1970, 2070, 2134, 2169, 2246,

Clarke, continued: 2354, 2358, 2389, 2567, 2734, 2744, 2778, 3065, 3400, 3426, 3628, 3930, 4271, 4273, 4434, 4577, 4678, 5715, 5880, 5918, 6377, 6386, 6387, 6415
Claverhouse, 3719
Clay, 498, 5911
Clayton, 831
Clear, 3726
Cleland, 4837. *See also* M'Clelland.
Clemenger, 5240
Clement, 1407
Clements, 487, 954, 1203, 1383, 1727, 3745, 3973, 4026, 4134, 4191, 4986, 5571, 6411
Clendinning, 4586
Clifford, 4616
Clifton, 822
Clogher, 299, 703, 1265, 1469, 2561, 2604, 3370, 4511, 4608, 4991, 6034
Clonbrock, 4274
Clonfert, 894
Clonmacnoise, 1032
Close, 95, 323, 3646, 4274, 4639, 4737, 5679, 6331
Cluff, 2359, 3627, 3653
Clugston, 2828
Coane, 5544
Coard, 4152
Coates, 443, 5691
Cobb, 105, 613
Cobbe, 3185
Cobett, 2543
Coburn, 946
Cochran, 1832, 2894, 3866, 5449
Cochrane, 640, 1270, 1871, 2631, 2989, 3786, 4438. *See also* Cockran.
Cockburn, 2282, 2379, 5350
Cockran, 151. *See also* Cochrane.
Cockshot, 6426
Coffey, 559, 5339
Coffy, 3261
Cohen, 2954
Colclough, 1531
Cole, 3026, 3372, 3584, 3679, 4186, 4722, 5652
Coleman, 2805, 3013, 3747, 5335, 6086, 6274
Colgan, 1875

Colhoun, 144, 1319, 1527, 1715, 1841, 5012, 5044, 5191. *See also* Calhoun, *and* Colquhoun.

Collingwood, 5745

Collins, 93, 285, 362, 1506, 2914, 3362, 3800, 4249, 4702, 4804, 5230, 5253, 5844. *See also* Collyns.

Collum, 1100, 3007, 3114, 3267, 3968, 4713, 5279, 5399, 5591, 5639

Collyns, 457, 4290. *See also* Collins.

Colmonell, 3605

Colony, 3045

Colquhoun, 2926

Colvan, 463, 3851. *See also* Colvin.

Colvil, 4377

Colvill, 5091

Colvin, 3258. *See also* Colvan.

Conan, 2395

Cone, 4834

Conly, 1569. *See also* Connolly, *and* Conolly.

Conn, 1136, 1535

Connell, 3621. *See also* M'Connell, *and* O'Connell.

Connolly, 237, 1979, 2184, 2286, 4015, 5945. *See also* Conly, *and* Conolly.

Connor, 539, 555, 1405, 1997, 2082, 3846, 3895, 4763, 4833, 5855, 6242. *See also* O'Connor.

Conolly, 654, 2250. *See also* Conly, *and* Connolly.

Conry, 543, 4329, 5388

Constable, 2783

Conway, 5207

Conyers, 3378

Cook, 3269

Cooke, 332, 341, 1256, 1572, 1609, 1673, 1836, 3126, 3189, 3302, 3975, 4615, 4754, 5764

Cookson, 5883

Cooper, 349, 3496, 3537, 3577, 4333, 4739, 4970, 5075, 5436

Coote, 57, 1282, 1295, 1553, 3090, 3184, 3668, 4087, 4160, 5027, 5402, 5498, 5953

Cope, 801, 1722, 1743, 1880, 2669, 2983, 3960, 4271, 4422

Copeland, 1583, 2654, 4526, 5317, 5566

Copland, 5663, 6024, 6446

Copley, 1322

Corbett, 2807

Corbitt, 6272

Cordner, 1146, 2243, 5036, 6306

Cordukes, 3189

Corfield, 4151, 4200

Cork, 488

Cork, Cloyne and Ross, 6117

Corner, 2685

Cornforth, 1274

Corr, 1506, 4490, 5714, 6011, 6290

Corrigan, 82, 254, 1117, 1504, 1972, 2073, 2229, 2248, 5458

Corry, 67, 132, 213, 483, 684, 1126, 1336, 1957, 3006, 3070, 4090, 4327, 4592, 5342, 5676, 5802

Corscadden, 1362

Corscaden, 941, 978, 3333

Corvan, 4800

Costelloe, 6356

Cottenham, 5746

Cotter, 4223

Cotterell, 5846

Cottingham, 3400

Cotton, 2075, 4813

Coulson, 1166, 2141, 3935, 4348

Coulter, 2148, 4453, 4482, 5031, 6179, 6391

Courtenay, 1815, 5893

Courtney, 5480, 5497

Courtown, 4281

Couser, 405. *See also* Cowser.

Coutts, 1274, 5694, 5766

Cowan, 348, 2183, 2989, 4236, 4599. *See also* Cowen.

Cowdy, 2471

Cowell, 2311, 5315

Cowen, 4652. *See also* Cowan.

Cowser, 2948. *See also* Couser.

Cox, 1148, 2121, 2548, 2784, 3667, 5847

Coyle, 4531, 4835, 4884, 5758

Coyne, 1989, 2907, 3158, 5486

Crabbs, 2953

Craham, 5322

Craig, 14, 61, 876, 1186, 2049, 2369, 2902, 3928, 4029, 4461, 4710

Crane, 400

Cranley, 4027

Chapter 3: Index of Surnames

Cranston, 4149
Cranstown, 4129
Craven, 3613
Crawford, 30, 154, 184, 730, 800, 871, 1136, 1205, 1466, 2079, 2416, 2454, 2497, 2509, 2947, 3847, 3963, 3990, 4026, 4734, 4786, 4858, 4868, 4992, 5259, 5268, 5619, 5798, 5921, 6163, 6267
Crawley, 415, 3644
Creagh, 884, 902
Creaghe, 6401
Creden, 5331
Creer, 3660
Creery, 4063, 5978
Cregan, 4904
Creighton, 1397, 1646
Cremorne, 5953
Crichton, 2864, 3017
Crilly, 2919
Croagan, 2721
Croft, 4601
Crofton, 432, 3581, 3700
Croker, 3468, 4085
Crolly, 633, 2313, 4069
Croly, 331, 3432, 4507
Crommelin, 360, 701, 3005
Cromrie, 3427
Crone, 1601, 4460
Cronin, 2583
Crook, 1780
Crooke, 1177, 1178
Crooks, 199
Crookshank, 5515
Crosbie, 4391, 4479, 4942, 4956, 5303, 5604
Crosier, 1230. *See also* Crozier.
Cross, 412, 521, 654, 1655, 3298, 3556, 4213
Crossle, 1653, 2646, 4188, 5343
Crossley, 4175
Crosslie, 3014
Crothers, 70, 185, 227, 628, 681, 1013, 1149, 2792, 2872. *See also* Carruthers, *and* Caruthers.
Crow, 6035
Crowe, 420, 563, 1059, 4992
Crozier, 291, 935, 2128, 4550, 5427, 5651, 5942, 6361. *See also* Crosier.

Crumley, 873
Crump, 454
Cubitt, 2058
Cuddy, 2891, 4048
Culberton, 2916
Culbertson, 2732
Cullen, 1012, 3489, 4295, 4848, 5029, 5252
Cully, 85. *See also* M'Cully.
Cultra, 4325
Cuming, 73, 373, 664, 2090, 3391, 4074, 4274, 4312, 5412
Cumming, 1150, 2398, 3471, 3999, 4217, 4966, 5285
Cummins, 221, 1628, 3702, 4220
Cunningham, 1631, 2138, 2666, 3557, 4026, 4255, 4462, 5616, 5803
Cuppadge, 5431
Cuppage, 2365, 3635, 4825, 6077
Cupples, 2318
Curran, 16, 3551, 5161
Currans, 3315
Curri, 3231
Currie, 203
Curry, 436, 611, 2107, 2177
Curties, 4343
Curtis, 174, 4207
Cusack, 3271
Cussen, 3910
Cust, 2414, 4027, 5883
Cuthberston, 695
Cuthbert, 697, 4961, 5431, 6191
D'Alten, 5878
D'Arcy, 591, 2235, 2517, 3310, 4057, 5200
D'Evelyn, 3607
D'Evlyn, 1208
Dale, 300, 1470
Dales, 3161
Dallas, 1204
Dalton, 3958
Daly, 2950, 3153, 3706, 4233, 5054, 5369
Dalzall, 2653
Dalzell, 1231
Dane, 482, 961, 993, 1353, 1974, 2043, 3549, 3951, 5193, 6408
Daniell, 6149

Darby, 539, 555

Darcus, 3134

Dargan, 1850

Darley, 641, 753, 2101, 2194, 3933, 4282, 4438, 5204

Darragh, 2206

Daveney, 3959

Davidson, 231, 282, 418, 856, 2012, 2049, 2174, 2684, 3379, 3784, 4103, 4183, 4205, 4265, 4432, 4435, 4837, 5869

Davies, 3350

Davis, 335, 551, 791, 1337, 3481, 3645, 3704, 3748, 4101, 4265, 4280, 4296, 4546, 4921, 4997, 5048, 6112

Davison, 157, 567, 1076, 1450, 1737, 1866, 4990, 6338

Davock, 4233

Dawes, 2651

Dawson, 72, 139, 206, 359, 595, 736, 752, 890, 1707, 1976, 2276, 2387, 2476, 2700, 3003, 3062, 3250, 3671, 4000, 4964, 5530, 5701, 6369

Day, 4401, 5848

De Barnardo, 2988

de Boudry, 1685

De Butts, 1880, 2669, 4625, 6087

De Grasse, 5961

de Grey, 1792

De Kay, 2462

de la Barca, 6007

de La Poer, 5997

De La Willis, 2277

De Latour, 6186

De Renzy, 2927

De Rinzy, 2929

Deane, 2301

Death, 4337

Debenham, 3607

DeCourcy, 892

Deering, 217, 220, 240, 371, 999, 3509

Deery, 1564, 5235

Delacherois, 4246

Delamere, 2649

Delany, 5771

Delap, 2750, 3591

Delaware, 3922

Denham, 3353, 3474, 4251, 4921, 5583

Denniss, 5265

Denny, 4028, 5182, 5194, 6079, 6308, 6360

Denroach: *See* Denroche.

Denroche, 5468

Denvir, 5520, 5644, 6101

Dermott, 26. *See also* M'Dermot, M'Dermott, *and* M'Diarmid.

Derry, 2294, 2796, 3656, 4167, 4362, 5405, 5609

Derry and Raphoe, 4235, 5609

Despard, 3891, 5788

Desvoeux, 4908

Devenport, 1788

Devers, 1048

Devlin, 389, 476, 671, 674, 3213, 3865, 4302, 5408, 5626

Devlyn, 1963

Dick, 267, 374, 1907, 1925, 2991

Dickenson, 864, 1165, 4594

Dickey, 1950, 2027

Dickie, 2577, 3282, 4190, 4771

Dickinson, 2733, 4356

Dickson, 114, 216, 230, 520, 797, 818, 1090, 1107, 1123, 1249, 1372, 1682, 1728, 1744, 1908, 2240, 3162, 4369, 4817, 4933, 4934, 5134, 5233, 5643, 6171, 6370, 6429

Digby, 275, 573

Dill, 577, 2432, 3311, 3610, 4350, 5710, 6358

Dillon, 117, 1052, 2238, 3077, 3151, 3234, 3556, 3720, 3899, 4590

Dimsdale, 2414

Dinning, 3805

Dinorben, 423, 6157

Dinsmore, 3777

Disney, 61, 82, 206, 248, 254, 567, 621, 805, 831, 842, 1038, 1504, 4441, 4466, 4744, 5163, 5360

Dix, 1993

Dixon, 452, 6065

Dobbin, 109, 552, 694, 832, 1163, 1561, 2064, 2449, 2468, 2911, 3043, 3158, 3213, 3410, 3691, 3851, 4033, 4307, 4431, 4664, 4723, 4952, 4998, 5062, 5137, 5285, 5494, 5502, 5640, 5734, 5806, 6218

Dobbs, 4548

Dobson, 1697, 5950

Dodd, 1951, 3424, 3825, 3956, 4710, 6058
Dohera, 6327
Doherty, 865, 2083, 2085, 2478, 2525, 4509, 4534, 6307, 6341, 6450. *See also* Dougherty, O'Doherty, *and* O'Dougherty.
Dolling, 4516
Dombraine, 1919
Don, 221
Donaghey, 3338. *See also* Donaghy.
Donaghmore, 395
Donaghy, 366, 1807. *See also* Donaghey.
Donald, 1092, 3038
Donaldson, 84, 457, 635, 1063, 1454, 1492, 1549, 2063, 2433, 3241, 4090, 4432, 4478, 4626, 5625, 5703, 6359
Donally, 1312. *See also* Donelly, *and* Donnelly.
Donegal, 1548, 2179
Donelan, 584. *See also* Donnelan.
Donelly, 190, 4556. *See also* Donally, *and* Donnelly.
Donlevy, 3287
Donnelan, 751, 854. *See also* Donelan.
Donnell, 1478. *See also* M'Donel, M'Donnell, O'Donel, O'Donnell, *and* O'Donnoll.
Donnellan, 1847
Donnelly, 952, 1234, 2372, 3158, 3336, 5245, 5790. *See also* Donally, *and* Donelly.
Donninem, 4460
Donoughmore, 1542, 5038
Donovan, 3240, 3773. *See also* O'Donovan.
Doran, 3340, 5492
Dorehill, 2173
Dornin, 5216
Dorrian, 930
Doudney, 3447, 3450
Dougal, 5093. *See also* Dugall, *and* M'Doughall.
Dougan, 571, 1897, 3113, 3307, 4773
Dougherty, 4234, 4531, 4788. *See also* Doherty, O'Doherty, *and* O'Dougherty.
Douglas, 258, 1280, 1554, 2351, 2730, 2860, 3012, 3113, 3836, 4197, 4703, 4723, 5082, 5434, 5786.
Dowan, 989
Dowdall, 187, 576
Dowling, 4405
Down, 3869, 3885

Down and Connor, 2149, 3642, 4369, 5994
Down and Connor and Dromore, 3219
Downey, 205, 2731, 6228
Downing, 576, 1060
Downman, 5901
Downton, 2727
Dowse, 5907
Doyle, 4631, 6433
Drakely, 3777
Drennan, 2145, 2151
Drew, 298, 1544, 1987, 6192, 6230
Dromore, 1272, 4122, 5115, 5256, 5889, 5955
Druit, 86
Druitt, 1730, 3980, 4922
Drummond, 3398
Drury, 5844
Dublin, 576, 632, 1952, 2857, 3195, 3495, 4806, 6331
Duckett, 6378
Dudden, 361, 346, 416, 1479, 1903, 2319, 3886, 4389
Duff, 298, 332, 341, 2547, 3337, 4672
Duffan, 1824
Duffin, 3266
Duffy, 922, 3419, 3518
Dugall, 4808. *See also* Dougal, *and* M'Doughall.
Duggan, 903, 1492, 3797
Duke, 6181
Dunbar, 1019, 1697, 1754, 2635, 3068, 5011, 6025, 6452
Duncan, 14, 407, 451, 470, 1058, 1509, 2433, 3028, 3154, 3266, 4126, 4784, 6439. *See also* Dunkin.
Dundas, 2325, 2733, 4758
Dungannon, 692
Dunkin, 260. *See also* Duncan.
Dunlop, 487, 599, 639, 739, 2373, 3263, 4073
Dunn, 2416, 6057
Dunphy, 2083
Dunsmore, 5600
Dunsterville, 4525
Durnion, 2878
Dwyer, 3615, 4677, 5852. *See also* O'Dwyer.
Dyer, 1476, 1767
Eagar, 3373, 4320

Eager, 3288, 5099
Eakin, 5113, 6199
Earl, 6182
Earles, 2031
Earls, 1131, 1179, 2327, 2735, 2913
Eastwood, 3918
Eaton, 2847, 5317
Eccles, 601, 1338, 2361, 4739, 4820, 5255, 6241
Echlin, 1752, 2076, 3109
Eden, 6435
Edgar, 100, 116, 405, 519, 1505, 1755, 2679, 3639, 3851, 3867, 4944
Edge, 2949, 3929
Edgeworth, 28, 2698
Edie, 622, 2413
Edinburgh, 3621
Edmonson, 6363
Edwardes, 3942
Edwards, 1439, 1936, 2740, 3864, 4695, 4958, 5385, 5913, 5957
Eeles, 5823
Egan, 389, 1979, 2145, 4166, 4987
Egar, 3448
Egerton, 829
Eggar, 2537
Eglinton, 6186
Eglintoun, 1761
Ekin, 932
Elden, 4583
Elder, 376, 1414
Eldon, 6348
Elgee, 4672
Elliot, 116, 134, 1445, 1956, 2588, 2705, 5496
Elliott, 77, 142, 253, 626, 873, 1012, 1142, 1361, 1689, 2507, 2636, 2728, 3934, 4238, 4383, 4757, 4948, 5366, 5751, 5831, 5890, 5985, 6395
Ellis, 1773, 2283, 2305, 2856, 3304, 3395, 3396, 4250, 4767, 5481, 6355
Ellison, 2734, 4002, 4748, 5702, 5730
Elly, 2960. *See also* Ely.
Elphin, 3601
Elrington, 430, 1987, 2986, 3264, 3391, 4161, 5675, 5697, 5964, 6214
Elsmere, 5509

Ely, 632. *See also* Elly.
Emerson, 6413
Emerson Tennent, 5174
Emly, 6273
Emmett, 841
Emslie, 108
Ennis, 460, 3457
Enniskillen, 5, 425, 1056, 2886, 3558, 4383, 4566
Eppes, 3122
Erne, 1466, 2369, 2864, 3017, 4573, 5041
Errol, 2542
Erskin, 1307, 5132
Erskine, 5769, 6398
Erwin, 2888
Evans, 97, 106, 560, 1038, 1940, 2505, 2582, 3048, 3456, 3469, 3657, 4007, 4091, 4207, 4460, 4472, 4957, 5560, 6040
Evatt, 1184
Evlyn, 1042
Ewart, 2681, 5814
Ewing, 1103, 1342, 1539, 2125, 2301, 4518
Exshaw, 5732
Eyre, 776, 783, 792, 899, 1718, 1745, 3582, 5354
Fairley, 679, 1095, 1768
Fairly, 1819
Fairs, 5915
Falkner, 5920
Falloon, 131, 3209, 4650
Falls, 1685, 2930, 4294. *See also* Faulds, *and* Fawls.
Fannin, 632
Fannon, 2
Farebrother, 5118
Faren, 3266, 4342
Faris, 1384, 3734
Farley, 523, 669
Farmar, 5803
Farmer, 2753, 3066, 5379
Farquhar, 5016
Farrell, 604, 4078, 4475, 4833, 5248, 6405. *See also* O'Farrell.
Fatherston, 1437
Faulds, 925. *See also* Falls, *and* Fawls.
Faulkner, 307, 1060, 4352, 4388

Fausset, 1613, 1652, 2808, 4567, 5078
Faussett, 1118, 1808, 2424, 4224
Fawcett, 1165, 1408, 5576, 5778, 6172
Fawcitt, 1571
Fawls, 2533. *See also* Falls, *and* Faulds.
Fay, 2130
Fee, 4225
Feeney, 5408
Feeny, 865
Fegan, 1666, 2772, 2918, 5406
Fenton, 1488, 1929, 2665, 4094, 5007, 6091
Fenwick, 771, 1739, 2986, 3264, 5624, 5834
Fergus, 4668
Ferguson, 417, 436, 527, 696, 1092, 1098, 1505, 2009, 2579, 3016, 3696, 3728, 5523, 5681, 6083, 6319
Ferns, 1987, 3055, 4572
Ferrier, 6109
Ferris, 862, 3850
Fetherston, 195
Fetherstonhaugh, 3247
Ffolliott, 3983
Fforde, 337, 2961, 5018
Field, 2610
Filgate, 6082
Fimenger, 3044
Finch, 770, 1139, 1517, 1731, 1789, 2887, 3039, 4243, 4791, 5608, 6303, 6323
Finley, 2051
Finn, 683
Finnegan, 3186
Fisher, 1689, 3120, 3249, 3360, 3401, 4116
Fitzgerald, 270, 330, 677, 1074, 1278, 1323, 1984, 2418, 2472, 3238, 3396, 3398, 3444, 4529, 5435, 5615, 6010
Fitzgerald and Vesci, 5119
Fitzpatrick, 652, 1795, 1883, 5012, 5409, 5596
Fitzsimmons, 4568
Fitzsimon, 2062, 3060
Fivey, 1217, 5557
Flack, 1882
Flanagan, 1202, 1466, 1521, 1721, 1948, 3181, 3351, 3515, 3657, 4092, 4399, 4471, 4711, 5323, 6246
Flanigan, 3306
Flannagan, 4233, 5776

Flavel, 2038
Flavell, 2495, 5847
Flavelle, 5244
Fleming, 237, 614, 791, 862, 1200, 1255, 1373, 1452, 1945, 2080, 2368, 2449, 2547, 2644, 2751, 3030, 3335, 3480, 3555, 3847, 3851, 4274, 4461, 4484, 4602, 4794, 5100, 5185, 5470, 5471, 5605, 5764, 6096. *See also* Flemming.
Flemming, 1806. *See also* Fleming.
Fletcher, 201, 2175, 3876
Fleury, 672, 1993, 2651
Flood, 1408, 1441, 1826, 2140, 2613, 3180
Floyd, 5820
Flynn, 5035, 6325. *See also* Flynne, *and* O'Flinn.
Flynne, 4616
Foley, 3685, 5493
Foot, 32, 550, 1551, 3769
Foott, 2581
Forbes, 3095
Ford, 1998, 2587, 3183, 5010, 5734
Forde, 1422, 2053, 2622, 4306, 4627, 4939, 6436
Forest, 686
Forrester, 483, 3651
Forster, 994, 1220, 1370, 3147, 4736, 5817
Forsyth, 4307
Forsythe, 2631, 2742, 3545
Fortescue, 3709
Foster, 17, 482, 507, 928, 2549, 2729, 3374, 3776, 5580
Fottrell, 6300
Foulis, 1486
Foulston, 4080
Fowler, 503, 4935
Fox, 1673, 1986, 2312, 2876, 3513, 3567, 4460, 5012
Foxall, 493
Foy, 4282
Foyle, 4535, 5949
Francis, 5685, 5888
Franklin, 1617
Franks, 3644, 4071
Fraser, 2857, 3730, 5260, 5704
Frazer, 23, 2001, 2300, 3583, 4615, 5503
Frazier, 766
Freel, 2426

Freeman, 5034
Freiland, 4674
French, 660, 2057, 2152, 3566, 4954
Frith, 535, 823, 1514, 1729, 2034, 2477, 3764, 4072, 4274, 4365, 4490, 4636, 4694, 4799, 5524
Frizel, 1657
Frizell, 2939, 3986, 4267, 4274, 4384, 5285
Frizelle, 3797
Frizzell, 4096
Frood, 4094
Fulcher, 6438
Fullagar, 5679
Fullarton, 2777. *See also* Fullerton.
Fuller, 1295, 3090
Fullerton, 208, 301, 377, 489, 576, 697, 1132, 1530, 6240. *See also* Fullarton.
Fulton, 313, 1713, 2273, 3587, 4830
Funston, 4134
Furey, 4796
Furlonge, 5796
Furness, 4193
Fust, 5455
Fyffe, 2964
Gabbett, 896, 3581, 4038, 5848, 6328
Gaddis, 1911
Gage, 605, 675, 722, 2414, 2951, 3372, 3373, 3672, 3917, 4971, 5152, 5228
Gaily, 1975
Gainsborough, 5962
Galagher, 1557
Galbraith, 15, 1241, 1618, 1693, 2952, 3235, 3473, 3688, 3981, 4569, 5606
Gallagher, 3206, 4326, 6009, 6200
Galleway, 3675. *See also* Galwey.
Galley, 3914
Gallogly, 2569, 4899, 5426, 6069, 6083, 6414
Gallwey, 1745. *See also* Galleway.
Galna, 2356
Galt, 3103, 6284
Gamble, 320, 592, 698, 1658, 1703, 1861, 2411, 2520, 2588, 2636, 2895, 3093, 3401, 3939, 5052, 5296, 5366, 5667
Gant, 600
Garden, 2697
Gardiner, 5542

Gardner, 219, 380, 553, 1600, 2703, 2946, 4506, 5556, 5956
Garland, 1722, 1848, 1880
Garmany, 936
Garmoney, 3639
Garmony, 5498
Garnett, 3795
Garr, 2706
Garraway, 882
Gartlan, 471, 5592
Gartland, 1469, 4568
Garvin, 1700
Gaskin, 119, 991, 4717
Gaston, 4869
Gault, 2881, 6089.
Gaussen, 1446
Gaut, 600
Gawen, 5492
Gawlers, 5972
Gayer, 585
Geary, 6145
Geddes, 1710, 2108, 2109
Geddings, 351
Geddis, 4359, 4889
Gee, 132, 1467, 2060. *See also* M'Gee, *and* M'Ghee.
Gelston, 5215
George, 6016
George II, 5768
Geraghty, 193, 565, 1893, 3377
Gerahty, 5443
Gerraghty, 3183
Gerrard, 748, 1694, 4340
Gervais, 3128, 6437
Getty, 1556, 4912
Gibbins, 5195
Gibson, 662, 921, 1357, 1409, 1514, 1818, 2108, 2146, 2343, 3343, 3451, 4125, 4555, 4674, 5122, 5295, 5706, 6147, 6399
Giland, 4436
Gilbert, 1286, 2909, 3209, 4169, 5595, 6396
Gildea, 371
Gile, 3396
Giles, 4956, 5001
Gilkey, 4108

Gillespie, 1382, 2008, 5824
Gillis, 2776, 3610
Gillman, 1528
Gillmore, 1733
Gilmor, 2415
Gilmore, 97, 218, 411, 1692, 2026, 2786, 2891, 4392, 5494, 5866, 6392
Gilmour, 1386, 1790, 3090
Gilpin, 2435, 3558, 4135, 4477
Girvan, 198, 6418
Girvin, 459, 1124, 3707, 4518, 5885
Girwood, 1163
Givan, 3041, 4960
Given, 1823, 2609, 4432, 4688
Glascock, 5935
Glasgow, 599, 827, 4699
Glass, 3042, 5480, 5497, 6168
Glen, 1447, 4052
Gleney, 3955. *See also* Glenny.
Glenfell, 4284
Glengall, 799
Glenn, 20, 334, 340, 603
Glenny, 164, 226, 3752, 5547, 5812. *See also* Gleney.
Glover, 2353, 3997
Goben, 5627
Godber, 5079
Godbert, 5688
Godfrey, 1944
Godkin, 5844
Godley, 5439
Goff, 4203
Golding, 3347, 5575
Goldshmidt, 5433
Goldsmith, 3444, 5184
Golland, 204
Gomm, 5265
Goodwin, 5217
Goold, 1044
Gordon, 113, 531, 760, 1135, 1556, 1705, 2200, 2680, 2912, 2916, 3088, 3091, 3260, 3724, 3794, 3797, 4124, 4463, 4740, 5314, 5510, 5603
Gore, 1967, 2150, 3958, 5957
Gorman, 4332

Gosford, 2468, 2512, 3350, 3591, 4274, 4776
Goslett, 5573
Gosling, 4345
Gossett, 3095
Goudy, 3606. *See also* Gowdy.
Gough, 5334, 6413
Gourley, 2390
Gowan, 4711. *See also* M'Gowan, MacGowan, *and* Magowan.
Gowdy, 3833. *See also* Goudy.
Grace, 6131
Gracey, 3516, 6130
Graham, 38, 90, 234, 548, 947, 1308, 1438, 1518, 1520, 1529, 1686, 1738, 1784, 1830, 2169, 2634, 2913, 3179, 3302, 3382, 3883, 3952, 4001, 4030, 4043, 4282, 4399, 4532, 4644, 4731, 4746, 4769, 4801, 5064, 5371, 5528, 5582, 5623, 5712, 5719, 5865, 5923, 5933, 6223, 6275, 6415
Grahan, 4691
Grainger, 2164
Grant, 386, 2683. *See also* O'Grant.
Grattan, 39, 2959, 3835, 6207
Graves, 29, 1058, 1476, 1869, 2329, 4796, 5555
Gray, 9, 1141, 1218, 1293, 1369, 1751, 2071, 2280, 2367, 2811, 3451, 4995, 5133, 5508, 5705, 6057, 6062, 6171. *See also* Grey.
Graydon, 1075, 3809
Greacen, 343, 1404, 1659, 3300
Greame, 6091
Green, 38, 1515, 1760, 1978, 2009, 2799, 2812, 3876, 4474, 5505
Greenaway, 828
Greene, 931, 2152, 5815
Greenfield, 2815, 4723
Greenville, 4912
Greenwood, 1973
Greer, 101, 414, 440, 1143, 1146, 1491, 1630, 1846, 1964, 2175, 2180, 2292, 2915, 3978, 4683, 4857, 4871, 5070, 5310, 5537, 5608, 5970, 6041
Greeves, 6020
Gregg, 964, 1708, 1975, 3048, 3283, 5049
Gregory, 3727
Greham, 4162
Grendon, 2551

Grenier, 5211
Gresson, 3714, 5218, 6204
Gretton, 5974
Greville, 1112
Grey, 5788. *See also* Gray.
Gribben, 138, 3798
Grierson, 4423, 6351
Griffin, 1084, 1662, 1788, 2834, 3072, 3158, 4413, 4538, 4551, 6114, 6335
Griffith, 453, 460, 1471, 1679, 2136, 2204, 3323, 3422, 4164, 4530
Grimshaw, 1762, 2578
Grinless, 6120
Groves, 1378
Gruithusion, 5804
Guard, 3652
Gubbins, 4926
Guillamore, 3919
Guillemard, 2829, 3791, 6195
Gulley, 2454
Gully, 6418
Gumley, 2048
Gunne, 816
Gunning, 825, 2019, 4689
Gurd, 3501
Gurley, 1680
Gustavus, 6115
Guthridge, 3569
Guthrie, 2609
Guttridge, 5149
Guy, 846, 4237, 5939
Gwyn, 2014
Gwynn, 5446, 5859
Gyles, 1665
Hacket, 3023
Hackett, 2415, 3841
Haddock, 1968
Haffarman, 4460
Hagan, 2406, 3630, 4191. *See also* Hagen, *and* O'Hagan.
Hagen, 2619
Hague, 2446
Haig, 68, 77, 235, 328, 414, 553, 603, 633, 731, 788, 900, 910, 955, 2991
Haimans, 4261

Hainen, 953
Hains, 4280
Haire, 5575, 5933. *See also* Hare.
Halahan, 1697, 4753
Hale, 1960, 4327, 5153, 5340
Haliday, 2297. *See also* Halliday.
Halkett, 5005
Hall, 247, 266, 284, 609, 1140, 1252, 1314, 1562, 1684, 1688, 2185, 2635, 2722, 3354, 3385, 3830, 4292, 4431, 4711, 5330, 5693, 5695, 5708, 6345
Hallam, 4313
Hallelwell, 6107
Hallewell, 4847
Halliday, 1418, 1426. *See also* Haliday.
Halligan, 6132
Halpin, 1717, 2085, 3230, 3534
Halsted, 1788
Hamerton, 1464, 2487
Hamill, 2112, 3051, 3125, 3163, 3171
Hamilton, 171, 248, 292, 495, 538, 564, 882, 939, 949, 1012, 1171, 1182, 1298, 1308, 1438, 1440, 1513, 1556, 1607, 1821, 1937, 2095, 2102, 2106, 2241, 2242, 2347, 2391, 2395, 2480, 2494, 2520, 2544, 2546, 2549, 2552, 2648, 2763, 2819, 2943, 2949, 3093, 3199, 3205, 3211, 3220, 3222, 3265, 3348, 3440, 3498, 3558, 3562, 3568, 3699, 3821, 3874, 3913, 3929, 4151, 4218, 4289, 4380, 4528, 4574, 4694, 4754, 4765, 4824, 4832, 4854, 4967, 4984, 4994, 5050, 5271, 5319, 5440, 5464, 5475, 5568, 5641, 5709, 5799, 5807, 5850, 5916, 5930, 5946, 6154, 6196, 6206, 6208, 6234, 6318
Hamlin, 4228
Hammersley, 1699
Hammond, 165, 1113
Hancock, 271, 918, 1740, 2556, 3787, 4911, 5398, 5466, 5867. *See also* Handcock.
Hand, 2271, 2278, 3517, 4746, 5114, 5480, 5497
Handcock, 117, 2140, 2535, 5546. *See also* Hancock.
Handy, 320, 648, 2605
Hanington, 531. *See also* Hannyngton.
Hanley, 1712, 2654, 3749. *See also* Hanly.
Hanlon, 3198. *See also* O'Hanlon.
Hanly, 4536. *See also* Hanley.

Hanna, 253, 259, 654, 1161, 4238, 4902, 5053, 5076, 5583, 5735

Hannagh, 737

Hannah, 1641, 4852

Hannay, 2440

Hannyngton, 757, 2119. *See also* Hanington.

Hanover, 5878

Hansard, 5205

Hanson, 1214, 1357, 1756, 2350

Happur, 1820

Harbison, 4552

Harcourt, 164, 2731

Hardcastle, 1444, 6140

Hardcourt, 3586

Harden, 852, 2045, 2264, 4502

Hardinge, 392

Hardman, 1988, 3913

Hardwicke, 3498

Hardy, 368, 567, 596, 1257, 1354, 2264, 2490, 2627, 3200, 3277, 3617, 4022, 4268, 4323, 4932, 4999, 5152, 5299, 5606, 5729

Hare, 3984, 5227. *See also* Haire.

Harkin, 4696

Harkness, 2348, 2726, 3734

Harley, 3390

Harman, 149, 246, 2602

Harper, 1050, 2862, 4020, 4317, 5312, 6220

Harpur, 145, 779, 1000, 2560, 2562, 3732

Harris, 536, 695, 914, 1331, 1546, 1683, 2215, 3226, 3733

Harrison, 191, 3119, 3975, 4198, 4614, 4622, 4678

Hart, 1860, 2097, 2313, 5124, 5618

Harte, 75, 1755, 2555, 6235

Hartford, 2770

Hartland, 4329

Hartness, 4090

Hartrick, 2325, 5286, 5849

Harvey, 401, 546, 2161, 2632, 2732, 3548, 4240, 4641, 6244

Haslett, 3645

Hassan, 3706

Hassard, 324, 333, 545, 690, 691, 853, 858, 1223, 1254, 3127, 3508, 3840, 4179, 4965, 5383

Hassett, 5158, 5180

Hatchell, 734, 5332, 5654

Hatrick, 3375

Haughton, 1352, 1728

Haverfield, 4545

Haverty, 5020

Hawkins, 430, 794, 3344, 5192, 5846

Hawks, 1387

Hawkshaw, 2864, 3017

Hawthorne, 834

Hay, 300, 3075, 3560, 5014, 5847. *See also* Hayes, *and* Hays.

Hayden, 3656

Haydon, 1935

Hayes, 2143, 2764, 3139, 3927, 4878, 5052, 6106

Hays, 2266

Hazelton, 1667, 2860

Hazleton, 2028

Hazlett, 241, 1627

Hazlette, 5071

Heacock, 4752

Healy, 911, 3616

Heaney, 2444

Heard, 4200

Hearn, 3811, 4932. *See also* Heron, *and* Herron.

Heath, 5809

Heather, 6330

Hedley, 5953

Heke, 5788

Hemming, 4023

Hempton, 3529

Henderson, 92, 133, 357, 408, 737, 917, 1439, 1687, 2012, 2041, 2056, 2081, 2412, 2650, 2816, 3233, 3243, 3426, 3515, 3537, 3949, 4145, 4607, 4722, 4795, 4858, 4865, 4894, 4937, 5853, 5887, 6042, 6052, 6380

Hendley, 3580

Hendren, 3326, 4428, 6056

Henley, 6003

Hennesey, 5387, 5499

Henning, 4922

Henry, 46, 94, 253, 267, 365, 416, 494, 616, 985, 1262, 1291, 1343, 1376, 1391, 1522, 1785, 1994, 2467, 2538, 2694, 3039, 3300, 3619, 3887, 3892, 4045, 4069, 4114, 4279, 4296, 4344, 4345, 4458, 4591, 4888, 4973, 5374, 5896, 5948, 5971, 6092

Henville, 256
Henzell, 3655
Hepburn, 5262
Herbert, 1130, 3737
Herd, 3094, 6190
Hereford, 3087
Heron, 110, 2586, 2611, 3074, 3159. *See also* Hearn, *and* Herron.
Herron, 6025
Hertford, 4984
Hertslet, 1567
Hervey, 495
Heslan, 2587
Hetherington, 1382, 2328
Hewetson, 5956
Hewett, 458
Hewison, 4021
Hewitt, 491, 599, 1708, 2339, 3591
Heygate, 4971
Heyland, 1251, 2329, 2394
Heyns, 3210
Hickey, 4418, 6105
Hickland, 64
Hicks, 4032
Higgin, 2801
Higginbotham, 3099, 5530. *See also* Higginbottom, Higinbotham, *and* Hinginbotham.
Higginbottom, 2686
Higgins, 2936, 3896, 6420
Higginson, 4329, 4858
Highland, 1507
Highmore, 6212
Higinbotham, 2797, 5850
Hildebrand, 5068
Hill, 387, 689, 1135, 1448, 1461, 1525, 1608, 1620, 1834, 2145, 2352, 3207, 3446, 3984, 4014, 4210, 4260, 4780, 5563, 5595, 5662, 6080
Hilliard, 1742. *See also* Hillyard.
Hills, 5881
Hillyard, 633. *See also* Hilliard.
Hilton, 4654
Hinchey, 2126
Hincks, 459

Hind, 2191. *See also* Hinds, *and* Hynds.
Hindlay, 3172
Hinds, 704, 1578, 3731, 5351
Hinginbotham, 5682. *See also* Higginbotham, Higginbottom, *and* Higinbotham.
Hirsch, 4033
Hitchcock, 2188
Hoare, 5745. *See also* Hore.
Hobbs, 3141, 3621
Hobhouse, 4913
Hobson, 149, 2715, 3773, 4241, 5290
Hodgens, 709, 1192, 4537, 4739, 6068
Hodson, 2987, 3276
Hoey, 1664, 3321
Hogan, 84, 85, 458, 806, 1331, 1755, 1827, 2548, 4462, 4831
Hogg, 1065, 1295, 4553, 5882, 6044
Hole, 698
Holland, 84, 1111, 2805, 3644, 4114, 5203, 6442
Holmes, 607, 634, 773, 775, 1385, 1864, 2084, 2206, 3527, 4604, 4874, 5636, 5741, 6243, 6417, 6449. *See also* Homes.
Homan, 4019
Homes, 3258. *See also* Holmes.
Hood, 2061, 4307, 5745
Hook, 5880
Hooks, 3197, 4492
Hoops, 5835
Hope, 1173
Hopkins, 1555, 2225, 3921
Hopps, 5508
Hore, 3072, 4016, 5197. *See also* Hoare.
Horgan, 3518
Horne, 444
Horner, 444, 5940
Hornidge, 2251
Hort, 3114, 3448
Hotham, 2234
Houghton, 3674
Houston, 107, 944, 1675, 1756, 1965, 2363, 2513, 2662, 3130, 3465, 6321. *See also* Hueston, *and* Huston.
Howard, 505, 3445, 5622
Howden, 1949, 3806, 5199
Howe, 2895, 4430, 5130, 5156, 5680, 5888

Chapter 3: Index of Surnames

Howell, 2352
Howey, 866
Howson, 6397
Hoy, 2610, 5903
Huddleston, 6313
Hudson, 302, 690, 1358, 1784, 2267, 3727, 4959, 5347
Hueston, 5222. *See also* Houston, *and* Huston.
Huey, 2710, 3725, 4402, 5391
Huffman, 6382
Huggins, 3168, 4006, 4747
Hughes, 2, 12, 22, 423, 862, 922, 1015, 1034, 1077, 1175, 1234, 1453, 1638, 1663, 1835, 1863, 2448, 2521, 2858, 2907, 3004, 3012, 3013, 3555, 3954, 3969, 4219, 4305, 4414, 4491, 4798, 5409, 5413, 5490, 5553, 5554, 5644, 6157, 6219, 6272
Hull, 1573, 2352, 4328, 5053, 5184
Hume, 3248, 4530, 4654, 4889
Humes, 3470
Humphreys, 102, 547, 3093, 3698, 4235, 4598, 4751, 5873
Humphries, 1333, 4346
Humphris, 2310
Humphrys, 3636, 5699
Huniford, 863
Hunt, 1846, 2826, 3057, 6256, 6330
Hunter, 568, 711, 796, 1132, 1150, 1226, 1382, 2146, 2178, 2558, 2769, 3047, 3189, 3736, 3846, 3895, 4211, 4236, 4833, 5074, 5254, 5266, 5531
Huntington, 2581
Hurson, 2345
Hurst, 380, 592, 1247, 1584, 2047, 2231, 3442, 4615, 4659, 5179
Huson, 3393
Huston, 433, 1742, 5160, 6255. *See also* Houston, *and* Hueston.
Hutcheson, 2158, 4102, 4372, 4585
Hutchinson, 105, 315, 395, 759, 3504, 5038
Hutton, 6390
Hyatt, 1597
Hyde, 945, 1156
Hynds, 2182. *See also* Hind, *and* Hinds.
Hyslop, 4661
Incontri, 692

Incoutri, 692
Ingham, 5126
Inglis, 3044
Ingoldsby, 2587
Ingram, 582, 1813, 2771, 4143
Innes, 352, 5551
Innis, 2411
Ireland, 1382, 4380
Irlam, 4900
Irvin, 867, 1961
Irvine, 7, 62, 239, 381, 382, 406, 467, 591, 618, 692, 693, 757, 847, 1087, 1233, 1508, 1757, 2153, 2170, 2326, 2450, 2452, 2906, 3291, 3411, 3461, 3802, 3896, 4170, 4375, 4637, 4707, 4813, 4982, 5397, 5494, 5593, 5724, 6412, 6416, 6421
Irving, 3539
Irwin, 51, 68, 255, 363, 364, 429, 454, 478, 663, 703, 720, 733, 781, 807, 904, 920, 962, 969, 1118, 1173, 1272, 1308, 1317, 1405, 1458, 1622, 1769, 1781, 1947, 2107, 2223, 2347, 2489, 2541, 2601, 2708, 2958, 3019, 3047, 3133, 3330, 3490, 3494, 3500, 3519, 3760, 3855, 3868, 4035, 4037, 4266, 4267, 4274, 4324, 4353, 4412, 4544, 4624, 4749, 4900, 4919, 5115, 5285, 5499, 5632, 5635, 5708, 5812, 5840, 5849, 6140, 6273, 6353, 6357, 6384
Irwine, 2928, 4832
Isdell, 3891, 6381
Jackman, 1855
Jackson, 78, 135, 268, 427, 730, 776, 785, 956, 1072, 1101, 2203, 2221, 2594, 3117, 3804, 3824, 3909, 4903, 5325, 6406
Jacob, 663, 2963, 4503
Jacobs, 3029
James, 2126, 2346, 3144, 4054, 4195, 4819
James II, 5023
James VI, 2468
Jameson, 1996, 4607
Jamieson, 2529
Jamison, 207, 208, 1505, 3242
Janes, 5730
Jardine, 2924
Jarvis, 3855
Jauvenir, 5013
Jebb, 1425, 2024, 2155, 2766, 3217, 4523, 4873

Jebson, 1146
Jeffares, 4049
Jeffcott, 4070
Jeffers, 2469
Jeffrey, 1776, 2580, 6123
Jeffreys, 2224
Jeffry, 2518
Jellet, 27
Jellett, 4870, 5077
Jelly, 4860
Jenkins, 109, 468, 694, 1492, 3303, 5130, 5255, 5549, 5921. *See also* Jinkins.
Jennings, 3399, 4042, 4555
Jephson, 4236
Jermy, 4400
Jervis, 3556
Jervois, 3058
Jervoise, 3081
Jessop, 1287, 3002
Jinkins, 749. *See also* Jenkins.
Jocelyn, 1280, 4913, 5789
John, 6006
Johns, 539, 555
Johnson, 670, 1479, 2920, 3115, 3143, 3795, 5206, 6148
Johnston, 168, 283, 405, 436, 644, 651, 907, 908, 1037, 1061, 1228, 1340, 1379, 1380, 1385, 1443, 1457, 1462, 1536, 1541, 1635, 1636, 1658, 1674, 1721, 1746, 1786, 1836, 1856, 1874, 1876, 1900, 1907, 1908, 1941, 1983, 1990, 1991, 2079, 2087, 2148, 2202, 2228, 2245, 2376, 2422, 2450, 2458, 2707, 2757, 2917, 3001, 3049, 3275, 3422, 3469, 3516, 3582, 3604, 3607, 3680, 3756, 3757, 3909, 3916, 3925, 3941, 3953, 3988, 4059, 4096, 4146, 4159, 4234, 4256, 4299, 4359, 4379, 4494, 4495, 4496, 4614, 4649, 4651, 4726, 4733, 4797, 4830, 4859, 4886, 4895, 4924, 5069, 5127, 5135, 5150, 5162, 5196, 5198, 5285, 5381, 5452, 5601, 5775, 5828, 5951, 5997, 6056, 6058, 6224, 6344, 6430
Johnstone, 25, 216, 1734, 2826, 4061, 4719, 4879, 5337
Johnton, 1465
Joint, 3790. *See also* Joynt.
Jolly, 3238
Jones, 106, 214, 281, 331, 880, 2180, 2263, 2366, 2371, 2511, 2891, 3182, 3235, 3377, 3588,

Jones, continued: 3877, 4070, 4091, 4647, 4969, 5154, 5702, 6181
Joplin, 1045
Jordan, 529, 2537, 3349
Joy, 2199
Joyce, 1196, 1930, 2016, 2040, 2054, 2135, 4718, 5447, 5610
Joynt, 3493, 4727. *See also* Joint.
Junk, 1786
Jupp, 5992
Kane, 5684. *See also* O'Kane.
Kavanagh, 4882. *See also* Cavanagh, *and* O'Cavanagh.
Kawaii, 5788
Kawiti, 5788
Kay, 3623, 3818. *See also* M'Cay, M'Kay, Mackay, *and* Mackey.
Kean, 4314. *See also* Keane, Keene, *and* M'Keane.
Keane, 4752, 5590.
Keaney, 1720
Keany, 1862
Kearney, 120, 667, 1933, 2937, 3599, 4890
Keatinge, 1453, 2561, 2604, 3055
Keegan, 646, 905, 1332, 1611
Keenan, 1244, 1616, 3439
Keene, 802, 1746. *See also* Kean, Keane, *and* M'Kean.
Keeran, 2026
Kehoe, 2657. *See also* Keogh, *and* M'Keogh.
Keightly, 3418
Keirs, 2495
Kellet, 3197
Kellett, 1351, 1872, 4341
Kelly, 764, 977, 1807, 2214, 2767, 3272, 3498, 3673, 3820, 4362, 4497, 4620, 5355, 5459, 5590, 5592, 6049, 6143, 6274. *See also* O'Kelly.
Kelsey, 4133, 5887
Kelso, 2425, 2903, 2921, 4287, 5453
Kemble, 1912
Kemmis, 3003
Kempston, 4945
Kendal, 3373
Kenedy, 134

Kennedy, 274, 682, 1002, 1547, 1804, 1989, 2080, 2755, 2889, 2914, 2984, 3289, 3301, 3306, 3363, 3876, 4092, 4488, 4508, 4572, 5186

Kennely, 4460

Kenny, 1345. *See also* M'Kenney, *and* M'Kenny.

Kent, 883, 2955, 4264, 4943

Kenyon, 5190

Keogh, 566. *See also* Kehoe, *and* M'Keogh.

Keown, 3602. *See also* M'Keown, *and* Makeown.

Kernaghan, 5411, 5943, 6043, 6407

Kernahan, 705

Kernan, 5721. *See also* M'Kernan.

Kerns, 2985

Kerr, 355, 392, 506, 610, 1232, 1469, 1808, 1991, 2268, 2591, 2861, 2935, 3105, 3116, 3776, 3808, 3931, 4527

Kerrigan, 2465, 4835

Kerrin, 2985

Kershaw, 3678

Kersteman, 4328

Keshan, 5220

Kesteman, 4328

Kettlewell, 5009

Kettyle, 4686

Keys, 812, 1067, 1242, 1398, 1597, 2417, 2506, 2530, 4707

Kidd, 58, 89, 200, 512, 518, 527, 528, 1147, 1992, 2810, 3303, 3391, 3522, 3928, 4274, 4586, 4730, 5039, 5277, 5285, 5382, 5629, 5756, 5788, 5797, 6286. *See also* Kydd.

Kidney, 277, 995, 1170, 5765

Kieran, 4396

Kiernan, 2183

Kilbee, 6291

Kildare, 5631

Killala, 3662, 5957

Killaloe, 4958, 5779, 6436

Killen, 437, 3239

Kilpatrick, 808, 809, 4181, 4206, 4608. *See also* Kirkpatrick.

Kinahan, 1560, 1965

Kincaid, 197, 503, 4227. *See also* Kinkade, *and* Kinkead.

Kinch, 5112

King, 413, 464, 1200, 1322, 1591, 2008, 2453, 2473, 2849, 2952, 3449, 4265, 4652, 4877, 5041, 5068, 5112, 5491, 5727, 5871

Kingsbury, 3662

Kingsmill, 2007

Kinkade, 5712. *See also* Kincaid, *and* Kinkead.

Kinkead, 163, 444, 1495

Kinley, 2106. *See also* M'Kinlay, *and* M'Kinley.

Kinnar, 1859

Kinnear, 261, 2430, 2474, 3778, 3824, 4132

Kinsale, 892

Kirk, 1416, 2133, 3520, 4576, 5611

Kirkpatrick, 2151, 2508, 3871, 5708. *See also* Kilpatrick.

Kirwan, 560, 1331

Kirwood, 3632

Kisby, 4071

Kitson, 98, 511, 826, 2479, 5177

Kittson, 1178, 2717, 4319, 5830

Klophel, 329, 3476

Knight, 903, 3160, 5501. *See also* M'Knight.

Knipe, 1091, 1261, 4242

Kniting, 2660

Knowles, 1273, 3045, 5590

Knox, 71, 383, 712, 763, 1565, 1774, 1790, 1966, 2614, 2628, 2836, 2847, 3213, 3219, 3232, 3642, 3651, 3885, 4106, 4167, 4201, 4203, 4209, 4772, 5212, 5333, 5336, 5762, 5779, 5994

Krauge, 3448

Krause, 4550

Kronheim, 6198

Kurleander, 5456

Kyan, 3435

Kydd, 1741, 4724. *See also* Kidd.

Kyffin, 4493, 4520, 5315

Kyle, 488, 1291, 1801, 5080, 6117

L'Estrange, 5436

La Nauze, 6032, 6226. *See also* Lanauze.

La Touche, 3246, 5439. *See also* Latouche.

Labarte, 5736

Labatt, 2925, 3558, 4263

Lacey, 256

Lacy, 256

Ladley, 2897, 3732

Lafferty, 808. *See also* Laverty.
Lagan, 1779
Laidler, 1392
Laing, 4157. *See also* Lang.
Laird, 2531, 3101, 5145, 5534, 5984
Lake, 546, 3353
Lalor, 3361, 4404
Lamar, 4131
Lamb, 613, 1761, 2783, 3682
Lambart, 5908
Lambert, 5877
Lanauze, 2910, 4164. *See also* La Nauze.
Lane, 83, 916, 1650, 1932, 2147, 3967, 4120, 5874, 5881, 6041
Lanesborough, 4215, 5254
Lang, 4051, 4710. *See also* Laing.
Langlands, 614
Langton, 1922
Langtree, 1619
Langtry, 1, 3, 402, 755, 2336, 2956, 3085
Lanktree, 2850, 3286, 3327, 4300
Lanyon, 4011
Laphan, 4475
Lappan, 174
Larcom, 311
Larmour, 844, 3169
Lathem, 301. *See also* Leathem.
Latimer, 3608, 5037
Latouche, 5558. *See also* La Touche.
Laughlin, 2926. *See also* Loughlin, M'Glaughlin, M'Laughlin, M'Lochlin, M'Loughlin, O'Loghlen, *and* O'Loughlin.
Laverty, 503, 3194. *See also* Lafferty.
Law, 3976, 4510, 4991, 5033
Lawder, 2048
Lawless, 2863, 4460
Lawlor, 1109, 3675
Lawrence, 5548, 5722
Lawrenson, 4669
Lawrin, 3019
Lawson, 1684, 1688, 4998
Lawther, 2564
Lay, 6242. *See also* Ley.
Layton, 6242
Le Fanu, 4677

Lea, 4836
Leach, 2020. *See also* Leech, Leeche, *and* Leitch.
Leard, 6271
Leathem, 2447, 4267, 5210, 5421, 5753. *See also* Lathem.
Leckie, 4358
Lecky, 1581, 2105, 2207, 2413, 3441, 6365
Ledger, 6250
Lediard, 5961
Ledlie, 1195, 3371, 3989, 5966
Lee, 69, 1320, 3044, 3705, 4918, 4946
Leebody, 880, 5886, 6402
Leech, 265, 518, 767, 825, 1477, 2691, 4593. *See also* Leach, Leeche, *and* Leitch.
Leeche, 456
Leeper, 287, 2404, 5230
Lees, 5597
Lefroy, 5846
Leggatt, 4693. *See also* Liggat.
Leigh, 4089
Leighlin, 1060, 3547, 3670
Leitch, 1568, 2416, 6261. *See also* Leach, Leech, *and* Leeche.
Leith, 5262
Lemon, 176, 4334
Lendrum, 575, 1010, 2258, 2284, 4846, 4881, 5247
Lennon, 556, 1185, 2129, 5257, 5902
Lepper, 1307, 1530, 2673, 3221, 3643, 4665
Leslie, 80, 189, 747, 965, 1710, 3525, 4274, 4439, 5026, 5474, 6171
Lester, 316, 997, 2457, 4738, 5258, 5814
Lett, 4401, 5288
Lever, 5118, 5909
Levingston, 3589
Lewers, 4349, 4934, 5318, 5338, 5980
Lewis, 299, 809, 1128, 5781, 5863
Lewisham, 4692
Ley, 4104. *See also* Lay.
Liggat, 4152, 5344. *See also* Leggatt.
Lilburn, 700, 3157
Lilburne, 2061
Limerick, 2614, 3622, 3881, 4958
Lind, 3215, 4864, 5433
Lindesay, 1852, 2851

Lindsay, 273, 415, 851, 1636, 2527, 3819, 4267, 4562, 4609, 4785, 4947, 4997, 5531, 5631, 5749

Lindsell, 3299

Lingard, 4735

Lingen, 6390

Linton, 303

Lions, 929. *See also* Lyon, *and* Lyons.

Lipsett, 118, 153, 1490, 1605, 2934, 5760

Lismore, 1987

Lispett, 1451, 3479

Lister, 1594

Little, 69, 147, 526, 866, 887, 1457, 2111, 2166, 2782, 2911, 2940, 3046, 4662, 4877, 4931, 5521, 5624. *See also* Lyttle.

Litton, 3285, 4805

Llewellen, 4284

Lloyd, 155, 1503, 1766, 1938, 1939, 2172, 2249, 3071, 3231, 5923, 6357

Lochrane, 4131. *See also* Loughran.

Lockhart, 1243, 3318, 3915, 5532

Lockwood, 6079

Lodge, 502, 1637, 1951, 3265

Loftus, 632, 710, 4565

Logan, 2099, 4378, 6350

Logier, 3848

London, 5846

Loney, 5608

Long, 3893, 4390

Longworth, 2696

Lonsdale, 4670

Lord, 3561, 3800

Lord Lieutenant of Ireland, 3024, 5883

Lord Primate of Ireland, 1019, 1754. *See also* Primate of All Ireland.

Loudon, 3661, 3708

Lough, 2287

Loughead, 687

Lougheed, 1812

Loughlin, 1386, 2741, 5067. *See also* Laughlin, M'Glaughlin, M'Laughlin, M'Lochlin, M'Loughlin, O'Loghlen, *and* O'Loughlin.

Loughran, 174, 1550, 2589, 3829. *See also* Lochrane.

Loughrey, 2008, 3351

Louth, 2791, 3600

Love, 37, 855, 2523, 3177, 5231

Lovelace, 6371

Lover, 6237

Low, 3146, 3329

Lowe, 1149, 6292

Lowry, 561, 750, 1160, 1305, 1658, 2399, 2760, 2853, 2858, 3025, 3453, 3465, 4070, 4683, 4907, 5091, 5711, 5755, 5794, 5862, 5983

Lowther, 5854

Lucan, 971

Lucas, 951, 2281, 5658, 6082, 6231

Lundie, 789

Lupton, 2471

Lurgan, 1707, 2804

Luther, 5284

Lutton, 963

Lyle, 345, 1283, 1401, 2668, 2786, 3354

Lynch, 2084, 3910, 4993

Lyndon, 6276

Lyon, 3398. *See also* Lions, *and* Lyons.

Lyons, 2965, 3235, 3718, 5648

Lysaght, 1662

Lyttle, 2192, 3115, 5577. *See also* Little.

M'Adam, 419, 3623, 4394

M'Afee, 2553, 5003

M'Aleer, 1374, 5096

M'Alister, 379, 738, 886, 1259, 1663, 4274, 5231, 5318, 5430, 6418. *See also* M'Callister.

M'Allen, 257, 657. *See also* Allan, *and* Allen.

M'Aloon, 5937

M'Anally, 1330, 1469, 2302, 2703, 5140

M'Ardle, 2585, 6143

M'Aree, 2086

M'Arthur, 4169

M'Ashee, 1934

M'Askie, 4344

M'Auly, 1811

M'Avoy, 372, 641

M'Beale, 3848

M'Birney, 3573, 5620. *See also* Berney, Birney, Birnie, *and* M'Burney.

M'Blain, 5952. *See also* Blain.

M'Bride, 104, 128, 1008, 1036, 3576, 3871, 3956, 4201, 5744, 6416

M'Burney, 601. *See also* Berney, Birney, Birnie, *and* M'Birney.

M'Cabe, 4326
M'Cadim, 4583
M'Cafferey, 6014. *See also* Caffrey.
M'Cafferty, 3334
M'Caherry, 5057
M'Calden, 4871. *See also* M'Caldin, Macaldan, Macalden, *and* Macaldin.
M'Caldin, 1302, 4325, 5678
M'Callen, 5168
M'Callister, 3032. *See also* M'Alister.
M'Camey, 1995
M'Candless, 4972
M'Cann, 1435, 3971, 5926, 6064, 6277. *See also* Macan.
M'Canna, 1939
M'Carron, 3234
M'Carten, 4416
M'Carter, 1214, 4086, 4512, 6269, 6400. *See also* Carter.
M'Cartney, 1202. *See also* Macartney.
M'Caul, 455
M'Cauley, 4435, 4436. *See also* Macauley.
M'Causland, 699, 728, 1186, 1347, 1386, 2042, 2384, 2892, 2951, 3672, 3983, 4111, 4826, 4841, 5004, 5509
M'Caw, 1047, 1953, 2105, 2726, 3402, 4191, 4912, 5687
M'Cay, 697, 1434. *See also* Kay, M'Kay, Mackay, *and* Mackey.
M'Chappan, 885
M'Christal, 3851. *See also* M'Chrystal, M'Chrystall, *and* M'Crystal.
M'Chrystal, 4274
M'Chrystall, 4897
M'Clatchy, 2486. *See also* Maclatchey, *and* Maclatchy.
M'Claverty, 5169
M'Clean, 173, 302, 3357, 5307, 5364, 6295. *See also* M'Lean, *and* Maclean.
M'Clearn, 3064
M'Cleery, 1151, 4995. *See also* M'Clery.
M'Clelland, 297, 532, 544, 721, 886, 2252, 2736, 3331, 3774, 3893, 4173, 4360, 4377, 4636, 4810, 5885, 6127, 6208, 6314. *See also* Cleland.
M'Clenahan, 1837
M'Clery, 885. *See also* M'Cleery.

M'Clintock, 140, 447, 1993, 2947, 3273, 3670, 3695, 6445
M'Closkey, 3061, 3761, 4835, 6090. *See also* M'Clusky.
M'Cloy, 407
M'Clung, 6118
M'Clure, 495, 986, 1213, 3375, 3729, 4597, 4771, 5495, 6440
M'Clusky, 2954. *See also* M'Closkey.
M'Coan, 4464
M'Collough, 2553, 3043. *See also* M'Cullach, M'Cullagh, M'Cullough, M'Culla, M'Cullow, *and* Maculla.
M'Collum, 2754
M'Comb, 1301
M'Combe, 2877
M'Combie, 6134, 6311
M'Conkey, 5274
M'Connell, 122, 1276, 1951, 2547, 3096, 3097, 3755, 4062, 4325, 4838, 5187, 5617, 5649, 6440. *See also* Connell, *and* O'Connell.
M'Conville, 4499
M'Cord, 795, 4526
M'Cormick, 1005, 1606, 1932, 2027, 4501, 4554, 4725, 5295, 5437
M'Cosh, 3408
M'Court, 2274, 6320
M'Coy, 4656, 5177
M'Cracken, 95, 1262, 1369, 3828
M'Crea, 1511, 1934, 2967, 3606
M'Creaght, 4519
M'Creary, 5432. *See also* M'Creery, *and* Macreery.
M'Creery, 909, 1576, 6359
M'Creight, 1425, 2224, 3354, 5538
M'Crossan, 1388, 2908
M'Crum, 3499
M'Crystal, 2274. *See also* M'Cristal, M'Chrystal, *and* M'Chrystall.
M'Culla, 3563. *See also* M'Collough, M'Cullach, M'Cullagh, M'Cullough, M'Cullow, *and* Maculla.
M'Cullach, 3251
M'Cullagh, 933, 2431, 2518, 5014, 5625
M'Cullough, 689, 1346, 2580, 2942, 5348, 5545
M'Cullow, 6334

Chapter 3: Index of Surnames

M'Cully, 1229, 3694, 6389. *See also* Cully.
M'Cune, 2593, 3693, 4975, 5990
M'Curdy, 3084, 3834, 3859, 3887
M'Cutchan, 4684
M'Cutcheon, 2117, 3131, 5759
M'Dermot, 1893. *See also* Dermott, M'Dermott, *and* M'Diarmid.
M'Dermott, 5383
M'Devitt, 930
M'Diarmid, 6347
M'Donagh, 2277, 2977, 3654, 4981, 5250, 5646. *See also* M'Donough.
M'Donald, 800, 1412, 1445, 1478, 2072, 2198, 2954, 3561, 5920. *See also* Macdonald, *and* MacDonald.
M'Donel, 331. *See also* Donnell, M'Donnell, O'Donel, O'Donnell, *and* O'Donnoll.
M'Donnell, 1881, 2160, 2227, 2503, 2583, 3397, 5281, 5380, 5635, 6355
M'Donough, 2814. *See also* M'Donagh.
M'Doughall, 3608. *See also* Dougal, *and* Dugall.
M'Dowal, 759, 1169
M'Dowall, 1364, 1370
M'Dowel, 25
M'Dowell, 393, 1775, 1977, 5525
M'Effer, 2762
M'Elhone, 1835
M'Elivee, 2204
M'Elles, 6187
M'Elrath, 4675. *See also* M'Ilrath.
M'Elroy, 2460, 2637, 5123, 5270, 5525. *See also* M'Ilroy.
M'Elwain, 401, 5320. *See also* M'Ilwaine, *and* M'Ilwaine.
M'Elwee, 1193. *See also* M'Ilwee.
M'Endow, 620, 1259
M'Entee, 4121, 4571
M'Entire, 2968, 5301. *See also* M'Intire, M'Intyre, Macintyre, *and* Mackintyre.
M'Evoy, 389
M'Ewan, 4837
M'Ewen, 1233, 3329, 3330
M'Fadden, 3803, 3826. *See also* Macfadden, MacFaden, *and* Macfadin.
M'Fall, 3993, 6362
M'Farlan, 3381. *See also* M'Parlan.

M'Farland, 243, 356, 1554, 2233, 2273, 2572, 3175, 3641, 3892, 4434, 6116, 6150. *See also* M'Parland.
M'Garel, 2124
M'Garry, 6174
M'Gauran, 3218
M'Geagh, 1538, 1953, 2392, 4933, 5316, 6075, 6337
M'Gee, 3069. *See also* Gee, *and* M'Ghee.
M'Gerr, 160
M'Gettigan, 4898
M'Gettrick, 1835
M'Ghee, 4547. *See also* Gee, *and* M'Gee.
M'Gill, 1475
M'Ginn, 2190
M'Ginnity, 3259
M'Glade, 4798
M'Gladery, 5894
M'Glaughlin, 3541. *See also* Laughlin, Loughlin, M'Laughlin, M'Lochlin, M'Loughlin, O'Loghlen, *and* O'Louglin.
M'Glinchy, 1296
M'Goldrick, 1394, 4548
M'Gonigle, 1289
M'Gowan, 2686, 2932, 4095, 4680, 4916, 5238, 6197. *See also* Gowan, MacGowan, *and* Magowan.
M'Greale, 3713
M'Grew, 4280
M'Grotty, 4725
M'Guckin, 6356
M'Guiness, 6095. *See also* Magenis, Magennis, Maginness, Maginnis, Maginniss, *and* Maguiniss.
M'Guskian, 4798
M'Gusty, 248
M'Harg, 3174
M'Hinch, 2050
M'Hugh, 1296, 1413
M'Illre, 466
M'Ilrath, 2596. *See also* M'Elrath.
M'Ilree, 599
M'Ilroy, 1066, 3673. *See also* M'Elroy.
M'Ilveen, 6259
M'Ilwain, 640, 687, 885. *See also* M'Elwain, *and* M'Ilwaine.

323

M'Ilwaine, 390, 775, 1157, 1877, 2125, 3493, 3980, 4194, 5055, 6278

M'Ilwee, 181, 362. *See also* M'Elwee.

M'Intire, 1797, 2612. *See also* M'Entire, M'Intyre, Macintyre, *and* Mackintyre.

M'Intosh, 2660. *See also* Mackintosh.

M'Intyre, 1801, 5514

M'Iver, 2638. *See also* MacIvor.

M'Kay, 3091, 3945, 4341, 5094. *See also* Kay, M'Cay, Mackay, *and* Mackey.

M'Kean, 5114, 5293, 5311. *See also* Kean, Keane, *and* Keene.

M'Kee, 172, 400, 735, 1245, 1279, 1330, 1599, 1899, 2178, 2293, 2727, 3463, 3559, 3624, 3751, 3759, 4716

M'Kell, 650

M'Kells, 5852

M'Kelvey, 2953, 4232, 5647, 5989

M'Kendrick, 3102

M'Kendry, 6293. *See also* M'Kindry.

M'Kenna, 21, 366, 1807, 3352, 3829, 3995, 5644, 5979

M'Kenney, 1388. *See also* Kenny, *and* M'Kenny.

M'Kenny, 2701, 2745, 3212, 3641, 5165

M'Kenzie, 3094, 4708, 6151. *See also* Mackenzie, *and* Makenzie.

M'Keogh, 6342. *See also* Kehoe, *and* Keogh.

M'Keown, 673, 1969, 2987. *See also* Keown, *and* Makeown.

M'Kernan, 4499. *See also* Kernan.

M'Kindry, 4039. *See also* M'Kendry.

M'Kinlay, 6119. *See also* Kinley, *and* M'Kinley.

M'Kinley, 3184, 3606

M'Kinney, 2448. *See also* Kenny, *and* M'Kinny.

M'Kinny, 2686, 4496

M'Kinstry, 3496, 3851, 3941, 4274, 4336, 4845, 5285, 6379

M'Kitterick, 3957

M'Knight, 689, 4040, 4041. *See also* Knight.

M'Lannahan, 4288. *See also* Maclannahan.

M'Laughlin, 2086, 2618, 4759, 5543. *See also* Laughlin, Loughlin, M'Glaughlin, M'Lochlin, M'Loughlin, O'Lochlen, *and* O'Loughlin.

M'Lean, 1470, 1557. *See also* M'Clean, *and* Maclean.

M'Leod, 48, 748. *See also* MacLeod.

M'Lernon, 932

M'Lochlin, 379

M'Lorinan, 931, 1663

M'Loughlin, 1611, 5574. *See also* Laughlin, Loughlin, M'Glaughlin, M'Laughlin, M'Lochlin, O'Lochlen, *and* O'Loughlin.

M'Loy, 1862

M'Mahon, 252, 782, 901, 1402, 1770, 1992, 2004, 2386, 3550, 3703, 3845, 3850, 3910, 5108, 5129, 5257, 5383, 5829. *See also* MacMahon, *and* Mahon.

M'Manns, 3417

M'Manus, 2656, 3417, 5982

M'Master, 1785, 2455, 3407, 4115, 4190

M'Math, 5626. *See also* MacMath.

M'Meehan, 5564. *See also* Meahan, *and* Meehan.

M'Menamy, 376

M'Millen, 2989, 4169, 4304

M'Minn, 5252

M'Morran, 3442, 3962

M'Mullan, 403, 5202, 5373, 5707

M'Mullen, 471, 508, 636, 1233, 2510, 2692, 4458, 4979, 5073

M'Mullin, 3164

M'Munn, 5752, 6206. *See also* Munn.

M'Murdy, 5703

M'Murn, 6280

M'Murray, 1676, 1699, 4095, 5906. *See also* Murrary, *and* M'Murry.

M'Murry, 379

M'Naghten, 3183. *See also* M'Naghton, M'Naughtan, *and* Macnaghtan.

M'Naghton, 2350

M'Nally, 4136, 5429

M'Namara, 1735

M'Naughtan, 4377

M'Naul, 5269

M'Neece, 2116, 3369, 5713. *See also* M'Niece, *and* MacNeece.

M'Neely, 1260, 3011. *See also* Neely, *and* Neilly.

M'Neight, 824, 5886

M'Neilance, 5612

M'Neill, 3583, 3920. *See also* Macneill, O'Neal, O'Neil, O'Neile, O'Neill, *and* Neill.

M'Nesty, 2641

Chapter 3: Index of Surnames

M'Nicholl, 4577
M'Niece, 2032
M'Nulty, 4571
M'Parlan, 6110. *See also* M'Farlan.
M'Parland, 6110. *See also* M'Parland.
M'Phillips, 2634. *See also* Philips, *and* Phillips.
M'Quade, 276, 3640, 3879, 6110
M'Quaide, 3477
M'Quilkin, 6267
M'Quillion, 2746
M'Quin, 2456. *See also* O'Quin, Quin, *and* Quinn.
M'Reynolds, 346. *See also* Rennolds, *and* Reynolds.
M'Seveney, 5201
M'Shane, 1051, 2716, 5032, 5416
M'Sharry, 136
M'Sorely, 1849, 3801, 4707, 4935
M'Sweeny, 5205. *See also* Sweany, Sweeney, Swiney, *and* Swiny.
M'Tear, 2625
M'Veagh, 1115
M'Veigh, 3319, 4533
M'Vicker, 3584
M'Vittee, 3178
M'Voy, 2345
M'Waters, 5420. *See also* M'Watters, Waters, *and* Watters.
M'Watters, 4267, 4712
M'Watty, 3442
M'Whinny, 5441. *See also* MacWhinny, Mawhiney, *and* Mawhinny.
M'William, 2138, 4642, 4679. *See also* M'Williams, *and* Williams.
M'Williams, 587, 593, 901, 1004, 1785, 2955, 3343, 3854, 3898, 3911, 4815, 5171
Macaldan, 1172. *See also* M'Calden, M'Caldin, Macalden, *and* Macaldin.
Macalden, 2410
Macaldin, 705
Macan, 3116. *See also* M'Cann.
Macarthey, 6172
Macartney, 637, 967, 1007, 1399, 2802, 3227, 3433, 3801, 4558. *See also* M'Cartney.
Macauley, 2461. *See also* M'Cauley.

Macclesfield, 3633
Macdonal, 2307. *See also* Donnell, M'Donell, MacDonnell, O'Donell, O'Donnell, *and* O'Donnoll.
Macdonald, 2804, 4142. *See also* M'Donald, *and* MacDonald.
MacDonald, 3729
MacDonnell, 4259
Macfadden, 668, 2407. *See also* M'Fadden, MacFaden, *and* Macfadin.
MacFaden, 4616
Macfadin, 869, 2714, 3870
MacGowan, 2083. *See also* Gowan, M'Gowan, *and* Magowan.
Macguire, 1661
Machan, 2637
Machoney, 506. *See also* Mahony.
Macintyre, 118. *See also* M'Entire, M'Intire, M'Intyre, *and* Mackintyre.
MacIvor, 5162. *See also* M'Iver.
Mack, 5336
Mackay, 408, 1274, 1805, 2552, 2758, 3196. *See also* Kay, M'Cay, M'Kay, *and* Mackey.
Macken, 6174
Mackenzie, 3290. *See also* M'Kenzie, *and* Makenzie.
MacKeon, 2381
Mackey, 1493, 3038, 3894, 4953. *See also* Kay, M'Cay, M'Kay, *and* Mackay.
Mackie, 4722, 5652
Mackintosh, 3875. *See also* M'Intosh.
Mackintyre, 1696. *See also* M'Entire, M'Intire, M'Intyre, *and* Macintyre.
Macklin, 1878
Maclannahan, 761. *See also* M'Lannahan.
Maclatchey, 1474. *See also* M'Clatchy, *and* Maclatchy.
Maclatchy, 748, 1361, 1635, 2912, 2913
Maclaurin, 70
Maclean, 1090, 1851, 3050, 3072, 3937, 4258, 4896, 5052, 5401. *See also* M'Clean, *and* M'Lean.
MacLeod, 6007. *See also* M'Leod.
Maclin, 598
MacMahon, 3900. *See also* M'Mahon, *and* Mahon.

Macmath, 884, 902. *See also* M'Math.

Macnaghtan, 5159. *See also* M'Naghten, M'Naghton, *and* M'Naughtan.

MacNeece, 5558. *See also* M'Neece, *and* M'Niece.

Macneill, 2823. *See also* M'Neill, O'Neal, O'Neil, O'Neile, O'Neill, *and* Neill.

Maconchy, 2944

MacOrmond, 1850

Macoun, 4339, 4681, 5094

Macpherson, 824

Macready, 5113, 6071. *See also* Macredy, *and* Mecredy.

Macredy, 4675

Macreery, 1910. *See also* M'Creary, *and* M'Creery.

Macrory, 5780

Maculla, 3683. *See also* M'Collough, M'Cullach, M'Cullagh, M'Cullough, M'Culla, *and* M'Cullow.

MacWhinny, 2453. *See also* M'Whinny, Mawhiney, *and* Mawhinny.

Macworth, 6098

Madden, 805, 895, 2036, 2290, 4612

Maddison, 5922

Maddock, 1260

Maffet, 815

Maffett, 2728

Maffit, 4378

Magaffin, 3751

Magallon, 6007

Magan, 547

Magarry, 764

Magauran, 810

Magee, 24, 59, 104, 457, 653, 782, 1155, 1722, 1724, 1880, 2616, 3013, 3195, 3386, 4899, 5302, 5850

Magenis, 3924. *See also* M'Guiness, Magennis, Maginess, Maginness, Maginnis, Maginniss, *and* Maguiniss.

Magennis, 930

Magill, 452, 659, 2193, 2554, 2650, 4068, 4264

Magilligan, 5897

Maginess, 4429

Maginn, 2294, 5633

Maginness, 2118

Maginnis, 4119, 5142

Maginniss, 3767, 4809

Maginnity, 1709

Magovern, 3056

Magowan, 1389, 5390. *See also* Gowan, M'Gowan, *and* MacGowan.

Magrath, 4276, 5557

Maguiniss, 6451. *See also* M'Guiness, Magenis, Magennis, Maginess, Maginness, Maginnis, *and* Maginniss.

Maguire, 810, 1166, 1612, 2472, 2636, 2863, 2884, 3078, 3204, 3206, 3926, 4053, 4193, 4476, 4650, 5269, 5614, 5814, 5947

Mahaffy, 3665. *See also* Mehaffy.

Mahon, 3272. *See also* M'Mahon, *and* MacMahon.

Mahony, 556, 4003. *See also* Machoney.

Mahood, 1909, 3532, 4221, 4635, 6404

Maidstone, 3160

Main, 3242, 5973. *See also* Maine, *and* Mayne.

Maine, 3471

Maingay, 4327

Mair, 5637

Mairs, 3162

Maitland, 4258

Major, 218, 2960, 4450

Makenzie, 5998. *See also* M'Kenzie, *and* Mackenzie.

Makeown, 3383. *See also* Keown, *and* M'Keown.

Malcolm, 2018

Malcolmson, 3964

Malcomson, 2104, 4797

Mallagh, 4339

Mallen, 4618

Malley, 2216. *See also* O'Malley.

Mallin, 1453, 5116

Mallon, 2499, 2907, 4075, 4196

Malone, 366, 883

Malony, 1030. *See also* Molony.

Manchester, 1130, 3427, 3455, 5109, 5878

Mande, 3421, 3874

Mandeley, 3743

Manders, 3609

Mandeville, 4155, 5878

Mangan, 501, 1587, 2800, 4887, 6036

Mangin, 6194

Manners, 799

Manson, 694, 1029

Mant, 97, 1615

Mantell, 6316

Manyard, 3997

Mapei, 409

Maphett, 5425

March, 4827

Markey, 2659

Marks, 2789

Marlay, 1266, 2500

Marmion, 2663

Marr, 2153, 2170, 6080

Marron, 1544, 5437

Marsh, 124

Marshall, 609, 789, 1114, 1299, 2212, 3107, 3538, 4518, 4563, 5121, 5275, 5386, 5508

Martin, 18, 123, 149, 198, 459, 741, 1164, 1201, 1225, 1533, 1669, 2142, 2167, 2680, 2995, 3302, 3538, 3734, 3799, 3863, 3898, 3911, 4272, 4274, 4406, 4792, 4889, 5435, 6146, 6332

Masaroon, 1039, 1092

Mason, 819, 1537, 1596, 3752, 3893, 5915

Massey, 3452, 6081

Matchet, 2168

Matchett, 26, 1026, 3332, 3598, 4595

Mathers, 931

Mathews, 332, 339, 341, 3316, 4457, 5184, 5629. *See also* Matthews.

Mathias, 1909, 2325, 2859, 3015, 3252, 3733, 4706. *See also* Matthias.

Matthews, 828, 879, 959, 2277, 3987. *See also* Mathews.

Matthewson, 1414

Matthias, 2107, 2516. *See also* Mathias.

Maturin, 11, 388, 1654, 4667

Maude, 2165, 3223, 4745, 4811, 4991, 5439, 5728, 5841, 6205, 6209

Maudeley, 3743

Maudsley, 5824

Mauleverer, 312, 360, 768, 943, 1326, 4274

Maunsel, 6417. *See also* Maunsell, *and* Monsell.

Maunsell, 530, 3981, 3982, 4009, 4283, 5260, 5709

Maveety, 2976

Mawhiney, 2849. *See also* M'Whinny, MacWhinny, *and* Mawhinny.

Mawhinny, 2473, 4435

Maxwell, 141, 194, 270, 1129, 1360, 1577, 2144, 2496, 3946, 4581, 4742, 4816, 4896, 5028, 5418, 5547, 5609, 5710, 5887, 5986, 6031, 6354, 6392

May, 28, 975, 1089, 1219, 3319, 4728, 6160

Mayberry, 3497

Mayers, 3015

Mayne, 1441, 2080, 2870, 3294, 3677, 4031, 5550, 5670, 6008. *See also* Main, *and* Maine.

Mayor, 282

Meade, 4831

Meagher, 6279

Meahan, 1290. *See also* Meehan, *and* M'Meehan.

Meares, 1787

Meason, 660

Meath, 2171, 2468, 3224, 4594, 6084, 6304, 6428

Mecredy, 6122. *See also* Macready, *and* Macredy.

Medcalf, 4309. *See also* Metcalf, *and* Metcalfe.

Medill, 3825

Meegan, 36

Meehan, 3237. *See also* Meahan, *and* M'Meehan.

Meeke, 4675

Mehaffy, 4500. *See also* Mahaffy.

Meharry, 1631, 5638

Melville, 4277

Menagh, 6276

Menary, 5498

Meneely, 2300

Mercer, 1163, 2788, 5605, 5800

Meredith, 574, 1778, 2498, 2584, 3325, 4726, 5130

Meredyth, 4836

Metcalf, 744, 3647, 4520. *See also* Medcalf, *and* Metcalfe.

Metcalfe, 2803

Metge, 708, 4929

Meyler, 6372

Middlemore, 4370

Miles, 3875

Millar, 589, 1271, 1519, 1648, 2149, 2276, 2392, 3318, 3774, 3775, 3940, 4366, 4554, 5605

Miller, 416, 502, 832, 1040, 1472, 1561, 1878, 1906, 2204, 2720, 2871, 3350, 3394, 4554, 4682, 4709, 5161, 5454, 5967, 6174

Millett, 4031

Milligan, 1700, 2835, 2844, 4897, 5770, 6386, 6387

Milliken, 45, 4906

Milling, 1152, 1789, 2866

Mills, 289, 1097, 2327, 2498, 3176, 3257, 4197, 4575, 4588, 5022, 5950, 6201, 6288

Milnes, 4995

Milns, 3557

Miltown, 4836

Minchin, 3195

Mines, 2629

Minnis, 6322

Minton, 1476

Mitchel, 25, 1794, 2452, 3538

Mitchell, 1375, 1412, 1639, 1817, 2029, 2173, 2474, 2512, 3115, 3350, 3625, 3697, 4073, 5047, 5090, 5669, 6004, 6005

Moamberlaine, 4848

Mockler, 5002

Moffat, 110, 2089, 5587

Moffatt, 2246, 3075, 4519, 5117, 5119

Moffit, 1365, 1380

Moffitt, 3138

Molesworth, 875

Mollan, 1816, 4955, 5672

Molloy, 482, 985, 1059, 2011, 2534, 3225. *See also* Mulloy.

Molony, 1428, 2723, 5594, 5607, 6100. *See also* Malony.

Molyneaux, 948, 2876, 4437

Molyneix, 3303

Molyneux, 566, 572, 647, 660, 835, 1325, 2875, 3513, 4230, 4274, 4580, 4934, 5113, 5278, 5784

Monaghan, 1388, 2254, 4789, 5703

Monahan, 5635

Monck, 2110, 5997. *See also* Moncks, *and* Monk.

Moncks, 5417

Moneypenny, 6156. *See also* Monypenny, *and* Monypeny.

Monk, 2550. *See also* Monck, *and* Moncks.

Monsell, 3704, 5405. *See also* Maunsel, *and* Maunsell.

Montagne, 1234

Montagu, 3427, 3455

Montanban, 6282

Monteague, 865

Monteith, 4029, 5649

Montgarret, 197

Montgomerie, 1761. *See also* Montgomery.

Montgomery, 183, 640, 682, 768, 981, 1003, 1230, 1259, 1329, 1562, 1602, 1741, 2017, 2310, 2854, 2973, 3135, 3295, 3614, 3730, 4584, 4673, 5185, 5661, 5912, 6135, 6215, 6388. *See also* Montgomerie.

Montmorres, 365

Monypenny, 4097, 5870. *See also* Moneypenny, *and* Monypeny.

Monypeny, 1328, 1873

Moody, 1510, 6266, 6296

Moon, 7, 3040

Moondooey, 3492

Mooney, 197, 1506, 3423, 4609, 5257

Moore, 54, 79, 107, 350, 515, 533, 642, 736, 783, 792, 857, 912, 937, 1164, 1350, 1501, 1521, 1610, 1633, 1698, 1867, 1926, 2089, 2098, 2178, 2219, 2315, 2362, 2483, 2518, 2519, 2580, 2623, 2761, 2813, 2914, 2963, 2990, 3083, 3259, 3317, 3356, 3443, 3453, 3742, 3897, 4137, 4168, 4174, 4199, 4360, 4399, 4632, 4866, 5103, 5114, 5139, 5305, 5367, 5404, 5418, 5504, 5562, 5613, 5743, 5839, 6298, 6310

Moorhead, 460, 1202, 1466, 2288, 6172. *See also* Morehead.

Moran, 2577, 3563, 4774

Morant, 6121

Morehead, 1460. *See also* Moorhead.

Moreland, 2321

Morell, 600, 727, 1634, 2833, 3623, 3705, 4166, 4599, 4933, 5643, 5885

Moreton, 2226

Morewood, 2899

Morgan, 20, 111, 408, 1484, 2285, 2631, 3041, 3894, 4069, 4584, 4739, 5764, 6081, 6213

Morison, 105. *See also* Morrison.

Morphy, 1387, 1825, 3780, 4163, 5904. *See also* Murphy.

Morris, 3758, 5066, 6254

Morrison, 192, 455, 465, 662, 933, 1213, 1789, 2052, 2347, 2397, 2488, 3257, 3555, 5579, 5827, 6158, 6309. *See also* Morison.

Morrow, 188, 1033, 1114, 1207, 2822, 3193, 4445, 5417, 5882, 6175

Mortimer, 375, 713, 1359

Morton, 1403, 1415, 1465, 1842, 2246, 6179

Moses, 1655

Moss, 2908, 4154

Moubray, 3857, 5189

Mountgarret, 4514, 2487, 3590

Moutray, 3010, 5297

Mulgan, 5681

Mulheron, 2688, 6385

Mulholland, 5368

Mullen, 3975, 4834, 5417. *See also* Mullin, *and* Mullins.

Mulligan, 568, 1532, 2096, 2274, 2838, 2909, 3425, 4941, 5437, 6013

Mullin, 4196, 5096. *See also* Mullen, *and* Mullins.

Mullins, 4187

Mulloy, 747, 1531, 4212, 6385. *See also* Molloy.

Mulreany, 325, 1772, 2267, 4898, 4914

Mulreny, 1296

Mulvany, 554, 5700

Mulveny, 6002

Munn, 5053. *See also* M'Munn.

Munro, 3145, 3196, 4574

Murdoch, 1609, 3132

Murdock, 681, 1210, 1417, 5842

Murphy, 50, 883, 1709, 2345, 2442, 2526, 3367, 3888, 4123, 4274, 4977, 5096, 5246, 5737, 6126. *See also* Morphy.

Murray, 849, 1186, 1411, 1690, 2094, 2124, 2149, 2197, 2378, 2504, 2583, 2701, 2757, 3314, 3397, 3404, 3424, 3580, 3620, 4436, 4465, 4753, 4812, 5162, 5165, 5230, 5296, 5300, 5569, 6026, 6352. *See also* M'Murray, *and* M'Murry.

Mussen, 3359, 6299

Nagle, 4460

Nangle, 4194

Napier, 256, 3384, 4629

Napoleon, 6282

Napper, 4842

Nash, 625, 889

Naulty, 3996

Nazim, 6216

Needham, 438, 923

Neely, 696, 806, 4834. *See also* M'Neely, *and* Neilly.

Neill, 844, 5021, 5116. *See also* M'Neil, MacNeill, O'Neal, O'Neil, O'Neile, *and* O'Neill.

Neilly, 270

Nelis, 5030

Nelmes, 2842, 4633

Nelson, 442, 1069, 1108, 1190, 1222, 1600, 5152, 5745, 6335

Nesbit, 1263

Nesbitt, 1215, 1346, 1362, 1540, 2997, 5786

Nettleton, 5363

Nevill, 5379

Neville, 1620, 2784

Nevin, 1546

New, 5842

Newcombe, 1744, 6241

Newcome, 617

Newell, 1201, 3537, 3921, 4880

Newenham, 901

Newport, 422

Newry, 5734

Newton, 505, 586, 998, 1073, 2123, 2270, 3970, 4393, 5358, 5754, 5993

Niblock, 1081, 1342, 1706, 3192, 4344

Nichols, 2620

Nicholson, 198, 1022, 2748, 2893, 3328, 5283, 5980, 6141

Nixon, 103, 321, 897, 964, 983, 984, 1199, 1455, 1695, 1782, 2189, 3690, 3723, 3738, 3822, 3939, 4068, 4148, 4171, 4229, 5110, 5414, 5638, 5767, 5865, 6088

Noble, 158, 288, 380, 924, 4398, 5152, 5575

Noel, 5642

Nolan, 333, 2160, 2612, 3405, 5599

Norris, 676, 1896, 2150, 5346

North, 220, 240

Northland, 2010, 2904

Norton, 5228

Novelli, 6072

Nucella, 5090

Nugent, 68, 1557, 2171, 3425, 3771, 3789, 4351, 4671, 4867, 5783, 5808, 5949, 6046

Nunn, 5845, 5900

O'Brian, 2, 372. *See also* Brien, Bryan, *and* O'Brien.

O'Brien, 12, 60, 205, 1487, 1569, 2296, 3296, 3552, 4118, 4460, 4611, 5650, 5757

O'Callaghan, 4822, 5517, 5898. *See also* Callaghan.

O'Cavanagh, 2289. *See also* Cavanagh, *and* Kavanagh.

O'Connell, 396, 2279, 2485, 3497, 3803. *See also* Connell, *and* M'Connell.

O'Connor, 4301. *See also* Connor.

O'Crady, 3443

O'Doherty, 2966. *See also* Doherty, Dougherty, *and* O'Dougherty.

O'Donel, 2307. *See also* Donnell, M'Donel, M'Donnell, O'Donnell, *and* O'Donnoll.

O'Donnell, 2066, 2714, 3110, 3863, 3938, 4151

O'Donnoll, 3938

O'Donovan, 3420, 3497, 6169. *See also* Donovan.

O'Dougherty, 1569. *See also* Doherty, Dougherty, *and* O'Doherty.

O'Driscoll, 2025, 2969, 2970, 4473, 6051

O'Dwyer, 5996. *See also* Dwyer.

O'Farrell, 4552. *See also* Farrell.

O'Flaherty, 4331

O'Flinn, 5960. *See also* Flynn, *and* Flynne.

O'Grady, 3919

O'Grant, 3456. *See also* Grant.

O'Hagan, 3531, 6422. *See also* Hagan, *and* Hagen.

O'Hanlon, 2869, 3425, 4739. *See also* Hanlon.

O'Hara, 1810, 3595

O'Kane, 2349, 2908, 4696. *See also* Kane.

O'Keeffe, 4107

O'Kelly, 3272. *See also* Kelly.

O'Loghlen, 4347. *See also* Laughlin, Loughlin, M'Glaughlin, M'Laughlin, M'Lochlin, M'Loughlin, *and* O'Loughlin.

O'Loughlin, 1611, 2985, 3213, 5161

O'Malley, 5403. *See also* Malley.

O'Meara, 273, 4204

O'Neal, 2683. *See also* M'Neill, Macneill, Neill, O'Neil, O'Neile, *and* O'Neill.

O'Neil, 1881, 3564, 5991, 6066

O'Neile, 1057

O'Neill, 1115, 1341, 2522, 2731, 2910, 3020, 3399, 3908, 4362, 4917, 5535, 6023

O'Quin, 619. *See also* M'Quin, Quin, *and* Quinn.

O'Reilly, 1870, 1920, 2484, 2999, 5819, 5928, 5941, 6428. *See also* Reilly.

O'Richards, 643

O'Rourke, 1275, 2587

O'Sullivan, 1117, 1232, 1655, 3121. *See also* Sullivan.

O'Tool, 683. *See also* O'Toole, *and* Toole.

O'Toole, 1955, 4589

Oakman, 202, 945

Obre, 175, 1726, 2738

Ochiltree, 1406, 6275

Ogilby, 1857, 3166, 3232, 4883

Ogle, 91, 161, 848, 2011, 2333, 3542

Oldham, 900, 5208

Oliver, 339, 3491, 4555, 4584, 4775, 5745, 5813, 6257

Olphert, 605, 1316, 1510, 3322

Olpherts, 260, 1007, 4076, 4527, 4606

Onslow, 4027

Orange Jenny: *See* 'Quinton, Jane', 5668

Ord, 6019

Orde, 5232

Ormonde, 5686

Ormsbey, 969

Ormsby, 742, 2419, 4167, 6375

Orr, 230, 402, 1046, 1231, 1311, 1327, 1604, 1623, 1786, 1972, 2303, 2827, 3047, 3112, 3316, 4275, 5067, 5112, 5142

Osborn, 4988, 5071

Osborne, 541, 562, 4284, 5384

Osburn, 461

Ossory, 292, 2928, 4281, 6234

Ossory *and* Ferns, 1589

Ossulton, 3455

Otway, 4542, 5558

Ould, 1283

Oulton, 130, 344, 1113, 1990, 2685, 2846, 3304, 3345, 3395, 3736, 3737, 3850, 4651, 5072, 5434

Ovenden, 146, 428, 729, 1352, 2873, 5393
Ovens, 44, 1215, 1911, 2502, 2520, 2668, 3124
Overend, 279, 782, 860, 2606, 2711, 4067, 4427, 5291, 6359
Overstoke, 5024
Owens, 877, 1901, 3398, 6307
Paget, 5119, 5261
Paine, 5298. *See also* Payne.
Paisley, 3222. *See also* Pasley.
Palmer, 133, 266, 2182, 3807, 5467, 5527, 5979, 6251, 6315
Park, 579, 839, 1506, 1843, 2391, 3478, 5922
Parke, 1793
Parker, 960, 1643, 1749, 3897, 4395, 5752
Parkinson, 836, 1001, 6233
Parkman, 6306
Parks, 702, 4428
Parmer, 5489
Parr, 2543, 6108
Parry, 28, 3884, 5892. *See also* Perry.
Parsons, 3522
Pasley, 4669. *See also* Paisley.
Passavant, 2787
Patchell, 3210
Paterson, 2329, 5736. *See also* Patterson, Patteson, *and* Pattison.
Paton, 262, 1913, 4274, 4896, 5163, 5285, 6419, 6432. *See also* Patton.
Patterson, 254, 1054, 1591, 1799, 1814, 1877, 2196, 2494, 2756, 3403, 3559, 3750, 3786, 4195, 4270, 4505, 4955, 5102, 5173, 5637, 6271. *See also* Paterson, Patteson, *and* Pattison.
Patteson, 1419
Pattison, 2992
Patton, 1555, 2467, 3470, 3849, 4264, 4459, 5751, 6045. *See also* Paton.
Paul, 245, 577, 733, 834, 1030, 1094, 2222, 2392, 3209, 3313, 3331
Payne, 3309, 3983. *See also* Paine.
Peacock, 2885, 3965, 5853
Peacocke, 4993
Pearce, 3412. *See also* Pierce.
Pears, 3983
Pearson, 1106, 2582
Peebles, 296, 3428

Peel, 3563, 3565, 4060, 4310
Pelling, 5438
Penn, 1062
Pennefather, 1300, 2839, 3147, 3427, 4281
Pentland, 2332, 4899, 4968, 5774, 5899
Penton, 235, 845
Peoples, 2357, 3492, 6173
Pepper, 314, 2565, 5711
Peppey, 1658
Perceval, 3346
Percey, 4849
Percival, 2169, 3496
Percy, 5232, 6054
Perkins, 804, 6142, 6268
Perrin, 734, 792, 4750
Perry, 1656, 2341, 2396. *See also* Parry.
Persse, 11, 3082
Petrie, 4291
Pettigrew, 308, 793, 5185
Peyton, 2226, 2536, 4141, 6054
Philips, 2265, 2794, 3526, 4279, 4296, 5157. *See also* M'Phillips, *and* Phillips.
Phillips, 334, 340, 1203, 2104, 4050, 4151, 4924, 6033
Philson, 1796
Pierce, 2895. *See also* Pearce.
Pigot, 2149
Pike, 3414, 3437, 3488, 4116, 4138
Pillar, 518, 1147, 2715
Pim, 2798, 5095
Pinching, 2633
Pine, 5788
Pinniger, 1722
Platt, 116
Player, 5607
Plunket, 5717, 5815
Plunkett, 3444, 5204
Pocock, 1818
Poe, 222, 2454
Pogue, 526
Pollock, 361, 587, 1582, 2890, 4828
Ponsonby, 2796, 3137, 5609
Poolar, 1456
Poole, 3240, 3716, 4870

Pooler, 1942
Pooley, 5089
Pope, 1952
Porter, 130, 302, 639, 665, 758, 963, 1215, 1467, 1577, 1741, 2100, 2151, 2570, 3126, 3156, 3236, 3301, 3403, 3648, 3849, 3860, 4024, 4034, 4321, 4653, 4723, 4727, 4748, 4795, 4821, 4893, 5091, 5142, 5212, 5394, 6021
Posnett, 3994
Pott, 1181
Potter, 179, 1668, 1894, 4322
Potterton, 3979
Potts, 1620
Pounder, 4970
Powel, 3118
Powell, 713, 1918, 4652
Power, 183, 622, 731, 3104, 4081, 4408, 6393
Praeger, 5229
Pratt, 531, 3941, 4283, 4306, 5273
Prentice, 89, 756, 1465, 1750, 2223, 4127, 4274, 4430, 4461, 5111
Prescott, 2266, 5362, 5548
Preston, 238, 2059, 3903
Price, 236, 1127, 1599, 1619, 1765, 3559, 3977, 6178, 6245
Priestly, 446, 4093
Primate of All Ireland, 617, 633, 1019, 1062, 2313, 4836, 5058, 5059. *See also* Lord Primate of Ireland.
Primate of All Ireland (Roman Catholic), 174. *See also* Lord Primate of Ireland.
Primate of All Ireland: *See also* Rev. Dr. Croly, 331.
Prince, 1680
Pring, 6207
Pringle, 391, 730, 972, 1896, 2781, 3852, 4132, 4621, 4634, 5465, 5584
Prior, 622, 2917
Probyn, 5733
Proctor, 1473, 1747, 4339, 5246, 6215
Puckle, 4203
Pugin, 6063
Purcell, 1420, 3397, 4018, 4746
Purdon, 4463
Purdy, 1946, 2554
Quain, 96, 2243, 3040, 3671, 3750, 5203

Quale, 3801
Quarry, 125, 4570
Quay, 2828
Queen Elizabeth, 3272
Quick, 4526
Quigley, 2089, 3399
Quigly, 6161
Quill, 2900
Quin, 58, 278, 746, 1382, 1616, 1649, 1884, 2030, 2135, 3415, 4254, 4696, 4911, 5574. *See also* M'Quin, O'Quin, *and* Quinn.
Quinan, 762
Quinn, 132, 362, 1009, 1332, 2227, 2340, 3781, 4499, 4898, 4914
Quintin, 2550, 5251
Quinton, 378, 786, 1586, 2239, 4083, 5428, 5668, 5895
Radcliffe, 756, 1472, 3795, 5256. *See also* Ratcliffe.
Rafferty, 5720. *See also* Raverty.
Raikes, 171
Rainsford, 2519
Ralph, 732
Ram, 3907
Ramsay, 1393, 2021, 2105, 2370, 3366, 3992, 4238, 5083, 5324, 5761
Ramsey, 1454, 2207
Ranfurley, 1062, 4203, 5994
Ranfurly, 2010, 3642
Rankin, 817, 1438, 1895, 2430, 4770
Ranson, 1039, 4967, 5793
Raphoe, 771, 2986, 3264
Rarnwell, 3000
Ratcliffe, 938. *See also* Radcliffe.
Rathborne, 2696
Raubb, 5964
Raven, 5140
Raverty, 4497. *See also* Rafferty.
Rawdon, 623, 6369
Ray, 3111. *See also* Rea.
Raynes, 5378, 5389
Rea, 2765, 4747, 5146. *See also* Ray.
Read, 1294. *See also* Reade, Reed, *and* Reid.
Reade, 3123, 3939, 4920
Ready, 6438

Redington, 2576, 4017

Redman, 519

Redmond, 431

Reed, 1519, 2438, 2448, 2802, 3872, 3912, 4437, 4751. *See also* Read, Reade, *and* Reid.

Reeves, 355, 1950, 2607, 4115, 4752

Reford, 5589

Reid, 87, 711, 740, 1632, 1660, 1838, 2028, 2109, 2713, 2826, 3021, 3376, 3429, 3777, 3894, 3955, 4202, 4206, 5665, 5795. *See also* Read, Reade, *and* Reed.

Reilly, 74, 962, 1363, 1981, 2057, 2338, 2655, 3185, 3775, 3803, 3826, 3947, 5097, 5868. *See also* O'Reilly.

Remington, 1463, 2894, 3091

Rennick, 435, 1345, 2990. *See also* Renwick.

Rennolds, 5239. *See also* M'Reynolds, *and* Reynolds.

Renwick, 6308, 6360. *See also* Rennick.

Reynell, 1542

Reynolds, 1188, 2573, 4025, 4187, 4901, 5385, 5511, 5655. *See also* M'Reynolds, *and* Rennolds.

Rhind, 2678

Ribton, 1598

Rice, 2360, 3160, 4354, 5380

Richardson, 236, 242, 326, 542, 830, 861, 1064, 1275, 1390, 1461, 2186, 2675, 3510, 3674, 4245, 4449, 4487, 4640, 4756, 5061, 5141, 5438, 6039

Richey, 2393, 2894, 3074, 3076, 3237, 3371, 3511. *See also* Ritchie.

Rickard, 40, 549, 1701, 3706, 5104

Rickards, 40

Riddall, 335, 342, 553, 1898, 4267

Riddle, 1747, 2206

Ridge, 2180

Ridgway, 5472

Rigby, 5797

Rigg, 1989

Riggs, 2946, 3851, 4267

Riley, 3293

Rimington, 2010

Ringland, 1657, 2643

Ringwood, 5677, 5698

Ripon, 5056

Risk, 2344

Ritchie, 1342, 3560, 3849, 4963, 4972, 6333. *See also* Richey.

Riversdale, 4958

Riverston, 5023

Roach, 3752. *See also* Roche.

Robb, 1272, 2049, 5115, 6215

Roberison, 4189

Roberts, 716, 2164, 4079, 4714, 5793

Robertson, 3484, 3678

Robinson, 76, 356, 454, 587, 695, 831, 943, 962, 1011, 1339, 1431, 1481, 1674, 2012, 2232, 2295, 2320, 2396, 2401, 2437, 2633, 2635, 3236, 3241, 3582, 3712, 3773, 3851, 4004, 4099, 4139, 4153, 4274, 4527, 4583, 4754, 4772, 4850, 5151, 5285, 5353, 5365, 5818, 6055, 6078, 6125, 6232

Robson, 464

Roche, 1879, 2734, 3739. *See also* Roach.

Rochfort, 4467

Rocks, 888

Roddy, 5282

Roden, 1280, 4913, 6212

Rodgers, 1138, 1250, 1321, 1716, 2209, 3027, 5155, 5408, 5416, 5417, 5539. *See also* Rogers.

Rodney, 4334, 5961

Rodwell, 3622

Roe, 286, 1297, 1743, 2551

Rogar, 4028

Rogers, 251, 479, 811, 1645, 1704, 1803, 2093, 2227, 2230, 2581, 2836, 2950, 3202, 3307, 3365, 3703, 3827, 3976, 4373, 4414, 4521, 4724, 5172, 5345, 5367, 6384. *See also* Rodgers.

Roleston, 2126. *See also* Rolestone, Rolleston, Rolston, Roulston, *and* Roulstone.

Rolestone, 1405

Rolleston, 3409

Rolston, 2615, 3619, 3831, 5260, 5458

Roney, 2938, 4481, 5093

Rook, 3702, 4814

Rooke, 5054

Rooney, 4483, 6176

Roper, 1032, 2931, 4165, 5105

Rosborough, 1396

Roscommon, 3816
Rose, 5253
Roskell, 2279
Ross, 98, 111, 156, 1187, 1231, 2094, 3030, 3252, 3483, 3487, 3517, 3576, 3646, 3674, 3729, 3950, 4311, 4340, 4984, 5176, 5495, 5653, 5702, 5730, 5838, 6076, 6265
Rossborough, 1531, 3118
Rossmore, 3966, 4540, 5214, 6424
Rotch, 5722
Rotherham, 1115
Roulston, 6431. *See also* Roleston, Rolestone, Rolleston, Rolston, *and* Roulstone.
Roulstone, 3375
Rowan, 85, 1263, 3100, 4306, 4704, 4978, 5514
Rowe, 103, 1480
Rowland, 803
Rowley, 3505
Roy, 2975
Ruddell, 4266
Ruddy, 5015
Rule, 2292
Runnett, 3684
Running, 1748, 3038
Rush, 3640, 3829, 4400
Rusk, 3094
Russell, 186, 520, 1609, 1919, 2733, 2855, 3263, 3447, 3450, 3520, 3609, 4032, 4480, 4498, 4549
Rutherfoord, 3495
Rutherford, 184, 2015, 5924, 6185
Rutledge, 1385, 1477, 1910, 2441, 2649, 4134, 5706
Rutton, 3943
Ruxton, 3254
Ryan, 1809, 1989, 2575, 2739, 3902, 6427
Ryder, 3580, 3958, 4150
Ryves, 5360
Sadleir, 4367, 6091, 6329
Salley, 60
Sample, 3345
San Adrien, 6007
Sanders, 4747, 4926. *See also* Saunders.
Sanderson, 349, 1974. *See also* Saunderson.
Sandes, 3018

Sandford, 2945
Sands, 3274
Sankey, 4165, 5959
Saul, 2981
Saunders, 643, 4262, 4608, 6043, 6211. *See also* Sanders.
Saunderson, 2205, 2429, 5581. *See also* Sanderson.
Saurin, 963, 1673, 3113, 4429, 5889
Savage, 5380, 6074
Savile, 4541
Scarlett, 310, 1480
Schoales, 772
Scholefield, 4957
Schomberg, 821, 940
Scott, 96, 155, 219, 414, 469, 497, 557, 813, 882, 1078, 1342, 1895, 1937, 1943, 1973, 2306, 2337, 2482, 2645, 2682, 2719, 2728, 2787, 2859, 3464, 3571, 3649, 3848, 3870, 4672, 5255, 5285, 5448, 5861, 6024
Scriven, 1905, 3208
Scudamore, 5658
Scully, 5225
Seafield, 3456
Searight, 517, 586, 1030, 1154, 3341, 6262
Sears, 6412
Seaton, 5810, 6281
Seaver, 347, 370, 449, 1023, 1188, 1212, 1598, 2298, 3930, 4066, 5792, 5955
Seawright, 4830
Sebastiani, 6217
Seed, 2035, 6260
Seers, 934
Sefton, 2642
Seller, 5843
Selss, 4799
Semple, 1449, 3426, 6366
Sergeant, 5256
Sewell, 534, 3737
Seymour, 3328, 3677, 5025
Shankey, 4855, 5105
Shanks, 3940, 6269
Shannon, 673, 2752, 2787, 4201, 6240
Sharkey, 2946, 3491, 3851, 4030, 4274, 4358, 5285, 6078

Sharp, 1924

Sharpe, 1268, 2877, 3862, 4184, 5773

Shaw, 45, 112, 196, 244, 308, 365, 410, 599, 854, 2327, 2871, 3349, 3726, 4208, 4777, 5258, 5401, 5434, 5723, 5739

Sheal, 3150. *See also* Sheals, Sheil, Sheilds, *and* Sheill.

Sheals, 4393

Sheane, 59

Sheckleton, 985. *See also* Shekeleton, *and* Shekleton.

Shee, 4077

Sheehan, 1085

Shegog, 1371, 4862

Sheil, 221, 4158, 4531, 4708, 4764, 4859, 5732, 5987. *See also* Sheal, Sheals, Sheilds, *and* Sheill.

Sheilds, 3669

Sheill, 4198

Shekeleton, 5074. *See also* Shekleton, *and* Sheckleton.

Shekleton, 211, 1273, 5306, 5796

Sheldon, 1148

Shelton, 4501

Shepherd, 6212

Sheppard, 1110, 1773, 2346, 2445, 4676, 6138

Shepphard, 688

Sherard, 2817. *See also* Sherrard.

Sheridan, 1346, 5054, 6012

Sheriff, 348, 4036

Sherrard, 872, 881, 4774, 4905, 5496. *See also* Sherard.

Sherry, 5416

Shiel, 5017, 5536

Shields, 81, 624, 5000, 5125, 5213

Shillington, 282, 1157, 5285, 5463

Shirley, 1049

Shoales, 1381

Shone, 2371

Short, 4428

Shuldham, 46

Shuter, 250

Shuttleworth, 3400

Siddons, 5590

Sidley, 5069, 5395. *See also* Sydney.

Sidney, 3942

Sifton, 6266

Silcock, 1964

Sim, 2586, 4044, 5146, 5219. *See also* Sims, *and* Syms.

Simcock, 4202

Simon, 1888

Simpson, 123, 304, 481, 934, 1162, 1206, 1753, 2120, 2154, 2177, 2632, 2877, 2947, 3302, 3515, 4178, 4192, 4364, 4770, 4773, 5138, 5265. *See also* Simson.

Sims, 284, 3233, 5712. *See also* Sim, *and* Syms.

Simson, 2079. *See also* Simpson.

Sinclair, 56, 629, 681, 825, 1096, 1267, 1497, 1791, 2348, 2821, 3216, 3402, 4382, 4386, 4493, 4520, 4903

Singer, 3581, 5234, 5848

Singleton, 486, 790, 3890, 6448

Sinnamon, 129, 163, 1080, 1094, 1829, 4414, 4698

Sinnott, 2764. *See also* Synnot.

Sinton, 458, 613

Skelton, 514, 2213, 3592

Skene, 6047

Skiffington, 6346

Skipton, 4109

Slacke, 1335, 2111

Slade, 3205, 3220

Slane, 4196

Sleith, 3330

Sligo, 6367

Sloan, 2680, 2681, 2898, 6389

Sloane, 358, 2820, 3352, 4856, 5512, 5630, 5710

Smallon, 6414

Smart, 5682

Smedley, 1860

Smith, 225, 570, 731, 1016, 1225, 1260, 1360, 1400, 1441, 1507, 1509, 1801, 1891, 2025, 2029, 2471, 2501, 2599, 2661, 2690, 3018, 3194, 3281, 3643, 3659, 3956, 4047, 4072, 4489, 4500, 4571, 4572, 4610, 4782, 4869, 4885, 4925, 4955, 5054, 5089, 5309, 5483, 5625, 5704, 5837, 5891, 6027, 6111, 6172, 6183. *See also* Smyth, *and* Smythe.

Smylie, 5927, 6070

Smyly, 3095

Smyrl, 3052

Smyth, 103, 124, 410, 612, 926, 942, 1216, 1238, 1475, 1651, 2134, 2388, 2600, 2713, 2800, 3735, 3877, 3937, 3980, 4071, 4501, 4721, 4814, 4915, 5084, 5259, 5316, 5952, 6037, 6123, 6423, 6439. See also Smith, and Smythe.

Smythe, 1618, 1675, 2403, 2578

Snodgrass, 2039

Snowdon, 212

Soden, 1093

Sodor and Man, 1049

Solomon, 6180

Somers, 492, 6289. See also Summer.

Somerville, 125, 5750

Sotheren, 218

Sothergill, 4930

Sparks, 6302

Sparrow, 2468

Spear, 474, 484, 509, 5965

Speer, 1887, 3260, 3416, 3546

Spence, 334, 340, 347, 4636, 5287

Spencer, 1664

Spinks, 2067

Spotswood, 4109

Spratt, 1644, 5529

Sproule, 1288, 2557, 3444, 3540, 5131, 5188

Srubsole, 615. See also Subsole.

St. Alban's, 3720

St. Clair, 5510

St. Felix, 919

St. George, 126, 778, 1380, 2087, 2395, 2712, 3451, 4084, 4112, 4237, 4274, 4424, 4447, 4832, 5791

St. Leger, 6329

Stack, 309, 356, 384, 1978, 3009, 3579, 3972, 4561, 4562, 5055, 5747, 6305

Stacke, 3763

Stackhouse, 4401

Stackpoole, 6202

Stacpoole, 5046

Stafford, 450, 768, 5627

Standfield, 2451

Stanfield, 2846

Stanley, 43, 55, 76, 199, 426, 443, 513, 594, 706, 880, 958, 1020, 1021, 1428, 1928, 1935, 2658,

Stanley, continued: 3182, 3762, 3792, 4177, 4267, 5285, 5415, 5479, 6252

Stannus, 4984

Stanton, 3402

Staples, 661, 5686, 5768, 5851

Star, 167

Starke, 822

Staunton, 1428

Steed, 4776

Steel, 1471, 3326, 4252, 4539

Steele, 1747, 2749, 4888, 5851, 6265

Steen, 2181, 4991

Steinhelt, 5679

Stephens, 1133, 1886, 2996, 3492, 3518, 4005, 4214, 4253, 4421, 4695, 5822

Stephenson, 1427, 1915, 2317, 2559, 3544, 5598. See also Stevenson.

Stepney, 1931, 2205, 3346

Sterne, 778, 898, 2436, 3562, 5239, 5246, 5352

Stevenson, 1647, 2226, 2317, 2409, 2432, 2773, 2801, 3736, 3751, 3961, 4032, 4115, 5094, 5377, 6199. See also Stephenson.

Stewart, 96, 100, 209, 321, 510, 519, 630, 653, 778, 1025, 1275, 1489, 1635, 1656, 2088, 2374, 2679, 3125, 3194, 3257, 3353, 3376, 3380, 3446, 3612, 3631, 3735, 3745, 4318, 4358, 4387, 4452, 4504, 4527, 4638, 4749, 4802, 5070, 5186, 5262, 5559, 5743, 5842, 5857, 5875, 5985, 5988, 6059, 6103, 6127, 6185. See also Stuart.

Stinson, 297, 655, 970, 1248, 2431

Stirling, 605, 832, 4205

Stitt, 130, 1281, 2824, 2880, 3343, 5392

Stoddart, 2568, 6073. See also Studdert.

Stokes, 1253, 3161, 5718

Stone, 6, 229, 239, 1292, 2309, 2550, 3261, 4285, 4935, 5656

Stoops, 77

Stopford, 2171, 6084

Storey, 1510, 2724, 6339

Story, 215, 2674, 3190, 3647, 4113, 5570, 5795

Stothers, 1938

Stover, 2176

Strachan, 3507, 3570, 3618

Strain, 800, 5586

Straker, 4193

Strandford, 3327

Strangways, 4298

Strawhorne, 4676

Streatfield, 5883

Strickland, 2729

Stringer, 5681

Strong, 2636

Stronge, 1931, 3297, 3670, 4274, 4690, 6449

Stuart, 180, 312, 743, 943, 1017, 1055, 1062, 1082, 1904, 2094, 2162, 3292, 3813, 5091, 5820. *See also* Stewart.

Stubbs, 715, 2262, 3842

Studdert, 187, 2994. *See also* Stoddart.

Sturdy, 1563, 2852

Sturgeon, 2245, 4605

Stutton, 1763

Subsole, 606. *See also* Srubsole.

Suffern, 2922, 2923, 3871

Sugden, 6238

Suirdale, 5038

Sullivan, 283, 4697, 6054, 6242. *See also* O'Sullivan.

Summer, 3054. *See also* Somers.

Sussex, 253, 259, 1496

Sutcliffe, 3798

Sutter, 4205

Swan, 223, 1512, 4657

Swanzy, 299

Sweany, 863

Sweden, 6115

Sweeney, 104, 396, 1384. *See also* M'Sweeny, Sweeny, Swiney, *and* Swiny.

Sweeny, 2574, 3345, 4168

Swinerton, 3048

Swiney, 4093. *See also* M'Sweeny, Sweeney, Sweeny, *and* Swiny.

Swiny, 566

Sydney, 3466. *See also* Sidney.

Syme, 2353, 2848

Symington, 417

Syms, 5086. *See also* Sim, *and* Sims.

Synge, 703

Synnot, 754, 1211, 1833, 1906, 3502, 4868, 5645. *See also* Sinnott.

Taaffe, 3167

Tackaberry, 1134

Tackeray, 923. *See also* Thackeray.

Tagerty, 2704

Taggart, 170

Talbot, 2595, 3906, 4587

Talbot de Malahide, 3906

Tanchell, 5263

Tankerville, 3455

Taplay, 2172

Tassey, 5014

Tate, 664, 3689, 5978

Tavers, 1719

Taylor, 1, 3, 235, 321, 619, 714, 868, 1743, 1757, 1767, 2181, 2211, 2346, 2370, 2459, 2598, 2604, 2632, 2682, 3596, 4433, 4663, 5690, 5918, 6085, 6108, 6340

Tease, 1568

Tecey, 920

Tecy, 1758

Teevan, 1180

Tegg, 580, 581, 6294

Temmins, 1498. *See also* Timmons.

Temple, 25, 5348, 6166

Templeton, 714, 1144

Tener, 5144

Tenison, 25, 1324, 2205, 2739

Teriney, 3681

Tertius, 3672

Thacker, 3493, 5092

Thackeray, 1273. *See also* Tackeray.

Thetford, 2316

Thetfort, 2069

Thistle, 369

Thom, 6242

Thomas, 2103

Thompson, 14, 270, 300, 312, 360, 435, 947, 1024, 1091, 1145, 1307, 1377, 1588, 1844, 1858, 1890, 2003, 2005, 2009, 2163, 2269, 2278, 2314, 2352, 2630, 2633, 2687, 2688, 2718, 2759, 2861, 2862, 3034, 3098, 3173, 3197, 3212, 3263, 3327, 3364, 3460, 3594, 3634, 3639, 3641, 3727, 3817, 3844, 3877, 4028, 4247, 4295, 4350, 4368, 4448, 4551, 4564, 4638, 4650, 4823, 4892, 4897, 4915, 4927, 4938, 5177, 5178, 5328, 5352, 5450, 5507, 5541, 5594, 5626, 5778, 5782, 5805, 5855, 5879, 5905, 5934, 5951, 6000, 6193, 6317, 6368

Thomson, 1243, 1543, 2291, 2608, 3042, 3478, 4300, 4460, 5689, 6123, 6210

Thormond, 3655

Thornberry, 4491

Thornley, 717, 2139, 3033, 3129

Thornly, 3741

Thornton, 878, 3458, 4274, 4363

Thorp, 86

Thursby, 5817

Tickell, 4274

Tidy, 1306

Timmerman, 2326

Timmons, 5317. *See also* Temmins.

Tippett, 5707

Tipping, 2941, 4278, 4308, 4343, 5289

Tisdale, 5237

Tisdall, 3728, 5582

Tisdan, 2915

Titterington, 2451

Toan, 645

Tobias, 210, 5588

Todd, 370, 1164, 1545, 2194, 2495, 2865, 2883, 3449, 3703, 3923, 3932, 3976, 4761, 5176, 5913, 6028, 6058, 6144

Toel, 6376

Tomney, 1035

Tone, 2566

Toner, 6229

Toole, 2304. *See also* O'Tool, *and* O'Toole.

Torrens, 840, 4806, 5081, 6216

Totten, 2553, 5798, 6038

Tottenham, 688, 1265, 3370, 4417, 4573, 4603, 5013, 5030, 5091, 5748

Tower, 2179

Towesland, 2837

Townley, 923

Townsend, 125, 6084, 6304

Toye, 4777

Tracy, 3687, 3851, 5833, 6227

Trail, 1698

Travers, 3075, 4286

Traynor, 2394

Treacy, 5879

Treanor, 5982

Tredennick, 5292, 5302

Trenar, 2617

Trench, 438, 5141

Trimble, 269, 604, 1361, 2132, 2156, 3731, 4068

Tronson, 829, 1112, 1174

Trotter, 988, 1939, 2893, 5166

Troup, 108

Troy, 452, 453, 4274, 5457

Trumble, 4923

Tuam, 704, 1625, 2443, 3454, 5815

Tucker, 5040, 5313

Tuft, 3626, 4969, 6094

Tupper, 27

Turle, 101

Turner, 98, 541, 732, 777, 920, 1116, 2563, 2737, 2829, 3024, 3847, 5496, 5914, 6236

Turney, 4980

Turnly, 4172

Turtle, 1827

Tuthill, 118, 178, 221, 1845, 3802, 6225

Tutthill, 353, 354

Twible, 891

Twigg, 982, 1657, 2061, 5713

Twinam, 1601

Twiss, 2592

Tydd, 2524, 3092

Tyke, 1383, 1407

Tyrconnell, 2066

Uprichard, 3342

Ure, 6097

Urwick, 45, 3678, 4739, 5968

Usher, 1896, 2125, 5917

Ussher, 415, 1429, 4901, 5066

Vallely, 160, 966, 3611

Vance, 603, 1633, 4132

Vauce, 1610

Vaughan, 829, 1018, 1112, 2951

Vercker, 3998. *See also* Vereker.

Verdon, 2585

Vereker, 5845. *See also* Vercker.

Verner, 499, 602, 1191, 1548, 2127, 2179, 3014, 3827, 4596

Vernon, 111, 1368, 2972, 3079

Verschoyle, 480, 1433, 1906, 2329, 2549, 4088

Verulam, 1318, 5602

Chapter 3: Index of Surnames

Vesey, 1552, 1962
Vessey, 758
Victor, 855
Victoria, 5768
Vignoles, 3974
Vigors, 5737
Villiers, 3557
Vincent, 5832
Vint, 1246, 1702, 2786
Vogan, 169, 2028, 6203
Waddel, 1187
Waddell, 294, 1348, 2664, 5785
Waddle, 856
Waddrington, 4381
Waddy, 2671
Wade, 520, 1403, 1415, 1543, 1554, 1597, 1672, 1783, 1802, 2390, 2779, 3012, 3067, 3112, 3851, 3914, 3928, 4274, 4410, 4491, 4783, 5095, 5285, 5357, 5526, 5594, 5666, 5816, 6133, 6178, 6275, 6414
Wadsworth, 2432
Waldron, 4295, 5440, 6099
Wale, 1952, 3305
Wales, 3978
Walker, 1, 3, 228, 231, 537, 711, 726, 784, 1071, 1120, 1362, 1672, 1691, 2091, 2695, 3019, 3033, 3258, 3663, 3856, 3905, 4029, 4206, 4443, 4951, 5161, 5359, 5929
Walkingshaw, 3239
Walkington, 5731
Wall, 3201, 4868, 5063
Wallace, 13, 808, 824, 870, 886, 2002, 2147, 2577, 2689, 2832, 3159, 3326, 3387, 3585, 3782, 4130, 4494, 4702, 4720, 4749, 5101, 5202, 5264, 5533, 5659, 6162
Wallen, 3470
Waller, 5932
Walmisley, 6364
Walpole, 2915
Walsh, 1420, 1427, 1467, 2408, 2892, 3424, 4005, 4433, 4844, 5604, 6336
Walshe, 1520
Walter, 5981
Walton, 3236
Wann, 1670, 2463, 3401, 3746, 4117, 4799, 5045

Ward, 427, 798, 1344, 2010, 2023, 2027, 4093, 5076
Wardlaw, 1810
Wardwell, 1923
Waring, 766, 883, 3307, 3691, 4122
Warnell, 4976
Warner, 4619
Warnock, 13, 207, 3610, 4569, 4774
Warrell, 1603
Warren, 1113, 1261, 1771, 2775, 4949
Warring, 1116
Wason, 1632
Waterford, 3044, 5997
Waters, 831, 4985. *See also* M'Waters, M'Watters, *and* Watters.
Watkins, 3873, 4956, 5685, 6099
Watson, 347, 688, 1406, 1839, 1885, 1977, 1978, 2353, 2611, 3572, 3620, 3874, 4341, 4646, 6081
Watt, 1859, 2001, 2350, 3815, 5400, 6102
Watters, 4770. *See also* M'Waters, M'Watters, *and* Waters.
Watts, 3431, 4768, 5321, 6165
Wattson, 1973
Wauchob, 843, 2780
Waugh, 41, 950, 3016, 3076, 3182, 5085
Wauhop, 4293
Wearing, 1699
Webber, 3818
Webster, 35, 903, 1310, 4524, 5147, 5682, 6182
Weir, 456, 790, 980, 2377, 3036, 4033, 5764
Welch, 134
Weld, 31, 6053
Weldon, 4559
Wellington, 4105, 6292, 6310
Wells, 814
Welsh, 11, 255, 493, 947, 1166, 1358, 1877, 2159, 3281, 4030, 4072, 4433, 4598, 5117
Wemys, 842
Wentworth, 5860
Wesley, 210, 894, 2498, 2713, 2720, 5007, 5100
West, 263, 2272, 2405, 3191, 3305, 3770, 3955, 4257, 4651, 4715, 4950, 5401, 5856
Westenra, 1183, 1766, 3966, 4540, 5214, 6424
Westlake, 3506

Westmeath, 5023, 5783
Westminster, 5981
Westwater, 6314
Whateley, 2857
Whately, 5976
Whealan, 6443. See also Whelan.
Wheeler, 946, 4231
Whelan, 4455. See also Whealan.
Whitaker, 3912. See also Whittaker.
White, 71, 99, 107, 123, 305, 319, 392, 393, 455, 485, 525, 705, 719, 788, 873, 1189, 1263, 1474, 1568, 1828, 2131, 2974, 3234, 3259, 3454, 3560, 3609, 3664, 3696, 3722, 3787, 3873, 4362, 4570, 4607, 5008, 5476, 6030, 6276. See also Whyte.
Whitehead, 1978
Whitel, 4953
Whiteside, 612, 5056
Whitestone, 884, 1059, 1150, 1198, 3347, 4165
Whitla, 233
Whitley, 1197, 4993
Whitsitt, 1954
Whittaker, 176, 592, 1027, 1285, 1808, 1936, 2146, 2845, 3543, 4374, 5375. See also Whitaker.
Whittington, 1979
Whyte, 3445. See also White.
Wiggins, 1403, 1415
Wighton, 806
Wiglesworth, 5733
Wigney, 4573
Wilcocks, 4056. See also Willcocks.
Wiles, 6188
Wiley, 1264, 1642, 2635
Wilford, 82, 6124
Wilkin, 558, 2335, 4415
Wilkins, 238
Wilkinson, 2917, 4091, 5516
Wilkison, 3436
Willcocks, 5705. See also Wilcocks.
Willey, 1366. See also Wylie, Wyllie, and Wylly.
Williams, 504, 517, 538, 586, 643, 1621, 1732, 1902, 1935, 2351, 2730, 2948, 3106, 3358, 3423, 3530, 3583, 3929, 4189, 4613, 4728, 4983, 5273, 5473, 5674, 5880, 6358. See also M'William, and M'Williams.

Williamson, 807, 981, 1708, 2548, 4865, 4969, 5242, 5798, 5843, 6094
Willis, 339, 397, 2183, 2277, 2670, 3186, 3316, 3828, 4709
Willoughby, 2394, 4568
Willshire, 2725
Wilson, 19, 34, 61, 133, 143, 162, 165, 196, 253, 259, 385, 441, 456, 673, 702, 715, 745, 766, 809, 872, 881, 883, 932, 987, 1058, 1148, 1149, 1359, 1417, 1427, 1455, 1475, 1496, 1519, 1534, 1555, 1591, 1595, 1966, 1974, 1975, 1980, 2077, 2088, 2095, 2108, 2112, 2176, 2328, 2355, 2371, 2464, 2588, 2608, 2639, 2747, 2847, 2882, 2955, 3074, 3125, 3159, 3184, 3192, 3233, 3244, 3260, 3329, 3374, 3403, 3445, 3491, 3658, 3710, 3832, 3882, 3979, 4156, 4194, 4330, 4357, 4380, 4440, 4492, 4599, 4613, 4637, 4676, 4773, 4875, 5087, 5203, 5230, 5298, 5376, 5826, 6056, 6067, 6394, 6414
Wilton, 2910, 3985
Wiltshire, 3392, 4355
Winchelsea and Nottingham, 3160
Winchester, 3054
Wingfield, 2127
Winning, 1344, 2237
Winslow, 222, 810, 1310
Winter, 3676
Wintoun, 6281
Wisely, 1530
Withers, 184
Wolesworth, 3344
Wolf, 2109
Wolfe, 5768
Wolfenden, 5143
Wolff, 1499
Wolseley, 900, 1473, 2991. See also Wolsley, Woolsely, Woolsey, and Woolsey.
Wolsley, 964, 984, 1985, 4133, 4728
Wood, 850, 1176, 2084, 2647, 3312, 4226, 4915, 5224, 6270. See also Woods.
Woodhouse, 283, 399, 487, 1121, 2044, 2264, 2439, 3165, 3793, 4485, 4490, 4839, 6264
Woodley, 1892
Woodright, 2208. See also Woodwright.
Woodroffe, 3452
Woods, 2610, 3744, 4497, 4649, 5327, 5410, 5853, 6040, 6388. See also Wood.

Chapter 3: Index of Surnames

Woodside, 4570

Woodwright, 1479, 2208. *See also* Woodright.

Woolsely, 2948. *See also* Wolseley, Wolsley, Woolsey, *and* Woolsley.

Woolsey, 758, 3517, 4266

Woolsley, 6441

Workman, 578, 1011, 2037

Worlingham, 2468

Worrall, 5966

Wray, 280, 1118, 1652, 3092, 3422, 6258

Wright, 25, 95, 496, 1685, 1723, 1938, 2241, 3191, 3395, 3629, 3828, 3838, 4324, 4378, 4384, 4486, 4528, 4701, 5529, 5886, 6038, 6040, 6391

Wrightson, 162, 612, 759, 1688, 1972, 2677, 3344, 5116, 5458

Writeson, 461

Wrixon, 1684, 3846

Wylie, 2831, 3014, 3648, 3775. *See also* Willey, Wyllie, *and* Wylly.

Wyllie, 614

Wylly, 4809

Wynne, 10, 1436, 1452, 1480, 1806, 2790, 3346, 4065, 4576, 5072, 5148

Wyon, 5170

Wyse, 4887, 5811

Yates, 1455

Yeats, 1728, 5572

Yeoman, 5058

York, 778, 807, 6310

Young, 47, 65, 747, 829, 1303, 1418, 1721, 1953, 2085, 2364, 2892, 3155, 3191, 3562, 3671, 3692, 3715, 4434, 4577, 4736, 4859, 4962, 4967, 5236, 5399, 5461, 5515, 5529, 5787, 6176, 6177, 6184, 6437

Yule, 1621

4. INDEX OF PLACE NAMES

Country and County not named:
Biddasoa: 4213
Bloomfield: 3236
Busaco: 4213
Cazal Nova: 3484
Coa: 4213
Douglass: 2713
Ervatris, parish of: 3809
Everton: 1370
Ferry: 204
Foz d'azouce: 4213
Fuentes d'Onor: 4213
Grange, The: 6221
Jenet's-pass: 6384
Kingston; Scots Church: 5708
Lesaco Bridge: 4213
Mizanda de corvo: 4213
Newcastle: 1507
Norwood; Thenwood-cottage [Surrey?]: 1764
Oporto: 6244
Pombal: 4213
Redina: 4213
Rodrigo: 4213
St. Anne's Church: 5796
St. George's Church: 2785
St. Nicholas's Church: 713
Trawmese: 3899
Vittoria: 4213

Africa:
Country or city not named: 927, 1942, 3478
Calahar: 1817

America: *See* U.S.A.
Antigua: 3677, 3752
Arctic: 3252
At Sea: 546, 915, 1196, 1817, 2753, 2849, 3081, 3120, 3465, 3790, 3917, 4119, 4175, 4629, 4809, 5106, 5339, 6028, 6119
Australasia: 3466

Australia:
Morpeth: 6278
Poekataroo: 5781
Victoria; Melbourne: 5750, 5756, 5788
Australia, diocese of: 1429
Australia *var.* New South Wales; Port Philip: 3290
Australia: *See also* N.S. Wales, New South Wales, *and* South Australia: 5184

Austria:
Silesia; Bohmischdorf: 1045
Vienna: 3906

Batavia; Benjoemas: 5958

Belgium:
Antwerp: 3959
Brussels: 3690, 4910, 5208, 6290
Liege: 6170
Malines: 3959
Ostend: 5133
Waterloo: 1862, 2796, 4213, 5309, 6292

Bermuda: 546

Brazil; Buenos Ayres *var.* Buenos Aires: 4665

British Guyana; Demerara; Georgetown: 5925

Canada: 27, 1382, 2468. *See also* Canada East, Canada West, and Canadian Provinces.

Canada East:
Town or city not named: 1204, 2806, 2849, 3120
Hemmingford: 609
Montréal: 249, 1414, 2037, 2920, 3106, 3818, 4735, 5164, 5683, 6306
Montréal; Berthier: 5683
Québec: 608, 4044, 4849, 5768
Québec; Saint Clare: 5268
Québec; St. Peter's Church: 4849
Standstead-plain: 131

Canada West:
Albion; Sandhill: 4034
Barrie: 1204
Bathurst District; Lanark: 3961
Beechmount: 3952
Bytown *var.* Ottawa: 3866
Cavanville: 27
Churchville: 4597
Coburg; Moira Cottage: 27
Colborne District: 1346
Dundas: 5156
Etobicoke: 369
Gore District; Capefield: 2125
Grand River: 6112
Haldimand County; Caynga [Cayuga?]: 6113
Hamilton: 3522, 4174

The Armagh Guardian, 1844–1852 (Vol. I.) Births, Marriages, and Deaths

Canada West, continued:
Home District: 568
Kingston: 933, 4270
London: 3716
Niagara: 213, 770, 4574, 5246
Niagara; Stamford: 213
Ottamby: 244
Ottawa: 3866
Peterboro' *var.* Peterborough: 797, 818, 1346, 6361
Petersburgh [*var.* Peterborough?]: 797
Port Robinson: 2139
St. Clair: 1443
St. Thomas's *var.* St. Thomas: 3831
Sydenham; Brooklands: 4228
Thorald: 5337
Toronto: 228, 369, 568, 695, 1467, 2073, 2229, 2248, 2571, 3780, 4960, 6452
Trafalgar: 3855
York: 6112
See also Upper Canada.

Canadian Provinces: 1060

Cape of Good Hope:
Town or city not named: 3998, 4363, 5322
Stellingsbosch *var.* Stellenbosch: 5960

Ceylon; Galle; Badagamo Church: 1973

China:
Town or city not named: 179, 6242.
Amoy: 6242
Foo-chou-foo: 4763
Shanghae *var.* Shanghai: 2753
Shanghai: 2753
See also Hong Kong.

Cuba: 4044
Denmark; Copenhagen: 6335

East Indies *var.* India:
Town or city not named: 4257
Agra: 4760
Decca: 2372
Hyderabad: 1460
Kamptee: 5089
Mooltan: 2317
Salem: 1592
Simla: 4468
See also India.

Egypt: 6310

England:
Town or city not named: 618, 1045, 3026, 3026, 5974
Askern: 6129
Axminster: 3268
Aylesbury: 4351
Barnes, near London: 2851
Barnstaple: 5249
Barton-under-Needwood: 3565
Bath: 323, 948, 1106, 1129, 1287, 1377, 1493, 1915, 2079, 2582, 2662, 2947, 3058, 3104, 3264, 3588, 3813, 4381, 6133, 6194
Bath; Bathwick; St. Mary's Church: 3264
Bath; Portland Chapel: 2582
Bath; Walcot: 4381
Bath; Walcut *var.* Walcot: 2582
Baydon: 6372
Beachy Head: 6119
Bedale: 4185
Bedfordshire; Cockayne Hatley: 5883
Bedfordshire; Silso: 682
Bedfordshire; Southill: 3116
Beighton: 2612
Bentley: 2537
Berks *var.* Berkshire; Hungford: 3073
Berkshire; Hungford: 3073
Berkshire; Mersenden: 1658
Berkshire; Runnymede: 5795
Birkenhead: 459, 3086, 3482, 3488, 3615, 4361, 5483
Birkenhead; Parkfield: 3488
Birmingham: 903, 2614, 5522
Birmingham; Beech's Railway Hotel: 2614
Bishopwearmouth: 5980
Bockin: 3642
Bolton: 2543
Bridgewater: 1356, 3843
Bridgewater; Barford House: 1356, 3843
Bridlington: 3045
Brighton: 424, 2791, 4077, 4213, 4573, 5170, 5837, 6001
Brighton; Richmond-villa: 5837
Brighton [Beighton?]: 2612
Bristol: 778, 898, 1967, 3682, 4023, 4365, 5239, 5607
Bristol; Ashley Court: 5607
Bristol; Montpellier; St. Andrew's Church: 5607
Bromptom *var.* Brompton; Michael's Grove: 4259
Brompton; Michael's Grove: 4259
Brompton Church: 5813

Chapter 4: Index of Place Names

England, continued:
Buckinghamshire; Grove: 3147
Buckinghamshire; Richings Park: 4355
Bucks *var.* Buckinghamshire; Grove: 3147
Bucks *var.* Buckinghamshire; Richings Park: 4355
Bury St. Edmund's; Farnham Hall: 799
Byfield House, Barnes, near London: 2851
Calton: 6310
Cambridge: 2801, 2829, 3682, 6152, 6313, 6397
Cambridge; Trinity College: 2801
Cambridgeshire; Shelford: 1952
Cambridgeshire; Weaken Hall: 3607
Carlisle: 5985
Charlton, near Dover: 6209
Chatham: 1315, 2727, 4022
Chatham; St. John's Church: 2727
Chelsea: 1978
Cheltenham: 1226, 2561, 2604, 4328, 4368, 4573, 4779, 4847, 4847, 4957, 4957, 5236, 5953, 5997
Cheltenham; St. Mary's Church: 4573, 5953
Cheltenham; St. Paul's Church: 4328
Chertsey; Ashford House: 2725
Cheshire; Chester: 1870
Cheshire; Gore Hall: 2150
Cheshire; Hollywood: 132
Cheshire; Mobberley: 1965
Cheshire; Norley Hall: 2264, 4485
Cheshire; Norton Priory: 6221
Cheshire; Roslin Villa: 3899
Cheshire; Rudy: 4900
Chester; North Gate-street House: 1920
Chesterfield: 5147
Chichester: 5705
Circencester: 5961
Clifton: 1967, 4918, 4946, 6364
Conisborough: 5685
Conisbrough *var.* Conisborough: 5685
Cornwall: 4274
Cornwall; Fowey: 717
Cornwall; Padztow Church: 1383, 1407
Crewe: 2103, 6318
Cumberland; Camerton Church, St. Helens, Maryport: 2135
Cumberland; Lonninghead: 3621
Cumberland; Maryport: 2135
Cumberland; St. Helens, Maryport: 2135
Darenth: 5954
Dart Court: 3160

Deddington: 5090
Derby: 6003
Derbyshire; Calwish Calwich Abbey: 2390
Derbyshire; Denby: 1089
Devenport *var.* Devonport: 3281
Devonport: 1596, 3281, 4072, 5624
Devonport; Stoke Church: 5624
Devonshire; Arlington-court: 5341
Devonshire; Ham: 5253
Devonshire; Hathersage Church: 3400
Devonshire; Hathersage Hall: 3400
Devonshire; Kingsbridge: 892
Devonshire; Newport: 698
Devonshire; Pilton House: 3445
Devonshire; Ringrove House, near Kingsbridge: 892
Devonshire; Swimbridge: 698
Devonshire; Torquay: 1967, 6109
Devonshire; Trehill: 4104
Devonshire; Wembury: 3796
Devonshire: *See also* North Devon.
Doncaster: 6173
Dorset; Lulworth Castle: 31
Dorset; Weymouth: 3983
Dorset; Wyke Regis, near Weymouth: 3983
Dorsetshire; Shroton House: 5360
Dover: 3160, 4203, 4400, 5768, 5784, 6209
Dover; St. James's Church: 4203, 4400
Dulwich: 1860, 6072
Dulwich; Woodhouse: 6072
Durdham Down; Grove House: 4999
Durham: 2168
Durham; Carr House, Stranton, West Hartlepool: 1824
Durham; Gateshead: 1387
Durham; Hartlepool: 903
Durham; St. Hilda's Catholic Church, Hartlepool: 903
Durham; Stranton, West Hartlepool: 1824
Durham; West Hartlepool: 1824
Edgbaston: 5810, 6180
Elympton: 5090
Essex; Belcamp, St. Paul's: 5492
Essex; Foxearth, parish of: 2582
Essex; Leyton: 6152
Essex; Michaelstown Hall: 1722, 1880
Essex; Mountnessing Church: 6438
Essex; Shenfield-place: 2179
Essex; Southend: 4971
Essex; St. Paul's: 5492
Essex; Stratford-green: 3920

England, continued:
Essex; Terling: 3398
Farnham Castle: 3054
Forquay *var.* Torquay: 143
Friary, Newark: 4847
Fryern Barnet; St. James's Church: 1387
Gateacre: 2279
Gloucester, county of, *var.* Gloucestershire; Wotton-under-Edge: 1476
Gloucestershire; Greet, near Winchcombe: 5153
Gloucestershire; Stratford House, Stroud: 6107
Gloucestershire; Stroud: 6107
Gloucestershire; Tockington: 576
Gloucestershire; Winchcombe: 5153
Gloucestershire; Wotton-under-Edge: 1476
Gosport: 6067
Gravesend: 579
Great Yarmouth: 5976
Greenwich: 689, 1678, 1678, 5071, 5799
Grimsby: 1685
Halifax Church: 1173
Ham Green: 3385
Hampshire; Andover: 5972
Hampshire; Ashe: 5846
Hampshire; Batramsley Lodge, Lymington: 5803
Hampshire; Ewshot-house: 5846
Hampshire; Hale Park: 4203
Hampshire; Lymington: 5803
Hampshire; Merchistoun-hall: 256
Hampshire; Portsea: 2125
Hampshire; Ramridge Cottage, Andover: 5972
Hampshire; Wymering: 256
Hampstead: 6212
Hants *var.* Hampshire, for which see Hampshire.
Harrow-on-the-hill; Byron House: 2951
Haslar Hospital, Gosport: 6067
Hastings: 3053, 3150, 6285
Healing: 1685
Heddon-on-the-Wall: 5264
Henley-on-Thames; South-hill: 5881
Hereford: 6055
Herefordshire; Kent-church-court: 5658
Hertfordshire; Bushey: 5891
Heslington, near York: 6129
Highwood Writtle; Parsonage: 2668
Hornsey Church: 5642
Hounslow: 6152
Hove; Seafield-lodge: 660

Huddersfield: 4900, 5056
Hull: 804, 1853, 2075
Huyton: 6302
Ipswich: 5675
Isle of Ely; Surton: 617
Isle of Wight: 117, 1085, 1491, 2779, 5491, 5963
Isle of Wight; Parkhurst: 5491, 5963
Isle of Wight; Ryde; Trinity Church: 2779
Isle of Wight; St. Laurence, parish of: 117
Isle of Wight; Shanklen: 1085
Isle of Wight; Ventnor; St. Anne's Cottage: 1491
Kent; Eltham: 6195
Kent; Goodmersham: 3160
Kent; Greenhithe: 6203
Kent; Hawley-house: 6211
Kent; Lewisham: 5590
Kent; Somerhill: 1958
Kent; Swanscombe: 5954
Kent; Tonbridge-wells *var.* Tunbridge Wells: 3073
Kent; Woolwich: 4033, 4431, 4645, 5777, 5901, 6124
Kentish Town; St. Alben's Villas: 5805
Keswick; Groswaith Church: 3374
Keswick; Hadds-house: 3374
Kewstoke, near Weston-super-Mare: 4261
Keynsham, near Bath: 1915
Kilburn House, near London: 4610
Kimbolton Castle: 3455
Kingston: 4446
Knightsbridge; St. Paul's Church: 2829
Lancashire; Accrington House: 3565
Lancashire; Blackburn Church: 5884
Lancashire; Burnley: 6378
Lancashire; Everton: 2783
Lancashire; Leagram Hall, near Preston: 31
Lancashire; Preston: 31, 6426
Lancashire; Worsley: 5440
Lancaster: 2670, 2801
Lancaster; St. Thomas's Church: 2801
Leamington: 617
Leamington Hastings, near Southam: 5817
Leeds: 1173, 1607, 1781, 1853, 2544, 5434, 6042, 6091
Leeds; Mansten *var.* Manston Parsonage: 2544
Leeds; Manston Parsonage: 1607
Leicester; Humstone: 3672
Leicestershire; Ansty Church: 1409
Leicestershire; Charley hall: 1409

Chapter 4: Index of Place Names

England, continued:
Leicestershire; Roecliffe: 4971
Lillies: 4351
Lincoln's-inn: 3104
Lincolnshire; Holbeach: 1465
Lincolnshire; Thonock Hall: 5567
Liverpool: 28, 123, 131, 226, 348, 409, 409, 506, 506, 754, 952, 1049, 1174, 1416, 1576, 1657, 1680, 2279, 2336, 2370, 2805, 3103, 3215, 3249, 3471, 3482, 3832, 3894, 4036, 4092, 4133, 4280, 4287, 4362, 4393, 4393, 4462, 4530, 4654, 4654, 5162, 5322, 5547, 5754, 5917, 6141, 6268, 6302, 6309, 6397
Liverpool; Abercomby-square: 754
Liverpool; Birkenhead: 1416
Liverpool; Foxleth Park [Toxteth Park?]: 1680
Liverpool; Kirkdale: 5917
Liverpool; Rock Ferry: 4287
Liverpool; St. Augustine's Church: 6268
Liverpool; St. George's Presbyterian Church: 6309
Liverpool; St. John's Church: 131, 4133
Liverpool; St. Peter's Church: 4092
Liverpool; St. Philip's Church: 4280
Liverpool; St. Stephen's Church: 6141
Liverpool; St. Thomas's Church: 1680
Liverpool; Wesleyan Chapel: 409
London: 5, 16, 78, 154, 215, 318, 333, 368, 580, 581, 602, 658, 660, 682, 692, 757, 801, 823, 835, 944, 1019, 1062, 1071, 1130, 1182, 1211, 1235, 1293, 1301, 1303, 1412, 1441, 1504, 1548, 1566, 1567, 1707, 1722, 1754, 1761, 1792, 1818, 1833, 1880, 2003, 2046, 2064, 2147, 2161, 2179, 2312, 2326, 2342, 2387, 2491, 2528, 2537, 2614, 2747, 2804, 2810, 2829, 2851, 2876, 2890, 2951, 2991, 3056, 3068, 3121, 3154, 3223, 3229, 3240, 3246, 3348, 3370, 3412, 3415, 3454, 3467, 3485, 3495, 3502, 3534, 3551, 3557, 3566, 3642, 3679, 3720, 3807, 3818, 3827, 3869, 3881, 3922, 3980, 4104, 4105, 4345, 4426, 4431, 4464, 4501, 4507, 4566, 4592, 4610, 4625, 4692, 4716, 4780, 4811, 4827, 4828, 4859, 4879, 4954, 4957, 4966, 4988, 4994, 5011, 5062, 5174, 5205, 5224, 5232, 5254, 5261, 5305, 5325, 5327, 5341, 5392, 5450, 5482, 5602, 5686, 5689, 5701, 5726, 5728, 5737, 5776, 5795, 5810, 5813, 5828, 5846, 5854, 5892, 5959, 5981, 5983, 5992, 6017, 6024, 6063, 6079, 6086, 6119, 6139, 6167, 6186, 6205, 6236, 6254, 6256, 6287, 6294,

London, continued: 6296, 6308, 6316, 6360, 6371, 6382, 6390, 6399, 6438, 6446, 6449
London; All Souls' Church, Langham Place: 2876
London; Battersea: 2732
London; Bayswater: 5892
London; Bedford-square: 2747, 2991
London; Belgrave-square: 1211
London; Berkeley-square: 1062, 4692
London; Bloomsbury: 3557
London; Bryanston-square: 3642
London; Bryanstone-square: 4879, 5846
London; Cadogan Place: 1833, 1548
London; Camden Town: 4966, 6017
London; Carlton-terrace: 2342
London; Carpenter's-hall: 5992
London; Cavendish-square: 16
London; Cheapside: 580, 581, 6294
London; Chelsea: 5392, 6449
London; Chesham-place: 3229
London; Chester-square: 6316
London; Chesterfield House: 2491, 4426
London; Clapham: 3502
London; Curzon-street Chapel: 5846
London; Dalston: 5776
London; Devonshire-place: 682
London; Doctors' Commons: 6382
London; Eaton-square: 1182, 4811, 5341, 5728, 5981
London; Fitzroy-square: 333
London; Governnesses' Home: 6186
London; Grove Cottage: 1293
London; Hammersmith: 6063
London; Hanover-square: 660, 1707, 2326, 2804, 2991, 4913, 5254, 5737
London; Hyde Park: 2829, 4625
London; Hydepark-gate: 660
London; Hydepark-square: 1722, 1880
London; Islington: 4780, 4994
London; Kensington: 6256
London; Kew: 5828
London; Knightsbridge: 5854
London; Langham Place: 2876, 3827
London; Lowndes-square: 3246, 4345, 4827
London; Manchester-square: 2951
London; Montague-square: 3869
London; Nelson lodge, Chelsea: 6449
London; Paddington: 5795
London; Pall Mall: 3818
London; Piccadilly: 4105
London; Pimlico: 2179, 3412

347

England, continued:
London; Portman-square: 835
London; Putney-park: 6390
London; Regent's Park: 3223, 3534, 3557
London; Roman Catholic Chapel: 5813
London; Royal Mews, Pimlico: 3412
London; Russell-square: 4988
London; Soho-square: 1567
London; South Hackney: 6079
London; St. Benet's: 4507
London; St. George's Church, Bloomsbury: 3557
London; St. George's Church, Hanover-square: 660, 1707, 2804, 2991, 4913, 5254, 5737
London; St. James's: 1754
London; St. James's Chapel: 5232
London; St. James's Church: 944, 5261
London; St. James's Church, Paddington: 5795
London; St. James's Church, Westminster: 4957
London; St. James's-square: 1019, 1792, 3068, 5011
London; St. John's Church, Wapping: 5892
London; St. John's Wood: 2046, 3467
London; St. Martin's Church: 3240
London; St. Martin's-in-the-Fields: 6086
London; St. Marylebone Church: 3827
London; St. Mary's Church, Battersea: 2732
London; St. Mary's Church, Bryanston-square: 3642, 5846
London; St. Pancras *var.* St. Pancras' Church: 1818, 3454
London; St. Paul's Church: 757
London; St. Paul's Church, Knightsbridge: 5854
London; St. Peter's Church: 6308
London; St. Peter's Church, Eaton-square: 5981
London; St. Peter's Church, Pimlico: 2179
London; St. Stephen's: 4507, 5325
London; Strand: 1235, 5828
London; Tabernacle: 4431
London; Tavistock-place: 1818
London; Upper Chelsea: 1441
London; Upper Clapton: 6167
London; Wapping: 5892
London; Westminster: 78, 4957
London; Whitehall: 6287
London, Diocese of: 5846
London-bridge: 5118
Lullworth: 6315

Manchester: 97, 490, 1322, 1953, 2103, 2351, 2351, 2425, 2581, 2612, 3801, 3877, 3975, 4068, 4738, 5040, 5068, 5146, 5219, 6041, 6066, 6220
Manchester; Ducie Chapel: 2612
Manchester; Eccles: 3877
Manchester; Richmond Hill: 1322
Manchester; Salford: 6066
Manchester; St. John's Church: 2581
Manchester; St. Mary's Church: 6041
Manchester Cathedral: 1455
Margaret Roding: 6212
Marleborough: 6372
Middlesborough-on-Tees: 4323
Middlesex; Chelsea: 2824
Middlesex; Darley-house, Sunbury: 6106
Middlesex; Ealing: 6237
Middlesex; Finchley: 6209
Middlesex; Heston: 5880
Middlesex; Sunbury: 6106
Middlesex; Twyford Abbey: 1879
Milton, near Gravesend: 579
Mortlake; Ladon-house: 4354
Muckinge: 6211
Newark: 4847
Newcastle: 194
Newcastle-on-Tyne *var.* Newcastle-upon-Tyne: 198, 712, 2513, 4193, 5531, 6255, 6321
Newcastle-upon-Tyne; Clavering-place Congregation: 6255
Newcastle-upon-Tyne; Priory: 6321
Newcastle-upon-Tyne; Walker Cottage: 5531
Newton-on-Trent: 5378, 5389
Nicholson House: 5980
Norfolk; Feltwell Church: 3607
Norfolk; Hargham-hall: 4400
Norfolk; Harpley: 5140
Norfolk; Hockwood Hall: 617
Norfolk; Manor House, Feltwell: 3607
Norfolk; Raveningham Hall: 2809, 5567
Norfolk; Stanfield-hall: 4400
Norfolk; Summerfield: 5140
Norfolk; Wallington Hall: 4060
North Devon; Bideford: 1860. *See also* Devonshire.
Northampton: 451
Northamptonshire; Oundle: 384
Northamptonshire; Welgrave: 1148
Northamptonshire; Winford: 1973
Northumberland; Meldonpark: 5883
Northumberland; Westwood Hall: 5232

Chapter 4: Index of Place Names

England, continued:
Norton: 3973, 4986
Norton, near Askern; Wesleyan Chapel: 6129
Norwich: 4167
Norwich; St. James's Church: 4167
Nottinghamshire; Southwell: 498
Notts *var.* Nottinghamshire; Southwell: 498
Oxford: 581, 1049, 4143, 4957, 5892, 6372, 6410
Oxfordshire; Entham-hall: 3633
Oxfordshire; Garsington: 4143
Oxfordshire; Hensington House: 3503
Oxfordshire; Woodeaton: 1318
Oxon. *var.* Oxfordshire; Garsington: 4143
Oxon. *var.* Oxfordshire; Kirtlington: 2829
Oxon. *var.* Oxfordshire; Trinity College, University of Oxford: 4143
Paignton: 6201
Plumstead Church: 391
Plymouth: 3299, 4751, 5031, 5253, 5931, 5961, 6071
Plymouth; Royal Navy Hospital, Stone-house: 5031
Plymouth; St. Andrew's Church: 5253
Poole: 4099
Portsea: 1626, 5013
Portsmouth: 2101, 2194, 3152, 3324, 5013
Portsmouth; Anglesey Barracks: 3324
Portsmouth; Great Salterns: 5013
Portsmouth; Southsea: 3152
Preston: 4089
Ramsgate: 3147, 4444, 6063
Reading: 6019
Redcar: 6091
Richmond Hill: 3942
Rochdale: 6281
Scarborough; St. Mary's Church: 5056
Selby: 5259
Sheffield: 6128, 6173
Sheffield; Bradfield Church: 2010
Shropshire: 6357
Shropshire; Ludlow: 4596
Shropshire; Market-drayton: 1957
Shropshire; Marlow Lodge, near Ludlow: 4596
Shropshire; Pradoe, The: 5190
Shropshire; Wenlock: 5957
Shropshire; Wrodwardine Church: 822
Somersetshire; Brislington: 2876
Somersetshire; Heath House, Brislington: 2876
Somersetshire; Taunton: 3998
South Shields; St. Stephen's Church: 5985
Southam: 5817

Southampton: 80
Southampton; Holyrood Church: 1620
Southwell: 5685
Spithead: 804
St. Leonards-on-Sea: 1810
Staffordshire; Bellamour Hall: 900
Staffordshire; Blymhill: 5140
Staffordshire; Newcastle; St. George's Church: 1476
Staffordshire; St. Mary's Colton: 900
Staffordshire; Walsall: 3613
Staffordshire; Wolseley *var.* Wolsely: 900, 2991
Stanford: 3607
Stephen's Walbroke: 3432
Stockton on Tees; Stranton Church: 903
Stockwell; Most House: 5118
Stoke-next-Guildford: 5200
Streatham: 6287
Suffolk: 3682
Suffolk; Harkstead: 4345
Suffolk; Kensingham; Vicarage: 5346
Suffolk; Lowestoft: 2325
Suffolk; Lowestroft *var.* Lowestoft: 3733
Suffolk; Sibton: 4116
Suffolk; Sudbury: 5962
Suffolk; Worlingham: 2468
Surrey; Clapham: 5663, 5881
Surrey; Clapham; St. Mary's Church: 5881
Surrey; Cobham: 5321
Surrey; Compton: 5846
Surrey; Croydon: 3450
Surrey; Ewell Church: 2147
Surrey; Lavender Hill: 2732
Surrey; Leatherhead: 6294
Surrey; Mitcham: 505
Surrey; Petersham Church: 3942
Surrey; Phipsbridge, Mitcham: 505
Surrey; Richmond: 3788
Surrey; Shirley Park: 6348
Surrey; Thames Ditton: 5914
Surrey; Woodcote Grove: 1722, 1880
Sussex: 1496
Sussex; Dulany House: 5254
Sussex; Eastbourne: 6369
Sussex; New Shoreham: 5360
Sussex; Udimore, parish of: 3150
Sutton; Byron Hotel: 4244
Sutton: 4244
Sutton-on-Hone: 6211
Tamworth; Bonehill House: 4310

England, continued:
Tharnham-curra-Holme: 5140
Thistleton, near Hull: 804
Todmorden: 5179
Tonbridge Wells *var.* Tunbridge Wells: 1499, 4099
Torquay: 143, 3804
Tunbridge Wells: 6021
Tunbridge-wells *var.* Tunbridge Wells: 1499, 4099
Twickenham; Shirley House: 3503
Ventnor: 6318
Wakefield: 4222
Wallasey Church: 3471
Warrington: 87, 2810
Warwickshire; Balsall Heath: 3236
Warwickshire; Barton-on-the-Heath: 4957
Warwickshire; Wall-end: 271
Watford; Grove: 5006
Weedon: 4732
Wembury Church: 3796
Wenbury *var.* Wembury Church: 3796
West Twyford Church: 1879
Westbury-upon-Tyne: 4999
Weston-super-Mare: 4261
Willenhall: 6365
Wilts *var.* Wiltshire; Chippenham: 1722
Wilts *var.* Wiltshire; Dauntsey: 2986
Winchelsea and Nottingham: 3160
Winchester, Diocese of: 3054
Windsor: 391
Woolwich: 4431, 6124
Woolwich; English Presbyterian Church: 4033
Woolwich; Rectory Place: 4645
Worcester: 4277
Writtle: 3398
Writtle; Highwood Vicarage: 3398
York: 5685, 6129
York, Archdiocese of: 778
Yorkshire; Bridlington: 5818
Yorkshire; Broomhead Hill: 2010
Yorkshire; Carnaby, near Bridlington: 5818
Yorkshire; East Riding: 5818
Yorkshire; Knaresborough Church: 2826
Yorkshire; Thorpe Hesley Glebe: 2778
Yorkshire; Wadworth: 427
Yorkshire; Wakefield: 3740
Yorkshire; Wakefield Church: 3877
Yorkshire; West Bank: 6173

France:
Town or city not named: 742, 2326, 4469, 6315
Agean: 395
Bayonne: 5658
Boulogne-Suer-Mer *var.* Boulogne-sur-Mer: 3254
Boulogne-sur-Mer: 1726, 1854, 2119, 3254, 3298
Caën: 225
Cape Barfleur: 6222
Isle of France: 5894
Marseilles: 5211
Nive: 4213
Nivelle: 4213
Orthes *var.* Orthez: 3484, 4213, 6310
Paris: 3432, 4327, 5722, 5783, 6082, 6164, 6443
Paris; British Embassy: 4327, 6082
Paris; St. Cloud: 6282
Pas de Calais; Aire: 4909
Pau: 619
Sauveterra: 3484
Sedan: 5662
St. Omer: 6233
St. Omer's *var.* St. Omer: 6233
Tarbes: 3484, 4213
Toulouse: 938, 3484, 4213, 6310
Via Bigorre: 3484

Gambia: 5299

Germany:
Baden Baden: 710
Frankfort on the Maine, or Frankfort-on-the-Main: 5986, 6180
Frankfort *var.* Frankfurt: 5679, 6301
Frankfurt: 5679, 6301
Hamburgh *var.* Hamburg: 3041, 5034, 5133, 5433
Hanover; Palace Chapel: 5878
Heidelberg: 4805
Homberg *var.* Hamburg: 5034
Munich: 5804
Strasbourg: 5926
Westphalia; Coasfeld *var.* Coesfeld: 4799
Westphalia; Coesfeld: 4799

Greece; Corfu: 3036, 3378, 4338, 4746
Grenada: 5925
Guernsey; New Ground: 6344
Holland: 6310. *See also* Netherlands, the.

Hong Kong: 5339. *See also* China.

India:
Town or city not named: 260, 1196, 3917, 4257, 4629, 4910, 5265, 5824
Agra: 4760
Allahabad: 4247
Bellary: 189
Bengal: 663, 900, 2372, 4809, 6216
Bengal; Barrackpore: 499
Bengal; Chillakall, Zillah Rungpore: 5959
Bengal; Zilla Rungpore: 5959
Bengal Presidency; Simla: 829
Bombay: 3305, 4114, 6212
Bombay Presidency; Ahmednuggur: 3421
Calcutta: 2749, 5322, 5431, 5492, 5975, 6216
Calcutta; Bishop's Palace: 5975
Calcutta; St. Paul's Cathedral: 5431
Decca: 2372
Ferozepore: 3044
French Rocks: 4276
Hyderabad: 1460
Kamptee: 5089
Kurrachee: 1978
Lucknow: 2708
Maderia: 4891
Madras: 1345, 2376, 3984
Madras; Darwar: 189
Madras; Ellichpoor: 1696
Madras; Poonamalla: 3901
Madras; Secunderabad: 562
Madras; St. George's Cathedral: 3984
Madras Presidency; Hullyhall, near Darwar: 189
Mangalore: 4693
Meerat: 171
Mooltan: 2317
Nolapore: 31
Punjaub: 3942
Punjaub; Lahore: 5419
Salem: 1592
Scinde: 1978. *See also* Upper Scinde.
Simla: 1112, 4468, 5265
Upper Scinde; Sukkur: 3384. *See also* Scinde.
See also East Indies.

Ionian Island: 3378

Ireland:
County and townland not named: 5251, 5459, 5590, 5644
County not named:
Ardagh Church: 2727
Ardshill-house: 3497
Ashfield: 3828
Aughnahone: 2705
Ballina: 3699, 4877
Ballinagh: 2067
Ballinasloe: 4752
Ballinderry: 1997
Ballintockan: 1374
Ballyconnell: 2852, 3468
Ballymore Church: 3092
Ballymore, parish of: 3454
Ballytigue: 2818
Bantry Church: 935
Beech Hill: 1347
Bell-hill: 152
Belleek: 275
Bergin Place, Grand Canal: 4719
Berwick Hall: 4448
Brackley: 98
Breaky: 866
Broomhill: 212
Bryansfort: 567
Cahir: 2180
Carmagh: 1116
Carrick: 1421
Cathedral of Clogher *var.* Clogher Cathedral: 2370
Cherry Hill: 2023
Church Hill: 5625
Churchhill: 1222, 5160
Clarlemont [Charlemont, co. Armagh?]: 4998
Clogher: 3879
Clonmel: 5315
Clonor: 453
Clough Church: 2848
Cor: 61
Cove House, Kingstown: 3484
Crokstown [Cookstown?]: 1616
Cucklehill Presbyterian Meeting-house: 3619
Daminy: 2632
Derrydaragh: 4440
Donaghmore: 2964, 5913
Donelony: 3375
Donoughmore *var.* Donaghmore: 1319

Ireland, county not named, continued:
Dromarky Cottage: 2159
Dromore: 1937
Dromore Church: 2395
Drumbunyon House: 1963
Drumetre: 636
Drummond: 3185
Drumsagh [Drumragh?]: 746
Dundrum: 5049
Dungarvan: 4391, 4956
Dunmore Cottage: 2082
Edenderry: 4262
Fenagh: 1911
Garrohill [Garvoghill, co. Fermanagh?]: 103
Gawin: 4978
George's Church: 3317
Glencan: 5982
Gortin: 2618
Grand Canal: 4719
Greenisland: 3165
Hibernian Lodge: 4613
Ivey Farm: 69
Kilderry: 2097
Kililea Church: 2892
Killileagh: 3107
Killylea: 2498, 4183
Killyman: 1066
Kilmore: 285
Kilmore Church: 2391
Kingstown: 3484, 3577
Knappagh: 3094
Lake View Cottage: 5625
Lakeview: 1601
Lara: 6444
Longford Hotel: 3798
Longford Lodge, near Kingstown: 3577
Lough Water: 4205
Lydia Villa: 346
Maghery: 1601
Maydown: 521
Middleton: 3556
Milburn Cottage, Carmagh: 1116
Millbrook: 3673
Millmount: 1584
Milltown: 3424
Moat: 5385
Mossvale: 1016
Mount Drummond: 4669
Mount Shannon: 3322
Mountainview: 599

Mountpleasant: 2362, 2891
Mullaghmen [Mullaghmeen?]: 1489
New Market: 247
New Park: 3850
Newport: 3396
Norton Cottage: 2969
Orange Lodge: 781
Oughterard: 466
Outerarde *var.* Oughterard: 466
Parsonstown: 6374
Peat Hill: 1492
Philipstown: 1886
Redhill: 2300
Renshaw: 5735
Rockmount: 4090
Rodeny: 4134
Roosky: 4880
Rusky *var.* Roosky: 4880
Sally Vale: 730
Saltertown-house: 362
Sandville: 291
Shanetamny: 2682
Sheephill: 2109
Slatmulrony: 1101
St. Andrew's Church: 2915
St. Ann's church: 711, 1767, 3238
St. Anne's Church: 622, 1675
St. George's Church: 1341, 3093, 3845, 4208, 5593
St. Mark's Church: 4755
St. Mary's Church: 133, 333, 3728, 5230, 5533
St. Mathias' Church: 2551
St. Michael's Church: 4958
St. Patrick's Cathedral: 133
St. Paul's Church: 2911, 4677
St. Peter's Church: 132, 371, 703, 831, 1251, 1744, 2947, 3448, 4401, 5711
St. Thomas's Church: 124, 482, 985, 1531, 4071
Tartalaghan [*var.* Tartaraghan?] Rectory: 1727
Tempo House, Killyman: 1066
Timahoe, parish of: 3799
Townelea House: 2182
Trew Cottage: 1189
Trinity Church: 5229
Tullamore: 744, 1812, 2798, 4012
Tullamore Church: 2613
Tullyrod: 4307
Water Hill: 2370
Waterhill House: 4948
Willymaddy [Killymaddy?]: 5503

Chapter 4: Index of Place Names

Antrim, county of:
Townland not named: 270, 2124
Aghagallon: 6396
Aghalee, parish of: 5595
Ahoghill: 489, 795, 1811, 2902, 4597, 5693
Antrim: 589, 1325, 2082, 2151, 2509, 3822
Antrim Church: 931, 2152
Aughagallon *var.* Aghagallon, near Lurgan: 6396
Ballinderry: 1968, 2642
Ballinderry Presbyterian Church: 5886
Ballintoy Castle: 576
Ballybentra: 3836
Ballycastle: 376, 2112, 2677, 2882, 3125, 3487, 3796, 5707
Ballyclare: 711, 1048, 4778
Ballycloughan, near Ballymena: 3125
Ballykeel, Ballymena: 3239
Ballylesson Church: 6210
Ballylinney, parish of: 2403
Ballymacash: 3795
Ballymacash, near Lisburn: 2037
Ballymacilrany: 930
Ballymacilreny *var.* Ballymacilrany: 930
Ballymartin, Templepatrick: 3163
Ballymena: 27, 59, 109, 355, 1366, 1556, 2027, 2082, 2275, 2293, 2317, 2449, 2564, 2596, 3043, 3125, 3130, 3200, 3239, 3271, 3351, 3383, 3471, 3522, 3557, 3617, 3624, 3694, 3759, 3999, 4073, 4103, 4115, 4205, 4210, 4307, 4311, 5137, 5169, 5294, 5420, 5578, 5756, 5788, 5869, 6118, 6218, 6255, 6321
Ballymena Church: 355
Ballymoney: 791, 1862, 3660, 3719, 3725, 3754, 3880, 4202, 4658, 5514, 5922, 6355
Ballymoney Church: 1862
Ballynafeigh: 3302
Ballynure, parish of: 5446
Ballysillan Presbyterian Church: 4377
Beechfield: 5113
Beechmount, Belfast: 5589
Belfast: 20, 48, 96, 97, 101, 108, 110, 130, 181, 190, 191, 192, 210, 235, 331, 344, 390, 408, 414, 440, 441, 443, 483, 520, 537, 542, 669, 849, 855, 877, 879, 882, 917, 927, 930, 946, 957, 975, 1025, 1039, 1103, 1104, 1105, 1123, 1136, 1163, 1219, 1246, 1250, 1263, 1291, 1301, 1332, 1334, 1369, 1426, 1430, 1439, 1450, 1486, 1592, 1594, 1611, 1615, 1619, 1663, 1689, 1702, 1730, 1751, 1762, 1763, 1767, 1777, 1790, 1801, 1836, 1837, 1861, 1877, 1878, 1892, 1939, 1949, 1950, 1953,

Belfast, county Antrim, continued: 1966, 1968, 1969, 1977, 2001, 2048, 2081, 2130, 2151, 2191, 2195, 2196, 2197, 2276, 2291, 2297, 2300, 2303, 2304, 2311, 2321, 2325, 2336, 2412, 2416, 2444, 2461, 2512, 2525, 2526, 2553, 2560, 2567, 2578, 2631, 2659, 2678, 2681, 2706, 2715, 2723, 2728, 2730, 2736, 2742, 2752, 2783, 2786, 2801, 2816, 2821, 2832, 2840, 2847, 2858, 2867, 2868, 2869, 2897, 2898, 2901, 2922, 2923, 2930, 2985, 2987, 3035, 3037, 3069, 3102, 3119, 3126, 3143, 3161, 3162, 3172, 3173, 3189, 3213, 3227, 3235, 3266, 3271, 3301, 3302, 3319, 3327, 3349, 3350, 3352, 3364, 3368, 3401, 3410, 3446, 3460, 3493, 3507, 3524, 3540, 3560, 3567, 3570, 3575, 3584, 3587, 3671, 3680, 3732, 3735, 3755, 3790, 3800, 3831, 3833, 3846, 3849, 3851, 3871, 3894, 3898, 3909, 3911, 3931, 3949, 3969, 3975, 3978, 3980, 3994, 4011, 4039, 4048, 4054, 4062, 4110, 4119, 4172, 4194, 4219, 4239, 4279, 4296, 4300, 4321, 4342, 4345, 4370, 4377, 4380, 4380, 4498, 4533, 4552, 4553, 4559, 4584, 4609, 4614, 4615, 4649, 4674, 4696, 4702, 4709, 4721, 4723, 4739, 4754, 4772, 4777, 4798, 4817, 4833, 4834, 4840, 4899, 4921, 4938, 4963, 4977, 5016, 5040, 5044, 5051, 5055, 5060, 5070, 5087, 5101, 5106, 5116, 5142, 5159, 5161, 5162, 5167, 5185, 5199, 5201, 5229, 5281, 5286, 5313, 5335, 5339, 5367, 5387, 5438, 5450, 5472, 5485, 5512, 5531, 5583, 5588, 5589, 5594, 5605, 5626, 5630, 5630, 5644, 5649, 5717, 5762, 5764, 5814, 5832, 5855, 5863, 5864, 5867, 5903, 5920, 5921, 5931, 5952, 5956, 5971, 6005, 6006, 6018, 6026, 6027, 6039, 6081, 6119, 6127, 6158, 6192, 6207, 6210, 6230, 6260, 6269, 6323, 6338, 6414, 6419
Belfast; Alfred-place Presbyterian Church: 2868
Belfast; Alfred-street Church: 3349
Belfast; All Saints Church: 5051
Belfast Barracks: 1751
Belfast District: 2276
Belfast Reformed Presbyterian Church: 5971
Berry Street Presbyterian Church, Belfast: 957
Birch-hill: 2547
Botanic-view, Belfast: 3575
Bridgehill, Lisburn: 2625
Broadisland: 3192
Brookville, Ballymena: 2027
Broughshane: 3125

County Antrim, continued:
Broughshane, Ballymena: 2275
Bunker's-hall, Belfast: 5101
Burnside, near Antrim: 589
Bushmills: 2177, 2466, 2770, 2771, 2787, 5269, 6151
Bushmills Presbyterian Church: 2112
Bushyfield: 6103
Cairnlough, Glenarm: 3286
Cargan House, Toomebridge: 2499
Carmoney [Carnmoney?]: 3735
Carmoney *var.* Carnmoney Church: 3735
Carnmoney: 298, 2578, 3163
Carnmoney, parish of: 2403
Carnmoney Church: 298, 2578, 3163
Carrick Hill, Belfast: 3931
Carrickfergus: 393, 539, 555, 2183, 3162, 3320, 3482, 3876, 4411, 4570, 4704, 5067, 5446, 5691, 5855, 5965. *See also* Carrickferguss.
Carrickfergus; Barn Cottage: 2183
Carrickfergus Church: 539, 555
Carrickfergus Presbyterian Church: 4570
Carrickferguss *var.* Carrickfergus Church: 555
Cathedral of Connor *var.* Connor Cathedral: 4638
Clady Cottage, Dunadry: 4702
Clenavy Glebe [Glenavy?]: 2155
Clenone [Glenone?], Portglenone: 3706
Cliftonville: 5749
Clogher, near Ballymena: 4311
Clough, near Ballymena: 3694
Coleman's Hotel, Portrush: 5501
Connor: 149, 642
Connor Church: 149
Corn Market, Belfast: 5814
Coslett's-bridge, near Lisburn: 645
Craig, near Bushmills: 2466
Craigbilly: 1810
Cranfield: 2153
Crescent, Belfast: 2752, 3189
Crescent, Portstewart: 1109
Crevillyvalley, near Ballymena: 3271
Croagh: 2177
Cromac Lodge, Belfast: 2871
Cromore: 3427
Crookedstone: 2178
Crossan House, Lisburn: 5161
Crosshill, near Crumlin: 877
Crumlin: 877, 1836, 2178, 6018
Cullybackey: 1556

Cushendall: 131, 1223, 3741
Cushendun: 3216
Derriaghy *var.* Derryaghy: 2164, 4638
Derriaghy *var.* Derryaghy, near Lisburn: 4551
Derryaghy: 2164, 4638
Derryaghy, near Lisburn: 4551
Derrykeighan Glebe: 1208
Dervock: 3076
Dunadry: 4563, 4702, 6016
Dunandry [Dunadry?]: 2871
Duncairn: 5780
Dunfane, near Ballymena: 5169
Dunluce: 4584
Dunluce, parish of: 2899
Dunluce Rectory: 2899
Dunseverick, near Bushmills: 6151
Edenderry: 5202
Elm Grove, Belfast: 4584
Falls, Belfast: 3302
Finaghy House: 5998
Finvoy: 2495
Finvoy Presbyterian Church: 2495
First Presbyterian Church, Ahoghill: 4597
First Presbyterian Church, Ballymena: 4311
First Presbyterian Church, Islandmagee: 3192
First Presbyterian Church, Larne: 5966
First Presbyterian Meeting-house, Belfast: 3301
Fisherwick-place Church, Belfast: 408, 2631, 3041, 4584
Friends' Meeting House, Belfast: 2783
Furze Lodge, Glenavy: 630
Garden-hill, Belfast: 3173
Giant's Causeway: 612
Glebe, Glenavy: 4873
Glenalina, Belfast: 4614
Glenarm: 567, 3286, 4818
Glenavy: 630, 1865, 2642, 4873
Glenavy Church: 5951
Glenbank, Belfast: 3894
Glenbrook: 2483
Glendaragh Cottage, Crumlin: 2178
Glendarragh: 1251
Glenmore: 3674
Glenmore, near Lisburn: 236, 1064
Glenview, Carrickfergus: 5691
Glenwherry *var.* Glenwhirry: 3239
Glenwhirry: 3239
Gloonan Lodge, Ahoghill: 1811
Gracehill, near Ballymena: 1366
Grange, Toome Bridge *var.* Toomebridge: 6293
Gransha, Islandmagee: 3192

County Antrim, continued:
Green Island, Carrickfergus: 3162
Greenhill, near Ballymena: 2317
Grove-green, Lisburn: 3876
Hilden, Lisburn: 6042
Hillhall Presbyterian Church: 6042
Hopefield, Belfast: 2821
Independent Chapel, Belfast: 4739
Independent Meeting-house, Belfast: 5952
Island of Rathlin *var.* Rathlin Island: 675
Islandmagee: 3192
Jennymount: 583
Kilcurry, near Aboghill [Ahoghill?]: 2902
Killagan, near Ballymoney: 3725
Killead: 2178, 5206
Killead Presbyterian Church: 4675
Killealy: 2178
Kilroot: 5446
Kilwaughter, near Larne: 377
Klinty, near Ballymena: 4205
Knocknacarry: 5993
Lambeg: 1461, 4865
Larne: 377, 1029, 2124, 5966
Laurel Hill, near Lisburn: 5778
Layde, parish of, Cushendall: 131
Leighinmore: 1950
Lenagh: 6080
Ligoneil, Belfast: 6127
Linenhall-street Presbyterian Church, Belfast: 1790, 2736, 3213
Linfield, near Belfast: 1762
Lisburn: 111, 165, 233, 236, 270, 308, 645, 989, 1064, 1065, 1155, 1390, 1923, 2037, 2175, 2198, 2439, 2556, 2625, 2650, 2744, 2987, 3174, 3321, 3328, 3359, 3396, 3537, 3566, 3587, 3727, 3736, 3876, 4093, 4329, 4551, 4559, 4638, 4858, 4984, 5161, 5432, 5495, 5867, 5887, 6042, 6068, 6299, 6448
Lisburn Cathedral: 111, 270, 2987, 3396
Lisburn Presbyterian Church: 3537, 5887
Lisnarrick: 2450
Longwood, Belfast: 2578
Lower Malone: 798
Magheragal Church: 3674
Magheragall: 5886
Maghcrintendry: 2177
Malone: 1547
Malone Church, Knappagh: 3094
Malone, Belfast: 5199
Manse, Ballymena: 6218
Markstown, near Cullybackey: 1556

Mary-street Presbyterian Church, or Meeting-house, Belfast: 1836, 1977, 3126, 3302
May-street Church, Belfast: 2786, 4754
Millform, Killead: 4675
Milltown, near Ballyclare: 4778
Moore Fort: 2219
Mosside Presbyterian Church: 6317
Mount Charles: 5921
Mount Collyer Park: 1687, 4894
Mount Collyer Park, Belfast: 408, 917
Mount-pottinger, Belfast: 3560
Mountain Lodge, near Belfast: 4649
Mountgilbert: 6269
Moyrusk, Lisburn: 1923
Muckamore: 718
Muckrim: 6335
Oakfield, near Carrickfergus: 3482
Ohoghill *var.* Ahoghill: 795
Old Park: 6190
Orangefield, Belfast: 2730
Palace, near Belfast: 1615
Parkmore: 3508
Parkmore, Cushendall: 1223
Parsonage, Belfast: 5286
Plantation, Lisburn: 5887
Port Stewart: 6185. *See also* Portstewart.
Portglenone: 1810, 3706
Portrush: 2805, 5501, 5705, 5948, 6039, 6355
Portrush Church: 3373
Portstewart: 1109, 5743, 5752, 6185. *See also* Port Stewart.
Prospect, Belfast: 5485
Ramoan Rectory: 5405
Randalstown: 46, 2170, 6080, 6297
Randalstown Presbyterian Church: 2153
Rasharkin, near Ballymena: 5420
Rashee: 3903
Rathlin Island *var.* Island of Rathlin: 675, 3917
Reformed Presbyterian Church, Belfast: 3584
Registrar's Office, Belfast: 4674
Registrar's Office, Lisburn: 308
Rose Lodge, Belfast: 3994
Rosebrooke, Carrickfergus: 5446
Rosedermot: 4307
Rosedernot *var.* Rosedermot: 4307
Rosemary-street Church, Belfast: 2681, 4772, 5583
Rosevale, near Cromlin *var.* Crumlin: 1836
Rosevale, near Lisburn: 6068
Rosstula: 4219
Royal Hotel, Belfast: 1892

County Antrim, continued:
Sandy-lodge, Ballymena: 4103
Scotchmount, Malone: 1547
Seaview Cottage, Belfast: 3364, 3460
Second Presbyterian Church or Meeting-house, Belfast: 1861, 2151, 4723
Silverstream, Whiteabbey: 3735
Slaght: 2449
Slat *var.* Slaght: 2449
Slavney *var.* Slievenaghy, Finvoy: 2495
Smithfield: 4761
Solderstown *var.* Soldierstown Church, parish of Aughalea *var.* Aghalee: 5595
Soldierstown Church, parish of Aghalee: 5595
Springfield: 3674, 5077
Springvale, Ballyclare: 711
St. Anne's, or St. Ann's, Church, Belfast: 130, 390, 443, 855, 946, 1136, 1250, 1877, 1878, 1950, 2149, 2204, 2311, 2325, 3266, 3350, 3446, 3493, 3898, 3911, 4899, 5055, 5201, 5229, 5814, 5921, 5956, 6005, 6006
St. George's Church, Belfast: 3980, 4194
St. Malachi's Roman Catholic Church, Belfast: 5644
St. Michael's Church, Belfast: 3327
Strand Presbyterian Church, Belfast: 2416
Templepatrick: 1430, 3163
Templepatrick Church: 3319
The Abbey, Belfast: 6338
Third Presbyterian Congregation, Ballymena: 3383
Toomebridge: 2499, 6293
Tullyinamullin *var.* Tullynamullan: 6080
Tullynamullan: 6080
Wesleyan Church, Belfast: 1619, 3732, 5754, 6269
Whiteabbey: 2786, 3735
Whiteabbey Presbyterian Church: 332, 341
Woodburn Cottage, Carrickfergus: 5855

Ardagh, Diocese of: 3056, 6048
Ardfert and Aghadoe, Diocese of: 5099

Armagh, county of:
Townland not named: 87, 91, 899, 1009, 1491, 2172, 2302, 2476, 2776, 2884, 5114
Achavilly: 405
Acton: 4144
Acton Church: 320, 698
Acton Glebe: 539, 555
Aghanlig *var.* Aghinlig: 2615

County Armagh, continued:
Aghinlig: 2615
Ahorey *var.* Aghory: 808, 809, 2548, 4969
Aghory: 2548, 4969
Aghory Meeting-house: 808, 809
Ahory *var.* Aghory, near Richhill: 6094
Albert Hotel, Armagh: 1666, 3598, 4595
Alistragh: 104, 3956
Altinamoichan *var.* Altnamackan: 5549
Altinamorichan *var.* Altnamackan, Newtownhamilton: 468
Anagh *var.* Annagh, near Portadown: 339, 5798
Annaclare, near Armagh: 1484
Annacramp *var.* Annacramph, near Grange: 358
Annagh House, Portadown: 2277
Annagh-house: 3316
Annagh *var.* Anagh, near Portadown: 339, 445, 5798
Annahill *var.* Annahilt: 1, 3
Annahue Cottage: 266
Annslough, near Middletown: 174
Annvale, Keady: 5255
Ardgonnell: 4403, 4412, 4953
Ardgonnell, near Middletown: 2334
Ardrea, parish of Loughgall: 4462
Ardress: 282, 1737
Ardross: 202
Argory: 661
Armagh: 2, 4, 9, 12, 22, 26, 39, 40, 41, 43, 46, 55, 58, 60, 68, 73, 74, 76, 77, 83, 89, 100, 101, 112, 113, 114, 115, 116, 122, 127, 135, 136, 136, 138, 158, 162, 166, 167, 169, 177, 199, 205, 219, 223, 224, 231, 235, 253, 254, 257, 258, 260, 262, 268, 278, 280, 288, 303, 312, 315, 316, 331, 342, 343, 360, 364, 365, 367, 372, 373, 379, 386, 405, 411, 412, 414, 415, 418, 419, 427, 430, 435, 440, 448, 463, 483, 496, 501, 507, 516, 519, 522, 528, 543, 549, 551, 553, 567, 574, 577, 584, 593, 594, 597, 603, 606, 608, 614, 615, 616, 620, 633, 647, 651, 652, 656, 657, 664, 674, 679, 684, 700, 701, 714, 715, 731, 751, 756, 765, 767, 777, 784, 788, 811, 812, 820, 825, 826, 836, 837, 845, 854, 856, 862, 874, 880, 900, 911, 919, 920, 924, 943, 949, 959, 962, 965, 966, 968, 973, 974, 986, 997, 1001, 1002, 1005, 1006, 1021, 1022, 1025, 1026, 1033, 1034, 1036, 1040, 1041, 1042, 1057, 1067, 1076, 1077, 1093, 1097, 1119, 1152, 1153, 1156, 1175, 1200, 1209, 1216, 1230, 1236, 1250, 1257,

Armagh (city), continued: 1259, 1271, 1276, 1279, 1320, 1337, 1339, 1360, 1372, 1378, 1389, 1390, 1403, 1404, 1411, 1415, 1452, 1456, 1465, 1481, 1483, 1484, 1493, 1494, 1500, 1502, 1505, 1522, 1532, 1543, 1550, 1554, 1561, 1570, 1597, 1600, 1622, 1637, 1638, 1649, 1659, 1663, 1666, 1672, 1678, 1691, 1692, 1698, 1701, 1704, 1721, 1723, 1749, 1783, 1802, 1806, 1858, 1863, 1874, 1882, 1883, 1884, 1897, 1913, 1914, 1928, 1941, 1955, 1979, 1984, 1988, 1989, 1994, 2028, 2030, 2057, 2064, 2080, 2090, 2091, 2168, 2184, 2185, 2230, 2264, 2269, 2274, 2313, 2345, 2384, 2390, 2396, 2397, 2398, 2417, 2456, 2458, 2481, 2521, 2522, 2547, 2589, 2627, 2631, 2633, 2680, 2699, 2702, 2703, 2716, 2737, 2759, 2765, 2777, 2800, 2811, 2829, 2841, 2879, 2917, 2918, 2919, 2920, 2946, 2950, 3005, 3012, 3066, 3067, 3077, 3096, 3097, 3112, 3117, 3185, 3300, 3322, 3331, 3352, 3391, 3392, 3472, 3491, 3496, 3499, 3521, 3548, 3550, 3555, 3563, 3564, 3598, 3605, 3611, 3629, 3639, 3664, 3683, 3705, 3708, 3753, 3773, 3783, 3791, 3792, 3847, 3851, 3851, 3852, 3856, 3867, 3910, 3914, 3937, 3941, 3953, 3954, 3985, 4074, 4075, 4096, 4120, 4127, 4128, 4146, 4159, 4177, 4180, 4196, 4242, 4266, 4267, 4274, 4297, 4298, 4303, 4325, 4346, 4358, 4363, 4364, 4384, 4410, 4411, 4413, 4414, 4415, 4416, 4439, 4442, 4444, 4461, 4465, 4484, 4491, 4515, 4521, 4529, 4532, 4537, 4556, 4575, 4576, 4580, 4589, 4595, 4600, 4601, 4607, 4608, 4632, 4639, 4639, 4712, 4722, 4731, 4737, 4742, 4792, 4800, 4816, 4819, 4822, 4838, 4850, 4851, 4856, 4890, 4896, 4897, 4927, 4928, 4959, 4973, 4974, 4975, 4976, 4990, 4997, 5016, 5039, 5048, 5058, 5072, 5084, 5104, 5108, 5111, 5138, 5139, 5146, 5151, 5163, 5173, 5177, 5178, 5219, 5231, 5245, 5281, 5285, 5318, 5338, 5348, 5357, 5367, 5374, 5379, 5380, 5388, 5390, 5406, 5408, 5409, 5412, 5413, 5416, 5417, 5418, 5429, 5444, 5457, 5471, 5477, 5479, 5488, 5489, 5504, 5509, 5511, 5540, 5553, 5554, 5555, 5556, 5585, 5601, 5617, 5618, 5621, 5629, 5652, 5672, 5690, 5702, 5708, 5730, 5744, 5754, 5764, 5801, 5803, 5814, 5853, 5869, 5919, 5944, 5964, 6022, 6078, 6093, 6113, 6138, 6155, 6166, 6228, 6257, 6275, 6277, 6328, 6354, 6363, 6377, 6380, 6381, 6402, 6409, 6410, 6414, 6416, 6418, 6430, 6439, 6448

County Armagh, continued:
Armagh, borough of: 1229
Armagh, parish of: 955, 1987, 2986, 5285, 5847, 6078
Armagh Cathedral: 101, 360, 414, 919, 1250, 1271, 1320, 1360, 1561, 1637, 2064, 3117, 4298, 4521, 4887, 4896, 5072, 6078, 6093, 6414
Armagh Poor Law Union: 965, 986, 1156, 1483, 3112
Armagh, Presbytery of: 116
Armaghbeague *var.* Armaghbreague: 2654
Armaghbrague *var.* Armaghbreague Church: 4090
Armaghbreague: 457, 1492, 5625, 6359
Armaghbreague, parish of: 5703
Armaghbreague Church: 457, 1492, 4090, 5625, 5703, 6359
Artabrackagh, Portadown: 878
Artabracken *var.* Artabrackagh, Portadown: 878
Artgonnell *var.* Ardgonnell: 4403, 4412, 4953
Artgonnell *var.* Ardgonnell, near Middletown: 2334
Ash Trees, near Tandragee: 613
Ashfort: 536
Athol Cottage, near Tandragee: 828
Aughacommon *var.* Aghacommon, Lurgan: 4266
Aughagallon, near Lurgan: 5595
Aughanlig *var.* Aghinlig, near Moy: 5458
Aughantarragh and Corr: 1846, 1848
Aughataragh *var.* Aughantarragh and Corr: 472
Aughaterra [*var.* Aughantarragh and Corr?]: 1846, 1848
Aughnagurgan: 6359
Avon Lodge, Armagh: 112, 551, 1337, 5048
Balaghey *var.* Ballaghy: 1261
Ballaghy, near Armagh: 4242
Balleer: 740
Ballinacor *var.* Ballynacor, near Lurgan: 2909
Ballinahone House, near Armagh: 1637, 6381
Ballintagart *var.* Ballintaggart: 2883
Ballintagert *var.* Ballintaggart, near Portadown: 491, 4698
Ballintaggart: 1939
Ballintate House: 563
Ballintegart *var.* Ballintaggart, Portadown: 4698
Ballsmill: 142
Ballyards, near Armagh: 4178, 4192

County Armagh, continued:
Ballybreagh: 1755
Ballybreagh House, Richhill: 5060
Ballydonaghy: 4429
Ballydougherty: 5735
Ballyhagan: 646, 1611
Ballyhagan, near Loughgall: 905, 4241
Ballyknock, Tandragee: 6442
Ballylane: 1669
Ballyloughan, Richhill: 4206
Ballymacnab: 3077, 4483, 4589
Ballymacome *var.* Ballymacone, near Keady: 2386
Ballymacone: 1402
Ballymacone, near Keady: 901
Ballymagerney *var.* Ballymagerny: 402, 730
Ballymagerny: 402
Ballymagerny, near Loughgall: 1623, 4903
Ballymagirney *var.* Ballymagerny, near Loughgall: 1623, 4903
Ballymagorman House: 834
Ballymartrim: 3831
Ballymascanlan: 6142
Ballymascanlon *var.* Ballymascanlan Church: 6142
Ballymore: 846
Ballymore-house, Tandragee: 5977
Ballymorrin *var.* Ballymoran: 4607
Ballymoyer: 4849
Ballymoyer *var.* Ballymyre: 1906, 3332, 3502, 5645
Ballymoyer *var.* Ballymyre Church: 4868
Ballymoyer *var.* Ballymyre Glebe: 3201, 5063
Ballymurrin *var.* Ballymoran, near Armagh: 1505
Ballymyre: 1906. *See also* Ballymoyer.
Ballynacor: 2909
Ballynahone, near Armagh: 4601
Ballynary: 1233
Ballynerary [Ballynary?]: 1233
Ballynewry: 809, 4636
Ballyrath, near Armagh: 315
Ballyreagh-house: 5482
Ballytrue: 5051
Ballytyrone, near Loughgall: 1120
Ballyworkan House: 314, 2565
Balteagh: 5052
Barn Hill: 335, 1747
Barrack hill *var.* Barrack-hill and Barrackhill, Armagh: 656, 826, 5177
Beechhill: 123

Belaghyl: 5498
Bellaghy *var.* Ballaghy, near Armagh: 4242
Bellview: 402, 3318
Bellview, near Richhill: 2956
Belmont, Forkill: 426
Belmount *var.* Belmont, Forkhill *var.* Forkill: 958
Belmount, Forkill: 958
Belteagh *var.* Balteagh: 5052
Beresford Arms, Armagh: 1279, 3392
Blackwatertown: 142, 185, 253, 259, 293, 342, 462, 540, 571, 988, 1013, 1031, 1149, 1207, 1405, 1989, 2372, 2792, 3158, 5417, 6406
Bloomvale, near Lurgan: 119
Bondville: 99, 238
Bondville House, Middletown: 3779
Bottlehill: 1938
Brackley: 662
Brackley, Keady: 4437
Bracknagh Hill: 1261
Breagh, parish of Seaford [Seagoe?]: 5231
Breakley *var.* Brackley, near Keady: 3961
Brookley, Armagh: 6257
Broomfield: 5678
Cabra Grove, Tandragee: 4206
Cabra *var.* Cabragh: 370
Cabra *var.* Cabragh, near Markethill: 4694
Callan Lodge, Loughgall: 3663
Callan-bridge *var.* Callanbridge and Callan Bridge: 244, 5260
Callin-Turlagh, near Charlemont: 2615
Camagh, near Keady: 1927
Camlough: 174
Canary: 6240
Cariff: 3116
Carnagh: 4435
Carnagh House: 478, 1317, 2489
Carnagh House, Keady: 4353, 5840
Carnagh, near Keady: 1580
Carrick: 3614
Carrickgollaghy *var.* Carrickgallogly: 6110
Castle Dillon *var.* Castledillon: 566, 614, 835, 948, 1235, 2876, 4580, 5784
Castletown: 4597
Cavan, Belaghyl: 5498
Cavanaca *var.* Cavanacaw: 1716
Cavanacaw: 1716
Cavanaghagrove *var.* Cavanaghgrove: 379
Cavanaghgrove: 379
Cavenacaw *var.* Cavanacaw, near Armagh: 6166

County Armagh, continued:
Chantilly Lodge: 175
Charlemont: 61, 82, 206, 210, 254, 403, 595, 609, 752, 805, 1096, 1117, 1232, 1357, 1453, 1504, 2073, 2229, 2615, 3158, 3277, 3355, 3619, 4231, 4381, 4952, 4998, 5325, 5502, 5767, 5806
Charlemont Arms Hotel, Armagh: 2521, 5490, 5553
Charlemont Church: 61, 82, 206, 254, 805, 1504
Charlemont Fort: 4541
Clady Beg: 1233
Cladybeg *var.* Clady Beg, near Markethill: 3538, 3625
Cladybegg *var.* Clady Beg: 1233
Clanacle *var.* Clonakle: 487
Clanmore: 683
Clanrolla, near Lurgan: 5094
Clanticlay: 2266
Clantilew: 1726, 2738
Clare: 1231, 1427, 5678
Clare Church, near Tandragee: 1427
Clare Presbyterian Meeting-house: 1231
Clare, near Lurgan: 5022
Clarke's-bridge: 6415
Clark's bridge, near Newtownhamilton: 738
Clonakle *var.* Clanacle: 487
Cloncore: 4583
Clonmacash: 4583
Clounagh *var.* Clownagh, near Portadown: 755
College, Armagh: 3791
Colone *var.* Calone, near Markethill: 2632
Coolkarn [Culkeeran?]: 3184
Coolkiln *var.* Coolkill, Middletown: 866
Copney: 1189, 1684
Copney, near Loughgall: 2435
Copney, near Moy: 1252
Copney, near Verner's Bridge: 3187
Corcrain House, Portadown: 4922
Cordrummond, near Markethill: 431
Corhammock: 98
Cornamucklagh: 863
Corneymuckley *var.* Cornamucklagh: 863
Corr and Dunavally: 805
Cottage, Lurgan: 3345
Course Lodge, near Rich-hill *var.* Richhill: 1231
Cram Island-House: 1688
Crayfield: 2170
Creeve: 4452

Creggan: 4679
Creggan, parish of: 4557, 5552
Cremore: 800, 3729
Cremore Meeting-house, Mountnorris: 4518
Cremore Presbyterian Church: 3729
Cronkill, near Verner's-bridge *var.* Verner's Bridge: 2032
Crossdall: 4428
Crossmaglen: 524, 1665, 1666, 4604, 5741
Crow Hill, Lurgan: 5579
Crunsaught [*var.* Crunagh?], near Mountnorris: 6295
Culkeeran: 3184
Cullentragh: 4607
Cullintra *var.* Cullentragh: 4607
Culloville: 554, 556
Curlust *var.* Corlust, near Tandragee: 6092
Curryhews: 4436
Dahliavale, Lurgan: 2033
Daisyhill: 2497
Daisyhill, Mountnorris: 2828
Darkley House: 2810
Darkly House, Keady: 2877
Dartry: 967, 1007
Deanery, Armagh: 430, 5964
Dennyhara *var.* Dinnahorra: 933
Derry Ore, near Verner's Bridge: 1667
Derryadd, Verner's Bridge: 1673
Derrybroughas House, Portadown: 5115
Derrycary *var.* Derrycorry, Verner's bridge: 805
Derrycorry: 6417
Derrycrew, near Loughgall: 5905
Derryhale House, Portadown: 3182
Derryhaw: 644
Derryhaw, near Tynan: 168
Derryloughan: 1938
Derrymacash Chapel: 6213
Derryraine: 527
Derryran: 495
Derryrane *var.* Derryraine: 527
Derryscholop *var.* Derryscollop: 456
Derryscollip *var.* Derryscollop: 1972
Derryscollop: 456, 1972, 5458
Derryvane: 3014
Derryvore House, Portadown: 963
Desert, Armagh: 205
Dinnahorra: 933
Dougha [Dougher?]: 3113
Dougher: 3113
Dromanargoole: 2281

County Armagh, continued:
Drumadd: 5318
Drumanan: 2738
Drumard: 6181
Drumart: 613, 1354
Drumart House, Tandragee: 2490
Drumatee: 347, 4636
Drumbanagher: 302, 350, 5743, 6331
Drumbanagher Church: 3646
Drumcairn *var.* Drumcarn, near Armagh: 6228
Drumcree: 336, 394, 578, 813, 863, 1348, 5115, 5519
Drumcree, parish of: 1251, 2826, 4208
Drumcree Church: 336, 863, 1747, 5115
Drumcree grave-yard: 394
Drumcreve *var.* Drumcree: 336
Drumcullen, near Blackwatertown: 1207
Drumgar: 1846
Drumgreenagh: 920
Drumhillary *var.* Drumhillery, near Middletown: 1830
Drumhillery Presbyterian Church, near Keady: 4435, 4436
Drumhillery, near Keady: 3379
Drumhillery, near Middletown: 1830
Drumilly: 1722, 1880. *See also* Drummilly.
Druminis *var.* Drumminis: 1992
Druminis *var.* Drumminis Presbyterian Meeting-house: 527
Drumlargue *var.* Dunlarg, near Keady: 1017
Drumman Beg: 4608
Drummannon: 283
Drummanon *var.* Drummannon: 283
Drummilly: 801, 2669, 3960, 4271. *See also* Drumilly.
Drumminis Presbyterian Church: 527
Drummonbeg *var.* Drumman Beg: 4608
Drummond, near Armagh: 74, 2057
Drummond, near Keady: 1511
Drummonmore, near Armagh: 4346
Drumnargoole-house *var.* Drumnargoole House: 320, 648, 698
Drumnasoo Cottage: 2891
Drumnasoo, near Loughgall: 1311, 1327
Drumorgan: 490
Drumrush [Drumrusk?]: 883
Drumrusk: 883
Drumsallan: 1116, 1261, 1846
Drumsallan Church: 766, 883, 3307, 4096
Drumsallan Parish Chapel: 883
Drumsallen *var.* Drumsallan Church: 766, 1846, 3307

Drumsallon *var.* Drumsallan: 883
Drumsallon *var.* Drumsallan Church: 883, 1261
Dundrum House, Keady: 2810
Dundrum, near Keady: 200, 3303
Eagralougher: 1598
Eden Villa, Portadown: 1217
Edenderry-House, Portadown: 782
Edenderry, Portadown: 4646, 6125, 6383
Eglish: 2228, 3338
Eglish Church: 1674
Eglish Mills: 366
Egre Lougher *var.* Eagralougher: 1598
Elm Cottage, Portadown: 64
Elmpark: 323
Fairlawn House: 875
Fairview: 963
Fairview House, Ballytrue: 5051
Fairview, near Richhill: 3429
Farm Lodge, Lurgan: 1163, 5800
Farmacaffly, near Armagh: 3985
Farmhill, Keady: 2948
Feagey, parish of Tartaraghan: 2266
Feduff: 5385
Fellows-hall *var.* Fellowshall, near Tynan: 1053
Fellowshall: 2169
Firgrove, Tanderagee *var.* Tandragee: 92
Firgrove, Tandragee: 92
First Presbyterian Church or Meeting-house, Armagh: 862, 1200, 1452, 2080, 3847, 3849, 4461, 5318, 5338, 5348, 5708
First Presbyterian Church, Keady: 1259, 5255
First Presbyterian Church, Markethill: 5495
First Presbyterian Meeting-house, Newtownhamilton: 5401
Forkhill Lodge: 2476
Forkhill *var.* Forkill: 267, 1210, 1410, 3425, 5437, 5437, 5726, 6177
Forkhill *var.* Forkill, parish of: 226
Forkhill *var.* Forkill Church: 76
Forkill: 76, 267, 426, 958, 1210, 1410, 3425, 5437, 5644, 5726
Forkill, parish of: 226, 6177
Forkill Church: 76
Fortwilliam, near Portadown: 2948, 3358, 4728
Foxpark, Loughgall: 487, 4839
Foy: 863
Freeduff: 4478
Friends' Meeting-house, Lurgan: 5778
Friends' Meeting-house, Richhill: 4342
Fruithill: 105

Chapter 4: Index of Place Names

County Armagh, continued:
Gate Cottage, Deanery, Armagh: 5964
Glasdrummond *var.* Glassdrummond: 4518
Glasdrumond *var.* Glasdrummond, near Markethill: 2880
Glassdrummond: 4518
Glenaghy, near Portadown: 550, 1551, 3769
Glenaul House: 4008
Glenaul House, near Benburb: 3127
Glenaule: 1061
Glenburn, Keady: 3039
Gosford Castle: 2468, 2512, 3591, 4776
Grange: 358, 414, 3185, 4363
Grange Church: 3185
Grange Church, near Armagh: 4608
Grange Oneiland: 6085
Grange O'Neiland *var.* Grange Oneilland: 2653
Grange, near Armagh: 647, 3792, 4608, 5690
Graymount: 5133
Green Hall: 314, 488, 4361
Greenman *var.* Greenan, Loughgall: 4608
Greenvale, Keady: 1124
Hackney, near Charlemont: 3158
Harrybrook: 852, 2045, 2264, 2264, 4502
Hawthorn Hill: 1624, 3889, 5515
Hawthorn Hill, Armagh: 767, 1988
Hawthorn Lodge, near Lurgan: 2685
Hawthorn-hill *var.* Hawthorn Hill: 6177
Heath Hall: 1188, 5955
Heathhall *var.* Heath Hall: 3930
Hermitage, Keady: 1200
Hill-head, Tynan: 1291
Hockley, near Charlemont: 5502
Hoophill-house, Lurgan: 3940
Infirmary House, Armagh: 1339
Jennyfield, near Armagh: 1749
Jonesboro *var.* Jonesborough: 1926
Jonesborough: 6142
Jonesborough, parish of: 89
Jonesborough Chapel: 1926
Jonesborough Church: 267
Keady: 24, 93, 109, 128, 200, 283, 287, 457, 557, 599, 601, 694, 749, 882, 901, 1017, 1029, 1036, 1078, 1124, 1200, 1259, 1511, 1580, 1680, 1927, 2012, 2138, 2245, 2293, 2351, 2386, 2680, 2810, 2812, 2877, 2948, 3039, 3098, 3303, 3379, 3844, 3961, 4201, 4353, 4435, 4436, 4437, 4497, 4555, 4605, 4730, 5233, 5255, 5540, 6118
Keady, parish of: 1425, 2079, 2224, 2947, 3354
Keady Church: 2877

Keady Cottage: 304
Keady Presbyterian Meeting-house: 694
Keady Rectory: 481
Keadymore: 3330
Kearn House: 1272
Kearn House, near Portadown: 4170
Kilcarron: 5335
Kildarton: 5640
Killalea Presbyterian Church: 1295
Killcannon, near Markethill: 4102
Killeen Cottage: 58
Killevie Castle: 493
Killilea *var.* Killylea: 4617, 4863
Killowen, near Armagh: 1505
Killuney: 77
Killycairn *var.* Killycarn: 81
Killycarn: 81
Killycarron *var.* Killycarn: 3108
Killycopple: 495
Killylea: 379, 1116, 1186, 4617, 4863, 5498, 5509
Killylea Church: 1186
Killyleagh: 4539
Killymadday *var.* Killymaddy: 766
Killymaddy: 766
Killyman, parish of: 5163
Killyquin: 1453
Kilmacrie, near Markethill: 1533
Kilmore: 1, 3, 105, 613, 1938, 1939, 2172, 2891, 3132, 3182, 5608, 6085
Kilmore Church: 1, 3, 105, 613, 1938, 1939, 2172, 2891, 3182, 5608
Kilmore, near Lurgan: 2358, 4681, 5094
Kiltubbrid: 1457
Kiltubrid *var.* Kiltubbrid, near Middletown: 2488
Kiltubride *var.* Kiltubbrid: 1457
Kilvergan: 991
Kingsmill Presbyterian Church: 1000
Kinneary: 4903
Kinneary, near Armagh: 825
Kinneary, near Charlemont: 1096
Kinnego: 3619
Knappa *var.* Knappagh: 1674, 1746, 2228, 3049, 4096
Knappa *var.* Knappagh Meeting-house: 5498
Knappagh: 1674, 1746, 2228, 2826, 3049, 4096, 4160
Knappagh Presbyterian Church or Meeting-house: 3090, 5498
Knockbawn: 747, 2364

County Armagh, continued:
Knocknashane, near Lurgan: 3594
Lake View: 497
Laraghshankill, near Blackwatertown: 571
Laraghshankle *var.* Laraghshankill, near Blackwatertown: 571
Lattery: 662
Lawnmount, near Lurgan: 2909
Lebawn Cottage, Tynan: 4729
Legacorry: 6056
Legarhill: 61
Legor Hill *var.* Legarhill: 61
Leslie Hill: 747
Leslie-hill, Armagh: 1622
Levaghy, near Portadown: 4481
Limnagore: 455
Linenvale: 927, 1095, 1768, 1819
Lisdown, near Armagh: 679
Lisdrumchor: 3329
Lisdrumwhor *var.* Lisdrumchor: 3329
Lislea: 1806, 4065
Lislea Bleach Works, near Armagh: 4576
Lislea House: 1452, 5072
Lislea, near Keady: 599
Lislooney: 1452, 4079
Lislooney Meeting-house: 866
Lislooney, near Tynan: 3343
Lisnadill: 519, 1770, 2789, 3188, 3203
Lisnadill Church: 4192
Lisnadill Electoral Division: 986
Lisnadill, near Armagh: 1042
Longfield-house, Forkhill *var.* Forkill: 5644
Looneystown, near Richhill: 3097
Loughgall: 249, 266, 358, 368, 402, 419, 487, 674, 726, 730, 838, 905, 1120, 1311, 1327, 1371, 1427, 1623, 1664, 1712, 1743, 1791, 1828, 1880, 2420, 2435, 2956, 2983, 3663, 4241, 4271, 4386, 4422, 4477, 4536, 4608, 4670, 4903, 4932, 5606, 5729, 5905
Loughgall, parish of: 4462, 5714, 5847
Loughgall Church: 266, 402, 730, 5606
Loughgilly, parish of: 2549
Loughgilly Church: 2549
Low Mills, Lurgan: 4717
Lurgaboy: 347, 3649
Lurgan: 12, 115, 119, 131, 148, 241, 271, 313, 465, 508, 563, 569, 610, 653, 814, 819, 859, 918, 931, 991, 1024, 1047, 1094, 1113, 1122, 1136, 1137, 1163, 1243, 1245, 1286, 1428, 1627, 1628, 1698, 1707, 1730, 1740, 1839, 1990, 2000, 2028, 2033, 2332, 2338, 2339,

Lurgan, continued: 2358, 2365, 2440, 2553, 2643, 2644, 2658, 2666, 2685, 2751, 2773, 2774, 2804, 2846, 2865, 2883, 2909, 3209, 3304, 3314, 3318, 3328, 3340, 3345, 3363, 3386, 3395, 3404, 3431, 3594, 3595, 3635, 3665, 3736, 3737, 3850, 3876, 3915, 3940, 3964, 4007, 4115, 4197, 4220, 4266, 4457, 4554, 4650, 4651, 4681, 4682, 4717, 4821, 4825, 4922, 4938, 4968, 5022, 5066, 5071, 5072, 5094, 5137, 5363, 5398, 5438, 5466, 5506, 5532, 5543, 5579, 5595, 5605, 5687, 5731, 5774, 5800, 5843, 5899, 5917, 5994, 6038, 6041, 6077, 6343, 6396
Lurgan Church: 131, 1113, 2685, 2846, 3209, 3304, 3345, 3395, 3736, 3737, 3850, 4650, 4651, 5731
Lurgan Cot, near Richhill: 206
Lurgan Poor Law Union: 819
Lurgan Presbyterian Church or Meeting-house: 313, 1698, 3318, 5532
Maddan: 920, 1587, 4887
Maddan, parish of: 2800
Maddan Chapel: 5554
Maddan Church: 920
Madden *var.* Maddan: 920, 4887
Madden *var.* Maddan, parish of: 2800
Madden *var.* Maddan Chapel: 5554
Madden *var.* Maddan Church: 920
Madden *var.* Maddan Rectory: 1587
Madden *var.* Maddan, near Armagh: 501
Magarity: 739
Magarity, parish of Tartaraghan: 2652
Magheralin Church: 2909
Maghery: 5052
Maghery, Verner's Bridge: 3013
Mall Presbyterian Meeting House, Armagh: 6418
Manse, Armagh: 5471
Maralin *var.* Magheralin Church: 2909
Market Hill *var.* Markethill: 1055
Market-hill *var.* Markethill: 666, 1055, 1231
Markethill: 52, 98, 370, 431, 449, 624, 662, 666, 667, 933, 1023, 1051, 1055, 1121, 1212, 1231, 1330, 1533, 1670, 1895, 2138, 2162, 2210, 2298, 2302, 2512, 2880, 3163, 3164, 3216, 3350, 3401, 3463, 3538, 3625, 3746, 3753, 3852, 3937, 4102, 4117, 4274, 4274, 4490, 4694, 4872, 5045, 5140, 5201, 5495, 5669, 5763, 5827, 6110, 6156
Marlacco *var.* Marlacoo: 6140
Marlacoo: 6140
Marlycoo *var.* Marlacoo: 588

County Armagh, continued:
Marorkin: 475
Meigh Church: 1598
Middletown: 99, 168, 174, 455, 866, 942, 1037, 1125, 1237, 1258, 1405, 1417, 1457, 1558, 1830, 1970, 2245, 2334, 2354, 2488, 3326, 3779, 4131, 5196, 5381, 6056, 6276
Middletown Church: 99, 1405
Middletown Glebe: 1326
Middletown Presbyterian Church: 1417, 2245, 3326, 4428, 6056
Milford, near Armagh: 5318
Millmount, Markethill: 5495
Millmount, Portnorris: 3729
Milltown Church, near Verner's Bridge: 3014
Millview, Keady: 2293
Monbrief, near Lurgan: 5543
Moneycree: 2790
Moore Vale *var.* Moorevale: 3752
Moorebrook: 3317, 3443
Moorebrooke *var.* Moorebrook: 2519
Moorevale: 5812
Moorvale *var.* Moorevale: 226, 912
Moss Spring *var.* Moss-spring, near Charlemont: 82, 1117, 1504, 2073, 2229
Moss View, near Portadown: 2788
Moughan *var.* Mowhan, near Markethill: 2210. *See also* Mowhan.
Mount Caulfield, or Mountcaulfield: 298, 332, 341
Mount Irvin [Irwin?]: 1961
Mount Irwin: 663, 720, 1622, 3868, 4900
Mount Irwin, near Tynan: 1458, 4037
Mountain Lodge: 4703
Mountain Lodge, Keady: 2351
Mountain-lodge: 936
Mountcaulfield: 4672. *See also* Mount Caulfield.
Mounthill: 4204
Mountnorris: 480, 582, 2158, 2828, 2932, 4518, 6295, 6442
Mountnorris Presbyterian Church: 1233, 3329, 3330
Mowhan, Mountnorris: 6442
Mowhan, near Markethill: 5763. *See also* Moughan.
Moynagh, parish of: 299
Mullabrack *var.* Mullaghbrack: 2247, 4799. *See also* Mullaghbrack.
Mullabrack *var.* Mullaghbrack, parish of: 449, 1614, 4910
Mullabrack *var.* Mullaghbrack Church: 347, 370, 4384, 4490, 4636, 4694
Mullaghbawn: 3425
Mullaghbrack: 347, 370, 1330, 2247, 4274, 4384, 4490, 4636, 4694, 4799
Mullaghbrack, parish of: 449, 1614, 2247, 4274, 4910
Mullaghbrack Church: 347, 370, 1330, 4490, 4636, 4694
Mullaghlgass: 3989
Mullaghmore: 6011
Mullaglass *var.* Mullaghglass: 3989
Mullahead: 1881, 2318
Mullahead house, Tandragee: 2227, 5635
Mullalagon *var.* Mullyleggan, near Blackwatertown: 988
Mullalelish: 4871
Mullaletragh, near Richhill: 5460
Mullaloughran: 2702
Mullentine *var.* Mullantine, near Portadown: 3186, 4904, 4939
Mulleoghran *var.* Mullyloughran: 4411
Mullyleggan, near Blackwatertown: 988
Mullyloughran: 4411
Nall *var.* Naul, near Killylea: 5498
Naul: 3639
Naul, near Killyleagh *var.* Killylea: 4539
Newtownhamilton: 196, 317, 468, 738, 1495, 1671, 1714, 1971, 3774, 3893, 3955, 4033, 4290, 4441, 4466, 5107, 5401, 5665, 5856, 5999, 6110, 6156, 6188, 6196, 6234
Newtownhamilton, parish of: 567, 1038, 4384, 5163
Orange-hill, Tandragee: 3660
Palace, Armagh: 5058, 5059
Palnagh *var.* Pollnagh, near Killiliea *var.* Killylea: 4617
Palnagh *var.* Pollnagh: 2457, 4738
Palnagh *var.* Pollnagh, near Killylea: 4617
Park View or Parkview, near Tandragee: 1431, 2295, 3604
Pavilion, Armagh: 3005
Pluck Mills, near Eglish: 3338
Port-Nelligan: 3556
Portadown: 64, 129, 144, 150, 163, 165, 253, 279, 314, 336, 339, 390, 397, 399, 443, 445, 458, 491, 513, 550, 578, 599, 706, 755, 782, 813, 860, 878, 945, 963, 1030, 1080, 1089, 1094, 1144, 1157, 1193, 1217, 1266, 1551, 1560, 1611, 1673, 1747, 1779, 1829, 2044, 2183, 2204, 2204, 2277, 2320, 2500, 2523,

Portadown, continued: 2670, 2788, 2874, 2948, 3019, 3085, 3182, 3186, 3316, 3323, 3341, 3358, 3499, 3541, 3769, 3793, 3828, 3979, 4069, 4097, 4170, 4305, 4325, 4339, 4357, 4397, 4429, 4481, 4585, 4646, 4698, 4728, 4860, 4868, 4884, 4904, 4922, 4939, 5115, 5298, 5454, 5574, 5595, 5619, 5641, 5798, 5860, 6035, 6120, 6125, 6160, 6213, 6215, 6259, 6262, 6264, 6309, 6309, 6353, 6383, 6402

Portadown Church: 163, 165, 314, 339, 3316, 3828

Portadown Presbyterian Church: 4585

Portnorris: 3729

Poyntzpass: 698, 764, 834, 3703, 4093, 6266

Presbyterian Meeting-house, Armagh: 1806

Prospect House, Tandragee: 349, 5581

Providence Chapel, Lurgan: 3328

Queen's Arms, Portadown: 6035

Raughlan: 337, 2961

Rawes, the: 4492

Raws, the *var.* the Rawes: 4492

Rectory, Lurgan: 5994

Rectory, Newtownhamilton: 4466

Red Rock *var.* Redrock Presbyterian Church or Meeting-house: 495, 2632, 4240

Redrock Presbyterian Church: 495, 2632, 4240

Retreat, near Armagh: 4731

Reughlin [Raughlin?]: 5018

Rich-Hill *var.* Richhill: 1192, 1231

Richhill: 84, 85, 206, 458, 1054, 1192, 1231, 1331, 1672, 1748, 1755, 1827, 1898, 1900, 2400, 2548, 2956, 3038, 3050, 3097, 3429, 3586, 4206, 4271, 4325, 4342, 4462, 4586, 4674, 4739, 4871, 4969, 5060, 5678, 6094, 6275

Richhill Church: 458, 1331, 1755, 1827, 2548, 4462, 4969

Richhill Presbyterian Church or Meeting-house: 1054, 3038, 4325, 4871, 5678

Richmount: 394

Richmount, near Portadown: 578, 599

Roan: 4090

Roan Mills: 5885

Rock-cottage, Aughnagurgan: 6359

Rockmount, near Keady: 694, 1029

Rokeby-green, Armagh: 4267

Roman Catholic Chapel, Armagh: 6414

Rosebrook, near Armagh: 331

Rosemount, parish of Tartaraghan: 2373

Ross View Cottage, near Charlemont: 3619

County Armagh, continued:

Roxboro' *var.* Roxborough: 5136, 5527

Roxborough: 5527

Sandy Mount, near Richhill: 3050

Scotch Establishment, Armagh: 714

Seaford [Seagoe?], parish of: 5231

Seago *var.* Seagoe: 3019, 6213

Seago *var.* Seagoe Church: 963, 1673

Seagoe: 125, 1272, 1473, 1673, 1985, 2948, 3019, 3113, 4266, 4429, 4728, 6213

Seagoe, parish of: 5231

Seagoe Church: 963, 1272, 2948, 3113, 4266, 4429, 4728

Second Presbyterian Church or Meeting-house, Armagh: 116, 405, 519, 1505, 3639, 4607, 4722

Second Presbyterian Church, Drumbanagher: 302

Second Presbyterian Meeting-house, Markethill: 662

Segahan *var.* Seagahan, near Armagh: 986

Sevaghen, near Portadown: 1673

Seven Houses, Armagh: 2345, 4363

Shankhill *var.* Shankill, parish of: 1113, 4122

Shankill, parish of: 1113, 4122

Silverwood: 3113

Solitude, Lurgan: 2000

Southwark, Newry: 5893

Spring-hill, Tynan: 3878

St. John's Church, Middletown: 4953

St. Mark's Church, Armagh: 68, 77, 127, 199, 235, 260, 331, 365, 419, 553, 567, 603, 633, 731, 756, 777, 788, 874, 880, 955, 962, 1152, 1403, 1415, 1543, 1554, 1597, 1672, 1783, 1913, 2168, 2223, 2264, 2390, 2800, 2946, 3012, 3112, 3491, 3499, 3914, 3928, 4180, 4267, 4267, 4274, 4297, 4358, 4491, 4896, 5163, 5281, 5285, 5379, 5816, 6275

St. Mark's Church, Portadown: 1030, 2183, 4339, 5298, 5798, 6215

St. Patrick's Cathedral, Armagh: 58, 115, 219

St. Patrick's Chapel, Armagh: 5408, 6277

Storm-hill: 5382

Summer Hill: 169. *See also* Summerhill.

Summer Island: 3930

Summerhill: 5684. *See also* Summer Hill.

Tagnavin *var.* Taghnevan, near Lurgan: 3404

Tanagh, Killalea *var.* Tannagh, Killylea: 1116

Tanderagee *var.* Tandragee: 92

Tandragee: 92, 137, 163, 339, 349, 517, 596, 613, 704, 808, 828, 846, 876, 1088, 1272, 1390, 1427, 1431, 1735, 2038, 2227, 2295,

Tandragee, continued: 2324, 2443, 2490, 2495, 2893, 3211, 3278, 3604, 3660, 3781, 4013, 4206, 4570, 4585, 4649, 4830, 4961, 4997, 5036, 5166, 5198, 5581, 5635, 5733, 5929, 5977, 6092, 6266, 6442
Tandragee Castle: 5109
Tandragee Church: 828, 4649, 4830
Tandragee Presbyterian Meeting-house: 1735
Tandragee School House: 4961
Tannagh, Killylea: 1116
Tartaraghan: 283, 487, 3165, 4583, 6232
Tartaraghan, parish of: 11, 1427, 2266, 2373, 2652, 6078
Tartaraghan Church: 283, 487, 4583
Tartaraghan Glebe: 4004, 5353, 6232
Tartaraghan Rectory: 954, 1727
Tarthlogue: 1228
Tartlogue *var.* Tarthlogue: 1228
Tassagh: 1992, 3039, 3303, 3624, 5681, 5829
Tassagh Presbyterian Church or Meeting-house: 3039, 3303
Tassagh, near Keady: 882, 2680
Tassah *var.* Tassagh: 5681
Tassah *var.* Tassagh, near Keady: 2680
Teagury, near Loughgall: 838
Tegnavin *var.* Taghnevan, near Lurgan: 1047, 5687
Terryskean: 253
Third Presbyterian Church, Armagh: 3851, 5231
Timakeel, near Portadown: 2523, 5231
Timikeel *var.* Timakeel, near Portadown: 2523
Timmakeel *var.* Timakeel, near Portadown: 1144
Tiregerty, near Blackwatertown: 293, 631
Toll Bridge: 609
Tullyallan Presbyterian Church: 3538
Tullyallen Presbyterian Church: 3108
Tullybrick: 1125, 1237
Tullybrick Nursery, near Middletown: 1125, 1237
Tullybrone, near Keady: 283
Tullycairn, Markethill: 624
Tullycalliday *var.* Tullycallidy: 635
Tullycallidy: 635
Tullydoey *var.* Tullydowcy: 776
Tullydowey: 776
Tullyelmer: 115, 2800, 4887
Tullygally, near Lurgan: 4220
Tullyherron Chapel: 6110
Tullymacone House, near Keady: 128, 1036

Tullymore: 1849, 3928
Tullynaglush: 400
Tullynickle: 60
Tullyroan: 629, 1684, 1688, 4135, 4382
Tullyroan, near Loughgall: 1791, 4386, 4477
Tullyrone *var.* Tullyroan: 629, 1684, 1688, 4135
Tullyrone *var.* Tullyroan, near Loughgall: 4386
Tullyvallan: 2646, 6415
Tullyvallen *var.* Tullyvallan: 1063, 6415
Two-mile-Flush: 3257
Tynan: 107, 168, 433, 455, 1053, 1291, 1458, 1931, 2169, 2521, 3343, 3878, 3907, 4037, 4729, 5052, 5608
Tynan, parish of: 174, 3072, 3937, 4896, 5013
Tynan Abbey: 1931, 3670, 4729, 6449
Tynan Church: 107, 455, 2169, 5052
Tyranny *var.* Tyrhanny: 4492
Tyregarty *var.* Tiregerty: 631
Tyregarty *var.* Tiregerty, near Blackwatertown: 293
Tyrhanny: 4492
Tyrone's-ditches *var.* Tyrone's Ditches: 81, 2460, 3703
Tyross: 1456, 1942
Umgola: 469
Urker: 4071
Urker Park, Crossmaglen: 1665
Vallenbrook, Newtownhamilton: 1495
Verner's Bridge: 805, 1204, 1667, 1673, 2032, 3013, 3014, 3187, 6154
Vicar's Hill, Armagh: 9, 177, 219, 516, 606, 615, 811, 973, 1378, 1502, 1704, 2841, 3944, 3954, 4521, 5413, 6410
Victoria House, Armagh: 2080
Watkinshaw's Grove: 5538
Wesleyan Chapel, Armagh: 4997, 6439
Wheatfield, Richhill: 4586
Whengrove: 266
White-hill, Poyntzpass: 834
Willmount: 105
Willmount, near Markethill: 5827
Willowbank, Keady: 749
Wood Park: 4775
Woodbine Cottage, Lurgan: 2553
Woodbine-cottage, Tandragee: 4570
Woodford Cottage, Armagh: 5412
Woodford, near Armagh: 2398, 4074
Woodlawn House, Richhill: 4674
Woodpark: 126, 5997
Woodview, near Richhill: 1748, 3038

The Armagh Guardian, 1844–1852 (Vol. I.) Births, Marriages, and Deaths

Armagh, Archdiocese of:
Parish not named: 5994
Clonoe, parish of: 5089
Derrynoose, parish of: 5089

Armagh, Diocese of:
Parish not named: 1620
Ballygawley: 295
Ballymascanlan, parish of: 969
Balymascanlon *var.* Ballymascanlan, parish of: 969
Clonoe and Derrynoose, united parishes of: 2029
Derver, parish of: 5410
Donaghendry, parish of: 565
Donaghmore, parish of: 3199
Killyman Church: 2266
Kilmore: 1283
Loughgall, parish of: 4775
Madden, parish of: 663
Middletown: 312
Newtownhamilton, parish of: 1174
Tartarahan *var.* Tartaraghan, parish of: 11
Tynan, parish of: 1090

Carlow, county of:
Ballyconnell: 6443
Bunbury Lodge: 5462
Burton Hall: 1766
Carlow: 1473, 3527, 4622, 6062
Cloydagh, parish of: 4381
Cloydagh Church: 4361
Croan: 4848
Erindale: 5737
Font Hill: 6206
Johnstown: 5823
Kilbride: 566
Leighlin-Bridge; Deanery House: 3547
Nurney, parish of: 2613
Rutland, near Carlow: 6062

Cashel, Diocese of; Kilbragh, parish of: 6193

Cavan, county of:
Townland not named: 509, 1285, 1869, 3056, 3677, 3981, 3982, 5375, 5737, 6012, 6014, 6280
Annagh: 1870
Annagh Abbey: 1920
Ardlogher Cottage: 2072
Arva *var.* Arvagh: 1869, 2635

County Cavan, continued:
Arvagh: 1642, 1869, 2459, 4025
Ashfield: 4967, 5439
Ashfield Lodge: 3745
Ashfield, near Cootehill: 3883
Bailieboro' *var.* Bailieborough: 1998, 3729
Bailieborough: 1468, 1998, 3197, 3729, 3785, 4054, 4221, 4819, 5710, 6340
Ballieborough *var.* Bailieborough: 5710
Bailieborough Poor Law Union;
 Greaghnaquinna *var.* Greaghnacunnia: 3065
Ballinacargy: 4214, 4253
Ballinagh: 4098, 5928
Ballinamallard: 5397
Ballintemple: 2661
Ballintemple, parish of: 2690
Ballyconnel *var.* Ballyconnell: 203, 3388
Ballyconnell: 203, 477, 1871, 2034, 3231, 3231, 3388, 3764, 6069
Ballyconnell House: 4545
Ballyhaise: 439, 1873, 4747, 6175
Ballyhaise House: 102, 547, 3636, 3698, 5699
Ballyjamesduff: 1795, 2362, 4454, 5882
Ballyjamesduff Circuit: 2700
Ballymacrue House: 4399
Bawnboy: 5383
Bawnboy House: 333
Bellamont Forest, Cootehill: 1553, 5402, 5953
Bellamount *var.* Bellamont Forest, Cootehill: 1553
Bell's-grove, Mountnugent: 2979
Belturbet: 466, 1091, 1139, 1950, 2048, 2246, 2533, 2852, 2999, 3336, 3420, 4316, 4519, 4549, 4930, 5824, 6065, 6169
Belturbet Church: 1091, 2048
Berrymount: 1689
Bingfield: 215, 3190, 3647, 5795, 6339
Black Lion or Black-Lion *var.* Blacklion: 787, 1711 4470
Blacklion: 787, 1269, 1408, 1445, 1711, 1725, 1826, 1858, 2385, 3738, 4383, 4407, 4470, 4581, 4603, 4749, 5319, 5366, 5399, 6263
Bonebrooke: 810
Broghan: 1384
Broghan House: 1384
Broghan Presbyterian Church: 1384
Broomfield: 1328, 5870
Broomfield, Ballyhaise: 1873
Butlersbridge: 3459, 3803, 3826
Cabra Lodge: 5273
Cabra *var.* Cabragh, near Cootehill: 3142

County Cavan, continued:
Campstown, near Cootehill: 665
Carnavica: 6108
Carne Cottage: 3574
Carrig Glebe: 514
Castle Hamilton: 2240, 2943
Castlerahan: 2656
Cavan: 238, 1091, 1102, 1508, 1739, 1981, 2036, 2059, 2065, 2098, 2188, 2265, 2331, 2380, 2427, 2446, 2655, 2714, 2764, 2889, 2911, 2915, 2998, 3184, 3206, 3423, 3453, 3658, 3681, 3710, 3742, 3743, 3803, 3826, 3925, 3926, 3996, 4176, 4216, 4326, 4498, 4549, 4602, 4677, 4799, 4866, 4892, 5128, 5132, 5156, 5351, 5486, 5507, 5533, 5696, 5757, 6398, 6452
Cavan Church: 238, 3453
Cavan Poor Law Union: 1102, 3681, 5550
Cavan Presbyterian Church or Meeting-house: 3184, 4602
Cavan, near Ballinamallard: 5397
Cleggan, near Blacklion: 5319
Cleggean *var.* Cleggan, near Blacklion: 5319
Clifton: 5243, 5272
Cloncovie: 1437
Clonervy: 195, 5243, 5272
Clonturkhill, near Swanlinbar: 3138
Cloverhill: 4795
Cootehill: 401, 665, 668, 869, 1074, 1420, 1553, 1554, 1639, 1798, 1817, 1996, 2029, 2407, 2408, 2485, 2714, 2794, 2877, 3099, 3142, 3562, 3798, 3870, 3883, 3888, 4031, 4184, 4282, 4438, 4571, 4616, 4967, 5001, 5204, 5371, 5383, 5402, 5550, 5561, 5577, 5710, 5738, 5773
Cootehill, parish of: 3933
Cootehill Church: 1420, 4282
Coothill *var.* Cootehill: 1817
Corgariff: 246
Corr House: 3734
Cortober: 2797
Cranaghan Glebe, Ballyconnell: 2034, 3764
Croghan *var.* Croaghan: 104
Crohan *var.* Croaghan, near Killeshandra: 4168, 4199
Crossdoney: 3561
Culturbet [Belturbet?]: 466
Dartey, near Cootehill: 5577
Denn: 86
Derrygara-house or Derrygara House, Butler's-bridge *var.* Butlersbridge: 3803, 3826
Derrylane, parish of: 2048

Drumacarrow Lodge: 4293
Drumads, near Cavan: 2427
Drumbannon Cottage, Bailieborough: 3785
Drumeena Church: 4795
Drumheel: 4047, 4885
Drumheel House: 1891, 6291
Drumkilroosk: 5882
Drumlane, parish of: 4519
Drumlane Church: 2246
Drummully House: 2240
Drumyarkin, near Cootehill: 5550
Dunglave, near Swanlinbar: 3806
Dunseverick: 5978
Enniskeen, parish of: 1344
Erne Hill: 1091
Farragh House: 5119
Farrenconnel-house *var.* Farren Connell House, Cavan: 2171, 3771, 4671, 5808, 6046
Farrenconnell: 3789
Farrenseer: 3734
Fort Lodge House: 5300
Fort William: 57
Gartinardress: 5787
Glenfarm-Hall, Blacklion: 4603
Gortnaneau [Gortnaneane?]: 4967
Greaghnacunnia: 3065
Greenville: 3458
Hackwood, Killeshandra: 6033
Kildallen Church: 4747
Kill: 4164, 4571
Killeshandra: 104, 1384, 1731, 1787, 1804, 1873, 2142, 2167, 2381, 2484, 2574, 2616, 3474, 3734, 3799, 4168, 4199, 4455, 6033. *See also* Killishandra.
Killeshandra Church: 1787
Killibandrick: 4368
Killinagh Church: 1858
Killinkere Church: 6108
Killinure: 926
Killinure House: 2848
Killishandra *var.* Killeshandra: 2574, 2142, 2167, 3799. *See also* Killeshandra.
Kilmore: 5240
Kilmore Church: 3561, 5119
Kilmore House: 1368
Kilnaleck: 3811
Kingscourt: 2237, 3805, 3823
Kingscourt Church: 1344
Knockatampul *var.* Knocktemple, Virginia: 3908
Lakeview: 4602

County Cavan, continued:
Lara *var.* Larah Church: 1307
Laragh: 3948
Larah *var.* Laragh: 3948
Larchfield, Kingscourt: 2237
Largay: 643, 6211
Lavey, parish of: 5643
Lavey Church: 5643
Lisball: 6108
Lissagoan House: 4288
Loughlan House: 121
Lurgan Lodge: 5638
Lurgan, near Blacklion: 4407
Modubawn, near Cootehill: 5738
Mountnugent: 2979
Mountpleasant, Ballyconnel *var.* Ballyconnell: 477, 3388
Mullaghbawn, near Black Lion *var.* Blacklion: 1445, 4383
Mullintra: 4283
Mullyare, Blacklion: 1826
Munterconnaught, parish of: 1115
Newgrove, near Cootehill: 3888
Nixon Lodge: 5865
Omard: 2910
Plush, near Butlersbridge: 3459
Pottle, near Bailieboro' *var.* Bailieborough: 4221
Prospect: 5119
Quivvy *var.* Quivey, Belturbet: 4316
Quivy Lodge: 4215
Rakenny: 5571
Rantavan: 1351
Ravenswood: 1307, 2205
Rectory House, Killyshandra *var.* Killeshandra: 2142
Rectory, Bailleborough: 1468
Rectory, Templeport: 6226
Redhills: 5126, 5888
Retreat: 5836
Reville Lodge, Ballyhaise: 4747
Rice Hill: 4755
Riversdale House, Belturbet: 6065
Rock-view: 5427
Rockfield: 4560
Rockville: 5882
Rockville, Ballyjamesduff: 4454
Royal School, Cavan: 3742
Quivey, Belturbet: 4316
Shinan House: 4755
Stradone House: 780, 2697, 3597

Sugarloaf: 1517
Summerhill: 5582
Swanlinbar: 907, 1340, 1514, 2051, 2145, 2202, 2887, 2959, 3138, 3406, 3806, 4166, 4987, 5127
Swanlinbar Church: 2145, 3138
Temple Port *var.* Templeport Church: 2910
Templeport: 2910, 6032, 6226
Templeport, parish of: 3218
Templeport Church: 2910
Templeport Rectory: 6032
Thornhill: 983
Thornhill, near Black Lion *var.* Blacklion: 3738
Toam, near Black Lion *var.* Blacklion: 1269, 1858, 2385
Tome *var.* Toam, Blacklion: 5399, 6263
Tomregan, parish of: 3764
Tully: 768
Tully, Killesandra *var.* Killeshandra: 104, 2616
Tullyvin: 2754
Tunnyinn: 4571
Virginia: 3908
Wesleyan Chapel, Cootehill: 4967
Woodville: 4243, 4791

Clare, county of:
Townland not named: 2524
Bath [Rath?]: 6194
Birdhill near Killaloe: 5158, 5180
Carrigorae: 5615
Clare, Union of: 3995
Clondigad: 3210
Drumconra, Ennis: 4347
Ennis: 763, 1477, 2486, 2691, 3210, 4347
Glebe, Kilkeedy: 6231
Hermitage: 2524
Kilkea: 3885
Kilkeedy: 6231
Killaloe: 5180, 5530
Killaloe Cathedral: 5530
Rath: 6194
Tullaker *var.* Tullaher: 6202

Clogher, Diocese of: 1265, 1469, 2561, 2604, 3370, 4511
Clogher Poor Law Union: 3712
Clones Poor Law Union: 1003, 2069, 2438
Clonfert, Diocese of: 894
Clonmacnoise, Diocese of: 1032

Cloyne, Diocese of:
Kilmanhan, parish of: 3655
Kilshannick, parish of: 2722

Connor, Diocese of:
Ballymartin, parish of: 2403
Glebe-house, Ballymartin: 2403

Cork, county of:
Aghadown Glebe: 5838
Aghamarta Castle: 3919
Ballinagaragh: 405
Ballyhooly: 3581
Baltimore: 125
Bandon: 1295, 1439, 1528, 1889, 2933, 3058, 3090, 4286, 4695, 5879
Bantry: 3121, 4081, 6393
Berehaven: 3977, 4741
Blackpool House: 4719
Blackrock: 32
Blackrock, near Cork: 2900
Breeny Beg, near Bantry: 3121
Brewery House, Kinsale: 5674
Brewery-house, Bandon: 1528
Buttevant: 216, 4223
Buttevant, parish of: 4223
Buttevant Barracks: 216
Carlton-villas: 5386
Carrigaline: 2945
Carrigallen *var.* Carrigaline: 2945
Castletown, Berehaven: 3977, 4741
Charleville: 4926
Charleville, parish of: 2722
Clonakilty Church: 125
Cloyne: 5960
Cork: 1590, 1767, 1916, 2175, 2900, 2969, 3415, 3647, 3718, 3726, 3737, 3912, 3934, 4068, 4189, 4207, 4463, 4707, 4777, 5215, 5821, 5947, 5963, 5991
Cork, West Riding of: 5879
Cove: 1312
Cove of Cork: 1082, 4667
Deer Park, Charleville: 4926
Donoughmore: 6010
Donoughmore *var.* Donaghmore Rectory: 709
Drishane: 5750
Fermoy: 909, 3452
Flynnville, near Cloyne: 5960
Glanmire: 5526
Glengarro: 4744

County Cork, continued:
Glenville: 4959
Grove-hill or Grove Hill: 692, 3291
Independent Chapel, Cork: 3726
Kildinan: 1879
Killileagh: 2581
Kilmanhan: 3655
Kinsale: 672, 1364, 3272, 4200, 5674
Kinsale Barracks: 1314
Leslee Court: 703
Little Island House: 2839
Macroom: 6250
Mallow: 2581
Milltown: 4320
Moviddy Rectory: 3772
Newmarket: 4463
Passage: 4979
Passage West: 4334
Queenstown: 5517
Queenstown Church: 3452
Rathclarin Church: 5879
Rathcormac *var.* Rathcormack, parish of: 3580
Rathcormack, parish of: 3580
Rathpeacon: 4719
Scots Church, Bandon: 1295
Scots Church, Cork: 4068
Shandon: 4207
Spike Island, Cove: 1312
Springfort House, Mallow: 2581
St. Mary's Church, Shandon: 4207
St. Mary's Church, Youghal: 1987
Sun Lodge: 5813
Templebrady *var.* Templebready Glebe, Carrigallen *var.* Carrigaline: 2945
Templebready Glebe, Carrigaline: 2945
Trabolgan: 1879
Tureen House, Passage West: 4334
Woodfort, Fermoy: 3452
Youghal: 1987, 2071, 2367
Youghal, parish of: 1987

Cork, Diocese of: 488

Cork, Cloyne and Ross, Diocese of: 6117

Derry, county of:
Townland not named: 407, 1620, 3612, 3695, 4268
Aghadoey *var.* Aghadowey Meeting-house: 407
Aghadowey, parish of: 3651

County Derry, continued:
Aghadowey Meeting-house: 407
Aghanloo Glebe: 3095
Ahanloo *var.* Aghanloo, parish of,
  Newtownlimavady: 882
Ardmore, near Derry: 1238
Ardnargle: 3166
Aughdoey *var.* Aghadowey, parish of: 3651
Ballinahedin *var.* Ballyhanedin: 2817
Ballinderry: 250
Ballinderry, parish of: 5237
Ballinderry, near Magherafelt: 702
Ballindreat, Derry: 2494
Ballongery *var.* Balloughry, near Derry: 824
Ballybritton: 1226
Ballycumlargy *var.* Ballycomlargy,
  Moneymore: 1616
Ballygallon *var.* Ballygallin, Coleraine: 5826
Ballygoney Presbyterian Church: 3074
Ballyhanedin: 2817
Ballykelly: 2787
Ballymoghan: 702
Ballymoughan *var.* Ballymoghan: 702
Ballymuckle-cur: 2096
Ballymulderg, near Magherafelt: 932
Ballynacross: 2694
Ballyoughry: 4588
Ballyougry *var.* Ballyoughry: 4588
Ballyrashane Church: 4073
Ballysally: 3103
Balteagh, parish of: 2914
Banagher Glebe: 3483
Banagher, near Bellaghy: 1944
Beech-hill: 4109
Bellaghy: 1135, 1582, 1705, 1944, 2063, 2322,
  2449, 2693, 3270, 3489, 4109
Bellaghy Castle: 1135, 1525, 1834, 2219, 5662
Bellaghy Church: 1135, 2063
Bellarena: 722, 4971
Boom hall, near Londonderry: 1958
Boreva [Bovevagh?]: 1631
Bovea [Bovevagh?] Meeting-house: 1475
Boveedy: 3090
Bovevagh: 1475, 1631
Braehead, Londonderry: 3992
Burbuoy Cottage, Moneymore: 3210
Burnfoot, near Newtownlimavady: 2049
Burt: 5421
Burt, near Derry: 5210
Cabin-hill, Dervock: 6317
Campsie House: 2340

Carndaisy: 746, 5186
Carrick: 1568
Castle-dawson *var.* Castledawson: 6356
Castledawson: 1132, 1279, 1472, 1676, 1699,
  1700, 1707, 2387, 2486, 2497, 2844, 3003,
  3088, 4114, 4740, 5441, 5732, 6356
Castledawson Presbyterian Church: 1472
Cathedral Church of St. Columb's,
  Londonderry: 3651
Cathedral, Londonderry *var.* Derry Cathedral:
  5682
Cavanreagh, near Draperstown: 3526
Chapel of Ease, Derry: 1840
Churchhill, near Ballykelly: 2787
Clabber, near Coleraine: 3872
Claudy: 4218, 4972
Clondermot, parish of: 1641
Cloughfin: 2494
Clover Hill: 3651
Coach, near Moneymore: 2819
Coleraine: 13, 302, 401, 404, 705, 848, 1109,
  1157, 1172, 1283, 1373, 1463, 1756, 1790,
  1805, 2022, 2134, 2139, 2410, 2609, 2668,
  2710, 2755, 2894, 2950, 3074, 3076, 3091,
  3140, 3351, 3651, 3798, 3872, 4073, 4233,
  4317, 4725, 4767, 5336, 5391, 5445, 5758,
  5826, 5918, 6038, 6134, 6151, 6284, 6311,
  6355
Coleraine Church: 1283, 6038
Coleraine Poor Law Union: 1373
Comber House: 3372
Commercial Hotel, Derry: 1606
Coolafinny: 1867
Coolkeiragh House: 3155, 4962
Cottage, Derry: 4186
Crescent, Derry: 6051
Culnady: 2096
Cumber: 4972
Cumber Upper Church: 3372
Cumber-house: 2092
Curragh, Macosquin: 2695
Derry: 35, 90, 197, 300, 503, 824, 1143, 1175,
  1213, 1214, 1227, 1238, 1242, 1386, 1394,
  1398, 1407, 1509, 1534, 1557, 1606, 1640,
  1774, 1797, 1840, 1855, 1866, 2025, 2095,
  2294, 2487, 2494, 2506, 2529, 2530, 2532,
  2621, 2628, 2688, 2736, 2748, 2989, 3134,
  3148, 3176, 3193, 3194, 3195, 3234, 3334,
  3353, 3387, 3474, 3529, 3590, 3645, 3661,
  3695, 3810, 4026, 4086, 4186, 4195, 4287,
  4350, 4350, 4527, 4535, 4577, 4661, 4667,

Chapter 4: Index of Place Names

Derry (city), continued: 4725, 4762, 4763, 4787, 4809, 4869, 4915, 5028, 5171, 5210, 5583, 5692, 5770, 5786, 5850, 5906, 5971, 6051, 6240, 6267, 6368, 6440. *See also* Londonderry.
Derry Cathedral: 197, 503, 1386, 1509, 2025, 3194, 3643, 4195, 4501, 4869, 5609, 5850, 6240
Derry, Walls of: 2694
Derrylane, near Dungiven: 1475
Dervock: 6317
Desertmartin: 4167
Draperstown: 2600, 3526
Draperstown Presbyterian Church: 5316
Dromore Church: 1699
Drumachose, parish of: 605
Drumachose Church: 5228
Drumbane, near Newtownlimavady: 2982
Drumcorrin: 3774
Drummond, near Moneymore: 2348
Dullaghy: 1132
Dunboe Rectory: 3656
Dunbrock, Newtownlimavady: 6090
Dunduan House, Coleraine: 2609
Dungiven: 1475, 3061, 3449, 5253, 6076, 6258
East Wall Wesleyan Chapel, Londonderry: 4169
Fairview House, near Castledawson: 4114
Faughanvale: 1867, 2483
Faughanvale, parish of: 2960
First Presbyterian Church, Coleraine: 2894, 3076
First Presbyterian Church, Derry or Londonderry: 300, 824, 1213, 3645
First Presbyterian Church, Glendermott *var.* Clondermot: 3774
First Presbyterian Church, Moneymore: 3371
Fort William: 1647
Foyle-view, Derry: 3645
Fruit Hill *var.* Fruithill: 3672
Fruithill: 2181, 2951
Garvagh: 3812, 5160
Gayfield, Muff: 6183
Glendermott: 3774
Glendermott *var.* Clondermot: 1641, 2802
Glenleary, Coleraine: 4317
Glenone Glebe: 2542
Gortnamoyagh: 2329
Gortnessy: 6440
Gortree: 6366
Gravesend Villa: 2329

County Derry, continuted:
Greenhill: 1472
Greenview, Castle-dawson *var.* Castledawson: 1279
Grove, Londonderry: 6392
Hervey Hill: 4842
Inch, near Derry: 5692
Jackson-hall, Coleraine: 2668
Kilcronaghan Glebe: 536, 2648
Killred: 6015
Killyberry, Castledawson: 2486
Killyfaddy, near Magherafelt: 670
Kilrea: 302, 915
Knockadoo: 5186
Knockcloghrim Church: 5979
Knockinkerragh *var.* Knocknakeeragh, near Coleraine: 5445
Knockintarn *var.* Knockantern: 3354
Knockintern *var.* Knockantern: 1401
Knocktarns *var.* Knockantern: 1283
Labby, near Draperstown: 2600
Labbyvale, near Draperstown: 5316
Lakeview House: 1446
Lakeview House, near Magherafelt: 659
Lakeview, Castledawson: 5441
Learmount: 3486, 5088
Learmount Castle: 3378, 3614
Lisachrin: 1132
Lisaghrin *var.* Lisachrin: 1132
Lisalbanagh, Magherafelt: 2681
Lisbuney *var.* Lisbunny: 1396
Lisbunny: 1396
Liscall: 1646
Lismacarrol: 4841
Lismacarroll *var.* Lismacarrol: 5004
Londonderry: 13, 843, 844, 1362, 1383, 1392, 1419, 1448, 1464, 1605, 1708, 1796, 1818, 1958, 2014, 2020, 2118, 2147, 2238, 2425, 2527, 2917, 3233, 3249, 3584, 3645, 3651, 3693, 3766, 3815, 3983, 3992, 4169, 4175, 4178, 4192, 4362, 4473, 4501, 4512, 4771, 5682, 5881, 6244, 6392. *See also* Derry.
Londonderry, registration district of; Registrar's Office, Londonderry: 2989
Lower Tamlaght, parish of: 2542
Luney, near Magherafelt: 2201
Macosquin: 2695, 5160
Macosquin Presbyerian Church: 1756
Maghera: 1977, 2134, 2687, 3100, 4201
Maghera, parish of: 4167
Maghera Church: 4201

371

County Derry, continued:
Magherafelt: 19, 362, 363, 659, 670, 673, 702, 807, 932, 982, 996, 1058, 1168, 1429, 1472, 1529, 1962, 2006, 2078, 2088, 2176, 2201, 2292, 2329, 2433, 2681, 2752, 3047, 3360, 3866, 3993, 4126, 4445, 4801, 6140, 6362
Magherafelt Church: 363, 1359
Magherafelt Poor Law Union: 996, 2201
Magherafelt Presbyterian Church: 673, 932
Magilligan: 2414
Magilligan, parish of: 4043
Magilligan, parish of *var.* Tamlaghtard: 1686, 4052
Magilligan Church: 2414
Magilligan Glebe: 90
Manor House, Kilrea: 915
Molenan: 3893, 5418
Moneyhaw House, Moneymore: 5574
Moneymore: 735, 1279, 1428, 1616, 1708, 1906, 2348, 2681, 2713, 2727, 2736, 2819, 2831, 3159, 3210, 3284, 3371, 3402, 3839, 4324, 4716, 5186, 5574
Moneymore Church: 1428
Muff: 3375, 6183
Mulkeeragh: 1475
Mulkereagh *var.* Mulkeeragh: 1475
Myroe: 1655, 5638
Myroe Presbyterian Church: 1631
Newtownlimavady: 605, 882, 1510, 1535, 1555, 1648, 1650, 1801, 1823, 2049, 2163, 2181, 2951, 2982, 3453, 3672, 3967, 4120, 4193, 5102, 5269, 5874, 6089, 6090
Newtownlimavady Church: 1510
Newtownlimavady Poor Law Union: 2163
Newtownlimivady *var.* Newtownlimavady: 2049
Nn-Limavady *var.* Newtownlimavady: 605, 1650, 5269
Nn-Limavady *var.* Newtownlimavady Church: 605
Prehen-House, Derry: 1774
Quilly, Coleraine: 2755
Redcastle: 4788
River View, Derry: 2748
Rockspring, near Moneymore: 3371
Roe Park: 699
Roe-house: 1510
Roman Catholic Chapel, Moneymore: 5574
Rose Lodge, Magherafelt: 1168, 2078
Rowesgift: 576, 1060
Rush-hall: 5267

Rushfield, Moneymore: 3402
Scots Church, Derry: 3353
Spring-bank, Moneymore: 3159
Springbank: 110, 3074
Springlane, Magherafelt: 2088
St. Columb's, Londonderry: 1448
St. John's Church, Moneymore: 1708, 4324
St. Peter's Church, Derry: 3195
Strieve: 605
Strieve-hill: 5228
Summerhill: 5923
Tamlaght O'Crilly, parish of: 4842
Tamlaght, Newtownlimavady: 6089
Tamlaghtard: 4971
Tamlaghtard, parish of: 2951
Tamlaghtard, parish of, *var.* Magilligan: 4052
Tamlaghtard Church: 4971
Tamlaghtocrilly *var.* Tamlaght O'Crilly, parish of: 4842
Tamnadace *var.* Tamnadeese, near Castledawson: 1700
Tamnadeese: 1700
The Lodge, Newtownlimavady: 1535
The Lodge, NN-Limavady *var.* Newtownlimavady: 1535
Tillinkerry, near Magherafelt: 3047
Tircrevan: 4052
Tiverevan *var.* Tircreven, parish of Tamlaghtard: 4052
Tubbermore: 1529, 2682
Tullybrisland, parish of Faughanvale: 2960
Tullybuoy: 1428
Upper Comber *var.* Cumber Upper Church: 3372
Warbleshinny, parish of Glendermott *var.* Clondermot: 1641
Warwick Lodge: 1341
Waterside, Derry: 1214, 3234
Waterside, Londonderry *var.* Derry: 2014
Woodbank, near Coleraine: 2134

Derry, Diocese of:
Parish not named: 2254, 2796, 4167, 4201, 4362, 5405
Ardstraw, parish of, near Newtownstewart: 889
Derg, parish of: 2763
Donagh, parish of: 5121
Donagh Glebe: 5121
Lower Cumber, parish of: 6253
Tamlaghtard, parish of: 1686

Chapter 4: Index of Place Names

Derry and Raphoe, Diocese of: 4235, 5609

Donegal, county of:
Townland not named: 392, 2054, 2250, 2307, 3651, 5447, 6173, 6356
Admiran: 1471, 5984
Admiran, Stranorlar: 1593, 2055
Admirand *var.* Admiran: 1471, 5984
Admirand *var.* Admiran, Stranorlar: 1593, 2055
Aghanunshin Church: 1118
Allsaints, parish of: 1414
Allsaints and Taughboyne: 3518
Altameenagh: 2549
Archdall Lodge, Bundoran: 6047
Ardara: 1540
Ardnamona: 280
Ards: 2953
Ards House: 3612
Arran Arms Hotel, Donegal: 1052
Aughalane *var.* Aghalaan House, Pettigo: 4424
Aughalane *var.* Aghalaan, near Pettigo: 4447
Aughinunshin *var.* Aghanunshin Church: 1118
Ayr Hill, Ramelton: 1856
Ballgreen: 3376
Ballintra: 941, 1515, 3333, 3857, 3858, 4227, 5600, 5712
Ballintra Church: 5712
Ballyare House: 1799, 1814, 3786
Ballybegly: 1885
Ballybigly *var.* Ballybegly: 1885
Ballyboe, near Manorcunningham: 3688
Ballybofey: 17, 2531, 3418, 5534, 5984, 6229
Ballyconnell: 1868
Ballyconnell House: 1316, 4606
Ballyhenny, Ramelton: 6199
Ballyholly *var.* Ballyholey, near Raphoe: 1485
Ballylennon Presbyterian Church: 1214
Ballylin, Ramelton: 1796
Ballymore: 6004
Ballyshannon: 8, 118, 153, 178, 392, 717, 1131, 1133, 1158, 1179, 1289, 1305, 1365, 1381, 1422, 1451, 1490, 1605, 1696, 1706, 1760, 1935, 2009, 2031, 2083, 2262, 2263, 2277, 2282, 2379, 2934, 2996, 3033, 3110, 3129, 3312, 3411, 3479, 3480, 3481, 3654, 3692, 3842, 3864, 3938, 4021, 4158, 4187, 4234, 4245, 4269, 4315, 4387, 4421, 4513, 4531, 4548, 4648, 4680, 4757, 4764, 4981, 4996, 5223, 5238, 5241, 5250, 5350, 5535, 5536, 5544, 5599, 5760, 5822, 5823, 5871, 5987, 6165, 6246, 6350
Ballyshannon, parish of: 221
Ballyshannon Church: 118, 221, 392
Barkhall, Letterkenny: 6261
Bedford: 248
Birdstown: 4896, 5609, 5986
Bonny Glen, Donegal: 844
Bridge Cottage, Carndonagh, Gawin: 4978
Brown-hall: 6318
Bunbeg, Gweedore: 2126
Buncrana: 743, 1082, 1794, 2294, 2671, 3083, 3645, 3777, 4064, 4869
Buncrana Castle: 2194
Buncrana Presbyterian Church: 4064
Bundoran: 179, 324, 1313, 1422, 1668, 1894, 1909, 2218, 2376, 3124, 3151, 3439, 3666, 3874, 4250, 5100, 5969, 6047, 6200
Burt: 3126
Burt Church: 5753
Cabry Church: 5494
Calhame: 1568
Carnagrave: 345
Carndonagh: 4567, 4978
Carraduffy: 1951
Carrickart Church: 2917
Carricknahorna, near Ballyshannon: 4757
Carrigart *var.* Carrickart Church: 2917
Carrowcannon: 429
Carrycastle, Ramelton: 1975
Carthage-House, Culdaff: 1565
Cashel-house: 1907
Cashel, near Ballyshannon: 3479
Castlefin: 1656, 2467, 2496, 3084, 3093, 3859, 5212, 5712
Castlemunay, near Dunkaneely *var.* Dunkineely: 1397
Claggan, near Culdaff: 2508
Cloghaneely: 2426, 5894
Clondavaddog Church: 301
Clondevanddock *var.* Clondavaddog Church: 301
Clonmany Church: 2085
Close, Raphoe: 5761
Convey *var.* Convoy: 2624
Convoy: 1603, 2624, 2645
Convoy House: 2647
Conyburry *var.* Coneyburrow, near Lifford: 2402
Coraduffy *var.* Carraduffy: 1951
Cottage, Donegal: 1512
Covehill, near Letterkenny: 3863
Coxtown: 1075

County Donegal, continued:
Crossroads: 3211
Crossroads, Donegal: 1584
Culdaff: 1565, 2508
Culdaff, parish of: 3150, 4859
Curraughmoan, Stranorlar: 4835
Desertegy: 2802
Dingledycooch Lodge, Bundoran: 3666
Donegal: 231, 844, 978, 1052, 1296, 1342,
  1362, 1512, 1539, 1583, 1584, 1772, 2238,
  2301, 2360, 2626, 3234, 3258, 3265, 3274,
  3652, 3863, 4035, 4344, 4522, 4720, 4736,
  4876, 5564, 5646, 5930, 5966, 6235, 6243
Donegal Church: 2301
Dooish: 1471, 2049
Doolish [Dooish?]: 1471
Dountinny: 6206
Drimnahoagh *var.* Drumnahoagh, Letterkenny:
  2077
Dromore, near Letterkenny: 1632, 6199
Drumboe: 3927
Drumholme *var.* Drumhome: 6385
Drumhome: 6385
Drumlogher: 1447
Drumnahoagh, Letterkenny: 2077
Dsimnacrosh: 2507
Dunfanaghy: 388, 847, 1632, 2047, 2113, 2954,
  3233, 3325, 3436, 3536, 4232, 4829, 6349
Dunfanaghy Presbyterian Church: 1632
Dungloe: 5998
Dungloe Church: 4151, 4200
Dunkaneely *var.* Dunkineely: 1260, 3011
Dunkineely: 1260, 1397, 3011, 4005
Dunlewey House: 3447, 3450
Dunlewvey *var.* Dunlewey House: 1919
Dunwilley: 1530
Dysertegney *var.* Desertegny, parish of: 2802
Dysertegney *var.* Desertegny Church: 2802
Eddnaharnon Cottage, Letterkenny: 6431
Fahan: 4787
Fahan Church: 5923
Falcaragh *var.* Falcarragh, Dunfanaghy: 2047
Falcarragh: 4527
Fanet: 301
Figart House, Dunfanaghy: 4232
Finner Church, Bundoran: 1894
Fintra House: 3265, 3558
Fintra House, near Killybegs: 2480, 3063
First Presbyterian Church, Stranorlar: 1471
Fort Royal: 4542
Fort Stewart: 5743

Fortwilliam: 5292, 5302
Fox-hall *var.* Foxhall: 66
Foxhall, Letterkenny: 5120
Foyle View: 3643
Fyfannan house, Killybegs: 4835
Fyfannon *var.* Faiafannan, Killybegs: 3761
Glebe-house, Kilteevock *var.* Kilteevogue:
  3366
Glen House: 2085
Glen Lodge: 3248
Glenalla: 1860
Glencar, near Letterkenny: 2769
Glenfin Church, parish of Kelteevack *var.*
  Kilteevogue: 1454
Glenfin, parish of Kilteevogue: 1454
Gortlee: 1343
Gortlee Covenanting Church: 1343
Graffy, near Strabane: 2465
Green Cottage, Manorcunningham: 1527
Greencastle: 2966, 3717
Greenfort: 5663
Greenhill: 771
Grove, the: 3786
Gweedore: 2126, 3447
Higginstown House, Ballyshannon: 5544
Horn Head *var.* Hornhead: 4802
Hornhead: 4504
Inishkeel, parish of: 1215
Inniskeel *var.* Inishkeel, parish of) 1215
Inver, parish of: 2017
Inver Church: 844, 6206
Inver House: 2017
Kilbarron Church, Ballyshannon: 4234
Kilcar, parish of: 3558
Kildeney *var.* Kildoney Glebe, near
  Ballyshannon: 6350
Kill, near Dunfanaghy: 2113
Killaghtee: 1215, 3424, 4005
Killaghtee, parish of: 3281
Killaghtee Church: 1215, 3281, 3424, 4005
Killaughlig, near Letterkenny: 2430
Killemard *var.* Killymard Church: 6265
Killult Church: 429, 1584, 2126, 4527
Killybegs: 1148, 1159, 1951, 2267, 2480, 2954,
  3063, 3265, 3405, 3424, 3462, 3558, 3761,
  4835
Killybegs Church: 1951, 3558
Killygordon: 3631
Killylastion *var.* Killylastin, Letterkenny: 1975
Killymard: 4002
Killymard Church: 1342, 6265

Chapter 4: Index of Place Names

County Donegal, continued:
Kilmacrenan: 4373, 6045
Kilmacrenan, Barony of: 285
Kilteevogue: 3366
Kilteevogue, parish of: 1454, 3366
Kiltiferigle *var.* Kiltyfergal: 3470
Kiltyfergal: 3470
Kimmid: 3241
Kincraige: 3525
Kinnycally: 3778
Knowhead: 4350
Lackagh: 1577, 2100
Laghey *var.* Laghy: 1654, 6385
Laghy: 6385
Legnathraw: 2559
Letterkenny: 865, 1260, 1434, 1435, 1568, 1632, 1975, 2007, 2021, 2077, 2166, 2192, 2357, 2430, 2474, 2769, 3101, 3233, 3422, 3612, 3778, 3863, 3892, 5120, 5145, 5172, 5890, 5896, 6009, 6199, 6261, 6431
Letterkenny Church: 1260
Lettershambo *var.* Lettershanbo: 3470
Lettershanbo: 3470
Lifford: 1376, 1388, 1391, 1488, 1850, 2008, 2363, 2402, 3447, 4200, 4931
Lifford Church: 2008
Lifford Common: 3650
Lisnabert: 3606
Lisnenan, near Letterkenny: 2021
Lough Eske: 47, 4736, 5236
Lough Salt: 4151
Loughnaginn, near Letterkenny: 2474
Lupta, near Ballyshannon: 5871
Manorcunningham: 1329, 1478, 1527, 1602, 1800, 2558, 3289, 3688
Marblehill House: 5025
Mason Lodge: 4195
Meenlecklanore Cottage: 4151
Mevagh, parish of: 2917, 5516
Milford: 1591, 3560
Millfield, Buncrana: 1794
Moncllan: 3591
Moneltan *var.* Monellan: 2750
Moneygregin *var.* Moneygreggan, near Newtowncunningham: 1591
Monreagh: 3064, 3893
Moor, Donegal: 1539
Mooreview House, near Kilmacrenan: 4373
Moorview, Letterkenny: 5172
Mountcharles: 325, 1388, 2368, 3520, 4898, 4914, 5216, 5611, 5624
Moville: 2086, 2966
Moyaugh, near Rathmelton *var.* Ramelton: 3530
Muff: 4788
Muff Church: 4915
Mullaghderg, parish of: 4151
Mullanboy, near Castlefin: 1656
Munglas: 3591
Murlog *var.* Murlough, near Lifford: 2363
Murlog *var.* Murlough Catholic Chapel: 2008
Murlough: 2008
Murlough Catholic Chapel: 2008
Murvagh, Ballintra: 4227
Newtowncunningham: 1591, 3518, 4808
Nn. Cunningham *var.* Newtowncunningham: 4808
Oak Park: 1118, 1652, 3092, 3756
Oak Park, Letterkenny: 3422
Pettigo: 285, 1069, 1284, 1612, 1937, 2654, 3078, 3204, 3241, 3874, 4424, 4432, 4447, 4790, 4807, 5759, 6385
Pettigo Church: 285, 1937, 3620, 3874
Pettigo Presbyterian Church: 3241, 4432
Port Nassau *var.* Portnassau, near Ballyshannon: 4158, 4387, 5536, 5987
Portballyraine, Letterkenny: 865
Portsalon: 4940
Ramelton: 11, 1429, 1591, 1796, 1856, 1876, 1975, 2984, 3233, 3376, 3778, 3894, 4072, 4488, 4508, 6185, 6199
Ramelton Church: 11
Raphoe: 14, 1485, 1513, 1513, 2608, 3492, 3644, 4195, 4227, 4448, 5516, 5761
Raphoe Presbyterian Church: 2608, 4448
Rashin *var.* Roshin, near Dunfanaghy: 1632
Rathmelton: 3530
Rathmullan: 1375, 3232
Rathmullan Church: 2089
Rathmullen House: 5779
Ray: 703
Ray, near Manor-Cunningham *var.* Manorcunningham: 1329, 1602
Raymochey *var.* Raymoghy Church, Mannorcunningham: 1478
Raymocky *var.* Raymoghy, parish of: 6357
Raymoghy: 1800
Raymoghy, parish of: 6357
Raymoghy Church, Manorcunningham: 1478
Rectory, Letterkenny: 2007
Red Castle: 4531
Registrar's Office, Ballyshannon: 4548

County Donegal, continued:
Registrar's Office, Donegal: 3258
Registrar's Office, Stranorlar: 3470
Rochfort, Buncrana: 743
Rock Park: 3620, 4911
Rockfort: 3813
Rockfort, Buncrana: 1082
Rockhill, Letterkenny: 3612
Rockville, Ballyshannon: 5535
Rosehill, Fahan: 4787
Roshine Lodge, Donegal: 4736
Rossvoyland Lodge, near Donegal: 5930
Roughan, parish of Allsaints: 1414
Rowantree Hill: 1165
Rubleshaney [*var.* Urbalshinny?], near Milford: 1591
Scarnamallagh Glebe: 2121
Scots' Church, Ramelton: 3233
Sea-view: 4994
Second Presbyterian Church, Ramelton: 1975
Sharon, near Manorcunningham: 1800
Sheephaven, Coast Guard district of: 6004
Shellfield: 5559
Spamount, Dunkaneely *var.* Dunkineely: 4005
Spamount, Dunkineely: 4005
Sprackburn, Letterkenny: 2166
Springfield, Bundoran: 1668
St. John's Point: 1362, 2089
St. Johnston: 34, 2193
Stranorlar: 1471, 1530, 1593, 2055, 2667, 3470, 4534, 4835
Stranorlar Church: 1530
Swanmount: 1215, 3136, 3156, 3225
Swilly View, near Letterkenny: 6009
Tarmon House: 4151
Taughboyne: 3518
Templecarne, parish of: 1284, 3874
Templecarne Glebe, near Pettigo: 1284
Templecrone, parish of: 4151
Templemore, parish of: 1813
Terhomin: 2430
Three Trees: 3221
Trumman, Donegal: 3258
Trummen *var.* Trumman, Donegal: 3258
Tulloughobegley, parish of: 429
Tullydonnell: 2645
Tullydonnet *var.* Tullydonnell, near Convoy: 2645
Ture Castle: 3020
Tyrconnell: 4151
Urbalshinny: 1591

Wesleyan Chapel, Donegal: 4035
Wesleyan Methodist Chapel, St. John's Point: 1362
White House, Killybegs: 1148
Whitecastle: 611
Willsbrook, near Ballyshannon: 221
Wood Lodge, Mountcharles: 2368
Woodhill, near Ardara: 1540

Down, county of:
Townland not named: 2128, 4119, 4701, 5566, 5641
Agnesville: 133
Anahilt *var.* Annahilt: 4944
Anahilt *var.* Annahilt, parish of: 3867
Annahill Meeting-house: 1146
Annahilt: 2679, 4944
Annahilt Meeting-house: 1146
Ardbrin, near Banbridge: 2397
Ardglass: 1919, 6332
Ardtrin: 3751
Arnol's Vale *var.* Arno's Vale, Rostrevor: 1625
Arno's Vale: 4343
Artanna *var.* Ardtanagh, Seaforde: 5628
Ashton, Newry: 2333
Aughnacavan: 2580
Aughnacavan, Donaghmore, near Newry: 1741, 2518
Backnamulough: 5432
Ballee: 207
Balling-house, Banbridge: 3963
Balloo House: 5283
Balloo, Bangor: 639
Ballyblack: 2050
Ballyboley, near Greyabbey: 3559
Ballybranagh, near Downpatrick: 2938
Ballycopeland Presbyterian Church: 2050
Ballydown: 184
Ballydugan House: 3602
Ballyesborough: 207, 208
Ballygilbert: 5344
Ballygilbert Presbyterian Church: 4152
Ballyhalbert: 208, 576
Ballyhemlin: 2827
Ballyhomra, near Hillsborough: 1336
Ballykelly, near Banbridge: 6370
Ballylimp: 5202
Ballymacarrett: 5832
Ballymacarrett Presbyterian Church: 2300
Ballymagarick *var.* Ballynagarrick, Gilford: 3186
Ballynagarrick: 4429

Chapter 4: Index of Place Names

County Down, continued:
Ballynahinch Church: 157
Ballynaskea: 5176
Ballyobegan, Ballywalter: 2827
Ballyobican *var.* Ballyobegan, Ballywalter: 2827
Ballyrussell, Comber: 639
Ballytrim House: 2760
Ballywalter: 2827
Ballyward, parish of Drumgooland: 1406
Banbridge: 157, 184, 568, 708, 950, 1418, 1878, 1960, 2143, 2174, 2388, 2397, 2838, 2894, 2903, 2921, 2924, 3042, 3242, 3364, 3368, 3460, 3516, 3744, 3905, 3963, 3976, 3980, 4173, 4356, 4360, 4377, 4642, 4675, 4743, 4782, 4871, 4878, 4921, 4929, 5074, 5340, 6025, 6127, 6179, 6329, 6361, 6370, 6391, 6413
Banbridge Poor Law Union: 2924
Banford House, Gilford: 1728
Bangor: 639, 1419, 4925, 5626, 6189
Bangor, parish of: 6189
Bangor Church: 5626
Bank Lodge, Downpatrick: 3109
Barbacon Cottage, Bryansford: 4147
Barnmeen: 2772
Bellmount, Banbridge: 6127
Bessmount, near Dundonald: 2156
Black Causeway: 3321
Black-causeway, Strangford: 363
Blairs *var.* Blaris: 2864
Blaris: 2864, 3017
Boardmills: 2828
Briansford *var.* Bryansford: 3758
Brookfield, Banbridge: 4782
Bryansford: 415, 1896, 2988, 3758, 4147, 4901, 5978
Bryansford Church: 415, 1896, 5978
Bunkerhill House: 3895
Buskhill, Donaghmore: 886
Cabra House: 471
Camperdown, Comber: 4723
Cargycreevy: 2888
Carmeen: 2795
Carnmeen: 4482
Carpenham: 2102
Carradare [*var.* Carrowdare?] Castle: 360
Carrowdore Castle: 3005
Castle-hill, Rathfriland: 3921
Castle, Dundrum: 2540
Castlewellan: 1406, 2151, 2510, 2611, 4626

Castlewellan Presbyterian Church: 4626
Clare, near Moira: 3244
Clare, Waringstown: 4197, 5950
Clonallan, parish of: 2836
Clonallen *var.* Clonallan, parish of: 2836
Clough: 2611, 5820, 6358
Clough Presbyterian Church or Meeting-house: 1406, 5820
Cloverhill, near Loughbrickland: 721
Comber: 639, 3239, 4723, 5142
Corbally: 1964
Craigavad: 2871
Craigavad, near Holywood: 3131
Crawfordsburn: 4734, 6322
Creevy: 849
Derryaghy: 3380
Derrycraw, near Newry: 5380
Divernagh *var.* Duvernagh, Newry: 3787
Donaghadee: 825, 2050, 4246
Donaghmore: 123, 642, 886, 1164, 1741, 2518, 2580, 3703, 3976
Donaghmore Presbyterian Church or Meeting-house: 123, 3897
Donaghmore, Newry: 4724
Donoughmore *var.* Donaghmore: 1164
Donoughmore *var.* Donaghmore, parish of: 4514
Donoughmore *var.* Donaghmore Presbyterian Church: 3897, 1263, 1600, 1747, 2076, 2200, 2593, 2720, 2938, 2980, 2981, 3109, 3555, 3693, 3782, 4306, 5035, 5073, 5990
Downpatrick Poor Law Union: 5035
Downshire Road Presbyterian Church or Meeting-house, Newry: 3825, 3956, 5853, 6058
Dromara: 3865, 4461, 5628
Dromore: 1617, 2389, 2395, 4122, 4614, 4614, 4793, 4832
Dromore, parish of: 4264
Dromore Cathedral: 4264, 4614
Dromore Church: 4832
Drumbane, near Moira: 1277
Drumbeg, near Lisburn: 2151
Drumbo: 308
Drumgooland, parish of: 1406
Drumnagally: 6391
Drumnahall: 985
Drumnavaddy House, Banbridge: 1960
Drumnikelly: 2993
Dundonald: 2156, 4590
Dundonald, parish of: 4590

377

County Down, continued:
Dundrum: 2540, 2993
Dunsford Church: 1964
Ebenezer Chapel, Newry: 1201
Edenderry, Loughbrickland: 3626
Edenderry, Scarva: 4969, 6094
Edentrillick: 5432
Edentrillie *var.* Edentrillick: 5432
Elmdale, near Newry: 2997
Elmfield, Gilford: 1728
Elsinore, Rostrevor: 1355
Emyvale *var.* Emyville, Newry: 4865
Emyville, Newry: 4937
Finnis, Dromara: 5628
First Presbyterian Church, Saintfield: 4837
First Presbyterian Meeting-house, Newry: 3957
Fort Hill, Banbridge: 2894
Fourtowns: 302, 834
Fourtowns Presbyterian Church: 834
Gilford: 1543, 1728, 2148, 2269, 3186, 3342, 3943, 4266, 4879, 4889, 5033, 5178, 5221, 5449, 5875, 5951, 6025, 6179, 6272
Glascar: 3703, 3976, 4724, 5345, 5735
Glascar Presbyterian Church: 3703, 3976, 4724
Glastry: 207, 208, 5202
Glebe House, Bangor: 6189
Glebe, Dundonald: 4590
Glebe, Strangford: 3724, 5314
Glen Chapel: 5380
Greenfield: 3876
Greyabbey: 3135, 3559
Harrymount: 1815
Hazel-bank: 4510
Hazel-bank, near Banbridge: 3516
Heartsfort, Rosstrevor: 1675
Heartsfort, Rosstrevor *var.* Rostrevor: 1675
Heath Hall, Newry: 5792
Hillhall: 5074
Hillhall, near Lisburn: 100
Hillsboro' *var.* Hillsborough: 3914, 5920
Hillsborough: 97, 1336, 2451, 2650, 2773, 3311, 3396, 3914, 3921, 4101, 5920, 6082, 6404
Hillsborough Church: 97, 2773
Hillsborough Presbyterian Church: 2650
Hilltown Glebe: 3170
Holywood: 1735, 2027, 2833, 3119, 3131, 3846, 3895, 3975, 3977, 4905, 5124, 5275, 5434, 5779, 5994, 6432
Holywood Church: 2027, 3846, 3895, 5779
Holywood Mills: 6432

Kate's-bridge: 1418
Kescum: 5345
Kilbroney, parish of: 3048
Kilbroney, Rosstrevor *var.* Rostrevor: 1038
Kilbroney, Rostrevor: 1038
Kilkeel: 95, 2893, 3167, 3646, 5053, 5679, 5781, 5820, 5858
Kilkeel Church: 95, 5053
Killaghy, near Donaghadee: 2050
Killaughy *var.* Killaghy, near Donaghadee: 2050
Killinchy: 212, 5649
Killowen, near Rosstrevor *var.* Rostrevor: 706
Killowen, near Rostrevor: 706
Killroney, Rostrevor: 2582
Killyleagh: 459
Killyleagh Church: 459
Kilmacrew House: 3751
Kilmacrue *var.* Kilmacrew House: 3751
Kilmood: 1964
Kircubbin *var.* Kirkcubbin: 500, 5076, 5513, 5671, 5723, 5739
Kirkcubbin *var.* Kircubbin: 2657, 3553, 5076, 5723, 5723, 5739
Knockbreda: 5849
Lakemount: 2395, 4832
Lakeview, near Newry: 2743
Laurel Lodge: 2673
Laurencetown, Banbridge: 6413
Lawrencetown House: 3614
Legacurry Presbyterian Church: 2012
Legmore, Derriaghy *var.* Derryaghy: 3380
Legmore, Derryaghy: 3380
Lesize-house: 5337
Lisadian: 1000, 2825
Lisban, Kirkcubbin *var.* Lisbane, Kircubbin: 2657
Lisburn: 100, 2012, 2151
Lisnadian [*var.* Lisadian?]: 1000
Lisnagannon, near Loughbrickland: 5586
Lisnastrain *var.* Lisnastrean, near Lisburn: 2012
Lisnastrean, near Lisburn: 2012
Lissidian [Lisadian?] House: 2825
Locust Lodge: 4615
Longhorne *var.* Loughorne: 123
Loughagery *var.* Loughaghery: 100
Loughaghery: 2679, 3867
Loughaghery Presbyterian Church or Meeting-house: 2679, 3867
Loughaghny [*var.* Loughagery?] Meeting-house: 2679

Chapter 4: Index of Place Names

County Down, continued:
Loughaghry *var.* Loughaghery: 2650
Loughaghry *var.* Loughaghery Presbyerian Church: 3867
Loughans, Gilford: 6179
Loughborne *var.* Loughorne: 1164
Loughbrickland: 721, 3242, 3626, 5586
Loughbrickland Presbyterian Church: 3242
Loughoine *var.* Loughorne: 2580
Loughorne: 123, 1164, 2518, 2580
Magheralin: 4516, 5438
Magheralin, parish of: 5681
Magherally: 1243, 3042
Magherally Presbyterian Church: 1243
Marine, Holywood: 2027
Maryvale: 2580
Maxwell Court: 1359
Maze House: 2836
Mill Isle: 642
Millisle *var.* Mill Isle: 642
Millmount, Banbridge: 2143, 4878
Millvale, Rostrevor: 5587, 5929
Moira: 281, 1277, 1480, 3244, 4640
Money Carragh *var.* Moneycarragh: 3491
Moneycarragh: 3491
Morne: 790, 6278
Morne Rectory, Kilkeel: 3646, 5679
Mount Kearney: 3897
Mountnorris: 1433
Moyallen: 1
Moygannon: 1999
Moygannon, Rosstrevor *var.* Rostrevor: 756
Moygannon, Rostrevor: 756
Mullertown House, near Kilkeel: 5858
Mutton-hill, Banbridge: 184
Narrow Water: 6064
Narrowater *var.* Narrow Water: 6064
New Church of Magheralin, near Lurgan, co. Armagh: 5438
Newcastle: 2664, 3758, 3788, 4901, 5519
Newry: 42, 88, 95, 132, 164, 174, 186, 226, 290, 348, 357, 389, 408, 410, 444, 486, 503, 517, 541, 637, 654, 689, 723, 760, 790, 829, 848, 870, 872, 881, 886, 913, 922, 937, 945, 946, 957, 992, 1000, 1009, 1030, 1112, 1126, 1146, 1195, 1201, 1281, 1336, 1532, 1598, 1661, 1709, 1732, 1741, 1778, 1816, 2011, 2018, 2058, 2081, 2099, 2103, 2130, 2161, 2261, 2333, 2337, 2452, 2554, 2577, 2650, 2683, 2689, 2731, 2743, 2758, 2820, 2842, 2863, 2884, 2885, 2942, 2992, 2997, 3006,

Newry, continued: 3070, 3159, 3171, 3197, 3243, 3371, 3399, 3563, 3583, 3632, 3787, 3808, 3825, 3890, 3897, 3923, 3932, 3956, 3957, 3965, 4136, 4137, 4145, 4157, 4174, 4233, 4514, 4553, 4591, 4592, 4619, 4669, 4710, 4724, 4774, 4830, 4865, 4937, 4955, 5016, 5019, 5173, 5252, 5256, 5342, 5352, 5380, 5400, 5425, 5437, 5520, 5537, 5545, 5561, 5614, 5635, 5648, 5672, 5676, 5693, 5734, 5769, 5792, 5812, 5853, 5893, 5939, 6028, 6052, 6058, 6074, 6130, 6144, 6197, 6227, 6274, 6286, 6376, 6384, 6422
Newry Barracks: 4633
Newry Cathedral: 4137
Newry Poor Law Union: 937, 4553
Newtownards: 1359, 2117, 2120, 3559, 3585, 4770
Newtownbreda: 1965
Ogle's Grove, Hillsborough: 4101
Omeath, near Newry: 723
Orange-hill, Banbridge: 6179
Orangefield: 1965, 2662
Parochial House, Dromara: 3865
Parsonage, near Kirkcubbin *var.* Kircubbin: 3553
Portaferry: 5887
Purdysburn, Belfast: 3037
Rathfriland: 387, 828, 1201, 1480, 1608, 2664, 3245, 3360, 3689, 3851, 3921, 3987
Rathfryland *var.* Rathrfriland: 387
Reformed Presbyterian Congregation of Newry: 886
Registrar's Office, Banbridge: 1418
Ringclare, Donaghmore: 3703, 3976
Ringclave *var.* Ringclare, Donaghmore: 3976
Ringford, near Ardglass: 6332
Rose Hall: 2162
Rosemount Cottage, Gilford: 2148
Rosstrevor *var.* Rostrevor: 389, 916, 1625, 1940, 2120, 2721
Rosstrevor *var.* Rostrevor Church: 1940
Rostrever *var.* Rostrevor: 2120
Rostrevor: 186, 322, 389, 706, 756, 916, 1038, 1355, 1940, 2102, 2582, 2721, 2858, 3048, 3059, 3231, 3782, 3931, 4343, 5081, 5557, 5929
Rostrevor Church: 1038, 1940, 3048
Roughfort, near Banbridge: 3242
Saintfield: 1765, 2464, 3940, 4042, 4837, 6178
Saintfield House: 1127, 1765
Sandys-street Church, Newry: 2081

County Down, continued:
Sandys-street Presbyterian Church, Newry: 790, 2577, 4774
Saul Rectory: 859
Scarva: 4206, 4889, 4969, 5635, 5868, 6094
Scarva Presbyterian Church: 4889
Seafield, Kilkeel: 2893
Seaford *var.* Seaforde: 3471
Seaforde: 3471, 5628
Seaview, near Rostrevor: 5081
Second Presbyterian Church, Bangor: 1419
Second Presbyterian Church, Newry: 3808
Second Presbyterian Church, Rathfriland: 3689
Spring Hill, near Waringstown: 5778
Springvale, Gilford: 4266
St. John's Church, Moira: 1480
St. Mary's Church, Newry: 226, 348, 517, 586, 864, 945, 3583, 5256, 5734
Stramore House: 6141
Strandtown, near Belfast: 849
Strangford: 363, 2374, 3724, 3896, 5314
Toughblane, near Hilsborough *var.* Hillsborough: 6404
Tremount: 1674
Trevor Hill: 91, 3691
Trevor Hill, Newry: 5019
Tromara, near Moira: 281
Tullycairne: 4264
Tullyconnaught: 4941, 5368
Tullyconnaught House, near Banbridge: 2838
Tullylish: 1243, 1728, 2148, 3257, 3516, 3980, 4197, 5950, 6141, 6179, 6413
Tullylish, parish of: 5572
Tullylish Church: 1728, 3257, 6413
Tullylish Church, near Banbridge: 3980
Tullylish Presbyterian Meeting-house: 2148
Tullylish-house, Gilford: 5221
Tullylisk *var.* Tullylish: 4197
Tullymore Park: 1280
Tullynakill: 4963
Tullyrain: 4360
Tullyraine *var.* Tullyrain: 4360
Tyrella: 1755
Unitarian Meeting-house, Newry: 2452
Waringston *var.* Waringstown: 3257
Waringstown: 3257, 4095, 4122, 4197, 5778, 5950
Warrenpoint: 335, 688, 791, 1008, 1098, 1110, 1154, 1217, 1773, 1816, 1850, 1922, 1999, 2441, 2649, 2793, 3030, 3924, 3945, 3947, 4044, 4091, 4341, 4627, 4710, 4803, 4951, 4955, 5094, 5340

Warrenpoint Church: 335, 688, 791, 1773, 4091, 4341, 5094
Warrenpoint Presbyterian Church: 4710
Wellington Lodge, near Hillsborough: 3921
Wesleyan Chapel, Newry: 164
Willmount, Ranbridge [Millmount, Banbridge?]: 2143
Willowbrook, Scarva: 5635
Windsor Hill, Newry: 957, 1732
Woodside: 4837

Down, Diocese of:
Parish not named: 3869, 3885
Kilmore: 344

Down and Connor, Diocese of: 2149, 3642, 4369, 5994

Down and Connor and Dromore, Diocese of: 3219

Dromore, Diocese of:
Parish not named: 2836, 3865, 5889
Clonduff, parish of: 3170

Dublin, county of:
Townland not named: 5510
Allerton: 4813
Anne Vale, Golden Bridge: 6054
Ashbrook, Cullenswood: 2002
Ashtown: 6174
Auburn: 30
Balbriggan: 2546, 2665
Balbriggan Church: 2665
Ballygallbeg: 1038
Ballyowen: 3377
Belle Villa, Dublin: 3287
Belle Vue: 3727
Belmont House, Stillorgan: 6423
Belview: 5510
Blackrock: 120, 895, 922, 1921, 3801, 3814, 3816, 3891, 4107, 4547, 6196, 6234
Blanchardstown: 6174
Booterstown: 3801, 3891, 5095, 5484, 5926
Booterstown Church: 3801, 3891, 5095
Canal basin: 1349
Capel-street Presbyterian Church, Dublin: 3871
Cary's-fort *var.* Carysfort Lodge, Stillorgan Park: 2545
Carysfort Lodge, Stillorgan Park: 3149
Castle, Dublin: 5877, 5908
Castleknock: 2550, 3261, 4285, 6109
Castleknock Church: 2550, 3261, 6109

Chapter 4: Index of Place Names

County Dublin, continued:
Cenchoeur Cottage, Howth: 2567
Centenary Chapel, Stephen's-green, Dublin: 3848
Chapel Royal, Dublin: 2110
Church of St. Nicholas Without, Dublin: 4753
Claremont: 4080, 4249
Clonliff: 4292
Clonliffe *var.* Clonliff: 4292
Clonskeagh: 3144
Clontarf: 350, 621, 1581, 2028, 2711, 2733, 2995, 3129, 4094, 4529, 4750, 5132, 6448
Clontarf Church: 2028, 2733, 4094, 4529, 4750
Cloragh: 4551
Coolock: 506, 753
Coolock Church: 506
Cork Abbey: 2127
Corn Market, Dublin: 201
Crumlin: 5217
Cullenswood: 2002
Dalkey: 3250
Dalymount, Phibsborough: 5771
Diswellstown: 6238
Dodderbank: 328, 2991
Dollymount: 5230
Donnybrook: 512, 1746, 2011, 2575, 3348, 3449, 4690, 4836, 5117, 5913
Donnybrook Church: 1746, 2011, 5913, 5924
Drayton Lodge, Monkstown: 5009
Drumcondra: 2803, 3382, 5291
Drumcondra Hill, Dublin: 385
Dublin: 6, 25, 28, 33, 38, 45, 53, 58, 59, 62, 86, 94, 96, 102, 117, 133, 154, 172, 183, 187, 196, 201, 203, 213, 214, 220, 229, 237, 240, 273, 296, 309, 311, 319, 326, 328, 360, 367, 385, 389, 412, 421, 442, 446, 460, 467, 484, 488, 493, 502, 504, 506, 508, 515, 532, 534, 538, 540, 544, 547, 552, 566, 572, 585, 604, 605, 625, 632, 641, 653, 663, 676, 724, 725, 734, 736, 747, 762, 767, 769, 782, 802, 817, 832, 842, 843, 871, 879, 889, 900, 910, 912, 953, 961, 964, 967, 969, 972, 984, 984, 999, 1007, 1007, 1011, 1012, 1020, 1039, 1040, 1085, 1090, 1092, 1095, 1107, 1108, 1111, 1117, 1149, 1164, 1165, 1178, 1186, 1188, 1208, 1253, 1255, 1279, 1282, 1292, 1300, 1314, 1338, 1426, 1455, 1473, 1501, 1516, 1519, 1531, 1542, 1555, 1561, 1564, 1573, 1577, 1585, 1617, 1618, 1624, 1630, 1658, 1662, 1675, 1677, 1697, 1717, 1722, 1734, 1744, 1752, 1775, 1799, 1800, 1809, 1814, 1844, 1845, 1847, 1851, 1888, 1902, 1912, 1920, 1932, 1935, 1936, 1953, 1954, 1974, 1979,

Dublin (city), continued: 1987, 1988, 1993, 2068, 2080, 2085, 2085, 2111, 2124, 2130, 2149, 2160, 2188, 2191, 2208, 2225, 2226, 2228, 2241, 2242, 2289, 2296, 2318, 2329, 2347, 2366, 2383, 2384, 2417, 2419, 2421, 2467, 2478, 2511, 2519, 2534, 2542, 2550, 2551, 2562, 2563, 2575, 2583, 2606, 2607, 2633, 2651, 2660, 2663, 2729, 2734, 2739, 2757, 2764, 2780, 2800, 2803, 2823, 2858, 2863, 2875, 2905, 2914, 2935, 2940, 2943, 2952, 2959, 2963, 2972, 2973, 2986, 2994, 3003, 3007, 3009, 3016, 3020, 3025, 3033, 3034, 3048, 3049, 3072, 3080, 3106, 3114, 3117, 3139, 3141, 3143, 3153, 3182, 3215, 3230, 3247, 3252, 3256, 3259, 3262, 3267, 3277, 3287, 3294, 3306, 3309, 3317, 3334, 3343, 3347, 3361, 3369, 3374, 3382, 3391, 3415, 3423, 3443, 3447, 3448, 3450, 3495, 3503, 3513, 3523, 3525, 3542, 3556, 3579, 3581, 3597, 3605, 3609, 3615, 3616, 3632, 3634, 3644, 3655, 3662, 3670, 3676, 3678, 3687, 3697, 3713, 3723, 3732, 3734, 3768, 3801, 3803, 3817, 3835, 3848, 3849, 3862, 3863, 3870, 3871, 3873, 3874, 3877, 3884, 3913, 3978, 3979, 3981, 4002, 4003, 4045, 4046, 4049, 4066, 4067, 4070, 4078, 4140, 4161, 4165, 4169, 4171, 4174, 4179, 4204, 4217, 4236, 4251, 4257, 4263, 4281, 4283, 4291, 4299, 4301, 4309, 4312, 4331, 4333, 4335, 4367, 4376, 4401, 4419, 4430, 4450, 4456, 4475, 4478, 4487, 4489, 4493, 4506, 4520, 4528, 4538, 4549, 4550, 4551, 4558, 4561, 4594, 4609, 4610, 4611, 4612, 4628, 4650, 4664, 4668, 4669, 4673, 4700, 4701, 4707, 4708, 4713, 4715, 4739, 4745, 4750, 4752, 4759, 4773, 4781, 4796, 4804, 4836, 4859, 4867, 4868, 4870, 4875, 4887, 4932, 4935, 4943, 4968, 4980, 4997, 5003, 5008, 5038, 5042, 5054, 5066, 5091, 5092, 5095, 5136, 5141, 5143, 5144, 5150, 5193, 5204, 5217, 5218, 5220, 5225, 5230, 5234, 5235, 5244, 5248, 5305, 5317, 5328, 5334, 5360, 5372, 5396, 5404, 5407, 5415, 5419, 5434, 5438, 5467, 5469, 5510, 5515, 5518, 5546, 5552, 5557, 5569, 5593, 5606, 5615, 5631, 5668, 5670, 5697, 5699, 5700, 5704, 5710, 5711, 5713, 5725, 5742, 5745, 5748, 5751, 5755, 5771, 5780, 5785, 5788, 5794, 5797, 5806, 5811, 5815, 5841, 5844, 5845, 5848, 5877, 5900, 5908, 5915, 5920, 5924, 5932, 5935, 5943, 5966, 5967, 5983, 5996, 6002, 6006, 6043, 6061, 6065, 6087, 6099, 6132, 6145, 6159, 6162, 6172, 6175, 6177, 6196,

Dublin (city), continued: 6204, 6207, 6214, 6233, 6234, 6241, 6247, 6249, 6252, 6253, 6267, 6273, 6300, 6309, 6319, 6330, 6339, 6342, 6344, 6374, 6380, 6388, 6405, 6408, 6425, 6436, 6439, 6441, 6450
Elm Grove: 643
Elm Grove, Ranelagh: 3419
Elm Lodge, Sandymount: 2140
Fair House: 2535
Fairview, Clontarf: 2995
Finglass: 3727
Finglass Church: 3727
Fitzwilliam Lodge, Blackrock: 3816
Fortfield House, Rathfarnham: 3636, 3698
Four Courts, Dublin: 5771
Glasnevin: 3946
Glasnevin House, Dublin: 5631
Glassnevin *var.* Glasnevin: 3946
Glassthule: 2997
Glenageary *var.* Glenagarey: 4423
Glengeary *var.* Glenagarey, Kingstown: 6351
Golden Bridge: 6054
Grand Canal, Dublin: 5007, 6425
Grangegorman: 4164
Grangegorman, parish of: 3799
Grangegorman Church: 4164
Granite Lodge: 1620
Greenfield, Coolock: 753
Haddington Cottage, Dublin: 3117
Hammersmith, Dublin: 2563
Harold's Cross: 732, 4083
Harold's-cross Church, Dublin: 4551
Herbert House, Booterstown: 5926
Hilton Lodge, Rathmines: 6043
Home Ville, Rathmines: 4794
Hospital for Incurables, Dublin: 3817
Howth: 2567
Island-bridge, Dublin: 94
Kilcreagh House: 2941
Killiney: 5105
Kilmainham: 2235, 6435
Kilmashogue Cottage: 1070
Kingstown: 63, 193, 484, 577, 786, 1370, 2118, 2595, 2723, 2931, 3016, 3057, 3139, 3193, 3715, 4467, 4504, 4802, 4890, 4943, 4965, 5046, 5194, 5860, 6060, 6117, 6351
Kingstown Hill: 785
Kingstown Scots Church: 577
Knockmaroon: 6109
Larchhill, Santry: 506
Larkhill: 4194

Laurel Lodge, Kingstown: 3297
Lucan: 951, 971, 1014
Lusk Church: 3979
Malahide: 723, 3906, 4345
Malahide Church: 4345
Marino: 3079
Marino Cottage, Clontarf: 2711
Marymount, Blackrock: 3801
Mary's Abbey, Dublin: 6374
Mary's-abbey Presbyterian Church, Dublin: 1953
Mespil House, Dublin: 1085
Miltown House, Dublin: 154
Miltown Park, Donnybrook: 4690
Monkstown: 488, 643, 743, 768, 1060, 1370, 1425, 1906, 1935, 1988, 2351, 2356, 2864, 2925, 3017, 3279, 3297, 3346, 3795, 4051, 4165, 4283, 4390, 4528, 4812, 4814, 5009, 5054, 5681, 5704, 5955, 6055, 6126, 6331
Monkstown Church: 488, 643, 768, 1060, 1425, 1906, 1931, 1935, 2351, 2864, 3017, 3346, 3795, 4165, 4283, 4528, 4814, 5681, 5704, 5955, 6055, 6331
Monkstown Church, Kingstown: 1370
Monkstown House: 560
Mount Jerome Cemetery, Dublin: 2384
Mount Vernon, Dollymount: 5230
Mountjoy: 6030
Newtown-park or Newtown Park: 5515, 6331
Old Men's Asylum, Dublin: 4309
Ormond-quay Presbyterian Church, Dublin: 4773
Palmerston, near Dublin: 5038
Palmyra: 1070, 5092
Phibsborough: 5771, 6161
Phibsborough Church: 3978, 3863
Phipsborough *var.* Phibsborough Church, Dublin: 3978
Phoenix-park or Phoenix Park: 311, 2576, 4017, 4714, 5308, 5654
Pleasant Ville, Rathgar: 5362
Portobello: 4268
Ranelagh: 3419, 3609
Rathfarnham: 3636, 3698
Rathgar: 3082, 5143, 5362, 5967
Rathmines: 1426, 2734, 3145, 3685, 3743, 4155, 4214, 4253, 4268, 4561, 4581, 4794, 4831, 5935, 5968, 6043
Rich View, Clonskeagh: 3144
Richmond: 1683, 3226
Rogerstown, Rush: 3979

Chapter 4: Index of Place Names

County Dublin, continued:
Rosemount, Drumcondra: 2803
Rosetta Cottage: 4630
Royal Barracks, Dublin: 2366
Royal Hospital, Kilmainham: 6435
Rus in Urbe, Kingstown: 4890
Rush: 3979
Rutland House, Grand Canal, Dublin: 6425
Saggart House: 2549, 4088
Salt Hill Hotel, near Dublin: 3513
Sandford Church, Dublin: 4066
Sandford Grove: 1432
Sandymount: 2140, 3034, 4715, 5117, 5746, 6183
Sandymount Cottage, near Dublin: 1902, 5144
Sanford Church: 6273
Santry: 506
Scots Church, Dublin: 1519
Scots Church, Mary's Abbey, Dublin: 6374
Scripplestown House: 2696, 3261
Sheep Hill: 4984
Ship-street Barracks, Dublin: 3309
Sidney Lodge: 5095
Somerton: 2110
Springfield, Blackrock: 3891
St. Andrew's Church, Dublin: 5751, 5797, 5915
St. Anne's Church, Dublin: 38, 196, 1090, 1165, 1618, 1722, 1974, 3447, 3450, 5845
St. Audeon's Church, Dublin: 4668, 5317
St. Bride's Church, Dublin: 2519
St. Bridget's Church, Dublin: 5844
St. Edmondsbury: 923
St. George's Church, Dublin: 86, 183, 237, 502, 736, 767, 832, 964, 984, 1011, 1658, 1936, 1993, 3443, 3676, 4549, 4550, 4673, 6436
St. Mark's Church, Dublin: 273, 1617, 2111, 3306, 4204, 5920
St. Mary's Church, Donnybrook: 3348,: 5117
St. Mary's Church, Dublin: 663, 3423, 3870, 4609, 6267
St. Mary's parish, Dublin: 3713
St. Matthias, Dublin: 5848
St. Michan's, Dublin: 2551
St. Patrick's Cathedral, Dublin: 5915
St. Patrick's Church, Dublin: 538
St. Peter's Church, Dublin: 117, 220, 240, 309, 460, 504, 566, 632, 734, 1012, 1426, 1473, 1932, 2225, 2329, 2551, 2633, 2651, 2803, 3347, 3581, 3609, 3647, 3670, 3801, 3873, 4281, 4520, 4561, 4707, 4752, 4870, 4935, 4968, 5141, 5143, 5204, 5713, 5755, 5780, 5794, 5815, 5983, 6043, 6175, 6241, 6273, 6330, 6441
St. Thomas's Church, Dublin: 59, 747, 782, 1149, 3114, 3556, 3644, 3913, 4430, 4932, 5515, 6177
Stephen's-green, Dublin: 3848
Stillorgan: 1614, 1952, 2515, 6423
Stillorgan Church: 1952
Stillorgan Park: 2545, 3149
Stone-House: 3347
Summerhill: 3928
Summerhill, Dublin: 2228
Swords: 5230
Swords, parish of: 3445
Swords Church: 3445
Tallaght, parish of: 1011
Tallaght Church: 454, 4813
Taney Church: 576, 2914
Tivoli House, Kingstown Hill: 785
Under Secretary's Lodge, Phoenix Park: 2576, 4017
Victoria Lodge, Donnybrook: 2575
Virgemont: 2414
Waltersland, Stillorgan: 1614
Watersland *var.* Waltersland, Stillorgan: 2515
Wesleyan Centenary Chapel, Dublin: 1092
Whitehall, Blackrock: 922
Whitehall, Crumlin: 5217
Woodley: 6070
Woodtown-house: 2199
Woodview, Blackrock: 4107
York-street Chapel, Dublin: 45

Dublin, Archdiocese of: 1952, 2857, 3195, 4806
Dublin, Diocese of; St. Dolough's, parish of: 2994
Emly, Diocese of: 6273

Fermanagh, county of:
Townland not named: 618, 896, 3388, 4735, 5369, 5369, 5375
Aghadrum: 1469
Aghalurcher, parish of: 4489
Aghamore: 4687, 5664
Aghavea: 406, 4030, 4678
Aghavea Church: 406, 778, 4678
Annaghard, near Clones: 1956
Annamartin: 736
Ardress: 1381

County Fermanagh, continued:
Ardress Glebe: 4565
Ardverney: 1381
Arney Lodge: 4525
Aughadrum *var.* Aghadrum: 1469
Aughalurcher: 4476
Aughamore *var.* Aghamore: 5664
Aughavea *var.* Aghavea: 1757
Aughavea Church *var.* Aghavea Church: 406
Aughaward: 2735
Ballaghmore: 5895
Ballicassidy *var.* Ballycassidy: 1426
Ballinamallard: 428, 1508, 1636, 3438, 3543, 4494, 4861, 5995
Ballinamallard, parish of: 5660
Ballinamallard Church: 428, 1636, 4494
Ballycassidy: 473
Ballycassidy, Lowtherstown: 5043
Ballyho-bridge and Ballyho Bridge *var.* Ballyhobridge, near Clones: 699, 3628
Ballyho-bridge *var.* Ballyhobridge: 669
Ballyhobridge: 669, 3628
Ballymakenny: 1202
Ballymullen, near Newtownbutler: 4686
Beacho *var.* Beagho: 558
Beagho: 558
Beleek *var.* Belleek: 4548
Bella Hill: 4609
Bella-hill, near Brookeborough: 1575
Bellanalack: 1309
Bellanalack Church: 1309
Belleek: 4548
Belleisle: 5394
Bellevue: 1409. *See also* Belview.
Belnaleck House: 2043
Belnaleck *var.* Bellanalack: 5936
Belnaleck *var.* Bellanalack Church: 1309
Belnaleck *var.* Bellanalack, near Enniskillen: 3549
Belview: 5510. *See also* Belleview.
Benmore Church: 1438, 5365, 5916
Benmore, Churchhill: 292
Boa Island: 3241
Boho, parish of: 1936, 2502, 2636, 2845
Boho Church: 1808
Brackagh: 1520
Brocka *var.* Brockagh, near Lowtherstown: 2255
Brockagh, near Lowtherstown: 2255
Brookboro' *var.* Brookeborough: 4936, 5469
Brookborough *var.* Brookeborough: 2016, 4855, 5117, 5246, 5622

Brookeboro' *var.* Brookeborough: 2419
Brookeborough: 176, 263, 406, 618, 1196, 1352, 1575, 1757, 1769, 2016, 2419, 2422, 2436, 4398, 4433, 4855, 4936, 5105, 5117, 5123, 5246, 5469, 5622, 5938
Brookview Lodge, Enniskillen: 3873
Broughas: 1166
Bungalo, Lowtherstown: 4660
Bungola *var.* Bungalo, Lowtherstown: 4843
Bunn: 4032
Caldwell View Cottage: 1454
Cappy: 264, 1831, 2423
Cappy House, Enniskillen: 4869
Capy *var.* Cappy, near Enniskillen: 1521
Cara House: 2203, 2221
Carnaguiltaugh *var.* Carrownagiltagh, near Tempo: 1982
Carneyharne *var.* Carneyhome: 134
Carneyhome: 134
Carrick House: 1991
Carrickreagh: 2335
Castle Archdall: 1166, 1358, 1520, 2159, 2860, 3008, 4467, 5518, 5969
Castle Archdall Church: 1166, 1520
Castle Caldwell: 591, 232, 692, 757, 2326
Castlearchdall *var.* Castle Archdall: 1358
Castletown: 4000
Cavanagarvin: 1758
Cavanaleck: 4279
Cavanaleck Meeting-house: 4279, 4296
Cherrymount: 3951
Churchhill: 292, 1808, 2093
Clintivern: 1358
Cloghan: 5037
Cloncorie: 669
Clonelly: 5615
Clones Church: 134
Colebroke *var.* Colebrooke: 4425
Colebrook Church: 286
Colebrooke: 591, 2327, 2676, 4425
Colebrooke Church: 2327
Coolcaughal *var.* Coolcoghill: 4398
Coolcoghill: 4398
Cooltrain Church: 4433, 6172
Coragh, near Lisnaskea: 2990
Corkhill: 1010
Corkhill Lodge, Enniskillen: 5247
Corkill *var.* Corkhill Lodge, Enniskillen: 4881
Corracloon, parish of Inishmacsaint: 2636
Corrylongford *var.* Corralongford, near Fivemiletown: 4797

Chapter 4: Index of Place Names

County Fermanagh, continued:
Corsenchin, near Lisnaskea: 4032
Cosbystown: 5365
Cragheen Cottage, near Ballinamallard: 4861
Cran, near Fivemiletown: 1693
Cranbrook: 4433
Cranbrooke *var.* Cranbrook: 2211, 2604
Crievehill: 1256
Crocknacrieve: 6326
Crom: 1466
Crom Castle, Newtownbutler: 1466, 2369, 2864, 3017, 4278, 4573, 5041
Croughrim *var.* Croaghrim, near Florencecourt *var.* Florence Court: 5481
Croughrim, near Florence Court: 5481
Curran-hill: 4494
Curran-hill, Enniskillen: 3275
Curren *var.* Currin, near Enniskillen: 1636
Danesford, Holly Well: 2704
Derryargan: 1345
Derrybrusk: 220, 240, 371, 3509
Derrybrusk, parish of: 1974
Derrybrusk Glebe: 354, 914
Derryconnelly: 2015, 1438, 1642, 2520, 3939, 5830
Derrygonnelly *var.* Derryconnelly: 2015
Derrygore: 239, 1173
Derryhillagh: 4637, 5376
Derryinch: 5524
Derrylee: 1690
Derrylin: 5542
Derryscobe: 1562
Derryvolan, parish of: 1546
Derryvolan Church: 591, 787, 4637, 4749
Derryvoland *var.* Derryvolan: 591, 787
Derryvoland *var.* Derryvolan, parish of: 1546
Derryvoland *var.* Derryvolan Church: 591, 787, 4637
Derryvollan *var.* Derryvolan: 6079
Derryvulland *var.* Derryvolan: 6079
Derryvullen *var.* Derryvolan, parish of: 4401
Derryvullen *var.* Derryvolan Church: 4749
Doon, near Tempo: 5423, 5521
Doone *var.* Doon: 2327
Doonin: 5271
Doonin Cottage: 5850
Dresternan: 222
Dresternan House: 810
Dromard: 1353
Dromore: 2377
Drumack: 4399

Drumall: 1520
Drumanure, Derrygonnelly: 3939
Drumard: 993
Drumbad: 2635
Drumbad, Lisnaskea: 1521
Drumboe *var.* Drumbo, near Lowtherstown: 106
Drumcaw, near Lisnaskea: 2855
Drumcose, near Enniskillen: 2939
Drumcrew: 1202, 2568
Drumcrew House, Lisnaskea: 1399
Drumcrew, near Lisnaskea: 3433
Drumcrow: 2636
Drumcullion, near Ballinamallard: 3543
Drumderg: 2895
Drumderge *var.* Drumderg: 2895
Drumduff: 1911
Drumkeen: 1983, 2793, 4803
Drumkeeran: 3730
Drumkeeran, parish of: 354
Drumkeeran Church: 3730
Drumlught: 4711
Drummacoorin: 2636
Drummadooran *var.* Drummacoorin, parish of Boho: 2636
Drummainy: 2299
Drummee, Inishmore Island: 787
Drummee, Innishmore *var.* Inishmore: 2115, 2323
Drumrella *var.* Drumralla, Newtownbutler: 3191
Drumscambly *var.* Drumskimly, near Derrygonnelly *var.* Derryconnelly: 2015
Drumskimly, near Derryconnelly: 2015
Eagle Mount, Lisnaskea: 1757
Eagle-mount *var.* Eagle Mount, Lisnaskea: 4375
Eaglemont *var.* Eagle Mount, Lisnaskea: 2906
Eden, Enniskillen: 151
Edensap *var.* Edenasop, near Tempo: 1924
Ederney: 1901, 1983
Ely Lodge: 4225
Enniskillen: 38, 44, 146, 149, 151, 159, 176, 182, 209, 239, 246, 247, 264, 269, 272, 277, 307, 321, 351, 352, 378, 381, 391, 406, 485, 509, 510, 511, 535, 592, 604, 618, 626, 678, 705, 729, 748, 775, 817, 823, 850, 896, 897, 904, 995, 1018, 1027, 1028, 1068, 1099, 1100, 1170, 1176, 1177, 1178, 1197, 1199, 1241, 1248, 1256, 1268, 1274, 1278, 1285, 1306, 1309, 1346, 1361, 1377, 1387, 1442, 1474,

Enniskillen, continued: 1514, 1518, 1521, 1546, 1578, 1583, 1586, 1635, 1636, 1644, 1693, 1724, 1729, 1742, 1782, 1803, 1825, 1894, 1909, 1910, 1911, 1991, 2013, 2019, 2052, 2062, 2072, 2107, 2132, 2160, 2186, 2189, 2190, 2237, 2239, 2244, 2259, 2268, 2272, 2309, 2310, 2328, 2328, 2375, 2394, 2401, 2411, 2428, 2450, 2469, 2477, 2492, 2501, 2502, 2514, 2516, 2520, 2568, 2569, 2572, 2587, 2588, 2601, 2602, 2623, 2636, 2637, 2638, 2639, 2717, 2735, 2781, 2815, 2845, 2853, 2854, 2859, 2873, 2895, 2912, 2913, 2939, 2985, 3015, 3031, 3046, 3046, 3114, 3181, 3275, 3312, 3337, 3365, 3400, 3405, 3439, 3514, 3532, 3544, 3549, 3558, 3569, 3696, 3723, 3775, 3873, 3882, 3939, 3968, 4005, 4040, 4068, 4118, 4148, 4162, 4163, 4181, 4226, 4229, 4230, 4251, 4252, 4285, 4352, 4359, 4374, 4453, 4476, 4522, 4524, 4526, 4558, 4568, 4587, 4634, 4635, 4662, 4689, 4705, 4706, 4707, 4820, 4869, 4881, 4882, 4892, 4897, 4915, 4921, 4982, 4993, 5056, 5122, 5129, 5149, 5154, 5195, 5247, 5278, 5279, 5331, 5349, 5355, 5377, 5393, 5411, 5414, 5426, 5428, 5453, 5478, 5523, 5524, 5551, 5591, 5598, 5616, 5623, 5633, 5639, 5667, 5673, 5673, 5694, 5695, 5721, 5765, 5766, 5790, 5802, 5895, 5934, 5937, 5943, 6073, 6083, 6102, 6112, 6233, 6249, 6412
Enniskillen, parish of: 2913, 3938
Enniskillen Church: 705, 823, 1583, 2107, 2859, 3015, 3046
Enniskillen Poor Law Union: 1018, 1100, 3882, 3951
Enniskillen Presbyterian Church: 775, 5598
Fair Wood Park, Enniskillen: 4251
Farnacassidy: 1180
Floraville, Enniskillen: 4005
Florence Court: 425, 1056, 2024, 2283, 2305, 2886, 4383, 4523, 5079, 5100, 5481, 5688
Florence-court *var.* Florence Court: 5688
Florence-court *var.* Florence Court Churchyard: 4383
Florencecourt *var.* Florence Court: 425, 2283, 2305, 5100
Fort Hill: 2613
Galoon, parish of: 4687
Garvary: 2588
Garvary Lodge: 2914
Garvery *var.* Garvary: 2588
Garvoghill: 103

Glasmullagh, near Lowtherstown: 141
Gledstown, Maguiresbridge: 5941
Glenarn, near Lack: 106
Glencunny, parish of Rossorry: 2895
Glenlevan: 2520
Glenleven *var.* Glenlevan: 2520
Goblusk: 4001, 5322
Gola: 898
Gola Castle: 5239, 5352
Gola House: 778
Gortahurk, Holywell: 2936
Gortatole: 4009
Gorthaloghan *var.* Gortaloughan, near Enniskillen: 159
Gortmessen, parish of Enniskillen: 2913
Gortmesson: 1393
Gortra: 4550
Gortra House: 291
Gortra, Newtownbutler: 5942
Gransagh: 2310
Greenhill: 382
Greenhill, near Brookeborough: 618
Grogy: 3434
Halfway House, Drumbad: 2635
Halfway House, Drumbed *var.* Drumbad: 2635
Holly Well: 2704. *See also* Holywell.
Hollybrook: 216, 1249, 1682
Hollyhill, Enniskillen: 1583
Holywell: 2936. *See also* Holly Well.
Imperial Hotel, Enniskillen: 182, 5478
Inishmacsaint, parish of: 1438, 2636, 5916
Innishmore: 2115, 2323, 3308
Inishmore Island: 787
Innishmore *var.* Inishmore, Island of, Lough Erne: 75
Innismacsaint *var.* Inishmacsaint, parish of: 1438, 5916
Island-view, Enniskillen: 535
Jamestown: 5247
Johnstown: 467
Johnstown House: 5593
Kesh: 1171, 2707, 3763, 6265
Kesh Glebe: 242
Kilgartnaleague: 428
Kilgortnaleague *var.* Kilgartnaleague: 428
Killalahard: 2141
Killard: 1690
Killeshar *var.* Killesher, Florence-Court: 2024
Killesher: 4676
Killesher, parish of: 2268
Killesher Church: 4676

County Fermanagh, continued:
Killesher, Florence Court: 2024
Killesher, Florencecourt *var.* Florence Court: 4523
Killester [Killesher?]: 4676
Killester [Killesher?] Church: 4676
Killgrania *var.* Killygrania: 4637
Killikeran, Brookeboro' *var.* Killykeeran, Brookeborough: 5938
Killilahard *var.* Killalahard: 2141
Killygrania: 4637
Killyhevlin: 482, 1974
Killyvilly: 2588
Kilmalanophy: 1635
Kilmelanafy *var.* Kilmalanophy: 1635
Kilmore: 1822, 3952
Kilskeery: 3802, 5394
Kilskeery Church: 3802, 5394
Kilskeery *var.* Kilskeery Church: 3802
Kilskerry Glebe: 4748
Kilskery *var.* Kilskeery Church: 5394
Kilturk: 655
Kinawley, parish of: 810
Kinawley Glebe: 1986
Knockballymore: 5041
Knockmanowl: 4644
Lack: 106, 1380, 1380
Lakeview House: 1736
Lanachran *var.* Lanaghran, near Enniskillen: 3939
Legg, Churchhill: 1808
Lenaghan: 2411, 5366
Levaghey House: 5043
Levaghy: 1223, 5656
Levaghy, near Enniskillen: 2309
Levahy *var.* Levaghy: 5656
Levahy *var.* Levaghy, near Enniskillen: 2309
Levelly Glebe: 3123
Lisbellaw: 1643, 1910, 1998, 2053, 3390, 4272, 4663, 5010, 5317, 5399, 5941, 6388
Lisbellaw Church: 5399
Lisbellaw Presbyterian Church: 4272
Lisbofin: 1118, 2424, 4224
Lisdeverick *var.* Lisdivrick, parish of Killesher: 2268
Lisnarrick: 2603
Lisnaskea: 216, 380, 520, 1075, 1202, 1221, 1399, 1521, 1721, 1757, 2327, 2855, 2906, 2990, 3433, 3515, 4030, 4032, 4375, 4399, 4711, 5057, 5365, 5474, 5637, 5751, 5933
Lisnaskea, parish of: 1466

Lisnaskea Church: 380, 520, 1075, 1202, 1466, 1721, 3515, 4399, 4711
Lisnaskea Glebe: 1948, 4471
Lisnaskea Glebe, near Enniskillen: 3181
Lisnaskea Poor Law Union: 1140, 1221
Littlehill, near Maguiresbridge: 103
Littlemount: 71
Lough Erne: 75
Lowry: 4234
Lowtherstown: 106, 141, 428, 693, 908, 1563, 1574, 1753, 2255, 2768, 2860, 3385, 3515, 4660, 4749, 4843, 5043, 5706, 5786, 5995, 6421
Macknagh, near Lisnaskea: 5057
Magheracross, parish of: 1442, 5098
Magheramena *var.* Magheramenagh: 4886, 5452
Magheramenagh: 5452
Magherestaphena: 1421
Maguire's Bridge *var.* Maguiresbridge: 6251
Maguires-bridge *var.* Maguiresbridge Presbyterian Church: 3343
Maguiresbridge: 103, 286, 438, 994, 1181, 1220, 1721, 2116, 2640, 3034, 3308, 3343, 5528, 5941, 6251, 6395
Manor Highgate: 140
Manorwater House: 4901
Manorwater-house *var.* Manorwater House: 5655
Marlbank, near Enniskillen: 5496
Millwood: 154
Miltate, near Lisbellaw: 1643
Miltown, near Newtownbutler: 774
Monea Church: 3939
Moneymakin *var.* Moneymakinn: 1140
Moneymakinn: 1140
Montgibbon: 3801
Moybane, near Enniskillen: 4558
Mullaghdun Church: 1408
Mullaghmeen: 1489
Mullaghy, near Enniskillen: 2401
Mullinagoan House: 3118
Mullmagoan House: 1531
Mullyare: 1165, 1408
Munville: 155
Necairn Castle: 591
Newtownbutler: 774, 1313, 1466, 2369, 2432, 2505, 2864, 2990, 3017, 3191, 4035, 4207, 4573, 4686, 5041, 5802, 5942
Nursery Park, near Enniskillen: 3569, 5149
Nutfield, Lisnaskea: 5474

County Fermanagh, continued:
Oakfield: 981
Oakfield, near Enniskillen: 2854
Pettigo: 4688
Portnacloyduff: 2635
Portnacloyduff *var.* Portnacloyduff: 2635
Prospect: 964, 984, 4171
Prospect Hill: 4813
Prospect House: 4053
Pubble, near Tempo: 3535
Registrar's Office, Enniskillen: 1910, 1911, 1991, 2244, 2310, 2328, 2520, 2588, 2636, 2735, 2895
Riversdale: 822, 4643, 5394
Riverstown: 434
Rockfield: 62, 3461
Rosbick *var.* Rossbrick: 134
Ross: 1309
Ross, near Enniskillen: 1894
Rossaa: 4676
Rossahilly, near Enniskillen: 1644
Rossbrick: 134
Rossfad: 861, 5061
Rossinin *var.* Rossinnan: 1166
Rossinnan: 1166
Rosslea: 2634
Rosslen: 1498
Rossorry: 321, 1358, 2411, 4072, 4359, 5366
Rossorry, parish of: 2370, 2895
Rossorry Church: 321, 1358, 2411, 4072, 4359, 5366
Rossory Glebe: 868
Rossory *var.* Rossorry, parish of: 2370
Rossory *var.* Rossorry Church: 321, 4359
Rossoy [Rossaa?]: 4676
Rushen *var.* Rushin: 23
Russian *var.* Rushin, Enniskillen: 5154
Saint Catherine's, near Churchhill: 2093
Salaghey *var.* Sallaghy, parish of Galloon: 4687
Sallaghey, parish of Galloon: 4687
Sallaghy: 1493, 1690, 2990, 4032, 5664
Sallaghy Church: 1493, 1690, 2990, 4032
Sallybank, near Enniskillen: 2815
Sandhill-cottage, near Derrygonnelly: 1438
Scotch *var.* Scots Church, Enniskillen: 1361
Scots Church, Enniskillen: 748, 1474, 1635
Shanmullagh, near Ballycassidy: 473
Shebeg House: 3714
Silverhill: 980, 2636
Silverhill, near Enniskillen: 1178

Sion Hill: 5274
Skea: 1254
Skea House: 545
Slavan [Slawin?] Church: 2635
Summerhill: 4756, 5141
Summer-hill House: 3510
Sydaire: 1742
Tattymacall, near Lisbellaw: 1998, 5010
Templemaghery: 106
Templemaghery Church: 106
Templemahery *var.* Templemaghery Church: 106
Tempo: 176, 592, 643, 772, 775, 1385, 1703, 1924, 1982, 2084, 2146, 3535, 4134, 4797, 5423, 5521, 5706, 6083, 6271, 6411
Tempo Church: 176, 592, 2146, 6083
Tempo Presbyterian Church: 1385, 2084, 4134, 4797
Tettymacall [*var.* Tattymacall?], near Enniskillen: 775
The Cross: 823
Trillic *var.* Trillick: 1385
Trillick: 1385, 2244
Trinity Church, Crom: 1466
Trory: 239, 1765, 2310
Trory Church: 239
Trory Glebe: 5634
Trory Glebe, Enniskillen: 2514
Tubbrid: 309, 3972
Tubbrid Church: 309
Tubbrid, Kesh: 3763
Tubrid *var.* Tubbrid: 309, 1978, 3972
Tubrid *var.* Tubbrid Church: 309
Tubrid *var.* Tubbrid, Kesh: 3763
Tully, near Florencecourt *var.* Florence Court: 5079
Tullyavey: 1742
Tullycleagh Glebe: 5288
Tullycreevy: 2450
Tullyharney, Lisbellaw: 5399
Tullyhommon House, Pettigo: 4432
Tullyreagh: 1784
Tunnylummon: 6245
Waternerry: 3832
Watternerry *var.* Woaghternerry: 2913
Waughternerry *var.* Woaghternerry, Enniskillen: 2735
Welshtown Cottage: 1454
Wesleyan Chapel, Enniskillen: 1742
Whitehall: 6088
Whitepark: 1352
Windmill-Hill, Enniskillen: 2160
Woaghternerry: 2913

Ferns, Diocese of:
Parish not named: 1987, 3055
Ferns, Diocese of; Ballyrahan: 6182

Galway, county of:
Ardbear house, Clifden: 3377
Ardrahan Church: 1743
Athenry, parish of: 792
Atherney *var.* Athenry, parish of: 792
Ballinasloe: 4418
Ballydugan: 5916
Cappard: 1618, 2952
Castle Taylor: 1743, 2983, 4422
Castleblakeney: 4631
Castleblakeney, parish of: 4631
Castlekelly: 3272
Cathedral Church, Clonfert: 783
Clifden: 3377, 4150
Clifden Castle: 4057
Clifden Church, Connemara: 4150
Clonfert: 783, 792, 1743
Clonfert Cathedral: 792
Collegiate Church of St. Nicholas, Galway: 3981, 3982
Connemara: 4150
Custom-house, Galway: 5297
Earcourt [Eyrecourt?]: 5792
Eyrecourt: 783, 1718
Eyrecourt Castle: 792, 1745, 3582, 5354
Eyrecourt Church: 1745
Flower Hill: 5023
Galway: 2157, 3981, 3982, 4340, 4359, 5297, 5431, 6164, 6197, 6325, 6420
Gregg Castle: 4954
Kilbannon *var.* Kilbennan Church: 5296
Kilbennan: 5296
Killinan Church: 2952
Kilmacduagh: 1743
Leegan Lodge: 3686
Newborough House: 3686
Prospect House, Eyrecourt: 1718
Rectory, Castleblakeney: 4631
Roscrea: 1743
Salthill: 6036
Shannon View: 783, 792
Thornfield: 3272
Tooloobane: 3276
Tuam: 5606, 6114

Kerry, county of:
Blennerville: 3137
Caherciveen: 3518

County Kerry, continued:
Callinafercy: 1621
Cleedy Cottage, Kenmare: 3497
Crotto: 3137
Derry: 4319
Ferriter, parish of: 2818
Kenmare: 3497
Killarney: 633, 2583, 2818
Listowel Church: 3018
Meanus: 1987
Milltown: 1621
Park, Killarney: 2583
Rectory, Tralee: 5182
Scots Church, Tralee: 1621
Tralee: 1621, 2253, 2709, 2741, 2758, 3137, 3780, 4340, 4529, 4579, 5099, 5182, 5904
Tralee Church: 3137, 4340
Valencia: 2418

Kildare, county of:
Castletown, Celbridge: 2250
Celbridge: 365, 2250, 5240
Convent of Mercy, Naas: 1779
Crowhill: 4848
Downing's House: 6163
Fairview: 2944
Gilltown: 3662
Halverstown: 3397
Kilcullen Church: 5496
Monasterevan *var.* Monasterevin: 2914
Monasterevin: 2914
Naas: 1779
Narraghmore, parish of: 4806
Narraghmore Rectory: 4806
Rathangan: 688
Strawberry Lodge: 3609
Tullylast: 2798
Vicar's Hall: 3995

Kildare, Diocese of: 5631

Kilfenora, Diocese of: 1359

Kilkenny, county of:
Townland not named: 4836
Ballyquin house: 117, 3556, 3899
Castlecomer: 6038
Danesfort: 842
Dunmore Cottage: 1449
Gowran, parish of: 5851
Gowran Church: 5851
Inistioge: 5946

County Kilkenny, continued:
Kells Church: 833
Kilfane Glebe: 867
Kilkenny: 222, 770, 1589, 1750, 2074, 3345, 4332, 4335, 5184, 5293, 5311, 5360, 5468, 6365, 6403
Kiltorcan: 3873
Mount Geale: 5755, 5794
Palace, Kilkenny: 1589

Killala, Diocese of: 3662, 5957

Killaloe, Diocese of:
Parish not named: 2994, 4958, 5779
Bath [Rath?], parish of: 6194
Kilkeedy and Inchicronan, parish of: 6231
Rath, parish of: 6194

Kilmallock Poor Law Union: 4926

Kilmore, Diocese of:
Dromlease *var.* Drumlease, parish of: 3346
Kildrumferton, parish of: 514
Killinagh: 1752

King's (Offaly), county of:
Ballinakill *var.* Ballynakill, near Edenderry: 2692
Ballyboy Church: 2173
Clara: 3638, 5541
Clonlohan House: 187
Durrow Abbey: 2205
Edenderry: 2429, 2692, 5165
Ferbane: 3002
Frankford: 2173
Kilduff House: 220, 240
Kilduffe *var.* Kilduff House: 220
Killadrown: 2858
Kincor: 3002
Kinnitty, parish of: 5732
Parsonstown: 699, 831, 2042, 3669, 4073, 4985
Philipstown Rectory: 2220
Sharavogue: 1183
Tullamore: 456

Laois, or Laoix, county of: 462
See also Queens, county of.

Leitrim, county of:
Townland not named: 4141, 4598, 6181, 6342,
Annadale: 1335, 2111
Annaduff, parish of: 2140
Annaduff Church: 6181

County Leitrim, continued:
Aughavass Cottage: 1771
Avilly: 3552
Ballinamore: 237, 1370, 2587, 3206, 4015, 4616, 5945
Blacklion: 3180
Blackpark, Manorhamilton: 1695
Brook Hill: 3422, 3756
Bushhill: 748, 1694, 4340
Carrick-on-Shannon: 1893, 5069, 5232, 6054
Carrickfad: 5719
Carrigallen: 1689
Castlecar: 4295
Cleen Cottage, Dromahair *var.* Drumhaire: 5988
Cleen Cottage, Drumhaire: 5988
Clogher, Drumsna: 2391
Cloone: 4715
Cloone Glebe: 6044
Commons, Manorhamilton: 1526
Drumhaire: 5988
Drumlease: 3346
Drumshambo *var.* Drumshanbo: 2587, 3637, 4668
Drumshanbo: 2587, 4668, 2391, 6099
Fanagh *var.* Fenagh, parish of: 2048
Fenagh, parish of: 2048
Fenagh Glebe: 1482
Friarstown House: 3582
Glenade: 5819
Greyfield House: 2307
Hermitage: 5329
Inishmagrath: 907, 2707
Innismagrath *var.* Inishmagrath: 907
Killarga Church: 3731
Killogue: 2182
Killogue, parish of: 2182
Killogue Church: 2182
Kinlough Church: 2087
Kinlough House: 1541, 2087, 4726
Laheen: 4141
Lakefield, Mohill: 432
Lakeview: 2051
Lakeview Cottage, Blacklion: 3180
Lurganboy: 3205, 3220
Manorhamilton: 981, 1012, 1341, 1526, 1695, 2051, 2182, 2347, 2356, 2383, 2896, 2977, 3430, 3457, 3645, 3747, 4068, 4295, 4494
Manorhamilton Church: 2347, 4295
Mohill: 432, 2721, 5835
Mough House: 2048

Chapter 4: Index of Place Names

County Leitrim, continued:
Rectory, Carrick-on-Shannon: 5232
Rosinvere *var.* Rossinver, parish of: 2087
Ross, near Manorhamilton: 2896
Rossinver, parish of: 2087
Skreeny: 1012, 5029
Sorrelfield, Manorhamilton: 4068
Springfield, Mohill: 5835
Strand Hill: 1571
Streamstown, Ballinamore: 1370
Summerhill: 6054
Woodville: 1744

Limerick, county of:
Townland not named: 2826, 5847
Anglesboro' *var.* Anglesborough House, Mitchelstown: 6324
Anglesborough House, Mitchelstown: 6324
Ardcanny, parish of: 4248
Ash Hill Towers: 3456
Askeston: 3910
Ballynacourty: 4752
Ballyneale: 2784
Beechmount, Rathkeale: 2249
Bruree: 2784
Cahirline, near Castleconnell: 4038
Castleconnell: 4038
Castlerea: 322
Doon, parish of: 6273
Glin: 884, 902
Kilfrush: 4926
Kilmallock: 3456
Kilrush *var.* Kilfrush: 4926
Limerick: 796, 1055, 1260, 2175, 2594, 2911, 3622, 3704, 3739, 3910, 3998, 4207, 4248, 4363, 4546, 4586, 4587, 4831, 5130, 5207, 5324, 5733, 5833, 6328
Limerick Cathedral: 4248
Melton, near Kilmallock: 3456
Mitchelstown: 6324
Newcastle, parish of: 3622
Rathkeale: 2249, 2592
St. Michael's Church, Limerick: 3704
Tullybracky Rectory: 330
Wesleyan Chapel, Limerick: 5130

Limerick, Diocese of: 2614, 4958

Longford, county of:
Townland not named: 1108
Abbeylara Church: 4653
Ardagh Church: 735
Ballinamuck: 6112
Ballymacormac *var.* Ballymacormick: 1599
Ballymacormick Church: 1599
Ballymahon: 6223
Carrickadurhis: 6013
Cartronard: 99
Castroneard: 1854
Cloncaulfield: 3118
Cloncaulfield House: 1531
Colehill-house: 183
Edgeworthstown: 2698, 4652, 5727
Edgeworthstown, parish of: 5442
Edgeworthstown Church: 4652
Killashee [Kilnashee?]: 573, 1599
Lisbrack: 4329
Longford: 438, 4329, 4653, 4677, 4898, 4914, 4992, 4993
Longford Church: 438, 4329
Moat House: 2183
Moigh House: 46
Nicholson's-court: 3118

Louth, county of:
Townland not named: 2663, 2784, 2947, 3250
Ardee: 2503, 2746, 4076, 6369
Ardree *var.* Ardee: 1043
Ballymascanlan Church: 6142
Ballymascanlan, parish of: 969
Ballyoonan: 4857
Bellurgan: 5289
Bellurgan Park: 4308, 4343
Black Rock, Dundalk: 5592
Blackrock: 6050
Blackrock *var.* Black Rock, Dundalk: 211
Boyne Lodge, Drogheda: 921
Bridge of Crin *var.* Bridgeacrin Chapel: 6143
Bridgeacrin Chapel: 6143
Brohatua: 4528
Cardistown: 1043
Carlingford: 337, 523, 1501, 1665, 5103, 5613
Carnally: 2622
Castlebellingham: 707, 3262, 3517
Castlering: 3904
Castletown: 3918
Castleview, Carlingford: 5613
Charlestown: 260, 3322
Charlestown Glebe: 260
Charlestown Glebe, Ardee: 4076
Charleville: 3728
Christian's Town *var.* Christianstown: 935
Christiantown *var.* Christianstown: 5651

391

County Louth, continued:
Clonmore, parish of: 4094
Collon: 6341
Cookstown House, Ardee: 1043
Cookstown House, Ardree *var.* Ardee: 1043
Derver, parish of: 5410
Drogheda: 174, 921, 1544, 2137, 2551, 2622, 2693, 3251, 3296, 3608, 4202, 4228, 4475, 4768, 5230, 5926
Drumshallon: 3655
Dundalk: 49, 211, 741, 816, 923, 1059, 1273, 1323, 1665, 1709, 1921, 1926, 1993, 2026, 2257, 2274, 2352, 2577, 2585, 2731, 2734, 2745, 2823, 2893, 3033, 3089, 3207, 3259, 3306, 3464, 3709, 3829, 3918, 4092, 4094, 4137, 4543, 5306, 5356, 5410, 5517, 5547, 5575, 5592, 5793, 5898, 5949, 6050, 6064, 6097, 6101, 6137, 6274, 6277, 6320, 6426, 6427
Dundalk Church: 923, 2893
Dungooley: 2476
Dunleer: 327
Dunneny-House: 1251
Endowed School, Dundalk: 5573
Enniskeen *var.* Inniskeen: 3531
Glinn House, Carlingford: 337
Gyle's Castle, Carlingford: 1665
Heynstown: 1906
Heynstown Rectory: 3394
Inniskeen: 3531
Killincool: 5091
Killencool Rectory: 3292
Killincool, parish of: 1904
Lannatt: 5592
Legavoreen, Drogheda: 4475
Lodge: 1209
Louth: 1905, 3208, 3946
Louth Hall: 2791, 3600
Lurgangreen: 2209, 2230
Mellifont: 2224, 3354
Mellifont Church: 2224
Mellifont Glebe: 6001
Milesdown: 758
Millifont *var.* Mellifont Church: 3354
Mountain House: 447
Mountpleasant, Dundalk: 2823
Newton House: 6445
Nootka, Carlingford: 5103
Omeath: 4553
Omeath Church: 4553
Rathcoole House: 5582

Rathdonnell *var.* Rathdaniel, near Collon: 6341
Rathrowel *var.* Rathroal, Dundalk: 5410
Rectory, Louth: 1905, 3208
Registrar's Office, Dundalk: 1709
Richardstown: 3613
Richmond House, Dundalk: 3918
Roachdale: 4190
Rockland, near Carlingford: 523
Shortstone: 6143
St. Nicholas's Church, Dundalk: 1273, 1665
Stickillen: 985
Thistle House, Dundalk: 1926
Woodvill, near Lurgangreen: 2230

Mayo, county of:
Achillbeg *var.* Island of Achill: 4194
Ballina: 1294, 2630, 3237, 4727, 6239, 6283
Bellmullet: 3348, 5493, 5533
Bingham Castle: 3253
Carrakelly *var.* Carrowkelly: 3237
Carrowkelly: 3237
Castlebar: 2216, 2672, 2866
Castletown, Cong: 2517
Cherry Cottage, Westport: 5068
Cloncormick House: 371
Cong: 2517
Erris: 3062, 5493
House of Castlebar: 5444
Island of Achill: 4194
Killala: 3662
Kilmore, parish of: 3062
Mullafarry Church: 3237
Mullafary *var.* Mullafarry Church: 3237
Newcastle: 5403
Rossport House, Erris: 5493
Westport: 604, 1152, 1789, 3589, 4106, 5068
Westport House: 6367

Meath, county of:
Townland not named: 2466
Adamstown: 4466
Agher: 3676
Aghera: 1872
Aghera, parish of: 1872
Ardbraccan: 6304
Ardbraccan Church: 2171
Athboy Church: 1115
Bensfort House: 286
Brittas: 5593
Clope: 86
Cruisetown: 4208

County of Meath, continued:
Curraghtown House: 4079
Drewstown: 1115
Dunboyne: 6159
Dunshaughlin, parish of: 3655
Friermore: 1115
Furz Park: 161
Glebe House, Aghera: 1872
Kells: 851, 3505
Kieran House: 2150
Laracoe *var.* Laracor, parish of: 5812
Laracor, parish of: 2541
Laracor Glebe: 2541
Lismullin Park: 3820
Lodge, Navan: 4783
Loughcrew Church: 6178
Mosserath, Kells: 3505
Moyglere, parish of: 1204
Navan: 4783, 6428
New Haggard Cottage: 320
Painstown, parish of: 4628
Rathkenny, parish of: 248
Ratoath: 2079
Skreen, parish of: 3795
Skyrne *var.* Skreen, parish of: 3795
Slane: 6288
Slane Church: 248
Stirling House: 1011
Summersea: 3795
Sylvan Park: 3835
Thomastown: 5009
Trim: 704
Waterloo Lodge, Trim: 704

Meath, Diocese of:
Parish not named: 2171, 3224, 4594, 4628, 6084, 6304, 6428
Ardagh, parish of: 1647
Loughcrew: 1275

Monaghan, county of:
Townland not named: 3517, 3950, 4270, 4327, 4450, 4622
Aghabog: 2674. *See also* Ahabog.
Aghabog Glebe: 4113
Aghnamullen: 4388
Aghnamullen Church: 4166
Ahabog: 5570. *See also* Aghabog.
Ahafin: 4050
Analore: 2315, 5114
Analore Mills: 2315, 3356
Anketell Grove: 338, 1086, 2122, 3533, 4666, 5657

Anketell-grove *var.* Anketell Grove: 4582
Annahean: 4620
Anneville, Castleblayney: 4045
Archdeaconry, Clontibret: 6034
Aughakist: 4773
Aughnamullen *var.* Agnhamullen: 4388
Aughnamullen *var.* Aghnamullen Church: 4166
Ballibay *var.* Ballybay: 1218, 4199, 4954
Ballibay *var.* Ballybay, parish of: 632, 1697
Ballibay *var.* Ballybay Church: 1697
Ballidian *var.* Balladian, near Ballybay: 2597
Ballinode: 2208, 3191, 3562, 5529
Ballinode Church: 531, 2208, 3191, 3562, 5529
Ballinode Mills: 3191, 5529
Ballyalbany Presbyterian Church: 1895
Ballybay: 928, 1218, 1634, 1697, 2280, 2539, 2597, 2795, 2833, 3505, 3872, 4166, 4168, 4199, 4878, 4954, 5643, 5793
Ballybay, parish of: 632, 1697
Ballybay Church: 1697, 5793
Ballybreen Cottage: 2634
Ballymackey, near Carrickmacross: 6149
Ballynode *var.* Ballinode Church: 2208
Bath Hill: 6143
Bellevu: 3644
Bessmont *var.* Bessmount Park: 4673
Bessmount: 5332
Bessmount Park: 682, 768
Bessmount-park *var.* Bessmount Park: 183
Billis: 4655
Bloomfield, Castleblayney: 599
Bourdaution *var.* Burdautien, near Clones: 2278
Brandrum House: 3668, 5027
Brewery, Monaghan: 4949
Brookmount: 4934
Brookvale: 5150
Camla: 1766, 3966
Camla Vale: 4540, 6424
Carrickmacross: 435, 471, 1145, 1350, 1811, 2352, 2762, 3197, 3640, 3845, 3958, 4125, 4331, 4966, 5295, 5383, 6121, 6149
Carrickmacross, parish of: 2633
Carrickmacross Church: 435, 2352, 3197
Carrickmacross Poor Law Union: 2352
Castleblaney *var.* Castleblayney: 884, 891, 902, 960, 1599, 1899, 2187, 2187, 3659, 4853, 5464
Castleblaney *var.* Castleblayney Church: 884
Castleblayney: 69, 400, 570, 599, 795, 884, 891, 902, 960, 1059, 1150, 1198, 1492, 1599,

393

Castleblayney, continued: 1610, 1633, 1899, 2187, 2470, 2562, 2814, 3399, 3442, 3573, 3659, 3832, 3962, 4045, 4198, 4591, 4708, 4853, 4862, 4919, 4934, 5464, 5575, 5620, 5824, 6303
Castleblayney, parish of: 3442
Castleblayney Church: 884, 902, 1150,: 3442
Castleshane: 951, 971, 5658, 6082
Clencorn: 3804
Clinculland: 526
Clinkirk *var.* Clonkirk, near Clones: 2278
Clonavilla: 3238
Cloncaw: 4256
Clones: 50, 252, 255, 412, 420, 460, 492, 526, 529, 654, 677, 873, 894, 929, 947, 1003, 1141, 1161, 1162, 1167, 1224, 1247, 1420, 1467, 1579, 1613, 1956, 2004, 2069, 2278, 2285, 2286, 2287, 2308, 2314, 2316, 2438, 2573, 2724, 2740, 2808, 3043, 3283, 3356, 3490, 3517, 3628, 3648, 3809, 3825, 3838, 3950, 4288, 4349, 4598, 4746, 4795, 5015, 5114, 5125, 5270, 5480, 5497, 5514, 5680, 5775, 6223, 6298, 6451
Clones, parish of: 1032
Clones Church: 255, 1467, 2278, 3517, 4598, 4746, 5114, 5480, 5497, 5680
Clones Rectory: 2271
Clonkee [Clonkeen?], near Clones: 6298
Clontibret: 299, 1081, 1128, 2035, 3303, 4000, 4437, 4934, 6034
Clontibret, parish of: 1128
Clontibret Church: 299
Clough: 526
Cloverhill: 294
Coolderry: 5817
Cormeen: 4388, 5711
Cornaho: 2169
Corovahan *var.* Corvaghan, near Clones: 3283
Cortamlet: 6415
Creigance [Creighans?]: 3330
Creighans: 3330
Cremorne: 3909
Crieve House: 4673, 6135
Cumry Lodge, Ballibay *var.* Ballybay: 5643
Cumry Lodge, Ballybay: 5643
Currin, parish of: 5680
Derrigolin Glebe, Carrickmacross: 1145
Derryhallagh: 301
Derrylavin: 1932
Derrylusk: 3030
Derryvalley: 3909

Donagh: 436
Drum: 1467, 2060, 4034, 4786, 5924
Drum Presbyterian Church: 4786
Drumaconnor: 2288
Drumbraine House: 680
Drumgole: 4786
Drumkeen: 1756
Drumloo Cottage: 482
Drumloo Cottage, Newbliss: 2729
Drummaconnor *var.* Drummaconor: 6172
Drummaconor: 6172
Drummuck: 3183
Drummullen: 525
Drumnail: 4428
Drumneil: 598
Drumnoland: 4656
Drumroo: 4341
Drumskelt, Ballibay *var.* Ballybay: 2539
Drumskelt, Ballybay: 2539
Drumsnatt Church: 1479
Drunreaske: 6005
Emyvale: 1169, 1807, 1864, 1992, 3673, 3916, 4378, 6040
Emyvale Presbyterian Church: 1992
Errigal Glebe: 2231
Errigal Trough: 6437
Errigle *var.* Errigal Glebe: 2231
Errigle *var.* Errigal Glebe, Aughnacloy: 4659
Errigle Trough *var.* Errigal Trough: 6437
Fairview: 727
Fairview, Ballybay: 4166
Falkland: 1129
First Presbyterian Church or Meeting-house, Monaghan: 444, 1404, 2453
Fort Frederick, near Ballybay: 3505
Fort Johnston *var.* Fortjohnston: 1719
Fortjohnston: 1719, 3941
Frankford Cottage, Castleblayney: 4591
Galina *var.* Gallina, 3030
Gallina, near Monaghan: 1945
Garmany's Grove, Castleblayney: 1610
Germany's *var.* Garmany's Grove, Castleblaney *var.* Castleblayney: 1633
Glasslough: 80, 623, 815, 1773, 1946, 3757, 3852, 3941, 4256, 4845, 5113, 5168, 5465, 5487, 5500, 5584, 5842, 6040, 6379
Glasslough Church: 3941, 4306, 6040
Glebe, Monaghan: 2620
Glenan *var.* Glennan: 4495
Glenan *var.* Glennan Presbyterian Meeting-house: 2610

Chapter 4: Index of Place Names

County Monaghan, continued:
Glenan *var.* Glennan, near Glasslough: 4256
Glennan: 2610, 6224
Glennan Presbyterian Meeting-house: 2610
Gola House: 2208, 5559
Gortnawinny Cottage: 947
Grange House: 696
Granshaw *var.* Gransha, Clones: 5680
Hill Cottage, Monaghan: 803
Hillhall: 3326
Hillton *var.* Hilton: 2290
Hilton: 2290
Hiltown *var.* Hilton: 895
Island Cottage, near Clones: 3950
Ivy-hill: 287, 5750
Kalmacklay: 525
Killaneel: 4495
Killenan: 4165
Killevan Church: 5575
Killifargy *var.* Killyfargy, parish of Currin: 5680
Killyfargy, parish of Currin: 5680
Kilmore: 821
Kilmore, parish of: 940
Lakeview: 1441, 3018
Laragh: 2812
Laurel Hill: 4888
Legnakelly, near Clones: 2287
Lisabuck, near Clones: 677
Lisanisk: 5295
Lisaniske *var.* Lisanisk: 5295
Liscarney: 5176
Lisinisk *var.* Lisanisk, Carrickmacross: 4125
Lisnavane *var.* Lisnaveane: 1187, 1348
Lisnaveane: 1187, 1348
Lough Bawn: 3578, 5065
Lough Dona: 5296
Loughbawn *var.* Lough Bawn: 3578
Loughmorne: 4773
Monaghan: 2, 25, 156, 160, 190, 343, 444, 537, 548, 791, 803, 815, 887, 1071, 1185, 1187, 1307, 1314, 1404, 1412, 1507, 1659, 1893, 1896, 1912, 1943, 1945, 1977, 2070, 2111, 2216, 2319, 2330, 2353, 2404, 2406, 2437, 2453, 2473, 2482, 2504, 2538, 2620, 2718, 2719, 2728, 2766, 2827, 2849, 2856, 3138, 3217, 3335, 3417, 3477, 3512, 3610, 3640, 3829, 4041, 4121, 4378, 4490, 4511, 4598, 4619, 4623, 4652, 4652, 4733, 4874, 4949, 4953, 4983, 5047, 5086, 5090, 5105, 5242, 5470, 5473, 5653, 5727, 6008, 6095, 6175, 6187

Monaghan, parish of: 2931, 4165
Monaghan Poor Law Union: 2718, 4983
Mossview House, Emyvale: 3673
Mount Carmel: 504
Mount Salem, Clones: 894
Mount-Louise: 1184
Muckna, Castleblayney: 1492
Mulladuff *var.* Mullaghduff: 2610
Mulladuff *var.* Mullaghduff, near Glasslough: 5487, 5500
Newbliss: 217, 1063, 1302, 2314, 2729, 3115, 3294, 5670
Newbliss House: 5580
Newgrove: 3562, 4330
Orchard Vale: 1507
Parsonage, Newbliss: 217
Poplar Vale: 830, 2675, 4449
Pound-hill, Clones: 1141
Rectory, Aghabog: 2674
Rectory, Ahabog *var.* Aghabog: 5570
Rectory, Castleblayney: 1198
Registrar's Office, Castleblayney: 400
Registrar's Office, Clones: 526
Retreat: 2133
Rockcorry: 196, 213, 1980, 2813, 3039, 6352
Rockfield: 299
Rocksfield: 3845
Rockville House: 3178
Rooskey *var.* Roosky: 3051
Rosefield: 1479
Rosefield, near Monaghan: 2319
Roslea: 1072, 1101
Roslea Manor: 4612
Rosslea *var.* Roslea: 1072
Sancho Errigle *var.* Shanco Errigal: 287
Seceding Congregation, Garmany's Grove, Castleblaney *var.* Castleblayney: 1610
Shanco Errigal Church: 287
Shanoho: 4572
Shelvins: 6056
Smithborough: 5831, 5985
Stone-bridge Presbyterian Meeting-house: 525, 873
Summer-hill: 242
Tanagh: 72
Teledon *var.* Tilledon Cottage, Glasslough: 3852
Teravera *var.* Tiravera: 3326
The Hill, Monaghan: 791
Thornford House: 884, 902
Thornhill: 25, 1479, 1479, 1903, 6148

County Monaghan, continued:
Tilledon Cottage, Glasslough: 5584
Tinary, Newbliss: 1302
Tiravera: 3326
Townview, Monaghan: 25
Tullaree, Glasslough: 5842
Tulledon *var.* Tilledon Cottage, Monaghan: 1896
Tullnageer *var.* Tullynageer: 3639
Tully House, Monaghan: 1314
Tullycaghny: 400
Tullycahey *var.* Tullycaghny: 400
Tullycorbet, parish of: 4870, 5227
Tullynageer: 3639
Tydavnet, parish of: 6437
Tydavnet Church: 6437
Tyhollan, parish of: 5515
Tyledon *var.* Tilledon Cottage: 4621
Watt's Bridge: 3133
Williamstown, Clones: 5775
Woodstock: 2610

Ossory, Diocese of:
Parish not named: 292, 2928, 4281, 6234
Poleroan: 422

Ossory and Ferns, Diocese of: 1589

Queen's (Laoix), county of:
Townland not named: 462
Abbeyleix: 1773
Altavilla: 5284
Ballickmoyler: 4014
Ballintoher: 1993
Cappaloughan: 2584
Castletown: 2613
Coolbanagher Church: 4308
Dairy Hill: 4678
Donmore: 661
Harristown: 5851
La Bergerie: 1677
La Bergerie, Portarlington: 540
Lea Church, near Portarlington: 2369
Maryborough: 1092, 1780, 4058
Mountmellick: 1686, 2803, 2858
Mountrath Church: 4572
New Park: 4572
Portarlington: 462, 540, 1031, 2369, 3974, 4024, 4273, 4908, 4984
Portrane: 5029
Raheenduff: 4381

Rearyvalley: 2584
Rock of Dunamace *var.* Dunamase: 4404
Rock of Dunamase: 4404
Rosenalis Church: 2584
St. Michael's Church, Portarlington: 4273
Stradbally: 4405

Raphoe, Diocese of:
Parish not named: 771, 2986
Killea Rectory: 2843
Killymard, parish of: 531
Raymoghy, parish of: 1800
Tullaghobegley, parish of: 3409

River Boyne: 5668

Roscommon, county of:
Townland not named: 3146, 3444, 5787
Ardcarne Church: 3422
Ashfort House: 4295, 5440
Athlone: 3444, 5131
Boyle: 2472, 2536, 3118, 3667, 6267
Castle Tenison: 1324
Castlerea: 2361
Cloon-hill: 2548
Cloonequin: 5141
Clover Hill, Boyle: 3667
Fortland: 5297
Keadew: 1324
Keadue *var.* Keadew: 1324
Killukin Rectory: 3601
Kilronan Castle: 2205
Kiltoom: 3444
Longfield: 3444
Mount Plunkett, near Athlone: 3444
Oatlands, near Boyle: 2536
Rahara House, near Athlone: 5131
Roscommon: 6342
St. Peter's Church: 3444
Strokestown, parish of: 2226

Sligo, county of:
Townland not named: 867, 1918, 1976, 1976, 2972, 5576, 6342
Abbeyview: 4924
Abbeyview, Sligo: 5157
Ahamlish Church: 4070
Ballinode *var.* Bellanode: 2978
Ballintain: 3593
Ballisodare: 2732
Ballisodare, near Sligo: 4322
Ballyglass: 4392

County Sligo, continued:
Ballymote: 1835, 2347, 2799, 4474, 5505
Bellanode: 2978
Calry Church, Sligo: 2415
Calry Glebe, Sligo: 1733
Castle Baldwin: 1889
Chaffpool: 6289
Cloonamahon: 4726
Cloonerar [Cloonarara?]: 1918
Cloonlough *var.* Cloonlurg Cottage, Ballymote: 2799
Cloonlurg Cottage, Ballymote: 4474, 5505
Collooney: 2346
Collooney Abbey: 2586
Coloony *var.* Collooney: 2346
Cooper-hill *var.* Cooper's Hill: 3496
Cooper's Hill: 4336
Cooper's-hill *var.* Cooper's Hill: 5436
Cummin: 742
Daskey [Easky?] Vicarage: 3062
Dromaid: 384
Dromard Rectory, Ballisodare, near Sligo: 4322
Easkey Church *var.* Easky Church: 1976
Easkey Vicarage: 3062
Easky: 1929, 1976
Easky Church: 1976
Eoskey *var.* Easky: 1976
Fortland: 2511
Hazlewood: 10, 1436
Hermitage: 5148
Keybrook: 3118
Lissadill House: 742
Lungy: 4406
Lynn's Place, Sligo: 5312
Markree Castle: 3577
Mount Edward: 214, 4091
Mullaghmore: 353
Oldrock: 4923
O'Donnell-place, Thornhill, Sligo: 1959
Powellsborough House: 3118
Rathbraghan: 4996
Rathbrogan: 2009
Riversdale: 713
Riverstown: 5436
Riverstown Church: 3496
Rusheen: 2346
Rusheen, near Sligo: 2598
Saltport: 3837
Scarden: 2454
Screen: 1225
Skreen: 6031
Sligo: 299, 1084, 1134, 1225, 1420, 1477, 1576, 1733, 1959, 2070, 2107, 2267, 2307,

Sligo (town), continued: 2370, 2371, 2415, 2454, 2471, 2475, 2586, 2598, 2599, 2834, 2916, 2940, 2973, 2974, 2975, 2976, 3021, 3022, 3023, 3028, 3029, 3493, 3524, 3574, 3576, 3582, 3675, 3784, 3790, 3794, 3814, 3887, 4018, 4019, 4152, 4234, 4238, 4322, 4344, 4451, 4593, 4647, 4854, 5157, 5312, 5323, 5359, 5395, 5494, 6158, 6375, 6394, 6407
Sligo, borough of: 6289
Somertown: 5436
St. John's Church, Sligo: 2371, 2916, 3582, 3675
Streamstown: 703
Streeda: 4070
Tanragee: 867
Temple House: 3346
Thornhill, Sligo: 1959
Tobercurry: 3079
Tobercurry, parish of: 2391
Tower Hill: 4506
Tubbercurry *var.* Tobercurry: 3079
Tubbercurry *var.* Tobercurry, parish of: 2391

Tipperary, county of:
Barnane: 2697
Borrisokane: 2767
Borrisoleigh: 5724
Bourney Glebe: 6225
Cahir Barracks: 2939
Carrick-on-Suir: 4155, 4408, 5742, 5809
Cashel: 559, 719, 2651, 5227, 5476
Castletown Cambie: 5296
Clerkhill *var.* Clarkill, near Borrisokane: 2767
Clifton: 688
Cloghjordan: 6168
Clonmel: 577, 1201, 2442, 3797, 3841, 4123, 4408, 5736
Cloughjordan: 4578, 5085
Farrenrory: 1766
Johnstown: 6099
Knocklofty: 5038
Landaff Lodge, Thurles: 4409
Liseahill: 3891
Millbrook: 4031
Nenagh: 4697, 4945
Newpark, Cashel: 5227
Outeragh, parish of: 690
Palace, Cashel: 5476
Rathbeg: 4920
Rectory, Templetuohy: 6193

County Tipperary, continued:
Redmonstown: 6328
Redmount: 3092
Roscrea: 59
Springfield, Clonmel: 5736
St. Mary's Church, Clonmel: 3797
Templemore: 1766, 5480, 5497
Templetuohy: 6193
Templetuohy and Loughmore, united parishes of: 6193
The Priory: 1766
Thurles: 4409, 5258, 6131
Thurles Church: 5258
Tipperary: 3448
Tipperary, parish of: 768
Toomevara: 2349

Tuam, Diocese of:
Parish not named: 704, 1625, 2952, 3454, 5815
Atherney, parish of: 734
Kilkerrin, parish of: 3105

Tyrone, county of:
Townland not named: 37, 143, 509, 745, 789, 2421, 3403, 3452, 3651, 3978, 4191, 4530, 4654, 5028, 5164, 5315, 5594, 5755, 6314
Abercorn Arms Hotel, Strabane: 284
Aghaloo, parish of: 21
Aghintain: 3256
Ahgadullagh: 4237
Aldohol *var.* Altdoghal: 2273
Allan Rock, Dungannon: 3403
Alt Presbyterian Church: 1656
Altdoghal: 2273
Altmore: 4805
Altnaveagh: 297
Anaghbeg: 1667
Anahoe House: 5343
Anahoe House, Ballygawley: 4188
Anglies, near Cookstown: 1240
Anketell Lodge, Stewartstown: 6434
Annagh House, Clogher: 5083
Annaghroe: 640
Annaghroe House: 1270
Annaginny: 65
Annaginny, Dungannon: 6184
Annaguinea *var.* Annaginny, near Dungannon: 65
Annahavil: 2684
Annaquinnea *var.* Annaginny, Dungannon: 6184

Annaro *var.* Annaghroe: 640
Annaroe *var.* Annaghroe House: 1270
Annesley Lodge, Coal Island *var.* Coalisland: 413
Annesley Lodge, Coalisland: 413
Arboe: 4917
Arboe, parish of: 3369
Arboe Glebe: 3369
Ardagarvan *var.* Artigarvan, parish of Leckpatrick: 5212
Ardarva-House: 17
Ardstraw: 3426, 3776
Ardstraw, parish of: 37, 2686
Ardstraw-bridge: 2416
Ardtrea, near Cookstown: 417
Armagh House: 1275
Artigarvan Lodge: 3398
Artigarvan-lodge *var.* Artigarvan Lodge: 2668
Artigarvan, parish of Leckpatrick: 5212
Artigarvon *var.* Artigarvan, near Strabane: 1459
Aughacloy: 4659
Aughadullagh *var.* Aghadullagh: 4237
Aughafadd *var.* Aghafad, near Clogher: 4769
Aughareny *var.* Aghareany, near Dungannon: 51
Aughentain *var.* Aghintain: 4797
Aughentain *var.* Aghintain Mills: 5979
Augher: 1469, 1470, 3161, 6053
Augher Castle: 5175, 5189
Aughnacloy: 149, 227, 361, 436, 461, 474, 587, 640, 687, 857, 885, 901, 1004, 1151, 1206, 1229, 1569, 1660, 1785, 1995, 2154, 2206, 2448, 2683, 2807, 2870, 3015, 3315, 3416, 3702, 3711, 3751, 3854, 3855, 4294, 4685, 4731, 4995, 5661, 6136, 6389, 6444
Aughnacloy Church: 361, 361, 587, 901, 1785
Aughnacloy Presbyterian Church or Meeting-house: 640, 687, 885, 3751
Aughtentain *var.* Aghintain: 3256
Badoney: 1385
Badoney Cottage: 5706
Badoney, near Trillick: 6271
Badony *var.* Badoney: 1385
Ballagh, parish of Clogher: 5525
Ballinahatty: 479
Ballinassagart: 3620, 5297
Ballough *var.* Ballagh, Clogher: 489
Ballycloy: 5483
Ballycolman, Strabane: 3175
Ballycushy, near Fintona: 533

County Tyrone, continued:
Ballygawley: 375, 696, 1820, 1887, 2080, 2579, 3032, 4188, 4302, 5012, 5716, 6176, 6312
Ballygawley Presbyterian Church or Meeting-house: 696, 2579
Ballygawly *var.* Ballygawley: 696
Ballygawly *var.* Ballygawley Meeting-house: 696
Ballymagorry: 1395, 2756
Ballymagorry, near Strabane: 2756
Ballymagowan: 2878
Ballymagrame *var.* Ballymagrane Presbyterian Church: 3315
Ballymagrane: 3315, 4685
Ballymagrane Presbyterian Church: 4685
Ballymenagh, Cookstown: 1616, 4499
Ballyreagh: 2104, 6057
Ballysudden, near Cookstown: 1308
Ballywhilon *var.* Ballywholan: 1357
Ballywholan: 1357
Bantry *var.* Brantry: 5435
Bar Church, parish of Fintona: 1784
Bar, Parsonage, Fintona: 5347
Beachmount: 5447. *See also* Beechmount.
Bealmount, Dungannon: 372
Beech-hill, near Omagh: 4691
Beechgrove: 3414, 3437
Beechmount: 1930, 5610. *See also* Beachmount.
Beechmount, Strabane: 2040
Bellevue: 564
Belnaclogh: 5718
Belnesagart: 474
Benburb: 162, 369, 461, 607, 612, 759, 766, 773, 776, 806, 987, 1230, 1360, 1363, 1367, 1496, 1523, 1595, 1741, 1989, 2144, 2372, 3014, 3072, 3127, 3158, 3307, 3684, 4016, 4599, 4618, 4640, 5197, 5260, 6171, 6417
Benburb Castle: 776, 899
Benburb Church: 162, 461, 759, 806, 1989, 3072, 3158, 5260, 6417
Benburb Presbyterian Church: 1230, 1741
Benoan: 5282
Beragh: 306, 1203, 1374, 1881, 1908, 2227, 2233, 2341, 3202, 3781, 4434, 4569, 4785, 5096, 5155
Beragh, near Dungannon: 6020
Beragh, Omagh: 4211
Berney Glebe, Strabane: 1400
Bogisland, near Castlcaulfield *var.* Castlecaulfield: 1859

Bogisland, near Castlecaulfield: 1859
Bolton's Walls, near Caledon: 4132
Bovain House: 206
Bovain *var.* Bovean, near Moy: 800
Bovean, near Moy: 800
Brackagh: 274
Brackaville, near Coalisland: 1308
Brantry: 5287, 5435, 5919
Brantry Church: 5919
Breakly: 437
Breen, near Strabane: 2590
Brookfield, Moy: 5482
Brydge Hall: 3041
Bunnynubber, near Omagh: 75
Bush, The; Killyman, near Dungannon: 5364
Bush Mount, near Dungannon: 1015
Cairnteel *var.* Carnteel House: 587
Caledon: 15, 79, 161, 170, 173, 223, 235, 502, 538, 676, 789, 793, 934, 972, 990, 1151, 1244, 1333, 1664, 1838, 1896, 2212, 2260, 2355, 2431, 2835, 3499, 3538, 3707, 3721, 3852, 4132, 4182, 4208, 4539, 4657, 4995, 5014, 5185, 5287, 5333, 5651, 6276, 6414
Caledon Church: 161, 934, 1151, 1664
Caledon Hill, Caledon: 3721
Caledon Presbyterian Church: 5014
Cammowen Green: 4434
Camus: 2686, 5927
Camus Juxta Mourne, parish of: 6111
Camus, near Strabane: 1142
Canal Stores, Caledon: 2260, 4182
Cappagh: 75, 4260
Cappagh, parish of: 3469, 6191
Cappagh Church: 75, 3469
Cappagh, near Omagh: 2555
Carlan *var.* Carland Presbyterian Church: 6057
Carland: 1114, 2393, 6057
Carland Presbyterian Church or Meeting-house: 1114, 6057
Carland, near Dungannon: 454
Carlin House: 4324
Carnahinny, near Clogher: 3511
Carnalay: 1466
Carndreen: 2861, 2862
Carniheny *var.* Carnahinny, near Clogher: 3511
Carntall: 334, 340, 737, 1203
Carntall Presbyterian Church or Meeting-house: 334, 340, 737, 1203
Carntall Meeting-house, Clogher: 4238
Carnteel: 561, 587
Carnteel House: 587, 901, 2955, 4815

County Tyrone, continued:
Carnteel House, near Aughnacloy: 3854
Carrickmore: 2712, 4084, 4112, 4129, 4149, 5070
Carrickmore, Termon *var.* Termonmaguirk: 5791
Carrickmore, Termonmaguirk: 5791
Carrygullon *var.* Carrigullin, near Strabane: 1842
Cashel-house: 4254
Castle Stewart: 312, 943
Castle Stuart *var.* Castle Stewart: 312
Castle, Dungannon: 2119
Castlecaulfield: 733, 1634, 1859, 2106, 2619, 3199, 3494, 3498, 3519, 4824, 6176
Castlecaulfield Church: 733, 3498
Castlecaulfield Presbyterian Church or Meeting-house: 1634, 3519
Castledawson: 3285
Castlederg: 1296, 1413, 1536, 2465, 2496, 3426
Castletown House: 1424
Castletown Lodge, Fintona: 5384
Cavanalee: 1934
Cecil: 3128, 6437
Chapel House, Clogher: 3988
Claggan: 2105, 2207, 2726, 3402, 4191, 4912
Claggan Presbyterian Church: 2105, 2726, 4191, 4912
Claggin *var.* Claggan: 2105, 3402
Claggin *var.* Claggan Presbyterian Church: 2105, 2726, 4191, 4912
Clananees *var.* Clananeese: 1859
Clananeese: 750, 1859, 2399, 3465, 3778, 3824, 4132
Clananeese Presbyterian Church: 261
Clananeese, Carnteel: 561
Claudy *var.* Clady: 1656
Claudy *var.* Clady, Strabane: 3834
Clenanees *var.* Clananeese, Carnteel: 561
Clennanese *var.* Clananeese Presbyterian Church: 261
Clew *var.* Crew Bridge: 282
Clogher: 36, 199, 276, 297, 407, 437, 489, 737, 761, 1190, 1545, 2104, 2112, 2114, 2251, 2256, 2878, 3511, 3610, 3712, 3988, 4059, 4238, 4366, 4769, 4991, 5083, 5373, 5957
Clogher, parish of: 5525
Clogher Cathedral or Clogher Cathedral Church: 297, 437, 4991
Clogher Presbyterian Church: 2104, 3610

Clogherney *var.* Clogherny Church: 4434
Clogherny: 4434
Clogherny Church: 4434
Cloghog House: 69
Clohog *var.* Cloghog, near Omagh: 6147
Clonfeacle: 366, 883, 2907
Clonfeacle, parish of: 21, 366, 759, 806, 1662, 3072, 6039, 6219
Clonfeacle Glebe: 4538
Clonfecle *var.* Clonfeacle: 883
Clonfeele *var.* Clonfeacle, parish of: 21
Clonghore, near Castlederg: 1413
Clougherney *var.* Clougherny: 4344
Clougherny: 4344
Coagh: 245, 775, 2108, 2153, 2170, 2206, 3052, 4393, 5636
Coagh Presbyterian Church: 5636
Coal Island: 464. *See also* Coalisland.
Coal Island Mills *var.* Coalisland Mills, Dungannon: 4877
Coal Island *var.* Coalisland: 683
Coalhill, near Dungannon: 2108
Coalisland: 413, 464, 683, 1308, 1322, 1369, 2105, 2207, 3004, 3441, 3701, 5068, 5257, 5299, 5705. *See also* Coal Island.
Coalisland Church: 1369
Coalisland House: 4056
Coalisland Mills: 464, 4877, 5068
Coalisland Mills, Dungannon: 1322
Coalisland-house: 1369
Coldrum: 2623
Colreagh *var.* Coolreaghs, Cookstown: 3402
Commercial Hotel, Dungannon: 865
Commercial Hotel, Stewartstown: 5740
Commercial House, Cookstown: 3706
Cookhill, near Dungannon: 4925
Cookstown: 19, 416, 417, 586, 590, 671, 853, 858, 1030, 1073, 1087, 1239, 1240, 1275, 1303, 1308, 1321, 1423, 1450, 1476, 1519, 1538, 1552, 1610, 1616, 1633, 1710, 1775, 1953, 2123, 2135, 2180, 2222, 2344, 2392, 2406, 2445, 2684, 3074, 3215, 3263, 3313, 3331, 3367, 3402, 3504, 3627, 3653, 3706, 3800, 4420, 4499, 4554, 4699, 4830, 4864, 4893, 4912, 4933, 5026, 5106, 5160, 5276, 5310, 5316, 5430, 5441, 5764, 5982, 6075, 6100, 6337
Cookstown Church: 1275
Cookstown Poor Law Union: 3367
Cookstown Presbyterian Meetng-house: 416
Coolhill: 2479

County Tyrone, continued:
Coolkill, near Dungannon: 970
Cootehill [Coolhill?], near Dungannon: 2479
Corcreevy-house, near Fivemiletown: 2236
Corcrevey-house *var.* Corcreevy-house, near Fivemiletown: 2459
Corderry: 885
Coreany *var.* Corrainy, Dungannon: 452
Corkhill: 575, 2258, 4846
Corr, near Benburb: 4618
Corrylongford, near Fivemiletown: 4797
Cottage-hill, Aughnacloy: 857
Court-house, Clogher: 4059
Craig, near Claudy co. Derry: 4218
Creeduff House: 3802
Creevagh, near Dungannon: 2393, 3193
Creggan House, Cookstown: 2135
Crevagh *var.* Creevagh, Dungannon: 3193
Crevenagh House, Omagh: 33
Crew: 2686
Crew Bridge: 5463
Crew Church, parish of Ardstraw: 2686
Crew Cottage, Ballygauley *var.* Ballygawley: 295
Crew Cottage, Ballygawley: 295
Crew, Ballygawley: 1820
Crievagh: 2726
Crilly-house: 5185, 5912
Crosh House, Newtownstewart: 1715
Crossdernot-House: 2061
Crossteely: 3465
Culcairn *var.* Culkeeran, near Benburb: 1496
Culkearn, Moy: 228
Culkeeran: 518
Culkeeran, near Benburb: 1496
Culkeeran, near Moy: 1147
Culkeerane House, Moy: 1741
Culkeerin: 2715
Culkerin *var.* Culkeeran, Moy: 2715
Culligan, near Caledon: 4539
Cumber, Fintona. 4265
Curlagh: 223
Curlough *var.* Curlagh, near Caledon: 223, 4657
Curnavathan, Cookstown: 19
Curr, near Beragh: 4434
Curran: 1367
Curren *var.* Curran: 461
Daisy-hill, Clogher: 4366
Darraghmore: 3821
Deerpark, near Omagh: 4577

Derrabard House: 758
Derrihore *var.* Derryhoar, near Dungannon: 3349
Derrybard: 2258
Derrycortrevy *var.* Derrygortrevy Church: 218
Derryfubble: 450, 1264
Derryfubble, near Benburb: 3014
Derrygonan House: 612
Derrygortreavy *var.* Derrygortrevy Church: 282
Derrygortrevy Church: 218, 282
Derryhoar: 3349
Derryloran, parish of, Cookstown: 1030, 5607
Derryloran Rectory, Cookstown: 6100
Derrypubble *var.* Derryfubble: 450
Derryvale: 4138
Derryvole: 3488
Desart Glebe: 4826
Desertcreat: 3403
Desertcreat, parish of: 5091
Desertcreat Church: 3403
Desertcreight *var.* Desertcreat, parish of: 5091
Donacavey, parish of: 5030
Donagheady: 2217
Donaghendry: 427. *See also* Donahendry.
Donaghendry Church, Stewartstown: 427
Donaghendry Rectory: 5443
Donaghmore: 854, 1357, 1417, 1634, 1821, 2350, 2763, 2937, 2958, 2971, 3494, 3519, 4458, 5144, 5475
Donaghmore, parish of: 2106
Donaghmore Church: 854
Donaghmoyne Glebe: 4417
Donahendry *var.* Donaghendry Rectory: 5443
Donamoine *var.* Donaghmoyne Glebe: 4417
Donemana: 4029
Donemony *var.* Dunamony: 3824
Donoughmore: 5044
Donoughmore Church: 2242
Donoughmore *var.* Donaghmore: 2242
Doogory House, Omagh: 1908
Douglasbridge: 1947
Dreenan: 2862
Dromerin [*var.* Drumearn?]: 1569
Dromore: 1380, 1635, 2432, 4237, 4255, 4569
Dromore, parish of: 3610
Dromore Church: 1380
Dromore Rectory: 778
Drum, near Omagh: 3000
Drumacmay *var.* Dunmacmay, parish of Aghaloo: 21
Drumanney [Drumanuey?]: 1147

County Tyrone, continued:
Drumanuey: 1147
Drumardnagross: 1738
Drumcairn, Stewartstown: 2088, 2434
Drumcann: 2679
Drumconnis House, Omagh: 5031
Drumcraw: 4499
Drumcullion, near Ballygawley: 2579
Drumglas *var.* Drumglass House, Dungannon: 5632
Drumglass, parish of: 3671
Drumglass House: 5632
Drumglass House, near Dungannon: 3760, 4832
Drumglass House, Tullycullen *var.* Tullycullion, near Dungannon: 3500
Drumgrannon, near Moy: 685
Drummond: 107
Drumnabuoy *var.* Drumnaboy, near Strabane: 5927
Drumnafin *var.* Drumnafern, near Dungannon: 3824
Drumnakilly: 230, 728, 1908
Drumnakilly House: 4111
Drumnakilly parsonage, Omagh: 5839
Drumquin: 1343, 3861, 4265, 5603
Drumquin Meeting-house: 2049
Drumragh: 746
Drumragh, parish of: 1907, 5780
Drumraw: 2908
Drumrawn, near Drumquin: 5603
Drumreagh: 2094
Drumsallan: 766
Drumshambo Glebe: 1379
Dullaghan, Dromore: 4255
Dunamony: 3824
Dundiven Glebe: 530
Dungannon: 7, 29, 51, 56, 65, 130, 160, 187, 193, 206, 250, 261, 326, 355, 359, 372, 398, 419, 451, 452, 453, 454, 464, 470, 476, 505, 532, 544, 559, 560, 587, 600, 603, 683, 687, 733, 797, 818, 865, 888, 890, 939, 969, 970, 979, 998, 1015, 1044, 1114, 1123, 1138, 1147, 1234, 1262, 1322, 1404, 1416, 1460, 1549, 1634, 1657, 1685, 1786, 1832, 1835, 1904, 2061, 2094, 2106, 2108, 2119, 2136, 2243, 2252, 2270, 2275, 2345, 2378, 2393, 2409, 2479, 2629, 2822, 2907, 2915, 2965, 3004, 3013, 3040, 3059, 3157, 3168, 3193, 3280, 3293, 3339, 3349, 3357, 3377, 3393, 3403, 3440, 3473, 3500, 3539, 3542, 3567, 3623,

Dungannon, continued: 3630, 3671, 3700, 3705, 3740, 3750, 3760, 3778, 3808, 3824, 3846, 3853, 3895, 3901, 3902, 3933, 3964, 3970, 3986, 3991, 4006, 4087, 4139, 4156, 4196, 4265, 4275, 4289, 4302, 4379, 4438, 4480, 4493, 4517, 4520, 4544, 4552, 4599, 4641, 4785, 4789, 4798, 4832, 4877, 4883, 4911, 4925, 4933, 5032, 5082, 5096, 5134, 5144, 5203, 5222, 5226, 5257, 5307, 5358, 5364, 5370, 5408, 5629, 5632, 5636, 5648, 5677, 5698, 5705, 5713, 5852, 5885, 5982, 5993, 6020, 6184, 6346, 6429
Dungannon Castle: 757
Dungannon Church: 2243
Dungannon Circuit: 2248
Dungannon Poor Law Union: 4517
Dunlow: 4464
Dunmore: 2726
Dyan: 1664
Eary: 2968, 5301
East Langfield: 4133
Ecclesgreen: 2552
Ecclesgreen, Fintona: 5050
Ecclesville: 6241
Edenderry, near Benburb: 987, 3307
Effernen: 6271
Eglish, Dungannon: 3853
Elm Lodge, Dungannon: 3159
Errigal Glebe, Aughnacloy: 4659
Fair View, Dungannon: 398
Fairlawn, near Moy: 1267, 1497
Fairview, Aughnacloy: 1995
Fardross, near Clogher: 2251
Fareagh, near Omagh: 4459
Favour Royal: 5189
Feglish, near Lowtherstown: 693
Fimore *var.* Fymore: 297
Fintona: 533, 758, 872, 881, 976, 1046, 1524, 1559, 1636, 1759, 2086, 2405, 2552, 2641, 2830, 3545, 4009, 4226, 4265, 4577, 4774, 4905, 5030, 5347, 5361, 5384, 5562, 5709
Fintona, parish of: 1784
Fintona Church: 758, 4009, 5030, 5709
Fintona Presbyterian Church or Meeting-house: 872, 881
First Presbyterian Church, Clenanees *var.* Clananeese: 2399
First Presbyterian Church or Meeting-house, Dungannon: 600, 3623, 3705, 4599
First Presbyterian Church, Newtownstewart: 2273
First Presbyterian Church, Omagh: 2455

Chapter 4: Index of Place Names

County Tyrone, continued:
First Presbyterian Church, Strabane: 3606
First Presbyterian Congregation, Cookstown: 1321
Fivemiletown: 334, 340, 520, 603, 788, 893, 906, 1190, 1203, 1489, 1693, 1973, 2084, 2104, 2236, 2284, 2459, 2532, 3526, 3528, 3830, 4279, 4296, 4797, 5330, 5529
Flush House, Augher: 6053
Flushtown, near Strabane: 2254
Friends Meeting-house, Grange: 2715
Furlough House: 326
Fyfin, near Castlederg: 3426
Fymore: 297
Garvaughey House: 6416
Garvey: 640
Garvey, Aughnacloy: 5661
Gillygooly: 2455
Glasmullagh, near Omagh: 5539
Glebe, Clonfeacle: 1662
Glencoppagagh, near Plumbridge: 243
Glencrew, near Aughnacloy: 2807
Glencull, Aughnacloy: 1004
Glencush: 2967
Glenelly Presbyterian Church: 2713
Glengun: 1784
Glenhoy: 4492, 5718
Glenhoy Presbyterian Church: 3161
Glenhoy, near Augher: 3161
Glentimon, parish of Urney: 383
Goerstown-house *var.* Gorestown-house, Moy: 1050
Goerstown, Moy *var.* Gorestown: 145
Goland: 2432
Gorestown, Moy: 145, 779
Gortaclare: 306
Gortalowry, Cookstown: 1610, 1633
Gortanelly, near Caledon: 538
Gortin: 1886, 2926, 3381, 6045, 6116, 6150
Gortindoragh *var.* Gortindarragh, near Castlederg: 1536
Gortmarron: 5816
Gortmerron-house: 4957
Gortmore: 2908
Gortmore, Omagh: 3935, 4348
Gortnagross, near Killeter: 5188
Gorton House, Dungannon: 5358
Grange: 417, 1022, 2374, 2715, 4683, 5799
Grange Foyle: 4535
Grange Park: 2605
Greenhill: 2161

Greenmount: 1643
Greenmount, near Omagh: 251, 1645
Grenville, Aughnacloy: 1785
Grouse Lodge: 4324
Grove hill or Grove-hill, near Omagh: 5647, 5989
Grove Hill, near Strabane: 4124
Halftown, Aughnacloy: 436
Harlough, Dungannon: 1904
Hotel, Trillick: 4843
Independent Chapel, Donaghmore: 2350
Independent Chapel, Donoughmore *var.* Donaghmore: 1357
Kildress: 2109, 2359
Kildress, parish of: 1275
Killay, near Pomeroy: 827
Killeeshil: 47, 234. *See also* Killishil and Killishill.
Killen: 1440
Killeter: 2861, 2862, 4235, 5188
Killishil Cottage: 234, 4082
Killishil *var.* Killeeshil: 47
Killishill Cottage: 5064
Killishill *var.* Killeeshil Rectory: 5940.
Killybrack: 3469
Killyclogher: 3389
Killycolp: 1679
Killycolp, Dungannon: 2136
Killymaddy: 1672
Killymaddy House, near Dungannon: 733
Killymaddy, Castlecaulfield: 6176
Killyman: 96, 641, 1117, 1232, 1504, 1655, 2266
Killyman Church: 96, 1117, 1232, 1655
Killyman House: 600
Killyman, Moy: 2229
Killyman, near Dungannon: 5307, 5364
Killymeal: 2378
Killymoon: 3745
Killymore, near Newtownstewart: 4318
Killymorgan, Ballygawley: 6176
Kilmaslee: 1114
Kilrail House: 697
Kilrudden: 2892
Kilskeery: 4992, 5259, 6416
Kilskeery, parish of: 758
Kilskeery Church: 6416
Kilskerry *var.* Kilskeery Church: 6416
Kilvin, near Omagh: 6153
King William Hotel, Aughnacloy: 2807
Kinneary, near Moy: 1712

403

County Tyrone, continued:
Knockmany: 310
Knockmoyle: 3990
Knockmoyle, near Omagh: 3214
Lackagh: 1440, 4237
Lackaugh *var.* Lackagh: 1440
Lake View, Aughnacloy: 2870
Lakeview Cottage, Dungannon: 3157
Lammy: 4577
Lamy *var.* Lammy, near Dungannon: 5982
Lara Vale *var.* Laragh Vale: 361
Laragh Vale: 361
Larch Mount, Dungannon: 464
Latbeg: 4991
Laught, near Dungannon: 4265
Leckpatrick, parish of: 5212
Legnacash: 2684
Letbeg *var.* Latbeg: 4991
Letterbratt: 2713
Lime Park: 2560
Liscleen: 4029
Liscreevaghan, Strabane: 6111
Lisdhu: 180, 312, 943
Lisferty *var.* Lisfearty, near Aughnacloy: 1660
Liskey, near Strabane: 5857
Lismulreavey, near Dungannon: 3986
Lisnacrieve House: 3819, 4947
Lisnagir, near Omagh: 1299
Lisnamallard: 1046
Lisnedin, Dromore: 1635
Lisonally House, near Omagh: 2131, 3722
Lisroan: 218, 1790
Lisrone *var.* Lisroan: 218, 1790
Lissane: 5686
Longfield West: 1440
Loughry: 1852, 2851
Lower Badoney, parish of: 309
Lower Badony *var.* Lower Badoney, parish of: 309, 5609
Lower Clananees *var.* Clananeese Presbyterian Church: 1859
Lower Clananeese: 261, 3778, 3824, 4132
Lower Clananeese Presbyterian Church: 1859, 3824
Lower Clenanees *var.* Clananeese Presbyterian Church: 3824
Lower Clenanees *var.* Clananeese, Dungannon: 3778
Lower Clenanees *var.* Lower Clananeese: 3824
Lower Clenaneese *var.* Lower Clananeese: 4132

Lower Clennanese *var.* Lower Clananeese, near Dungannon: 261
Lower Drumney, near Strabane: 1776
Lower Longfield *var.* Longfield West Church: 1440
Lyme Park Lodge: 3347
Magheracolton: 2416
Magheraglass, near Cookstown: 3627, 3653
Magherakellaghan, near Claudy *var.* Clady, Strabane: 3834
Magir, near Strabane: 5320
Maydown, near Benburb: 776
Mayne House: 697
Melmount, Strabane: 1581
Mill View, Aughnacloy: 1206
Milltown or Miltown House or Miltown-house, Dungannon: 1685, 4751, 5873
Milltown, parish of Ardstraw: 37
Milltown, Strabane: 2039
Miltown-house, Strabane: 4235
Miltown, Ballymagorry, near Strabane: 1395
Minterburn: 3362, 4132, 4995, 5508, 6057, 6171
Minterburn Presbyterian Church: 4132, 4995, 5508
Minterburn, near Caledon: 5287
Moneyveagh *var.* Mineveigh, near Dungannon: 2409
Moss-spring: 254
Mossfield, near Strabane: 3860
Mount Pleasant: 4362
Mount Pleasant, near Clogher: 1545
Mount Pollock, near Dungannon: 2252
Mount Stewart, near Clogher: 36
Mount-stewart *var.* Mount Stewart, near Clogher: 36
Mountfield Church: 697
Mountjoy: 3984
Moy: 18, 45, 70, 78, 145, 227, 228, 254, 265, 410, 456, 518, 542, 627, 628, 649, 650, 661, 681, 685, 686, 716, 779, 784, 794, 800, 825, 875, 974, 1035, 1050, 1079, 1143, 1147, 1200, 1252, 1262, 1267, 1363, 1497, 1684, 1688, 1712, 1713, 1714, 1741, 1972, 2229, 2248, 2399, 2434, 2715, 2872, 3013, 3428, 3465, 3726, 3849, 4505, 4724, 4810, 4963, 5116, 5135, 5458, 5482, 5767, 5852, 5950, 6113
Moy, parish of: 3344
Moy Church: 410, 456, 518, 542, 661, 825, 1684, 1972, 3344, 5116
Moyard: 634
Moyard, Benburb: 607, 773

County Tyrone, continued:
Moyle Glebe: 625, 889
Moyle Rectory: 5162
Muff Glebe, Cookstown: 1087, 5276
Muff, near Cookstown: 3504
Mullaghboy, near Moy: 1363
Mullaghmena *var.* Mullaghmenagh, near Omagh: 3177
Mullaghmore: 305, 437, 6191
Mullaghmore, near Omagh: 4389
Mullaghriffy: 6176
Mullans, near Fintona: 2405
Mullicarnon *var.* Mullcarnon, Caledon: 4995
Mullin: 5919
Mullinaveigh *var.* Mullynaveigh, near Caledon: 3707
Mullycrunnett: 2350
Mullyrodden, near Caledon: 1838
Mulvin: 4010, 6037
Mulvyn *var.* Mulvin: 4010
New Mills *var.* Newmills Church: 943
Newmills: 312, 943, 6214
Newmills Church: 312
Newtownsaville: 3767, 889, 1214, 1304, 1715, 2273, 2686, 3038, 3115, 3260, 3776, 4318, 4916, 5167, 6037, 6111
Newtownstewart Church: 3260, 6037, 6111
Nn-stewart *var.* Newtownstewart: 1214
Nockmany *var.* Knockmany: 310
Nowtownsaville *var.* Newtownsaville: 3767
Omagh: 33, 75, 155, 188, 230, 243, 251, 329, 356, 374, 689, 695, 715, 1213, 1234, 1290, 1299, 1312, 1332, 1360, 1443, 1462, 1588, 1629, 1645, 1890, 1907, 1908, 1925, 1933, 2131, 2213, 2214, 2232, 2555, 2571, 2617, 2701, 2908, 3000, 3001, 3115, 3177, 3211, 3212, 3213, 3214, 3273, 3295, 3316, 3389, 3407, 3445, 3452, 3469, 3475, 3476, 3592, 3641, 3643, 3722, 3892, 3935, 3936, 3971, 4028, 4108, 4153, 4154, 4211, 4280, 4348, 4389, 4394, 4396, 4459, 4562, 4577, 4684, 4691, 4696, 4960, 5000, 5012, 5030, 5031, 5055, 5069, 5165, 5187, 5192, 5213, 5448, 5539, 5565, 5594, 5647, 5659, 5666, 5720, 5747, 5807, 5839, 5872, 5970, 5989, 6000, 6147, 6153, 6305, 6308, 6360
Omagh Church: 356, 689, 1907, 3641, 5594
Omagh Poor Law Union: 3476
Orritor Presbyterian Church: 4095
Parkanaur: 3498
Parkanour *var.* Parkanaur: 4879
Parkenore *var.* Parkanaur: 3498

Parkmount, Dungannon: 355
Parochial House, Beragh: 5096
Parsonage, Fintona: 5347
Parsonage, Moy: 265
Planting Lodge, Cookstown: 5160
Plumbridge: 243
Plumtree Cottage, Mullaghmore: 305
Pomeroy: 494, 827, 1785, 2448, 3198, 4130, 4458, 4496, 5096
Pomeroy House: 5755, 5794
Pomeroy Presbyterian Church: 2448
Porthall, Strabane: 5918
Prospect Hill, Cookstown: 1423
Prospect, near Strabane: 2570
Rahorran, near Fivemiletown: 3528
Raveagh: 5957
Ravengh *var.* Raveagh: 5957
Registrar's Office, Cookstown: 1308
Registrar's Office, Dungannon: 451, 470, 1147, 1262
Richmond Glebe: 3010
Rochdale *var.* Rockdale House: 5983
Rockdale: 4683, 5711, 5862
Rockdale House: 1160, 1658, 4070, 4907, 5091, 5862, 5983
Rose Hill, near Strabane: 2054
Rose Vale, Dungannon: 3853
Roughan House: 5415
Sandholes Presbyterian Church: 1710, 2108, 2109, 5982
Scran: 3546
Second Presbyterian Church, Omagh: 4108
Second Presbyterian Church, Strabane: 1609
Second Presbyterian Meeting House, Dungannon: 3159
Sedennan, near Omagh: 5970
Seskanore *var.* Seskinore: 2552
Seskinore: 306, 2552, 2892
Seskinore Lodge: 6445
Seskinore *var.* Seskanore Mills: 4844
Sherrigrim: 737
Sherrygroom *var.* Sherrigrim: 737
Silverbrook: 5209
Sion, Strabane: 5717
Sixmilecross: 1319, 1655, 1786, 3027, 4496
Sixmilecross Presbyterian Church: 1786
Skinbuoy *var.* Skinboy, near Douglasbridge: 1947
Springhill House: 3461
Springhill, Strabane: 6447
Springtown: 2525

County Tyrone, continued:
St. Anne's Church, Dungannon: 2061, 2413, 3040, 3671
St. Ann's *var.* St. Anne's Church, Dungannon: 2061, 2106, 4911
St. Thomas's Church, Dungannon: 1657
Stewardstown [Stewartstown?]: 839, 1506, 1843
Stewartstown: 69, 147, 346, 416, 427, 638, 839, 1506, 1537, 1777, 1793, 1843, 1967, 2088, 2392, 2434, 2782, 3076, 3546, 3886, 4100, 4108, 4589, 5257, 5280, 5740, 5902, 6434
Stiloga, near Benburb: 1523
Strabane: 3, 161, 284, 775, 977, 1015, 1142, 1288, 1343, 1349, 1388, 1395, 1400, 1459, 1474, 1487, 1572, 1581, 1604, 1609, 1651, 1776, 1841, 1842, 1875, 1933, 1934, 2039, 2040, 2041, 2054, 2056, 2083, 2095, 2125, 2129, 2134, 2217, 2226, 2254, 2465, 2557, 2570, 2590, 2608, 2660, 2686, 2756, 2860, 3168, 3169, 3175, 3222, 3263, 3269, 3353, 3469, 3520, 3568, 3606, 3657, 3834, 3860, 3861, 3980, 4124, 4209, 4235, 4371, 4472, 4479, 4486, 4500, 4509, 4588, 4665, 4852, 4902, 4942, 5080, 5112, 5142, 5303, 5320, 5494, 5560, 5612, 5712, 5717, 5857, 5859, 5861, 5897, 5918, 5927, 6037, 6111, 6146, 6208, 6307, 6334, 6400, 6447
Strabane Church: 284, 1933, 1934, 2134, 4500, 5112
Straghery: 3571
Stragullen: 4124
Stranghroy *var.* Straughroy, near Omagh: 2571
Strangmore *var.* Stangmore, near Dungannon: 3964
Straughroy: 4260
Summerview: 3911
Summerview-house: 3898
Tamlaght: 1014
Tamlaght Glebe: 1681
Tamlaght, Coagh: 2153, 2170
Tamnaghmore: 3071
Tamnamore House *var.* Tamnaghmore House: 1503
Tamnamore *var.* Tamnaghmore: 3071
Tatnagole: 5268
Tattykeeran, Beragh, Dungannon: 4785
Terman *var.* Termon Rectory: 3228
Termon Rectory: 3228, 3255, 4385
Termon Rectory, Dungannon: 5226
Termon *var.* Termonmaguirk: 5791
Termonamongan, parish of; Killeter: 4235

The Bush, Killyman, near Dungannon: 5307
Thorehill: 5713
Thornhill: 622, 2413
Tirnaskea: 4140
Togherdoo: 3451
Trew, Killyman: 1117
Trillic *var.* Trillick: 2847, 4992
Trillick: 1205, 2847, 2881, 3634, 4134, 4660, 4843, 4992, 5181, 5259, 5259, 6248, 6271
True Hill, near Moy: 3013
Tullaclena House, Dromore: 4569
Tullaclena House, parish of Dromore: 3610
Tully O'Donnell, Dungannon: 4544
Tullyallen: 6049
Tullyarm: 306
Tullyarn *var.* Tullyaran: 2350
Tullyblerty, Aughnacloy: 4995
Tullybryan, Ballygawley: 1887
Tullycullen *var.* Tullycullion, near Dungannon: 3500
Tullydoey *var.* Tullydowey, near Blackwatertown: 6406
Tullydoey, near Blackwatertown: 6406
Tullygoney: 806, 6417
Tullygoney, near Benburb: 4640
Tullyharm: 5461
Tullyhogue: 2128
Tullylagan: 2180
Tullylegan *var.* Tullylagan: 1974
Tullylegan *var.* Tullylagan, Cookstown: 5310
Tullylern, near Benburb: 766
Tullyneskin *var.* Tullyniskin Church: 505
Tullyniskin Church: 505
Tullynure Lodge: 1720
Tullynure, near Omagh: 5187
Turleenan, Moy: 5950
Twyford: 641
Tyrconnelly: 4029
Tyrooney: 1786
Tyrooney, Sixmilecross: 4496
Upper Clananeese: 750, 3465
Upper Clananeese Presbyterian Church: 561
Upper Clenanees *var.* Clananeese Presbyterian Church: 561
Upper Clenaneese *var.* Upper Clananeese Presbyterian Church: 3465
Upper Clennanees *var.* Upper Clananeese: 750
Upper Langfield Glebe: 2447
Urney: 5762
Urney, parish of: 383
Urney Park, near Strabane: 4209

Chapter 4: Index of Place Names

County Tyrone, continued:
Waterloo Cottage, Cookstown: 4864
Wellbrook: 2082, 2708, 4095, 5499. *See also* Willbrooke.
Wesleyan Chapel, Dungannon: 5852
Willbrooke: 5849. *See also* Wellbrook.
Woodbrook: 3222
Woodend: 1362

Ulster, province of: 4924

Waterford, county of:
Affane: 622
Ballytera *var.* Balleighteragh, near Dungarvan: 6327
Bonmahon: 3447, 3450
Clonmel: 5284
Dungarvan: 2066, 6327, 6420
Dungarvan Church: 4956
Glebe House, near Waterford: 3748
Kilcronan, parish of: 5002
Kilmacthomas: 3104
Lismore Cathedral: 5002
Macollup Castle: 1987
Passage: 6336
Tramore: 2928, 3958
Waterford: 422, 690, 691, 1361, 1444, 2803, 2929, 3020, 3733, 3748, 4395, 4408, 4503, 4814, 5017, 5258, 5876
Waterford Cathedral: 3733
Waterford, Diocese of: 3044

Westmeath, county of:
Townland not named: 5023
Athlone: 2696, 4718, 4964, 5054
Auburn: 4758
Belmont, Kilbeggan: 5541
Belmore place: 5755
Bloomfield: 3676
Castle Reynell: 1542
Castlepollard: 289
Castletown Delvin: 4212
Correa: 4932
Drumraney *var.* Drumreany Glebe: 63
Drumreany Glebe: 63
Dunboden Park: 3577
Grange: 5582
Kilbeggan: 5541
Killybrook: 764
Lough Glore, near Castlepollard: 289
Moate: 3501
Mount Temple Church: 4993

County Westmeath, continued:
Mullingar: 4415, 4653
Newcastle: 3261
Portlick Castle: 4814
Prospect: 3728
Rochfort: 4467
Rockbrook: 3891
St. Mary's Church, Athlone: 3075
Tyrellpass *var.* Tyrrellspass: 4349
Tyrrellspass: 492, 5095
Tyrrels-pas *var.* Tyrrellspass: 492

Wexford, county of:
Arthurstown: 396, 5715
Ballyrahan: 6182
Barondown: 5907
Clohamon house: 566
Duffry Hall: 1531
Enniscorthy: 3055, 4970
Ferns, parish of: 3072
Gorey: 5290, 5844, 6182
Growtown: 1828
Hilltown: 769
Hollyfort Cottage, Gorey: 5290
Horetown Church: 5435
Kilmuckridge: 4700
Millpark House, Enniscorthy: 4970
Monomolin Glebe: 3060
Moreton: 4920
Moyne: 4337
Mulrankin: 2998
New Ross: 2152, 4624
Newtownbarry: 2519
Newtownbarry, parish of: 5326
Park Cottage, near Wexford: 2005
Prospect: 5711
Raheenduff: 5435
Rainsford Lodge, Newtownbarry: 2519
Taghmon: 2657
Techmon *var.* Taghmon: 2657
Tintern Abbey: 1531
Wexford: 1828, 2005, 2963, 3020, 3491, 3491, 5277
Yorkville: 6105

Wicklow, county of:
Townland not named: 2775, 5510, 5604
Avonview, Rathdrum: 4085
Ballygannon: 3929
Ballyhenry: 4823
Bellfield: 3840

407

County Wicklow, continued:
Belview: 5439
Blesinton *var.* Blessington: 54, 3288, 6345
Blessington: 54, 3288, 6345
Bray: 218, 5604, 5848
Bray Church: 5604, 5848
Carnew: 4935
Castle Howard: 2493
Castlemacadam: 3749
Clonmannon: 768
Cookstown, Enniskerry: 6122
Delgany: 690, 691, 2534, 5439
Delgany Church: 690, 691, 5439
Delgany Glebe: 3770, 4950
Donard: 782
Donoughmore Glebe: 2739
Dromin: 5997
Drumdangan: 2949
Enniskerry: 6122
Fairview, near Delgany: 2534
Fort Faulkner: 1060
Kilbride: 54
Kilpipe Church: 3773
Kiltegan: 4094
Methodist Chapel, Rathdrum: 2949
Miltown: 5496
Powerscourt: 2775
Rathdrum: 2949, 3929, 4085, 4430, 6386
Rathdrum Wesleyan Chapel: 3929
Rockstown: 3929
Spring Farm: 690
Stratford: 133
Tubberpatrick: 3773
Westbrook House: 3506
Wicklow: 4673
Woodstock: 1265

Isle of Man:
Town or city not named: 1049
Douglas: 1518, 1619, 3095
Douglas; St. George's Church: 3095
Ramsey: 796
Sodor and Man, Diocese of: 1049

Italy:
Arco, Tyrol: 2467
Castellamare, near Naples: 4258
Florence: 423
Naples: 409, 3190, 4258
Naples; Penne: 409
Rome: 4469, 6217

Italy, continued:
Sicily: 4179, 4629
Sicily; Catania: 4179
Sienna: 4313

Jamaica:
Town or city not named: 546, 1058, 4981, 5250, 6057
Elim: 3147
Kingston: 191
Mount Zion: 229
Newcastle: 3122
Port Antonio: 1446
St. Thomas in the East; St. Mary's Chapel: 349
Trelawney: 349

Jersey:
Town not named: 2761, 5263, 5736
St. Helier's: 1448

Kalunga: 5824

Malta: 2234, 2468, 5834

Mauritius: 5266

N.B. *var.* New Brunswick:
St. David: 2776
Portland, St. John's *var.* St. John: 4370
St. John's *var.* St. John: 772, 2083, 3629, 4316
See also New Brunswick.

N.B. *var.* North Britain:
Stirling: 1789
Balbirnie: 6453
Myreton: 3478
Rickarton: 5262
Whitehaugh: 5262
See also Scotland.

N.S. Wales *var.* New South Wales; Sydney: 4443. *See also* New South Wales *and* Australia.

Netherlands, the: 3235. *See also* Holland.

New Brunswick:
Portland, St. John: 4370
St. David: 2776
St. John: 34, 772, 2083, 3629, 4316, 4370, 5576, 6027, 6307
St. John's *var.* St. John: 34, 5576, 6027, 6307
St. Malachi's Church, St. John: 6307
See also N.B. *var.* New Brunswick.

New South Wales:
 Town or city not named: 5925
 Cecil Hill: 2560
 Darlinghiush, near Sydney: 3466
 Parramatta: 3310
 Patena: 4061
 Port Philip: 3290, 4218
 Port Philip; Geelong: 4218
 St. James Church, Sydney: 1429
 Sydney: 1429, 2006, 3111, 3466, 4443, 5999
 Sydney, Diocese of: 3466
 See also Australia and N.S. Wales.

New Zealand: 5788

Newfoundland: 546, 4049

Nicaragua; San Juan del Sur: 6407

Nile River: 5745, 5894

North America:
 Davenport: 3585
 var. Canada West; Niagara: 5246
 var. Canada West; Kingston: 4270
 var. United States of America; Virginia; Lynchburgh: 261

North Britain *var.* Scotland; Lindertis: 660
See also N.B. *var.* North Britian *and* Scotland.

Nova Scotia; Hallifax *var.* Halifax: 1916

Peru; Lima: 5911

Poland; Prague: 5456

Port Leopold: 3252

Portugal:
 Town or city not named: 5881
 Cape St. Vincent: 5894
 Foz d'Aronce: 3484
 Madeira; Funchal: 3414, 3437, 4621
 Madeira: 840, 2904, 3900, 4621
 Pombal: 3484
 Redinha: 3484
 Sabugal: 3484
 Sabugal: 4213
 Torres Vedras: 3484

Québec *var.* Canada East: 2806, 2849, 3120
See also Canada East.

River Muris: 3651

River Nile: 6335

River Tweed: 3651

Russia:
 Town or city not named: 3235
 Archangel: 6332
 St. Petersburg: 6399

Scotland:
 Town or city not named: 2961, 2962, 3719, 4880, 5590, 5596, 5766, 6281
 Aberdeen: 108, 4771
 Aberdeenshire; Bankhead: 5014
 Aberdeenshire; Hunly: 3044
 Aberdeenshire; Lethenty: 6047
 Alloa: 1789
 Athol Staneford, New Mains: 2730
 Ayr: 262, 3605, 5637
 Ayrshire; Kilmun: 5782
 Ayrshire; Kilwinning: 3648
 Ayrshire; Mauchline: 5568
 Balbirnie: 6453
 Barracks, Dundee: 2927
 Beith: 925
 Blackadder Castle: 944
 Bridgeton: 5563
 Bute; Ashburn House: 4464
 Campbell field, near Ayr: 5637
 Campsie: 4023
 Clune's-vennal, Newtown: 4895
 Cromarty; Poyntzfield House: 3196
 Dumfries: 2343, 6347
 Dumfriesshire; Annan: 4719
 Dundee: 2927
 Dundee; Spalding House: 1382
 Dundonald Presbyterian Church: 198
 Duntogher: 714
 Edinburgh: 25, 313, 1192, 1274, 1298, 1484, 2009, 2165, 2306, 2353, 2609, 2730, 2857, 3413, 4076, 4131, 4369, 4438, 4480, 4564, 4765, 5005, 5021, 5183, 5336, 5424, 5451, 5788, 5847, 6123, 6270, 6328, 6373
 Edinburgh; Canonmills: 5021
 Edinburgh; Churchhill: 6270
 Edinburgh; Grange Bank: 4480
 Edinburgh; Leith-links: 4564
 Edinburgh; Morning side, Grange Bank: 4480
 Edinburgh; Ratho: 2306
 Edinburgh; St. John's Chapel: 2857, 5847
 Edinburgh; St. Peter's Episcopal Chapel: 2009
 Edinburgh, Diocese of: 3621
 Forfarshire; Rossie Castle: 2804

Scotland, continued:
Gilcomston Free Church: 4771
Girvin: 3696
Glasgow: 298, 332, 341, 711, 722, 956, 1188, 1274, 1484, 1512, 2291, 2563, 2586, 2591, 3282, 3648, 3875, 4236, 4674, 5257, 5336, 5782, 5865, 6023, 6310
Glasgow; Gartnavel: 3875
Glasgow; Gwmgad House: 3875
Glasgow; St. Jude's: 3875
Greenock: 70, 681, 5159
Gretna Green: 1455
Gretnagreen *var.* Gretna Green: 1455
Haddington, county of: 2468
Harris: 6007
Honeybark: 108
Huntley: 6025
Inch: 108
Inverallort: 4055
Inverness: 3408
Inverness; Balloch, Culloden: 5704
Inverness; Culloden: 5704
Isle of Bute: 1287, 4096
Isle of Bute; Rothesay: 1287
Isle of Bute; Rothsay *var.* Rothesay: 1287, 4096
Isle of Skye: 376
Isle of Skye; Knock: 376
Jura: 3920
Jura; Ardlussa: 3920
Kilberney: 4722, 5652
Kirkcudbrightshire; Balmaghie House: 531
Lanarkshire; Braehead: 5440
Lanarkshire; Stevenston: 3238
Langholm: 3621
Lauriston Castle: 6185
Leith: 5922
Lindertis: 660
Loch Lomond: 4063
Longwood, Langholm: 3621
Maines of Brighton, near Montrose: 614
Malross: 3651
Mauchiline *var.* Mauchline: 2962
Mauchline: 2962, 5597
Monteith: 5649
Montrose: 614, 3618, 4322
Montrose; Paradise Cottage: 3618
Morningside: 5304
Morningside; Churchhill: 5304
Myreton: 3478
Nairnshire; Glenferness: 5093

Nairnshire; Glenferness House: 5093
Newtown: 4895
Orkney: 4464
Orkney; Hescombe: 4464
Orkney Islands: 6446
Paisley: 417, 856, 1509, 3222, 5752
Peeblesshire; Kippet: 1297
Perth: 1529, 2848
Perthshire; Achrader [Auchterarder?]: 919
Perthshire; St. Martin's: 2804
Pitfirrane: 5005
Portlehew: 5973
Portpatrick: 3920
Raddery: 4142
Renfrewshire; Houston: 300
Renfrewshire; Kilbarchan: 4361
Rickarton: 5262
Rosshire: 3290
Rosshire; Tain: 1237
Rothesay: 2292
Rothsaye *var.* Rothesay: 2292
Roxburghshire; Ladhope: 2857
Selkirk: 4629
Shetland Islands; Lerwick: 6446
Shetland Islands; Noss, Island of: 6446
Skirling: 3190
St. Andrew's: 1382
St. Paul's Chapel: 3621
Stirling: 1241, 1789, 2952
Stirling; Allan Park: 1241
Stirling; Balgair: 2952
Symington: 4239
Whitebog, near Raddery: 4142
Whitehaugh: 5262
Zetland *var.* Shetland Islands; Lerwick: 6446

Sierra Leone:
Town not named: 5880
Free-Town: 6333

Singapore: 5339

South Africa:
Cape Town: 469
Waterkloof: 5346

South America; Valparaiso: 1488

South Australia:
Town or city not named: 5184
Adelaide: 5252, 5400, 5833
North Adelaide: 5184, 5252

South Australia, continued:
  Port Adelaide: 5184
  See also Australia.

South Wales:
  Glamorganshire; Cardiff: 3240
  Kilwendeage: 5889
  See also Wales.

Spain:
  Town or city not named: 6007
  Badajoz: 3484, 6292
  Bilboa: 2988
  Cadiz: 3484
  Canary Islands; Teneriffe: 5894
  Coranna *var.* Corunna: 6310
  Corunna: 4213, 6310
  Madrid: 3484
  Malaga: 6084
  Pyrenees: 938, 4213, 6310
  Salamanca: 938, 3484, 6310
  San Muñoz: 4213
  Trafalgar: 5745, 6335
  Vera: 4213
  Vittoria: 938, 6310

St. Domingo: 6222

St. Helena: 179

St. Lucia: 5925

Sweden:
  Christiana: 6115
  Stockholm: 5433

Switzerland; Canton de Vaud: 2243

Tasmania *var.* Van Dieman's Land: 915
See also Van Dieman's Land.

Turkey; Constantinople: 225

U.C. *var.* Upper Canada: *See* Canada West.

United States of America:
  Town or city not named: 1017, 2462, 3215, 3867, 4020, 4672, 5911, 6399
  Alabama: 3204
  Albany: 1835, 3561
  Albany, New York: 2688
  Alexandria: 4672
  Alleghany City: 2787
  Allegheny City, Pennsylvania: 4526

United States of America, continued:
  Ann Arbor, Michigan: 654
  Athens: 4131, 4131
  Baltimore: 695, 2175, 4784, 5317, 5528, 6412
  Bayou Sara, Louisiana: 4875
  Biloxi, Mississippi: 5843
  Boston: 2083, 3775, 5433, 5548, 6009, 6306, 6307
  Bridgeport, Connecticut: 5702, 5730
  Brooklin *var.* Brooklyn: 6280
  Brooklyn: 6280
  Brooklyn, New York: 2539, 3107, 3783, 5381, 5596
  Buffalo, New York: 5792
  Bunker's Hill: 5891
  California; town or city not stated: 3886
  Charleston, South Carolina: 4358, 5269, 5269
  Cincinatti *var.* Cincinnati: 2055, 2057, 3084, 3084, 3176, 3401, 5534
  Cincinnati: 2055
  Cincinnatti *var.* Cincinnati: 2337, 3177
  Clifton, Staten Island: 5016
  Clinton, Alleghany county, Pennsylvania: 3537
  Columbus, Ohio: 6145
  Conington, Kentucky: 2755
  Dayton, Ohio: 2526
  Elizabeth Town, New Jersey: 5948
  Evansville, Indiana: 2057
  Fairfax, Virginia: 5528
  Fincastle, Virginia: 5525
  Floyd's Fork, Jefferson County: 5627
  Franklinville: 4031
  Galena, Illinois: 5001
  Georgetown, Pennsylvania: 2566
  Greenville, Tennessee: 5233
  Harrisburg, Pennsylvania: 4408
  Highland County, Ohio: 5024
  Hollydaysburgh, Pennsylvania: 5368
  Jersey City: 6303
  King's Chapel, Boston: 6306
  Kingstown, N.H. *var.* New Hampshire: 1310
  Kingstown, New Hampshire: 1310
  Knox, Ohio: 1256
  Lancingburg, New York: 4555
  Louisiana; town or city not named: 673
  Louisville: 4575
  Louisville, Kentucky: 5206
  Lynchburgh, Virginia: 261
  Madison: 5849
  Malone, New York: 2461
  Manavunk, Pennsylvania: 3235

United States of America, continued:
Matamoras: 6303
Mobile: 5731
Mukwonago, Wisconsin: 3235
Nachetoehes: 4902
Nashota; Sylvanus Church: 1912
Natches: 4672
New Haven, Connecticut: 1225
New Orleans: 1168, 1861, 2235, 2304, 4175, 5015, 5843, 5949, 6362
New York City: 28, 236, 841, 1230, 1788, 1793, 1888, 2381, 2659, 2856, 2953, 2954, 2957, 3027, 3078, 3110, 3130, 3232, 3435, 3677, 3790, 3880, 4042, 4119, 4132, 4239, 4266, 4623, 4730, 4764, 4834, 4888, 4905, 4921, 4941, 5016, 5097, 5133, 5164, 5267, 5361, 5442, 5646, 5702, 5714, 5730, 5949, 6010, 6011, 6012, 6013, 6014, 6015, 6055, 6219, 6243, 6376, 6384
Newport: Kentucky 3096
North Ford, Sacramento, California: 6144
Northeastern Diocese; Sylvanus Church: 1912
Norwich: 4315
Orange County, New York: 3880
Oyden, Monroe County, New York: 1153
Paris, Tennessee: 5684
Pennsylvania; town or city not named: 1062
Petersburgh, Virginia: 1801
Philadelphia: 236, 1299, 2926, 3000, 3232, 3235, 3554, 3800, 4193, 4317, 5000, 5603, 5856, 5888, 6059, 6258, 6412
Philadelphia; Salem Church: 5000
Pike township, Knox County, Ohio: 1256
Pittsburg *var.* Pittsburgh; 1st English Evangelical Lutheran Church: 2787
Pittsburg *var.* Pittsburgh: 4563
Pittsburgh: 2787, 3289, 4563, 5014, 5525
Providence, Rhode Island: 3775
Rodney, Mississippi: 5842
Rye, Westchester County, New York: 1788
Sacramento, California: 4460, 6144
Salisbury Mills, Orange County, New York: 3880
San Francisco, California: 4460, 5106, 5411, 5459
Scioto River: 6145
South Brooklyn, New York: 2539
Springfield, Massachusetts: 4977
St. John's Church, Buffalo, New York: 5792
St. John's Church, New York: 6384
St. Louis, Missouri: 4669, 5234

Staten Island; Clifton: 5016
Sweet Springs: 5525
Texas: 4902
Three Springs, Ohio: 2645
Washington: 6007
Westchester County, New York: 1788
Yorkville, South Carolina: 2217
Youngstown, Ohio: 3859, 3887

Upper Canada *var.* Canada West:
Barrie: 1204
Etobicoke, near Toronto: 369
Hamilton: 3522
Kingston: 933
Neilson; St. Anne's: 3288
Ottamby: 244
Toronto: 1467, 2229
Port Robinson: 2139
See also Canada West.

Van Dieman's Land:
Town or city not named: 915.
Jamestown; Perth Church: 921
Launceston: 5645
New Norfolk; Stanfield: 6279
South Esk; Glasslough: 921
See also Tasmania.

Wales:
Town or city not named: 4008
Aberystwyth: 2678
Baglan-hall, Glamorganshire: 4284
Beach Rhyl: 6157
Breconshire; Tymaur: 822
Cardiff, Glamorganshire: 3240
Carmarthenshire; Lougharne: 822
Glamorganshire; Baglan-hall: 4284
Glamorganshire; Cardiff: 3240
Glen Uske, Monmouthshire: 6098
Holyhead: 2742, 5322, 5868
Kilwendeage: 5889
Kinmel-park: 6157
Lougharne, Carmarthenshire: 822
Maesteg-house, near Swansea: 4284
Monmouth: 5772
Monmouthshire; Glen Uske: 6098
Monmouthshire; Newport: 5880
Monmouthshire; Pontypool: 5733
Montgomeryshire; Trowscoed Hall: 6357
Newport, Monmouthshire: 5880
Penrhos Point, near Holyhead: 5322

Wales, continued:
 Pontypool, Monmouthshire: 5733
 Radnorshire; Presteign: 631
 Swansea; St. Mary's Church: 4284
 Swansea: 2678, 4284
 Tregeyd Hay *var.* Tregoyd Hay: 3087
 Tregoyd Hay: 3087
 Trowscoed Hall, Montgomeryshire: 6357
 See also South Wales.

West Indies:
 Island or city not named: 3484, 3677, 4892
 St. Thomas: 2934
 Tobago: 745. 2837
 Trinidad; 2100; 5925
 Trinidad; Port-au-Prince: 5974
 Trinidad; San Fernando: 5159
 See also Jamaica.

5. INSTITUTION & PUBLICATION INDEX

Abercorn Arms Hotel (Strabane), 284
African (ship), 5894
Albert Hotel (Armagh), 166, 291, 3598, 4595
Alceste (ship), 5106
Amazon (French frigate), 6222
American Citizen (newspaper), 3554
Analore Mills, 2315
Anglo Celt (newspaper), 2036, 3423
Anson (ship), 5961
Ards Yeoman Infantry, 5076
Armagh Boarding and Day School, 316
Armagh Company of Volunteers, 6257
Armagh County Infirmary, 25, 1481, 2396, 4850, 5151
Armagh Foundry, 4358
Armagh Gaol, 25, 837, 1034, 2091, 2737
Armagh Guardian, 1858, 2759, 4927
Armagh Loan Fund, 463
Armagh Observatory, 2633, 6363
Armagh Union Workhouse, 965, 1156, 1483, 3112
Arran Arms Hotel (Donegal), 1052
Asia (ship), 5887
Asylum (Armagh), 135, 268
Bailieborough National School, 1998
Ballymagorry Mills, 2756
Ballyshannon Yeomanry Corps, 3479
Banbridge Union Workhouse, 2924
Bank of England, 5208, 6019
Bank of Ireland, 1464, 1750, 2595, 3715, 4340, 4796, 5396, 5484, 6328
Banks, Foster & Co. (Keswick, England), 3374
Banner of Ulster (newspaper), 108, 2300
Baptist Society, 4578
Battle of Bunker's Hill, 5891
Beech's Railway Hotel (Birmingham), 2614
Belfast and Ballymena Railway, 5067
Belfast Bank, 444, 4733
Belfast Banking Company, 1334, 4543
Belfast Chronicle (newspaper), 1486
Belfast College, 669, 1123, 1291, 1777

Belfast Commercial Chronicle (newspaper), 2867
Belfast Natural History and Philosophical Society, 5450
Belfast News-Letter (newspaper), 1025, 2303
Belle Poule (ship), 5894
Benevolent Society of St. Patrick, 1897, 4180
Bengal Civil Service, 900, 2372
Bengal Medical Service, 663
Beresford Arms Hotel (Armagh), 1279, 3392
Blackwood and Sons, Messrs. (Edinburgh), 5424
Board of Emigration (Londonderry), 3992
Board of Green Cloth, Royal Household, 4780
Board of Guardians, Coleraine Poor Law Union, 1373
Board of Public Works, 2757
Bolling, Messrs. E. & W., 2543
Boot and Shoe Depot (Armagh), 4146
Boyd & Watts (Lurgan), 3431
Boyd, William, Messrs. & Co. (Armagh), 6166
Bradshaw & Co., 2626
Bradshaw and Co. (Donegal), 4522, 1583
Bradshaw and Co. (Enniskillen), 1583, 4522
Brantry Parochial School, 5287
British Army [corps not stated], 5891, 6066. *See also* Hon. East India Company Army.

British Army:
- 1st (or Grenadier) Regiment of Foot Guards, 944, 1707
- 1st (Royal) Regiment of Dragoons, 1810, 3081
- 1st (The Royal) Regiment of Foot, 127, 3158, 4431, 5817, 3260, 3690, 4998, 5502, 5817
- 1st Regiment of Life Guards, 5854
- 2d Garrison Battalion, 842
- 2d Regiment of Dragoons, 938
- 3d (Buffs) Regiment of Foot, 794, 1597, 1751, 1915, 2074, 2173, 2578, 5194
- 3d Garrison Battalion, 6314
- 3d West India Regiment, 1903, 4892, 5299
- 4th (King's Own) Regiment of Foot, 238, 1315, 2396, 2785, 3324, 4732, 5696
- 4th (Royal Irish) Dragoon Guards, 3306, 4092, 4506
- 4th Regiment of Light Dragoons, 1518

British Army, continued:
- 5th (Royal Inniskilling) Dragoon Guards, 3613, 4030
- 5th Carbineers, 5974
- 5th Fusileers [might have been the Army of the Hon. East India Company], 275
- 5th Regiment of Dragoons, 636
- 6th (Inniskilling) Regiment of Dragoons, 324, 798, 938, 4897, 5275, 6386, 6387
- 6th (Royal 1st Warwickshire) Regiment of Foot, 1987, 5346
- 6th Regiment of Dragoon Guards (Carabiniers), 1541
- 7th (The Queen's Own) Regiment of (Light) Dragoons (Hussars), 3577
- 8th (The King's Royal Irish) Regiment of (Light) Dragoons (Hussars), 1639, 1817, 1940, 2029, 5824, 6187
- 9th Regiment of Foot, 2018, 2058, 2103, 3646
- 9th Regiment of Light Dragoons, 504
- 10th Regiment of Foot, 3044, 4328
- 12th Regiment of Foot, 4493, 4520, 5315
- 13th (1st Somersetshire) (Prince Albert's Light Infantry) Regiment of Foot, 1739, 1778, 4091
- 14th Regiment of Foot, 822
- 14th Regiment of Light Dragoons, 2003
- 15th Regiment of Foot, 1023, 4363
- 16th (The Queen's) Regiment of (Light) Dragoons (Lancers), 3082, 5799
- 16th Regiment of Foot, 4338, 5088
- 17th Regiment of Foot, 2806, 3496, 3984, 4336
- 18th (The Royal irish) Regiment of Foot, 5492
- 19th Regiment of Dragoons, 1191
- 19th Regiment of Foot, 630
- 20th Regiment of Foot, 2477
- 20th Regiment of Light Dragoons, 656
- 21st Dragoons [var. 21st Regiment of (Light) Dragoons], 4363
- 21st Fusiliers [var. 21st Regiment of Foot (Royal North British Fuzileers)], 3196, 3621, 3827, 4596, 5422, 5792, 6386, 6387
- 21st Regiment of (Light) Dragoons, 4363
- 22d Regiment of Foot, 935, 2434, 4629, 5651
- 22d Regiment of Infantry, 31
- 25th Regiment of Foot, 2376

- 27th (Enniskillen) Regiment of Foot, 1734, 2005, 3268, 3998, 4551, 6265
- 28th Regiment of Foot, 2173, 3299, 6107
- 31st Regiment of Foot, 1719, 2696, 5355, 5477, 6140
- 32d Regiment of Foot, 127, 361, 2317
- 33d Regiment of Foot, 3305, 3305
- 34th Regiment of Foot, 3820, 6392
- 35th Regiment of Foot, 2814
- 36th Regiment of Foot, 672, 546, 194, 2701, 5491
- 37th Regiment of Foot, 5784
- 38th Regiment of Foot, 1250, 1510, 2413, 3977
- 39th Regiment of Foot, 1083, 3310, 1916
- 41st Regiment of Foot, 1950, 3934
- 42d (Royal Highland) Regiment of Foot, 2311, 2761, 5262
- 43d Regiment of Foot, 4932
- 43d Regiment of Light Infantry, 2235
- 44th Regiment of Foot, 732, 1403, 1415, 2234, 2761, 2806, 3588, 4753, 5622, 6344
- 45th Regiment of Foot, 2568, 5662, 6073
- 46th Regiment of Foot, 4363, 6313, 256, 6106, 6268, 6418
- 47th Regiment of Foot, 4746, 5081
- 48th Regiment of Foot, 1376, 1391, 5792
- 49th Regiment of Foot, 2620, 5823
- 50th Regiment of Foot, 329, 3358, 4061
- 51st Regiment of Foot, 1377
- 52d (Oxfordshire) Regiment of Foot (Light Infantry), 778, 3670, 4213, 6292, 6375
- 53d Regiment of Foot, 1764
- 54th Regiment of Foot, 350, 759, 1314, 1364
- 57th Regiment of Foot, 44, 1925, 2065, 2186, 3548, 4836, 6350
- 58th Regiment of Foot, 3588, 4022, 4551, 5805, 3247
- 60th Regiment of Foot (The King's Royal Rifle Corps), 602, 2366, 2427, 3309, 4141
- 61st Regiment of Foot, 499
- 62d Regiment of Foot, 171, 5953
- 63d Regiment of Foot, 5530
- 64th Regiment of Foot, 3057
- 65th Regiment of Foot, 3835
- 66th Regiment of Foot, 3877
- 67th Regiment of Foot, 3236, 3422

British Army, continued:
- 68th (Durham) Regiment of Foot (Light Infantry), 3298, 3937, 4402
- 70th Regiment of Foot, 2223, 2225, 4327, 5535
- 71st (Highland) Regiment of Foot (Light Infantry), 6172
- 72d (Highlanders) Regiment of Foot, 4365
- 73d Regiment of Foot, 3580
- 74th (Highlanders) Regiment of Foot, 1880, 3952, 4055
- 75th Regiment of Foot, 5825
- 76th Regiment of Foot, 1479, 5276, 5834
- 77th Regiment of Foot, 2101, 2194, 3938
- 81st Regiment of Foot, 2733
- 82d Regiment of Foot, 5246, 5246
- 83d Regiment of Foot, 2241, 2929
- 84th Regiment of Foot, 3901
- 85th Regiment of Foot, 1106, 3147
- 86th Regiment of Foot, 2805
- 87th (Prince of Wales' Irish) Regiment of Foot, 1099, 1917
- 88th Regiment of Foot, 454, 3695, 3702, 4956
- 89th Regiment of Foot, 4719
- 90th Regiment of Foot, 124, 4093
- 94th Regiment of Foot, 3484
- 96th Regiment of Foot, 3290, 5009, 5093, 5419
- 97th Regiment of Foot, 4984, 5266
- 98th Regiment of Foot, 4328
- Armagh Regiment of Militia, 91, 2302, 2468, 4514
- Cambridge Regiment of Militia, 6313
- Carbineers, 1280, 2276
- Donegal Regiment of Militia, 392
- Dragoon Guards, 5232
- Dublin County Regiment of Militia, 5510
- Enniskillen Dragoons: *See* British Army, 5th (Royal Inniskilling) Dragoon Guards.
- Enniskillen Dragoons: *See* British Army, 6th (Inniskilling) Regiment of Dragoons.
- Fermanagh Regiment of Militia, 896, 618
- Grenadier Guards [*var.* 1st (or Grenadier) Regiment of Foot Guards], 1707
- Hants Light Infantry Regiment of Militia, 5228
- Inniskilling Dragoons: *See* British Army, 6th (Inniskilling) Regiment of Dragoons]

- K.R. Rifles: *See* British Army, 60th Regiment of Foot (The King's Royal Rifle Corps)
- Leitrim Militia: *See* British Army, Leitrim Regiment of Militia
- Leitrim Regiment of Militia, 4141, 4598, 6181
- Londonderry Regiment of Militia, 3695
- Louth Regiment of Militia, 4228
- Monaghan Militia: *See* British Army, Monaghan Regiment of Militia
- Monaghan Regiment of Militia, 3517, 3950, 6187
- Rifle Brigade (The), 139
- Roscommon Regiment of Militia, 3146
- Rothesay and Caithness Fencibles, 326
- Royal Artillery: *See* British Army, Royal Regiment of Artillery
- Royal Canadian Rifle Regiment, 4574
- Royal Dragoons, 1810
- Royal Engineers, 311, 1745, 2020
- Royal Horse Artillery, 653, 2029, 5841, 5914
- Royal Irish Artillery [*var.* Royal Regiment of Irish Artillery], 6245
- Royal Meath Regiment of Militia, 2466
- Royal Newfoundland Corps, 4049
- Royal North British Fusiliers: *See* British Army, 21st Regiment of Foot (Royal North British Fuzileers)
- Royal North Down Regiment of Militia, 2128
- Royal Regiment: *See* British Army, 1st (The Royal) Regiment of Foot
- Royal Regiment of Artillery, 256, 353, 1640, 2744, 3145, 3777, 3802, 4541, 5253, 5264, 6033, 6124, 6178, 6328, 6330
- Royal Regiment of Irish Artillery, 6245
- Royal Tyrone Regiment of Militia, 789, 3452, 4366, 4493, 4520, 5315
- Royal West India Rangers, 4719
- Royal West Middlesex Regiment of Militia, 5135
- Royal York Rangers, 5099
- Sligo Regiment of Militia, 867, 1918. *See also* Hon. East India Company Army.

British Consulate (Bayonne, France), 5658

British Embassy (Paris), 4327, 6082

Brookeborough Dispensary and Fever Hospital, 1352

Brown, Messrs. Hugh & Co. (Glasgow), 3648

Buffalo (ship), 804
Burnfoot National School, 2049
Byron Hotel (Sutton, England), 4244
Bytown Orange Lily (newspaper), 3866
Cambrian Institution for the Deaf and Dumb (Swansea, Wales), 2678
Camillus (ship), 4175
Canal Stores (Caledon), 2260
Cambridge University: *See* University of Cambridge.
Canterbury Tales (Mrs. Lee), 4918
Capital City Fact (newspaper), 6145
Carrickmacross Endowed School, 3958
Carrickmacross Union Workhouse, 2352
Cathedral School (Armagh), 1378
Cavan Union Workhouse, 1102, 3681
Celin (ship), 1817
Ceylon (ship), 5894
Charlemont Arms Hotel (Armagh), 2521, 5490, 5553
Church Missionary Society, 2753, 5431
Cistercian Order (France), 6315
Clantilew Volunteers, 2738
Clare Journal (newspaper), 763
Claremont Deaf and Dumb Institution (Monkstown), 2356, 4249
Clogher Union Workhouse, 3712
Clones Union Workhouse, 1003, 2069, 2438
Coal Island [*var.* Coalisland] Mills, 464, 4877, 5068
Coast Guards, 1375, 3758, 4200, 5930, 6004
Coleman's Hotel (Portrush), 5501
Coleraine Chronicle (newspaper), 2710, 5391, 6134
College (Armagh), 2829, 3791
College of Physicians (Edinburgh), 25
Collegiate Institution (Liverpool), 6397
Collegiate Manor of Slatmulrony, 1101
Coleraine Poor Law Union, 1373
Commercial Hotel (Armagh), 597
Commercial Hotel (Derry), 1606, 4725
Commercial Hotel (Dungannon), 865, 865
Commercial Hotel (Londonderry), 4501
Commercial Hotel (Stewartstown), 5740
Commercial Hotel (Tandragee), 6266

Common Pleas Office, 289
Convent of Mercy (Naas), 1779
Cookstown Union Workhouse, 3367
Cork District Lunatic Asylum, 5991
Corps de Garde (France), 2326
Corpus Christi College, University of Oxford, 3682
County Antrim Infirmary, 270
County Down Infirmary, 4701
Courier (newspaper), 3121
Court for the Relief of Insolvent Debtors, 4078
Court of Queen's Bench, 4750
Crowhill Corps of Yeomanry, 2738
Crow-street Theatre (Dublin), 1888
Culloden (ship), 5894
Cumber Mills (co. Derry), 4972
Daily Express (newspaper), 5785
Derry Standard (newspaper), 4577
Diocesan School (Armagh), 731
District Lunatic Asylum (Limerick), 2594
District Lunatic Asylum (Maryborough), 4058
District Model School (Bailieborough, co. Cavan), 3729
Dooish National School, 2049
Down Gaol, 5566
Downpatrick Union Workhouse, 5035
Drelincourt School (Armagh), 1097, 4575
Drogheda Argus (newspaper), 1544
*Drogheda Conservative Jo*urnal (newspaper), 2137, 3608
Dromahaire (emigrant vessel), 3790
Dublin and Enniskillen Royal Mail Coach, 3439
Dublin Evening Mail (newspaper), 1085, 4274
Dublin Evening Packet (newspaper), 4301
Dublin Independent College, 1095
Dublin Society, 4268
Dublin Theological Institution, 4739
Dumfries Courier (newspaper), 6347
Dundalk (steamer), 4372
Dundalk and Enniskillen Railway Company, 5362
Dundalk Endowed School, 2257
Dundalk Patriot (newspaper), 1709
Dundalk Poor Law Union, 3207
Dungannon Union Workhouse, 4517

Dungannon Volunteers, 326
Eagle Iron Foundry, 1194
Edinburgh Original Secession Hall, 1484
Edinburgh Review (journal), 6123
Eliza Morrison (ship), 2849
Emigrants' Friend Society (Philadelphia), 3554, 5528
Emyvale Flour Mills, 3916
Endowed School (Dundalk), 5573
Enniskillen Protestant Yeomen, 1177
Enniskillen Share Coach, 6319
Enniskillen Union Workhouse, 1018, 1100, 3882
Enniskillen Yeomanry, 6112
Enterprise (ship), 3252
Envoy (barque), 1392
Established Church of Ireland, 3391
European (screw steamer), 5130
Fair Trader Coach, 2130
Family Hotel (Lisnaskea), 4030
Felon (newspaper), 3361
Fermanagh Reporter (newspaper), 269, 604, 1361
Foudroyant (ship), 5894
Freeman's Journal (newspaper), 4611, 5020
Freemasons' Tavern, 2422
Frequented Village (poem; W.L. Fletcher), 201
Furet (ship), 6222
Galway Mercury (newspaper), 2157
Garrick (packet-ship), 6028
Gas-works (Belfast), 3735
General Post Office, 4906, 5328, 6285, 6401
General Post Office (Liverpool), 3832
Glasgow College, 1512
Globe (newspaper), 3121
Globe and Traveller (newspaper), 2528
Grand Canal Company (Ireland), 6002
Grand Canal Company (Portobello), 4268
Green and Ward (firm), 6254
Green, Messrs. James, & Co. (Keady), 2812
Greta Works (England), 3374
H.M.S. Bellerophon (ship), 5031
H.M.S. Bombay (ship), 1196
H.M.S. Castor (ship), 5788
H.M.S. Superb (ship), 67

Halifax Guardian (newspaper), 2776
Hart's Army List, 4213
Hartlepool West Harbour and Docks, 903
Haslar Hospital (Gosport, England), 6067
Hawk (ship), 6222
Hon. East India Company [HEIC], 260, 842, 1055, 1345, 1959, 3423, 3580, 4314, 4327, 4727, 5110, 6078, 6141, 6209, 6212, 6305
HEIC Army:
- 3d Regiment of Nizam's Light Cavalry, 1696
- 8th Lancers, 2376; 38th Regiment of Native Infantry, 5089
HEIC, **Bengal Army**, 663, 1682, 3676, 4468
- 1st Bengal Fusiliers, 1112
- 1st Regiment of Bengal Native Infantry, 4276
- 2d Fusiliers, 4760
- 2d Regiment of Bengal Native Infantry (Grenadiers), 1330
- 10th Regiment of Bengal Native Infantry, 2708
- 26th Regiment of Bengal Native Infantry, 4247
- 69th Regiment of Bengal Native Infantry, 5265
- Bengal Horse Artillery, 5265
HEIC, **Bombay Army**:
- 1st Bombay Lancers [*var.* 1st Regiment of Bombay Light Cavalry (Lancers)], 5110
- 1st Grenadier Regiment (Scinde Contingent), 5499
- 1st Regiment of Bombay Light Cavalry (Lancers), 4999, 5110
- 2d (Grenadier) Regiment of Bombay Native Infantry, 829
- 3d Regiment of Bombay Native Infantry, 3384
- 7th Bombay Regiment of Native Infantry, 3421
- 24th Regiment of Bombay Native Infantry, 1978
- Bombay Artillery, 4999
- Bombay Horse Artillery, 5264
HEIC, **Madras Army**:
- 5th Regiment of Madras Native Infantry, 180
- 13th Regiment of Madras Native Infantry, 1345
- 23d Regiment of Madras Light Infantry, 3917
- 25th Regiment of Madras Native Infantry, 1592
- 33d Regiment of Madras Native Infantry, 6037, 6111
- 35th Regiment of Madras Native Infantry, 189, 4693

HEIC, Madras Army (continued):
- 37th (Grenadier) Regiment of Madras Native Infantry, 1460
- 40th Regiment of Madras Native Infantry, 562
- 42d Regiment of Native Infantry, 1441
- 43d Regiment of Madras Native Infantry, 4158
- 44th Regiment of Madras Native Infantry, 4891
- Madras Horse Artillery, 1696

Her Majesty's Mint, 5170
Hibernian Bank, 3596, 6300
Hibernian Foundry, 3755
High Court of Admiralty, 1441
Hints to Small Farmers (William Blacker), 4274
Historical Sketches of the Native Irish (Christopher Anderson), 5451
Holy Trinity (Dublin), 3877
Holywood Mills, 6432
Honourable Society of the Inner Temple (London), 2951
Hospital for Incurables (Dublin), 3817
Hughes, Messrs. John & Co. (Coalisland), 3004
Hull Rockingham (newspaper), 804
Impartial Reporter (newspaper), 2132
Imperial Hotel (Enniskillen), 182, 5478
Independent Society, 3050
Inner Temple [*var.* Honourable Society of the Inner Temple] (London), 2951
Inverness Advertiser (newspaper), 3408
Irish Church Missions Society (London), 4150
Irish Commissariat, 3382
Irish Melodies (Thomas Moore), 2289
Irish Volunteers, 1286, 4534, 5077, 6068
Irish Volunteers (1781), 3903
Island Mills (Lisburn), 1390
Keady Dispensary, 24, 287
Kerry Evening Post (newspaper), 2253, 5099
Kilkeel Parochial School, 3167
Kilkenny Moderator (newspaper), 5468
Kilmallock Board of Guardians, 4926
King & Newton (Coal Island Mills), 464
King William Hotel (Aughnacloy), 2807
King William III. Arms Hotel (Clones), 2724
King's County Chronicle (newspaper), 3669
Knights Templar of Ireland, 25
Lady Consbrook (ship), 4119

Lancet (newspaper), 5788
Laragh Mills, 2812
Le Rhin (frigate), 5745
Leeds Mercury (newspaper), 1853
Legion of Honor [*var.* Légion d'Honneur] (France), 619, 2326
Leopard (ship), 5894
Letters of Junius (attr. Sir Philip Francis), 5685
Lifford Gaol, 1488
Limerick Chronicle (newspaper), 330
Linen Hall Hotel, 5245
Lislea Bleach Works (co. Armagh), 4576
Lisnaskea Union Workhouse, 1221
Literary Gazette (journal), 2537
Lloyds Bank, 4099
London and North-Western Railway, 6302
London Missionary Society, 5034
Londonderry and Dublin Coach Company, 1394
Londonderry Journal (newspaper), 4661
Londonderry Standard (newspaper), 824
Longford Hotel, 3798
Loughgall Dispensary, 1371
Lurgan Chronicle (newspaper), 4007
Lurgan Union Workhouse, 819
M'Culla and Ferris (Armagh), 862
Macedonian (frigade), 2462
Magherafelt Union Workhouse, 996, 2201
Mars (ship), 5745
Mary Stewart (ship), 3693
Masonic Order, 25
Matthew King (ship), 6332
Mayda (ship), 915
Medals of Creation (Gideon Algernon Mantell), 6316
Methodist Society, 2314
Middle Temple (England), 5327, 5980
Middletown Infirmary and Fever Hospital, 942
Middletown Mills, 1558
Model School (Armagh), 731
Molyneux Blind Asylum (Dublin), 2651
Monaghan Union Workhouse, 2718, 4983
Moore, Messrs. Robert and Co. (Armagh), 5504
Moore's Melodies, var. Thomas Moore's *Irish Melodies*, 2289
Moringo (ship), 5894

Morning Chronicle (newspaper), 5020
Municipal Corporations Act, 3718
Nation (Dublin), 3361, 3775
National Institute for the Deaf and Dumb (Claremont), 4080
National School (Manorhamilton), 2977
Nenagh Guardian (newspaper), 4945
Neptune (ship), 6067
New Orleans Delta (newspaper), 2304
Newry Academy, 5693
Newry Commercial Telegraph (newspaper), 2885, 3243, 4145, 4865, 4937, 5425, 6052
Newry Examiner and Louth Advertiser (newspaper), 1323
Newry Navigation, 5635
Newry Union Workhouse, 937, 4553
Newtownhamilton Dispensary, 6156
Newtownlimavady Union Workhouse, 2163
North Devon Journal (newspaper), 5249
Northern Bank Branch (Magherafelt), 1058
O'Connell Tribute (The), 6161
O'Connor and Moore (Dublin), 5305
Observatory (Armagh), 2633, 6363
Old Men's Asylum (Dublin), 4309
Omagh and Fintona Corps of Voluneers, 4577
Omagh Gaol, 1312
Omagh Union Workhouse, 3476
Orange Association (Bytown, Canada West), 3866
Orange Lodge, 306, 655, 1830, 2740, 1363, 4388, 4465
Orange Lodge 672, 3572
Orange Lodge No. 86, 358
Order of Saint Louis, 619
Ordnance Survey Department, 3605, 3740
Orien (ship), 3920
Oscar (screw steamer), 6119
Otter (ship), 5894
Oxford University: *See* University of Oxford.
Park Theatre (New York), 1888
Pilot (ship), 5339
Pomeroy Dispensary, 494
Presbyterian Church of Ireland, Ahoghill Presbytery, 5693
Presbyterian Church of Ireland, Remonstrant Synod of Ulster, 6018

Presbyterian Secession Church of Ireland, 3867
Primitive Wesleyan Methodist Society, 3337, 4738, 6251
Pro-Corn-Law Tracts (William Blacker), 4274
Protective Union (Boston, U.S.A.), 3775
Protestant Journal (newspaper), 181
Protestant Orphan Society, 4332
Provincial Bank of Ireland, 35, 689, 796, 909, 968, 1109, 1629, 2071, 2216, 2262, 2353, 2367, 2699, 2714, 2942, 3075, 3446, 3472, 3507, 3570, 3618, 3704, 3733, 3794, 3842, 3936, 4018, 4073, 4189, 4234, 4391, 4463, 4479, 4480, 4546, 4579, 4707, 4956, 4970, 5086, 5293, 5311, 5386, 5545, 5682, 5872, 5876, 5879, 6022
Queen's Arms (Portadown), 6035
Queen's College (Belfast), 3126, 4345
Queen's College (Cork), 3647
Queen's College (Galway), 6197
R. Moore & Co. (Armagh), 1698
Racer (Revenue Cutter), 1159
Ranters [*var.* Primitive Methodists], 4323
Richardson & Co., Messrs., 1461
Robert Bradford (barque), 5322
Roscommon Messenger (newspaper), 2361
Royal Academical Institution (Belfast), 2291
Royal Academy, 4077
Royal Botanic Garden (Belfast), 2901
Royal College (Belfast), 3271
Royal College of Physicians, 2215
Royal College of Surgeons in Ireland, 107, 3449, 5913
Royal County Limerick Regiment, 2826
Royal Dublin Agricultural Society, *var.* Royal Agricultural Society, 4274
Royal Engineer Department, 1847, 5127, 5129
Royal Exchange (London), 3566
Royal Free Grammar School, 6372
Royal George (ship), 804
Royal Hibernian Academy, 2757
Royal Hospital (Greenwich, England), 689
Royal Hospital (Kilmainham), 2235, 6435
Royal Hotel (Belfast), 1892
Royal Hotel (Holyhead, Wales), 5868
Royal Irish Academy, 2241, 2757
Royal Lunatic Asylum (Gartnavel, Glasgow), 3875

Royal Navy, 83, 131, 140, 498, 531, 641, 821, 855, 916, 976, 1012, 1235, 1303, 1476, 1626, 1676, 1699, 1851, 1953, 2001, 2101, 2116, 2120, 2125, 2325, 2733, 2785, 2917, 3056, 3116, 3190, 3210, 3265, 3344, 3398, 3446, 3558, 3581, 3661, 3733, 3796, 3983, 3992, 4005, 4238, 4665, 4704, 4770, 4811, 4849, 4948, 5013, 5031, 5266, 5562, 5709, 5728, 5745, 5756, 5788, 5803, 6027, 6047, 6057, 6073, 6308, 6360. *See also* Coast Guards; Royal Navy, Coast Guards; *and,* Royal Navy, Royal Marines.

Royal Navy (Portugal), 5881

Royal Navy Hospital (Plymouth), 5031

Royal Navy, Coast Guards, 4854

Royal Navy, Royal Marines, 524, 1012, 1708, 3083, 5961, 6067, 6335

Royal Observatory (Greenwich), 1678

Royal School (Armagh), 836

Royal School (Cavan), 3742

Royal School of Dungannon, 2094, 3933, 4438

Royal Zoological Gardens (Phoenix Park), 5308

Salt Hill Hotel (near Dublin), 3513

Sarah Sanda (ship), 3120

Saunders's News Letter (newspaper), 446, 4268, 4309

Savings' Bank (Armagh), 4

Scottish Guardian (newspaper), 1298

Sea-King (ship), 393

Seskanore Mills, 4844

Seskinore Yeomanry, 306

Shamrock (steamer), 42

Signet (journal), 5847

Sligo Chronicle (newspaper), 4322

Sligo Guardian (newspaper), 2940, 3493

Sligo Infirmary, 1976

Sligo Regiment of Militia, 1918

Sly's African Journal, 469

Society for Promoting Christianity Among the Jews, 5810, 6198

Society for the Propagation of the Gospel in Foreign Parts, 5846

Society of Friends, 2442, 4503, 5827

Spanish Legation (Washington, U.S.A.), 6007

St. Clare's Convent (Newry), 6227

St. Patrick, Benevolent Society of, 1897

Stock Exchange (London), 6438

Streetsville Weekly Review (newspaper), 4034

Swanlinbar Dispensary, 2051, 2887

Tandragee School, 4961

Tape-a-bord (ship), 6222

Thames (steamer), 546

The Life of Lord Charlemont (Henry W. Hardy), 3277

The Times (newspaper), 5327

Theatre Royal (Limerick), 4587

Theological College of the Irish General Assembly, 3126

Thomas (brig), 4044

Tipperary Free Press (newspaper), 3841

Tontine Rooms (Armagh), 2168

Toronto Christian Guardian (newspaper), 2248

Travels in the Holy Land, &c. (Dr. William Wilson), 2747

Treatise on the Climate of Pau (Taylor), 619

Trinity College (Dublin), 625, 641, 889, 967, 1007, 1090, 1255, 1314, 1531, 1555, 1662, 1912, 1920, 1987, 2417, 2542, 2562, 2994, 3072, 3581, 3734, 3874, 3877, 3981, 4331, 4367, 4401, 4430, 4456, 4538, 4868, 4870. *See also* University of Dublin.

Trinity College (Oxford): *See* University of Oxford, Trinity College.

Trinity College, University of Cambridge: *See* University of Cambridge, Trinity College.

Tullybrick Nursery, 1125, 1237

Tullyvin Endowed School, 2754

Tyrawly Herald (newspaper), 3237

Tyrone Constitution (newspaper), 5030

Tyrone County Infirmary, 5028

Tyrone Infirmary (Omagh), 1588

Tyrone Militia, 1st Strule Corps of Yeomanry, 37

Ulster Bank, 2222, 2509, 2643, 3313, 3295, 3331, 3562, 3754, 4658, 4675, 5387, 5507, 5532

Ulster Branch Bank, 465

Ulster Canal Carrying Company, 1167

Ulster Conservative (newspaper), 184

Ulster Gazette (newspaper), 1093

Ulster Institution for the Deaf and the Dumb and the Blind (Belfast), 3302

Ulster Railway, 2869, 4271, 4897, 4963, 5764

Unicorn (ship), 6222

United Colleges of St. Salvador and St. Leonard's (Scotland), 1382
United Irishmen, 5169
University of Cambridge, 2801, 2829; Christ's College, 6397; Pembroke College, 2829; Queen's College, 6152; Trinity College, 2801, 4143
University of Dublin, 1208, 1800, 2986, 3369, 3391, 3713, 4750, 5234, 6214. *See also* Trinity College (Dublin).
University of Glasgow, 1484, 2291, 5782
University of Oxford, 4143, 6410; Brasenose College, 5892; Christ Church, 2468; Pembroke College, 581, 6372; Trinity College, 4957, 5054, 5360, 5704, 5848, 6172, 6388
Variations of Popery (Samuel Oliver Edgar), 3867
Venus (ship), 5894
Verner's Bridge Dispensary, 1204
Victoria Hotel (Armagh), 1863, 5409
Victoria Hotel (Banbridge), 4642
Ville de Paris (ship), 5961
Vindicator (newspaper), 930
Volunteers of '82, 294
Volunteers of 1780, 593
Volunteers of 1782, 5102, 5131
Warder (newspaper), 4630
Waring Bank (Clogher), 761
Waterford Guardian (newspaper), 3020
Waterford Mail (newspaper), 6336
Waterloo, battle of, 1862
Wesleyan Methodist Society, 51, 128, 686, 812, 836, 1001, 1712, 1738, 1822, 2400, 2498, 3569, 3572, 4222
Wesleyan Times (journal), 5062
Western Herald (newspaper), 2253
Widow and Orphan's Fund, 5205
William M'Arthur & Co., 1557
Wonders of Geology (Gideon Algernon Mantell), 6316
Worshipful Company of Carpenters, 5992
Yeoman Cavalry, Cookstown Corps, 2406
Yeomanry Corps of Derry, 3148

6. JOHN THOMPSON, PROPRIETOR AND EDITOR

John Thompson was trained up in the newspaper business by William Trimble (1802–1886), the proprietor and editor of *The Impartial Reporter and Farmers' Journal*, published at Enniskillen, in the county Fermanagh.

On December 3, 1844, Mr. Thompson launched his own newspaper, a weekly entitled, *The Armagh Guardian*, from his office at 63, English-street, Armagh. Originally a six-column, four page publication, Thompson enlarged the journal twice between 1844–1852: first, on February 7, 1848, to a seven-column format; and, second, to a six-column, eight-page format on March 20, 1852. By the end of 1852, Thompson had moved his operation to 41, English-street, head of College-street.

In his first editorial article[1], Mr. Thompson outlined the philosophical and political orientation of his new journal. His first object was to support the *status quo* of the social classes. Accordingly, *The Armagh Guardian* would "assist in spreading that knowledge ... which is admitted to be essential for the better understanding of each individual in the present well-ordered arrangements of society." Espousing the virtues of the present landlord-tenant system as a great "bulwark of British glory," Mr. Thompson pledged to advocate for "the just and inalienable rights of the landlord." Though he would not be party to any oppression of the tenantry through the medium of his journal, yet the Irish should "devote themselves to that employment for which nature has so peculiarly adapted them, rather than following the phantoms of independence." Mr. Thompson's second, but "more important trait of the character of this Journal is its *religious* sentiments. They are strictly Protestant." After lamenting the current appetite for expediency, popularity, and novelty over principle, Mr. Thompson declared his third objective, that is, the political stance of his newspaper: "We are Conservative—the cause is good—and as such we enter the political arena." However, while guarding the principles of Conservatism, he did not wish to "increase the stock of prejudices," and so, would endeavour to depend "upon the force rather than the number of our arguments," and to "soften the asperities of manner." Finally, *The Armagh Guardian* would champion the "great agricultural and other resources" of the county of Armagh, the profile of which, he asserted, would be enhanced "by the introduction of railways." Mr. Thompson called on his readers to expand their minds, their duties enlarged, because: "the importance of this county, both as a nucleus of agriculture, and the focus of trade for a great tract of country, may not any longer be kept secret."

In the *Literary and Educational Year Book* for 1859, Mr. Thompson submitted an entry, describing his paper as "the advocate of Conservative Progress," with particular attention "given to the Great Question of Education." In provincial directories and other sources, Thompson identified himself as a printer and stationer.

Thompson published other works, including *A Record of the City of Armagh*, by Edward Rogers, in 1861. Arguably, the most notable of Thompson's undertakings was *A Memoir Introductory to the History of the Primacy of Armagh*. Originally circulated in Thompson's newspaper, in weekly portions of four pages each, in 1854 Robert King reprinted the series as

---

[1] See *Transcript of John Thompson's editorial article, from the inaugural edition of The Armagh Guardian, published December 3, 1844*, in Chapter 2, page 296.

a book. Thompson's efforts and support did not go unnoticed, as the following accolade, which appeared in the 1855 edition of *The Ulster Journal of Archaeology*, attests: "The Editor of the *Armagh Guardian*, in which the Memoir first appeared, has reason to congratulate himself on having been chosen to convey to the public a work of which any periodical in the empire might be proud."

A review of the advertising columns in *The Armagh Guardian* reveals that Mr. Thompson diversified his income as a sales agent for such goods as E.D. Lines & Company's Metallic Inks, and for life and fire assurance policies indemnified by the Norwich Union company. He was also the sales representative in Armagh for a number of pharmaceutical products, a representative sample of which follow:

- Measam & Co.'s (London) Medicated Cream for rheumatism, gout, and cutaneous diseases, erysipelas, childblain, ringworm, scorbutic humours, stings, and sprains;
- Kearsley's (London) Original Widow Welch's Female Pills for "effectually removing Obstructions, and relieving all other Inconveniences to which the Female Frame is liable;"
- Norton's Chamomile Pills for "Indigestion and all stomach complaints;"
- Dr. Locock's Pulmonic Wafers to give "instant relief, and a rapid Cure of Asthma, Consumption, Coughs, Colds, and all disorders of the Breath and Lungs," and also Dr. Locock's "Antibilious Wafers" and "Female Wafers;"
- Thomas Parrs' (London) Life Pills for indigestion, gout, rheumatism, rheumatic gout, liver complaints, jaundice, cutaneous eruptions on the skin, scurvy, and scorbutic affections;
- Professor Holloway's (London) Pills, for the "cure of a disordered liver and stomach, when in a most hopeless state;"
- "The Silent Friend," a book available in six languages and in its fortieth edition by 1851, promoted as a "practical work on the Exhaustion and Physical Decay of the System, produced by excessive indulgence, the consequences of infection, or the abuse of mercury;" and,
- "On Nervous and Generative Diseases," a book, also containing "the newly-discovered preventive lotion [with respect to] Manhood: the causes of its Premature Decline."

John Thompson and Family – Biographical Notes:

John Thompson was born in 1815 in Enniskillen, county Fermanagh, the son of Mr. William Henry Thompson and the former Miss Copeland of the same county. John Thompson had one sibling, a sister, who died rather young, at the home of John Copeland, Esq., Hollyhill, Enniskillen. The Thompsons had their origins near the town of Donegal, once holding landed property there – the ownership of which, and social position appertaining thereto, John Thompson had hoped to regain in his lifetime.

In about 1820, John Thompson's father gave up his commercial interests in Ireland, to emigrate with his family to America. There, the elder Thompson pursued a clerical calling in the Episcopalian church, was ordained by the Right Rev. Bishop Hobart, in Christ Church, April 19th, 1821, and admitted to the holy order of priests by the Right Rev. Bishop White at St. Peter's Church, Philadelphia, May 8th 1822. The Rev. Mr. W.H. Thompson concluded his career as the minister for Trinity Church in Pittsburgh, Pennsylvania; he died at Rye, Westchester County, New York, August 26th 1830.

Chapter 6: John Thompson, Proprietor and Editor

After a residence of ten years in the United States, John Thompson returned to Enniskillen. Mr. Thompson was first employed by his uncle, Mr. John Copeland, in the Agricultural Bank, becoming manager of the branch in that town.

A few years after setting up his newspaper shop in the city of Armagh, John Thompson married Eliza Brackin, daughter of Hugh Brackin and Elizabeth Copeland. The event was recorded in the August 21, 1848 edition of Thompson's newspaper:

> On the 17th inst., in Killinagh Church, county Cavan, by the Rev. James Armstrong, John Thompson, Esq., Proprietor of *The Armagh Guardian*, to Eliza, only daughter of Hugh Brackin, Esq., of Toam, near Black Lion, in said county.

Births were noticed, first, for a son, in the June 22, 1849 edition of the newspaper and second, for a daughter, on August 16, 1851. The son was William Copeland Bracken Thompson, who was named for his maternal uncle. One more son and three more daughters were born to Mr. and Mrs. Thompson.

An entry in *The Irish Law Times and Solicitors' Journal* reveals that Thompson's financial affairs were in distress during the 1860s. A petition to declare him an insolvent had been filed on August 11, 1869, and the hearing was scheduled at Armagh for October 30th of that year. The same volume shows that Thompson was discharged October 20th, suggesting that an arrangement had been concluded to the satisfaction of the creditors.

After an illness of several months, John Thompson died February 5th, 1880, at Armagh. In the obituary published in *The Armagh Guardian* on February 13th, in language typical of that used for writing such notices in the mid-nineteenth century, it was stated that:

> In private life the late Mr. John Thompson was a most hospitable and friendly companion. He seldom entered personally into public affairs, being of a very retiring, unassuming manner. In religion he was a sound Protestant, but free from all taint of intolerance, and not much caring who preached Christ providing Christ was preached. In politics he was a strict Conservative, and those who knew him best sometimes thought he was too aristocratic a Conservative; for he never forgot the respectability of his family and family relations in Fermanagh, Cavan, and Donegal, and the family relations of his father's second marriage, after the demise of his own mother. As a husband he was faithful and affectionate; as a parent deeply attached and tender. In every relation of life he bore an upright character; and all who had experience of his sterling worth will long keep his memory alive in their hearts, while deeply sympathising in the bereavement of his widow and children, for whose earnest prayer will ascend to the Throne of Him who is the Father of the fatherless.

The chief mourners included Mr. Thompson's two sons, William C.B. Thompson and Hugh B. Thompson, their two uncles Mr. James Bracken, J.P., and Mr. William C. Bracken, of Blacklion, county Cavan, and Mr. Hugh A. Bradshaw and Mr. William Arthur, of Enniskillen. Mr. Thompson's remains were accompanied by a "large concourse of citizens" from his home at 41, English-street, to the rail station in Armagh. From thence, the funeral cortège continued by rail car to Enniskillen, where a funeral service was read at the Church, and Mr. Thompson's body consigned to a tomb in the church-yard.

Mr. Thompson's son, William Copeland Bracken Thompson, was the executor of his father's estate. A merchant by trade, William succeeded his father at the helm of *The Armagh Guardian*, assisted by his younger brother, Hugh. In 1888, Hugh Thompson departed for Africa, to take up missionary work, and thus, the burden of managing the newspaper's affairs fell solely to his brother, William.

Suffering from a "delicate constitution," William Thompson succumbed to worry and strain, dying at his residence, 41, English-street, on January 3rd, 1892. Attended by his cousins and chief mourners, Mr. Hugh Bracken and Mr. William Bracken, Mr. Thompson's remains were interred in the family vault in Killesher grave-yard, county Fermanagh. His estate was administered by two of his sisters, Emily Jane Thompson and Amelia Caroline Thompson.

After William Thompson's death, Mr. Samuel Delmege Trimble (1857–1947), the proprietor and publisher of *The Donegal Independent and Sligo, Leitrim and Fermanagh Advertiser* newspaper, purchased *The Armagh Guardian*.

Three of William Thompson's sisters lived as spinsters, in Belfast: Elizabeth Anna (1851–1911), Mary Sophia in (1853–1920), and Amelia Caroline (1861–1902). Emily Jane (1856–1921) married Cecil Sheridan Forwood (1878–1966), son of Ernest Harrison and Mabel Forwood, of Cheshunt, Hertfordshire, at Centenary Church, St Stephen's Green, Dublin, on March 18th, 1901. No children were born of the marriage, and on June 9th, 1921, Emily Forwood *née* Thompson died at Altamont, Bangor, county Down.

In 1903, Hugh Bracken Thompson married Margaret Churchill at Kingston, Surrey. The couple resided at Altamont, no. 23, Downshire Road in Bangor, county Down, and raised three daughters: Norah Margaret Elizabeth, Aileen Mary Felicia, and Kathleen Caroline Churchill. Hugh Thompson died on the December 6th, 1924. In his will, Mr. Thompson bequeathed £300 "to the Editors of 'Echoes of Service,' to be distributed among servants of the Lord who have been labouring for Him in the Foreign Mission Field for thirty years or more."

:: :: ::

BIBLIOGRAPHY

Blacker, Henry Beaver. *Brief sketches of the parishes of Booterstown and Donnybrook, in the county of Dublin*. Dublin: George Herbert, 1874.

Bolton, Robert. *History of the Protestant Episcopal Church, in the County of Westchester*. New York: Stanford & Swords, 1855.

"Bracken, Ireland and Lancashire," post to the Bracken surname board by 'Soopy464' (July 9, 2010), hosted by *Ancestry*, online at boards.ancestry.com.au.

Burke, Bernard, Sir. *A Genealogical and Heraldic History of the Landed Gentry of Great Britain and Ireland*, Volume I. London: Harrison, Pall Mall.

Coke, Charles Anthony. *Census of the British Empire: compiled from official returns for 1861, Part II—Scotland, Ireland, and the British Colonies*. London: Harrison, 1864.

Crisp, Frederick Arthur, ed. *Visitation of England and Wales*, Vol. XV. Privately printed, 1908.

Cunningham, John B. *Oscar Wilde's Enniskillen: Fermanagh in mid Victorian times 1864-71*. Belleek, county Fermanagh: Davog Press, 2002.

"Death of Mr. John Thompson," in *The Armagh Guardian*, 13 February 1880.

"Death of Mr. W.C.B. Thompson, in *The Armagh Guardian*, 6 January 1892.

General Register Office (England). England and Wales Civil Registration Indexes. London, England: General Register Office. Transcriptions hosted online, www.freebmd.org.uk, by The Trustees of FreeBMD (accessed 7 July 2013).

General Registry Office of Ireland. *Death records of Ireland, 1864-1870, with index of deaths, 1864-1921*; *Quarterly returns of births in Ireland, 1864-1955, with indexes to births, 1864-1921*; and, *Marriage records, 1845-1970, with indexes to marriages, 1845-1911*. Records microfilmed, transcribed, and posted to *Family Search*, online at www.familysearch.org (accessed 7 July 2013).

Great Britain, Parliament. "Macken Case," in *Reports from Committees: Sixteen Volumes (12.), Volume XVI: Orange Lodges in Ireland*. House of Commons Papers, Session 19 February – 10 September 1835. Ordered, by the House of Commons to be printed, 6 August 1835 (pp. 226–231*ff*).

Haydn, Joseph Timothy. "Remarkable and memorable trials during the last hundred years," in *Dictionary of Dates, and Universal Reference relating to all ages and nations*. London: Edward Moxon, 1841.

Holt, Sarah K. *Genealogy Pages*. Online at www.sarahkholt.com (accessed 7 July 2013).

"Hugh Bracken & Elizabeth Copeland," posts by Soopy46@aol.com and Valerie BW to FERMANAGH-GOLD-L mailing list (August 20, 2011), hosted by RootsWeb, online at archiver.rootsweb.ancestry.com.

Ireland, Registrar General. *General Alphabetical Index to the Townlands and Towns, Parishes and Baronies, of Ireland*. Dublin: A. Thom for H.M.S.O., 1861; reprinted, Baltimore, Maryland: Genealogical Publishing Co., Inc., 2006.

Liverpool Record Office. *Liverpool Registers*. Liverpool, England. Records microfilmed, indexed, and posted to *Ancestry* www.ancestry.ca (accessed 7 July 2013).

Mac Annaidh, Séamus. *Fermanagh books, writers and newspapers of the nineteenth century*. Marmara Denzi, 1999.

Malcolmson, A.P.W. *The pursuit of the heiress: Aristocratic marriage in Ireland, 1750–1820*. Ulster Historical Foundation, 1982.

Medical Directory for Scotland 1854. London: John Churchill, 1854.

Mitchell, Brian. *A New Genealogical Atlas of Ireland*, 2nd ed. Baltimore, Maryland: Genealogical Publishing Co., Inc., 2002.

Murphy, Edward William. *Chloroform: its properties and safety in childbirth*. London: Walton and Maberly, 1855.

National Archives, London, England. *Census returns of England and Wales, 1911*. Kew, Surrey, England: The National Archives of the United Kingdom, 1911. Microfilmed, digitised, and hosted online by Ancestry www.ancestry.ca (accessed 7 July 2013).

"Notice of Charitable Bequest (Hugh Bracken Thompson)." *The Belfast Gazette*, 15 May 1925.

Principal Probate Registry. *Calendar of the Grants of Probate and Letters of Administration made in the Probate Registries of the High Court of Justice in England*. London, England. Digitised and hosted online by Ancestry www.ancestry.ca (accessed 7 July 2013).

Public Record Office of Northern Ireland [PRONI]. *Will Calendars*. Digitised and hosted online by the PRONI, www.proni.gov.uk (accessed 7 July 2013).

The Church of Jesus Christ of Latter Day Saints. *Family Search*. Online at www.familysearch.org (accessed, various dates, 2011–2013).

The Irish Law Times, and Solicitors' Journal, Vol. III. Dublin: John Falconer, 1869.

The National Archives of Ireland. *Census of Ireland, 1901 and 1911*. Digitised, indexed and contextualised in partnership with Library and Archives Canada. Online at www.census.nationalarchives.ie (accessed 7 July 2013).

Thompson, John, editor. *The Armagh Guardian*. Armagh, Ireland: John Thompson, December 3, 1844 – December 30, 1852.

Vincent, Benjamin. "Executions of Remarkable Criminals," in *Haydn's Dictionary of Dates relating to all ages and nations for Universal Reference*, 12th edition. London: Edward Moxon and Co., 1866.

Wakley, Thomas, editor. "Case of a Woman Pregnant with Five Children," published originally in the *Dublin Journal* (Jan. 1840); reprinted in, *The Lancet: A journal of British and foreign medicine*, Vol. I. London: George Churchill, Feb. 8, 1840.

Wakley, Thomas H. and Thomas Wakley, jun., editors. "Centenarianism in Ireland," in *The Lancet*, vol. 1889 (Sept. 21, 1889, pg. 609). London: Wakley & Son, 1889.

www.ingramcontent.com/pod-product-compliance
Lightning Source LLC
Chambersburg PA
CBHW060505300426
44112CB00017B/2549